MARKETING RESEARCH
Methodological Foundations
Sixth Edition

MARKETING RESEARCH
Methodological Foundations
Sixth Edition

Gilbert A. Churchill, Jr.

Arthur C. Nielsen, Jr., Chair of Marketing Research
University of Wisconsin

The Dryden Press
Harcourt Brace College Publishers

Fort Worth   Philadelphia   San Diego   New York   Orlando   Austin   San Antonio
Toronto   Montreal   London   Sydney   Tokyo

Publisher Elizabeth Widdicombe
Acquisitions Editor Lyn Hastert
Developmental Editor Glenn E. Martin

Project Management Elm Street Publishing Services, Inc.

Compositor The Clarinda Company
Text Type 10/12 Times Roman

Address for Editorial Correspondence
The Dryden Press, 301 Commerce Street, Suite 3700, Fort Worth,
TX 76102

Address for Orders
The Dryden Press, 6277 Sea Harbor Drive, Orlando, FL 32887
1-800-782-4479, or 1-800-433-0001 (in Florida)

ISBN: 0-03-098366-5

Library of Congress Catalog Number: 93-74358

Printed in the United States of America
    6 7 8 9 0 1 2 3 039 9 8 7 6 5 4 3

The Dryden Press
Harcourt Brace College Publishers

THE DRYDEN PRESS SERIES IN MARKETING

INTENDED MARKET

The basic objective that motivated the first five editions of this book serves as the impetus for the sixth edition as well. The book is designed for the introductory sequence in marketing research and attempts to structure the discipline of marketing research for students.

The topic of marketing research is a complex one. It requires answers to a number of questions and a number of decisions about the technique or techniques to be used to solve a research problem. Without some overriding framework, students often become so overwhelmed by the bits and pieces that they fail to see the interrelationship of the parts to the whole. This distorted vision can be detrimental to both the aspiring manager and the aspiring researcher, for in a very real sense marketing research is one big trade-off. Decisions made about one stage in the research process have consequences for the other stages. Managers must appreciate the subtle and pervasive interactions among the parts of the research process in order to be appropriately confident about a particular research result. Researchers also need to appreciate the interactions among the parts. The parts serve as ''pegs'' on which to hang knowledge accumulated about research methods, but researchers must avoid becoming enamored of the parts to the detriment of the whole.

This book attempts to serve both the aspiring manager and the aspiring researcher through its basic organization around the stages of the research process. The research process is a sequence of steps that must be completed when answering a research question. The six parts of the book parallel these specific stages:

1. Formulate the problem
2. Determine the research design
3. Design the data collection method and forms
4. Design the sample and collect the data
5. Analyze and interpret the data
6. Prepare the research report

Moreover, the stages are broken into smaller parts, and a given stage is typically discussed in several chapters and appendixes. Not only does this allow students to see the forest for the trees, but it also provides instructors a great deal of latitude about what is covered. An instructor's decision on what to cover will depend, of course, on the background, interests, and maturity of the students and on the time provided in the curriculum for marketing research. Because *Marketing Research: Methodological Foundations,* Sixth Edition, provides instructors great flexibility in the level of depth with which to cover any particular stage in the research process, it can be used in a variety of introductory marketing research course sequences: one- or two-quarter sequences or in semester courses. The first five editions of the book have been used to advantage at both the undergraduate and graduate levels by simply covering more material at a higher level of sophistication in the graduate courses.

ORGANIZATION

Part 1, on formulating the problem, consists of three chapters. Chapter 1 provides an overview of marketing research, including the kinds of problems for which it is used, who is doing research, and how it is organized. It also discusses some of the career opportunities available in marketing research. Chapter 2 provides an overview to the various ways of gathering marketing intelligence. It emphasizes the increasingly important role played by decision support systems in providing business and competitive intelligence, and contrasts the information system approaches to the project emphasis approach taken in the book. The appendix to Chapter 2 discusses various ethical frameworks for viewing marketing research techniques. Chapter 3 overviews the research process in terms of the kinds of decisions to be made at each stage and then discusses in some detail the problem formulation stage of the research process. One question to be asked whenever research is being considered is whether the research is likely to be worth the money it will cost. The appendix to Chapter 3 discusses how Bayesian analysis can be used to make this judgment.

Part 2 consists of two chapters and deals with the nature of the research design. It emphasizes ensuring that the research addresses the appropriate questions and treats them in an efficient manner. Chapter 4 overviews the roles of various research designs and also discusses two basic designs, the exploratory and the descriptive, at some length. Chapter 5 discusses the role and conceptual logic of experiments.

The four chapters in Part 3 delve into methods of data collection and design of data collection forms. Chapter 6 focuses on secondary data as an information resource and includes a discussion of commercial marketing information services. The appendix to Chapter 6 discusses the many sources of published secondary data. Chapter 7 discusses the two main methods of data collection, observation and communication, and Chapter 8 covers the construction of questionnaires and observation data collection forms. Chapter 9 explains the general topic of attitude measurement using scales and discusses some of the more common types of attitude scales. The important but often neglected topic of developing measures for marketing constructs of interest is discussed in one of the three appendixes to Chapter 9. Multidimensional scaling and conjoint analysis are explained in the other two.

Part 4, which consists of three chapters, is concerned with the actual collection of data needed to answer questions. Chapter 10 discusses the various types of sampling plans that can be used to determine the population elements from which data should be collected. Chapter 11 treats the question of how many of these elements are needed, so that the problem can be answered with the required precision and confidence in the results. Chapter 12 discusses the many errors that can arise in completing this data collection task from a perspective that allows managers to better assess the quality of the information they receive from research.

Once data have been collected, emphasis in the research process logically turns to analysis, which amounts to searching for meaning in the collected information. The search for meaning involves many questions and several steps. The five chapters and several appendixes in Part 5 attempt to overview these steps and questions. Chapter 13 reviews the preliminary analysis steps of editing, coding, and tabulating the data. The main questions that must be resolved before statistical examination of the data can begin are covered in Chapter 14. Next, Chapters 15, 16, and 17 review the statistical techniques most useful in the analysis of marketing data. Chapter 15 discusses the procedures appropriate for examining the differences among and between groups; Chapter 16 covers the assessment of association; and Chapter 17 examines the multivariate techniques of discriminant, factor, and cluster analysis.

Part 6 consists of one chapter and an epilogue. Chapter 18 discusses a critical part of the research process, the research report, which often becomes the standard by which the research effort is assessed. Chapter 18 discusses the criteria a research report should satisfy and the form it can follow to contribute positively to the research effort. This chapter also discusses some of the graphical means that can be used to communicate the important findings more forcefully. The epilogue ties together the elements of the research process by demonstrating in overview fashion their interrelationships.

The organization of the book around the stages in the research process produces several significant benefits. First, it demonstrates and continually reinforces how the ''bits'' of research technique fit into a larger whole. Students can see readily, for example, the relationship between statistics and marketing research, or where they might pursue additional study to become research specialists.

Second, the organization permits great flexibility. For example, instructors with only a single, one-quarter introductory course in marketing research faced with the need to develop some appreciation for the basic questions addressed in research might choose to overview the research process at an elementary level. One way to accomplish this would be to omit Chapter 5 on causal research designs, Chapter 9 on attitude measurement, and Chapter 11 on sample size, and to cover only Chapter 13 from among the five analysis chapters. This approach would serve to present the process and at the same time to avoid some of the more technical questions of research design, measurement, and sampling, and the statistical analysis of the collected data.

On the other hand, instructors who wish to emphasize, say, the questions of analysis or measurement would have ample materials to do so. There is, for example, one database in the textbook itself and a number of other databases in the *Instructor's Manual* that instructors can have students analyze using one of the standard statistical packages. Each of these databases is available both in hard copy and on computer disk to all who adopt the book. The database in the book involves buying through catalogs. It is used to demonstrate everything from the coding of data to the most involved statistical techniques. The appendixes to appropriate chapters contain sample computer output and discuss the interpretation of that output in light of the notions discussed in the chapter. One of the appendixes also lists and describes the command structures for an SPSS/PC+ run. These appendixes provide students a direct connection between statistical concepts and the application of these concepts. The database is rich enough for students to perform their own analyses, thereby increasing their comfort level with the statistical techniques discussed. The specific portions of the book that should be used to produce this emphasis or several other emphases are discussed in the *Instructor's Manual,* which contains suggested outlines for organizing courses to achieve different emphases in different time frames.

Each part (except Part 6) concludes with cases that illustrate many of the major issues raised in the section. The cases represent actual situations, although many of them have disguised names and locations to protect the identity of the sponsors. The cases afford students the opportunity to apply what they have learned by critically evaluating what others have done, thereby increasing their analytic skills.

CHANGES IN THE SIXTH EDITION

Although it looks similar to the first five editions, the new edition contains some major changes. One change is an increased emphasis on the international aspects of marketing research, which is reflected both in the text discussion and in the examples used to illustrate the concepts. There is also a greater emphasis on marketing research in service settings and marketing to organizational buyers.

Another change focuses on a major revision of the cases. More than 25 percent of the cases are new and another 30 percent have been revised. Moreover, a video case has been added to this edition. The video case, which uses an original script and professional actors, is written in such a way as to allow the viewing of short segments that illustrate the points being discussed at a specific point in time. There is a special icon at the end of the chapters that indicates the questions that might be asked after students view a segment of the video case. The video case should make for a very interactive learning environment.

Readers will also be happy to know that a number of features incorporated in the fifth edition are being retained and expanded for this edition because they were so well received. Foremost among these is the extensive treatment of ethics in marketing research. This edition continues to present a conceptual framework for viewing ethical choices early on (Appendix 2A) and more ethical scenarios that students need to address in subsequent chapters. This organization resolves the problem of how to treat the topic of ethics. It is difficult to treat it early because students do not yet have the technical sophistication to appreciate alternative ways to approach ethical problems. Treating it late, as most books do for this reason, makes ethics appear as an afterthought. Treating the conceptual foundations early in the book and then interweaving ethical dilemmas with technical issues allow students to more readily appreciate the social consequences of proceeding in particular ways.

As part of the revision plan for the sixth edition, all of the chapters have been subjected to thorough scrutiny and rewrite. There has also been a major updating of the examples, for instance. There are many more in-text examples and Research Realities than were found in the fifth edition, and the examples are as up-to-date as possible. For example, this edition contains more than 85 Research Realities and 25 percent of them are new.

SPECIAL FEATURES

As readers might suspect from the previous chapter descriptions, the level and difficulty of the material varies. Certain parts, such as the discussion of commercial information services in the secondary data chapter, are purely descriptive. Others, such as the notion of measurement, are by their nature abstract and, as such, are difficult for students not used to thinking in abstract terms. This, though, is the nature of marketing research, and this book does not avoid topics simply because they are difficult. Rather, the posture has been to include those topics that are vital to understanding the nature of the research process, while attempting to simplify complex ideas into their basic elements. Throughout, the emphasis is placed on conceptual understanding of the material rather than on mathematical niceties or discussion of interesting but unimportant tangents. The purpose here is to walk the middle ground between the two kinds of introductory textbooks currently available. One type discusses the concepts of marketing research without providing sufficient detail about some of the important, but perhaps more difficult, stages in the process. The other kind goes to the opposite extreme of discussing some technically difficult stages in great detail while omitting the basic structure of the process, and at other stages providing only cursory coverage of some of the more elementary, but critically important, methods. *Marketing Research: Methodological Foundations,* Sixth Edition, is designed to avoid such extremes by providing the student with a thorough treatment of the important concepts, both simple and complex.

The general approach employed throughout is not only to provide the student with the pros and cons of the various methods with which a research problem could be addressed, but also to develop an appreciation of why these advantages and disadvantages arise. The hope is that through this appreciation, students will be able to creatively apply and critically evaluate the procedures of marketing research.

This book contains a number of features designed to help students develop their creative and analytical marketing research skills. Some of the more important features follow.

- **Cases**   The cases at the end of each part are included to assist students in developing their evaluation and analytical skills. The cases are also useful in demonstrating the universal application of marketing research techniques. The methods of marketing research can be used not only by distributors of products, as is commonly assumed, but also to address other issues in the private and public sectors. The cases include such diverse entities or issues as the Big Brother program, marketing management education programs, banking services, and theatre, among others. Moreover, raw data for six of the cases are available to allow students the opportunity to do their analyses to answer the questions posed, and in the process, develop their data analysis skills.

- **Video Case**   The video case allows for an interactive learning environment. Students can be shown segments of the video, and class discussion can then be structured to identify the issues and determine what should be done next. In this sense, the video case parallels the type of situation students are likely to encounter in the workplace. It also helps show how decisions made at one stage of the research process affect decisions made at later stages.

- **Computer-based Experiential Exercises**   The *Instructor's Manual* contains suggestions for computer-based exercises for a number of chapters. These exercises, which are available on disk to adopters and which have been developed by D. A. Schellinck and R. N. Maddox, can be assigned to illustrate chapter content and tend to be very involving for students.

- **Ethical Dilemmas**   The ethical dilemmas present students with scenarios that arise when making marketing research choices. They are presented along with discussion of the technical choices, so that students can not only see the advantages and disadvantages of proceeding in particular ways but the social consequences of doing so as well.

- **Research Realities**   The Research Realities illustrate what is going on in the world of marketing research today, both in general and at specific companies such as Clorox, General Mills, and Gillette.

- **Problems**   The problems at the end of each chapter allow students the opportunity to apply the concepts discussed in that chapter to very focused situations, thereby developing firsthand knowledge of the strengths and weaknesses of the various techniques.

- **NFO Coffee Study**   The questionnaire, coding form, and raw data from a study on ground coffee conducted by NFO are used to frame a number of application problems. These problems, which are denoted by a special icon at the end of the chapters, allow students the opportunity to work with "live" data in honing their skills in translating research problems into data analysis issues and in interpreting computer output. Moreover, the database is rich enough for instructors to design their own application problems/exercises, thereby allowing even more opportunity for hands-on learning.

- **Exercises**   There are also exercises for each chapter in the *Instructor's Manual*. The exercises direct students to do small-scale projects using particular techniques. The exercises develop students' in-depth understanding of the techniques, including their proper application.

SUPPLEMENTS TO THE TEXTBOOK

The *Instructor's Manual* to the textbook completes a comprehensive teaching package. It includes a preface that offers suggestions on how the book and *Instructor's Manual* can be used most effectively. The preface is followed by suggested outlines on how to teach the course to achieve desired emphases within different time frames. Next are the chapter-by-chapter resource materials, which include the following for each chapter:

1. Learning objectives
2. List of key terms
3. Detailed outline

Gilbert A. Churchill, Jr., DBA (Indiana University), is the Arthur C. Nielsen, Jr., Chair of Marketing Research at the University of Wisconsin–Madison. He joined the Wisconsin faculty in 1966 and has taught there since, except for one year that he spent as a visiting professor at Bedriftsokonomisk Institutt in Oslo, Norway. Professor Churchill was named Distinguished Marketing Educator by the American Marketing Association in 1986, only the second individual so honored. The award recognizes and honors a living marketing educator for distinguished service and outstanding contributions in the field of marketing education. He was also named Marketing Educator of the Year by the Academy of Marketing Science in 1993 for his significant scholarly contributions.

Professor Churchill is a past recipient of the William O'Dell Award for the outstanding article appearing in the *Journal of Marketing Research* during the year. He has also been a finalist for the award five other times. He was named Marketer of the Year by the South Central Wisconsin Chapter of the American Marketing Association in 1981. He is a member of the American Marketing Association and has served as vice-president of publications and on its board of directors as well as on the association's Advisory Committee to the Bureau of the Census. In addition, he has served as consultant to a number of companies, including Oscar Mayer, Western Publishing Company, and Parker Pen.

Professor Churchill's articles have appeared in such publications as the *Journal of Marketing Research, Journal of Marketing, Journal of Consumer Research, Journal of Retailing, Journal of Business Research, Decision Sciences, Technometrics,* and *Organizational Behavior and Human Performance,* among others. He is a co-author of several other books, including *Sales Force Management: Planning, Implementation, and Control,* Fourth Edition (Homewood, Ill.: Irwin, 1993) and *Salesforce Performance* (Lexington, Mass.: Lexington Books, 1984), and is also the author of *Basic Marketing Research,* Second Edition (Fort Worth, Tex: Dryden Press, 1992). He is a former editor of the *Journal of Marketing Research* and has served on the editorial boards of the *Journal of Marketing Research, Journal of Marketing, Journal of Business Research,* and *Journal of Health Care Marketing.* Professor Churchill currently teaches undergraduate and graduate courses in marketing research and sales management. He has been recognized for his teaching as the recipient of the Lawrence J. Larson Excellence in Teaching Award.

CONTENTS

PART 2 **DETERMINE RESEARCH DESIGN**   143

4 **RESEARCH DESIGN**   144

5 **CAUSAL DESIGNS**   190

PART 3   DESIGN DATA COLLECTION METHOD AND FORMS   269

6   **DATA COLLECTION: SECONDARY DATA   270**

8 DATA COLLECTION FORMS   396

12 COLLECTING THE DATA: FIELD PROCEDURES AND NONSAMPLING ERRORS 652

PART 5 ANALYSIS AND INTERPRETATION OF DATA 735

13 DATA ANALYSIS: PRELIMINARY STEPS 736

PART *6*   THE RESEARCH REPORT   1079

18   THE RESEARCH REPORT   1080

Fundamental Criterion of Research Reports   1081
Writing Criteria   1082
   Completeness   1082
   Accuracy   1082
Research Realities 18.1: An Example of Inept Phrasing and Its Consequences   1084
   Clarity   1084
   Conciseness   1085
Research Realities 18.2: Some Suggestions When Choosing
   Words for Marketing Research Reports   1086
Forms of the Report   1087
   Title Page   1088
   Table of Contents   1088
   Summary   1088
   Introduction   1089
   Body   1090
   Conclusions and Recommendations   1092
   Appendix   1094
Research Realities 18.3: Are American Students Really
   Lost in Math and Science?   1095
The Oral Report   1097
   Preparing the Oral Report   1098
   Delivering the Oral Report   1099
Graphic Presentation of the Results   1100
   Pie Chart   1101
   Line Chart   1102

MARKETING RESEARCH, THE RESEARCH PROCESS, AND PROBLEM DEFINITION

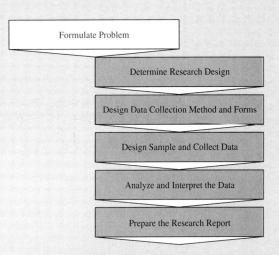

Formulate Problem

Determine Research Design

Design Data Collection Method and Forms

Design Sample and Collect Data

Analyze and Interpret the Data

Prepare the Research Report

Part 1 gives an overview of marketing research. Chapter 1 looks at the kinds of problems for which it is used, who is doing it, and how it is organized. Chapter 2 discusses alternative ways of providing marketing intelligence, through marketing information systems or decision support systems or through projects designed to get at specific issues. This book takes a project approach to the provision of marketing intelligence. The appendix to Chapter 2 discusses some of the ethical questions that can arise when gathering information. Chapter 3 then provides an overview of the research process and discusses in detail the problem formulation stage of that process.

1

MARKETING RESEARCH: A PERVASIVE ACTIVITY

Many people have a mistaken identity about marketing research. They believe it is simply asking ultimate consumers what they think or feel about some product, ad, or issue. While marketing research does make use of consumer surveys, it involves much more than that. Consider the following examples.[1]

Example To keep track of the benefits of event sponsorship, researchers at John Hancock Financial Services, whose company sponsors the John Hancock Bowl, scour magazines and newspapers across the country, counting the number of stories about the bowl game and crunching numbers on column inches, circulation, and ad rates. They determine the company's TV exposure value from factors such as the precise number of times the football announcers mention John Hancock and the amount of time their name is on the screen in pre-game promotions and during the broadcast. Burroughs Wellcome Co., a pharmaceutical company, has also experimented with athletic-event sponsorship. The company sponsored a women's tennis tournament to market a new sunscreen lotion. By distributing coupons at the match and then tracking how many were redeemed, the company found that the tennis events reached the target audience of upscale women, aged thirty and older.[2]

Example Three communications giants — AT&T, Telecommunications Inc., and US West — are working with 300 Littleton, Colorado, residents in an experiment that may determine the future of home movie viewing. 150 residences are being hooked up to a "movie on demand" service called "Take One," and another 150 are being connected

---

[1]Do not worry if some of the terms and data collection methods mentioned in the examples are unfamiliar, as they are described later in the book. The intent in the examples is simply to provide some flavor of the types of problems that marketing research is used to address and some of the approaches that are used.

[2]Michael McCarthy, "Keeping Careful Score on Sports Tie-Ins," *The Wall Street Journal* (April 24, 1991), pp. B1, B5.

to an enhanced pay-per-view service called "Hits at Home." Since the purpose is to determine what people will watch and how often, test homes pay no installation fee and no monthly base rate. Customers are charged only for what they watch: $3.99 for movies-on-demand and $2.99 for enhanced pay-per-view.

Take One customers can select movies from a guide listing over 1,000 titles and can then either order them by remote-control from prompts on their TV screens or call in their order. Within five minutes, the movie begins playing on the customer's TV. Hits at Home is equivalent to having 24 movie channels (most cable customers now have only two or three). The same movie will play on four channels at 30-minute intervals, so viewers do not have to wait as long to see a movie as they do with more limited movie-channel service. At the control center, orders are entered into a computer terminal, and the computer handles the routing. For a Take One video, the clerk must find the movie video and manually load it into one of 120 VCRs. Hits at Home orders are routed solely by computer. The decision as to which is more promising will depend partly on the demand generated by each service.[3]

Example Researchers with stopwatches from the Food Marketing Institute followed shoppers through supermarkets and found that no matter what size the store was, customers only spend about forty minutes cruising the aisles before checking out. The researchers also discovered that most consumers shop less than half of a typical supermarket. Only one in three, for example, stop at an in-store bakery, and just one in five is likely to make a deli purchase. The Food Marketing Institute uses observations like these to help design supermarkets and to select the right mix of goods and services.[4]

Example Quaker Direct, a direct-marketing program established by Quaker Oats, sent out packets of coupons to some 18 million homes. A household identification number was embedded in the bar code of each coupon. Within four months, Quaker's research department was able to understand how well the promotion worked by tracking exactly which coupons each household redeemed. All of the information gathered by household is appended to a data base recording specific transactions. Quaker executives call this "household management" because they know exactly which coupons were redeemed by which household. Using this information, the company is able to target future mailings, offering higher incentives to resistant shoppers or dropping from the packet products consumers are not interested in.[5]

Example Nickelodeon, the cable TV network for kids, has made research a top priority. Its primary research vehicle is focus groups. Nickelodeon typically begins by using

---

[3]"AT&T, US West, TCI Test Two Enhanced Home Movie Services," *Marketing News,* 26 (November 9, 1992), p. 5.

[4]Richard Gibson, "Planning Supermarkets to Maximize Temptation," *The Wall Street Journal* (May 9, 1991), p. B1.

[5]Millie Neal, "Quaker's Direct Hit," *Direct Marketing,* 9 (January 1991), pp. 52, 53, 70; Kathleen Deveny, "Segments of One: Marketers Take Aim at the Ultimate Narrow Target: The Individual," *The Wall Street Journal* (March 22, 1991), p. B4.

focus groups to discuss rudimentary concepts for shows or to brainstorm with kids. Moderators ask the targeted audience questions such as how they spend their time, what their favorite movies are, and what video games they enjoy playing. From this information, they can get some ideas on directions worth pursuing. After learning in a focus group that kids enjoy being scared, the network searched for a scary show that did not rely on blood and gore. The result was a live-action pilot called "Are You Afraid of the Dark?" Nickelodeon finds it beneficial to use the same kids over and over in focus groups. These "expert" groups are used throughout the development process for a given show. Expert groups were used in developing the game show "Double Dare." Kids viewing the first "Double Dare" pilot said it was "too predictable" because the physical challenge always came last. Based on this feedback, the producers changed "Double Dare" to allow the grease-and-goo antics to occur any time.[6]

Example   Kraft USA, realizing the growing importance of using research for store-specific marketing, staged an experiment combining a demographic profile of cream cheese buyers with data showing which supermarkets drew most of those shoppers. Kraft pinpointed 30 stores where people frequently bought items from special displays and installed coolers in them, tailoring the types of cream cheese in each to the tastes of the store's shoppers. Shoppers in a big Midwestern city found extra rows of strawberry-flavored cream cheese at one supermarket. Just miles away, another store had almost no strawberry cream cheese but lots of diet versions. Still another had mostly large, 12-ounce cartons of Philadelphia cream cheese. Sales in these supermarkets jumped 147 percent over the previous year. Such experiments are possible due to the new insights provided by checkout scanners, which are generating more sophisticated data on consumers' buying habits.[7]

Example   Chrysler Corporation, as part of the introduction of its new LH lines of cars, spent $30 million to re-educate the more than 100,000 employees in its dealerships. Chrysler wants to win back younger, more affluent buyers with the Chrysler Concorde, Dodge Intrepid, and Eagle Vision. In simulated test drives, Chrysler will use microphones to see how salespeople treat different types of customers (played by trainers). Chrysler trainers will coach the dealership staffers on better ways to present both the new cars and older models. The company is offering cash incentives to dealers with high customer-satisfaction scores.[8]

The previous examples just scratch the surface regarding the scope of marketing research activities. This book will provide a better perspective on how marketing research is and can be used. For the moment, note that it does involve more than simply

---

[6]Joseph M. Winski, " 'Addicted' to Research, Nick Shows Strong Kids' Lure: Agency Exec Says Net Hits the Hot Button," *Advertising Age,* 63 (February 10, 1992), pp. S2, S22.

[7]Michael J. McCarthy, "Marketers Zero In On Their Customers," *The Wall Street Journal* (March 18, 1991), p. B1.

[8]Bradley A. Stertz, "Autos: For LH Models, Chrysler Maps New Way to Sell," *The Wall Street Journal* (June 30, 1992), p. B1.

asking individual consumers about their likes and dislikes. While consumer surveys are an important marketing research tool, other methods are also used. The choice depends on the problem to be solved. The fundamental point is that marketing research is a pervasive activity that can take *many forms* because its basic purpose is to help managers make better decisions in any of their areas of responsibility.

MARKETING MANAGER'S ROLE REVISITED

The marketing concept suggests that the central focus of the firm should be the customer's satisfaction. The marketing manager can control a number of factors in attempting to satisfy consumer desires. Labeled the marketing mix, these factors have been categorized in various ways. One of the better-known classifications is the four P's of product, price, place, and promotion.[9] The marketing manager's essential task is to combine these variables into an effective and profitable marketing program, a program in which all the elements of the marketing mix are conceived and implemented as part of a cohesive and interrelated whole.

The marketing manager's task would be much simpler if all the elements that potentially affect customer satisfaction were under the manager's control and if consumer reaction to any contemplated change could be predicted. Unfortunately, neither of these things usually happens. The behavior of individual consumers is largely unpredictable. Further, a number of factors affecting the success of the marketing effort are beyond the marketing manager's control, including the internal resources and objectives of the firm and the competitive, technological, economic, cultural and social, and political and legal environments.

Figure 1.1 summarizes the task of marketing management. Customers (C) are at the center because they are the focus of the firm's activities. Their satisfaction is achieved through simultaneous adjustments in the elements of the marketing mix, but the results of these adjustments are uncertain because the marketing task takes place within an uncontrollable environment. Thus, as director of the firm's marketing activities, the marketing manager has an urgent need for information; marketing research is traditionally responsible for this intelligence function. Marketing research is the firm's formal communication link with the environment. It generates, transmits, and interprets feedback information originating in the environment relating to the success of the firm's marketing plans and the strategies employed in implementing those plans.

The communication link that marketing research serves is becoming increasingly critical and difficult as the world moves to a global economy. What works in one environment does not necessarily work in another. See Research Realities 1.1.

MARKETING RESEARCH ROLE

Marketing research can help the manager with each of the sectors in Figure 1.1. Table 1.1 summarizes the latest survey of marketing research activities conducted by the

---

[9]E. Jerome McCarthy and William D. Perreault, Jr., *Basic Marketing: A Managerial Approach,* 11th ed. (Homewood, Ill.: Richard D. Irwin, 1993).

FIGURE 1.1   **Task of Marketing Management**

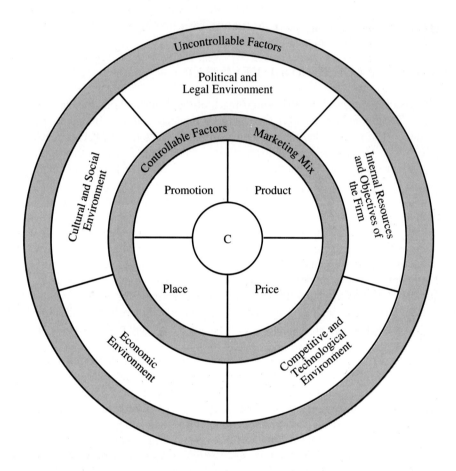

Source: Adapted from E. Jerome McCarthy and William D. Perreault, Jr., *Basic Marketing: A Managerial Approach,* 11th ed. (Homewood, Ill.: Richard D. Irwin, Inc., 1993), p. 57. Copyright 1993, adapted with permission.

American Marketing Association.[10] Although the table is organized around problem areas, the ties between the research activity descriptions and Figure 1.1 are evident. Much research is done to measure consumer wants and needs, for example, or to assess

---

[10] Thomas C. Kinnear and Ann R. Root, *1988 Survey of Marketing Research* (Chicago: American Marketing Association, 1988). This survey is the eighth in a series begun in 1947. This latest survey was sent to 2,401 marketing research executives, and the tabulation in Table 1.1 is based on the returns from the 587 usable questionnaires.

Research Realities 1.1

International Missteps Caused by Environmental Differences

Example An American manufacturer of cornflakes tried to introduce its product in Japan but failed miserably. Since the Japanese were not interested in the general concept of breakfast cereals, how could the manufacturer expect them to purchase cornflakes?

Example After learning that ketchup was not available in Japan, a U.S. company is reported to have shipped the Japanese a large quantity of its popular brand-name ketchup. Unfortunately, the firm did not first determine why ketchup was not already marketed in Japan. The large, affluent Japanese market was so tempting that the company feared any delay would permit its competition to spot the "opportunity" and capture the market. A marketing research study would have revealed the reason behind the lack of availability of ketchup: soy sauce is the preferred condiment in Japan.

Example Unilever was forced to withdraw temporarily from one of its foreign markets when it learned the hard way that the French were not interested in frozen foods.

Example CPC International met some resistance when it first tried to sell its dry Knorr soups in the United States. The company had test-marketed the product by serving passersby a small portion of its already prepared warm soup. After the taste test, the individuals were questioned about buying the product. The research revealed U.S. interest, but sales were very low once the packages were placed on grocery store shelves. Further investigation uncovered that the market tests had not taken into account the American tendency to avoid dry soups. During the testing, those individuals interviewed were unaware that they were tasting a dried soup. Finding the taste quite acceptable, the interviewees indicated they would be willing to buy the product. Had they known that the soup was sold in a dry form and that the preparation required 15 to 20 minutes of occasional stirring, they would have lost interest in the product. In this case, the soup's method of preparation was extremely important to the consumer, and the company's failure to test for this unique product difference resulted in an unpredicted sluggish market.

Example Warner encountered difficulties when it tried to sell a cinnamon-flavored FRESHEN-UP gum in Chile. Because the gum's taste was unacceptable there, the product fared poorly in the marketplace. Coca-Cola also had little success in marketing a product in Chile. When the company attempted to introduce a new grape-flavored drink, it soon discovered that the Chileans were not interested. Apparently, the Chileans prefer wine as their grape drink.

Example Chase and Sanborn met resistance when it tried to introduce its instant coffee in France. In the French home, the consumption of coffee plays a more significant role than in the English home. Since the preparation of "real" coffee is a ritual in the life of the French consumer, he or she will generally reject instant coffee because of its impromptu characteristics.

Source: David A Ricks, *Blunders in International Business* (Cambridge, Mass.: Blackwell Publishers, 1993), pp. 133–136.

---

the impact of past or contemplated adjustments in the marketing mix (the two inner rings of Figure 1.1). Some of the research, though, deals directly with the environment — for example, studies of legal constraints on advertising and promotion, social values and policy studies, and studies of business trends.

Another way to view the types of marketing intelligence that research provides is to assess the use to which management puts the information. Some marketing research is

TABLE **1.1**   **Research Activities of 587 Companies**

	Percentage Doing		Percentage Doing
A. Business/Economic and Corporate Research		**D. Distribution**	
1. Industry/market characteristics and trends	83%	1. Plant warehouse location studies	23%
2. Acquisition/diversification studies	53	2. Channel performance studies	29
3. Market share analyses	79	3. Channel coverage studies	26
4. Internal employee studies (morale, communication, etc.)	54	4. Export and international studies	19
B. Pricing		**E. Promotion**	
		1. Motivation research	37%
1. Cost analysis	60%	2. Media research	57
2. Profit analysis	59	3. Copy research	50
3. Price elasticity	45	4. Advertising effectiveness	65
4. Demand analysis:		5. Competitive advertising studies	47
a. Market potential	74		
b. Sales potential	69	6. Public image studies	60
c. Sales forecasts	67	7. Sales force compensation studies	30
5. Competitive pricing analyses	63	8. Sales force quota studies	26
		9. Sales force territory structure	31
C. Product		10. Studies of premiums, coupons, deals, etc.	36
1. Concept development and testing	68%		
2. Brand name generation and testing	38	**F. Buying Behavior**	
3. Test market	45	1. Brand preference	54%
4. Product testing of existing products	47	2. Brand attitudes	53
		3. Product satisfaction	68
5. Packaging design studies	31	4. Purchase behavior	61
6. Competitive product studies	58	5. Purchase intentions	60
		6. Brand awareness	59
		7. Segmentation studies	60

Source: Thomas C. Kinnear and Ann R. Root, *1988 Survey of Marketing Research*, 1988, p. 43. Reprinted with permission from 1988 Survey of Marketing Research, published by the American Marketing Association, Chicago, IL 60606.

used for planning, some for problem solving, and some for control. Marketing research, when used for planning, deals largely with marketing opportunities. The emphasis is on determining those opportunities that are viable and those that are not promising for the firm, as well as on providing estimates of the viable opportunities so that marketing management can better assess the resources needed to develop them. Problem-solving marketing research focuses on the short- or long-term decisions that the firm must make with respect to the elements of the marketing mix, while control-oriented marketing research helps management to isolate trouble spots and to keep abreast of current operations. The kinds of questions addressed by marketing research with regard to the planning, problem-solving, and control decision functions are listed in Table 1.2. The ties between the marketing manager's responsibilities and the typical questions dealt with by marketing research are again evident.

Firms operating in the international arena often use marketing research to get a perspective on what it is like to do business in specific countries. Some of the questions they might use marketing research to investigate are listed in Table 1.3.

TABLE 1.2 Kinds of Questions Marketing Research Can Help Answer

I. Planning
  A. What kinds of people buy our products? Where do they live? How much do they earn? How many of them are there?
  B. Are the markets for our products increasing or decreasing? Are there promising markets that we have not yet reached?
  C. Are the channels of distribution for our products changing? Are new types of marketing institutions likely to evolve?
II. Problem Solving
  A. Product
    1. Which of various product designs is likely to be the most successful?
    2. What kind of packaging should we use?
  B. Price
    1. What price should we charge for our products?
    2. As production costs decline, should we lower our prices or try to develop higher quality products?
  C. Place
    1. Where, and by whom, should our products be sold?
    2. What kinds of incentives should we offer the trade to push our products?
  D. Promotion
    1. How much should we spend on promotion? How should it be allocated to products and to geographic areas?
    2. What combination of media — newspapers, radio, television, magazines — should we use?
III. Control
  A. What is our market share overall? In each geographic area? By each customer type?
  B. Are customers satisfied with our products? How is our record for service? Are there many returns?
  C. How does the public perceive our company? What is our reputation with the trade?

TABLE 1.3   Questions about Foreign Markets That Marketing Research Might Be Used to Answer

- What is the nature of competition in the foreign market?
- Who are the major direct and indirect competitors?
- What are the major characteristics of the competition?
- What are the firm's competitive strengths and weaknesses in reference to such factors as product quality, product lines, warranties, services, brands, packaging, distribution, sales force, advertising, prices, experience, technology, capital and human resources, and market share?
- What attitudes do different governments (domestic and foreign) have toward foreign trade?
- Are there any foreign trade incentives and barriers?
- Is there any prejudice against imports or exports?
- What are different governments doing specifically to encourage or discourage international trade?
- What specific requirements — for example, import or export licenses — have to be met to conduct international trade?
- How difficult are certain government regulations for the firm?
- How well-developed are the foreign mass communication media?
- Are the print and electronics media abroad efficient and effective?
- Are there adequate transportation and storage or warehouse facilities in the foreign market?
- Does the foreign market offer efficient channels of distribution for the firm's products?
- What are the characteristics of the existing domestic and foreign distributors?
- How effectively can the distributors perform specific marketing functions?
- What is the state of the retailing institutions?

Source: Vinay Kothari, "Researching for Export Marketing," in Michael Czinkota, ed., *Export Promotion: The Public and Private Sector Interaction* (New York: Praeger Publishers, 1983), pp. 169–172.

DEFINITION OF MARKETING RESEARCH

The American Marketing Association defines **marketing research** as the

> function which links the consumer, customer, and public to the marketer through information — information used to identify and define marketing opportunities and problems; generate, refine, and evaluate marketing actions; monitor marketing performance; and improve understanding of marketing as a process. Marketing research specifies the information required to address these issues; designs the method for collecting information; manages and implements the data collection process; analyzes the results; and communicates the findings and their implications.[11]

There are several important elements in the definition. First, the definition is broad. Marketing research deals with all phases of the marketing of either goods or services. It

---

[11]Peter D. Bennett, ed., *Dictionary of Marketing Terms* (Chicago: American Marketing Association, 1988), pp. 117–118.

involves the application of research techniques to the solution of marketing problems of any sort, be they planning, problem-solving, or control issues. The fundamental requirement is that they involve marketing questions. Note that the definition encompasses more than simply the application of research techniques to applied marketing problems. It also involves understanding marketing as a process. Finally, the definition indicates that marketing research is not simply collecting data specified by someone else. Rather, in addition to its role in the actual collection of the data and their analysis, marketing research plays an important role in determining the information that is needed to address specific issues as well as the implications of what the collected information suggests.

WHO DOES MARKETING RESEARCH?

Marketing research, as a significant business activity, owes its existence to the shift from a production-oriented to a consumption-oriented economy that occurred in this country at the end of World War II. However, some marketing research was conducted before the war, and the origins of formal marketing research predate the war by a good number of years.

> More by accident than foresight, N. W. Ayer & Son applied marketing research to marketing and advertising problems. In 1879, in attempting to fit a proposed advertising schedule to the needs of the Nichols-Shepard Company, manufacturers of agricultural machinery, the agency wired state officials and publishers throughout the country requesting information on expected grain production. As a result, the agency was able to construct a crude but formal market survey by states and counties. This attempt to construct a market survey is probably the first real instance of marketing research in the United States.[12]

There were even formal marketing research departments and marketing research firms before World War II.[13] However, marketing research really began to grow when firms found they could no longer sell all they could produce but rather had to gauge market needs and produce accordingly. Marketing research was called upon to estimate these needs. As consumer discretion became more important, there was a concurrent shift in the orientation of many firms. Marketing began to assume a more dominant role and production a less important one. The marketing concept emerged and along with it a reorganization of the marketing effort. Many marketing research departments were born in these reorganizations. The growth of these departments was stimulated by a number

---

[12]From Lawrence C. Lockley, "History and Development of Marketing Research," p. 1–4, in Robert Ferber, ed., *Handbook of Marketing Research.* Copyright © 1974 by McGraw-Hill, 1974. Used with permission of McGraw-Hill Book Company.

[13]The Curtis Publishing Company is generally conceded to have formed the first formal marketing research department with the appointment of Charles Parlin as manager of the Commercial Research Division of the Advertising Department in 1911. The A. C. Nielsen Company, the largest marketing research firm in the world, began operation in 1934. For a detailed treatment of the development of marketing research, see Robert Bartels, *The Development of Marketing Thought* (Homewood, Ill.: Richard D. Irwin, 1962), pp. 106–124, or Jack J. Honomichl, *Marketing Research People: Their Behind-the-Scenes Stories* (Chicago: Crain Books, 1984), especially Part II on pages 95–184, which deals with the evolution and status of the marketing research industry.

of factors, including past successes, increased management sophistication, and the data revolution created by the computer. The success of firms with marketing research departments caused still other firms to establish departments.

The growth in the formation of new marketing research departments has abated somewhat recently. Yet the firm that does not have a formal department, or at least a person assigned specifically to the marketing research activity, is now the exception rather than the rule (see Figure 1.2). Marketing research departments are prevalent among industrial and consumer manufacturing companies, but they also exist in other types of companies. Publishers and broadcasters, for example, do a good deal of research. Most of this research involves the generation of market coverage statistics to measure the size of the audience reached by the message and to provide a demographic

FIGURE 1.2   Organization for Marketing Research

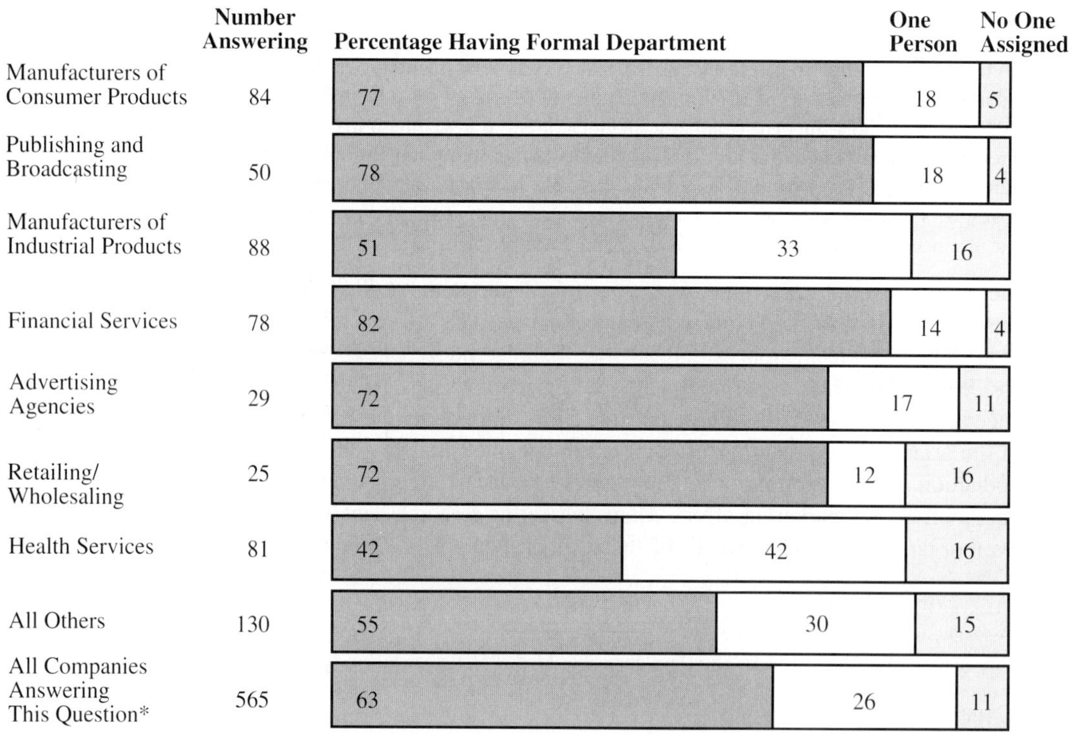

	Number Answering	Percentage Having Formal Department	One Person	No One Assigned
Manufacturers of Consumer Products	84	77	18	5
Publishing and Broadcasting	50	78	18	4
Manufacturers of Industrial Products	88	51	33	16
Financial Services	78	82	14	4
Advertising Agencies	29	72	17	11
Retailing/ Wholesaling	25	72	12	16
Health Services	81	42	42	16
All Others	130	55	30	15
All Companies Answering This Question*	565	63	26	11

*Excludes marketing research and consulting firms.

Source: Thomas C. Kinnear and Ann R. Root, *1988 Survey of Marketing Research* (Chicago: American Marketing Association, 1988), p. 10.

profile of this audience. These data are then used by the communication medium to sell advertising space or time.

Financial service companies also use marketing research. Much of the research done by these departments involves forecasting, measurement of market potentials, determination of market characteristics, market share analyses, sales analyses, location analyses, and product mix studies.[14]

Many advertising agencies have formal research departments. Much of the research conducted by these agencies deals directly with the advertising function, involving such things as studying the effectiveness of alternative copy or alternative advertisements. However, many of the agencies also do marketing research for their clients — for example, measuring the market potential of a product or the client firm's market share.

The enterprises included in the "all others" category shown in Figure 1.2 include public utilities, transportation companies, and trade associations, among others. Public utilities and transportation companies often provide their customers with useful marketing information, particularly statistics dealing with area growth and potential. Trade associations often collect and disseminate operating data gathered from members.

The entire spectrum of marketing research activity also includes specialized marketing research and consulting firms, government agencies, and universities. Whereas most specialized research firms are small, a few are large. Research Realities 1.2 offers a brief description of the activities of the world's ten largest marketing research firms and depicts their revenues as well as the proportion of revenues generated outside the United States. Some firms provide syndicated research; they collect certain information on a regular basis, which they then sell to interested clients. The syndicated services include such operations as A. C. Nielsen, which provides product movement data for grocery stores and drug stores, and the NPD, which operates a consumer panel. The syndicated services are distinguished by the fact that their research is not custom designed, except in the limited sense that the firm will perform special analyses for the client from the data it regularly collects. Other research firms, though, specialize in custom-designed research. Some of these provide only a field service; they collect data and return the data-collection instruments directly to the research sponsor. Some are limited-service firms that not only collect the data but also analyze them for the client. And some are full-service research suppliers that help the client in the design of the research as well as in collecting and analyzing data.

Government agencies provide much marketing information in the form of published statistics. As a matter of fact, the federal government is the largest producer of marketing facts through its various censuses and other publications.[15]

Much university-sponsored research of interest to marketers is produced by the marketing faculty or by the bureaus of business research found in many schools of business.

---

[14]Thomas C. Kinnear and Ann R. Root, *1988 Survey of Marketing Research* (Chicago: American Marketing Association, 1988).

[15]Some government publications containing useful marketing information are reviewed in the appendix to Chapter 6.

Research Realities 1.2

The World's Ten Largest Marketing Research Firms

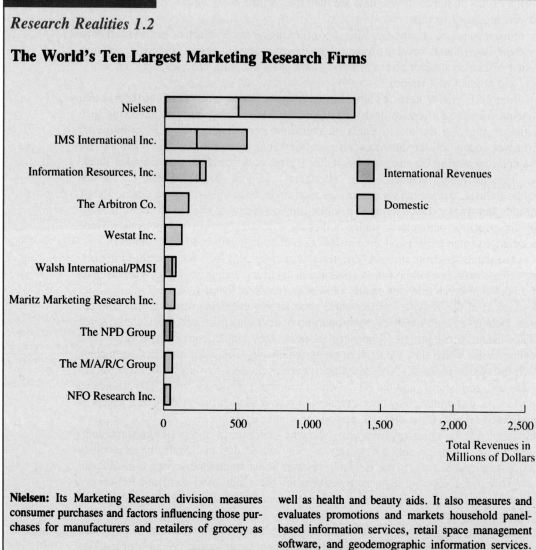

Source: Developed from Jack Honomichl, "1993 Honomichl Business Report on the Marketing Research Industry," *Marketing News*, 27 (June 7, 1993), pp. H1–H10.

Nielsen: Its Marketing Research division measures consumer purchases and factors influencing those purchases for manufacturers and retailers of grocery as well as health and beauty aids. It also measures and evaluates promotions and markets household panel-based information services, retail space management software, and geodemographic information services. Its media research division measures television viewing and prepares the Nielsen TV ratings.

IMS International Inc.: Specializing in the pharmaceutical industry, IMS measures consumption of pharmaceutical and other health-care products, evaluates physicians' prescription patterns, and provides services that help pharmaceutical marketers target the efforts of their sales forces and promotional materials.

Information Resources, Inc.: Operates InfoScan, a syndicated market tracking service based on a sample of grocery, drug, and mass merchandiser stores, where product movement data are captured via UPC scanning. Also operates BehaviorScan, a group of eight so-called "single-source" mini-markets, where in addition to measuring product movement, IRI has the ability to target TV commercials to specific households in a controlled environment.

The Arbitron Co.: Arbitron develops syndicated local market radio and TV audience measurements and advertising expenditure information. It also markets a line of proprietary software systems for PC use at local TV and radio stations for analytical processing of audience data.

Westat Inc.: Westat does large-scale survey research projects for agencies of the federal government using its own telephone interviewing, field interviewing, and data editing staffs to execute the studies.

Walsh International/PMSI: Walsh/PMSI concentrates on research and promotional services to the pharmaceutical/health-care industry through a variety of syndicated services. Its Alpha Rx Data Service accesses a network of 25,000 pharmacy computer terminals to build a data base that now has over 1.6 billion prescriptions by doctor and by product. Another service, SOURCE Territory Manager, provides prescription data by zip code, while PRO Monitor is a menu-driven system to analyze promotion efforts.

Maritz Marketing Research Inc.: One MMRI group specializes in providing general marketing research and customer satisfaction measurement. Another group provides syndicated, custom, and large-scale customer satisfaction studies for the auto industry. Its services include product clinics, consumer and dealer research, and Quality Function Deployment/Voice of the Consumer studies.

The NPD Group: The NPD Group is organized into several business units. Its syndicated services unit provides tracking data bases covering store movement, consumer purchasing, and consumer attitude/awareness to industries such as toys, apparel, textiles, sporting goods, athletic footwear, petroleum products, home electronics, and cameras, among others. Its customer services unit operates a household panel for pretest marketing, new product simulations, and custom tracking.

The M/A/R/C Group: The Marketing and Research Counselors unit of M/A/R/C engages in custom marketing research and also offers market simulation and modeling services. Its Quality Strategies unit specializes in customer satisfaction measurement programs, while its Targetbase Marketing unit creates targeted data base and related marketing programs.

NFO Research Inc.: NFO maintains the largest consumer panel in the United States with over 425,000 households (over 1 million individuals). Panel households are categorized by demographics and product ownership, allowing for mail and/or telephone surveys of target groups. NFO's National Yellow Pages Monitor division is the leading provider of syndicated yellow pages audience measurement services.

Faculty research is often reported in marketing journals, whereas research bureaus often publish monographs on various topics of interest.

ORGANIZATION OF MARKETING RESEARCH

The marketing research function has no single form of organization. Rather, organizational form depends very much on the size and organizational structure of the company itself. Small firms are much less likely to have a research department, and it is much more likely to be a one-person operation than a full department when they do have one. In these cases, of course, there are few organizational questions other than determining to whom the research director shall report. Most often this will be the sales or marketing manager, although some marketing research managers report directly to the president or the executive vice-president.

Larger research units present more organizational problems. Again, there appears to be no general form of organization, although three types are common:

1. by area of application, such as by product line, brand, market segment, or geographic area;
2. by marketing function performed, such as field sales analysis, advertising research, or product planning; and
3. by research technique or approach, such as sales analysis, mathematical and/or statistical analysis, field interviewing, or questionnaire design.

Many firms with very large marketing research departments combine these "pure" organizational structures still further into a hybrid approach.

The organizational structure of the firm itself — particularly whether it is centralized or decentralized — also affects the organization of the marketing research function. With decentralized companies, the fundamental question is whether each division or operating unit should have its own marketing research department, whether a single department in central headquarters should serve all operating divisions, or whether there should be research departments at both levels. The primary advantages of a corporate-level location are greater coordination and control of corporate research activity, economy, increased capability from an information system perspective, and greater usefulness to corporate management in planning. The primary advantage of a division or group-level location is that it allows research personnel to acquire valuable knowledge about divisional markets, products, practices, and problems. Even though shifting between the corporate and divisional structures occurs quite frequently, the recent trend is toward a mixed arrangement in an attempt to secure the advantages of each.

For example, Kodak has a combination centralized/decentralized marketing research function. The people in the divisions work directly with managers of those business units. The centralized group is responsible for staying abreast of industry trends and changing technology, because changes here could affect numerous business units. Researchers assigned to corporate marketing research are also responsible for competitive analysis to ensure the most objective view. Finally, the centralized group serves as a quality control center for the research activity. Division-initiated projects are passed before this group for possible changes in method. One benefit of this review is that it provides better ways to approach specific tasks. Kraft also uses a hybrid organization structure. It assigns research groups to each customer group (e.g., grocery, refrigerated products, frozen products, and food service), and it has a corporate group of researchers as well. Some of the advantages Kraft realizes from the centralized group are the consistent application of research methods, opportunities to share key information across departments and customer bases, the potential to minimize duplication in spending of research funds, and an improved ability to produce actionable, cost-effective research across all of the firm's customer bases.[16]

The Japanese are more likely to view research as a "line" function performed by all involved in the decision process rather than as a "staff" function performed by professional marketing researchers. Those involved in the decision team might play a role in gathering and interpreting information. For example, in developing its "Pro Mavica" professional still-video system, which, unlike conventional 35mm still cameras, records images on a two-inch square floppy disk, Sony did extensive marketing research. This research involved a mail survey, personal and telephone interviews, and on-site tests to elicit user response to the product during its development. A unique aspect was that the Pro Mavica task force included both engineers and sales/marketing representatives from Sony's medical systems and broadcast units. In addition to working with their marketing peers, Sony's engineers gained insights from talking with prospects; they then incorporated user comments into product modifications.[17]

The most appropriate summary comment about the organization of the marketing research function is that this organization might be expected to be dynamic and ever-changing. It will depend on the relative importance of the marketing research function within the firm, on the scale and complexity of the research activities to be undertaken, and on the firm's philosophy as to how marketing research should interface with the firm's decision making. The data indicate that large firms, for example, are likely to spend a larger proportion of the marketing budget on research than are small firms. Among firms with sales of $25 million and over, approximately 3½ percent of the average marketing budget is spent on research, whereas among smaller firms, only about 1½ percent of the average marketing budget is spent on research.[18] As Figure 1.3 indicates, a few firms spend a very large proportion of their total marketing budget on research. As the firm's size and market position change, the emphasis and organization of the marketing research function must also change so that it is continually tailored to suit the firm's information needs.

One important change that has been occurring in marketing research in recent years is the transition from a specific problem perspective to a total marketing intelligence perspective. This perspective is usually called a **marketing information system (MIS)**

[16]Larry Stanek, "Keeping Focused on the Consumer While Managing Tons of Information," *Presentations from the 9th Annual Marketing Research Conference* (Chicago: American Marketing Association, 1988), pp. 62–70.

[17]Michael Czinkota and Masaaki Kotabe, "Product Development the Japanese Way," *The Journal of Business Strategy,* 11 (November/December 1990), p. 36.

[18]A. Parasuraman, "Research's Place in the Marketing Budget," *Business Horizons,* 26 (March–April 1983), pp. 25–29.

Figure 1.3   Share of Marketing Budgets Allocated to Research

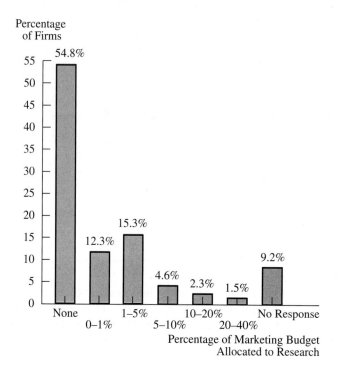

Source: Developed from data in A. Parasuraman, ''Research's Place in the Marketing Budget,'' *Business Horizons,* 26 (March–April 1983), pp. 25–29.

or **decision support system (DSS)**.[19] The emphasis in such systems is on diagnosing the information needs of each of the marketing decision makers so that these people have the kinds of information they need, when they need it, to make the kinds of decisions they must make.

An important impetus behind this change is the literal explosion in information that is available to aid in making business decisions. This information explosion is

[19]Information systems can be discussed at both the functional and corporate levels. When discussing corporate information systems, MIS stands for *management* information system, and it is understood that DSS refers to the structure of the decision support system for the whole company. Since our interest is marketing intelligence, we will use the term MIS to refer to the *marketing* information system and DSS to refer to the structure of the information system to support marketing decision making. Some writers use MRIS to distinguish the marketing information system from MIS, the management information system.

due in part to technology and in part to the increasing complexity of the world's economic system. For example, it has been estimated that the typical firm selling its products through supermarkets needed 0.5 gigabytes of memory (1 gigabyte equals 1,000,000,000 bytes) to manage its marketing data bases in 1985 when its main source of product movement information was retail audits. By 1989, with scanning data, it needed 3.5 gigabytes and by 1991, 38.0 gigabytes, almost 100 times as much.[20] We shall have more to say on marketing intelligence systems in the next chapter.

JOB OPPORTUNITIES IN MARKETING RESEARCH

It is hard to generalize about the kinds of tasks a marketing researcher might perform. As previously suggested, the tasks will depend on the type, size, organizational structure, and philosophy of the firm with which the individual is employed. They will also depend on whether the person works for a research supplier or for a consumer of research information. The responsibilities of a marketing researcher could range from the simple tabulation of questionnaire responses to the management of a large research department. Research Realities 1.3 lists some common job titles and the functions typically performed by occupants of these positions. Figure 1.4 on page 21 illustrates what these people are likely to be paid and how that compares with salaries of those in similar positions in 1983.

As you can tell from these job descriptions, there are opportunities in marketing research for people with a variety of skills. One could find a career as a technical specialist, such as a statistician, or as a research generalist managing others, such as a research director. The skills required to perform each job satisfactorily will, of course, vary.

The typical entry-level position in consumer goods companies is analyst, most usually for a specific brand. While learning the characteristics and details of the industry, the analyst will receive on-the-job training from a research manager. The usual progression of responsibilities is to senior analyst, research supervisor, and research manager for a specific brand, after which time the researcher's responsibilities broaden to include a group of brands.

The typical entry-level position among research suppliers is that of research trainee, a position in which the person will be exposed to the types of studies in which the supplier specializes and procedures that are followed in completing them. Quite often, trainees will spend some time actually conducting interviews, coding completed data collection forms, or possibly even assisting with the analysis. The idea is to expose trainees to the processes that are followed in the firm so that when they become account representatives, they will be sufficiently familiar with the firm's capabilities to be able to

---

[20]David Sharp, "The Evolving Dialogue With the Global Customer," paper presented at the Marketing Science Institute's conference on "The Changing World of Marketing," Boston, October 24–25, 1991. Retail audits and scanners are discussed in Chapter 6.

Research Realities 1.3

Marketing Research Job Titles and Responsibilities

1. **Research Director/Vice-President of Marketing Research:** This is the senior position in research. The director is responsible for the entire research program of the company. Accepts assignments from superiors or from clients or may, on own initiative, develop and propose research undertakings to company executives. Employs personnel and exercises general supervision of research department. Presents research findings to clients or to company executives.

2. **Assistant Director of Research:** This position usually represents a defined "second in command," a senior staff member having responsibilities above those of other staff members.

3. **Statistician/Data Processing Specialist:** Duties are usually those of an expert consultant on theory and application of statistical technique to specific research problems. Usually responsible for experimental design and data processing.

4. **Senior Analyst:** Usually found in larger research departments. Participates with superior in initial planning of research projects and directs execution of projects assigned. Operates with minimum supervision. Prepares or works with analysts in preparing questionnaires. Selects research techniques, makes analyses, and writes final report. Budgetary control over projects and primary responsibility for meeting time schedules rest with the senior analyst.

5. **Analyst:** The analyst usually handles the bulk of the work required for execution of research projects. Often works under senior analyst's supervision. The analyst assists in preparation of questionnaires, pretests them, and makes preliminary analyses of results. Most library research or work with company data is handled by the analyst.

6. **Junior Analyst:** Working under rather close supervision, junior analysts handle routine assignments. Editing and coding of questionnaires, statistical calculations above the clerical level, and simpler forms of library research are among the duties. A large portion of the junior analyst's time is spent on tasks assigned by superiors.

7. **Librarians:** The librarian builds and maintains a library of reference sources adequate to the needs of the research department.

8. **Clerical Supervisor:** In larger departments, the central handling and processing of statistical data are the responsibility of one or more clerical supervisors. Duties include work scheduling and responsibility for accuracy.

9. **Field Work Director:** Usually only larger departments have a field work director, who hires, trains, and supervises field interviewers.

10. **Full-Time Interviewer:** The interviewer conducts personal interviews and works under direct supervision of the field work director. Few companies employ full-time interviewers.

11. **Tabulating and Clerical Help:** The routine, day-to-day work of the department is performed by these individuals.

Source: Thomas C. Kinnear and Ann R. Root, *1988 Survey of Marketing Research*, p. 4 of the Appendix. Reprinted with permission from *1988 Survey of Marketing Research*, published by the American Marketing Association, Chicago, IL 60606.

develop intelligent responses, perhaps in the form of formal quotations, to client needs for research information.

In order to enter marketing research, an individual needs human relations, communication, conceptual, and analytical skills. Marketing researchers must be able to interact effectively with others, for they rarely, if ever, work in isolation. They should be able to communicate well both orally and with the written word. If researchers can't communicate the results and discuss what the results mean, it makes little difference what they

FIGURE 1.4   **Mean Compensation for All Marketing Research Positions**

Position	Number of Positions		Compared with 1983 Mean ($000)	Percent Change
Directors	314	$61,300	51.0	+20%
Assistant Directors	58	$50,700	44.7	+13
Senior Analysts	185	$40,300	34.0	+19
Statisticians	56	$45,400	30.7	+48
Analysts	175	$31,100	25.1	+24
Field Work Directors	10	$32,300	23.5	+37
Librarians	25	$31,200	20.8	+33
Junior Analysts	94	$24,900	18.8	+32
Clerical Supervisors	19	$22,600	16.8	+35
Full-Time Interviewers	8	$17,000	13.1	+30
Tabulating and Clerical Help	124	$19,700	14.0	+41
Total Number of Positions	1,068			

Source: Thomas C. Kinnear and Ann R. Root, *1988 Survey of Marketing Research* (Chicago: American Marketing Association, 1988), p. 62.

know or how good the research is.[21] They need to understand business in general and marketing processes in particular.[22] When dealing with brand, advertising, sales, or other managers, they must understand the issues with which these managers contend and the types of mental models they use to make sense of the situations. Marketing researchers

---

[21]Jack Honomichl, ''CEOs Perceive a Shortage of People Worth Hiring,'' *Marketing News,* 26 (October 12, 1992), p. 11.

[22]Mary Brownell, ''Surveying the Changing Research Environment and Its Effect on Us,'' *Journal of Advertising Research,* 29 (October/November 1989), pp. RC-3 to RC-10.

also should have some basic numerical and statistical skills, or at least they should be capable of developing those skills. They must be comfortable with numbers and with the techniques of marketing research. Their growth as professionals and their advancement within their organization will depend on their use of these skills and their acquisition of other technical, management, and financial skills.

The American Marketing Association's skills matrix for marketing researchers, which is used to structure its professional development program, provides a useful overview of the set of technical skills needed for a career in marketing research (see Table 1.4). As the matrix indicates, general managerial and financial skills become more important as researchers move up in the research department.

TABLE 1.4   Skills Needed by Marketing Researchers

	Entry/Junior Level (Less than 3 years experience)	Mid-Level (3–7 years experience)	Senior Level (More than 7 years experience)
Technical Skills			
Computer literacy	*	*	*
Numerical skills	*	*	*
Sample design	*	*	*
Statistical analysis	*	*	*
Data base management		*	*
Model building		*	*
Project management		*	*
Research knowledge		*	*
System design		*	*
Marketing processes			*
Project conceptualization			*
Managerial Skills			
Communicating	*	*	*
Statistical analysis	*	*	*
Reporting	*	*	*
Coordinating projects	*	*	*
Coordinating people		*	*
Motivating		*	*
Defining tasks		*	*
Training/development		*	*
Planning/strategy			*
Financial administration			*

Source: *The American Marketing Association's Professional Development Program* (Chicago: American Marketing Association, 1988), p. 9.

An increasingly common career path for those working in divisional structures is a switch from the research department to product or brand management. One advantage these people possess is that after working intimately with marketing intelligence, they often know as much or more about customers, the industry, and the competitors as anyone in the company with the same amount of experience. Researchers desiring this switch need more substantive knowledge about marketing phenomena and greater business acumen in general than those planning on staying in marketing research, although all researchers need a good foundation of business and marketing knowledge if they are going to succeed.

Successful marketing researchers tend to be proactive rather than reactive; that is, they identify and lead the direction in which the individual studies and overall programs go rather than simply responding to explicit requests for information. Successful marketing researchers realize that marketing research is conducted for only one reason — to help make better marketing decisions. Thus, they are comfortable making recommendations to others rather than having responsibility for the decisions themselves.

SUMMARY

This chapter presented an overview of marketing research's nature, its usefulness in marketing decision making, the extent to which it is currently being used and by what types of companies, and the organization of the research function. By definition, marketing research is the function that links the consumer, customer, and public to the marketer through information, which is used to identify and define marketing opportunities and problems; generate, refine, and evaluate marketing actions; monitor marketing performance; and improve understanding of marketing as a process.

Marketing research is indeed a pervasive activity. Marketing research departments exist in most larger firms and among most types of companies. Marketing research has been employed, at least by some companies, in each of the domains of the marketing manager's responsibility.

No one form of organization dominates the marketing research function. Rather, the research activity is typically organized to reflect the specific firm's unique needs. Two factors that bear heavily on this organization are the firm's size and the degree of centralization/decentralization of its operations.

Job opportunities in marketing research are good and are getting better. Although there is variety in the positions available and in the skills needed for them, most positions require analytical, communication, and human-relations skills. Marketing researchers must be comfortable working with numbers and statistical techniques and must be familiar with a great variety of marketing research methods and techniques.

Questions

1. What is marketing management's task? What is marketing research's task? Is there any relation between the two tasks?

2. How is marketing research defined? What are the key elements of this definition?

3. Who does marketing research? What are the primary kinds of research done by each enterprise?

4. How would you explain the fact that production research started in the 1860s but that marketing research did not develop formally until the 1910s and did not experience real growth until after World War II?

5. What factors influence the internal organization of the marketing research department and its reporting location within the company?

6. In a large research department, who would be responsible for specifying the objective of a research project? For deciding on specific procedures to be followed? For designing the questionnaire? For analyzing the results? For reporting the results to top management?

7. What are the necessary skills for employment in a junior or entry-level marketing research position? Do the skills change as one changes job levels? If so, what new skills are necessary at these higher levels?

Applications and Problems

1. Discuss whether or not marketing research would be valuable for the organizations that follow. If you believe that marketing research would be valuable, describe in detail how it would be used to aid in decision making.
   a. A bank
   b. A multinational oil company
   c. A retail shoe store with only one outlet
   d. A Mercedes dealership in Lafayette, LA
   e. A candidate for the U.S. Congress, representing a district in Chicago, IL
   f. The Los Angeles Lakers
   g. A distributor of large-screen televisions, operating in Mexico City
   h. The English Department at your university
   i. A wheat farmer in Nebraska with 850 acres

2. What do the two following research situations have in common?

   Situation I: The SprayIt Company marketed a successful insect repellent. The product was effective and a leader in the market. The product was available in blue aerosol cans with red caps. The instructions were clearly specified on the container in addition to a warning to keep the product away from children. Most of the company's range of products were also produced by competitors in similar containers. The chief executive officer (CEO) was worried because of declining sales and shrinking profit margins. Another issue that perturbed him was that companies such as his were being severely criticized by government and consumer groups for their use of aerosol cans. The CEO contacted the company's advertising agency and asked it to do the necessary research to find out what was happening.

   Situation II: In April of this year, the directors of University Z were considering expanding the business school because of increasing enrollment during the past ten years. Their plans included constructing a new wing, hiring five new faculty members, and increasing the number of scholarships from 100 to 120. The funding for this ambitious project was to be provided by private sources, internally generated funds, and the state and federal governments. A previous research study completed five years earlier, using a sophisticated forecasting method, indicated that student enrollment would have peaked last year. Another study, conducted three years ago, indicated that universities could expect gradual declining enrollments during the next ten years. The directors were concerned about the results of the later study and the talk it stimulated about budget cuts by the state and federal governments. A decision to conduct a third and final study was made to determine likely student enrollment.

3. What do the two following research situations have in common?

   Situation I: The sales manager of CanAl, an aluminum can manufacturing company, was wondering whether the company's new cans, which would be on the market in two months, should be priced higher than the traditional products. He confidently commented to the vice-president of marketing, "Nobody in the market is selling aluminum cans with screw-on tops; we can get a small portion of the market and yet make substantial profits." The product manager disagreed with this strategy. In fact, she was opposed to marketing these new cans. The cans might present problems in preserving the contents. She thought, "Aluminum cans are recycled, so nobody is going to keep them as containers." There was little she could do formally because these cans were the president's own idea. She strongly recommended to the vice-president that the cans should be priced in line with the other products. The vice-president thought a marketing research study would resolve this issue.

   Situation II: A large toy manufacturer was in the process of developing a tool kit for children in the 5–10 year age group. The tool kit included a small saw, screwdriver, hammer, chisel, and drill. This tool kit was different from the competitors' as it included an instruction manual, "101 Things to Do." The product manager was concerned about the safety of the kit and recommended the inclusion of a separate booklet for parents. The sales manager recommended that the tool kit be made available in a small case, as this would increase its marketability. The advertising manager recommended a special promotional campaign be launched to distinguish this tool kit from the competitors'. The vice-president thought that all the recommendations were worthwhile but the costs would increase drastically. He consulted the marketing research manager, who further recommended that a study be conducted.

4. Evaluate the research in the following example.

   The HiFlyer Airline company was interested in altering the interior layout of its aircraft to suit the tastes and needs of an increasing segment of its market — business people. Management was planning to reduce the number of seats and install small tables to enable business people to work during long flights. Prior to the renovation, management decided to do some research to ensure that these changes would suit the needs of the passengers. To keep expenses to a minimum, the following strategy was employed.

   The questionnaires were completed by passengers during a flight. Due to the ease of administration and collection, the questionnaires were distributed only on the short flights (those less than one hour). The study was conducted during the second and third weeks of December, as that was when flights were full. To increase the response rate, each flight attendant was responsible for a certain number of questionnaires. The management thought this was a good time to acquire as much information as possible; hence, the questionnaire included issues apart from the new seating arrangement. As a result, the questionnaire took 20 minutes to complete. After the study, management decided that the study would not be repeated, as the information was insightful enough.

5. Specify some useful sources of marketing research information for the following situation:

   Dissatisfied with the availability of ingredients for his favorite dishes, Albert Lai would like to open his own retail ethnic grocery store. Based on the difficulty of finding many specialty ingredients, Albert realizes the need for a local wholesale distributor specializing in hard-to-find ethnic foodstuffs. He envisions carrying items commonly used in Asian and Middle-Eastern recipes.

With the help of a local accountant, Lai prepared a financial proposal that revealed the need for $150,000 in start-up capital for Lai's Asian Foods. The proposal was presented to a local bank for review by their commercial loan committee, and Lai subsequently received the following letter from the bank:

> Mr. Lai:
>
> We have received and considered your request for start-up financing for your proposed business. While the basic idea is sound, we find that your sales projections are based solely on your own experience and do not include any hard documentation concerning the market potential for the products you propose to carry. Until such information is made available for our consideration, we have no choice but to reject your loan application.

Albert does not wish to give up on his business idea because he truly believes that there is a market for these ethnic food products. Given his extremely limited financial resources, where and how might he obtain the needed information? (Hint: First determine what types of information might be useful.)

6. Suppose that you have decided to pursue a career in the field of marketing research. In general, what types of courses should you take in order to help achieve your goal? Why? What types of part-time jobs, internships, and/or volunteer work would look good on your resume? Why?

 Thorndike Sports Equipment Video Case

1. If you were interviewing for a position as a research analyst with Thorndike Sports Equipment, what company research would you do to prepare for the meeting with Thorndike's president?

2. Would Joyce Hernandez's position be described as marketing research? Explain.

3. Imagine that Luke, the president of Thorndike Sports, is boasting to you that the company is customer-driven because of the existence of an 800 telephone number. How would you respond to this statement?

4. What changes to the customer service department are necessary to make it an integral part of the research department?

ALTERNATIVE APPROACHES TO MARKETING INTELLIGENCE

It was suggested in the last chapter that the fundamental purpose of marketing research is to help marketing managers make decisions they face each day in their various areas of responsibility. As directors of their firms' marketing activities, marketing managers have an urgent need for information or marketing intelligence. They might need to know about the changes that could be expected in customer purchasing patterns, the types of marketing intermediaries that might evolve, which of several alternative product designs might be the most successful, the shape of the firm's demand curve, or any of a number of other issues that could affect the way they plan, solve problems, or evaluate and control the marketing effort. We suggested that marketing research is traditionally responsible for this intelligence function. As the formal link with the environment, marketing research generates, transmits, and interprets feedback regarding the success of the firm's marketing plans and the strategies and tactics employed to implement those plans.

This book views providing marketing intelligence from a project perspective. The project view discusses the steps that need to be taken to solve a specific problem faced by a marketing manager. The next chapter overviews these steps, and the remainder of the book discusses each one in detail. It should be pointed out beforehand, though, that the project emphasis to research is just one way of providing marketing intelligence. Two other ways are through marketing information systems (MISs) and decision support systems (DSSs). This chapter provides some appreciation for the differences between the project emphasis to research highlighted throughout this book and these alternative schemes. First, the philosophical difference between a project emphasis and the alternative approaches is explained. The next sections discuss the essential nature of marketing information systems and decision support systems. These discussions culminate in a discussion of the complementary roles of projects and information systems in providing marketing intelligence.

FUNDAMENTAL DIFFERENCE

The difference in perspective between a project emphasis to research and an emphasis on information systems was highlighted years ago in a useful analogy that compares a flash bulb and a candle.

> The difference between marketing research and marketing intelligence is like the difference between a flash bulb and a candle. Let's say you are dancing in the dark. Every 90 seconds you are allowed to set off a flash bulb. You can use those brief intervals of intense light to chart a course, but remember everybody is moving, too. Hopefully, they'll accommodate themselves roughly to your predictions. You might get bumped and you may stumble every so often, but you can dance along.
>
> On the other hand, you can light a candle. It doesn't yield as much light but it's a steady light. You are continually aware of the movements of other bodies. You can adjust your own course to the courses of others. The intelligence system is a kind of candle. It's no great flash on the immediate state of things, but it provides continuous light as situations shift and change.[1]

Historically, one of the problems of the research project emphasis has been its nonrecurring nature. A project is often devised in times of crisis and carried out with urgency, and this has led to an emphasis on data collection and analysis instead of the development of pertinent information on a regular basis. One suggestion for closing the gap is to think of management in terms of an ongoing process of decision making that requires a flow of regular input rather than in terms of crisis situations. Both MIS and DSS represent ongoing efforts over the last few decades to provide pertinent decision-making information to marketing managers on a regular basis.

MARKETING INFORMATION SYSTEMS

The earliest attempts at providing a steady flow of information inputs (i.e., candlelight) focused on the **marketing information system (MIS)**, which was defined as "a set of procedures and methods for the regular, planned collection, analysis, and presentation of information for use in making marketing decisions."[2] The key word in the definition is "regular," since the emphasis in MIS is the establishment of systems that produce

---

[1]Statement by Robert J. Williams, who was the creator of the first recognized marketing information system at the Mead Johnson division of the Edward Dalton Company. "Marketing Intelligence Systems: A DEW Line for Marketing Men," *Business Management* (January 1966), p. 32.

[2]Donald F. Cox and Robert E. Good, "How to Build a Marketing Information System," *Harvard Business Review,* 45 (May–June 1967), pp. 145–154. See also Keith Fletcher, Alan Buttery, and Ken Deans, "The Structure and Content of the Marketing Information System: A Guide for Management," *Marketing Intelligence and Planning,* 6 (No. 4, 1988), pp. 27–35; Allan Potter and Richard Laska, *The EIS Book: Information Systems for Top Managers* (Homewood, Ill.: Dow-Jones Irwin, 1990).

information needed for decision making on a recurring basis rather than for one-time research studies.

In designing marketing information systems, the thrust is a detailed analysis of each decision maker who might use the system in order to secure an accurate, objective assessment of each manager's decision-making responsibilities, capabilities, and style. The types of decisions each decision maker is called on to make and the types of information each person needs to make those decisions are determined. MIS analysis looks at the types of information the individual receives regularly and the special studies that are periodically needed. It considers the improvements decision makers would like to see in the current information system, not only in the types of information they receive but also in the form in which they receive it.

Given these information specifications, designers then attempt to specify, get approval for, and subsequently generate a series of reports that go to the various decision makers.[3] Research Realities 2.1, for example, shows the types of sales analysis, sales expense, and margin reports that were developed for a sales information system for a consumer food products company while the author was serving as a consultant. This Research Reality indicates that the purpose and form of each report typically meant designing it so that it might serve a number of managers with similar job titles. System support people spent a lot of time working with individual decision makers in order to develop good report formats. Efficient systems were also developed for use in extracting and combining information from the various data banks. The development of such formats and systems is a typical occurrence when designing MISs. It is not unusual to have separate data banks for general sales data, market data, product data, sales representative data, and consumer data in an MIS.[4]

Although it might not be obvious from Research Realities 2.1, there are several things that had to be done to develop this, or similar, information systems. First, the decision makers affected by the planned system had to be identified. Then, after determining the type of information each person needed and the form in which they could best use it, it was necessary to specify the data that would be input to the system, how that data could be secured and stored, how the data in separate data banks would be

---

[3]See Raymond McLeod, Jr., and John C. Rogers, "Marketing Information Systems: Their Current Status in Fortune 1000 Companies," *Journal of Management Information Systems*, 1 (Spring 1985), pp. 57–75, for the results of a survey conducted among the executives of the Fortune 1000 that highlights the relative emphasis on marketing information systems and their use by management in the reporting firms. The paper also provides a historical perspective on the development and use of marketing information systems. See also Steve Johnston and Sarah Woodward, "Marketing Management Information Systems — A Review of Current Practice," *Marketing Intelligence and Planning,* 6 (No. 2, 1988), 27–29; David Jobber and Martin Watts, "User Attitudes Towards Marketing Information Systems — A UK Survey of Manufacturing Companies," *Marketing Intelligence and Planning,* 6 (No. 2, 1988), pp. 30–35, for discussions of British experience.

[4]See Van Mayros and D. Michael Werner, *Marketing Information Systems* (Radnor, Penn.: Chitton, 1982), for detailed list of the elements that might go into each one of these data banks. See also Robert J. Thierauf, *Group Decision Support Systems for Effective Decision Making: A Guide for MIS Practitioners and End Users* (New York: Quorum Books, 1989).

Research Realities 2.1

Sales Analysis, Sales Expense, and Margin Reports in a Consumer Food Products Company

Report Name	Purpose	Frequency	Distribution*
A. Sales Analysis Reports			
Region	To provide sales information in units and dollars for each sales office or center in the region as well as a regional total.	Monthly	One copy of applicable portions to each regional manager.
Sales Office or Center	To provide sales information in units and dollars for each district manager assigned to a sales office.	Monthly	One copy of applicable portions to each sales office or center manager.
District	To provide sales information in units and dollars for each account supervisor and retail salesperson reporting to the district manager.	Monthly	One copy of applicable portions to each district manager.
Salesperson Summary	To provide sales information in units and dollars for each customer on whom the salesperson calls.	Monthly	One copy of applicable portions to each salesperson.
Salesperson Customer/ Product	To provide sales information in units and dollars for each product for each customer on whom the salesperson calls.	Monthly	One copy of applicable portions to each salesperson.
Salesperson/Product	To provide sales information in units and dollars for each product that the salesperson sells.	Quarterly	One copy of applicable portions to each salesperson.

*To understand the report distribution, it is useful to know that salespeople were assigned accounts in sales districts. Salespeople were assigned one or, at most, a couple of large accounts and were responsible for all the grocery stores, regardless of geography, affiliated with these large accounts, or they were assigned a geographic territory and were responsible for all of the stores within that territory. All sales districts were assigned to sales offices or sales centers. The centers were, in turn, organized into regions.

accessed and combined, and what the report formats would look like. Only after these analysis and design steps were completed could the system be constructed, which was essentially a programming task. Programmers wrote and documented the programs that made data retrieval as efficient as possible in terms of use of computer time and mem-

Report Name	Purpose	Frequency	Distribution*
Region/Product	To provide sales information in units and dollars for each product sold within the region. Similar reports would be available by sales office and by district.	Monthly	No general distribution; used for special sales analysis when needed.
Region/Customer Class	To provide sales information in units and dollars for each class of customer located in the region. Similar reports would be available by sales office and by district.	Monthly	No general distribution; used for special sales analysis when needed.

B. Sales Expense and Margin Reports

Salesperson Compensation and Expense Report	To provide a listing of salesperson compensation and expenses by district.	Monthly	District managers
Salesperson Sales Expense Report	To provide comparative information regarding the ability of the salespeople to manage their expenses.	Monthly	District managers
Salesperson Margin Report	To highlight the contribution to profit being made by the various salespeople.	Monthly	District managers
Sales Office and Center Margin Report	To highlight the profitability of the various districts within a sales office or center.	Monthly	Center managers
Region Margin Report	To highlight the profitability of the various centers within a region.	Monthly	Region managers

ory. When all the procedures were debugged so that the system was operating correctly, it was put on line. Once on line, any of the authorized managers could ask for any of the previously defined reports. In the earliest days of MISs, these requests would go through the computer or information systems departments, which would issue a hard copy or printed report. Today, managers can access these reports directly through computer terminals on their desks.

DECISION SUPPORT SYSTEMS

When they were first proposed, MISs were held up as an information panacea. The reality, however, often fell short of the promise. The primary reasons are as much behavioral as they are technical. People tend to resist change, and with MISs the changes are often substantial. Many decision makers are reluctant, for example, to disclose to others what factors they use and how they combine these factors when making a decision about a particular issue, and without such disclosure it is next to impossible to design reports that will give these people the information they need in the form they need it. Even when managers are willing to disclose their decision-making calculus and information needs, there are problems.

Different managers typically emphasize different things and, consequently, have different data needs. There are very few report formats that are optimal for different users. Either the developers have to design ''compromise'' reports that are satisfactory for a number of users, although not ideal for any single user, or they have to engage in the laborious task of programming to meet each user's needs, one program at a time. Sometimes top management provides less than enthusiastic support for the changes that necessarily accompany MIS, a condition that seems to be particularly common among the more unsuccessful attempts to develop MISs. Equally troublesome, though, are the problems associated with underestimating the costs and time required to establish such systems. This is caused by underestimating the size of the task, changes in organizational structure, key personnel, and the electronic data processing systems they require. By the time these systems can be developed, the personnel for which they are designed often have different responsibilities, or the economic and competitive environments around which they are designed have changed. Thus, they are often obsolete soon after being put on line, meaning that the whole process of analysis, design, development, and implementation has to be repeated anew.

Another fundamental problem with MIS is that the systems do not lend themselves to the solution of ill-structured problems — the most common kind of problems managers face. The notion of ill-structured problems can be understood through Simon's description of decision making as a process involving the three stages of intelligence, design, and choice.[5]

> Intelligence refers to the gathering of information from the decision-making system's environment and exploring that information in an effort to recognize the existence of problems. Design refers to the clarification of a problem, to the creation of potential solutions to the problem, and to the assessment of a potential solution's feasibility. Finally, the choice stage involves the act of choosing one of the feasible solutions and investigating the implementation of that solution. . . . If a problem encountered in decision making cannot be fully

---

[5]Herbert A. Simon, *The New Science of Management Decisions* (New York: Harper & Row, 1960).

clarified and if the exploration of potential solutions cannot be completed before a choice must be made, then the problem is said to be ill-structured. Otherwise, the problem is well-structured and can (in principle, at least) be programmed.[6]

Many of the activities performed by managers cannot be programmed, nor can they be performed routinely or delegated to someone else, because they involve personal choices. Since a manager's decision making is often *ad hoc* and addressed to unexpected choices, standardized reporting systems lack the necessary scope and flexibility to be useful. Nor can managers, even if they are willing to, specify in advance what they want from programmers and model builders, because decision making and planning are often exploratory. As decision makers and their staffs learn more about a problem, their information needs and methods of analysis evolve. Further, decision making often involves exceptions and qualitative issues that are not easily programmed.

As these problems with MIS became more apparent, the emphasis in supplying marketing intelligence on a more regular basis changed from the production of preformatted, batch reports to a **decision support system (DSS)** mode, where a DSS has been defined as "a coordinated collection of data, systems, tools, and techniques with supporting software and hardware by which an organization gathers and interprets relevant information from business and the environment and turns it into a basis for marketing action."[7]

A DSS concentrates on the design of data systems, model systems, and dialog systems that can be used interactively by managers. See Figure 2.1.[8]

Data System

The **data system** in a DSS includes the processes used to capture and the methods used to store data coming from marketing, finance, and manufacturing, as well as information coming from any number of external or internal sources. The typical data system will have modules containing customer information, general economic and demographic information, competitor information, and industry information, including market trends.

---

[6]Robert H. Bonczek, Clyde W. Holsapple, and Andrew B. Whinston, "Developments in Decision Support Systems," undated manuscript, Management Information Research Center, Krannert Graduate School of Management, Purdue University, pp. 3–4.

[7]John D. C. Little, "Decision Support Systems for Marketing Managers," *Journal of Marketing,* 43 (Summer 1979), p. 11. See also Martin D. Goslar and Stephen W. Brown, "Decision Support System Models," *Information Processing and Management,* 2 (1988), pp. 429–448; Blair Peters, "The 'Brave New World' of Single Source Information," *Marketing Research: A Magazine of Management and Applications,* 2 (December 1990), pp. 13–21.

[8]Figure 2.1 and the surrounding discussion are adapted from the excellent treatment of the subject by Ralph H. Sprague, Jr., and Eric D. Carlson, *Effective Decision Support Systems* (Englewood Cliffs, N.J.: Prentice-Hall, 1982), Chapters 1 and 2. See also Jitender S. Deogun, "A Conceptual Approach to Decision Support Systems: Advantage in Consumer Marketing Settings," *Journal of Consumer Marketing,* 3 (Summer 1986), pp. 43–50; Alan J. Greco and Jack T. Hogue, "Developing Marketing Decision Support Systems in Consumer Goods Firms," *Journal of Consumer Marketing,* 7 (Winter 1990), pp. 55–64.

FIGURE 2.1   **Components of a Decision Support System**

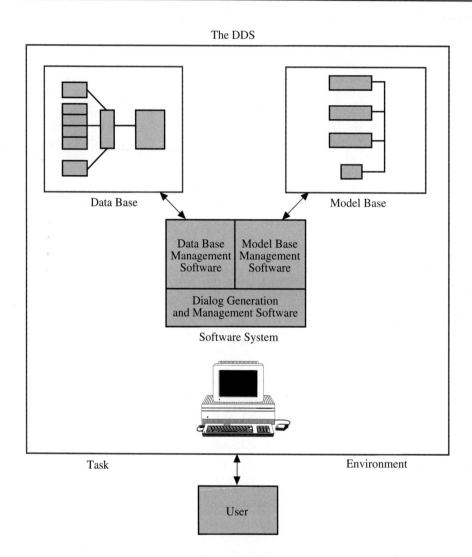

The DDS

Data Base

Model Base

Data Base Management Software

Model Base Management Software

Dialog Generation and Management Software

Software System

Task

Environment

User

Source: Adapted from Ralph H. Sprague, Jr., and Eric D. Carlson, *Building Effective Decision Support Systems,* © 1982, p. 29. Adapted by permission of Prentice Hall, Inc., Englewood Cliffs, New Jersey.

The customer information module typically contains information on who buys and who uses the product, where they buy and use it, when, in what situations and quantities, and how often.[9] It could also include information on how the purchase decision is made, the most important factors in making that decision, the influence of advertising or some sales promotion activity on the decision, the price paid, and so on. Marketing research as discussed in this book would typically supply some of the information input to the customer information module of the data system. Other input might come from the purchase of syndicated commercial marketing information, as discussed in Chapter 6. Still others might come from specifically designed processes to generate consumer purchase data, as in Research Realities 2.2.

The module containing general economic and demographic information attempts to capture some of the most relevant facts about what is happening in the external environment. These might be facts about national or international economic activity and trends or might concern interest rates, unemployment, or changes in GNP. The demographic facts would concern changes in population, changes in the rate of household formation, or any of the other factors that could potentially affect the future success of the firm. Much of this input would come from government data, primarily from the various censuses, discussed in more detail in Chapter 6.

Research Realities 2.2

Generating Consumer Purchase Data

Hoping to show what it can do with personalized promotions, Quaker Oats Company is teaming up with CBS for the first round of a broad direct-mail campaign. In the program, called Quaker Direct, the Chicago-based food company will mail packages of coupons, each coded with household identification numbers, beginning in the fall. When consumers redeem the coupons, the grocery stores' electronic scanners will automatically send detailed information about the purchase back to Quaker. With that data, Quaker can then determine who has a dog, say, or a child, and can then specifically target the next round of coupons it mails to that particular household. For its part, CBS will shoulder part of the cost and will include fliers on its fall-season television shows.

Quaker has three mailings planned, and will spend more than $18 million for them. The second and third mailings will have different partners, but the cereal maker wouldn't disclose who. "This is an opportunity to talk with consumers one on one and to talk to them in a way where they can answer," says Daniel Strunk, director of promotions at Quaker. "In return, we can listen and respond over time with better-tailored promotions."

Source: "For You, Sally Smith, Coupons and Comedies," *The Wall Street Journal* (January 22, 1990), p. B1.

---

[9]For specific suggestions on constructing the consumer information data base, see Robert C. Blattberg and John Deighton, "Interactive Marketing: Exploiting the Age of Addressability," *Sloan Management Review*, 33 (Fall 1991), pp. 5–14.

One module could contain information on specific competitors. What are their names and market shares? In which market niches do they operate? What is their percentage of sales by product? What are their distribution methods? Where are their production facilities located? How big are they? What are their goals? What are their unique capabilities?

The industry information and market trend module would contain general information on what is happening in the industry. This might mean financial information about margins, costs, research and development activities, and capital expenditures. It could mean trends in manufacturing or technology, either with respect to raw materials or processes. The industry module could contain information on new technologies that might affect the production process or create new product substitution capabilities. It would also contain information on marketing trends, such as changing distribution patterns or product consumption.

One of the important trends in the development of DSS is the explosion in the last few years in data bases that provide information on customers, competitors, industries, or general economic and demographic conditions. There are over 3,000 data bases now that can be accessed on line via computer, as compared to fewer than 900 in 1980. Some 200 to 300 of these apply to the information needs of business. The insights that marketing managers can gather from commercially available data bases are almost mind-boggling. They certainly dwarf the possibilities of even a half-dozen years ago. Research Realities 2.3 describes the experience of how the Mead Corporation is staying abreast of developments in its industry. Similarly, Table 2.1 describes some of the issues and relevant sources of information that allow a company to stay tuned into its competitors. Increasingly, companies are setting up systems to track and capture this information regularly.[10]

Much of the most recent emphasis is on global competitive intelligence data systems. For example, Digital Equipment launched its Competitive Information System (CIS) in 1984. Initially, the system was used to collect and distribute data on domestic competitors. After four years, though, it became truly global. CIS contains product descriptions and announcements, internal and external competitive analyses, market analyses, company strategies, policies, and overviews, and includes a direct feed from an external news wire. Digital uses CIS both for strategic and tactical purposes. While its higher-level executives use CIS for strategic decision making and planning, its sales representatives use other pieces of CIS data to formulate sales tactics. The system currently has more than 10,000 registered employee users and generates more than 100,000 log-ins worldwide.[11] Because of the increasing importance of global competitive intelli-

---

[10]Some of the most important information sources are described in Chapter 6. For a general discussion of the design of business intelligence systems, see Benjamin Gilad and Tamar Gilad, *The Business Intelligence System: A New Tool for Competitive Advantage* (New York: American Management Association, 1988); Kirk W. M. Tyson, *Competitor Intelligence Manual and Guide: Gathering, Analyzing, and Using Business Intelligence* (Englewood Cliffs, N.J.: Prentice Hall, 1990). For an overview of what industry is actually doing, see Howard Sutton, *Competitive Intelligence* (New York, The Conference Board, 1988).

[11]Kate Bertrand, ''The Global Spyglass,'' in F. Maidment, ed., *Annual Editions: International Business* (Guilford, Conn.: Dushkin Publishers, 1992), pp. 90–92.

Research Realities 2.3

An Experience of the Mead Corporation with an On-Line Information Search

Dennis Rediker, director of strategy and planning at the Mead Corporation, uses on-line research to explore and track developments in the forest products industry, which is the company's core business. Although papermaking is an ancient process, there have recently been rapid developments in pulp production abroad that are of keen interest to the company.

The company wants to obtain quality pulp of a sort never before used in papermaking. It also wants to find sources for this pulp in many different countries. The company recognizes that fast-growing trees can be cost-effectively converted into quality pulp, which can give a paper manufacturer a considerable cost advantage.

New technology has made this possible for Rediker's company. He went on line, for example, to scan the big global NEXIS data base for information about eucalyptus pulp. An article in *The Economist* produced leads to companies using the special technology needed to mass-produce paper from this raw material. In particular, Rediker learned that B.A.T. Industries' subsidiary, Wiggins-Teape, had purchased Celulosa de Asturias, a Spanish eucalyptus pulper.

He next did a search on B.A.T. Industries in the

Viewpoint Library Files of the Exchange service. A 1984 report by an analyst in the investment firm of Phillips & Drew produced useful information and led him to other companies involved in producing eucalyptus pulp, such as Aracruz Cellulose of Brazil.

Following these leads, Rediker identified several contacts in companies around the world with whom he could exchange views on this subject. Further research in the Dialog and NEXIS data bases brought up statistics on production and investments. Of particular interest was the discovery that many companies are linked through relationships not widely known. Rediker passed this intelligence along to the company's senior international vice-president, James Van Vleck, who established new contacts with people who could help explore the options available to the company as well as the likely effect of future pulp development on the company's business.

After the initial research, Rediker established a procedure for following future developments continuously through ECLIPSE (automatic electronic clipping service) searches on NEXIS. "Planning," says Rediker, "is the most external, information-conscious function in a company, so it's not surprising that external data bases are playing an increasingly important role for us planners. In fact, the same thing is happening with top management."

Source: James McGrane, "Using On-Line Information for Strategic Advantage," *Planning Review* (November–December 1987), p. 29.

gence, a debate is developing over whether U.S. spy agencies should become involved. (See Research Realities 2.4.)

As the number of data bases has expanded, so too has public concern with the issue of privacy, and if and how people's rights to privacy are being violated in the generation and sharing of these data bases. For example, Panel A in Research Realities 2.5 describes a project for which AT&T received public criticism, and Panel B discusses the controversy over the generation and sale of license plate data. The sharing of financial data seems to have generated the most controversy. For example, because of public outcry, Citicorp abandoned its plans to sell information it gathers from its Visa card holders. Similarly, Equifax, the giant credit reporting company, decided to abandon its controversial practice of selling direct mail companies target lists it draws from confidential credit files, and Lotus Development Corporation dropped its plans to sell a

TABLE **2.1**   **Conducting a Competitive Analysis: Issues and Sources of Information**

Outline of a Competitor Profile	Selected Sources of Competitor Information
Background	
Company identification; location; description; brief history; state of incorporation.	General business directories, in part or on line; industry-specific directories.
Affiliates. How is the company organized? How often has it altered its structure?	Corporate press releases, Business Wire (Nexis), PR Newswire (Nexis, Dialog), Dun & Bradstreet (D&B), America's Corporate Families; Corporate Affiliations data base.
Number of shares outstanding; ownership (insiders, institutions, major shareholders).	CDA Spectrum reports based on Securities and Exchange Commission (SEC) filings; D&B reports.
Finance	
Statistics and performance analyses (revenue, earnings, growth); sales by division; profitability by business unit/product line.	SEC filings (Disclosure), Compustat, brokerage reports (Investext, Exchange).
Banks/investment banking firms used.	Directories, tombstone ads, SEC filings, D&B reports.
Stock market data; current market value.	Dow Jones News Retrieval.
Ratios and industry comparisons. Do they track, lead, or lag the industry?	Prentice-Hall, RMA, D&B, Media General, Investext.
Cash flow analysis; assets and return on assets; capitalization; working capital; internal rate of return on investment.	Compustat.
Products	
Description of products and services offered (product mix — depth and breadth of product line) and market position by product; product strength and weaknesses (individually and the line as a whole). How committed is the firm to a particular product line?	Directories. Attend trade shows and conventions to obtain product literature; send for product catalogs; clip advertisements.
Analysis of new product introductions.	Press releases, new product announcement data base (Predicasts). Have your sales force query your customers.
R&D expenditures and apparent interests of technical personnel; an analysis of the company's design and development process.	Scan technical journals for articles authored by employees of competitors.
Patents held/pending; product standards (specs), quality and technical analysis.	World Patent Index (Dialog), Derwent, IFI/Plenum Claims data bases. Have your engineers analyze competitors' products.
Pricing policies (Who decides flexibility in pricing levels?). Note special selling arrangements (Are they competing for your customers?).	Note trade discounts offered.
Licensing and joint venture agreements.	Corporate press releases tracked on PR Newswire and Business Wire.

TABLE **2.1** *Continued*

Outline of a Competitor Profile	Selected Sources of Competitor Information
Markets	
Market segmentation and customer analysis; customer base (markets targeted, regional sales analysis, penetration, importance to the firm, dominance of market); profiles of markets/customers (including product mix and sales data by product line); market growth and potential for future growth; market share by product line.	Press releases, public documents, industry analyses by investment banking firms or consulting groups (scan Investext, Exchange, FIND/SVP data bases or Harfax directories). Check data bases for announcements of large customer purchases. Use your sales force to assess customer loyalties.
How does the company view the direction of the industry?	Employment ads in newspapers (What type of positions are they seeking to fill and does this indicate a new direction for the firm?).
Market and geographic area targeted for expansion; marketing tactics.	Check acquisition and divestiture announcements for trends.
Distribution network/channels of distribution.	Press releases by wholesalers and independent reps.
Advertising/marketing/sales efforts, including budgets and firms used.	Standard Directory of Advertisers.
Foreign trade analysis. Recent orders; government contracts. Analysis of sales force (experience, compensation); T&E practices.	Trade press, DIOR reports, Commerce Business Daily, DMS.
Facilities	
Location, size, domestic vs. foreign.	Directories.
Capacity, capacity utilization, announced capacity expansions.	Check plans for plant expansions and closings (press releases and local press).
Product mix by plant; shipments and profitability data; unit cost/price.	Industry consultants.
Capital investments; equipment purchases; key suppliers.	Press releases.
Number of production lines and shifts.	Business Dateline (Data Courier), local newspapers, Vutext, regional business press (PROMT).
Regulatory issues.	Note investigations by government agencies (Newsnet, Nexis).
Personnel	
Employees — total, management, R&D staffing, engineers (number, education, training, experience).	Directories, public documents.
Biographies of senior management, including employment contracts, incentive (bonus) programs, and golden parachute agreements.	D&B, Standard & Poor's (S&P) directories, public documents.
Description of the members of the board of directors.	D&B, S&P directories, public documents; *Who's Who* series.

(continued)

TABLE **2.1** *Continued*

Outline of a Competitor Profile	Selected Sources of Competitor Information
Consultants used by the firm. Labor union information (relations with management, results of recent negotiations with other firms in the industry, date of next contract renegotiation).	Check labor contract expiration dates and strikes in the trade press.
Detailed corporate structure. Who has P&L responsibility?	Changes in who reports to whom and their responsibilities are often detailed in press releases.
Safety information (accidents) and government/industry regulations violations.	OSHA, ERISA, EEOC compliance (Nexis, Newsnet).
Management style and flexibility.	General business press, management journal articles.
Fringe benefits and compensation practices.	Use your human resources department's contacts and data bases. Do you have any employees who worked for your competitor?
Track managerial changes for indications of disputes in upper management (turnover of personnel).	Listings in business and trade journals; classifieds.

Apparent Strategic (Long-Range) Plans

Detail of acquisition and divestiture strategy.	Dow Jones, Investext.
New products on the horizon (Does it indicate a new direction for the firm?).	New Product Announcement data base, press releases.
Statements of plans to enter new markets or improve market position (increase share of market).	Presentations to Wall Street analysts.
Apparent strategic objectives; corporate/divisional/subsidiary company priorities; business unit/segment goals; basic business philosophy/targets.	General business press, letters to the shareholders.
Analysis of company's decision-making process. Overall corporate image and reputation.	SEC filings, such as exhibits to 10-Ks and proxy statements.
Assess company's ability to adapt/change; how will the company look/perform in the future?	
Anti-takeover measures instituted; shareholder actions; lawsuits pending.	
What are the firm's key successes and failures? Why has it been successful? Overall corporate strengths and weaknesses.	
Attitudes toward risk.	

Note: The acronyms denote the producers of the various data bases. Many of them are company names, e.g., FIND/SVP, and a few are abbreviations of well-known data suppliers, e.g., Dun & Bradstreet (D&B).

Source: Barbie E. Kaiser, "Practical Competitor Intelligence," *Planning Review* (September–October 1987), pp. 17–18. Reprinted with permission. See also Klaus Brockhoff, "Competitor Technology Intelligence in German Companies," *Industrial Marketing Management*, 20 (May 1991), pp. 91–98 for discussion of the most common practices German companies use to keep track of competitors' technology.

Research Realities 2.4

Should the CIA Provide Competitive Intelligence?

The Clinton Administration will review whether economic intelligence gathered by U.S. spy agencies should be shared with private companies or individuals. CIA Director R. James Woolsey told a Senate committee: "[This issue is] the hottest current topic in intelligence policy." The review will examine the complexities, legal difficulties, and foreign policy difficulties of passing along important commercial secrets learned in the course of routine intelligence work to private firms.

Analysts expect that the review will fuel the debate about the CIA's potential role in helping U.S. companies combat foreign competition. The previous director of Central Intelligence, Robert M. Gates, had strongly opposed authorizing the sharing of commercial secrets with private firms, stating that "the U.S. intelligence community does not, should not, and will not engage in industrial espionage."

Some business organizations have urged the government to reverse that decision, citing increased efforts by foreign intelligence organizations to obtain industrial secrets from U.S. corporations. Others feel strongly about setting an international example, keeping spying and business separate, and avoiding what surely would become special and preferential treatment of individual firms.

Source: Adapted from R. Jeffrey Smith, "Administration to Consider Giving Spy Data to Business," *The Washington Post* (February 3, 1993), p. 1.

---

software product containing shopping habits and personal data on approximately 120 million U.S. households.[12] There is little doubt that as the ability to gather and organize individual level data expands, so will the controversy regarding individual versus company rights. Companies planning on entering particular types of data in their data systems need to be sensitive to privacy issues.

Beyond a sensitivity to public concerns, an important criterion as to whether a particular piece of data might find itself in the data bank is whether it is useful for marketing decision making. The basic task of a DSS is to capture relevant marketing data in reasonable detail and to put that data in a truly accessible form. It is crucial that the data base management capabilities built into the system can logically organize the data the same way a manager does, regardless of the form that organization assumes.

Model System

The **model system** includes all the routines that allow the user to manipulate the data to conduct the kind of analyses the individual desires. Whenever managers look at data,

---

[12]Michael W. Miller, "Citicorp Creates Controversy With Plan to Sell Data on Credit-Card Purchases," *The Wall Street Journal* (August 21, 1991), pp. B1, B6; Michael W. Miller, "Equifax to Stop Selling Its Data to Junk Mailers," *The Wall Street Journal* (August 9, 1991), pp. B1, B8; Michael W. Miller, "Lotus Likely to Abandon Consumer-Data Project," *The Wall Street Journal* (January 23, 1991), p. B1; Cyndee Miller, "Privacy vs. Direct Marketing," *Marketing News,* 27 (March 1, 1993), pp. 1, 14–15.

Research Realities 2.5

Some Controversies over the Generation and Sale of Consumer Behavior Data

Panel A: AT&T

How private are your phone records? That unsettling question has arisen recently on two fronts: a high-stakes lobbying campaign and a fight over an unusual new American Telephone & Telegraph Co. venture. In both cases, the issue is causing anxiety because few laws protect the privacy of phone records even as the technology to collect and search the records is advancing rapidly.

The AT&T project is an ordinary-sounding series of specialty 800-number directories. The first, "Gifts, Catalogs and Celebrations," was published in October. AT&T plans to put out a book of toll-free travel numbers in January and is contemplating 10 other directories after that.

What isn't so ordinary is AT&T's method of selecting the households that will receive the books. The phone giant is searching its electronic phone records for frequent callers of each 800-number category. Thus, AT&T could promise advertisers that the first book will reach consumers with a guaranteed appetite for gift and catalog phone services.

Source: Panel A: Michael W. Miller, "Lobbying Campaign, AT&T Directories Raise Fears About Use of Phone Records," *The Wall Street Journal* (December 13, 1991), pp. B1, B4; Panel B: Michael W. Miller, "Debate Mounts Over Disclosure of Driver Data," *The Wall Street Journal* (August 25, 1992), p. B1.

The project is drawing criticism because it's a rare case of phone company marketers exploiting their unique knowledge of the numbers their customers call. "This particular application seems to be innocent enough . . . but you cannot easily distinguish it from more intrusive forms of combing through phone records for marketable nuggets," says Eli Noam, a Columbia University specialist in telecommunications and law. He dreams up a more offensive example: Compiling a list of frequent callers of divorce lawyers and selling it to dating services.

AT&T has also come under fire from an unlikely defender of privacy: the direct-marketing industry. After the directories were described in the trade weekly DM News, the Chicago Association of Direct Marketing branded the phone books an "invasion of privacy." The 2,800-member group demanded that AT&T cancel the project or get written permission from customers to have their call records searched. Direct marketers have an economic reason for fearing AT&T's plan: They do a lucrative business selling their own lists of their most frequent callers.

AT&T dismisses the suggestion that its directories pose a threat to privacy. "We're trying to use this information to help our customers save money or make money or save time," says David Williams, the publisher of AT&T's 800 directories. He compares searching for frequent 800-number callers to other ways that AT&T analyzes customers' calling patterns

they have a preconceived idea of how something works and, therefore, what is interesting and worthwhile in the data. These ideas are called models.[13] Most managers also want to manipulate data to gain a better understanding of a marketing issue. These manipulations are called procedures. The routines for manipulating the data may run the

[13]John D. C. Little and Michael N. Cassettari, *Decision Support Systems for Marketing Managers* (New York: American Management Association, 1984), p. 14.

for marketing purposes. For instance, the company might offer discounts to volume long-distance callers or a special deal on calls to a particular foreign country.

Panel B: Automobile License-Plate Data

"You can use license plate numbers to track down a lot of information," writes Joseph Scheidler in "Closed: 99 Ways to Stop Abortion." His suggestion number 60: Jot down the license-plate numbers of cars that park at an abortion clinic. Go to the motor vehicle bureau and find out the name and address of the cars' owners. Send them letters and picket their homes.

In more than 20 states, this is simple and perfectly legal. Most privacy-minded Americans with unlisted numbers and addresses don't know that motor vehicle bureaus will sell their name, address, and sometimes even height and weight to anyone who pays a few dollars' fee. Today, some states even sell computer tapes of their entire files to marketers, insurance companies, and other curious businesses.

Now a fight is brewing over the privacy of personal information stored in state drivers' data bases — just one battleground in a mounting debate over privacy and public records. Computerized data bases of real-estate filings, police "rap sheets," and workers-compensation claims have all provoked similar disputes.

Spurred by anti-abortion protesters' rising use of the license-plate tactic, Rep. James Moran (D., Va.) is pushing a bill making it illegal for states to disclose drivers' data without the subject's consent. Rep. Moran has already run into opposition from one big group that relies heavily on drivers' data: private detectives. "I check these files to locate lost clients, defendants, witnesses, plaintiffs, loan skips, and non-paying fathers," complained Dallas private investigator Marc Smith in a letter to the congressman. The bill also worries junk-mailers, who routinely use drivers' records to create target marketing lists. Sears, Roebuck & Co., for instance, has used state records on height and weight to pick prospects for its "Big and Tall" men's catalog.

State motor-vehicle officials point to all sorts of other legitimate uses that the Moran bill could crimp. A private school bus company can check out the record of someone applying to be a driver. A car owner can locate the kid who bashed his fender. Even some civil libertarians have misgivings about the bill. "Whenever the government keeps secrets, a little red light should go off," says Mike Godwin, staff counsel of the Electronic Frontier Foundation, a civil-liberties group. He supports tight privacy for commercial transactions such as credit-card purchases and video rentals. But when it comes to government data, he says access for the press and the public should often outweigh the right to privacy.

gamut from summing a set of numbers to conducting a complex statistical analysis to finding an optimization strategy using some kind of nonlinear programming routine. At the same time, "the most frequent operations are basic ones: segregating numbers into relevant groups, aggregating them, taking ratios, ranking them, picking out exceptional cases, plotting and making tables."[14]

---

[14]*Ibid.*, p. 15.

The explosion in recent years in the number of data bases available and the size of some of them has triggered a commensurate need for ways to analyze them efficiently. For example, the estimates suggest that marketing managers in packaged goods companies are inundated with 100 to 1,000 times more bits of data than they had even a few years ago because of the adoption of scanner technology (discussed in Chapter 6) in their channels of distribution. The huge quantities of information they receive every week require a great amount of time in order for even an astute analyst to provide simple summaries showing the major trends. In response, a number of firms have been working on the development of **expert systems,** computer-based artificial intelligence systems that attempt to model how experts process information to solve the problem at hand.

For example, Figure 2.2 displays the type of output provided by CoverStory, an expert system developed by Information Resources, Inc., for the analysis of its scanner-generated data.[15] CoverStory can provide highlights of the performance of a brand (as well as competing brands) within minutes. It can sort through all the data and provide a comparison of current and past results by brand and by category as well as by markets, regions, or key accounts. Moreover, as Figure 2.2 indicates, it can even produce a memo highlighting the major findings.

Expert systems or formal models that attempt to capture the issues managers deem most relevant when making particular decisions have been directed at various types of problems and affect various decision levels in organizations. Figure 2.3. depicts the use of marketing decision models in *Fortune* 1000 companies. The credit approval and sales-person routing models could be considered operational models. Operational models are usually used by lower-level managers to support the short time-horizon (e.g., daily or weekly) decisions that they are usually called on to make. These models normally use internal company data in their operation.

The pricing, sales territory assignment, and advertising media selection models could be considered more tactical. Tactical models are commonly used by middle managers to allocate and control the firm's resources. The time horizon built into tactical models is typically longer than that built into operational models, ranging from several months up to a couple of years. Although they too make use of internal, objective data for the most part, they also rely on subjective and external data.[16]

---

[15]For a description of CoverStory, see John D. Schmitz, Gordon D. Armstrong, and John D. C. Little, "CoverStory — Automated News Finding in Marketing," *Interfaces,* 20 (November/December 1990), pp. 29–38. For general discussions of expert systems, see Judy Bayer and Rachel Harter, " 'Miner,' 'Manager,' and 'Researcher': Three Modes of Analysis of Scanner Data," *International Journal of Research in Marketing,* 8 (April 1991), pp. 17–27; Paul Alpar, "Knowledge-Based Modeling of Marketing Managers' Problem Solving Behavior," *International Journal of Research in Marketing,* 8 (April 1991), pp. 5–16; Arvind Rangaswamy, Bari A. Harlam, and Leonard M. Lodish, "INFER: An Expert System for Automatic Analysis of Scanner Data," *International Journal of Research in Marketing,* 8 (April 1991), pp. 29–40.

[16]For an example of tactical models for making sales promotion decisions, see Maged M. Abraham and Leonard M. Lodish, "Promoter: An Automated Promotion Evaluation Decision," *Marketing Science,* 6 (Spring 1987), pp. 101–123. For discussion of the models available to assist in advertising decisions, see Robert Lorin Cook and John M. Schleade, "Application of Expert Systems to Advertising," *Journal of Advertising Research,* 28 (June/July 1988), pp. 47–56; Raymond R. Burke, Arvind Rangaswamy, and Jerry Wind, "A Knowledge-Based System for Advertising Design," *Marketing Science,* 9 (Summer 1990), pp. 212–229.

FIGURE 2.2   Example Report Produced by the Expert System CoverStory

To: **Director of Marketing**

From: **CoverStory**

Date: **01/18/90**

Subject: **XYZ Cereal Brand Summary for Four Weeks Ending December 29, 1989**

XYZ Cereal's volume share in Total United States was 16.6 in the Total Cereal category for the four weeks ending 12/28/89. This is a decrease of 1.3 share points from a year earlier up by .4 from last period, (4 week ending Nov. 30, 1989). This reflects volume sales of 8.1 million equiv. ounces - down 6.2 percent since last year.

Category volume (currently 48.8 million equiv. ounces) rose 1.4% from a year earlier. Display activity and unsupported price cuts rose over the past year - unsupported price cuts from 31 points to 47. Price fell during the year by .16 dollars to 2.20. Featuring (30 ACV points) and distribution (100 percent of ACV) remained about the same level as a year earlier.

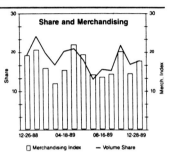

Components of XYZ Cereal Volume

Within the XYZ Cereal line, share decreases have been sustained by:

- 9 oz. off 1.1 share points from last year to 8.2

- 13 oz off .3 share points to 5.4

- Variety pak off .2 to 3.0

XYZ Cereal 9 oz. share decrease may be partly attributed to 6.6 pts of ACV decrease in distribution versus year ago.

Competitor Summary

Among XYZ Cereal's major competitors, the principal gainers are:

- **Corn Krunch:** up .3 share points from last year to 8.5 (but down .2 since last period).

- **Sun Cereal:** up 2.6 share points from year ago to 6.8.

and loser:
- **Oats Plus:** down .7 to 4.8

XYZ Cereal's share is 16.6 - down 1.3 points from the same period last year.

Corn Krunch share increase may be partly attributed to supported price cuts (up 10 points to 28). Sun Cereal share increase may be partly attributed to 8.0 pts of ACV increase in distribution versus year ago.

Geographic Highlights

XYZ Cereal posted significant gains relative to a year ago in:

- **Philadelphia:** up 2.6 share points from last year to 18.9. This may be attributed to 6.5 pts of ACV distribution vs. year ago and 13.4 points increase in displays since last year.

but posted losses in:
- **Atlanta:** down 1.8 to 13.2 This may be partly attributed to 20.5 ACV points decrease in featuring versus a year ago and 9.1 points decrease in displays versus year ago.

Source: Courtesy of Information Resources, Inc.

The new product evaluation and product deletion models could be considered more strategic in nature. Strategic models tend to be broad in scope. Many of the data for them comes from external sources and may be subjective in nature. These models are used by top managers to execute their strategic planning responsibilities and, consequently, use years, rather than months or days, for the appropriate time horizon.

FIGURE 2.3   **Use of Marketing Decision Models in *Fortune* 1000 Companies**

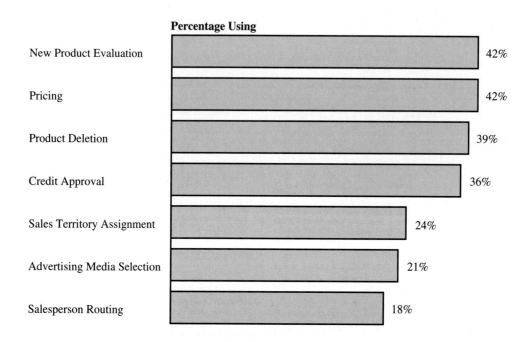

Percentage Using

New Product Evaluation	42%
Pricing	42%
Product Deletion	39%
Credit Approval	36%
Sales Territory Assignment	24%
Advertising Media Selection	21%
Salesperson Routing	18%

Source: Developed from information in Raymond McLeod, Jr., and John C. Rogers, "Marketing Information Systems: Their Current Status in *Fortune* 1000 Companies," *Journal of Management Information Systems*, 1 (Spring 1985), pp. 57–75.

Dialog System

The **dialog systems,** also called language systems, are most important and clearly differentiate DSSs from MISs. The dialog systems permit managers who are not programmers themselves to explore the data bases, using the system models to produce reports that satisfy their own particular information needs. The reports can be tabular or graphical, and the report formats can be specified by individual managers. The dialog systems can be passive, which means that the analysis possibilities are presented to the decision makers for selection via menu, a few simple key strokes, light pen, or a mouse device, or they can be active, requiring the users to state their requests in a command mode. A key feature is that instead of funneling their data requests through a team of programmers, managers can conduct their analyses by themselves (or through one of their assistants) sitting at a computer terminal using the dialog system. This allows them to target the information they want rather than being overwhelmed with irrelevant data. Managers can ask a question and, on the basis of the answer, can ask a subsequent question, and then another, and another, and so on.

> With the right DSS, for example, a marketing VP evaluating the sales of a recently introduced test instrument could "call up" sales by month, then by the year, breaking them out *at his option* by, say, customer segments. As he works at his CRT terminal, his inquiries could go in several directions, depending on the decision at hand. If his train of thought raises questions about monthly sales last year compared to forecasts, he wants his information system to follow along and give him answers immediately.
>
> He might see that his new product's sales were significantly below forecast. Forecasts too optimistic? He compares other products' sales to his forecasts, and finds that the targets were very accurate. Something wrong with the product? Maybe his sales department is getting insufficient leads, or isn't putting leads to good use? Thinking a minute about how to examine that question, he checks ratios of leads converted to sales — product by product. The results disturb him. Only 5% of the new product's leads generate orders compared to the company's 12% all-product average. Why? He guesses that the sales force isn't supporting the new product enough. Quantitative information from the DSS perhaps could provide more evidence to back that suspicion. But already having enough quantitative knowledge to satisfy himself, the VP acts on his intuition and experience and decides to have a chat with his sales manager.[17]

As the availability of on-line data bases has increased, so too has the need for better dialog systems. The dialog systems are what put data at the managers' fingertips. Even though that sounds simple enough, it is a difficult task because of the large amount of data that are available, the speed with which the data hit a company, and the fact that data come from various sources. Bringing the data together from the disparate data sources into meaningful reports is no small feat.

> Large data base services typically provide their customers with a hard copy of the data (usually the size of a large phone book) and a magnetic tape with the data for loading on a mainframe. (They) give you the tapes in their format. You have to be able to read it and load it, which is not an easy task. The documentation that some of the services give you to load the data is sketchy.
>
> Some of the data comes in basically as flat, sequential files, and it is pretty easy to decode and load that in a day or two. But if you are trying to load it into a formal data base, that can take several days or weeks because you are trying to figure out all the indexing structures (for efficient retrieval) and are writing some pretty custom code.[18]

To compound things, the geographic boundaries used by the data suppliers differ from each other and most often from the firm's own geographic territories. Further, the services typically collect data on different time cycles. Some might provide it weekly, whereas others might provide it twice a month, monthly, or even less often. The discrepancies must be reconciled in a meaningful way if the various inputs are going to be combined into effective decision making.

---

[17]Michael Dressler, Ronald Beall, and Joquin Ives Brant, "What the Hot Marketing Tool of the '80s Offers You," *Industrial Marketing,* 68 (March 1983), pp. 51 and 54.

[18]Bob Goligoski, "Brand Leaders," *Business Computer Systems,* 5 (June 1986), pp. 26–33.

A relatively new way to handle these problems is through distributed network computing. These systems rely on workstations that are linked together. Because the workstations are linked, users do not have to worry where the information is stored in the network of computers. Networking is usually found in the largest corporations. More importantly, the systems used to access and manipulate the data make use of a common interface or server. Through that server, the analyst can enter data, query data, do spreadsheet analyses, plots, or statistical analyses, or can even prepare reports, all through some very simple commands (see Figure 2.4). For example, one popular sys-

FIGURE 2.4   Use of Dialog Systems with Common Server or Interface Using Simplified, Standardized Instructions to Perform Multiple Tasks

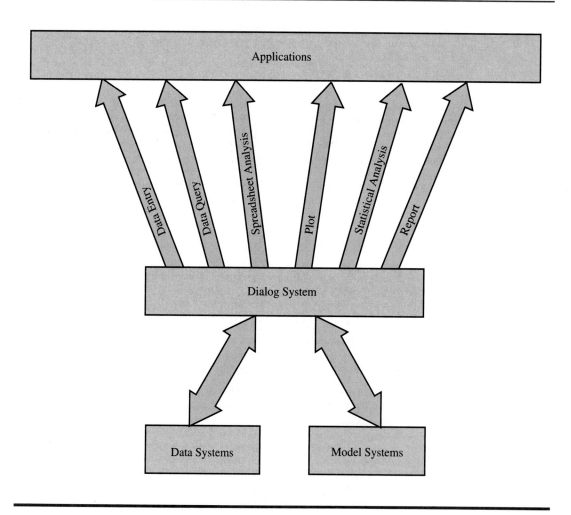

tem, Metaphor, uses a mouse-driven graphic front end.[19] Users simply need to point and click the mouse to access the documents they need. Further, they can formulate complex queries through simple instructions. They can join data elements simply by drawing a line between two boxes. Thus, to look at sales in the southeast region, for example, users can simply draw a line between the data element marked ''sales'' and the box labeled ''southeast region.'' They can build more elaborate routines by flowing data through a series of the available tools (word processing, spreadsheet, and graphics, for instance). They can specify sequences of operations by drawing arrows from one routine to the next. Once created, they can store these routines and launch similar analyses in the future with a single click of the mouse. Once recalled, they can modify and restore them. Thus, managers are able to continuously improve their modeling of the problems they face without needing to become computer experts, or even very knowledgeable about what goes on behind the scenes.

Research Realities 2.6 describes the experiences of Clorox before and after installing the Metaphor dialog system.

DSS VERSUS MIS

From the previous discussion, it should be obvious that DSS and MIS are both concerned with improving information processing so that better marketing decisions can be made. Yet DSS differs from MIS in a number of ways.[20] First, DSS tends to be aimed at the less well-structured, underspecified problems that managers face rather than at those problems that can be investigated using a relatively standard set of procedures and comparisons. Second, DSS attempts to combine the use of models and analytical techniques and procedures with the more traditional data access and retrieval functions. Third, such systems specifically incorporate features that make them easy to use in an interactive mode by noncomputer people, including such things as menu-driven procedures for doing an analysis and graphical display of the results. Regardless of how the interaction is structured, DSS systems have the ability to respond to users' *ad hoc* requests in ''real time,'' that is, the time available for making the decision. Fourth, these systems emphasize flexibility and adaptability. They can accommodate different decision makers with diverse styles as well as changing environmental conditions.

THE FUTURE OF DSS VERSUS TRADITIONAL MARKETING RESEARCH

There is no question that the explosion in data bases and computer software for accessing those data bases is changing the way marketing intelligence is obtained. Not only are

---

[19]Some other popular systems are Express, Marksman, and Decision Master. For a general discussion on the use of these systems, see Valerie Free, ''The Marketing War Gets Automated,'' *Marketing Communications,* 13 (June 1988), pp. 40–48, 79.

[20]For discussion of the features that differentiate DSS from MIS, see Sprague and Carlson, *Effective Decision Support Systems;* and Bonczek, Holsapple, and Whinston, ''Developments in Decision Support Systems.''

Research Realities 2.6

Experience at Clorox in Using the Metaphor Dialog System

Getting all the data on computer systems at Clorox once taxed the company's MIS department beyond its resources. With new volumes of data rolling in all the time, it was too complex and time-consuming to load all the information on mainframes. But that was often the only way that data from different geographic areas and time periods could be reconciled.

Before Clorox acquired the Metaphor system, brand managers sometimes would come to the MIS department "with requests that certain product data be looked at," according to Sean F. McKenna, Clorox's systems and data base administrator for Metaphor systems. He recalls that it sometimes took so long to honor the request that by the time the brand manager got the data, "no one was interested in looking at it anymore."

Today, Clorox brand managers are able to use all the data bought from the major services because Met-

aphor has written conversion routines that allow these data to be quickly loaded.

Tim Hensley, director of business systems, information services, and McKenna have found that marketing teams for Clorox's many brands require little MIS support because the marketing personnel develop their own applications. "We give the brand people a 25-hour training course for the system, but we find that they can learn to use it for all practical purposes in five hours or so," says McKenna.

Clorox officials decline, for competitive reasons, to discuss how the Metaphor system is being used with any specific brands. But they talked generally about how it was employed when Kingsford with Mesquite charcoal was introduced last year.

The company got into the charcoal briquet business in 1973 when it acquired Kingsford Company. Kingsford later became the leading national charcoal briquet brand. In 1981, Clorox introduced Match Light, an instant-lighting charcoal that has a commanding lead in that niche.

When Clorox planned the introduction of Kingsford with Mesquite charcoal (briquets laced with

Source: Bob Goligoski, "Brand Leaders," *Business Computer Systems*, 5 (June 1986), pp. 26–33.

more companies building decision support systems, but those that have them are becoming more sophisticated in using them for general business and competitive intelligence. (See Research Realities 2.7 for an example.) This, in turn, has produced some changes in the organization of the marketing intelligence function. One relatively recent but important change has been the emergence of the position of Chief Information Officer, or CIO.[21]

The CIO's major role is to run the company's information and computer systems like a business. The CIO serves as the liaison between the firm's top management and its information systems department. He or she has the responsibility for planning, coordi-

[21]For general discussions of the office of CIO, see P. Declan O'Riordan, "The CIO: MIS Makes Its Move into the Executive Suite," *Journal of Information Systems Management* (Summer 1987), pp. 54–56; and Jim Sielski, "Evolving Post of Chief of Info," *Chicago Tribune* (November 20, 1988), pp. 33–35.

mesquite wood to impart a mesquite flavor to food), it wanted to determine if Mesquite sales would siphon off sales from its two other charcoal brands. If so, the company could end up spending money for promotion and advertising without increasing its overall share of the \$418 million U.S. market (1985) for charcoal briquets. That share stood at about 42 percent, according to analysts.

Kingsford with Mesquite charcoal was launched last year in about half the country and was not initially sold in many states where Clorox's two other charcoal brands were marketed. Sales data were then collected from all states, and marketers found that sales of Kingsford and Match Light declined only slightly in areas where Mesquite was being sold.

Further analysis of the sales data (on the Metaphor system) of competing charcoal brands disclosed that in areas where Mesquite was being sold, the sale of generic charcoal brands marketed by several large supermarket chains was declining. Clorox's overall share of the market rose several percentage points, and Mesquite was introduced nationally early in 1986.

When following sales of a mostly seasonal product like charcoal briquets, brand managers have to access data, such as weather conditions, that may affect sales. That type of information can be easily retrieved and integrated with other data for analysis by Metaphor users at Clorox.

Hensley, who oversees business systems managers, client services, and user training and education at Clorox, is not readily given to endorsing vendor products. But his enthusiasm for the Metaphor system underscores many of his comments, especially when he discusses the graphics capabilities of the system:

Metaphor has a graphics capability that other systems don't have. Prior to getting the system, our graphics were done primarily for presentations. You knew the answer. You just wanted to get it up graphically to show to someone else.

Now, production of graphics is so simple, they can be used for analysis. You can take something and in maybe five seconds construct the graphic. You can turn it and look at it six different ways graphically and do in two or three minutes what it would take hours to do with another system. This has been made so easy that the system has become a true tool, not just a decision-support system.

nating, and controlling the use of the firm's information resources and is much more concerned with the firm's outlook than the daily activities of the department. CIOs typically know more about the business in general than the managers of the information systems department, who are often more technically knowledgeable. In many cases, the managers of the information systems department will report directly to the CIO.

The explosion in data bases and DSSs has not eliminated the need for traditional marketing research projects in gathering marketing intelligence. This is because the two approaches are not competitive mechanisms for marketing intelligence but, rather, complementary ones. Even though a DSS provides valuable input for broad strategic decisions, allows managers to stay in tune with what is happening in their external environments, and serves as an excellent early warning system, it sometimes does not provide enough information about what to do in specific instances, such as when the firm is faced with a new product introduction, a change in distribution channels, the effectiveness of a new promotion campaign, and so on. When actionable information is required to address

Research Realities 2.7

Casinos Leave Nothing to Chance: Gambling Houses Use Consultants, Data Bases, and Questionnaires to Learn More about Their Customers

Casinos don't like to gamble — not with their marketing dollars. Instead, gambling houses are going to great lengths to learn more about their customers. Through computerized cards, questionnaires, and the watchful eyes of employees, casinos are developing highly specialized data bases that profile the gambling preferences and life-styles of their customers.

This type of primary data allows casinos to tailor marketing plans to individual regions and customers. In particular, the data have come in handy with perks, the industry's most popular form of self-promotion. In the past, casinos used a "shotgun" approach, indiscriminately awarding customers free show tickets and hotel rooms. Now, through consumer analysis, casinos can determine who is worthy of freebies and who is not.

One of the most advanced forms of data collection is computerized cards that are used by customers and feed data bases with personal information. At the Claridge Hotel in Atlantic City, just one of many casinos that use this system, players at slot machines are offered incentives to "register" their play on personalized cards. Before they pull the lever, players insert their cards into the machine. Then a computer tracks every movement of the machine, and the information is stored in the casino's data base. Through these cards, casinos learn everything about customers' playing habits.

Detailed questionnaires are another solid source of consumer information. Customers are given discounts on services or the chance to win a cash prize as an incentive for filling them out. These questionnaires reach well beyond a customer's gambling habits to gather information about his or her income, life-style, and even favorite sports. The whole process is designed to match a customer to a market segment so that the casino can design specific promotions based on customer preferences.

The data received also tell casinos where customers are from and how they'll be traveling to the hotel, a critical factor in the business. By analyzing customers' zip codes, casinos can concentrate advertising dollars and, perhaps more importantly, learn where they need to expand transportation lines. Busing programs, for example, are a major part of the marketing effort in Atlantic City, where the industry concentrates on recreational gamblers.

Having a detailed data base on all of their customers has allowed casinos to pursue a much more efficient and lucrative marketing strategy. Whereas casinos once focused their efforts solely on luring back the high rollers, they are now aggressively pursuing the middle market. Says Nancy Bauer, senior vice-president of marketing at Trump Castle in Atlantic City, "The middle-market gamblers may spend less, but in aggregate, they're worth more."

Source: Warren Berger, "Casinos Leave Nothing to Chance," *Adweek's Marketing Week,* 30 (January 9, 1989), pp. 19–20.

specific marketing problems or opportunities, the research project will probably continue to play a major role.[22]

In sum, both traditional (or project-based) and DSS-based approaches to marketing intelligence can be expected to grow in importance.[23] In an increasingly competitive world, information is vital, and a company's ability to obtain and analyze information will largely determine the company's future. The light from both flash bulbs and candles is necessary.

SUMMARY

This book takes a project-based approach to the provision of marketing intelligence. The difference between a project emphasis to research or the alternative MIS or DSS emphasis is that both of the latter rely on the continual monitoring of the firm's activities, its competitors, and its environment, whereas the former emphasizes the in-depth but non-recurring study of some specific problem or environmental condition.

A marketing information system was defined as a set of procedures and methods for the regular planned collection, analysis, and presentation of information for use in making marketing decisions. The thrust in designing an MIS is the detailed analysis of each decision maker who might use the system in order to secure an accurate, objective assessment of each manager's decision-making responsibilities, capabilities, and style, and, most important, each manager's information needs. Given the specifications for information needs, system support people develop report formats and efficient systems for extracting and combining information from various data banks. In the early days of MISs, information requests would go through the computer department, which would issue a hard copy or printed report. Now managers can get a copy of one of the standard report formats directly on a computer terminal.

Although MISs did provide more regular marketing intelligence than had been true when firms relied on marketing research projects, such systems suffered from some other problems. They required managers to disclose their decision-making processes, which many managers were reluctant to do. Further, the report formats were typically

---

[22]Even with respect to the activity of providing competitive intelligence, a project-based approach can complement the insights gathered through ongoing monitoring. For a comparison of the benefits and costs of using each approach, see John E. Prescott and Daniel C. Smith, ''A Project-Based Approach to Competitive Analysis,'' *Strategic Management Journal,* 8 (September–October 1987), pp. 411–423. For discussion of the role for project-based research in the information environment of the future, see Verne B. Churchill, ''The Role of Ad Hoc Survey Research in a Single Source World,'' *Marketing Research: A Magazine of Management and Applications,* 2 (December 1990), pp. 22–26.

[23]For discussion of the trends in DSS and marketing research, see M. C. Er, ''Decision Support Systems: A Summary, Problems, and Future Trends,'' *Decision Support Systems,* 4 (September 1988), pp. 355–363. For a look at the factors affecting the usage of DSSs, see George M. Zinkhan, Erich A. Joachimsthaler, and Thomas C. Kinnear, ''Individual Differences and Marketing Decision Support Systems Usage and Satisfaction,'' *Journal of Marketing Research,* 24 (May 1987), pp. 208–214; and Tom Eisenhart, ''Computer-Aided Marketing: After 10 Years of Marketing Decision Support Systems, Where's the Payoff?'' *Business Marketing,* 75 (June 1990), pp. 46–51.

compromises that tried to satisfy the different styles of the different users. And, the development time required for these systems often meant that they quickly became obsolete.

DSSs are replacing MISs in many companies. A DSS is a coordinated collection of data, systems, tools, and techniques with supporting software and hardware by which an organization gathers and interprets relevant information from business and the environment and turns it into a basis for marketing action. A DSS concentrates on the design of data systems, model systems, and dialog systems. The data systems include the processes used to capture and store information useful for marketing decision making. A marketing research project might be one input to a data system. The model system includes all the routines that allow users to manipulate data to conduct the kinds of analyses they desire. The dialog systems are most important and most clearly differentiate DSSs from MISs. They allow managers to conduct their own analyses while they or one of their assistants sit at a computer terminal. This allows managers to analyze problems using their own personal insight into what might be happening in a given situation, relying on their intuition and experience rather than on a series of prespecified reports. Not only does this eliminate a lot of irrelevant data, but it also saves time because managers can program the analysis themselves rather than waiting for the computer department to process their request for some specific information.

Questions

1. What is a marketing information system? How does a project emphasis to marketing research differ from an information systems emphasis?

2. What are the steps in MIS analysis? In developing an MIS system?

3. What are the main differences between a marketing information system and a decision support system?

4. In a decision support system, what is a data system? A model system? A dialog system? Which of these is most important? Why?

5. What is (are) the likely future approach(es) to marketing intelligence? Will there be a change in the relative importance of traditional research and MIS and DSS systems?

Applications and Problems

1. Twenty years ago the marketing information system was emphasized as being the solution to a host of problems arising from irregular research efforts. The promise was never realized, and current emphasis is on the design of decision support systems rather than marketing information systems. How do you account for the gap between the promise and delivery of the MIS? Do you think DSSs will suffer the same fate as MISs? Why or why not?

2. You are responsible for deciding whether to adopt an MIS or DSS system for the following situations. Which system approach would you choose? Why?
   a. Production of profit and loss statements for Kool Aid sugar-free flavored drink mixes.
   b. Introduction of a new product line extension for Smucker's preserves and jellies.
   c. Determination of seasonal pricing schedules for Johnson outboard motors.
   d. Identification of the amount of time spent on hold by consumers on a toll-free, customer-service assistance telephone line.

3. In each of the following scenarios, identify the general type of DSS model (operational, tactical, or strategic) that the decision maker is likely to use and explain the choice.
   a. Sharon Baker is brand manager for Sappy Maple Syrup. It is her responsibility to decide where a series of ads should be placed. The advertising agency that designed the ads has suggested that they be run over a nine-month period.
   b. Greg Martin is a district sales manager for Affiliated Grocery Wholesalers. His largest customer, Fred's Fine Foods, has informed him that it will need increased salesperson contact over the next month due to its "Super Silver 25th Anniversary Sale." Martin must decide how to rearrange sales-call schedules to provide increased contact with Fred.
   c. Erika Porter is vice-president of marketing for Ferret Industries, a pet products company. Sales of one of Ferret's product lines have been decreasing steadily for the last five years. Porter must decide whether the product line has the potential to be rescued, or if it should be phased out of production.

4. Your company is in the process of installing its first DSS. The system has been designed, the hardware installed, and it is due to be up and running in two weeks. Your task is to provide system users with orientation and training. It is your feeling that the company's managers will initially be resistant to using the DSS. To help overcome this resistance, what specific capabilities of the DSS will you emphasize in your initial orientation presentation?

5. You are a vice-president of international marketing for a consumer packaged-goods company. In a recent board of directors meeting, it was decided that you would head the development of a competitive information system (CIS) for your organization. You have been asked to write a brief description of the types of data to be stored in the CIS along with possible uses of the data by employees within your company. Write a clear and concise paragraph describing your recommendations.

APPENDIX 2A

Marketing Research Ethics

Much of this text discusses the techniques for doing marketing research. Most of the time, the act of choosing a particular research technique will involve an implicit judgment about the ethics of the proposed procedure. **Ethics** are the moral principles and values that govern the way an individual or group conducts its activities. Ethics apply to all situations in which there can be actual or potential harm of any kind (e.g., economic, physical, or mental) to an individual or group. **Marketing ethics** are the principles, values, and standards of conduct followed by marketers.

Many marketing researchers (and managers as well) fail to confront the issue of whether it is morally acceptable to proceed in a particular way or whether they are acting in a socially responsible manner by doing so. Many take the view that if it is legal, it is

---

Source: This appendix is based largely on the unpublished paper by Jacqueline C. Hitchon and Gilbert A. Churchill, Jr., "The Three Domains of Ethical Concern for the Marketing Researcher."

ethical. They fail to appreciate that there can be differences between what is ethical and what is legal. Even among those who do appreciate the distinction, there is often a reluctance to evaluate the ethical implications of their decisions because they feel ill-equipped to do so. Like most professionals, they simply do not know how or where to start.[1]

Although ignorance may seem like bliss, the dangers to individual researchers and the marketing research profession itself of ignoring ethical issues simply because they are difficult are real and growing. For one thing, there have been a number of recent cases in which members of the profession face litigation for alleged unethical practices. Atkinson Research was sued for using a survey questionnaire to rig TV ratings in Minneapolis on behalf of its client, KARE-TV.[2] The questionnaire contained instructions for respondents to watch a particular TV channel as often as possible for a week, ostensibly so that the firm could assess viewer reactions. The suit charged that the "survey" was taken during the May Nielsen ratings period to deliberately manipulate the TV ratings. In another instance, Beecham Products sought more than $24 million in court from the research company Yankelovich Clancy Shulman for negligent misrepresentation of research findings, because its market share forecasts were not upheld during the 1986 launch of Delicare, a detergent for fine fabrics.[3] A further cause for concern resides in the increasing use of telephone "surveys" as a guise for sales ploys or fundraising.[4] This troublesome trend has resulted in the introduction of legislation in a number of states in the last few years that would entirely ban various forms of unsolicited telephone calls, including genuine research calls.

As mentioned, behaving ethically is not simply a matter of complying with laws and regulations. Rather, a particular act may be legal but not ethical. For example, although legal, many find abortion on demand unethical. Similarly, even though it is perfectly legal to observe people without their consent when they are shopping, some would argue that it is unethical to do so. Ethics are more proactive than the law. They attempt to anticipate problems, whereas most laws and regulations emerge from social pressure for change in a slow, reactive fashion. Ethics are concerned with the development of moral standards by which situations can be judged. They focus on those situations in which there can be actual or potential harm of some kind (for example, economic, physical, or mental) to an individual or group. They are concerned with the development of moral standards that can be applied to those situations. They focus on issues such as the following:

- Is the action or anticipated action arbitrary or capricious? Does it unfairly single out an individual or group?

---

[1]Karen Berney, "Finding the Ethical Edge," *Nation's Business,* 75 (August 1987), pp. 18–24.

[2]Gregg Cebrzynski, "TV Station Sued Over Alleged 'Phoney' Survey," *Marketing News,* 21 (August 28, 1987), pp. 1 and 42.

[3]Ellen Neuborne, "Researchers See Chill from Suit," *Advertising Age,* 58 (July 20, 1987), pp. 3, 50.

[4]Martha Brannigan, "Pseudo Polls: More Surveys Draw Criticism for Motives and Methods," *The Wall Street Journal* (January 27, 1987), p. 27.

- Does the action or anticipated action violate the moral or legal rights of any individual or group?
- Does the action or anticipated action conform to accepted moral standards?
- Are there alternative courses of action that are less likely to cause actual or potential harm?[5]

Marketing researchers need to recognize that (1) the effective practice of their profession depends a great deal on the goodwill of and participation by the public, and (2) currently, the American public is becoming more and more protective of its privacy. This makes it more difficult and costly to approach, recruit, and survey participants. "Bad" research experiences that violate the implicit trust of the participants in a study can only accentuate the trend. In addition to moral fairness issues, then, self-preservation issues dictate that marketing researchers develop a sense for the ethical issues involved in particular choices. The fact that good ethics is good business is one of the reasons associations whose members are involved in marketing research have developed codes of ethics to guide the behaviors of their members.[6] Table 2A.1, for example, contains the code of ethics for the New York Chapter of the American Marketing Association (AMA). This code is particularly clear on some of the issues that are especially troublesome to practicing researchers.

The purpose of this appendix is to provide marketing researchers with a framework and some guidelines for making ethical judgments. To this end, the appendix first reviews two main approaches from moral philosophy for making ethical judgments — deontology and teleology. The two approaches offer different perspectives on ethical problems. They serve to illustrate that a judgment about the ethicality of some approach depends not only on the researcher's awareness of the ethical dilemma but also on his or her philosophical orientation or value system.[7] Then the appendix discusses some of the major ethical issues that arise within the researchers' three domains of ethical responsibility (pictured in Figure 2A.1): (1) the researcher–participant relationship, (2) the researcher–client relationship, and (3) the researcher–research team relationship. It is recognized that all these interactions take place within a larger environment and that they have potential implications for society as well as for the research profession itself.

One of the many things that make ethical decisions difficult is that the researcher's duties and responsibilities toward one party in the three domains often conflict with the individual's responsibilities toward another, including one's self. The individual then must somehow balance these opposing obligations. Consider, for example, the dilemma

---

[5]Robert A. Cooke, *Ethics in Business: A Perspective* (Chicago: Arthur Andersen & Co., 1988), p. 2.

[6]For an empirical study of how people's views on ethical behaviors in research affect their participation, see Eleanor Singer, "Public Reactions to Some Ethical Issues of Social Research," *Journal of Consumer Research,* 11 (June 1984), pp. 501–509.

[7]This appendix approaches ethics from the micro, or individual, level. It can also be approached from a macro perspective in which the focus is on the ethical rightness or wrongness of the system itself or from a company or firm perspective. For discussion of the types of questions that arise from these alternative perspectives, see Cooke, *Ethics in Business.*

TABLE **2A.1**   **A Personal Code for Practicing Market and Opinion Research**

A. My commitment to scientific practice

1. I WILL follow the principles and use the methods of scientific investigation in the research I do. Research, as I define it, means seeking knowledge through scientific study. It can be practiced at many levels of complexity and precision and through many approaches, but to fit my definition it must have a serious purpose, use orderly and objective thinking, and show a respect for data. Whatever research I do will reflect, in these qualities, its scientific orientation.

2. I will do research in the framework of the scientific method.

— Serious research is a process that follows the scientific method. It starts with defining the problem and ends with challenging the results through testing and reanalysis.

3. I will use scientific techniques that fit the individual problem.

— In the collection and analysis of information, research may use procedures from a variety of scientific disciplines. I cannot master all of the available approaches, but I will understand and use a range of techniques. I will put the best tools I can against the problem at hand.

4. I will present each research study for what it is and claim for it the precision and significance it deserves to have.

— In the field of market and opinion research, even the best designs are imperfect and the best results approximations. The data are estimates, the methods are affordable compromises; there usually are none of the external checks or the critical discussion that might come with open publication.

— In these circumstances the burden of objectivity is on the researcher to provide a professional explanation appropriate to the way the research was done and the way it will be used.

— I will put each study I do into perspective, assess its reliability and application, and say how its technical aspects affect its meaning.

5. I will encourage users to make independent evaluations of my research.

— I will question and check and challenge the work that others do for me and hope that those I work for will follow the same practice.

— I will urge users to go beyond checking for consistency and plausibility, since regularity over time or between small samples can result from intensive measurements or undisclosed smoothing of the data and may say little or nothing about how well the research was done.

— I see rigorous examination and ventilation as the best tests of good research and the best incentives for doing it.

6. I will give the users of my research the information they need to understand it.

— I respect the rights of those who pay for my research and, if the research is published, of all who use it, to be told how the research was conducted, in such detail that a good researcher could redo the study without further information.

— Additionally, I will provide such information as the rates of sample completion, the results of field validations, the statistical error limits, and possible sources of other errors, when this is relevant and would help users understand the research.

— I will conceal or misrepresent nothing with a serious bearing on how the research was done, how good it is, or what it means.

My commitment to scientific practice gives me the approach, the tools, the point of view, and the challenge I need for productive study. It is what identifies me, at least to myself, as a professional in the practice of research.

B. My commitment to honest research

1. I AM committed to honest research and to honest research information. I see simple honesty as basic to the research concept and honest counts and honest meaning as fundamental to research practice. Most of the research I do is used to make money, or support a point of view, or strengthen an argument. I believe that honest research can be done toward such objectives, but only if the research is objectively designed, im-

TABLE 2A.1   *Continued*

partially conducted, and delivered free of cosmetic alteration or biased interpretation.

2. I will base research on honest plans, set up to get germane and honest answers.
— Honest research is not designed to mislead or misrepresent, or to use measurements made under abnormal or manipulated conditions as representations of the public's normal behavior.

3. I will work insistently for sound field operations, for the collection, in the field, of honest information.
— Whether or not a good design translated into honest data depends on how the data are gathered.
— I have seen how easily research can be corrupted by failures to follow instructions, by invented responses, or by misrepresentation of how or from whom the data were collected. I know how often such problems are linked to unworkable questionnaires and unfair time and productivity demands from those conducting the survey.
— I will instead make a conscious effort to understand the realities of field operations. I will insist on the careful selection of field people. I will provide positive incentives for quality work, and check the work I get with an objective and rigorous system of validations.

4. I will resist temptations to shade results, to overstate their significance, and to reach conclusions that go beyond the findings.
— I will not alter the findings of research to protect my income or my reputation.
— I believe it is my duty, as a researcher, to draw as much meaning as I can from collected information. But I will not go beyond honest analysis in an effort to give sponsors what they want to hear or what they have paid for.
I will personally guarantee the integrity of whatever data I report. I will accept responsibility for the conclusions I draw. If I cannot do research honestly, I will not do it at all.

C. My commitment to fair business dealings

1. I WILL protect the interests of those I serve

and deal fairly with people and organizations who do research or perform research functions. Those who pay for research, and those who do it, have a right to seek a profit from their research operations. But this has to be accomplished through businesslike and responsible conduct. If the findings of my research are to be above suspicion, the business practices involved in the research must also be above suspicion.

2. I will treat all of the information involved in my research as privileged.
— I will protect the confidentiality of unpublished proprietary research and of anything I learn from a sponsor about the sponsor's business.
— I will expect that a research plan or proposal submitted in confidence will be treated as proprietary and not used or disclosed without approval outside the company to which it was submitted.

3. I will keep my relations with those I work for professional and responsible.
— I will make it a point to discuss with sponsors any problems in conducting research as the problems are encountered.
— I will not add unrelated questions to a study without the sponsor's consent.
— I will fit the scope of any research I do to the importance of the insights and the need for precision in the information the research is designed to provide.

4. I will compete fairly against others who do research and deal fairly with those who do or sell research services.
— I support active competition for research assignments and believe researchers should compete on terms or conditions as well as the quality of their skills and the excellence of their thinking. But I will not buy or sell research at terms or conditions or with specifications that make honest work impossible or with commitments to do work or to produce results that cannot be honored.

(continued)

TABLE 2A.1   *Continued*

—I will keep the agreements I make with interviewers and other research workers and pay them promptly when their work is completed. I will not contract for research unless I can pay for that work.

—I consider kickbacks and other illicit favors given in return for research business to be incompatible with research and below the minimum levels of research ethics.

—I will get and give full value for the money spent through me for research or research services.

In the practice of research, I will hold to the highest standards of legality and business ethics, and beyond that, I will do whatever is necessary to ensure the confidence of those I work for, and those who provide me with help or information.

D. My commitment to the public interest

1. I WILL protect the rights of respondents and the general public to fair treatment from the research I do. I recognize that my research may intrude on the time and privacy of those who give me information. But I will make every effort to minimize their discomfort, protect their identity, and make sure their views are heard and reported.

2. I will do research without harming, embarrassing, or taking unfair advantage of respondents.

—I believe that, with care and imagination, participation in an honest and productive survey can be made a positive experience for most respondents, and I believe this can be accomplished without compromising the interests of the sponsor or the scientific integrity of the research.

—I will not drain the public's goodwill and cooperation through unnecessarily long interviews or poorly designed questioning procedures. And I will not tolerate those who use the pretense of conducting research to get money from, exploit, propagandize, or otherwise take advantage of people.

3. I will protect the right to privacy by guarding the identity of individual respondents.

—I will not release the names of respondents to anyone for any purpose other than legitimate validation, because the guarantee of anonymity is the respondent's only insurance against the disclosure of personal matters.

4. I will encourage sponsors to do research that seeks out and effectively represents the needs and views of the public.

—It is my responsibility, as a researcher, to listen for the voice of the people and to make it heard.

—Research serves its highest purpose when it speaks for the citizen or the consumer, when it brings the wants and wishes and ideas of people to light, not for manipulation or exploitation, but for translation into needed products and laws and services.

E. I stand, by my own election, as an honest broker between those who give their money for research and those who give their information. I will assure a fair exchange between the parties. I will practice research to serve the public as well as the private interest.

Source: Courtesy of the New York Chapter, American Marketing Association.

faced by a researcher deciding whether to expose the true purpose of a study to potential respondents. The researcher believes that exposing the true purpose beforehand would increase noncooperation and would lower the accuracy and reliability of the data collected from those who participate. The researcher's obligation to the client suggests that the research purpose should be disguised. That could be unfair to respondents. As a compromise, the researcher might decide to withhold the purpose initially but then to debrief each respondent after securing the data. Even though that might be perceived as

FIGURE 2A.1 **A Structure for Evaluating Ethical Dilemmas**

	Participant	Client	Member of Research Team
Deontological-Based Analysis Impact of the contemplated action on the rights of each individual			
Teleological-Based Analysis Benefits or consequences to be realized from the contemplated action			

being more fair than keeping the purpose hidden, it might also cause some of the respondents to feel that they had been duped. That, in turn, could cause them to refuse to participate in any research investigations in the future, thereby hurting the profession.

ETHICAL FRAMEWORKS

As mentioned previously, there are currently two major traditions providing different bases for evaluating the ethics of a given act that tend to dominate ethical reasoning in general and marketing ethics in particular: **deontology** and **teleology**.[8]

---

[8]For general discussions of the differences between the perspectives, see Cooke, *Ethics in Business;* O. C. Ferrell and Larry G. Gresham, "A Contingency Framework for Understanding Ethical Decision Making in Marketing," *Journal of Marketing,* 49 (Summer 1985), pp. 87–96; Shelby D. Hunt and Scott Vitell, "A General Theory of Marketing Ethics," *Journal of Macromarketing,* 6 (Spring 1986), pp. 5–16; and Donald P. Robin and R. Eric Reidenbach, "Social Responsibility, Ethics, and Marketing Strategy: Closing the Gap between Concept and Application," *Journal of Marketing,* 51 (January 1987), pp. 44–58. For descriptions of other frameworks, see one of the general books on ethics, such as Richard De George, *Business Ethics,* 2nd ed. (New York: Macmillan); or Manuel Velasquez, *Business Ethics,* 2nd ed. (Englewood Cliffs, N.J.: Prentice-Hall, Inc., 1982). For a general treatment of ethics in marketing, including separate discussions of ethics in advertising, field sales, and marketing research, see Gene R. Laczniak and Patrick E. Murphy, eds., *Marketing Ethics: Guidelines for Managers* (Lexington, Mass.: D.C. Heath, 1985).

Deontology

Deontological ethics focus on the welfare of the individual and emphasize means and intentions for justifying an act. Deontologists believe that features of the act itself make it right or wrong. Deontological thinking rests on two fundamental principles — the rights principle and the justice principle. The *rights principle* focuses on two criteria for judging an action: (1) universality, which means that every act should be based on principles that everyone could act on; and (2) reversibility, which means that every act should be based on reasons that the actor would be willing to have all others use, even as a basis for how they treat the actor. The rights principle is the philosophical source of specific, generally acknowledged rights in society, such as the "right to know." Several rights have acquired the force of law and have become established in the literature with respect to the treatment of research participants.[9]

The *justice principle* reflects three categories of justice: (1) distributive, whereby resources are distributed according to some evaluation of just desserts; (2) retributive, whereby the wrongdoer is punished proportionally to the wrong, provided that it was committed knowingly and freely; and (3) compensatory, whereby the injured party is restored to his or her original position. An example of the justice principle applied in a marketing research setting concerns the compensatory measures that researchers take in debriefing research participants who have been significantly changed by the research experience.

With its emphasis on the issue that every individual has a right to be treated in ways that ensure the person's dignity, respect, and autonomy, the deontological model is sometimes referred to as the rights, or entitlements, model.

Teleology

The most well-known branch of teleological ethics is **utilitarianism,** which focuses on society as the unit of analysis and stresses the consequences of an act in evaluating its ethical status rather than the intentions behind it.[10] The utilitarian model emphasizes the consequences that an action may have on all those directly or indirectly affected by it. The utilitarian perspective holds that the correct course of action is the one that promotes "the greatest good for the greatest number." Utilitarianism requires that a social cost/benefit analysis be conducted for the contemplated action. All benefits and costs to all persons affected by the particular act need to be considered to "the degree possible and summarized as the net of all benefits minus all costs. If the net result is positive, the act is morally acceptable; if the net result is negative, the act is not."[11] Net benefits can be assessed by focusing on the questions listed in Table 2A.2.

---

[9]Alice M. Tybout and Gerald Zaltman, "Ethics in Marketing Research: Their Practical Relevance," *Journal of Marketing Research,* 11 (November 1974), pp. 357–368.

[10]The various teleological theories differ on the issue of whose good it is that one ought to promote. Whereas utilitarianism focuses on the net benefits to society, ethical egoism holds that individuals ought to focus on their own self-interests when evaluating the consequences of an act.

[11]Robin and Reidenbach, "Social Responsibility, Ethics, and Marketing Strategy," p. 46.

TABLE 2A.2   **Questions That Need Asking to Apply the Utilitarian Model**

What are the viable courses of action available?	Who is directly harmed? Who is indirectly harmed?
What are the alternatives?	Who is directly benefited? Who is indirectly benefited?
What are the harms and benefits associated with the course of action available?	What are the social and/or economic costs attached to each alternative course of action?
Can these harms and benefits be measured? Can they be compared?	Which alternatives will most likely yield the greatest net benefit to all individuals affected by the decision? Or, if no alternative yields a net benefit, which one will lead to the least overall harm?
How long will these harms and benefits last?	
When will these harms and benefits begin?	

Source: Robert A. Cooke, *Ethics in Business: A Perspective* (Chicago: Arthur Andersen & Co., 1988), p. 5.

Historically, social scientists for the most part have assumed that a cost/benefit analysis is appropriate in deciding whether or not to conduct a research study.[12] Usually, the costs of conducting the study, in terms of time, money, and harm to participants, are weighed against its benefits in terms of useful and valid information to society. Marketing researchers have operated similarly, but they have typically focused on the benefits to the client rather than to society as a whole. Both have tended to neglect or have operated as if they are seemingly unaware of other ethical perspectives, or that the decision reached from applying a utilitarian perspective could conflict with one reached from applying some other perspective. A case in point is illustrated in the ethical dilemmas in Table 2A.3, which capture nicely the difference in emphasis between the deontological and teleological perspectives.

The utilitarian (teleological) perspective, with its focus on the greatest good for the greatest number, would suggest that both the sheriff and the CEO acted correctly. By acting the way they did, they saved the other eleven. The deontological view, with its emphasis on fairness and justice to the individual, would suggest that both acted unethically. The dilemmas illustrate one of the fundamental problems with the utilitarian view—namely, that individuals or small groups can suffer major harm because their ''large costs'' are averaged with small gains to a large number of other people, with the result that the net benefit for the act is positive.

Partly because small segments can pay a high price for a slight benefit to large numbers, the suggestion has recently been made that utilitarianism is only appropriate to very general planning when no specific harm to individuals is expected and that marketing activities having a foreseeable and potentially serious impact on individuals should

---

[12]Louise H. Kidder and Charles M. Judd, *Research Methods in Social Relations,* 5th ed. (New York: Holt, Rinehart and Winston, 1986), pp. 452–510.

TABLE 2A.3   **Contrasting Ethical Applications of Deontological and Teleological Analysis**

Consider one situation in which a small-town sheriff is confronted with the following in a "grade B" Western movie: Twelve men have been arrested for murder. The town is upset, and a mob threatens to kill all 12, unless the individual who committed the heinous crime comes forward. The sheriff can't stop the mob, so one person is chosen at random and turned over to the crowd, thus saving the other 11.

Or consider this case: The CEO of a company is under attack because the company recently experienced some setbacks caused entirely by external circumstances. Stockholders stand to lose much of their investment, and the entire leadership of the company is threatened. At random and without any foundation or reason the CEO decides to blame one of the vice-presidents. The entire company is saved.

Here's the issue: Did the sheriff or CEO act ethically in either or both cases?

Source: Taken from the comments made by Myles Brand, Provost and Vice-President for Academic Affairs at the Ohio State University, while serving as a moderator for the session "Academia: Fostering Values" at the Fourth Biannual W. Arthur Cullman Symposium, The Ohio State University, Columbus, Ohio, April 25, 1988.

be regulated by deontological reasoning.[13] This implies that since research participants, clients, and team members are identifiable individuals and the effect of the research on them can be anticipated, the criteria of universality and reversibility should be applied rather than a broad cost-benefit analysis.

Readers also need to be aware that although the two frameworks emphasize different perspectives by which the ethicality of some contemplated act can be evaluated, neither approach provides precise answers to ethical decisions. In a utilitarian analysis, for example, one still needs to quantify costs and benefits; in deontological reasoning, one needs to evaluate the seriousness of a right's infringement. What constitutes ethical conduct in the eyes of the profession is ultimately going to be a matter of consensus. That consensus can be reached only if individual researchers think about ethical issues and exchange views.

In part to redress the balance in a field dominated by a utilitarian approach to ethical decision making, deontological reasoning underlies the remainder of the discussion in this appendix — specifically, identifying rights violations and conflicts and evaluating their severity. As students of marketing research, you should form the habit of interpreting a rights violation, as identified here, as a cost to be integrated into a utilitarian cost/benefit analysis. Interpreting the issues from both perspectives should make you more informed researchers who are better able to see and to evaluate the ethical trade-offs in particular situations.

RESEARCHER–RESEARCH PARTICIPANT RELATIONSHIP

One useful way of viewing the ethical dilemmas that arise in the domain of the researcher–research participant relationship is by categorizing them according to the five

---

[13]Robin and Reidenbach, "Social Responsibility, Ethics, and Marketing Strategy."

rights of research participants to which they are most strongly related.[14] The advantage of discussing these issues within such a framework is that the emphasis is on identifying why a procedure might be unethical (e.g., it violates participants' right to safety) and learning which procedures in the past have caused ethical controversy. Researchers are then in a better position to generalize to new situations as they arise.

On March 15, 1962, President Kennedy delivered a special message on protecting consumers' interests in which he outlined the Consumers' Bill of Rights, enumerating the right to safety, the right to be informed, the right to choose, and the right to be heard. These four rights were given the force of law in the Privacy Act of 1974, which applies to the abuse of respondents in federal government surveys.[15] Moreover, because most marketing research participants are acting in their role as consumers, these rights are ethically (even where they are not legally) applicable to our discussion. Other rights have since been advocated by various interest groups (e.g., the right to a consumer education, the right to representation, the right to a healthy physical environment), but one right in particular has been generally accepted and seems appropriate within the domain of the researcher–research participant relationship: the right to redress.[16]

In many research instances, a violation of one right may also involve a violation of another. Not all rights violations are grievous, however, so once an infringement has been identified, subjective judgment is required to evaluate the seriousness of the offense. For example, many researchers have pointed out that the degree of deception involved in concealing the true purpose of an experiment (and disregarding the subjects' right to be informed) is usually of the same trivial order as the degree of deception involved in the "white lies" that are an inherent part of everyone's social and family life. Still, even minor deceits can contribute to the growing atmosphere of distrust of marketing researchers in society and might better be minimized.

Table 2A.4 lists the eight areas of ethical concern that seem most relevant to the domain of the researcher–research participant relationship.[17] Each key issue primarily

---

[14]This procedure is consistent with the approach used by Tybout and Zaltman. Their analysis concentrated on three of the four rights then established, rather than the five rights discussed here. See Tybout and Zaltman, "Ethics in Marketing Research: Their Practical Relevance."

[15]Cynthia J. Frey and Thomas C. Kinnear, "Legal Constraints and Marketing Research: Review and Call to Action," *Journal of Marketing Research*, 16 (August 1979), pp. 295–302.

[16]David A. Aaker and George S. Day, "A Guide to Consumerism," in David A. Aaker and George S. Day, eds., *Consumerism: Search for the Consumer Interest* (New York: Macmillan Publishing Co., Inc., 1982), pp. 4–8; and Lee E. Preston and Paul N. Bloom, "The Concerns of the Rich/Poor Consumer," in Paul N. Bloom and Ruth Belk Smith, eds., *The Future of Consumerism* (Lexington, Mass.: D. C. Heath and Co., 1986), pp. 38–40.

[17]For background on the various rights of research participants, see Herbert C. Kelman, "Human Uses of Human Subjects: The Problem of Deception in Social Psychological Experiments," *Psychological Bulletin*, 67 (January 1967), pp. 1–11; Charles Mayer and Charles White, Jr., "The Law of Privacy and Marketing Research," *Journal of Marketing*, 33 (April 1969), pp. 1–4; Herbert C. Kelman, "The Rights of the Subject in Social Research: An Analysis in Terms of Relative Power and Legitimacy," *American Psychologist*, 27 (November 1972), pp. 989–1016; Tybout and Zaltman, "Ethics in Marketing Research;" "Ethical Principles of Psychologists," *American Psychologist*, 36 (June 1981); pp. 633–638; Robert Rosenthal and Ralph L. Rosnow, *Essentials of Behavioral Research: Methods and Data Analysis* (New York: McGraw-Hill, 1984); and Kidder and Judd, *Research Methods in Social Relations*.

TABLE 2A.4   **Eight Key Problem Areas of Ethical Concern within the Domain of the Researcher–Research Participant Relationship**

Ethical Issues	Rights Violations	Rights Compensation
1. Preserving participants' anonymity	Right to safety	
2. Exposing participants to mental stress	Right to safety	Right to be heard
3. Asking participants questions detrimental to their self-interest	Right to safety	
4. Use of special equipment and techniques	Right to safety	Right to redress
5. Involving participants in research without their knowledge	Right to be informed	Right to redress
6. Use of deception	Right to be informed	Right to be heard; right to redress
7. Use of coercion	Right to choose	
8. Depriving participants of their right to self-determination	Right to choose	

violates one of three rights: the right to safety, to be informed, or to choose. The fourth right, the right to be heard, is violated whenever a participant is not allowed to ask questions during and after the research procedure or to voice anxieties and misgivings. Moreover, compliance with the right to be heard by the researcher can sometimes compensate for an infringement of other rights, the most pertinent example being the compensatory use of debriefing procedures after experiments. Whereas the right to be heard stresses the fundamental need for self-expression, the right to redress emphasizes restoration to an original or comparable position. Although it can be argued that compensatory measures are desirable in all eight situations, Table 2A.4 lists the use of the right to be heard and the right to redress where they seem to be most pertinent.

Preserving Participants' Anonymity

Maintaining subjects' anonymity ensures that their identity is safe from invasions of privacy. The preservation of participants' anonymity is often a more serious obligation in the field of marketing research than in other behavioral disciplines, because the information obtained by marketing researchers can be extremely useful to other agents. Purchase-related data, for example, are of interest to all kinds of sellers. As previously noted, one of the currently widespread abuses of telephone surveys regards the sale to direct-mail marketers of information obtained from telephone respondents under the guise of research. Further, knowledge of participants' identities is often desirable for the client who wishes to compile a mailing list of survey respondents, particularly those who feel favorably disposed to the product concept being tested. Unless respondents agree ahead of time to have their identities disclosed to the sponsor, however, such information should not be provided.

Exposing Participants to Mental Stress

An effort should be made at all times to minimize any mental stress that the research procedures may inflict on participants. On an everyday procedural level, this includes arriving punctually for a prearranged interview, showing the subject consideration and respect, and promptly fulfilling one's commitments (e.g., payment for participating). In addition, subjects may be exposed to stress as a result of the idiosyncratic subject matter of an experiment. For example, taste tests can be humiliating for participants who pride themselves on their ability to identify a certain brand when they find themselves unable to do so in a blind taste test.

Debriefing is usually recognized as essential if the research experience is stressful or if deception is used, but it can be undertaken in other circumstances because it is consistent with the subject's right to be heard. Its main purpose is to give participants the opportunity to voice their views on the research experience and to have any anxieties dispelled. Ideally, subjects should be debriefed individually to reduce embarrassment and facilitate honesty, and efforts should be made to outline the main features of the research project, to convey the researcher's sincere belief in its importance, and to emphasize the value of the subject's own contribution. A second purpose of debriefing is to provide the researcher with insights concerning unforeseen problems in the procedure. This stage in the debriefing process is best accomplished by someone unconnected with the study in the subject's eyes so that the participant can be frank about the experience without fear of disappointing the research staff. Although it will be too late to correct most problems, the insights may be useful in interpreting the results and interacting more productively with subjects in the future.

Asking Participants Questions Detrimental to Their Self-Interest

Consider the situation in which a marketing researcher is employed to ask respondents how acceptable certain prices are for a product, when the client's objective is to raise the current price to the highest acceptable level. If respondents are informed of the purpose of the research and its sponsor, they are likely to hedge in their answers, which will reduce the quality of the research. If, on the other hand, they are not informed about the purpose and sponsor, their responses may be against their own self-interests, thereby violating their right to safety. Situations like this that put the researcher's ethical standards against his or her technical standards are particularly distressing. Although the simplest solution may be to refuse to undertake the project, it is up to the individual to consider all the issues involved and reach an informed decision with which he or she feels comfortable.

Use of Special Equipment and Techniques

Special equipment and techniques may violate rights other than participants' right to safety, and these items deserve separate mention largely because they threaten subjects' safety in ways that other procedures do not. One class of equipment, recording devices, makes later identification of individual subjects much easier and thus threatens their anonymity. The potential audience for a participant's response is also broadened when recordings are used. In certain cases, such techniques may even render blackmail a possibility. For example, a sympathetic and interested researcher may prompt a salesperson to reveal expense account abuses or sales ploys inconsistent with his employer's policies, disclosure of which might deprive him of his job, bonus, and so on. In short, the researcher must take active responsibility for the correct use of audio- and videotapes and for their safe storage. Another class of special techniques that causes ethical concern is projective techniques, the renewed use of which is currently being advocated in consumer research.[18] Projective techniques are believed to be a means of revealing unconscious thoughts and motives. In situations where the subject is not even aware of what he or she is revealing, it is evident that the researcher is doubly obliged to act discreetly and responsibly.

If safety is interpreted primarily in physical rather than privacy terms, equipment that is used to measure participants' physiological reactions can also violate the right to safety. Although most measures in marketing research have traditionally been either self-report or human observational, there is growing interest in the use of physiological measures, particularly to measure the response to advertising.[19] When testing physiological reactions, the researcher is obligated to ensure that the machines are used and maintained properly so that there is no threat to the participant's physical safety. In addition, it is important that the subject be psychologically comfortable with the procedure, which usually entails explaining how the equipment functions and how it should feel to the subject.

Involving Participants in Research without Their Knowledge

The importance of gaining subjects' "informed, expressed consent" was first articulated at the Nuremburg Trials in protest against the inhuman treatment of prisoners involved in research in Nazi concentration camps. The criterion of "informed, expressed consent" has subsequently been incorporated into many codes of ethics and was amended to allow incompletely informed consent, provided that (a) the research involves minimal risk to subjects, and (b) the research could not be practically carried out otherwise. The grim source of the "informed, expressed consent" rule lends it particular importance; moreover, the general concept gives rise to two further areas of ethical concern: the use of coercion and the use of deception.

Three common procedures exist that involve subjects in research without their knowledge and therefore without their consent:

---

[18]David G. Mick, "Consumer Research and Semiotics: Exploring the Morphology of Signs, Symbols, and Significance," *Journal of Consumer Research*, 13 (September 1986), pp. 196–213.

[19]David W. Stewart, "Physiological Measurement of Advertising Effects," *Psychology and Marketing*, 1 (Spring 1984), pp. 43–48; John T. Cacioppo and Richard E. Petty, "Physiological Responses and Advertising Effects: Is the Cup Half Full or Half Empty," *Psychology and Marketing*, 2 (Summer 1985), pp. 115–126; Joanne M. Klebba, "Physiological Measures of Research: A Review of Brain Activity, Electrodermal Response, Pupil Dilation and Voice Analysis Methods and Studies," in *Current Issues and Research in Advertising* (Ann Arbor: University of Michigan, 1985), pp. 53–76; and Scott S. Liu, "Picture-Image Memory of TV Advertising in Low-Involvement Situations: A Psychophysiological Analysis," in *Current Issues and Research in Advertising* (Ann Arbor: University of Michigan, 1986), pp. 27–60.

The first, *participant observation*, is the name given to procedures in which the researcher participates in the activity of interest in order to observe people's behavior in their natural environment. A relevant example would be a marketer living among and studying young, white American males (18–25 years old) for 18 months in order to better understand their consumption behavior. One class of error to which participant observation is especially sensitive is a "control effect," which occurs when the measurement process itself causes the phenomenon to change. This often happens when the researcher discloses his or her identity and purpose, at which time the people who are being observed alter their behavior. The control effect can be, and usually is, reduced by incognito participation, which then becomes a source of ethical problems. The concerted move toward greater use of qualitative methods among researchers renders the ethical questions inherent in participant observation more urgent.

Few clear guidelines exist on how participant observers should balance ethical concerns against greater validity in observation. One suggestion is to reveal one's true identity and purpose to subjects once the data have been collected and to allow them to read the final report on their activities.[20] This course of action is consistent with participants' right to be heard. It rests on the hope that they will endorse the researcher's efforts and conclusions. If they do not support the study's findings, however, the researcher is faced with two competing obligations: promoting the use of the research versus respecting the subject's right to redress (i.e., to refuse to participate after the fact).

A second procedure, *observing people in public places*, is less intrusive than participant observation and is also more common among marketing researchers. It is helpful to watch shoppers' reactions to new floor displays in a store, for example. For many researchers, any activity or conversation occurring in a public place is fair game and arouses no ethical scruples. Strictly speaking, however, the research participants are being involved without their knowledge or consent, and their rights are being infringed on. If the research cannot be practically carried out by any other means, the violation can be minimized in two ways: (1) by posting an obvious notice over the whole area (e.g., the store) stating that it is under observation by researchers, or (2) by approaching subjects individually once the data have been collected and asking their permission to use the information. The latter procedure gives people the opportunity to refuse to participate after the fact and is consistent with their right to redress.

Withholding benefits from control groups is an issue of particular concern in running field experiments. Indeed, Burroughs-Wellcome's AIDS-combating drug AZT was recently released for general use before testing was complete, precisely because it seemed ethically indefensible to deprive test control groups of the hope of delaying the disease's progress.[21] Less dramatic examples of field experiments that would deprive control groups of benefits include sales force management studies in which the experimental groups receive increased incentives and the control group does not, or market tests of

---

[20]Elizabeth C. Hirschman, "Humanistic Inquiry in Marketing Research: Philosophy, Method, and Criteria," *Journal of Marketing Research*, 23 (August 1986), p. 244.

[21]D. Grady, "Look, Doctor, I'm Dying. Give Me the Drug," *Discover* (August 1986), pp. 78–86.

promotional tools in which the control group does not receive the sales promotion. Issues to consider in deciding whether to run a field experiment with a control group include the importance of the benefit to the participants and the crucial nature of the information to be provided by running the study.

Use of Deception

Deception is commonly used in research with human participants in the belief that subjects try to guess what behavior the researcher is expecting to see, and they then alter their behavior accordingly.[22] Even procedural information can provoke dysfunctional responses. If the researcher announces that a recall test will be given later, for example, subjects may make a conscious effort to memorize the stimuli, whereas the recall test may well have been intended to tap noneffortful remembrance. Because of such concerns, most research is given a cover story or guise, and subjects in experiments are not informed about what kinds of tests will be given to them later.

These precautions seem sensible from the point of view of preserving the validity of the research, but they violate the subjects' right to know what is going to happen to them and the real context in which their responses are being made. Once again, there is no single correct decision that can be generalized for all research. However, a legal framework is available in this instance to supplement other frameworks. The 1981 amendment to the Privacy Act sanctions incompletely informed consent, provided that the research involves minimal risk to the subject and cannot be practically carried out any other way. Whenever deception is used, it is essential that, during debriefing, participants are informed why deception was necessary and are reassured that their believing the cover story does not mean that they have been made fools of.

Use of Coercion

The use of coercion by Nazi doctors in World War II concentration camps to get subjects for their research experiments has been well publicized. Less overt forms of coercion operate frequently in today's research with human subjects, and the legitimate researcher needs to be alert to them.

Captive Subject Pools   Unlike many social scientists, marketers usually do not recruit prisoners or hospital patients, subjects who tend to think that it will count against them in their own institution if they refuse to participate. But marketing researchers do commonly use employees who may think that their success in the company is partially dependent on their compliance. Researchers investigating sales force performance issues, for example, have been known to obtain access to the salespeople through their manager. One incentive that has been used to encourage salespeople to participate in the study is to note in their personnel files (which are used by the manager to evaluate them)

---

[22]Alan G. Sawyer, "Demand Artifacts in Laboratory Experiments," *Journal of Consumer Research*, 1 (March 1975), pp. 20–30; and Leonard Berkowitz and Edward Donnerstein, "External Validity Is More than Skin Deep: Some Answers of Criticisms of Laboratory Experiments," *American Psychologist*, 37 (March 1982), pp. 245–257.

whether or not they participated. In general, substantial incentives tend to have coercive aspects. Church groups also have been used by marketing researchers, because they represent a convenient sample of adults of various ages. In such cases, care should always be taken to ensure that the church or other institutional members do not feel coerced, particularly if the researcher makes a donation for each participant who complies.

Persistent Harassment   Telephone interviewing currently is the most popular data collection technique among marketing researchers. In a recent Walker Industry Image Study, for example, 73 percent of the respondents indicated that they had participated in a research study in the past, and 70 percent of those who had participated previously had done so via a telephone interview.[23] Unfortunately, its high usage level has provoked an ethical dispute in the profession that may lead to government regulation. Consumers are being harassed by an overload of telephone surveys, many of which are merely sales ploys in disguise and an increasing number of which, though genuine, comprise irritatingly impersonal computer-voiced interviews. As with all forms of coercion used in recruiting research subjects, harassment by telephone tends to result not only in an ethical dilemma but also in poor data. If people agree to answer questions, they will do so resentfully and without due care; it is also likely that many will refuse to participate at all, with the result that the final sample of respondents will be skewed and will have been relatively costly to obtain.[24] Moreover, if a given profession cannot solve its own ethical problems, government eventually steps in with regulations that tend to cover more than the original problem.

Status of the Researcher   As an expert and authority figure, the researcher can use this status as another subtle source of coercion.[25] Sometimes individuals who agreed to take part in the research initially may wish to change their minds later on but are too intimidated to voice their reluctance. Marketing researchers need to be particularly sensitive to this issue when dealing with children, the elderly, the poor, or the uneducated.

Depriving Participants of Their Right to Self-Determination

The experience of participating in research will often have some effect on the individual, but usually it is of a trivial nature, such as when a person, to kill time for ten minutes before supper, fills in a questionnaire about preferred retail outlets. In some instances, however, the subject is substantially changed by the research experience in ways that he or she could not have foreseen and has thereby been deprived of choice in the matter of self-development. For example, the objective of taste tests is to find the alternative that is preferred by most people, or a particular segment of subjects, not to demonstrate to subjects that many of them cannot identify their "favorite" brand when the typical identification symbols (such as the label) have been removed. One nagging question is

---

[23]*Industry Image Study*, 8th Edition (Indianapolis: Walker Research, Inc., 1988), p. 3.

[24]Brannigan, "Pseudo Polls."

[25]Tybout and Zaltman, "Ethics in Marketing Research."

what this does to the individual's self-confidence. In situations like this, it is the experimenter's responsibility to restore the subject to his or her original condition or to a comparable condition, an obligation that is consistent with compensatory justice.

RESEARCHER–CLIENT RELATIONSHIP

The ethical issues surrounding the researcher's interactions with the study's subjects are difficult in their own right, and they become even more troublesome when the researcher's obligations to the client are introduced into the picture. Many times, the demands of how to best serve the client will compete with the demands placed on the researcher regarding the moral rights of participants. Ethical concerns in the domain of the marketing researcher–client relationship can be usefully organized around four main issues: confidentiality, technical integrity, administrative integrity, and research utilization.

Confidentiality

The researcher is obliged to be discreet in at least two respects: (1) in not revealing one client's affairs to another client who is a competitor, and (2) in some circumstances, in not revealing the sponsor of the research to participants. In both cases, the researcher's loyalties can be torn and compromises may be necessary.

It is difficult to serve well several clients who have similar business interests. Even if one keeps one's list of clients confidential so that overt inquiries from one customer about another are avoided, it is not always possible to keep information acquired about one client's interests from affecting work for another client. The collection of basic demographic and socioeconomic information in a particular area is a case in point. What if that information, gathered for one client, is useful in designing a study for another client? Should the researcher ignore the knowledge he or she has when this can raise the quoted cost of the research to the second client and thereby jeopardize the business for the researcher? Because of the need for client confidentiality, the issue of when "background knowledge" stops and an ethical conflict begins is a real one for independent research agencies, as the following comment attests:

> I get involved in a number of proprietary studies. The problem that often arises is that some studies end up covering similar subject matter as previous studies. Our code of ethics states that you cannot use data from one project in a related project for a competitor. However, since I often know some information about an area, I end up compromising my original client. Even though upper management formally states that it should not be done, they also expect it to be done to cut down on expenses. This conflict of interest situation is difficult to deal with. At least in my firm, I don't see a resolution to the issue. It is not a one-time situation, but rather a process that perpetuates itself. To make individuals redo portions of studies which have recently been done is ludicrous, and to forgo potential new business is almost impossible from a financial perspective.[26]

---

[26]Shelby D. Hunt, Lawrence B. Chonko, and James B. Wilcox, "Ethical Problems of Marketing Researchers," *Journal of Marketing Research,* 21 (August 1984), p. 314.

Another issue of client confidentiality concerns whether the researcher should even make known the clients for whom he or she is working. Many researchers believe that their list of clients is good advertising for their research competence and do not wish to be secretive on the subject. At the same time, exposing the list of clients for whom one works violates their confidentiality to a degree and could in some instances compromise their operations. This can happen particularly if the researcher has such a specialized competency that simply listing the client for whom he or she is working tips off competitors as to what the firm may be doing.

A conflict of loyalties also exists if the sponsor of the research does not want to be identified to the research participants, for fear of biasing their responses or indirectly tipping off a competitor. Participants' right to be informed, however, includes knowledge of the research sponsor as well as of the research purpose. Not every obligation can be fulfilled in this instance, and the researcher must make decisions tailored to each situation. For example, greater weight can be given to participants' rights if they are providing information that could be used against their interests.

Technical Integrity

As Research Realities 2A.1 indicates, marketing researchers personally feel that maintaining research integrity is the most difficult ethical problem they face. Violations of research integrity extend from designing studies without due care through the unnecessary use of complex analytical procedures, to the deliberate fudging of data. It cannot be emphasized enough that in this pioneering stage of the profession's development, researchers must maintain the strictest technical integrity if they are to have credibility as professional experts. It is not only unethical but also short-sighted to take advantage of the client's lack of expertise in research design and methodology, because where trust fails, funding eventually does also. Specific recommendations include choosing the simplest appropriate methodology, as opposed to unnecessarily sophisticated and costly techniques; expressing oneself in simple and generally accessible language rather than in intimidating jargon; making explicit mention of the limitations of the research; and refusing any project in which personal problems or conflicts will lead to inadequate performance.

Administrative Integrity

Research Realities 2A.1 indicates that treating clients fairly is also a difficult ethical problem for marketing researchers. Unfair practices that have received particular mention can be generally grouped under the term *administrative integrity,* as distinguished from *technical integrity,* which refers to the honest application of one's professional skills. For independent research agencies, passing on hidden charges to the client, regardless of their source, and conflicts in pricing are common problems. As one senior consultant comments:

> Our firm encourages us to sell clients retainer-type services, rather than fixed-price contracts. Under the "retainer-type" situation, clients are charged however many hours it takes to complete a study and more often than not this turns out to be more expensive (than contracts).

Research Realities 2A.1

Researchers' Own Perceptions of the Four Most Difficult Ethical Problems They Face*

Activity	Examples	Frequency
Maintaining their research integrity	Deliberately withholding information, falsifying figures, altering research results, misusing statistics, ignoring pertinent data	33%
Treating outside clients fairly	Passing hidden charges to clients, overlooking violations of the project requirements when subcontracting parts of the project	11
Maintaining research confidentiality	Sharing information among subsidiaries in the same corporation, using background data developed in a previous project to reduce the cost of a current project	9
Balancing marketing and social considerations	Conducting research for companies that produce products hazardous to one's health, or research that improves the effectiveness of advertising to children	8

*Based on responses to the question, "In all professions (e.g., law, medicine, education, accounting, marketing, etc.), managers are exposed to at least some situations that pose a moral or ethical problem. Would you briefly describe the job situation that poses the *most difficult* ethical or moral problem for you?"

Source: Developed from the information in Shelby D. Hunt, Lawrence B. Chonko, and James B. Wilcox, "Ethical Problems of Marketing Researchers," *Journal of Marketing Research*, 21 (August 1984), pp. 309–324.

What to do? Recommend the "retainer" or act in the best interests of the client and recommend the contract approach?[27]

Research Utilization

A researcher's ethical obligations to the client extend beyond the mere completion of the project. After the project is finished, the researcher has the responsibility to promote the correct use of the research and to prevent the misuse of the findings. To some extent, these obligations are fulfilled if the contributions and limitations of the research are clearly articulated in the research report. In addition to inadvertent misuse, however, the client might deliberately suppress or distort the research results. Empirical evidence, for example, indicates that dishonesty in reporting to higher-ups is perverting the results of market tests and that potentially successful products have been dropped and unwanted

[27]Hunt, Chonko, and Wilcox, "Ethical Problems of Marketing Researchers," p. 314.

ones have been introduced because of the manipulation of marketing research results.[28] Distortion of the findings can create a serious dilemma for the researcher, because it raises the issue of with whom the researcher's loyalties rest: the manager who hired the researcher and to whom the research report was delivered but who is now distorting the findings to support his or her own preconceived beliefs, or the firm for which the manager works. In situations like this, the researcher will often want to set the record straight because it is the firm's (not the manager's) money that paid for the research, and the researcher's own integrity and reputation are also at stake.

RESEARCHER–RESEARCH TEAM RELATIONSHIP

Up to now it appears that researchers operate as individuals when making research decisions. That is incorrect. Rather, an authority structure that constrains the individual researcher's decision-making latitude is likely to exist. When subordinates are acting according to instructions, the supervisor is partly responsible for their ethical conduct. Moreover, in addition to the official hierarchy, there exists an unofficial sphere of influence that renders every team member partially responsible for the others' moral behavior. Three areas of primary concern in the domain of the researcher–research team are the individual's own belief system, association with others at work, and the opportunity to behave unethically.[29]

Own Beliefs

Surprisingly, only a small correlation has been found between people's ethical behavior in organizations and their own ethical beliefs. Indeed, association with other people who are behaving unethically and the opportunity to behave likewise are better predictors of an individual's conduct than his or her own belief system.[30]

Association with Others

Many studies indicate that superiors have a great deal of influence over subordinates' ethical conduct. In fact, actions of top management have been found to be the best predictor of perceived ethical problems for marketing researchers.[31] The source of the boss's influence probably resides in subordinates' fear of reprisals for not conforming

---

[28]Calvin L. Hodock, ''Intellectual Dishonesty Is Perverting the Results from Various Market Tests,'' *Marketing News,* 18 (January 1984), p. 1.

[29]Ferrell and Gresham, ''A Contingency Framework for Understanding Ethical Decision Making in Marketing.''

[30]Mary Zey-Ferrell and O. C. Ferrell, ''Role-Set Configurations and Opportunities as Predictors of Unethical Behavior in Organizations,'' *Human Relations,* 35 (July 1982), pp. 587–604; and O. C. Ferrell, Mary Zey-Ferrell, and Dean Krugman, ''A Comparison of Predictors of Ethical and Unethical Behavior among Corporate and Agency Advertising Managers,'' *Journal of Macromarketing,* 3 (Spring 1983), pp. 19–27.

[31]Hunt, Chonko, and Wilcox, ''Ethical Problems of Marketing Researchers.''

and in their acceptance of legitimate authority. As a consequence of the poor examples they see, marketing practitioners do not see themselves as being under pressure to improve their own ethics.[32] Indeed, they view themselves as more ethical than their peers, top management, and corporate policy. Based on these findings, and consistent with the Ethical Principles of Psychologists,[33] it appears that, in general, the chief investigator of the research project should recognize responsibility for the ethical behavior of juniors and collaborators and take steps to monitor their actions and overtly encourage strict moral integrity.

A caveat is in order here, however: When frequency of contact with superiors is low, peers will have more influence than superiors on ethical conduct. This finding underlines the need for managers who find themselves unable to interact frequently with their staffs to be able to trust all members of the staff. Each member will not only affect the quality of work for which he or she is responsible but will also influence the other team members and the quality of their work.

Opportunity

Evidence suggests that the opportunity to engage in ethical behavior affects its occurrence; more behaviors are likely to be unethical when there is greater opportunity to engage in unethical behavior.[34] Moreover, the opportunity to behave unethically is greater for marketing researchers than for many workers because of their boundary-spanning roles. Marketers, in general, span the boundary between the company and the public; marketing researchers, specifically, bridge the gap between the participant and the client, and there is a great deal of room for dishonesty while playing the go-between. Punishments and rewards might be used to reduce the attractiveness of opportunities for unethical conduct, such as a special raise for acting ethically or a delayed promotion for acting unethically. Management could also issue a corporate code of ethics to announce its concern with ethical issues and to voice standards of conduct that it considers desirable. For codes of ethics to be effective, however, they need to be well integrated into the management team's decision making. Otherwise, they make little difference in researchers' perceptions of ethical problems.[35] Other suggestions to reduce the acceptability of unethical conduct within the organization include the use of consultants and seminars on ethics.[36]

---

[32]O. C. Ferrell and K. Mark Weaver, "Ethical Beliefs of Marketing Managers," *Journal of Marketing,* 42 (July 1978), pp. 69–73.

[33]"Ethical Principles of Psychologists," *American Psychologist,* 36 (June 1981), pp. 633–638.

[34]Zey-Ferrell and Ferrell, "Role-Set Configurations and Opportunities"; Ferrell and Gresham, "A Contingency Framework for Understanding Ethical Decision Making."

[35]Hunt, Chonko, and Wilcox, "Ethical Problems of Marketing Researchers."

[36]Patrick Murphy and Gene R. Laczniak, "Marketing Ethics: A Review with Implications for Managers, Educators and Researchers," in Ben M. Enis and Kenneth J. Roering, eds., *Review of Marketing 1981* (Chicago: American Marketing Association, 1981), pp. 251–266.

NEEDED: A BALANCED PERSPECTIVE

You are probably sensitive by now to the fact that ethical issues are indeed difficult to deal with. Even when one wants to do what is morally right, it is not always intuitively obvious what the correct course of action is. Actions that might benefit one of the parties in the three domains might harm another. Whose rights or what benefits should take precedence? There are no easy answers to this question, but there are some things researchers can do to assure themselves that they are operating ethically when making decisions on techniques.

Sensitivity to the issue helps in itself. Asking oneself about the ethical implications of each contemplated course of action is a useful posture in its own right. Those who do that regularly should behave more ethically because their actions then entail explicit rather than implicit judgments. It is also useful to develop experience and expertise in handling difficult ethical situations. To that end, each of the following chapters contains two or more ethical situations that you are asked to evaluate. These Ethical Dilemmas are strategically placed within the chapters to expose you to the technical elements of the techniques before confronting you with the ethical issues.

You are strongly urged to evaluate each of these Ethical Dilemmas formally using both deontological and teleological moral philosophies, taking into account the typical parties with which researchers deal. Figure 2A.1 offers a structure that you might find useful for conducting these analyses. When applying deontological philosophy to clients and research team members, you might find it helpful to focus on the individuals involved within the client's organization and the research team and to think about their rights in similar terms to the rights identified for participants in research (the right to be informed, the right to be heard, and so on).

SUMMARY

In this appendix, a philosophical base for evaluating the ethics involved in using various marketing research techniques is established. Ethics is concerned with the development of moral standards that can be applied to situations in which there can be actual or potential harm of any kind (economic, physical, or mental) to an individual or group. When contemplating some action, the marketing researcher needs to be concerned with at least three parties: participants or subjects, clients, and members of the research team.

There are two major traditions providing different bases for evaluating the ethics of a given act that tend to dominate marketing ethics: deontology and teleology. Deontological ethics focus on the welfare of the individual and emphasizes means and intentions in justifying an act. Deontologists argue that every individual has certain rights, and it is the features of the act itself with regard to how the act affects these rights that make the act right or wrong.

Teleological ethics focus on the benefits to be derived from the act. The various teleological theories differ on the issue of whose benefits to focus on. The most well-known branch of teleological ethics, utilitarianism, focuses on society as the unit of analysis. It holds that the correct course of action is the one that promotes the greatest good for the greatest number.

From a deontological perspective, participants have the right to safety, the right to be informed, the right to choose, the right to be heard, and the right to redress.

A researcher's most difficult ethical problems in dealing with clients include the problems of maintaining confidentiality, maintaining technical and administrative integrity, and making sure that the research is used correctly. When dealing with other research team members, it is not only the researchers' own beliefs that affect how ethically they behave, but also the ethics of the others with whom they associate and the number of opportunities they face for unethical behavior.

If researchers are to behave ethically, they need to be vigilant. They must be aware that the use of certain techniques in certain instances may be morally questionable. A recommended posture is to evaluate each contemplated action from both the deontological and the teleological perspectives. That, at least, will make the judgment explicit rather than implicit.

Questions

1. The opinion has sometimes been voiced, "If it's legal, it's ethical." Is there any difference between what is legally right and what is morally right? Explain.

2. What are the essential differences between the deontological and teleological ethical perspectives? Which do you embrace? Why?

3. What questions would need to be asked to apply the teleological perspective?

4. What are the basic rights of participants in research?

5. What are the areas of most ethical concern within the domain of the researcher–research participant relationship from a deontological perspective? What rights are at issue in each area?

6. What are the chief ethical concerns of marketing researchers when dealing with clients?

7. What factors most affect a researcher's ethics when dealing with other research team members? What are the implications for how researchers behave?

3

THE RESEARCH PROCESS AND PROBLEM FORMULATION

Chapter 1 highlights the many kinds of problems that marketing research can be used to solve. It emphasizes that marketing research is the firm's communication link with the environment and that it can help the marketing manager in planning, problem solving, and control, although few companies use marketing research for exactly the same activities.

A company's philosophy of how marketing research fits into its marketing plan determines its *program strategy* for marketing research.[1] Some companies may use marketing research on a continuous basis to track sales or to monitor the firm's market share. Others may resort to marketing research only when a problem arises or an important decision — such as the launching of a new product — needs to be made. A program strategy specifies the types of studies that are to be conducted and their purposes. Research Realities 3.1, for example, outlines the types and purposes of the various studies that are conducted by Gillette Company in its constant endeavor to maintain its 60 percent share of the blade and razor market. The design of the individual studies themselves defines the firm's *project strategy* — for example, the use of personal interviews in the national consumer studies, mail questionnaires in the brand tracking studies, and telephone interviews when measuring brand awareness.

Wendy's restaurants' experience is helpful in distinguishing between a program strategy and a project strategy. To help with positioning questions, Wendy's annually conducts in-store surveys. These are conducted over a four-day period in each restaurant in the chain and involve interviews conducted with 200 customers who are asked 20 questions each. The questions cover such things as "demographics, what the customers would order, how often they come to Wendy's, how often they visit a competitors'

---

[1]Walter B. Wentz, *Marketing Research: Management and Methods* (New York: Harper & Row Publishers, 1972), pp. 19–24. For an example of a program strategy for marketing research, see Robert Johnson, "In the Chips: At Frito-Lay, the Consumer is an Obsession," *The Wall Street Journal* (March 22, 1991), pp. B1–B2.

Research Realities 3.1

Major Thrusts of Marketing Research at Gillette Company

1. **Annual National Consumer Studies**

   The objectives of these annual studies are to determine what brand of razor and blade was used for the respondents' last shave, to collect demographic data, and to examine consumer attitudes toward the various blade and razor manufacturers. These studies rely on personal interviews with national panels of male and female respondents, who are selected by using probability sampling methods.

2. **National Brand Tracking Studies**

   The purpose of these studies is to track the use of razors and blades so as to monitor brand loyalty and brand switching tendencies over time. These studies are also conducted annually and use panels of male and female shavers. However, the information for them is collected via mail questionnaires.

3. **Annual Brand Awareness Studies**

   These studies are aimed at determining the "share of mind" Gillette products have. This in-

formation is collected by annual telephone surveys that employ unaided as well as aided recall of brand names and advertising campaigns.

4. **Consumer Use Tests**

   The key objectives of the use-testing studies are to ensure that "Gillette remains state of the art in the competitive arena, that our products are up to our desired performance standards, and that no claims in our advertising, packaging, or display materials are made without substantiation." At least two consumer use tests are conducted each month by Gillette. In these tests, consumers are asked to use a single variation of a product for an extended period of time, at the end of which their evaluation of the product is secured.

5. **Continuous Retail Audits**

   The purpose of the retail audits is to provide top management with monthly market share data, along with information regarding distribution, out-of-stock, and inventory levels of the various Gillette products. This information is purchased from the commercial information services providing syndicated retail audit data. The information is supplemented by special retail audits, which Gillette conducts itself, that look at product displays and the extent to which Gillette blades and razors are featured in retailer advertisements.

Source: Adapted from "Mature Products Remain as the Mainstays in the Gillette Company," *Marketing News,* 17 (June 10, 1983), p. 17. Adapted with permission from Marketing News, published by the American Marketing Association, Chicago, IL 60606. Gillette is using different methods to assess consumer preferences in Eastern Europe. See Lourdes Lee Valeriano, "Marketing: Western Firms Poll Eastern Europeans to Discern Tastes of Nascent Consumers," *The Wall Street Journal* (April 27, 1992), p. B1.

---

establishment, and what they like and dislike about Wendy's and its competitors."[2] The *program strategy* issue is whether or not the assessment of these various customer characteristics is worthwhile and should be continued. If the answer is yes, the *project strategy* issue is how, specifically, to go about this. Should the emphasis on data collection, for example, continue to be in-store surveys using personal interviews? Or should it be switched to self-administered, printed questionnaires or perhaps one of the newer

---

[2]"Wendy's to Use Research Positioning to Direct Growth," *Marketing News,* 14 (January 25, 1980), p. 7. See also James W. Near, "Manager's Journal: Wendy's Successful Mop Bucket Attitude," *The Wall Street Journal* (April 27, 1992), p. A14.

electronic interviewing devices? Should a larger or smaller sample be taken within each store? Should the period of time during which the data are collected be changed? In sum, project strategy deals with how a study should be conducted, whereas program strategy addresses the question of what type of studies the firm should conduct and for what purposes.

All research problems require their own special emphases and approaches. Since every marketing research problem is unique in some ways, the research procedure typically is custom tailored. Nonetheless, there is a sequence of steps, called the **research process** (see Figure 3.1), that can be followed when designing the research project.[3]

FIGURE 3.1   **Relationship among the Stages in the Research Process**

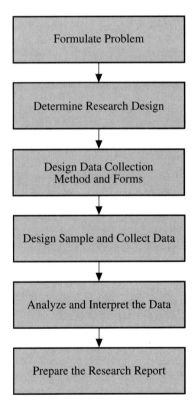

---

[3]Our diagram of the research process is similar to the statement of Claire Selltiz, Lawrence S. Wrightsman, and Stuart W. Cook, *Research Methods in Social Relations,* 3rd ed. (New York: Holt, Rinehart and Winston, 1976), p. 13, and also to that of Harper W. Boyd, Jr., Ralph Westfall, and Stanley F. Stasch, *Marketing Research: Text and Cases,* 7th ed. (Homewood, Ill.: Richard D. Irwin, 1989), pp. 38–48.

This chapter reviews the research process and discusses the first step—formulating the problem.

MARKETING RESEARCH—SEQUENCE OF STEPS

Formulate Problem

One of the more valuable roles marketing research can play is helping to define the problem to be solved. Only when the problem is carefully and precisely defined can research be designed to provide pertinent information. Part of the process of problem definition includes specifying the *objectives* of the specific research project or projects that might be undertaken. Each project should have one or more objectives, and the next step in the process should not be taken until these can be explicitly stated.

Determine Research Design

The sources of information for a study and the research design go hand in hand. They both depend on how much is known about the problem. If relatively little is known about the phenomenon to be investigated, exploratory research will be warranted. Exploratory research may involve reviewing published data, interviewing knowledgeable people, conducting focus groups, or investigating trade literature that discusses similar cases. One of the most important characteristics of exploratory research is its flexibility. Since researchers know little about the problem at this point, they must be ready to follow their intuition about possible areas of investigation or tactics to adopt. If, on the other hand, the problem is precisely and unambiguously formulated, descriptive or causal research is needed. In these research designs, data collection is not flexible but is rigidly specified, with respect to both the data-collection forms and the sample design.

Design Data Collection Method and Forms

Quite often, the information needed to solve the problem cannot be found in the firm's own sales data or other internal records or in published documents such as government census reports or industry sales trends. The research then must depend on **primary data,** which are collected specifically for the study. The research questions here are several. Should the data be collected by observation or questionnaire? Should the form be structured as a fixed set of alternative answers, or should the responses be open-ended? Should the purpose be made clear to the respondent, or should the study objectives be disguised? There are more questions, but these should serve to illustrate the basic concerns at this stage of the research process.

Design Sample and Collect Data

In designing the sample, the researcher must specify, among other things (1) the sampling frame, (2) the sample selection process, and (3) the size of the sample. The **sampling frame** is the list of population elements from which the sample will be drawn. Although we often assume that the frame is implicit in the research problem and thus take it for granted, the assumption can be dangerous.

Take the case of the manufacturer of dog food . . . who went out and did an intensive market study. He tested the demand for dog food; he tested the package size, the design, the whole advertising program. Then he launched the product with a big campaign, got the proper distribution channels, put it on the market and had tremendous sales. But two months later, the bottom dropped out — no follow-up sales. So he called in an expert, who took the dog food out to the local pound, put it in front of the dogs — and they would not touch it. For all the big marketing study, no one had tried the product on the dogs.[4]

As this old but classic example illustrates, the dog population was not part of the sampling frame, probably because it is people who buy dog food and not the dogs themselves. Nevertheless, the careless specification of population elements had dire consequences. While the results may not be as severe, we need to realize that when we sample from, say, a phone book or a mailing list, we are not sampling from the population as a whole but are sampling only from people whose names appear in the phone book or on the mailing list.

The sample selection process requires that the form of the sample be specified. Will it be a probability sample, in which each population element has a known chance of being selected, or will it be a nonprobability sample? Will the probability sample, if one is indicated, be simple or complex? If a nonprobability sample is used, will it be one of convenience, judgment, or some kind of quota system?

The decision on sample size involves determining how many people, households, business firms, or whatever it is necessary to study in order to get answers to the problem that are sufficiently accurate and reliable for the decision being made, without exceeding the time and money budgeted for the project.

Once the dimensions of the sample design are specified, data collection can commence. Data collection will require a field force of some type, although field methods will be largely dictated by the kinds of information to be obtained and the sampling requirements. The use of personnel to collect data raises a host of questions with respect to selection, training, and control of the field staff — questions that must be anticipated in designing the research.

Analyze and Interpret the Data

Researchers may amass a mountain of data, but these data are useless unless the findings are analyzed and the results interpreted in light of the problem at hand. Data analysis generally involves several steps. First, the data-collection forms must be scanned to be sure that they are complete and consistent and that the instructions were followed. This process is called **editing.** Once the forms have been edited, they must be coded. **Coding** involves assigning numbers to each of the answers so that they may be analyzed,

---

[4]Joseph R. Hochstim, ''Practical Uses of Sampling Surveys in the Field of Labor Relations,'' *Proceedings of the Conference on Business Application of Statistical Sampling Methods* (Monticello, Ill.: The Bureau of Business Management, University of Illinois, 1950), pp. 181–182. As should be obvious from the example, researchers need to access both constituencies (dogs and dogs' purchasing agents) when assessing the appeal of a product like dog food. See Nancy J. Church, ''Get the Dog's Opinion When Researching Dog Food,'' *Marketing News,* 22 (August 29, 1988), p. 41, for suggestions on how to go about this.

typically by computer. The final step in analyzing the data is **tabulation.** This refers to the orderly arrangement of data in a table or other summary format achieved by counting the frequency of responses to each question. It is common to also cross classify the data against other variables. For example, researchers may have asked women if they liked a certain kind of new cosmetic. Their responses could be analyzed by age group, income level, and other characteristics.

The coding, editing, and tabulation functions are common to most research studies. The statistical tests applied to the data, if any, are somewhat unique to the particular sampling procedures and data-collection instruments used in the research. These tests should be anticipated before data collection is begun, if possible, to assure that the data and analyses will be appropriate to the problem as specified.

Prepare the Research Report

The research report is the document submitted to management that summarizes the research results and conclusions. It is all that many executives will see of the research effort, and it becomes the standard by which that research is judged. Thus, it is imperative that the research report be clear and accurate, since no matter how well all previous steps have been completed, the project will be no more successful than the research report. One empirical study that investigated the factors determining the extent to which research results are used by firms found that the research report was one of the five most important determinants.[5]

Additional Comments

Even though the preceding discussion should provide some understanding of the steps in the research process, five points need to be made. First, each step in the process is more complex than the discussion suggests. Each involves numerous issues rather than a single decision or even a few decisions. Table 3.1 lists some of the typical questions that need resolving for each stage.

Second, the stages in the research process serve to structure the remainder of this book. The remainder of this chapter, for example, deals with stage 1, problem formulation, and each of the remaining stages warrants a special section in the book.

Third, the stages in the research process can also be used to direct additional study in research methodology. The aspiring research student needs more sophistication in at least some of the stages than this book could possibly provide. The sections and chapters should provide some indication of where in-depth study might be most useful.

Fourth, the stages have been presented as if one would proceed through them in a lockstep fashion when designing a research project. Nothing could be further from the truth. Rather, Figure 3.1 could be drawn with a number of feedback loops suggesting a

---

[5]Rohit Deshpande and Gerald Zaltman, "A Comparison of Factors Affecting Researcher and Manager Perceptions of Market Research Use," *Journal of Marketing Research,* 21 (February 1984), pp. 32–38. See also Michael Y. Hu, "An Experimental Study of Managers' and Researchers' Use of Consumer Marketing Research," *Journal of the Academy of Marketing Science,* 14 (Fall 1986), pp. 44–51.

possible need to rethink and revise the various elements in the process as the study proceeds. The process would begin with problem formulation, but after that anything could happen. The problem might not be specified explicitly enough to allow the development of the research design, in which case the researcher would need to return to stage 1 to delineate the research objectives more clearly. Alternatively, the process may proceed smoothly to the design of the data-collection forms, the pretest of which may require a revision of the research objectives or the research design. Still further, the sample necessary to answer the problem as specified may be cost prohibitive, again requiring a revision of the earlier steps. Once the data are collected, no revision of the procedure is possible. It is possible, though, to revise the earlier steps on the basis of the *anticipated* analysis, and it is imperative that the methods used to analyze the data are determined before the data are collected. Although it is hard for beginning researchers to understand, the steps in the research process are highly interrelated. A decision made at

TABLE **3.1** **Questions to Be Addressed at the Various Stages of the Research Process**

Stage in the Process	Typical Questions
Formulate problem	What is the purpose of the study — to solve a problem? Identify an opportunity?
	Is additional background information necessary?
	What information is needed to make the decision?
	How will the information be used?
	Should research be conducted?
Determine research design	How much is already known?
	Can a hypothesis be formulated?
	What types of questions need to be answered?
	What type of study will best address the research questions?
Determine data collection method and forms	Can existing data be used to advantage?
	What is to be measured? How?
	What is the source of the data?
	Are there any cultural factors that need to be taken into account in designing the data-collection method? What are they?
	Are there any legal restrictions on the collection methods? What are they?
	Can objective answers be obtained by asking people?
	How should people be questioned?
	Should the questionnaires be administered in person, over the phone, or through the mail?
	Should electronic or mechanical means be used to make the observations?
	What specific behaviors should the observers record?
	Should structured or unstructured items be used to collect the data?
	Should the purpose of the study be made known to the respondents?
	Should rating scales be used in the questionnaires?

(continued)

TABLE **3.1**   *Continued*

Stage in the Process	Typical Questions
Design sample and collect the data	What is the target population? Is a list of population elements available? Is a sample necessary? Is a probability sample desirable? How large should the sample be? How should the sample be selected? Who will gather the data? How long will the data gathering take? How much supervision is needed? What operational procedures will be followed? What methods will be used to ensure the quality of the data collected?
Analyze and interpret the data	Who will handle the editing of the data? How will the data be coded? Who will supervise the coding? Will computer or hand tabulation be used? What tabulations are called for? What analysis techniques will be used?
Prepare the research report	Who will read the report? What is their technical level of sophistication? Are managerial recommendations called for? What will be the format of the written report? Is an oral report necessary? How should the oral report be structured?

one stage affects decisions at each of the other stages, and a revision of the procedure at any stage often requires modifications of procedures at each of the other stages. Unfortunately, it seems that this lesson is understood only by those who have experienced the frustrations and satisfactions of being involved in an actual research project.

Fifth, the important error to note when designing a research project is the *total error* likely to be associated with the project. All the steps are necessary and vital. Errors can arise in any one of them, and it is dangerous to emphasize one to the exclusion of others. Many beginning students of research, for example, argue for large sample sizes to reduce sampling error. What they fail to realize is that sample size is a decision made with respect to one subset of one stage in the process. Although the increase in sample size reduces sampling error, it often leads to an *increase* in the *total error* of the research effort, because other errors increase more than proportionately with sample size. To keep the study within budget, the larger sample size may dictate fewer follow-ups with those who did not respond to the initial contact. The larger this nonresponse problem, the greater the question of whether the responses that are secured are representative of the selected sample. Response errors can also increase when the sample size is increased. The larger sample will typically mean the use of more interviewers if the study is being done by phone or in person. This raises a host of issues with respect to the selection and training of the interviewers so that they all handle the interviews in the same way. Otherwise, the different responses that are secured can be as much a function of the interviewers collecting the data as they are differences in respondents. Thus, researchers frequently face a dilemma because of normal budget and time constraints. Should they select a large sample to minimize sampling error, or should they select a smaller sample, thereby ensuring better interviewer controls, more accurate responses, and a higher response rate among those contacted? In one study that investigated the incidence of sampling and nonsampling errors by comparing respondent replies against known data, the consistent finding was "that nonsampling error is the major contributor to total survey error, while random sampling error is minimal."[6] The fact that nonsampling error far outweighed sampling error led the authors to conclude that the "emphasis on methods to reduce random sampling error by emphasizing large samples may be misplaced."[7]

ETHICAL DILEMMA 3.1

A manufacturer of bolts and screws approaches you and outlines the following problem: "My friend owns a hardware store, and you used a technique called multidimensional scaling to produce what I think he called a 'perceptual map,' which positioned his operation in relation to his competitors and showed him where there was space in the market to expand his business. I don't understand the details of it, but I was very impressed with the map and I want you do to the same for me."

- What have you learned about the manufacturer's research problem?
- Is it likely that the development of a perceptual map will be useful to the manufacturer of bolts and screws?
- Is it ethical to agree to his proposal?

PROBLEM FORMULATION

An old adage says, "A problem well defined is half-solved." This is especially true in marketing research, for it is only when the problem has been clearly defined and the objectives of the research precisely stated that research can be designed properly.

---

[6]Henry Assael and John Keon, "Nonsampling vs. Sampling Errors in Survey Research," *Journal of Marketing,* 46 (Spring 1982), p. 114. We will say more about the various errors that can arise when conducting research when discussing each of the stages in the research process.

[7]*Ibid.,* p. 121.

''Properly'' here means not only that the research will generate the kinds of answers needed but that it will do so efficiently.

Problem definition is being used in the broadest sense of the term here. It refers to those situations that might indeed represent real problems to the marketing decision maker as well as those situations that might be better described as opportunities. To understand the problem-definition stage of the process, it is helpful to have some appreciation as to how problems and opportunities arise.

There are three fundamental sources for marketing research problems or opportunities: (1) unanticipated change, (2) planned change, and (3) serendipity in the form of new ideas.[8] Change in one form or another is by far the most important source.

One of the great sources of unanticipated change is the environment in which firms operate. There are simply many elements in a firm's external environment that can create problems or opportunities. These include demographic, economic, technological, competitive, political, and legal changes that often can significantly affect the marketing function. How the firm responds to the new technology or to the new product introduced by a competitor or to the change in demographics or life-styles largely determines whether the change turns out to be a problem or an opportunity. For example, ''General Foods' entry of Maxim was the first freeze-dried instant coffee. This put Nestlé under considerable pressure. Nestlé responded with Taster's Choice freeze-dried instant coffee and soon dominated Maxim in the market.''[9] An example of a political/legal change is the deregulation of the financial services industry. Firms like Fidelity capitalized on this environmental change by introducing enhanced-services packages including discount brokerage service. Unanticipated change can also arise within the firm's internal environment. The firm may be losing market share or its sales might not be as high as forecast. The firm may find itself losing key salespeople or its best distributors to competitors. In situations of unanticipated change, a key issue is finding exactly *what* is happening and *why*. Marketing research often plays a role in answering such questions.

Not all change is unanticipated; much of it is planned. Most firms want business to grow and contemplate various marketing actions for helping it do so. These include the introduction of new products, improved distribution, and more effective pricing and advertising strategies. Planned change is oriented more toward the future, whereas unanticipated change is oriented more toward the past. The basic question surrounding planned change is *how* the firm may bring about the desired change. The role of marketing research here involves investigating the feasibility of the alternatives being considered.

A third source of marketing problems or opportunities is serendipity, or chance ideas. The new idea might come from a customer in a complaint letter or by some other means. For example, Rubbermaid makes it a practice for its executives to read customer letters to find out how people like the company's products. These letters often lead to new product ideas. Complaints about the difficulty of storing traditional rack-and-mat

---

[8]William O'Dell, Andrew C. Ruppel, Robert H. Trent, and William J. Kehoe, *Marketing Decision Making: Analytic Framework and Cases,* 4th ed. (Cincinnati: South-Western Publishing Co., 1988).

[9]Glen L. Urban, John R. Hauser, and Nikhilesh Dholakia, *Essentials of New Products Management* (Englewood Cliffs, N.J., Prentice-Hall, Inc., 1987), p. 6.

sets because of their bulk led the company to develop a one-piece dish drainer for washing dishes by hand, for example. Strict attention to detail, including suggestions like this, has allowed the company to introduce about 100 new products a year, and over 30 percent of the company's sales in recent years have come from new products.[10] What is especially remarkable is that approximately one-third of the new products are developed from the ground up, yet the company claims a success rate of 90 percent. Marketing research plays an important role in the company's development process. Besides customers, other sources for good ideas are salespeople and their call reports. Comments from the trade might serve as the impetus for a decision problem, for which research might play a role.

Regardless of how decision problems or opportunities arise, most of them will require additional information for resolution. This information must be identified and approaches for securing it determined. This requires good communication between decision makers and marketing researchers. The decision makers need to understand what research can and cannot accomplish. The researchers need to understand the nature of the decision the managers face and what they hope to learn from research (i.e., the project objectives).

Researchers must avoid simply responding to requests for information. To do so is akin to allowing a patient who is seeing a doctor make his or her own diagnosis, and to cap it off, allow the patient to prescribe the treatment as well. Rather, the researcher needs to work with the manager much like a patient works with a doctor; both need to be open in their communication as they translate symptoms into underlying causal factors.

There is a tendency to assume that managers have a clear understanding of the problems they face and that the only difficulty lies in communicating that understanding. That is false. To many managers, the research problem is seen primarily as a lack of important facts. They tend to define it as a broad area of ignorance. "They say in effect: 'Here are some things I don't know. When the results come in, I'll know more. And when I know more, then I can figure out what to do.' "[11] Research results based on such a mode of operation most often turn out to be "interesting" but not very actionable. The research reduces the level of uncertainty, but it provides little understanding of the true decision problem. Both managers and researchers need to recognize that marketing research does not produce answers or strategies. It produces data — data that must be interpreted and converted into action plans by management. For the interpretation to be on target, the research needs to reflect management's business priorities and concerns, for "It is far better to resolve the right decision problem partially than to resolve the wrong problem fully."[12]

Managers must play an active role in communicating their information needs to researchers. They also need to be semiactive participants in the research process itself,

---

[10]Andrew Kupfer, "Why the Bounce at Rubbermaid," *Fortune*, 115 (April 13, 1987), pp. 77–78; Zachary Schiller, "At Rubbermaid, Little Things Mean a Lot," *Business Week* (November 11, 1991), p. 126.

[11]Alan R. Andreasen, " 'Backward' Market Research," *Harvard Business Review*, 63 (May–June 1985), p. 176.

[12]O'Dell et al., *Marketing Decision Making*, p. 14.

interacting with the researchers when necessary to ensure that the process provides the information they truly need to help them make the decisions they face. Sometimes this means using their own intuition when interpreting the research findings, as Research Realities 3.2 demonstrates.

In other cases, managers need to get directly involved in the research process. For example, one of the factors that plays an important part in Japan's new-product development is that the Japanese consider marketing research to be a line function executed by all participants in the product development process rather than a staff function per-

---

Research Realities 3.2

Managers as Active Participants in the Research Process

In the early days of pay-cable services, a television company was considering the establishment of a cultural cable channel as a logical extension of its business. A company executive commissioned a survey to determine the demand for such a channel, which would have carried a monthly fee similar to that charged by Home Box Office (HBO), at the time the only existing pay-cable outlet.

The survey appeared to give a green light to the project, indicating that 20 percent of all cable users would subscribe. But the executive, even though he could find no technical flaw in the questionnaire or the sampling technique, remained skeptical of the results. He remembered from his years of experience how focus group participants would often claim to be fans of public television but would rarely admit to watching "Dallas," "Dynasty," or other top-rated network shows. This phenomenon suggested to him that the survey data might not be realistic.

Pursuing his hunch, the executive hired another research firm to investigate the channel's potential. This firm knew that consumers have been known to tell "white lies" to an interviewer. They tend, for example, to exaggerate their involvement in socially desirable activities such as voting. Similarly, they are apt to overestimate their willingness to purchase attractive or glamorous new products or services. They may

wish to please the interviewer, to appear open to new experiences, to appear financially capable of purchasing the offering, or — as in the case of the cable station — to appear intelligent and cultured. The new research team constructed its study to account for such tendencies.

Although the researchers asked many of the same questions that appeared in the first survey, they also included seemingly unrelated questions about respondents' recent participation in a range of activities, from attending the opera to going to the zoo to watching a ball game. Again, 20 percent said they were willing to pay for the cultural channel. But when respondents who had never before patronized cultural events were eliminated from the "yea sayers" — on the assumption that they were unlikely to undergo a sudden metamorphosis into highbrows — the research predicted that less than 1 percent of cable users were likely to subscribe. The company scrapped its plan for the station.

How did this cable executive avoid a calamity? First, his understanding of the market allowed him to recognize potential shortcomings in the initial research. Second, he was able to find a research company experienced in gauging consumers' real interest in new products. Obviously, had he commissioned the research only to support a decision he had already made, he would never have questioned the encouraging findings of the first study. His success underscores the importance of management's direct involvement in market research.

Source: Robert S. Duboff, "The Real Magic of Market Research," *Viewpoint*, 17 (Summer 1988), pp. 19–20.

formed only by marketing researchers. One upshot of this perspective is a more hands-on approach that looks at the context in which things occur and that places more emphasis on softer, less-formal data collection methods. For example, Toyota sent a group of its engineers and designers to southern California to observe how women got into and operated their cars. Their observations suggested that women with long fingernails had trouble opening the door and operating various knobs on the dashboard. On the basis of this knowledge, they were able to redraw some of their automobile and interior designs.[13]

A proper understanding of the basic structure of decision problems can help researchers interact with management to better specify research issues. The simplest decision situations can be characterized by the following conditions.

1. A decision maker *(D)* is operating in some environment *(E)* in which there is a problem.
2. There are at least two courses of action, A_1 and A_2, that *D* can follow.
3. If *D* chooses to follow A_1, for example, there are at least two possible outcomes of that choice (O_1 and O_2), and *D* prefers one of these outcomes to the other.
4. There is a chance, but not an equal chance, that each course of action will lead to the desired outcome. If the chances are equal, the choice does not matter.[14]

In sum, a person faces a decision situation if he or she has a problem, has several good (but not equally good) ways of solving it, and is unsure about which course of action to select. Research can assist in clarifying any of these characteristics of the decision situation. Let us briefly consider how.

The Decision Maker and the Environment

A critical element for the researcher in defining the problem is understanding the decision maker and the environment in which that person is operating. The researcher needs to ensure that the description of the management decision provided by the decision maker is accurate and indeed reflects the appropriate areas of concern. To this end, it typically helps if the researcher understands the genesis of the manager's problem or opportunity. What is the background on the business? What factors have led to the manager's concerns with the issues? What information would help the decision maker in dealing with these issues? What would the decision maker do with the information?[15]

If the decision maker's original posture will not change regardless of what is found, the research will be wasted. Surprisingly, research is sometimes simply "conscience

---

[13]Michael Czinkota and Masaaki Kotabe, "Product Development the Japanese Way," *The Journal of Business Strategy* (November/December 1990), pp. 31–36.

[14]See Russell L. Ackoff, *The Art of Problem Solving* (New York: John Wiley & Sons, Inc., 1978).

[15]Sue Jones, "Problem Definition in Marketing Research: Facilitating Dialog between Clients and Researchers," *Psychology and Marketing*, 2 (Summer 1985), pp. 83–92; W. Steven Perkins and Ram C. Rao, "The Role of Experience in Information Use and Decision Making by Marketing Managers," *Journal of Marketing Research*, 27 (February 1990), pp. 1–10.

money''; the research results are readily accepted when they are consistent with the decision the individual ''wants to make'' or with the person's perceptions of the environment or the consequences of alternative actions. When the research results conflict with the decision maker's original position, however, the results are questioned at best and discarded as being inaccurate at worst. The reason, of course, is that the individual's view of the decision problem is so strongly held that research will do little to change it. When this situation prevails, research will be a waste of the firm's resources. To avoid wasting resources because of the ''confirmed prejudice,'' ''I know better,'' or ''don't bother me with the facts'' traps (see Research Realities 3.3, for example), researchers need to assess the situation before doing the research, not after. This means determining

---

Research Realities 3.3

Instances in Which Research Will Be a Waste of Time and Resources

The ''I Know Better'' Trap

A challenger to IBM in the personal computer market rejected research that clearly demonstrated that although users of its product preferred it to IBM's on virtually every technical attribute, they continued to believe that IBM had a superior product overall. The company's managers dismissed the data, deciding that the technical superiority of their product would eventually translate into a rejection of IBM; two years later, they're still waiting for their wish to come true.

The Confirmed Prejudice Trap

In the early 1970s, a cigarette manufacturer noted a trend: consumers wanted natural products. Excited over the possibility of a new market niche, the company spent a fortune to develop an ''all-natural'' cigarette, Real, and then commissioned research to support its decision. Despite successful concept and taste tests, the product failed.

The fate of the venture should have been obvious from the outset to all concerned. After all, naturalness

is valued for its connotations of good health, and, as studies have shown, smokers are far less concerned about health than are other consumers. A broad-based research project — or an unbiased ''reality test'' on the part of management — would have uncovered this fatal flaw.

The ''Don't Bother Me With the Facts'' Trap

One reason Horst W. Schroeder was ousted as president of Kellogg Company was that he overrode the company's tradition of collegiality and often was unwilling to listen to subordinates. In one case, Schroeder became convinced that Pro-Grain, a ''he-man cereal'' popular with Australians, would make a big hit in the United States. When company researchers armed with market data disagreed, he is said to have exploded in anger. Worse, he ordered them to keep their conclusion quiet. ''We were told it should be kept confidential,'' says a former marketing official. ''Schroeder wanted to keep the results to himself.''

When Pro-Grain was introduced in the United States in 1987, it did even worse than the researchers had warned. Within a few months, Kellogg took it off the market. Schroeder escaped blame; a product development official was demoted.

Source: Robert D. Duboff, ''The Real Magic of Market Research,'' *Viewpoint,* 17 (Summer 1988), p. 18; Richard Gibson, ''Personal 'Chemistry' Abruptly Ended Rise of Kellogg President,'' *The Wall Street Journal* (November 28, 1989), pp. A1, A6.

the decision maker's objectives and finding out how the decision might change if certain results were found.

A rather surprising example of such pointless research was cited in a survey of financial service companies that had been undertaken by the Advertising Research Foundation. Financial service companies — banks, brokers, insurers, and so forth — have begun to advertise on television almost as much as beer and wine marketers. However, unlike brewers and other consumer goods industries, who routinely spend upwards of $500,000 annually to test the effectiveness of their ads, financial service companies have paid surprisingly little attention to advertising research. In fact, the Advertising Research Foundation found that the median annual research budget was $28,300 at banks, $45,800 at diversified financial companies, and only $22,500 at insurance companies. What is even more startling was the finding that, of the 60 percent of this group who bothered to test at all, fully 58 percent admitted that the results of such research did not play an important part in their marketing decision making.[16] Unless financial service advertisers come to value the insights that advertising research might offer, even the small sums that they currently allot to such research could be considered money wasted.

Often the task of determining how the management decision might change with research information is complicated by the fact that the researcher's contact is not the final decision maker but a liaison. Yet, this determination must be made if the researcher is to design a cost-effective attack on the problem.

The researcher also needs to understand the environment in which the decision maker operates. What are the constraints on that person's actions? What are the resources at the decision maker's disposal? What is the time frame in which the manager is operating? It does little good to design a study, however accurate, that costs $20,000 and takes six months to complete when the decision maker needs the results within one month and has only $2,000 for the research. Obviously, some compromises must be made, and it is the researcher's responsibility to anticipate them by carefully examining the decision environment.

Researchers also need to be aware that the corporate culture can affect decision making and, consequently, research that supports that decision making. Things simply happen differently at different institutions. In some firms, the process by which decisions are made is dominant, whereas in other firms, the personality of management might be more important. At General Mills, for example, the emphasis is on research that evaluates alternatives, and the culture at General Mills tries to force all information requests into action alternatives. Instead of focusing on the question "What proportion of potato chips are eaten at meals?", the emphasis would be on translating the question into "How can I advertise my potato chips for meal consumption?" or "Will a 'meal commercial' sell more chips than my present commercial?" To design the most effective

---

[16]Bill Abrams, "Financial Service Advertisers Seen Neglecting Ad Research," *The Wall Street Journal* (August 8, 1983), p. 23. See also Harry P. Polly, "Advertising Tips for the Financial Services Industry," *Secured Lender*, 45 (January/February 1989), pp. 22, 24.

research, researchers need to be aware of the general corporate culture regarding how decisions are made and what role research plays when making those decisions.[17]

Alternative Courses of Action

Research can be properly designed only when the alternative courses of action being considered are known. The more obvious ones are typically given to the researcher by the decision maker, and the researcher's main task here is to determine whether the list provided indeed exhausts the alternatives. Quite often, some of the options will remain unstated. Yet, if the research is to be germane to all the alternatives, implicit options must be made explicit. Thus, it is important that the decision maker and the researcher work together to come up with a complete list of the alternative courses of action being considered.

Let us consider an example of the types of alternative courses of action that a company may consider. The Campbell Soup Company has a strong commitment to keeping pace with consumer and technological trends. As part of its ongoing research, the company's product managers team up with in-house and outside researchers to probe for openings in the market. In addition to Campbell's traditional family market, the research teams have investigated the eating habits and flavor preferences of career women, Hispanics, consumers over age 55, and owners of microwave ovens — each of these groups suggesting an alternative course of action. And after the company's "Soup is Good Food" campaign was well established, the team began work on positioning soup as a convenient snack food. Some of the other alternatives the company is considering are creating other value-added food items, advertising heavily to attract consumers to try Campbell's products, and being a low-cost producer.[18]

Researchers at times must be detectives to uncover the hidden agendas and alternatives lurking beneath the surface in any decision situation. If a critical piece of information remains undiscovered, even the most sophisticated research techniques cannot solve the problem. Attempting to impress the company president, researchers at Pillsbury discovered this fact belatedly — to their embarrassment:

> The late Bob Keith, then president of the Pillsbury Company, was once persuaded by Pillsbury's operations researchers to review one of his major marketing decisions using a formal

---

[17]Joel Levine, while vice-president of marketing research at The Pillsbury Company in Minneapolis, suggested that awareness of the corporate culture is one of the most important factors that distinguishes researchers who affect strategic marketing decisions from those who do not. See "Six Factors Mark Researchers Who Sway Strategic Decisions," *Marketing News*, 17 (February 4, 1983), p. 1. See also Bernie Whalen, "Researchers Stymied by 'Adversary Culture' in Firms," *Marketing News*, 16 (September 17, 1982), pp. 1 and 7. For discussion of how changes in the corporate culture are affecting research at Sony, see Elizabeth Rubinfien, Yamiko Ono, and Laura Lundro, "A Changing Sony Aims to Own the 'Software' That Its Products Need," *The Wall Street Journal* (December 30, 1988), pp. A1 and A4.

[18]"Soup Maker Bets Future on Monitoring Technological Consumption Changes," *Marketing News*, 18 (October 12, 1984), pp. 44. See also Anthony Bianco, "Marketing's New Look: Campbell Leads a Revolution in the Way Consumer Products Are Sold," *Business Week* (January 26, 1987), pp. 64–69; Richard Gibson and Kathleen Deveny, "Health: Americans' Ignorance About Nutrition Hinders Efforts to Improve Nations Diet," *The Wall Street Journal* (November 13, 1991), p. B1.

decision model. He agreed to the outcomes, their values, and their probabilities, and chose the decision rule he felt most appropriate. The computer then calculated the expectations, compared them, and reported the alternative that should be chosen according to that rule. Mr. Keith disagreed, noting that another alternative was obviously the only correct choice — indeed, it was the choice that *had* been made not long before. "How can that be?" the researchers asked. "You accepted all the values and probabilities and chose the decision rule yourself. The rest is just arithmetic." "That's fine," Keith replied, "but you forgot to ask me about a few other things that were more important."[19]

Objectives of the Decision Maker

One of the more basic facts of decision making is that individuals differ in their attitudes toward risk, and these differences influence their choices. Some people are risk takers; they are willing to assume a good deal of risk for the chance of a big gain.[20] Some are risk evaders; they are willing to assume little risk, even when the size of the potential gain is large, if the chance of loss also exists. Some individuals simply walk a middle ground. A person's attitude towards risk is not always consistent. It changes with the situation and the magnitude of the potential consequences. Thus, a person may be a risk taker, even when the chances of things turning out badly are reasonably high, if that person feels secure and if the consequences of his or her actions would not be catastrophic. That same person may avoid risks if his or her position in the company is insecure or if the consequences would be disastrous if things were to turn out wrong.

It is the researchers' task to discover as best they can the type of decision maker with whom they are dealing. Very often some hint of the decision maker's posture can be gained from intensive probing, using "what-if" hypothetical outcomes of the research.

Closely allied to the need to determine the decision maker's attitude toward risk is the need to determine the decision maker's specific objectives. It is unfortunate, but true, that these are rarely explicitly stated.

> Despite a popular misconception to the contrary, objectives are seldom given to the researcher. The decision maker seldom formulates his objectives accurately. He is likely to state his objectives in the form of platitudes which have no operational significance. Consequently, objectives usually have to be extracted by the researcher. In so doing, the researcher may well be performing his most useful service to the decision maker.[21]

The researcher must transform the platitudes into specific operational objectives that the research can be designed to serve.

---

[19]Charles Raymond, *The Art of Using Science in Marketing* (New York: Harper & Row, 1974), p. 17.

[20]The types of decision makers are more formally defined in decision theory literature. See, for example, the classic work by Howard Raiffa, *Decision Analysis: Introductory Lectures on Choices under Uncertainty* (Reading, Mass.: Addison-Wesley, 1968), pp. 51–101.

[21]Russell L. Ackoff, *Scientific Method* (New York: John Wiley, 1962), p. 71. A useful technique for uncovering objectives is to get the decision maker to agree to a single-sentence statement specifying the objective to guide the research. See Randall G. Chapman, "Problem-Definition in Marketing Research Studies," *Journal of Consumer Marketing*, 6 (Spring 1989), pp. 51–59.

One effective technique for uncovering these objectives consists of confronting the decision maker with each of the possible solutions to a problem and asking him whether he would follow that course of action. Where he says "no," further probing will usually reveal objectives which are not served by the course of action.[22]

Once the objectives for the research are finally decided on, they should be committed to writing. This often produces additional clarity in communication and thinking. The decision maker and researcher should then agree formally on their written expression (by each initialing each statement of purpose, by initialing the entire document, or by some other means). This tends to prevent later misunderstandings. The formal endorsement of objectives also helps to ensure that the research will not treat symptoms but rather the problem that produced the symptoms.

Consequences of Alternative Courses of Action

A great deal of marketing research is intended to determine the consequences of various courses of action. Much of the research highlighted in Chapter 1 in Tables 1.1 and 1.2, detailing the uses of marketing research, for example, deals with the effect of manipu-

---

ETHICAL DILEMMA 3.2

The president of a small bank approaches you with plans to launch a special program of financial counseling and support for women and asks you to establish whether there is sufficient public interest to justify starting the program. No other bank in the city caters specifically to women, and you think that professional women, in particular, might be enthused. If news of the plan leaks out, the president believes that competitors may try to preempt him, so he asks you to keep the bank's identity secret from respondents and to inquire only into general levels of interest in increased financial services for women. However, as you read through the literature that he has left on your desk, you notice that the bank is located in the most depressed area of the city, where women might be harassed and feel unsafe.

- Would it be unethical to research the general problem of how much demand exists for a women's banking program, when the bank in question will interpret the demand as encouragement to launch such a program itself?
- What might be the costs to the researcher in voicing misgivings about the suitability of this particular bank's launching of the program? Would you voice your misgivings?
- Does it violate respondents' rights if you do not reveal the identity of the research sponsor? If so, is it a serious violation in this case? Is there a conflict of interest here with respect to respondents' right to be informed versus the client's right to confidentiality?

---

[22]Ackoff, *Scientific Method*, p. 71.

lating one of the Ps in the marketing mix. This is not surprising because, as we have seen, the marketing manager's task basically involves manipulating the elements of the mix to achieve customer satisfaction. What is a more natural marketing research activity than seeking answers to such questions as: What will be the change in sales produced by a change in the product's package? If we change the sales compensation plan, what will be the effect on the sales representatives' performance and on their attitudes toward the job and company? Which ad is likely to generate the most favorable customer response?

Researchers are primarily responsible for designing research that accurately assesses the outcomes of past or contemplated marketing actions. In this capacity, they must gauge the actions against all the outcomes management deems relevant. Management, for example, may want to know the impact of the proposed change on sales and on consumer attitudes. If the research addresses only consumer attitudes, management will most assuredly ask for the relationship between attitudes and sales. Embarrassing questions of this nature can be avoided only if researchers painstakingly probe for all relevant outcomes before designing the research.

DECISION PROBLEM TO RESEARCH PROBLEM

A detailed understanding of the total decision situation should enable researchers working in consort with managers to translate the decision problem into a research problem. A research problem is essentially a restatement of the decision problem in research terms. Consider, for example, the new product introduction for which sales are below target. The decision problem faced by the marketing manager is deciding what to do about the shortfall. Should the target be revised? Was it too optimistic? Should the product be withdrawn? Should one of the other elements in the marketing mix, such as advertising, be altered? Suppose the manager suspects that the advertising campaign supporting the new-product introduction has been ineffective. This suspicion could serve as the basis for a research problem. The product manager who believed that advertising was not creating sufficient customer awareness for a successful new-product launch might wish to have some evidence that either confirmed or denied that suspicion before changing the advertising program. The research problem would then become the assessment of product awareness among potential customers.

Some illustrations of the distinctions between decision problems and research problems can be found in Table 3.2. Although the two problems are related, it should be apparent that they are not the same. The decision problem involves what needs to be done. Research can provide the necessary information to make an informed choice, and the research problem essentially involves determining what information to provide and how that information can best be secured.

In making this determination, the researcher must make certain the real decision problem, not just the symptoms, is being addressed. There have been many cases in which poor problem definition led to poor research problem definition with unfortunate consequences, some more dire than others. The debacle with Coca Cola Classic is well known. What is perhaps less well known is that Miller did not invent Lite Beer. Rather,

TABLE **3.2**   **Examples of the Relationship between Decision Problems and Research Problems**

Decision Problems	Research Problems
Develop package for a new product	Evaluate effectiveness of alternative package designs
Increase market penetration through the opening of new stores	Evaluate prospective locations
Increase store traffic	Measure current image of the store
Increase amount of repeat purchasing behavior	Assess current amount of repeat purchasing behavior
Develop more equitable sales territories	Assess current and proposed territories with respect to their potential and workload
Allocate advertising budget geographically	Determine current level of market penetration in the respective areas
Introduce new product	Design a test market through which the likely acceptance of the new product can be assessed
Expand into other countries	Assess market potential for firm's products in each of the countries being considered
Select foreign distribution channels	Evaluate current channel structures and channel members in each of the countries being considered

it was first developed by Meister Brau.[23] Further, the taste tests indicated that people liked the beer. When the product was introduced by Meister Brau, though, it failed. The company, in turn, sold it to Miller, who defined the decision problem, and subsequently the research problem, as something more than having a preferred taste. Rather, Miller's research suggested that big beer drinkers tried to project macho images, and the very concept of a diet beer connoted "wimp." Miller's emphasis thus became one of changing the image of the brand through its use of famous sports personalities. Another not-so-well-known example involved the Muppets. The producer of the show, Bernie Brillstein, originally pitched the show to CBS. CBS's marketing research indicated that there was "no way to win an audience with a show having a *frog* for a host. The frog was Kermit; he and his fellow Muppets became a hugely successful syndication."[24] In this case, neither the decision makers nor the researchers at CBS took into account the fact that every new show has to form a chemistry with its viewers, and that takes time.

Still another example of poor problem definition involves the fax machine. The fax machine is American in invention, technology, design, and development. Yet not one fax machine offered for sale in the United States today is American-made. A primary reason is that marketing research convinced American manufacturers that there was no

[23]Wayne A. Lemburg, "Past AMA President Hardin, Head of Market Facts, Looks Back at the Early Days of Marketing Research," *Marketing News,* 20 (December 19, 1986), p. 9.

[24]Dennis Kneale, "CBS Frantically Woos Hollywood to Help It Win Back Viewers," *The Wall Street Journal* (February 9, 1989), p. A10.

need for such a piece of equipment. The manufacturers looked at the issue as the cost differential between communicating via a machine and sending the communication via regular mail. With fax machines allowing one to send, for $1 a page, the same letter that the post office would deliver for 25 cents at the time, they concluded that the market was not of sufficient size to bother pursuing. However, the Japanese defined the problem differently. "They did not ask, 'What is the market for this *machine*?' Instead, they asked, 'What is the market for what it does?' And they immediately saw, when looking at the growth of courier services such as Federal Express in the '70s and early '80s, that the market for the fax machine had already been established."[25]

How does one avoid the trap of researching the wrong decision problem? The main way is by refusing to respond to requests for information without developing a proper appreciation for the decision problem. The difference in response perspectives is highlighted in the Parkay margarine example in Research Realities 3.4. There is an old saying: "If you do not know where you want to go, any road will get you there." It is the same in decision making. If you do not know what you want to accomplish, any alternative will be satisfactory. If the decision maker does not know what he or she wants to achieve, the research study won't accomplish it. Instead of going off to prepare a research proposal outlining the methods to be used when a research request first comes in, which is the typical procedure, researchers are well advised to take the time to probe the situation carefully until they have acquired the necessary appreciation for (1) the decision maker and the environment, (2) the alternative courses of action, (3) the decision maker's objectives, and (4) the consequences of alternative actions. As Figure 3.2 indicates, even marketing managers believe that researchers should take an active role in helping to define the decision problem and in specifying the information that will be useful for solving it.

There are several mechanisms available for making sure that the true decision problem will be addressed by the research. One way is to execute a "research request step."[26] The research request step requires that the decision maker and researcher have a meeting in which the decision maker describes the problem and the information that is needed. The researcher then drafts a statement describing his or her understanding of the problem. The statement should include, but is not limited to, the following items:

1. **Action** — the actions that are contemplated on the basis of the research.
2. **Origin** — the events that led to a need for the decision to act; even though the events may not directly affect the research that is conducted, they help the researcher understand more deeply the nature of the research problem.

---

[25]Peter F. Drucker, "Marketing 101 for a Fast-Changing Decade," *The Wall Street Journal* (November 20, 1990), p. 17.

[26]Paul W. Conner, " 'Research Request Step' Can Enhance Use of Results," *Marketing News,* 19 (January 4, 1985), p. 41. See also Paul D. Boughton, "Marketing Research and Small Business: Pitfalls and Potential," *Journal of Small Business Management,* 21 (July 1983), pp. 36–42; and Charles D. Cowan, "Write Your Questions Down Before You Pay for Your Research," *Marketing Research: A Magazine of Management & Applications,* 4 (March 1992), pp. 65–68.

Research Realities 3.4

Alternative Responses to an Information Request and Their Likely Effects

I would like you to meet someone — research analyst X, . . . (who has) been at Kraft for a little more than two years now and is well regarded by the marketing group he works with.

One morning analyst X receives a phone call from the marketing manager of Parkay margarine. The marketing manager tells our analyst that the R & D lab has been working on a new improved flavor for Parkay margarine and that they've finally come up with one that he thinks is acceptable.

Before he authorizes full production with the new formula, he thinks it would be prudent to conduct a taste test to determine if consumers will react favorably to the new flavor. Actually, he is calling to find out how much product would be required for such a test. He adds that it's very important that this research be initiated quickly since a competitor, Blue Bonnet, has just come out with a new improved version of its product.

Analyst X decides to conduct personal interviews in central location mall facilities. Basically, these will be blind taste tests.

Then analyst X determines that he wants to use a triangular discrimination taste test to determine if respondents can detect differences between the products. That will be followed by a sequential monadic evaluation of each product to obtain additional diagnostic rating data and preference.

You might be saying that this design sounds pretty good. . . . Sequential approach so you don't waste

time and money if the new flavor is not as good as everyone thinks, adequate sample sizes for both stick and soft versions, two phases for the evaluation, a triangle discrimination to see if respondents can detect differences between the formulas, and sequential monadic to obtain diagnostic evaluations.

But let me introduce research analyst Y. She has the same credentials as analyst X and is faced with the same initial phone call. The marketing manager wants to know how much product is needed for a taste test.

Analyst Y responds that before she can design any research, she needs a little more information. Sounds like analyst X, right? Just listen. Analyst Y is not sure a taste test is exactly what is needed. She suggests they discuss the project.

Analyst Y begins to review the information she has been given and lists some of the questions she will want to ask the marketing manager when they get together. She looks up the most recent SAMI information to see how well Blue Bonnet has been performing since the introduction of its new flavor. She checks to see if Parkay has been affected by this change. She reviews the historical project files to review any prior test research for Parkay.

When analyst Y meets the marketing manager she asks the following questions:

- Why are we considering a new formula? Blue Bonnet doesn't seem to have hurt our franchise with its new flavor.
- If we do utilize the new flavor, what do we hope to accomplish? Do we expect to pull in new users or do we want to minimize the chances of our consumers converting over to Blue Bonnet?
- How will we announce the new flavor?

Source: Larry P. Stanek, "Bad Design Leads Managers to Doubt Value of Research," *Marketing News*, 11 (January 1980), p. 12. Reprinted with permission from Marketing News, published by the American Marketing Association, Chicago, IL 60606.

- Does the new formula taste more like butter or affect aftertaste, spreadability, or cooking uses?
- Can we obtain product from a regular facility? So often R & D's controls are much more stringent than those of our production plants. I would rather use product for this test that closely resembles the product consumers would receive.

Analyst Y then works out a research design. She also recommends a two-phase study, but her objectives are to determine Parkay users' responses to the new flavor in terms of usage and preference and to determine competitive users' response to the new flavor versus the new Blue Bonnet flavor.

Analyst Y also will interview 600 female respondents who are heads of household, primary grocery shoppers, between 18 and 60, and who have used Parkay in the past month. Respondents in the first phase of the research must be regular users of Parkay. In the second phase, they must be regular users of competitive margarines.

The research will involve personal sequential monadic in-home placements. In the first phase, 300 respondents will evaluate Parkay's current formula and the new one. In the second, 300 respondents will compare Parkay's new formula and Blue Bonnet's formula. In both phases, half the sample will evaluate sticks, the other half will evaluate soft products.

There are several clear differences between this research design and the first example, all the differences being dependent on the problem definition phase.

Analyst X is a research taker or research technician. He basically responded to the marketing manager's request for a taste test without considering the marketing situation that prompted the request.

His research design was quite sound, given the information he had. He would have obtained answers, and those answers probably would have been correct. Unfortunately, both he and the marketing manager would be wondering why they were receiving consumer complaint letters about the new flavor from long-time Parkay users.

Research analyst Y is an internal marketing consultant — a true marketing research professional. Her approach was to attempt to clearly understand the marketing situation, in order to understand marketing decisions that would be based on this research.

Her research design was fundamentally sound as well, but it was a more costly and time-consuming approach than that of analyst X. Why? Because she understood the risks involved as well as the potential gains that could be realized.

In both instances, the marketing manager could make a decision based on data obtained from a research study. The difference is that one manager now suspects marketing research because it failed to predict some Parkay users' negative responses. The other is even more confident in using marketing research.

We marketing research professionals must strive to go beyond simple problem solving. We must insist on being internal marketing consultants. That is the only way we can be assured that our research designs, techniques, and statistical analyses will continue to be valid. It is the only way marketing management will become more confident in its use of marketing research.

FIGURE 3.2   Percentage of Research Users Who Believe that Researchers "Absolutely Must" or "Preferably Should" Engage in the Activity

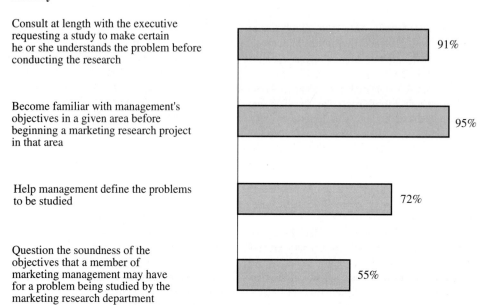

Activity

Consult at length with the executive requesting a study to make certain he or she understands the problem before conducting the research — 91%

Become familiar with management's objectives in a given area before beginning a marketing research project in that area — 95%

Help management define the problems to be studied — 72%

Question the soundness of the objectives that a member of marketing management may have for a problem being studied by the marketing research department — 55%

Source: Developed from the information in James R. Krum, Pradeep A. Rau, and Stephen K. Keiser, "The Marketing Research Process: Role Perceptions of Researchers and Users," *Journal of Advertising Research,* 25 (December 1987/January 1988), p. 14.

3. **Information** — the questions that the decision maker needs to have answered in order to take one of the contemplated courses of action.

4. **Use** — a section that explains how each piece of information will be used to help make the action decision; supplying logical reasons for each piece of the research ensures that the questions make sense in light of the action to be taken.

5. **Targets and subgroups** — a section that describes from whom the information must be gathered; specifying the target groups helps the researcher design an appropriate sample for the research project.

6. **Logistics** — a section that gives approximate estimates of the time and money that are available to conduct the research; both of these factors will affect the techniques finally chosen.

This written statement should be submitted to the decision maker for his or her approval. The approval should be formalized by having the decision maker initial and date the entire document or each section of it. One interesting thing about signatures or initials is that they commit managers to an agreement much stronger than word of mouth. Lawrence Blagman, the director of marketing research for MasterCard International, discovered this out early in his research career. As he reports: "I learned a very big lesson once when conducting a communication test. The objectives for testing were not written, the results of the test came back, and when I proceeded to show how and why the advertising failed to communicate the intended message, the agency and marketing group were quick to point out all the other things that were communicated. Now although these other issues were of lesser importance and were not the purpose of the advertising, marketing proclaimed the test to be a success."[27] Consequently, the research department at MasterCard International requires those requesting research to sign the research request form prepared by the researchers before the department will even undertake the formal development of the procedures for the research.

Another way of ensuring that the true decision problem is addressed in the research is through the use of scenarios that attempt to anticipate the contents of the final report. The researcher is primarily responsible for preparing the scenarios. Based on his or her understanding of the total decision situation, the researcher tries to anticipate what the final report could look like and prepares hypothetical elements, admittedly in relatively crude form. The researcher then confronts the decision maker with tough questions such as, "If I come up with this cross-tabulation with these numbers in it, what would you do?"[28] One of the biggest payoffs from this exercise is improved communication between research and manager as to the exact parameters of the study. For example, one large electronics company wished to determine the knowledge of and preferences for stereo components among young consumers. It was only after the researchers prepared mock tables showing preference by age and sex that the client's wishes became truly clear. Based on their prior discussions, the researchers specified the age breakdowns for the tables as 13 to 16 and 17 to 20. Only after presenting this scenario to the company's managers did the researchers learn that to the client, young meant children aged 10 or more. The client further believed that preteens are very volatile and undergo radical changes from year to year, especially as they approach puberty. Thus, not only was the contemplated research wrong from the standpoint of the age groups it would attempt to access, but the planned cross-tabulations were too gross to capture the client's basic concerns. Without the scenarios, the client's expectations may not have surfaced until the research was too far underway to change it.

The use of either a formal research request or hypothetical scenarios can help ensure that the *purpose* of the research is agreed on before the research is designed.

---

[27]Lawrence H. Blagman, "Managing Information," in *Presentations from the 9th Annual Marketing Research Conference* (Chicago: American Marketing Association, 1988), p. 134.

[28]Andreasen, " 'Backward' Market Research," p. 180.

THE RESEARCH PROPOSAL

Once the purpose and scope of the research are agreed on, researchers can turn their attention to choosing the *techniques* that will be used to conduct the research. The techniques decided on should also be communicated to the decision maker before the research begins. Typically this is done via a formal research proposal, which allows the researcher another opportunity to make sure that the research being contemplated will provide the information necessary to answer the decision maker's problem.

Research proposals can take many forms.[29] Some will be very long and detailed, running 20 pages or more. Others will be short and to the point. Much depends on the detail with which the various parts are described. Table 3.3 contains a sample form that can be followed in preparing a research proposal or plan. Again, the decision maker's approval for the plan should be sought and formalized by having him or her sign and date the proposal.

Research Realities 3.5 contains portions of an actual research plan (with some authorization and budget information removed) that was prepared by the research department at General Mills. Note the clearly stated criteria that will be used to interpret the results and the carefully crafted action standards, specifying what will be done depending on what the research results indicate. The effort expended by the marketing research department in translating information requests into specific, action-oriented statements like this helps account for the wide acceptance of and enthusiastic support for the research function at General Mills.

IS MARKETING RESEARCH JUSTIFIED?

Although the benefits of marketing research are many, it is not without its drawbacks, and the question of whether the research costs are likely to exceed the research benefits always needs to be asked. There is no denying that the research process is often time-consuming and expensive, and, if done incorrectly, it can hurt more than help a company. In some ways "research is like fire — it can illuminate and comfort: but if not managed properly, it can burn and hurt," badly in some instances, as was the case with CBS and the Muppets.[30] Even when done correctly, there are situations in which marketing research cannot provide answers a company seeks, or poses risks that outweigh its possible advantages. The benefits of testing a new product, for example, must be weighed against the risk of tipping off a competitor, who can then rush into the market with a similar product at perhaps a better price or some other added product advantage. Similarly, it may be worthwhile to forego research if there is little financial risk associated with the decision. The expense and effort of marketing research may also not be

---

[29]For suggestions on preparing proposals, see Ron Tepper, *How to Write Winning Proposals for Your Company or Client* (New York: John Wiley, 1989).

[30]Blagman, "Managing Information," p. 126.

1. *Tentative project title.*
2. *Statement of the marketing problem.* This is a brief statement that outlines or describes the general problem under consideration. Its brevity gives the reader a general sense of the reason for the project before reading the proposal in detail.

This section also sums up preliminary discussions that have taken place between the decision maker and the writer. From it the decision maker can determine whether the researcher comprehends the problem and the decision maker's information needs accurately. It is a good way for both parties to make sure they understand each other before committing further time and money to the project.

3. *Purpose and limits of the project.* In this section the writer states the purpose(s) and scope of the project. *Purpose* refers to the project's goals or objectives. Often a *justification* for the project — a statement of why it is important to pursue research on this topic — is included here. *Scope* refers to the actual limitations of the research effort (in other words, what is *not* going to be investigated). In this section the writer spells out the various hypotheses to be investigated or the questions to be answered. At this point the writer may also want to address what effect time and money constraints may have on the project or what the potential limitations are of the applicability of the project's findings. Far from being a hedge, documenting these issues early in the project may help in avoiding misunderstandings and disagreements when the project is completed.

4. *Data sources and research methodology.* The types of data to be sought (primary or secondary) are briefly identified here, and a brief explanation is given about how the necessary information will be gathered (e.g., surveys, experiments, library sources). *Sources* for data may be government publications, company records, actual people, and so forth.

If measurements, such as consumer attitudes, will be involved, the techniques to be used should be stated. Since this proposal is designed to be read by management, not fellow researchers, the language used in describing these techniques should be as nontechnical as possible. The nature of the problem will probably indicate the types of techniques to be employed.

The population or sample to be studied and its size should be described. The writer should mention whether the group will be divided into segments (i.e., rather than studying 1,000 teenagers, a study may focus only on those who own cars). The writer should also justify why that kind of sampling strategy is necessary.

The kinds of data-collection forms the researcher plans to use should be discussed and included in the plan if possible. Depending on the nature of the study, these may be questionnaires, psychological tests, or observation forms. The proposal should indicate the reliability and validity of the measure to be used.

5. *Estimate of time and personnel requirements.* The number of people required to complete the study should be listed, along with an indication of their level of responsibility and rate of pay. The various phases of the study, and the amount of time required for each, should also be made clear. An example follows:

1. Preliminary investigation: two months;
2. Final test of questionnaire: one month;
3. Sample selection: one month;
4. Mail questionnaire, field follow-up, etc.: four months.

As mentioned earlier, if the project is to be completed under serious time constraints, the researcher may wish to indicate what effect this circumstance may have on the study's results.

6. *Cost estimates.* The cost of the personnel required should be combined with expenses for travel, materials, supplies, computer charges, printing and mailing costs, and overhead charges, if applicable, to arrive at a total cost for the project. As mentioned with regard to time, if the project is to be completed under serious financial constraints, the effect of this should be made clear at this point. It is better to face these potential problems early in the project than to run out of money or miss a deadline once a project has begun. The researcher, not the client, is usually the one to bear the responsibility for such shortcomings.

Source: Adapted from J. Paul Peter and James H. Donnelly, Jr., *A Preface to Marketing Management*, 6th ed. (Homewood, Ill.: Richard D. Irwin, Inc., 1994), pp. 50–51. Copyright 1994, adapted with permission.

Research Realities 3.5

A Sample Proposal at General Mills for Research on *Protein Plus* Cereal

1. *Problem and Background.* Protein Plus has performed below objectives in its test market. New product and copy alternatives are being readied for testing. Three alternative formulations — Hi Graham (A), Nut (B), and Cinnamon (C) — which retain the basic identity of current Protein Plus but which have been judged to be sufficiently different and of sufficient potential, have been developed for testing against current (D).

2. *Decision Involved.* Which product formulations should be carried into the concept fulfillment test?

3. *Method and Design.* Monadic in-home product test will be conducted. Each of the four test products will be tested by a separate panel of 150 households. Each household will have purchased adult ready-to-eat (RTE) cereal within the past month and will be interested in the test product as measured by the selection of Protein Plus as one or more of their next ten cereal packages they would like to buy. They will be exposed to Protein Plus in a booklet that will also contain an ad for several competitive products, such as Product 19, Special K, Nature Valley, and Grape Nuts. A Protein Plus ad will be constructed for each of the four test products, differing primarily in the kind of taste reassurance provided. Exposure to these various executions will be rotated

so that each of the four test panels are matched on RTE cereal usage.

The study will be conducted in eight markets. Product will be packaged in current Protein Plus package flagged with the particular flavor reassurance for that product.

The criterion measure will be the homemakers' weighted post share, adjusted to reflect the breadth of interest in the various Protein Plus communications strategies.

Rather than trust a random sampling procedure to represent the population at large, a quota will be established to ensure that the sample of people initially contacted for each panel will conform as closely as possible to the division of housewives under 45 (56%) and over 45 (44%) in the U.S. population.

4. *Criteria for Interpretation.* Each formulation generating a higher weighted homemaker share than standard will be considered for subsequent testing. If more than one formulation beats standard, each will be placed in concept fulfillment test unless one is better than the other(s) at odds of 2:1 or more.

5. *Estimated Project Expense:* Within ±500: $22,000.

6. Individual who must finally approve recommended action: _____ .

7. Report to be delivered by _____ if authorized by _____ and test materials shipped by _____ .

Source: Used with permission of General Mills, Inc.

worthwhile if the results will not influence subsequent decisions. Such was the case in our earlier example of financial service advertisers.

The appendix to this chapter outlines a formal process by which the potential value of research can be determined and a comparison with its costs made. Whether or not the formal process is followed is immaterial. What matters is that the fundamental question be asked and answered before research is begun: Will the research be worth it? Do potential benefits exceed anticipated costs?[31] These questions demand that the "criterion of adequacy" be applied: By what standard will the research be judged? Will the objective be to explore the impact of a prespecified set of alternatives or to discover which decision options are potentially viable? The objectives of the research very much depend on what is known about the decision problem, a question explored more fully in Part 2.

CHOOSING AND USING A RESEARCH SUPPLIER

Most sizable business organizations today have formal marketing research departments. However, except for the very largest consumer products companies, these departments tend to be small — sometimes consisting of one person. In such cases, the firm's researcher may spend less time conducting actual research than supervising projects undertaken by research suppliers hired by the firm. Marketing managers in many large companies also use outside suppliers.

There are many advantages to using research suppliers. If the research work load tends to vary during the year, the firm may find it less expensive to hire suppliers to conduct specific projects when needed than to staff an entire in-house department that may sit idle between projects. Also, the skills required for various projects may differ. By hiring outside suppliers, the firm can match the project to the vendor with the greatest expertise in the particular area under investigation. In addition, hiring outside suppliers allows the sponsoring company to remain anonymous and to avoid problems that might arise with regard to internal politics.

Although it has become increasingly common to buy marketing research, many managers are uncertain as to how one goes about selecting a research supplier. Perhaps the first step is to decide when research is really necessary. There is no simple formula for assessing this need, but most managers turn to research when they are unsure about their own judgment and other information sources seem inadequate. Before contacting research suppliers, it is important for the managers to identify the most critical areas of uncertainty and the issues that would benefit most from research.

Once a manager has determined the most critical areas for research, he or she is ready to seek the right supplier for the job. The selection process is not easy, for there are thousands of qualified marketing research companies in the United States. Some are full-service "generalist" companies; others are specialists in qualitative research, advertising-copy testing, concept testing, and so on; and still others are services that only conduct interviews, process data, or work with statistics.

The manager must carefully evaluate the capabilities of suppliers in light of the company's research needs. Some issues require small-scale qualitative studies whereas others require large-scale quantitative research projects. It is essential that the vendor

---

[31]See J. Walker Smith, "Beyond Anecdotes: Toward a Systematic Model of the Value of Marketing Research," *Marketing Research: A Magazine of Management & Applications,* 3 (March 1991), p. 3–14, for an example.

selected understands the firm's information needs and has the expertise required to conduct the research.

Experts suggest that managers should seek proposals from at least three companies. They also urge that the research user talk with the persons at the supplier company who will be processing and analyzing the data, writing the report, supervising the interviewers, and making presentations to management.

Marketing research is still an art, not a science. It benefits from heavy involvement of senior research professionals, who provide insights that come only from years of training and experience. A research firm's most important asset is the qualification of the research professional(s) who will be involved in the design, day-to-day supervision, and interpretation of the research.

The research user's responsibility is to communicate effectively with the prospective vendor and provide the necessary background and objectives for the study. Research users should also ask about the supplier's quality-control standards. Most research firms are pleased when clients show concern about the quality of their work and will gladly explain their quality-control steps in the areas of field work, coding, and data processing.

After reading the proposals and meeting key personnel, the manager should perform a comparative analysis. He or she should use the proposals to evaluate each vendor's understanding of the problem, how each will address it, and the cost and timing estimate of each. In making this evaluation, the manager needs to keep in mind that the value of the information is determined by its use, not its mere presence. Thus, the manager must be forthright in addressing how he or she would use the information provided by executing the various proposals.

Many firms have formal evaluation systems with specified criteria for evaluating suppliers.[32] This is particularly true among those companies who use suppliers on a regular basis. Land O'Lakes, Inc., the dairy producer, for example, uses the criteria shown in Table 3.4 to evaluate the research suppliers it uses. The company has a formal set of written guidelines that it shares with potential research suppliers that spells out these criteria in more detail. Further, at the completion of each project, a research analyst, manager, or the research director evaluates the supplier in terms of whether the provider was excellent, very good, good, fair, or poor in terms of each of the criteria. There is also a comment section for each criterion where the evaluator can explain the basis of the evaluations. The firm applies as many of these criteria as it can when evaluating the proposals of new suppliers.

When evaluating suppliers that seem equally competent, a manager must rely on his or her intuitive assessment regarding the soundness of the research design proposed, the supplier's responsiveness to the manager's specific questions, and the vendor's understanding of the subtler aspects of the marketing problem.

---

[32]For a list of the criteria used by DowBrands Inc., see Robert M. Smith, "Research Provider Partnerships: Do They Consider the Client's Real Needs?" *Marketing Research: A Magazine of Management & Applications,* 4 (June 1992), pp. 24–26.

TABLE 3.4   **Criteria Used by Land O'Lakes, Inc. to Evaluate Research Suppliers**

General attitude and responsiveness: enthusiastic, helpful, prompt replies on costs estimates, proposals, etc.
Marketing insight: informative, understands study objectives, has ability to analyze data, provides
                     recommendations
Fundamental design: questionnaire, study instructions, test plan, etc.
Questionnaire construction: format, order and wording of questions, appropriate scales
Tabulation design: format, accuracy
Day-to-day serving: responsive and informative on study progress, problems, etc.
Analysis: thorough, relates to objectives
Quality of report writing: concise, clear, accurate, executive summary
Presentation: well-planned, concise, materials organized, verbal skills
Delivery time: topline, tables, report
Cost: over, under, justified
Overall performance
   Excellent: outstanding performance in all phases of the project
   Very good: acceptable performance on all phases of the project
   Good: work is satisfactory; however, could improve performance in one or two phases of the project
   Fair: performance fell short in one or more phases of the project
   Poor: performance and quality of the work is unacceptable

Source: Courtesy of Stephen Lauring, Marketing Research Manager, Land O'Lakes, Inc.

SUMMARY

A company's philosophy of how marketing research fits into its marketing plan determines its program strategy for marketing research. A program strategy specifies the types of studies that are to be conducted and determines their purposes. The design of the individual studies themselves defines the firm's project strategy.

Although each research problem imposes its own special requirements, a marketing research project can be productively viewed as a sequence of steps — the research process — that includes the following: (1) formulate problem, (2) determine research design, (3) design data collection method and forms, (4) design the sample and collect data, (5) analyze and interpret the data, and (6) prepare the research report. These steps are so highly interrelated that they can rarely be performed consecutively but rather require a good deal of iteration between and among the various steps. These steps organize the remainder of this book, since each section elaborates a stage. The stages also indicate the potential areas of expertise needed by the aspiring researcher. The research process highlights the key error in designing a research project, which is total error. This means that a larger error may have to be accepted at some specific stage, such as sampling, so that the total error associated with the project may be minimized.

The first stage in the research process is problem formulation. In defining the decision problem, the researcher and the manager each need to be open and honest in their communications with each other. Decision problems or opportunities can arise from three sources: unplanned change; planned change; and serendipity, or chance ideas. The simplest decision problem is characterized by an individual operating in an environment who wants something, has alternative ways of pursuing it, and is in doubt about which course of action to take, because the available options will not be equally efficient. The decision problem is what to do in this situation. To determine whether research can assist the decision maker in making the choice, it is necessary to translate the decision problem into a research problem that addresses the questions of what information to provide for the decision problem and how that information can best be secured. If the decision problem was triggered by unplanned change, the typical emphasis will be on determining what happened and why. If it is a result of planned change, the research emphasis will probably be on how to bring about the desired result. Chance ideas could produce either kind of research emphasis.

It is absolutely imperative that the research address the "real" decision problem and not some visible, but incorrect, specification of it. For this to happen, the researcher working on the problem must develop sufficient understanding of the decision maker and the environment, the alternative courses of action being considered, the decision maker's objectives (including the person's attitude toward risk), and the potential consequences of the alternative courses of action. One useful mechanism for ensuring that the actual decision problem will be addressed by the research is for the researcher to prepare a written statement of the problem after meeting with the decision maker. Another way is by preparing scenarios that anticipate the contents of the final report, including the planned cross-tabulations, and asking the decision maker what he or she would do with the results. In either case, it is useful to secure signed agreement from the decision maker that the written statement correctly captures the situation. After such agreement is obtained, the researcher should prepare a research proposal, which describes the techniques that will be used to address the problem. The research proposal should include some perspective on how each stage in the research process will be handled, as well as the time and cost estimates.

Before going ahead with the research, the potential gains to be derived should always be specified explicitly and compared with the costs to ensure that the research is likely to be worthwhile.

Questions

1. What is the difference between a program strategy for research and a project strategy?
2. What is the research process?
3. What is the most important error in research? Explain.
4. What are the sources of marketing problems or opportunities? Does a source change typically trigger a change in research emphasis? Explain.
5. What is the basic nature of a decision problem?
6. What are the fundamental characteristics of decision problems?
7. What is involved in a research request step? What is included in the written statement?
8. What is involved in using scenarios to help define the decision problem?

9. What is the purpose of a research proposal? What goes into the various parts?

10. Why would firms want to use outside suppliers for their research? How should decision makers go about choosing an outside supplier for some research?

Applications and Problems

1. Given the following decision problems, identify the research problems:
   a. what pricing strategy to follow for a new product
   b. whether to increase the level of advertising expenditures on print
   c. whether to increase in-store promotion of existing products
   d. whether to expand current warehouse facilities
   e. whether to change the sales force compensation package
   f. whether to change the combination of ticket price, entertainers, and security at the Indiana State Fair
   g. whether to revise a bank's electronic payment service

2. Given the following research problems, identify corresponding decision problems for which they might provide useful information:
   a. design a test market to assess the effect on sales volume of a particular discount scheme
   b. evaluate the stock level at the different warehouses
   c. evaluate the sales and market share of grocery stores in a particular location
   d. develop sales forecasts for a particular product line
   e. assess the level of awareness among students, faculty, and staff of the benefits of IBM PS/2 ownership
   f. assess attitudes and opinions of customers toward existing theme restaurants

3. Briefly discuss the difference between a decision problem and research problem.

4. In each of the following situations, identify the fundamental source of the marketing problem or opportunity, a decision problem arising from the marketing problem or opportunity, and a possible research problem.
   a. Cool Pool Supply is a manufacturer of swimming pool maintenance chemicals. Recently, a malfunction of the equipment that mixes anti-algae compound resulted in a batch of the product that not only inhibits algae growth but also causes the pool water to turn a beautiful shade of light blue (with no undesirable side effects).
   b. The MBA director of a local college recently extended offers to 20 promising students. Only 5 offers were accepted. In the past, acceptance rates have averaged 90 percent. A survey of non-acceptors conducted by the director revealed that the primary reason students declined the offer was their perception that the college's course requirements are too "restrictive."
   c. Chocoholic Candy Company has enjoyed great success in its small regional market. Management attributes much of this success to Chocoholic's unique distribution system, which ensures twice-weekly delivery of fresh product to retail outlets. The directors of the company have instructed management to expand Chocoholic's geographical market if it can be done without altering the twice-weekly delivery policy.

5. You are the marketing manager of a mid-sized manufacturing firm. Recently you solicited proposals for an upcoming research project from three outside marketing research suppliers. You have the formal proposals in hand and must choose which supplier to use. In general, what criteria should you use in making your decision?

6. The chapter discussed the research problem and the problem formulation step in research design. Take a step back for a moment and consider the following question: In the absence of company problems, is there any need to conduct marketing research?

7. Describe three situations in which marketing research should not be undertaken. Explain why this is true.

Thorndike Sports Equipment Video Case

1. What is the problem in Thorndike's racquetball division?

2. As research analyst for Thorndike, you have been assigned the project of solving "the Graph-Pro racquet problem." Outline the steps you would take in order to understand the scope of the problem. What types of research would you propose to Thorndike's president?

APPENDIX 3A

Bayesian Decision Theory

Once the decision problem has been defined, the manager or researcher must determine whether research will or will not be employed to help solve it. Bayesian decision theory is a particularly useful scheme for structuring the research decision so that the proper choice can be made; further, when research is the indicated choice, Bayesian analysis also provides for the systematic evaluation of alternative research strategies. Even though the rudiments of Bayesian statistical method are quite old, the technique has only recently become popular. This appendix shows how Bayesian decision theory can be used to determine whether research should be conducted or whether the decision should be made with the available information.[1] A proper discussion of this question requires that we first review some basic notions associated with decision making and probability.

---

[1] The technique has its origins in a paper by Reverend Thomas Bayes, "An Essay Toward Solving a Problem in the Doctrine of Chance," *Philosophical Transactions of the Royal Society,* 1763. Bayes suggested that probability judgments based on hunches can and should be combined with traditional probabilities based on relative frequencies through the use of a theorem he designed. Robert Schlaifer's book, *Probability and Statistics for Business Decisions* (New York: McGraw-Hill, 1959), probably did more than any other work to popularize Bayesian decision theory. For a number of interesting case studies regarding its potential usefulness, see Robert D. Behn and James W. Vaupel, *Quick Analysis for Busy Decision Makers* (New York: Basic Books, Inc., 1982).

BASIC NOTIONS OF DECISION MAKING

Probability

Suppose I was holding a coin in my hand and I asked you, "What is the probability of getting a head when I toss this coin?" You might reply, "Fifty percent, or one-half." Would it make any difference to you, though, if I told you that the coin was not a fair coin? According to classical probability theory, you could not provide the probability of a head turning up if the coin was not fair. In classical statistics, probability refers to relative frequency in the long run. If the coin was fair, one could extrapolate from past experience. If the coin was not fair, one would have to toss the coin a great number of times under controlled conditions and record the relative proportion of heads. **Classical probabilities** are thus seen to be limited to cases in which one can safely extrapolate from past information or in which one can run a controlled experiment.

Bayesian probability assumes a different perspective. Instead of viewing probabilities as long-run relative frequencies, Bayesians view them as more akin to betting odds. Thus, when asked for the probability of getting a head in one toss of the coin, you would have to judge for yourself whether the coin was fair or not, and if you did consider it likely to be biased, by how much.

Bayesians hold that this view of probability is more appropriate to the problems the business decision maker faces than is classical probability. When introducing a new product, for example, the decision maker cannot simply argue that the chance of success for this product is 60 percent because, historically, 60 percent of all the products introduced have been successful. At a minimum, the economic environment, consumer demand, and the competitive frame will be different, and these factors must be taken into account in assessing the likelihood of success. Certainly the decision maker can rely on past experience in making probability judgments, much as you might rely on your knowledge about me and the likelihood of my cheating you when tossing the coin. The fact remains, however, that each new product introduction is unique, and the probability estimates associated with the product's success must be **personal** or **subjective probabilities,** since they cannot be generated in the classical sense.

Each of us makes these subjective judgments all the time, although we most often do it implicitly. Poker players, for example, well recognize the need for subjective judgments. Even though good poker players may know the objective probability of getting four of a kind in a game of five-card stud, when they are betting they must decide whether the person sitting across the table actually has the four of a kind necessary to beat their own full house. It is doubtful that they would simply use objective probabilities. Rather, they will take into account the other cards that are showing on the table and the way the person is betting and what they know about that person's betting behavior. Does the other player bluff? Or only bet heavily on a good hand? The particular hand in question is a unique event, but poker players need to form, and will form, some personal estimate of their chances of winning the hand. Similarly, many of you are probably already assessing the likelihood of getting an A, B, and so on in each of your courses. One can, and most of us do, assign personal probabilities to events, and Bayesians hold that these probability judgments need to be made explicit in framing our decisions.

Payoff Table

Another important ingredient in the decision theory approach to problem solving is the **payoff table.** The payoff table and the important role played by Bayesian analysis in marketing research are best illustrated by an example.

Consider the problem facing the marketing manager who is responsible for pricing a new product. Suppose the manager is considering whether to use a skim- or penetration-pricing strategy, or whether to price the product somewhere in between the two extremes. That is, suppose three price alternatives are under consideration:

- A_1 — skim-pricing strategy (price per unit is \$12.50);
- A_2 — intermediate price (\$10.00 per unit);
- A_3 — penetration strategy (price per unit, \$7.50).

The marketing manager recognizes that the desirability of each price depends on the demand that develops for the product. Suppose that the possible levels of product demand and associated consequences are as depicted in Table 3A.1.

Table 3A.1 is a payoff table depicting the decision situation. The example is somewhat limited; it contains only three alternatives and three possible states of nature. Either the alternatives or the states of nature, or both, could have been expanded. The only difference this would have made would have been an increase in the amount of computation.

Note that the payoff table contains three elements: alternatives, states of nature, and consequences. The alternatives, sometimes called acts, are options open to the decision maker. The states of nature are uncontrollable elements in the environment in which the manager operates. These elements may be of two types — those beyond the decision maker's influence and those that can be influenced. General economic conditions are typically a given for most firms and are of the first type. Competitive reactions are often influenced by the decisions of the firm and illustrate the second type. Because both types are beyond the decision maker's control, they are logically considered states of nature or environmental variables, and not decision options. The example treats the demand materializing for the product, not the decision maker's brand, as the states of nature. There is a consequence associated with each decision alternative, given each potential state of nature.

Table 3A.1 is read as follows. If the decision maker selects the skimming price (A_1), and low demand for the product actually results, the company can be expected to

TABLE 3A.1   **Payoff Table for Pricing Decision**

Alternative	State of Nature		
	Light Demand, S_1	Moderate Demand, S_2	Heavy Demand, S_3
Skimming price — A_1	100	50	−50
Intermediate price — A_2	50	100	−25
Penetration price — A_3	−50	0	80

realize a profit of $100.[2] If there is intermediate demand, the resulting profits could be expected to be $50, and with high demand, the firm could be expected to incur a loss of $-\$50$. You may wonder why the example is cast in this way — that is, why the firm could be expected to lose money under conditions of high product demand and to make money under conditions of low product demand. Note two things. First, the entries themselves are unimportant for illustrating the Bayesian approach. They will affect the computations and possibly the decision, but not the procedure. If you take issue with the numbers, rest assured that any other numbers could serve as well in illustrating the technique. Second, the numbers do reflect some traditional wisdom about when skimpricing and penetration-pricing strategies are warranted. For example, it is generally held that all other things being equal, a penetration strategy is better when there is high potential demand for the product, as this gives the firm some opportunity to keep out competition and thereby get a larger share of the market. A skimming strategy under conditions of high product demand would be an enticement for competitors. With low product demand, on the other hand, a penetration strategy could be disastrous. It might not allow the firm to recover its investment, whereas a skimming strategy would afford the possibility of quicker capital recovery. The numbers used for the consequences are designed to reflect these kinds of considerations. In practice, they would be generated from the best available information. The important thing for now is to note that a payoff table contains alternatives, states of nature, and the consequences of each alternative given each state of nature — the essential elements in decision problems. The payoff table, then, provides a formal structure for the traditional decision problem. The structure is productive in determining the best course of action.

Which pricing decision is optimal? If the marketing manager is 100 percent certain that there will be low product demand, alternative A_1 (skimming price) is clearly the preferable choice, because it provides higher profits than either A_2 or A_3. If the manager is 100 percent certain that there will be high product demand, the penetration strategy A_3 is best. The intermediate price A_2 is best if the decision maker expects a moderate level of demand. Clearly, then, the individual's choice of alternatives depends on which state of ature is expected. This suggests the assignment of probabilities to the various states of nature.

Suppose, on the basis of the company's past experience, some past marketing research, and the company's knowledge of available substitute products, that the decision maker expects this product to attract a limited market segment. In particular, the probabilities associated with each state of nature are assessed as follows:[3]

---

[2]The entries in the table should be, or at least could be, considered as discounted future returns reflecting the cost of capital. They could also be treated as thousands or millions of dollars, or whatever unit is appropriate. The example is framed in dollars to keep the mathematics simple.

[3]One could argue that the numbers actually assigned to the probabilities for the states of nature should depend on the action considered, because economic theory suggests that product demand is influenced by the price charged. This presents no new conceptual difficulties, although it does make the discussion and calculations somewhat more cumbersome. We will assume, for discussion purposes, that the probabilities for the states of nature and the alternatives being considered are independent.

- light demand (S_1): $P(S_1) = 0.6$;
- moderate demand (S_2): $P(S_2) = 0.3$;
- heavy demand (S_3): $P(S_3) = 0.1$.

Different decision makers, given the same information, might assess these probabilities differently, just as two experienced poker players might assess the likelihood of the same player having four of a kind differently. This is why these probabilities are personal or subjective. In all other ways, though, they follow the normal rules and definitions of probabilities.

PRIOR ANALYSIS

Now that the preliminary notions connected with payoff tables and probability have been reviewed, we are in a position to address the question of whether research should or should not be conducted. In essence, this question can be reduced to a comparison of the value of the decision without research to the anticipated value of the decision, assuming that research were to be conducted. If the anticipated value is higher with research, the research is warranted; if the cost of research exceeds its potential contribution to the managerial decision, research is not justified.

Expected Value

A criterion that has been used for comparing the potential value of the decision with research to the potential value without research is that of expected value. **Expected value** is simply a weighted average of the various consequences in the payoff table, where the weights are the probabilities assigned to each of the possible states of nature. Expected value is defined for each alternative or act i. Further, when (1) the alternative has n outcomes, (2) the probability of the jth outcomes is p_j, and (3) the value of the jth outcome given the ith alternative is V_{ij}, then the expected value of the ith alternative is

$$EV_i = \sum_{j=1}^{n} p_j V_{ij}.$$

The expected value of the three pricing alternatives is thus determined to be:

$$EV(A_1) = (0.6)(100) + (0.3)(50) + (0.1)(-50) = 70.0.$$
$$EV(A_2) = (0.6)(50) + (0.3)(100) + (0.1)(-25) = 57.5.$$
$$EV(A_3) = (0.6)(-50) + (0.3)(0) + (0.1)(80) = -22.0.$$

Alternative A_1 (the skim-pricing strategy) offers the highest expected value. It would be the best choice, assuming that the decision maker's goal is to maximize expected returns. The decision maker, to be sure, may have other goals. He or she might, for example, be interested in minimizing any potential loss, in which case alternative A_2, with a maximum loss of \$25, would be preferred. The decision theory apparatus can be adapted to reflect other decision criteria.

Let us assume, though, that the decision maker does desire to maximize expected return, in which case the expected value of the optimal act without research is $70. This means that in the absence of any further information, the decision maker would choose a skim-pricing strategy with an expected return of $70.

PREPOSTERIOR ANALYSIS

Suppose that, before making the pricing decision, the decision maker has the opportunity to commission a marketing research study. Should it be done, or should the pricing decision be made with the present information? To make the choice between research and no research, it seems reasonable *to compare the expected value of the optimal act before the research and the expected value of the optimal act after the research, taking into account the cost of the research itself.*

Value of Perfect Information

One way of generating a quick comparison is to determine the greatest possible increase in expected value. This would occur, of course, if the research information perfectly predicted the state of nature — level of product demand — that would actually result. The decision maker could then simply price the product accordingly.

For instance, if the research indicated that the demand for the product would be light, the decision maker would choose the skimming price with a return of $100, because this return is higher than the $50 return associated with an intermediate price and the $50 loss associated with the penetration price. Similarly, if the research indicated that the demand for the product would be moderate, the intermediate price would be optimal, and if product demand should be indicated to be heavy, the penetration price would be best.

How likely is it that the decision maker would select each alternative price and realize the gain associated with that price? This likelihood is given by the probability that the individual will be told that a given state of nature will result; for if S_1 results, the manager makes decision A_1; if S_2 results, decision A_2 is chosen; and if S_3 results, decision A_3 is picked. The best estimates of these probabilities are the probabilities assigned to each state of nature, since the individual is not given a choice about which state of nature will result but is only told in advance which one will happen. Once the decision maker is told this, though, there is no question about its validity, because the information is perfect. One can proceed with certainty in the choice of alternatives.

Expected value under certainty is found by multiplying the probability that the decision maker will be told a given state of nature will occur by the value associated with the *optimal act* given that particular state of nature. Expected value under certainty for the example problem is

$$EV(C) = (0.6)(100) + (0.3)(100) + (0.1)(80) = 98,$$

where the consequences reflect, respectively, alternative A_1 with S_1, alternative A_2 with S_2, and alternative A_3 with S_3.

The difference between the expected value under certainty and the expected value of the optimal act under uncertainty (recall that this was A_1) is the **expected value of perfect information;** that is,

$$
\begin{aligned}
EV(PI) &= EV(C) - EV \text{ (optimal act under uncertainty)} \\
&= \$98 - \$70 \\
&= \$28.
\end{aligned}
$$

The perfect information calculation indicates that the cost of the contemplated research cannot exceed \$28, as this is the net benefit that results with perfect information, a result the research is unlikely to produce. If the research project costs more than \$28, it should not be undertaken and the pricing decision should be made with the information currently available. This means that the skimming price would be selected.

Value of Sample Information

It would be extremely helpful if the decision maker could buy research information that would allow the pricing decision to be made under conditions of certainty. It is also true that such information is generally unavailable. However, the decision maker usually does have the option of buying imperfect sample information. Should this be done? This is the question to which we now turn.

Disregarding the cost of the research for the moment, suppose that the firm is considering test marketing the product. It intends to use test market results to predict eventual product demand, although it recognizes the hazards associated with test marketing. Sometimes the product will sell poorly in a test market and yet be highly successful when introduced nationally. The reverse may also be true. Suppose, on the basis of past product performances, the company is able to anticipate certain correlations between test market results and product performance nationally. Let

- Z_1 — disappointing or only slightly successful test market,
- Z_2 — moderately successful test market, and
- Z_3 — highly successful test market,

and suppose past experience provided the estimates contained in Table 3A.2.

Table 3A.2 is read by row within a given column. This means, for example, that 0.7 of those products that eventually produced only light demand nationally also performed poorly in the test market, whereas 0.2 of them were moderately successful in the test market and 0.1 were highly successful in the test market. On the other hand, most products that were successful nationally (generated heavy demand) also had highly successful test markets (0.6), whereas a few national successes had moderately successful test markets (0.3), and a small percentage even had disappointing test markets (0.1). In other words, the test market was a relatively good but not perfect barometer of success. Products that performed poorly in the test market generally performed poorly nationally and vice versa, although there were exceptions.

One of the key factors in deciding whether or not to conduct research is finding out how the managerial decision might change as a result of the research. If the managerial

TABLE 3A.2   **Conditional Probabilities of Getting Each Test Market Result, Given Each State of Nature**

Test Market Result	Light Demand, S_1	Moderate Demand, S_2	Heavy Demand, S_3
Disappointing or only slightly successful — Z_1	0.7	0.2	0.1
Moderately successful — Z_2	0.2	0.6	0.3
Highly successful — Z_3	0.1	0.2	0.6
	1.0	1.0	1.0

decision will be the same regardless of the research findings, the research is not worthwhile. There must be some research results, perhaps extreme, that would alter the managerial decision. This means that the first step in evaluating the worth of sample information (research results) must be revision of the initial probabilities on the basis of the research results that might occur. Someone, usually the research director, must directly assess the question of how the probabilities surrounding the various states of nature would change if the results of the contemplated test market are disappointing (Z_1), moderately successful (Z_2), or highly successful (Z_3).

The revision of prior probabilities in the light of additional information is the very essence of **Bayes' rule.** The right-hand column of Table 3A.3 contains the revised probabilities associated with each state of nature.[4] There are three sets of these probabilities, one for each possible test market result.

The top section of Table 3A.3, for example, contains the revised probabilities for each of the states of nature, given that the test market results were disappointing. A disappointing performance of the product in the test market would imply that the probability of light demand for the product should be revised upward to 0.858 from its initial value of 0.6, that the probability of moderate demand should be revised downward to 0.122 from its initial value of 0.3, and that the probability of heavy demand should be revised downward to 0.020 from its initial value of 0.1.

Note two things about these calculations. First, the calculations can be performed before doing the research. The possible research results are simply *anticipated,* and the prior probabilities are revised systematically employing Bayes' rule on the basis of what might happen. Second, two people given the same test market results might arrive at different final probabilities for the states of nature. This is because the posterior probabilities depend on both the test market results and the initial assessment of the prior probabilities. There is nothing very unusual about different people arriving at different conclusions on the basis of the same set of evidence. Most experienced researchers have

---

[4]See Schlaifer, *Probability and Statistics,* for the development of the logic and calculations of how prior probabilities are systematically revised with new information.

TABLE 3A.3   **Revision of Prior Probabilities in Light of Possible Test Market Results**

j (1)	State of Nature S_j (2)	Prior Probability $P(S_j)$ (3)	Conditional Probability $P(Z_k|S_j)$ (4)	Joint Probability $P(Z_kS_j)$ (5) = (3) × (4)	Posterior Probability $P(S_j|Z_k)$ (6) = (5) ÷ Sum of (5)
	Z_1—Disappointing or Only Slightly Successful Test Market				
	1 Light demand—S_1	0.6	0.7	0.42	0.858
	2 Moderate demand—S_2	0.3	0.2	0.06	0.122
	3 Heavy demand—S_3	0.1	0.1	0.01	0.020
				0.49	1.000
	Z_2—Moderately Successful Test Market				
	1 Light demand—S_1	0.6	0.2	0.12	0.364
	2 Moderate demand—S_2	0.3	0.6	0.18	0.545
	3 Heavy demand—S_3	0.1	0.3	0.03	0.091
				0.33	1.000
	Z_3—Highly Successful Test Market				
	1 Light demand—S_1	0.6	0.1	0.06	0.333
	2 Moderate demand—S_2	0.3	0.2	0.06	0.333
	3 Heavy demand—S_3	0.1	0.6	0.06	0.333
				0.18	1.000

met the decision maker who argues, "I don't care what your research says, I know better. We have been doing things this way successfully for ten years, and I do not see any reason to change, particularly on the basis of one research study, which must be in error anyway." What this decision maker is really saying is that his or her prior probabilities are such (for example, so close to 1) that the research is not substantial enough to warrant any significant change in them.

One interesting example of the effect of prior probabilities on the desirability of doing research involves the Allied Mills Company. In this instance, the product manager and the research manager disagreed about whether a market test should be run before introducing a new product. The research manager favored a market test, whereas the product manager did not. The disagreement became so heated that "the research manager accused the product manager of misleading management. The product manager in turn accused the research manager of not recognizing a sound new product idea when he saw one."[5] The disagreement finally narrowed down to a difference in their prior assess-

[5]Donald S. Tull and Del I. Hawkins, *Marketing Research: Measurement and Method*, 3rd ed. (New York: Macmillan, 1984), p. 47.

ments about the likely success of the new product. Given this basic difference, the research made sense to the research manager but did not make sense to the product manager. It is only when the two parties agreed to commit these prior estimates to paper that the basis for the dispute became clear. Whenever a decision maker's prior probabilities are so strong that research will do little to change them, the research will be wasted. If this is anticipated before the research is begun, unnecessary research costs can be avoided.

These arguments demonstrate that the first step in evaluating the worth of some proposed research is to calculate how the prior probabilities would be revised on the basis of the possible anticipated research results. The second step involves calculation of the value of the research on the basis of the optimal decision, given each possible research result and the likelihood that the result will indeed occur. In other words, the second step requires that *the optimal decision be determined for each potential research outcome*.

The expected value of each alternative pricing strategy is calculated for each sample result in Table 3A.4. If the test market is unsuccessful, the skim-pricing strategy (A_1) is optimal because it offers the highest expected return. On the other hand, if the test market is either moderately or highly successful, the intermediate pricing strategy (A_2) would be optimal. The penetration strategy (A_3) would not be called for regardless of the test market outcome. Although this finding may at first be surprising, the explanation is straightforward. The only time the penetration strategy is optimal is when heavy product

TABLE **3A.4   Expected Value of Each Alternative, Given Each Research Outcome**

Z_1 — *Disappointing or Only Slightly Successful Test Market*
Revised probabilities: $P(S_1) = 0.858$; $P(S_2) = 0.122$; $P(S_3) = 0.020$
$EV(A_1) = 100(0.858) + 50(0.122) + (-50)(0.020) = 90.9$
$EV(A_2) = 50(0.858) + 100(0.122) + (-25)(0.020) = 54.6$
$EV(A_3) = (-50)(0.858) + 0(0.122) + 80(0.020) = -41.3$

Z_2 — *Moderately Successful Test Market*
Revised probabilities: $P(S_1) = 0.364$; $P(S_2) = 0.545$; $P(S_3) = 0.091$
$EV(A_1) = 100(0.364) + 50(0.545) + (-50)(0.091) = 59.1$
$EV(A_2) = 50(0.364) + 100(0.545) + (-25)(0.091) = 70.4$
$EV(A_3) = (-50)(0.364) + 0(0.545) + 80(0.091) = -10.9$

Z_3 — *Highly Successful Test Market*
Revised probabilities: $P(S_1) = 0.333$; $P(S_2) = 0.333$; $P(S_3) = 0.333$
$EV(A_1) = 100(0.333) + 50(0.333) + (-50)(0.333) = 33.3$
$EV(A_2) = 50(0.333) + 100(0.333) + (-25)(0.333) = 41.6$
$EV(A_3) = (-50)(0.333) + 0(0.333) + 80(0.333) = 10.0$

demand can be expected. The prior probability of heavy product demand materializing was initially so low that heavy demand would never become the dominant state of nature, regardless of the test market results. Consequently, the penetration strategy would never be optimal, at least on the basis of the proposed research.

Given a choice, the decision maker would prefer test market result Z_1 because this allows the opportunity to maximize the expected return. Given a Z_1 result, the individual would simply choose A_1 with a return of $90.90. Unfortunately the decision maker will not have a choice of test market results, because these will be governed by consumer response to the product. The decision maker can, however, anticipate the *likelihood of getting each possible test market result*. These projections can then be used in conjunction with the optimal acts to determine the potential value of the proposed research.

The probability of obtaining each test market result (that is, the probability of each Z_k) is given as

$$P(Z_k) = \sum_{j=1}^{n} P(S_j)P(Z_k|S_j),$$

and for $k = 1$, for example, the probability is found to be

$$P(Z_1) = P(S_1)P(Z_1|S_1) + P(S_2)P(Z_1|S_2) + P(S_3)P(Z_1|S_3)$$
$$= (0.6)(0.7) + (0.3)(0.2) + (0.1)(0.1)$$
$$= 0.49.$$

This probability is given in the tabular computation form as the sum of the elements in Column 5, Table 3A.3. Table 3A.3 thus indicates that the probabilities associated with each test market outcome are $P(Z_1) = 0.49$, $P(Z_2) = 0.33$, and $P(Z_3) = 0.18$.[6]
The expected value of the test-marketing procedure is found by weighting each expected value of the optimal act, given each research result, by the probability of receiving that expected value. Thus, although the decision maker cannot be assured of obtaining a Z_1 test market result, the probability of receiving the $90.90 expected value from making decision A_1 is 0.49. Similarly, the manager can anticipate the $70.40 associated with making decision A_2, given test market result Z_2, 33 percent of the time, and the $41.60 associated with making decision A_2, given test market result Z_3, 18 percent of the time. The expected value of the proposed research is thus found to be

$$EV(\text{research}) = (90.90)(0.49) + (70.40)(0.33) + (41.60)(0.18)$$
$$= 75.26,$$

---

[6]The probabilities sum to 1, as they should, because one of the three test market outcomes must result.

because, in general, **the expected value of a research procedure** *is the sum of the products of the probability of obtaining the kth research result and the expected value of the preferred decision given the kth research result.*

Should the research be undertaken? The answer is yes, as long as it costs less than $5.26. The $5.26 represents the *increment* in expected value with the research. The expected value of the best decision in the absence of research was $70, whereas the expected value with the proposed research was $75.26. If the expected value with the research were less than $70, the research would not be warranted.

REVIEW OF PROCEDURE

Because determining the value of research involves a number of steps and calculations, a review of the overall procedure is helpful. We have essentially calculated three quantities: (1) the expected value of the decision without research, (2) the expected value of perfect information, and (3) the expected value of some proposed research. The first two quantities provide ready benchmarks to which the value of the research can be compared. The benefits of the research must exceed (1), and the cost must be less than (2).

Figure 3A.1 diagrams the situation. Assuming that the benefits and costs are both measured in the same units, the 45-degree line separates the area into situations in which

FIGURE 3A.1   Value of Research Information

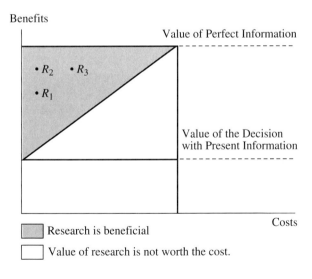

research is beneficial and those in which it is undesirable. The value of the decision with present information is given by the expected value of the optimal act without research. The expected value of each act is, in turn, determined by weighting the consequences by the probabilities of obtaining each consequence.

Perfect information provides an easily calculated upper benchmark for the value of research. The ease with which it can be calculated is its primary value, because research does not produce perfect information. The value of perfect information is given by the difference between the expected value under certainty and the expected value of the optimal decision without research. The expected value under certainty is, in turn, determined by weighting the value of the optimal act under each assumed state of nature by the probability of obtaining that value — that is, by the probability associated with the state of nature.

Determining the value of proposed research requires the calculation of several quantities, including:

1. how the prior probabilities would be revised on the basis of the research results;
2. the expected value of the optimal act, given each potential research result, and the revised probabilities surrounding the states of nature;
3. the probability of obtaining each research result and thereby realizing the return associated with the optimal act.

These calculations were all made on the basis of what might be expected to happen and, as such, are anticipated quantities.

The anticipated results of the research can be used to compare alternative research strategies as well as to determine whether research should or should not be conducted. Figure 3A.1 contains three hypothetical research strategies, labeled R_1, R_2, and R_3. All of these are beneficial in that the assumed value of the research exceeds the value of the decision without research. R_2 is best; it costs the same as R_1 but has greater benefits; it has the same benefits as R_3, but costs less.

DECISION TREE

An alternative way of approaching what we have been doing is by using a decision tree. A **decision tree** is simply a decision flow diagram, in which the problem is structured in chronological order. The tree has branches, which are connected by decision forks or chance forks. A decision fork or node is typically depicted as a small square and a chance fork is depicted as a small circle. The important thing in decision tree analysis is to lay out the problem completely before attempting to solve it by pruning, or crossing off, the undesirable branches.

Figure 3A.2 shows a decision tree for the pricing decision. All numbers have been left off on purpose, to throw the basic structure of the tree into bolder relief. The decision maker's initial decision, reading from left to right, is whether to conduct research or to select a pricing strategy on the basis of the data at hand. The choice will

FIGURE 3A.2   Decision Tree for Pricing Decision Problem

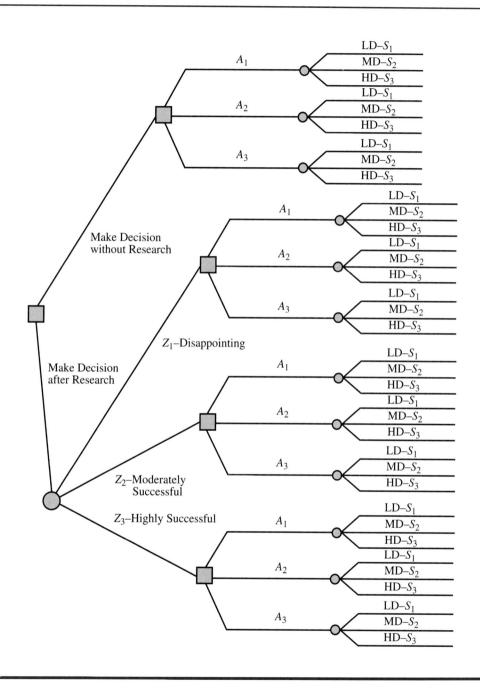

depend on the expected value of the two options, quantities that can be determined by solving the tree. Disregarding the solution for a moment, if the decision maker decides to make the decision with the data at hand, he or she is immediately confronted with another decision, shown by the square fork — the particular price to use. If research is the indicated option, the next node is a chance fork representing the various research results that might occur because the decision maker cannot control the test market results. Given any of the three possible test market results, the decision maker will then have to choose a particular price, and thus the next junction in each case is a square representing a decision fork. The decision can be good or bad in any case. It depends on the product demand that actually results, and this, of course, is beyond the decision maker's control.

The decision tree is solved from right to left. The solution involves determining the expected value associated with each alternative. The alternative that is optimal at each decision node is then carried backward, and the nonoptimal ones are simply crossed off, most commonly by putting a double line through each undesirable alternative.

Consider the upper branch. The expected value of each alternative is calculated as before, by weighting the consequences by the probabilities associated with attaining each consequence. We already have all the necessary numbers, so we need not repeat the calculations. Decision A_1 is optimal, and alternatives A_2 and A_3 are pruned. Because decision A_1 had an expected value of $70, the value of the decision without research is also $70. Figure 3A.3 contains the entries.

Consider the lower branch. The expected value of each pricing alternative will now change, since the probabilities associated with each state of nature will change, depending on the test market results. Proceeding as before, we first enter the expected value of each pricing option reflecting the *new probabilities* at the right-hand side of the tree, and the undesirable alternatives are deleted. The value of the optimal act is then carried back to the decision node. All that remains, then, is the weighting of each value at the decision node by the probability that the value will be obtained — that is, by the probability of going down the branch in question. The sum of the products of probabilities and values, 75.26, is entered at the chance node to indicate the value of the decision with research. Because this quantity exceeds that associated with the upper branch, the upper branch will be crossed off, and the decision will be to go ahead with the research, assuming that it costs no more than $5.26. Although the whole analysis could be carried out with the cost of the research entered directly as a net subtraction from the values in the payoff table, it is done this way to demonstrate the maximum value of the research, given the potential research outcomes.

It is not necessary to formally solve the decision tree to benefit from it. The decision tree is a most useful device for conceptualizing a problem and communicating its basic structure to others. Diagramming the problem forces a focus on the interrelationships of the decisions that need be made. This helps illuminate the role of research in the decision and encourages communication between decision maker and researcher. Whether or not a formal Bayesian analysis is undertaken to determine whether potential research benefits justify the costs, constructing a tree of the decision problem can cast such problems in bold relief.

FIGURE 3A.3   **Solution to Decision Tree for Pricing Decision Problem**

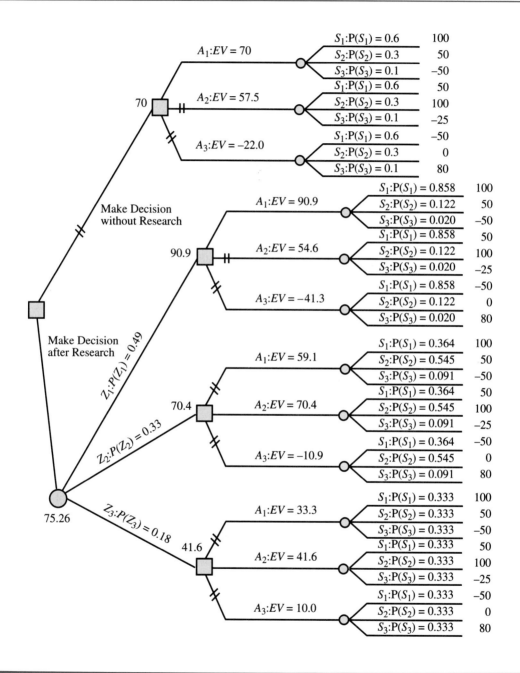

ADDITIONAL CONSIDERATIONS

Even though the basic concept behind the decision theory approach is simple enough — compare the expected value of the optimal decision without research to the expected value of the research results — calculations for even the simplest of examples can get tedious. The previous example is basic in several respects, not the least of which are (1) the limited states of nature and alternatives it considers, (2) the assumption that the decision maker possesses a "linear utility function," and (3) the certainty associated with the payoffs. There is no conceptual problem in introducing refinements. The basic approach remains the same, but there are more calculations to perform.

Additional States of Nature and/or Alternatives

Only three pricing alternatives and three states of nature are treated in the example. This is unrealistic in actual decision problems. At a very minimum, the states of naturecan be expanded to include the economic environment, competitive reactions, and consumer demand. This expansion can create problems in the assignment of prior probabilities. Probabilities for states of nature such as "competitor introduces product at lower price when demand is strong and economy is booming" or "at same price" will have to be assessed under these conditions. These probability assignments can become complex, involving, as they do, joint probabilities. Someone will have to take special pains to ensure that the states of nature are indeed mutually exclusive and exhaustive.

The expansion of alternatives simply entails a greater number of expected value calculations. The problem here is again one of ensuring that all viable alternatives are entered in the decision calculations and that they are expressed as mutually exclusive options.

Nonlinear Utility Functions

The example uses an expected value criterion. The expected value criterion is appropriate when potential gains or losses are "within bounds" — that is, when none of the returns is psychologically overwhelming to the decision maker.

If the decision maker in the example cannot tolerate the loss of $50, because it will ruin the business or produce great financial strain, the expected value criterion will not apply. The expected value criterion is an average, and averages obscure. The decision maker who cannot tolerate a loss of $50 can never be expected to select pricing strategies A_1 or A_3 because of the probability that each of these could result in such a loss.

There are alternatives to the expected value criterion. One of the more popular approaches is to construct an index that reflects the decision maker's attitude toward risk and to employ the index values in the payoff table. All calculations then proceed as before, but now the criterion is one of expected utility, taking account of the riskiness of the situation rather than expected value.[7]

Uncertain Payoffs

The consequences in the payoff table are shown as single numbers. Thus, if the skimming price is selected and light demand materializes, the payoff is $100, no more, no less. The more likely situation is that the payoffs will be estimated with some uncertainty, and rather than the single figure of $100; the estimate might be that there is a 50 percent chance of realizing a $100 return; but the return might also go as low as $75 or as high as $125.

An estimate with a range of values can be incorporated in the decision structure. However, such an estimate entails an assessment of the likely returns and the probability associated with each return. The average return, which is then calculated by weighting the returns by the respective probabilities, is entered in the payoff table, and the calculations proceed as before.

BAYESIAN ANALYSIS AND MARKETING RESEARCH

It is clear from this simplified example that Bayesian analysis has much to offer decision and research analysts. It facilitates communication between them because of the conceptual structuring of the decision problem it provides, particularly when the tree diagram is constructed. Bayesian analysis is demanding of each of them as well. It demands that decision makers make their judgments clear, both with respect to what they anticipate might happen and also with respect to the probabilities they attach to the states of nature. It also requires that decision makers clarify the alternatives they are considering and the consequences they anticipate for each of the alternatives, given their assessment of the environment. Not all decision makers will be willing to expose their decision calculus in detail.

Bayesian analysis also demands much of the researcher. It requires taking on a computational burden, demonstrating finesse in extracting the decision maker's judgments so that the implicit alternatives and states of nature are completely enumerated and the appropriate decision criterion is used, and paying attention to detail so that the

---

[7]A number of authors discuss the construction of these utility indices. See, for example, Howard Raiffa, *Decision Analysis: Introductory Lectures on Choices under Uncertainty* (Reading, Mass.: Addison-Wesley, 1968), pp. 51–101, for a particularly helpful discussion. See also Paul J. H. Schoemaker, "The Expected Utility Model: Its Variants, Purposes, Evidence, and Limitations," *Journal of Economic Literature,* 20 (July 1982), pp. 529–563; and Paul J. H. Schoemaker, *Experiments on Decisions Under Risk: The Expected Utility Hypotheses* (Boston: Kluwer-Nijhoff Publishing, 1980).

problem is correctly structured and the decision maker's subjective judgments are correctly translated into probabilistic statements.[8]

These problems are not insurmountable, as reported applications attest.[9] Although some decision makers might not be willing to employ the entire decision theory apparatus, the fundamental questions need to be asked and answered before research is begun: "Will the research be worth it? Do potential benefits exceed anticipated costs?"

■
Questions

1. What is the basic nature of a payoff table?
2. What is the role of marketing research with respect to the elements of a payoff table?
3. How is the maximum value of any contemplated research determined?
4. What is meant by perfect information? How is the value of such information determined?
5. Outline the procedure necessary to determine the value of imperfect research information.
6. What is Bayesian analysis? What role does it play in evaluating the contribution of research to the decision problem?
7. What is the difference between objective and subjective probabilities? How is the difference important for business decision making?
8. What is a decision tree? How is it constructed? How is it "solved"?

■
Applications and Problems

1. Karen Horner, an antique dealer, had been selling antiques at the Tecumseh Antique Mall for the past five years. Karen recently decided to expand her part-time business into a full-time venture and is preparing to open her own store in the neighboring town of Manchester. She is trying to decide whether or not to use an advertising campaign to announce her store's opening. Based on her past experience in the antique business, Karen believes that the probabilities associated with each state of nature are as follows:

$$\text{Light Demand } (S_1): P(S_1) = 0.20$$
$$\text{Fair Demand } (S_2): P(S_2) = 0.55$$
$$\text{Heavy Demand } (S_3): P(S_3) = 0.25$$

[8]For a review of the evidence regarding the elicitation of subjective probabilities, see Thomas S. Wallsten and David V. Budescu, "Encoding Subjective Probabilities: A Psychological and Psychometric Review," *Management Science,* 29 (February 1983), pp. 151–173.

[9]For specific assessments of the use of decision theory in evaluating contemplated marketing research, see Gert Assmus, "Bayesian Analysis for the Evaluation of Marketing Research Expenditures," *Journal of Marketing Research,* 14 (November 1977), pp. 562–568; G. S. Albaum, D. S. Tull, and J. Hansen, "The Expected Value of Information: How Widely Is It Used in Marketing Research?" in Neil Beckwith, Michael Houston, Robert Mittelstaedt, Kent B. Monroe, and Scott Ward, eds., *1979 Educators' Conference Proceedings* (Chicago: American Marketing Association, 1979), pp. 32–34; and D. J. Brownlie, "A Case Analysis of the Cost and Value of Marketing Information," *Marketing Intelligence and Planning,* 9 (No. 1, 1991), pp. 11–18.

The following payoff table depicts Karen's decision situation:

	State of Nature		
Alternative	**Light Demand,** S_1	**Fair Demand,** S_2	**Heavy Demand,** S_3
Don't Advertise Opening	$-$6,000	$-$4,000	$-$2,000
Low-Key Advertising	$-$ 6,500	2,000	4,000
Normal Advertising	$-$ 7,000	4,000	8,000
Intensive Advertising	$-$ 9,000	6,000	14,000

a. Diagram the decision tree for Karen's decision problem.
b. Calculate the expected value of each of the four advertising campaign alternatives.
c. For the most likely state of nature, what is Karen's most profitable advertising selection?
d. If Karen is extremely risk adverse, which advertising selection reduces her exposure to losses?
e. What is the expected value of her decision problem under certainty?
f. If Lew's Research Company offers to do a research project for Karen for $1,700 that will predict her store's sales for the next five years, should she hire Lew? Why?

2. Mr. Bullis has decided that he is ready to enter the auto parts business. Mrs. Bullis is sure that the store will be successful and convinces her husband that the probability of the store's being successful is 65 percent. Mr. Bullis agrees but is wondering whether he should do some marketing research. If he does the research with the aid of some students, the cost will be only $1,000. On the other hand, he can get reliable results from Dependable Research Results, Inc., but this will cost him $4,000.
   Assume the following payoff table:

	State of Nature	
Alternative	**Successful (High Demand)** 1	**Not Successful (Low Demand)** 2
Open the Store (A_1)	$400,000	$-$170,000
Do Not Open the Store (A_2)	0	0

Also assume the following conditional probabilities of survey results, where Z_1 indicates high demand or success, and Z_2 indicates low demand or failure:

Research by:	**Conditional Probabilities**
Mr. Bullis	$P(Z_1/S_1) = P(Z_2/S_2) = 0.70$
	$P(Z_1/S_2) = P(Z_2/S_1) = 0.30$
Dependable Research Results, Inc.	$P(Z_1/S_1) = P(Z_2/S_2) = 0.90$
	$P(Z_1/S_2) = P(Z_2/S_1) = 0.10$

a. What is the expected value of each alternative without research? Which alternative is preferred assuming that Mr. Bullis wants to maximize expected returns?

b. What is the expected value of perfect information? What does this indicate?

c. Revise the prior probabilities to capture the anticipated results by completing the following table:

State of Nature	Prior Probabilities	Conditional Probabilities	Joint Probabilities	Posterior Probabilities

Mr. Bullis's Research

Z_1: Research results indicate high demand or success.

    S_1: successful (high demand)

    S_2: unsuccessful (low demand)

Z_2: Research results indicate low demand or failure.

    S_1: successful (high demand)

    S_2: unsuccessful (low demand)

Research Agency

Z_1: Research results indicate high demand or success.

    S_1: successful (high demand)

    S_2: unsuccessful (low demand)

Z_2: Research results indicate low demand or failure.

    S_1: successful (high demand)

    S_2: unsuccessful (low demand)

d. Compute the expected value for the two research options.

e. Should Mr. Bullis do any research? If yes, which research option should he choose? If no, why not?

3. For Problem 2, prepare the appropriate decision trees for the three options: (a) no research, (b) Mr. Bullis does the necessary research, and (c) Dependable Research Results, Inc., does the necessary research.

4. Battleground Manufacturing Company, a maker of hooked rugs, is considering raising the price of one of the more popular styles, fireplace rugs, from $349.95 to $399.95. Bee Crostreet, Battleground's marketing manager, recently attended a conference at which several papers on Bayesian decision theory were presented. Bee is quite enamored with the technique and thinks it might be appropriate for the pricing decision now facing her. She has called on you to help her with her analysis. She particularly wants help in determining the following:

   a. whether she should make the price-change decision on the basis of the information that she has; or

   b. whether she should secure some marketing research information before making the decision.

   The company's best projection of the future discounted profits of this item is $600,000 if the price is not changed. If the price is changed, the estimated return is much more uncertain, because it depends on consumer reaction to change. If there is little negative reaction, the discounted future returns are projected at $1,600,000; returns are projected at $800,000 if there is some negative reaction and $200,000 if there is a strong negative reaction.

   Bee thinks that the most likely state of affairs will be some consumer resistance to the price hike, but that consumer reaction will not be strongly negative and that there is even a possibility of no negative reaction at all to the price increase. When pressed, Bee attached these probabilities to the various consumer reactions.

   - S_1: little or no negative reaction   probability = 0.3
   - S_2: some negative reaction   probability = 0.5
   - S_3: strong negative reaction   probability = 0.2

   The research being considered by Bee for reducing the uncertainty surrounding the decision is a small test market, in which the price of the product will be raised to $399.95 and the change in sales monitored. The company has had some previous experience with research of this kind, and although the results are not directly generalizable, they do provide a good indication of what might happen. There have been instances, though, in which the test-market results overestimated and other cases in which the test market underestimated what happened nationally. Prior experience suggests the following contingencies in particular between eventual market demand and the test-market results.

	General Reaction		
Test Market Result	**Little or None,** S_1	**Some Negative Reaction,** S_2	**Strong Negative Reaction,** S_3
T_1: little change in sales	0.6	0.2	0.1
T_2: some sales decrease	0.3	0.6	0.4
T_3: significant sales decrease	0.1	0.2	0.5

   The entry 0.6 in the second row, second column, suggests, for instance, that 60 percent of the time in which there was some negative reaction to the price boost nationally, there was also some decrease in the quantity sold in the test market; the entry in the third row, second column, indicates that 20 percent of the time in which there was some negative reaction nationally, there was a significant sales decrease in the test market; and the entry in the first row, second column, indicates that 20 percent of the time there was little change in sales of the product in the test market, although the price boost did occasion some negative reaction when implemented nationally. The costs associated with market-testing the price change total $180,000.

a. Should Bee make the price-change decision on the basis of the information she has now, or should she pay to have the market-test experiment conducted?

b. Diagram Bee's dilemma in the form of a decision tree.

c. Calculate the value of perfect information to Bee.

d. Calculate the value of the market-test information to Bee.

CASE 1.1
Big Brothers of Fairfax County

Big Brothers of America is a social-service program designed to meet the needs of boys ages six to eighteen from single-parent homes. Most of the boys served by the program live with their mothers and rarely see or hear from their fathers. The purpose of the program is to give these boys the chance to establish a friendship with an interested adult male. Big Brothers of America was founded on the belief that an association with a responsible adult can help program participants become more responsible citizens and better adjusted young men.

The program was started in Cincinnati in 1903. Two years later, the organization was granted its first charter in New York State through the efforts of Mrs. Cornelius Vanderbilt. By the end of World War II, there were 30 Big Brothers agencies. Today there are 300 agencies across the United States, and 120,000 boys currently are matched with Big Brothers.

The Fairfax County chapter of Big Brothers of America was founded in Fairfax in 1966. In 1971, United Way of Fairfax County accepted the program as part of its umbrella organization and now provides about 85 percent of its funding. The remaining 15 percent is raised by the local Big Brothers agency.

Information about the Big Brothers program in Fairfax County reaches the public primarily through newspapers (feature stories and classified advertisements), radio, public service announcements, posters (on buses and in windows of local establishments), and word-of-mouth advertising. The need for volunteers is a key message emanating from these sources. The agency phone number is always included so that people wanting to know more about the program can call for information. Those calling in are given basic information over the telephone and are invited to attend one of the monthly orientation sessions organized by the Big Brothers program staff. At these meetings, men get the chance to talk to other volunteers and to find out what will be expected of them should they decide to join the program. At the end of the session, prospective volunteers are asked to complete two forms. One is an application form and the other is a questionnaire in which the person is asked to describe the type of boy he would prefer to be matched with, as well as his own interests.

The files on potential Little Brothers are then reviewed in an attempt to match boys with the volunteers. A match is made only if both partners agree. The agency stays in close contact with the pair and monitors its progress. The three counselors for the Big Brothers program serve as resources for the volunteer.

The majority of the inquiry calls received by the Fairfax County agency are from women who are interested in becoming Big Sisters or from people desiring information on the Couples Program. Both programs are similar to the Big Brothers program and are administered by it. In fact, of 55 calls concerning a recent orientation meeting, only 5 were from males. Only 3 of the 5 callers actually attended the meeting, a typical response.

Although the informational campaigns and personal appeals thus seemed to have some effect, the results were also generally disappointing and did little to alleviate the shortage of volunteer Big Brothers. There are currently 250 boys waiting to be matched with Big Brothers, and the shortage grows weekly.

Big Brothers of Fairfax County believed that a lack of awareness and accurate knowledge could be the cause of the shortage of volunteers. Are there men who would volunteer if only they were made aware of the program and its needs? Or is the difficulty a negative program image? Do people think of Little Brothers as problem children, boys who have been in trouble with the law or who have severe behavioral problems? Or could there be a misconception of the type of man who would make a good Big Brother? Do people have stereotypes with respect to the volunteers — for example, that the typical volunteer is a young, single, professional male?

Questions

1. What is (are) the marketing decision problem(s)?
2. What is (are) the marketing research problem(s)?
3. What types of information would be useful to answer these questions?
4. How would you go about securing this information?

CASE 1.2
Supervisory Training at the Management Institute

University of Wisconsin-Extension is the outreach campus of the University of Wisconsin System. Its mission is to extend high-quality education to people who are not necessarily ''college students'' in the normal sense. The Management Institute (MI) is one of the departments within UW-Extension. It conducts programs aimed at providing education and training in at least a dozen areas of business and not-for-profit management.

The supervisory training area within the Management Institute designs and conducts continuing education training programs for first-level supervisors. The training programs are designed to improve a trainee's managerial, communication, decision-making, and human relation skills. They consequently cover a broad range of topics.

A continuing decline in enrollments in the various programs during the past several years had become a problem of increasing concern to the three supervisory program directors. They were at a loss to explain the decline, although informal discussions among the supervisors raised a number of questions to which they did not know the answers. Have people's reasons for attending supervisory training programs changed? What are their reasons for attending them? Was the decline caused by economic factors? Was it because of increased competition among continuing education providers? Was it due to the content or structure of MI's programs themselves? Was it because of the way the programs were structured or promoted? Were the programs targeted at the right level of supervisor?

Typically, the major promotion for any program involved mailed brochures that described the content and structure of the course. The mailing list for the brochures was all past attendees of any supervisory training program conducted by the Management Institute.

Questions

1. What is the decision problem?
2. What is (are) the research problem(s)?
3. How would you recommend MI go about addressing the research problem(s)? That is, what data would you collect and how might those data be used to answer the research question(s) posed?

CASE 1.3
Department of Administration

Consistent with its general policy of stimulating economic development in the area, the Department of Administration (DOA) of a U.S. state wishes to give more state business to small vendors. Assuming that state contracts benefit small businesses financially, it should be within the power of the DOA to help small businesses prosper by facilitating the procurement of state contracts on their behalf. To explore this idea further, the DOA solicits bids from the local marketing research firms — themselves small businesses — to investigate the issue.

Hobbes Research is a newly formed company in the region with a small, specialized staff. Hobbes is not a "full-service" marketing firm in that it does not employ its own telephone interviewers or field workers. Rather, it concentrates on the planning and supervision of research projects. Hobbes Research is eager to submit a proposal for the DOA's small-business development scheme, based upon the following information obtained during discussions with the DOA.

BACKGROUND INFORMATION

The general problem of promoting small-business development by means of the procurement of state contracts seemed to encompass several subproblems. The DOA had no idea what the financial impact of selling to the state was for small businesses. It seemed likely that small vendors would make less profit from their dealings with the state than with private companies, but no actual data were available, and there was no indication whether small businesses were satisfied with their dealings with the state. Similarly, the DOA was ignorant of any problem small vendors encountered in obtaining state contracts. Presumably, there must be advantages in selling to the state, but these were likewise unclear.

Hobbes Research felt that exploratory interviews with small-business owners, DOA personnel, and perhaps one or two academics in the field might clarify these issues. In addition, the State Bureau of Procurement provided information packets for small-business owners, and annual reports of the state's purchasing activities were published regularly, all of which might be informative.

Meanwhile DOA staff were happy to impart their preliminary ideas about state small-business interactions. They believed that being a vendor to the state had positive impact on small businesses and that the level of economic impact on individual businesses varied. They were also convinced that small businesses bid lower for state deals than for private-industry contracts and that profit margins on sales to the state were lower than profit margins on other sales. Finally, they felt that small businesses derived satisfaction from dealing with the state but that they experienced recurring, common problems in procuring state contracts.

Hobbes Research needed some clarification of definitional issues before they could plan further. It appeared that a business that reported less than $1.5 million in gross sales in the 1993 calendar year could officially be classified as small. Moreover, such a business would only be termed a current vendor to the state in the eyes of the DOA if it had sold to the state during the 1993 fiscal year (July 1, 1992–June 30, 1993). For 1,000 out of an estimated 2,500 firms thus qualifying as small vendors, the DOA wanted gross sales and profit figures for 1993 and wished to know the number of employees hired for the express purpose of working on state contracts in 1993.

Listings of relevant companies were available on state tapes. Specifically, the State Department of Revenue possessed one tape listing the addresses of all businesses located in the state and another that contained gross sales figures for all businesses situated in the state. Further, the State Bureau of Procurement kept a purchase-order tape that identified vendors to the state for any given year.

The DOA wanted to work closely with whichever marketing research firm they selected to undertake the study. They were enthusiastic about having their staff help with administrative duties such as typing and printing and requested that their premises be considered the research center. Indeed, they were glad to provide an office equipped with personal computers for the purposes of data analysis. In addition, the DOA was adamant that its staff would need to see an interim report before any large-scale study commenced. In this way, they could review the questionnaire and have a clear idea of the tabulations that the researchers were planning to generate.

It was already January 6, 1994, and the DOA wanted the entire project completed and a full, written report by the end of April 1994. The closing date for submission of proposals was January 15. They promised that they would announce their choice of marketing research firm by the end of that month.

Questions

1. Prepare a research proposal to submit to the DOA on behalf of Hobbes Research.
2. Evaluate your approach to data collection versus other approaches that could be used.

CASE 1.4
Wisconsin Power & Light (A)[1]

Recent changes in the utility industry have led to a more deregulated and competitive environment. In response, Wisconsin Power & Light (WP&L) has been shifting its focus from that of a product-driven to more of a market- and information-driven company. Management has increasingly relied on information from marketing studies and has been incorporating the external data in their decision-making processes. WP&L's espousal of a market-sensitive mentality has helped to shape the company's overall business strategies. One current area of concern for WP&L involves environmental issues, so much so that one of the company's goals, is "to be a responsible corporate citizen, promoting the social, economic, and environmental well-being of the communities that it serves."

WP&L, in an effort to realize its environmental goals, developed several programs for its residential, commercial, and industrial customers to foster the conservation of energy. The programs, which were classified under the BuySmart umbrella of WP&L's Demand-Side Management Programs, consisted of specific programs such as Appliance Rebates, Energy Analysis, Weatherization Help, and the Home Energy Improvement Loan (HEIL) program. All previous marketing research and information gathering focused primarily on issues from the customer's perspective, such as an evaluation of net program impacts in terms of energy and demand savings and an estimation of the levels of free ridership (individuals who would have undertaken the conservation actions promoted by the program, even if there was no program in place). In addition, a study has been designed and is currently being conducted to evaluate and identify customer attitudes and opinions concerning the design, implementation, features, and delivery of the residential programs. Having examined the consumer perspective, WP&L's current goal

[1]The contributions of Kavita Maini and Paul Metz to the development of this case are gratefully acknowledged as is the permission of Wisconsin Power & Light to use the material included.

is to focus on obtaining information from other participants in the programs, namely employees and lenders.

The next task for the management of WP&L to undertake is a study of the Home Energy Improvement Loan (HEIL) program of the BuySmart umbrella. The HEIL program was introduced in 1987 and was designed to make low-interest-rate financing available to residential gas and electric WP&L customers for conservation and weatherization measures. The low-interest guaranteed loans are delivered through WP&L account representatives in conjunction with participating financial institutions and trade allies. The procedures for obtaining a loan begin with an energy "audit" of the interested customer's residence to determine the appropriate conservation measures. Once the customer decides on which measures to have installed, the WP&L representative assists in arranging the low-interest-rate financing through one of the participating local banking institutions. At the completion of the projects, WP&L representatives conduct an inspection of the work by checking a random sample of participants. Conservation measures eligible under the HEIL program include the installation of natural gas furnaces/boilers, automatic vent dampers, intermittent ignition devices, heat pumps, and heat pump water heaters. Eligible structural improvements include the addition of attic/wall/basement insulation, storm windows and doors, sillbox insulation, window weather-stripping, and caulking.

PURPOSE

The primary goal of the current study is to identify ways of improving the HEIL program from the lenders' point of view. Specifically, the following issues need to be addressed:

- Identify the lenders' motivation for participating in the program.
- Determine how lenders get their information regarding various changes/updates in the program.
- Identify how lenders promote the program.
- Assess the current program with respect to administrative and program features.
- Determine the type of credit analysis conducted by the lenders.
- Identify ways of minimizing the default rate from the lenders' point of view.
- Identify lenders' opinions of the overall program.
- Assess the lenders' commitment to the program.
- Identify if the reason for loan inactivity in some lending institutions is due to lack of a customer base.

Question

1. Prepare a research request that will address WP&L's study objectives.

CASE 1.5
The Williams Company

The Williams Company is a regional manufacturer of soft drinks in flavors such as grape, cherry, and orange. Top management has recently become concerned about the erosion of its competitive position and is now considering plans for a summer promotional campaign. The special promotion would cost $100,000, and management is concerned about whether it should contract for an expenditure of this magnitude, because it has little past experience against which to measure the possible success of such efforts. If consumer reaction is extremely favorable (over a 10 percent increase in market share), the company stands to make an incremental profit of $400,000; if it is favorable (5 to 10 percent increase in market share), the projected profits are $100,000; and if it is unfavorable (no appreciable change in market share), the company stands to incur an incremental loss of $100,000 — the cost of the campaign. The marketing manager's best estimates of the likelihood of these occurrences are as follows:

- S_1: extremely favorable consumer reaction   probability = 0.3
- S_2: favorable consumer reaction   probability = 0.4
- S_3: unfavorable consumer reaction   probability = 0.3

The Williams Company is considering contracting for a marketing research study to assess the potential effectiveness of the planned campaign. The research study would cost $25,000 and would include laboratory copy tests to measure attention-getting power and field studies to assess consumer attitudes toward the advertisements. On the basis of its past experience, the Surveys Unlimited research company has suggested the following relations between its assessments of an ad's effectiveness and the ultimate success of the advertisement.

Surveys Unlimited's Experience	Consumer Reaction		
	Extremely Favorable	**Favorable**	**Unfavorable**
Strongly positive	0.7	0.2	0.0
Moderately positive	0.3	0.6	0.2
Slightly positive	0.0	0.2	0.8

The table is read row within column. Thus, for example, the entry in the first row, first column indicates that 70 percent of those advertisements that created an extremely favorable customer reaction also elicited a strongly positive reaction in the research.

Questions

1. Should the decision on the special promotion be made without the research, or should the proposed research be conducted? Construct a payoff table for the promotion decision option without the research.

2. Diagram the total decision, including the research option, in the form of a decision tree.

3. Evaluate the value of perfect research information. Evaluate the value of the research information to be provided by Surveys Unlimited.

DETERMINE RESEARCH DESIGN

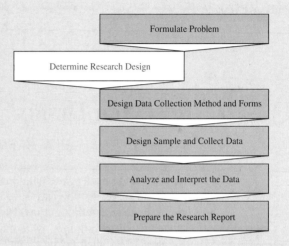

Formulate Problem

Determine Research Design

Design Data Collection Method and Forms

Design Sample and Collect Data

Analyze and Interpret the Data

Prepare the Research Report

Part 2 deals with the general nature of designing research so that it addresses the appropriate questions efficiently. Chapter 4 is an overview of the role of various research designs and also discusses two of the basic designs — the exploratory and the descriptive — at some length. Chapter 5 discusses the role of experiments in marketing research.

RESEARCH DESIGN

The preceding chapters present some of the kinds of problems that marketing research can help to solve. As you may have noticed, there can be great variation in the nature of the questions research might investigate. Some can be very specific: for example, if we change the advertising mix, what might happen to sales? Others are much more general: why have sales fallen below target? How do customers feel about the product? As you may have guessed, different formulations of a problem can lead to different research approaches to answer it.

This chapter introduces the notion of research design and discusses the basic types and their interrelations. It also reviews two of the design types — the exploratory and the descriptive — in some detail. The next chapter deals with the nature of causal or experimental designs.

PLAN OF ACTION

A **research design** is simply the framework or plan for a study, used as a guide in collecting and analyzing data. It is the blueprint that is followed in completing a study. It resembles the architect's blueprint for a house. Even though it is possible to build a house without a detailed blueprint, doing so will more than likely produce a final product that is somewhat different than what was orginally envisioned by the buyer. A certain room is too small; the traffic pattern is poor; some things really wanted are omitted, other less important things are included; and so on. It is also possible to conduct research without a detailed blueprint. The research findings, too, will probably differ widely from what was desired by the consumer or user of the research. "These results are interesting, but they do not solve the basic problem" is a common lament. Further, just as the house built without a blueprint is likely to cost more because of midstream alterations in construction, research conducted without a research design is likely to cost more than research properly executed using a research design.

Thus a research design ensures that the study (1) will be relevant to the problem and (2) will use economical procedures. It would help the student learning research methods if there were a single procedure to follow in developing the framework or if there were a single framework to be learned. Unfortunately, this is not the case.

> There is never a single, standard, correct method of carrying out research. Do not wait to start your research until you find out *the* proper approach, because there are many ways to tackle a problem — some good, some bad, but probably several good ways. There is no single perfect design. A research method for a given problem is not like the solution to a problem in algebra. It is more like a recipe for beef stroganoff; there is no one best recipe.[1]

Rather, there are many research design frameworks, just as there are many unique house designs. Fortunately, though, just as house designs can be broken into basic types (for example, ranch, split level, two-story), research designs can be classified into some basic types as well. One very useful classification is in terms of the fundamental objective of the research: exploratory, descriptive, or causal.[2]

TYPES OF RESEARCH DESIGN

The major emphasis in **exploratory research** is on the discovery of *ideas* and *insights*.[3] The soft drink manufacturer faced with decreased sales might conduct an exploratory study to generate possible explanations. The **descriptive research** study is typically concerned with determining the *frequency* with which something occurs or the relationship between two variables. The descriptive study is typically guided by an initial hypothesis. An investigation of the trends in the consumption of soft drinks with respect to such characteristics as age, sex, geographic location, and so on, would be a descriptive study. A **causal research** design is concerned with determining *cause-and-effect* relationships. Causal studies typically take the form of experiments, because experiments are best suited to determine cause and effect. For instance, our soft drink manufacturer may be interested in ascertaining the effectiveness of different advertising appeals. One way for the company to proceed would be to use different ads in different geographic areas and investigate which ad generated the highest sales. In effect, the company would perform an experiment, and if it was designed properly, the company would be in a position to conclude that one specific appeal caused the higher rate of sales.

Having stated the basic general purpose of each major type of research design, three important caveats are in order. First, although the suggested classification of design types is useful for gaining insight into the research process, the distinctions are not absolute. Any given study may serve several purposes. Nevertheless, certain types of research designs are better suited to some purposes than others. The crucial tenet of

---

[1]Julian L. Simon, *Basic Research Methods in Social Science: The Art of Empirical Investigation* (New York: Random House, 1969), p. 4.

[2]Claire Selltiz, Lawrence S. Wrightsman, and Stuart W. Cook, *Research Methods in Social Relations,* 3rd ed. (New York: Holt, Rinehart and Winston, 1976), pp. 90–91. See also Fred N. Kerlinger, *Foundations of Behavioral Research,* 3rd ed. (New York: Holt, Rinehart and Winston, 1986), pp. 347–390.

[3]The basic purposes are those suggested by Selltiz, Wrightsman, and Cook, *Research Methods.*

research is that *the design of the investigation should stem from the problem*. Each of these types is appropriate to specific kinds of problems.

Second, in the remainder of this chapter and in the next chapter, we shall discuss in more detail each of the design types. The emphasis will be on their *basic characteristics* and *generally fruitful approaches*. Whether or not the designs are useful in a given problem setting depends on how imaginatively they are applied. Architects can be taught basic design principles; whether they then design attractive, well-built houses depends on how they apply these principles. So it is with research. The general characteristics of each design can be taught. Whether they are productive in a given situation depends on how skillfully they are applied. There is no single best way to proceed, just as there is no single best floor plan for, say, a ranch-type house. It all depends on the specific problem to be solved. Research analysts, then, need an understanding of the basic designs so that they can modify them to suit specific purposes.

Third, the three basic designs can be looked at as stages in a continuous process. Figure 4.1 shows the interrelations. Exploratory or formulative studies are often seen as the initial step. When researchers begin an investigation, it stands to reason that they lack a great deal of knowledge about the problem. Consider, for example, the following problem: "Brand X's share of the disposable diaper market is slipping. Why?" This statement is too broad to serve as a guide for research. To narrow and refine it would logically be accomplished with exploratory research, in which the emphasis would be on finding possible explanations for the sales decrease. These tentative explanations, or hypotheses, would then serve as specific guides for descriptive or causal studies. Suppose the tentative explanation that emerged was that "Brand X is an economy-priced diaper, originally designed to compete with low-cost store-brand diapers. Families with children have more money today than when the brand was first introduced and are willing to pay more for higher quality baby products. It stands to reason that our market share would decrease." The hypothesis that families with small children have more real income to spend, and that a larger proportion of that money is going toward

FIGURE 4.1   Relationships among Research Designs

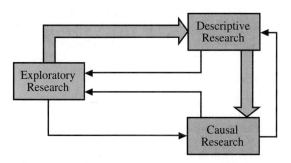

baby products, could be examined in a descriptive study of trends in the baby products industry.

Suppose that the descriptive study did support the hypothesis. The company might then wish to determine whether mothers were, in fact, willing to pay more for higher quality diapers and, if so, what features (such as better fit or greater absorbency) were most important to them. This might be accomplished partially through a test marketing study, a causal design.

Each stage in the process thus represents the investigation of a more detailed statement of the problem. Although we have suggested that the sequence would be from exploratory to descriptive to causal research, alternative sequences might occur. The "families with small children have more money to spend on baby products" hypothesis might be so generally accepted that the sequence would go from exploratory directly to causal. The potential for conducting research in the reverse direction also exists. If a hypothesis is disproved by causal research (e.g., the product bombs in the test market), the analyst may then decide that another descriptive study, or even another exploratory study, is needed. Also, not every research problem will begin with an exploratory study. It depends on how specific researchers can be in formulating the problem before them. A general, vague statement leads naturally to exploratory work, whereas a specific cause-effect hypothesis lends itself to experimental work.

Research Realities 4.1, for instance, lists some of the individual projects that were conducted by PepsiCo to support the conception and introduction of its successful O'Grady's potato chips. In this instance, the examination of the potato chip category with respect to market shares and trends, the ideation sessions, and the focus groups to help develop meaningful ways to describe a thick potato chip could all be classified as exploratory research. The diary panel that was set up to measure trial and repeat purchase behavior would be considered descriptive, and the market simulation test and the test of the commercial would be considered causal.

EXPLORATORY RESEARCH

As previously stated, the general objective in exploratory research is to gain insights and ideas. The exploratory study is particularly helpful in breaking broad, vague problem statements into smaller, more precise subproblem statements, hopefully in the form of specific hypotheses. A **hypothesis** is a statement that specifies how two or more measurable variables are related.[4] A good hypothesis carries clear implications for testing stated relationships. In the early stages of research, we usually lack sufficient understanding of the problem to formulate a specific hypothesis. Further, there are often several tentative explanations for a given marketing phenomenon. For example: sales are off because our price is too high; our dealers or sales representatives are not doing the job they should; our advertising is weak; and so on. Exploratory research can be used to establish

---

[4]See Kerlinger, *Foundations of Behavioral Research,* for a discussion of the criteria of good hypotheses and of the value of hypotheses in guiding research.

Research Supporting the Development and Introduction of O'Grady's Potato Chips

As a first step, Frito-Lay examined whether or not a consumer need existed for a different type of potato chip. An inventory was made of the potato chip product. There were relatively few options available. Potato chips on the market were either flat or ridged, unflavored or cheese flavor or flavored with sour cream and onion. Yet, Frito-Lay knew that consumers seek variety and often differentiate between products on a textural basis.

At the corporate level, a number of hurdle criteria were set: a $100 million-plus business, it had to add incremental volume, it had to have broad national appeal, and it had to be a unique, not easily replicated product.

To start with, new product ideas were developed through a number of sources. Ideation sessions were conducted with scientists, the marketing department, home economists, and consumers. Recipe books were collected, and the industry's packaged potato snack products were purchased from stores and studied for differentiation opportunities, for needs that weren't being filled.

Four distinct product ideas resulted from this exercise: a "better Pringles," which was dropped on judgment due to Pringles' lack of success; a "potato Frito," a thicker, processed chip that later became "crunch chips"; a super-crispy chip that became Ta-Tos; and a bite-sized, latticed chip — a small, thin, fragile O'Grady's forerunner. The ideas were exposed to consumers through product evaluation groups, which provided direction on product refinement and positioning issues. The results suggested that development should continue on all three, although the crunch chips and the Ta-Tos were the most well received at this stage. The O'Grady's product was de-emphasized because consumers saw it as too light and thin.

Even though the Ta-Tos and Crunchy's were well-received and eventually went to test market, they did not fit with the business objective of being a new potato chip. Despite its consumer rejection, the lattice chip, which was to become O'Grady's, offered the most differentiable potato chip. O'Grady's was then taken from thin and crispy to the other end of the spectrum — thicker, heavier, and crunchier. The lattice cut gave it a unique appearance. The thickness gave it a unique texture (crunchiness) and taste (more potato taste). Home-use tests confirmed that the shift to thickness was positive, and focus group research was conducted to help develop meaningful, motivating ways of describing a thick potato chip. *Crunchy, hearty,* and *more potato taste* seemed to be most appealing.

From a market simulation test, the interest-generating ability of the concept and the fit of the product with the concept, as well as the trial and repeat and volume potential of the brand, were determined. Only two sizes and a plain flavor were tested. The results were positive, but they indicated that the product wouldn't surpass the corporate hurdle rate. So, an additional au gratin cheese flavor was developed and was selected via further home-use tests. At the same time, focus group copy development research led Frito-Lay to emphasize or embody simplicity, small-town values, implied wholesomeness, and heartiness. This commercial, opening with a potato plant, was found to be positively intrusive and memorable and to elicit positive consumer reactions with appropriate images being conveyed.

While in test market, a full range of research was conducted to monitor O'Grady's performance. An awareness and trial study was conducted. A diary panel was set up to measure trial, repeat, and depth of repeat. An image study was set up to make sure the desired positioning was conveyed. Finally, distribution checks helped monitor distribution and out-of-stock levels. These test market data allowed for fine tuning of the national program and also provided standards against which to measure O'Grady's performance during expansion.

Source: Keynote talk by Norman Heller, president and chief executive officer, PepsiCo Wines & Spirits International, at the Association of National Advertisers' New Product Marketing Workshop, October 16, 1984. See also "Spotting Competitive Edges Begets New Product Success," *Marketing News,* 18 (December 21, 1984), p. 4. For other examples of Frito-Lay's use of marketing research to understand the potato chip category, see Robert Johnson, "In the Chips: At Frito-Lay, the Consumer Is an Obsession," *The Wall Street Journal* (March 22, 1991), p. B1.

priorities in studying these competing explanations. The priorities would be established because a particular hypothesis discovered in the exploratory study appears to be promising. They might also arise because the exploratory study generates information about the practical possibilities of researching specific, conjectural statements.

The exploratory study is also used to increase the analyst's familiarity with the problem. This is particularly true when the analyst is new to the problem arena (for example, a marketing research consultant going to work for a company for the first time).

The exploratory study may be used to clarify concepts. For instance, management is considering a change in service policy that will, it is hoped, result in improved dealer satisfaction. An exploratory study could be used to clarify the notion of dealer satisfaction and to develop a method by which dealer satisfaction could appropriately be measured.

When Congress discusses revising the tax code in order to make it ''more fair'' (so as to increase taxpayer compliance), a problem that often surfaces is how to determine what fairness in the tax code means. Is it tax enforcement that bothers people? Tax avoidance by other people? The way tax laws are written? Tax rates? That people believe their tax dollars are being poorly spent? Exploratory research would play a particularly important role in clarifying a concept such as this.

In sum, an exploratory study is used for any or all of the following purposes:[5]

- formulating a problem for more precise investigation or for developing hypotheses;
- establishing priorities for further research;
- gathering information about the practical problems of carrying out research on particular conjectural statements;
- increasing the analyst's familiarity with the problem;
- clarifying concepts.

In general, exploratory research is appropriate to any problem about which little is known. Exploratory research then becomes the foundation for a good study.

Because knowledge is lacking when an inquiry is begun, exploratory studies are characterized by *flexibility* with respect to the methods used for gaining insight and developing hypotheses. ''Formal design is conspicuous by its absence in exploratory studies.''[6] Exploratory studies rarely use detailed questionnaires or involve probability sampling plans. Rather, investigators frequently change the research procedure as the vaguely defined initial problem is transformed into one with more precise meaning. Investigators follow where their noses lead them in an exploratory study. Ingenuity, judgment, and good luck inevitably play a part in leading to the one or two key hypotheses that, it is hoped, will account for the phenomenon. Notwithstanding the flexibility, research experience has demonstrated that literature surveys, experience surveys, focus

---

[5]Selltiz, Wrightsman, and Cook, *Research Methods,* p. 91.

[6]Harper W. Boyd, Ralph Westfall, and Stanley F. Stasch, *Marketing Research: Text and Cases,* 7th ed. (Homewood, Ill.: Richard D. Irwin, 1989), p. 93.

FIGURE 4.2   **Types of Exploratory Studies**

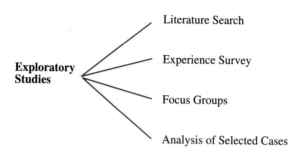

groups, and the analysis of selected cases are particularly productive in exploratory research.[7] See Figure 4.2.

Literature Search

One of the quickest and cheapest ways to discover hypotheses is in the work of others, through a **literature search.** The search may involve conceptual literature, trade literature, or, quite often, published statistics.

Stouffer's, for example, relied very heavily on the search of a variety of literature and published statistics when developing its Lean Cuisine low-calorie frozen entree line. "After studying medical and consumer literature for about seven years, Stouffer launched an intensive study of the entire diet food market . . . Consumer media were studied to determine what people were buying, reading and doing about their diet. Stouffer scrutinized trends such as jogging."[8]

The literature that is searched depends, naturally, on the problem being addressed. Miller Business Systems Inc. of Dallas, for example, routinely monitors trade literature to keep track of its competitors. The information on each competitor is entered into the "competitor profiles" that it keeps in its data base. The company regularly scans these profiles for insights on what the competition might be doing. One such scan indicated that one competitor had hired nine furniture salesmen in a ten-day period. This was a

---

[7]Selltiz, Wrightsman, and Cook, *Research Methods;* Chapter 4 has a particularly informative discussion of the types of research that are productive at the exploratory stages of an investigation.

[8]Anna Sobczynski, "Reading the Consumer's Mind," *Advertising Age,* 55 (May 3, 1984), p. M16. See also Kevin Higgins, "Meticulous Planning Pays Dividends at Stouffer's," *Marketing News,* 17 (October 28, 1983), pp. 1 and 20; and Alix M. Freedman, "Glamour of Upscale Frozen Foods Fades as Buyers Return to Basics," *The Wall Street Journal* (December 15, 1987), p. 29.

tip-off to a probable push by the competitor in the office furniture market. With this early notice, Miller was able to schedule its salespeople to make extra calls on their accounts, thereby blunting the competitor's sales drive.[9]

Sometimes conceptual literature is more valuable than trade literature. For example, a search of conceptual literature would be warranted for a firm whose management believes that its field sales force is largely dissatisfied. The search would include works on psychology, sociology, and personnel, in addition to marketing journals. The focus would be on the factors determining employee satisfaction–dissatisfaction. The analyst would keep a keen eye out for those factors also found in the company's environment. The question of how to measure an employee's satisfaction would also be researched at the same time.

Suppose the problem is one that typically triggers much marketing research: "Sales are off. Why?" Exploratory insights into this problem could easily and cheaply be gained by analyzing published data and trade literature. Such an analysis would quickly indicate whether the problem was an industry problem or a firm problem. Very different research is in order if the firm's sales are down but (1) the company's market share is up, because industry sales are down further; (2) the company's market share has remained stable; or (3) the company's market share has declined. The last situation would trigger an investigation of the firm's marketing-mix variables, whereas the first condition would suggest an analysis to determine why industry sales are off. The great danger in omitting exploratory research is obvious from the preceding example; without the analysis of secondary data as a guide, there is a great danger of researching the wrong "why."

A company's own internal data should be included in the literature examined in exploratory research, as Mosinee Paper Company found to its pleasant surprise. The company was contemplating dropping one of its products because of its dismal sales performance. Before doing so, though, the company tallied sales of the product by salesperson and found that only a single salesperson was selling that specific grade of industrial paper. On further investigation, Mosinee discovered how the buyers "were using the paper — an application that had been known only to the one salesman and his customers. This information enabled management to educate its other salesmen as to the potential market for the paper and sales rose substantially."[10]

It is important to remember that in a literature search, as in any exploratory research, the major emphasis is on the discovery of ideas and tentative explanations of the phenomenon and not on demonstrating which explanation is *the* explanation. The demonstration is better left to descriptive and causal research. Thus, the analyst must be alert to the hypotheses that can be derived from available material, both published material and the company's internal records.

---

[9]Steven P. Galante, "More Firms Quiz Customers for Clues About Competition," *The Wall Street Journal* (March 3, 1986), p. 17.

[10]Jon G. Udell and Gene R. Laczniak, *Marketing in an Age of Change* (New York: John Wiley & Sons, 1981), p. 154.

Experience Survey

The **experience survey,** sometimes called the *key informant survey,* attempts to tap the knowledge and experience of those familiar with the general subject being investigated. For example, Clearwood Building Inc. of San Francisco focused on architects and designers when trying to get a handle on its competitors. They asked these people to describe the traits of builders that tended to turn off buyers of expensive homes. Some of the answers included bad manners, workers who tracked dirt across carpets, and beat-up construction trucks, which buyers objected to having parked in their driveways. The company used these insights for a major repositioning of its business to the Bay Area's upper crust. "The company bought a new truck and kept it spotless. Its estimators donned jackets and ties. And its work crews, now impeccably polite, began rolling protective runners over carpets before they set foot in clients' homes. In less than two years, Clearwood's annual revenue jumped to $1 million from $200,000."[11]

In studies concerned with the marketing of a product, anyone who has any association with the marketing effort is a potential source of information. This would include the top executives of the company, sales manager, product manager, and sales representatives. It would also include wholesalers and retailers who handle the product as well as consumers who use the product. It might even include individuals who are not part of the chain of distribution but who might, nevertheless, possess some insight into the phenomenon. For example, a publisher of children's books investigating a sales decrease gained valuable insights by talking with librarians and schoolteachers. These discussions indicated that an increased use of library facilities, both public and school, coincided with the product's sales decline. These increases were, in turn, attributed to a very sizable increase in library holdings of children's books resulting from federal legislation that provided money for this purpose.

Usually, a great many people know something about the general subject of any given problem. However, not all of them should be contacted.

> Research economy dictates that the respondents in an experience survey be carefully selected. The aim of the experience survey is to obtain insight into the relationships between variables rather than to get an accurate picture of current practices or a simple consensus as to best practices. One is looking for provocative ideas and useful insights, not for the statistics of the profession. Thus the respondents must be chosen because of the likelihood that they will offer the contributions sought. In other words, a *selected* sample of people working in the area is called for.[12]

One *does not,* therefore, use a probability sample in an experience survey. It is a waste of time to interview those who have little competence or little relevant experience. It is also a waste of time to interview those who cannot articulate their experience and knowledge. It is important, though, to include people with differing points of view. The following were all interviewed with varying degrees of success when the children's

---

[11]Galante, "More Firms Quiz Customers."

[12]Selltiz, Wrightsman, and Cook, *Research Methods,* p. 94.

books sales decline was being researched: company executives, key people in the product group, sales representatives, managers of retail outlets in which the books were sold, teachers, and librarians.

The interviews were all unstructured and informal. The emphasis in each interview among those immediately concerned with the distribution of the product was "How do you explain the sales decrease? In your opinion, what is needed to reverse the downward slide?"[13] Most of the time in each interview was then devoted to exploring in detail the various rationales and proposed solutions. A number of sometimes conflicting hypotheses emerged. This provided the researchers with an opportunity to "bounce" some of the hypotheses off groups with differing vantage points and, in the process, get a feel for which of the hypotheses would be most fruitful to research. The interviews with librarians and teachers were divorced from the immediate problem. Here the emphasis was on discovering changes in children's reading habits.

The respondents were given a great deal of freedom in choosing the factors to be discussed. This is consistent with the notion that the emphasis in exploratory research is on developing tentative explanations and not on demonstrating the viability of a given explanation.

This emphasis, as well as the conduct of the experience survey, is reflected in the experience of the industrial goods manufacturer described in Research Realities 4.2, who used this technique to gain insight into a declining sales situation. The insight from these interviews was used to focus more personal interviews investigating its general truth, and the notion of continued growth was indeed supported.[14]

Focus Groups

Focus groups are another useful method for gathering ideas and insights.[15] In a **focus group,** a small number of individuals are brought together in a room to sit and talk about some topic of interest to the focus group sponsor. The discussion is directed by a

---

[13]Selltiz, Wrightsman, and Cook suggest that it is often useful in an exploratory study to orient questions towards "what works." That is, they recommend that questions be of the following form: "If (a given effect) is desired, what influences or what methods will, in your experience, be most likely to produce it?" (p. 95).

[14]For further discussion about the general conduct and uses of experience surveys, see Michael J. Houston, "The Key Informant Technique: Marketing Applications," in Thomas V. Greer, ed., *Conceptual and Methodological Foundations of Marketing* (Chicago: American Marketing Association, 1974), pp. 305–308; John Siedler, "On Using Informants: A Key Technique for Collecting Qualitative Data and Controlling Measurement Error in Organization Analysis," *American Sociological Review,* 39 (December 1974), pp. 816–831; Lynn W. Phillips, "Assessing Measurement Error in Key Informant Reports: A Methodological Note on Organizational Analysis in Marketing," *Journal of Marketing Research,* 18 (November 1981), pp. 395–415; George John and Torger Reve, "The Reliability and Validity of Key Informant Data from Dyadic Relationships in Marketing Channels," *Journal of Marketing Research,* 19 (November 1982), pp. 517–524; Douglas M. Lambert, Howard Marmorstein, and Arun Sharma, "Industrial Salespeople as a Source of Market Information," *Industrial Marketing Management,* 19 (May 1990), pp. 141–148.

[15]Focus groups grew out of focused interviews. For discussion of their origin and evolution, see Robert K. Merton, "The Focused Interview and Focus Groups: Continuities and Discontinuities," *Public Opinion Quarterly,* 51 (Winter 1987), pp. 550–566.

Research Realities 4.2

Use of an Experience Survey to Gain Insight into a Declining Sales Situation

Even though the company had earlier experienced ten years of revenue and profit growth, the last several years of declining revenues had caused the firm's board of directors to question the advisability of continuing with one line of business. A review of internal sales records revealed that their market for the service line was limited to approximately thirty large packaged goods manufacturers. No significant external secondary data sources were located. Executives of the firm were then asked to identify the three most knowledgeable persons in the country with respect to the service-line characteristics, its market, and the capabilities of competitive suppliers. All three persons nominated were executives of present or past customers of the firm. Appointments for personal interviews were made with each nominee by telephone, using the firm's president as a reference.

Each of the three personal interviews was conducted at the informant's place of business and lasted

Source: William E. Cox, Jr., *Industrial Marketing Research* (New York: John Wiley & Sons, 1979), pp. 25–26.

from 1½ to 3½ hours. The sessions ranged over a wide variety of topics. Informants were asked to assess the past, current, and probable future developments of the service line, the market, and the comparative strengths and weaknesses of the major suppliers of the service line, including the research sponsor.

The findings revealed that there had been no decline in market activity during the past two years. There had been, however, a concerted effort by a number of packaged goods manufacturers to divert business to two new service suppliers during the period. This was done to ensure additional sources of supply and capacity in order to handle a significant expansion of demand that was expected to occur within two years. As a result, established suppliers were allocated less business during the period but could expect a resumption of their previous growth in the near future. The manufacturers were reluctant to divulge these plans to the established suppliers for fear that they would add excess capacity and act to limit the competitiveness of the new suppliers.

---

moderator. The moderator attempts to follow a rough outline of the issues under consideration, while at the same time making sure that the comments made by each person present are included in the group's discussion. Each individual is thereby exposed to the ideas of the others and submits his or her ideas to the group for consideration.

Focus groups are currently one of the most frequently used techniques in marketing research; they have proved to be productive for a variety of purposes, including the following:

1. to generate hypotheses that can be further tested quantitatively;
2. to generate information helpful in structuring consumer questionnaires;
3. to provide overall background information on a product category;
4. to secure impressions on new product concepts.

For example, American Express used the insights gathered from focus groups as an important input when developing the program that extended manufacturers' warranties on products that were bought with an American Express card.[16] Similarly, Ray-O-Vac found through a series of focus groups that people wanted brighter, more modern, and more dependable flashlights. The company also discovered that people were willing to pay for added durability. These insights led to the development of their line of Workhorse flashlights, which regenerated a mature market.[17] Research Realities 4.3 discusses the insights Oscar Mayer and the Buick Division of General Motors gleaned from focus groups.

Although focus groups do vary in size, most consist of eight to twelve members. Smaller groups are too easily dominated by one or two members; with larger groups, frustration and boredom can set in, as individuals have to wait their turn to respond or get involved. Respondents are generally selected so that the groups are relatively homogeneous, minimizing both conflicts among group members on issues not relevant to the study objectives and differences in perceptions, experiences, and verbal skills. Differences that are too great with respect to any of these characteristics can intimidate some of the group participants and stifle discussion. For example, the group for a project that involved a mixed group of architects, roofing contractors, and building owners included a person whose company was called Tony the Roofer. "Tony had all the experience and involvement with the product category the other participants had. But he was so intimidated by all the other people, he just would not say anything. Every so often we would ask what *he* thought of some subject, but he just would mumble that he agreed with what one of the 'bigger' people had said."[18]

Most firms conducting focus groups use screening interviews to determine the individuals who will compose a particular group. One type they try to avoid is the individual who has participated before in a focus group, since some of these people tend to behave as "experts." Their presence can cause the group to behave in dysfunctional ways as they continually try to make their presence felt. As focus groups have become more popular, problems in recruiting rookies have intensified. Firms also try to avoid groups in which some of the participants are friends or relatives, because this tends to inhibit spontaneity in the discussion as the acquaintances begin talking to each other.

Given that the participants in any one group should be reasonably homogeneous, how can a firm ensure that it is getting a wide spectrum of insights? The key way is by having multiple groups. Not only can the characteristics of the participants vary across groups, but so can the issue outline. Ideas discovered in one group session can be introduced in subsequent group sessions for reaction. A typical project has four groups, but some may have up to twelve. The guiding criterion is whether the later groups are generating additional insight into the phenomenon under study. When they show diminishing returns, the groups are stopped.

---

[16]Jeffrey A. Trachtenberg, "Listening, the Old-Fashioned Way," *Forbes,* 140 (October 5, 1987), pp. 202, 204.

[17]Jennifer Riddle, "Complaining Customers Get Firms' Attention," *Wisconsin State Journal* (June 22, 1986), p. 2.

[18]Robert C. Inglis, "In-Depth Data: Using Focus Groups to Study Industrial Markets," *Business Marketing,* 72 (November 1987), p. 80.

Research Realities 4.3

Experiences of Oscar Mayer and the Buick Division of General Motors with Focus Groups

Oscar Mayer   When Oscar Mayer found that its "Select Slices" line of lunch meats was not meeting sales projections and was actually declining in sales, it launched a series of focus group studies to get some idea of why. One insight from the focus groups was that people perceived luncheon meats as being very high in calories. For example, participants in general estimated that a single ham slice had between 150 and 250 calories, which was more than they perceived a Snickers bar to have (in fact, the ham slice had fewer than 30).

Using this research as a basis, Oscar Mayer decided to launch a new line of low-fat cold cuts by repositioning many of its existing products from the Select Slices product line. The repositioning involved some new packaging, including adding a blue shield to the packaging that mentions the fat-free content of the cold cuts (e.g., 96 percent fat free for its corned beef); new flavors; grouping the products together on the supermarket shelves; and a new ad program emphasizing that, in addition to tasting great, the product was low in fat and calories.

Buick Division of General Motors   The Buick Division of General Motors used focus groups to help develop the Regal two-door, six-passenger coupe it introduced in 1987. The effort had begun more than five years earlier, when Buick held about 20 focus groups across the country and asked what features customers wanted in a new car. Who were the customers? They were people with incomes of $40,000 or more per year, people who could afford a $14,000 price tag — at that time, $1,000 to $2,000 more than the cost of the average new car. All the participants, gathered in every major geographic region of the country, had purchased new cars within the last four years.

"What these groups told us was that the customers wanted a legitimate back seat, at least 20 miles per gallon, and 0-to-60-miles-acceleration in 11 seconds or less," says Jay Qualman, Buick's general director of advertising. "They wanted a stylish car, but they didn't want it to look like it had just landed from outer space."

After Buick engineers created clay models of the car and mock-ups of the interior, the company went back to yet another focus group of target buyers. What the customers didn't like were the oversized bumper and the severe slope of the hood. What they did like were the four-wheel disk brakes and the four-wheel independent suspension.

Focus groups also helped to refine the advertising campaign for the Regal. Participants were first asked which competing cars most resembled the Buick in terms of image and features. The answer was Oldsmobile, a sister General Motors division. "That made us realize we had to separate the two in the minds of the public," says Qualman. "So we repositioned Buick above Oldsmobile. How? By focusing on comfort and luxury features such as full six-passenger seating, wood grain instrument panels, velour-type fabrics, and special stereo systems. We also learned that the driving experience was more important to Buick owners."

Buick and its agency, McCann-Erickson, created twenty ad concepts, which were later narrowed down to four. Next, focus groups were shown various TV commercials and printed ad slicks. Participants then voiced their reactions as to which were most effective. "Among the things we were concerned with was selecting a music sound track that would attract younger customers without turning off their parents," says Qualman. The theme: "The new Buick Regal. There's nothing like it on the American road."

Source: Mary Jung, "Oscar Mayer Repositions Failing Line to Attract Health-Conscious Consumers," *Marketing News,* 22 (August 15, 1988), p. 6; and Jeffrey A. Trachtenberg, "Listening, the Old Fashioned Way," *Forbes,* 140 (October 5, 1987), pp. 202, 204.

The typical focus group session lasts from 1½ to 2 hours. Groups can be arranged at various sites, including the client's home office, a neutral site, the office of the research agency, or even one of the respondent's homes. Each site has its own advantages and disadvantages with respect to the ability to recruit respondents, the costs of the session, the rapport that can be established, and the ability to record the interviews for later transcription and analysis.[19]

The trend is to hold four groups at facilities designed especially for them. One advantage of these facilities is that they can incorporate the latest in technology because of the large number of groups held there. For example, video-conferencing technology can be used to link groups in different locations, allowing participants at the various locations to interact directly with each other. This technology makes global groups truly possible. See Research Realities 4.4.

The moderator in the focus group has a key role.[20] For one thing, the moderator typically translates the study objectives into a discussion guide. To do so, he or she needs to understand the background of the problem and the most important information the client hopes to glean from the research process. The moderator also needs to understand the parameters of the groups in terms of their number, size, and composition, as well as how they might be structured to build on one another. Moreover, the moderator must lead the discussion so that all objectives of the study are met, and do so in such a way that *interaction* among the group members is stimulated and promoted. The focus group session should not be allowed to dissolve into nothing more than a set of concurrent interviews in which the participants each take turns responding to a predetermined set of questions. This is an extremely delicate role. It requires someone who is intimately familiar with the purpose and objectives of the research and at the same time possesses good interpersonal communication skills. One important measure of a focus group's success is whether the participants talk to each other, rather than the moderator, about the items on the discussion guide.

Some of the key qualifications moderators must have are described in Table 4.1. Moderating an industrial focus group is even more difficult than moderating one involving a consumer product. A moderator for a consumer good typically knows something about the product or service at issue. After all, moderators are consumers too. This is not so with many industrial goods. This means that the moderator's briefing for an industrial good has to be longer and more detailed. It also means that many of the group

---

[19]Goldman and McDonald discuss the pros and cons of the various sites as well as a number of other operational questions that arise with the conduct of focus groups. See Alfred E. Goldman and Susan Schwartz McDonald, *The Group Interview: Principles and Practice* (Englewood Cliffs, N.J.: Prentice-Hall, 1987). See also *Focus Groups: Issues and Approaches,* prepared by the Qualitative Research Council of the Advertising Research Foundation, 1985; David W. Stewart and Prem N. Shamdasani, *Focus Groups: Theory and Practice,* (Newbury Park, CA: Sage Publications, 1990).

[20]Thomas L. Greenbaum, *The Practical Handbook and Guide to Focus Group Research* (Lexington, Mass.: D. C. Heath and Company, 1988) has a particularly useful discussion on the requirements for moderators and how to go about selecting them. For a list of professional moderators and facilities, see "1992 Marketing News Directory of Focus Group Facilities & Moderators," *Marketing News,* 26 (January 6, 1992), pp. FG3–FG15.

Research Realities 4.4

Global Focus Groups

It is now possible for companies to find out how consumers perceive their products in London and New York — at the same time. Thanks to video-conferencing technology, marketing researchers can conduct focus groups in two different locations, with participants interacting with each other.

"It's a big opportunity, but people don't know it exists," said Thomas L. Greenbaum, executive vice president of Clarion Marketing and Communications, Greenwich, Connecticut. The technique allows marketers to compare regional perspectives without travel. Clarion set up a global focus group for a telecommunications company that sought representation from Europe and the United States. Focus groups were held in London and New York, with a moderator in each city.

FocusVision Network, Inc., of Newport Beach, California, plans to unveil an international network of focus facilities. The system, already in place in the United States, has the capability to broadcast live focus-group interviews from FocusVision facilities to a client's office. International expansion is a "logical and important application of video-conferencing," said John J. Houlahan, president of FocusVision. "Instead of making the industry come to the technology, we're taking the technology to the industry," Houlahan said.

Computer companies, telecommunications firms, and other high-tech companies will lead the way because their target audiences are "separated by the miles and different cultures but they inhabit similar worlds and have similar needs," said Hank Bernstein, senior vice president and director of consumer information services at DMB & B, Inc., New York. According to Bernstein, who participated in the London–New York focus group, once the participants got used to the technology, "they really did talk to each other across the continent."

Source: Cyndee Miller, "Anybody Ever Hear of Global Focus Groups?" *Marketing News,* (May 27, 1991), p. 14.

participants will know a great deal more about the product or service being discussed than the moderator. Directing group discussion under these conditions can be a taxing job indeed.[21]

Sponsors can realize several advantages from the proper conduct of focus groups. For one thing, they allow for serendipity. Ideas can simply drop "out of the blue" during a focus group discussion. Further, the group setting allows them to be developed to their full significance, because it allows for snowballing. The comment by one individual can trigger a chain of responses from other participants. Often after a brief introductory warm-up period, respondents can "turn-on" to the discussion. They become sufficiently involved that they want to express their ideas and expose their feelings.

[21]Inglis, "In-Depth Data," has a useful discussion of the extra difficulties moderators of industrial focus groups face. For discussions of the use of focus groups for industrial goods, see Edward F. McQuarrie and Shelby H. McIntyre, "Focus Groups and the Development of New Products by Technologically Driven Companies: Some Guidelines," *Journal of Product Innovation Management,* 3 (March 1986), pp. 40–46; Curtis J. Fedder, "Biz-to-Biz Focus Groups Require a Special Touch," *Marketing News,* 24 (January 8, 1990), p. 46.

TABLE 4.1 Ten Criteria of Good Focus Group Moderators

1. Quick Learner Moderator must be able to learn quickly and incorporate new material into his or her normal thinking and vocabulary. Must be able to absorb the content of the client briefing quickly and understand what the client is seeking to generate from the focus group sessions. Must be able to quickly absorb and understand the inputs from the group participants.

2. A "Friendly" Leader Moderator can develop rapport with group respondents quickly (within ten minutes). Should be viewed by the group as the authority figure; also as the type of person with whom they would like to have a casual conversation. If moderator is perceived as being friendly, he or she will elicit more honest, in-depth responses from the group than one who is dictatorial or threatening.

3. Knowledgeable But Not All-Knowing Moderator will communicate to the group that he or she has some knowledge about the subject at hand but is not an expert. If group members feel the moderator is an expert, they will ask questions about the topic rather than provide answers or discussion of their views. Participants also might respond to the moderator's direction from the perspective of an expert rather than that of the consumer, user, or potential customer for the product, service, or idea being covered, to impress the moderator with their knowledge.

4. Excellent Memory Moderator needs to have a good memory to be able to tie together inputs that are generated during the early part of the session with others that come up toward the end. Must be able to recall key information volunteered by each participant throughout the session so that statements made later can be cross-checked for the consistency of the participants' viewpoints.

5. Good Listener Moderator must be a good listener. Must have the ability to remember key information that individual participants say during the group and the ability to hear all the information that people say, in terms of both content and implication.

6. A Facilitator, Not a Performer The objective of the group is to secure information from the participants rather than entertain the clients in the observation room. Some moderators perform for the clients who are observing the session. Observing focus groups can be tedious, particularly if one is participating in a series of groups, and comic relief can pass the time more quickly, but too much moderator-generated humor will result in less-than-satisfactory inputs from the participants.

7. Flexible Moderator must be flexible during the session with regard to the flow of the discussion. Some adhere so closely to their moderator's guide that they disrupt the natural flow of group discussion to ensure that each point on the outline is covered before going on to the next item. The guide is simply an outline, and it is often much more effective to deviate from the prearranged order to capitalize on the inputs of valuable discussion. An effective moderator is sufficiently flexible to do this.

8. Empathic Moderator should be an empathic individual. Must be able to relate to the nervousness that some group respondents have as a result of being asked to talk before the others. If respondent believes that the moderator understands his or her situation, this person is much more likely to participate actively in the group discussions.

9. A "Big Picture" Thinker Moderator must be able to separate the important observations on a group session from the less significant inputs. At the conclusion of each group session, the moderator must be able to draw together all the inputs received and be able to communicate to the client the overall ("big picture") message generated by the discussion.

10. Good Writer Most clients who use the focus group technique require written reports to summarize the results of the groups. Therefore, the moderator should be skilled in writing clear, concise summaries of the sessions that provide clients with meaningful and action-oriented conclusions and recommendations.

Source: Reprinted with the permission of Lexington Books, an imprint of Macmillan Publishing Company, from *The Practical Handbook and Guide to Focus Group Research* by Thomas L. Greenbaum, pp. 50–54. Copyright © 1988 by Lexington Books. See also Naomi Henderson, "Trained Moderators Boost the Value of Qualitative Research," *Marketing Research: A Magazine of Management & Applications,* 4 (June 1992), pp. 20–23.

Some feel more secure in the group environment than if they were being interviewed alone, since they soon realize that they can expose an idea without necessarily having to defend or elaborate on it. Consequently, responses are often more spontaneous and less conventional than they might be in a one-on-one interview.

Group interviews do offer certain benefits not obtainable with individual depth interviews, but they also have their weaknesses. (See Table 4.2.) Although group interviews are easy to set up, they are difficult to moderate and to interpret. It is easy to find

TABLE 4.2   The Advantages/Disadvantages of Focus Groups versus Individual Depth Interviews

Advantages of Individual Depth Interviews

- They permit the moderator to delve much deeper into a topic, because all the attention during the 1½-hour session is concentrated on one individual rather than a group of ten.
- They allow more candid discussion on the part of the interviewee, who might be intimidated to talk about a particular topic in a group of his or her peers. This is particularly the case for sensitive topics such as personal-care products, financial behavior, or attitudes toward sex, religion, and politics.
- They eliminate negative group influences that can occur in a focus group. Because there is only one person being interviewed in the room, it is not possible for the individual's comments to be influenced by others.
- They are essential for certain situations where competitors would otherwise be placed in the same room. For example, it might be very difficult to do an effective focus group with managers from competing department stores or restaurants. Therefore, research with these people must be done on a one-to-one basis.

Limitations of Individual Depth Interviews

- They are typically much more expensive than groups, particularly when viewed on a per-interview basis. This is because the time of the moderator, which is the biggest cost in qualitative research, is the same for a two-hour focus group as it is for two hours of one-on-ones.
- They generally do not get the same degree of client involvement as focus groups. It is difficult to convince most clients to sit through multiple hours of one-on-ones; this can be a problem if one of the objectives is to get the clients to view the research so they benefit firsthand from the information.
- They are physically exhausting for the moderator, so it is difficult to cover as much ground in one day as can be covered with groups. Most moderators will not do more than four or five interviews in a day, yet in two focus groups they can cover 20 people.

Advantages of Focus Groups

- They are a much more cost- and time-effective way to generate qualitative research information. For the same budget, the client gains input from significantly more people, increasing the reliability of the information.
- They give the moderator the ability to leverage the dynamics of the group to obtain reactions that might not otherwise be generated in a one-on-one session.
- There are only a few situations in which participants would be intimidated by the subject and would be unwilling to share their views.

Source: Thomas L. Greenbaum, ''Focus Groups vs. One-on-Ones: The Controversy Continues,'' *Marketing News,* 25 (September 2, 1991), p. 16. Reprinted with permission of American Marketing Association.

evidence in one or more of the group discussions that supports almost any preconceived position. Because executives have the ability to observe the discussions through one-way mirrors or the opportunity to listen to tape recordings of the sessions, focus groups seem more susceptible to executive and even researcher biases than do other data-collection techniques, although sometimes the ability to study the tapes can be an advantage. Not only does the systematic study of the tapes allow those doing so to get a first-hand sense of what the target group is feeling, but the tape also provides a vehicle for communicating that feeling to others. For example, Time Inc. used focus groups when it noticed signs of rising dissatisfaction with customer service, which threatened renewal rates.

> Readers who had received poor service were invited to hour-long sessions to voice their complaints.
>
> "All of the people had some complaint about what had happened to them," McDonald (the director of research) said. "A premium promised but not delivered, a mix-up in billing, a payment not credited, an erroneous referral to a collection agency."
>
> Because of the bad service, he said, the readers were furious.
>
> McDonald taped the focus groups, edited the tape to a 25-minute video, and used it as a propaganda device to change the attitudes of the customer service staff.
>
> "Its impact upon the Time Inc. staff was incredibly powerful," he said. "Suddenly, all of the faceless millions had faces. The customers became real people rather than abstractions."[22]

Putting faces on the faceless worked to advantage for Time, but it can just as easily become a disadvantage, for it makes it very easy to forget that the discussion, and consequently the results, are greatly influenced by the moderator and the specific direction he or she provides. Moderators possessing all of the desired skills listed in Table 4.1 are extremely rare. One has to remember that the results are not representative of what would be found in the general population, and thus are *not* projectable. Further, the unstructured nature of the responses makes coding, tabulation, and analysis difficult. Focus groups should *not* be used, therefore, to develop head counts of the proportion of people who feel a particular way. Focus groups are better for *generating* ideas and insights than for systematically examining them.[23]

Analysis of Selected Cases

The **analysis of selected cases** is sometimes referred to as the analysis of "insight-stimulating examples." By either label, the approach involves the *intensive study of selected cases* of the phenomenon under investigation. Examination of existing records,

[22]Scott C. McDonald, Nancy E. Dince, and Larry P. Stanek, "Focus Groups Being Subverted by Clients," *Marketing News,* 18 (August 28, 1987), p. 48.

[23]For an empirical assessment of the relative ability of individual interviews versus focus groups of various sizes and composition to generate ideas, see Edward F. Fern, "The Use of Focus Groups for Idea Generation: The Effects of Group Size, Acquaintanceship, and Moderator on Response Quantity and Quality," *Journal of Marketing Research,* 19 (February 1982), pp. 1–13. See also Wendy Sykes, "Validity and Reliability in Qualitative Market Research: A Review of the Literature," *Journal of the Market Research Society,* 32 (July 1990), pp. 289–328.

observation of the occurrence of the phenomenon, unstructured interviewing, or some other approach may be used. The focus may be on entities (individual people or institutions) or groups of entities (sales representatives or distributors in various regions).

The method is characterized by several features.[24] First, the attitude of the investigator is key. The proper attitude is one of alert receptivity, of seeking explanations rather than testing explanations. The investigator is likely to make frequent changes in direction as new information emerges. This may include the search for new cases. More often it will mean a change in the data collected in a given case. Second, the success of the method depends heavily on the investigator's integrative powers. The analyst must be able to assemble many diverse bits of information into a unified interpretation. Finally, the method is characterized by its intensity. The analyst attempts to obtain sufficient information to characterize and explain both the unique features of the case being studied and the features that it has in common with other cases.

> In one study to improve the productivity of the sales force of a particular company, the investigator studied intensively two or three of the best sales representatives and two or three of the worst. Data was collected on the background and experience of each representative and then several days were spent making sales calls with them. As a result, a hypothesis was developed. It was that checking the stock of retailers and suggesting items on which they were low were the most important differences between the successful and the poor sales representatives.[25]

In this example, the key insight good sales representatives had in common, and the way in which they differed from poor sales representatives, was that they checked retailer inventory.

Some situations that are particularly productive of hypotheses are the following:

1. Cases reflecting changes and, in particular, abrupt changes. The adjustment of a market to the entrance of a new competitor can be quite revealing of the structure of an industry, for example.

2. Cases reflecting extremes of behavior. The example of the best and worst sales representatives was cited previously. Similarly, if one wanted to gain some idea of what factors account for the variation in company territory performance, one would be well advised to compare the best and worst territories, rather than looking at all territories.

3. Cases reflecting the order in which events occurred over time. For example, in the territory performance question, it may be that in one territory sales are handled by a branch office where they were formerly handled by a manufacturer's agent, whereas in another, the sales branch office replaced an industrial distributor.

---

[24]These features are detailed further in Selltiz, Wrightsman, and Cook, *Research Methods,* pp. 98–99. See also Thomas V. Bonoma, "Case Research in Marketing: Opportunities, Problems, and a Process," *Journal of Marketing Research,* 22 (May 1985), pp. 199–208; and Robert K. Yin, *Case Study Research: Design and Methods* (Beverly Hills, Calif.: Sage Publications, 1989).

[25]Harper W. Boyd, Ralph Westfall, and Stanley F. Stasch, *Marketing Research: Text and Cases,* 6th ed. (Homewood, Ill.: Richard D. Irwin, 1985), p. 51.

Which cases will be most valuable depends, of course, on the problem in question. It is generally true, though, that cases that display *sharp contrasts* or have *striking features* are most useful. This is because minute differences are usually difficult to discern. Thus, instead of trying to determine what distinguishes the average case from the slightly above-average case, we contrast the best and worst to magnify whatever differences may exist.

ETHICAL DILEMMA 4.1

Prompted by an increasing incidence of homes for sale by owner, the president of a local real estate company asks you to undertake exploratory research to ascertain what kind of image realtors enjoy in the community. Unbeknownst to your current client, you undertook a similar research study for a competitor two years ago and, based on your findings, have formed specific hypotheses about why some homeowners are reluctant to sell their houses through realtors.

- Is it ethical to give information obtained while working for one client to another client who is a competitor? What should you *definitely* not tell your current client about the earlier project?
- Is it ethical to undertake a research project when you think that you already know what the findings will be? Can you generalize findings from two years ago to today?
- Should you help this company define its problem, and, if so, how?

DESCRIPTIVE RESEARCH

A great deal of marketing research can be considered descriptive research. Descriptive research is used when the purpose is as follows:

1. To describe the characteristics of certain groups. For example, based on information gathered from known users of our particular product, we might attempt to develop a profile of the ''average user'' with respect to income, sex, age, educational level, and so on.
2. To estimate the proportion of people in a specified population who behave in a certain way. We might be interested, say, in estimating the proportion of people within a specified radius of a proposed shopping complex who would shop at the center.
3. To make specific predictions. We might be interested in predicting the level of sales for each of the next five years so that we could plan for the hiring and training of new sales representatives.

Descriptive research encompasses an array of research objectives. The fact that a study is a descriptive study, however, does not mean that it is simply a fact-gathering expedition.

Facts do not lead anywhere. Indeed, facts, as facts, are the commonest, cheapest, and most useless of all commodities. Anyone with a questionnaire can gather thousands of facts a day — and probably not find much real use for them. What makes facts practical and valuable is the glue of explanation and understanding, the framework of theory, the tie-rod of conjecture. Only when facts can be fleshed to a skeletal theory do they become meaningful in the solution of problems.[26]

The researcher should not fall prey to the temptation of beginning a descriptive research study with the vague thought that the data collected should be interesting. A good descriptive study presupposes much prior knowledge about the phenomenon studied. It rests on one or more specific hypotheses. These conjectural statements guide the research in specific directions. In this respect, a descriptive study design is very different from an exploratory study design. Whereas an exploratory study is characterized by its flexibility, descriptive studies can be considered rigid. Descriptive studies require a *clear specification* of the *who, what, when, where, why,* and *how* of the research.

Consider a chain of food convenience stores planning to open a new outlet. The company wants to determine how people come to patronize the new outlet. Consider some of the questions that would need to be answered before data collection for this descriptive study could begin. Who is to be considered a patron? Anyone who enters the store? What if they do not buy anything but just participate in the grand-opening prize giveaway? Perhaps a patron should be defined as anyone who purchases anything from the store. Should patrons be defined on the basis of the family unit, or should they be defined as individuals, even though the individuals come from the same family? What characteristics of these patrons should be measured? Are we interested in their age and sex, or perhaps in where they live and how they came to know about our store? When shall we measure them — while they are shopping, or later? Should the study take place during the first weeks of operation of the store, or should the study be delayed until the situation has stabilized somewhat? Certainly if we are interested in word-of-mouth influence, we must wait at least until that influence has a chance to operate. Where shall we measure the patrons? Should it be in the store, or immediately outside of the store, or should we attempt to contact them at home? Why do we want to measure them? Are we going to use these measurements to plan promotional strategy? In that case the emphasis might be on measuring how people become aware of the store. Or are we going to use them as a basis for locating other stores? In that case the emphasis might shift more to determining the trading area of the store. How shall we measure them? Shall we use a questionnaire, or shall we observe their purchasing behavior? If we use a questionnaire, what form will it take? Will it be highly structured? Will it be in the form of a scale? How will it be administered? By telephone? By mail? Perhaps by personal interview?

---

[26]Robert Ferber, Donald F. Blankertz, and Sidney Hollander, Jr., *Marketing Research* (New York: The Ronald Press Co., copyright 1964), p. 153. See also, "Marketing Research Needs Validated Theories," *Marketing News,* 17 (January 21, 1983), p. 14; Mick Alt and Malcolm Brighton, "Analyzing Data: Or Telling Stories?" *Journal of the Market Research Society,* 23 (October 1981), pp. 209–219.

These questions are not the only ones that would be or should be asked. Certainly, some of the answers will be implicit in the hypothesis or hypotheses that guide the descriptive research. Others, though, will not be obvious. The researcher will only be able to specify them after some labored thought or even after a small pilot or exploratory study. In either case, the researcher is well advised to delay collecting that first item of information with which to test the hypotheses until clear judgments of the who, what, when, where, why, and how of descriptive research have been made.

The researcher should also delay data collection until a determination can be made on how the data are to be analyzed. Ideally, one would have a set of dummy tables developed before beginning the collection process. A **dummy table** is a table that is used to catalog the data collected. It is a statement of how the analysis will be structured and conducted. It is complete in all respects save for filling in the actual numbers; that is, it contains a title, headings, and specific categories for the variables making up the table. All that remains after collecting the data is to count the number of cases of each type. Table 4.3 illustrates a table that might be used by a women's specialty store investigating whether it is serving a particular age segment and whether this segment differs from that of its competitors.

Note that the table lists the particular age segments the proprietor wishes to compare. It is crucial that this specification of variables and categories be made before data collection begins. The statistical tests that will be used to uncover the relationship between age and store preference should also be specified before data collection begins. Inexperienced researchers often question the need for such hard, detailed decisions before collecting the data. They assume that delaying these decisions until after the data are collected will somehow make the decisions easier. Just the opposite is true, as any experienced researcher will attest.

> Most difficult for the beginning researcher to anticipate will be the analytical problems he may face after the data are gathered. He tends to believe that a wide variety of facts will be enough to solve anything. Only after struggling with sloppy, stubborn, and intractable facts, with data not adequate for the testing of hypotheses and with data that are interesting but incapable of supporting practical recommendations for action will he be fully aware that the big "mistakes" of research usually are made in the early stages. Each definition of a problem or problem variable will create different facts or findings, and a formulation once made serves

TABLE 4.3   Dummy Table: Store Preference by Age

Age	Prefer A	Prefer B	Prefer C
Less than 30			
30–39			
40 or more			

to restrict the scope of analysis. No problem is definitively formulated until the researcher can specify how he will make his analysis and how the results will contribute to a practical solution.[27]

Once the data have been collected and analysis is begun, it is too late to lament, "If only we had collected information on that variable" or "If only we had measured the *Y* variable using a finer scale." Rectifying such mistakes at this time is next to impossible. Rather, the analyst must account for such contingencies when planning the study. Structuring the tables used to analyze the data makes such planning easier.

An alternative way of ensuring that the information collected in a descriptive study will address the objectives motivating it is to specify in advance the objective each question addresses, the reason the question is included, and the analysis in which the question will be used, although not going as far as laying out all of the cross-classification tables. Table 4.4, for example, contains specifications for several questions in a study for a meat packer investigating the market potential of a new sport-related hot dog. Although output planning like this is extremely valuable, there is added merit in specifying all anticipated dummy tables in advance, as we have suggested previously. The dummy tables are particularly valuable in providing clues on how to phrase the individual questions and code the responses.

Figure 4.3 is an overview of the various types of descriptive studies. The basic division is between longitudinal and cross-sectional designs. The **cross-sectional study** is the most common and most familiar. It typically involves a sample of elements from the population of interest. Various characteristics of the elements or sample members are measured once. **Longitudinal studies,** on the other hand, involve panels. A **panel** is a fixed sample of elements. The elements may be stores, dealers, individuals, or other entities. The panel or sample remains relatively constant through time, although there are periodic additions to replace dropouts or to keep it representative. The sample members in a panel are measured repeatedly, as contrasted to the one-time measurement in a cross-sectional study. Both cross-sectional and longitudinal studies have weaknesses and advantages. Because they are both common, let us briefly review the principal advantages and disadvantages of each.

Longitudinal Analysis

True longitudinal studies rely on panel data and panel methods. As mentioned, a panel is a fixed sample of subjects that is measured repeatedly. There are two types of panels: true panels and omnibus panels. **True panels** rely on repeated measurements of the same variables. Nielsen maintains a panel of 40,000 households nationwide as a basis of its SCANTRACK service. The panel households use a hand-held scanner to record every item they purchase. They simply pass the scanner across the Universal Product Codes on the packages of the purchased items when they return from shopping and then answer a programmed set of questions (e.g., store where purchased, price paid) by responding to

---

[27]Ferber, Blankertz, and Hollander, *Marketing Research*, p. 171.

TABLE 4.4 Output Planning Module for Several Questions in a Food Study

Question Number(s) and Variable Name(s)

Questions #5.0 and 5.1 asking number of packages of hot dogs consumed per month by household and usual number of hot dogs per package plus number of loose links per month.

Information Content of Question(s)

Computer coding will multiply number of packages per month by dogs per package plus links to obtain the total household usage of hot dogs per month.

Reasons for Including Question(s)

These questions provide information needed in order to segment the population of hot dog users into submarkets based on usage level. Usage volume can serve as an excellent predictor of future purchase patterns, may be related to interest in proposed new hot dog product and may support media selection that will reach high-usage households at least cost.

Primary Analysis and Information Value

I. *Frequency Distribution:* Indicates number of dogs used per month for all respondents. These will be coded into three categories: *Light, Moderate,* and *Heavy Users.*

II. *Relation to Demographics:* Usage types will be cross-tabulated with size of household, age of household shopper, total income, sex, and education of shopper in order to identify the characteristics of the three user segments. Statistic — Chi square.

III. *Relation to Price:* Usage will be systematically related to responses on purchase probability under different pricing conditions. This will tell us the importance of price for the user segments and help in estimating volume of sales at different price points.

Additional Analysis and Information Value

Relation to Importance of Product Features: User segments will be compared in terms of their mean responses to the 10-point importance-attribute scales including package, brand name, quality, contents, taste, texture, smell, shape, and color of the hot dogs. This will provide information on the relative importance of attributes and assist in formulating advertising approaches for the target segments.

Source: Benjamin D. Sackmary, "Data Analysis & Output Planning Improve Value of Marketing Research," *Marketing News,* 17 (January 21, 1983), p. 6. Published by the American Marketing Association.

a series of prompts from the machine. Similarly, National Purchase Diary Panel (NPD) maintains a consumer panel of families who record their purchases in a paper diary when they return from shopping. The operations of these panels will be detailed when discussing secondary sources of information in Chapter 6. The important point to note now is that each sample member is measured with respect to the same characteristics at each time — purchases.

In an **omnibus panel,** a sample of elements is still selected and maintained, but the information collected from the members varies. At one time, it may be attitudes about a new product. At another time, the panel members might be asked to evaluate alternative advertising copy. In each case, a sample might be selected from the larger group, which is, in turn, a sample of the population. The subsample might be drawn randomly. More

FIGURE 4.3   **Classification of Descriptive Studies**

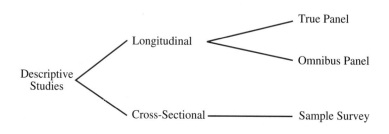

than likely, though, participants with the desired characteristics will be chosen from a total panel. For example, the Parker Pen Company maintains a panel of 1,100 individuals who were chosen because they expressed some interest in writing instruments and, of course, because of their willingness to participate. Parker Pen will often use selected members of this panel to evaluate new writing instruments. If the new instrument is a fountain pen, they will often choose individuals who prefer fountain pens to test the products. Those chosen and the information sought will vary from project to project.

R. J. Reynolds uses ability criteria rather than interest criteria in selecting its panel members. The company maintains a panel of 350 of its employees whose job it is to provide information for quality control and new brand development.[28] Only those employees who can successfully pass a screening test in which they smoke three cigarettes and can then identify which two were alike are allowed in the panel. As members of the panel, the employees are called on to smoke, sniff, feel, and draw on unlit cigarettes and then provide their sensory evaluations. Although the information that is collected is fairly standardized, the cigarettes being evaluated vary from test to test.

Nickelodeon, the children's cable television network, uses a panel of children to help it evaluate its programming and magazine ideas. In an especially interesting twist, it uses on-line computer connections to gather their reactions. See Research Realities 4.5.

The distinction between the true panel and the omnibus panel is important. True longitudinal analysis, also called time series analysis, can only be performed on the first type of data, with repeated measurements of the same entities over time. We shall see why when we discuss the method of analysis unique to panel data — the turnover table. The turnover table can only be used when individuals and variables are held constant through time. This is not to deny the value of omnibus panels. Rather, the purpose is simply to erect a caution flag because in other respects (for example, sample design, information collection, and so forth), both types of panels have about the same advan-

---

[28]Margaret Loeb, "Testers of Cigarettes Find On-Job Puffing Really Isn't a Drag," *The Wall Street Journal* (August 22, 1984), pp. 1 and 15.

Research Realities 4.5

Use of an On-Line Computer Panel by Nickelodeon

After reading an article in a new magazine, a child pans it, calling the article "stupid." Another says: "It was boring." A third: "A lot of it was a little too weird for me." For market researchers, these sorts of spontaneous comments are priceless, but they're tough to obtain, because kids are often intimidated when they talk to adults. Now Nickelodeon, the children's cable television network, has gotten around that problem by setting up one of the first consumer product testing panels established over a computer network.

"It's a great tool because it gives a real sense of immediacy with the kids," says Michael Hainey, an editor of the *Nickelodeon Magazine* prototype that was skewered by the children. "We liked it because it was a sounding board for kids across the country." The children responded favorably to the magazine overall, Hainey says, but "We'll be rethinking" parts, such as a confusing table of contents and an article on a boy from North Dakota.

The children — 75 of them between the ages of 8 and 12 in a dozen areas from Boston to Los Angeles — have been recruited for a two-year stint as participants in "Get hooked on Nick" by Nickelodeon's researchers. Nickelodeon wants to make sure that TV shows, often created by childless New Yorkers, will actually appeal to boys and girls of all races who are between the ages of 2 and 14 and who come from all over the country.

Other TV and movie people also are getting in touch with their fans on services such as CompuServ, Prodigy, and GEnie. Show publicists and directors sometimes go on-line to see how people reacted to a show that ran the night before. In other fields, computer software companies have been doing market research on-line in CompuServ forums for years, asking early testers to report problems as they find them.

But Nickelodeon seems to be the first network to formalize on-line research. The children that it selected all had computers and VCRs. Half are minorities, and half are girls. Family incomes in the group range from $20,000 to $120,000.

The children, who aren't paid, can go on-line and chat informally with each other or with Nickelodeon researchers three afternoons a week. Sometimes, they post jokes on a bulletin board or contribute a sentence to a fantasy story started by one child. When Nickelodeon wants reaction to a new show or to the magazine, it sends videos or a prototype to 20 kids and asks them to sign on to a special conference at a set time for one to two hours.

If a special research project comes up, the children are there. In one case, Nickelodeon sent 12 children videotapes of a new show called "The Tomorrow People" and then asked them their opinions. One conclusion: Many children didn't realize that action was shifting among several countries. Producers inserted graphics in the show to clarify the changes in location.

In December, when the network had just started the on-line project, it used the kids' group to decide whether to produce a special news show on Somalia. Researchers found that the children already understood the issues, and Nickelodeon dropped the idea.

On-line isn't perfect, Nickelodeon researchers concede. "You'd prefer to see them in person," says Hainey. On-line "tends to be a lot of monosyllabic typing." It also doesn't work for younger children, who reveal more by their body language than by their spoken or written words.

Therefore, Nickelodeon continues more traditional research, including analyzing Nielsen and Arbitron ratings, in-person focus groups, interviews at schools, and tracking letters and calls about shows. But the on-line group eliminates travel costs and lets people in New York get reaction in a few hours to questions such as preferred sneaker styles or what music children consider oldies — "Beatoven," one boy replied. It has already become "an unbelievable research resource to us," says Rande Price, manager of research.

Source: William M. Bulkeley, "Nickelodeon Sets Up Online Focus Group," *The Wall Street Journal* (March 29, 1993), p. B4. Reprinted by permission of Wall Street Journal, © Dow Jones & Company, Inc. All Rights Reserved Worldwide.

TABLE **4.5**   **Number of Families in Panel Purchasing Each Brand**

Brand Purchased	During First Time Period, t_1	During Second Time Period, t_2
A	200	250
B	300	270
C	350	330
D	150	150
Total	1,000	1,000

tages and disadvantages when compared to cross-sectional studies. Consequently, we shall treat both types together when discussing these general advantages.

Probably the single most important advantage of panel data is analytical. Suppose we are presently subscribing to the type of service that generates consumer purchase data from a panel of 1,000 families. Suppose further that we are interested in determining the effect of a recent package design for our Brand A and that our brand has two main competitors, B and C, and a number of other smaller competitors. Let us classify all these smaller, miscellaneous brands in a single catch-all category, labeled Brand D, and let us consider the performance of our brand at time t_1, before the change, and time t_2, after the package change.

We could perform several types of analyses on these data.[29] We could look at the proportion of those in the panel who bought our brand in period t_1. We could also calculate the proportion of those who bought our brand in period t_2. Suppose these calculations generated the data shown in Table 4.5. Table 4.5 indicates that the package change was successful. Brand A's market share increased from 20 percent to 25 percent. Further, Brand A seemed to make its gains at the expense of its two major competitors, whose market shares decreased.

But that is not the whole story or even a completely accurate picture of the market changes that occurred. Look at what happens when, in assessing the effect of the package change, the identity of the sample members is maintained. Since we have repeated measures of the same individuals, we can count the number of families who bought Brand A in both periods, those who bought B or C or one of the miscellaneous brands in both periods, and those who switched brands between the two periods. Suppose that Table 4.6 resulted from these tabulations. Table 4.6, which is a **turnover table** (also

---

[29]Hans Zeisel, *Say It with Figures,* 5th ed. (New York: Harper & Row, 1968), pp. 200–239, has a highly readable version of the analyses that can be performed with panel data. See also David Rogosa, "Comparisons of Some Procedures for Analyzing Longitudinal Panel Data," *Journal of Economics and Business,* 32 (Winter 1980), pp. 136–151; Frank J. R. van de Pol, *Issues of Design and Analysis of Panels* (Amsterdam, The Netherlands: Sociometric Research Foundation, 1989).

TABLE 4.6   Number of Families in Panel Buying Each Brand in Each Period

		During Second Time Period, t_2				
		Bought A	**Bought B**	**Bought C**	**Bought D**	**Total**
During First Time	Bought A	175	25	0	0	200
Period, t_1	Bought B	0	225	50	25	300
	Bought C	0	0	280	70	350
	Bought D	75	20	0	55	150
	Total	250	270	330	150	1,000

called a **brand-switching matrix**), contains the same basic information as Table 4.5. That is, we see that 200 (or 20 percent) of the families bought Brand A in period t_1, and that 250 (or 25 percent) did so in period t_2. But Table 4.6 also shows that Brand A did not make its market share gains at the expense of Brands B and C, as originally suggested, but rather captured some of the families who previously bought one of the miscellaneous brands: 75 families switched from the catch-all category, Brand D, which they purchased during period t_1, to Brand A in period t_2. And, as a matter of fact, Brand A lost some of its previous users to Brand B during the period: 25 families switched from Brand A in period t_1 to Brand B in period t_2.

Table 4.6 also allows the calculation of brand loyalty. Consider Brand A, for example; 175, or 87.5 percent of the 200 who bought Brand A in period t_1, remained "loyal" to it (bought it again) in period t_2. By dividing each cell entry by the row or previous period totals, one can assess these brand loyalties and can also throw the basic changes that occurred in the market into bolder relief. Table 4.7, produced by such calculations, suggests for example that among the three major brands, Brand A elicited the greatest buying loyalty and Brand B the least. This is important to know because it indicates whether families like the brand when they do try it.[30]

Whether those who switched from one of the miscellaneous brands to Brand A were induced to do so by the package change is open to question for reasons that will be discussed in the next chapter. The point is that turnover or brand-switching analysis can only be performed when there are *repeated* measures, over time, for the same variables

---

[30]Table 4.7 can also be viewed as a transition matrix, because it depicts the brand-buying changes occurring from period to period. Knowing the proportion switching allows early prediction of the ultimate success of some new product or some change in market strategy. See, for example, Seymour Sudman and Robert Ferber, *Consumer Panels* (Chicago: American Marketing Association, 1979), pp. 19–27, which also provides an excellent review of the literature on such facets of consumer panels as their uses, sampling and sampling biases, data collection methods, conditioning, data processing and file maintenance, costs of operating, and choosing a consumer panel service. See also Scott Menard, *Longitudinal Research* (Newbury Park, CA: Sage Publications, Inc., 1991).

TABLE **4.7**   **Brand Loyalty and Brand Switching Probabilities among Families in Panel**

		During Second Time Period, t_2				
		Bought A	**Bought B**	**Bought C**	**Bought D**	**Total**
During First Time Period, t_1	Bought A	.875	.125	.000	.000	1.000
	Bought B	.000	.750	.167	.083	1.000
	Bought C	.000	.000	.800	.200	1.000
	Bought D	.500	.133	.000	.367	1.000

for the same subjects. It is *not* appropriate for omnibus panel data, in which the variables being measured are constantly changing, nor is it appropriate for cross-sectional studies, even if successive cross-sectional samples are taken.

> The turnover table is the heart of panel analyses because the raw data it generates admit all sorts of elaborations. Any analysis that does not start with a turnover table is overlooking the unique contribution that panels can make to the study of change, and the use of sophisticated statistical algorithms cannot compensate for this shortcoming. From an economic point of view, when we analyze panel data without constructing and using a turnover table, the cost per bit of information conveyed to management will probably be excessive in comparison to the cost of trend or time series studies.[31]

Considering that information is available from panels for multiple periods, the unique advantage of longitudinal analysis becomes obvious. One can look at changes in individual entity behavior and attempt to relate them to a succession of marketing tactics — for example, advertising copy changes, package changes, price changes, and so on. Further, because the same subjects are measured before and after changes in marketing variables, small changes in the criterion variable are more easily identified than if separate studies were made using two or more independent samples. Variation of the criterion variable in the latter case may be due to changes in the composition of the sample.

Although the major advantage of a panel is analytical, panels also have some advantages in terms of the information collected in a study. This is particularly true with respect to classification information, such as income, education, age, and occupation. In

---

[31]Francesco M. Nicosia, "Panel Designs and Analyses in Marketing," in Peter D. Bennett, ed., *Marketing and Economic Development* (Chicago: American Marketing Association, 1965), pp. 222–243. For applications of brand switching or turnover analysis, see Alan R. Andreason, "Potential Marketing Applications of Longitudinal Methods," and Robert W. Pratt, Jr., "Understanding the Decision Process for Consumer Durable Goods: An Example of the Application of Longitudinal Analysis," both of which can also be found in Bennett on pp. 261–275 and pp. 244–260, respectively. See also Gregory P. Markus, *Analyzing Panel Data* (Beverly Hills, Calif.: Sage Publications, 1979); Jacques A. Hagenaars, *Categorical Longitudinal Data: Log-Linear, Trend, and Cohort Analysis* (Newbury Park, CA: Sage Publications, Inc., 1990).

many studies, there is a great deal of classification information that we would like to secure, as this allows more sophisticated analysis of the results. Unfortunately, cross-sectional studies are limited in this respect. Respondents being contacted for the first and only time typically do not stand still for lengthy, time-consuming interviews. The situation is different in panels because panel members are usually compensated for their participation; thus, the interviews can be longer and more exacting, or there can be several interviews. Also, the sponsoring firm can afford to spend more time and effort securing accurate classification information, because this information can be used in a number of studies.

Panel data are also believed to be more accurate than cross-sectional data, because panel data tend to be freer from the errors associated with reporting past behavior.[32] Errors arise in reporting past behavior because humans tend to forget, partly because time has elapsed but partly for other reasons. In particular, research has shown that events and experiences are forgotten more readily if they are inconsistent with attitudes or beliefs that are important to the person, or threaten the person's self-esteem. Because behavior is recorded as it occurs in a panel, less reliance is placed on a respondent's memory. When diaries are used to record purchases, the problems should be virtually eliminated because the respondent is instructed to record the purchases immediately upon returning home. When other behaviors are of interest, respondents are asked to record those behaviors as they occur, thus minimizing the possibility that they will be forgotten or distorted when they are eventually asked about. Table 4.8, for example, shows a page out of an Arbitron radio listening diary. These diaries, which are used to determine radio station listening audiences, are used by the stations to make programming decisions and by advertisers to figure out what to buy. Every person over the age of 12 in each of the participating households receives a new diary for each week they participate. A key advantage of the diary is that it is completely portable and can be filled out anywhere, which tends to increase its accuracy.

Errors also occur because the interviewer and the respondent have distinct personalities and different social roles. Very often respondents say what they think the interviewers *want* to hear or what they feel the interviewers *should* hear. The panel design helps

---

[32]The arguments as to why panel data are less susceptible to these problems are developed in detail in Granbois and Engel, "The Longitudinal Approach." The errors due to these sources are elaborated in the chapters on measurement and data collection. For some empirical evidence, see Seymour Sudman and Robert Ferber, "A Comparison of Alternative Procedures for Collecting Consumer Expenditure Data for Frequently Purchased Products," and Robert A. Wright, Richard H. Beisel, Julia D. Oliver, and Michele C. Gerzowski, "The Use of a Multiple Entry Diary in a Panel Study on Health Care Expenditure," both of which can be found in Robert Ferber, ed., *Readings in Survey Research* (Chicago: American Marketing Association, 1978), on pp. 487–502 and pp. 503–512, respectively; Yoram Wind and David Lerner, "On the Measurement of Purchase Data: Surveys versus Purchase Diaries," *Journal of Marketing Research,* 16 (February 1979), pp. 39–47; John McKenzie, "The Accuracy of Telephone Call Data Collected by Diary Methods," *Journal of Marketing Research,* 20 (November 1983), pp. 417–427; and Rie Irving and Martin C. J. Elton, "The Use of Diaries to Measure Discretionary Behavior: Hypotheses and Results," *Evaluation Review,* 10 (February 1986), pp. 95–113; Ian Plewes, Rosemary Creeser, and Ann Mooney, "Reliability and Validity of Time Budget Data: Children's Activities Outside School," *Journal of Official Statistics,* 6 (No. 4, 1990), pp. 411–419.

TABLE 4.8 Arbitron Radio Listening Diary

	Time		Station			Place			
			Call letters or station name. *Don't know? Use program name or dial setting.*	Check (√) one		Check (√) one			
	Start	Stop		AM	FM	At Home	In a Car	At Work	Other Place
→ **Early Morning** (from 5 AM)									
→ **Midday**									
→ **Late Afternoon**									
→ **Night** (to 5 AM Friday)									

THURSDAY

Time   Station   Place

If you didn't hear a radio today, please check here. ☐

Source: © 1994 The Arbitron Company.

reduce this interaction bias. First, respondents come to trust the interviewer to a greater degree because of repetitive contact. Second, more frequent contact creates rapport.

The main disadvantage of panels is that they are nonrepresentative. The agreement to participate involves a commitment on the part of the designated sample member. Some individuals refuse this commitment. They do not wish to be bothered with filling out consumer diaries or testing products or evaluating advertising copy or whatever else may be involved with the panel operation. Consumer panels that require households to keep a record of their purchases, for example, generally have cooperation rates of about 60 percent when participants are contacted in person and lower participation rates if telephone or mail is used for the initial contact.[33]

The better ongoing panel operations select prospective participants systematically. The sponsoring organization attempts to generate and maintain panels that are representative of the total population of interest with respect to such characteristics as age, occupation, education, and so on. Quite often the organization will use quota samples so that the proportion of those in the sample with a particular characteristic (e.g., sex) equals the proportion in the population.[34] All the research organization can do, though, is designate the families or respondents that are to be included in the sample. It cannot force individuals to participate, nor can it require continued participation from those who initially choose to cooperate. It often encourages participation by offering some premium or by paying panel members for their cooperation. Nevertheless, a significant percentage of individuals designated for inclusion refuse to cooperate initially or quickly drop from the panel. Depending on the type of cooperation needed, the refusal and attrition rates might run over 50 percent.[35] Of course, not all panel attrition is due to quitting. Some individuals move away and others die. In any case, the question arises whether the panel is then indeed representative of the population, since those designated to participate are not participating. Further, the payment of a reward for cooperation raises the question of whether particular types of people are attracted to such panels.

It seems, for example, that "panel cooperation appears to be best in households with more than two members, in households having wives in the younger age groups, and in households with more education."[36] Of course, this nonrepresentative quality may not be a problem in every study. It depends on the purpose of the study and the particular variables of interest.

In one of the more extensive studies investigating the "representativeness" of a continuing household panel, Market Facts compared survey results on specific issues

---

[33]See Sudman and Ferber, *Consumer Panels,* p. 31. See also B. Golany, F. Y. Phillips, and J. J. Rousseau, "Few-Wave vs. Continuous Consumer Panels: Some Issues of Attrition, Bias, and Variance," *International Journal of Research in Marketing,* 8 (September 1991), pp. 273–280.

[34]Quota samples are explained in Chapter 10.

[35]Sudman and Ferber, *Consumer Panels,* p. 31. Winer demonstrates the biasing effects of attrition on the parameters of models fit to panel data. See Russell S. Winer, "Attrition Bias in Econometric Models Estimated with Panel Data," *Journal of Marketing Research,* 20 (May 1983), pp. 177–186. See also Jennifer Waterton and Denise Lievesley, "Attrition in a Panel Study of Attitudes," *Journal of Official Statistics,* 3 (No. 3, 1987), pp. 267–282.

[36]Sudman and Ferber, *Consumer Panels,* p. 32.

when the data were gathered using their mail panel against the data gathered from randomly selected telephone samples. Research Realities 4.6 shows that the differences were very small with respect to such issues as travel outside the United States, beer consumption, households with heart-attack sufferers, and households with cigarette smokers. However, the study goes on to point out that "experimentation of this kind has revealed instances of significant differences between data generated by mail panel and data generated through telephone interviewing. . . . What these experiments strongly

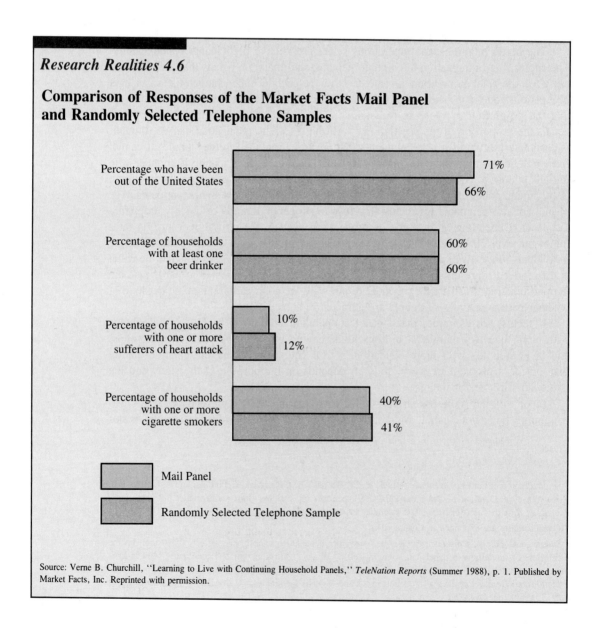

Research Realities 4.6

Comparison of Responses of the Market Facts Mail Panel and Randomly Selected Telephone Samples

Percentage who have been out of the United States
71%
66%

Percentage of households with at least one beer drinker
60%
60%

Percentage of households with one or more sufferers of heart attack
10%
12%

Percentage of households with one or more cigarette smokers
40%
41%

Mail Panel

Randomly Selected Telephone Sample

Source: Verne B. Churchill, "Learning to Live with Continuing Household Panels," *TeleNation Reports* (Summer 1988), p. 1. Published by Market Facts, Inc. Reprinted with permission.

suggest, therefore, is that great care must continue to be exercised in the selection of research method, when methodological options exist. But they also suggest that many . . . marketing questions can be addressed very effectively through controlled mail panels. . .''[37] The trouble with bias that is due to unrepresentativeness, of course, is that one never knows in advance whether it will affect the results, much less how.

Cross-Sectional Analysis

The cross-sectional study is the best known and most important type of descriptive design, as measured by the number of times it is used in comparison to other methods. The cross-sectional study has two distinguishing features. First, it provides a snapshot of the variables of interest at a single point in time, as contrasted to the longitudinal study, which provides a series of pictures that, when pieced together, provide a movie of the situation and the changes that are occurring. Second, the sample of elements is typically selected to be representative of some known universe. Therefore, a great deal of emphasis is placed on selecting sample members, usually with a probability sampling plan. That is one reason that the technique is often called a **sample survey.** The probability sampling plan allows the sampling error associated with the statistics generated from the sample, but used to describe the universe, to be determined. The "large" number of cases usually resulting from a sample survey also allows for cross-classification of the variables.

The objective of cross-classification analysis is to establish categories so that classification in one category implies classification in one or more other categories. The method of cross-classification analysis will be detailed later, in the discussion of tabulation. For the moment, simply note that it involves counting the *simultaneous occurrence* of the variables of interest. For example, suppose that management believes that one's occupation is an important factor in determining the consumption of its product. Further, suppose that the proposition to be examined is that white-collar workers are more apt to use the product than blue-collar workers. This hypothesis could be examined in a cross-sectional study. Measurements would be taken from a representative sample of the population with respect to occupation and use of the product. In cross tabulation, researchers would count the number of cases that fell in each of the following classes:

- white-collar and use the product
- blue-collar and use the product
- white-collar and do not use the product
- blue-collar and do not use the product.

That is, the emphasis would be on the relative frequency of occurrence of the joint phenomenon — white-collar occupation and user of the product. If the hypothesis is to be supported by the sample data, the proportion of white-collar workers using the product should exceed the proportion of blue-collar workers using the product.

---

[37]Verne B. Churchill, "Learning to Live with Continuing Household Panels," *Telenation Reports* (Summer 1988), p. 2.

As the chapters on analysis should illustrate, cross-classification analysis is a bread-and-butter technique that marketing researchers use to make sense out of survey data. One type of cross-classification analysis that is particularly effective for descriptive research arises when there is a series of "properly spaced" surveys, because this allows cohort analysis of the data. The **cohort,** which refers to the aggregate of individuals who experience the same event within the same time interval, serves as the basic unit of analysis in such studies. A very common analysis emphasis is on birth cohorts, or groups of people born within the same time interval.[38] The potential usefulness of cohort analysis can be seen when using the age-based per capita soft drink consumption data shown in Table 4.9. What do you think such data portend for the future of the soft drink industry? A typical interpretation would suggest dire consequences as the large but young cohorts grow older and are replaced by smaller cohorts because of declining birthrates in the United States. As a matter of fact, most people, on seeing these data, might be inclined to agree with the *Business Week* article that stated, ". . . by 1985, there will be four million fewer persons in the thirteen-to-twenty-four age group. And these four million persons would have consumed some 3.3 billion cans of soft drinks annually."[39]

A birth cohort analysis of soft drink consumption data would focus on the changing consumption patterns of identifiable groups as they age — for example, all those born between 1940 and 1949. Table 4.10, for example, shows the percentage of people in each age cohort born between 1900 and 1969 who consume soft drinks on a typical day. Note that Table 4.10 is constructed so that the interval between any two surveys or measurement periods corresponds approximately to the age-class interval that is used to

TABLE **4.9**   **Per Capita Consumption of Soft Drinks by Various Age Categories**

Age	Per Capita Consumption, 1979
20–29	48 gallons
30–39	42 gallons
40–49	35 gallons
50+	24 gallons

Source: Joseph O. Rentz, Fred D. Reynolds, and Roy G. Stout, "Analyzing Changing Consumption Patterns with Cohort Analysis," *Journal of Marketing Research,* 20 (February 1983), p. 12. Published by the American Marketing Association.

---

[38]Joseph O. Rentz, Fred D. Reynolds, and Roy G. Stout, "Analyzing Changing Consumption Patterns with Cohort Analysis," *Journal of Marketing Research,* 20 (February 1983), pp. 12–20; Joseph O. Rentz and Fred D. Reynolds, "Forecasting the Effects of an Aging Population on Product Consumption: An Age-Period-Cohort Framework," *Journal of Marketing Research,* 28 (August 1991), pp. 355–360.

[39]"The Graying of the Soft Drink Industry," *Business Week* (May 23, 1977), p. 68.

TABLE **4.10** **Consumption of Soft Drinks by Various Age Cohorts (Percentage Consuming on a Typical Day)**

Age	1950	1960	1969	1979	
8–19	52.9	62.6	73.2	81.0	
20–29	45.2	60.7	76.0	75.8	C8
30–39	33.9	46.6	67.7	71.4	C7
40–49	28.2	40.8	58.6	67.8	C6
50+	18.1	28.8	50.0	51.9	C5
		C1	C2	C3	C4

C1 — cohort born prior to 1900　　　　　C5 — cohort born 1931–1940
C2 — cohort born 1901–1910　　　　　　C6 — cohort born 1940–1949
C3 — cohort born 1911–1920　　　　　　C7 — cohort born 1950–1959
C4 — cohort born 1921–1930　　　　　　C8 — cohort born 1960–1969

Source: Joseph O. Rentz, Fred D. Reynolds, and Roy G. Stout, "Analyzing Changing Consumption Patterns with Cohort Analysis," *Journal of Marketing Research,* 20 (February 1983), p. 12. Published by the American Marketing Association.

define the age cohorts used in the study (ten years in this case). Because of this, the consumption of the various age cohorts over time can be determined by reading down the diagonal. Consider Cohort C5, for example, which refers to all those born between 1931 and 1940. The C5 diagonal indicates that 52.9 percent of the people in this age group who were interviewed in 1950 consumed soft drinks on a typical day; by 1960 that percentage had increased to 60.7 percent, to 67.7 percent by 1969, and to 67.8 percent by 1979. A complete analysis of the cohort data in Table 4.10 that looks at the percentage of people consuming soft drinks and other data that show the amount consumed per capita suggests just the opposite conclusion of the *Business Week* article.

> Specifically, each succeeding cohort has increased its consumption and once the level is established consumption will remain relatively stable over the life course. Thus consumption in the cohort aged 20–29 will not decrease as the cohort ages. Further, total soft drink consumption would increase as the larger and younger cohorts (whose per capita consumption is high) replace the smaller and older cohorts (whose per capita consumption is lower).[40]

Not only does cross-classification analysis serve, then, as a basic analytic technique in descriptive research studies, but when there is a series of properly spaced surveys, cohort analysis, or a special form of cross-classification analysis, can be used to advantage.

----

[40]Rentz, Reynolds, and Stout, "Analyzing Changing Consumption," p. 13. This article explains cohort analysis and uses it to analyze the effects of aging and cohort succession on consumption of a product class. For general discussion of the use of cohort analysis in forecasting, see Joseph L. Bonnici and William B. Fredenberger, "Cohort Analysis — A Forecasting Tool," *Journal of Business Forecasting,* 10 (Fall 1991), pp. 9–13.

The sample survey has several disadvantages. These include superficial analysis of the phenomenon, high cost, and the technical sophistication required to conduct survey research. Let us consider each disadvantage in turn.

One common criticism of survey data is that they typically do not penetrate very deeply below the surface, since breadth is often emphasized at the expense of depth. There is ordinarily an emphasis on the calculation of statistics that efficiently summarize the wide variety of data collected from the sometimes large cross section of subjects. Yet the very process of generating summary statistics to describe the phenomenon suggests that the eventual ''average'' might not accurately describe any individual entity making up the aggregate. The situation is much like that of ''the guy who slept with his feet in the refrigerator and his head in the stove and who, on the average, was comfortable.''

Second, a survey is expensive in terms of time and money. It will often be months before a single hypothesis can be tested because of the necessary preliminaries so vital to survey research. The entire research process — from problem definition through measuring instrument development, design of the sample, collecting the data, and editing, coding, and tabulating the data — must be executed before an analyst can begin to examine the hypotheses that guide the study. As parts of the remainder of this book will show, each of these tasks can be formidable in its own right. Each can require large investments of time, energy, and money.

Survey research also requires a good deal of technical skill. The research analyst must either have the skills required at each stage of the process or have access to such skills in, say, the form of technical consultants. It is the rare individual indeed who has the technical sophistication both to develop an attitude scale and to design a complex probability sample.

ETHICAL DILEMMA 4.2

Marketing Research Insights was asked to carry out the data collection and analysis procedures for a study designed by a consumer goods company. After studying the research purpose and design, a consultant for Marketing Research Insights concluded that the design was poorly conceived. First, he thought that the design was more complex than was necessary, inasmuch as some of the data could be obtained through secondary sources, precluding the necessity of much primary data collection. Second, the proposed choice of primary data collection would not produce the kinds of information sought by the company.

Although the consultant advised the company of his opinions, the company insisted on proceeding with the proposed design. Marketing Research Insights' management was reluctant to undertake the study, as it believed that the firm's reputation would be harmed if its name was associated with poor research.

- What decision would you make if you were a consultant for Marketing Research Insights?
- In general, should a researcher advance his or her opinion of a proposed design, or should the researcher remain silent and simply do the work?
- Is it ethical to remain silent in such situations?

SUMMARY

A research design is the blueprint for a study that guides the collection and analysis of data. Just as different blueprints reflect differing degrees of detail, so research designs vary in their specificity. Some are very detailed and involve the investigation of specific ''if-then'' relationships, whereas others simply provide a picture of the overall situation. Figure 4.4 summarizes the important features of the different designs.

Exploratory research is basically ''general picture'' research. It is quite useful for becoming familiar with a phenomenon, for clarifying concepts, for developing but not testing ''if-then'' statements, and for establishing priorities for further research. Exploratory studies are characterized by their flexibility. The investigator's imagination and ingenuity will guide the pursuit, although literature searches, experience surveys, focus groups, and selected cases have proved to be useful for gaining insight into a phenomenon.

Descriptive studies are anything but flexible. Rather, they are rigid in requiring a precise specification of the who, what, when, where, why, and how of the research. Descriptive studies rest on one or more specific hypotheses. They are used when the research is intended to describe the characteristics of certain groups, to estimate the proportion of people who behave in a certain way, or to make predictions.

Descriptive studies are of two types: longitudinal and cross-sectional. Longitudinal studies rely on panel data. A panel is simply a fixed sample of individuals or some other entities from whom repeated measurements are taken. There are two different kinds of panels — panels in which the same measurements are taken in each measurement period (true panels) and those in which different measurements are taken in each measurement period (omnibus panels). The turnover table, a most informative method of analysis that is unique to panel data, is only applicable to panels in which the same variables are measured over time.

Cross-sectional studies, or sample surveys, rely on a sample of elements from the population of interest that are measured at a single point in time. A great deal of emphasis is placed on the scientific generation of the sample so that the members are representative of the population of interest. A typical sample survey involves summarizing and generalizing the data collected. The analysis of sample survey results rests heavily on the cross-classification table, which is used to report the joint occurrence of the variables of interest.

Cohort analysis is a special type of cross-classification analysis that can be used when there is a series of surveys and the spacing between them corresponds to a natural, or cohort, division of the population, where a cohort refers to the aggregate of individuals who experience the same event within the same time interval.

Questions

1. What is a research design? Is a research design necessary to conduct a study?
2. What are the different types of research designs? What is the basic purpose of each?
3. What is the crucial tenet of research?
4. What are the basic uses for exploratory research?
5. What is the key characteristic of exploratory research?

FIGURE 4.4   **Types of Research Designs**

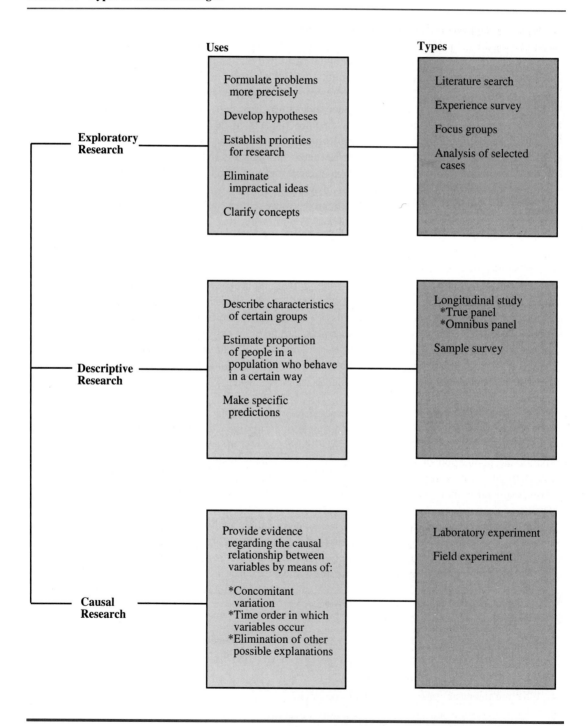

6. What are some of the more productive types of exploratory research? What are the characteristics of each type?

7. What are the basic uses of descriptive research?

8. What is the key characteristic of descriptive research?

9. What are the main types of descriptive studies, and what do their differences mean?

10. What are the basic types of panels, and of what importance are the differences that exist?

11. What is the turnover table? How is it read? What kinds of analyses does a turnover table allow that cannot be done with other types of studies?

12. What is the fundamental thrust of a sample survey? What are its advantages and disadvantages?

13. What are the basic types of cross-sectional studies? How do they compare in terms of advantages and disadvantages?

14. What is a cross-tabulation table? What is the objective of cross-classification analysis?

15. What is a cohort? What is cohort analysis?

Applications and Problems

1. Industrial Health Technologies, Ltd. (IHT), located on the East Coast, is a manufacturer of industrial respirators. The Research and Development (R&D) department recently designed a prototype respirator for the asbestos-abatement industry that is battery powered and would extend the operating life of current models from 8 to 30 hours without recharging. A similar model introduced by Deep Mine Safety Apparatus (DMSA) four months earlier was marginally successful. However, both IHT's and DMSA's models suffered from a technical flaw. It was found that use of the respirators for 30 hours without recharging required 18 hours of recharging to return the batteries to a state of full charge. Notwithstanding this technical flaw, IHT's management team, headed by Chuck Montford, was excited about R&D's efforts. Chuck and Carl Corydon, IHT's marketing manager, had decided to do a sample survey to gauge customer reaction to the new battery capability. A random sample of 100 asbestos-abatement firms was to be chosen from a list of East Coast federally licensed asbestos-abatement firms. Mail questionnaires were designed to determine respondents' attitudes and opinions towards this new respirator.

   In this situation, is the research design appropriate? If yes, why? If no, why not?

2. Emilie Malti, president of Jamaican Specialties, a specialty food marketing firm, was convinced that the target audience for her line of Caribbean conserves in mango, lime, passion fruit, and papaya consisted of women, ages 25 to 44, with household incomes of $30,000 and up. Jamaican Specialties' major competitor's (Pacific Flavor) market segment appeared to be more widely dispersed with respect to both age and income. Emilie and her marketing vice-president, Ruth Marion, attributed this difference to the type of magazines in which Pacific Flavor advertised. Emilie and Ruth decided to conduct a study to determine the socioeconomic characteristics of their firm's market segment. They formed a panel of 800 women ages 18 and up. Mail questionnaires would be sent to all panel members. One month after receiving all questionnaires, the company would again send similar questionnaires to all of the panel members. In this situation, is the research design appropriate? If yes, why? If no, why not?

3. Telephonic was a large supplier of residential telephones and related services in the southwestern United States. The research and development department of Telephonic recently designed a prototype with a memory function that can store the number of calls and the contents of the calls for a period of 48 hours. A similar model, introduced by Telephonic's competitor three months earlier, was marginally successful. However, both models suffer from a technical flaw. It has been found that a call lasting more than 20 minutes would result in a loss of the dial tone for 90 seconds. This was mainly attributable to the activation of the memory function. Notwithstanding the flaw, management was excited about the efforts of the research and development department. They decided to do a field study to gauge consumer reaction to the memory capacity. A random sample of 1,000 respondents was to be chosen from three major metropolitan areas in the Southwest. The questionnaires were designed to uncover respondent's attitudes and opinions toward the new phone.

   In this situation, is the research design appropriate? If yes, why? If no, why not?

4. A medium-sized manufacturer of high-speed copiers and duplicators was introducing a new desk-top model. The vice-president of communications had to decide between two advertising programs for this product. He preferred advertising program gamma and was sure it would generate more sales than its counterpart, advertising program beta. The next day he was to meet with the senior vice-president of marketing and planning to decide on an appropriate research design for a study that would aid in the final decision about which advertising program to implement.

   What research design would you recommend? Justify your choice.

5. Gettings & Gettings, a father-and-son insurance agency in Lafayette, Indiana, was concerned with improving its service. In particular, the firm wanted to assess if customers were dissatisfied with current service and the nature of this dissatisfaction. What research design would you recommend? Justify your choice.

6. Greg Martin is the owner of a pizza restaurant that caters to college students. Through informal conversations with his customers, Greg has begun to suspect that a video-rental store specifically targeting college students would do quite well in the local market. While his informal conversations with students have revealed an overall sense of dissatisfaction with existing rental outlets, he hasn't been able to isolate specific areas of concern. Thinking back to a marketing research course he took in school, Greg has decided that focus group research would be an appropriate method to gather information that might be useful in deciding whether to pursue further development of his idea (e.g., a formal business plan, store policies, etc.).
   a. What is the decision problem and resulting research problem apparent in this situation?
   b. Who should Greg select as participants in the focus group?
   c. Where should the focus group session be conducted?
   d. Who should be the moderator of the focus group?
   e. Develop a discussion outline for the focus group.

7. The Federal Reserve (the Fed) controls currency in the United States. Recently, the Fed has been considering some changes in the currency that circulates. One change involves paper money, which is currently all the same size and shape (no matter what the denomination of the bill). Some members of the Fed believe that money would be easier for consumers to handle if it came in different colors. For example, the one dollar bill could remain green, the five dollar bill could be printed on blue paper, the ten dollar bill could

be red, and so on. In addition, the Fed is considering changing the size of the bills, so that the five dollar bill would be larger than the one, the ten would be larger than the five, and so on.

Before making these changes, the Fed believes that it might be useful to conduct some marketing research. Thus, Madison Marketing Research, Inc. (MMR) is contacted by the Fed and asked to collect some information to help forecast whether or no these changes will be successful and popular with consumers. What research should Madison Marketing Research propose? Be specific when describing alternative research designs.

8. The leadership of the Boy Scouts of America (BSA) is concerned about several issues related to their membership. These issues include low retention rates among members (e.g., many scouts quit after only one or two years); high turnover rates among leaders; and declining membership in some regions (e.g., in large urban areas). Design a marketing research program to assist BSA in assessing and reversing these trends.

9. The Pen-Lite Company is a manufacturer of writing instruments such as fountain pens, ballpoint pens, soft-top pens, and mechanical pencils. Typically, these products have been retailed through small and large chains, drug stores, and grocery stores. The company recently diversified into the manufacture of disposable cigarette lighters. The distribution of this product was to be restricted to drug stores and grocery stores. The reason was that management believed that its target market of low- and middle-income consumers would use these outlets. Your expertise is required to decide on an appropriate research design to determine if this would indeed be the case.

What research design would you recommend? Justify your choice.

10. Airways Luggage is a producer of cloth-covered luggage, one of the primary advantages of which is its light weight. The company distributes its luggage through major department stores, mail-order houses, clothing retailers, and other retail outlets such as stationery stores, leather-goods stores, and so on. The company advertises rather heavily, but it also supplements this promotional effort with a large field staff of sales representatives, numbering around 400. The numbers vary because one of the historical problems confronting Airways Luggage has been the large number of sales representatives' resignations. It is not unusual for 10 to 20 percent of the sales force to turn over every year. Because the cost of training a new person is estimated at $5,000 to $10,000, not including the lost sales that might result because of a personnel switch, Ms. Brooks, the sales manager, is rightly concerned. She has been concerned for some time and, therefore, has been conducting exit interviews with each departing sales representative. On the basis of these interviews, she has formulated the opinion that the major reason for this high turnover is general sales representatives' dissatisfaction with company policies, promotional opportunities, and pay. But top management has not been sympathetic to Ms. Brooks' pleas regarding the changes needed in these areas of corporate policy. Rather, it has tended to counter Ms. Brooks' pleas with arguments that too much of what she is suggesting is based on her gut reactions and little hard data. Top management desires more systematic evidence that job dissatisfaction in general and these dimensions of job dissatisfaction in particular are the real reasons for the high turnover before they would be willing to change things. Ms. Brooks has called on the Marketing Research Department in Airways Luggage to assist her in solving her problem.
    a. As a member of this department, identify the general hypothesis that would guide your research efforts.
    b. What type of research design would you recommend to Ms. Brooks? Justify your answer.

11. Fred Spears, director of advertising for *Competitive Farming*, is responsible for selling advertising space in the magazine. The magazine deals primarily with farming and the marketing of agricultural products and is distributed solely by subscription. Major advertisers are agricultural equipment manufacturers and production input suppliers, since the magazine is primarily directed at farmers, ranchers, and those persons employed in marketing agricultural products.

    Because the size and composition of the target audience for *Competitive Farming* are key concerns for prospective advertisers, Mr. Spears is interested in collecting more detailed data on the readership. Although he presently has total circulation figures, he believes that these understate the potential exposure of an advertisement in *Competitive Farming*. In particular, he thinks that for every subscriber to *Competitive Farming,* there are several others on the farm or employed within the various firms who also read *Competitive Farming*. Fred wishes to determine how large this secondary audience is and also wishes to develop more detailed data on readers, such as degree of training in various areas, including pesticide handling, equipment repair, and commodity marketing. He believes that this detail would be helpful in influencing potential clients to commit their advertising dollars to *Competitive Farming*. Fred has asked you to assist him in solving his problems.

    a. Does Fred have a specific hypothesis? If yes, state the hypothesis.

    b. What type of research design would you recommend? Justify your answer.

12. Investment Services, Inc., is a real estate developer headquartered in Florida but operating throughout the southeastern United States. One of the military bases located in one of the cities within Investment Services' market area recently closed, and the forty housing units for military people located at the base were put up for public sale. The housing units, which were all duplexes, were somewhat run-down because the decision to phase out the base had been made some time ago. Only minimum maintenance was conducted after the fateful decision.

    Investment Services' management thinks that these units will command only a very low price at the public sale because of their dilapidated condition. The developers believe that because of this low price, the units could be repaired and sold at a nice profit.

    Before bidding on the contract, though, Investment Services' management is interested in determining what kind of demand there might be for these units. It has asked you to assist in determining this reaction. What kind of research design would you suggest? Why?

13. The Wisconsin Ice Cream Co. of Mount Horeb, Wisconsin, a regional manufacturer of gourmet ice cream and frozen novelties, conducted a study in 1993 to assess how its brand of gourmet ice cream was faring in the market. Mail questionnaires were sent to a panel of 1,575 households. Wisconsin Ice Cream has three major competitors: Baumgardt's Food Co. of State College, Pennsylvania; Doug's Ice Cream of Michigan City, Indiana; and Guyer Foods of Charlevoix, Michigan. A similar study conducted in 1992 had indicated the following market shares: Wisconsin, 29.84 percent (i.e., 470 families); Baumgardt's, 22.54 percent (355 families); Doug's, 26.03 percent (410 families); and Guyer's, 21.59 percent (340 families). The present study indicated that Wisconsin's market share had not changed during the one-year period. Results of the study indicated that Baumgardt's market share had decreased to 20 percent (315 families), Doug's market share had decreased to 20.32 percent (320 families), and Guyer's market share had increased to 29.84 percent (470 families). Wisconsin Ice Cream Co. managers decided that they had little to worry about.

The 1993 study revealed some additional facts. Over the one-year period, 80 families had switched from Doug's and 50 families had switched from Guyer's to Wisconsin Ice Cream. Ten families had switched from Wisconsin and 15 families had switched from Doug's to Baumgardt's Ice Cream. Results also indicated that although none of Baumgardt's families had switched to Doug's Ice Cream, 40 of the Wisconsin and 5 of Guyer's families now purchased Doug's Ice Cream. It was revealed that Guyer's current customers comprise 80 families formerly purchasing Wisconsin Ice Cream, 65 families formerly purchasing Baumgardt's Ice Cream, and 40 families formerly purchasing Doug's Ice Cream.

a. Do you think that Wisconsin's management team is accurate in analyzing the situation? Justify your answer.

b. You are called on to do some analysis. From the preceding data construct the brand switching matrix. (Hint: begin by filling in the row and column totals.)

c. Indicate what this matrix reveals for each of the brands over the one-year period.

d. Complete the brand loyalty and switching possibilities matrix below.

		At Time t_2 (1993)				
		Bought Wisconsin	**Bought Baumgardt's**	**Bought Doug's**	**Bought Guyer's**	**Total**
At Time t_1 (1992)	Bought Wisconsin					
	Bought Baumgardt's					
	Bought Doug's					
	Bought Guyer's					
	Total					

e. What can be said about the degree of brand loyalty for each of the four products?

14. Peppy Pet Company, a large manufacturer of pet food products, conducted a study in 1993 in order to assess how its brand of dog food was faring in the market. Questionnaires were mailed to a panel of 1,260 families with a dog. The Peppy Pet brand had three major competitors: Brand A, Brand B, and Brand C. A similar study conducted in 1992 had indicated the following market shares: Peppy Pet, 31.75 percent (i.e., 400 families); Brand A, 25 percent (315 families); Brand B, 32.54 percent (410 families); and Brand C, 10.71 percent (135 families). The present study indicated that Peppy Pet's market share had not changed during the one-year period. However, Brand B increased its market share to 36.5 percent (460 families). This increase could be accounted for by a decrease in Brand A's and Brand C's market shares (Brand A now had a share of 22.23 percent, or 280 families; Brand C now had a share of 9.52 percent, or 120 families). The management of the Peppy Pet Company decided it had little to worry about.

The 1993 study also revealed some additional facts. Over the one-year period, 70 families from Brand A and 30 families from Brand C had switched to Peppy Pet. Five families from Brand B and 30 families from Brand C had switched to Brand A, while none of the Peppy Pet users had switched to Brand A. These facts further reassured management. Finally, 45 families switched from Brand B to Brand C, but none of the families using Peppy Pet or Brand A had switched to Brand C. Brand C's loyalty was estimated to be .556.

   a. Do you think that the management of the Peppy Pet Company was accurate in its analysis of the situation? Justify your answer.

   b. You are called upon to do some analysis. From the preceding data, construct the brand-switching matrix.

   c. Indicate what this matrix reveals for each of the brands over the one-year period.

   d. Complete the following table and compute brand loyalties.

   e. What can be said about the degree of brand loyalty for each of the four products?

| | **At Time (t_2)** | | | | |
	Bought Peppy Pet	**Bought A**	**Bought B**	**Bought C**	**Total**
At Time (**t₁**)					
Bought Peppy Pet					
Bought A					
Bought B					
Bought C					

15. The LoCalor Company is a medium-sized manufacturer of highly nutritional food products. The products have been marketed as diet foods with high nutritional content. Recently, the company was considering marketing these products as snack foods but was concerned about their present customers' reaction to the change in the products' images. The company has decided to assess customers' reaction by conducting a study using one of the established consumer panels.

     What type of panel would you recommend in the preceding situation? Why?

 Thorndike Sports Equipment Video Case

   1. Where should Ted look first for information on the kinds of racquets players desire?

   2. If primary research is warranted, what projects would you propose to Luke Thorndike? What role would secondary research play in your primary research plans?

   3. Looking at the primary research that you have decided is necessary in order to understand the problem in the racquetball division, how much will it cost Thorndike Sports Equipment to complete this project?

   4. List three questions that you would ask retailers and/or players. Explain the rationale for asking these questions.

   5. After informally speaking to a number of retailers and players, would you be able to provide solutions to the problem? Why or why not?

   6. If the information gained from talking to these people cannot be used to solve the problem, is there still value in talking to these people?

7. As the researcher for Thorndike, you have been asked to construct a discussion guide for additional focus groups. Write up a discussion guide for the moderator to follow.

8. Should focus group participants be told the objective of the group? Why?

9. What are the benefits of doing qualitative research? How can findings from this type of research be used? What are the limitations of this type of research?

10. Ted has received valuable information from his focus group. Can he now reliably propose a solution to the racquet problem? Why or why not?

11. Ted mentions that he has videotaped the focus group sessions. What are some of the reasons for videotaping a focus group? What are some of the drawbacks to videotaping a focus group?

12. Is it ethical to videotape a group without telling participants that they are being taped? Is is ethical to make an audio tape of focus groups without telling the participants?

5

CHAPTER

CAUSAL DESIGNS

Many times, the marketing manager has one or more specific *X-causes-Y* hypotheses that need to be examined: for example, a 5 percent increase in the price of the product will have no appreciable impact on the quantity demanded by customers, or that redesigning the cereal package so that it is shorter and less likely to tip over will improve consumer attitudes toward the product. When the research question can be framed this explicitly, the researcher is dealing with a situation ripe for causal analysis. Descriptive research can be used for testing hypotheses. However, descriptive designs are not as satisfactory as experiments for establishing causality. The reasons require an understanding of the notion of causality, the types of evidence that establish causality, and the effect of extraneous variables in a research setting. In addition to explaining experimental design, this chapter deals with these concepts.

CONCEPT OF CAUSALITY

The concept of causality is complex, and a detailed discussion of it would take us too far afield. However, a few essentials will allow us to properly determine the role of the experiment in establishing the validity of an *X-causes-Y* statement.

The scientific notion of causality is very different from the common-sense, everyday notion.[1] First, the common-sense notion suggests that there is a single cause of an event. The everyday interpretation of the statement *X* is the cause of *Y* implies that *X* is indeed *the* cause. The scientific notion holds that *X* would only be one of a number of determining conditions.

Another difference between the common-sense and scientific notions of causality is that while the everyday interpretation implies a completely deterministic relationship, the

---

[1]See Claire Selltiz, *et al., Research Methods in Social Relations,* rev. ed. (New York: Holt, Rinehart and Winston, 1959), pp. 80–82, for a brief but lucid discussion of the differences between the common-sense and scientific notions of causality. See also David A. Kenny, *Correlation and Causality* (New York: John Wiley & Sons, 1979), especially Chapter 1.

scientific notion implies a probabilistic relationship. That is, the common-sense notion suggests that for X to be a cause of Y, X must always lead to Y. The scientific notion suggests that X can be a cause of Y if the occurrence of X makes the occurrence of Y more likely or more probable.

Finally, the scientific notion implies that we can *never prove* that X is a cause of Y. Rather, we always *infer* but never prove that a relationship exists. The inference is typically based on some observed data, perhaps acquired in a very controlled experimental setting. Nevertheless, the scientific notion recognizes the fallibility of such procedures. This begs the question of what kinds of evidence can be used to support scientific inferences. There are three basic kinds of evidence: concomitant variation, time/order of occurrence of variables, and elimination of other possible causal factors.[2]

Concomitant Variation

Consider the statement "X is a cause of Y." Evidence of concomitant variation as to the validity of this statement refers to the extent to which X and Y occur together or vary together in the way predicted by the hypothesis. Two cases can be distinguished — the qualitative and the quantitative.

Consider the qualitative case first. Suppose that the causal factor X was "dealer quality" and the effect factor Y was the company's market share, and suppose that we were interested in examining the statement, "The success of our marketing efforts is highly dealer dependent. Where we have good dealers, we have good market penetration, and where we have poor dealers, we have unsatisfactory market penetration." Now, if X is to be considered a cause of Y, we should expect to find the following: In those territories where our good dealers are located, we would expect to have satisfactory market shares, and in those territories where our poor dealers are located, we would expect to have unsatisfactory market shares. However, if we found that the proportion of territories with unsatisfactory market shares was higher where the good dealers were located, we would conclude that the hypothesis was untenable.

Consider Table 5.1, in which the 100 dealers in each of the company's sales territories have been classified as good or poor. Suppose that the research department has also investigated the firm's market penetration in each sales territory and has categorized these market shares using some criteria supplied by management as being either satisfactory or unsatisfactory. This table provides evidence of concomitant variation. Where we find the presence of X, a good dealer, we also find the presence of Y, satisfactory market share, and where X is lacking, we are more likely to find a territory where our market share is unsatisfactory. Stating it another way, 67 percent of the good dealers are found in territories where our market share is satisfactory. However, only 25 percent of the poor dealers are located in territories where the market share is satisfactory.

Perfect evidence of concomitant variation would be provided, of course, if all good dealers were located in territories with satisfactory market shares and all poor dealers

---

[2]Selltiz, *et al.*, *Research Methods*, pp. 83–88.

TABLE **5.1**   **Evidence of Concomitant Variation: Qualitative Case**

| | Market Share — *Y* | | |
Dealer Quality — *X*	Satisfactory	Unsatisfactory	Total
Good	40 (67%)	20 (33%)	60 (100%)
Poor	10 (25%)	30 (75%)	40 (100%)

were located in territories with unsatisfactory market shares. The "pure" case will rarely be found in practice, as other causal factors will produce some deviation from a one-to-one correspondence between *X* and *Y*. So we search for the proportion of cases having *X* that also possess *Y* and compare that to the proportion of cases not having *X* that possess *Y*.

When the cause and effect factors can logically be considered continuous variables, the approach is similar. Now, though, the evidence should be consistent with regard to the amount of *X* in comparison to the amount of *Y*. Consider the relationship between advertising effort and sales. The firm's dollar expenditure on advertising is logically considered the cause, *X*, and sales the effect, *Y*. Further, the hypothesis would probably state that the higher the level of advertising expenditure, the greater the sales. Quantitative evidence of concomitant variation would be provided by finding evidence consistent with this hypothesis in that *X* was higher in those territories or in those years where *Y* was also greater. Again, the relationship could not be expected to be perfect, because that would deny the existence of other sales-determining factors. However, we would expect to find some positive relationship between the variables.

Suppose that an analysis of the relationship between *X* and *Y* provided supporting evidence of concomitant variation. What can we say? All we can say is that *the association makes the hypothesis more tenable; it does not prove it.*[3] Similarly, the absence of an association between *X* and *Y* cannot be taken in and of itself as evidence that there is no causal relationship between *X* and *Y*, because we are always inferring, rather than proving, that a causal relationship exists.

Consider first the case in which positive evidence of concomitant variation was provided. Table 5.2, which might be of interest to a candy manufacturer, suggests that candy consumption is affected by marital status.[4] Single people are more likely than

---

[3]In Chapter 13 we will discuss the various conditions that can arise when looking at evidence of concomitant variation. For the moment, we simply wish to emphasize through example that association between *X* and *Y* does not mean there is causality between *X* and *Y* and that the absence of such association does not mean there is no causality.

[4]The example is adapted from Hans Zeisel, *Say It with Figures*, 5th ed., rev. (New York: Harper & Row, 1968), pp. 137–139. This classic book is recommended reading for all who are faced with the task of analyzing data.

TABLE 5.2   **Evidence of Concomitant Variation between Marital Status and Candy Consumption**

| Marital Status — X | Candy Consumption — Y | | Total |
	Eat Candy Regularly	Do Not Eat Candy Regularly	
Single	750 (75%)	249 (25%)	999 (100%)
Married	1,265 (63%)	745 (37%)	2,010 (100%)

Source: Adapted from *Say It with Figures,* 5th ed., rev. by Hans Zeisel, after Table 9–8 (p. 138). Copyright © 1968 by Harper & Row, Publishers, Inc. By permission of Harper & Row, Publishers, Inc.

married people to eat candy regularly. Seventy-five percent of the single people in the sample ate candy regularly, whereas only 63 percent of the married people were regular consumers. Further, the evidence is not to be taken lightly, because it was taken from a rather large sample of 3,009 cases. On the basis of this evidence, can we safely conclude that marriage causes a decrease in candy consumption? Or are there other possible explanations? What about the effects of age? Married people are usually older than single people, and perhaps older people eat less candy. Table 5.3 shows the relationship between candy consumption and marital status for different age segments of the population — up to 25 years, and 25 years and over. This is equivalent to holding the effects of age constant. As Table 5.3 suggests, there is little difference in the candy-eating habits of married and single people; up to 25 years of age, 79 percent of the singles and 81 percent of the marrieds eat candy regularly. For those over 25 years of age, 60 percent of the singles and 58 percent of the marrieds eat candy regularly. In effect, Table 5.3

TABLE 5.3   **Candy Consumption by Age and Marital Status**

| | Up to 25 Years | | | 25 Years and Over | | |
	Eat Candy Regularly	Do Not Eat Candy Regularly	Total	Eat Candy Regularly	Do Not Eat Candy Regularly	Total
Single	632 (79%)	167 (21%)	799 (100%)	120 (60%)	80 (40%)	200 (100%)
Married	407 (81%)	96 (19%)	503 (100%)	873 (58%)	634 (42%)	1,507 (100%)

Source: Adapted from *Say It with Figures,* 5th ed., rev. by Hans Zeisel, after Table 9–6 (p. 138). Copyright © 1968 by Harper & Row, Publishers, Inc. By permission of Harper & Row, Publishers, Inc.

TABLE 5.4 Lack of Evidence of Concomitant Variation between Age and Listening to Classical Music

| Age — X | Listening to Classical Music — Y | | |
	Listen	Do Not Listen	Total
Below 40	390 (64%)	213 (36%)	603 (100%)
40 and Over	433 (64%)	243 (36%)	676 (100%)

Source: Adapted from *Say It with Figures,* 5th ed., rev. by Hans Zeisel, after Table 8–7 (p. 123). Copyright © 1968 by Harper & Row, Publishers, Inc. By permission of Harper & Row, Publishers, Inc.

suggests that a person's candy consumption is unaffected by the individual's marital state. The original association suggested by Table 5.2 was spurious.

Consider now the case of the absence of initial evidence of concomitant variation and why that does not imply that there is no causation between X and Y. Table 5.4 suggests that there is no relationship between a person's listening to classical music and the individual's age; in a sample of 1,279 cases, 64 percent of those under 40 and 64 percent of those over 40 listen to classical music.[5] For a record manufacturer interested in delineating market segments, this is a finding of considerable import. It is also somewhat unexpected. Consider what happens, though, when educational level is also introduced as an additional explanatory variable. As Table 5.5 reveals, there is an association between age and listening to classical music. Take college-educated people. As they get older, they display a higher propensity to listen to classical music; 78 percent of those 40

TABLE 5.5 Listening to Classical Music by Age and Education

| Age | College | | | Below College | | |
	Listen	Do Not Listen	Total	Listen	Do Not Listen	Total
Below 40	162 (73%)	62 (27%)	224 (100%)	228 (61%)	151 (39%)	379 (100%)
40 and Over	195 (78%)	56 (22%)	251 (100%)	238 (56%)	187 (44%)	425 (100%)

Source: Adapted from *Say It with Figures,* 5th ed., rev. by Hans Zeisel, after Table 8–8 (p. 124). Copyright © 1968 by Harper & Row, Publishers, Inc. By permission of Harper & Row, Publishers, Inc.

---

[5]The example is taken from Zeisel, *Say It with Figures,* pp. 123–125.

and over listen, whereas only 73 percent of the under-40 respondents listen. The reverse situation occurs among those who do not have a college education; whereas 61 percent of the under-40 age group listen to classical music, only 56 percent of the 40-and-over age group do so. The relationship between age and listening to classical music was originally obscured by the effect of education. When education was properly held constant, the relationship became visible.

The situations illustrated are not the only ones that can occur. A more complete picture will be presented in Chapter 13. For the moment, you should simply be aware that concomitant variation is one type of evidence that supports the existence of a causal relationship between X and Y. However, it is not the whole story. It may be that there is a causal relationship when there is no initial evidence of concomitant variation, or that there is no causal relationship when there is initial evidence. Further evidence of the existence of a causal relationship can be provided by looking at the order of occurrence of variables and by eliminating other possible sources of explanation.

Time Order of Occurrence of Variables

The time order of variables' occurrence as evidence of a causal relationship between two variables is conceptually simple.

> One event cannot be considered the "cause" of another if it occurs *after* the other event. The occurrence of a causal factor may precede or may be simultaneous with the occurrence of an event; by definition, an effect cannot be produced by an event that occurs only after the effect has taken place. However, it is possible for each term in the relationship to be both a "cause" and an "effect" of the other term.[6]

Although conceptually simple, the application of this type of evidence to support causality requires an intimate understanding of the time sequence governing the phenomenon.

Consider the relationship between a firm's annual advertising expenditures and sales. This relationship is frequently used as evidence of the effect of advertising on sales for a given product. However, many companies follow a rule of thumb that uses past sales in allocating resources to advertising — for example, 10 percent of last year's sales. This practice begs the question of which way the relationship runs. Does advertising lead to higher sales, or do higher sales lead to an increased ad budget? An intimate understanding of the way the company establishes the ad budget should resolve the dilemma in this situation.

Elimination of Other Possible Causal Factors

The elimination of other possible causal factors is very much like the Sherlock Holmes approach to analysis. Just as Sherlock Holmes holds that "when you have eliminated the

---

[6]Selltiz, *et al.*, *Research Methods*, p. 85.

impossible, whatever remains, however improbable, must be the truth,''[7] this type of evidence of causality focuses on the elimination of possible explanations other than the one being studied. This may mean physically holding other factors constant, or it may mean "adjusting" the results to remove the effects of factors that do vary.

Take the situation of the divisional manager of a chain of supermarkets investigating the effects of end displays on apple sales. Suppose that the manager found that per-store sales of apples increased during the past week and that a number of stores were using end displays for apples. To reasonably conclude that the end displays were responsible for the sales increase, the manager would need to eliminate such explanatory variables as price, size of store, and apple type and quality. This might involve looking at apple sales for stores of approximately the same size, checking to see if the prices were the same in stores having an increase in sales and stores with no increase, and checking to determine if the type and quality of apples were consistent with those of the previous week.

An interesting example of eliminating other possible causal factors by adjusting the results occurred with the 1983 Nielsen television ratings. A study, commissioned by the National Association of Broadcasters and dealing with people's attitudes toward advertising, indicated that people were dissatisfied with the offerings on broadcast TV and were spending less time watching it. At the same time, Nielsen data suggested otherwise. In fact, the Nielsen ratings were so high for that season that many were questioning the numbers, particularly since 1983 marked the first year that Nielsen reported the ratings based on its larger metered sample of 1,420 households versus the 1,260 it had used previously. Were the Nielsen data wrong? If not, what could account for the dramatic increase in broadcast TV viewership? Several of the most promising explanations were an increase in the amount of special-event programming, the weather, economic conditions, a change in the proportion of working women, and a change in the number of pay cable homes. Through systematic investigation of each of these factors, it was discovered that broadcast TV viewing was indeed up and the most likely explanation was the abnormal weather the country experienced in 1983, particularly in the East, Central, Pacific, and Northeast states.[8]

The testing of new products illustrates the need for and the problems associated with trying to eliminate other possible causal factors in order to conclude that the result was attributable to the variable in question. When testing new products, manufacturers often wish to determine whether the product has any differential advantages in consumers' minds (e.g., it is of superior quality or taste or has a desirable special feature). Yet when consumers are given a product to test, their responses can be affected by awareness of the manufacturer of the product. This results in respondents rating the product higher or lower than they might have if the brand name was unavailable because of their attitudes toward the manufacturer. That makes it difficult to determine whether respondents indeed liked or disliked the product itself. To overcome such bias, letters rather than brand names are often used to label the products presented to respondents. That, in turn, raises

---

[7]Arthur Conan Doyle, "The Sign of the Four," in *The Complete Sherlock Holmes* (Garden City, N.Y.: Garden City Publishing Company, Inc., 1938), p. 94.

[8]Kevin Burns, "TV Viewing Up — Maybe," *Media Message: An Ogilvy & Mather Commentary on Media Issues* (October 1983), pp. 1–7.

the issue of whether the evaluations might be affected by the letters that are used. Research Realities 5.1 describes one of the more extensive investigations of whether respondents might systematically favor products identified by particular letters.

The accompanying figure displays the average mean rating of each letter across the total sample. While not shown, there was a great deal of consistency in the rank order of the letters, although some minor differences exist among the versions. In particular, the top third of the letters are the same in all versions, as are the bottom third. Thus, it appears that the order in which the letters were presented had little effect on the ratings.

With a few notable exceptions, letters near the beginning of the alphabet tended to be rated higher than those near the end. Letters A and B were rated the highest in all versions, and letters U through Z were among the lowest. However, the letters M and S (and, to a lesser extent, L, R, and T) were rated high, and letters F and Q were rated low in all versions.

Because some letters were consistently perceived as being more favorable than others, care should be exercised in the selection of letters as brand labels. Choosing letters that are relatively similar with respect to their ratings may help to minimize bias caused by the product labels. Letters G through P (except L and M) were relatively homogeneous in their ratings. Of course, the letters used should not suggest or appear to be abbreviations for the actual brand names.

Role of the Evidence

We shall see shortly that the controlled experiment provides all three types of evidence of causality. It allows us to check for concomitant variation and time order of occurrence of variables, secure in the fact that if the experiment has been designed correctly, many of the other possible explanations will have been eliminated. However, even in an experiment, not all other explanations will have *necessarily* been eliminated. There is also the possibility that in concluding that *X* caused *Y*, we may have neglected another factor that is associated with *X* and, in fact, caused *Y*. Alternatively, we may be wrong when we conclude that *X* did not cause *Y*, because we have neglected some condition under which *X* is indeed a determiner of *Y*.

The correct posture towards these three types of evidence is that they provide a reasonable basis for believing that *X* is, or is not, a cause of *Y*. We can never be absolutely sure, though, that the relationship has been conclusively demonstrated. Study replication along with knowledge of the problem are fundamental in increasing our confidence in the conclusion. The accumulation of studies pointing to a specific conclusion increases our confidence in its correctness. Similarly, an intimate knowledge of the phenomenon under investigation, in conjunction with a pattern of evidence, serves as a more reasonable basis for interpreting the results of research than does an examination of the evidence by one untrained in the subject matter of concern. Method knowledge is not a substitute for conceptual knowledge.

EXPERIMENTATION

As mentioned, an **experiment** is capable of providing more convincing evidence of causal relationships than are exploratory or descriptive designs. This is why experiments

Using Letters to Identify Products or Brands

To determine if some letters are perceived more favorably than others, Market Facts sent questionnaires to 4,000 households in its Consumer Mail Panel. Each subsample of 1,000 was balanced to be nationally representative with respect to geographic region, population density, age, and income. Approximately 3,000 questionnaires were returned.

The instructions given to the respondents were as follows:

When some people look at different letters of the alphabet, they may feel that certain letters have a more favorable meaning than other letters. For each letter shown below, please check the response that best describes how you feel about any meaning of the letter.

Source: "Using Letters to Identify Products or Brands," *Research on Research*, No. 16 (Chicago: Market Facts, Inc., undated). Reprinted with permission.

The 26 letters were then listed in one of four sequences:

1. Alphabetical order
2. Reverse alphabetical order
3. Random order:
   TJENXBFHZOGPACRWLQKDSIVYMU
4. Reverse random order

The responses available to the respondents were as follows:

Very Favorable	(200)
Somewhat Favorable	(100)
No Meaning	(0)
Somewhat Unfavorable	(−100)
Very Unfavorable	(−200)

The numbers in parentheses are the values assigned to the responses for the analysis of the data (and were not shown to the respondents).

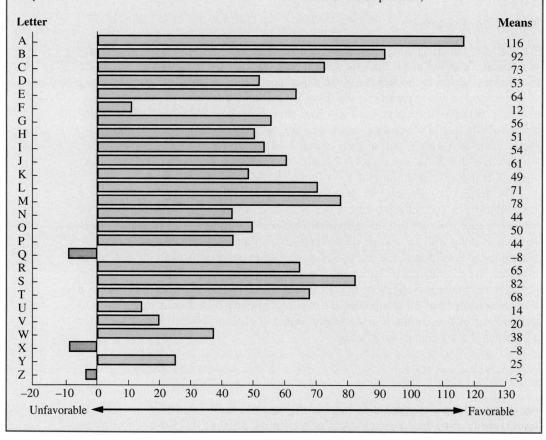

Letter	Means
A	116
B	92
C	73
D	53
E	64
F	12
G	56
H	51
I	54
J	61
K	49
L	71
M	78
N	44
O	50
P	44
Q	−8
R	65
S	82
T	68
U	14
V	20
W	38
X	−8
Y	25
Z	−3

Unfavorable ◄―――――――――――► Favorable

are often called causal research. An experiment has greater ability to supply evidence of causality because of the *control* it affords investigators.

> An *experiment* is taken to mean a scientific investigation in which an investigator manipulates and controls one or more independent variables and observes the dependent variable or variables for variation concomitant to the manipulation of the independent variables. An *experimental design,* then, is one in which the investigator *manipulates* at least one independent variable.[9]

Because investigators are able to control at least some manipulations of the presumed causal factor, they can be more confident that the relationships discovered are "true" relationships.

Both exploratory and descriptive designs are distinguished from **experimental designs** in that they are examples of *ex post facto* research. *Ex post facto* literally means "from what is done afterward." In *ex post facto* research, the criterion variable *Y* is observed. The analyst then attempts to find one or more causal variables, *X*s, which afford plausible explanations as to why *Y* occurred. This kind of retrospective analysis affords little control of the *X*s and therefore contains great potential that the occurrence of *Y* is attributable to some other *X*s than the ones being investigated. One is limited to supplying evidence of concomitant variation in *ex post facto* research. The lack of evidence about the time/order of occurrence of variables and the systematic exclusion of other possible explanations of the phenomenon make such designs suspect for establishing causality.

Laboratory and Field Experiments

Two types of experiments can be distinguished — the laboratory experiment and the field experiment. Because each has its own advantages and disadvantages, research analysts need to be familiar with both.

A **laboratory experiment** is one in which an investigator creates a situation with the desired conditions and then manipulates some variables while controlling others. The investigator is consequently able to observe and measure the effect of the manipulation of the independent variables on the dependent variable or variables in a situation in which the effect of other relevant factors is minimized. A **field experiment** is a research study in a realistic or natural situation, although it, too, involves the manipulation of one or more independent variables under as carefully controlled conditions as the situation will permit. For example, Kmart has learned through numerous field experiments over the years just what kinds of products it should promote in its "blue light specials."[10]

The laboratory experiment is distinguished from the field experiment, then, primarily in terms of environment. The analyst creates a setting for a laboratory experiment,

---

[9]Fred N. Kerlinger, *Foundations of Behavioral Research,* 3rd ed. (New York: Holt, Rinehart and Winston, 1986), p. 293. See also Geoffrey Keppel, *Design and Analysis: A Researcher's Handbook,* 2nd ed. (Englewood Cliffs, N.J.: Prentice-Hall, 1982), especially Chapter 1 for a description of the essential ingredients in experiments.

[10]Melinda Grenier Guiles, "Attention Shoppers: Stop that Browsing and Get Aggressive," *The Wall Street Journal* (June 16, 1987), pp. 1, 17.

whereas a field experiment is conducted in a natural setting. The distinction is not always a clear one, since it is more one of degree than of kind, as both involve control and manipulation of one or more presumed causal factors. The degree of control and precision afforded by each type varies, however.[11] A specially designed or artificial situation provides more control.

The distinction can perhaps best be made by seeing how each is used to investigate the effects of the same causal variable. Price is particularly interesting in this regard, as a number of laboratory and field experiments have investigated the effect of price on the quantity sold. The following investigation was designed to ascertain the closeness with which the price-demand estimates generated in a laboratory experiment correspond to the estimates generated in a field experiment.[12]

The laboratory experiment consisted of a set of simulated shopping trips. In each, subjects chose the brand they preferred to purchase from a full assortment of prepriced brands of cola and coffee. The relative prices of the different brands were changed for each of the eight simulated purchase trips for each subject. These price changes were communicated to each subject by index cards listing the available brands and their corresponding prices.[13] Each subject was free to switch brands to obtain the best product for the money. The trial purchase was not unlike an actual purchase in this respect. These simulated shopping trips were administered in the homes of a systematic sample of 135 homemakers in a small town in Illinois. The laboratory experiment followed a field experiment also designed to test the effect of price on the demand for different brands of cola and coffee.

The prices of the brands were also manipulated in the field experiment. The field experiment was conducted in two small towns in Illinois, ten miles apart. The manipu-

---

[11]Laboratory and field experiments typically play complementary roles in providing managerially useful marketing information. For a discussion of their respective roles, see Alan G. Sawyer, Parker M. Worthing, and Paul E. Sendak, "The Role of Laboratory Experiments to Test Marketing Strategies," *Journal of Marketing,* 43 (Summer 1979), pp. 60–67. For discussion of the increasing use of lab experiments by economists to test their theories of marketplace behavior, see Jerry E. Bishop, "Lab Experiments Test Old Economic Rules, Raising New Questions," *The Wall Street Journal* (November 25, 1986), pp. 1, 24.

[12]John R. Nevin, "Using Controlled Experiments to Estimate and Analyze Brand Demand," unpublished Ph.D. dissertation, University of Illinois, 1972. See also John R. Nevin, "Laboratory Experiments for Estimating Consumer Demand: A Validation Study," *Journal of Marketing Research,* 11 (August 1974), pp. 261–268. Another area in which laboratory and field experiments have been used to examine the same phenomenon is comparative advertising. See George E. Belch, "An Examination of Comparative and Noncomparative Television Commercials: The Effects of Claim Variation and Repetition on Cognitive Response and Message Acceptance," *Journal of Marketing Research,* 18 (August 1981), pp. 333–349; and William R. Swinyard, "The Interaction between Comparative Advertising and Copy Claim Variation," *Journal of Marketing Research,* 18 (May 1981), pp. 175–186. For comparison of consumer choice processes in a laboratory versus an actual grocery store, see Raymond R. Burke, Barbara E. Kahn, and Leonard M. Lodish, "Comparing Dynamic Consumer Choice in Real and Computer-Simulated Environments," *Journal of Consumer Research,* 19 (June 1992), pp. 71–82.

[13]The laboratory experiment also included a paired-preference experiment. The paired-preference experiment required each subject to make preference choices among all possible pairs of brands in a single-merchandise classification with each brand listed at its regular price. Subjects were also asked to indicate how much the price of the preferred brand would have to increase before they would switch to the original nonpreferred brand.

lations here, though, involved actual changes in price for the respective brands. Four supermarkets were used in all, two from each town. Two units in one town were designated as control stores, where the price of each brand was maintained at its regular level throughout the experiment. In the experimental town, the prices were systematically varied in the two stores during the experiment. Prices were marked on the package of each brand to be clearly visible but not conspicuous. After each price change, a cooling-off period was introduced to offset any surplus accumulated by consumers. The effect of the price change was monitored by recording weekly sales for each brand. This allowed brand market shares for each price condition to be determined. No displays, special containers, or other devices were used to draw consumer attention to the fact that the relative prices of the brands had been altered. All other controllable factors were also held as constant as possible.

Note the distinction between the two studies. In the field experiment, no attempt was made to set up special conditions. The situation was accepted as found, and manipulation of the experimental variable — price — was imposed in this natural environment. The laboratory experiment, on the other hand, was contrived. Subjects were told to behave as if they were actively shopping for the product. The prices of the respective brands were varied for each of these simulated shopping trips. Whereas the simulated shopping trips generated reasonably valid estimates of consumers' reactions to "real life" (field experiment) price changes for brands of cola, they produced relatively invalid estimates for brands of coffee, because they tended to overstate the effects of the price changes.[14]

Internal and External Validity

There are certain advantages and disadvantages that result from the different procedure in the two types of experiments. The laboratory experiment typically has greater internal validity because of the greater control it affords. To the extent that we are successful in eliminating the effects of other factors that may obscure or confound the relationships under study, either by physically holding these other factors constant or by allowing for them statistically, we may conclude that the observed effect was due to the manipulation of the experimental variable. That is, we may conclude that the experiment is internally

---

[14]Nevin, "Laboratory Experiments," p. 266. In a related study, Stout compared the ability of three techniques to estimate price-quantity relationships for four different products: (1) a field or in-store experiment in which different prices were employed in different stores; (2) a laboratory experiment in which homemakers were asked to go through a trailer set up as a "store" and to select products as if they were on a regular shopping trip; and (3) personal interviews in which homemakers were interviewed on their way to the store, were shown different products at the different prices, and were asked what purchases they would make if they saw the same items while on an actual shopping trip. Only the in-store experiment produced the expected negative relationship between price and quantity for all four products and relationships that were statistically significant. Neither the laboratory experiment nor the personal interviews produced results similar to the in-store test. Roy G. Stout, "Developing Data to Estimate Price-Quantity Relationships," *Journal of Marketing,* 33 (April 1969), pp. 34–36. For a general review of the evidence regarding the investigation of the price-demand relationship, see Vithala R. Rao, "Pricing Research in Marketing: The State of the Art," *Journal of Business,* 57 (January 1984), pp. 539–560.

valid. Thus, **internal validity** refers to our ability to attribute the effect that was observed to the experimental variable and not to other factors. In the pricing experiment, internal validity focused on the need to obtain data demonstrating that the variation in the criterion variable—brand demanded—was the result of exposure to the treatment or experimental variable—relative price of the brand—rather than other factors, such as advertising, display space, store traffic, and so on. These other factors were nonexistent in the simulated shopping trip.

Whereas the laboratory experiment is generally believed to be more internally valid, the field experiment is typically more externally valid.[15] **External validity** focuses on the problems of collecting data that demonstrate that the changes in the criterion variable observed in the experiment as a result of changes in the predictor variables can be expected to occur in other situations. Can the effect be generalized? Because laboratory experiments are more artificial than field experiments, it is questionable whether the results can be generalized to other populations and settings.[16] In the simulated shopping trip, no real purchase takes place. Further, we may suppose that the experimenter's calling attention to the price may induce people to be more price conscious than they would be in a supermarket.[17] They may attempt to act more "rationally" than they normally would. Further, those who agreed to participate in the laboratory experiment may not be representative of the larger population of shoppers, either because the location of the study was atypical or because those who willingly participate in such a study may be systematically different from those who decline to participate. This would seriously jeopardize the external validity of the findings.

The example in Research Realities 5.2 illustrates the difference between internal and external validity. Internal validity addresses the questions of whether the auto editor of the *Boston Globe* actually experienced a 25 percent increase in miles per gallon, and if he did, whether the improvement could be attributed to using Tufoil in the crankcase. External validity refers to whether that result could be generalized to other drivers, other cars, and other situations.

---

[15]Cook and Campbell distinguish four types of validity: (1) statistical conclusion, (2) internal, (3) construct, and (4) external. Their definitions of internal and external validity parallel ours. Statistical conclusion validity addresses the extent and statistical significance of the covariation that exists in the data; construct validity examines the operations used in the experiment and attempts to assess whether they indeed capture the construct they were supposed to measure. We will have more to say on construct validity in the measurement chapters and statistical conclusion validity in the analysis chapters. Thomas D. Cook and Donald T. Campbell, *Quasi-Experimentation: Design and Analysis Issues for Field Settings* (Chicago: Rand McNally College Publishing Company, 1979), pp. 37–94.

[16]For a general discussion of how the usefulness of experimental results is affected by the researcher's treatment of unmanipulated background factors in the experiment, see John G. Lynch, Jr., "On the External Validity of Experiments in Consumer Research," *Journal of Consumer Research,* 9 (December 1982), pp. 225–244.

[17]Mark I. Alpert, *Pricing Decisions* (Glenview, Ill.: Scott, Foresman, 1971), p. 104. Chapter 4 on "Demand Curve Estimation" discusses in more detail the use of the laboratory experiment and field experiment in estimating price-quantity relationships. See also Sidney J. Bennett and J. B. Wilkinson, "Price-Quality Relationships and Price Elasticity Under In-Store Experimentation," *Journal of Business Research,* 2 (1974), pp. 27–38; Kent B. Monroe, *Pricing: Making Profitable Decisions* (New York: McGraw-Hill, 1979); Kent B. Monroe and William B. Dodd, "A Research Program for Establishing the Validity of the Price-Quality Relationship," *Journal of the Academy of Marketing Science,* 16 (Spring 1988), pp. 151–168.

Research Realities 5.2

Illustration of Internal and External Validity

Some technical breakthroughs sound too good to be true. With so many new devices and gadgets on the market that purport to save fuel, for example, it can be difficult to tell an effective product from a fraud.

The case of Tufoil, a popular motor-oil additive that's supposed to improve a car's gasoline mileage an average 10% to 20%, shows how difficult making a judgment can be.

. . . Tufoil's basic technology is a suspension of tiny particles of Teflon-like materials that reduces friction. Dudley Fuller and Glenn Rightmire, engineering professors at Columbia University, say the technology "shows promise." At the request of *The Wall Street Journal,* they read Tufoil's patent description and other technical documents.

. . . Tufoil has had rave reviews in several newspapers. In May, the *New York Times* cited testimonials from police departments and race-car drivers, and concluded: "Tufoil apparently does just what it says it does." The *Boston Globe's* auto editor wrote about a test he did on his own car.

"It worked!" wrote the editor. "We have good records on the car. We have kept track of every dime spent and every drop of gas put into it." With Tufoil in the crankcase, he said, the car got 12.5 miles to the gallon, compared with 10 before. Said the editor, "That's a 25% increase."

So it is. But tests performed by consumers, even those who are as expert as racers and auto editors, generally prove little. "There's a placebo effect," says William Haynes, an attorney for the Federal Trade Commission. "If you put a product in your car that you think will improve gas mileage, you may subconsciously change your driving habits."

Changes in temperature and humidity can alter a car's mileage significantly, too. "There are just so many variables" in such tests, Mr. Haynes says, that the only way to be certain is to test a product in a laboratory on a number of cars hooked to a dynamometer, an apparatus that measures engine power. Other authorities say dynamometer tests should be supplemented by tests on whole fleets of cars on the road, in which none of the drivers knows if the car has the product.

. . . This summer, the Energy Department finally ran limited dynamometer tests on Tufoil and other products, including three special motor oils made by major oil companies. Fuel economy improved 2.8% to 5% for Tufoil, 4.1% for Arco Graphite and 3.6% for Mobil 1; Exxon Uniflo made no difference. Mr. Reick believes the results for Tufoil were low because the car was a small four-cylinder Pontiac. But an Energy Department engineer involved in the tests says a 5% improvement is impressive for a lubricant.

Double-digit savings from additives don't make sense, other experts say. Peter Hutchins, who tests energy-saving devices for the Environmental Protection Agency, says only about 25% to 30% of the energy in a typical automobile engine is lost to friction. Thus, he reasons, "even if you eliminate all the friction in an engine — which is impossible — the best you could hope for is about a 25% improvement in fuel economy."

That's true for most cars, concedes Mr. Reick. But he insists Tufoil can work wonders in engines with acute friction caused by sticking piston rings and other problems.

Meanwhile, the Federal Trade Commission is complaining about some of Tufoil's advertising claims. The agency questions such language in Tufoil brochures as "average 10% to 20% better mileage," and "fully guaranteed and insured."

Though Mr. Reick bristles at the FTC criticisms, he also concedes he has "reservations" about some of the techniques being used to promote Tufoil. Indeed, if he could have his way, he would avoid the business end of Tufoil's operation: "I'd just stay in my lab in my garage and invent things."

Source: Paul Blustein, "Fuel-Saver Additive Gets Raves, but Claims Are Tougher to Prove," *The Wall Street Journal* (August 29, 1980), p. 15. Reprinted by permission of *The Wall Street Journal,* © Dow Jones & Company, Inc. 1980. All Rights Reserved Worldwide. For discussion of the controversy surrounding the claims of other devices for autos to save fuel and to reduce undesirable exhaust emissions, see Gregory A. Patterson, "Unusual Claims About Magnets Attract Suits," *The Wall Street Journal* (September 24, 1991), pp. B1–B2.

The distinction between internal validity and external validity is an important one, in that the controls needed for each often conflict. A control or procedure required to establish internal validity will often jeopardize representativeness, and vice versa for reasons that should become obvious from the discussion that follows of the various types of experimental designs and the account they take of extraneous influences. Both internal and external validity are matters of degree rather than all-or-nothing propositions.

ETHICAL DILEMMA 5.1

The promotions manager of a soft drink company asks you to help him run an experiment to determine whether he should start advertising in cinemas showing "R," "X," and higher-rated movies. He explains that he has read a journal article indicating that viewers' responses to upbeat commercials are more favorable if the commercials follow very arousing film clips, and he believes that his soft drink commercial will stimulate more sales of the drink in the cinema if it follows previews of very violent or erotic films, such as are shown before the main feature film.

- If you ran a laboratory experiment for this client, what kinds of manipulations would you use, and what are the ethical issues involved in their use?
- Is it feasible to run a field experiment, and would the ethical issues change if a field experiment were run rather than a laboratory experiment?
- If you found that increasing viewers' arousal levels did indeed make them more favorably disposed toward products advertised through upbeat commercials, what are the ultimate ethical implications for influencing television programming?

EXPERIMENTAL DESIGN

A common terminology will facilitate the discussion of the basic types of experimental designs.[18]

Let *X* refer to the exposure of an individual or group to an experimental treatment; an *experimental treatment* is the alternative whose effects are to be measured and compared. The experimental variables may be alternative prices, package designs, advertising themes, or any of a number of other variables. Certainly, the possible experimental treatments in marketing would include all the elements of the marketing mix.

Let *O* refer to the process of observation or measurement of the test units. The *test units* are the individuals or other entities whose responses to the experimental treatments are being

---

[18]The basic symbolism follows Donald T. Campbell and Julian C Stanley, *Experimental and Quasi-Experimental Designs for Research* (Chicago: Rand McNally, 1966). It is also used by Seymour Banks, *Experimentation in Marketing* (New York: McGraw-Hill, 1965).

studied. The test units could be stores, dealers, sales representatives, consumers, or any of the many other entities that serve as objects for a firm's marketing efforts.

Further, let movement through time be represented by a horizontal arrangement of Xs and Os. Thus the symbolic arrangement

$$X \quad O_1 \quad O_2$$

would indicate that one or more test units were exposed to an experimental variable and that their response was then measured at two different points in time. Let a vertical arrangement of Xs and Os reflect simultaneous exposure or measurement of different test units. The symbolic arrangement

$$X_1 \quad O_1$$
$$X_2 \quad O_2$$

would then indicate that there are two different groups of test units; that each group of test units was exposed to a different experimental treatment but at the same time; and that the response of the two groups was also simultaneously measured.

Extraneous Variables

We worry about experimental design because we want to be able to conclude that the observed response was due to our experimental manipulations. The key ingredient affecting our ability to do this is advance planning. In particular, we need to design the study so as to be able to rule out extraneous factors as possible causes. These extraneous factors fall into several categories.

History **History** refers to the specific events, external to the experiment but occurring at the same time, that may affect the criterion or response variable. Suppose that one of the major appliance manufacturers was interested in investigating consumers' price sensitivity in regard to refrigerators. Suppose that the company conceived the following experiment to take place in Gary, Indiana, a big steel-producing center.[19] Refrigerator sales at regular prices would be monitored for a four-week period. Then the price of all units would be cut 10 percent and these sales monitored for four weeks. The measure of price sensitivity would derive from comparing per-week sales at the lower price with per-week sales at the higher price. The experiment would be diagrammed as

$$O_1 \quad X \quad O_2.$$

---

[19]The experiment is admittedly bad. The issue was purposely presented this way to demonstrate the history effect more vividly.

Now suppose that soon after the price reduction, the union contract with the steel industry expired, and there was a strike. What do you think would happen to refrigerator sales? Since major appliance purchases are usually postponable, it could be expected that there would be fewer sales at the lower price than at the higher one. Would we therefore conclude that the demand curve for refrigerators is upward sloping — that is, the higher the price, the greater the number of units that could be sold? Obviously not, for we know that there were extenuating circumstances in the experiment that caused the observed aberration.

Unfortunately, the effects of history on a research conclusion are rarely so obvious. There are always a great many variables that can and do affect what we observe and whose effect is subtle and hidden. What we need is some way of isolating the effects of history, as we are rarely in a position to physically control it. This is particularly true in the field experiment, because laboratory experiments often give us some control in this regard.

Maturation   Although similar to history, **maturation** specifically refers to changes occurring within the test units that are not due to the effect of the experimental variable but result from the passage of time. Thus, when the test units are people, maturation refers to the fact that people get older, become tired, or perhaps become hungry. Measured changes in attitude toward a product, for example, may occur simply because people have become older while using the product and not because of the reinforcement advertising to which they were exposed. Similarly, it may turn out that individuals who belong to a consumer panel changed their consumption of our brand over time not because of any changes in our marketing strategy but simply because of some change in them. They matured, so to speak, in that their tastes changed, or perhaps their marital status or family status changed.

Maturation effects are not limited to test units composed of people. Organizations also change. Dealers grow, become more successful, diversify, and so on. Stores change. Store traffic increases, its composition changes, the store's physical makeup decays; and then the store is perhaps renovated.

Of course, the type of maturation effect depends on the timing of the specific experiment in question. It would be hard to justify the argument that the people whose response was measured changed significantly as a result of, say, age maturation in an experiment that lasted a week. On the other hand, if the interview securing their responses lasted a couple of hours, they could very well have grown tired or have become hurried for some reason; for example, their spouses will be home from work in one-half hour and they have not yet started preparing dinner. Thus, their responses to the later questions may differ from those to the former simply because their own personal situation has changed, and for no other reason.

Testing   The **testing effect,** which can be of two types, is concerned with the fact that the process of experimentation itself may affect the observed response. The *main testing effect* is the effect of a prior observation on a later observation. For example, students taking achievement and intelligence tests for the second time usually do better than those taking the tests for the first time, even though the second test is given without any information about the scores or items missed in the first one.[20] The first administration in and of itself is responsible for the improvement. In many situations, this main testing effect will manifest itself in respondents' desire to be consistent. Thus, in successive administrations of an attitude questionnaire, respondents reply in a consistent manner even though there has been some change in their attitudes. Alternatively, in a single administration, they answer later questions so that their replies parallel their replies to similar early questions as best they can recall them; that is, their responses to the latter part of the questionnaire are not made independently but are conditioned by their responses to the early questions.

The main testing effect may also be reactive; there are very few things in social science, that can be measured, in which the process of measurement does not itself change what is being measured. The very fact that persons report their attitudes to someone else may change those attitudes. Similarly, the very fact that a person is a member of a consumer panel that reports purchasing behavior may change that person's purchasing behavior.

There is also an *interactive testing effect,* which means that a prior measurement affects the test unit's response to the experimental variable. People who are asked to indicate their attitudes toward Chevrolet may become much more aware of the Chevrolet ads than those who are not queried. Yet if we are interested in the attitude impact of the ads, we are interested in their effect on the population as a whole and not simply on those individuals composing our sample.

The results of the two testing effects are different. The main effect manifests itself in the relation between observations and can be depicted as

$$O_1 \quad X \quad O_2$$

that is, the process of measurement O_1 in turn affects the measurement O_1 or the later measurement O_2. The interactive testing effect, on the other hand, can be diagrammed as

$$O_1 \quad X \quad O_2$$

that is, the process of measurement O_1 results in some change in the test unit's reaction to the experimental stimulus. The distinction is an important one, because the main testing effect usually exerts its greatest impact on the internal validity of an experiment, whereas the interactive testing effect most typically affects the external validity of a conclusion.

Instrument Variation Any and all changes in measuring instruments that might account for differences in measurements are referred to as **instrument variation.** The

---

[20]Campbell and Stanley, *Experimental and Quasi-Experimental Designs,* p. 9.

change may occur in the instrument itself, or it may result from variations in its administration. When there are many observers or interviewers, there can be significant instrument variations, because it is difficult indeed to ensure that all the interviewers will ask the same questions with the same voice inflections, with the same probes, with the same rapport, and so on. Thus, the recorded differences between the awareness level of, say, two respondents may not actually reflect a true difference in awareness but rather a difference that arose because each interviewer handled the interview slightly differently. Of course, the same thing can occur with interviews conducted by the same interviewer. It is highly unlikely that each situation will be handled in exactly the same way. Interviewers may become more adept at eliciting the desired responses, or they may become bored with the project and tired of interviewing. In either case, part of the difference in the reported scores will be due to the way each assignment is handled.

The measuring instrument may also undergo some modification during the course of an investigation. Modifications may be major or minor. If major (for example, a completely new set of attitude statements), the responses to each questionnaire would probably be analyzed separately. Sometimes, though, a minor modification is needed, such as a slight change in wording of a specific question that makes it more understandable without changing its meaning. Although slight, this kind of change could cause variations in the reported answers, and the analyst is well advised to be aware of this.

Statistical Regression   The tendency of extreme cases of a phenomenon to move closer to the average during the course of experiment is called **statistical regression.** The test units may be extreme by happenstance, or they may have been specifically selected because of their extreme positions. For example, people may be chosen for investigation because they exhibit extreme behavior, say, in their alcohol consumption. Suppose a consumer panel is formed of these test units. It is likely that in subsequent monitoring, their *reported* alcohol intake would be closer to the average.

Alternatively, a cross-sectional study investigating the use of one brand of orange juice might reveal several families who used ten cans in a week. This may be because they had house guests, and thus it would not be surprising that in a subsequent observation their orange juice consumption would be more typical.

There is always some variation in behavior, attitudes, knowledge, and so on, and it stands to reason that the most extreme cases of the phenomenon have the most room in which to vary. Statistical regression is concerned with the occurrence of this phenomenon.[21]

Selection Bias   Sometimes bias arises from the way in which test units are selected and assigned in an experiment. **Selection bias** is said to be in evidence when there is no way of certifying that groups of test units were equivalent before being tested.

The following example typifies the problem of selection bias. "Many say the President has at least convinced them that the energy crisis is real or that the problems are

---

[21]For discussion of its effects on panel data, see Huik van de Stadt and Tom Wanskeek, "Regression Effects in Tabulating from Panel Data," *Journal of Official Statistics,* 6 (No. 3, 1990), pp. 311–317.

more serious than they thought. In an Associated Press–NBC poll last week, 60% of those who heard the President's speech agreed that there is a world-wide crisis, while 46% of those who didn't hear the speech believe the crisis is real.''[22] The fallacy in the argument is that there is no way of determining if those who saw the President's speech had similar attitudes, before viewing, to those who did not see it. What typically occurs is that exposure to some mass communication has been voluntary, and thus the exposed and unexposed groups inevitably possess a systematic difference on the factors determining the choice. Republicans listen to the speeches of Republican candidates; Democrats listen to those of Democratic candidates; those who have a favorable attitude toward a product pay more attention to the product's ads; and so on. If we are to conclude that exposure to the experimental stimulus (TV special, speech, ad, and so on) was responsible for the observed effect, we must somehow ensure that the comparison groups were equal before exposure.

The prior equality of comparison groups is established in two main ways: matching and randomization. Suppose there are twenty stores in total, ten to be designated for an experimental group and ten for a control group, and suppose that an experiment is designed to examine the effect of a special aisle display on sales of, say, ketchup. Now, we would certainly expect the sales of ketchup in any store to be associated with the store's traffic. We could, therefore, be far off in our conclusion if we somehow ended up with most of the large stores in one group and most of the small stores in the other group. To prevent this, we could consider matching the stores according to some external criterion, such as annual sales or square feet of floor space, and then assign one store from each matched pair to each group.

Alternatively, we could assign the twenty stores at random to each of the groups, using a table of random digits. In general, randomization is the preferred procedure in assuring the prior equality of the comparison groups.[23] First, it is hard to match test units on any but a few characteristics, so the test units may be equal in terms of the variables chosen but unequal in terms of others. In addition, if the matched characteristic is not an important determinant of the response, the researcher has wasted time and money in matching the test units. The general principle is as follows: ''Whenever it is possible to do so, randomly assign subjects to experimental groups and conditions and randomly assign conditions and other factors to experimental groups.''[24] Randomization does not play its usually productive role when the sample of test units is small, because randomization only produces groups that are ''equal on the average'' when the sample is large enough to allow the positive and negative deviations about the average to balance.

---

[22]''For Most Americans Saving Energy Isn't a Patriotic Principle,'' *The Wall Street Journal* (July 23, 1979), p. 1. A similar, and very common, instance of selection bias when studying marketing phenomena occurs when evaluating the impact of advertising. A typical argument for a successful campaign centers around how those who claim they saw ads for the company's products feel versus those who do not remember seeing the ads. For an example, see Joseph B. White, ''GM's New Ad Campaign Puts a Shine On Its Image — but Not Yet a Deep One,'' *The Wall Street Journal* (October 8, 1990), pp. B1, B7.

[23]See Kerlinger, *Foundations,* pp. 288–289, for a general discussion of the pros and cons associated with matching.

[24]*Ibid.,* p. 288.

With small samples, matching becomes a complement to, and not a substitute for, randomization, in that matched test units should then be randomly assigned to treatment conditions.[25]

Experimental Mortality   The loss of test units during the course of an experiment is called **experimental mortality.** It is a problem because there is no way of knowing if the test units that were lost would have responded to the experimental stimulus in the same way as those that were retained.

Consider again the special aisle display and ketchup sales example. Suppose that during the course of the experiment, two managers of stores in the experimental group decided to use the display for another product. This would reduce the number of experimental stores to eight, and even though our major interest would be on average store sales in the experimental group in comparison to average store sales in the control group, we would have no way of knowing if this average would have been higher or lower if the two dropout stores had continued participating. We *cannot* simply *assume* that their sales would have been like those in the other experimental stores. They might have been, but again they might have been vastly different. The problem with experimental mortality, as with all of these other extraneous sources of variation, is not that they have indeed operated but rather that we *do not know whether or not they have operated* and whether or not they have affected the criterion variable. The key then becomes one of designing investigations so that this doubt can be eliminated.

SPECIFIC DESIGNS

Three types of experimental designs are commonly distinguished: preexperimental designs, true experimental designs, and quasi-experimental designs.[26] True experimental designs are the most effective in eliminating the doubt that can arise in interpreting research results, as they provide the most control over the various extraneous factors. Unfortunately, not all marketing problems allow the use of true experimental designs. An understanding of their features, though, should allow a more scientific interpretation of the results, with due allowance for the necessary caveats when preexperimental or quasi-experimental designs are used.

Preexperimental Designs

A preexperimental design is distinguished by the fact that the researcher has very little control over both the *when* and the *to whom* of exposure to experimental stimuli and over the *when* and *to whom* of measurement.

---

[25]Cook and Campbell suggest that "perhaps the best way of reducing the error due to differences between persons is to match *before* random assignment to treatments" with the best matching variables being those "that are most highly correlated with posttest scores." *Quasi-Experimentation*, p. 47.

[26]See Campbell and Stanley, *Experimental and Quasi-Experimental Designs*, for an extensive discussion of the three types.

The One-Shot Case Study   A useful point of departure for discussing experiments is the one-shot case study. The one-shot case study can be diagrammed

$$X \qquad O.$$

A single group of test units is exposed to an experimental variable, and its response is observed once. There is no random allocation of test units in the group; rather, the group is self-selected or is selected arbitrarily by the experimenter. For example, we might interview a convenience sample of those who read a particular trade journal for their reaction to our product. The experimental stimulus here would be the ad.

The one-shot case study is of little value in establishing the validity of hypothesized causal relationships (the ad was responsible for creating a favorable attitude toward our product) because it provides too little control over the extraneous influences. It provides no basis for comparing what happened in the presence of X with what happened when X was absent. Yet the minimum demands of scientific inquiry require that such comparisons be made.

The one-shot case study is more appropriate for exploratory than conclusive research. It is appropriately used to suggest hypotheses; it is not appropriate for testing their validity.

The One-Group Pretest–Posttest Design   The one-group pretest–posttest design

$$O_1 \qquad X \qquad O_2$$

adds a pretest to the one-shot case study design. In effect, the convenience sample of designated respondents is interviewed for their attitudes toward our product before the ad is placed. They are also interviewed after the ad is run, and the effectiveness of the ad is taken as the difference in their attitudes before and after exposure to the ad:

$$d = O_2 - O_1.$$

Although widely used to argue the effectiveness of marketing strategies, the one-group pretest–posttest design's failure to control extraneous error nullifies its conclusions. Consider just some of the factors that might be responsible for the $O_2 - O_1$ difference, aside from the experimental variable X. First, history is uncontrolled. There may have been other ads, trade journal articles, some firsthand experience with the product, or any of a host of other factors occurring simultaneously with the experiment that caused the attitude change observed in a particular respondent. The respondent's position may have changed. Because of a change in the individual's status, the respondent may have been more responsive to the product in question at O_2 than at O_1 (maturation). Both the interactive and main testing effects might be at work. Because respondents were interviewed to secure O_1, they paid more attention to the trade journal ad than the normal reader might (interactive testing effect), so the $O_2 - O_1$ difference cannot be generalized to the population of interest. In addition, respondents might attempt to appear consistent with their O_1 score (main testing effect). Perhaps the respondents' initial responses created an extreme attitude score in either a positive or negative direction; then statistical regression is likely to have occurred with the O_2 scores. Suppose there is some experimental mortality. Would the $O_2 - O_1$ difference have been larger or smaller if the lost participants were included? We do not know. Further, the sample was a convenience sample, and the result probably could not be generalized to the larger population. Even if the intial sample had been a probability sample, all of the other extraneous sources of error could still have affected the results.

The Static-Group Comparison   The static-group comparison is a design in which there are two groups, one that has experienced X and another that has not. A key feature is that the groups have not been created by randomization. The static-group comparison is diagrammed

$$\text{EG:} \quad X \qquad O_1$$

$$\text{CG:} \qquad\qquad O_2.$$

To continue with our previous example of the effectiveness of a particular ad, the static-group comparison would be conducted as follows: After the ad is run, interviews would be conducted among a sample of readers. Those who remembered seeing the ad would be considered the "experimental group," EG. Those who did not recall seeing the ad would be considered the "control group," CG. The attitudes of each group toward the product would be measured, and the effectiveness of the ad would be taken to be

$$d = O_1 - O_2,$$

that is, the difference in attitudes between those seeing the ad and those not seeing it.

There are two fundamental sources of extraneous error in the static-group comparison. First, there is no way of ensuring that the groups were equivalent prior to the comparison. Those who have favorable attitudes toward a product often pay more attention to ads for the product than those who have unfavorable attitudes. It may be that the $O_1 - O_2$ difference reflects the initial attitude of the two groups and is not in any way attributable to the ad.

The second fundamental weakness of the static-group comparison involves its representativeness. It may be that the two groups were indeed equal at some previous time. Now, however, not all individuals contacted are willing to supply their attitudes toward the product. The design suffers experimental mortality as a result of this nonresponse, since the question of what the O_2 and O_1 scores would have been if all those designated to participate had indeed cooperated is unanswered.

True Experimental Designs

Randomization makes the data from true experimental designs more valid than data from any preexperimental design. The true experimental design is distinguished by the fact that the experimenter can randomly assign treatments to randomly selected test units. In effect, the experimenter can control the *when* and *to whom* of exposure. The experimenter can also control the *when* and *to whom* of measurement. To distinguish the true experiment, let us denote a random assignment of test units to treatments by (R).

Before–After with Control Group Design   The before–after with control group design was considered an experimental ideal for a number of years. The design can be diagrammed

$$EG: \quad (R) \quad O_1 \quad X \quad O_2$$

$$CG: \quad (R) \quad O_3 \qquad O_4.$$

Although it diagrams quite simply, this design imposes a number of requirements on the researcher. First, the division of the test units is under the researcher's control. The researcher alone is able to decide which test units will receive the experimental stimulus and which will not. It is *not* up to the test units to self-select whether they will be members of the control or experimental groups, as they did in the preexperimental designs. Further, the experimenter cannot arbitrarily assign test units to the experimental and control groups. He or she must do this randomly. The experimenter may match the test units on some external criterion and then assign one member from each of the matched pairs to the experimental and control groups, but this final assignment is made randomly. Finally, each of the test units in both groups is measured before and after the introduction of the experimental stimulus.

Consider the problem faced by an in-house credit union in promoting the credit union idea among the company's workers. Suppose that the company is considering the effectiveness of a rather expensive brochure, ''Know Your Credit Union,'' in creating awareness and understanding of the functioning of the credit union. Let the brochure be the experimental stimulus X. The use of the before–after with control group design to investigate the effectiveness of the brochure would proceed along the following lines: First, a sample of the firm's employees would be selected at random; second, one-half of these employees would be randomly assigned to the experimental group receiving the brochure, while the other half would form the control group; third, each of the respondents selected for the sample would be measured, using some scale or questionnaire to ascertain the employee's knowledge of the credit union; and fourth, the brochure would be mailed to those respondents who were designated for the experimental group.[27] After the lapse of some appropriate time interval (say, one to two weeks), the knowledge scale or questionnaire would again be administered to each of the sample respondents.

Now consider this design in terms of the various sources of extraneous error. The difference O_4 minus O_3 reflects the effects of the extraneous influences. For instance, consider the possibility that during the course of the experiment there was a change in

---

[27]The brochure would be mailed if that were the normal way of distributing it. If some other method of distribution were commonly used, the experimental procedure would also follow this mode of distribution.

the bank prime lending rate and credit became more expensive. This history effect would be partially responsible for any differences in O_4 and O_3. However, it would also exert a similar influence on those belonging to the experimental group. Thus, if we were to consider the effect of the experimental variable to be E and the effect of these extraneous or uncontrolled sources of variation to be U, the impact of the experimental stimulus X could be secured as follows:

$$\frac{\begin{array}{ll} O_2 - O_1 & = E + U \\ O_4 - O_3 & = \quad U \end{array}}{(O_2 - O_1) - (O_4 - O_3) = E} \quad .$$

But note that this calculation applies to the following sources of extraneous variation: history, maturation, main testing effect, statistical regression, and instrument variation. All these influences should affect both groups approximately equally. Selection bias, of course, was eliminated by the random assignment of individuals to groups. The design can suffer from experimental mortality, however, if some of the employees designated for the study refuse to participate.

Assuming that proper procedures were employed to eliminate experimental mortality, one can readily appreciate why this design was long considered ideal. But this changed with the discovery that the design may not control for the interactive testing effect. The pretest can make the experimental subjects respond to X, wholly or partially, because they have been sensitized. Yet the key question for credit union management is how employees in general, not just those pretested, respond to the brochure.

The situation in calculating the impact of the experimental stimulus then becomes

$$\frac{\begin{array}{ll} O_2 - O_1 & = E + U + I \\ O_4 - O_3 & = \quad U \end{array}}{(O_2 - O_1) - (O_4 - O_3) = E + I} \quad ,$$

where I measures the interactive effect of testing. The analyst is unable to determine the impact of the experimental stimulus when the interactive effect of testing is present in the before–after with control group design. His or her calculation of the net difference provides a result, but this result has two components — a component due to the experimental stimulus and a component due to the interactive testing effect.

A classic example of the interactive testing effect occurred in a United Nations education campaign.[28] The study employed a sample of 2,000 individuals split into two equivalent groups of 1,000 each. Each member of the first group was interviewed to determine his or her knowledge of and attitudes toward the United Nations. This was followed by a publicity campaign of several months' duration, in turn followed by inter-

---

[28]S. A. Star and H. M. Hughes, "Report on an Educational Campaign: The Cincinnati Plan for the United Nations," *American Journal of Sociology*, 40 (1949–1950), p. 389.

views with the second sample. A comparison of the two sets of scores produced practically no results; the members of the second sample were no better informed and did not have any more favorable attitudes than the first sample. The second sample was not even generally aware that the publicity campaign had been going on. In terms of the population of interest, the campaign was indeed a failure. Yet when the first sample was reinterviewed, there was a decided change in the members' attitudes toward and information about the United Nations. They had been sensitized to watch for and pay more attention to United Nations publicity.[29] The same kind of testing effect can operate in a before–after with control group design.

Four-Group Six-Study Design In many research problems, the prior measurement is of such a nature that the test units are not sensitized to the experiment. In cases such as these, the before–after with control group design provides an estimate of the effect of the experimental variable. When an interactive testing effect is likely to be present, the four-group six-study design is a good choice.

The four-group six-study design can be diagrammed as

$$EG \quad I: \quad (R) \quad O_1 \quad X \quad O_2$$

$$CG \quad I: \quad (R) \quad O_3 \quad \quad O_4$$

$$EG \quad II: \quad (R) \quad \quad X \quad O_5$$

$$CG \quad II: \quad (R) \quad \quad \quad O_6.$$

Consider again the problem of measuring the effect of the "Know Your Credit Union" brochure. The four-group six-study design would impose the following requirements on the researcher. First, a sample of the firm's employees would be selected at random. Second, the sample would be randomly divided into four groups. Those designated for the first experimental and control groups would be measured, using some appropriate instrument, for their knowledge of the credit union. The brochure would then be mailed to those designated as belonging to the first and second experimental groups. Then all four groups would be measured on their knowledge of the credit union. There are thus six measurements in all, as suggested by the name of the design.

One can readily appreciate the control afforded by the four-group six-study design. Selection bias is handled by the random assignment of test units to groups. The other extraneous sources of error are handled much as they were in the before–after with control group design — that is, by making the logical assumption that factors such as history, maturation, and so on should affect all groups. By thus looking at the "difference in differences," the impact of these extraneous factors should be netted out.

---

[29]For a discussion of the procedures that can be used to minimize sensitization effects, see Anthony Greenwald, "Within-Subjects Designs: To Use or Not to Use?" *Psychological Bulletin,* 83 (No. 2) (1976), pp. 314–320.

Further, although there is a possible interactive testing effect with the first experimental group, there can be none with the second experimental group, because there is no prior measurement to sensitize the respondents. The lack of a prior measurement raises the question of how to calculate the effect of X in the second experimental and control groups. One thing that can be done is to estimate what the prior measurements would have been. The most logical estimate is one that takes account of the random assignment of the test units to groups, assuming that, except for sampling variations, the four groups were equal *a priori* in their knowledge of the credit union. Thus, the best estimate of the "before measurement" for the second experimental and control groups is the average of the before measurements actually taken; that is, $\frac{1}{2}(O_1 + O_3)$.

On substituting this estimate, the various differences between after and before measurements are as follows:

$$\text{EG} \quad \text{I:} \quad O_2 - O_1 \qquad\qquad = E + U + I$$

$$\text{CG} \quad \text{I:} \quad O_4 - O_3 \qquad\qquad = \qquad U$$

$$\text{EG} \quad \text{II:} \quad O_5 - \tfrac{1}{2}(O_1 + O_3) = E + U$$

$$\text{CG} \quad \text{II:} \quad O_6 - \tfrac{1}{2}(O_1 + O_3) = \qquad U.$$

What is the impact of the experimental stimulus? Clearly, it is determined by comparing the second experimental and control groups and is given specifically by the calculation

$$[O_5 - \tfrac{1}{2}(O_1 + O_3)] - [O_6 - \tfrac{1}{2}(O_1 + O_3)] = [E + U] - [U] = E.$$

However, that is not the only estimated effect provided by the four-group six-study design. This design also allows the effect of the uncontrolled extraneous factors on the response to be estimated, and it provides for an estimate of the magnitude of the interactive testing effect. Two independent estimates of extraneous error are in fact provided, one by each of the control groups. An estimate of the size of the interactive testing effect is provided by comparing Experimental Groups I and II through the calculation

$$[O_2 - O_1] - [O_5 - \tfrac{1}{2}(O_1 + O_3)] = [E + U + I] - [E + U] = I.$$

One need only look at the estimates of the various effects to appreciate why the four-group six-study design has become a conceptual ideal. Its practical application in marketing is somewhat limited, however, because the design is expensive in terms of time and money.[30] Further, marketing samples are not always so large as to afford the luxury of dividing the samples of test units into four equal groups. If the group samples

---

[30]For an example of its use, see Richard W. Mizerski, Neil K. Allison, and Stephen Calvert, "A Controlled Field Study of Corrective Advertising Using Multiple Exposures and a Commercial Medium," *Journal of Marketing Research*, 17 (August 1980), pp. 341–348.

are small, it is unlikely that they will, in fact, be equal even if assigned randomly. Rather, the equality-of-groups assumption depends on the operation of the statisticians' "law of large numbers." Nevertheless, the isolation of the various effects afforded by the four-group six-study design makes it a standard against which other designs may be compared.

After-Only with Control Group Design   The careful reader will have observed that the researcher can estimate the impact of the experimental stimulus in the four-group six-study design simply by comparing Experimental Group II to Control Group II, which raises the question of why Experimental Group I and Control Group I are included. They are certainly *not* needed to generate an estimate of a "before measurement" for Experimental Group II and Control Group II, because regardless of what this measurement is, it cancels in the basic calculation of the effect of the experimental variable; that is,

$$[O_5 - \tfrac{1}{2}(O_1 + O_3)] - [O_6 - \tfrac{1}{2}(O_1 + O_3)] = O_5 - O_6.$$

Thus, the before measurements are not needed to estimate the effect of the experimental stimulus. They do allow the researcher to study individual cases of change and to develop better methodology, because they enable study of the experimental variable under different conditions. If the researcher's sole interest is estimating the impact of the experimental variable, though, as is often the case, this estimate can be provided by studying the last two groups of the four-group six-study design in an after-only with control group design.

The after-only with control group design can be diagrammed

EG: (R) X O_5

CG: (R) O_6

where the observations have been subscripted with a 5 and 6 to indicate that these groups are the unpretested groups in the four-group six-study design. To use this design to investigate the effect of the "Know Your Credit Union" brochure, the researcher would again select a random sample of employees. One-half would be randomly assigned to the experimental group, and the other half would form the control group. Neither group would be premeasured, and the brochure would be mailed to all those in the experimental group. After some appropriate time lapse, both groups would be measured for their knowledge, and the estimated effect of the brochure would be provided by the difference O_5 minus O_6.

One can readily appreciate how the extraneous sources of error are eliminated in this experiment. The main extraneous factors are assumed to affect both groups, and thus their influence is eliminated by calculating the difference between O_5 and O_6. There is no interactive testing effect since there is no pretest. The experimental test units should behave much like the larger population of employees, in that some might read the brochure carefully, some might read it casually, and some might simply throw it away without reading it. This is as it should be, and the results can therefore be generalized to the population of employees.

There are two very important caveats, though, with respect to the after-only with control group design. This design is very sensitive to problems of selection bias and experimental mortality. The prior equality of the groups is assumed because of the random assignment of test units to groups. There is no before measurement, however, so the assumption cannot be checked. It must be taken on faith, and this faith demands that the assignment of test units to groups was indeed random. Further, the design is highly sensitive to experimental mortality. There is simply no way of determining whether those who refuse to cooperate or drop out of the experimental group are similar to those dropping out of the control group. Experimental mortality, if it exists, calls into question the foundation on which the after-only with control group design rests — namely, that the groups are equal save for the impact of the experimental stimulus.

Be aware that the after-only with control group design does not allow the investigation of individual cases of change. This can sometimes be of real concern. For example, the design would not allow credit union management to investigate the effect of the "Know Your Credit Union" brochure on those who already had a good working knowledge of the credit union versus those who had little awareness and knowledge. The design affords no way of determining an employee's prior knowledge. Both the before–after with control group design and the four-group six-study design are superior in this respect. However, if the individual cases of change are not of interest, the after-only with control group design is a viable one. As a matter of fact, it is probably the most frequently used experimental design in marketing research, because it possesses a number of sample size, cost, and time advantages, involving as it does only two groups and two measurements.

An example of the use of the after-only with control group design is AT&T's experience when investigating the effectiveness of two different advertising appeals. Even though AT&T's "Reach Out" campaign had been quite successful, the company was somewhat disappointed with the amount of long-distance calling by light users of the system. In searching out reasons for the light use, the company discovered through an attitude survey that light users were overestimating the costs of long-distance calls by as much as 50 percent.

> In response, AT&T developed its alternative campaign called "Cost of Visit," which emphasized making use of the economy of "off-peak" hours.
>
> To test this campaign as an alternative to the proven Reach Out theme, AT&T chose to conduct a split-cable experiment. Over 15 months, one group of cable TV subscribers received the Reach Out campaign, while the second group in the same community and watching the same television shows saw the Cost of Visit commercials. AT&T obtained records of telephone use from the telephone company's billing system.
>
> The Cost of Visit strategy produced more long-distance calling during experimentation than the Reach Out strategy, especially among light users. The company estimated that the new copy could generate additional revenue of nearly $100 million over a five-year period at no additional cost to the phone company.[31]

---

[31]Leonard M. Lodish and David Rubstein, "New Gold Mines and Minefields in Market Research," *Harvard Business Review*, 64 (January/February 1986), p. 169.

Quasi-Experimental Designs

We have just seen that the true experimental design is distinguished by the control it affords the researcher. The researcher is able to determine who will be exposed to the experimental stimulus, when the exposure will occur, who will be measured, and when that measurement will take place. In some cases, the investigator simply will not have control of the "when" and "whom" of exposure. The researcher will not be able to schedule the experimental stimuli or randomly assign test units to groups. If the researcher does have control of the "when" and "whom" of measurement, though, a quasi-experimental design results.

There are a number of quasi-experimental designs, although we will discuss only the time-series experiment.[32] The discussion should indicate the emphasis in quasi-experimental designs. The time-series experiment was selected because it is uniquely suited to some types of marketing data that are routinely generated.

Time-Series Experiment The time-series experiment can be diagrammed as

$$O_1 \quad O_2 \quad O_3 \quad O_4 \quad X \quad O_5 \quad O_6 \quad O_7 \quad O_8.$$

This diagram suggests that a group of test units is observed over some time, that an experimental stimulus is introduced, and that the test units are again observed for their reaction. A change in the previous pattern of observations is taken as the effect of the experimental stimulus.[33]

The time-series experiment demands that researchers have repeated access to the same test units. Further, while researchers cannot schedule the exposure of these test units to the experimental stimulus, they can control when the units will be measured. Panel data conform nicely, then, to the time-series experiment. Further, there are a number of panels supplying marketing data routinely. This is why the time-series experiment is one of the most important quasi-experimental designs for the marketing researcher.

Of course, our interest when using the time-series experiment is in establishing that the observed effect is due to the experimental variable. This requires that we eliminate other plausible hypotheses for the occurrence of the phenomenon. Now, the time-series experiment bears some resemblance to the preexperimental one-group pretest–posttest design. The resemblance is superficial, since the series of observations affords additional

---

[32]Campbell and Stanley, *Experimental and Quasi-Experimental Designs,* pp. 36–64, and Banks, *Experimentation in Marketing,* pp. 37–45; both present a number of useful quasi-experimental designs.

[33]Lehmann, for example, reports a natural experiment in which knowledge, attitude, intention to buy, and confidence in judgment were measured at four different points in the time before and after an advertising campaign for a new product. Donald R. Lehmann, "Responses to Advertising a New Car," *Journal of Advertising Research,* 17 (1977), pp. 23–27. For an example of the use of a time-series experiment to evaluate service quality, see James H. Drew and Ruth N. Bolton, "A Longitudinal Analysis of the Impact of Service Changes on Customer Attitudes," *Journal of Marketing,* 55 (January 1991), pp. 1–9.

control. Consider some of the possible patterns of responses that may result, as illustrated in Figure 5.1.

Note first of all that the pattern of responses, rather than any single observation, is key in interpreting the data from a time-series experiment. Consider, say, the impact of a package change, X, on the firm's market share. On the basis of the plot of the data points in Figure 5.1, it would seem logical to conclude that the package change:

1. exerted a positive impact in situation A (it raised the firm's market share);
2. had a positive impact in situation B (it halted a decline in market share);
3. had no long-run impact in situation C (sales in Period 5 seem to be borrowed from sales in Periods 6 and 7);
4. had no impact in situation D (the firm's market share growth remained steady);
5. had no impact in situation E (the observed fluctuation after the introduction of the experimental variable is no greater than what was previously observed).

FIGURE **5.1   Some Possible Outcomes in a Time-Series Experiment When Introducing an Experimental Variable** X

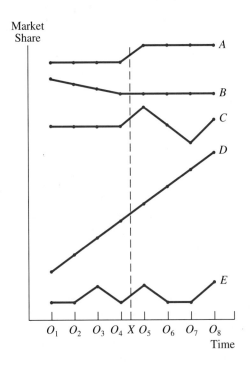

Of course, we would be interested in testing for the statistical significance of any observed changes.

Consider now the additional control afforded by the time-series experiment versus the one-group pretest–posttest design in interpreting the after and before measurements. First, maturation can be partially ruled out as causing the difference in O_5 and O_4 because it is unlikely that it would only operate in this one instance. Rather, it would logically have an effect on a number of other observations. Instrument variation, statistical regression, and the main testing effect would be similarly avoided. Selection bias can be reduced by the random selection of test units. Experimental mortality can, hopefully, be controlled by paying some premium to maintain cooperation. Of course, we saw in Chapter 4 that the ability to solicit and maintain cooperation in panels presents some problems, and a panel may not completely control the problems of selection bias and experimental mortality. These are conditions that also occur in the one-group pretest–posttest preexperimental design.

The failure to control history is the most fundamental weakness of the time-series experiment. Despite this, a carefully executed time-series experiment can provide some useful insight. If the careful examination of, say, consumer panel data before, during, and after introducing the experimental variable fails to turn up any unusual competitive reaction, and if researchers also record other environmental changes as they occur, the researchers are in a position to make a valid assessment of the effect of the experimental stimulus. Of course, researchers can never be as sure that the impact of history has been ruled out in a quasi-experimental design as they can in a true experimental design. However, a repeatable stimulus, such as a cents-off coupon program, will afford greater certainty, because the effect of history will not be the same each time.

Another weakness of the time-series experiment is that it may be influenced by the interactive testing effect. There may be some peculiarity in the experimental stimulus so that it affects only those sampling units subjected to repeated testing.

Experimental versus Nonexperimental Designs

By now you should appreciate that exploratory and descriptive designs are not particularly useful in establishing the existence of causal relationships. They simply do not provide the control necessary to infer that a causal relationship does indeed exist. Exploratory studies are less of a problem in this regard, since they are rarely used to make causal statements. Unfortunately, the same thing cannot be said about descriptive studies. Frequently, the evidence of a cross-sectional survey is employed to argue that X caused Y or the evidence from some time-series data is analyzed using, say, regression analysis to establish X as causing Y.

The error in such arguments can be appreciated by dissecting the typical descriptive study. A random sample of respondents is selected. The respondents are measured with respect to some effect or response variable Y. Next they are queried about the hypothesized causal factor X. If it is then found that those who possess X also possess Y and those who lack X also lack Y, the truth of the assertion that "X causes Y" is established. The research is *ex post facto,* because the researcher is starting with the observation of a dependent or criterion variable and is retrospectively searching for plausible explanations.[34]

A problem arises in descriptive studies with respect to all three types of evidence used to support causality. Concomitant variation is observed. However, there is no way of knowing that those who did and did not possess *Y* were at some prior time equivalent with respect to both *Y* and *X*. In the experiment, the researcher is able to establish this equivalence by the random assignment of test units to groups. The researcher also knows quite accurately who was exposed to *X* and does not have to rely on a respondent's memory. The analyst is thus able to determine whether *Y* occurs more frequently among the subjects who have been exposed to *X* than it does among those who have not.

The researcher is also better able to establish the time order of occurrence of variables in an experiment. The experimental and control groups are set up in such a way that it is reasonable to assume they did not differ in terms of the response variable before exposure to the experimental stimulus. With some experimental designs, the researcher actually measures the test units with respect to the criterion variable before exposing them to the experimental stimulus. In descriptive studies, the researcher simply has to assume that prior equality exists.

The descriptive study affords little control in eliminating other possible explanations. All the factors that affect experimental results also operate in descriptive research, but the analyst has no way of removing their effects. The analyst ends up in the awkward position of asserting it is this *X* and no other *X* that is causing *Y*. This assertion rests on a great deal of faith.

ETHICAL DILEMMA 5.2

The regional sales manager for a large chain of men's clothing stores asks you to establish whether increasing his salespeople's commission will result in better sales performance. Specifically, he wants to know whether increasing the commission on limited lines of clothing will result in better sales on those lines along with the penalty of fewer sales on the remaining lines, and whether raising the commission on all lines will produce greater sales on all lines. Suppose that you think that the best way to investigate the issue is through a field experiment in which some salespeople receive increased commission on a single line, others receive increased commission across the board, and still others make up a control group whose members receive no increase in commission.

- Are there ethical problems inherent in such a design?
- Is the control group being deprived of any benefits?

---

[34]Kerlinger, *Foundations*, pp. 347–360, has a particularly illuminating discussion of the problems of interpretation in *ex post facto* research.

This is not to deny the important role played by descriptive designs in marketing research. They are, after all, the dominant form. Rather, the reader must be aware of the dangers of using descriptive designs to establish causal linkages between variables.

EXPERIMENTATION IN MARKETING RESEARCH

Experiments in marketing were rare before 1960, but their growth since then has been steady. One of the most important growth areas has been in market testing, or test marketing.[35] Although some writers make a distinction between the terms, the essential feature of the **market test** is that "it is a controlled experiment, done in a limited but carefully selected part of the marketplace, whose aim is to predict the sales or profit consequences, either in absolute or relative terms, of one or more proposed marketing actions."[36] Very often the action in question is the marketing of a new product or an improved version of an old product. For example, Research Realities 5.3 describes Wendy's experience in developing the "Big Classic" hamburger.

Notwithstanding previous tests of the product concept, the product package, the advertising copy, and so on, the test market is still the final gauge of consumer acceptance of the product. A. C. Nielsen data, for example, indicate that roughly three out of four products that have been test marketed succeed, whereas four out of five that have not been test marketed fail.[37] An example of the benefits to be gained from test marketing is provided by Green Giant's experience in developing Oven Crock baked beans, which came already sweetened in the can. On the basis of blind taste tests, the executives at Green Giant thought they had a certain success. "We did a series of blind taste tests and had a significant winner over bland pork and beans by a 3-to-1 or 4-to-1 preference margin. . . . But Oven Crock was a disaster in a test market. Surveys later showed that people who ate heavily flavored baked beans added their own fixings to the bland variety, and didn't want somebody to do it for them." As John M. Stafford, a

---

[35]For recent assessments of what is happening in the test marketing arena, see *Sales and Marketing Management* magazine's annual coverage of the topic, which typically appears in the March issue. See also "To Test or Not to Test Seldom the Question," *Advertising Age,* 55 (February 20, 1984), pp. M10–M11, and Leslie Brennen, "Meeting the Test," *Sales and Marketing Management,* 142 (March 1990), pp. 57–65.

[36]Alvin R. Achenbaum, "Market Testing: Using the Marketplace as a Laboratory," in Robert Ferber, ed., *Handbook of Marketing Research* (New York: McGraw-Hill, 1974), pp. 4–31 to 4–54. See also "Some Methodological Issues in Product Testing," *Research on Research,* No. 41 (Chicago: Market Facts, Inc., undated); James F. Donues, "Marketplace Measurement: The Evolution of Market Testing," *Journal of Advertising Research,* 27 (December 1987/January 1988), pp. RC-3–RC-5; Madhav N. Segal and J. S. Johar, "On Improving the Effectiveness of Test Marketing Decisions," *European Journal of Marketing,* 26 (No. 4, 1992), pp. 21–33.

[37]"Test Marketing: What's in Store," *Sales and Marketing Management,* 128 (March 15, 1982), pp. 57–85. See also "New Product Debuts Reach Record Levels, Creating Market Pressures," *The Wall Street Journal* (June 11, 1987), p. 1; Richard Gibson, "Pinning Down Costs of Product Introductions," *The Wall Street Journal* (November 26, 1990), p. B1.

Research Realities 5.3

Research Conducted by Wendy's for the "Big Classic" Hamburger

To find out what people want, Wendy's spent $1 million over nine months doing taste tests with 5,200 people in six cities. They tested:

- Nine different buns: some hard, some soft; with sesame seeds or poppy seeds; cold, toasted, or warmed; square or round; and even croissants.

- Forty special sauces, including steak sauce, hot sauce, mustard, and salad dressing.

- Three types of lettuce: chopped, shredded, and leaf.

- Two sizes of tomato slices.

- Four boxes in ten earth-tone colors.

The final product is a quarter-pound square beef patty topped with leaf lettuce, two tomato slices, raw onion rings, dill pickles, and extra dabs of ketchup and mayonnaise on a corn-dusted, hearth-baked kaiser bun. It comes in an almond-colored styrofoam box with a dome sculpted to resemble the bun's top. It can cost up to 10 cents more than the old burger, which is still on the menu.

A significant research finding was that the order of the condiments "makes a tremendous difference to consumers," said Denny Lynch, a spokesperson for Wendy's. "Which is why the Big Classic will taste different rightside up or upside down, depending on the way the toppings hit your taste buds."

Wendy's came up with a color code to help its employees remember the correct order: white, red, green, white, red, green (mayonnaise, ketchup, pickle, onion, tomato, lettuce).

Source: "Wendy's Discovers — Old Burger," *The Wisconsin State Journal* (September 19, 1986), p. 6. Reprinted with permission.

---

former executive vice-president at Pillsbury commented, "Our beans were terrific, but they were a solution to no known problem."[38]

Test marketing is not restricted to testing the sales potential of new products but has been used to examine the sales effectiveness of almost every element of the marketing mix. Market tests, for example, have also been employed to measure the sales effectiveness of a new display, the responsiveness of food sales to supermarket shelf space changes, the impact of a change in retail price on the product's market share, the price elasticity of demand for a product, the effect of different commercials on sales of a product, and the differential effects of price and advertising on demand.

Experimentation is not restricted to test marketing. Rather, it can be used whenever the manager has some specific mix alternatives to consider (for example, package design A versus B) and when the researcher can control the conditions sufficiently to allow an adequate test of the alternatives. Experiments are often used, therefore, when testing

---

[38]Lawrence Ingrassia, "A Matter of Taste: There's No Way to Tell If a New Food Product Will Please the Public," *The Wall Street Journal* (February 26, 1980), pp. 1 and 23. See also Steve Blount, "Test Marketing: It's Just a Matter of Time," *Sales and Marketing Management*, 144 (March 1992), pp. 32–43.

Research Realities 5.4

Experience of National Geographic Society in Marketing *Journey Into China*

The Society had set aside $1.8 million to sell 380,000 copies of the new book to its members and subscribers. The offer included a separate wall map of China.

Before putting all $1.8 million into a mass mailing, the Society conducted a test mailing. One thing it wanted to find out was which of three prices to sell the book for: $19.95, $22.95, or $24.95. In addition, for the first time, it offered the option of buying a more expensive deluxe edition for an extra $10.

The test also sought to determine which of the two brochure covers would work best. One displayed a photograph of a person carrying two baskets through a deep-green rice paddy, bannered with the caption "Take a spectacular tour of today's China." The other cover was red, with a small color photograph of a pagoda and a waterfall; its caption read "Take a family tour of China for only (book's price)."

The brochure was accompanied by a perforated order card and a blue and black two-tone photograph of the Forbidden City in Peking. A four-page sales letter on National Geographic Society letterhead used the blue and black ink for alternating paragraphs. The package was completed with a half-page letter from the publisher folded inside a small map of China.

The version with the photograph of the rice paddy achieved the best response in the test, so it was chosen for the mass mailing. And the most profitable price turned out to be $19.95.

The results were stunning. It was the second most successful direct-mail campaign for a single book in the Society's history. The original mailing to Society members produced sales of more than 410,000 (a 4.28 percent response), well above the goal of 380,000. Moreover, 30 percent requested the deluxe edition. Since only 420,000 copies were printed in the first run, two additional press runs of 50,000 were required that year to fill later orders resulting from an insert card sent out with bills and from the Society's Christmas catalog.

Source: Reprinted with permission of *Direct Marketing*, November, 1983, p. 76.

---

product or package concepts and advertising copy, although they have also been used to determine the optimal number of sales calls to be made on industrial distributors.[39]

An interesting example of the use of experimentation to examine the appeal of a new product while simultaneously fine tuning the other elements of the marketing mix can be found in the experience of the National Geographic Society in marketing *Journey Into China*, a 518-page book with 400 full-color illustrations, which is reported in Research Realities 5.4.

---

[39]There are several references that provide useful overviews of the use in marketing of experiments in general and test markets in particular. In addition to the Banks reference previously cited, one should also see David M. Gardner and Russell W. Belk, *A Basic Bibliography on Experimental Design in Marketing* (Chicago: American Marketing Association, 1980); and John R. Dickinson, *The Bibliography of Marketing Research Methods*, 3rd ed. (Lexington, Mass.: Lexington Books, 1990), pp. 148–150.

FUTURE AND PROBLEMS OF EXPERIMENTATION

Although it is probably true that marketing experiments will be used more frequently in the future, particularly when the research problem is one of determining which is the best of an available set of limited marketing alternatives, experimentation is not without its problems. Test marketing is a useful vehicle for illustrating these problems, because it has been characterized as a double-edged sword (although to a greater or lesser extent the problems are present in other types of experiments). As Larry Gibson, a former director of corporate marketing research for General Mills, commented about test marketing: "It costs a mint, tells the competition what you're doing, takes forever, and is not always accurate. . . . For the moment, it's the only game in town."[40] Three of the more critical problems with experimentation in general and test marketing in particular are cost, time, and control.

Cost

A major consideration in test marketing has always been cost. There are the costs of the experiment itself with which to contend. These include the normal research costs associated with designing the data-collection instruments and the sample, as well as the wages paid to the field staff that collects the data. The direct research costs are often substantial, and other costs must be borne as well. For instance, the test market should reflect the marketing strategy to be employed on the national scale if the results are to be useful, so the test also includes marketing costs for advertising, personal selling, displays, and so on. Philip Morris, for example, test marketed Like, its 99 percent caffeine-free cola, in eight cities. Its ad budget for those eight cities, which contain approximately 5 percent of the U.S. population, was $2.3 million. That amounts to $45 million on a national basis, which is more than Pepsi or Coke spend. The market test also included coupons, free samples, and other promotions, the cost of which was approximately equal to the ad budget.[41] With new-product introductions, there are also the costs associated with producing the merchandise. To produce the product on a small scale is typically inefficient. Yet to gear up immediately for large-scale production can be tremendously wasteful if the test market indicates that the product is a failure. Given all of these various expenses, the fact that it typically costs $3.1 million to take a new product from research and development through test marketing in only 2 percent of the United States should not be too surprising.[42]

---

[40]"To Test or Not to Test Seldom the Question," pp. M10–M11.

[41]"Seven-Up's No-Caffeine Cola," *The Wall Street Journal* (March 25, 1982), p. 27.

[42]Eleanor Johnson Tracy, "Testing Time for Test Marketing," *Fortune,* 110 (October 29, 1984), pp. 75–76. See also Christopher Power, "Will It Sell in Podunk? Hard to Say," *Business Week* (August 10, 1992), pp. 46–47.

Time

The time required for an adequate test market can be substantial. For example, it took Procter & Gamble nine years to go national with Pampers disposable diapers after they were first introduced in Peoria, Illinois.[43] One reason for extending the length of time for test markets is that empirical evidence indicates their accuracy increases directly with time. According to A. C. Nielsen data, after two months, forecast accuracy is only one out of seven, in the sense that when test market results are compared to national sales figures, the test market statistics only predict national sales in 13 percent of the cases. The odds steadily increase, though, to five out of six after ten months.[44] Consequently, a year is often recommended as a minimum period before any kind of go–no go decision is made to account for seasonal sales variations and repeat purchasing behavior. Experiments continued over long periods, however, are costly and raise additional problems of control and competitive reaction. Experiments conducted over short periods do not allow for the cumulative effect of the marketing actions.[45]

Control

The problems associated with control manifest themselves in several ways. First, there are the control problems in the experiment itself. What specific test markets will be used?[46] How will product distribution be organized in those markets? Can the firm elicit the necessary cooperation from wholesalers? From retailers? Can the test markets and control cities be matched sufficiently to rule out market characteristics as the primary determinant of the different sales results? Can the rest of the elements of the marketing

---

[43]Julie B. Solomon, "P&G Rolls Out New Items at Faster Pace, Turning Away from Long Marketing Testing," *The Wall Street Journal* (May 11, 1984), p. 25. See also Dan Koeppel, "Will K-C Ever Get Once Overs Out of Missouri?" *Adweek's Marketing Week* (February 27, 1989), p. 62.

[44]"How to Improve Your Chances for Test-Market Success," *Marketing News,* 18 (January 6, 1984), pp. 12–13.

[45]Some work has been done on early prediction of a new product's success, but these efforts still must have sufficient time to allow assessment of repeat purchasing tendencies. See Chakravarthi Narasimhan and Subrata K. Sen, "New Product Models for Test Market Data," *Journal of Marketing,* 47 (Winter 1983), pp. 11–24 for a review of a number of these models. For an empirical comparison of the predictive power of five of them, see Vijay Mahajan, Eitan Muller, and Subhash Sharma, "An Empirical Comparison of Awareness Forecasting Models of New Product Introduction," *Marketing Science,* 3 (Summer 1984), pp. 179–197. For a report on the extent of their use see Vijay Mahajan and Jerry Wind, "New Product Models: Practice, Shortcomings and Desired Improvements," *Journal of Product Innovation Management,* 9 (June 1992), pp. 128–139.

[46]See, for example, Leonard Lodish and Dov Pekelman, "Increasing Precision of Marketing Experiments by Matching Sales Areas," *Journal of Marketing Research,* 15 (August 1978), pp. 449–455; Eileen Norris, "Product Hopes Tied to Cities with the 'Right Stuff,' " *Advertising Age,* 55 (February 20, 1984), pp. M10, M39, and M40; and Mitchell J. Shields, "Screening the Nation for the Four-Star Audience," *Advertising Age,* 54 (February 21, 1983), pp. M9, M31, and M32, for discussion of conceptual issues. See Pat Seelig, "All Over the Map," *Sales and Marketing Management,* 142 (March 1989), pp. 58–69, for a list of frequently used test markets.

strategy be controlled so as not to induce unwanted aberrations in the experimental setting? A common problem that firms have to overcome when test marketing products is the problem of too much control. Precisely because the product is being test marketed, it receives more attention in the test market in the form of always-stocked shelves, extra effort from the sales force, and so on, than can ever be given to it on a national scale. Moreover, evidence suggests that overattention and the establishment of unrealistic in-store conditions, along with incorrect volume estimates, account for more than three out of four new product failures.[47] One reason given for the failure of Pringles potato chips, which was very successful in test market but bombed nationally, is that quality slipped when the project was mass produced on the necessarily larger scale.[48]

There are control problems associated with competitive reaction. Although the firm might be able to coordinate its own marketing activities and even those of intermediaries in the distribution channel so as not to contaminate the experiment, it can exert little control over its competitors. Competitors can, and do, sabotage marketing experiments by cutting the prices of their own products, by gobbling up quantities of the test market-er's product (thereby creating a state of euphoria and false confidence on the part of the test marketer), and by other devious means. It has been called the most dangerous game in all of marketing because of the great opportunity it affords for misfires, as attested by the examples in Research Realities 5.5.

One could argue that the misfire reflected in Example 5 (Research Realities 5.5) represents one of the fundamental reasons that one test markets products. Indeed, it seems better to find out about product performance problems like this in test market than after a product is introduced nationally. Consider, for example, the losses in company prestige that would have resulted if the following problems had not been discovered in test markets:

1. Because packages would not stack, the scouring pads fell off the shelf.
2. A dog food changed color on the store shelves.
3. In cold weather, baby food separated into a clear liquid and a sludge.
4. In hot weather, cigarettes in a new package dried out.
5. A pet food gave the test animals diarrhea.
6. When it was combined with a price reduction, a product change in a liquid detergent was thought by consumers to be dilution with water.
7. Because of insufficient glue, over half of the packages came apart during transit.
8. Excessive settling in a box of paper tissues caused the box to be one-third empty at purchase.

---

[47]"How to Improve Test Marketing," *Research on Research,* No. 21 (Chicago: Market Facts, Inc., undated).

[48]Damon Darden, "Faced with More Competition, P&G Sees New Products as Crucial to Earnings Growth," *The Wall Street Journal* (September 13, 1983), pp. 37 and 53. For discussion of the general problems of overcontrolling the marketing effort in test markets, see "How to Keep Well-Intentioned Research from Misleading New-Product Planners" and "How to Improve Your Chances for Test-Market Success," *Marketing News,* 18 (January 6, 1984), pp. 1 and 8, and pp. 12 and 13, respectively.

Research Realities 5.5

Examples of Test-Marketing Misfires

Example 1: When Campbell Soup first test marketed Prego spaghetti sauce, Campbell marketers say they noticed a flurry of new Ragu ads and cents-off deals that they believe were designed to induce shoppers to load up on Ragu and to skew Prego's test results. They also claim that Ragu copied Prego when it developed Ragu Homestyle spaghetti sauce, which was thick, red, flecked with oregano and basil, and which Ragu moved into national distribution before Prego.

Example 2: Procter & Gamble claims that competitors stole its patented process for Duncan Hines chocolate chip cookies when they saw how successful the product was in test market.

Example 3: A health and beauty aids firm developed a deodorant containing baking soda. A competitor spotted the product in test market, rolled out its own version of the deodorant nationally before the first firm completed its testing, and later successfully sued the product originator for copyright infringement when it launched its deodorant nationally.

Example 4: When Procter & Gamble introduced its Always brand sanitary napkin in test market in Min-

nesota, Kimberly-Clark Corporation and Johnson & Johnson countered with free products, lots of coupons, and big dealer discounts, which caused Always not to do as well as expected.

Example 5: A few years ago, Snell (Booz, Allen, and Hamilton's design and development division, which does product development work under contract) developed a temporary hair coloring that consumers used by inserting a block of solid hair dye into a special comb. "It went to market and it was a bust," the company's Mr. Schoenholz recalls. On hot days when people perspired, any hair dye excessively applied ran down their necks and foreheads. "It just didn't occur to us to look at this under conditions where people perspire," he says.

Example 6: Campbell Soup spent 18 months developing a blended fruit juice called Juiceworks. By the time the product reached the market, three competing brands were already on store shelves. Campbell dropped its product.

Example 7: Spurred by its incredible success with Fruit 'N Juice Bars, Dole worked hard to create a new fruity ice cream novelty product with the same type of appeal. Company officials expected that the product resulting from this development activity, Fruit and Cream Bars, which it test marketed in Orlando, Florida, would do slightly less well because it was more of an indulgence-type product. The test market results were so positive, however, that Dole became the number-one brand in the market within three months. The company consequently shortened the test market to six months. When it rolled out the product, though, the company unhappily found four unexpected entrants in the ice cream novelty category. Because of the intense competition, product sales fell short of expectations.

Source: Example 1 — Betsy Morris, "New Campbell Entry Sets Off a Big Spaghetti Sauce Battle," *The Wall Street Journal* (December 2, 1982), p. 31; Example 2 — Eleanor Johnson Tracy, "Testing Time for Test Marketing," *Fortune,* 110 (October 29, 1984), pp. 75–76; Example 3 — Kevin Wiggins, "Simulated Test Marketing Winning Acceptance," *Marketing News,* 19 (March 1, 1985), pp. 15 and 19; Example 4 — Damon Darden, "Faced with More Competition, P&G Sees New Products as Crucial to Earning's Growth," *The Wall Street Journal* (September 13, 1983), pp. 37 and 53; Example 5 — Roger Recklefs, "Success Comes Hard in the Tricky Business of Creating Products," *The Wall Street Journal* (August 23, 1978), pp. 1 and 27; Example 6 — Annetta Miller and Dody Tsiantor, "A Test for Market Research," *Newsweek,* 110 (December 28, 1987), pp. 32–33; and Example 7 — Leslie Brennan, "Test Marketing Put to the Test," *Sales and Marketing Management,* 138 (March 1987), pp. 65–68.

9. Sunlight dishwashing liquid was confused with Minute Maid lemon juice by at least 33 adults and 45 children, who became ill after drinking it.

10. When a large packaged goods company set out to introduce a squirtable soft-drink concentrate for children, it held focus groups to monitor user reaction. In the sessions, children squirted the product neatly into cups. Yet once at home, few could resist the temptation to decorate their parents' floors and walls with the colorful liquid. After a flood of parental complaints, the product was withdrawn from development.[49]

Examples 1 through 4 and 6 and 7 in Research Realities 5.5 are of a different sort. By exposing the product to competitors through a test market, each of the firms lost much of its differential development advantage. The simple point is that the marketing manager contemplating a market test must weigh the costs of such a test against its anticipated benefits. Sometimes firms may want to avoid test markets expressly because of the threat of competitive reaction, which was General Mills' rationale for doing so when introducing Total Oatmeal. Arthur Schulze, executive vice-president, said "It's somewhat risky, but we didn't want another company to see our oatmeal in a test market and preempt us. We also wanted to be in national distribution by fall and winter, when hot cereal sales are strongest."[50] Even though the market test may serve as the final yardstick for consumer acceptance of a product, perhaps more careful early product testing in the form of need-satisfaction studies and in-home product performance tests would indicate that the market test is not warranted in particular instances.

Types of Test Markets

Figure 5.2 shows the most commonly used **standard test markets.** A standard market is one in which companies sell the product through their normal distribution channels. The results are typically monitored by one of the standard distribution services discussed in the next chapter. An alternative to the standardized test market is the **controlled test market,** which is sometimes called the forced-distribution test market. In the controlled market, the entire test program is conducted by an outside service. The service pays retailers for shelf space and therefore can guarantee distribution to those stores, which represent a predetermined percentage of the marketer's total food store sales volume. The service also positions the product in the best location in the store with the right number of shelf facings; it stocks the store shelves and coordinates any trade promotion

---

[49]Problems 1–8 are discussed in Jay E. Klompmaker, G. David Hughes, and Russell I. Haley, "Test Marketing in New Product Development," *Harvard Business Review,* 54 (May–June 1976), pp. 135–136; Problem 9 is found in Lynn G. Reiling, "Consumers Misuse Mars Sampling for Sunlight Dishwashing Liquid," *Marketing News,* 16 (September 3, 1982), pp. 1 and 12; and Problem 10 is discussed in Annetta Miller and Dody Tsiantor, "A Test for Market Research," *Newsweek,* 110 (December 28, 1987), pp. 32–33.

[50]*The Wall Street Journal* (June 25, 1987), p. 27.

FIGURE 5.2   **Most Popular Standard Test Markets**

Akron, OH	Columbus, OH	Huntsville, AL	Oklahoma City, OK	San Diego, CA
Albany, NY	Corpus Christi, TX	Hutchinson, KS	Omaha, NE	San Francisco, CA
Albuquerque, NM	Council Bluffs, IA	Indianapolis, IN	Orange, TX	Savannah, GA
Ann Arbor, MI	Dallas, TX	Jacksonville, FL	Orlando, FL	Schenectady, NY
Anniston, AL	Dayton, OH	Kalamazoo, MI	Pensacola, FL	Scranton, PA
Appleton, WI	Daytona Beach, FL	Kansas City, KS	Peoria, IL	Seattle, WA
Asheville, NC	Decatur, IL	Kansas City, MO	Philadelphia, PA	Shreveport, LA
Atlanta, GA	Denver, CO	Knoxville, TN	Phoenix, AZ	Sioux Falls, SD
Augusta, GA	Des Moines, IA	Lansing, MI	Pittsburgh, PA	South Bend, IN
Austin, TX	Detroit, MI	Las Vegas, NV	Pittsfield, MA	Spartanburg, NC
Bakersfield, CA	Dubuque, IA	Lexington, KY	Poland Spring, ME	Spokane, WA
Baltimore, MD	Duluth, MN	Lincoln, NE	Port Arthur, TX	Springfield, MA
Bangor, ME	Durham, NC	Little Rock, AK	Portland, ME	Springfield, MO
Baton Rouge, LA	Eau Claire, WI	Los Angeles, CA	Portland, OR	Springfield, IL
Battle Creek, MI	El Paso, TX	Louisville, KY	Poughkeepsie, NY	Stockton, CA
Beaumont, TX	Elkhart, IN	Lubbock, TX	Providence, RI	Superior, MN
Binghamton, NY	Erie, PA	Lynchburg, VA	Pueblo, CO	Syracuse, NY
Birmingham, AL	Eugene, OR	Macon, GA	Quad Cities: Rock Island & Moline, IL;	Tacoma, WA
Boise, ID	Evansville, IN	Madison, WI	Davenport & Bettendorf, IA	Tallahassee, FL
Boston, MA	Fargo, ND	Manchester, NH	Raleigh, NC	Tampa, FL
Boulder, CO	Flint, MI	Marion, IN	Reading, PA	Toledo, OH
Buffalo, NY	Fort Collins, CO	Melbourne, FL	Reno, NV	Topeka, KS
Canton, OH	Fort Lauderdale, FL	Memphis, TN	Richmond, VA	Troy, NY
Carson City, NV	Fort Smith, AR	Miami, FL	Roanoke, VA	Tucson, AZ
Cedar Rapids, IA	Fort Wayne, IN	Midland, TX	Rochester, NY	Tulsa, OK
Champaign, IL	Fort Worth, TX	Milwaukee, WI	Rockford, IL	Washington, DC
Charleston, SC	Fresno, CA	Minneapolis, MN	Rome, GA	Waterloo, IA
Charleston, WV	Grand Junction, CO	Mobile, AL	Sacramento, CA	West Palm Beach, FL
Charlotte, NC	Grand Rapids, MI	Modesto, CA	St. Louis, MO	Wichita, KS
Chattanooga, TN	Green Bay, WI	Monterey, CA	St. Paul, MN	Wilkes-Barre, PA
Chicago, IL	Greensboro, NC	Montgomery, AL	St. Petersburg, FL	Winston, NC
Cincinnati, OH	Greenville, NC	Nashville, TN	Salem, NC	Yakima, WA
Cleveland, OH	Harrisburg, PA	New Haven, CT	Salem, OR	York, PA
Colorado Springs, CO	Hartford, CT	New Orleans, LA	Salinas, CA	Youngstown, OH
Columbia, SC	High Point, NC	New York, NY	Salt Lake City, UT	
Columbus, GA	Houston, TX	Newport News, VA	San Antonio, TX	

Source: Data from Pat Seelig, ''All Over the Map,'' *Sales and Marketing Management*, 142 (March 1989), pp. 65–66.

programs. A number of firms operate controlled test markets, including Audits & Surveys and Burgoyne.[51]

An increasingly popular variation of the controlled test market is the **electronic test market.** Electronic test markets differ from traditional controlled test markets in several ways. First, providers of the service recruit a panel of households in the test market area from which they secure a great deal of demographic information. People in these households are given identification cards, which they show when checking out at grocery

---

[51]For a full list of the research firms operating controlled test markets and the cities that they use, see Pat Seelig, ''All Over the Map.''

stores. Everything they purchase is automatically recorded and associated with the household through scanners found in all supermarkets in the area. Second, suppliers of these services are capable of monitoring each household's television-viewing behavior. They thus can correlate exposure to test commercials with purchase behavior, which in turn allows users of the service to test not only consumer acceptance of a new or modified product but also various other parts of the marketing program. Del Monte, for example, uses electronic test markets for media weight, pricing, and promotion tests, in addition to new-product evaluations.[52] The leading suppliers of electronic test marketing services are Nielsen and BehaviorScan. Research Realities 5.6 describes how the link between the demographic information of households and their purchase behavior can be used to advantage.

Another relatively recent variation when test marketing products is for firms to engage in **simulated test marketing (STM)** as a prelude to a full-scale market test. Most STM studies operate similarly. First, consumers are interviewed in shopping malls or sometimes in their homes. During the interview, they are exposed to the new product and are asked to rate its features. Then they are shown commercials for it and for competitors' products. In a simulated store environment, they are then given the opportunity to buy the product using seed money or cents-off coupons to make the purchase. Those not purchasing the test product are typically given free samples. After a use period, follow-up phone interviews are conducted with the participants to assess their reactions to the product and their repeat-purchase intentions. All the information is fed into a computer model, which has equations for the repeat purchase and market share likely to be achieved by the test model. The key to the simulation is the equations built into the computer model. Validation studies indicate that most STM models can come within 10 percent of actual sales in 80 percent of the cases.[53]

A prime advantage of STMs is the protection from competitors they provide. They are good for assessing trial- and repeat-purchasing behavior. They are faster and cheaper than full-scale tests and are also particularly good for spotting weak products, which allows firms to avoid full-scale testing of these products. The Achilles heel of STMs is that they do not provide any information about the firm's ability to secure trade support for the product or about what competitive reaction is likely to be. Thus, they are more suited for evaluating product extensions than for examining the likely success of radically different new products.

Controlled test markets are more expensive than simulated test markets but less costly than standard test markets. One reason they cost less is that the supplier secures

---

[52]Jacob Kendathel, "The Advantages of Electronic Test Markets: An Advertiser View Based on Experience," *Journal of Advertising Research,* 25 (December 1985/January 1986), pp. RC11–RC12. See also Aimee L. Stern, "Test Marketing Enters a New Era," *Dun's Business Month,* 126 (October 1985), p. 86.

[53]"Simulated Test Marketing Winning Acceptance," *Marketing News,* 19 (March 1, 1985), pp. 15 and 19. See also Allan D. Shocker and William G. Hall, "Pretest Market Models: A Critical Evaluation," *Journal of Product Innovation Management,* 3 (September 1986), pp. 86–107; and Kevin J. Clancy and Robert S. Shulman, "It's Better to Fly a New Product Simulator than Crash the Real Thing," *Planning Review,* 20 (July/August 1992), pp. 10–17.

Research Realities 5.6

Use of an Electronic Test Market by Ocean Spray

In an attempt to be perceived more broadly, Ocean Spray developed a totally new fruit beverage, Mauna La'I Hawaiian Guava Drink. The product represented a significant departure for Ocean Spray, in that it was different in color, taste, and aroma from any other fruit drink on the market.

Concerned about how consumers might respond to the product, Ocean Spray decided to test market it using BehaviorScan's facilities in Eau Claire, Wisconsin, and Midland, Texas. Ocean Spray believed that the target market for Mauna La'I was similar to that for its cranberry drink: older children and adults with average education and income.

After six months in test market, initial trial for Mauna La'I was good, but the rate of repurchase was far below what was needed to be profitable. It did not appear that Mauna La'I would survive the test to go

national. But on analyzing BehaviorScan's data more closely, Ocean Spray found a few surprises: (1) the buyer base was smaller than expected, but these consumers were buying the product more frequently than was projected; (2) the product was not selling to the target market — yuppies (young urban professionals) were buying the Mauna La'I.

After analyzing this pattern for nearly a year, Ocean Spray decided that it would be profitable to market the product as long as it was marketed towards the heavily beverage-consuming yuppies. Mauna La'I's media plan was altered to reach the more upscale market, and the juice was rolled out nationally. After only three months in the national market, consumer demand was so high that Ocean Spray started to produce a 64-ounce size. John Tarsa, Ocean Spray's Manager of Marketing Research, believes that the use of an electronic test market was key to Mauna La'I's success. "In a traditional test market, we wouldn't be rolling with Mauna La'I at all, because our repeat number was no good. The electronic test market was instrumental in helping us decide what we needed to change to make it a success."

Source: Leslie Brennan, "Test Marketing Put to the Test," *Sales and Marketing Management,* 138 (March 1987), p. 68; and David Kiley, "Small Firms Grow Strong on Steady Diet of Data," *Adweek's Marketing Week* (May 16, 1988).

distribution. The manufacturer does not need to use its own sales force to convince the trade that stocking the product is worthwhile. The manufacturer can rest assured that the new product will obtain the "right" level of store acceptance, will be positioned in the "correct" aisle in each store, will receive the "right" number of facings on the shelf, will have the "correct" everyday price, will not experience any out-of-stock problems, and will receive the planned level of trade promotion displays and price features.

The "perfect" implementation of the marketing plan also represents one of the weaknesses of the controlled test market. Acceptance or rejection of the new product by the trade is typically critical to any new product's success.[54] When the manufacturer does not need to worry about this because the new product fits in nicely with the existing line for which the company already has distribution, the controlled test market works

---

[54]Andrew M. Tarskis, "Natural Sell-In Avoids Pitfalls of Controlled Tests," *Marketing News,* 20 (October 14, 1986), p. 14.

FIGURE 5.3   **A Perspective on the Various Types of Test Markets**

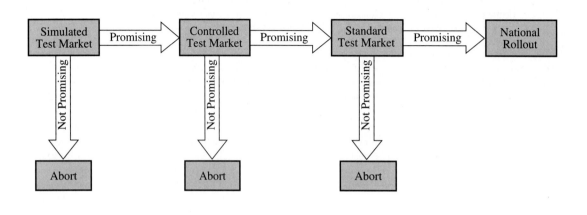

well. However, the problem of over-control of the marketing effort still needs to be taken into account. The normal situation is going to involve out-of-stocks, poor aisle locations, inadequate displays, and less-than-perfect cooperation from the trade on pricing and promotions. When the manufacturer has sufficient experience to make these adjustments, the controlled test market provides a useful laboratory for testing acceptance of the product and for fine-tuning the marketing program. When the product is novel or represents a radical departure for the manufacturer, the question of trade support is much more problematic, and the controlled test is much less useful under these circumstances.

The traditional test market provides a more natural environment than either simulated or controlled test markets. The standard test market plays a more vital role when the following situations apply:

1. It is important for the firm to test its ability to actually sell to the trade and get distribution for the product.

2. The capital investment is substantial, and the firm needs a prolonged test market to accurately assess its capital needs or its technical ability to manufacture the product.[55]

3. The firm is entering new territory and needs to build its experience base so that it can play for real, but it wants to learn how to do so on a limited scale.

---

[55]John R. Blair, "Volumetric Estimation: Review of Approaches the Pros Use — Packaged Goods Emphasis," paper presented at American Marketing Association's 7th Annual Marketing Research Conference, Orlando, Florida, September 29, 1986; and Dwight R. Riskey, "Test Market Decisions . . . Under Pressure," *Journal of Data Collection,* 27 (Spring 1987), pp. 9–13.

Choosing a Test Market Procedure

Those faced with the need to test market a new product or to fine-tune another element of the marketing program need to choose which type of test market to use. One useful way to view that choice is to look at the alternatives as stages in a sequential process, with simulated test markets preceding controlled test markets, which in turn come before standard test markets. See Figure 5.3. The sequence is not always as pictured, though. A very promising STM or controlled market test can cause a firm to skip one or more intermediate stages and perhaps move directly to national rollout.

SUMMARY

The emphasis in this chapter was on the third basic type of research design — causal design. The notion of causality was reviewed, and according to the scientific interpretation of the statement ''*X* causes *Y*,'' it was found that (1) we could never prove that *X* caused *Y,* and (2) if the inference that it did was supported by the evidence, *X* was one factor that made the occurrence of *Y* more probable, but it did not make it certain.

Three types of evidence support the establishment of causal linkages. Concomitant variation implies that *X* and *Y* must vary together in the way predicted by the hypothesis. The time order of occurrence of variables suggests that *X* must precede *Y* in time if indeed it is to be considered a cause of *Y.* The elimination of other factors requires the analyst to design the investigation so that the results do not lend themselves to a number of conflicting interpretations.

Experiments provide the most convincing evidence of the three types of causal linkages. An experiment is simply a scientific investigation, in which an investigator manipulates and controls one or more predictor variables and observes the response of a criterion variable. There are two general types of experiments: the laboratory experiment, in which an investigator creates an artificial situation for the manipulation of the predictor variables; and the field experiment, which allows these manipulations to take place in a natural setting. The greater control afforded by a laboratory experiment allows the more precise determination of the effect of the experimental stimulus. There is also, however, a greater danger of generalizing the results of a laboratory experiment because of its artificial nature.

In either type of experiment, the investigator has to be on guard against extraneous sources of error that may confound interpretation: history, maturation, testing (both main and interactive), instrument variation, statistical regression, selection bias, and experimental mortality. True experimental designs are particularly useful in controlling, or at least removing from the observed results, the impact of these errors. True experimental designs are distinguished from preexperimental and quasi-experimental designs by the fact that they allow the investigator to decide who are to be exposed to the experimental stimulus and to control when they are to be exposed.

Although experiments were rarely used in marketing before 1960, their growth since then has been steady. The market test to establish the sales potential of new products has become standard practice for some companies, and test marketing is being used more and more to determine the effectiveness of contemplated changes of any elements of the marketing mix. Two increasingly popular variations when market testing new products are the controlled test, in which the distribution of the product is guaranteed by the service provider, or the simulated test market (STM), in which reactions from users of the product are used in a series of equations to predict the repeat-purchase behavior and market share likely to be realized by the test product. Despite causal designs' growing use, descriptive designs are still the dominant form of marketing research investigations. This is partly due to tradition, but it also reflects the cost, time, and control problems associated with experimental research.

Questions

1. How do the scientific notions and common-sense notions of causality differ?
2. What types of evidence can be employed to support an inference of causality?
3. What is an experiment?
4. What is the distinction between a laboratory and a field experiment?
5. What is the difference between internal and external validity?
6. What are the basic extraneous variables that can affect the outcome of a research investigation?
7. What is the difference between the main testing effect and the interactive testing effect? Why is the distinction important?
8. What are the main ways of establishing the prior equality of groups? Which method is preferred, and why?
9. What are the distinctions between preexperimental, true experimental, and quasi-experimental designs?
10. What are the basic types of preexperimental designs?
11. What are the main types of true experimental designs? What are the key issues or problems associated with each of these designs?
12. How is the effect of the experimental stimulus determined in a before–after with control group design? In a four-group six-study design? In an after-only with control group design?
13. How does the true experimental, after-only with control group design differ from the preexperimental, static-group comparison research design?
14. When would one want to employ a four-group six-study design instead of a before–after with control group design, and vice versa?
15. When would one want to employ a before–after with control group design or a four-group six-study design in lieu of an after-only with control group design, and vice versa?
16. What is the basic nature of the time-series experiment? How does the time-series experiment differ from the preexperimental, one-group pretest–posttest design? What is the importance of this difference?
17. Compare descriptive research and true experimental design with respect to the ability of each to control or allow for extraneous factors.

18. How would you explain marketing's infrequent use of experimental research before 1960 and its steadily increasing use since then?

19. What is a test market? For what kinds of investigations can test markets be used? What are the problems associated with test markets?

20. What is the primary difference between a standard test market and a controlled test market?

21. How does an electronic test market work? What are its advantages compared to a traditional test market?

22. How does simulated test marketing (STM) work? What are its main advantages and disadvantages compared to full market tests?

23. Under what conditions is a standard test market a better choice than either simulated or controlled test markets?

Applications and Problems

1. Charlie Sharp is the national sales manager of Hitech Inc. Charlie recently hypothesized that "Hitech's increase in sales is due to the new sales personnel that we recruited from the vocational school over the last several years. Sales of the new salespeople are up substantially, whereas sales for longer-term salespeople have not increased."

Identify the causal factor X and the effect factor Y in the preceding statement.

2. To gather support for his conclusion, Charlie asked the research department of Hitech to investigate the sales of each of the company's salespeople. Using criteria supplied by management, the department categorized territory sales changes as "increased substantially," "increased marginally," or "no increase." Consider the following table, in which 260 sales personnel have been classified as old or new:

	Territory Sales Change			
Salesperson Assigned	**Increased Substantially**	**Increased Marginally**	**No Increase**	**Total**
New	75	30	5	110
Old	50	40	60	150

a. Does this table provide evidence of concomitant variation? Justify your answer.

b. What conclusions can be drawn about the relationship between X and Y on the basis of the preceding table?

3. Consider the following statement: "The increase in repeat-purchase frequency is due to retailers' decisions to stock our product in the gourmet food section of supermarkets during the last nine months. Repeat purchases from the gourmet section are up as much as 50 percent from our previous store location."

Identify the causal factor X and the effect factor Y in the preceding statement.

4. The research department of the company in Question 3 investigated the change in repeat-purchase frequency for each store location. Using criteria supplied by management, the department categorized repeat-purchase frequency changes as *increased substantially, increased marginally,* or *no increase.* Consider the following table, in which 624 store locations have been classified as *old* or *gourmet:*

| | **Repeat-Purchase Frequency** | | | |
Store Location	Increased Substantially	Increased Marginally	No Increase	Total
Gourmet	180	72	12	264
Old	120	96	144	360

   a. Does this table provide evidence of concomitant variation? Justify your answer.
   b. What conclusions can be drawn about the relationship between X and Y on the basis of the preceding table?

5. Six months later, the research department in Question 4 investigated the situation once again. However, a new variable was considered in the analysis — namely, the size of the package. More specifically, they considered if repeat-purchase frequency was affected depending on whether the package was a 14 or 18 ounce size. The following table summarizes the research department's findings:

| | **14-Ounce Package** | | | |
Store Location	Increased Substantially	Increased Marginally	No Increase	Total
Gourmet	84	24	—	108
Old	65	19	—	84

| | **18-Ounce Package** | | | |
Store Location	Increased Substantially	Increased Marginally	No Increase	Total
Gourmet	6	12	6	24
Old	24	48	24	96

   a. If the size of package is ignored, does this table provide evidence of concomitant variation between a change in repeat purchases and in-store location? Justify your answer.
   b. If the size of package is considered, does the table provide evidence of concomitant variation between repeat purchases and in-store location? Justify your answer.

   Several experimental designs are described in Questions 6 through 10. For each design, answer the following questions or complete the following tasks:

   (i) What type of design is being used? Explain.
   (ii) Diagrammatically represent the design.
   (iii) Discuss the threats to internal and external validity for the design.

6. A leading manufacturer of frozen food products decided to test the effectiveness of an in-store display. Four large supermarkets, located near the company's main office, were selected for the experiment. The display was set up in two of the stores, and sales were monitored for a period of two weeks. The sales of the other two stores were also recorded, but no displays were used. Sales volume for the frozen food products increased 2 percent more in the stores that used the in-store displays than in the stores that did not use the displays.

7. A branch of Alcoholics Anonymous wanted to test consumer attitudes toward an anti-drinking advertisement. Two random samples of respondents in Piscataway, New Jersey, were selected for the experiment. Personal interviews relating to consumer attitudes toward alcoholism were conducted with both samples. One of the samples was shown the anti-drinking advertisement, and following this, personal interviews were conducted with both samples in order to examine consumer attitudes toward alcoholism.

8. A manufacturer of a line of office equipment, based in Houston, Texas, marketed its products in the southwest United States. The region consisted of 30 geographic divisions, each headed by a divisional manager who had a staff of salespeople. The firm's management wanted to test the effectiveness of a new sales training program in which the sales personnel in five of the divisions typically participated. The divisional managers of these five divisions were instructed to monitor sales for each salesperson for each of the five months before and after the training program. The results were to be sent to the vice-president of sales in Houston, who planned to compare them against sales changes in the other divisions.

9. A new manufacturer of women's cosmetics was planning to retail the firm's products through mail order. The firm's management was considering the use of direct-mail advertisements to stimulate sales of their products. Prior to committing themselves to advertising through direct mail, management conducted an experiment. A random sample of 1,000 housewives was selected from Memphis, Tennessee. The sample was divided into two groups, with each subject being randomly assigned to one of the two groups. Direct-mail advertisements were sent twice over a period of one month to respondents of one of the groups. Two weeks later, respondents of both the groups were mailed the company's catalog of cosmetics. Sales to each group were monitored.

10. Milbar Corporation, a specialty hand-tool company located in Chagrin Falls, Ohio, was considering introducing a new style of snap ring pliers. Before it went ahead with production of the pliers, Jack Bares, CEO, decided that the company should test the effectiveness of its sales promotion campaign. Jack chose four disparate cities in which to run the experiment. In two of the randomly chosen cities, Binghamton, New York, and Manderville, Louisiana, Milbar first questioned mechanics and parts people on their attitudes toward snap ring pliers. Next, Milbar ran the new pliers sales promotion campaign in the randomly chosen Binghamton and Medford, Oregon. Then Milbar went back to all four cities — Binghamton, Manderville, Medford, and Omaha, Nebraska — and measured mechanics' and parts people's attitudes toward the new and old snap ring pliers.

11. The product development team at Flameglo Log Company has been working on several modifications of Flameglo's highly successful line of fireplace logs. The most promising development is a new log that burns in several different colors. Based on favorable feedback from a few employees who have tested the product in their homes, management feels that the new log has the potential to become a major seller.

At a recent strategy meeting, the vice-president of marketing suggested a test-marketing program before committing to introduction of the new log. He pointed out that a test market would be a good way to evaluate the effectiveness of two alternative advertising and promotional campaigns that have been proposed by Flameglo's ad agency. He feels that effectiveness should be evaluated in terms of the trial and repeat-purchasing behavior engendered by each program. He also wants to gauge Flameglo's current distributors' acceptance of the new product.

The CEO of Flameglo, however, is not very enthusiastic about the idea of test marketing. She is concerned that Flameglo's competitors could easily duplicate the new log; that the company is nearing the limit of its budgeted costs for developing the new log; and that the seasonal nature of log sales makes it imperative to reach a "go–no go" decision on the new log by early April, only four months away.

The director of marketing research stated that she felt a test-marketing plan could be devised that would satisfy both the vice-president of marketing and the CEO. She was instructed to submit a preliminary proposal at the next strategy meeting.

a. What information should be obtained from the test market in order to satisfy the vice-president of marketing?

b. Under what constraints must the test-marketing plan operate in order to satisfy the CEO?

c. Given your answers to a and b above, what method of test marketing should the director recommend? Why?

 Thorndike Sports Equipment Video Case

1. After looking at the study constructed to test the effects of different strings, what do you think are the problems with this design?

2. Devise a study that overcomes the weaknesses you have identified in the previous question.

CASE 2.1
Rumstad Decorating Centers (A)

In 1929, Joseph Rumstad opened a small paint and wallpaper supply store in downtown Rockford, Illinois. For the next 45 years the store enjoyed consistent, although not spectacular, success. Sales and profits increased steadily but slowly as, to keep pace with the competition, the original line of products was expanded to include unpainted furniture, mirrors, picture framing material, and other products. In 1974, because of a declining neighborhood environment, Jack Rumstad, who had taken over management of the store from his father in 1970, decided to close the downtown store and open a new outlet on the far west side of the city. The west side was chosen because it was experiencing a boom in new home construction. In 1992, a second store was opened on the east side of the city, and the name of the business was changed to Rumstad Decorating Centers. The east side store was staffed with sales clerks but was basically managed by Rumstad himself from the west side location. All ordering, billing, inventory control, and even the physical storage of excess inventory were concentrated at the west side store.

In 1993, the east side store was made an independent profit center. Rumstad personally took over the management of the outlet and hired a full-time manager for the west side store. With the change in accounting procedures occasioned by this organizational change, it became possible to examine the profitability of each outlet separately.

Rumstad conducted such an examination early in 1994, using the profit and loss figures in Table 1, and became very concerned with what he discovered. Both stores had suffered losses for 1993, and, although he had anticipated incurring a loss during the first couple of years of operation of the east side store, he was not at all prepared for a second successive loss at the west side outlet. He blamed the 1992 loss on the disruptions caused by the change in organizational structure. Further, from 1992 to 1993, the east side had a 25 percent increase in net sales, a 25 percent increase in gross profits, and an 8 percent increase in total direct costs. Also, although the east side store still showed a net loss, it was 80 percent less than the previous year's loss. The west side store, on the other hand, had shown a 21 percent decrease in net sales, a 31 percent decrease in gross profit, an 11 percent decrease in direct costs, and a 136 percent increase in net loss. Rumstad is very concerned about the survival of the business and is particularly

TABLE 1 **Profit and Loss Statement for Rumstad Decorating Centers**

	East Side Store		West Side Store	
	1993	**1992**	**1993**	**1992**
Total Sales	$114,461	$91,034	$ 87,703	$108,497
Cash sale discounts	4,347	2,971	4,165	2,930
Net sales	110,114	88,063	83,538	105,567
Beginning inventory	53,369	49,768	1,936	0
Purchases	64,654	56,528	163,740	59,366
Total	118,023	106,206	165,676	59,366
Ending inventory	51,955	53,369	115,554	1,936
Cost of sales	66,068	52,837	50,122	57,430
Gross profit or loss	44,046	35,226	33,416	48,137
Direct Costs				
Salaries	24,068	19,836	24,549	26,583
Payroll taxes	2,025	1,814	1,764	2,060
Depreciation — furniture and fixtures	92	92	92	92
Freight	6	43	511	800
Store supplies	694	828	607	4,153
Accounting and legal expenses	439	433	439	433
Advertising	2,977	4,890	4,820	5,252
Advertising — yellow pages	1,007	618	1,387	956
Convention and seminar expenses	0	33	83	216
Insurance	226	139	1,271	1,643
Office expense and supplies	4,466	4,393	5,327	5,010
Personal property tax	139	139	140	140
Rent	7,000	7,000	4,900	4,900
Utilities	2,246	1,651	2,746	2,359
Total direct costs	45,385	41,909	48,636	54,597
Profit or loss	(1,339)	(6,683)	(15,220)	(6,460)

concerned with the west side store. He has called you in as a research consultant to help him pinpoint what is happening so that he might take corrective action.

WEST SIDE STORE

The west side store is located in the heart of the census tract with the highest per capita income in the city. Most of the residents in the area are professional people or white-collar workers. The store is a freestanding unit located on a frontage road with the word "Rumstad" printed across the front. Since Rumstad's transfer to the east side store, there has been a succession of managers at the west side store. The first one lasted for six months and the second and third for four months. The current manager, previously a sales clerk at the store for four years, has held the job for ten months. Even though the products carried and the prices charged are the same in both stores, there is some difference in advertising emphasis. The west side store does all of its advertising in the *Shopper's World,* a weekly paper devoted exclusively to advertising, which is distributed free to all households in the community. Delivery is by and large door-to-door, although it is quite typical for a group of newspapers to be placed at the entrance to apartment buildings and for residents to pick up a copy if they so choose.

EAST SIDE STORE

The east side store is located in a predominantly blue-collar area. Most of the residents in the immediate vicinity work for one of the various machine tool manufacturers that compose one of the basic industries in Rockford. The store is located in a small shopping center. It has a large window display area with a readily visible ''Rumstad Decorating Center'' sign above the store. The east side store advertises periodically in the *Rockford Morning Star* in addition to its yellow pages advertising.

Question

1. How would you proceed to answer Rumstad's problem?

CASE 2.2
HotStuff Computer Software (A)[1]

Simpson, Edwards and Associates has had considerable success with a computer software package that it designed to enable government agencies to manage their data base systems. The firm is currently developing a second product, a more specialized version of its first endeavor. Called HotStuff, its latest computer software concept is targeted at the firefighting industry. Researchers at Simpson, Edwards and Associates have a hunch that fire departments are a prime market for data base software because of their extensive information-handling responsibilities — equipment inventories, building layouts, hazardous materials data, budget records, personnel files, and so on.

   At this embryonic stage in the new product's development, the company is following the same game plan that helped it launch its previous success. Responsibilities have been broadly divided: Jean Edwards has assumed command of the production side and Craig Simpson has taken charge of marketing and promotion. Craig's first move was to reassemble the original team of staff members who had researched the market for

[1]The contributions of Jacqueline C. Hitchon to the development of this case are gratefully acknowledged.

government agency software. At their first orientation meeting, he submitted the following objectives for their deliberation:

1. Determine market potential.
2. Identify important product attributes.
3. Develop an effective promotional strategy.
4. Identify competitors in the market.

By the close of discussion, the group had decided that its first task would be exploratory research. Specifically, it decided to conduct experience surveys involving local fire chiefs, informal telephone interviews with state and national fire officials, and literature search. Based on findings from the exploratory research effort, it hoped to be able to pursue descriptive research to fulfill the four objectives.

EXPLORATORY RESEARCH

The first finding to emerge from the exploratory research affected the target market for HotStuff. There are two broad categories of fire departments: municipal departments with full staffs of paid firefighters, and volunteer departments consisting of a paid chief and remaining members who may or may not be paid firefighters. The team quickly discovered that the two kinds of departments differ in two important ways. First, from the point of view of funding, municipal departments receive the majority of their funds from taxes, so the money is tightly controlled and tends to be earmarked for specific uses. Volunteer fire departments, on the other hand, rely heavily on donors and special events as sources of income, to the extent that fundraising may account for more than 50 percent of their total receipts. Since money obtained through fundraising is not technically part of the budget, it is not subject to budgetary controls per se.

The second key difference between municipal and volunteer departments concerned purchasing procedures. Local municipal departments tended to route all purchases through a central purchasing agent, who would then apply for approval from the data processing center at city hall before acquiring computer hardware and software. Fire chiefs interviewed in volunteer departments, however, reported that they had sole authority to purchase any hardware or software required.

Telephone calls to out-of-state fire officials indicated that these differences were consistent across the nation. As a result, Simpson, Edwards and Associates decided to restrict its target market to volunteer fire departments.

A second finding uncovered in the exploratory research concerned the extent to which the needs of the target market were already being met. Inquiries within the state revealed that only a few volunteer departments had already purchased computers. Further, those with computers had not possessed them for long and were still in the process of automating manual data bases. The general feeling among fire officials was that computerization would be an inevitable development in the industry in the near future. Indeed, four specialized software packages were already being advertised in fire prevention journals: Chief's Helper, Fire Organizer, Spread Systems, and JLT Software. Spread Systems differed from the others in that it consisted of separate programs, each of which sold individually and covered a particular information type, such as inventory records or hazardous materials. The strategy followed by Spread Systems allowed fire departments to reduce their expenditure on software because they could select only those programs that they neeeded. It was conjectured at Simpson, Edwards and Associates that specific programs for specific functions may help overcome initial consumer caution toward spending several thousand dollars for computer software, because the expenditure would not be made all at one time. It was also believed that some makers of generic software packages that perform spreadsheet or data base management analysis should be included in the list of competitors, although users of generic software packages needed some proficiency with computers in order to tailor these basic packages to their specific applications.

A third finding of interest from the exploratory research was that the term *volunteer* was offensive to departments officially classified as volunteer because they thought that it implied a lack of professionalism. In fact, their staffs were as well-trained as members of municipal departments. This sentiment led the researchers to conclude that the label *volunteer* should not be used in the future promotion of HotStuff.

Based on what it had learned from the exploratory research, Simpson, Edwards and Associates decided to conduct a more formal investigation to address the following objectives:

1. Determine the market potential for its new software by
   a. establishing the incidence of computer use and planned computer purchases in volunteer fire departments, and
   b. obtaining more information about volunteer fire departments' funding and authority structures.
2. Identify important product attributes — that is, the types of information that needed to be handled by volunteer fire departments and that therefore needed to be incorporated into the software.
3. Secure ideas for promotional strategy by
   a. determining which fire publications are read by the target market, and
   b. determining which association conventions are most well-attended by the target market.
4. Identify competitors in the market by
   a. establishing which brands of software are currently used in volunteer fire departments, and
   b. establishing how satisfactory existing software packages are perceived to be.

STUDY DESIGN

Simpson, Edwards and Associates' researchers believed that the best way to address these objectives was through a national survey of volunteer fire departments. They decided on a structured–disguised telephone survey using team members as interviewers. The state fire marshall informed the group that most volunteer fire departments were located in communities with populations under 25,000. Consequently, it was decided to sample towns with populations under 25,000 that were situated within a 20-mile radius of cities of at least 100,000 people. Volunteer fire departments within those towns could then be contacted by telephone by means of directory assistance. Two large cities were randomly selected from each state in the United States, excluding Alaska and Hawaii, and then a town located near each city was randomly selected. An atlas and the 1990 Census were used to identify cities and towns of the right specification.

A questionnaire was devised and pretested twice. The first pretest was conducted through personal interviews and was meant to test the questionnaire; the second pretest was performed by telephone and was meant to test the mode of administration. In each case, inquiries were directed to the fire chiefs as representatives of the departments. The actual survey was conducted between April 13 and April 24. It would have taken less time to administer the survey had there not been a national fire convention the week that the phone survey began. Because the national fire convention coincided with Easter week, many fire chiefs were not at their departments; they attended the convention with their families, as their children did not have school. Nonetheless, the interviewer team was able to increase the response rate to 85 percent by numerous callbacks.

Questions

1. Evaluate Simpson, Edwards and Associates' decision to focus on volunteer fire departments as its target market, based on the exploratory research.

2. Do you consider that exploratory research was productive in this case? Do you think that further useful insights could have been gained without significantly greater expenditure of resources? If so, what and how?

3. Comment on the differences between the four objectives as originally formulated and as reformulated after exploratory research.

4. Was the choice of phone interviews a good one?

CASE 2.3
Chestnut Ridge Country Club (A)[1]

The Chestnut Ridge Country Club has long maintained a distinguished reputation as one of the outstanding country clubs in the Elma, Tennessee, area. The club's golf facilities are said by some to be the finest in the state, and its dining and banquet facilities are highly regarded as well. This reputation is due in part to the commitment by the Board of Directors of Chestnut Ridge to offer the finest facilities of any club in the area. For

[1]The contributions of David M. Szymanski to the development of this case are gratefully acknowledged.

example, several negative comments by club members regarding the dining facilities prompted the board to survey members to get their feelings and perceptions of the dining facilities and food offerings at the club. Based on the survey findings, the board of directors established a quality control committee to oversee the dining room, and a new club manager was hired.

Most recently, the board became concerned about the number of people seeking membership to Chestnut Ridge. Although no records are kept on the number of membership applications received each year, the board sensed that this figure was declining. They also believed that membership applications at the three competing country clubs in the area — namely, Alden, Chalet, and Lancaster — were not experiencing similar declines. Because Chestnut Ridge had other facilities, such as tennis courts and a pool, that were comparable to the facilities at these other clubs, the board was perplexed as to why membership applications would be falling at Chestnut Ridge.

To gain insight into the matter, the board of directors hired an outside research firm to conduct a study of the country clubs in Elma, Tennessee. The goals of the research were: (1) to outline areas in which Chestnut Ridge fared poorly in relation to other clubs in the area; (2) to determine people's overall perception of Chestnut Ridge; and (3) to provide recommendations for ways to increase membership applications at the club.

RESEARCH METHOD

The researchers met with the board of directors and key personnel at Chestnut Ridge to gain a better understanding of the goals of the research and the types of services and facilities offered at a country club. A literature search of published research relating to country clubs uncovered no studies. Based solely on their contact with individuals at Chestnut Ridge, therefore, the research team developed the survey contained in Figure 1. Because personal information regarding demographics and attitudes would be asked of those contacted, the researchers decided to use a mail questionnaire.

The researchers thought it would be useful to survey members from Alden, Chalet, and Lancaster country clubs in addition to those from Chestnut Ridge for two reasons. One, members of these other clubs would be knowledgeable about the levels and types of services and facilities desired from a country club, and, two, they had at one time represented potential members of Chestnut Ridge. Hence, their perceptions of Chestnut Ridge might reveal why they chose to belong to a different country club.

No public documents were available that contained a listing of each club's members. Consequently, the researchers decided to contact each of the clubs personally to try to obtain a mailing list. Identifying themselves as being affiliated with an independent research firm conducting a study on country clubs in the Elma area, the researchers first spoke to the chairman of the board at Alden Country Club. The researchers told the chairman that they could not reveal the organization sponsoring the study but that the results of their study would not be made public. The chairman was not willing to provide the researchers with the mailing list. The chairman cited an obligation to respect the privacy of the club's members as his primary reason for turning down the research team's request.

1. *Of which club are you currently a member?* _____
2. *How long have you been a member of this club?* _____
3. *How familiar are you with each of the following country clubs?*

Alden Country Club?

_____ very familiar (I am a member or I have visited the club as a guest)
_____ somewhat familiar (I have heard about the club from others)
_____ unfamiliar

Chalet Country Club

_____ very familiar
_____ somewhat familiar
_____ unfamiliar

Chestnut Ridge Country Club

_____ very familiar
_____ somewhat familiar
_____ unfamiliar

Lancaster Country Club

_____ very familiar
_____ somewhat familiar
_____ unfamiliar

4. *The following is a list of factors that may be influential in the decision to join a country club. Please rate the factors according to their importance to you in joining your country club. Circle the appropriate response, where 1 = not at all important and 5 = extremely important.*

Golf facilities	1	2	3	4	5
Tennis facilities	1	2	3	4	5
Pool facilities	1	2	3	4	5
Dining facilities	1	2	3	4	5
Social events	1	2	3	4	5
Family activities	1	2	3	4	5
Number of friends who are members	1	2	3	4	5
Cordiality of members	1	2	3	4	5
Prestige	1	2	3	4	5
Location	1	2	3	4	5

5. *The following is a list of phrases pertaining to Alden Country Club. Please place an X in the space that best describes your impressions of Alden. The ends represent extremes; the center position is neutral.* Do so even if you are only vaguely familiar with Alden.

Club landscape is   Club landscape is
attractive.   :__:__:__:__:__:__:__: unattractive.

FIGURE 1 *Continued*

Clubhouse facilities are poor. :___:___:___:___:___:___:___: Clubhouse facilities are excellent.

Locker room facilities are excellent. :___:___:___:___:___:___:___: Locker room facilities are poor.

Club management is ineffective. :___:___:___:___:___:___:___: Club management is effective.

Dining room atmosphere is pleasant. :___:___:___:___:___:___:___: Dining room atmosphere is unpleasant.

Food prices are unreasonable. :___:___:___:___:___:___:___: Food prices are reasonable.

Golf course is poorly maintained. :___:___:___:___:___:___:___: Golf course is well maintained.

Golf course is challenging. :___:___:___:___:___:___:___: Golf course is not challenging.

Membership rates are too high. :___:___:___:___:___:___:___: Membership rates are too low.

6. *The following is a list of phrases pertaining to Chalet Country Club. Please place an X in the space that best describes your impressions of Chalet. Do so even if you are only vaguely familiar with Chalet.*

Club landscape is attractive. :___:___:___:___:___:___:___: Club landscape is unattractive.

Clubhouse facilities are poor. :___:___:___:___:___:___:___: Clubhouse facilities are excellent.

Locker room facilities are excellent. :___:___:___:___:___:___:___: Locker room facilities are poor.

Club management is effective. :___:___:___:___:___:___:___: Club management is ineffective.

Dining room atmosphere is pleasant. :___:___:___:___:___:___:___: Dining room atmosphere is unpleasant.

Food prices are unreasonable. :___:___:___:___:___:___:___: Food prices are reasonable.

Food quality is excellent. :___:___:___:___:___:___:___: Food quality is poor.

Golf course is poorly maintained. :___:___:___:___:___:___:___: Golf course is well maintained.

Golf course is challenging. :___:___:___:___:___:___:___: Golf course is not challenging.

Tennis courts are in excellent condition. :___:___:___:___:___:___:___: Tennis courts are in poor condition.

There are too many tennis courts. :___:___:___:___:___:___:___: There are too few tennis courts.

Membership rates are too high. :___:___:___:___:___:___:___: Membership rates are too low.

(continued)

FIGURE 1 *Continued*

7. **The following is a list of phrases pertaining to Chestnut Ridge Country Club. Please place an X in the space that best describes your impressions of Chestnut Ridge.** *Do so even if you are only vaguely familiar with Chestnut Ridge.*

Club landscape is attractive.	:___:___:___:___:___:___: Club landscape is unattractive.
Clubhouse facilities are poor.	:___:___:___:___:___:___: Clubhouse facilities are excellent.
Locker room facilities are excellent.	:___:___:___:___:___:___: Locker room facilities are poor.
Club management is ineffective.	:___:___:___:___:___:___: Club management is effective.
Dining room atmosphere is pleasant.	:___:___:___:___:___:___: Dining room atmosphere is unpleasant.
Food prices are unreasonable.	:___:___:___:___:___:___: Food prices are reasonable.
Food quality is excellent.	:___:___:___:___:___:___: Food quality is poor.
Golf course is poorly maintained.	:___:___:___:___:___:___: Golf course is well maintained.
Tennis courts are in poor condition.	:___:___:___:___:___:___: Tennis courts are in excellent condition.
There are too many tennis courts.	:___:___:___:___:___:___: There are too few tennis courts.
Swimming pool is in poor condition.	:___:___:___:___:___:___: Swimming pool is in excellent condition.
Membership rates are too high.	:___:___:___:___:___:___: Membership rates are too low.

8. **The following is a list of phrases pertaining to Lancaster Country Club. Please place an X in the space that best describes your impression of Lancaster.** *Do so even if you are only vaguely familiar with Lancaster.*

Club landscape is attractive.	:___:___:___:___:___:___: Club landscape is unattractive.
Clubhouse facilities are poor.	:___:___:___:___:___:___: Clubhouse facilities are excellent.
Locker room facilities are excellent.	:___:___:___:___:___:___: Locker room facilities are poor.
Club management is ineffective.	:___:___:___:___:___:___: Club management is effective.
Dining room atmosphere is pleasant.	:___:___:___:___:___:___: Dining room atmosphere is unpleasant.
Food prices are unreasonable.	:___:___:___:___:___:___: Food prices are reasonable.
Food quality is excellent.	:___:___:___:___:___:___: Food quality is poor.
Golf course is poorly maintained.	:___:___:___:___:___:___: Golf course is well maintained.

FIGURE 1 *Continued*

Tennis courts are in poor condition.	:___:___:___:___:___:___:	Tennis courts are in excellent condition.
There are too many tennis courts.	:___:___:___:___:___:___:	There are too few tennis courts.
Swimming pool is in poor condition.	:___:___:___:___:___:___:	Swimming pool is in excellent condition.
Membership rates are too high.	:___:___:___:___:___:___:	Membership rates are too low.

9. *Overall, how would you rate each of the country clubs? Circle the appropriate response, where 1 = poor and 5 = excellent.*

Alden	1	2	3	4	5
Chalet	1	2	3	4	5
Chestnut Ridge	1	2	3	4	5
Lancaster	1	2	3	4	5

10. *The following questions are designed to give a better understanding of the members of country clubs.*

Have you ever been a member of another club in the Elma area?
_____ yes   _____ no

Approximately what is the distance of your residence from your club in miles?
_____ 0–2 miles   _____ 3–5 miles   _____ 6–10 miles
_____ 10+ miles

Age: _____ 21–30   _____ 31–40   _____ 41–50
_____ 51–60   _____ 61 or over

Sex: _____ male   _____ female

Marital status: _____ married   _____ single   _____ widowed
_____ divorced

Number of dependents including yourself:
_____ 2 or less   _____ 3–4   _____ 5 or more

Total family income:
__ Less than $20,000
__ $20,000–$29,999
__ $30,000–$49,999
__ $50,000–$99,999
__ $100,000 or more
__ Do not know/Refuse to answer

Thank you for your cooperation!

The researchers then made the following proposal to the board chairman: in return for the mailing list, the researchers would provide the chairman a report on Alden members' perceptions of Alden Country Club. In addition, the mailing list would be destroyed as soon as the surveys were sent. The proposal seemed to please the chairman, for he agreed to give the researchers a listing of the members and their addresses in exchange for the report. The researchers told the chairman they must check with their sponsoring organization for approval of this arrangement.

The research team made similar proposals to the chairmen of the boards of directors of both the Chalet and Lancaster country clubs. In return for a mailing list of the club's members, they promised each chairman a report outlining their members' perceptions of their clubs, contingent on their securing approval from their sponsoring organization. Both agreed to supply the requested list of members.

The researchers subsequently met with the Chestnut Ridge Board of Directors. In their meeting, the researchers outlined the situation and asked for the board's approval to provide each of the clubs with a report in return for the mailing lists. The researchers emphasized that the report would contain no information regarding Chestnut Ridge nor information by which each of the other clubs could compare itself to any of the other clubs in the area, in contrast to the information to be provided to the Chestnut Ridge Board of Directors. The report would only contain a small portion of the overall study's results. After carefully considering the research team's arguments, the Board of Directors agreed to the proposal.

MEMBERSHIP SURVEYS

A review of the lists subsequently provided by each club showed Alden had 114 members, Chalet had 98 members, and Lancaster had 132 members. The researchers believed that 69 to 70 responses from each membership group would be adequate. Anticipating a 70 to 75 percent response rate because of the unusually high involvement and familiarity of each group with the subject matter, the research team decided to mail 85 to 90 surveys to each group, a simple random sample of members was chosen from each list. In all, 87

TABLE 1   Average Overall Ratings of Each Club by Club
Membership of the Respondent

Club Rated	Club Membership			Composite Ratings across All Members
	Alden	Chalet	Lancaster	
Alden	4.57	3.64	3.34	3.85
Chalet	2.87	3.63	2.67	3.07
Chestnut Ridge	4.40	4.44	4.20	4.35
Lancaster	3.60	3.91	4.36	3.95

TABLE 2 **Average Ratings of the Respective Country Clubs across Dimensions**

	Country Club			
Dimension	**Alden**	**Chalet**	**Chestnut Ridge**	**Lancaster**
Club landscape	6.28	4.65	6.48	5.97
Clubhouse facilities	5.37	4.67	6.03	5.51
Locker room facilities	4.99	4.79	5.36	4.14
Club management	5.38	4.35	5.00	5.23
Dining room atmosphere	5.91	4.10	5.66	5.48
Food prices	5.42	4.78	4.46	4.79
Food quality	a	4.12	5.48	4.79
Golf course maintenance	6.17	5.01	6.43	5.89
Golf course challenge	5.14	5.01	a	4.77
Condition of tennis courts	b	5.10	4.52	5.08
Number of tennis courts	b	4.14	4.00	3.89
Swimming pool	b	b	4.66	5.35
Membership rates	4.49	3.97	5.00	4.91

[a]Question not asked.
[b]Not applicable.

members from each country club were mailed a questionnaire (348 surveys in total). Sixty-three usable surveys were returned from each group (252 in total) for a response rate of 72 percent.

Summary results of the survey are presented in Tables 1 through 3. Table 1 gives people's overall ratings of the country clubs, and Table 2 shows people's ratings of the

TABLE 3 **Attitudes toward Chestnut Ridge by Members of the Other Country Clubs**

Dimension	**Alden**	**Chalet**	**Lancaster**
Club landscape	6.54	6.54	6.36
Clubhouse facilities	6.08	6.03	5.98
Locker room facilities	5.66	5.35	5.07
Club management	4.97	5.15	4.78
Dining room atmosphere	5.86	5.70	5.41
Food prices	4.26	4.48	4.63
Food quality	5.52	5.75	5.18
Golf course maintenance	6.47	6.59	6.22
Condition of tennis courts	4.55	4.46	4.55
Number of tennis courts	4.00	4.02	3.98
Swimming pool	5.08	4.69	4.26
Membership rates	5.09	5.64	4.24

various clubs on an array of dimensions. Table 3 is a breakdown of attitudes toward Chestnut Ridge by the three different membership groups: Alden, Chalet, and Lancaster. The data are average ratings of respondents. Table 1 scores are based on a five-point scale, where one is poor and five is excellent. Tables 2 and 3 are based on seven-point scales in which one represents an extremely negative rating and seven an extremely positive rating.

Questions

1. What kind of research design is being used? Is it a good choice?
2. Do you think it was ethical for the researchers not to disclose the identity of the sponsoring organization? Do you think it was ethical for the board of directors to release the names of their members in return for a report that analyzes their members' perceptions toward their own club?
3. Overall, how does Chestnut Ridge compare to the other three country clubs (Alden, Chalet, and Lancaster)?
4. In what areas might Chestnut Ridge consider making improvements to attract additional members?

CASE 2.4
N–Rich Coffee Creamer

N–Rich, a powdered, nondairy coffee creamer, was originally introduced in 1965, but a series of events during the 1990s led to a reconsideration of the product's marketing strategy. While discussing this revised marketing strategy in early 1994, John Bendt, marketing manager, and Gregg Ostrander, the N–Rich product manager, directed their attention to the results of a study regarding a new package for the product. They had definitely decided a new package was in order and had narrowed the choice to two alternatives. The only question that still remained was which alternative they should adopt.

N–Rich, like its competitors, had historically been packaged in glass jars with screw tops. Both of the new containers under consideration were cylinder-shaped cardboard canisters. The cardboard package was lighter, unbreakable, and most important, cheaper to make. The primary problem was to convince consumers of the benefits of cardboard containers and to persuade them to change their habit of using glass jars.

The two alternatives differed primarily in their tops. Alternative Y had an aluminum pull top with a resealable plastic lid, much like the top of a tennis ball can. Alternative X had a plastic twist top with two openings, much like the top of a parmesan cheese container. The small opening in Package X enabled the user to pour the creamer, whereas the larger opening in Package Y allowed the user to spoon out the creamer, the traditional way of serving with the glass jars.

To assist in the package choice, the company that owns N–Rich had commissioned a marketing research study by an independent marketing research organization. The purposes of the study were to determine which alternative was preferred and to measure consumer reaction to the cardboard containers versus the glass containers. The study results, which Bendt and Ostrander were now reviewing, had been generated in an in-home product usage test in Fresno, California.

THE SAMPLE

Four large grocery stores were judgmentally chosen from the larger population of grocery stores in Fresno. Two of the stores had discount, lower-price images and two of the stores had higher-quality images. One store was chosen from each side of town to balance the study geographically.

As shoppers entered each store, they were asked in a screening interview if anyone in their household used powdered, nondairy creamer. If they answered yes, they were then asked how often they used creamers, what brand(s), and why. All those households that used creamer more than two or three times per week were then asked to participate in a marketing research study. Approximately 20 percent of those asked to participate declined to do so. Those who did agree to cooperate were given a free sample of each package and were asked to use the samples interchangeably until they received a questionnaire in two weeks' time. Fifty households were chosen in this fashion from each store for a total sample of 200 households.

THE USE TEST

The product samples that the participating households received were full-sized, 16-ounce creamer containers with a plain brown exterior and no graphic design. The only labeling was a sticker listing the manufacturer and the ingredients that the creamer contained. The only differences between the two packages were the tops; an "X" was placed on the pour top, and a "Y" was placed on the pull top.

Each participating household was mailed a copy of the questionnaire in Figure 1 two weeks after the initial store contact. Each was then called three days after the

FIGURE 1   **Coffee Creamer Questionnaire**

**Two weeks ago you were provided with coffee creamer samples "X" and "Y."
Please provide us with your reactions to each of the samples by answering the
following questions in the space provided.**

   *1. Has your household had a chance to try each of the two sample products given to
   you at the grocery store two weeks ago?*

   _____ Yes
   _____ No

(continued)

FIGURE 1   *Continued*

2. **Please rate each product on the following attributes by circling the appropriate number.** *(1 is poor, 2 is fair, 3 is o.k., 4 is good, 5 is excellent)*

	Product X	Product Y	Your Brand
Taste	1 2 3 4 5	1 2 3 4 5	1 2 3 4 5
Whitening power	1 2 3 4 5	1 2 3 4 5	1 2 3 4 5
How the product dissolves	1 2 3 4 5	1 2 3 4 5	1 2 3 4 5
Creaminess	1 2 3 4 5	1 2 3 4 5	1 2 3 4 5

3. **For each of the following, please check the space that best describes the packages X and Y.**

	Hard to Open	Moderately Hard to Open	Neutral	Moderately Easy to Open	Easy to Open
Package X	_____	_____	_____	_____	_____
Package Y	_____	_____	_____	_____	_____

	Inconvenient to Use	Moderately Inconvenient	Neutral	Moderately Convenient	Convenient to Use
Package X	_____	_____	_____	_____	_____
Package Y	_____	_____	_____	_____	_____

	Looks Unattractive	Looks Moderately Unattractive	Neutral	Looks Moderately Attractive	Looks Attractive
Package X	_____	_____	_____	_____	_____
Package Y	_____	_____	_____	_____	_____

	Messy to Use	Moderately Messy to Use	Neutral	Moderately Unmessy to Use	Not at All Messy to Use
Package X	_____	_____	_____	_____	_____
Package Y	_____	_____	_____	_____	_____

	Difficult to Get Product Out with Spoon	Moderately Difficult to Get Product Out with Spoon	Neutral	Moderately Easy to Get Product Out with Spoon	Easy to Get Product Out with Spoon
Package X	_____	_____	_____	_____	_____
Package Y	_____	_____	_____	_____	_____

FIGURE 1   *Continued*

	Product Gets Lumpy	**Product Doesn't Get Lumpy**
Package X	_____	_____
Package Y	_____	_____

4. *Please rate Packages X and Y according to how you feel they protect the quality of the product.*

	Poor	**Fair**	**O.K.**	**Good**	**Excellent**
Package X	_____	_____	_____	_____	_____
Package Y	_____	_____	_____	_____	_____

5. *Did your household prefer one of the sample packages?*
   _____ Prefer Package X   _____ No Package Preference
   _____ Prefer Package Y

6. *If your household prefers one of the sample packages, why?*

7. *Does your household prefer one of the sample packages over the glass container of the brand you usually buy?*
   _____ Prefer Package X   _____ Prefer the Glass Container
   _____ Prefer Package Y   _____ No Package Preference

8. *What are the reasons for your answer to Question #7?*

9. *Does your household prefer one of the sample products over the brand of coffee creamer you usually buy?*
   _____ Prefer Package X   _____ Prefer Usual Brand
   _____ Prefer Package Y   _____ No Preference

10. *What are the reasons for your answer to Question #9?*

11. *Would you buy one of the sample products over the brand you usually buy?*
   _____ Would Buy Product X   _____ Will Continue to Buy Usual Brand
   _____ Would Buy Product Y

12. *What are the reasons for your answer to Question #11?*

questionnaires were mailed to ascertain whether they had received it and to remind them to send it back promptly. Those households that were not reached by telephone on the first try were called back at a different time or on a different day. However, telephone contact was not made with approximately one-quarter of the households. Some of these households, as well as some of those households that were contacted, did not return the questionnaire within the two-week cut-off period established for the study.

The results Bendt and Ostrander were reviewing were based on the 136 questionnaires that were received in time to be tabulated.

Questions

1. What kind of research design is being used?
2. Evaluate the design with respect to each of the extraneous influences that can affect experiments.

CASE 2.5
Bakhill Foods

Michelle Gill, the marketing manager for Bakhill Foods, was discussing the future advertising strategy for Bakhill Coffee with the firm's advertising agency when the discussion turned to magazine ads and the copy for those ads.

Gill had recently been to a conference on psychological perception. At that conference, it was pointed out that in spite of the old adage "you can't judge a book by its cover," we do just that in our interpersonal relations; an individual's initial perception of and reaction to another individual is affected by the physical attractiveness of the other person. Further, a fair summary statement of that research is "what is beautiful is good." The evidence cited at the conference supporting this proposition was impressive. What particularly impressed Gill, though, was that the positive attributes one associates with a physically attractive person do not depend on actual contact with that person. They arise when the judge is simply shown photographs of physically attractive and unattractive individuals but is otherwise unaware of subjects' traits.

Gill thought that this knowledge could be used to advantage in the advertising copy for Bakhill Coffee. She proposed that the product be shown with a physically attractive female. The advertising agency countered with the argument that it would be better to employ physically unattractive people in the ads to make the ads more believable and effective by making them less "romantic," since coffee is not a romantic product. Further, the agency suggested it might be better to employ males in the ads rather than females. After considerable discussion, the advertising agency proposed and conducted the following research to answer two questions: Should physically attractive or unattractive individuals be used in the ads? Should male or female models be employed?

THE DESIGN

Four different advertisements were prepared. The copy was the same in each ad; only the person holding the coffee was changed. The four ads included an attractive male, an attractive female, an unattractive male, and an unattractive female. The attractiveness of each model was determined by having a convenience sample of subjects view photographs of twenty different models — ten of each sex — and rate each model on a seven-point scale where "1" was unattractive and "7" was attractive. The male and female models with the highest and the lowest mean scores were then selected as the stimulus persons for the experiment.

A color ad with each of the four models and the planned copy was then developed. A sample of subjects for the experiment was developed by random sampling from the New York City telephone book. Contacted subjects were asked to participate in a marketing research experiment. The subjects were paid for their participation, and they were also reimbursed for their travel to the agency's headquarters.

On their arrival at the ad agency, the 96 subjects who agreed to participate were randomly assigned to one of the advertisements. The 48 males and 48 females were first divided randomly into 12 groups of four persons each, and one member of each group was then assigned to one of the four ads. Each saw one, and only one, test ad. However, three other dummy ads were also used to disguise the particular ad of interest. The dummy ads were the same for each subject. Each subject was introduced to the experiment with the following instructions:

> We are interested in obtaining your opinions concerning particular test advertisements. You will be shown four ads, one at a time, and after each showing, you will be asked several questions about your reaction to the ad and the particular product depicted in the ad. You should note that this is *not* a contest to see which ad is better, so please do *not* compare the four ads in making your evaluations. Each ad should be judged by itself, without reference to the other ads.

After answering any questions, the experimenter gave the first ad to the subject. When the subject had read the advertisement, it was taken away, and the experimenter then handed the subject a copy of the data collection sheet (Figure 1). After completion of this form, the experimenter handed the subject a copy of the second ad, and the process was repeated. At no time were subjects allowed to look back at the advertisements once they had surrendered them to the researcher. To allow subjects time to warm up to the task, the experimenter always placed the test ad third in the sequence of four.

THE SCALE

The items in the scale contained in Figure 1 were chosen in order to tap all three components (cognitive, affective, and conative) of attitude. *A priori,* it was thought that the cognitive component would be measured by the *believable, informative,* and *clear* items; that the affective or liking component would be effectively tapped by the items *interesting, appealing, impressive, attractive,* and *eye-catching;* and that the conative component would be captured by the three behavioral-intention items at the bottom of the questionnaire.

These *a priori* expectations were not strictly confirmed. A basic item analysis suggested that the term "interesting" was not related to any of the three components, and it

FIGURE 1   **Sample Questionnaire for Bakhill Coffee Study**

On each of the scales below, please check the space that you feel best describes the advertisement you just read.

Interesting	:___:___:___:___:___:___:	Dull
Unappealing	:___:___:___:___:___:___:	Appealing
Unbelievable	:___:___:___:___:___:___:	Believable
Impressive	:___:___:___:___:___:___:	Unimpressive
Attractive	:___:___:___:___:___:___:	Unattractive
Uninformative	:___:___:___:___:___:___:	Informative
Clear	:___:___:___:___:___:___:	Confusing
Not eye-catching	:___:___:___:___:___:___:	Eye-catching

What is your overall reaction to this advertisement?

Unfavorable :___:___:___:___:___:___: Favorable

With regard to the product itself, how do you feel this product compares to similar products put out by other manufacturers?

Distinctive :___:___:___:___:___:___: Ordinary

Would you like to try this product?

No — Definitely not :___:___:___:___:___:___: Yes — Definitely

Would you buy this product if you happened to see it in a store?

Yes — Definitely :___:___:___:___:___:___: No — Definitely not

Would you actively seek out this product in a store in order to purchase it?

No — Definitely not :___:___:___:___:___:___: Yes — Definitely

---

was dropped from the analysis.[1] Responses to the remaining items in each component were summed to produce a total score for each component. The analysis of these scale scores indicated that[2]

1. The attractive male model produced the highest cognition scores for the ad among females and males.
2. The attractive male model produced the highest affective scores among female subjects, whereas the attractive female model produced the highest affective scores among males.

---

[1]The rationale for and method of conducting an item analysis is explored more fully in Chapter 9 and Appendix C to that chapter.

[2]The analysis of this kind of data is elaborated in the appendix to Chapter 15.

3. The attractive male model produced the highest conative scores toward the product for female subjects, whereas the unattractive male model produced the highest conative scores among male subjects.

On the basis of these results, the advertising agency suggested that the attractive male model be employed in the advertisement.

Questions

1. What kind of design is being employed in this investigation?
2. Evaluate the design.

CASE 2.6
Madison Gas and Electric Company (A)[1]

Madison Gas and Electric Company (MG&E) is a public utility that generates and distributes electric power and natural gas for the city of Madison, Wisconsin, and surrounding towns and villages. Providing service to approximately 200,000 customers over a 750-square-mile area, the company's load profile includes such diverse entities as government, manufacturers, wholesalers, retailers, agriculture, and private housing. Since government is the largest employer in the area, MG&E's loads are not seriously affected by fluctuations in the economy at large. As a consequence, load growth over the company's history has been stable and manageable.

In recent years MG&E's advertising has been largely educational. The company has tried in particular to provide its customers with information on how to conserve energy and how to use electricity and natural gas safely. One of the advertisements, for example, featured ''free energy audits.'' Any customer in MG&E's service area could call a special number to schedule a free energy audit. The company would send two company representatives who would thoroughly examine the dwelling unit and would make specific recommendations for ways the household could save money on its energy costs. The recommendations would include approximate cost estimates for the recommended changes (e.g., more insulation in the attic, weatherstripping on the doors) as well as the savings likely to be realized and the payback period. MG&E's corporate executives believed that customers benefited directly from such information because it allowed them to better control their energy costs. The company also profited, because reduced energy demand permitted it to use its existing facilities, thereby deferring new plant construction until further in the future. Customer reaction to the advertising (which is primarily television, although it includes radio and print media) had thus far been very favorable.

[1]The contributions of Thomas Noordewier to the development of this case are gratefully acknowledged.

Recently, the state of Wisconsin passed legislation stating that a public utility may not charge its ratepayers for any expenditure for advertising unless the advertising contains a disclaimer explaining that the expenditure is ultimately charged to the utility's ratepayers. According to the law, the disclaimer must be conspicuous in relation to how the advertisement is presented. More specifically, the law stated that the "written disclaimer shall be located in a conspicuous place in the advertising and shall appear in conspicuous and legible type in contrast by typography, layout or color with other printed matter in the advertising." Although committed to its safety and conservation advertising, MG&E's management was concerned about possible adverse customer reactions to advertisements containing such disclaimers. It was thought that inclusion of a rider alerting customers to the fact that they were paying for the advertising might have a negative effect on viewers' evaluations of the presented message.

RESEARCH STUDY

To address this concern, the company commissioned a study to examine how customers' perceptions of advertisements would be affected by disclaimers. The basic design of the research to be used was straightforward. A sample of 450 adult MG&E customers from each of three research sites was to be selected. More particularly, 150 subjects were to be selected at each of the three major Madison-area shopping centers: East Towne, West Towne, and South Towne. Located at the outskirts of Madison, these three shopping centers attract shoppers from the city of Madison as well as surrounding towns and villages included in MG&E's service area. All three shopping centers were used because each caters to a somewhat different clientele. The West Towne center was located in the higher income area of the city and served mainly professionals and other white-collar workers. The East Towne center was located in the lower income area and served primarily blue-collar workers. The South Towne center served a mix of the two groups.

Three different treatment levels were then randomly assigned to the groups. The three treatment levels consisted of presenting subjects television advertising messages without any disclaimer, presenting them messages with disclaimers, or presenting them messages both with and without disclaimers. The objective of the research was to ascertain whether differences in evaluations of the advertisements existed among subjects assigned to each of the three treatment levels.

The following procedures to select subjects were decided on. First, the interviewers were assigned specific spots in the corridors of each mall. They were instructed to stop adults going by the designated spots at irregular intervals. They were to ask each adult whether he or she had heard, seen, or read any utility advertising in the past few months and whether the person was an MG&E customer. If the adult said yes to both questions, the person was considered to be qualified to serve as a study subject. All others were thanked for their cooperation and dismissed.

Each qualified subject was then assigned to one of three treatment conditions. In each treatment condition, the subject was exposed to four ads and was asked to rate each commercial immediately after having seen it using a scale that ran from "highest rating" to "worst rating" with respect to how "helpful," "informative," "necessary," and "believable" the ad was. After viewing all four ads, each subject was asked to provide an overall (summary) evaluation of the commercials, using "excellent" to "poor" descriptors. In addition, each subject was asked to indicate which ad he or she liked the "best" and the "least" and why. Finally, each subject was asked to respond to a set of demographic and socioeconomic questions so that the representativeness of the sample could be checked. See Figure 1 for a copy of the questionnaire (in this case, the one used at South Towne).

FIGURE 1   **Viewing Questionnaire (South Towne, Treatment A)**

Subject is shown one commercial at a time and is asked after viewing each:

1. How would you evaluate this commercial in terms of the following characteristics (1 = highest rating, 2 = next highest, 3 = average, 4 = below average, 5 = worst rating, 6 = not sure)

Commercial #1
Home Energy Audit

	1	2	3	4	5	6
a. helpful	[ ]	[ ]	[ ]	[ ]	[ ]	[ ]
b. informative	[ ]	[ ]	[ ]	[ ]	[ ]	[ ]
c. necessary	[ ]	[ ]	[ ]	[ ]	[ ]	[ ]
d. believable	[ ]	[ ]	[ ]	[ ]	[ ]	[ ]

Commercial #2
Congratulations for Conserving Energy

	1	2	3	4	5	6
a. helpful	[ ]	[ ]	[ ]	[ ]	[ ]	[ ]
b. informative	[ ]	[ ]	[ ]	[ ]	[ ]	[ ]
c. necessary	[ ]	[ ]	[ ]	[ ]	[ ]	[ ]
d. believable	[ ]	[ ]	[ ]	[ ]	[ ]	[ ]

Commercial #3
Gas Safety

	1	2	3	4	5	6
a. helpful	[ ]	[ ]	[ ]	[ ]	[ ]	[ ]
b. informative	[ ]	[ ]	[ ]	[ ]	[ ]	[ ]
c. necessary	[ ]	[ ]	[ ]	[ ]	[ ]	[ ]
d. believable	[ ]	[ ]	[ ]	[ ]	[ ]	[ ]

(continued)

Figure 1   *Continued*

Commercial #4
Commercial Energy Audit

	1	2	3	4	5	6
a. helpful	[ ]	[ ]	[ ]	[ ]	[ ]	[ ]
b. informative	[ ]	[ ]	[ ]	[ ]	[ ]	[ ]
c. necessary	[ ]	[ ]	[ ]	[ ]	[ ]	[ ]
d. believable	[ ]	[ ]	[ ]	[ ]	[ ]	[ ]

Interviewer: Ask the following *after* showing all the commercials.

2. *Overall, how would you rate these MG&E television commercials?*

Excellent	[ ]	Not very good	[ ]
Very good	[ ]	Poor	[ ]
Average	[ ]	Not sure	[ ]

3. *Of the four commercials you saw, which one did you like the most?*

| Commercial 1 | [ ] | Commercial 3 | [ ] |
| Commercial 2 | [ ] | Commercial 4 | [ ] |

*Why?*_____

_____

_____

_____

_____

_____

_____

4. *Of the four commercials you saw, which one did you like the least?*

| Commercial 1 | [ ] | Commercial 3 | [ ] |
| Commercial 2 | [ ] | Commercial 4 | [ ] |

*Why?*_____

_____

_____

_____

_____

_____

_____

_____

Now we would like to ask you just a few more questions for classification purposes.

FIGURE 1 *Continued*

5. **Which of the following categories includes your age?**

18–24	[ ]	50–64	[ ]
25–34	[ ]	65 and over	[ ]
35–49	[ ]		

6. **What is your education level?**

Grade school or less	[ ]	College graduate	[ ]
High school graduate	[ ]	Graduate degree	[ ]
Some college	[ ]		

7. **Are you male or female?**

Male [ ]   Female [ ]

8. **Are you presently a university student?**

Student [ ]   Not a student [ ]

9. **Do you own or rent your residence?**

Own	[ ]
Rent	[ ]
Live with parents/friends/relatives	[ ]
Other	[ ]

10. **Do you pay the electric and gas bill for the household, or is it paid for by someone else?**

I pay	[ ]
Landlord pays	[ ]
Another member of the household pays	[ ]
Someone else pays	[ ]
It depends	[ ]

11. **What is your main source of your home heating? Do you heat your residence with gas, oil, electricity, coal, or how?**

Gas	[ ]	Wood	[ ]
Oil	[ ]	Other	[ ]
Electricity	[ ]	Not sure	[ ]
Coal	[ ]		

12. **To the best of your knowledge, what was the approximate amount of your gas and electric bill last month?**

Under $10.00	[ ]	$51–$75	[ ]
$11–$20	[ ]	$76–$100	[ ]
$21–$30	[ ]	$101–$200	[ ]
$31–$40	[ ]	Over $200	[ ]
$41–$50	[ ]	Not sure	[ ]

(continued)

FIGURE 1   *Continued*

---

13. **Which of the following categories includes your total family income for last year, before *taxes*?**

$7,500 or less	[ ]
$7,501 to $15,000	[ ]
$15,001 to $25,000	[ ]
$25,001 to $35,000	[ ]
$35,001 to $50,000	[ ]
$50,001 and over	[ ]
Not sure	[ ]

14. **How would you describe the area in which you live?**

City	[ ]
Suburb	[ ]
Town/rural	[ ]

15. **The Public Service Commission now requires all utility advertising to carry a disclaimer saying that the cost of advertising is included in customers' rates. What is your reaction to having MG&E's advertising carry this disclaimer?**

16. **Is there anything you'd like to add regarding MG&E's overall performance?**

TABLE 1   **Summary of Treatment Conditions***

	Shopping Center/Treatment Group								
Commercial	**South Towne**			**West Towne**			**East Towne**		
Number	**A**	**B**	**C**	**A**	**B**	**C**	**A**	**B**	**C**
1	DW/O	DW	FW	EW/O	EW	FW/O	FW/O	FW	FW
2	EW/O	EW	DW/O	GW/O	GW	DW/O	DW/O	DW	DW
3	FW/O	FW	GW	DW/O	DW	GW	GW/O	GW	GW/O
4	GW/O	GW	EW/O	FW/O	FW	EW	EW/O	EW	EW/O

*The various symbols are:
  D: home energy audit ad;
  E: congratulations for conserving energy ad;
  F: gas safety ad;
  G: commercial energy audit ad;
  W: with the disclaimer;
  W/O: without the disclaimer.

The treatment conditions differed with respect to the types of ads shown to the subjects. While the basic content of all four ads was the same for each treatment group (for example, one discussed the availability of a home energy audit, another a commercial energy audit, a third gas safety, and a fourth offered congratulations for conserving energy), the ads differed with respect to whether or not they contained the disclaimer. All those in Treatment Condition A were shown videotaped television commercials without any disclaimers. All those in Treatment Condition B were shown the same four ads with the disclaimer "the cost of this message is included in MG&E's rates" inserted at the end of the message. Those in Treatment Condition C saw two ads with the disclaimers attached and two ads without disclaimers. The ads to which the disclaimers were attached varied by shopping center, and the order in which the ads were seen also varied by shopping center. The complete design is displayed in Table 1.

Questions

1. What kind of research design is being used?
2. Evaluate the design with respect to its control of the various extraneous factors that might affect the interpretation of the research results.
3. Are there any logical reasons for changing the order of the ads and mixing up which ads contain the disclaimer and which ones do not?
4. What do you think of the way the subjects were selected?

3

DESIGN DATA COLLECTION METHOD AND FORMS

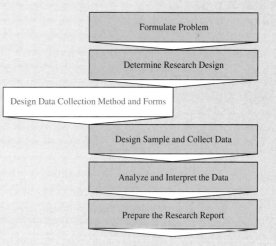

Formulate Problem

Determine Research Design

Design Data Collection Method and Forms

Design Sample and Collect Data

Analyze and Interpret the Data

Prepare the Research Report

Part 3 treats the third stage in the research process — designing the methods of data collection and the data collection forms. Chapter 6 focuses on secondary data as an information resource, while the appendix to Chapter 6 describes the contents of some of the most useful sources of published information. Chapter 7 discusses observation and communication, the main methods of data collection. Chapter 8 deals with the construction of questionnaires and observational data collection forms. Chapter 9 discusses the general topic of attitude measurement using scales and reviews the many types of attitude scales. The appendixes to Chapter 9 discuss perceptual mapping, conjoint measurement, and some basic notions about psychological measurement.

6
CHAPTER

DATA COLLECTION: SECONDARY DATA

Once the research problem is defined and clearly specified, the research effort logically turns to data collection. The natural temptation for beginning researchers is to advocate some sort of survey among appropriate respondent groups. This should be a last, rather than a first, resort. "A good operating rule is to consider a survey akin to surgery — to be used only after other possibilities have been exhausted."[1] First attempts at data collection should logically focus on secondary data.

Secondary data are statistics not gathered for the immediate study at hand but for some other purpose. **Primary data,** in contrast, are originated by the researcher for the purpose of the investigation at hand. The purpose, therefore, defines the distinction. If General Electric Company collected information on the demographic characteristics of refrigerator purchasers to determine who buys the various sizes of refrigerators, this would be primary data. If they secured this same information from internal records gathered for other purposes (for example, warranty information) or from published statistics, the information would be considered secondary data.

USING SECONDARY DATA

Beginning researchers are apt to underestimate the amount of secondary data available. Table 6.1, for example, lists some of the information on people and households that is available in the published literature for small geographic areas because of the census of population. Not searching for the secondary data that are available on a topic is unfortunate, as secondary data possess some important advantages over primary data. Further, because of the recent "information explosion," such an oversight will be even more consequential in the future.

---

[1]Robert Ferber and P. J. Verdoorn, *Research Methods in Economics and Business* (New York: Macmillan, 1962), p. 208.

TABLE 6.1   **Information Items Available from the 1990 Census of Population**

Population	Housing
100-Percent Component	
Household relationship	Number of units in structure
Sex	Number of rooms in unit
Race	Tenure — owned or rented
Age	Vacancy characteristics
Marital status	Value of owned unit or rent paid
Hispanic origin	
Sample Component	
Education — enrollment and attainment	Source of water and method of sewage disposal
Place of birth, citizenship, and year of entry	Autos, light trucks, and vans
Ancestry	Kitchen facilities
Language spoken at home	Year structure built
Migration	Year moved into residence
Disability	Number of bedrooms
Fertility	Farm residence
Veteran status	Shelter costs, including utilities
Employment and unemployment	Condominium status
Occupation, industry, and class of worker	Plumbing
Place of work and commuting to work	Telephone
Work experience and income in 1989	Utilities and fuels

Note: Subjects covered in the 100-percent component will apply to all persons and housing units. Those covered by the sample component will apply to a portion of the population and housing units.

Advantages of Secondary Data

The most significant advantages of secondary data are the cost and time economies they offer the researcher. If the required information is available as secondary data, the researcher simply needs to go to the library, locate the appropriate source or sources, and extract and record the information desired. This should take no more than a few days and would involve little cost. If the information were to be collected in a field survey, the following steps would have to be executed: data collection form designed and pretested; field interview staff selected and trained; sampling plan devised; data gathered and checked for accuracy and omissions; data coded and tabulated. As a conservative estimate, this process would take two to three months and could cost several thousand dollars, since it would include expenses and wages for a number of additional field and office personnel. With secondary data, these expenses have been incurred by the original source of the information and do not need to be borne by the user. Expenses are shared by the users of commercial sources of secondary data, but even here the user's costs will be much less than they would be if the firm collected the same information itself.

These time and cost economies prompt the general admonition: *Do not bypass secondary data. Begin with secondary data, and only when the secondary data are exhausted or show diminishing returns, proceed to primary data.* Sometimes secondary data may provide enough insight by themselves that there will be no need to collect primary data on the topic. This will be particularly true when all the analyst needs is a ballpark estimate, which is often the case. For example, a common question that confronts marketing research analysts is, "What is the market potential for the product or service?" Are enough people or organizations interested in it to justify providing it? Research Realities 6.1 illustrates how secondary data were used to advantage to answer this question. In this case, a manufacturer of pet food used secondary data to assess the potential demand for a dog food that included both moist chunks and hard, dry chunks.

Research Realities 6.1

Use of Secondary Data by a Manufacturer of Pet Foods to Assess the Potential Demand for a Dog Food That Included Both Moist Chunks and Hard, Dry Chunks

The question was, "Is there currently a significant number of persons who mix moist or canned dog food with dry dog food?" At this early stage in the exploration of this product concept, the firm did not want to expend funds for primary research. While an actual survey of pet owners would have yielded the best answer, such a survey would have required the expenditure of several thousand dollars. In addition, further development of the idea would have required a delay of several weeks to obtain the survey results. An effort to develop an acceptable first answer to the question of demand using secondary sources was initiated.

The firm identified the following information:

1. From published literature on veterinary medicine, the firm identified the amount (in ounces) of food required to feed a dog each day by type of food (dry, semimoist, moist), age, size, and type of dog.

2. From an existing survey conducted annually by the firm's advertising agency, the firm obtained information on
   a. the percentage of U.S. households owning dogs;
   b. the number, sizes, and types of dogs owned by each household in the survey;
   c. the type(s) of dog food fed to the dogs; and
   d. the frequency of use of various types of dog food.

It was assumed that dog owners who reported feeding their dogs two or more different types of dog food each day were good prospects for a product that provided premixed moist and dry food. Combining the information in the survey with the information from the literature on veterinary medicine and doing some simple multiplication produced a demand figure for the product concept. The demand exceeded 20 percent of the total volume of dog food sales, a figure sufficiently large to justify proceeding with product development and testing.

Source: David W. Stewart and Michael A. Kamins, *Secondary Research: Information Sources and Methods,* 2nd ed. (Newbury Park, Calif.: Sage Publications, 1993), p. 129. Reprinted by permission of Sage Publications, Inc.

As the example indicates, it is often necessary to make some assumptions when using secondary data in order to use the data effectively (e.g., the number of owners who were good prospects). The key is to make reasonable assumptions and to vary these assumptions to determine how sensitive a particular conclusion is to their variations. In the dog food example, ". . . altering the assumption regarding the number of owners who were good prospects for the new product to include as few as one-tenth of the original number did not alter the decision to proceed with the product. Under such circumstances, the value of additional information would be quite small."[2]

Even though it is rare when secondary data completely solve the particular problem under study, secondary data typically will (1) help to better state the problem under investigation, (2) suggest improved methods or data for better coming to grips with the problem, and/or (3) provide comparative data by which primary data can be more insightfully interpreted.

Disadvantages of Secondary Data

There are two problems that commonly arise when secondary data are used: (1) they do not completely fit the problem; and (2) there are problems with their accuracy.

Problems of Fit   Since secondary data are collected for other purposes, it will be rare when they fit the problem as defined perfectly. The problems of fit are particularly acute in cross-country studies, as the various censuses are inconsistent in the information they collect, when they collect it, and how they present it. (Research Realities 6.2 discusses this further.) In some cases, the fit will be so poor as to render them completely inappropriate. Secondary data are ill-suited to problems for three reasons: (1) units of measurement, (2) class definitions, or (3) publication currency.

It is not uncommon for secondary data to be expressed in units different from those deemed most appropriate for the project. Size of retail establishment, for instance, can be expressed in terms of gross sales, profits, square feet, and number of employees. Consumer income can be expressed by individual, family, households, and spending unit. So it is with many variables, and a recurring source of frustration in using secondary data is that the source containing the information presents that information in units of measurement different from those needed.

Assuming that the units are consistent, we find that the class boundaries presented are often different from those needed. If the problem demands income by individual in increments of $5,000 (0–$4,999, $5,000–$9,999, and so on), it does the researcher little good if the data source offers income by individual using boundaries $7,500 apart (0–$7,499, $7,500–$14,999, and so on).

---

[2]David W. Stewart, *Secondary Research: Information Sources and Methods* (Beverly Hills, Calif.: Sage Publications, 1984), p. 113. See also *Measuring Markets: A Guide to the Use of Federal and State Statistical Data* (Washington, D.C., U.S. Department of Commerce, 1979); Kathy Friedman, *Case Studies for Better Business Decisions* (Washington, D.C., U.S. Department of Commerce, 1992) for discussion of the marketing-related information that is available from the federal and state governments and how that information can be used for such marketing tasks as market potential estimation, establishing sales quotas, allocating advertising budgets, locating retail outlets, and so on.

Research Realities 6.2

Inconsistencies in the Information Collected in Country Censuses

Language

English-speaking countries, of course, present no language barriers to U.S. market researchers. And a number of nations offer bilingual census tabulations. Nations publishing census reports containing English include the Scandinavian countries, Japan, South Korea, Taiwan, Singapore, and Thailand.

Other countries offer only their native language. This is not too serious a problem if the language is French, Italian, Spanish, or Portuguese. Demographic terms in these languages are fairly close to English and the format of the tables, along with a little guesswork, is often enough to let researchers find what they need. German, Hungarian, Polish, and languages using different alphabets, such as Russian, are much more difficult to decipher unless one has been trained in these languages.

Data Content

What a researcher can get from a census depends on what is on the census form. The content is typically a mixture of traditional questions and some new items of interest to government bureaucrats and policy makers. These same forces, further modified by budget constraints, shape the form and content of the printed results.

European countries such as Switzerland and Germany print a good deal of information on noncitizens. Canada collects data on religion. Both of these topics are ignored in the U.S. censuses. What this suggests is that one cannot expect to find the same range of data topics from one country to the next; this can complicate a researcher's life enormously.

Consider income data, the lifeblood of most U.S. segmentation studies. Most nations do not include an income question in their censuses. Britain doesn't. Japan doesn't. Nor do France, Spain, and Italy. Among the few countries that have asked about income are

Canada, Australia, New Zealand, Mexico, Sweden, and Finland.

Educational attainment can be used for socioeconomic status. However, educational systems vary enough among countries that comparisons can be fairly crude. Some countries report graduates of vocational-technical schools, while in this country education is reported simply by the number of years of school attended.

Data concerning marital status also varies from country to country. Ireland, for example, recognizes only three marital statuses: single, married, and widowed. Other countries tabulate the separated population, but sometimes lump it in with divorced or married populations. Latin American censuses often have "cohabitating" or "consensual union" as marital categories. Sweden cross-tabulates its cohabiting population by marital status. Although most countries gather data on marital status, few cross-tabulate it with household headship. Nor is headship often cross-tabulated by educational attainment.

Census Frequency

The United States takes a census every ten years, which is the typical frequency. Japan and Canada conduct their censuses every five years, but the mid-decade counts are not as complete as the ones done at the end of each decade. France takes a census irregularly; since the 1960s, the interval has been about seven years. In what used to be West Germany, the most recent census was taken in 1987, but the previous one was in 1970, the same year of the last Dutch census.

Some northern and western European nations seem to be abandoning the census as a data collection tool. Instead, they hope to rely on population registers to account for births, deaths, and changes in marital status or place of residence. One result of this appears to be less hard-copy data. Assuming that government data bases can be tapped for market research purposes, this would present no serious problem where research budgets are robust. However, government bureaucrats aren't always friendly to market researchers.

Source: Donald B. Pittenger,"Gathering Foreign Demographics is No Easy Task," *Marketing News*, 24 (January 8, 1990), pp. 23, 25. Reprinted with permission of American Marketing Association.

Finally, secondary data quite often lack publication currency. The time from data collection to data publication is often long, sometimes as much as three years, as, for example, with much government census data. Even though census data have great value while current, this value diminishes rapidly with time, as many marketing decisions require current, rather than historical, information.

Problems of Accuracy   The accuracy of much secondary data is also questionable. As this book indicates, there are numerous sources of error possible in the collection, analysis, and presentation of marketing information. When the researcher collects the information, the individual's firsthand experience should allow the assessment of the accuracy of the information and its bounds of error. These bounds can be critical for marketing decisions that are based on the information. When using secondary data, the researcher is in no way relieved from assessing accuracy. It is still the researcher's responsibility, although the task is indeed more difficult.[3] The following criteria, though, should help the researcher judge the accuracy of any secondary data: they are the source, the purpose of publication, and general evidence regarding quality.[4]

Consider the source first. Secondary data can be secured from either a primary source or a secondary source. A **primary source** is the source that originated the data. A **secondary source** is a source that, in turn, secured the data from an original source. The *Statistical Abstract of the United States,* which is published each year, contains a great deal of useful information for many research projects. The researcher using the *Statistical Abstract* would be using a secondary source of secondary data, as none of what is published in the *Statistical Abstract* originates there. Rather, all of it is taken from other government and trade sources. The researcher who *terminated* the search for secondary data with the *Statistical Abstract* would violate the most fundamental rule in using secondary data — *always use the primary source of secondary data.*

There are two main reasons for this rule. First and foremost, the researcher will need to search for general evidence of quality (e.g., the methods of data collection and analysis). The primary source will typically be the only source that describes the process of collection and analysis, and thus it is the only source by which this judgment can be made. Second, a primary source is usually more accurate and complete than a secondary source. Secondary sources often fail ''to reproduce significant footnotes, or textual comments, by which the primary source had qualified the data or the definition of units.''[5]

---

[3]Jacob has a particularly helpful discussion on the various errors that are present in published data and what remedies are available to the analyst for treating these errors. See Herbert Jacob, *Using Published Data: Errors and Remedies* (Beverly Hills, Calif.: Sage Publications, 1984). The problem of accuracy in secondary data seems to be getting worse as the ability to generate and capture data expands; see William M. Bulkeley, ''Databases Are Plagued by Reign of Error,'' *The Wall Street Journal* (May 26, 1992), p. B6.

[4]For an alternative list of criteria, see Stewart, *Secondary Research,* pp. 23–33.

[5]Erwin Esser Nemmers and John H. Myers, *Business Research: Text and Cases* (New York: McGraw-Hill, 1966), p. 38. See also William G. Zikmund, *Business Research Methods,* 4th ed. (Chicago: The Dryden Press, 1994).

Research Realities 6.3

Using the Source to Evaluate the Accuracy of Secondary Data

A. Northwest Airlines
Airline passengers who fly Northwest appear to have a lot to complain about — and they did so in droves last year; in fact, complaints against Northwest increased 1,418 percent.

B. Security and Exchange Commission
The Security and Exchange Commission is studying the possibility of replacing stock certificates with a paperless electronic book-entry system. A major advantage of the electronic system is that it would speed up the way securities trades are processed, reducing

the period to settle short trades to three days from the current five. However, a study among 750 investors by Frederick/Schneiders, Inc. indicated that 81 percent were opposed to eliminating the stock certificates. A large majority of those surveyed cited the potential for computer error or the collapse of a brokerage firm as reasons for wanting to hold on to their certificates.

C. Home Handymen
Home handymen play a significant role in millions of purchasing decisions, a new study finds. According to the study, 18 million ''must-know'' men affect what is bought by as many as 85 million other consumers. The study says that such men — independent do-it-yourselfers who have a compulsion to know what makes things tick and enjoy fiddling with gadgets — are sought out for their advice by buyers of products in such areas as home improvement and electronics.

Source: Example A: ''If You Can't Lick 'Em, Just Call 'Em Names,'' *The Wall Street Journal* (March 30, 1988), p. 21; Example B: Sandra Block, ''SEC to Sponsor Discussions on a Plan to Make Stock Certificates Obsolete, Speed Up Settlement,'' *The Wall Street Journal* (November 27, 1990), pp. C1, C13; Example C: ''Just Ask the Man Who Has Taken One Apart,'' *The Wall Street Journal* (September 20, 1991), p. B1.

Errors in transcription can also occur in copying the data from a primary source. Once made, transcription errors seem to hold on tenaciously, as the following example illustrates. In 1901, Napoleon Lajoie produced the highest batting average ever attained in the American League when he batted .422 on 229 hits in 543 times at bat. In setting the type for the record book after that season, a printer correctly reported Lajoie's .422 average, but incorrectly reported his hits, giving him 220 instead of 229. A short time later, someone pointed out that 220 hits in 543 at bats yields a batting average of .405, and so Lajoie's reported average was changed. The error persisted for some 50 years until an energetic fan checked all the old box scores and discovered the facts.[6]

A second criterion by which the accuracy of secondary data can be assessed is the purpose of publication. Consider the examples in Research Realities 6.3. After reading them, do you think any of the following: (A) Northwest Airlines is a troubled carrier;

---

[6]*The Chicago Tribune,* September 19, 1960. If there had not been a cult of ''baseball superfans whose passion is to dig up obscure facts about the erstwhile national pastime,'' the error might never have been discovered. See ''You May Not Care But 'Nappie' Lajoie Batted .422 in 1901,'' *The Wall Street Journal* (September 13, 1974), p. 1.

(B) the SEC should reconsider its plan to go to an electronic book-entry system for stock transfers; (C) home handymen are an important group of innovators that marketers need to target in their communications? Are your reactions any different if you are told: Example A resulted from press releases prepared by the Tobacco Institute, which was upset over Northwest Airlines' announced ban on smoking on all of its domestic flights; the survey in Example B was sponsored by U.S. Banknote Corporation, a large printer of stock certificates; or the survey in Example C was sponsored by *Popular Mechanics* magazine? Do you now have the same confidence in the objectivity of the results? Probably not, suggesting one can use the source as a criterion to evaluate the accuracy of secondary data.

> Sources published to promote sales, to advance the interests of an industrial or commercial or other group, to present the cause of a political party, or to carry on any sort of propaganda are suspect. Data published anonymously, or by an organization which is on the defensive, or under conditions which suggest a controversy, or in a form which reveals a strained attempt at "frankness," or to controvert inferences from other data are generally suspect.[7]

This is not to say that data collected or sponsored by an interested party cannot be used by the researcher. Rather, it is simply to suggest that such data should be viewed most critically by the research user. A source that has no ax to grind but, rather, publishes secondary data as its primary function deserves confidence. If data publication is a source's *raison d'être,* high quality must be maintained. Inaccurate data offer such a firm no competitive advantage, and their publication represents a potential loss of confidence and eventual demise. The success of any organization supplying data as its primary purpose depends on the long-run satisfaction on the part of its users that the information supplied is indeed accurate.

The third criterion by which the accuracy of secondary data can be assessed is the general evidences of quality. One item of evidence here is the ability of the supplying organization to collect the data. The Internal Revenue Service, for example, has greater leverage in securing income data than an independent marketing research firm. Related to this issue, though, is the question of whether the additional leverage introduces bias. Would a respondent be more likely to hedge in estimating his or her income in completing a tax return or in responding to a consumer survey? In addition, the user needs to ascertain how the data were collected. A primary source should provide a detailed description of how the data were collected, including definitions, data collection forms, methods of sampling, and so forth. If it does not, researcher beware! Such omissions are usually indicative of sloppy methods.

---

[7]Nemmers and Myers, *Business Research,* p. 43. For other illustrations of how knowledge of the source provides insights into the accuracy of the data, see Marilyn Chose, "Mixing Science, Stocks Raises Question of Bias in the Testing of Drugs," *The Wall Street Journal* (January 26, 1989), p. Al; Michael Miller, "High-Tech Hype Reaches New Heights," *The Wall Street Journal* (January 12, 1989), p. B1; Jeff Bailey, "How Two Industries Created a Fresh Spin on the Dioxin Debate," *The Wall Street Journal* (February 20, 1992), pp. A1, A6; "Leading Researchers Invite Criticism — and They Get It," *Marketing News,* 26 (June 22, 1992), p. 5.

When the details of data collection are provided, the user of secondary data should examine them thoroughly. Was the sampling plan sound? Was this type of data best collected through questionnaire or by observational methods? What about the quality of the field force? What kind of training was provided? What kinds of checks of the field-work were employed? What was the extent of nonresponse due to refusals, to subjects not at home, and by item? Are these statistics reported? Is the information presented in a well-organized manner? Are the tables properly labeled, and are the data within them internally consistent? Are the conclusions supported by the data? As these questions suggest, the user of secondary data must be familiar with the research process and the potential sources of error. The remainder of this book should provide much of the needed insight for evaluating secondary data. For the moment, though, let us examine some of the main sources of secondary data.

ETHICAL DILEMMA 6.1

An independent marketing research firm was hired by a manufacturer of power equipment such as lawn mowers, snowblowers, and chain saws, to study the Minneapolis market. The manufacturer wanted to determine (1) whether there was sufficient market potential to warrant opening a new dealership, and (2) if so, where the dealership should be located in the metropolitan area. The research firm went about the task by scouring secondary data on the Minneapolis market, partic-ularly statistics published by the Census Bureau. In less than two months, the research firm was able to develop a well-documented recommendation as to what the power equipment manufac-turer should do.

Approximately six months after completing this study, the firm was approached by a manu-facturer of electric power tools to do a similar study concerning the location of a distribution center through which it could more effectively serve the many hardware stores in the area.

- Is it ethical for the research firm to use the information it has collected in the first study to reduce its cost quote to the client in the second?
- Does it make any difference if the firm making electric power tools also manufactures electric mowers and chain saws?
- Suppose some of the data were collected through personal interviews that the first client paid for. Should that affect the situation in any way?

TYPES OF SECONDARY DATA

There are several ways by which secondary data can be classified. One of the most useful is by source, which immediately suggests the classification of internal and exter-nal data. **Internal data** are those found within the organization for whom the research is being done, whereas **external data** are those obtained from outside sources. The exter-nal sources can be further split into those that regularly publish statistics and make them available to the user at no charge (e.g., the United States government) and the commercial organizations that sell their services to various users (e.g., A. C. Nielsen Company). In the remainder of this chapter, we will review some of the more important sources of commercialized statistics; Appendix 6A treats some of the main sources of published statistics. Together they represent some of the most commonly used sources of secondary data, the ones with which the researcher would typically commence the search. Figure 6.1 provides an overview of these sources.

Internal Secondary Data

Data that originate within the firm for which the research is being conducted are internal data. If they were collected for some other purpose, they are internal secondary data. The sales and cost data compiled in the normal accounting cycle represent promising

FIGURE 6.1   **Types of Secondary Data**

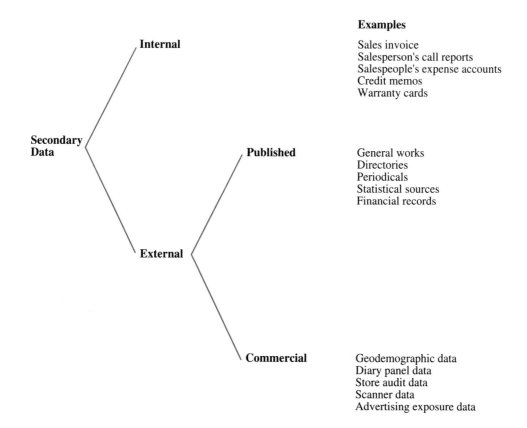

internal secondary data for many research problems. This is particularly true when the problem is one of evaluating past marketing strategy or of assessing the firm's competitive position in the industry. It is less helpful in future-directed decisions, such as evaluating a new product or a new advertising campaign. Even here, though, sales and cost data can serve as a foundation for planning this research.

Generally, the single most productive source document is the sales invoice. From this, the following information can usually be extracted:

- Customer name and location.
- Product(s) or service(s) sold.
- Volume and dollar amount of the transaction.
- Salesperson (or agent) responsible for the sale.
- End use of product sold.
- Location of customer facility where product is to be shipped and/or used.
- Customer's industry, class of trade, and/or channel of distribution.
- Terms of sale and applicable discount.
- Freight paid or to be collected.
- Shipment point for the order.
- Transportation used in shipment.

Other documents provide more specialized input. Some of the more important of these are listed in Table 6.2. Most companies are likely to use only two or three of these sources of sales information in addition to the sales invoice. The particular ones depend on the company and the types of analyses used to plan and evaluate the marketing effort. Even something as simple as a product registration card can be used to advantage for marketing intelligence, as Research Realities 6.4 indicates.

Another useful but often overlooked source of internal secondary data is previous marketing research studies on related topics. Even though each study typically addresses a number of specific questions, most also involve only one or two key items that have been learned. There can be great synergy when these key items are studied and combined. As Larry Stanek, who was then the director of marketing research at Kraft, commented:

> Combining key learnings can help you develop a competitive advantage for your company. By examining your combined learnings, you may discover things that other companies have yet to learn. Or you can learn to be more productive or cost effective and lower your research costs. Or you may learn something that helps you skip steps or speeds your development processes. . . .[8]

Two of the most important advantages associated with internal secondary data are their ready availability and low cost. Internal secondary data are the least costly of any

---

[8]Larry P. Stanek, "Keeping Focused on the Consumer While Managing Tons of Information," in *Presentations from the 9th Annual Marketing Research Conference* (Chicago: American Marketing Association, 1988), pp. 66–67. See also Joel D. Raphael and Richard Kitaeff, "The Research Information Center," *Marketing Research: A Magazine of Management & Applications* 2 (September 1990), pp. 50–52.

TABLE 6.2 **Some Useful Sources of Internal Secondary Data**

Document	Information Provided
Cash register receipts	Type (cash or credit) and dollar amount of transaction by department by salesperson
Salesperson's call reports	Customers and prospects called on (company and individual seen; planned or unplanned calls)
	Products discussed
	Orders obtained
	Customers' product needs and usage
	Other significant information about customers
	Distribution of salesperson's time among customer calls, travel, and office work
	Sales-related activities: meetings, conventions, etc.
Salesperson's expense accounts	Expenses by day by item (hotel, meals, travel, etc.)
Individual customer (and prospect) records	Name and location and customer number
	Number of calls by company salesperson (agents)
	Sales by company (in dollars and/or units, by product or service, by location of customer facility)
	Customer's industry, class of trade, and/or trade channel
	Estimated total annual usage of each product or service sold by the company
	Estimated annual purchases from the company of each such product or service
	Location (in terms of company sales territory)
Financial records	Sales revenue (by products, geographic markets, customers, class of trade, unit of sales organization, etc.)
	Direct sales expenses (similarly classified)
	Overhead sales costs (similarly classified)
	Profits (similarly classified)
Credit memos	Returns and allowances
Warranty cards	Indirect measures of dealer sales
	Customer service

type of marketing research, and if maintained in an appropriate form, internal sales data can be used to analyze the company's sales performance by product, geographic location, customer, channel of distribution, and so on. Cost data allow the further determination of the profitability of these segments of the business. We shall not go into the details of this type of analysis here because it is a somewhat specialized topic and is extensively reported elsewhere.[9] The aspiring researcher should not bypass this information but should begin most studies with internal secondary data.

---

[9] See, for example, Charles H. Sevin, *Marketing Productivity Analysis* (New York: McGraw-Hill, 1965); or Sanford R. Simon, *Managing Marketing Profitability* (New York: American Management Association, Inc., 1969) for two of the best treatments of sales and profitability analysis.

Research Realities 6.4

Targeting: It's in the Cards

When the Skil Corporation was launching a cordless power screwdriver, management was worried. It believed that the company had designed a useful product, but it wondered whether consumers would think the new tool was just a gimmick. Using information from product registration cards and follow-up interviews, Skil was quickly able to prove to itself that the screwdriver was not a fad.

The registration card research revealed something else, however. Although do-it-yourselfers were the primary market for the new product, a substantial portion of the purchasers were elderly people for whom the screwdriver's ease of operation was the chief advantage. "We hadn't realized the arthritis implications," says Skil's Ron Techter. In response, Skil began advertising in publications geared to older Americans.

Almost everyone has filled out a product registration card. As they slip the card into the mailbox, few consumers realize that they have just completed a questionnaire. Yet for National Demographics & Lifestyles (NDL), the information from product-registration cards has been pure gold. NDL compiles information from these "mini-questionnaires" to feed its comprehensive data base, which includes demographics and participation information covering 57 activities, interests, and life-styles.

According to Jock Bickert, the company's founder, NDL data offer no special advantage at a national level, because a marketer can survey 1,500 or 2,000 consumers to obtain national projections. However, NDL's data base is very powerful when one moves down to individual markets, neighborhoods, or even postal routes.

One company that has made effective use of NDL's data is Amana Appliance. One day Bill Packard, domestic sales manager for an independent Amana Appliance distributor in Fort Lauderdale, was talking with Amana's manager of marketing services, Dave Collins. Collins mentioned that Amana could provide Packard with profiles of Amana purchasers from his territory for the past year and a half, based on NDL product-registration cards. When the NDL profile arrived, Packard got an idea.

He took the information to the marketing director of a Boca Raton real estate developer who was trying to decide what brand of appliances to put into his $200,000 homes. Packard pointed out that the purchaser profile of high-end Amana products perfectly matched the developer's profile of potential customers. Initially skeptical, the marketing director polled 100 potential home buyers himself. These home-buyer profiles so closely matched Amana's that the developer decided to use Amana appliances in the kitchens.

"If you look at one of our completed questionnaires," says NDL's Jock Bickert, "you really begin to get a picture of the individual. You are able to say, 'This person is a likely candidate for these kinds of offers and promotions and appeals and is very unlikely for other kinds.' You can't do that if you are looking at demography alone."

Source: Wally Wood, "Targeting: It's In the Cards," *Marketing & Media Decisions*, 23 (September 1988), pp. 121–122.

Searching for Published External Secondary Data

There is such a wealth of published external data that beginning researchers typically underestimate what is available. The statement that there is *some relevant* external secondary data on almost any problem a marketer might confront is not an exaggeration. The fundamental problem is not availability; it is identifying and accessing what is there. Even those researchers who do have an inkling of how much valuable secondary data there is are typically unsure of how to go about searching for it. Figure 6.2 provides

FIGURE 6.2   **How to Get Started When Searching for Published Sources of Secondary Data**

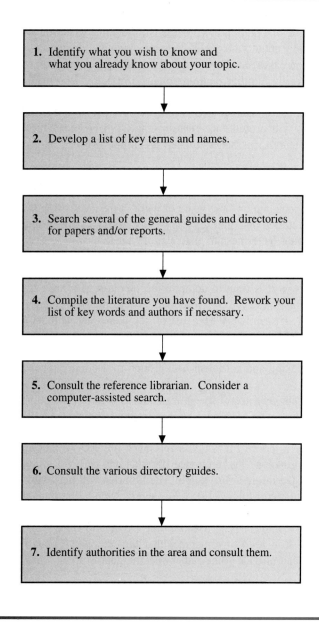

1. Identify what you wish to know and what you already know about your topic.

2. Develop a list of key terms and names.

3. Search several of the general guides and directories for papers and/or reports.

4. Compile the literature you have found. Rework your list of key words and authors if necessary.

5. Consult the reference librarian. Consider a computer-assisted search.

6. Consult the various directory guides.

7. Identify authorities in the area and consult them.

some general guidelines that can be used to get started on a search of secondary data on a particular topic.[10]

Step 1   The first step in the process is to identify what you wish to know and what you already know about your topic. This may include relevant facts, names of researchers or organizations associated with the topic, key papers and other publications with which you are already familiar, and any other information you may have.

Step 2   A useful second step is to develop a list of key terms and names. These terms and names will provide access to secondary sources. Unless you have a very specific topic of interest, it is better to keep this initial list long and quite general.

Step 3   In Step 3, you are ready to use the library for the first time. It is useful to begin your search with several of the directories and guides listed in Appendix 6A. Only look at the previous two or three years of work in the area, using three or four general guides. Some directories and indexes use a specialized list of key terms or descriptors. Such indexes often have thesauri that identify these terms. A search of these directories requires that your list of terms and descriptors be consistent with the thesauri.

Step 4   Now it is time to compile the literature you have found. Is it relevant to your needs? Perhaps you are overwhelmed by information. Perhaps you have found little that is relevant. If so, rework your list of key words and authors and expand your search to include a few more years and a few additional sources. Once again evaluate your findings. By the end of Step 4, you should have a clear idea of the nature of the information you are seeking and sufficient background to use more specialized sources.

Step 5   One very useful specialized source is a reference librarian. Reference librarians are specialists who have been trained to know the contents of many of the key information sources in a library, as well as how to search those sources most effectively. It is a rare problem indeed for which a reference librarian cannot uncover some relevant published information. The reference librarian can help you if you wish to consider a computer-assisted information search. The librarian will need your help, though, in the form of a carefully constructed list of key words. Some librarians will prefer to produce their own lists of key words or descriptors, but it is a good idea to verify that such a list is reasonably complete. The librarian may be able to suggest specialized sources related to the topic. You need to remember that the reference librarian cannot be of much help until you can provide some rather specific details about what you want to know.

---

[10] The figure and surrounding discussion are adapted from David W. Stewart, *Secondary Research: Information Sources and Methods* (Beverly Hills, Calif.: Sage Publications, 1984). See also Jac L. Goldstucker, *Marketing Information: A Professional Reference Guide,* 2nd ed. (Atlanta: College of Business Administration, Georgia State University, 1987).

Step 6   If you have had little success or your topic is highly specialized, consult one of the general guides to information listed in Appendix 6A. These are really directories of directories, which means that this level of search will be very general. You will first need to identify potentially useful primary directories, which will then lead you to other sources.

Step 7   If you are unhappy with what you have found or are otherwise having trouble, and the reference librarian has not been able to identify sources, use an authority. Identify some individual or organization that might know something about the topic. The various *Who's Who* publications, *Consultants and Consulting Organizations Directory, Encyclopedia of Associations, Industrial Research Laboratories in the United States,* or *Research Centers Directory* may help you identify sources. The Bureau of the Census puts out a list of department specialists who users can contact for information on any of the Bureau's studies. These people are often quite knowledgeable about related studies in their areas of expertise. Faculty at universities, government officials, and business executives can also be useful sources of information.

Some Key General Sources of External Secondary Data

In addition to the key role played by reference librarians, some other particularly important sources of external secondary data are associations, general guides to useful marketing information, and on-line computer searches.

Associations   Most associations gather, and often publish, detailed information on such things as industry shipments and sales, growth patterns, environmental factors affecting the industry, operating characteristics, and the like. Trade associations are often able to secure information from members that other research organizations cannot because of the working relationships that exist between the association and the firms that belong to it. Two useful sources for locating associations serving a particular industry are *Directories in Print* and the *Encyclopedia of Associations,* described in Appendix 6A.

General Guides to Secondary Data   Other useful sources for locating information on a particular topic are the general guides to secondary data described in Appendix 6A. Table 6.3, for example, lists what the *Encyclopedia of Business Information Sources* has to say about data sources on the electric appliance industry. Aspiring researchers are also well-advised to acquaint themselves with the more important general sources of marketing information so that they know what statistics are available and where they can be found. Many of the most important of these are listed and briefly described in Appendix 6A.

On-Line Computer Searches

On-line computer searches have become increasingly popular in the last 20 years for locating published information and data, as computer-readable storage systems for data bases have come into their own. Many public libraries, as well as college and university

TABLE **6.3**   **Sources of Data on the Electric Appliance Industry**

General Works

The Last Hundred Years: Household Technology. Daniel Cohen. M. Evans and Company, 216 E. 49th Street, New York, NY 10017. (212) 688-2810. 1982. $8.95.

Directories

Appliance — Appliance Industry Purchasing Directory. Dana Chase Publications, 1110 Jorie Blvd., CS-9019, Oakbrook, IL 60522 (312) 990-3484. Annual. $35.00

Appliance Manufacturer Buyers Guide. Corcoran Communications, Inc., 29100 Aurora Rd., Solon, OH 44139. (216) 349-3060. Annual. $25.00.

Directory of Consumer Electronics, Photography & Major Appliance Retailers & Distributors. Chain Store Guide Information Services, 425 Park Ave., New York, NY 10022. (212) 371-9400. Biennial. $199.00. Firms with a minimum of $250,000 in annual sales. Generally includes product lines, sales volume, year founded, key personnel, and related information.

Financial Ratios

Cost of Doing Business Survey. National Association of Retail Dealers of America, 10 E. 22nd St.,

No. 310, Lombard, IL 60148. (708) 953-8950. Annual. Members, $50,00; nonmembers, $75.00.

On-line Data Bases

Trinet Databases. Trinet, Inc., Nine Campus Dr., Parsippany, NJ 07054. (800) 874-6381 or (201) 267-3600. Current data on U.S. non-manufacturers and manufacturers. Updated several times a year. Inquire as to on-line cost and availability.

Periodicals and Newsletters

Appliance. Dana Chase Publications, 1110 Jorie Blvd., CS-9019, Oakbrook, IL 60522. (312) 990-3484. Monthly. $65.00 per year.

Appliance Manufacturer. Corcoran Communications, Inc., 29100 Aurora Rd., Solon, OH 44139 (216) 349-3060. Monthly. $50.00 per year.

Appliance Service News. Gammit Enterprises, Inc., 110 W. Saint Charles Rd., Lombard, IL 60148. (312) 932-9550. Monthly. $11.25.

Executive Update Newsletter. National Electrical Manufacturers Association, 2101 L St., N. W., Washington, DC 20037. (202) 467-8400. Monthly. $10.00 per year. Newsletter for managers in the electrical product manufacturing industries.

libraries, have invested in the equipment and personnel that are necessary to make data-base searching available to their patrons. Currently, there are more than 3,000 data bases to pick from, with 200 to 300 of them applying to business.

The operation of the on-line services is as follows: There is a data-base producer, a data-base vendor, and a data user. The data-base producer collects the information and edits it according to the organization's criteria. The producer then puts it on tape or compact disk and sells it to the vendor for a fee. The vendor mounts the tape or disk on a computer. The vendor might combine or split the information to fit his or her own needs. Thus, the same data base from different vendors might have different structures.

TABLE **6.3** *Continued*

NARDA News. National Association of Retail Dealers of America, 10 E. 22nd St., No. 310, Lombard, IL 60148. (708) 953-8950. Monthly. $48.00.

NEMA News Bulletin. National Electrical Manufacturers Association, 2101 L St., N. W., Washington, DC 20037. (202) 467-8400. Monthly. Membership newsletter.

Product Design and Development. Chilton Co., Chilton Way, Radnor, PA 19089. (800) 345-1214 or (215) 964-4000. Monthly. $35.00 per year.

Statistics Sources

Dealerscope. North American Publishing Co., 401 N. Broad St., Philadelphia, PA 19108. (215) 238-5300. Monthly. Free to qualified personnel. Formerly *Merchandising*.

Facts and Figures. National Electrical Manufacturers Association, 2101 L St., N. W., Washington, DC 20037. (202) 467-8400. Annual. Free. Produced by NEMA Statistical Department. Provides economic data relating to over 70 electrical products.

Major Household Appliances. U.S. Bureau of the Census, Washington, DC 20233. (301) 763-4100. Annual. $1.00.

Trade Associations and Professional Societies

Appliance Parts Distributors Association. 228 E. Baltimore St., Detroit, MI 48202. (313) 875-8455.

Association of Home Appliance Manufacturers. 20 N. Wacker Dr., Chicago, IL 60606 (312) 984-5800.

National Appliance Service Association. 406 W. 34th St., Suite 628, Kansas City, MO 64111. (816) 753-0210.

National Association of Retail Dealers of America. 10 E. 22nd St., Lombard, IL 60148. (312) 953-8950.

Other Sources

Small Household Appliances. Available from Off-the-Shelf Publications, Inc., 2171 Jericho Turnpike, Commack, NY 11725. (516) 462-2410. 1987. $795.00. Published by Business Trend Analysts. Market data. Covers toasters, coffeemakers, food processors, etc.

Value Line Investment Survey. Value Line, Inc., 711 Third Ave., New York, NY 10017. (212) 687-3965. Weekly. $495.00 per year. Published in three parts: (I) Summary & Index, (II) Selection & Opinion, (III) Ratings and Reports. Part III contains analyses of specific industries.

Source: James Woy, ed., *Encyclopedia of Business Information Sources*, 8th ed. (Detroit: Gale Research, Inc., 1991–1992), pp. 334–335.

The vendor also pays a fee every time the data base is used and pays a fee for all citations from it. The user pays when accessing the data base whether he or she gets the answer or not. The more information one gets, the more one pays. The user also pays for the use of the telephone lines, connect charges, and printing charges. Printing charges vary as a function of how much is printed and whether the printing occurs on-line or off-line at a more convenient time, in which case the output is mailed to the user. In sum, the costs of using a data base include: (1) planning and executing the search, (2) telephone line charges, (3) connect charges, and (4) citation and printing charges. The big advantage of on-line searching is time savings. Some of the more well-known data-base vendors are: BRS, Compuserve, Data-Star, Dialog, Easynet, Mead Data Central, Orbit, The Source, and Vu/Text.

Data bases are typically defined by the type of information they contain. For example, bibliographic data bases provide references to magazine or journal articles. They will list the name of the article, the author, the title of the journal, and the date of publication. They are also likely to include some key words that describe the contents of the article. Most bibliographic data bases also provide an abstract or summary of the article. Some of the useful data bases for marketers are those that contain the following:

- *Specific company or industry information* — The information in these data bases comes primarily from reports filed with the Securities and Exchange Commission, stockholder reports, and stock market information. The data bases cover financial, marketing, and product information, some company profiles, and the usual directory information such as name of the organization, its address, and its phone number. Typical examples are *Moody's Corporate Profiles* and *Standard and Poor's Corporate Descriptions*.

- *Mergers, affiliations, ownership information* — These data bases typically list the institutions and people that own a stock by name, and the ownership changes, including the mergers and acquisitions, that have taken place in the recent past or are pending. Typical examples are *Disclosure/Spectrum Ownership* and *Insider Trading Monitor*.

- *Company directory information* — There are a number of directories. These differ in the types of companies they cover (e.g., public or private), the size of the companies covered, and their geographic coverage. In addition to the name, address, and telephone number, many of the directories will list the primary and secondary Standard Industrial Classification (SIC) codes for the business. Typical examples are *D&B Dun's Market Identifiers* and *Standard and Poor's Corporate Register*.

- *U.S. government contract information* — These data bases are particularly useful to businesses dealing with the government. They contain information on whether a specific company has any government contracts and recent contract awards. Typical examples are *Commerce Business Daily* and *DMS Contract Awards*.

- *Economic information* — These data bases contain general economic and demographic information. Some of it comes from U.S. census materials and some from the private sector. Many of these data bases contain forecasts of future economic activity. Typical examples are *Cendata* and *PTS U.S. Forecasts*.

- *General business information* — These data bases cover companies, industries, people, and products. The information from them comes primarily from trade and business-oriented journals, selected newspapers, and various reports. Typical examples are *ABI/Inform* and *Harvard Business Review*.

- *Brand name/trade name information* — These data bases contain information on specific products, including what competitors might be doing with respect to new product introductions or expenditures on advertising and which company owns a specific trademark. Typical examples are *New Product Announcements* and *Thomas Register Online*.

TABLE 6.4   **How to Conduct a Data-Base Search**

Step 1: Specify the information to be sought and develop a "search strategy." The search strategy is a set of words that will be entered into the computer for the actual search. If the data base being searched is unfamiliar, it is often valuable to develop the search strategy with the help of a specialist familiar with the data base.

Step 2: Log on to the data base, either by loading the appropriate CD-Rom (read-only computer disk) disk or by dialing the data-base computer via a modem. If dialing, the data-base computer will ask for identification to determine whether the searcher is an authorized user of the system. The user will reply by typing in a code. If it is accepted, the data-base computer will ask for the name of the data base or file to be searched.

Step 3: Input the search strategy. When the search strategy has been entered, the computer will begin the search and will report the number of matches. If the number of matches is large, the user may wish to add further qualifications to the terms used in the search to find the specific information he or she needs.

Step 4: If the results are satisfactory, the user must decide the level of detail he or she wishes to see for each match made. The choices may include a simple bibliography, an annotated bibliography, a bibliography with abstracts, or the full text. The more detail the user wants, the more costly the search will be because of printing charges. Users doing a search via modem connections with the data-base computer will also need to decide whether to have the information printed at the computer site and delivered later by mail or United Parcel Service, or printed immediately at the terminal. Having the results delivered by mail or UPS is usually cheaper, since charges for the services are partially based on the amount of time the computer is connected to the user's terminal.

- *People information* — These data bases contain information on people who have been noted in the literature for their accomplishments in the arts, sciences, business, or other fields of endeavor. These data bases are used to track people in the business world or inventors and the patents they hold. Typical examples are *American Men & Women of Science* and *Standard & Poor's Register-Biographical.*

As the preceding list indicates, companies use on-line data bases to search for journal articles, reports, speeches, marketing data, economic trends, legislation, inventions, and many other types of information on a particular topic. Some especially useful guides to on-line data bases are described in Appendix 6A. Table 6.4 explains how to conduct a data-base search.

STANDARDIZED MARKETING INFORMATION SERVICES

The many standardized marketing information services that are available are another important source of secondary data for the marketing researcher. These services are available at some cost to the user and in this respect are a more expensive source of secondary data than published information. However, they are also typically much less expensive than primary data, because purchasers of these data share the costs incurred

---

ETHICAL DILEMMA 6.2

A marketing manager for a dog food manufacturer stumbled onto an important piece of competitive intelligence while visiting a local printer near the company's plant. While waiting to speak with the salesperson that handled the company's account, the manager noticed some glossy advertising proofs for one of its competitor's products. The ad highlighted some new low prices. When he mentioned the prices to the printer, he was told that they were part of a new advertising campaign. The marketing manager called a meeting of the company's own management on his return to headquarters. As a result of that meeting, the company initiated a preemptive, price-cutting campaign of its own that effectively neutralized the competitor's strategy.

- Did the marketing manager act ethically in reporting the information back to his own company?
- Would your judgment be different if the proofs were in a folder and the marketing manager somewhat casually but inadvertently opened the folder while standing there? What if he did so on purpose after noticing that the folder pertained to the competitor?
- Should information like this be entered into the firm's decision support system?

---

by the supplier in collecting, editing, coding, and tabulating them. Because it must be suitable for a number of users, though, what is collected and how the data are gathered must be uniform. Thus, the data may not always ideally fit the needs of the user, which is their main disadvantage over primary data.

This section reviews some of the main types and sources of standardized marketing information service data.

Profiling Customers

Market segmentation is common among businesses seeking to improve their marketing efforts. Effective segmentation demands that firms group their customers into relatively homogeneous groups. That enables them to tailor marketing programs to the individual groups, thereby making them more effective. A common segmentation base for firms selling industrial goods takes into account the industry designation or designations of its customers, most typically by means of the Standard Industrial Classification (SIC) codes. The SIC codes are a system developed by the U.S. Census Department for organizing the reporting of business information, such as employment, value added in manufacturing, capital expenditures, and total sales. Each major industry in the United States is assigned a two-digit number, indicating the group to which it belongs. The types of businesses making up each industry are further identified by additional digits. Figure 6.3 displays a partial breakdown of the construction industry.

One of the commercial services that is especially popular among industrial goods and service suppliers is Dun's Market Identifiers (DMI), a special name given by Dun & Bradstreet to its marketing information service. DMI is a roster of over 7 million

FIGURE 6.3   **Partial Breakdown of Standard Industrial Classification (SIC) Codes**

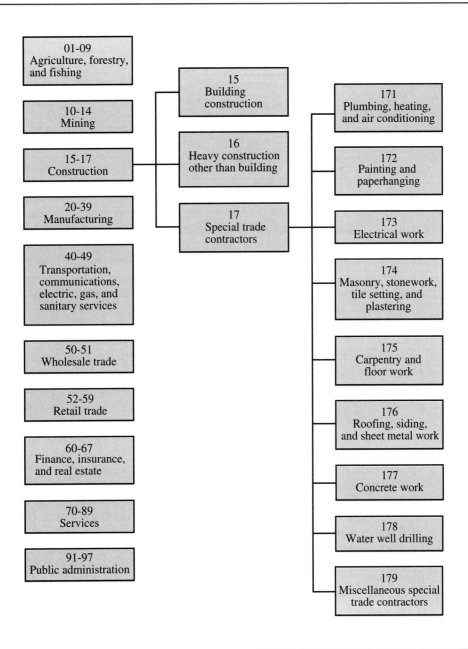

establishments that is updated monthly so that the record on each company is accurate and current. The records are available in hard copy or as computer files. Panel A of Figure 6.4 is an example of a $3'' \times 10''$ card record. Note its contents, particularly the ability to identify the industries that the company or plant serves by means of the SIC codes. The "Enhanced DMI" refers to a two-tiered expansion developed by Dun of the revised 1987 SIC codes. The expansion is structured similarly to the way the third and fourth digits of the code refine the basic two-digit major groups. Panel B of Figure 6.4 shows how the system works. The upshot of the additional digits is a dramatic expansion in the number of types of businesses. There are 1,006 four-digit categories as defined by the government's 1987 revisions, some 2,500 six-digit codes, and more than 15,000 eight-digit codes with the Enhanced DMI.

The enhanced system allows much more precise customer targeting. Suppose, for example, "that one of your targeted markets is food products machinery, and the product you sell into that segment is heat gauges, which are used on only three specific types of food machines — milk pasteurizing machinery, bakery ovens, and brewing equipment. By utilizing the Enhanced DMI of that one market segment, food products machinery can now be separated into the three distinct areas you need to target, with each measured, mailed, and analyzed on its own merits. Conversely, you can easily combine the performance of these three segments into one by using the first four digits of each, thereby allowing you to produce growth trends or compare sales performance with data from previous years."[11]

The DMI records on a company-by-company basis allow sales management to construct sales prospect files, define sales territories and measure territory potentials, and isolate potential new customers with particular characteristics. They allow advertising management to select prospects by size and location; to analyze market prospects and select the media to reach them; to build, maintain, and structure current mailing lists; to generate sales leads qualified by size, location, and quality; and to locate new markets for testing. Finally, they allow marketing research to assess market potential by territory, to measure market penetration in terms of numbers of prospects and numbers of customers, and to make comparative analyses of overall performance by districts and sales territories and in individual industries.

Firms selling consumer goods can ill afford to target individual customers, because no single customer is likely to buy much of any product or service. Rather, firms need to target groups of customers. Their ability to do this has increased substantially since the 1970 census, which was the first electronic census. Since that time, the Census Bureau has made available computer tapes of the facts that have been gathered and, more recently, optical disks, which also make the data usable by those with personal computers. Having the data available in electronic form allows their tabulation by arbitrary geographic boundaries, and an entire industry has developed since 1970 to take advantage of this capability. The "**geodemographers**," as they are most typically called, combine census data with their own survey data or data that they gather from administrative

---

[11]Jerry Reisberg, "The Next Generation in Direct Marketing," *Sales & Marketing Management,* 142 (May 1989), p. 62. See also Marydee Ojala, "Taking the Lead in Company Sales," *Link-Up* 19 (May/June 1992), pp. 22–23.

FIGURE 6.4   **Dun's Market Identifiers**

Panel A: Sample 3″ × 10″ Record

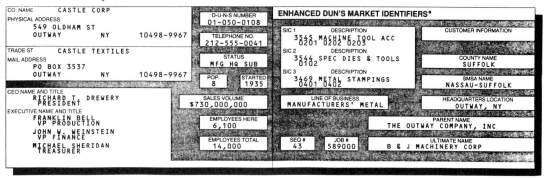

Panel B: How the Enhanced DMI System Works

To better explain how this system works, let's examine one of the two-digit manufacturing codes: SIC 35 — Industrial & Commercial Machinery and Computer Equipment.

This particular two-digit Major Group represents all machinery manufacturers, with a third digit defining the specific type of machinery — engines, farm machinery, construction, metal working, special industry machinery, office machinery, and so on. In this example, we'll use SIC 355 — Special Industry Machinery. By adding a fourth digit, we can further refine the type of machinery within the three-digit Special Industry category (food products, textiles, woodworking, paper, printing, etc.). For example, if we want to identify manufacturers of Food Products Machinery, we would look at SIC 3556. But this is as far as the government's system goes in its standard codings.

Enhanced DMI adds two additional two-digit codes to the four-digit SIC. Thus, continuing with this same example, we find that within SIC 3556 there are numerous types of food products machinery — dairy machinery, beverage machinery, meat-processing machinery, and more. The first two-digit extension would divide these other types of industries into major subgroups of six digits, with a second two-digit extension further refining each line of business, which, in the case of dairy machinery, would break down into cheese-making machinery, ice-cream machinery, milk-processing machinery, and other highly specific categories.

These subgroups are all identified and categorized independently, yet they are related at both the six-digit and four-digit levels, because each is a refinement of the previous code. What this means is that all food products machinery can be collapsed back into the three-digit category and even further back into the two-digit Major Group, which makes it possible to compare data on shipments and establishments with those produced by the federal government and other sources.

Source: Panel A: Dun's *Marketing Services,* Dun & Bradstreet, Inc. Panel B: Jerry Reisberg, ''The Next Generation in Direct Marketing,'' *Sales & Marketing Management,* 142 (May 1989), pp. 60–62.

records, such as motor vehicle registrations or credit transactions, to produce customized products for their clients.

For example: ''R. L. Polk has a product for retailers called the Vehicle Origin Survey. Polk gathers license-plate numbers from cars parked in shopping centers and matches them against Polk's National Vehicle Registration Database to find out where these retail customers live. The shopping center can then use plots of its customers' residences to determine its trading area.[12] Moreover, the locations can be matched with the Census Bureau's demographics for the area using its TIGER files, thereby providing a demographic profile of the people who shop there.[13]

Another thing that the geodemographers do is regularly update the census data through statistical extrapolation. The data can consequently be used with much more confidence during the years intervening between the censuses. Another value-added feature that has had a great deal to do with the success of the industry has been the analysis performed on the census data. Firms supplying geodemographic information have cluster-analyzed the census-produced data to come up with "homogeneous groups" that describe the American population. For example, Claritas Inc. (the first firm to do this and still one of the leaders in the industry) used over 500 demographic variables in its Prizm (Potential Ratings for Zip Markets) system when classifying residential neighborhoods. This system breaks the 250,000 neighborhood areas in the United States into 40 types based on consumer behavior and life-style. Each of the types has a fancy name that theoretically describes the type of people living there, such as Urban Gold Coast, Shotguns and Pickups, Pools and Patios, and so on. Claritas Inc. or the other suppliers will do a customized analysis for whatever geographic boundaries a client specifies. Alternatively, a client can send a tape listing the zip code addresses of some customer data base, and the geodemographer will attach the cluster codes. Figure 6.5 shows the type of maps that can be produced by these services, and Research Realities 6.5 depicts their use.

Measuring Product Sales and Market Share

A critical need in today's increasingly competitive environment is for firms to have an accurate assessment of how they are doing. A common yardstick for that assessment is sales and market share. Firms selling industrial goods or services typically track their own sales and market shares through analyses of their sales invoices. They also obtain feedback from the sales department in terms of how they did in various product or system proposal competitions. An alternative source that companies use to measure their market share is one of the on-line bibliographic data sources discussed previously. Many

---

[12]*Where & Who (Are The Customers)* (Detroit: R. L. Polk & Co., undated).

[13]For discussion of some of the marketing insights made possible by the availability of geodemographic data, see Martha Farnsworth Riche, "The Business Guide to the Galaxy of Demographic Products and Services," *American Demographics,* 7 (June 1985), p. 25. See also Eugene Carlson, "Population-Data Firms Profit by Pinpointing Special Groups," *The Wall Street Journal* (October 15, 1985), p. 33; Betsy Morris, "Marketing Firm Slices U.S. into 240,000 Parts to Spur Clients' Sales," *The Wall Street Journal* (November 3, 1986), pp. 1, 23; Lisa Del Priore, "Geomapping Tools for Market Analysis," *Marketing Communications,* 12 (March 1987), pp. 91–94; Joe Schwartz, "Why They Buy," *American Demographics,* 11 (March 1989), pp. 40–41; Howard Schlossberg, "Census Bureau's TIGER Seen as a Roaring Success," *Marketing News,* 24 (April 30, 1990), p. 2; and Richard K. Thomas and Russell J. Kirchner, *Desktop Marketing: Lessons from America's Best* (Ithaca, N.Y.: American Demographic Books, 1991).

Figure 6.5 Sample Geodemographic Map

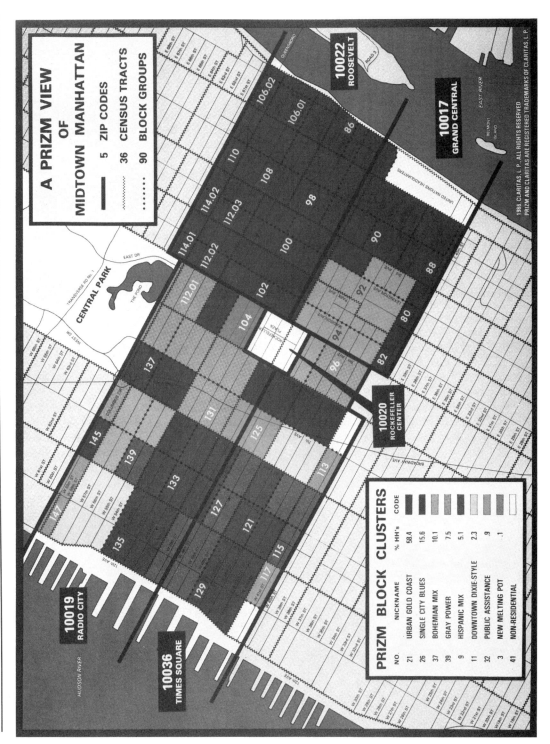

Source: Claritas, Inc.

Research Realities 6.5

Examples of Use of Geodemographic Data

I. Sears's Use of Geodemographic Analysis   Sears geocodes its credit-card customer base to find its best customers and identify growth segments to target. The analyses also can be used to determine which merchandise is best suited to an area's needs.

Sears recently announced the opening of two "intercept" stores in previously underrepresented locations in the Chicago area. Company spokeswoman Kathy Gucfa said the stores have been customized to match the life-styles of people in the market areas they serve.

One of the new Sears Ltd. stores is in Chicago's Old Town district, which has a heavy concentration of apartment dwellers and singles. The store features a Brand Central superstore; departments such as hardware, home improvements, and ready-to-assemble furniture; and concession services, such as a bakery and cafe, a floral shop, an optical department, and shoe repair.

The other new store, in the Ford City shopping center on Chicago's South Side, offers more clothing and a Kids & More department, which Sears describes as a collection of shops "built by moms and kids. . . for moms and kids" with a design based on the company's extensive research with mothers and children. The neighborhood area consists primarily of single-family households with children.

II. Use of Geodemographic Analysis by a Florida Supermarket   A Florida supermarket chain had seen its homogeneous market change radically with the influx of young, affluent residents. Identifying just who shops in the chain's stores involved a combination of low-tech legwork and high-tech data base segmentation. Focus groups and personal interviews were conducted to determine how various customer groups made buying decisions. License plates were counted in the stores of the chain and its competitors to determine the trading area for each specific store. SRI's Values and Life-styles classification system was linked to National Demographic Survey cluster definitions to provide a psychological profile of each census tract and its households. Further analysis of diary-panel data helped predict what products each segment was likely to purchase. Then two years' worth of scanner data was analyzed by store, category, product, and brand to understand the difference in sales for each store.

By segmenting each store into eight clusters of consumers, the chains suddenly could understand why the deli counter in one store had twice the volume of a store ten miles away, or why coffee in one store underperformed the chain average. That led, in turn, to separate promotions and marketing for each store, replacing a chain-wide system.

A special training program for sales personnel and recipe promotions tripled deli sales in ten months. In the area of promotion, three magazines were mailed out — each designed to appeal to a different buying group. Each magazine carried different recipes and coupons for the three market segments, and the coupons were coded to track redemption by household. Overall redemption rates surpassed national norms substantially.

Source: Example I is taken from Lynn G. Coleman, "Marketers Advised to 'Go Regional'," *Marketing News*, 23 (May 8, 1989), p. 1; and Example II is from Laurie Petersen, "Aiming at the Household," *Adweek's Marketing Week*, 30 (February 27, 1989), pp. 20–25.

times a search of an appropriate data base will turn up published studies containing product, company, and market information, including market-share statistics.

Manufacturers of consumer goods also monitor their sales by account through the examination of sales invoices. For them, though, that is only part of the equation to determine how they are doing. Using factory shipments as a sales barometer neglects the filling or depleting of distribution pipelines that may be occurring. The other part of the equation involves the measurement of sales to final consumers. Historically there are several ways that such measurements have been handled, including the use of diary panels of households and the measurement of sales at the store level.

Diary Panels   The diary panels operate similarly. For example, The NPD Group (NPD) national paper diary panel, which is the largest in the United States, comprises more than 16,000 monthly reporting households, who use a preprinted diary to record their monthly purchases in approximately 20 product categories. Figure 6.6 illustrates the sample diary for Toys & Games/Hobby & Craft Purchases. Note that the diary asks for considerable detail about the toy purchased, including the price paid, store where purchased, age and sex of both the recipient and the purchaser, as well as other specific characteristics of the purchase.

The households composing NPD are geographically dispersed but demographically balanced so they can be projected onto total U.S. purchasing. Panel members are recruited quarterly and are added to the active panel after they have satisfactorily met NPD's reporting standards. Households are recruited so that the composition of the panel mirrors the population of the United States. The panel is balanced with respect to size, age of female head of household, household income, and geography. Panel members are compensated for their participation with gifts, and households are dropped from the panel at their request or if they fail to return three of their last six diaries.

The diaries are returned to NPD monthly, the purchase histories are aggregated, and reports prepared. Using these reports, the subscribing company is able to assess (among other things) the following:

- the size of the market, the proportion of households buying over time, and the amount purchased per buyer;
- manufacturer and brand shares over time;
- brand loyalty and brand-switching behavior;
- frequency of purchase and amount purchased per transaction;
- influence of price and special price deals, as well as average price paid;
- characteristics of heavy buyers;
- impact of a new manufacturer or brand on the established brands; and
- effect of a change in advertising or distribution strategy.[14]

For example, the Toy Manufacturers of America, the industry trade group, found through analysis of NPD data that there is a fundamental shift occurring in where toys are purchased. There has been a decline in use of toy departments in department and discount stores and an increasing use of toy supermarkets like Toys ''R'' Us and Child World.

---

[14]See *Insights* (New York: NPD Research, Inc., undated) for discussion of these and other analyses using diary-panel data.

FIGURE 6.6 Sample Page from The NPD Group, Inc., Diary

PAGE 1

TOYS & GAMES/HOBBY & CRAFT
PURCHASES - For Children & Adults

Include ALL ELECTRONIC TOYS, VIDEO GAMES & TRADING CARDS.
Report ALL JUVENILE and CHILDREN'S BOOKS on Page 2.

SPECIAL OFFER CODES

1 Manufacturer Coupon
2 Store Coupon
3 Store Sale
4 Manufacturer Rebate
5 Other Special Offer

STORE CODES

01	Book Store	50	Electronics Store
10	Department Store	60	5 & 10/Variety
20	Mail Order House	70	Grocery/Food
21	Hobby Store		Supermarket
22	Gift/Card/Stationery	80	Drug
	Store	85	Catalog Showroom
28	Hardware	90	Door to Door
30	Discount	95	Warehouse/Price Club
40	Video Store	99	Home Shopping via TV
45	Toy Store		Other

CATEGORY CODES

10 Infant Toys: Rattles, Crib Toys, Activity Centers, Mobiles, Exercise Sets
14 Role Playing/Home Making: Doctor/Nurse Kits, Play Kitchens, Gardening Tools, Play Vanities, Cosmetics & Dress Up Sets, Play Appliances, Etc.
18 Talking/Sound Toys: Slide Viewers, Tape Recorders & Play Telephones, Musical Instruments/Radios
22 Dolls & Accessories: Fashion Dolls, Baby Dolls, Mini Dolls, Talking Dolls, Clothes & Accessories
26 Stuffed Toys: Stuffed Animals & Toys Including Talking, Musical & Animated Plush
30 Action Figures/Accessories: Robots, Warriors, Military & Space Figures, & Other Themed Figures
34 Guns: Laser Guns, Water Pistols, All Other Guns
38 Building & Construction Toys: Wood, Metal, Plastic Blocks/Interlocking Pieces
42 Remote Controlled Vehicles: Cars, Boats, Trucks, Aircraft Operated By A Remote (Connected) Mechanism
46 Radio Controlled Vehicles: Cars, Boats, Trucks, Aircraft That Are Radio Operated
48 Battery Powered Vehicles: Cars, Boats, Trucks, Aircraft That Require A Battery
54 Wind Up/Friction - Powered Vehicles: Cars, Boats, Trucks, Aircraft Powered By Rubber Bands, Wind Up Mechanism Or Friction
58 Other Vehicles: Non-Powered Cars, Boats, Trucks, Planes (Plastic, Wood, Metal)
62 Electric Cars/Trains & Accessories
66 Games/Puzzles: Trivia, Board, Word, Card & Puzzle Games, Chess, Checkers, Backgammon, Brain Teasers & Jigsaw Puzzles
67 All Children's VCR Videos
70 Electronic & Video Games/ Learning Aids: Educational Electronic Interactive TV Video Games, Software, Accessories, Computer Game Software, Electronic Handheld Games/ Software, and CD Video Games
74 Learning & Scientific Toys: (Non Electronic) Flash Cards, Alphabet Boards, Globes, Telescopes & Lab Sets
78 Creative Toys: Paint, Crayons, Markers, Sewing/Knitting Sets & Supplies, Model Kits & Other Design Toys
82 Activity Toys: Jacks, Marbles, Kites, Yo-Yos, Bubbles, Balloons
86 Junior Sports Equipment: (Indoor/Outdoor) Bats, Balls, Skates, Skateboards & Velcro Mitts
90 Ride Ons: Riding Toys Including Bikes, Trikes, Wagons, Scooters, Rocking Horses, Sleds, Battery Operated
99 All Other Toys: All Trading Cards, Children's Furniture, Plastic & Metal Playground Toys, Pools, Etc. & All Other Toys Not In Any Other Category

Date Of Purchase	Full Name Of Toy Or Game (Copy from label or box)	Manufacturer (Write in)	Manufacturer's Code	Model Number	Description Of Toy Or Game — Type of Toy or Game (Write in)	Category Code	How many of each kind did you buy?	Price — Total Price Paid (Exclude tax)	Where Purchased — Name of Store (Write in)	Store Code	Age & Sex Of Purchase	For What Age Was Item Purchased?	Special Questions
19	Doodle Draw	Active kids	68259 06233	6233	Design Toy	78	1	10 99 3	Fun Shop	45	33		4 03 3 4 1 2

SPECIAL QUESTIONS: Enter correct codes in far right columns above

A. How is the receiver(s) of this Toy/Book related to the buyer? (Write in all numbers that apply)

CODE		CODE	
01	Son	11	Bought for Myself/Ourselves
02	Daughter	12	Husband
03	Grandson	13	Wife
04	Granddaughter	14	Friend (No Relation)
05	Cousin	15	Do Not Know Recipient Yet
06	Niece	16	Son(s) and/or Daughter(s)
07	Nephew	17	Grandson(s) and/or Granddaughter(s)
08	Brother	99	Other
09	Sister		
10	Bought for Entire Family		

B. Did recipient influence purchase?

CODE
1 Asked for this Toy/Book by name
2 Asked for this type of Toy/Book
3 Had no direct influence

C. What MOST influenced the purchase decision? (Enter one code)

CODE
1 Manufacturer's Reputation
2 Magazine Advertisement
3 Newspaper Ad/Insert/Flyer
4 TV Advertisement
5 Store Display
6 Price
7 Recipient Asked for Toy/Book
8 Other Influence
9 No Particular Reason

D. Did you plan to buy this specific item in advance?

CODE
1 Yes
2 No

E. What was the occasion?

CODE
1 Christmas/Chanukah
2 Birthday
3 Other Special Occasion
4 No Special Occasion

Answer F and G for Juvenile Books Only

F. Is the book...

CODE
1 Hard Covered with Paper Pages inside?
2 Hard Covered with Board Pages inside?
3 Soft Covered?
4 A Boxed Set?

G. Is the item...

CODE
1 A Book?
2 A Book and Record Set?
3 A Book with Cassette Set?
4 A Book with Sound Pad?

Example: 68259 06233

Answer All Special Questions For Juvenile Books On Top Of Page 2.

Source: Courtesy of The NPD Group, Inc., Port Washington, NY.

Store Audits Another historically popular way of measuring sales to ultimate customers is at the store level, using either store audits or scanners. Scanners reflect the new way of measuring sales; store audits reflect the old. However, store audits are still used in many types of stores that do not yet use scanners, primarily because the products they sell do not lend themselves to scanner processing or because they have not made the investment in scanner equipment.

The basic concept of a store audit is very simple. The research firm sends field workers, called auditors, to a select group of retail stores at fixed intervals. On each visit the auditor takes a complete inventory of all products designated for the audit. The auditor also notes the merchandise moving into the store by checking wholesale invoices, warehouse withdrawal records, and direct shipments from manufacturers. Sales to consumers are then determined by the following calculation:

$$\text{Beginning inventory} + \text{Net purchases (from wholesalers and manufacturers)}$$
$$- \text{Ending inventory} = \text{Sales.}$$

The store audit was pioneered by the A. C. Nielsen Company and served as the backbone of the *Nielsen Retail Index* for many years. The method is still used to measure sales and to gather information on retail prices, store displays, and promotional activity for the drug stores, mass merchandisers, and liquor stores among the sample of outlets used to construct the *Nielsen Retail Index*. Sales of food stores in the sample of outlets, however, are now monitored by scanner. The company takes the auditing records and generates the following information for each of the brands for each of the products audited:

- sales to consumers;
- purchases by retailers;
- retail inventories;
- number of days' supply;
- out-of-stock stores;
- prices (wholesale and retail);
- special factory packs; and
- dealer support (displays, local advertising, coupon redemption).

Subscribers to the Nielsen service can get these data broken down by competitor, geographic area, or store type. Nielsen will also provide special reports to clients for a fee. These special reports include such things as the effect of shelf facings on sales, the sales impact of different promotional strategies, premiums or prices, or the analysis of sales by client-specified geographic areas. The stores pinpointed for inclusion in the panel are contacted personally to secure their cooperation. Further, the stores are compensated for their cooperation on a per-audit basis.

Scanners Since the late 1970s, Nielsen has been supplementing its Retail Index service with its SCANTRACK service. The SCANTRACK service emerged from the revolutionary development in the grocery industry brought about by the installation of scanning equipment to read Universal Product Codes. Universal Product Codes are 11-digit numbers imprinted on each product sold in a supermarket. The first digit, called the number system character, indicates the type of product it is (e.g., grocery or drug). The next five digits identify the manufacturer and the last five a particular product of the manufacturer, be it a different size, variety, or flavor. See Figure 6.7.

There is a unique 11-digit code for every product in the supermarket. As the product with its bar code is pulled across the **scanner,** the scanner identifies the 11-digit number, looks up the price in the attached computer, and immediately prints the description and price of the item on the cash register receipt. At the same time, the computer can keep track of the movement of every item that is scanned. The SCANTRACK service provides weekly sales data from a nationwide sample of scanner-equipped stores. The data allow clients to evaluate the effectiveness of short-term promotions, to evaluate pricing changes, to follow new product introductions, and to monitor unexpected events, such as product recalls and shortages.

Figure 6.7   **Universal Product Codes**

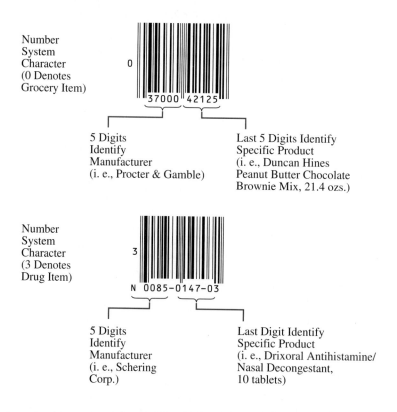

Scanners' effects on the collection of sales and market share data have been profound. For one thing, they have changed the locus of power in distribution channels. Research Realities 6.6 describes the nature of the change. Another important change wrought by scanners is an increased ability to link purchase behavior with demographic information. Before the advent of scanners, the link was made using diaries. A problem with diaries is that they depend for their accuracy on the conscientiousness of those in the panel to record their purchases as they occur. Scanner data are not subject to such recording biases. Several firms have developed systems over the last few years to take advantage of this fact, including Information Resources and Nielsen. A key feature of the new systems is the ability to link television-viewing behavior with product-purchasing behavior to produce what has become known as "single-source" data.

The basics of single-source research are straightforward. As an example, consider the operation of the Information Resources BehaviorScan system. In each of the markets in which BehaviorScan operates, more than 3,000 households have been recruited by Information Resources to present identification cards at each of the grocery or drug stores every time their members make a purchase. Almost all the supermarkets and drug stores in each area are provided scanners by Information Resources.[15] Each household member presents his or her identification card when checking out. The card is scanned along with the purchases, allowing Information Resources to relate a family's purchases by brand, size, and price to the family's demographic characteristics and the household's known exposure to coupons, newspaper ads, free samples, and point-of-purchase displays.

Information Resources also is able to direct different TV advertising spots to different households through the "black boxes" that have been attached to the television sets in each test household, in cooperation with the cable television systems serving the markets. This allows Information Resources to monitor the buying reactions to different advertisements or to the same advertisement in different types of households (e.g., whether the buying reactions to a particular ad are the same or different among past users and nonusers of the product). This targetable TV capability allows Information Resources to balance the panel of members for each ad test within each market according to the criteria the sponsor chooses (e.g., past purchasers of the product), thereby minimizing the problem of having comparable experimental and control groups.

Nielsen's system is designed to measure natural consumer behavior rather than test the effects of different promotions or advertising. Its SCANTRACK National Electronic Household Panel has 40,000 participating households whose purchases are measured through an electronic wand they are asked to pass over the UPC codes on products brought into the house. The electronic unit then queries them with respect to where purchase was made, age and sex of the shopper, price paid, deal type if any, among other things. The information from each household is downloaded once a week to

---

[15]Recently, Information Resources also began to offer BehaviorScan for testing in mass merchandisers such as WalMart, Kmart and Target, in addition to grocery and drug stores. See *Testing Services* (Chicago: Information Resources, undated).

Scanners Shift Balance of Power in Marketplace

The marketplace has always been a battleground. Manufacturers clamoring for shelf space are pitted against retailers struggling to offer a wide range of products to their customers. Until recently, manufacturers dominated the fray. They could extend their product line with new sizes, new flavors, and so on, relatively secure in the knowledge that retailers would willingly stock the new items. However, the widespread use of optical scanners has recently tipped the balance in the other direction.

Scanners at the checkout read the Universal Product Codes (UPC), which describe the brand, item, manufacturer, and pricing of each item sold. Wal-Mart, Sears, and Kmart have begun to install scanners in their stores. All Toys ''R'' Us stores are equipped with scanners, and the toy chain, which controls roughly one-quarter of the U.S. toy market, refuses to stock any item not marked with a UPC code.

Although the impact of scanning information is just beginning in most retail markets, it has already transformed the grocery store. Let's say that you have developed a new brand of yogurt that you would like to introduce nationally. The problem is that the grocer's shelves are already bursting with products, and by using scanner data the grocer knows pretty closely to the penny how much money can be made on each of the products on the shelves. However, the grocer has no evidence that your new product will sell half as much as the product that has to be removed from the shelf to make room for it.

To deal with this problem, retailers have begun charging slotting allowances, which are fees that retailers charge manufacturers for each space or slot on the shelf that a new product will occupy. A major retailer in Los Angeles might charge a slotting fee of $4,000 for the chain, per slot. If your brand of yogurt has 14 flavors, distribution in that one chain alone would cost $56,000, and shelf space in all five of L.A.'s major chains would cost a whopping $280,000.

But slotting fees are only one aspect of the new technology. One very powerful application of optical scanner data is Direct Product Profitability (DPP), which is just beginning to be applied in the marketplace. DPP is a financial model that allocates all the retailer's costs, item by item, to every item on the shelf to determine the net profit of each. The model factors in costs associated with purchasing, transportation, shelf inventory, and marketing as well as the general overhead of the store.

A good way to see what a powerful tool DPP can be is to look at a single product — for example, sugar. On a gross-profit basis, sugar looks like an important and profitable category, but by using DPP it becomes clear that on a net-profit basis, sugar is a money-loser for the retailer. Sugar is a big, bulky package, heavy and easily damaged, and the space it consumes in the warehouse and on the shelf, as well as the labor expenses for stocking it, cost more than the return the retailer is getting based on price and sales turnover. Retailers are obviously not going to pull sugar from their shelves. However, it seems reasonable that retailers will take a close look at how much space is devoted to sugar and which brands perform better than others.

Up until now, retailers have been the primary beneficiary of optical scanner information, but some are beginning also to help manufacturers while improving their own margins. For example, Safeway Stores, Inc., one of the world's leading food stores, has launched an optical scanner checkout network that helps manufacturers evaluate promotion effectiveness and identify potential new markets. Safeway Scanner Marketing Research Service (SMRS) uses scanner data to track sales of items stocked in two locations in a single store to see, for example, whether chewing gum sells better at the checkout stand or in the candy aisle. The company downloads summaries of weekly sales items onto floppy disks so that manufacturers can analyze the data. SMRS tracks coupon redemptions and helps manufacturers determine the effect of in-store sampling on sales and the most effective types of in-store displays. By using scanner data, SMRS can also track the effect on unit sales of a change in price. SMRS sells this information to manufacturers willing to use the service.

Sources: Spencer L. Hapoienu, ''The Struggle for a Place on the Shelf,'' *Viewpoint* (July/August 1988), pp. 3–9; ''Safeway Stores Double as Research Lab,'' *Marketing News*, 21 (August 28, 1987), p. 36; and Brent H. Felgner, ''Retailers Grab Power, Control Marketplace,'' *Marketing News*, 23 (January 16, 1989), pp. 1–2.

Nielsen's computer simply by transmitting the data over the telephone.[16] Some of the other types of analyses that are possible with SCANTRACK's National Household Panel Reports are described in Table 6.5.

The impact of single-source measurement on the conduct of marketing activities has been and promises to be so profound that it may "ultimately rival the importance of the microscope to scientists," according to a report by J. Walter Thompson USA.[17]

> A Campbell Soup Co. single-source experiment with its V-8 juice shows how the system works. Using an index of 100 for the average household's V-8 consumption, Campbell found that demographically similar TV audiences can consume vastly different amounts of V-8. In early 1987, for example, "General Hospital" had a below-average 80 index, while "Guiding Light" had an above-average 120 index. The results were surprising, because "General Hospital" actually had a slightly higher percentage of women 25 to 54 years old — the demographic groups most predisposed to buy V-8 — and so would ordinarily have been expected to be a better advertising forum to reach V-8 drinkers.[18]

While single-source measurement offers the opportunity for new market insights, firms subscribing to these services need to prepare themselves for the incredible amounts of data these services produce. Without proper planning, firms literally can drown in these data. That is why decision support systems for analyzing data (particularly expert systems, which were discussed in Chapter 2) are becoming increasingly important in marketing research.

Measuring Advertising Exposure and Effectiveness

Another area in which there is a great deal of commercial information available for marketers relates to the assessment of exposure to and effectiveness of advertising. Most suppliers of industrial goods advertise most heavily in trade publications. To sell space more effectively, the various trade publications typically sponsor readership studies, which they then make available to potential advertisers. Suppliers of consumer goods and services also have access to media-sponsored readership studies. In addition, a number of services have evolved to measure consumer exposure to the various media.

Television and Radio   The Nielsen Television Index is probably the most generally familiar commercial information service. The most casual television watcher has probably heard of the Nielsen ratings and the impact they have on which TV shows are

[16]*Nielsen Household Panel* (Northbrook, Ill.: A. C. Nielsen Company, undated).

[17]"Study Predicts Bigger Impact by Single-Source Data," *Marketing News,* 22 (February 1, 1988), p. 13.

[18]Joanne Lipman, "Single-Source Ad Research Heralds Detailed Look at Household Habits," *The Wall Street Journal* (February 16, 1988), p. 35. For examples of these and other kinds of analyses that single-source measurement systems allow, see Gerald J. Eskin, "Applications of Electronic Single-Source Measurement Systems," *European Research,* 15 (No. 1, 1987), pp. 12–20.

TABLE **6.5**   **Types of Analyses Possible Using SCANTRACK National Electronic Household Panel Reports**

Type	Purpose	Key Measures
Market Overview/Trend Analysis	To provide a general overview of consumer purchasing for a particular product category, its major segments, and major brands. Measures are compared between brands and over time to identify changes and developments in the marketplace. Data can be analyzed for any time period, can be looked at across/within outlet types, or can be looked at for specific consumer groups (e.g. heavy buyers, microwave owners, etc.).	Volume and market share. Percentage of households purchasing (penetration). Volume per buyer (buying rate). Volume per purchase occasion. Purchase occasion per buyer (frequency). Pricing (total, deal, nondeal). Percentage of volume on deal (coupon vs. store special). Distribution of volume by outlet (e.g. grocery, drug, club warehouse, etc.).
Demographic Analysis	To target advertising and promotional efforts most effectively by determining the demographic profile of particular buyer groups (e.g., brand buyers, heavy buyers, frequent commercial viewers). By evaluating the absolute sales importance of one demographic segment versus another, along with the importance of each demographic segment relative to the general population, the overall profile of each buyer group can be identified.	Across all demographic characteristics, the following measures are produced: Distribution of buyers. Distribution of volume. Market share (within demo group). Percentage of volume on deal (within demo group). Buyer Index (distribution of buyers — distribution of population). Volume Index (distribution of volume — distribution of population).
Loyalty/Combination Purchase Analysis	To understand the extent to which buyers are loyal to a brand; to determine the competitive set in which brands operate; and to identify size/flavor/form preference. The report also looks at the importance of price and dealing when buyers purchase competitive items.	Percentage of brand buyers purchasing competitive items. Percentage of brand volume accounted for by buyers who purchase competitive brands. Percentage of competitive brand volume purchased on deal by Brand A buyers. Price paid for competitive brand by Brand A buyers. Brand A buyers' total category volume (distribution). Interaction Index – index of Brand A's interaction with competitive brands versus expectations.

T<small>ABLE</small> **6.5** *Continued*

Type	Purpose	Key Measures
Brand Shifting Analysis	To identify the sources of growth or decline in a brand's sales. By looking at changes from period to period on a household-by-household basis, we can see if volume changes were attributed to consumers switching to/from other brands, increasing/decreasing their overall category purchasing, and/or entering/leaving the market.	Brand-shifting volume. Increased/decreased category purchasing. New/lost category buyers. Percentage of shifting gains/loss. Gain/loss index. Interaction index.
Trial and Repeat Analysis	Trial measures consumer interest in a new product by evaluating the percentage of households making at least one purchase of the product. Trial also measures the ability of a marketing plan to translate interest into purchasing. Repeat purchasing evaluates product satisfaction by determining the percentage of triers repurchasing the brand — the ability of a product to deliver on its promise.	Cumulative trial. Cumulative repeat. Depth of repeat. Package rate (volume on trial, on repeat). Percentage volume on deal (total on trial vs. on repeat) Market share (total from trial vs. from repeat).

Source: *Nielsen Household Panel* (Northbrook, Ill.: A. C. Nielsen Company, 1992).

canceled by the networks and which are allowed to continue. The index itself is designed to provide estimates of the size and nature of the audience for individual television programs. Until recently, the basic data were gathered through the use of audimeter instruments, which are electronic devices attached to the television sets in cooperating households. Each audimeter was connected to a central computer, which recorded when the set was on and to what channel it was tuned. Data was also gathered through written diaries used on occasion to determine *who* was watching TV when the audimeter indicated the set was on. Beginning in the fall of 1988, Nielsen started measuring TV audiences through the use of people meters. The switch was not without controversy, however, as Research Realities 6.7 indicates. **People meters** attempt to measure not only the channel to which a set is tuned, but who in the household is watching. Each member of the family has his or her own viewing number. Whoever turns on the set, sits down to watch, or changes the channel is supposed to enter his or her number into the people meter. All of this information is transmitted immediately to the central computer for processing.

Research Realities 6.7

Grousing about People Meters

When ABC Chairman Tom Murphy addressed more than 100 TV critics, he asked a leading question: "How many of you would conscientiously be pushing people meter's buttons after you'd had one in your home for several weeks?" Only two of the professional tube-watchers raised their hands. They aren't the only ones expressing skepticism about the A. C. Nielsen Company's switch from diaries and passive audimeters to a technology dependent on button pushers.

In the past, Nielsen measured TV audiences on the basis of written diaries filled out by scientifically selected families twice a year during "sweeps" month. Now these data are being gathered by high-tech people meters, and the change has a lot of broadcasters grousing. Many think that the new system is biased in favor of yuppies or "techies" and against those who feel uncomfortable with high-tech gadgetry. There is also widespread concern that the system underrepresents teens and kids.

Nickelodeon and MTV have been especially hard hit by the disinclination of young people to punch people-meter buttons. People-meter viewing levels for the two networks are routinely 20 to 40 percent below those shown by the Nielsen diary. MTV sales reps actually show a people meter to prospective advertisers to demonstrate how hard the device is to operate. According to Marshall Cohen, senior vice-president for MTV Networks, telephone coincidentals are the most consistently accurate form of kid and teen mea-

surement. But this process, which involves calling each and every household in the people-meter sample, is very expensive.

Yet people meters aren't without their supporters. Many smaller independent stations have found their market share boosted by the new people-meter data. With the old diary system, Nielsen families usually sat down at the end of the week and filled in the diary. When they wrote down what shows they watched, they tended to remember the most popular shows — most of which are shown on the networks. The rerun of "Happy Days" they may have watched while they folded laundry was less likely to make it into the diary.

In addition, some researchers believe that people meters more accurately differentiate between "core" viewers, who actively seek out a particular show, and "peripheral" viewers, who end up watching whatever happens to be on when they walk into the room. Thus, MTV may show more adult viewers, CNN more young people, and ESPN more women than before.

Although industry insiders may disagree about the relative merits of people meters, they do agree about one thing: a passive audience-measurement device is the only solution to accurately measuring an increasingly fragmented audience. Nielsen has been field testing an infrared-based passive meter, but no commercial use of that device has yet been scheduled.

"The desire is there on behalf of nearly everyone involved in TV buying to have access to a reliable passive-measurement system," says David Marans of J. Walter Thompson in New York. "It's just a matter of making the new technology less cumbersome."

Source: Richard Mahler, "Grousing about People Meters," *Adweek* (December 5, 1988), pp. F.K. 10–11; and Chuck Ross, "How Meters Matter in the Sweeps," *Adweek* (June 20, 1988), pp. B.T. 10–12.

Through the data provided by these basic records, Nielsen develops estimates of the number and percentage of all TV households viewing a given TV show. Nielsen also breaks down these aggregate ratings by ten socioeconomic and demographic characteristics, including territory, education of head of house, county size, time zones, household income, age of woman of house, color TV ownership, occupation of head of house, presence of nonadults, and household size. These breakdowns assist the network, of course, in selling advertising on particular programs, while they assist the advertiser in choosing programs to sponsor that reach households with the desired characteristics.[19]

Advertisers buying radio time are also interested in the size and demographic composition of the audiences they will be reaching. Radio-listening statistics are typically gathered using diaries that are placed in a panel of households. Arbitron, for example, generates telephone numbers randomly to ensure that it is reaching households with unlisted numbers. Those household members who agree to participate when called are sent diaries, similar to those illustrated in Chapter 4, in which they are asked to record their radio-listening behavior for a short period. Most radio markets are rated only once or twice a year, although some of the larger ones are rated four times a year. The April/May survey is conducted in every Arbitron market and consequently is known as the "sweeps" period. Radio ratings typically are broken down by audience age and sex and focus more on individual than household behavior, in contrast to television ratings.

Print Media   There are several services that measure exposure and readership to print media. For example, the Starch Readership Service measures the reading of advertisements in magazines and newspapers. Some 50,000 advertisements in 1,000 issues of consumer and farm magazines, business publications, and newspapers are assessed each year, using over 75,000 personal interviews.

The Starch surveys employ the "recognition method" to assess a particular ad's effectiveness. With the magazine open, the respondent is asked to indicate whether he or she has read *each ad*. Three degrees of reading are recorded:

1. noted — a person who remembered seeing any part of the advertisement in that particular issue;

2. associated — a person who not only "noted" the advertisement but also saw or read some part of it that clearly indicates the brand or advertiser;

3. read most — a person who read 50 percent or more of the written material in the ad.[20]

---

[19]Greater detail about the Nielsen television rating can be found in *The Nielsen Ratings in Perspective* (Northbrook, Ill.: A. C. Nielsen Company, undated). For discussion of the advantages and disadvantages of using people meters for TV audience measurement, see Richard Mahler, "Grousing about People Meters," *Adweek Special Report* (December 5, 1988), pp. F.K. 10–11; and Peter Barnes and Joanne Lipman, "Networks and Ad Agencies Battle over Estimates of TV Viewership," *The Wall Street Journal* (January 7, 1987), p. 21. For discussion of their accuracy, see Roland Soong, "The Statistical Reliability of People Meter Ratings," *Journal of Advertising Research,* 26 (February–March 1988), pp. 50–56; J. Ronald Milavsky, "How Good Is the A. C. Nielsen People-Meter System? A Review of the Report by the Committee on Nationwide Television Audience Measurement," *Public Opinion Quarterly,* 56 (Spring 1992), pp. 102–115. Nielsen is currently experimenting with a passive meter system that would require viewers to do nothing but turn on their sets. Those watching a particular program would be identified through computer-image recognition technology. For discussion of the opportunities and problems with this system, see Steve McClellan, "New Nielsen System Is Turning Heads," *Broadcasting,* 122 (May 18, 1992), p. 8.

[20]*The Starch Readership Report: Methodology and Use* (Mantaroneck, N.Y.: Starch INRA Hooper, undated).

During the course of the interview, data are also collected on the observation and reading of the component parts of each ad, such as the headlines, subheadings, pictures, copy blocks, and so forth.

Interviewing begins a short time after the issue of the magazine is placed on sale. For weekly and biweekly consumer magazines, interviewing begins three to six days after the on-sale date and continues for one to two weeks. For monthly magazines, interviewing begins two weeks after the on-sale date and continues for two weeks.

The interviews are conducted by a trained staff of field interviewers, who have the responsibility of selecting those to be interviewed, since a quota sample is employed. Each interviewer must locate within a particular area an assigned number of readers who are 18 years of age and over, with various occupations, family sizes, and marital and economic statuses. The quotas are determined so that different characteristics will be represented in the sample in proportion to their representation in the population. Readers are included in the sample when they conform to the specified demographic characteristics and when they reply in the affirmative when asked if they had read the particular magazine issue in question. The size of the sample varies by publication. Most Starch studies are based on a minimum of 100 issue readers.

Starch readership reports are compiled issue by issue and include three features: (1) labeled issue, (2) summary report, and (3) adnorm tables. The target ads in each issue are labeled to indicate overall readership level as well as the noting or reading of the major components of the ads. The summary report lists all the ads that were measured in the issue. The ads are arranged by product category and show the percentages for the three degrees of ad readership: noted, associated, and read most, allowing the comparison of the readership of each ad versus the other target ads in the issue. The adnorm tables enable one to compare the readership of an ad in a given issue with the norm for ads of the same size and color that are for the same product category for that publication.

Starch readership data allow advertisers to compare their ads with competitors' ads, current ads with prior ads, current ads against competitors' prior ads, and current ads against Starch adnorm tables. This process can be effective in assessing changes in theme, copy, layout, use of color, and so on.

Multimedia Services   The Simmons Media/Marketing Service uses a national probability sample of more than 19,000 respondents and serves as a comprehensive data source allowing the cross referencing of product usage and media exposure. Four different interviews are conducted with each respondent so that magazine, television, newspaper, and radio can all be covered by the Simmons Service. Information is reported for total adults and for males and females separately.[21]

The service conducts two personal interviews, which obtain measures of respondent readership of individual magazines and newspapers. A self-administered questionnaire is used to gather product purchase and use information for over 800 product categories, which remain relatively fixed from year to year. Television-viewing behavior is ascer-

---

[21]*Simmons Research: Your Key to Opportunity* (New York: Simmons Market Research Bureau, Inc., undated).

tained by means of a personal viewing diary, while radio-listening behavior is gathered through telephone and personal interviews.

A probability sample is used in selecting respondents for the study. All households receive a premium for participating, and a minimum of six calls is made in the attempt to interview previously unavailable respondents. A large number of demographic characteristics are gathered from each respondent included in the study, which permits firms to identify the heavy purchasers of various products. By also taking into account the purchasers' media habits, the firms are better able to segment and target the most promising groups. See Table 6.6 for an example.

Simmons determines magazine readership using the "through-the-book" or editorial interest method. In the "through-the-book" method, respondents are screened to determine which magazines they might have read during the past six months. They are then shown actual issues of magazines stripped of confusing material (for identification purposes), such as advertising pages and recurring columns and features. Nine feature articles unique to the issue are exhibited, and an indirect approach, asking respondents to select the articles they personally find especially interesting, is employed. At the end, a qualifying question is asked: "Now that you have been through this magazine, could you tell me whether this is the first time you happened to look into this particular issue, or have you looked into it before?" Respondents must affirm prior exposure to the issue to qualify as readers. Expressions of doubt or uncertainty would disqualify them.

Mediamark Research also makes available information on exposure to various media and household consumption of various products and services. Its annual survey of 20,000 adult respondents covers more than 250 magazines, newspapers, radio stations, and television channels and over 450 products and services.[22] Information is gathered from respondents by two methods. First, a personal interview is used to collect demographics and data pertaining to media exposure. Magazine readership is measured by a "recent reading" method that asks respondents to sort a deck of magazine logo cards according to whether they (1) are sure they have read, (2) are not sure they have read, and (3) are sure they have not read a given magazine within the previous six months.

Newspaper readership is measured using a "yesterday reading" technique in which respondents are asked which of the daily newspapers on the list of papers that circulate in the area were read or looked into within the previous seven days. For Sunday and weekend papers, a four-week time span is used. Radio listening is determined through a "yesterday" recall technique in which respondents are shown a list of five day-parts (or time periods) and are asked how much time was spent listening to a radio during each time period on the previous day. They are then asked what stations were listened to. Television audience data are collected in a similar manner.

On completion of the interview, interviewers then leave a questionnaire booklet with respondents. The booklet, which covers personal and household usage of approximately 3,500 product categories and services and 5,700 brands, is personally picked up

---

[22]*Knowledge Is Power* (New York: Mediamark Research, Inc., 1987). See also *Winning the Marketing Game: How Syndicated Consumer Research Helps Improve the Odds* (New York: Mediamark Research, Inc., 1987); and *Ready for the 90's* (New York: Mediamark Research, Inc., 1990), for descriptions of the types of analyses the media exposure and product-uses data bases allow.

TABLE 6.6 Sample Output from Simmons Media/Marketing Service

	TOTAL U.S. '000	ALL USERS A '000	B % DOWN	C % ACROSS	D INDX	HEAVY USERS SEVEN OR MORE TIMES A '000	B % DOWN	C % ACROSS	D INDX	TYPE: CREME RINSE A '000	B % DOWN	C % ACROSS	D INDX
TOTAL MALES	87118	33176	100.0	38.1	100	12224	100.0	14.0	100	11485	100.0	13.2	100
18–24	12577	5266	15.9	41.9	110	2345	19.2	18.6	133	1639	14.3	13.0	99
25–34	21739	9327	28.1	42.9	113	3999	32.7	18.4	131	3070	26.7	14.1	107
35–44	18402	7327	22.1	39.8	105	2685	22.0	14.6	104	2529	22.0	13.7	104
45–54	12383	4816	14.5	38.9	102	1679	13.7	13.6	97	1882	16.4	15.2	115
55–64	9899	3107	9.4	31.4	82	1019	8.3	10.3	73	1211	10.5	12.2	93
65 OR OLDER	12117	3333	10.0	27.5	72	497	4.1	4.1	29	1154	10.0	9.5	72
18–34	34316	14593	44.0	42.5	112	6344	51.9	18.5	132	4710	41.0	13.7	104
18–49	59213	24437	73.7	41.3	108	9977	81.6	16.8	120	8185	71.3	13.8	105
25–54	52525	21470	64.7	40.9	107	8363	68.4	15.9	113	7482	65.1	14.2	108
35–49	24896	9844	29.7	39.5	104	3633	29.7	14.6	104	3475	30.3	14.0	106
50 OR OLDER	27905	8739	26.3	31.3	82	2247	18.4	8.1	57	3301	28.7	11.8	90
GRADUATED COLLEGE	19148	6643	20.0	34.7	91	2621	21.4	13.7	98	1931	16.8	10.1	76
ATTENDED COLLEGE	16724	6607	19.9	39.5	104	2660	21.8	15.9	113	1821	15.9	10.9	83
GRADUATED HIGH SCHOOL	31493	12441	37.5	39.5	104	4712	38.5	15.0	107	5012	43.6	15.9	121
DID NOT GRADUATE HIGH SCHOOL	19752	7485	22.6	37.9	100	2231	18.3	11.3	80	2721	23.7	13.8	104
EMPLOYED FULL-TIME	64828	26159	78.8	40.4	106	10278	84.1	15.9	113	8777	76.4	13.5	103
EMPLOYED PART-TIME	3018	1046	3.2	34.7	91	391	3.2	13.0	92	*334	2.9	11.1	84
NOT EMPLOYED	19272	5971	18.0	31.0	81	1555	12.7	8.1	58	2375	20.7	12.3	93
PROFESSIONAL/MANAGER	17280	6237	18.8	36.1	95	2495	20.4	14.4	103	1980	17.2	11.5	87
TECHNICAL/CLERICAL/SALES	13671	5708	17.2	41.8	110	2262	18.5	16.5	118	1576	13.7	11.5	87
PRECISION/CRAFT	13576	5499	16.6	40.5	106	1928	15.8	14.2	101	2052	17.9	15.1	115
OTHER EMPLOYED	23319	9761	29.4	41.9	110	3986	32.6	17.1	122	3502	30.5	15.0	114
SINGLE	22432	8659	26.1	38.6	101	3840	31.4	17.1	122	2919	25.4	13.0	99
MARRIED	54550	20933	63.1	38.4	101	7141	58.4	13.1	93	7368	64.2	13.5	102
DIVORCED/SEPARATED/WIDOWED	10136	3584	10.8	35.4	93	1243	10.2	12.3	87	1199	10.4	11.8	90
PARENTS	26289	11419	34.4	43.4	114	4022	32.9	15.3	109	4015	35.0	15.3	116
WHITE	75302	28832	86.9	38.3	101	10845	88.7	14.4	103	9945	86.6	13.2	100
BLACK	9181	3386	10.2	36.9	97	1009	8.3	11.0	78	1189	10.4	13.0	98
OTHER	2635	958	2.9	36.4	95	*371	3.0	14.1	100	**352	3.1	13.4	101
NORTHEAST-CENSUS	18565	5930	17.9	31.9	84	2235	18.3	12.0	86	2824	24.6	15.2	115
MIDWEST	21107	9044	27.3	42.8	113	3149	25.8	14.9	106	3153	27.5	14.9	113
SOUTH	29369	11054	33.3	37.6	99	4013	32.8	13.7	97	3163	27.5	10.8	82
WEST	18077	7149	21.5	39.5	104	2827	23.1	15.6	111	2345	20.4	13.0	98
COUNTY SIZE A	36136	13597	41.0	37.6	99	5166	42.3	14.3	102	4471	38.9	12.4	94
COUNTY SIZE B	26297	9554	28.8	36.3	95	3643	29.8	13.9	99	3099	27.0	11.8	89
COUNTY SIZE C	13268	5103	15.4	38.5	101	2034	16.6	15.3	109	1930	16.8	14.5	110
COUNTY SIZE D	11417	4922	14.8	43.1	113	1381	11.3	12.1	86	1985	17.3	17.4	132
METRO CENTRAL CITY	27184	9780	29.5	36.0	94	3409	27.9	12.5	89	3155	27.5	11.6	88
METRO SUBURBAN	41416	15576	46.9	37.6	99	6334	51.8	15.3	109	5251	45.7	12.7	96
NON METRO	18517	7820	23.6	42.2	111	2482	20.3	13.4	96	3079	26.8	16.6	126
TOP 5 ADI'S	18949	7357	22.2	38.8	102	2897	23.7	15.3	109	2483	21.6	13.1	99
TOP 10 ADI'S	27261	10749	32.4	39.4	104	4389	35.9	16.1	115	3643	31.7	13.4	101
TOP 20 ADI'S	39408	15094	45.5	38.3	101	5744	47.0	14.6	104	5060	44.1	12.8	97
HSHLD. INC. $75,000 OR MORE	11355	3881	11.7	34.2	90	1711	14.0	15.1	107	1138	9.9	10.0	76
$60,000 OR MORE	19422	7217	21.8	37.2	98	2985	24.4	15.4	110	2272	19.8	11.7	89
$50,000 OR MORE	27605	10435	31.5	37.8	99	4156	34.0	15.1	107	3423	29.8	12.4	94
$40,000 OR MORE	38985	14775	44.5	37.9	100	5900	48.3	15.1	108	5207	45.3	13.4	101
$30,000 OR MORE	52579	20467	61.7	38.9	102	7765	63.5	14.8	105	7223	62.9	13.7	104
$30,000 – $39,999	13594	5692	17.2	41.9	110	1865	15.3	13.7	98	2017	17.6	14.8	113
$20,000 – $29,999	14483	5681	17.1	39.2	103	2214	18.1	15.3	109	2012	17.5	13.9	105
$10,000 – $19,999	13291	4760	14.3	35.8	94	1686	13.8	12.7	90	1370	11.9	10.3	78
UNDER $10,000	6764	2268	6.8	33.5	88	558	4.6	8.2	59	880	7.7	13.0	99
HOUSEHOLD OF 1 PERSON	9165	2615	7.9	28.5	75	1160	9.5	12.7	90	959	8.4	10.5	79
2 PEOPLE	28885	10358	31.2	35.9	94	3746	30.6	13.0	92	3385	29.5	11.7	89
3 OR 4 PEOPLE	35978	14221	42.9	39.5	104	5258	43.0	14.6	104	5450	47.5	15.1	115
5 OR MORE PEOPLE	13090	5982	18.0	45.7	120	2060	16.9	15.7	112	1691	14.7	12.9	98
NO CHILD IN HSHLD.	53687	18941	57.1	35.3	93	7227	59.1	13.5	96	6568	57.2	12.2	93
CHILD(REN) UNDER 2 YEARS	6492	2788	8.4	42.9	113	979	8.0	15.1	107	922	8.0	14.2	108
2 – 5 YEARS	11280	4898	14.8	43.4	114	1699	13.9	15.1	107	1661	14.5	14.7	112
6 – 11 YEARS	15823	7049	21.2	44.5	117	2491	20.4	15.7	112	2430	21.2	15.4	116
12 – 17 YEARS	16052	6793	20.5	42.3	111	2266	18.5	14.1	101	2317	20.2	14.4	109

*PROJECTION RELATIVELY UNSTABLE BECAUSE OF SAMPLE BASE-USE WITH CAUTION
**NUMBER OF CASES TOO SMALL FOR RELIABILITY-SHOWN FOR CONSISTENCY ONLY

TABLE 6.6 *Continued*

		TOTAL U.S. '000	ALL USERS A '000	B % DOWN	C % ACROSS	D INDX	HEAVY USERS SEVEN OR MORE TIMES A '000	B % DOWN	C % ACROSS	D INDX	TYPE: CREME RINSE A '000	B % DOWN	C % ACROSS	D INDX
TOTAL		87118	33176	100.0	38.1	100	12224	100.0	14.0	100	11485	100.0	13.2	100
OUTDOOR	QUINTILE 1	19093	7475	22.5	39.2	103	3166	25.9	16.6	118	2433	21.2	12.7	97
	QUINTILE 2	19548	7108	21.4	36.4	95	2694	22.0	13.8	98	2129	18.5	10.9	83
	QUINTILE 3	13400	5168	15.6	38.6	101	2098	17.2	15.7	112	1950	17.0	14.6	110
	QUINTILE 4	17076	6386	19.2	37.4	98	1981	16.2	11.6	83	2366	20.6	13.9	105
	QUINTILE 5	18000	7038	21.2	39.1	103	2286	18.7	12.7	91	2608	22.7	14.5	110
RADIO–DRIVE	QUINTILE 1	16639	6578	19.8	39.5	104	2491	20.4	15.0	107	2266	19.7	13.6	103
TIME	QUINTILE 2	17654	6993	21.1	39.6	104	2702	22.1	15.3	109	2380	20.7	13.5	102
	QUINTILE 3	18832	7274	21.9	38.6	101	2678	21.9	14.2	101	2415	21.0	12.8	97
	QUINTILE 4	16214	6222	18.8	38.4	101	2361	19.3	14.6	104	2193	19.1	13.5	103
	QUINTILE 5	17779	6108	18.4	34.4	90	1992	16.3	11.2	80	2231	19.4	12.5	95
RADIO–MID-	TERCILE 1	22963	9253	27.9	40.3	106	3264	26.7	14.2	101	3154	27.5	13.7	104
DAY	TERCILE 2	22821	8668	26.1	38.0	100	3205	26.2	14.0	100	3126	27.2	13.7	104
	TERCILE 3	41334	15255	46.0	36.9	97	5755	47.1	13.9	99	5206	45.3	12.6	96
RADIO-TOTAL	QUINTILE 1	17672	6977	21.0	39.5	104	2563	21.0	14.5	103	2417	21.0	13.7	104
	QUINTILE 2	17657	7063	21.3	40.0	105	2683	21.9	15.2	108	2407	21.0	13.6	103
	QUINTILE 3	17014	6588	19.9	38.7	102	2596	21.2	15.3	109	2231	19.4	13.1	99
	QUINTILE 4	18049	6671	20.1	37.0	97	2408	19.7	13.3	95	2324	20.2	12.9	98
	QUINTILE 5	16726	5877	17.7	35.1	92	1974	16.1	11.8	84	2107	18.3	12.6	96
TV–PRIME	QUINTILE 1	17076	6291	19.0	36.8	97	2171	17.8	12.7	91	2233	19.4	13.1	99
TIME	QUINTILE 2	17459	6602	19.9	37.8	99	2228	18.2	12.8	91	2111	18.4	12.1	92
	QUINTILE 3	17882	6237	18.8	34.9	92	2359	19 3	13.2	94	2301	20.0	12.9	98
	QUINTILE 4	16589	7086	21.4	42.7	112	2810	23.0	16.9	121	2552	22.2	15.4	117
	QUINTILE 5	18112	6960	21.0	38.4	101	2656	21.7	14.7	105	2288	19.9	12.6	96
TV-DAYTIME	TERCILE 1	23601	8684	26.2	36.8	97	3110	25.4	13.2	94	3119	27.2	13.2	100
	TERCILE 2	23634	9289	28.0	39.3	103	3637	29.8	15.4	110	3109	27.1	13.2	100
	TERCILE 3	39883	15203	45.8	38.1	100	5477	44.8	13.7	98	5257	45.8	13.2	100
TV-TOTAL	QUINTILE 1	17427	6259	18.9	35.9	94	2306	18.9	13.2	94	2157	18.8	12.4	94
	QUINTILE 2	17563	7114	21.4	40.5	106	2360	19.3	13.4	96	2505	21.8	14.3	108
	QUINTILE 3	17290	6351	19.1	36.7	96	2390	19.6	13.8	99	1981	17.2	11.5	87
	QUINTILE 4	17423	6704	20.2	38.5	101	2481	20.3	14.2	101	2424	21.1	13.9	106
	QUINTILE 5	17415	6748	20.3	38.7	102	2688	22.0	15.4	110	2419	21.1	13.9	105
YELLOW	QUINTILE 1	13397	6079	18.3	45.4	119	2184	17.9	16.3	116	1988	17.3	14.8	113
PAGES	QUINTILE 2	14023	5730	17.3	40.9	107	2276	18.6	16.2	116	1933	16.8	13.8	105
	QUINTILE 3	19063	7250	21.9	38.0	100	3020	24.7	15.8	113	2371	20.6	12.4	94
	QUINTILE 4	19294	7069	21.3	36.6	96	1982	16.2	10.3	73	2342	20.4	12.1	92
	QUINTILE 5	21340	7047	21.2	33.0	87	2762	22.6	12.9	92	2852	24.8	13.4	101
MAGAZINES–NEWSPAPERS: DUAL		24034	9728	29.3	40.5	106	3819	31.2	15.9	113	3274	28.5	13.6	103
MAGAZINE IMPERATIVE		20892	8755	26.4	41.9	110	3646	29.8	17.5	124	3102	27.0	14.8	113
NEWSPAPER IMPERATIVE		24336	7863	23.7	32.3	85	2452	20.1	10.1	72	2640	23.0	10.8	82
MAGAZINES–OUTDOOR: DUAL		19215	7761	23.4	40.4	106	3139	25.7	16.3	116	2669	23.2	13.9	105
MAGAZINE IMPERATIVE		25790	10438	31.5	40.5	106	3826	31.3	14.8	106	3779	32.9	14.7	111
OUTDOOR IMPERATIVE		27349	9712	29.3	35.5	93	3835	31.4	14.0	100	2916	25.4	10.7	81
MAGAZINES–RADIO: DUAL		19439	8068	24.3	41.5	109	3208	26.2	16.5	118	2698	23.5	13.9	105
MAGAZINE IMPERATIVE		26437	10379	31.3	39.3	103	3974	32.5	15.0	107	3545	30.9	13.4	102
RADIO IMPERATIVE		25509	9581	28.9	37.6	99	3575	29.2	14.0	100	3322	28.9	13.0	99
MAGAZINES–TELEVISION: DUAL		17584	7183	21.7	40.8	107	2618	21.4	14.9	106	2307	20.1	13.1	100
MAGAZINE IMPERATIVE		28628	11449	34.5	40.0	105	4665	38.2	16.3	116	3986	34.7	13.9	106
TELEVISION IMPERATIVE		26978	9480	28.6	35.1	92	3332	27.3	12.4	88	3339	29.1	12.4	94
MAGAZINES–YELLOW PGS: DUAL		16931	7296	22.0	43.1	113	2973	24.3	17.6	125	2334	20.3	13.8	105
MAGAZINE IMPERATIVE		30799	11693	35.2	38.0	100	4347	35.6	14.1	101	4071	35.4	13.2	100
YELLOW PGS IMPERATIVE		21137	8428	25.4	39.9	105	3223	26.4	15.2	109	2816	24.5	13.3	101
NEWSPAPERS–OUTDOOR: DUAL		20674	7707	23.2	37.3	98	2999	24.5	14.5	103	2350	20.5	11.4	86
NEWSPAPER IMPERATIVE		27249	9885	29.8	36.3	95	3190	26.1	11.7	83	3628	31.6	13.3	101
OUTDOOR IMPERATIVE		25038	9723	29.3	38.8	102	4040	33.0	16.1	115	3177	27.7	12.7	96
NEWSPAPERS–RADIO: DUAL		19333	7457	22.5	38.6	101	2682	21.9	13.9	99	2488	21.7	12.9	98
NEWSPAPER IMPERATIVE		29045	10348	31.2	35.6	94	3766	30.8	13.0	92	3646	31.7	12.6	95
RADIO IMPERATIVE		25079	10250	30.9	40.9	107	4108	33.6	16.4	117	3638	31.7	14.5	110
NEWSPAPERS–TELEVISION: DUAL		19805	7057	21.3	35.6	94	2381	19.5	12.0	86	2287	19.9	11.5	88
NEWSPAPER IMPERATIVE		29307	11001	33.2	37.5	99	4254	34.8	14.5	103	3735	32.5	12.7	97
TELEVISION IMPERATIVE		24358	9733	29.3	40.0	105	3769	30.8	15.5	110	3447	30.0	14.2	107
NEWSPAPERS–YELLOW PGS: DUAL		17003	6955	21.0	40.9	107	2640	21.6	15.5	111	2282	19.9	13.4	102
NEWSPAPER IMPERATIVE		32551	10949	33.0	33.6	88	3858	31.6	11.9	84	3772	32.8	11.6	88
YELLOW PGS IMPERATIVE		20075	8940	26.9	44.5	117	3674	30.1	18.3	130	2959	25.8	14.7	112
OUTDOOR-RADIO: DUAL		17644	6814	20.5	38.6	101	2621	21.4	14.9	106	2104	18.3	11.9	90
OUTDOOR IMPERATIVE		28923	10761	32.4	37.2	98	4428	36.2	15.3	109	3616	31.5	12.5	95
RADIO IMPERATIVE		27201	10766	32.5	39.6	104	3848	31.5	14.1	101	4079	35.5	15.0	114

*PROJECTION RELATIVELY UNSTABLE BECAUSE OF SAMPLE BASE-USE WITH CAUTION
**NUMBER OF CASES TOO SMALL FOR RELIABILITY-SHOWN FOR CONSISTENCY ONLY

Source: *1991 Study of Media & Markets* (New York: Simmons Market Research Bureau, Inc., 1991), pp. 4–5. All Rights Reserved.

TABLE 6.7   **A Controversy as to the Top Five Magazines Based on Total Adult Readership**

	In Millions
The Simmons List	
1. TV Guide	43.2
2. Reader's Digest	37.5
3. People	24.6
4. National Geographic	23.6
5. Time	23.2
The Mediamark List	
1. Reader's Digest	50.9
2. TV Guide	46.8
3. Better Homes and Gardens	35.5
4. People	30.4
5. National Geographic	30.3

Source: Joanne Lipman, "Readership Figures for Periodicals Stir Debate in Publishing Industry," *The Wall Street Journal* (September 2, 1987), p. 21.

by the interviewer after a short time period. The 20,000 respondents for the Mediamark reports are selected using probability sampling methods.

The difference in the procedures used by Simmons and Mediamark to measure media exposure, particularly magazine readership, can create a real dilemma for advertisers. Both firms interview approximately 20,000 people for each study, but the figures reported by them can be very different, as Table 6.7 indicates. In general, it seems that Mediamark's figures of readership are about 10 percent higher for weeklies and 35 percent higher for monthlies, but that can vary dramatically by publication.[23] This difference, of course, creates havoc for those attempting to buy media space in which to place ads.

Customized Measurements

In addition to the services mentioned previously, some firms supply customized rather than standardized marketing information. To discuss all of these suppliers of marketing intelligence would take us too far afield. We do wish to discuss mail panels, though, to

---

[23]Joanne Lipman, "Readership Figures for Periodicals Stir Debate in Publishing Industry," *The Wall Street Journal* (September 2, 1987), p. 21.

give readers a sense of their operation. Although they are not a true source of secondary data (because the data collected using them are specifically designed to meet the client's needs), the studies are sufficiently standardized and have enough features in common to warrant their inclusion here.

NFO Research, Inc., is one of the major independent research firms specializing in custom-designed consumer surveys using mail panels. NFO maintains representative panels drawn from a sampling frame of more than 400,000 households representing nearly one million consumers who have agreed to cooperate without compensation in completing self-administered questionnaires on a variety of subjects. The topics may include specific product usage; reaction to the product or advertising supporting it; reaction to a product package; attitude toward or awareness of some issue, product, service, or ad; and so on.

The national panel is dissolved and rebuilt every two years so that it matches current family population characteristics with respect to income, population density, age of homemaker, and family size for the continental United States and each of the nine geographic divisions in the census.

A current demographic profile is maintained for each family in the data bank. Included are such characteristics as size of family, education, age of family members, presence and number of children by sex, occupation of the principal wage earner, race, and so on. This information is used to generate highly refined population segments. If the user's needs require it, NFO can offer the client panels composed exclusively of mothers of infants, teenagers, elderly people, dog and cat owners, professional workers, mobile home residents, multiple car owners, or other specialized types. Each of these panels can be balanced to match specific quotas dictated by the client.[24]

The Consumer Mail Panel (CMP), operated as part of Market Facts, Inc., also represents a sample of households that have agreed to respond to mail questionnaires and product tests. Samples of persons for each product test or use are drawn from over 290,000 households in the CMP pool. The pool is representative of the geographical divisions in the United States and Canada and is broken down, within these divisions, according to census data on total household income, population density and degree of urbanization, and age of panel member.

According to CMP, its mail panel is ideally suited for experimental studies because the samples are matched. In particular, CMP is believed to be particularly valuable when

1. large samples are required at low cost because the size of the subgroups is large or there are many subgroups to be analyzed;
2. large numbers of households must be screened to find eligible respondents;
3. continuing records are to be kept by respondents to report such data as products purchased, how products are used, TV programs viewed, magazines read, and so on.

---

[24]More detailed information about the mail panel can be found in the company's publication *NFO* (Toledo, Ohio: NFO Research, Inc., undated).

CMP has recorded a number of other characteristics with respect to each participating household that allow for cross-tabulation of the client's criterion variable against such things as place of residence (state, county, and standard metropolitan area), marital status, occupation and employment status, household size, age, sex, home ownership, type of dwelling, and ownership of pets, dishwashers, washing machines, dryers, other selected appliances, and automobiles.[25]

SUMMARY

When confronted by a new problem, the researcher's first attempts at data collection should logically focus on secondary data. Secondary data are statistics gathered for some other purpose, in contrast to primary data, which are collected for the purpose at hand. Secondary data possess significant cost and time advantages, and it is only when their pursuit shows diminishing returns and the problem is not yet resolved that the researcher should proceed to primary data. The problem will typically not be resolved completely with secondary data, because secondary data rarely suit the problem perfectly. There are usually problems of appropriateness, and when the data are appropriate there still remain the problems of different units of measurement, class definitions, and publication currency than those required. Nevertheless, their diligent pursuit still typically offers the researcher a great deal of insight into the problem, information required to resolve it, and ways in which the information can be obtained. Sometimes secondary data will completely eliminate any need to collect primary data.

Secondary data can be found in either primary or secondary sources. A primary source is the source that originated the data, whereas a secondary source is a source that secured the data from an original source. The primary source should always be used. Further, the researcher should make some judgment about the quality and accuracy of secondary data by examining the purpose of publication, the ability of the organization to collect the data, and general evidence of careful work in their presentation and collection. Researchers should also become familiar with how to go about conducting an on-line computer search of existing data bases; this mode of inquiry promises to become more important as firms and individuals attempt to cope with the information explosion.

Secondary data include internal company data, published external secondary data, and data supplied by commercial marketing information services. Internal sales and cost data are a most inexpensive source of marketing information and can be used to gain a perspective on research problems. There is such a wealth of published external secondary data available that it is easy to overlook them, and the researcher is well advised to follow the process listed in Figure 6.1, or some variation of it, when locating secondary

---

[25]More detail about the Market Facts mail panel can be found in *Why Consumer Mail Panel is the Superior Option* (Chicago: Market Facts, Inc., undated); *Market Facts, Inc.: Data Collection and Analysis for Reducing Business Decision Risks* (Chicago: Market Facts, Inc., undated); and *Consumer Mail Panel Reference Guide* (Chicago: Market Facts, Inc., undated).

data. Further, aspiring researchers should personally examine the sources described in Appendix 6A so that their contents are familiar.

Standardized marketing information services can be an important adjunct to the researcher's data collection efforts. These services offer economies of scale because they serve a number of clients for a variety of purposes, and thus they are able to spread their costs of operation among clients. This means that if they are suitable for the clients' needs, they offer substantial time and cost advantages in the collection of primary data. Some common uses of the standardized marketing data bases are to profile customers, to measure product sales and market share, and to measure advertising exposure and effectiveness. Not all of the information services reviewed provide what we have called secondary data, since some of them (i.e., the mail panels) collect information of a specific nature for a specific client (primary data in the true sense of the word). Nonetheless, it was convenient to review them here along with the providers of more standardized marketing information.

Questions

1. What is the difference between primary and secondary data?

2. What are the advantages and disadvantages of secondary data?

3. What criteria can be employed to judge the accuracy of secondary data?

4. What is the difference between a primary source and a secondary source of secondary data? Which is preferred? Why?

5. What distinguishes internal secondary data from external secondary data?

6. How would you go about searching for secondary data on a particular topic?

7. How would you perform an on-line computer search? What types of information would you be hoping to find?

8. What is the basic operation of a store audit?

9. Describe how a type of business can be more successfully identified using the Enhanced DMI.

10. If you were a product manager for Brand X detergent and you needed up-to-date market share information by small geographical sectors, would you prefer National Purchase Diary Panel data or Nielsen data? Why?

11. For what types of studies would you prefer NPD consumer diary data rather than BehaviorScan consumption data? Vice versa?

12. What is the advantage of using single-source data?

13. How are Starch scores determined?

14. What is the basis for the Nielsen television ratings?

15. How do the "through-the-book" and "recent reading" methods for assessing magazine readership differ?

16. How do the multimedia services operate?

17. For what types of studies would you use mail panels?

Applications and Problems

1. List some major secondary sources of information for the following situations:
   a. The marketing research manager of a national soft-drink manufacturer has to prepare a comprehensive report on the soft-drink industry.
   b. Mr. Baker has several ideas for instant cake mixes and is considering entering this industry. He needs to find the necessary background information to assess its potential.
   c. Mr. Adams has heard that the profit margins in the fur business are high. The fur industry has always intrigued him, and he decides to do some research to determine if the claim is true.
   d. A recent graduate hears that condominiums are the homes of the 90s. She decides to collect some information on the condominium market.
   e. Owning a grocery store has been Mrs. Smith's dream. She finally decides to make this a reality. The first step she wishes to take is to collect information on the grocery business in her hometown.

2. Assume that you are interested in opening a fast-food Mexican restaurant in St. Louis, Missouri. You are unsure of its acceptance by consumers and are considering doing a marketing research study to evaluate their attitudes and opinions. In your search for information you find the following studies:

   Study A was recently conducted by a research agency for a well-known fast-food chain. To secure a copy of this study, you would be required to pay the agency $225. The study evaluated consumers' attitudes toward fast food in general based on a sample of 500 housewives for the cities of Springfield, Illinois; St. Louis and Kansas City, Missouri; and Topeka, Kansas. The findings indicated that respondents did not view fast food favorably. The major reason for the unfavorable attitude was the low nutritional value of the food.

   Study B was completed by a group of students as a requirement for an MBA marketing course. This study would not cost you anything, as it is available in your university library. The study evaluated consumers' attitudes toward various ethnic fast foods. The respondents consisted of a convenience sample of 200 students from St. Louis. The findings indicated a favorable attitude toward two ethnic fast foods, Italian and Mexican. Based on these results, one of the students planned to open a pizza parlor in 1990 but instead accepted a job as sales representative for General Foods Corporation.
   a. Critically evaluate the two sources of data.
   b. Which do you consider to be better? Why?
   c. Assume that you decide it will be profitable to become a franchisee in fast food. Identify five specific secondary sources of data and evaluate the data.

3. For many years, Home Decorating Products had been a leading producer of paint and painting-related equipment such as brushes, rollers, turpentine, and so on. The company is now considering adding wallpaper to its line. At least initially, it did not intend to actually manufacture the wallpaper but, rather, planned to subcontract the manufacturing. Home Decorating Products would assume the distribution and marketing functions.

   Before adding wallpaper to its product line, however, Home Decorating secured some secondary data assessing the size of the wallpaper market. One mail survey made by a trade association showed that, on the average, families in the United States wallpapered two rooms in their homes each year. Among these families, 60 percent did the task themselves. Another survey, which had also been done by mail but by one of the major home magazines, found that 70 percent of the subscribers answering the questionnaire had wallpapered one complete wall or more during the last twelve months. Among this 70 percent of the families, 80 percent had done the wallpapering themselves. Home Decorating Products thus has two sets of secondary data on the same problem, but the data are not consistent.

Discuss the data in terms of the criteria one would use to determine which set, if either, is correct. Assume that you are forced to make the determination on the basis of the information in front of you. Which would you choose?

4. Assume that your school is interested in developing a marketing plan to boost sagging attendance at major athletic events, particularly home football games. As an initial step in developing the new marketing plan, the athletic department has decided that it needs demographic and life-style profiles of people who currently attend games on a regular (season-ticket) basis. Fortunately, the ticket office maintains a listing of all season-ticket purchasers (including names and addresses) from year to year. What potential sources of internal secondary data might the athletic department first investigate before considering the collection of primary data?

5. Several scenarios follow. In each case, there exists a need for standardized marketing information. Recommend a service (or services) that could provide the required information. Explain your choice(s).

   a. As part of its advertising-sales strategy, radio station KMJC wants to stress the fact that their programming appeals to young adults between the ages of 19 and 25. The advertising salespeople need "numbers" to back up this claim.

   b. Imperial Sugar Company has developed a unique coupon and television campaign for its two-pound bag of brown sugar. The company needs to know the following in order to evaluate the campaign:

   (1) Are people more likely to use the coupon if they have also seen the television ad?

   (2) What is the median size of the household using the coupon?

   (3) What is the proportion of new purchasers to past purchasers among the users of the coupon?

   c. A national manufacturer of a pain remedy is considering a package change to a child-proof container specifically targeted to households with young children. The change will necessitate a 10 percent price increase. The manufacturer wants to know if its target market (parents with children under eight years of age) will perceive the price increase as justified since the new package is childproof.

   d. DLH Advertising Agency assured one of its clients that despite the $200,000 cost of placing a half-page ad in one issue of a national magazine, the actual cost of the ad per reader would be less than two cents. DLH is preparing a report to the client and needs data to back its assurance.

   e. Polybuild Software Inc. is introducing a software package that will make long-range forecasts of contaminant buildup levels in plants that manufacture polyester fibers. Polybuild needs a current listing of potential customers, organized by plant sales volume, in order to prioritize sales calls for the new package.

   f. WestTowne Shopping Center wishes to know the demographic characteristics of its patrons. However, the mall's retail tenants recently voted to ban marketing research interviews in or around the mall area, due to numerous customer complaints about harassment by interviewers. Where might the mall obtain the desired information?

Thorndike Sports Equipment Video Case

1. What type of research information is "piling up" in the room next to Luke's office?

2. It is obvious that Luke sees little value in the information that is gathering dust in the storage room. It is your job to persuade him that this information has value. How would you, as new research analyst, convince him of this?

3. **a.** The information that has been collected is in disarray. How would you organize this information in order to make it accessible to everyone in the company? Is a computer system necessary to keep the information in this room accessible?

   b. What procedures would need to be implemented to keep this information in order?

4. For each of the categories you have listed in Question 3, identify a research project in which the information could provide valuable information?

5. Briefly explain how computerized data bases and indexes can be used in market research? What are some of the difficulties encountered when using these systems? What steps can researchers take to avoid difficulties when looking for specific information relating to a research project?

6. If you were in Ted's position, what other search terms would you have used?

7. Where else should Ted have looked for information on racquets that are currently being used?

Secondary Data

There is so much published secondary data that it is impossible to mention all of it in a single appendix. For this reason, only a representative cross-section of the available material is presented.[1] These secondary sources are organized into six sections according to the type of information they contain. Several sources of electronic on-line search services are included. First, however, a brief discussion of governmental sources of secondary data is presented.

---

[1]For more detailed treatment, see H. Webster Johnson, Anthony J. Faria, and Ernest L. Maier, *How to Use the Business Library: With Sources of Business Information,* 5th ed. (Cincinnati: South-Western Publishing, 1984); Eleanor G. May, *A Handbook for Business on the Use of Federal and State Statistical Data* (Washington, D.C.: Department of Commerce, 1979); and David W. Stewart and Michael A. Kamins, *Secondary Research: Information Sources and Methods,* 2nd ed. (Beverly Hills, Calif.: Sage Publications, 1993).

CENSUS DATA AND OTHER GOVERNMENT PUBLICATIONS: OVERVIEW

The Bureau of the Census of the United States Department of Commerce is the largest gatherer of statistical information in the country. The original census was the Census of Population, which was required by the Constitution to serve as a basis for apportioning representation in the House of Representatives. The first censuses were merely head counts. Not only has the Census of Population been expanded, but the whole census machinery has also been enlarged. At this point there are nine different censuses, all of which are of interest to the marketing researcher. Table 6.1, for example, listed some of the most useful data on population and housing that are available in the Census of Population. Table 6A.1 lists some of the most useful data that are collected in the various economic censuses described in the following sections.

Census data are of generally high quality. Further, they are quite often available on the detailed level that the researcher needs. When not available in this form, researchers can purchase, for a nominal fee, either computer tapes or flexible diskettes to create their own tabulations from the Bureau of the Census. Alternatively, researchers can contract with one of the private companies that market census-related products for information on a particular issue. Not only does this allow the researcher to obtain information tailored to his or her specific needs, but it is also one of the fastest ways to get census data. Further, many of the private providers update the census data at a detailed geographic level for the between-census years.

There are two major drawbacks to the use of census data: (1) censuses are not taken every year, and (2) the delay from time of collection to time of publication is quite substantial, often two years or more. This last weakness, however necessary because of the massive editing, coding, and tabulation tasks involved, renders the data obsolete for many research problems. The first difficulty requires that the researcher supplement the census data with current data. Unfortunately, current data are rarely available in the detail the researcher desires. This is particularly true with respect to detailed classifications by small geographic area, unless one takes advantage of the services of a private provider with update capability.

The federal government also collects and publishes a great deal of statistical information in addition to the censuses. Some of this material is designed to supplement the various censuses and is gathered and published for this purpose (e.g., *Current Population Reports*), whereas other data are generated in the normal course of operations, such as collecting taxes, social security payments, claims for unemployment benefits, and so forth. Some publications also result from the desire to make the search for information more convenient.

COMPANY AND INDUSTRY INFORMATION

Almanac of Business and Industrial Financial Ratios **(Englewood Cliffs, N.J.: Prentice-Hall)**   This publication contains the number of establishments, sales, and selected operating ratios for various industries (e.g., food stores). The figures are derived

TABLE 6A.1   **Information Available from Economic Censuses**

Major Data Items	Retail Trade	Wholesale Trade	Service Industries	Construction Industries	Manufacturers	Mineral Industries
Number of Establishments and Firms:						
All establishments	X			X		
Establishments with payroll	X	X	X	X	X	X
Establishments by legal form of organization	X	X	X	X	X	X
Firms	X	X	X		X	X
Single-unit and multi-unit firms	X	X	X		X	X
Concentration by major firms	X	X	X		X	
Employment:						
All employees	X	X	X	X	X	X
Production (construction) workers				X	X	X
Employment size of establishments	X	X	X	X	X	X
Employment size of firms	X	X	X			
Production (construction) worker hours				X	X	X
Payrolls:						
All employees, entire year	X	X	X	X	X	X
All employees, first quarter	X	X	X	X	X	
Production (construction) workers				X	X	X
Supplemental labor costs, legally required and voluntary	X	X	X	X	X	X
Sales Receipts, or Value of Shipments:						
All establishments	X			X	X	X
Establishments with payroll	X	X	X	X		

TABLE **6A.1** *Continued*

Major Data Items	Retail Trade	Wholesale Trade	Service Industries	Construction Industries	Manufacturers	Mineral Industries
By product or line or type of construction	X	X	X	X	X	X
By class of customer	X	X				
By size of establishments	X	X	X	X	X	X
By size of firm	X	X	X			
Operating Expenses:						
Total	X	X	X			
Cost of materials, etc.	X	X		X	X	X
Specific materials consumed (quantity and cost)	X	X			X	X
Cost of fuels	X	X	X	X	X	X
Electric energy consumed (quantity and cost)	X	X	X		X	X
Contract work		X		X	X	X
Products bought and sold					X	X
Advertising	X	X	X			
Rental payments, total	X	X	X	X	X	X
Buildings and structures	X	X	X	X	X	X
Machinery and equipment	X	X	X	X	X	X
Communications services	X	X	X	X	X	X
Purchased repairs	X	X	X	X	X	
Capital Expenditures:						
Total	X	X	X	X	X	X
New, total	X	X	X	X	X	X
Buildings/equipment	X	X	X	X	X	X
Used, total	X	X	X	X	X	X
Buildings/equipment				X		X
Depreciable Assets, Gross Value Buildings/Equipment:						
End of 1981	X	X	X	X	X	X
End of 1982	X	X	X	X	X	X

(continued)

TABLE **6A.1** *Continued*

Major Data Items	Retail Trade	Wholesale Trade	Service Industries	Construction Industries	Manufacturers	Mineral Industries
Depreciation (total and detail for buildings/ equipment)	X	X	X	X	X	X
Retirements (total and detail for buildings/ equipment)	X	X	X	X	X	X
Inventories:						
End of 1986	X	X		X	X	X
End of 1987	X	X		X	X	X
Other:						
Value added	X	X		X	X	X
Specialization by type of construction/ manufacturing				X	X	
Central administrative offices and auxiliaries	X	X	X	X	X	X
Water use					X	X

Source: Adapted from *Guide to the 1987 Economic Censuses and Related Statistics* (Washington, D.C.: Bureau of the Census, U.S. Department of Commerce, 1989), p. 3.

from tax return data supplied by the Internal Revenue Service and are reported for twelve categories, based on assets, within each industry. The data thus allow the comparison of a particular company's financial ratios with competitors of similar size.

***Census of Agriculture* (U.S. Bureau of the Census: Government Printing Office)**
The *Census of Agriculture* was formerly taken in the years ending in "4" and "9." Since 1982, it is taken in years ending in "2" and "7." This census offers detailed breakdowns by state and county on the number of farms, farm types, acreage, land-use practices, employment, livestock produced and products raised, and value of products. It is supplemented by the annual publications *Agriculture Statistics* and *Commodity Yearbook*. In addition, the Department of Agriculture issues a number of bulletins, which often contain data not otherwise published.

Census of Construction Industries **(U.S. Bureau of the Census: Government Printing Office)**   Taken every five years (in the years ending with ''2'' and ''7''), this census covers establishments primarily engaged in contract construction, in construction for sale, or in subdividing real property into lots. Statistics are provided for such things as value of inventories, total assets, and employment by state.

Census of Government **(U.S. Bureau of the Census: Government Printing Office)**   The *Census of Government* presents information on the general characteristics of state and local governments, including such things as employment, size of payroll, amount of indebtedness, and operating revenues and costs. The census is authorized in the years ending in ''2'' and ''7.''

Census of Manufacturers **(U.S. Bureau of the Census: Government Printing Office)**   The *Census of Manufacturers* has been taken somewhat irregularly in the past, but it is now authorized for the years ending in ''2'' and ''7.'' It categorizes manufacturing establishments by type, using some 450 classes, and contains detailed industry and geographic statistics for such items as the number of establishments, quantity of output, value added in manufacture, capital expenditures, employment, wages, inventories, sales by customer class, and fuel, water, and energy consumption. The *Annual Survey of Manufacturers* covers the years between publications of the census, and *Current Industrial Reports* contains the monthly and annual production figures for some commodities.

Census of Mineral Industries **(U.S. Bureau of the Census: Government Printing Office)**   The *Census of Mineral Industries* is taken in the years ending in ''2'' and ''7.'' The information here parallels that for the *Census of Manufacturers* but is for the mining industry. The census offers detailed geographic breakdowns for some 50 mineral industries on such things as the number of establishments, production, value of shipments, capital expenditures, cost of supplies, employment, payroll, power equipment, and water use. The *Minerals Yearbook,* published by the Bureau of Mines of the Department of the Interior, supplements the *Census of Mineral Industries* by providing annual data, although the two are not completely comparable because they employ different classifications — an industrial classification for the Census Bureau data and a product classification for the Bureau of Mines data.

Census of Retail Trade **(U.S. Bureau of the Census: Government Printing Office)**   The *Census of Retail Trade,* which is taken every five years in the years ending in ''2'' and ''7,'' contains detailed statistics on the retail trade. Retail stores are classified by type of business, and statistics are presented on such things as the number of stores, total sales, employment, and payroll. The statistics are broken down by small geographic areas such as counties, cities, and standard metropolitan statistical areas. Current data pertaining to some of the information can be found in *Monthly Retail Trade.*

Census of Service Industries **(U.S. Bureau of the Census: Government Printing Office)**   The *Census of Service Industries* is taken every five years in the years ending in ''2'' and ''7.'' The service trade census provides data on receipts, employment, type of business (for example, hotel, laundry, and so on), and number of units by small geographic areas. Current data can be found in *Monthly Selected Services Receipts*.

Census of Transportation (U.S. Bureau of the Census: Government Printing Office)
The *Census of Transportation* is taken in the years ending in ''2'' and ''7.'' It covers three major areas: passenger travel, truck and bus inventory and use, and the transport of commodities by the various classes of carriers.

Census of Wholesale Trade (U.S. Bureau of the Census: Government Printing Office)   The *Census of Wholesale Trade*, which is taken every five years in the years ending in ''2'' and ''7,'' contains detailed statistics on the wholesale trade. For instance, it classifies wholesalers into over 150 business groups and contains statistics on the functions they perform, sales volume, warehouse space, expenses, and so forth. It presents these statistics for counties, cities, and standard metropolitan statistical areas. Current data can be found in *Monthly Wholesale Trade*.

Commodity Yearbook (New York: Commodity Research Bureau)   Published annually, this publication contains data on prices, production, exports, stocks, and so on for approximately 100 individual commodities.

Merchandising, "Statistical and Marketing Report" (New York: Billboard Publications)   This annual report, contained in the March issue, includes statistical information related to sales, shipments, imports, exports, and more, for certain consumer durables, including home electronics and major appliances.

Moody's Manuals (New York: Moody's Investors Service)   Published annually, these manuals — *Banks and Finance, Industrials, Municipals and Governments, Public Utilities,* and *Transportation* — contain balance sheets and income statements for individual companies and government units.

Predicast Forecasts (Cleveland: Predicasts, Inc.)   This quarterly publication provides short- and long-term forecasts for economic indicators, industries, and products and also serves as a guide to statistical information about companies and industries.

Standard & Poor's Corporate Records (New York: Standard & Poor's Corporation)
Corporate Records provides current financial statistics for companies as well as background information and news items.

Standard & Poor's Industry Surveys (New York: Standard and Poor's Corporation)
These surveys provide analyses of all major domestic industries, including outlooks for the industry, trends and problems, and statistical tables and charts. A basic analysis is published yearly and offers a comparative company analysis of the leading companies in an industry. Current analyses are published three times per year and include important developments and available statistics for the industry, market, and company, as well as investment outlook for the industry.

***Standard & Poor's Statistical Service* (New York: Standard and Poor's Corporation)** This publication presents monthly statistical data (current and historical) for several areas, including banking and finance, production and labor, and income and trade.

***U.S. Industrial Outlook* (Industrial Trade Administration, U.S. Department of Commerce: Government Printing Office)** Produced annually, this publication covers the recent trends and five-year outlook for more than 350 manufacturing and services industries.

***Worldcasts* (Cleveland: Predicasts, Inc.)** Published quarterly, *Worldcasts* provides worldwide forecast information for regions and for products. Forecast data are drawn from over 800 publications.

Related Indexes, Directories, and Guides

***Business Organizations, Agencies, and Publications Directory* (Detroit: Gale Research)** This directory serves as a guide to approximately 20,000 organizations, agencies, and publications related to business, trade, and industry in the areas of marketing, accounting, administration, human resources, and much more.

***Directory of Corporate Affiliations* (Wilmette, Ill.: National Register Publishing Company)** An annual publication, the *Directory of Corporate Affiliations* provides a listing of more than 4,000 major U.S. companies and their 48,000 subsidiaries, divisions, and affiliates. Both private and public firms are broken down by SIC code, by state (geography), and alphabetically. The publication includes a listing of mergers, acquisitions, and name changes since 1976.

***Fortune Directory* (New York: Time, Inc.)** Published annually by the editors of *Fortune* magazine, this directory provides information on sales, assets, profits, invested capital, and employees for the 500 largest industrial corporations in the United States.

***Guide to Industrial Statistics* (Washington, D.C.: U.S. Bureau of the Census)** A guide to the Census Bureau's programs relating to industry, including the type of statistics gathered and where these statistics are published.

***How to Find Information about Companies* (Washington, D.C.: Washington Researchers, 1992)** A useful guide to locating information about specific companies.

***International Directory of Corporate Affiliations* (Wilmette, Ill.: National Register Publishing Company)** Similar to the *Directory of Corporate Affiliations,* this annual publication contains information about the holdings of parent companies. However, it provides listings of the holdings of foreign companies by U.S. parent companies, as well as the U.S. holdings of foreign parent companies.

Million Dollar Directory (**New York: Dun & Bradstreet**)   Published annually by Dun & Bradstreet, this reference source lists the offices, products, sales, and number of employees for companies with assets of $500,000 or more.

Predicasts F & S Index — United States (**Cleveland: Predicasts**)   This index includes company, product, and industry information from over 750 sources, including financial publications, business newspapers, trade magazines, and special reports. Information is included on new products, technological developments, corporate acquisitions and mergers, and more. The index is published weekly, with monthly, quarterly, and annual compilations.

Standard Industrial Classification Manual (**Springfield, Va.: Office of Management and Budget, National Technical Information Service**)   The *Standard Industrial Classification Manual* provides the basic system used for classifying industries into 11 major divisions. The SIC system is used for federal economic statistics classified by industry.

Standard & Poor's Register of Corporations, Directors, and Executives (**New York: Standard and Poor's Corporation**)   This annual publication lists officers, products, sales, addresses, telephone numbers, and employees for more than 50,000 U.S. and Canadian corporations.

Thomas Register of American Manufacturers and Thomas Register Catalog File (**New York: Thomas Publishing Company**)   Published annually, this multi-volume publication lists the specific manufacturers of individual products and provides information on their addresses, branch offices, and subsidiaries.

Many of the listed sources are general. They contain information applicable to a wide number of research problems. They will typically provide a productive start in the search for secondary data. If this search results in a dead end, all is not lost by any means. The required secondary data may still be available in industry trade publications. The amount of data available on an industry-by-industry basis is extensive indeed, and researchers are well advised not to finish their search without reviewing the appropriate industry sources. Often the source of industry statistics will be the industry trade association; in other cases, it may be trade journals serving the industry.

MARKET AND CONSUMER INFORMATION

A Guide to Consumer Markets (**New York: The Conference Board**)   Issued annually, this publication contains data on the behavior of consumers in the marketplace. It includes statistics on population, employment, income, expenditure, and prices.

Aging America — Trends and Projections (**U.S. Senate Special Committee on Aging and the American Association of Retired Persons: Government Printing Office**)   This chartbook describes the sustained growth in America's elderly population expected during the next 30 years. Graphs and tables cover areas such as demographics, employment, health, and income.

Census of Housing **(U.S. Bureau of the Census: Government Printing Office)**   The *Census of Housing* is published decennially for the years ending in ''0.'' It was first taken in 1940 in conjunction with the *Census of Population* and lists such things as type of structure, size, building condition, occupancy, water and sewage facilities, monthly rent, average value, and equipment including stoves, dishwashers, air conditioners, and so on. For large metropolitan areas, it provides detailed statistics by city block. The periods between publications of the *Census of Housing* are covered by the bureau's annual *American Housing Survey*.

Census of Population **(U.S. Bureau of the Census: Government Printing Office)**   The *Census of Population* is taken every ten years, in the years ending with ''0.'' The census reports the population by geographic region. It also provides detailed breakdowns on such characteristics as sex, marital status, age, education, race, national origin, family size, employment and unemployment, income, and other demographic characteristics. The *Current Population Reports,* which are published annually and make use of the latest information on migrations, birth and death rates, and so forth, update the information in the *Census of Population*.

County and City Databook **(U.S. Bureau of the Census: Government Printing Office)**   Published once every five years, the *County and City Databook* serves as a convenient source of statistics gathered in the various censuses and provides breakdowns on a city and county basis. Included are statistics on such things as population, education, employment, income, housing, banking, manufacturing output and capital expenditures, retail and wholesale sales, and mineral and agricultural output.

County Business Patterns **(U.S. Department of Commerce: Government Printing Office)**   This annual publication contains statistics on a number of businesses by type and their employments and payrolls broken down by county. These data are often quite useful in industrial market potential studies.

Editor and Publisher Market Guide **(New York: Editor and Publisher Magazine)**   Published annually, this guide contains data on some 265 metropolitan statistical areas, including location, population, number of households, principal industries, retail sales and outlets, and climate.

Marketing Economics Guide **(New York: Marketing Economics Institute)**   Published annually, this publication provides detailed operating information on 1,500 retailing centers throughout the country on a regional, state, county, and city basis. It contains information on population, percent of households by income class, disposable income, total retail sales, and retail sales by store group.

Rand McNally Commercial Atlas and Marketing Guide **(Chicago: Rand McNally Company)**   Published annually, this atlas contains marketing data and maps for some 100,000 cities and towns in the United States. Included are such things as population, auto registrations, and retail trade.

Sales and Marketing Management Survey of Buying Power **(New York: Sales and Marketing Management)**   Published annually, this survey contains market data for states, a number of counties, cities, and standard metropolitan statistical areas. Included are statistics on population, retail sales, and household income, and a combined index of buying power for each reported geographic area.

State and Metropolitan Area Databook **(U.S. Department of Commerce: Government Printing Office)**   This book is a *Statistical Abstract* supplement put out by the Department of Commerce. It contains information on population, housing, government, manufacturing, retail and wholesale trade, and selected services by state and standard metropolitan statistical areas.

Related Indexes, Directories, and Guides

1990 Census of Population and Housing: User's Guide **(U.S. Bureau of the Census: Government Printing Office)**   The *User's Guide* provides information about how the data were collected and the scope of every subject, discusses how to locate all the statistics for a given geographical area, and provides a glossary of terms used in the census. An index to summary tape files is also available.

Data Sources for Business and Market Analysis, **3rd ed., Nathalie D. Frank (Metuchen, N.J.: Scarecrow Press, 1983)**   An annotated guide to original statistical sources arranged by source of information rather than by topic.

Measuring Markets: A Guide to the Use of Federal and State Statistical Data **(Washington, D.C.: U.S. Department of Commerce, 1979)**   This book serves as an excellent guide to both federal and state statistical data.

State Data and Database Sourcebook **(Chevy Chase, Md.: Information USA, Inc., 1989)**   This volume contains information on how to obtain data (including information that might be useful from a marketing perspective) from state offices. Information about available data, their cost, and so on are provided for each state.

GENERAL ECONOMIC AND STATISTICAL INFORMATION

Business Statistics **(U.S. Department of Commerce: Government Printing Office)**   Published every two years, this publication provides a historical record of the data series appearing monthly in the *Survey of Current Business.*

Economic Indicators **(Council of Economic Advisers: Government Printing Office)**   This monthly publication contains charts and tables of general economic data such as gross national product, personal consumption expenditures, and other series important in measuring general economic activity. An annual supplement presenting historical and descriptive material on the sources, uses, and limitations of the data is also issued.

Economic Report of the President (**U.S. Government: Government Printing Office**)
This publication results from the President's annual address to Congress about the general economic well-being of the country. The back portion of the report contains summary statistical tables using data collected elsewhere.

Federal Reserve Bulletin (**Washington, D.C.: Federal Reserve System Board of Governors**)   Published monthly, this publication is an important source of financial data, including statistics on banking activity, interest rates, savings, the index of industrial production, an index of department store sales, prices, and international trade and finance.

Handbook of Cyclical Indicators (**Washington, D.C.: U.S. Department of Commerce**)   Published monthly, this publication contains at least 70 indicators of business activity designed to serve as a key to general economic conditions.

Historical Statistics of the United States from Colonial Times to 1970 (**U.S. Bureau of the Census: Government Printing Office**)   This volume was prepared by the Bureau of the Census to supplement the *Statistical Abstract*. The *Statistical Abstract* is one of the more important general sources for the marketing researcher, since it contains data on many social, economic, and political aspects of life in the United States. One problem a user of *Statistical Abstract* data faces is incomparability of figures at various points in time because of the changes in definitions and classifications occasioned by a dynamic economy. *Historical Statistics* contains annual data on some 12,500 different series, using consistent definitions and going back to the inception of the series.

Monthly Labor Review (**U.S. Bureau of Labor Statistics: Government Printing Office**)   Published monthly, this publication contains statistics on employment and unemployment, labor turnover, earnings and hours worked, wholesale and retail prices, and work stoppages.

Statistical Abstract of the United States (**U.S. Bureau of the Census: Government Printing Office**)   This annual publication reproduces more than 1,500 tables originally published elsewhere that cover such areas as the economic, demographic, social, and political structure of the United States. The publication is intended to serve as a convenient statistical reference and as a guide to more detailed statistics. The latter function is fulfilled through references to the original sources in the introductory comments to each section, the table footnotes, and a bibliography of sources. The *Statistical Abstract* is a source with which many researchers begin the search for external secondary data.

Statistics of Income (**Internal Revenue Service: Government Printing Office**)   Published annually, this publication is prepared from federal income tax returns of corporations and individuals. There are different publications for each type of tax report — one for corporations, one for sole proprietorships and partnerships, and one for individuals. The *Corporate Income Tax Return* volume, for example, contains balance sheet and income statement statistics compiled from corporate tax returns and broken down by major industry, asset size, and so on.

***Survey of Current Business* (U.S. Bureau of Economic Analysis: Government Printing Office)**   This monthly publication provides a comprehensive statistical summary of the national income and product accounts of the United States. There are some 2,600 different statistical series reported, covering such topics as general business indicators, commodity prices, construction and real estate activity, personal consumption expenditures by major type, foreign transactions, income and employment by industry, transportation and communications activity, and so on. Most of the statistical series present data on the last four years.

***The Handbook of Basic Economic Statistics* (Washington, D.C.: Economic Statistics Bureau of Washington, D.C.)**   This monthly publication provides a compilation of more than 1,800 statistical series related to the national economy condensed from the volumes of information released by the federal government.

***United Nations Statistical Yearbook* (New York: United Nations)**   This annual United Nations publication contains statistics on a wide range of foreign and domestic activities, including forestry, transportation, manufacturing, consumption, and education.

***World Almanac and Book of Facts* (New York: Newspaper Enterprise Association)**   Issued annually by the Newspaper Enterprise Association, this publication serves as a well-indexed handbook on a wide variety of subjects. Included are industrial, financial, religious, social, and political statistics.

GENERAL GUIDES TO BUSINESS INFORMATION

In addition to the following sources, see ''Related Indexes, Directories, and Guides,'' in Sections One and Two of this appendix.

***A Handbook on the Use of Government Statistics* (Charlottesville, Va.: Taylor Murphy Institute)**   This publication is designed to assist the businessperson with the use of government statistics. A series of brief case descriptions are presented.

***A User's Guide to BEA Information* (U.S. Bureau of Economic Analysis: Government Printing Office)**   This booklet provides a directory for Bureau of Economic Analysis publications, computer tapes, diskettes, and other information sources.

***American Marketing Association Bibliography Series* (Chicago: American Marketing Association)**   Published periodically, each of the publications provides an in-depth annotated bibliography of a topic of interest in marketing.

***Business Information Sources,* revised ed., Lorna M. Daniells (Berkeley: University of California Press, 1985)**   A guide to the basic sources of business information organized by subject area.

***Business Information: How to Find It, How to Use It,* 2nd ed., Michael R. Lavin (Phoenix, Ariz.: Oryx Press, 1992)**   A general guide to searching for business information, this book provides useful information for the development of search strategies.

***Census Catalog and Guide* (U.S. Bureau of the Census: Government Printing Office)**   This catalog is an annual, cumulative publication describing all products (reports, maps, microfiche, computer tapes, diskettes, and on-line items) that the Census Bureau has issued since 1980, including information about how to order the information. Also included is an appendix that includes, among other things, a directory of telephone numbers of Census Bureau specialists by area of expertise.

***Encyclopedia of Business Information Sources,* 10th ed. (Detroit: Gale Research, 1994)**   A guide to the information available on various subjects, including basic statistical sources, associations, periodicals, directories, handbooks, and general literature.

***Factfinder for the Nation* (U.S. Bureau of the Census: Government Printing Office)**   Issued irregularly, this series of publications describes the range of Census Bureau materials that are available on a variety of subjects and suggests some of their uses. A few of the subjects included are population statistics, housing statistics, statistics on race and ethnicity, availability of census records about individuals, and more.

***Guide to American Directories,* 13th ed., Bernard Klein (Coral Springs, Fla.: Todd Publications, 1993)**   This guide provides information on directories published in the United States, categorized under 300 technical, mercantile, industrial, scientific, and professional headings.

***Guide to Foreign Trade Statistics* (Washington, D.C.: U.S. Bureau of the Census, 1991)**   A guide to the published and unpublished sources of foreign trade statistics.

***Guide to the 1987 Economic Censuses and Related Statistics* (U.S. Bureau of the Census: Government Printing Office)**   This reference provides general information about the uses, scope, content, coverage, legal authority and confidentiality, classification system, and geographic detail of the 1987 economic censuses. It describes each of the censuses, their related surveys, and special programs, with cross-references to other Census Bureau statistics.

***How to Win With Information or Lose Without It,* Andrew P. Garven and Hubert Bermont (Washington, D.C.: Bermont Books, 1980)**   This publication, written in nontechnical language especially for executives, discusses data banks and information retrieval services.

Statistics Sources, **18th ed., Paul Wasserman,** *et al.* **(Detroit: Gale Research, 1994)** A guide to federal, state, and private sources of statistics on a wide variety of subjects.

The Federal Database Finder **(Chevy Case, Md.: Information USA, Inc.)** This useful resource provides a directory of over 4,200 no-cost and fee-based data bases and data files that are available through the federal government.

Where to Find Business Information: A Worldwide Guide for Everyone Who Needs the Answers to Business Questions, **2nd ed., David M. Brownstone and Gorton Carruth (New York: John Wiley & Sons, 1982)** This publication lists over 5,000 books, periodicals, or data bases of current interest and contains subject, title, and publisher indexes.

INDEXES

In addition to the following sources, see ''Related Indexes, Directories, and Guides'' in Sections One and Two of this appendix.

American Statistics Index **(Washington, D.C.: Congressional Information Service)** Published annually and updated monthly, the publication is intended to serve as a comprehensive index of statistical data available to the public from any agency of the federal government.

Business Index **(Foster City, Calif.: Information Access Company)** The *Business Index* is a microform index to over 460 business periodicals, *The Wall Street Journal, Barrons,* the *New York Times,* and business information from more than 1,100 general and legal periodicals. Index entries are arranged by subject and author in alphabetic order.

Business Periodicals Index **(Bronx, N.Y.: The H. W. Wilson Company)** The *Business Periodicals Index* is a general purpose business index published monthly (with quarterly and annual compilations) and is composed of subject entries covering approximately 350 business periodicals.

Communications Abstracts **(Beverly Hills, Calif.: Sage Publications, Inc.)** *Communications Abstracts* provides an index to communications-related articles, books, and reports. It is issued quarterly and covers such topics as marketing, advertising, and mass communication.

Dissertation Abstracts International **(Ann Arbor, Mich.: University Microfilms International)** Issued monthly, this publication contains descriptions of doctoral dissertations from nearly 500 participating institutions in North America and around the world. The approximately 35,000 annual entries are divided into three divisions: the humanities and social sciences, the sciences and engineering, and European abstracts.

***Journal of Marketing, "Marketing Literature Review"* (Chicago: American Marketing Association)**   Each quarterly issue of the *Journal of Marketing* includes a "Marketing Literature Review" section that indexes a selection of article abstracts related to marketing from the business literature. Abstracts are drawn from over 125 business journals; entries are indexed under a variety of marketing subject headings.

***Social Sciences Citation Index* (Philadelphia: Institute for Scientific Information)**   Published three times yearly, with annual cumulations, this publication indexes all articles in about 1,400 social science periodicals and selected articles in approximately 3,300 periodicals in other disciplines.

***Statistical Reference Index* (Washington, D.C.: Congressional Information Service)**   Published monthly (with annual cumulations), this publication is intended to serve as a selective guide to American statistical publications from private organizations and state government sources.

***The Information Catalog* (New York: FIND/SVP)**   *The Information Catalog* is a bimonthly publication of FIND/SVP, a business information and research firm. This resource contains overviews of reports, directories, reference works, and so on, that may be of interest to businesses. The reports have been produced by FIND/SVP and other research companies, publishers, and brokerage firms.

***The Wall Street Journal Index* (Princeton, N.J.: Dow Jones Books)**   Published monthly, *The Wall Street Journal Index* provides a subject index of information appearing in *The Wall Street Journal* in two sections—general news and corporate news.

DIRECTORIES

In addition to the following sources, see "Related Indexes, Directories, and Guides" in Sections One and Two of this appendix.

***American Marketing Association International Membership Directory & Marketing Services Guide* (Chicago: American Marketing Association)**   This directory, produced annually, contains an international directory of AMA members and member companies as well as a guide to providers of marketing services.

***Business Organizations, Agencies, and Publications Directory* (Detroit: Gale Research)**   This directory serves as a guide to approximately 20,000 organizations, agencies, and publications related to business, trade, and industry in the areas of marketing, accounting, administration, human resources, and many more.

***Consultants and Consulting Organizations Directory*, 13th ed. (Detroit: Gale Research, 1992)**   This directory lists approximately 14,000 firms and individuals who are active in consulting and briefly describes their services and fields of interest.

***Directories in Print,* 12th ed. (Detroit: Gale Research, 1994)**   This directory, which is arranged by subject, lists, among other things, commercial and manufacturing directories; directories of individual industries, trades, and professions; and rosters of professional and scientific societies.

***Directory of American Research and Technology,* 27th ed. (New York: Bowker, 1992)**   A guide to research and development capabilities of more than 11,000 industrial organizations in the United States. It contains an alphabetical listing of the organizations, addresses of facilities, sizes of staffs, and fields of research and development.

***Directory of Online Databases* (Santa Monica, Calif.: Cuadra Associates, Inc.)**   Published quarterly, this publication describes more than 4,062 bibliographic and non-bibliographic data bases.

***Encyclopedia of Associations* (Detroit: Gale Research)**   Published annually, this encyclopedia lists the active trade, business, and professional associations, briefly describes each organization's activities, and lists their publications.

***Encyclopedia of Information Systems and Services,* 9th ed., Amy Lucas and Nan Soper (eds.), (Detroit: Gale Research 1989)**   This encyclopedia lists and describes over 2,500 organizations involved in data storage and retrieval. Included are data base producers and publishers, on-line vendors, information centers, research centers, and data banks.

***Federal Statistical Directory: The Guide to Personnel and Data Sources* (Phoenix, Ariz.: Oryx Press)**   The directory lists, by subject and by organizational unit within each agency, the names, office addresses, and telephone numbers of key personnel working with statistical programs and related activities of agencies in the executive branch of the federal government.

***FINDEX, The Directory of Market Research Reports, Studies and Surveys* (Bethesda, Md.: Cambridge Information Group)**   This publication provides a directory of more than 10,000 research reports produced by 500 top U.S. and international research firms.

***International Directory of Marketing Research Houses and Services* (New York: American Marketing Association, New York Chapter)**   This publication provides an alphabetic listing of domestic and international marketing research companies. A geographic listing is also provided, along with an index of principal personnel.

***Standard Directory of Advertisers* (Wilmette, Ill.: National Register Publishing Company)**   This annual directory lists over 25,000 companies with annual advertising allotments for advertising campaigns of more than $75,000. Included are individual listings containing information on type of business, address, key personnel, advertising agency relationship, products advertised, media utilized, and so on. The directory is published in two editions, one by product classification and one by geographic location.

***Standard Directory of Advertising Agencies* (Wilmette, Ill.: National Register Publishing Company)**   The *Standard Directory of Advertising Agencies* lists approximately 5,000 advertising agencies and provides information such as personnel by title, key accounts, addresses, and telephone numbers for the agencies. The directory is published three times each year.

***Who's Who in Consulting* (Detroit: Gale Research, 1983)**   This directory provides biographical information on consultants in a variety of fields, including their subject area and geographical location.

7

DATA COLLECTION: PRIMARY DATA

In Chapter 6, the point was made and emphasized that secondary data represents fast and inexpensive research information and that the researcher who gives secondary data only a cursory look is being reckless. However, it was also mentioned that rarely will secondary data provide a complete solution to a research problem. The units of measurement or classes employed to report the data will be wrong; the data will be somewhat obsolete by the time of its publication; the data will not be sufficiently complete, and so on. When these conditions occur, the researcher logically turns to primary data.

This chapter is the first of three dealing with primary data. It is intended as an introduction and is divided into four parts. Part 1 discusses the types of primary data generally obtained from and about subjects. Part 2 discusses the two main means employed — communication and observation — and the suitability of each method for securing the different kinds of primary data. Part 3 elaborates communication methods. In particular, it discusses the many types of questionnaires and means of administration. Part 4 does the same for observational methods.

TYPES OF PRIMARY DATA GENERALLY OBTAINED

Demographic/Socioeconomic Characteristics

One type of primary data of great interest to marketers is the subject's demographic and socioeconomic characteristics, such as age, education, occupation, marital status, sex, income, or social class. These variables are used to cross-classify the collected data and in some way make sense of them. We might be interested, for instance, in determining whether people's attitudes toward ecology and pollution are related to their level of formal education. Alternatively, a common question asked by marketers is whether the consumption of a particular product is related in any way to a person's (or family's) age, education, income, and so on, and if so, in what way. These are questions of market segmentation. Demographic and socioeconomic characteristics are often used to delineate market segments.[1]

Demographic and socioeconomic characteristics are sometimes called *states of being,* because they represent attributes of people. Some of these states of being, such as a respondent's age, sex, and level of formal education, can be readily verified. Some, such as social class, cannot be verified except very crudely, since they are relative and not absolute measures of a person's standing in society.[2] Income represents an intermediate degree of difficulty in verifiability. Although a person's income in any given year is some actual quantity, ascertaining the amount sometimes proves to be difficult.

Psychological/Life-Style Characteristics

Another type of primary data of interest to marketers is the subject's psychological and life-style characteristics in the form of personality traits, activities, interests, and values. **Personality** refers to the normal patterns of behavior exhibited by an individual. It represents the attributes, traits, and mannerisms that distinguish one individual from another. We often characterize people by the personality traits they display — aggressiveness, dominance, friendliness, sociability. Marketers are interested in personality because the traits people possess seem to be important in affecting the way consumers and others in the marketing process behave. The argument is often advanced, for example, that personality can affect a consumer's choice of stores or products or an individual's response to an advertisement or point-of-purchase display. Similarly, it is believed that certain characteristics, like extroversion or empathy, are more likely to be possessed by successful than by unsuccessful salespeople. Even though the empirical evidence on the ability of personality to predict consumption behavior or salesperson success is weak, personality remains a variable dear to the hearts of marketing researchers.[3]

---

[1]See Yoram Wind, "Issues and Advances in Segmentation Research," *Journal of Marketing Research,* 15 (August 1978), pp. 317–337; and T. P. Beane and D. M. Ennis, "Market Segmentation: A Review," *European Journal of Marketing,* 21 (No. 5, 1987), pp. 20–42.

[2]See James H. Myers and William H. Reynolds, *Consumer Behavior in Marketing Management* (Boston: Houghton Mifflin, © 1967), pp. 206–216, for a useful discussion of social class, its role in marketing-related phenomena, and the various ways in which it has been measured. See Charles M. Schaninger, "Social Class versus Income Revisited: An Empirical Investigation," *Journal of Marketing Research,* 18 (May 1981), pp. 192–208, for a comparison of the ability of social class and income to predict consumption of a number of household products; and see Gillian Stevens and Joo Hyun Cho, "Socioeconomic Indexes and the New 1980 Census Occupational Classification Scheme," *Social Science Research,* 14 (1985), pp. 142–168, for discussion of the measurement of socioeconomic status using occupation.

[3]For a review of the evidence regarding the relationship of personality to consumer behavior, see Harold H. Kassarjian, "Personality and Consumer Behavior: A Review," *Journal of Marketing Research,* 8 (November 1971), pp. 409–418. For a review of the evidence regarding the relationship between personality characteristics and salesperson success, see Gilbert A. Churchill, Jr., Neil M. Ford, Orville C. Walker, Jr., and Steve W. Hartley, "Selecting Successful Salespeople: A Meta-Analysis of Biographical and Psychological Selection Criteria," in Michael J. Houston, ed., *Review of Marketing 1987* (Chicago: American Marketing Association, 1987), pp. 98–134.

Personality is typically measured by one of the standard personality inventories that has been developed by psychologists.[4]

Life-style, or **psychographic, analysis** rests on the premise that the firm can plan more effective strategies to reach its target market if it knows more about its customers in terms of how they live, what interests them, and what they like. The thrust in psychographic research has been to develop a number of statements that reflect a person's activities, interests, and opinions (AIO) and consumption behavior. The statements might include such things as "I like to watch football games on television," "I like stamp collecting," "I am very interested in national politics." There would be a great many statements to which subjects are asked to respond.[5] For example, the advertising agency Needham, Harper, and Steers annually conducts a life-style study that includes 3,500 respondents answering 700 questions. Table 7.1 contains the list of characteristics that are usually assessed with AIO inventories. The attempt in the analysis is to identify groups of consumers who are likely to behave similarly toward the product or service and who have similar life-style profiles. Research Realities 7.1 provides life-style descriptions of the seven most common shopper types.

One problem that marketers experienced when using psychographics or AIO inventories was that the categories of users distinguished in one study focusing on one type of product would be very different from the categories of individuals identified in another study examining a different product. This meant that each product required a new data collection and analysis exercise. Because of the instability of profiles across products, it was also impossible to develop demographic descriptions of the various groups that would be useful when developing marketing strategies for new products or brands. The purpose of value and life-style research (VALS) is to avoid these problems by creating a

---

[4]There are a number of guides to the various personality inventories. Some of the more extensive ones are C. M. Bonjean, R. J. Hill, and S. D. McLemore, *Sociological Measurement: An Inventory of Scales and Indices* (San Francisco: Chandler, 1967); Ki-Taek Chun, Sidney Cobb, and J. R. P. French, *Measures for Psychological Assessment* (Ann Arbor, Mich.: Institute for Social Research, University of Michigan, 1975); D. G. Lake, M. B. Miles, and R. B. Earle, Jr., *Measuring Human Behavior: Tools for the Assessment of Social Functioning* (New York: Teachers College Press, Columbia University, 1973); and Delbert C. Miller, *Handbook of Research Design and Social Measurement,* 5th ed. (Newbury Park, CA: Sage Publications, 1991).

[5]One of the more popular lists in the 300-question inventory that appears in William D. Wells and Douglas Tigert, "Activities, Interests, and Opinions," *Journal of Advertising Research,* 11 (August 1971), pp. 27–35. For a general review of the origins, development, and thrust of life-style and psychographic research, see William D. Wells, ed., *Life Style and Psychographics* (Chicago: American Marketing Association, 1974). For evidence regarding the reliability and validity of psychographic inventories, see Alvin C. Burns and Mary Carolyn Harrison, "A Test of the Reliability of Psychographics," *Journal of Marketing Research,* 16 (February 1979), pp. 32–38; John L. Lastovicka, "On the Validation of Lifestyle Traits: A Review and Illustration," *Journal of Marketing Research,* 19 (February 1982), pp. 126–138; and Ian Fenwick, D. A. Schellinck, and K. W. Kendall, "Assessing the Reliability of Psychographic Analyses," *Marketing Science,* 2 (Winter 1983), pp. 57–74; and Thabet A. Edris and A. Meidan, "On the Reliability of Psychographic Research: Encouraging Signs for Measurement Accuracy and Methodology in Consumer Research," *European Journal of Marketing,* 24 (No. 3, 1990), pp. 23–41.

TABLE 7.1 **Life-Style Dimensions**

Activities	Interests	Opinions
Work	Family	Themselves
Hobbies	Home	Social issues
Social events	Job	Politics
Vacation	Community	Business
Entertainment	Recreation	Economics
Club membership	Fashion	Education
Community	Food	Products
Shopping	Media	Future
Sports	Achievements	Culture

Source: Adapted from Joseph T. Plummer, "The Concept and Application of Life Style Segmentation," *Journal of Marketing,* 38 (January 1974), p. 34. Published by the American Marketing Association. See also Ronald D. Michman, *Lifestyle Market Segmentation* (New York: Praeger Publishers, 1991).

standard psychographic framework that can be used for a variety of products.[6] Table 7.2, for example, shows the ten segments that have been identified from applying VALS in Japan.

Attitudes/Opinions

Some authors distinguish between attitudes and opinions, but others use the terms interchangeably. Most typically, **attitude** is used to refer to an individual's "preference, inclination, views or feelings toward some phenomenon," whereas **opinions** are "verbal expressions of attitudes." Since attitudes are typically secured from respondents by questioning, we shall not make the distinction between the terms but will treat attitudes and opinions interchangeably as representing a person's ideas, convictions, or liking with respect to a specific object or idea.

Attitude is one of the more important notions in marketing literature, because it is generally thought that attitudes are related to behavior.

---

[6]The original VALS was a typology of the American population developed by Arnold Mitchell to provide a model of societal values. It is described in his book, *The Nine American Lifestyles* (New York: MacMillan, 1983). It has been supplanted in the U.S. by VALS 2, which is much more focused on predicting consumer behavior. Other value-based classification schemes include Monitor, and The List of Values (LOV). For discussions of the use of value and life-style research, see Bickley Townsend, "Psychographic Glitter and Gold," *American Demographics,* 7 (November 1985), pp. 22–29; Lynn R. Kahle, Sharon E. Beatty, and Pamela Homer, "Alternative Measurement Approaches to Consumer Values: The List of Values (LOV) and Values and Life Style (VALS)," *Journal of Consumer Research,* 13 (December 1986), pp. 405–409; and Rebecca Piirto, *Beyond Mind Games: The Marketing Power of Psychographics* (Ithaca, N.Y.: American Demographic Books, 1991).

Research Realities 7.1

Life-Style Descriptions of the Seven Most Common Shopper Types

Inactive Shoppers (15% of all shoppers) have extremely restricted life-styles and shopping interests. Best characterized by their inactivity, Inactive shoppers do not engage in outdoor or do-it-yourself activities except for working in the yard or garden. They do not express strong enjoyment or interest in shopping, nor are they particularly concerned about such shopping attributes as price, employee service, or product selection.

Active Shoppers (12.8%) have demanding life-styles and are "tough" shoppers. They engage in all forms of outdoor activities and are usually do-it-yourselfers. "Actives" enjoy "shopping around," and price is a major consideration in their search. However, given their full range of interests outside of shopping, "Actives" appear to shop more as an expression of their intense life-styles than as an interest in finding bargains. Therefore, these shoppers probably balance price with quality, fashion, and selection in their search for value.

Service Shoppers (10%) demand a high level of in-store service when shopping. They usually seek convenient stores with friendly, helpful employees. Conversely, they quickly become impatient if they have to wait for a clerk to help them.

Traditional Shoppers (14.1%) share Active shoppers' preoccupation with outdoor activities but not their enthusiasm for shopping. They actively hike,

camp, hunt, and fish and are do-it-yourselfers who often work on their cars. In general, though, Traditional shoppers are not price sensitive, nor do they have other strong shopper requirements.

Dedicated Fringe Shoppers (8.8%) present clear motives for being heavy catalog shoppers. They are do-it-yourselfers and are more likely than average to try new products. They have almost a compulsion for being different. Dedicated Fringe shoppers are disinterested in extreme socializing. They have little interest in television and radio advertisements and exhibit limited brand and store loyalty. Therefore, the catalog represents a medium for obtaining an expanded selection of do-it-yourself and other products, and this reflects their individualism.

Price Shoppers (10.4%), as the name implies, are most identifiable by their extreme price consciousness. Price shoppers are willing to undertake an extended search to meet their price requirements, and they rely heavily on all forms of advertising to find the lowest prices.

Transitional Shoppers (6.9%) seem to be consumers in earlier stages of the family life cycle who have not yet formalized their life-style patterns and shopping values. They take an active interest in repairing and personalizing cars. Most participate in a variety of outdoor activities. They are more likely than average to try new products. Transitional shoppers exhibit little interest in shopping around for low prices. They are probably "eclectic shoppers" because they appear to make up their minds quickly to buy products once they become interested.

Source: Jack A. Lesser and Marie Adele Hughes, "The Generalizability of Psychographic Market Segments across Geographic Locations," *Journal of Marketing*, 50 (January 1986), p. 23.

TABLE **7.2** **Segments Identified Using VALS in Japan**

Dimension	Group	Percentage of Population	Description
Exploration	Integrators	4	Well-educated, modern people who enjoy the new and risky.
	Sustainers	15	People who resent changes.
Self-Expression	Self-Innovators	7	Young, active people who are interested in fashion and spend a lot of money on themselves.
	Self-Adapters	11	Shy people who are sensitive to others and pattern their buying after that of Self-Innovators.
Achievement	Ryoshiki ("social intelligence") Innovators	6	Career-oriented, highly educated, middle-aged people.
	Ryoshiki Adapters	10	Shy people who are sensitive to others and pattern their buying after that of Ryoshiki Innovators.
Tradition	Tradition Innovators	6	Middle-aged homeowners with middle-management jobs who are active in community affairs.
	Tradition Adapters	10	Affluent, young, well-educated managers who travel frequently.
Realist Orientation	High Pragmatics	14	Least likely to agree with any attitude statement; withdrawn; suspicious; unconcerned about self-improvement or preserving customs.
	Low Pragmatics	17	Attitudinally negative people with no psychological tendency who prefer inexpensive goods and established brands.

Source: Lewis C. Winters, "International Psychographics," *Marketing Research: A Magazine of Management & Applications* 4 (September 1992), pp.48–49. Reprinted with permission of American Marketing Association.

Obviously, when an individual likes a product he will be more inclined to buy it than when he does not like it; when he likes one brand more than another, he will tend to buy the preferred brand. Attitudes may be said to be the forerunners of behavior.[7]

Thus, marketers are often interested in people's attitudes toward the product itself, their overall attitudes with respect to specific brands, and their attitudes toward specific

---

[7]Fred L. Schreier, *Modern Marketing Research: A Behavioral Science Approach* (Belmont, Calif.: Wadsworth, 1963), p. 273. For a general discussion of the role of attitude in consumer behavior, see J. Paul Peter and Jerry C. Olson, *Consumer Behavior and Marketing Strategy,* 3rd ed. (Homewood, IL.: Irwin, 1993), especially pages 175–217.

aspects or features possessed by several brands. Attitude is such a pervasive notion in behavioral science, and particularly in marketing, that Chapter 9 is devoted to various types of instruments used to measure it.

Awareness/Knowledge

As used in marketing research, **awareness/knowledge** refers to what respondents do and do not know about some object or phenomenon. For instance, a problem of considerable importance is the effectiveness of magazine ads. One measure of effectiveness is the product awareness generated by the ad, using one of the three approaches described in Table 7.3. Although all three approaches are aimed at assessing the respondent's awareness of and knowledge about the ad, there is a definite increase in retention when knowledge is measured by recognition rather than by recall and by aided rather than unaided recall. This, of course, raises the question of which method is the "most accurate." There are problems with each method, not the least of which is separating true awareness from "bogus recall."[8] The important thing to note is that when marketers speak of a person's awareness, they often mean the individual's knowledge of the advertisement. A person "very much aware" or possessing "high awareness" typically knows a great deal about the ad.

Awareness and knowledge are also used interchangeably when marketers speak of product awareness. For example, Research Realities 7.2 discusses the use of recall data to assess the value of getting products in films. Marketing researchers are often interested in determining whether the respondent is aware of the following:[9]

- the product,
- its features,
- where it is available,
- its price,
- its manufacturer,
- where it is made,
- how it is used, and for what purpose, and
- its specific distinctive features.

---

[8]See Herbert E. Krugman, "Point of View: Measuring Memory — An Industry Dilemma," *Journal of Advertising Research,* 25 (August/September 1985), pp. 49–51; Charles E. Young and Michael Robinson, "Guideline: Tracking the Commercial Viewer's Wandering Attention," *Journal of Advertising Research,* 27 (June/July 1987), pp. 15–22; Murphy A. Sewall and Dan Sarel, "Characteristics of Radio Commercials and Their Recall Effectiveness," *Journal of Marketing,* 50 (January 1986), pp. 52–60; Myron Glassman and John B. Ford, "An Empirical Investigation of Bogus Recall," *Journal of the Academy of Marketing Science,* 16 (Fall 1988), pp. 38–41; and Robin Higie and Murphy A. Sewall, "Using Recall and Brand Preference to Evaluate Advertising Effectiveness," *Journal of Advertising Research,* 31 (April/May 1991), pp. 56–63.

[9]Schreier, *Modern Marketing Research,* pp. 269–273.

TABLE 7.3 **Approaches Used to Measure Awareness**

Unaided recall: Without being given any clues, consumers are asked to recall what advertisements they have seen recently. Prompting is not used because, presumably, even if prompting for the general category were used (for example, laundry detergents), respondents would have a tendency to remember more advertisements in that product category.
Aided recall: Consumers are given some prompting, typically in the form of questions about advertisements in a specific product category. Alternatively, respondents might be given a list showing the names or trademarks of advertisers that appeared in a particular magazine issue, along with names or trademarks that did not appear, and would be asked to check those to which they were exposed.
Recognition: Consumers are shown copies of actual advertisements and are asked whether or not they remember seeing each one.

Although framed in terms of awareness, these questions, to a greater or lesser degree, aim at determining the individual's knowledge of, or beliefs about, the product. For our purposes, then, knowledge and awareness will be used interchangeably to refer to what a respondent believes about an advertisement, product, retail store, and so on.

Intentions

A person's **intentions** refer to the individual's anticipated or planned future behavior. Marketers are interested in people's intentions primarily with regard to purchasing behavior. One of the better known studies concerning purchase intentions is that conducted by the Survey Research Center at the University of Michigan. The center regularly conducts surveys for the Federal Reserve Board to determine the general financial condition of consumers and their outlook with respect to the state of the economy in the near future. The center asks consumers about their buying intentions for big ticket items such as appliances, automobiles, and homes during the next few months. The responses are then analyzed, and the proportion of the sample that indicates each of the following is reported:

- definite intention to buy,
- probable intention to buy,
- undecided,
- definite intention not to buy.

Intentions receive less attention in marketing than do other types of primary data, largely because there is often a great disparity between what people say they are going to do and what they actually do. This is particularly true with respect to purchase behavior.

Figure 7.1, for example, describes the results of one investigation of the relationship. In the experiment, consumers were given a questionnaire that describes a new pricing option for a service to which customers already subscribed. The questionnaire asked them to circle a number that best indicated how likely they were to buy the service

Research Realities 7.2

CinemaScore Tests Moviegoers' Recall

Crocodile Dundee II grossed more than $70 million for Paramount Pictures, but how did it do for the products that negotiated their way into the hands of its stars and onto the movie screen? Enter Ed Mintz, whose CinemaScore has surveyed opening night audiences for more than a decade. After years of finding out whether people liked the movies they saw, Mintz became intrigued with the question of whether audiences remembered the products that were placed in motion pictures.

The system, which ultimately translates data into terms that a marketer can understand — cost per thousand — is based on an exit survey. The survey, designed to look like a ticket stub, has tabs that can quickly be torn to indicate the viewers' age, sex, those products they remembered seeing, and how well they liked the movie. CinemaScore runs the survey at different theaters and at different show times across the country to gather responses from a wide range of moviegoers.

From there, CinemaScore tallies it all up and applies a formula that uses audience recall and total box-office grosses to compute what the cost of that placement should be. The cost figure is then divided by the number of tickets sold to get a cost per thousand.

In *Dundee II*, Mintz found a mixed bag of winners and losers. Both Coca-Cola and Pepsi were in the film. With Coke, an average of 26 percent of those surveyed remembered seeing the product, whereas only 6 percent of the audience remembered seeing Pepsi.

But it wasn't just a flat case of "cola battle." Coke, it seems, had more of a starring role. In one scene, the star, Paul Hogan, throws a rock at a coke can — it's the focus of attention. Yet Pepsi was just one of several cans in the background. All those elements are taken into CinemaScore's final analysis.

In *Dundee II*, sources say General Foods paid at least $40,000 to put Sanka Coffee in the film. Did it get what it paid for? CinemaScore found that although the product was in the movie and the brand name was visible, the image was hardly recognizable. The exit survey put recall at just 12 percent.

"Once and for all it gives studios and corporate America a yardstick to measure the value of product placement in a film," says Marvin Cohen, who represents both studios and production companies in certain product-placement projects. "[CinemaScore] gives us hard, black-and-white figures that we can relate to, measuring not just the product, but the performance of the product," Cohen says. "We're all pleased to have something that equates the value of a service we can rest easy with."

Source: Betsy Sharkey, "How Many Noticed Sanka in 'Dundee II'? CinemaScore Polls Moviegoers," *Adweek's Marketing Week*, 29 (June 20, 1988), pp. 33–34. Product recall is also one of the measures used to assess the effectiveness of sports tie-ins. See Michael J. McCarthy, "Keeping Careful Score on Sports Tie-Ins," *The Wall Street Journal* (April 24, 1991), p. B1.

when it became available. The scale anchors ranged from 1 (definitely would not buy) to 10 (definitely would buy). As Figure 7.1 indicates, only 45 percent of those indicating that they definitely would buy the service did so within the first three months of its availability. Further, some of the respondents who indicated that they would not buy it did so.

Purchase intentions are most often used when studying the purchase of commodities requiring large outlays such as an automobile for a family, or plant and equipment for a business. The general assumption is that the larger the dollar expenditure, the more preplanning necessary and the greater the correlation between anticipated and actual

FIGURE 7.1 **Proportion of People Buying the Service versus Their Intention to Purchase It**

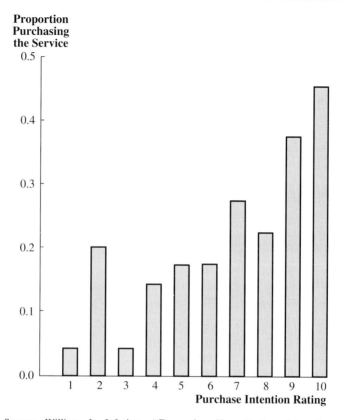

Proportion Purchasing the Service

Purchase Intention Rating

Source: William J. Infosino, "Forecasting New Product Sales from Likelihood of Purchase Ratings," *Marketing Science,* 5 (Fall 1986), p. 375.

behavior. Nevertheless, the evidence with regard to the predictive accuracy of intended purchasing behavior is still something less than encouraging.[10]

[10]Manohar U. Kalwani and Alvin J. Silk, "On the Reliability and Predictive Validity of Purchase Intention Measures," *Marketing Science,* 1 (Summer 1982), pp. 243–286; Murphy A. Sewall, "Relative Information Contributions of Consumer Purchase Intentions and Management Judgment as Explanations of Sales," *Journal of Marketing Research,* 18 (May 1981), pp. 249–253; Gary M. Mullett and Marvin J. Karson, "Analysis of Purchase Intent Scales Weighted by Probability of Actual Purchase," *Journal of Marketing Research,* 22 (February 1985), pp. 93–96; Linda F. Jamieson and Frank M. Bass, "Adjusting Stated Intention Measures to Predict Trial Purchase of New Products: A Comparison of Models and Methods," *Journal of Marketing Research,* 26 (August 1989), pp. 336–345; and Vicki G. Morwitz and David Schmittlein, "Using Segmentation to Improve Sales Forecasting Based on Purchase Intent: Which 'Definitely Will Buys' Will Buy?" working paper, Leonard N. Stern School of Business, New York University, 1991. Those organizations that collect purchase intentions data regularly often adjust the data based on their past experience as to how much bias a set of intentions data might contain.

TABLE 7.4   **Behavior Checklist**

	Purchase Behavior	Use Behavior
What		
How much		
How		
Where		
When		
In what situation		
Who		

Source: Adapted with permission from Fred L. Schreier, *Modern Marketing Research: A Behavioral Science Approach* (Belmont, Calif.: Wadsworth Publishing Company, 1963), p. 251. See also J. Paul Peter and Jerry C. Olson, *Consumer Behavior and Marketing Strategy*, 3rd ed. (Homewood, IL.: Irwin, 1993), p. 345.

Motivation

The concept of motivation seems to contain more semantic confusion than most terms in the behavioral sciences.

> Some writers insist that *motives* are different from *drives* and use the latter term primarily to characterize the basic physiological ''tissue'' needs (e.g., hunger, thirst, shelter, sex). Others distinguish between *needs* and *wants,* stating that needs are the basic motivating forces which translate themselves into more immediate wants which satisfy these needs (e.g., hunger needs give rise to wanting a good steak dinner).[11]

For our purposes a **motive** may refer to a need, a want, a drive, an urge, a wish, a desire, an impulse, or any inner state that directs or channels behavior toward goals.

A marketing researcher's interest in motives typically involves determining *why* people behave as they do. There are several reasons that explain this interest. In the first place, it is believed that a person's motives tend to be more stable than the individual's behavior, and, therefore, motives offer a better basis for predicting future behavior than does past behavior. Second, if we understand the motives behind a person's behavior, we better understand the behavior and, in turn, are in a better position to influence future behavior, or at least have offerings consistent with that anticipated behavior.

Behavior

Behavior concerns what subjects have done or are doing. Most typically in marketing, this means purchase and use behavior. Now, behavior is a physical activity. It takes place under specific circumstances, at a particular time, and involves one or more actors

---

[11]Myers and Reynolds, *Consumer Behavior,* p. 80.

or participants. The focus on behavior, then, involves a description of the activity with respect to the various components, and the marketing researcher investigating behavior is well advised to use Table 7.4 as a checklist in designing data collection instruments so that the key behavioral dimensions of interest are secured.[12] There are many subdimensions to each cell, and the researcher has to make a conscious inclusion-omission decision about each subdimension. Consider the *where,* for example. The "where of purchase" may be specified according to the kind of store, the location of the store by broad geographic area or specific address, the size of the store, or even the name of the store. So it is with each of the many cells. The study of behavior, then, involves the development of a description of the purchase or use activity, either past or current, with respect to some or all of the characteristics contained in Table 7.4.

BASIC MEANS OF OBTAINING PRIMARY DATA

The researcher attempting to collect primary data has a number of choices to make among the means that will be used. Figure 7.2 presents an overview of these choices. The primary decision is whether to employ communication or observation. **Communication** involves questioning respondents to secure the desired information using a data collection instrument called a questionnaire. The questions may be oral or written, and the responses may also be given in either form. **Observation** does not involve questioning. Rather, it means that the situation of interest is checked and the relevant facts, actions, or behaviors recorded. The "observer" may be a person or persons, or the data may be gathered using some mechanical device. For example, a researcher interested in the brands of canned vegetables the family buys might arrange a pantry audit in which the shelves are checked to see which brands the family has on hand.

Choosing a primary method of data collection implies several supplementary decisions. For example, should we administer questionnaires by mail, over the telephone, or in person? Should the purpose of the study be disguised or remain undisguised? Should the answers be open ended, or should the respondent be asked to choose from a limited set of alternatives? Even though Figure 7.2 implies that these decisions are independent, they are actually intimately related. A decision about method of administration, say, has serious implications regarding the degree of structure that must be imposed on the questionnaire.

Communication and observation each has its own advantages and disadvantages, and this section will review these general pluses and minuses. The next section then amplifies the supplementary decisions associated with the communication method, and the final section does the same for observational methods.

The communication method of data collection has the general advantages of versatility, speed, and cost, whereas observational data are typically more objective and accurate.

---

[12]The checklist is adapted from Schreier, *Modern Marketing Research,* p. 251. Schreier also has a productive discussion of the many kinds of questions that need to be answered to complete the checklist.

FIGURE 7.2   **Basic Choices among Means for Collecting Primary Data**

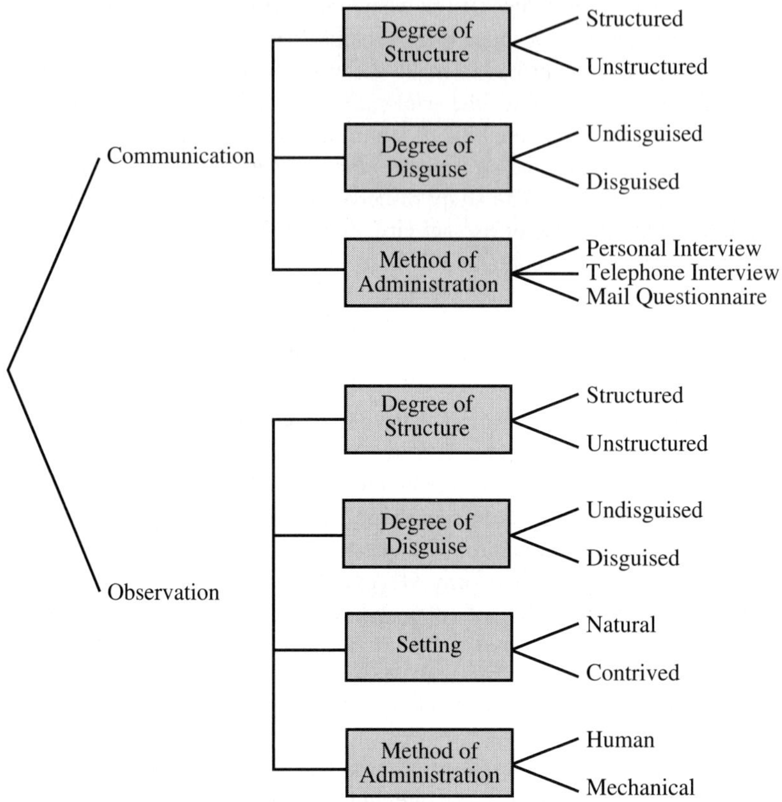

Versatility

Versatility refers to a technique's ability to collect information on the many types of primary data of interest to marketers. A respondent's demographic/socioeconomic characteristics and life-style, the individual's attitudes and opinions, awareness and knowledge, intentions, the motivation underlying the individual's actions, and even the person's behavior may all be ascertained by the communication method. All we need to do is ask, although there may be some problem with the accuracy of the replies.

Not so with observation. Observation is limited in scope to information about behavior and certain demographic/socioeconomic characteristics. But there are certain limitations to these observations. We are limited to observing present behavior, for example. We cannot observe a person's past behavior, nor can we observe the person's intentions as to future behavior. If we are interested in past behavior or intentions, we must ask.

Some demographic/socioeconomic characteristics can be readily observed. Gender is the most obvious example. Others can be observed but with less accuracy. A person's age and income, for example, might be inferred by closely examining the individual, including the person's mode of dress and purchasing behavior. Clearly, though, both of these observations may be in error, with income likely to be the farthest off. Other characteristics, such as social class, cannot be observed with any degree of confidence.

The other basic types of primary data cannot be measured by observation. We simply cannot observe an attitude or opinion, a person's awareness or knowledge, or motivation. Certainly we can attempt to make some inferences about these variables on the basis of the individual's observed behavior. For instance, if a person is observed purchasing a box of new XYZ detergent, we might infer that the person has a favorable attitude toward XYZ. There is a real question, though, as to the correctness of the inference. A great deal of controversy exists over whether attitudes precede behavior or behavior precedes attitude formation. Perhaps the latter explanation is correct, and the person, in fact, has no particular attitudes toward XYZ but just thought he or she would try it. The individual may not even have been aware of XYZ previously but just saw it for the first time on the shelf. Generalizing from behavior to states of mind is clearly risky, and researchers need to recognize this. Questioning clearly encompasses a broader base of primary data.

Speed and Cost

The speed and cost advantages of the communication method are closely intertwined. Assuming that the data lend themselves to either method, communication is a faster means of data collection than observation, because it provides a greater degree of control over data-gathering activities. Researchers are not forced to wait for events to occur with the communication method, as they are with the observation method. In some cases, it is impossible to predict the occurrence of the event precisely enough to observe it. For still other behaviors, the time interval can be substantial. For instance, an observer checking for brand purchased most frequently in one of several appliance categories might have to wait a long time to make any observations at all. Much of the time the observer would be idle. Such idleness is expensive, as the worker will probably be compensated on an hourly rather than a per-contact basis. Events of long duration also cause difficulty. An observational approach to studying the relative influence of a husband or wife in the purchase of an automobile would be prohibitive in terms of both time and money.

Objectivity and Accuracy

Balanced against these disadvantages of limited scope, time, and cost are the objectivity and accuracy of the observational method. Data that can be secured by either method typically will be more accurately secured by observation. This is because the observational method is independent of the respondent's unwillingness or inability to provide the information desired. For example, respondents are often reluctant to cooperate whenever their replies would be embarrassing or humiliating or would in some way place them in an unfavorable light.[13] Sometimes respondents conveniently forget embarrassing events; in other cases, the events are not of sufficient importance for them to remember what happened. Since observation allows the recording of behavior as it occurs, it is not dependent on the respondent's memory or mood in reporting what occurred.

Observation typically produces more objective data than does communication. The interview represents a social interaction situation. Thus, the replies of the person being questioned are conditioned by the individual's perceptions of the interviewer. The same is true of the interviewer, although the interviewer's selection and training affords the researcher a greater degree of control over these perceptions than those of the interviewee.

With observation, though, the subject's perceptions play less of a role. Sometimes people are not even aware that they are being observed. This removes the opportunity for them to tell the interviewer what they think the interviewer wants to hear or to give socially acceptable responses. The problems of objectivity are concentrated in the observer's methods, and this makes the task easier. The observer's selection, training, and control, and not the subject's perceptions of the field worker, become the crucial elements.

ETHICAL DILEMMA 7.1

A national department store chain with a relatively sophisticated image is planning to open a store in an area inhabited by wealthy professionals. The marketing research director of the company wants a detailed profile of the residents' characteristics and life-styles in order to tailor the new store to the tastes of this lucrative new market. He suggests that you, a member of his staff, contribute to the research effort by spending a month observing the residents going about their daily affairs of eating in restaurants, attending church, shopping in other stores, socializing with one another, and so on. You are then to prepare a report on what types of expenditures support their life-styles.

- Are there ethical problems involved in observing people in public places? Do the ethical problems become more serious if you socialize with your subjects?
- Who has ethical responsibility for your behavior: the marketing research director? you? both?

---

[13]Claire Selltiz, Lawrence S. Wrightsman, and Stuart W. Cook, *Research Methods in Social Relations,* 3rd ed. (New York: Holt, Rinehart and Winston, 1976), p. 293. See also Ed Blair, Seymour Sudman, Norman M. Bradburn, and Carol Stocking, "How to Ask Questions about Drinking and Sex: Response Effects in Measuring Consumer Behavior," *Journal of Marketing Research,* 14 (August 1977), pp. 316–321; Norman M. Bradburn and Seymour Sudman, *Improving Interview Method and Questionnaire Design: Response Effects to Threatening Questions in Survey Research* (San Francisco: Jossey Bass, 1979).

COMMUNICATION METHODS

As Figure 7.2 suggests, researchers must make a number of related decisions once they have chosen a method. Two of these involve structures and disguise, which we will discuss together.[14]

Structure is the degree of standardization imposed on the questionnaire. In a highly structured questionnaire, the questions to be asked and the responses permitted the subjects are completely predetermined. In a highly unstructured questionnaire, the questions to be asked are only loosely predetermined, and the respondents are free to respond in their own words. A questionnaire in which the questions are fixed but the responses are open ended would represent an intermediate degree of structure.

Disguise is the amount of knowledge about the purpose of a study communicated to a respondent. An undisguised questionnaire makes the purpose of the research obvious by the questions posed, whereas a disguised questionnaire attempts to hide the purpose of the study.

Structured–Undisguised Questionnaires

Structured–undisguised questionnaires are most commonly used in marketing research. With them, questions are presented with exactly the same wording, and in exactly the same order, to all respondents. The reason for standardizing them is to ensure that all respondents are replying to the same question. If one interviewer asks, "Do you drink orange juice?" and another asks, "Does your family use frozen orange juice?" the replies would not be comparable.

In the typical structured–undisguised questionnaire, the responses as well as the questions are standardized. **Fixed-alternative questions** in which the responses are limited to the stated alternatives are used. Consider the following question regarding the subject's attitude toward pollution and the need for more government legislation controlling it.

Do you feel the United States needs more or less antipollution legislation?

Needs more	[ ]
Needs less	[ ]
Neither more nor less	[ ]
No opinion	[ ]

No claim is made that this is a good question or even one that would be used. Rather, it is an example of a structured–undisguised question. The question's purpose is clear. It deals with the subject's attitudes toward antipollution legislation. The question is structured because respondents are limited to one of four stated replies.

---

[14]The simultaneous treatment of structure and disguise was suggested by Donald T. Campbell, "The Indirect Assessment of Social Attitudes," *Psychological Bulletin,* 47 (January 1950), pp. 15–38. A similar treatment can be found in Harper W. Boyd, Jr., Ralph Westfall, and Stanley F. Stasch, *Marketing Research: Text and Cases,* 7th ed. (Homewood, Ill.: Richard D. Irwin, 1989), pp. 215–221.

Probably the greatest advantages of the structured–undisguised question are that it is simple to administer and easy to tabulate and analyze.[15] Respondents should have little difficulty replying. Their responses should be reliable in that if they were asked the question again, they would respond in a similar fashion (assuming, of course, that their attitudes have not changed in the meantime).

The fixed-alternative question is reliable for several reasons. First, the frame of reference is often obvious from the alternatives. For example, consider the question, "How much do you watch television?" If no alternatives are supplied, one respondent might say "every day," another might say "regularly," and still another might respond with the number of hours per day. These responses would be more difficult to interpret than an alternative form that included the response categories "every day," "at least three times a week," "at least once a week," "less than once a week."

Providing alternative responses also often helps to make the question clear. The question "What is your marital status?" is more confusing than is the question, "Are you married, single, widowed, or divorced?" Providing the dimensions in which to frame the reply helps ensure the reliability of the question.

The reliability of fixed-alternative questions is sometimes associated with loss of validity, as the answers may not accurately reflect the true state of affairs. Fixed alternatives may force a response to a question on which the subject does not have an opinion. This is particularly true if the "no opinion" category is not provided as an alternative. Even when it is provided, there is often a tendency to keep the number of "no opinions" at a minimum. Thus the interviewer presses the respondent for a reply, which the person gives. Whether or not it accurately reflects the individual's attitude is another matter.

It may also be that the respondent has an opinion, but none of the response categories allows the accurate expression of that attitude. The example makes no allowance for distinguishing among those who feel that we definitely need a great deal more antipollution legislation (the "true" environmentalists) versus those who feel, though not too strongly, that something more should be done to clean up our air and water, and more legislation prohibiting pollution may be one answer.

Fixed-alternative responses may also lower validity when the response categories themselves introduce bias. This is particularly acute when an "appropriate" response is omitted because of an oversight or when insufficient prior research indicates that the response categories are appropriate. The provision of an "other" category does not eliminate this bias either, since there is a general reluctance on the part of subjects to respond in the "other" category. In using a fixed-alternative question, one must be reasonably certain that the alternatives adequately cover the range of probable replies.

The fixed-alternative question is thus most productive when possible replies are "well known, limited in number, and clear-cut. Thus they are appropriate for securing factual information (age, education, home ownership, amount of rent, and so on) and for eliciting expressions of opinion about issues on which people hold clear opinions."[16]

---

[15]This general discussion of advantages and disadvantages of the structured–undisguised question follows that of Selltiz, Wrightsman, and Cook, *Research Methods,* pp. 309–321.

[16]Selltiz, Wrightsman, and Cook, *Research Methods,* p. 316.

They are not very appropriate for securing primary data on motivations but certainly could be used (at least sometimes) to collect data on attitudes, intentions, awareness, demographic/socioeconomic characteristics, and behavior.

Unstructured – Undisguised Questionnaires

The unstructured – undisguised questionnaire is distinguished by the fact that the purpose of the study is clear but the response to the question is **open ended.** Consider the following question:

> *"How do you feel about pollution and the need for more antipollution legislation?"*

The initial stimulus (that is, question) here is constant. With it the interviewer attempts to get the subject to talk freely about his or her attitudes toward pollution. After presenting this initial stimulus, the interview becomes very unstructured. The respondent's initial reply, the interviewer's probes for elaboration, and the respondent's subsequent answers determine its direction. The interviewer may attempt to follow a rough outline. However, the order and the specific framing of the questions will vary from interview to interview. The specific content of each of these so-called **depth interviews** will therefore vary.

The freedom permitted the interviewer in conducting these depth interviews reveals the major advantages and disadvantages of the method. By not constraining the respondent to a fixed set of replies and by careful probing, an experienced interviewer should be able to derive a more accurate picture of the respondent's true position on some issue. This is particularly true with respect to sensitive issues in which there is social pressure to conform and to offer a "socially acceptable" response. Note the caveats — "experienced interviewer" and "careful probing" — contained in the preceding statement. The depth interview requires highly skilled interviewers. They are hard to find and are expensive when found. Further, the lack of structure allows the interviewer to influence the result. The interviewer's judgment about when to probe and how to word the probes can affect the response. Good depth interviews often take a long time to complete. This makes it difficult to secure the cooperation of respondents. It also means that a study using depth interviews, as opposed to fixed-alternative questions, may take longer to complete, will involve fewer observations, or will require a greater number of interviewers. The more interviewers there are, the greater the likelihood that the variation in responses will be partly interviewer-induced because of differences in administering the questionnaire.[17]

---

[17]Barbara Bailar, Leroy Bailey, and Joyce Stevens, "Measures of Interviewer Bias and Variance," *Journal of Marketing Research,* 14 (August 1977), pp. 337–343; and J. R. McKenzie, "An Investigation into Interviewing Effects in Market Research," *Journal of Marketing Research,* 14 (August 1977), pp. 330–331. A currently popular use of the depth interview is in laddering studies, in which the emphasis is on discovering the relationship between product attributes and consumer benefits and values, or means-ends chains. See, for example, Thomas J. Reynolds and Johnathan Gutman, "Laddering Theory, Method, Analysis and Interpretation," *Journal of Advertising Research,* 26 (February–March 1988), pp. 11–31; Jeffrey F. Durgee, "Depth Interview Techniques for Creative Advertising," *Journal of Advertising Research,* 25 (December 1985/January 1986), pp. 29–37; and Beth A. Walker and Jerry C. Olson, "Means-End Chains: Connecting Products with Self," *Journal of Business Research,* 22 (March 1991), pp. 111–118.

The depth interview also causes severe problems in analysis. The services of one or more skilled psychologists are typically required to interpret the responses. These people's services do not come cheaply. Further, the psychologist's own background and frame of reference will affect the interpretation. This subjectivity raises questions about both the reliability and validity of the results. It also causes difficulty in determining what the correct interpretation is and presents problems when tabulating the replies.[18]

Some of the problems with coding open-ended questions may be changing with new technology. Researchers are increasingly feeding respondents' answers into computers programmed to recognize a large vocabulary of words in their search for regularities in the replies. The computers are able to rank each word by the frequency of usage and then can print out sentences containing the key words. The detailed analysis of these sentences allows researchers to pick up on recurring themes.[19] Although these systems automate the coding of unstructured interviews, they leave interpretation to the individual analyst. Nevertheless, the systems can achieve in hours what a purely human review might take weeks to accomplish.

The depth interview is probably best suited to exploratory research, since it is productive with respect to just about all of the common purposes of exploratory research.

Unstructured–Disguised Questionnaires

Unstructured–disguised questionnaires lie at the heart of what has become known as motivation research.

> A person needs only limited experience in questionnaire type surveys to realize that many areas of inquiry are not amenable to exploration by direct questions. Many important motives and reasons for choice are of a kind that the consumer *will not* describe because a truthful description would be damaging to his ego. Others he *cannot* describe, either because he himself does not have the words to make his meaning clear or because his motive exists below the level of awareness. Very often such motives are of paramount importance in consumer behavior. If one tries to inquire into them with direct questions, especially categorical questions, one tends to get replies that are either useless or dangerously misleading.[20]

Researchers have circumvented the subjects' reluctance to discuss their feelings by developing techniques that are largely independent of the subjects' self awareness and willingness to reveal themselves. The main thrust in these projective methods has been

---

[18]Martin Collins and Graham Kalton, "Coding Verbatim Answers to Open Questions," *Journal of the Market Research Society,* 22 (October 1980), pp. 239–247.

[19]Formally, the procedure is known as content analysis. For discussion of how to go about conducting a content analysis, see Robert P. Weber, *Basic Content Analysis* (Beverly Hills, Calif.: Sage Publications, 1985). For discussion of recent advances in the automation of the analysis of verbatim responses, see David W. Stewart, "Making Use of Verbatim Response Analysis in Survey Research: New Solutions on the Horizon," paper presented at American Marketing Association's 2nd Advanced Research Techniques Forum, Beaver Creek, Colorado, June 16–19, 1991.

[20]F. P. Kilpatrick, "New Methods of Measuring Consumer Preferences and Motivation," *Journal of Farm Economics* (December 1957), p. 1314. See also Dennis Rook, "The Ritual Dimension of Consumer Behavior," *Journal of Consumer Research,* 12 (December 1985), pp. 251–264.

that of concealing the subject of inquiry by using a disguised stimulus. Though the stimulus is typically standardized, subjects are allowed to respond to it in a very unstructured form — thus the label "disguised–unstructured questionnaires." The basic assumption in **projective methods** is that an individual's organization of a relatively unstructured stimulus is indicative of the person's basic perceptions of the phenomenon and reactions to it.

> . . . the more unstructured and ambiguous a stimulus, the more a subject can and will project his emotions, needs, motives, attitudes, and values. The *structure* of a stimulus . . . is the degree of choice available to the subject. A highly structured stimulus leaves very little choice: the subject has unambiguous choice among clear alternatives. . . . A stimulus of low structure has a wide range of alternative choices. It is ambiguous: the subject can "choose" his own interpretation.[21]

In general terms, then, a **projective technique** involves the use of a vague stimulus that an individual is asked to describe, expand on, or build a structure around. Although almost any stimulus can serve, three common types of projective methods are word association, sentence completion, and storytelling.

Word Association With **word association** projective methods, subjects respond to a list of words read to them with the first word that comes to mind. The test words are dispersed throughout the list and are intermixed with some neutral words to conceal the purpose of the study. In the study of pollution, some of the key words might be the following:

Water	_____
Air	_____
Lakes	_____
Industry	_____
Smokestack	_____
City	_____

The subject's responses to each of the key words are recorded verbatim and later analyzed for their meaning. The responses are usually judged in three ways: by the frequency with which any word is given as a response, by the amount of time that elapses before a response is given, and by the number of respondents who do not respond at all to a test word after a reasonable period of time.

Some common responses will often emerge. These common responses when classified and grouped are then used to reveal patterns of interest, underlying motivations, or stereotypes. It is often possible to categorize the associations as favorable-unfavorable, pleasant-unpleasant, modern–old-fashioned, and so forth, depending on the problem.

---

[21]Fred N. Kerlinger, *Foundations of Behavioral Research,* 3rd ed. (New York: Holt, Rinehart and Winston, 1986), p. 471. For an overview of projective tests, see W. G. Klopfer and E. S. Taulkie, "Projective Tests," in M. R. Rosenweig and L. W. Porter, eds., *Annual Review of Psychology* (1976), pp. 543–567; and Sidney J. Levy, "Dreams, Fairy Tales, Animals, and Cars," *Psychology and Marketing,* 2 (Summer 1985), pp. 67–82.

The amount of time that elapses before a response is given to a test word is carefully determined. Sometimes a stopwatch is used, whereas in other cases the interviewer will count to herself or himself while waiting for a reply. Respondents who hesitate (operationally defined as taking longer than three seconds to reply) are judged to be sufficiently emotionally involved in the word that they do not provide their immediate reaction but an acceptable response. If they do not respond at all, their emotional involvement is judged to be so high as to block a response. An individual's pattern of responses, along with the details of the response to each question, are then used to assess the person's attitudes or feelings on the subject.

Sentence Completion   The **sentence completion** method requires the respondent to complete a number of sentences similar to the following:

> Many people behave as if our natural resources were _____ .
> A person who does not use our lakes for recreation is _____ .
> The number-one concern for our natural resources is _____ .
> When I think of living in a city, I _____ .

Again respondents are instructed to reply with the first thoughts that come to mind. The responses are recorded verbatim and are later analyzed.

In one study, Kassarjian and Cohen asked 179 smokers who believed cigarettes to be a health hazard why they continued to smoke. The majority gave responses such as, "Pleasure is more important than health," "Moderation is OK," "I like to smoke." One gets the impression that smokers are not dissatisfied with their lot. However, in a portion of the study involving sentence-completion tests, smokers responded to the question, "People who never smoke are _____ " with comments such as "better off," "happier," "smarter," "wiser," "more informed." To the question, "Teenagers who smoke are _____ ," smokers responded with "foolish," "crazy," "uninformed," "stupid," "showing off," "immature," "wrong." Clearly, the impression one gets from the sentence completion test is that smokers are anxious, uncomfortable, dissonant, and dissatisfied with their habit. This is quite different from the results of a probed open-end question.[22]

One advantage of sentence completion over word association projective methods is that respondents can be provided with a more directed stimulus. There should be just enough direction to evoke some association with the concept of interest. The researcher needs to be careful not to convey the purpose of the study or provoke the "socially accepted" response. Obviously, skill is needed to develop a good sentence completion or word association test.

Storytelling   The **storytelling** approach often relies on pictorial material such as cartoons, photographs, or drawings, although other stimuli are also used. These pictorial devices are descendants of the psychologists' **Thematic Apperception Test (TAT).** The

---

[22]Harold H. Kassarjian, "Projective Methods," in Robert Ferber, ed., *Handbook of Marketing Research* (New York: McGraw-Hill, 1974), p. 3–91. See also Eugene H. Fram and Elaine Cibotti, "The Shopping List Studies and Projective Techniques: A 40 Year View," *Marketing Research: A Magazine of Management & Applications*, 3 (December 1991), pp. 14–21.

TAT consists of a copyrighted series of pictures about which the subject is asked to tell stories. Some of the pictures are of ordinary events and some of unusual events; in some of the pictures the persons or objects are clearly represented, and in others they are relatively obscure. A respondent's interpretation of these events is employed to interpret the individual's personality; for example, whether the person is impulsive or shows intellectual control in interpreting the stimulus, whether the subject is creative or unimaginative, and so on.

When used in a marketing situation, the same pattern is followed. Respondents are shown a picture and asked to tell a story about the picture. The responses are used to assess attitudes toward the phenomenon rather than to interpret the subject's personality. For example:

> McCann-Erickson ad agency resorted to stick-figure sketches in research on its American Express Gold Card account. Focus group interviews hadn't made clear consumers' differing perceptions of gold-card and green-card holders.
>
>   The drawings, however, were much more illuminating. In one set, for example, the gold-card user was portrayed as a broad-shouldered man standing in an active position, while the green-card user was a "couch potato" in front of a TV set. Based on such pictures and other research, the agency decided to market the gold card as a "symbol of responsibility for people who have control over their lives and finances."[23]

With respect to the pollution example, the stimulus might be a picture of a city, and the respondent might be asked to describe what it would be like to live there. The analysis of the individual's response would then focus on the emphasis given to pollution in its various forms. If no mention were made of traffic congestion, dirty air, noise, and so on, the person would be classified as displaying little concern for pollution and its control.

Note that the various projective methods differ somewhat in their degree of structure of the stimulus. The word association and sentence completion methods involve presenting the stimuli to the respondent in the same sequence and in this sense are quite structured. They are unstructured as far as the response is concerned, as is the storytelling method. Respondents are free to interpret and respond to the stimuli in terms of their own perceptions and own words, and that is why these methods are typically categorized as disguised–unstructured techniques.

The unstructured nature of the projective methods produces many of the same difficulties encountered with the undisguised–unstructured methods of data collection. The greater standardization of the stimulus is a distinct advantage, but the problem with replies remains. The final interpretation of what was said often reflects the interpreter's frame of reference as much as it does the respondent's. Different interpreters often reach different conclusions about the same response. This raises havoc with the editing, coding, and tabulation of replies and suggests that projective methods are also more suited for exploratory research than for descriptive or causal research.

---

[23]Ronald Alsop, "Advertisers Put Consumers on the Couch," *The Wall Street Journal* (May 13, 1988), p. 17.

Structured–Disguised Questionnaires

Structured–disguised questionnaires are the least used in marketing research. They were developed in an attempt to secure the advantages of disguise in revealing subconscious motives and attitudes along with the advantages in coding and tabulation common to structured approaches. The arguments supporting the structured–disguised approach typically rest on some proposition regarding the role of attitude in the person's mental and psychological makeup.

One proposition holds that an individual's knowledge, perception, and memory are conditioned by the person's attitudes. Thus, in order to secure information about people's attitudes when a direct question would produce a biased answer, we can simply ask them what they know. Presumably, greater knowledge reflects the strength and direction of an attitude. Democratic voters could be expected to know more about Democratic candidates and the Democratic platform than those intending to vote Republican, for example. This argument is consistent with what we know about the operation of the selective processes — that individuals tend to selectively expose themselves, selectively perceive, and selectively retain ideas, arguments, events, and phenomena that are consistent with their own beliefs. Conversely, people tend to avoid, see differently, and forget situations and items that are inconsistent with their preconceived beliefs.

ETHICAL DILEMMA 7.2

Pharmaceutical Supply Company derives its major source of revenue from physician-prescribed drugs. Until recently, Pharmaceutical Supply had maintained a dominant position in the market. A new competitor had entered the market, however, and was quickly gaining market share.

In response to competitive pressure, Pharmaceutical Supply's management decided that it needed to conduct an extensive study concerning physician decision making with regard to selection of drugs. Janice Rowland, the marketing research director, decided that the best way to gather this information was through the use of personal and telephone interviews. Ms. Rowland directed the interviewers to represent themselves as employees of a fictitious marketing research agency, as she believed that a biased response would result if the physicians were aware that Pharmaceutical Supply was conducting the study. In addition, the interviewers were instructed to tell the physicians that the research was being conducted for their own purpose and not for a particular client.

- Was Ms. Rowland's decision to withhold the sponsor's true name and purpose a good one?
- Do the physicians have a right to know who is conducting the research?
- It has been argued that use of such deception prevents a respondent from making a rational choice about whether or not she or he wishes to participate in a study. Comment on this.
- What kind of results might have been obtained if the physicians knew the true sponsor of the study?
- What are the consequences for the research profession of using this form of deception?

This proposition suggests that one way of avoiding the socially acceptable response in securing a respondent's attitude toward pollution and the need for antipollution legislation would be to ask the person what he or she knows rather than how he or she feels. Thus, the researcher might frame questions such as the following: What is the status of the antipollution legislation listed below? A number of bills would be listed, some actual and some hypothetical, and the respondent would be asked to check the box that best describes the current status of the legislation. Some of the descriptions might be: "In committee," "Passed by the House but not the Senate," "Vetoed by the President," and so on. Respondents' attitudes toward the need for more legislation would then be assessed by the accuracy of their responses.

The main advantages of this approach emerge in analysis. Responses are easily coded and tabulated and an objective measure of knowledge quickly derived. Whether this measure of knowledge can also be interpreted as a measure of the person's attitude, though, is another matter. Is high legislative awareness indicative of a favorable or an unfavorable attitude toward the need for more antipollution legislation? Although this example raises some questions, a more imaginative approach might eliminate the confusion in interpretation. There is evidence to suggest, for instance, that the results obtained with structured–disguised approaches can be quite comparable to those obtained with unstructured–disguised approaches.[24]

QUESTIONNAIRES CLASSIFIED BY METHOD OF ADMINISTRATION

Questionnaires can also be classified by the method that will be used to administer them. The main methods are mail, phone, and personal interview.

A **personal interview** implies a direct face-to-face conversation between the interviewer and the respondent or interviewee. The interviewer asks the questions and records the respondent's answers, either while the interview is in progress or immediately afterward. The interview can take place in a home or office or at a control location like a mall, where shoppers are stopped (or intercepted) and asked to participate. The **telephone interview** means that this conversation occurs over the phone. The most normal administration of a **mail questionnaire** involves mailing the questionnaires to designated respondents with an accompanying cover letter. The respondents complete the questionnaire at their leisure and mail their replies back to the research organization.

The preceding descriptions suggest the most common or "pure" methods of administration. A number of variations are possible. Questionnaires for a "mail" administration may simply be attached to products or printed in magazines and newspapers. Similarly, questionnaires in a personal interview may be self-administered. When self-administered, respondents complete the questionnaire themselves. This might be done in

[24]Ralph Westfall, Harper Boyd, Jr., and Donald T. Campbell, "The Use of Structured Techniques in Motivation Research," *Journal of Marketing*, 22 (October 1957), pp. 134–139.

the interviewer's presence, in which case there would be an opportunity for the respondents to seek clarification on points of confusion from the interviewer. Alternatively, the respondents might complete the questionnaire in private for later pickup by a representative of the research organization, in which case the interaction would less resemble a personal interview. Another possibility is for the interviewer to hand the designated respondent the questionnaire personally but then have the respondent complete it in private and mail it directly to the research organization. In this case, the personal interview is indistinguishable from the mail questionnaire method. Similarly, telephone administration becomes very similar to mail administration when the telephone is used to fax the questionnaire to the respondent.[25]

Each of these methods of communication possesses some advantages and disadvantages. When discussing the pros and cons, the pure cases logically serve as a frame of reference. When a modified administration is used, the general advantages and disadvantages may no longer hold. They may also cease to hold in specific situations, in which case a general advantage may become a disadvantage, and vice versa. The advantages and disadvantages also may not apply when dealing with different countries with different cultures. For example, it is not culturally acceptable to answer questions from "strangers" over the telephone in Japan, while that is commonly done in the United States. Further, while the ability to develop a good mailing list is an important factor affecting the attractiveness of mail surveys in the United States, the Swedish government routinely publishes lists of every Swedish household, making mail studies very feasible there.[26] Therefore, it is not surprising that there are differences by country in the relative frequency with which the various data collection techniques are used. Figure 7.3, for example, highlights some of the country-by-country differences in Europe — differences that are particularly dramatic with respect to when and where personal interviews are conducted. In Sweden, personal interviews are used very seldom. In Switzerland and the United Kingdom, they almost always take place in a home or office. In France and The Netherlands, researchers typically rely on intercepting the respondent in a mall or on the street.

The specific problem and culture then will actually dictate the benefits and weaknesses that are associated with each method. Nevertheless, a general discussion of advantages and disadvantages serves to highlight the various methods, issues, and criteria that need to be considered in deciding on the manner in which the data will be collected. **Sampling control, information control,** and **administrative control** are definite points to consider when comparing the methods.

Sampling Control

Sampling control concerns the researcher's ability to direct the inquiry to a designated respondent and to get the desired cooperation from that respondent.

---

[25]John P. Dickson and Douglas L. MacLachlan, "Fax Surveys?" *Marketing Research: A Magazine of Management & Applications,* 4 (September 1992), pp. 26–30.

[26]Jeffrey Pope, *How Cultural Differences Affect Multi-Country Research* (Minneapolis, Minn.: Custom Research, Inc., 1991).

FIGURE 7.3   **Relative Use of Various Data-Collection Techniques in Selected European Countries**

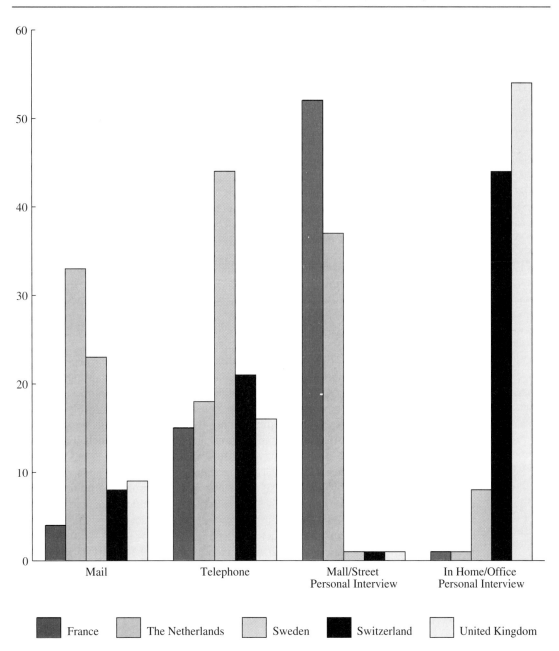

Source: Emanuel H. Demby, ''ESOMAR Urges Changes in Reporting Demographics, Issues Worldwide Report,'' *Marketing News* 24 (January 8, 1990), pp. 24–25. Reprinted with permission of American Marketing Association.

Table 7.5   **Summary of Studies of Demographic Factors Related to Telephone Ownership**

1. Telephone coverage is greater in urban areas than in rural areas, although in countries with very high overall telephone penetration (e.g., Canada, France, Denmark, and Norway) the difference is rather small.

2. In the United States, coverage is lower in the South. Similar regional differences prevail in at least some other countries (e.g., Ireland and Israel), but regional categorizations are country specific and are hard to compare cross-nationally.

3. In the United States, coverage is lower among nonwhites. No racial information was available from other countries.

4. Telephone coverage is always lower among those with lower incomes, the unemployed, those in manual or low-prestige occupations, and the less educated.

5. Telephone coverage is consistently lower for renters and people who live in apartments or trailers rather than in single family homes. Only the relationship with renting has data from both the United States and other countries.

6. Households without telephones tend to be headed by younger people, unmarried people, and perhaps males (data exists only for the United States, and even in the United States, the relationship is uncertain).

7. Nontelephone households tend to be either smaller than average or larger than average.

Source: Tom W. Smith, "Phone Home? An Analysis of Household Telephone Ownership," *International Journal of Public Opinion Research*, 2 (Winter 1990), p. 386.

Directing the Inquiry The direction of the inquiry is guided by the **sampling frame** — that is, by the list of population elements from which the sample will be drawn. With the telephone method, for example, one or more phone books typically serve as the sampling frame. Respondents are selected by some random method from the phone books serving the areas in which the study is to be done. Phone book sampling frames are inadequate in at least two important respects: They do not include those who do not have telephones or those who have unlisted numbers.

Of course, a great percentage of the U.S. population has phones — over 93 percent of all households in 1990.[27] Yet there is some variation by regions and by other demographic factors, both in the United States and worldwide. Research Realities 7.3 shows the distribution of telephone ownership worldwide, while Table 7.5 summarizes the evidence regarding the demographic factors affecting phone ownership. The differences in phone ownership by various demographic factors can bias the results of a telephone survey.

The proportion of households with telephones increases each year, however, and thus the problem of bias resulting from the exclusion of nontelephone households should diminish in the future.

[27]*Census of Housing*, Vol. 1 (Washington, D.C.: U.S. Bureau of the Census, 1991).

Research Realities 7.3   Map of Worldwide Telephone Ownership

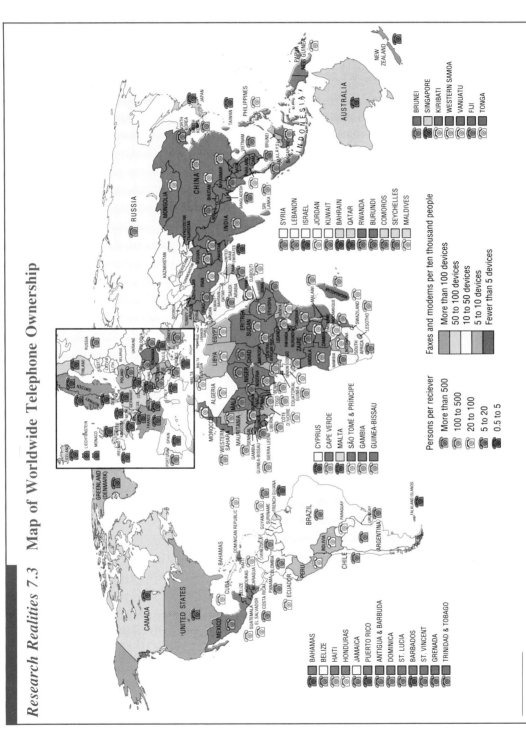

Source: Michael R. Czinkota, Ilkka A. Ronkainen, and Michael H. Moffett, *International Business*, 3rd. ed., (Fort Worth, Texas: Dryden Press, 1994). Chapter 13. Reproduced by permission of the publisher.

Studies that rely on phone book sampling frames underrepresent transient households. Anywhere from 12 to 15 percent of the residential numbers in a typical telephone directory are disconnected when called. Phone book sampling frames also do not include numbers that were assigned after the current directory was published, as well as the segment of the population that has requested an unlisted telephone number. The voluntary unlisted segment has been growing steadily and now represents over 28 percent of all residential phones in the United States.[28] The problem is particularly acute in urban areas in general, and some urban areas in particular. Figure 7.4, for example, shows the ten metropolitan areas in the United States with the highest population of unlisted numbers.

A comparison of unlisted versus listed households indicates that the following characteristics are associated with heads of unlisted households:

- younger;
- live in urban areas;
- nonwhite;
- more mobile;
- either very high or very low income[29]

One recent attempt at overcoming the sampling bias of unlisted numbers is **random digit dialing.** This approach simply entails the random generation of numbers to be called and often the automatic dialing of those calls as well. The calls are typically handled through one central interviewing facility employing the Wide Area Telephone Service (WATS).[30] This procedure allows geographically wide distribution or coverage. One problem with the random generation of phone numbers is that it can increase survey costs, since there are approximately 34,000 area-code prefix combinations in use in the continental United States. When the last four digits are generated randomly, there are approximately 340 million possible phone numbers that can be called. However, there are only about 80 million working residential telephone numbers in the United States. A simple comparison suggests that calling random telephone numbers will result in resi-

---

[28]"More Households Dial 'U' for Unlisted," *The Wall Street Journal* (May 7, 1991), p. B1.

[29]Tyzoon T. Tyebjee, "Telephone Survey Methods: The State of the Art," *Journal of Marketing,* 43 (Summer 1979), pp. 68–78; A. B. Blankenship, "Listed versus Unlisted Numbers in Telephone-Survey Samples," *Journal of Advertising Research,* 17 (February 1977), pp. 39–42; Patricia E. Moberg, "Biases in Unlisted Phone Numbers," *Journal of Advertising Research,* 22 (August–September 1982), pp. 51–55.

[30]G. J. Glasser and G. D. Metzger, "Random-Digit Dialing as a Method of Telephone Sampling," *Journal of Marketing Research,* 9 (February 1972), pp. 59–64; *The Use of Random Digit Dialing in Telephone Surveys: An Annotated Bibliography* (Monticello, Ill.: Vance Bibliographies, 1979); *Telephone Interviewing Bibliography* (Washington, D.C.: U.S. Bureau of the Census, 1981). Random-digit dialing is also being considered in other countries. For an assessment of its viability in the United Kingdom, see Jane Foreman and Martin Collins, "The Viability of Random Digit Dialing in the UK," *Journal of the Market Research Society,* 33 (July 1991), pp. 219–227.

FIGURE 7.4   **Ten Metro Areas with the Highest Proportion of Unlisted Telephone Numbers**

Source: "The Top 10 Unlisted MSA Markets," *The Frame* (March 1993), p. 2, published by Survey Sampling, Inc.

dential contacts only about one-fourth of the time.[31] An alternative scheme to random digit dialing is **Plus-One sampling,** in which a probability sample of phone numbers is

---

[31]Albert G. Swint and Terry E. Powell, "CLUSFONE Computer-Generated Telephone Sampling Offers Efficiency and Minimal Bias," *Marketing Today* (Elrick and Lavidge), 21 (1983). There is some evidence to suggest that certain sampling schemes can produce a higher proportion of working residential numbers without introducing any appreciable bias in the process. See, for example, Joseph Waksberg, "Sampling Methods for Random Digit Dialing," *Journal of the American Statistical Association,* 73 (March 1978), pp. 40–46; Robert Groves and Robert L. Kahn, *Surveys by Telephone* (New York: Academic Press, 1979); and Richard Pothoff, "Some Generalizations of the Mitofsky-Waksberg Technique of Random Digit Dialing," *Journal of the American Statistical Association,* 82 (June 1987), pp. 409–418. More sophisticated sampling schemes have also been used with random digit dialing to locate relatively rare segments of the population. See Johnny Blair and Ronald Czaja, "Locating a Special Population Using Random Digit Dialing," *Public Opinion Quarterly,* 46 (Winter 1982), pp. 585–590. For discussion of the services of firms supplying telephone samples, see Lewis C. Winters, "What's New in Telephone Sampling Technology," *Marketing Research: A Magazine of Management & Applications,* 2 (March 1990), pp. 80–82.

selected from the telephone directory and a single, randomly determined digit is added to each selected number.[32]

One or more mailing lists typically serve as the sampling frame in mail questionnaires. The quality of these lists determines the sampling biases. If the list is a reasonably good one, the bias can be small. For example, some firms have established panels that can be used to answer mail questionnaires and that are representative of the population in many important respects. Further, some mailing lists that may be ideally suited for certain types of studies can be purchased.

> Say you run a direct-mail business that specializes in selling monogrammed baby bibs. For a fee at any given time you can obtain a mailing list containing the names and addresses of up to one million pregnant women. And if it should suit your purposes, it's easy enough to get the list limited to women whose babies are expected in a certain month or who are expecting their first child.[33]

Sometimes the list is internally generated. Spurred on by technical advances, a number of firms are developing greater capabilities to target questionnaires or other mailings to specific households. For example, American Express, with its new image-processing technology, now is able to select all of its cardholders who made purchases from golf pro-shops, or who traveled more than once to Europe, or who attended symphony concerts, or who made some other specific purchase using their American Express card.[34]

The fact remains that the mailing list determines the sampling control in a mail study. If there is an accurate, applicable, and readily available list of population elements, the mail questionnaire allows a wide and representative sample, since it costs no more to send a questionnaire across country than it does to send one across town. Even ignoring costs, it is sometimes the only way of contacting the relevant population, such as busy executives who will not sit still for an arranged personal or telephone interview but may respond to a mail questionnaire. A key here, though, is the ability to address the questionnaire to a specific respondent rather than a position. As Research Realities 7.4 indicates, getting mail addressed to a person occupying a particular position is getting more difficult.

---

[32]E. Laird Landon, Jr., and Sharon K. Banks, "Relative Efficiency and Bias of Plus-One Telephone Sampling," *Journal of Marketing Research,* 14 (August 1977), pp. 294–299; and Madhav N. Segal and Firooz Hekmat, "Random Digit Dialing: A Comparison of Methods," *Journal of Advertising,* 14 (No. 4, 1985), pp. 36–43.

[33]"Mailing List Brokers Sell More than Names to Their Many Clients," *The Wall Street Journal* (February 19, 1974), pp. 1, 18; and Bob Davis, "Baby-Goods Firms See Direct Mail as the Perfect Pitch for New Moms," *The Wall Street Journal* (January 29, 1986), p. 31. For other discussions of how firms go about developing mailing lists and their value, see "Making a List, Selling It Twice," *The Wall Street Journal* (May 20, 1985), pp. 64–65; Michael W. Miller, "Data Mills Delve Deep To Find Information About U.S. Consumers," *The Wall Street Journal* (March 14, 1991), pp. A1, A12.

[34]Michael Finley, "Data-Base Marketing Alters Landscape," *Marketing News,* 22 (November 7, 1988), pp. 1–2. For discussion of some of the more important data bases about potential customers and how firms are using them, see Peter Francese and Rebecca Piirto, *Capturing Customers: How to Target the Hottest Markets of the '90s* (Ithaca, N.Y.: American Demographics, 1990).

Research Realities 7.4

Mail-Room Malady

The mail room at General Motors is saying no to bulk mail. GM's Flint Automotive Division has halted the delivery of bulk mail in an effort to reduce operating costs, and they are not alone. Hundreds of businesses nationwide are refusing to deliver third-class mail to their employees. As such decisions are becoming increasingly widespread, they are a source of real concern to direct marketers who want to reach employees where they work. Business-to-business advertisers whose mailings are targeted towards corporate managers are especially hard hit.

The Direct Marketing Association (DMA) has responded by setting up a task force to study the scope of the problem and devise possible solutions. The DMA recently surveyed mail-room supervisors of *Fortune 500* companies to determine mail-room practices. Preliminary results indicate that at least 30 percent of mail delivered to the companies is not received by the addressees.

Legally, there's nothing direct marketers can do about mail rooms throwing away bulk mail and nonsubscription magazines. The U.S. Postal Service has a longstanding policy declaring that mail addressed to an individual at a business is the property of that business. Another problem is that many corporations are requiring incoming mail to have mail-stops, or internal delivery codes, that identify various departments and speed sorting.

To make sure that they're reaching the right person, direct marketers need to follow up initial mail directly, perhaps via first-class mail. Another solution is for direct marketers and mail-room supervisors to work more cooperatively. One way is to ask mail-room supervisors to have employees fill out cards indicating what types of mail are beneficial.

Most important, marketers can keep the situation from worsening by frequently updating their mailing lists, says Gene Del Polito, executive director of the Direct Mail Association. "When you have sloppy mail practices and a lot of your mail is directed to people who aren't there . . . you're not creating the impression that the nature of your mail is very important," concludes Mr. Del Polito.

Source: Patricia Strnad, "Mail-Room Malady," *Advertising Age*, 60 (March 20, 1989), p. 62. See also Joanne Lipman, "Businesses to Junk Mailers: Take The Stuff and Toss It," *The Wall Street Journal* (October 26, 1989), pp. B1, B4.

It is estimated that the average consumer has his or her name on anywhere from 25 to 40 separate mailing lists and receives 80 pieces of unsolicited mail per year. All those who think unsolicited mail is a bother, however, can send one letter to the Direct Mail Marketing Association, a trade group of more than 2,600 direct mail marketers, and that organization will remove the name from every member's list. The statistics indicate, though, that for every person requesting to have his or her name removed, two more request that their names be added.[35]

Sampling control for the administration of questions via personal interview is conceptually difficult but practically possible. For some select populations (for example, doctors, architects, or firms), a list of population elements from which a sample can be

[35]Bruce Shawkey, "Mail Order Peddlers Pan Gold in Them Thar Lists," *Wisconsin State Journal* (July 31, 1983), pp. 1 and 4; Melinda Grenier Guiles, "Why Melinda S. Gets Ads for Panty Hose, Melinda F., Porsches," *The Wall Street Journal* (May 6, 1988), pp. 1 and 4; Ellen E. Schultz, "When It's the Wrong Time for Big Financial Decisions," *The Wall Street Journal* (October 29, 1991), pp. C1, C17.

drawn may be readily available in association or trade directories. For studies focused on consumer goods in which in-house interviews are to be conducted, however, there are few lists available, and those available are typically badly out-of-date. What is often done here is to use area sampling procedures. The general approach is dealt with in a later chapter. For now, simply be aware that it involves the substitution of areas and dwelling units for people as the sampling units. The substitution offers the advantage of accurate, current lists of sampling units, in the form of maps, for the generally inaccurate, unavailable lists of people. There remains the problem of ensuring that the field interviewer contacted the right household and person, but the personal interview does afford some sampling control in directing the questionnaire to specific sample units.

A currently popular alternative for conducting personal interviews among consumers is to use **mall intercepts.** The technique involves exactly what the name implies.[36] Interviewers intercept or stop those passing by and ask if they would be willing to participate in a research study. Those who agree are typically taken to the firm's interviewing facility that has been set up in the mall, where the interview is conducted.[37] With shopping mall intercepts, there are two issues affecting the ability to direct the inquiry to a randomly determined respondent. First, although a great many people do shop at malls, not everyone does. Only those who visit the particular mall in question have a chance of being included in the study. Second, a person's chances of being asked to participate depend on the likelihood of that person being in the mall. That, in turn, depends on the frequency with which he or she shops there. One thing that is commonly done with respect to this second source of variation in the selection probabilities is to weight the replies of the respondent by the reciprocal of the number of visits made to the mall in a set amount of time.[38]

Getting Cooperation Directing the inquiry to a specific respondent is one thing; getting a response from that individual is quite another. In this respect, the personal interview affords the most sample control. With a personal interview, the respondent's identity is known, and thus there is little opportunity for anyone else to reply. The problem

---

[36]For general discussions of the mall intercept as a data collection technique, see Roger Gates and Paul J. Solomon, "Research Using the Mall Intercept: State of the Art," *Journal of Advertising Research,* 22 (August/September 1982), pp. 43–50; Alan J. Bush and Joseph F. Hair, Jr., "An Assessment of the Mall Intercept as a Data Collection Method," *Journal of Marketing Research,* 22 (May 1985), pp. 158–167; Alan J. Bush, Ronald F. Bush, and Henry C. K. Chen, "Method of Administration Effects in Mall Intercept Interviews," *Journal of the Market Research Society,* 33 (October 1991), pp. 309–319.

[37]"Mall Research Facilities Directory," *Quirk's Marketing Research Review* (October–November 1988), contains a list of all shopping centers that have research facilities.

[38]The weighting technique was suggested by Seymour Sudman, "Improving the Quality of Shopping Center Sampling," *Journal of Marketing Research,* 17 (November 1980), pp. 423–431. For empirical assessments of the usefulness of the weighting, see Thomas D. Dupont, "Do Frequent Mall Shoppers Distort Mall-Intercept Survey Results," *Journal of Advertising Research,* 27 (August/September 1987), pp. 45–51; John P. Murry, Jr., John L. Lastovicka, and Guarav Bhalla, "Demographic and Life-style Selection Error in Mall-Intercept Data," *Journal of Advertising Research,* 27 (February/March 1989), pp. 46–52; Clifford Nowell and Linda P. Stanley, "Length-Biased Sampling in Mall Intercept Surveys," *Journal of Marketing Research,* 28 (November 1991), pp. 475–479.

TABLE 7.6   **Results of First Dialing Attempts**

Result	Number of Dialings		Probability of Occurrence
No answer	89,829		.347
Busy	5,299		.020
Out-of-service	52,632		.203
No eligible person	75,285		.291
Business	10,578		.041
At home	25,465		.098
Refusal		3,707	.014 (.146)*
Completion		21,758	.084 (.854)
Total	259,088		1.000

*Probability of occurrence *given* eligible individual is at home.

Source: Roger A. Kerin and Robert A. Peterson, "Scheduling Telephone Interviews." Reprinted from the *Journal of Advertising Research,* 23 (April/May 1983), p. 44. Copyright 1983 by the Advertising Research Foundation.

of nonresponse as a result of refusals to participate is also typically lower with personal interviews than with either telephone interviews or mail administered questionnaires. There is sometimes a problem with not-at-homes, but this can often be handled by calling back at more appropriate times.

Telephone methods also suffer from not-at-homes or no-answers. In one very large study involving more than 259,000 telephone calls, it was found that over 34 percent of the calls resulted in a no-answer.[39] What was even more disturbing was that the probability of making contact with an eligible respondent on the first call was less than one in ten (see Table 7.6). Fortunately, calling back is much simpler and more economical than following up personal interviews. The relatively low expense of a telephone contact allows a number of follow-up calls to secure a needed response, whereas the high cost of field contact restricts the number of follow-ups that can be made in studies employing personal interviews. Making sure the intended respondent replies is somewhat more difficult with telephone interviews than with personal interviews. So is the problem of determining which person in the household should be interviewed.[40]

---

[39]Roger A. Kerin and Robert A. Peterson, "Scheduling Telephone Interviews," *Journal of Advertising Research,* 23 (April/May 1983), pp. 41–47. See also Michael F. Weeks, Richard A. Kulka, and Stephanie A. Pierson, "Optimal Call Scheduling for a Telephone Interview," *Public Opinion Quarterly,* 51 (1987), pp. 540–549.

[40]Ronald Czaja, Johnny Blair, and Jutta P. Sebestik, "Respondent Selection in a Telephone Survey: A Comparison of Three Techniques," *Journal of Marketing Research,* 19 (August 1982), pp. 381–385; Diane O'Rourke and Johnny Blair, "Improving Random Respondent Selection in Telephone Interviews," *Journal of Marketing Research,* 20 (November 1983), pp. 428–432; Terry L. Childers and Steven J. Skinner, "Theoretical and Empirical Issues in the Identification of Survey Respondents," *Journal of the Market Research Society,* 27 (January 1985), pp. 39–53.

Mail questionnaires afford the researcher little control in securing a response from the intended respondent. The researcher can simply direct the questionnaire to the designated respondent and offer the individual some incentive for cooperating.[41] However, the researcher cannot control that cooperation. A great many subjects may refuse to respond. In many cases, only those most interested in the subject will respond. Some subjects will be incapable of responding because they are illiterate. For example, the International Reading Association estimates that some 20 million English-speaking, native-born American adults read or write so poorly that they have trouble holding jobs, and the author of *Illiterate America* suggests that 60 million adult Americans are illiterate.[42] Since many of these people have difficulty with everyday tasks like reading job notices, making change, or getting a driver's license, is it any wonder that they might not respond to a mail questionnaire that is at all complex! Whatever the reason, the nonresponse may cause a bias of indeterminate direction and magnitude. Also, it is not always clear who is responding in mail surveys, nor can the researcher exercise a great deal of control in this regard.

Information Control

The differing methods of data collection also permit a good deal of variation in the type of questions that can be asked and the amount and accuracy of the information that can be obtained from respondents.

The personal interview can be conducted using almost any form of questionnaire, from unstructured–undisguised through structured–disguised. The personal interaction between interviewer and respondent allows as stimuli the use of pictures or examples of advertisements, lists of words, scales, and so on. The use of the telephone rules out most aids, but the mail questionnaire allows the use of some of them. Personal interviews

---

[41]See Paul L. Erdos, *Professional Mail Surveys* (Malabar, Fla.: Robert E. Kreiger, 1983), or Donald A. Dillman, "The Design and Administration of Mail Surveys," *Annual Review of Sociology,* 17 (1991), pp. 225–249, for a discussion of the problem of sample control in mail surveys and what can be done to overcome respondent resistance. For general references on conducting telephone or mail surveys, see A. B. Blankenship, *Professional Telephone Surveys* (New York: McGraw-Hill, 1977); Donald A. Dillman, *Mail and Telephone Surveys: The Total Design Method* (New York: Wiley-Interscience, 1978); Paul J. Lavrakas, *Telephone Survey Methods* (Beverly Hills, Calif.: Sage Publications, 1987); Robert M. Groves, et al., eds., *Telephone Survey Methodology* (New York: Wiley-Interscience, 1988). For a bibliography of studies involving mail surveys, see Donald A. Dillman and Roberta L. Sangster, *Mail Surveys: A Comprehensive Bibliography, CPL Bibliography,* No. 272 (Chicago: Council of Planning Librarians, 1991).

[42]Daniel Machalaba, "Hidden Handicap: For Americans Unable to Read Well, Life is a Series of Small Crises," *The Wall Street Journal* (January 17, 1984), pp. 1 and 12; and Chris Martell, "Illiteracy Hurts All, Author Says," *Wisconsin State Journal* (April 3, 1985), pp. 1–2; Jock Elliott, "Our Inadequate, Uncompetitive System of Education," *Viewpoint* (July–August 1987), pp. 31–35; Janice C. Simpson, "A Shallow Labor Pool Spurs Businesses to Act to Bolster Education," *The Wall Street Journal* (September 28, 1987), pp. 1 and 19; and Mogens Nygaard Christofferson, "The Educational Bias in Mail Questionnaires," *Journal of Official Statistics,* 3 (No. 4, 1987), pp. 459–464. The illiteracy problem is also severe in England. See *Journal of the Market Research Society,* 26 (April 1984), for a number of articles on the subject and its consequences for survey research. The illiteracy problem has gotten so severe that many businesses are setting up their own in-house programs to combat it. See, for example, Helene Cooper, "Carpet Firm Sets Up an In-House School to Stay Competitive," *The Wall Street Journal* (October 5, 1992), pp. A1, A5.

allow the use of open-ended questions that require extensive probes. Mail questionnaires simply do not allow the use of questions requiring extensive probes for a complete response. Telephone interviews can incorporate them, but not nearly to the same extent. Personal interviews also allow the automatic sequencing of questions; for example, if the answer to question 4 is positive, ask questions 5 and 6, whereas if it is negative, ask questions 7 and 8. Although automatic sequencing is also possible with telephone interviews, mail questionnaires permit much less of it.

There is a greater danger of **sequence bias** with mail questionnaires than with questionnaires administered in person or over the phone. Respondents can see the whole questionnaire, and thus their replies to any single question may not be independently arrived at but are more likely to be conditioned by their responses to other questions than if either personal interviews or telephone interviews were used.

The mail questionnaire permits control of the bias caused by the interviewee's perception of the interviewer. With a mail questionnaire, respondents are also able to work at their own pace. This may produce better-thought-out responses than would be obtained in personal or telephone interviews, where there is a certain urgency associated with giving a response. A thought-out response, however, is no guarantee of an appropriate reply. If the question is ambiguous, the mail survey offers no opportunity for clarification. Each question must succeed or fail on its own merits. Because researchers cannot decipher differences in interpretation among respondents, they cannot impose a consistent frame of reference on the replies. Thus the responses to an open-ended question in a mailed questionnaire may be excessive or inadequate. With structured questions, the answers may simply reflect differences in the frame of reference being employed rather than any subject-to-subject variation in the particular characteristic being measured. The anonymity sometimes associated with a mailed questionnaire does afford people an opportunity to be more frank on certain sensitive issues (for example, sexual behavior).

Both personal and telephone interviews can cause interviewer bias because of the respondent's perception of the interviewer or because different interviewers ask questions and probe in different ways. Both of these biases can be more easily controlled in telephone surveys. There are fewer interviewer actions to which the respondent can react, and a supervisor can be present during telephone interviews to ensure that they are being conducted consistently. It is typically more difficult, though, to establish rapport over the phone than in person. The respondent in a telephone interview often demands more information about the purposes of the study, the credentials of the interviewer and research organization, and so on.

With regard to length of questionnaire or amount of information to be collected, the general rule of thumb is that long questionnaires can be handled best by personal interview and least well by telephone interview. So much, though, depends on the subject of inquiry, the form of the questionnaire, and the approach used to secure cooperation that a rigid interpretation of this advice would be unwarranted and hazardous.

As with so many things, computers are changing the way surveys are conducted. They were first used in the early 1970s to assist with telephone interviews. The early systems linked mainframe computers or mini computers to cathode-ray tube terminals (CRTs). Their essential function was to present on the terminal the questions that normally would have been on a paper questionnaire. Interviewers would read the questions as they came up on the CRT and would enter respondents' answers directly on the keyboard. The early systems generated such substantial savings in time and resources that they spawned a virtual revolution in data collection. Partly because of the advantages that accrue with CRT administration of questionnaires, telephone interviews have become the most popular data collection technique (see Research Realities 7.5). The revolution that CRT interviewing wrought was given further impetus with the development of the microcomputer.

Currently, there are at least four types of uses for microbased, stand-alone, computer-aided interviewing (CAI) software:

1. Telephone surveys in which each interviewer has a personal computer from which to ask questions;

2. In-person interviews in which the interviewer transports a portable lap-top computer to the interview site and uses it to interview the respondent, or places the computer in front of the respondent and lets the respondent answer questions as they appear on the screen;

3. Interviews in which the interviewee is sitting in front of the computer in a shopping mall or research laboratory and responds to questions as they are displayed on the monitor; and

4. Mail administration in which the questionnaire is sent by mail on diskette to respondents, who answer the questions using their own microcomputer and return the completed diskette by mail.[43]

One of the most important advantages of computer-assisted interviewing is the information control it allows. First, the computer displays each question exactly as the researcher intended. It will show only the questions and information that the respondent needs to or should see. Further, it will display the next question only when an acceptable answer to the current one is entered on the keyboard. If a respondent says that she or he bought a brand that is not available in that particular locale, for example, the computer can be programmed to reject the answer. This greatly simplifies skipping or branching procedures. The interviewer does not have to grapple with selecting the next question given the response to the current one; the computer does this automatically. This saves considerable time and confusion in administering the questionnaire and permits a more natural flow to the interview. It also ensures that there will be no variation in the sequence in which the questions are asked. Information control also manifests itself in the following:

1. Personalization of the questions. During the course of the interview, the computer is aware of all previous responses (e.g., name of wife, cars owned, supermarket patronized) and can customize the wording of future questions — for example, "When

---

[43]Edwin H. Carpenter, "Software Tools for Data Collection: Microcomputer Assisted Interviewing," *Applied Marketing Research,* 29 (Winter 1989), pp. 23–32. This article also compares the available CAI software packages with respect to their capabilities.

Research Realities 7.5

Among Those Participating in a Survey in a Year, the Percentage of People Participating in Various Types

Percentage

```
80 ┤    Telephone
   │    74      75      76
70 ┤    Mail              70      69      70
   │    65                        68      64
60 ┤                      56
   │                54
50 ┤
   │          45
40 ┤    Shopping
   │    Mall            35           34
   │    38      33    30      32
30 ┤
   │
20 ┤    Door-to-Door
   │    18              15
   │          14              10
10 ┤          11      11
   │
 0 ┼────┬──────┬──────┬──────┬──────┬──────
   1982  1984   1986   1988   1990   1992
                                        Year
```

Source: Adapted from *Industry Image Study: Research on Research,* 10th ed. (Indianapolis, IN: Walker Research, Inc., 1992), p. 2.

your wife, Ann, shops at the Acme, does she usually use the Fiat or the Buick?'' Such personalized questions can enhance rapport and thus provide for higher-quality interviews.

2. Customized questionnaires. Key information elicited early in the interview can be used to customize the questionnaire for each respondent. For example, only product attributes previously acknowledged by respondents as determinants of their decisions would be used to measure their brand perceptions, rather than using an *a priori* list of attributes common to all respondents.

In addition to the enhanced branching abilities and personalization of the questionnaires that they allow, computer-assisted interviews often produce increased accuracy in the results. There is evidence to suggest that people are more truthful when responding to a computer than to an interviewer or even when completing a self-administered, paper-and-pencil questionnaire. They seem to think that the computer is less judgmental and provides them greater anonymity. For example, Chevron's Ortho Consumer Products unit in San Francisco asked salespeople in two separate studies to assess the company's marketing strategy. Although both studies promised anonymity, salespeople had only kind words for their bosses when asked in the paper-and-pencil survey. ''When the questions were posed by computer, in contrast, 'not all the responses were so favorable to management,' says Edward Evans, manager of planning and analysis.''[44]

Computer-assisted interviewing certainly speeds the data collection and processing tasks. The preliminary tabulations of the answers are available at a moment's notice, because the replies are already stored in memory. One does not have the typical two-to-three-week delay caused by coding and data entry that happens when questionnaires are completed by hand.

Respondents also seem to enjoy the interviewing experience more when the questionnaire is administered by computer. That, in turn, seems to help response rates. For example, the return rate in disk-by-mail surveys often exceeds 50 percent.[45] Further, the whole notion of involving computers in the interviewing process has opened up some other capabilities with respect to managing the interviewing process. Table 7.7, for example, discusses the features common to computer-assisted telephone interviewing (CATI) systems.[46]

---

[44]Selwyn Feinstein, ''Computers Replacing Interviewers for Personnel and Marketing Tasks,'' *The Wall Street Journal* (October 9, 1986), p. 35. See also Sara Kiesler and Lee T. Sproull, ''Response Effects in the Electronic Survey,'' *Public Opinion Quarterly,* 50 (Fall 1986), pp. 402–413; John P. Liefeld, ''Response Effects in Computer Administered Questioning,'' *Journal of Marketing Research,* 25 (November 1988), pp. 397–404.

[45]''Disks-by-Mail,'' *Sawtooth News,* 5 (Spring 1989), pp. 4–5.

[46]For general overviews of the effect of CATI systems, see William L. Nicholls II and Robert M. Groves, ''The Status of Computer-Assisted Telephone Interviewing: Part I — Introduction and Impact on Cost and Timeliness of Survey Data,'' *Journal of Official Statistics,* 2 (No. 2, 1986), pp. 93–115; Robert M. Groves and William L. Nicholls II, ''The Status of Computer-Assisted Telephone Interviewing: Part II — Data Quality Issues,'' *Journal of Official Statistics,* 2 (No. 2, 1986), pp. 117–134; William E. Saris, *Computer-Assisted Interviewing* (Newbury Park, CA.: Sage Publications, 1991).

TABLE 7.7 **Common Features in CATI Software**

Questionnaire writing system. This allows the study author to create a computer-administered questionnaire. The software capabilities generally include the construction of complex skip patterns and logic branches, in which different answers to a question direct respondents to specific parts of the questionnaires, randomization of questions and answer alternatives, construction of long lists, entering of open-ends, restoration of previous answers into the text of the current question, and consistency checks.

Call management system. The call management system serves two functions. First, it is used to build the sample data base. This works by manually typing in the sample or by transferring the sample, in electronic form, from an existing data base. Second, it controls the flow of sample to the interviewing stations. It ensures that call-backs are made when scheduled, that busy numbers are redialed after a preset delay, that time zones are recognized, that exhausted sample is excluded, and that no part of the sample is overworked.

Quota control system. Quota control allows quota cells to be defined and quota limits be placed on the cells. The system tracks the quota while interviewing is in progress, closing out completed cells. In conjunction with the call management system, it prevents a sample corresponding to a closed cell from being sent to the interviewing stations if the respondents' qualifications are known in advance (for example, in a call-back situation in which the respondent has already been screened, or in a study in which a known sample is driving the study).

Call disposition monitoring system. Call disposition monitoring tracks each call attempt by its disposition (no answer, busy, immediate refusal, failed to qual-ify, call-back, complete, etc.). This is the richest source of information for tracking interviewing progress. The call disposition monitoring system is also used to calculate the incidence of qualified respondents so that it can be compared with the incidence that was assumed in constructing the cost quotation for the study.

Interviewer system. In addition to displaying the questionnaire for the interviewer system, CATI systems may determine which call to attempt next, provide call history information for the call before it is placed, dial the telephone number, automatically reschedule a ''no answer'' for another attempt, automatically determine when ''busy'' numbers are to be redialed, aid in scheduling call-backs, assist with assigning the call disposition codes, and increment the quota count for completed interviews. These features can eliminate most of the paperwork for the interviewer.

Reporting system. A valuable aspect of a CATI system is its ability to generate accurate and timely reports. These include quota reports, call disposition reports, incidence reports, top-line reports of respondent data, and interviewer productivity reports. Automatic reporting increases supervisor productivity and the overall quality of the data collection. Less time is spent compiling reports and more is spent on their interpretation and supervising the interviewing. Reports also give the study director and analysts an indication of whether the study is progressing according to plan.

Analysis capabilities. Some CATI systems include an integrated cross-tabulation and statistics package. This allows cross-tabs and statistics to be performed with a minimum of spec writing and retyping of text for annotating tables.

Source: Joseph Curry, ''Computer-Assisted Telephone Interviewing: Technology and Organizational Management'' (Ketchum, Idaho: Sawtooth Software, 1987), pp. 7–9. Reprinted with permission.

Even though computers have had a profound effect on interviewing techniques, they are not a panacea. There are limits to what the machines can do. They can't win over respondents with social chitchat or explain questions that are misunderstood. Unless the interviewees are good typists, the computers can't elicit lengthy responses. They can't recognize fuzzy or superficial answers and prod respondents to elaborate. They can't ask follow-up questions of interviewees who drop unexpected leads. And, the ones that ask questions by phone with mechanical voices have raised the ire of some people who consider unsolicited, randomly dialed calls an invasion of privacy.[47]

Further, disk-by-mail administration can only be used among those likely to own or to have access to a microcomputer. Therefore they can be quite useful in industrial surveys, because most business people have access to a machine, but they are more limited in general consumer surveys unless the product or service at issue involves a population likely to own a microcomputer (e.g., reaction to a new software program).

Administrative Control

The telephone survey is one of the quickest ways of obtaining information. A number of calls can be made from a central exchange in a short period, perhaps 15 to 20 per hour per interviewer if the questionnaire is short. An in-home personal interview affords no such time economies, because there is dead time between each interview in which the interviewer travels to the next respondent. If the researcher wishes to speed up the replies secured with in-home personal interviews, the size of the field force must be increased. This raises problems of interviewer-induced variation in responses because of slight differences in approach. Some of these can be reduced through proper selection and training of interviewers, but the personal interview still presents more formidable problems of control than the telephone interview, including control of interviewer cheating. With the telephone method, the researcher can also increase the speed with which replies are secured by increasing the number of interviewers. The researcher can supervise interviewers directly when they are making their calls, so problems of variation in administration and cheating should be much less acute, although the ability to monitor interviewers may be changing in response to worker complaints.[48] Mall interviews are similar to telephone interviews in this regard.

While the mail questionnaire represents a standardized stimulus and thus allows little variation in administration, it also affords little speed control. It often takes a couple of weeks to secure the bulk of the replies, at which time a follow-up mailing is often begun. It, too, will involve a time lapse of several weeks for the questionnaires to reach the respondents, be completed, and find their way back. Depending on the number of follow-up mailings required, the total time needed to conduct a good mail study can

---

[47]Feinstein, "Computers Replacing Interviewers," p. 35; Jack Honomichl, "Answering Machines Threaten Survey Research," *Marketing News* 24 (August 6, 1990), p. 11; Michael J. Havice and Mark J. Banks, "Live and Automated Telephone Surveys: A Comparison of Human Interviews and an Automated Technique," *Journal of the Market Research Society,* 33 (April 1991), pp. 91–102.

[48]Michael Allen, "Legislation Could Restrict Bosses from Snooping on Their Workers," *The Wall Street Journal* (September 24, 1991), pp. B1, B5.

often be substantial.[49] Of course, with a mail study the time required to secure a great many replies with a very large sample is little different from the time necessary for a small sample. This is not so with personal and telephone interviews, where there is a direct relationship between the number of interviews and the time required to complete them.

In-home personal interviews tend to be the most expensive per completed contact and the mail questionnaire tends to be the cheapest, but the subject and procedures of the inquiry can change the relative cost picture dramatically. For example, the per-contact cost of the mail questionnaire is generally low. However, if nonresponse is substantial, the cost per return may be quite high. For the most part, though, the mail, telephone, mall, and in-home personal interview methods require progressively larger field staffs, and the larger the field staff, the greater the problems of control. Good quality control costs money, and that is why the personal interview in the home is typically the most expensive data collection method. Table 7.8 summarizes the advantages and disadvantages of the primary communication methods.

Combining Methods

Each method of data collection thus has its uses, and none is superior in all situations. The problem as finally defined will often suggest one approach over the others, but the researcher should recognize that the approaches often can be used most productively in combination. In one home product-use test, for example, interviewers were employed to place the product, self-administered questionnaires, and return envelopes with the respondents, while telephone interviews were used for follow-up. The combination of methods produced telephone cooperation from 97 percent of the testing families, and 82 percent of the mail questionnaires were returned.[50]

Another example demonstrating advantages that can accrue through the creative use of a combination of data collection techniques is the locked box approach recommended for industrial surveys.[51] Surveying the industrial market is a relatively expensive proposition. One has to contend with busy executives who have better things to do with their

---

[49]Because of the need to send follow-up mailings to reduce the typically high incidence of nonresponse that occurs to any single mailing, researchers sometimes attempt to predict the ultimate response rate to a mailing based on the early returns. See Stephen J. Huxley, ''Predicting Response Speed in Mail Surveys,'' *Journal of Marketing Research,* 17 (February 1980), pp. 63–68; and Richard W. Hill, ''Using S-Shaped Curves to Predict Response Rates,'' *Journal of Marketing Research,* 18 (May 1981), pp. 240–242, for discussion of how this can be done.

[50]Stanley L. Payne, ''Combination of Survey Methods,'' *Journal of Marketing Research,* 1 (May 1964), p. 62. See also Kenneth C. Schneider and William C. Rodgers, ''Differences Between Nonrespondents and Refusers in Market Surveys Using Mixed Modes of Contact,'' *Journal of Business Research,* 21 (September 1990), pp. 91–107.

[51]David Schwartz, ''Locked Box Combines Survey Methods, Helps End Some Woes of Probing Industrial Field,'' *Marketing News,* 11 (January 27, 1978), p. 18. For studies that used the locked box, see Jerome E. Scott and Stephen K. Keiser, ''Forecasting Acceptance of New Industrial Products with Judgment Modeling,'' *Journal of Marketing,* 48 (Spring 1984), pp. 54–67; and Donald M. Fitch, ''Combination Technique Unlocks Hesitant Responses,'' *Marketing News,* 22 (January 4, 1988), p. 10.

TABLE **7.8**   **Primary Communication Methods of Data Collection:**
Advantages and Disadvantages

Advantages	Disadvantages
In-Home Personal Interview	
• Probably highest response rate	• Generally narrow distribution
• Best for getting response from specific, identified person	• Interviewer supervision and control difficult to maintain
• Allows use of any type of question/questionnaire	• Often difficult to identify individuals to include in sampling frame
• Sequencing of questions is easily changed	• Generally most expensive method of administration
• Allows probing of open-ended questions	
• Allows clarification of ambiguous questions	• Costly to revisit "not-at-homes"
• Permits easy use of visuals	• Relatively slow method of administration
	• Subject to interviewer bias
Mall Intercept (Same Advantages as In-Home Interview, PLUS):	
• Relatively short project completion time	• Sample control is more difficult than with in-home personal interview in terms of identifying a representative sample
• Less expensive than in-home interview	
• Much better interviewer supervision and control than in-home interview	• Interviews typically need to be shorter than in-home interview
Mail	
• May be only method able to reach respondent	• Very little control in securing response from specific individual
• Sampling frame easily developed when mailing lists are available	• Cannot secure response from illiterates

time than answer questionnaires, and with efficient secretaries and receptionists who prescreen executive mail, telephone calls, and personal visitors. Industrial surveys consequently produce very low response rates. The locked box has proved to be effective in getting through the prescreens and in generating executive cooperation. It is nothing more than a metal, shoe-sized box that is locked with a three-digit combination lock and that contains flash cards, interview exhibits, concept statements, or other survey materials. It is accompanied by a cover letter explaining the purpose of the survey and telling the respondent that an interviewer will be contacting him or her in a few days. The box becomes the gift for cooperating. However, it is of no use unless one knows the combination, information that is given the executive after he or she cooperates in the follow-up telephone interview. Thus, mail is used to deliver the box and the telephone to conduct the actual interview. At the same time, the box provides an opportunity to use stimuli such as pictures, examples, lists of words, scales, and so on, stimuli that otherwise might be restricted to personal interviews.

TABLE **7.8**   *Continued*

Advantages	Disadvantages
Mail	
• Not subject to interviewer bias	• Cannot control speed of response; long response time
• Respondents work at their own pace	
• Ensures anonymity of respondents	• Researcher cannot explain ambiguous questions
• Wide distribution possible	• Does not allow probing with open-ended questions
• Best for personal, sensitive questions	• Difficult to change sequence of questions
• Generally least expensive	• Sequence bias: respondents can view entire questionnaire as they respond
Telephone	
• Relatively low cost	• Difficult to establish representative sampling frame due to unlisted numbers
• Wide distribution possible	
• Interviewer supervision is strong; less interviewer bias	• Cannot use visual aids
• Relatively strong response rates (much higher than mail surveys)	• More difficult to establish rapport over the telephone than in person
• One of quickest methods of data collection	• Does not handle long interview well in most cases
• Less difficulty and cost in handling "call-backs" than in-home interviews	• Subject to some degree of interviewer bias (but much less than with personal interview)
• Allows easy use of computer support	• More difficult to determine that appropriate respondent is being interviewed than with personal interviews
• Sequence of questions is easily changed	

METHODS OF OBSERVATION

Observation is a fact of everyday life. We are constantly observing other people and events as a means of securing information about the world around us. Admittedly, some people make more productive use of those observations than others. One of the more interesting stories told about William Benton, one of the co-founders of the Benton and Boles advertising agency, concerned his walk along a street in Chicago during a hot day in 1929. Since it was hot, most of the windows were open, so he could hear the radios in the apartments he passed. What he mainly heard were the voices of the actors in *Amos and Andy,* one of the leading comedy programs at that time. Struck by this, Benton retraced his steps, this time counting the radios he could hear. He counted 23 of them in all, and found that 21 were tuned to *Amos and Andy*. Rushing back to his advertising firm, Benton suggested that they advertise one of their clients' products, Pepsodent toothpaste, on *Amos and Andy*. The sales of Pepsodent took off like a rocket, all because of Benton's first audience survey of radio listenership.[52]

Observation is also a tool of scientific inquiry. When used for that purpose, however, the observations are more systematically planned and recorded so that they relate to the specific phenomenon of interest. Although planned, they do not have to be sophisticated to be effective. They can be as basic as United Airlines' study of the garbage gathered from its various flights, which prompted the airline to discontinue serving butter on many of its short-range flights because few people were eating it, or the retailer who color-coded the promotional flyers it was sending according to zip code so that it could identify the trading area the store was serving by counting the flyers of each color that were returned.[53] This is a less sophisticated scheme than that used by many malls to determine their trading areas. Some malls use enumerators, who walk the parking lot recording every unique license number they find, 2,500 different numbers on a typical day. The data is then fed to R. L. Polk, which matches the license plates to zip code areas or census tracts and returns a color-coded map showing customer density from the various areas. At a cost of $5,000 to $25,000, these studies are not only less expensive, but they are quicker and more reliable than store interviews or examinations of credit card records.[54]

One of the reasons often cited for the Japanese's success in new product development is that they are masters of the art of observation. Japanese marketers spend a good deal of time studying consumers as they make use of the goods they buy.

> "I know of a Japanese shoe manufacturer who came to New York with a high-powered lens and a camera," says Johny K. Johansson, professor of marketing and international business at Georgetown University. "He rented a second-floor hotel room and took pictures of people's feet as they walked past." The hundreds of photographs the manufacturer took gave him a sense of how people walked.
>
> "This was New York City," Mr. Johansson says, "one of the biggest shoe markets in the world. The manufacturer wanted to see what kinds of shoes people wore who were in a hurry to get somewhere."[55]

Observation offers the researcher a number of possible approaches. Like communication methods, observational data may be gathered employing structured or unstructured methods that are either disguised or undisguised. Further, as Figure 7.2 shows, the observations may be made in a contrived or a natural setting and may be secured by a human or mechanical observer.

---

[52]Edward Cornish, "Telecommunications: What's Coming," paper delivered at the American Marketing Association's 1981 Annual Conference held in San Francisco, California, June 14–17, 1981.

[53]"Business Bulletin," *The Wall Street Journal* (August 11, 1983), p. 1.

[54]See James G. Barnes, G. A. Pym, and A. C. Noonan, "Marketing Research: Some Basics for Small Business," *Journal of Small Business Management,* 20 (July 1982), pp. 62–66; Steve Raddock, "Follow That Car," *Marketing and Media Decisions,* 16 (January 1981), pp. 70–71, 103; "I've Got Your Number," *The Wall Street Journal* (February 5, 1981), p. 21; and Martha Farnsworth Riche, "The Business Guide to the Galaxy of Demographic Products and Services," *American Demographics,* 7 (June 1985), pp. 22–33.

[55]Jeff Shear, "The Japanese Excel at Gauging Public Reaction to a New Product," *The Washington Times,* (March 15, 1990), p. C1.

Structured–Unstructured Observation

The distinction here parallels that for communication methods. Structured observation applies when the problem has been defined precisely enough to permit a clear *a priori* specification of the behaviors that will be observed and the categories that will be used to record and analyze the situation. Unstructured observation is used for studies in which the formulation of the problem is not specific; a great deal of flexibility is allowed the observers in terms of what they note and record.

Consider a study investigating the amount of deliberation and search that goes into a detergent purchase. On the one hand, the observers could be instructed to stand at one end of a supermarket aisle and record what they deem appropriate with respect to each sample customer's deliberation and search. This might produce the following record: "Purchaser first paused in front of ABC brand. He picked up a box of ABC, glanced at the price, and set it back down again. He then checked the label and price for DEF brand. He set that back down again, and after a slight pause, picked up a smaller box of ABC than originally looked at, placed it in his cart, and moved down the aisle." On the other hand, observers might simply be told to record the first detergent examined, the total number of boxes picked up by any customer, and the time in seconds that the customer spent in front of the detergent shelves by checking the appropriate boxes in the observation form. The last situation represents a good deal more structure than the first.

To use the more structured approach, it would have been necessary to previously decide precisely what was to be observed and the specific categories and units that would be used to record the observations. These decisions presuppose specific hypotheses, and the structured approach is again more appropriate for descriptive and causal studies. The unstructured approach would be useful in generating insights into the relevant dimensions of deliberation and search behavior. It would not be appropriate, however, for testing hypotheses about this kind of behavior, because of the many different kinds of behaviors that could be recorded and the difficulty of coding and quantifying the data in a consistent manner.

One way to develop consistency in coding is to use multiple coders who are extremely well-trained. This technique was used, for example, in an observational study examining the patterns of interactions between parents and children in making selections of breakfast cereals. The observers recorded verbatim the verbal exchanges between parent and child when making the choice. The coders then tried to assess the following:

1. which party initiated the selection episode;
2. how the other party responded;
3. the content and tone of the communication; and
4. the occurrence of unpleasant consequences, such as arguments or unhappiness.

The ultimate aim of the study was to determine if the child was unhappy with the resolution of the situation.[56]

---

[56]Charles K. Atkin, "Observation of Parent-Child Interaction in Supermarket Decision Making," *Journal of Marketing,* 42 (October 1978), pp. 41–45. Diaries have also been used to get at parent-child interactions when purchasing products and services. See Leslie Isler, Edward T. Popper, and Scott Ward, "Children's Purchase Requests and Parental Responses: Results from a Diary Study," *Journal of Advertising Research,* 27 (October/November 1987), pp. 28–39.

The advantages and disadvantages of structure in observation are very similar to those in communication. Structuring the observation reduces the potential for bias and increases the reliability of observations. However, the reduction in bias may be accompanied by a loss of validity, since the number of seconds spent in deliberation or the number of boxes of detergent picked up and examined may not represent the complete story of deliberation and search. What about the effort spent simply looking at what is available but not picking anything up, or the discussion between husband and wife about which detergent to select? A well-trained, highly qualified observer might be able to interpret these kinds of behavior and relate them in a meaningful way to search and deliberation.

> The major problem of behavioral observation is the observer himself. . . . In behavioral observation the observer is both a crucial strength and a crucial weakness. Why? The observer must digest the information derived from observations and then make inferences about constructs. . . . The strength and the weakness of the procedure is the observer's powers of inference. If it were not for inference, a machine observer would be better than a human observer. The strength is that the observer can relate the observed behavior to the constructs or variables of a study: he brings behavior and construct together.[57]

Nintendo, the computer game manufacturer, is one company that makes regular use of both structured and unstructured observation to keep abreast of playing trends and interests. The main mechanism by which it does this is through its Player-Support Program, which consists of "hotline" telephone numbers that provide tips on playing Nintendo games. In a typical week, some 16,000 people will call the toll-free number for recorded tips and another 84,000 people will speak to more than 250 game counselors. In addition, the game counselors will respond to another 8,000 letters per week. Nintendo uses these hotlines not only to enhance customer satisfaction but also as a source of marketing intelligence. As Peter Main, the vice-president of marketing, comments: "It has kept us in close contact with the end user. . . . We use the data we collect to absolutely ensure that our game developers are aware of what's hot and what's not."[58] The game counselors and the unstructured observations they make, along with structured observations of the number of calls made to the recorded tips on each game, allow Nintendo to monitor changing player interests.

Disguised–Undisguised Observation

Disguise in observational methods refers to whether or not the subjects know they are being observed. In the search and deliberation study, observers may assume a position well out of the way so shoppers are not aware that their behavior is being observed. In some cases, the disguise is accomplished by observers becoming part of the situation with the other participants unaware of this role. One firm, for example, uses observers disguised as shoppers to assess package designs. The observers record such things as how long shoppers spend in the display area, whether they have difficulty finding the

---

[57]Kerlinger, *Foundations,* p. 487.

[58]Joe Mandese, "Power Plays," *Marketing & Media Decisions,* 24 (March 1989), p. 104. See also Lucie Juneau, "No More Playing Around on Nintendo's Help Desk," *Computerworld,* 26 (June 1, 1992), p. 68.

product, and whether the information on the package appeared hard to read.[59] Other retailers are increasingly turning to on-site cameras not only to assess package designs but also to make general improvements in counter space and floor displays and to study traffic flows.[60] Still others are using paid observers disguised as shoppers to evaluate sales service with respect to promptness of service and the attitudes and courtesy of the employees.[61] Motel 6 uses its own representatives, who pose as soap salespeople, to stop guests at Motel 6 locations; they inform the guests they are trying to sell soap to the chain, "but, by the way, what do you think of the place?"[62]

The reason the observer's presence is disguised, of course, is to control the tendency for people to behave differently when they know their actions are being watched. There are at least two practical issues that can be raised about the disguised observation, though. First, it is often very difficult to disguise an observation completely, and second, identifying oneself as a research worker often increases one's ability to secure other relevant information, such as background data. There is also an ethical question associated with disguised observation.

> . . . the investigator who proposes to enter a situation without revealing his research purpose has an obligation to ask himself whether there is any possibility that his disguised activities will harm any of the people in the situation and if so, whether the potential results of his research are valuable enough to justify their acquisition under these circumstances.[63]

Disguised observations may be made *directly* or *indirectly*. An observer stationed at the checkout counter counting the number of boxes of each brand of detergent being purchased would be engaged in direct observation. However, an observer who counted inventory on hand by brand at the end of each day and adjusted the results for additions to inventory would be engaged in indirect observation. The key is that instead of observing the behavior itself, the researcher is observing the *effects* or *results* of that behavior.

There are many types of indirect observation.[64] One could, for example, derive measures of share of market for the various brands of detergent by conducting pantry

---

[59]David A. Schwartz, "Research Can Help Solve Packaging Functional and Design Problems," *Marketing News,* 9 (January 16, 1976), p. 8. For a general, how-to guide on participant observation, see Danny L. Jorgensen, *Participant Observation: A Methodology for Human Studies* (Beverly Hills, Calif.: Sage Publications, 1989).

[60]"On-Site's Cameras Focus on the Retail Marketplace," *Marketing News,* 18 (November 9, 1984), p. 46; "Planning Supermarkets to Maximize Temptation," *The Wall Street Journal* (May 9, 1991), p. B1.

[61]Larry Gulledge, "Evaluation Services Pay Off in Bigger Bottom Lines," *Marketing News,* 18 (October 12, 1984), p. 30; Karen Gershowitz, "Research Design Is Used to Evaluate Sales Reps," *Marketing News,* 21 (January 2, 1987), p. 6; Jolie Solomon, "Trying to Be Nice Is No Labor of Love," *The Wall Street Journal* (November 29, 1990), pp. B1, B6.

[62]Carol Hall, "King of the Road," *Marketing & Media Decisions,* 24 (March 1989), p. 86.

[63]Selltiz, Wrightsman, and Cook, *Research Methods,* p. 218. See also Martin Bulmer, ed., *Social Research Ethics: An Examination of the Merits of Covert Participant Observation* (New York: Holmes & Meier Publishers, 1982).

[64]For insight into some of the many ingenious ways that have been developed to make indirect measurements by observation, see Eugene J. Webb, et al., *Unobtrusive Measures: Nonreactive Research in the Social Sciences* (Chicago: Rand McNally, 1966); Lee Sechrest, *New Directions for Methodology of Behavior Science: Unobtrusive Measurement Today* (San Francisco: Jossey-Bass, 1979); and Thomas J. Bouchard, Jr., "Unobtrusive Measures: An Inventory of Uses," *Sociological Methods and Research* (February 1976), pp. 267–301.

audits. In a pantry audit, respondents' homes would be visited and permission would be sought to examine the "pantry inventory" and determine the presence and amount of various brands of detergent. Although one would typically not incur the expense of a pantry audit for a single product, the audit could be used to advantage to assess consumption of a prespecified set of products.

Over the years, many innovative, indirect measures of behavior have been developed. For example, a car dealer in Chicago checked the position of the radio dial of each car brought in for service. The dealer then used this as a proxy for share of listening audience in deciding upon the stations on which to advertise. Similarly, the number of different fingerprints on a page has been used to assess the readership of various ads in a magazine, and the age and condition of the cars in the parking lot has been used to gauge the affluence of the group patronizing the outlet.[65]

Observation is often more useful than surveys in sorting fact from fiction with respect to desirable behaviors. For example, a group of electric utilities secured permission from 150 households to put TV cameras into the homes when their projections of energy usage continually fell short of reality. The cameras, which were focused on the thermostat, revealed that what people said and what they did were vastly different. They said they set the thermostats at 68 degrees and left them there. It turned out that they fiddled with them all the time. "Older relatives and kids — especially teenagers — tended to turn them up, and so did cleaning ladies. Even visitors did it. In a lot of homes, it was guerrilla warfare over the thermostat between the person who paid the bill and everyone else."[66]

The advertising agency Young & Rubicam also used cameras along with personal observation to get a sense of what ice cream means to people, for its Breyers' ice cream account. "They photographed people lounging in their favorite chairs and taking that first scrumptious lick. They snooped in freezers, inspected bowls and utensils, watched people spoon on toppings and listened to one woman describe how she dims the lights and flips on her stereo before digging in. We learned about people's emotional response to ice cream and found that it's a very sensual, inner-directed experience," comments Robert Baker, marketing director for Breyers.[67]

Natural Setting–Contrived Setting Observation

Observations may be obtained either in natural or contrived settings. The former may be completely natural, or there may be an induced experimental manipulation. In the search and deliberation study, for example, we may simply choose to study the amount of these activities that normally go into the purchase of detergents. Alternatively, we might introduce some point-of-purchase display materials and might be interested in measuring

---

[65]See Bouchard, "Unobtrusive Measures," for a relatively detailed list of studies using indirect measures of behavior.

[66]Frederick C. Klein, "Researcher Probes Consumers Using 'Anthropological Skills,' " *The Wall Street Journal* (July 7, 1983), p. 21.

[67]Ronald Alsop, " 'People Watchers' Seek Clues to Consumers' True Behavior," *The Wall Street Journal* (September 4, 1986), p. 25.

their effectiveness. One measure of effectiveness might be the amount of search and deliberation they stimulate for the particular brand being promoted. Both of these studies could take place in a supermarket, which would be the natural setting. Alternatively, we could bring a group of people into a controlled environment, where they might engage in some simulated shopping behavior. We might have established a detergent display in this controlled environment and might study the degree of each participant's deliberation and search as he or she proceeds to make the purchase choices.

ETHICAL DILEMMA 7.3

A leading manufacturer of breakfast cereals was interested in learning more about the kinds of processes that consumers go through when deciding to buy a particular brand of cereal. To gather this information, an observational study was conducted in the major food chains of several large cities. The observers were instructed to assume a position well out of the shoppers' way, because it was thought that the individuals would change their behavior if they were aware they were being observed.

- Is it ethical to observe another person's behavior systematically without that person's knowledge? What if the behavior had been more private in nature? What if the behavior had been recorded on videotape?
- Does use of this method of data collection invade an individual's privacy?
- Even if there is no harm done to the individual, is there harm done to society?
- Does the use of such a method add to the concern over Big Brotherism?
- Can you suggest alternative methods for gathering the same information?

The advantage of the laboratory environment is that we are better able to control extraneous influences that might affect the interpretation of what happened. For example, shoppers in a natural setting pause to visit with their neighbors while deliberating over which detergent to buy; if we were measuring the time spent in deliberation, this interruption could raise havoc with the accuracy of the measurement. The disadvantage of the laboratory setting is that the contrived setting itself may cause differences in behavior and thus raise real questions about the external validity of the findings.

A contrived setting also tends to speed the data collection process, result in lower-cost research, and allow the use of more objective measurements. For example, Fisher-Price, which used to take toy prototypes to local homes to test reactions, now runs a free nursery at its corporate headquarters. The nursery handles five groups of children who come for six-week periods. Designers watch as children play with Fisher-Price toys and those of competitors.[68] Another advantage of the contrived setting is that the researcher does not need to wait for events to occur but can instruct the participants to engage in the

---

[68]"Fisher-Price Built on Reputation," *Wisconsin State Journal* (March 17, 1986), p. B3.

needed kind of behavior. This means that a great many observations can be made in a short period of time; perhaps an entire study can be completed in a couple of days or a week. This can substantially reduce costs.

The laboratory also allows the greater use of electrical and/or mechanical equipment than the natural setting does and thereby frees the measurement from the observer's selective processes. For example, IBM has set up "usability labs," in which customers try out software while programmers observe through a one-way mirror and "video cameras tape everything from fingers on keyboards to screens to facial expressions of participants."[69]

Human–Mechanical Observation

Much scientific observation is of the pencil-and-paper variety. One or more individuals are trained to systematically observe a phenomenon and to record on the observational form the specific events that took place.

DuPont, for example, relies on a human observer to deal with one of the most difficult problems it faces in its automotive paint division, color matching. It seems that no matter how much time and energy go into the metal repair work after an accident, the slightest difference in color shading upsets the customer. There is no problem in matching colors for domestic cars, since new models are introduced each fall in an orderly fashion, and factory color information is available well before the vehicles reach the showrooms. New models of imported cars reach dealer showrooms much more randomly throughout the year, however, and having paint shades available for their repair is a much greater problem. DuPont handles this problem through Charlie Smith, who operates out of a dockside laboratory in Jacksonville, Florida, the port of entry for thousands of imported cars each month. Smith not only has all the equipment that is necessary to mix colors to match the cars outside, but he also has a direct computer hook-up to DuPont's Troy, Michigan, laboratory, where the formulas for 17,000 different colors are stored.

> "DuPont has formulas to match almost any color I see coming ashore," reports Smith. "As each new color arrives, I spray out the DuPont formula on a test panel and compare it to the new car. If the spray-out matches the color, I report this to our Troy lab to verify the formula already in the computer. If it doesn't match, I go back to my lab and make adjustments in the formula."
>
> This may take a few hours or a few days, but once satisfied with the match, Smith relays the new formula directly to the Troy computer. This information then is distributed to body shops through DuPont's Refinish sales network.[70]

Electrical and/or mechanical observation also has its place in marketing research. Although it has been used for a long time, the development of new technologies is expanding the role and importance of electrical/mechanical observation. For example, in

---

[69]Aaron Bernstein, "Big Changes at Big Blue," *Business Week* (February 15, 1988), p. 96.

[70]"Mixing and Matching," *Special Report News from DuPont of Interest to the College Community,* 76 (November–December 1982), p.18.

an effort to improve service and sales, Kmart has been testing a new radar-like system that tracks customer traffic. The system relies on sensors mounted over the store entrance and at certain locations inside the store to count customers as they interrupt the beams of light the sensors emit. Kmart hopes to use the system "to improve service by sending salespeople to crowded departments and opening more checkout lanes before long lines form. . . . [It] also expects to be able to determine for the first time what percentage of shoppers actually make purchases. Until now, the company has only tracked transactions."[71]

Some of the earliest uses of electrical/mechanical observation focused on copy research and involved the galvanometer, tachistoscope, and eye camera. The **galvanometer** is used to measure the emotional arousal induced by an exposure to specific advertising copy. It belongs to the class of instruments that measure autonomic reactions, or reactions that are not under an individual's voluntary control. Because these responses are not controlled, it is not possible for individuals to mask or hide their "true" reactions to a stimulus. The galvanometer records changes in the electrical resistance of the skin associated with the minute degree of sweating that accompanies emotional arousal. For example, a subject could be fitted with small electrodes to monitor electrical resistance and then shown different advertising copy. The strength of the current induced would then be used to infer the subject's interest or attitude toward the copy.[72]

The **tachistoscope** is a device that provides the researcher timing control over a visual stimulus. The exposure interval may range from less than one hundredth of a second to several seconds. After each exposure, respondents are asked to describe everything they saw and what it meant. By systematically varying the exposure, the researcher is able to measure how quickly and accurately a particular stimulus (ad) can be perceived and interpreted. Note, though, that the use of a verbal reply implies that the tachistoscope is not a mechanical observer but rather a mechanical means of presenting stimuli.

The **eye camera** is employed to study eye movements while a respondent reads advertising copy. The original eye cameras utilized a light that was positioned to strike the cornea of the subject's eye, from which it was reflected to a moving film. The reflected light traced eye movements on the film. The researcher then had to project the film, frame-by-frame, while manually recording eye movements on a sheet of paper. Since the mid-1970s, though, computers have been developed that can automatically perform this analysis from videotape. There have also been important advances in the

---

[71]Francine Schwadel, "Kmart Testing 'Radar' To Track Shopper Traffic," *The Wall Street Journal* (September 24, 1991), pp. B1, B7.

[72]A review of 118 studies on involuntary responses to advertising found that pupil dilation, skin moisture, and heart rate are the most commonly used. See Paul J. Watson and Robert J. Gatchel, "Autonomic Measures of Advertising," *Journal of Advertising Research,* 19 (June 1979), pp. 15–26. See also David W. Stewart and David H. Furse, "Applying Psychophysiological Measures to Marketing and Advertising Research Problems," in James H. Leigh and Claude R. Martin, Jr., eds., *Current Issues and Research in Advertising* (Ann Arbor: University of Michigan, 1982), pp. 1–38; and Joanne M. Klebba, "Physiological Measures of Research: A Review of Brain Activity, Electrodermal Response, Pupil Dilation and Voice Analysis Methods and Studies," in James H. Leigh and Claude R. Martin, Jr., eds., *Current Issues and Research in Advertising,* vol. 1 (Ann Arbor: University of Michigan, 1985), pp. 53–76.

cameras themselves. Some of the new video cameras are now so small, weighing only a few ounces, that they can be clipped to a respondent's eyeglasses. The visual record produced as an individual reads an advertisement, for example, allows the detailed study of the person's behavior. What points did the individual perceive first? How long did the person linger on a given item? Did the individual read all the copy or part of it? The small video cameras that follow the path of the eye have also been used to analyze package designs, billboards, and displays in the aisles of supermarkets.[73]

Some of the newer electrical/mechanical observation devices include the optical scanner, which has automated the checkout process at many grocery stores and in the process revolutionized the marketing research function, and the people meter, which is used to develop TV viewing statistics. Both of these were discussed in the last chapter.

Two methods of mechanical observation that promise to provide useful supplementary information in telephone interviews — response latency and voice pitch analysis — owe their current popularity to mechanical/electronic recorders and the computer's ability to diagnose what is recorded. **Response latency** is the amount of time a respondent deliberates before answering a question. Since response time seems to be directly related to the respondent's uncertainty in the answer, it assists in assessing the individual's strength of preference when choosing among alternatives. Thus it provides an unobtrusive measure of, for example, brand preference or ambiguity experienced by a respondent in answering a particular question. The measure depends on a voice-operated relay that triggers an electronic stopwatch. When an interviewer approaches the end of a question, he or she simply presses a pedal that sets the stopwatch to zero and alerts the electronic mechanism to listen for the offset (end of the question) of the interviewer's voice. The stopwatch is automatically triggered at the offset. The moment the respondent begins answering, the watch is stopped by the voice-operated relay system, and a digital readout system indicates response latency to the interviewer, who can then record the deliberation time on the interview form. Note that there are several advantages in such a system. First, the method provides an accurate response latency measure without respondents being aware that this dimension of behavior is being recorded. Second, because the time is measured by an automatic device, the technique does not make the interviewer's task any more difficult, nor does it appreciably lengthen the interview. For example, DuPont, with little additional effort in an otherwise routine research survey,

---

[73]For discussions of the operation and use of eye camera technology to study the effectiveness of ads, packages, and displays, see J. E. Russo, "Eye Fixation Can Save the World," in H. K. Hunt, ed., *Advances in Consumer Research* (Ann Arbor, Mich.: Association for Consumer Research, 1978), pp. 561–570; J. Treistman and J. P. Gregg, "Visual, Verbal, and Sales Response to Print Ads," *Journal of Advertising Research,* 19 (August 1979), pp. 41–47; "Determining How Ads Are Seen," *Dun's Business Month,* 119 (February 1982), pp. 85–86; "Recall Scores Are Giving Short Shrift to Outdoor Ads, Study Finds," *Marketing News,* 18 (November 23, 1984), p. 16; Ronald Alsop, "Study of Magazine Ads Yields Some Eye-Opening Findings," *The Wall Street Journal* (December 5, 1985), p. 31; and Leo Bogart and B. Stuart Tolley, "The Search for Information in Newspaper Advertising," *Journal of Advertising Research,* 28 (April/May 1988), pp. 9–19.

used response latency to assess brand awareness and prospects' perception of quality of an industrial product for which there were many competitive brands.[74]

Voice pitch analysis relies on the same basic premise as the galvanometer: subjects experience a number of involuntary physiological reactions, such as changes in blood pressure, rate of perspiration, or heart rate, when emotionally aroused by external or internal stimuli. **Voice pitch analysis** examines changes in the relative vibration frequency of the human voice that accompany emotional arousal. All individuals function at a certain physiological pace, called the baseline. The baseline in voice analysis is established by engaging the respondent in unemotional conversation, which is recorded. Deviations from the baseline level indicate that the respondent has reacted to the stimulus question. These deviations can be assessed by special audio-adapted computer equipment that can measure the abnormal frequencies in the voice caused by changes in the nervous system, changes that may not be discernible to the human ear. A net reaction score can be generated by comparing the abnormal frequency produced by the stimulus to the person's normal frequency. The greater the difference, the greater the emotional intensity of the subject's reaction is said to be. Voice pitch analysis has at least two advantages over other **physiological reaction techniques.** First, these techniques measure the intensity but not the direction of feeling. With voice pitch analysis, the "recording of the physical phenomenon (voice pitch) occurs simultaneously with the subject's conscious interpretation of the attitude (verbal response); the direction (positive or negative) of the attitude is ascertained from the subject's self-report, while the intensity of the emotion is measured at the same time by mechanical means."[75] Second, whereas the measurement of blood pressure, pulse rate, psychogalvanic response, or other physiological reactions requires subjects be connected to the equipment, voice pitch analysis

---

[74]Robert C. Grass, Wallace H. Wallace, and Samuel Zuckerkandel, "Response Latency in Industrial Advertising Research," *Journal of Advertising Research,* 20 (December 1980), pp. 63–65. For general discussions of the use of response latency measures in marketing research, see James MacLachlan, John Czepiel, and Priscilla LaBarbera, "Implementation of Response Latency Measures," *Journal of Marketing Research,* 16 (November 1979), pp. 573–577; James MacLachlan and Priscilla LaBarbera, "Response Latency in Telephone Interviews," *Journal of Advertising Research,* 19 (June 1979), pp. 49–56; Tyzoon T. Tyebjee, "Response Latency: A New Measure for Scaling Brand Preference," *Journal of Marketing Research,* 16 (February 1979), pp. 96–101; David A. Aaker, Richard P. Bagozzi, James M. Carman, and James M. MacLachlan, "On Using Response Latency to Measure Preference," *Journal of Marketing Research,* 17 (May 1980), pp. 237–244; W. Jefferey Burroughs and Richard A. Feinberg, "Using Response Latency to Assess Spokesperson Effectiveness," *Journal of Consumer Research,* 14 (September 1987), pp. 295–299; John N. Bassili and Joseph F. Fletcher, "Response-Time Measurement in Survey Research: A Method for CATI and a New Look at Nonattitudes," *Public Opinion Quarterly,* 55 (Fall 1991), pp. 331–346.

[75]Nancy Nischwonger and Claude R. Martin, "On Using Voice Analysis in Marketing Research," *Journal of Marketing Research,* 18 (August 1981), pp. 350–355. For general discussions of the use of voice pitch analysis in marketing research, see Ronald G. Nelson and David Schwartz, "Voice Pitch Analysis," *Journal of Advertising Research,* 19 (October 1979), pp. 55–59; Glen A. Buckman, "Uses of Voice-Pitch Analysis," *Journal of Advertising Research,* 20 (April 1980), pp. 69–73; Linda Edwards, "Hearing What Consumers Really Feel," *Across the Board,* 17 (April 1980), pp. 62–67; and James Grant and Dean E. Allman, "Voice Stress Analyzer Is a Marketing Research Tool," *Marketing News,* 22 (January 4, 1988), p. 22.

allows a much more natural interaction between researcher and participant. This tends to make it less time-consuming and less expensive to use.

At the other extreme, **brain wave research,** which is in its infancy and which generates a good deal of controversy, requires a rather elaborate hookup of the subject to equipment. The purpose is to assess the stimuli that subjects find arousing or interesting. To do this, subjects are fitted with electrodes that monitor the electrical impulses emitted by the brain as the subject is exposed to various stimuli. The evidence suggests that the two hemispheres of the brain respond differently to specific stimuli, with the right hemisphere responding more to emotional stimuli and the left to rational stimuli.[76]

ETHICAL DILEMMA 7.4

You are running a laboratory experiment for the promotion manager of a soft drink company. The promotion manager has read a journal article indicating that viewers' responses to upbeat commercials are more favorable if the commercials follow very arousing film clips, and he is interested in testing this proposition with respect to his firm's commercials. To establish whether film clips that induce high levels of arousal result in more extreme evaluations of ensuing commercials than film clips that induce low levels of arousal, you are pretesting film clips for their capacity to arouse. To do this, you are recording subjects' blood pressure levels as they watch various film clips. The equipment is not very intrusive, consisting of a finger cuff attached to a recording device. You are satisfied that the procedure does not threaten the subject's physical safety in any way. In addition, you have made the subjects familiar with the equipment, with the result that they are relaxed and comfortable and absorbed in the film clips. On getting up to leave at the end of the session, one subject turns to you and asks, ''Is my blood pressure normal then?''

• Is it ethical to give respondents information about their physiological responses that they can interpret as an informed comment on the state of their health?

• What might be the result if you do not tell the subject the function of the equipment?

Three other electrical/mechanical observation techniques that are still in their infancy but seem to have the potential to significantly affect the measurement of particular consumer behaviors are Information Resources' VideoCart, Nielsen's videocassette ratings system, and Arbitron's passive people meters, described in Research Realities 7.6.

---

[76]For general discussions of the status of brain wave research, see F. Hansen, ''Hemispherical Lateralization: Implications for Understanding Consumer Behavior,'' *Journal of Consumer Research,* 8 (June 1981), pp. 23–36; A. Weinstein, ''A Review of Brain Hemisphere Research,'' *Journal of Advertising Research,* 22 (June/July 1982), pp. 59–63; Michael L. Rothschild, et al., ''Hemispherically Lateralized EEG as a Response to Television Commercials,'' *Journal of Consumer Research,* 15 (September 1988), pp. 185–198; Michael L. Rothschild and Yong J. Hyun, ''Micro Information Processing: Predicting Memory for Components of TV Commercials from EEG,'' *Journal of Consumer Research,* 16 (December 1989), pp. 7–61; Michael L. Rothschild and Yong J. Hyun, ''Predicting Memory for Components of TV Commercials from EEG,'' *Journal of Consumer Research,* 16 (March 1990), pp. 472–478; Jack Honomichl, '' 'Hypertargeting' Scenario Not As Far Fetched As It Seems,'' *Marketing News,* 26 (November 9, 1992), p. 11.

Research Realities 7.6

VideoCarts, Video Ratings, and Passive People Meters

VideoCarts

Market researchers want to know *everything* — what foods you pick up at the grocery store to snack on, and what you're watching while you eat them. Not only that, but some new technology is helping them get the information faster and more efficiently than ever before. Information Resources Inc. has just launched VideoCart, which will gather data as shoppers push it around the store. VideoCart, about the size of a laptop computer, is mounted on the handles of a shopping cart. Although designed primarily as an advertising medium, the carts also gather data as shoppers push them down the aisles. As a shopper pushes a VideoCart through the store, the manufacturers' ads for brands on the shelves being passed at that moment are triggered and appear on the flat, 6″ × 8″ liquid-crystal display. Tie-in promotion ads are also used; for instance, a hot-dog bun ad appears when the cart is near the hot dogs. Yet only 15 percent of VideoCart's display time is devoted to ads. The rest includes recipes, a continually changing video news magazine, store maps, and video games to play while waiting to check out.

Among data gathered are the VideoCart's own paths through the store, the time spent in various parts of the store, and shopper's opinions. For some applications, shoppers can interact with VideoCart through its touch-screen capability. Data obtained from "interrogating" each cart enables the grocer to analyze shopping patterns and the time spent shopping in each product category for optimal product placement and traffic management.

Source: "VideoCart Shopping Cart with Computer Screen Creates New Ad Medium that Also Gathers Data," *Marketing News*, 22 (May 9, 1988), pp. 1–2; Joanne Lipman, "Nielsen to Test Videocassette Rating System," *The Wall Street Journal* (August 17, 1988), p. 21; Cyndee Miller, "VideoCart Spruces Up for New Tests," *Marketing News*, 24 (February 1990), p. 19; and "Arbitron to Develop 'Pocket People Meter'," *Marketing News*, 27 (January 4, 1993), p. 12.

Video Ratings

While VideoCart tracks shopping patterns in the grocery store, A. C. Nielsen, the company that monitors TV viewing in the home, is expanding its rating services to include videocassettes. The company's new videocassette rating system will be piggybacked onto Nielsen's existing electronic TV ratings system. Currently 4,000 homes across the country are wired with "people meters," electronic devices that record which family members are watching television. About half of those homes also have videocassette recorders, which will be wired with a small box attached to the VCR. The box "reads" an electronic code on the videocassettes and tracks what part of the tape is — and isn't — viewed. Meanwhile, the people meter records who is watching the film. The box also kicks in when a TV program is taped, encoding the tape with information identifying what station is being watched at what time. Thus, the device can be used to track how often videotaped TV programs are watched and whether viewers fast-forward through the commercials.

Passive People Meters

A gadget will automatically gather information on TV viewership as well as on viewers who wear it, if plans pan out for Arbitron Co.'s "pocket people meter." Passive audience measuring devices have long been the dream of TV ratings services and their clients, which include the networks. Arbitron's proposed carry-around device, no larger than an electronic pager, would detect "a unique identifying code which broadcasters embed in the soundtrack of a radio or television program," the company said.

Any TV or radio broadcast audible to the device's wearer would be measured, instead of current technology's restriction to metered sets and diary systems in homes, Arbitron said. Data would be supplied to Arbitron either through a separate in-home modem or by mailing the meter back to the company. Arbitron hopes to use its new monitor to measure two U.S. media markets with the new system by the end of 1994.

Further, there are other potentially important developments in electronic measurement on the horizon.[77]

As mentioned, electrical/mechanical equipment frees the observation from the observer's selective processes. This is both its major strength and major weakness. Certainly recording when a TV set is turned on, to what channel it is tuned, and who is "watching" can be accomplished much more accurately by a people meter than by some other means. The fact that the set is tuned to a particular channel and that someone pushed the button indicating that he or she was in the room does not say anything, however, about the person's level of interest. A trained human observer's record might be more difficult to analyze, and it might be less objective, but his or her powers of integration could certainly produce a more valid assessment of what occurred. The essential point is that the marketing researcher needs to be aware of the electrical/mechanical equipment that is available so that he or she can make an informed choice about whether a piece of equipment might make a better observer than a human in a given instance (or vice versa) or whether a combination approach might be most productive.

SUMMARY

A researcher who cannot find the data needed in secondary sources resorts to primary data collection. The types of primary data of interest to marketing researchers include demographic/socioeconomic characteristics, psychological/life-style characteristics, attitudes/opinions, awareness/knowledge, intentions, motivation, and behavior of individuals and groups.

Communication and observation are the two basic means of obtaining primary data. Communication involves the direct questioning of respondents, whereas observation entails the systematic checking of appropriate facts or actions. Observation is the more limited approach. It can be used to secure behavioral primary data and some demographic/socioeconomic and life-style characteristics, and it has the advantage of accuracy over communication methods. Observation is not useful, though, for measuring attitudes, awareness, knowledge, intentions, or motivation. When these constructs are of interest, communication methods must be used, although mechanical devices are sometimes employed to assist in interpreting attitudes.

Communication methods may be classified by their degree of structure, degree of disguise, and method of administration. A structured questionnaire has a well-defined sequence and standardized response categories. It is most productively used for testing specific hypotheses, as would occur in descriptive or causal research. When the research is exploratory, unstructured questionnaires can be used. In an unstructured questionnaire, the response categories are not predetermined; the respondents are allowed to answer in their own terms.

---

[77]See, for example, Gregg Cebrzynski, "New Research Tools Provide 'Accurate' Attention Data," *Marketing News,* 20 (April 11, 1986), p. 1; "Big Boom in Electronic Research is Predicted," *Marketing News,* 22 (July 4, 1988), pp. 11 and 17; and Laurence N. Gold, "High Technology Data Collection for Measurement and Testing," *Marketing Research: A Magazine of Management & Applications,* 4 (March 1992), pp. 29–38.

The disguised questionnaire attempts to hide the purpose of the research from the respondent. This is particularly important when the respondent may be tempted to give the socially accepted response on sensitive issues.

Questionnaires can be administered by personal interviews in the home or a mall or some other convenient facility, over the phone, or by mail, using either paper-and-pencil questionnaires or computer-administered ones. Each approach has some general advantages and disadvantages, which may or may not occur in a specific study. The methods vary in terms of the control they offer the researcher with respect to sample, information, and administration. They are not mutually exclusive data collection methods and can often be used more productively in combination.

Observation methods can also be classified by several criteria, including degree of structure, degree of disguise, the naturalness of the setting, and whether human or mechanical devices are employed to secure the data. The arguments for structure and disguise here parallel those for communication methods.

Most observations in marketing research are probably obtained in a completely natural setting, although certain types of observations are regularly obtained in contrived or laboratory settings using electrical/mechanical equipment. The laboratory setting allows greater control of extraneous influences and thus may be more internally valid, although less externally valid. Electrical/mechanical measuring instruments permit more objective, reliable measurements by eliminating the opportunity for a human observer's selective processes to operate. They also eliminate the human observer's integrative powers, and in this respect may be less valid.

■
Questions

1. What types of primary data interest marketing researchers most? How are they distinguished?

2. What are the general advantages and disadvantages associated with obtaining information by questioning or by observation? Which method provides more control over the sample?

3. What is a disguised questionnaire? What is a structured questionnaire?

4. What are the advantages and disadvantages of structured–undisguised questionnaires? Of unstructured–undisguised questionnaires?

5. What is the rationale for employing unstructured–disguised stimuli? What is a word association test? A sentence completion test? A storytelling test?

6. What operating principle or assumption underlies the use of structured–disguised questionnaires? What are the advantages and disadvantages associated with structured–disguised questionnaires?

7. How do mail, telephone, and personally administered questionnaires differ with respect to the following:
   a. sampling control
   b. information control
   c. administrative control?

8. How can observational methods be classified? What are the key distinctions among the various types?

9. What principle underlies the use of a galvanometer? What is a tachistocope? What is an eye camera? What is an optical scanner?

10. What does response latency assess? How is it measured?

11. What is voice pitch analysis? What does it measure?

■

Applications and Problems

Should the communication or observational method be used in the situations described in Questions 1 and 2? (Justify your choice. Also specify the degree of structure and disguise that should be used.)

1. In 1993, the Metal Products Division of Geni Ltd. devised a special metal container to store plastic garbage bags. Plastic bags posed household problems, as they gave off unpleasant odors, looked disorderly, and provided a breeding place for insects. The container overcame these problems as it had a bag-support apparatus that held the bag open for filling and sealed the bag when the lid was closed. In addition, there was enough storage area for at least four full bags. The product was priced at $53.81 and was sold through hardware stores. The company has done little advertising and has relied on in-store promotion and displays. The divisional manager was wondering about the effectiveness of these displays. She has called on you to do the necessary research.

2. Cardworth is a national manufacturer and distributor of greeting cards. The company recently began distributing a lower-priced line of cards that was made possible by using recycled paper. Quality differences between the higher- and lower-priced cards did not seem to be noticeable to laypeople. The company followed a policy of printing its name and the price on the back of each card. The initial acceptance of the new line of cards convinced the vice-president of production, Bill Murray, that they should use this recycled paper for all their cards and increase their profit margin from 12.3 percent to 14.9 percent. The sales manager has strongly opposed this move and commented, "Bill, consumers are concerned about the quality of greeting cards; a price difference of 5 cents on a card does not matter." The vice-president has called on you to undertake the study.

Which survey method (mail, telephone, personal interview in the home or in a mall) would you use for the situations described in Questions 3 through 7? Justify your choice.

3. Administration of a questionnaire to determine the number of people who listened to the "100 Top Country Tunes in 1993," a program that aired on December 31, 1993?

4. Administration of a questionnaire to determine the number of households having a mentally ill individual and a history of mental illness in the household.

5. Administration of a questionnaire by a national manufacturer of microwave ovens in order to test people's attitudes and opinions toward a new model.

6. Administration of a questionnaire by a local drycleaner who wants to determine customers' satisfaction with a recent discount scheme.

7. Administration of a questionnaire by the management of a small hotel, which wants to assess customers' opinions of its service.

8. Several objectives for marketing research projects follow. For each objective, specify the type(s) of primary data that would be of use along with a possible method of data collection.
   a. Assess "people flow" patterns inside a shopping mall.
   b. Gauge the effectiveness of a new advertisement.

c. Gauge a salesperson's potential for success.

d. Segment a market.

e. Identify the shopper types that patronize a particular store.

f. Discover how people feel about a new package design.

Consider each of the following research projects (described in Questions 9 through 11). In each case, identify weak areas and describe how the research might have been improved to better attain its objectives. Be specific.

9. A local bank was interested in determining how it might better serve the needs of low-income households. It inserted a four-page survey into the monthly statement-of-account mailings of all account holders with less than $200 in their accounts. The survey was structured and undisguised; 1,200 surveys were mailed and 98 were completed and returned.

10. The Lee-Casey Lawn and Garden Company, which recently began business in a small midwestern city, has developed a special liquid fertilizer for a certain type of shrubbery. Lee-Casey is interested in determining whether there is a market for the product among homeowners, but it is unsure whether that particular type of shrubbery is popular in that area. In order to find out, Lee-Casey conducted a telephone survey of homeowners in the area. They were eventually able to reach about 75 percent of the homeowners; of these, 85 percent participated in the survey.

11. There are plans to open a new dress shop in a few months. The owners are unsure whether the new shop should be located in a shopping mall or at a downtown location. Since they think it would be best to simply ask shoppers for their preferences as to location, the owners contracted a local marketing research company to conduct a study. Using a structured, undisguised questionnaire format and the mall intercept method of administration, the research company was able to report to the owners of the new dress shop that most people prefer to shop for clothes in a shopping mall.

12. Quick-Stop Inc. recently opened a new convenience store in Northglenn, Colorado. The store is open every day from 7:00 A.M. to 11:00 P.M. In order to better plan the location of other units in the Denver metro area, management is interested in determining the trading area from which this store draws its customers.

    How would you determine this information by questionnaire method? By observation method? Which method would be preferred? Be sure to specify in your answer how you would define "trading area."

 Thorndike Sports Equipment Video Case

1. Thorndike Sports Equipment has decided to introduce three new racquets: a lightweight, a standard weight, and a heavyweight. The company wants to introduce these racquets with descriptive names that will tell the customer which weight category the racquet belongs to without simply using light, standard, and heavy as descriptors. Design a research study that will provide customer information on appropriate names for these new racquets. Your research plan can be a multiple-stage project, but you must provide estimated costs associated with your research proposal.

8
CHAPTER

DATA COLLECTION FORMS

In the previous chapter, the various types of questionnaires and observation forms and their methods of administration were discussed. The general advantages and disadvantages of using communication and observational methods, as well as the pros and cons associated with the many specific types of questionnaire or observational methods, were also dealt with. This chapter builds on that discussion. It reviews the procedures one should follow in developing a questionnaire or observational data collection form.

QUESTIONNAIRE DESIGN

Although much progress has been made, designing questionnaires is still an art and not a science. Much of the progress has come from admonitions such as "Avoid leading questions" or "Avoid ambiguous questions." It is much easier to embrace the admonitions than it is to develop questions that are indeed not leading or ambiguous. Nevertheless, Figure 8.1 offers a method that the beginning researcher can use to develop questionnaires. More experienced researchers would be expected to develop their own patterns, although the steps listed in Figure 8.1[1] would still be part of that pattern.

The stages of development are presented here in sequence, but researchers will rarely be so fortunate as to develop a questionnaire in step-by-step fashion. A more typical development will involve some iteration and looping. The researcher finds that the possible wordings of a response do not secure the content decided on, or that the content is not completely consistent with the information desired. This discovery, of course, requires a loop back to an earlier stage to make the necessary changes. Researchers should not be surprised, then, if they find themselves working back and forth among some of the stages. That is natural.

---

[1]This procedure is adapted from one suggested by Arthur Kornhauser and Paul B. Sheatsley, "Questionnaire Construction and Interview Procedure," in Claire Selltiz, Lawrence S. Wrightsman, and Stuart W. Cook, *Research Methods in Social Relations,* 3rd ed. (New York: Holt, Rinehart and Winston, 1976), pp. 541–573. See also Doug R. Birdie, John F. Anderson, and Martha A. Niebuhr, *Questionnaires: Design and Use,* 2nd ed. (Metuchen, N.J.: Scarecrow Press, 1986).

FIGURE 8.1 **Procedure for Developing a Questionnaire**

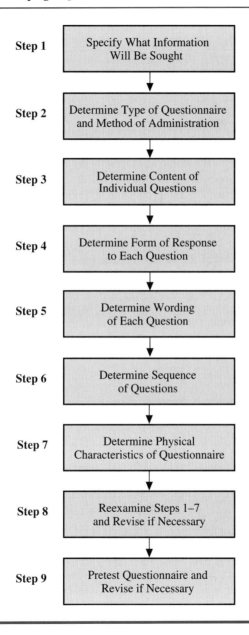

Step 1 — Specify What Information Will Be Sought

Step 2 — Determine Type of Questionnaire and Method of Administration

Step 3 — Determine Content of Individual Questions

Step 4 — Determine Form of Response to Each Question

Step 5 — Determine Wording of Each Question

Step 6 — Determine Sequence of Questions

Step 7 — Determine Physical Characteristics of Questionnaire

Step 8 — Reexamine Steps 1–7 and Revise if Necessary

Step 9 — Pretest Questionnaire and Revise if Necessary

Researchers should also be warned not to take the stages too literally. They are presented as a guide or a checklist. With questionnaires, the proof of the pudding is very much in the eating. Does the questionnaire produce accurate data of the kind needed? Blind adherence to procedure is no substitute for creativity in approach, nor is it any substitute for a pretest (Step 9 of Figure 8.1) with which one can discover whether the typical respondent indeed understands each question and is able and willing to supply the information sought.

Information Sought

Deciding what information will be sought is easy to the extent that researchers have been meticulous and precise at earlier stages in the research process. By the same token, if researchers have been sloppy and careless, the decision will prove to be difficult. Both descriptive and causal research demand sufficient prior knowledge to allow the framing of some specific hypotheses for investigation, which then guide the research. The hypotheses also guide the questionnaire. They determine what information will be sought and from whom, because they specify what relationships will be investigated. If researchers have heeded the earlier admonition to establish "dummy tables" to structure the data analysis, their job of determining what information is to be collected is essentially complete. Researchers must collect information on the variables specified in the dummy tables in order to investigate these hypotheses. Further, researchers must collect this information from the right people and in the right units. The hypotheses, then, will not only be a guide to what information will be sought but in large part will also determine the type of question and form of response used to collect it.

ETHICAL DILEMMA 8.1

As a new researcher for a large research supplier, you are told to design an attitude and usage questionnaire for a new customer, an appliance manufacturer. Before starting this project, your supervisor mentions that a similar study was completed 12 months ago and may provide some useful background information. Because you have no experience in durable consumer goods, you decide to use this previous report as a good source of secondary information.

After finding a copy of the previous study's final report, you discover that the report was completed for a competing appliance company. However, the report provides valuable background and competitive information. Because a questionnaire was developed and used successfully for this project, you decide to take a copy of the questionnaire and update it for the current client.

- Is it ethical for researchers to use questionnaires developed and paid for by prior clients on competitive client projects?
- Instead of using the questionnaire, would it have been legitimate to use the previous report as a source of secondary information to provide background information for the current project?
- Would the preceding situation be different if the prior research had been completed for a long-term, contract client?

This is not meant to deny that the preparation of the questionnaire itself may suggest further hypotheses and other relationships that might be investigated at slight additional effort and cost. A most important warning is in order here. If the new hypothesis is indeed vital to understanding the phenomenon, by all means include it and use it to advantage when designing the questionnaire. On the other hand (and we are repeating ourselves), if it simply represents one of those potentially ''interesting findings'' but is not vital to the research effort, forget it. The inclusion of ''interesting but not vital'' items simply lengthens the questionnaire, causes problems in administration and analysis, and often increases nonresponse. For example, Figure 8.2, which is based on data from more than one million interviews, shows what happens to refusal rates as the length of the interview increases.

The exploratory research effort is, of course, aimed at the discovery of ideas and insights and not at their systematic investigation. The questionnaire for an exploratory study is, therefore, loosely structured, with only a rough idea of the kind of information that might be sought. This is particularly true at the earliest stages of exploratory

FIGURE 8.2   Refusal Rate as a Function of Length of Interview

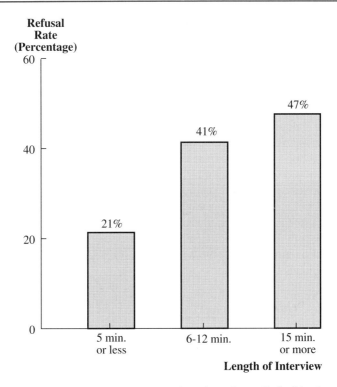

Source: Developed from information in *Industry Image Study,* 8th ed. (Indianapolis, Ind.: Walker Research, Inc., 1988).

research. It is also true, but to a lesser extent, at the later stages of exploratory research, when the emphasis is on determining the priorities that should be given to various hypotheses in guiding future research.

Type of Questionnaire and Method of Administration

After specifying the basic information that will be sought, the researcher needs to specify how it will be gathered. The *how* requires decisions about the structure and disguise to be used in the questionnaire and whether it will be administered by mail, telephone, or personal interviews. We saw in the last chapter that these decisions are not independent. If the researcher decides on a disguised–unstructured questionnaire using a picture stimulus storytelling format, this precludes straight telephone administration and raises serious questions about a mail administration of the instrument.[2] Similarly, mail administration is not recommended for unstructured–undisguised questionnaires with open-ended questions, particularly if they should have probes.

The type of data to be collected will have an important effect, of course, on the method of data collection, as will the culture of the country where the study is being done. (See Research Realities 8.1.) A researcher investigating the relationship between some behavior and a series of demographic characteristics in the United States (for example, how is dishwasher ownership related to income, age, family size, and so on) could use either mail, telephone, or in-home or mall personal interviews to gather the data. The methods would not be equally attractive because of cost and other considerations, but they all could be used. On the other hand, a researcher interested in measuring attitudes could not use all of the methods, although which ones could or could not be used would depend largely on previous decisions about structure and disguise. A decision to use a lengthy attitude scale, for example, would preclude a telephone administration, although it would allow the collection of data by either mail or personal interview. An open-ended questionnaire on attitudes would raise serious questions about mail administration. Thus, the researcher must specify precisely what primary data are needed, how these data might be collected, what degree of structure and disguise will be used, and how the questionnaire will be administered.

Figure 8.3 offers an example. The primary data at issue are use of caffeinated ground coffee and attitudes toward various brands. The questions are all very structured and undisguised. The questionnaire is to be administered by mail, using part of the NFO (National Family Opinion, Inc.) panel. Note the ease with which most of the responses could be tabulated.

Individual Question Content

The researcher's previous decisions regarding information needed, the structure and disguise to be imposed on its collection, and the method for administering the questionnaire

---

[2]The two methods might possibly be used in combination through the locked-box approach.

How Cultural Differences Affect Marketing Research in Different Countries

Willingness to Cooperate Compared with people around the world, Americans tend to be unusually helpful and friendly, which is reflected in their general willingness to cooperate in marketing research surveys. Quite often, Americans will answer the questions of a total stranger (in the research industry we call them "interviewers") about almost any subject — up to and including one's sex life. And Americans will agree to be interviewed anywhere: over the telephone, in a shopping mall, or at their place of business.

This climate of assumed cooperation can spoil Americans for doing research elsewhere in the world. Individual consumers in many other countries are less ready to answer any questions from an interviewer, let alone delicate or personal ones. Business people in many parts of the world have a more closed attitude than Americans about taking part in surveys.

In Korea, for example, business people are reluctant to answer any survey questions about their company — it is considered disloyal to divulge any type of information to "outsiders." And most Japanese business people are hesitant to take part in surveys during business hours — taking time away from your work for a survey is like "stealing" from your employer.

Differences in Research Costs The cost of doing exactly the same research can vary dramatically from country to country. Japan is generally regarded as the most expensive research market in the world; projects there usually cost several times what the same study would cost in the United States.

But even within a single region, such as the European community, costs can vary dramatically from country to country. ESOMAR, the European Society for Opinion and Marketing Research (the European equivalent of a combined American Marketing Association and Advertising Research Foundation), periodically studies differences in research costs from country to country within Europe. Here are examples of some of the cost differences ESOMAR found in its most recent study:

Examples of E.C. Research Cost Indices

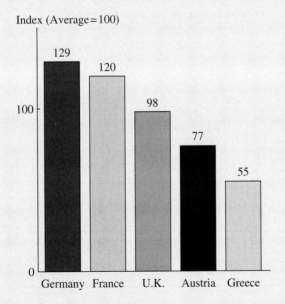

Index (Average = 100)

Germany 129, France 120, U.K. 98, Austria 77, Greece 55

Source: Jeffrey Pope, *How Cultural Differences Affect Multi-County Research* (Minneapolis, Minn.: Custom Research, Inc., 1991).

FIGURE 8.3   Cover Letter and Mail Questionnaire for Caffeinated Ground Coffee Study

``MARKET RESEARCH THROUGH REPRESENTATIVE HOUSEHOLDS``

NATIONAL FAMILY OPINION, INC.

P. O. Box 474   Toledo, OH 43654

TOLL-FREE NUMBERS
OUTSIDE OHIO: 1-800-537-4097
INSIDE OHIO: 1-800-472-4000

MONDAY THROUGH FRIDAY
8:00 A.M. TO 4:30 P.M.
EASTERN TIME

11519

Dear NFO Member,

Please give this questionnaire to the person in your household who is the Primary Coffee Drinker (this may be you). Thank you!

TO THE HOUSEHOLD MEMBER ANSWERING THIS QUESTIONNAIRE:

Today's questionnaire is about **caffeinated ground coffee**. Most of my questions can be answered by simply checking a box. However, where I've asked you to write in your opinions, please be as specific as possible.

When you have completed the questionnaire, please return it to me in the postage–paid envelope I've provided.

Thanks so much for your cooperation with this important study.

Sincerely,

Carol

Carol Adams

MEMBER OF AMERICAN MARKETING ASSOCIATION TOLEDO CHAMBER OF COMMERCE

Source: Courtesy of NFO Research, Inc.

FIGURE 8.3 *Continued*

1. What type of coffeemaker do you usually use to prepare you ground coffee at home? (CHECK *ONE* BOX)

      1☐ Automatic drip
      2☐ Electric percolator
      3☐ Stove top percolator
      4☐ Stove top dripolator
      ☐ Other (Specify: _____)

2. a. Check all the brands of regular ground coffee that you have ever used at home. (CHECK *ALL* THAT APPLY)
  b. Check the one brand you use most often. (CHECK *ONE* BOX)
  c. Check all the brands you currently have on hand. (CHECK *ALL* THAT APPLY)
  d. Check the one brand you will probably buy next. (CHECK *ONE* BOX)
  e. For each brand please indicate how much you like the brand overall on a scale of 1 to 10 with "1" meaning dislike it extremely and "10" meaning like it extremely. Rate each brand, whether you have used the brand or not.

	"A" Ever Used	"B" Use Most Often	"C" Have On Hand	"D" Will Buy Next	Brand Rating "1" Dislike It Extremely								"10" Like It Extremely
Folgers	1☐	1☐	1☐	1☐	01☐ 02☐ 03☐	04☐	05☐	06☐	07☐	08☐	09☐	10☐	
Hill Brothers ..	2☐	2☐	2☐	2☐	01☐ 02☐ 03☐	04☐	05☐	06☐	07☐	08☐	09☐	10☐	
Maxwell House Regular	3☐	3☐	3☐	3☐	01☐ 02☐ 03☐	04☐	05☐	06☐	07☐	08☐	09☐	10☐	
Maxwell House Master Blend	4☐	4☐	4☐	4☐	01☐ 02☐ 03☐	04☐	05☐	06☐	07☐	08☐	09☐	10☐	
Yuban	5☐	5☐	5☐	5☐	01☐ 02☐ 03☐	04☐	05☐	06☐	07☐	08☐	09☐	10☐	
Other (Specify:____	6☐	6☐	6☐	6☐	01☐ 02☐ 03☐	04☐	05☐	06☐	07☐	08☐	09☐	10☐	

3. What do you usually add to the coffee you drink? (CHECK *ALL* THAT APPLY)

      1☐ Nothing (I drink it black)
      2☐ A dairy creamer, like milk, cream, or Half and Half
      3☐ A non-dairy creamer, powdered or liquid
      4☐ Sugar
      5☐ Artificial sweetener
      ☐ Something else (Specify): _____

4. Are you the principal coffee purchaser for your household?

      1☐ Yes
      2☐ No

(continued)

FIGURE **8.3** *Continued*

5. *Please indicate how important it is to you that a ground coffee have each of the following characteristics.* (CHECK *ONE* BOX FOR *EACH* CHARACTERISTIC)

	Not At All Important								Extremely Important	
Rich taste	01☐	02☐	03☐	04☐	05☐	06☐	07☐	08☐	09☐	10☐
Always fresh	01☐	02☐	03☐	04☐	05☐	06☐	07☐	08☐	09☐	10☐
Gets the day off to a good start	01☐	02☐	03☐	04☐	05☐	06☐	07☐	08☐	09☐	10☐
Full-bodied taste	01☐	02☐	03☐	04☐	05☐	06☐	07☐	08☐	09☐	10☐
Rich aroma in the cup	01☐	02☐	03☐	04☐	05☐	06☐	07☐	08☐	09☐	10☐

	Not At All Important								Extremely Important	
Good value for the money	01☐	02☐	03☐	04☐	05☐	06☐	07☐	08☐	09☐	10☐
The best coffee to drink in the morning	01☐	02☐	03☐	04☐	05☐	06☐	07☐	08☐	09☐	10☐
Rich aroma in the can/bag	01☐	02☐	03☐	04☐	05☐	06☐	07☐	08☐	09☐	10☐
Smooth taste	01☐	02☐	03☐	04☐	05☐	06☐	07☐	08☐	09☐	10☐
Highest quality coffee	01☐	02☐	03☐	04☐	05☐	06☐	07☐	08☐	09☐	10☐

	Not At All Important								Extremely Important	
Premium brand	01☐	02☐	03☐	04☐	05☐	06☐	07☐	08☐	09☐	10☐
Not bitter	01☐	02☐	03☐	04☐	05☐	06☐	07☐	08☐	09☐	10☐
The coffee that brightens my day the most	01☐	02☐	03☐	04☐	05☐	06☐	07☐	08☐	09☐	10☐
Costs more than the other brands	01☐	02☐	03☐	04☐	05☐	06☐	07☐	08☐	09☐	10☐
Strong taste	01☐	02☐	03☐	04☐	05☐	06☐	07☐	08☐	09☐	10☐

	Not At All Important								Extremely Important	
Has no aftertaste	01☐	02☐	03☐	04☐	05☐	06☐	07☐	08☐	09☐	10☐
Economy brand	01☐	02☐	03☐	04☐	05☐	06☐	07☐	08☐	09☐	10☐
Rich aroma while brewing	01☐	02☐	03☐	04☐	05☐	06☐	07☐	08☐	09☐	10☐
The best ground coffee available	01☐	02☐	03☐	04☐	05☐	06☐	07☐	08☐	09☐	10☐
Enjoy drinking with a meal	01☐	02☐	03☐	04☐	05☐	06☐	07☐	08☐	09☐	10☐
Costs less than other brands	01☐	02☐	03☐	04☐	05☐	06☐	07☐	08☐	09☐	10☐

6. *On a scale of 0 to 10 with "0" meaning does not describe at all and "10" meaning describes completely, please indicate how well the following statements describe each of the coffee brands listed below. Rate each brand, whether you have used the brand or not. Please write in the number which indicates your answer on the lines provided.*

FIGURE **8.3**   *Continued*

	Folgers	Hills Brothers	Maxwell House Regular	Maxwell House Master Blend	Yuban
Rich taste	____	____	____	____	____
Always fresh	____	____	____	____	____
Gets the day off to a good start	____	____	____	____	____
Full-bodied taste	____	____	____	____	____
Rich aroma in the cup	____	____	____	____	____

	Folgers	Hills Brothers	Maxwell House Regular	Maxwell House Master Blend	Yuban
Good value for the money	____	____	____	____	____
The best coffee to drink in the morning ..	____	____	____	____	____
Rich aroma in the can/bag	____	____	____	____	____
Smooth taste	____	____	____	____	____
Highest quality coffee	____	____	____	____	____

	Folgers	Hills Brothers	Maxwell House Regular	Maxwell House Master Blend	Yuban
Premium brand	____	____	____	____	____
Not bitter	____	____	____	____	____
The coffee that brightens my day the most	____	____	____	____	____
Costs more than the other brands	____	____	____	____	____
Strong taste	____	____	____	____	____

	Folgers	Hills Brothers	Maxwell House Regular	Maxwell House Master Blend	Yuban
Has no aftertaste	____	____	____	____	____
Economy brand	____	____	____	____	____
Rich aroma while brewing	____	____	____	____	____
The best ground coffee available	____	____	____	____	____
Enjoy drinking with a meal	____	____	____	____	____
Costs less than other brands	____	____	____	____	____

7. *Please indicate your sex and age.*

      1□ Male

      2□ Female   Age:_____

will largely control the decisions regarding individual question content. But the researcher can and should ask some additional questions.[3]

Is the Question Necessary?   Suppose that an issue is important. The researcher then needs to ask whether the point has been adequately covered by other questions. If not, a new question is in order. The question should be framed to secure an answer with the required detail but not with more detail than needed. Very often in marketing, for example, we employ the concept of stage in the life cycle to explore family consumption behavior. Stage in the life cycle is a composite variable in which the various stages are defined in terms of marital status, presence of children, and the ages of the children. The presence of children is important because it indicates a dependency relationship, particularly if the youngest child is under 6, representing one type of responsibility, or is over 6 but under 17, representing another type of responsibility for the parents. In a study using stage in the life cycle as a variable, there is no need to ask the age of each child. Rather, all that is needed is one question aimed at securing the age of the youngest child if there are any children. Once again the role of the hypotheses and dummy tables is obvious when designing the questionnaire.

Are Several Questions Needed Instead of One?   There will often be situations in which several questions are needed instead of one. Consider the question, "Why do you use Crest?" One respondent may reply, "To reduce cavities," while another may reply, "Because our dentist recommended it." Obviously two different frames of reference are being employed to answer this question. The first respondent is replying in terms of why he is using it now, whereas the second is replying in terms of how she started using it. It would be better to break this one question down into separate questions that reflect the possible frames of reference that could be used; for example:

❑ *How did you first happen to use Crest?*

❑ *What is your primary reason for using it?*

Do Respondents Have the Necessary Information?   The researcher should carefully examine each issue to ascertain whether the typical respondent can be expected to have the information sought. Respondents will give answers. Whether the answers mean anything is another matter, however. In one public opinion survey, the following question was asked:[4]

Which of the following statements most closely coincides with your opinion of the Metallic Metals Act?

❑ It would be a good move on the part of the United States.

❑ It would be a good thing, but should be left to the individual states.

---

[3]These questions were suggested by Kornhauser and Sheatsley, "Questionnaire Construction." For a systematic treatment of questionnaire construction, see the classic work by Stanley L. Payne, *The Art of Asking Questions* (Princeton, N.J.: Princeton University Press, 1951). Other good general sources are Seymour Sudman and Norman M. Bradburn, *Asking Questions: A Practical Guide to Questionnaire Design* (San Francisco: Jossey-Bass, 1982); and Jean M. Converse and Stanley Presser, *Survey Questions: Handcrafting the Standardized Questionnaire* (Beverly Hills, Calif.: Sage Publications, 1986).

[4]Sam Gill, "How Do You Stand on Sin?" *Tide,* 21 (March 14, 1947), p. 72.

❏ It is all right for foreign countries, but should not be required here.

❏ It is of no value at all.

❏ No opinion.

The proportion of respondents checking each alternative was, respectively, 21.4 percent, 58.6 percent, 15.7 percent, 4.3 percent, and 0.3 percent. The second alternative captures the prevailing sentiment. Right? Wrong! There was no Metallic Metals Act, and the point of the example is that *most questions will get answers, but the real concern is whether the answers mean anything.*[5] For the answers to mean anything, the questions need to mean something to the respondent. This means that, first, the respondent needs to be informed with respect to the issue addressed by the question, and, second, the respondent must remember the information.

Consider the question, "How much does your family spend on groceries in a typical week?" Unless the respondent does the grocery shopping or the family operates with a fairly strict budget, he or she is unlikely to know. In a situation like this, it might be helpful to ask "filter questions" before this question to determine if the individual is indeed likely to have this information. An example filter question might be, "Who does the grocery shopping in your family?" It is not unusual, for example, to use filter questions of the sort, "Do you have an opinion on . . . ?" before asking about the specific issue in question in opinion surveys. The empirical evidence indicates that providing a filter like this will typically increase the proportion responding "no opinion" by 20 to 25 percentage points.[6]

Not only should the individual have the information sought, but he or she should remember it. Our ability to remember various events is influenced by the event itself and its importance, the length of time since the event, and the presence or absence of stimuli that assist in recalling it. Important events are more easily remembered than unimportant

---

[5]In a subsequent replication of the study on the Metallic Metals Act almost 40 years later, 64 percent of those interviewed had a definite opinion on the nonexistent act. See Daniel T. Seymour, "Numbers Don't Lie — Do They?" *Business Horizons,* 27 (November/December 1984), pp. 36–37. There are a number of other examples in the literature that report findings of people having opinions about totally fictional issues like the Metallic Metals Act. See, for example, George F. Bishop, Robert W. Oldendick, Alfred J. Tuchfarber, and S. E. Bennett, "Pseudo-Opinions on Public Affairs," *Public Opinion Quarterly,* 44 (Summer 1980), pp. 198–209; Herbert Schuman and Stanley Presser, "Public Opinion and Public Ignorance: The Fine Line Between Attitudes and Nonattitudes," *American Journal of Sociology,* 85 (March 1980), pp. 1214–1225; Del I. Hawkins and Kenneth A. Coney, "Uninformed Response Error in Survey Research," *Journal of Marketing Research,* 18 (August 1981), pp. 370–374; Kenneth C. Schneider, "Uninformed Response Rates in Survey Research: New Evidence," *Journal of Business Research,* 13 (August 1985), pp. 153–162; and George F. Bishop, Alfred J. Tuchfarber, and Robert W. Oldendick, "Opinions on Fictitious Issues: The Pressure to Answer Survey Questions," *Public Opinion Quarterly,* 50 (Summer 1986), pp. 240–250. The phenomenon is not unique to opinions. It also applies when measuring brand awareness, where it has been observed that the more plausible sounding a brand name, the more likely consumers are to claim they are aware of it even though it does not exist. See " 'Spurious Awareness' Alters Brand Tests," *The Wall Street Journal* (September 13, 1984), p. 29. See also Eric R. A. N. Smith and Peverill Squire, "The Effects of Prestige Names in Question Wording," *Public Opinion Quarterly,* 54 (Spring 1990), pp. 97–116.

[6]Herbert Schuman and Stanley Presser, "The Assessment of 'No Opinions in Attitude Surveys,'" in Karl F. Schnessler, ed., *Sociological Methodology, 1979* (San Francisco: Jossey-Bass, 1979), pp. 241–275. See also George F. Bishop, Robert W. Oldendick, and Alfred J. Tuchfarber, "Effects on Filter Questions in Public Opinion Surveys," *Public Opinion Quarterly,* 47 (Winter 1983), pp. 528–546; Otis Dudley Duncan and Magnus Stenbeck, "No Opinion or Not Sure?" *Public Opinion Quarterly,* 52 (Winter 1988), pp. 513–525.

events. Although many older adults might be able to remember who shot President John F. Kennedy, the year in which the assassination occurred, or what happened to the assassin, or might be able to recall the first car they ever owned, many of them will be unable to recall the amount of television or the particular shows they watched last Wednesday evening, or the first brand of mouthwash they ever used, when they switched to their current brand, or why they switched. The switching and use information might be very important to a *brand manager for mouthwashes,* but it is unimportant to most individuals, a condition we have to continually keep in mind when designing questionnaires. We need to put ourselves in the shoes of the respondent, not those of the product manager, when deciding whether the information is important enough for the individual to remember it.

We also need to recognize that an individual's ability to remember an event is influenced by how long ago it happened. While we might recall the television programs we watched last evening, we might have much greater difficulty remembering those we watched last week on the same evening and might find it all but impossible to recall our viewing pattern of a month ago. The moral of this is that if the event could be considered relatively unimportant to most individuals, we should ask about very recent occurrences of it.[7] For more important events, there are two effects operating in opposite directions that affect a respondent's ability to provide accurate answers about things that happened in some specified time period (for example, how many times the person has seen a doctor in the last six months); these are telescoping error and recall loss. **Telescoping error** refers to the fact that most people remember an event as having occurred more recently than in fact is the case. **Recall loss** means that they forget an event happened at all. The extent of the two sources of error on the accuracy of the reported information depends on the length of the reference period. For long periods, the telescoping effect is smaller while the recall loss effect is larger. For short periods, the reverse is true. "Thus, for short reference periods, the telescoping error may outweigh the recall loss, while for long periods the reverse will apply; in between there will be a length of reference periods at which the two effects counterbalance each other."[8] Unfortunately, there is no single reference period that can be used to frame questions for all events, because what is optimal depends on the importance of the event to those involved.

A third factor that affects our ability to remember is the stimulus we are given. As we saw in the last chapter, there is a definite increase in retention when a respondent's

---

[7]Bruce Buchanan and Donald G. Morrison, "Sampling Properties of Rate Questions with Implications for Survey Research," *Marketing Science,* 6 (Summer 1987), pp. 286–298. See also Adriana R. Silberstein, "Recall Effects in the U.S. Consumer Expenditure Interview Survey," *Journal of Official Statistics,* 5 (No. 2, 1989), pp. 125–142; Scot Burton and Edward Blair, "Task Conditions, Response Formulation Processes, and Response Accuracy for Behavioral Frequency Questions in Surveys," *Public Opinion Quarterly,* 54 (Spring 1991), pp. 50–79.

[8]Graham Kalton and Howard Schuman, "The Effect of the Question on Survey Responses: A Review," *Journal of the Royal Statistical Society, Series A,* 145 (Part 1, 1982), pp. 44–45. See also William A. Cook, "Telescoping and Memory's Other Tricks," *Journal of Advertising Research,* 27 (February/March 1987), pp. RC5–RC8; Norman M. Bradburn, Lance J. Rip, and Steven K. Shevell, "Answering Autobiographical Questions: The Impact of Memory and Inference on Surveys," *Science,* 236 (April 10, 1987), pp. 157–161; McKee J. McClendon, "Acquiescence and Recency Response Order Effects in Interview Surveys," *Sociological Methodology and Research,* 20 (August 1991), pp. 60–103.

memory is jogged using a recognition measure rather than an aided recall measure, and the aided recall measure, in turn, produces more "remembering" than an unaided recall measure.

Will Respondents Give the Information?   Even though respondents have the information, there is always a question of whether they will share it. Eastern Europeans are wonderful in this regard.

> . . . unlike blasé Western consumers, people in Eastern Europe are more than willing to answer questions. After years of directives from the top, people are flattered to be asked their opinions, even if they're just being asked about the taste of a toothpaste or the feel of a shaving cream. Gallup's Mr. Manchin [a regional vice-president] recounts how an old lady in Hungary thanked the interviewer at the end of an hour-long session. "It was such a wonderful experience to have a chance to talk to you for so long," she said. "How much do I pay you?"[9]

Researchers in many other parts of the world are not as fortunate and sometimes encounter situations in which respondents have the necessary information but they will not give it. Their willingness, in turn, seems to be a function of the amount of work involved in producing an answer, their ability to articulate an answer, and the sensitivity of the issue.

Even though a purchasing agent may be able to determine to the penny how much the company spent on cleaning compound last year or the relative amount spent on each brand bought, the agent is unlikely to take the time to look up these data to reply to an unsolicited questionnaire. Questionnaire developers need to be constantly mindful of the amount of effort it might take respondents to give the information sought. When the effort is excessive, they may have to settle for approximate answers, or they may be better off omitting the issue completely, since these types of questions tend to irritate respondents and damage their cooperation with the rest of the survey.

When respondents are unable to articulate their answers on an issue, they are likely to ignore it and also refuse to cooperate with the other parts of the survey. Such issues should be avoided, or else the researcher should use a good deal of creative energy designing a mechanism that allows respondents to articulate their views. Although respondents might not be able to express their preferences in car styling, for example, they should be able to indicate the style they like best when shown pictures of different body styles. General Motors used this picture scheme to determine preferences for grille designs when they found that respondents could not articulate their likes and dislikes. Similarly, J. C. Penney used pictures of its displays of women's clothing along with pictures of the displays of four of its competitors to determine its positioning in the market.[10]

---

[9]Lee Valeriano Lourdes, "Marketing: Western Firms Poll Eastern Europeans to Discern Tastes of Nascent Consumers," *The Wall Street Journal* (April 27, 1992), p. B1.

[10]Harper W. Boyd, Jr., Ralph Westfall, and Stanley F. Staasch, *Marketing Research: Text and Cases,* 6th ed. (Homewood, Ill.: Richard D. Irwin, 1985), p. 272; Gail Tom, Michelle Dragics, and Christi Holderegger, "Using Visual Presentation to Assess Store Positioning: A Case Study of J. C. Penney," *Marketing Research: A Magazine of Management & Applications,* 3 (September 1991), pp. 48–52.

When an issue is embarrassing or otherwise threatening to respondents, they are likely to refuse to cooperate. Such issues should be avoided whenever possible. If that is impossible because the issue is essential to the study, the researcher needs to pay close attention to how the issue is addressed, particularly with respect to question location and question phrasing.

In general, it is better to address sensitive issues later rather than earlier in the survey.[11] Most surveys will produce some initial mistrust in respondents. One has to overcome this skepticism and establish rapport. This is made easier when respondents have the opportunity to warm to the task by answering nonthreatening questions early in the interview, particularly questions that establish the legitimacy of the project.

When sensitive questions must be asked, it helps to consider ways to make them less threatening. Some helpful techniques in this regard include the following:[12]

1. Hide the question in a group of other more innocuous questions.

2. State that the behavior or attitude is not unusual before asking the specific questions of the respondent (e.g., "Recent studies show that one of every four households has trouble meeting monthly financial obligations"). This technique, known as the use of counterbiasing statements, makes it easier for the respondent to admit the potentially embarrassing behavior.

3. Phrase the question in terms of others and how they might feel or act (e.g., "Do you think most people cheat on their income tax? Why?"). Respondents might readily reveal their attitudes toward cheating when preparing income tax forms when asked these questions, but they might be very reluctant to do so if they were asked outright if they ever cheat on their taxes and why.

4. State the response in terms of a number of categories that the respondent may simply check. Instead of asking women for their age, for example, one could simply hand them a card with the age categories

    A: 20–29   B: 30–39   C: 40–49   D: 50–59   E: 60+

    and ask them to respond with the appropriate letter.

5. Use the **randomized response model,** which has the respondent answer one of several paired questions. The particular question is selected at random — for example, by having the respondent draw colored balls from an urn. The respondent is instructed to answer Question A if the ball is, say, blue, and Question B if the ball is red. The interviewer is unaware of the question being answered by the respondent, because he or she never sees the color of the ball drawn. Under these condi-

---

[11]Question sequence will be discussed more fully later in the chapter.

[12]For more extensive treatments on how to handle sensitive questions, see Kent H. Marquis, et al., *Response Errors in Sensitive Topic Surveys: Estimates, Effects, and Correction Options* (Santa Monica, Calif.: Rand Corporation, 1981); Thomas W. Mangione, Ralph Hingson, and Jane Barrett, "Collecting Sensitive Data: A Comparison of Three Survey Strategies," *Sociological Methods and Research,* 10 (February 1982), pp. 337– 346; D. A. Hay, "Does the Method Matter on Sensitive Survey Topics?" *Survey Methodology Journal,* 16 (June 1990), pp. 131–136; Linda Mooney and Robert Gramling, "Asking Sensitive Questions and Situational Framing: The Effects of Decomposing Survey Items," *Sociological Quarterly,* 32 (Summer 1991), pp. 289– 300.

tions the respondent is less likely to refuse to answer or to distort the answer he or she provides. A study to investigate the incidence of shoplifting might pair the sensitive question, "Have you ever shoplifted?" with the innocuous question, "Is your birthday in January?" The incidence of shoplifting can still be estimated by using an appropriate statistical model, because the percentage of respondents answering each question is controlled by the proportion of red and blue balls in the urn. Suppose, for example, that there are five red and five blue balls in the urn; thus the probability that the respondent will answer Question A, "Have you ever shoplifted?" is one-half. Further, the proportion of people whose birthdays fall in January is also known to be .05 from census data. Suppose that the proportion who answered "yes" to either Question A or B is .20. Using the standard laws of probability, we could then estimate that the proportion of the people in the sample who were responding "yes" to the sensitive question from the formula

$$\lambda = p\pi_S + (1 - p)\pi_A,$$

where

λ = the total proportion of "yes" responses to both questions,
p = the probability that the sensitive question is selected,
$1 - p$ = the probability that the innocuous question is selected,
π_S = the proportion of "yes" responses to the sensitive question, and
π_A = the proportion of "yes" responses to the innocuous question.[13]

Substituting the appropriate quantities indicates that

$$.20 = .50\pi_S + .50(.05)$$
$$\text{and } \pi_S = .35,$$

or that 35 percent of the respondents had shoplifted. Note, though, that the researcher cannot use the randomized response technique to determine specifically

---

[13]James E. Reinmuth and Michael D. Geurts, "The Collection of Sensitive Information Using a Two-Stage Randomized Response Model," *Journal of Marketing Research,* 12 (November 1975), pp. 402–407. For an elementary overview of the randomized response model, see Cathy Campbell and Brian L. Joiner, "How to Get the Answer Without Being Sure You've Asked the Question," *American Statistician,* 26 (December 1973), pp. 229–231. For reviews of its use, see D. G. Horvitz, B. G. Greenberg, and J. R. Abernathy, "Randomized Response: A Data Gathering Device for Sensitive Questions," *International Statistical Review* (August 1976), pp. 181–195; and Paul E. Tracy and James Alan Fox, "The Validity of Randomized Response for Sensitive Measurements," *American Sociological Review,* 46 (April 1981), pp. 187–200. For discussion of randomization devices and methodologies for self-administered and telephone interview applications of the randomized response method, see Donald E. Stem, Jr., and R. Kirk Steinhorst, "Telephone Interview and Mail Questionnaire Applications of the Randomized Response Model," *Journal of the American Statistical Association,* 79 (September 1984), pp. 555–564; Jamshid C. Hosseini and Robert L. Armacost, "Randomized Responses: A Better Way to Obtain Sensitive Information," *Business Horizons,* 33 (May/June 1990), pp. 82–86. For general treatments, see James Alan Fox and Paul E. Tracy, *Randomizing Response: A Method for Sensitive Surveys* (Beverly Hills, Calif.: Sage Publications, 1986); Arijit Chaudhuri and Rahul Mukerjee, *Randomized Response: Theory and Techniques* (New York: Marcel Dekker, Inc., 1987); U. N. Umesh and Robert A. Peterson, "A Critical Evaluation of the Randomized Response Model: Applications, Validations, and Research Agenda," *Sociological Methods and Research,* 20 (August 1991), pp. 104–138.

which respondents have shoplifted. This would preclude any opportunity to determine, for example, if shoplifting behavior was associated with any particular demographic characteristics.

ETHICAL DILEMMA 8.2

A financial institution has developed a new type of savings bond. The marketing director of this institution has requested that a local research supply company design a questionnaire that will help quantify target consumers' interest in this new bond. However, the marketing director is concerned about the possibility that competitors will hear about the new product concept because of the survey. He requests that the questionnaire be written in such a way that the true purpose of the study is masked.

To mask the actual purpose of the study, the questionnaire primarily asks respondents for details of their holiday plans and budgets. Because respondents are only asked questions about their finances after multiple vacation-related questions, it is hoped that respondents will assume the information is for a travel company. Moreover, the marketing director of the financial institution asks that interviewers tell respondents that the information is being gathered for a travel-related company.

- Discuss the implications of deceiving respondents on a questionnaire in this way.
- If the interviewers had not been told to explicitly tell respondents that the information was for a travel-related corporation, would the deception be acceptable?
- Are there ways of acquiring this type of information without resorting to deception while still protecting the institution's new product idea?
- Discuss the validity issues associated with respondents knowing the purpose of the survey as they are completing it.

Form of Response

Once the content of the individual questions is determined, the researcher needs to decide on the particular form of the response. Will the question be open-ended or fixed-alternative? If fixed-alternative, will it be a multichotomy, a dichotomy, or perhaps a scale?

Open-Ended Questions   Respondents are free to reply to **open-ended questions** in their own words rather than being limited to choosing from a set of alternatives. The following are examples:

*How old are you?*_____

*Do you think laws limiting the amount of interest businesses can charge consumers are needed?*_____

*Who sponsors the Monday night football games?*_____

*Do you intend to purchase an automobile this year?*_____

*Why did you purchase a Zenith brand color TV?*_____

*Do you own a VCR?*_____

*How many long distance phone calls do you make in a typical week?*_____

These questions span the gamut of the types of primary data that could be collected from demographic characteristics through attitudes, intentions, and behavior. The open-ended question is indeed a versatile device.

Open-ended questions are often used to begin a questionnaire. The general feeling is that it is best to proceed from the general to the specific in constructing questionnaires. So an opening question like, "When you think of television sets, which brands come to mind?" gives some insight into the respondent's frame of reference and could be most helpful in interpreting the individual's replies to later questions. The open-ended question is also often used to probe for additional information. The probes "Why? Why do you feel that way? Please explain" are often used to seek elaboration of a respondent's reply.

Multichotomous Questions   The **multichotomous question** is a fixed-alternative question; respondents are asked to choose the alternative that most closely corresponds to their position on the subject. Table 8.1, for example, presents some of the open-ended questions posed previously as multichotomous questions. Respondents would be instructed to check the box or boxes that apply.

The examples in Table 8.1 illustrate some of the difficulties encountered in using multiple-choice questions. None of the alternatives in the interest-ceiling legislation question, for example, may correctly capture the respondent's true feeling on the issue. The individual's opinion may be more complex, for one thing. He or she may believe that interest-ceiling legislation is needed, assuming that a number of provisos or contingent possibilities can be satisfied (for example, that business firms will not reduce the amount of credit available to customers nor shorten the length of the repayment period). If these conditions cannot be satisfied, the respondent may feel just the opposite. The multiple-choice question does not permit individuals to elaborate on their true position but requires them to condense their complex attitude into a single statement. Of course, a well-designed series of multiple-choice questions could allow for such elaborations. An exhaustive coverage of the potential qualifiers would also substantially increase the length of the questionnaire.

The interest-ceiling legislation question also illustrates a general problem in question design: Should respondents be provided with a "don't know" or "no opinion" option? There is no question that if a respondent truly does not know an answer or has no opinion on an issue that he or she should be allowed to state that when responding. However, the issue is whether that option should be *explicitly* provided the respondent in the form of a "don't know" or "no opinion" category by asking a filter question like "Do you have an opinion on . . . ?" The arguments regarding the provision of a neutral point or category revolve around data accuracy versus respondent cooperation. Those suggesting that a neutral point, or "no opinion," answer should not be provided argue that most respondents are not likely to be exactly neutral on an issue. Instead of providing them an easy way out, it is much better to have them think about the issue so

TABLE **8.1**   **Examples of Multichotomous Questions**

Age:	Television Purchase:

How old are you?
- [ ] Less than 20
- [ ] 20–29
- [ ] 30–39
- [ ] 40–49
- [ ] 50–59
- [ ] 60 or over

Why did you purchase a Zenith brand color TV?
- [ ] Price was lower than other alternatives
- [ ] Feel it represents the highest quality
- [ ] Availability of local service
- [ ] Availability of a service contract
- [ ] Picture is better
- [ ] Warranty was better
- [ ] Other

Interest-Ceiling Legislation:	Telephone-Use Behavior:

Do you think laws limiting the amount of interest businesses can charge consumers are needed?
- [ ] Definitely needed
- [ ] Probably needed
- [ ] Probably not needed
- [ ] Definitely not needed
- [ ] No opinion

How many long-distance telephone calls do you make in a typical week?
- [ ] Less than 5
- [ ] 5–10
- [ ] More than 10

that they can frame their preference, however slight it may be; that is certainly better than allowing the researcher to infer the majority opinion using only the responses from those taking a stand on the issue. Those who argue for including a neutral or "no opinion" category among the responses are inclined to suggest that forcing a respondent to make a choice when his or her preference is fuzzy or non-existent simply introduces response error into the results. Further, it makes it harder for respondents to answer and may turn them off to the whole survey. The jury is still out about which form better captures respondents' true position on an issue, although there is no question that the two alternatives can produce widely differing proportions of the number of respondents holding a neutral view, potentially in the range of 10 to 50 percent.[14] For example, Research Realities 8.2 reports the results of one study that used both four-point and five-point purchase intention scales. The scales were the same except for the provision of the neutral category in the five-point scale. The general conclusion emerging is that if one used only the extreme points (i.e., definitely will buy/definitely will not buy) for

---

[14]Kalton and Schuman, "The Effect of the Question on Survey Responses: A Review," pp. 51–52. See also Duncan and Stenbeck, "No Opinion or Not Sure?" pp. 513–525; Gail S. Poe, *et al.,* "Don't Know Box in Factual Questions in a Mail Questionnaire: Effects on Level and Quality of Response," *Public Opinion Quarterly,* 52 (Summer 1988), pp. 212–222.

Research Realities 8.2

A Comparison of the Use of Four-Point versus Five-Point Scales to Measure Purchase Intent

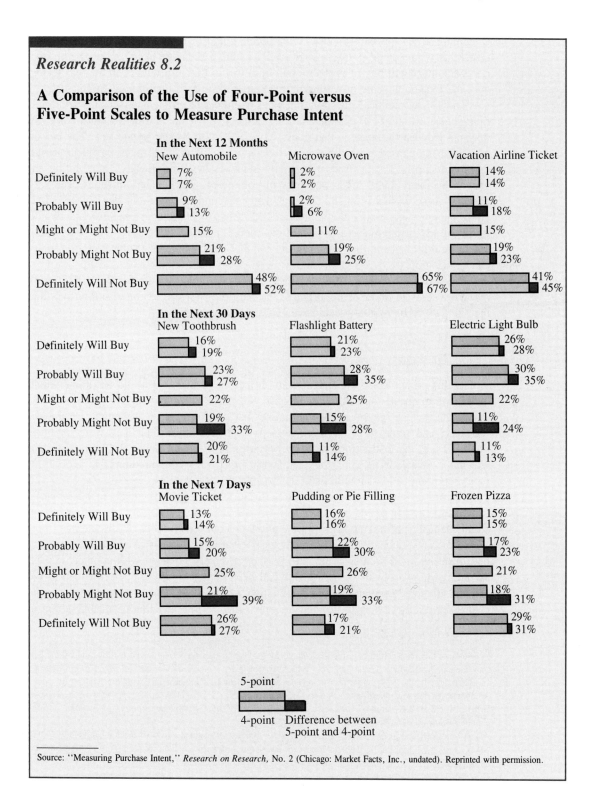

In the Next 12 Months

	New Automobile	Microwave Oven	Vacation Airline Ticket
Definitely Will Buy	7% / 7%	2% / 2%	14% / 14%
Probably Will Buy	9% / 13%	2% / 6%	11% / 18%
Might or Might Not Buy	15%	11%	15%
Probably Might Not Buy	21% / 28%	19% / 25%	19% / 23%
Definitely Will Not Buy	48% / 52%	65% / 67%	41% / 45%

In the Next 30 Days

	New Toothbrush	Flashlight Battery	Electric Light Bulb
Definitely Will Buy	16% / 19%	21% / 23%	26% / 28%
Probably Will Buy	23% / 27%	28% / 35%	30% / 35%
Might or Might Not Buy	22%	25%	22%
Probably Might Not Buy	19% / 33%	15% / 28%	11% / 24%
Definitely Will Not Buy	20% / 21%	11% / 14%	11% / 13%

In the Next 7 Days

	Movie Ticket	Pudding or Pie Filling	Frozen Pizza
Definitely Will Buy	13% / 14%	16% / 16%	15% / 15%
Probably Will Buy	15% / 20%	22% / 30%	17% / 23%
Might or Might Not Buy	25%	26%	21%
Probably Might Not Buy	21% / 39%	19% / 33%	18% / 31%
Definitely Will Not Buy	26% / 27%	17% / 21%	29% / 31%

5-point

4-point   Difference between 5-point and 4-point

Source: ''Measuring Purchase Intent,'' *Research on Research*, No. 2 (Chicago: Market Facts, Inc., undated). Reprinted with permission.

evaluating a new product or idea, *either* scale could be used. On the other hand, the researcher who wanted to use two categories as the percentage likely to buy the product (i.e., definitely will buy or probably will buy) would find a difference in the two scales, with the four-point scale providing more positive responses than the five-point scale.[15]

The TV-set purchase question illustrates a number of problems associated with multiple-choice questions. First, the list of reasons cited for purchasing a Zenith color TV may not exhaust the reasons that could have been used by the respondent. The person may have purchased a Zenith out of loyalty to a friend who owns the local Zenith distributorship or because she or he really practices the "buy locally" admonition advanced by many small town chambers of commerce. The "other" response category attempts to solve this problem. A great many respondents checking the "other" category, though, will render the study useless. Thus, the burden is on the researcher to make the list of alternatives in a multiple-choice question exhaustive. This may entail extensive prior research into the phenomenon that is to serve as the subject of a multiple-choice question.

Unless the respondent is instructed to check all alternatives that apply, or is to rank the alternatives in order of importance, the multiple-choice question also demands that the alternatives be mutually exclusive. The income categories

❑ $10,000–$20,000

❑ $20,000–$30,000

violate this principle. A respondent with an income of $20,000 would not know which alternative to check. A legitimate response with respect to the color TV purchase question might include several of the alternatives listed. The respondent thought the picture, warranty, and price were all more attractive on the Zenith than they were on other makes. Thus, the instructions would necessarily have to be "Check the most important reason," "Check all those reasons that apply," or "Rank all the reasons that apply from most important to least important."

A third difficulty with the TV purchase question is its great number of alternative responses. The list should be exhaustive, yet the alternative statements an individual can simultaneously process appears to be limited. In one early study, the researchers presented each respondent with a card with six alternative statements. After each respondent had made his or her choice, the card was immediately replaced with another. On the second card, two of the six statements had been changed, and one statement from the original list was omitted. Yet only one-half of the respondents "could identify the changes and a mere handful located the omission."[16] The meaning of all this is that in

---

[15]"Measuring Purchase Intent," *Research on Research, no. 2* (Chicago: Market Facts, Inc., undated). See also Gregory J. Spagna, "Questionnaires: Which Approach Do You Use?" *Journal of Advertising Research,* 24 (February/March 1984), pp. 67–70; and George F. Bishop, "Experiments with the Middle Response Alternative in Survey Questions," *Public Opinion Quarterly,* 51 (Summer 1987), pp. 220–232; Raphael Gillet, "The Top-Box Paradox," *Marketing Research: A Magazine of Management and Applications,* 3 (September 1991), pp. 37–39.

[16]Hadley Cantril and Edreta Fried, *Gauging Public Opinion* (Princeton, N.J.: Princeton University Press, 1944), chap. 1, as reported in Payne, *The Art of Asking Questions,* p. 93. For a discussion of people's limited information-processing abilities, see Jacob Jacoby, "Perspectives on Information Overload," *Journal of Consumer Research,* 10 (March 1984), pp. 432–435.

designing multiple-choice questions, the researcher should remain cognizant of human beings' limited data-processing capabilities. Perhaps a series of questions is more appropriate than one question. If there are a great many alternatives to a single question, they should be shown to respondents using cards and not simply read to them.

The fourth weakness of the TV purchase question is that it is susceptible to a potential order bias. The responses are likely to be affected by the order in which the alternatives are presented. Research Realities 8.3, for example, shows how the distribution of responses to the same behaviors was affected by the order in which the alternatives were listed on two versions of a mailed questionnaire. That the three questions produced statistically significant differences in the distributions of replies is especially noteworthy because order bias is least likely to occur in mail questionnaires because respondents can see all the response categories. In point of fact, response order bias is typically much greater in telephone surveys or interviews in which the structured responses are read to the respondents. The recommended procedure for combating this order bias is to prepare several forms of the questionnaire, or several cards, if cards are used to list the alternatives. The order in which the alternatives are listed is then altered from form to form. If each alternative appears once at the extremes of the list, once in the middle, and once somewhere in between, the researcher can feel reasonably comfortable that the possible effects of position bias have been neutralized.

The long-distance telephone call example in Table 8.1 illustrates another problem with multiple-choice questions when they are used to get at the frequency of various behaviors. The range of the categories used in the question seems to cue respondents about how they should reply. That is, the response scale categories themselves affect subjects' reports of the frequency with which they engage in the behavior. A scale with these three categories,

❑ Less than 10

❑ 10–20

❑ More than 20,

would likely produce a different picture of the frequency with which these same respondents make long-distance telephone calls than the one shown in Table 8.1. It seems that respondents make judgments about the researcher's knowledge or expectations from the categories and then respond accordingly. Specifically, they seem reluctant to report behaviors that are unusual in the context of the response scale — namely, those that constitute the extreme categories.[17] A general strategy for combating this tendency is to use open-ended answer formats when obtaining data on behavioral frequencies.

Dichotomous Questions   The **dichotomous question** is also a fixed-alternative question but one in which there are only two alternatives listed; for example:

---

[17]Norbert Schwarz, *et al.,* "Response Scales: Effect of Category Range on Reported Behavior and Comparative Judgments," *Public Opinion Quarterly,* 49 (Fall 1985), pp. 388–395; Norbert Schwarz, *et al.,* "The Range of Response Alternatives May Determine the Meaning of the Question: Further Evidence on Information Functions of Response Alternatives," *Social Cognition,* 6 (No. 2, 1988), pp. 107–117; Eric A. Greenleaf, "Measuring Extreme Response Style," *Public Opinion Quarterly,* 56 (Fall 1992), pp. 328–351.

Research Realities 8.3

How the Order in Which the Alternatives Are Listed Affects the Distribution of Replies

[Compared to a year ago] the amount of time spent watching television by my household is . . .

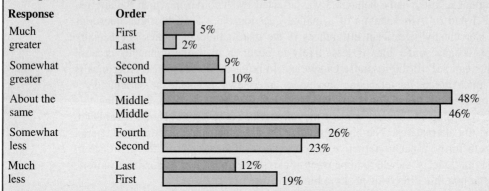

Response	Order	
Much greater	First	5%
	Last	2%
Somewhat greater	Second	9%
	Fourth	10%
About the same	Middle	48%
	Middle	46%
Somewhat less	Fourth	26%
	Second	23%
Much less	Last	12%
	First	19%

[Compared to a year ago] my household eats out at restaurants . . .

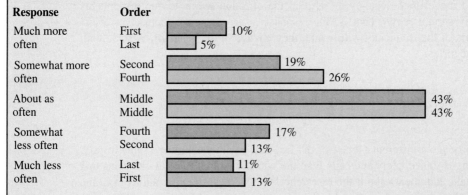

Response	Order	
Much more often	First	10%
	Last	5%
Somewhat more often	Second	19%
	Fourth	26%
About as often	Middle	43%
	Middle	43%
Somewhat less often	Fourth	17%
	Second	13%
Much less often	Last	11%
	First	13%

Most home repair or improvement projects completed in my home during the past years have been completed by . . . [Base: Those completing a project.]

Response	Order	
Hiring tradesmen	First	15%
	Last	11%
Tradesmen and household members	Middle	33%
	Middle	31%
Household members	Last	52%
	First	58%

Source: "An Examination of Order Bias," *Research on Research*, No. 1 (Chicago: Market Facts, Inc., undated). Reprinted by permission.

Do you think laws limiting the amount of interest businesses can charge consumers are needed?

❏ Yes

❏ No

Do you intend to purchase an automobile this year?

❏ Yes

❏ No

We have already seen how the first of these questions could also be handled as a multiple-choice question. The second could also be given a multichotomous structure. Instead of simply presenting the yes-no alternatives, the list could be framed as "Definitely intend to buy," "Probably will buy," "Probably will not buy," "Definitely intend not to buy," and "Undecided." Dichotomous questions can often be framed as multichotomous questions, and vice versa. (The two possess similar advantages and disadvantages, which were reviewed earlier when discussing structured questions. They will not be repeated here.) The dichotomous question offers the ultimate in ease of coding and tabulation, and this probably accounts for its being the most commonly used type of question in communication studies.

One special problem with the dichotomous question is that the response can depend on how the question is framed. This is true, of course, of all questions, but with the dichotomous question it represents a special problem. Consider two alternative questions:

Do you think that gasoline will be more expensive or less expensive next year than it is now?

❏ More expensive

❏ Less expensive

Do you think that gasoline will be less expensive or more expensive next year than it is now?

❏ Less expensive

❏ More expensive

Now, the questions appear identical, and certainly we might want to expand each to include categories for "No opinion" and "About the same." The fact remains, though, that the two questions will elicit different responses.[18] The simple switching of the positions of "More expensive" or "Less expensive" can affect the response an individual gives. Which, then, is the correct wording?

One generally accepted procedure for combating this order bias is to employ a split ballot. One phrasing is used on one-half of the questionnaires, and the alternative phrasing is employed on the other one-half of the questionnaires. The averaged percentages from the two forms should then cancel out any biases.

---

[18]Two of the best discussions of this are to be found in Payne, *The Art of Asking Questions,* and Howard Schuman and Stanley Presser, *Questions and Answers in Attitude Surveys* (Orlando: Academic Press, 1981), especially pp. 56–77.

Scales   Another type of fixed-alternative question is the question that employs a scale to capture the response. For instance, when inquiring about VCR use, the following question might be asked:

How often do you tape programs for later viewing with your VCR?

❑ Never

❑ Occasionally

❑ Sometimes

❑ Often

In this form, the question is a multichotomous question. However, the responses also represent a scale of use. The scale nature of the question would be more obvious perhaps if the following form were used to secure the replies:

Never	Occasionally	Sometimes	Often

The advantage of this scheme is that the descriptors could be presented at the top of the page, and types of programs could be listed along the left margin (for example, films, sporting events, network specials, and so on). The respondent would then be instructed to designate the frequency with which the VCR is used to record each type. The instruction would only need to be given once at the beginning, and thus a great deal of information could be secured from the respondent in a short period of time.

Decide on Question Wording

Step 5 in the questionnaire development process involves the phrasing of each question. This is a critical task, because poor phrasing of a question can cause respondents to refuse to answer it (even though they agreed to cooperate in the study) or to answer incorrectly, either on purpose or because of misunderstanding. The first condition, known as **item nonresponse,** can create a great many problems when analyzing the data. The second condition produces measurement error, in that the recorded or obtained score does not equal the respondent's true score on the issue.[19]

Experienced researchers know that the phrasing of a question can directly affect the responses to it. One humorous anecdote in this regard involves two priests, a Dominican and a Jesuit, who are discussing whether it is a sin to smoke and pray at the same time. "After failing to reach a conclusion, each goes off to consult his respective superior. The next week they meet again. The Dominican says, 'Well, what did your superior

---

[19]The notion of measurement error is defined more formally in Appendix 9C. For a review of the literature on the quality of questionnaire data, including item omission, see Robert A. Peterson and Roger A. Kerin, "The Quality of Self-Report Data: Review and Synthesis," in Ben Enis and Kenneth Roering, eds., *Annual Review of Marketing 1981* (Chicago: American Marketing Association, 1981), pp. 5–20; See also Floyd Jackson Fowler, Jr., "How Unclear Terms Affect Survey Data," *Public Opinion Quarterly,* 56 (Summer 1992), pp. 218–231.

say?' The Jesuit responds, 'He said it was all right.' 'That's funny,' the Dominican replied, 'my superior said it was a sin.' Jesuit: 'What did you ask him?' Reply: 'I asked him if it was all right to smoke while praying.' 'Oh,' says the Jesuit, 'I asked my superior if it was all right to pray while smoking.' "[20]

Even though it is recognized, then, that the wording of questions can affect the answers obtained, it is sometimes hard to develop good phrasings of questions, because there are few basic principles researchers can rely on when framing questions. Instead, the literature is replete with rules-of-thumb. While the rules-of-thumb are often easier to state than to practice, researchers need to be aware of the admonitions that surround the wording of questions.

Use Simple Words A "vocabulary problem" confronts most researchers. Because they are more highly educated than the typical questionnaire respondent, researchers are prone to use words familiar to them but not understood by many respondents. This is a difficult problem, because it is not easy to dismiss what one knows and put oneself in the respondent's shoes when trying to assess his or her vocabulary. A significant proportion of the population, for example, does not understand the word *Caucasian,* although most researchers do, and a very serious problem in designing questionnaires to survey Hispanics is in developing an unambiguous ethnic identifier.[21] The researcher needs to be constantly aware that the average person in the United States has a high school, not a college, education and that many people have difficulty in coping with usual tasks, such as making change, reading job notices, or completing a driver's application blank. A basic admonition is to keep the words simple. When there is a choice between more difficult and simpler wording, it is best to choose simplicity. There is always great potential for respondents to misunderstand what they are being asked even when simple words are used. Research Realities 8.4, for example, lists some problem words identified by Payne more than 40 years ago and explains why these words can cause difficulty. Payne identified more than 80 such words, which is one very important reason (and there are many) that those charged with the task of designing questionnaires would be well advised to read Payne's classic book.[22]

Avoid Ambiguous Words and Questions Not only should the words used be simple, but they also should be unambiguous. The same is true for the questions. Consider again the multichotomous question:

How often do you tape programs for later viewing with your VCR?

❑ Never

❑ Occasionally

---

[20]Sudman and Bradburn, *Asking Questions,* p. 1.

[21]Alan E. Bayer, "Construction of a Race Item for Survey Research," *Public Opinion Quarterly,* 36 (Winter 1972–1973), p. 596; Gonzola R. Soruco, "Sampling and Nonsampling Errors in Hispanic Population Telephone Surveys," *Applied Marketing Research,* 29 (Summer 1989), pp. 11–15.

[22]Payne, *The Art of Asking Questions.* For evidence regarding the words marketing research firms use most frequently in questionnaires, see John O'Brien, "How Do Market Researchers Ask Questions?" *Journal of the Market Research Society,* 26 (April 1984), pp. 93–107.

Research Realities 8.4

Some Multi-Meaning Problem Words Researchers Should Use with Caution

about

Among other uses, "about" is sometimes intended to mean somewhere near in the sense that both 48% and 52% are "about" half. It is also used to mean nearly or almost, in the sense that 48% is "about" half while 52% is "over" half. This small difference in interpretation may make a slight difference in the way various respondents answer certain questions.

all

Here is the first mention of a "dead giveaway" word, a term you will see frequently from here on.

Your own experience with true-false tests has probably demonstrated to you that it is safe to count almost every all-inclusive statement as false. That is, you have learned in such tests that it is safe to follow the idea that "all statements containing 'all' are false, including this one." Some people have the same negative reaction to opinion questions which hinge upon all-inclusive or all-exclusive words. They may be generally in agreement with a proposition, but nevertheless hesitate to accept the extreme idea of *all, always, each, every, never, nobody, only, none,* or *sure*.

Would you say that all cats have four legs?

Is the mayor doing all he can for the city?

It is correct, of course, to use an all-inclusive word if it correctly states the alternative. But you will usually find that such a word produces an overstatement. Most people may go along with the idea, accepting it as a form of literary license, but the purists and quibblers may either refuse to give an opinion or may even choose the other side in protest.

always

This is another dead giveaway word.

Do you always observe traffic signs?

Is your boss always friendly?

and

This simple conjunction in some contexts may be taken either as separating two alternatives or as connecting two parts of a single alternative.

Source: Stanley L. Payne, *The Art of Asking Questions.* Copyright 1951, Princeton University Press. © 1979 renewed by Princeton University Press. Excerpts, pp. 158–176, reprinted with permission of Princeton University Press.

Is there much rivalry among the boys who sell soda pop and crackerjack?

Some people will answer in terms of rivalry between two groups — those who sell pop and those who sell crackerjack. Others will take it as rivalry within the single group comprising both pop and crackerjack salesmen.

any

The trouble with this word is a bit difficult to explain. It's something like that optical illusion of the shifting stairsteps, which you sometimes seem to see from underneath and sometimes seem to see from above but which you aren't able to see both ways at the same time. The trouble with "any" is that it may mean "every," "some," or "one only" in the same sentence or question, depending on the way you look at it.

See whether you can get both the "every" and "only one" illusions from this question and notice the difference in meaning that results:

Do you think any word is better than the one we are discussing?

You could think, "Yes, I think just any old word (every word) is better." On the other hand, you might think, "Yes, I believe it would be possible to find a better word."

Another difficulty with "any" is that when used in either the "every" or the "not any" context it becomes as much a dead giveaway word as are "every" and "none."

bad

In itself the word "bad" is not at all bad for question wording. It conveys the meaning desired and is satisfactory as an alternative in a "good or bad" two-way question.

Experience seems to indicate, however, that people are generally less willing to criticize than they are to praise. Since it is difficult to get them to state their negative views, sometimes the critical side needs to be softened. For example, after asking, *What things are good about your job?*, it might seem perfectly natural to ask, *What things are bad about it?* But if we want to lean over backwards to get as many criticisms as we can, we may be wise not to apply the "bad" stigma but to ask, *What things are not so good about it?*

could

No fault is found with the word itself, but we are well advised to remember that it should not be confused with "should" or "might."

ever

This word tends to be a dead giveaway in a very special sense. "Ever" is such a long time and so inclusive that it makes it seem plausible that some unimpressive things may have happened.

Have you ever listened to the Song Plugger radio program?

"Yes — I suppose I must have at some time or other."

go

"Go" is given more space in the index of *The American Thesaurus of Slang* than any other word — a total of about 12½ columns.

When did you last go to town?

If the respondent takes this literally, it is a good question, but the "go to town" phrase has more than a dozen different slang meanings, including a couple that might get your face slapped.

heard

Sometimes these words are used in a very general sense *(Have you heard of . . . ?)* to include learning about not only through hearing but also through reading, seeing, etc. Unfortunately, however, some respondents apparently take such words literally. They don't say that they've heard when they've only seen, for instance. In one study, only half as many people said that they had "heard or read" anything about patents as reported having attended a patents exposition. Evidently, they considered whatever they learned from attendance as separate from hearing or reading.

less

This word is usually used as an alternative to "more," where it may cause a minor problem. The phrase "more or less" has a special meaning all its own in which some respondents do not see an alternative. Thus, they may simply answer "yes, more or less" to a question like:

Compared with a year ago, are you more or less happy in your job?

The easy solution to this problem is to break up the "more or less" expression by introducing an extra word or so to reverse the two:

Compared with a year ago, are you more happy or less happy in your job?

Compared with a year ago, are you less happy or more happy in your job?

like

This word is on the problem list only because it is sometimes used to introduce an example. The problem with bringing an example into a question is that the respondent's attention may be directed toward the particular example and away from the general issue which it is meant only to illustrate. The use of examples may sometimes be necessary, but the possible hazard should always be kept in mind. The choice of an example can affect the answers to the question — in fact, it may materially change the question, as in these two examples:

Do you think that leafy vegetables like spinach should be in the daily diet?

Do you think that leafy vegetables like lettuce should be in the daily diet?

you

The dictionary distinguishes only two or three meanings of "you" — the second person singular and plural and the substitution for the impersonal "one" — "How do you get there?" in place of "How does one get there?" In most questions "you" gives no trouble whatever, it being clear that we are asking the opinion of the second person singular. However, and here is the problem, the word sometimes may have a collective meaning as in a question asked of radio repairmen:

How many radio sets did you repair last month?

This question seemed to work all right until one repairman in a large shop countered with, "Who do you mean, me or the whole shop?"

Much as we might want to, therefore, we can't give "you" an unqualified recommendation. Sometimes "you" needs the emphasis of "you yourself" and sometimes it just isn't the word to use, as in the above situation where the entire shop was meant.

❏ Sometimes

❏ Often

For all practical purposes, the replies to this question would be worthless. The words *occasionally, sometimes,* and *often* are ambiguous. To one respondent, the word *often* might mean "almost every day." To another it might mean "yes, I use it when I have the specific need. This happens about once a week." The words *occasionally* and *sometimes* could also be interpreted differently by different respondents.[23] Thus, while the question would get answers, it would generate little real understanding of the frequency of use of the VCR to tape programs.

A much better strategy would be to provide concrete alternatives for the respondent, rather than the preceding ambiguous options. The alternatives might read, for example:

❏ Never use

❏ Use approximately once a month

❏ Use approximately once a week

❏ Use almost every day

Whether these would be the appropriate categories depends on the purpose of the study. The important thing is that the researcher has provided a consistent frame of reference for each respondent. Respondents are no longer free to superimpose their own definitions on the response categories.

An alternative way to avoid ambiguity in response categories when asking about the frequency of some behavior is to ask about the most recent instance of the phenomenon. The question might be framed in the following way, for example:

Did you tape any programs with your VCR in the last two days?

❏ Yes

❏ No

❏ Can't recall

The proportion responding *yes* would then be used to infer the frequency with which the VCR was used, and the follow-up question among all those responding yes, "For what purpose?" would give insight as to how respondents are using it. Some respondents who normally use their VCR might not have used it the last two days, but the opposite would be true for others. The same would be true with respect to purposes for which it was used. There might be some variation in comparison to what individuals normally do, but the variation should cancel out if a large enough sample of respondents was used. Thus, the aggregate sample should provide a good indication of the proportion of times the VCR is used and the proportion of times it is used to tape various types of programs. The researcher, in effect, relies on the sample to provide insight into the frequency of occurrence of the phenomenon, rather than a specific question that

---

[23]For empirical evidence of what happens with vague quantifiers, see Nora Cate Schaeffer, "Hardly Ever or Constantly? Group Comparisons Using Vague Quantifiers," *Public Opinion Quarterly,* 55 (Fall 1991), pp. 395–423.

may contain ambiguous alternatives. It is important that the sample be large enough in this instance so that the proportions can be estimated with the appropriate degree of confidence.

Avoid Leading Questions   A **leading question** is one framed to give the respondent a clue about how he or she should answer. Consider the question:

Do you feel that limiting taxes by law is an effective way to stop the government from picking your pocket every payday?

❑ Yes

❑ No

❑ Undecided

This was one of three questions in an unsolicited questionnaire that the author received as part of a study sponsored by the National Tax Limitation Committee. The committee intended to make the results of the poll available to members of Congress and to state legislators. Given the implied purpose, it is probably not surprising to see the leading words ''picking your pocket'' being used in this question, or the leading word ''gouge'' being used in another question. What is especially unfortunate is that it is unlikely the questions themselves accompanied the report to Congress. Rather, it is more likely that the report suggested that some high percentage (e.g., 90 percent of those surveyed) favored laws that limited taxes. Conclusion: Congress should pay attention to the wishes of the people and pass such laws.

One sees instances of this phenomenon everyday in the newspaper. While not seeing the questionnaire, the public is treated to a discussion of the results of this or that study concerning how the American people feel on issues. Yet the wording of a question makes a difference. One interesting report in this regard was published during New York City's financial crisis during the 1970s.

Question: What percentage of the American public favors federal aid for New York City? Choose one of the following: a. 69; b. 55; c. 42; d. 15; e. all of the above.

The correct answer is all of the above, because each of these results represented an outcome of a survey taken at the time.

One apparent key to the different responses was whether the aid was described as a ''bailout,'' ''federal funds,'' or ''the federal government guaranteeing loans.''[24]

The correct phrasing of this or almost any question could, of course, be argued. The important point for both researchers and managers to remember is that the phrasing finally chosen will affect the responses secured. If one truly wants an accurate picture of

---

[24]''Why the Polls Get Differing Results on Aid to New York,'' *Capital Times* (November 8, 1975), p. 2. See also Tom Smith, ''That Which We Call Welfare By Any Other Name Would Smell Sweeter: An Analysis of the Impact of Question Wording on Response Patterns,'' *Public Opinion Quarterly,* 51 (Spring 1987), pp. 75–83; Stephen Budiansky, *et al,* ''The Numbers Racket: How Polls and Statistics Lie,'' *U.S. News & World Report* (July 11, 1988), pp. 44–47.

Research Realities 8.5

Some Examples of Leading Questions

When Levi Strauss & Co. asked students which clothes would be most popular this year, 90 percent said Levi's 501 jeans. They were the only jeans on the list.

A survey for Black Flag said: "A roach disk . . . poisons a roach slowly. The dying roach returns to the nest and after it dies is eaten by other roaches. In turn

Source: Cynthia Crossen, "Studies Galore Support Products and Positions, But Are They Reliable," *The Wall Street Journal* (November 14, 1991), p. A1.

these roaches become poisoned and die. How effective do you think this type of product would be in killing roaches?" Not surprisingly, 79 percent said effective.

A Gallup poll sponsored by the disposable-diaper industry asked: "It is estimated that disposable diapers account for less than 2 percent of the trash in today's landfills. In contrast, beverage containers, third-class mail, and yard waste are estimated to account for about 21 percent of the trash in landfills. Given this, in your opinion, would it be fair to ban disposable diapers?" Eighty-four percent said no.

the situation, one needs to avoid leading the respondent. Research Realities 8.5 contains some examples of leading questions.

Avoid Implicit Alternatives An **implicit alternative** is one that is not expressed in the options. Consider the two following questions, which were used in two random samples of nonworking housewives to investigate their attitudes toward having a job outside the home.[25]

❑ *Would you like to have a job, if this were possible?*

❑ *Would you prefer to have a job, or do you prefer to do just your housework?*

Even though the two questions appear to be very similar, they produced dramatically different responses. For the first version, 19 percent indicated they would not like to have a job, whereas for the second, 68 percent suggested they would prefer not to have one, over three and one-half times as many. The difference in the two questions is that Version Two makes explicit the alternative implied in Version One.

As a general rule, one should avoid implicit alternatives unless there is a special reason for including them. Further, because the order in which the alternatives appear can affect the responses, one should rotate the order of the options in samples of questionnaires.

Avoid Implicit Assumptions Questions are frequently framed so that there is an **implied assumption** about what will happen as a consequence. The question "Are you in favor of placing price controls on crude oil?" will elicit different responses from indi-

---

[25]E. Noelle-Neumann, "Wanted: Rules for Wording Structured Questionnaires," *Public Opinion Quarterly,* 34 (Summer 1970), p. 200. See also Philip Gendall and Janet Hoek, "A Question of Wording," *Marketing Bulletin,* 1 (May 1990), pp. 25–36.

viduals, depending on their views of what that might produce in the way of rationing, long lines at the pumps, and so forth. A better way to state the question is to make explicit the consequence(s). Thus, the question would be altered to ask ''Are you in favor of placing price controls on crude oil if it would produce gas rationing?''

Figure 8.4 shows what can happen when the consequences are explicitly stated in a question. Version B makes the implied consequence in Version A explicit; the only way the seat belt law could be effective is if there were some penalty for not complying with it. Yet, when there was no explicit statement about what would happen if a person did not comply with the proposed law, 73 percent were in favor of it. When people faced the prospect of a fine for noncompliance, only 50 percent favored a mandatory seat belt law.

Avoid Generalizations and Estimates Questions should always be asked in specific rather than general terms. Consider the question, ''How many salespeople did you see last year?'' which might be asked of a purchasing agent. To answer the question, the agent would probably estimate how many salespeople call in a typical week and would multiply this estimate by 52. This burden should not be placed on the agent. Rather, a

FIGURE **8.4**   **Illustration of What Can Happen When an Implied Assumption Is Made Explicit**

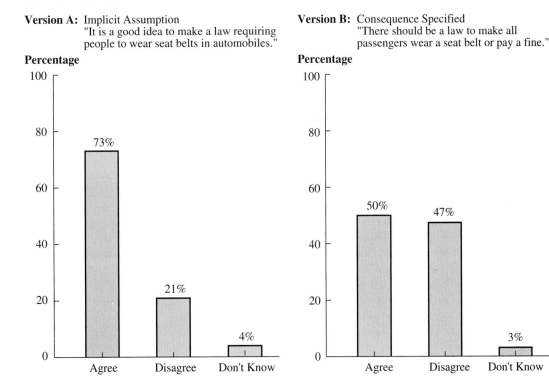

Source: Albert J. Ungar, ''Projectable Surveys: Separating Useful Data from Illusions,'' *Business Marketing,* 71 (December 1986), p. 90.

more accurate estimate would be obtained if the purchasing agent were asked, "How many representatives called last week?" and the researcher multiplied the answer provided by 52.

Avoid Double-Barreled Questions   A **double-barreled question** is one that calls for two responses and thereby creates confusion for the respondent. The question, "What is your evaluation of the price and convenience offered by catalog showrooms?" is asking respondents to react to two separate attributes by which such showrooms could be described. The respondent might think that the prices are attractive but the location is not, for example, and thereby is placed in a dilemma about how to respond. The problem is particularly acute if the individual must choose an answer from a fixed set of alternatives. One can and should avoid double-barreled questions by splitting the initial question into two separate questions. A useful indicator that two questions might be needed is the use of the word *and* in the initial wording of the question.

Decide on Question Sequence

Once the form of response and specific wording for each question have been decided, the researcher is ready to begin putting them together into a questionnaire. The researcher needs to recognize immediately that the order in which the questions are presented can be crucial to the success of the research effort. Again, there are no hard-and-fast principles but only rules-of-thumb to guide the researcher in this activity.

Use Simple, Interesting Opening Questions   The first questions asked the respondent are crucial. If respondents cannot answer them easily, find them uninteresting, or find them suspicious or threatening in any way, they may refuse to complete the remainder of the questionnaire. Thus, it is essential that the first few questions be simple, interesting, and in no way threatening to respondents. Questions that ask respondents for their opinion on some issue are often good openers, as most people like to think that their opinion is important. Sometimes it is helpful to use such an opener even when responses to it will not be analyzed, since opinion questions are often productive in relaxing respondents and getting them to talk freely.

Use Funnel Approach   The **funnel approach** to question sequencing gets its name from its shape, starting with broad questions and progressively narrowing down the scope. If respondents are to be asked "What improvements are needed in the company's service policy?" and also "How do you like the quality of service?" the first question needs to be asked before the second. Otherwise, quality of service will be emphasized disproportionately in the responses simply because it is fresh in the respondents' minds.

There should also be some logical order to the questions.[26] This means that sudden changes in topics and jumping around from topic to topic should be avoided. Transi-

---

[26]Jon A. Krosnik and Duane F. Alwin, "An Evaluation of a Cognitive Theory of Response Order–Effects in Survey Measurement," *Public Opinion Quarterly,* 51 (Summer 1987), pp. 201–219; McKee J. McClendon and David J. O'Brien, "Question-Order Effects on the Determinants of Subjective Well-Being," *Public Opinion Quarterly,* 52 (Fall 1988), pp. 351–364.

tional devices are sometimes necessary to smooth the flow when a change in subject matter occurs. Sometimes the simple insertion of appropriate filter questions will serve this purpose well, although the insertion of a brief explanation is the most commonly used bridge when a change in subject matter occurs.

Design Branching Questions with Care **Branching questions** are used to direct respondents to different places in the questionnaire, based on their response to the question at hand. Thus, for example, a respondent replying "yes" to the question of whether he or she bought a new car within the last six months would be directed to one place in the questionnaire where he or she might then be asked for specific details surrounding the purchase, whereas someone responding "no" to the same question would be directed elsewhere. Branching questions are used to reduce the number of alternatives that are needed in individual questions while simultaneously ensuring that the information needed is secured from those capable of supplying it. Those for whom a question is irrelevant are simply directed around it. Branching questions and directions are much easier to develop for surveys administered by telephone or in person, especially for those administered through computer-assisted interviewing, than for those sent through the mail. With mail questionnaires, the number of branching questions needs to be kept to an absolute minimum so that respondents do not become confused when responding or refuse to cooperate because the task becomes too difficult. Although they can be used more liberally with telephone and personal interview surveys, branching questions still need to be designed with care, since evidence indicates that branching instructions increase the rate of item nonresponse for items immediately following the branch.[27] When using branching questions, it is generally good practice to (1) develop a flow chart of the logical possibilities and then prepare the branching questions and instructions to follow the flow chart; (2) place the question being branched to as close as possible to the question causing the branching to minimize the amount of page flipping that is necessary; and (3) order the branching questions so that respondents cannot anticipate what additional information is required.[28] This last point suggests that the questionnaire should first ask, for example, whether the respondent owns any of the following small appliances before beginning to ask for the brand name, the store where purchased, and so on, for each appliance to which the respondent replied "yes." Otherwise, respondents will quickly recognize that "yes" answers to the ownership question lead to a number of other questions and that it is less taxing to say "no" in the first place.

Ask for Classification Information Last The typical questionnaire contains two types of information: basic information and classification information. Basic information refers to the subject of the study (for example, intentions or attitudes of respondents). Classification information refers to the other data that we collect to classify respondents in order to extract more information about the phenomenon of interest. For instance, we might be interested in determining if a respondent's attitudes toward the need for interest

---

[27]Donald J. Messmer and Daniel J. Seymour, "The Effects of Branching on Item Nonresponse," *Public Opinion Quarterly,* 46 (Summer 1982), pp. 270–277.

[28]Sudman and Bradburn, *Asking Questions,* pp. 223–227.

ceiling legislation are in any way affected by the person's income. Income here would be a classification variable. Demographic/socioeconomic characteristics of respondents are often used as classification variables for understanding the results.

The proper questionnaire sequence is to present questions securing basic information first and those seeking classification information last. There is a logical reason for this. The basic information is most critical. Without it, there is no study. Thus, the researcher should not risk alienating the respondent by asking a number of personal questions before getting to the heart of the study, since it is not unusual for personal characteristics to alienate respondents most. Respondents who readily offer their attitudes toward the energy crisis may balk when asked for their income. An early question aimed at determining their income may affect the whole tenor of the interview or other communication. It is best to avoid this possibility by placing the classification information at the end.

Place Difficult or Sensitive Questions Late in the Questionnaire   The basic information itself can also present some sequence problems. Some of the questions can be sensitive. Early questions should not be, for the reasons previously mentioned. If respondents feel threatened, they will turn off to the questionnaire. Thus, the sensitive questions should be relegated to the body of the questionnaire and intertwined and hidden among some not-so-sensitive ones. Once respondents have become involved in the study, they are less likely to react negatively or be turned off completely when delicate questions are posed. For example, one study investigating the impact of time and memory factors on response in surveys found that response bias becomes smaller as the interview progresses and that aided recall has no effect at the start of an interview but has a large effect late in the interview.[29]

Determine Physical Characteristics

The physical characteristics of the questionnaire can affect the accuracy of the replies that are obtained. For example, Figure 8.5 contains two versions of a question that was asked to determine which brands households had after it was determined that they had specific products. The letters are used instead of the actual brand names to protect the confidentiality of the data. The only fundamental difference in the questions was that a set of parentheses was provided in Form B for the "other brand" category, whereas Form A had a line where respondents wrote in the name of those brands not on the original list. The difference in results regarding the percentage of households owning Brands F and G among the 4,000 households surveyed was remarkable, as Table 8.2 indicates. Form B results were within a couple of percentage points of the results from the survey conducted one year earlier. It seems that respondents counted up from the bottom when checking the brand category, and the line on which the other brand was to

---

[29]Seymour Sudman and Norman M. Bradburn, "Effects of Time and Memory Factors on Response in Surveys," *Journal of the American Statistical Association,* 68 (December 1973), pp. 805–815. See also David Mingay and Michael T. Greenwell, "Memory Bias and Response-Order Effects," *Journal of Official Statistics,* 5 (No. 3, 1989), pp. 253–263.

FIGURE 8.5   **Two Forms of a Brand-Owned Question**

Form A

Important: For each type, if you have more than one, answer for the newest. 3a. What make or brand is it?

	Product X	**Product Y**	**Product Z**
Brand A	( ) 1	( ) 1	( ) 1
Brand B	( ) 2	( ) 2	( ) 2
Brand C	( ) 3	( ) 3	( ) 3
Brand D	( ) 4	( ) 4	( ) 4
Brand E	( ) 5	( ) 5	( ) 5
Brand F	( ) 6	( ) 6	( ) 6
Brand G	( ) 7	( ) 7	( ) 7
Other brand (Specify)	_____	_____	_____

Form B

3. What make or brand is the newest one?

	Product X	**Product Y**	**Product Z**
Brand A	( ) 1	( ) 1	( ) 1
Brand B	( ) 2	( ) 2	( ) 2
Brand C	( ) 3	( ) 3	( ) 3
Brand D	( ) 4	( ) 4	( ) 4
Brand E	( ) 5	( ) 5	( ) 5
Brand F	( ) 6	( ) 6	( ) 6
Brand G	( ) 7	( ) 7	( ) 7
Other brand	( ) 8	( ) 8	( ) 8

Source: Charles S. Mayer and Cindy Piper, "A Note on the Importance of Layout in Self-Administered Questionnaires," *Journal of Marketing Research,* 19 (August 1982), p. 390. Published by the American Marketing Association.

be entered in Form A was too close to the ruled line separating this question from the next one.[30]

The physical characteristics of a questionnaire can also affect how respondents react to it and the ease with which the replies can be processed. In determining the physical

---

[30]Charles S. Mayer and Cindy Piper, "A Note on the Importance of Layout in Self-Administered Questionnaires," *Journal of Marketing Research,* 19 (August 1982), pp. 390–391. See also Marie Elena Sanchez, "Effects of Questionnaire Design on the Quality of Survey Data," *Public Opinion Quarterly,* 56 (Summer 1992), pp. 206–217.

TABLE **8.2**   **Brand Share among Owners**

	Percentage Owning Brand		
	Form A	Form B	Net Difference
Product X			
Brand F	30	3	27
Brand G	47	71	24
Product Y			
Brand F	18	2	16
Brand G	27	41	14
Product Z			
Brand F	27	3	24
Brand G	35	58	23

format of the questionnaire, a researcher wants to do those things that help get the respondent to accept the questionnaire and that facilitate handling and control by the researcher.

Securing Acceptance of the Questionnaire   The physical appearance of the questionnaire can influence respondents' cooperation. This is particularly true with mail questionnaires, but it applies as well to questionnaires administered by personal interviews. If the questionnaire looks sloppy, for whatever reason, respondents are likely to think that the study is unimportant and refuse to cooperate, despite words to the contrary about its importance. If the study is important (and why conduct it if it is not?), make the questionnaire reflect that importance. This means that good-quality paper should be used for the questionnaires. It also means that the questionnaires should be printed, not mimeographed or otherwise photocopied.

The introduction to the research can also affect acceptance of the questionnaire. With mail questionnaires, the cover letter serves to introduce the study. It is very important that the cover letter convinces the designated respondent to cooperate. Good cover letters are rarely written in a hurry; rather, they usually require a series of painstaking rewrites to get the wording just so. Research Realities 8.6 lists important content considerations in the construction of cover letters.[31] With personal and telephone inter-

---

[31]Each of the parts listed in Research Realities 8.6 is discussed in detail in Paul L. Erdos, *Professional Mail Surveys* (Melbourne, Fla.: Robert E. Krieger Publishing Co., 1983), pp. 101–117. See also Bruce J. Walker, Wayne Kirchmann, and Jeffrey S. Conant, "A Method to Improve Response to Industrial Mail Surveys," *Industrial Marketing Management,* 16 (November 1987), pp. 305–314.

views, the introduction to the research is necessarily shorter. Nonetheless, the introduction needs to convince respondents about the importance of the research and the importance of their participation. Typically, this means describing how they can benefit from it, the fact that their replies will be confidential, and the incentive, if any, that they will receive for participating.

It is a good idea to include the name of the sponsoring organization and the name of the project on the first page or on the cover if the questionnaire is in book form. Both of these lend credibility to the study. However, since awareness of the sponsoring firm can often induce bias in respondents' answers, many firms use fictitious names for the sponsoring organization. This also helps eliminate phone calls or other inquiries from respondents asking for the results of the study.

Facilitate Handling and Control   Several things that facilitate handling and control by the researcher also contribute to acceptance of the questionnaire by respondents. These include such things as questionnaire size and layout and question sequencing.

Questionnaire size is important.[32] Smaller questionnaires are better than larger ones if (and this is a big if) they do not appear crowded. Smaller questionnaires seem easier to complete; they appear to take less time and are less likely to cause respondents to refuse to participate. They are easier to carry in the field and are easier to sort, count, and file in the office than larger questionnaires. If, on the other hand, smaller size is gained at the expense of an open appearance, these advantages are lost. A crowded questionnaire has a bad appearance, leads to errors in data collection, and results in shorter and less informative replies. For both self-administered and interviewer-administered questionnaires, for example, researchers have found that the more lines or space left for recording the response to open-ended questions, the more extensive the reply. Similarly, it has been found that giving respondents more detailed information about the type of information sought, through longer questions, improves reporting behavior.[33] Both of these techniques increase the physical size of the questionnaire needed for the study.

While postcard size probably represents the lower limit, letter size probably represents the upper limit to the size of an individual page in a questionnaire. When the questions will not all fit on the front and back of one sheet, multiple sheets need to be used. When this happens, the questionnaire should be made into a booklet rather than stapling or paper clipping the pages together. This not only facilitates handling but also reinforces an image of quality.

---

[32]A. Regula Herzog and Jerald G. Bachman, ''Effects of Questionnaire Length on Response Quality,'' *Public Opinion Quarterly,* 45 (Winter 1981), pp. 549–559; David Jobber, ''An Examination of the Effects of Questionnaire Factors on Response to an Industrial Mail Survey,'' *International Journal of Research in Marketing,* 6 (December 1989), pp. 129–140.

[33]Charles F. Cannell, Lois Oksenberg, and Jean M. Converse, ''Striving for Response Accuracy: Experiments in New Interviewing Techniques,'' *Journal of Marketing Research,* 14 (August 1977), pp. 306–315; Ed Blair, Seymour Sudman, Norman M. Bradburn, and Carol Stocking, ''How to Ask Questions about Drinking and Sex: Response Effects in Measuring Consumer Behavior,'' *Journal of Marketing Research,* 14 (August 1977), pp. 316–321; Andre Laurent, ''Effects of Question Length on Reporting Behavior in the Survey Interview,'' *Journal of the American Statistical Association,* 67 (June 1972), pp. 298–305.

Another thing that facilitates handling and also promotes respondent cooperation is numbering the questions. This is particularly true when branching questions are employed. Without numbered questions, instructions about how to proceed (e.g., "If the answer to Question 2 is yes, please go to Question 5") cannot be used. Even with numbered questions, though, it is helpful if the respondent can be directed by arrows to the appropriate next question after a branching question. Another technique researchers have found useful with branch-type questions is the use of color-coding on the questionnaire, where the next question to which the respondent is directed matches the color of the space in which the answer to the branching or filter question was recorded.

Numbering the questions makes it easier to edit, code, and tabulate the responses.[34] If the questionnaires themselves are numbered, it is easier to keep track of the questionnaires and to determine which ones, if any, are lost. It also makes it easier to monitor interviewer performance and to detect interviewer biases, if any. The research director will be able to develop a log that lists which questionnaires were assigned to which interviewers. Mail questionnaires are an exception to the principle that the questionnaires themselves should be numbered. Respondents often interpret an assigned number on a mail questionnaire as a mechanism by which their responses can be identified. The accompanying loss in anonymity is threatening to many of them, and they refuse to cooperate or otherwise distort their answers.

---

[34]These elementary steps, which are involved in the processing of all questionnaires, are discussed in Chapter 13.

Research Realities 8.6

Sample Cover Letter for a Mail Questionnaire

Panel A: Contents

1. Personal communication.
2. Asking a favor.
3. Importance of the research project and its purpose.
4. Importance of the recipient.
5. Importance of the replies in general.
6. Importance of the replies when the reader is not qualified to answer most questions.
7. How the recipient may benefit from this research.
8. Completing the questionnaire will take only a short time.
9. The questionnaire can be answered easily.
10. A stamped reply envelope is enclosed.
11. How recipient was selected.
12. Answers are anonymous or confidential.
13. Offer to send report on results of survey.
14. Note of urgency.
15. Appreciation of sender.
16. Importance of sender.
17. Importance of the sender's organization.
18. Description and purpose of incentive.
19. Avoiding bias.
20. Style.
21. Format and appearance.
22. Brevity.

Source: Paul L. Erdos, *Professional Mail Surveys* revised edition (Melbourne, Fla: Robert E. Krieger Publishing Co., Inc., 1983), pp. 102–103. Reprinted with permission.

Panel B: Sample*

PROFESSIONAL MAIL SURVEYS COMPANY —— 17
7432 East Court Avenue
Elveron, California   90101
(213) 991-5550

(Date)

1 —Dear Mr. Smythe:

2 —— Will you do us a favor?

3

We are conducting a nationwide survey among executives and
managers in the metalworking industries. The purpose of this research
3 — is to find out the opinion of yourself and other experts on the
advantages and disadvantages of using three new steel products. Your —— 1
5 — answers will enable steel manufacturers to be aware of the requirements
of the users and the opinions of nonusers of these items, and this
in turn will help them to design the products you need.   3

6   7

Your name appeared in a scientifically selected random sample. —— 11
5 — Your answers are very important to the accuracy of our research,
6 — whether or not your company is a user of one or more of the products
described.

8

9 —— It will take only a short time to answer the simple questions on the
enclosed questionnaire and to return it in the stamped reply envelope.— 10

12

Of course all answers are confidential and will be used only in
combination with those of other metalworking executives and managers —— 4
from all over the United States.

3 —

13 —— If you are interested in receiving a report on the findings of
this research, just write your name and address at the end of this
questionnaire, or if you prefer, request the results of the Survey on
Steel Products in a separate letter. We will be glad to send you a
complimentary report when ready.   12

14 —— Please return the completed questionnaire at your earliest
convenience. Thank you for your help.

Sincerely,

15

James B Jones —— 1

James B. Jones
Director —— 16

18 —P.S. The enclosed dollar bill is just a token of appreciation.

*Note: The numbers refer to the corresponding items in Panel A.

Reexamination and Revision of the Questionnaire

A researcher should not expect that the first draft will result in a usable questionnaire. Rather, reexamination and revision are the order of the day in questionnaire construction. Each question should be reviewed to ensure that the question is not confusing or ambiguous, potentially offensive to the respondent, leading or bias inducing, and also that it is easy to answer. How can one tell? An extremely critical attitude and good common sense should help. The researcher should examine each word in each question. The literature on question phrasing is replete with examples of how some seemingly innocuous questions produce response problems.[35] When a potential problem is discovered, the question should be revised. After examining each question — and each word in each question — for its potential meanings and implications, the researcher might test the questionnaire in some role-playing situations, using others working on the project as subjects. This role playing should reveal some of the most serious shortcomings and should lead to further revision of the instrument.

Pretesting the Questionnaire

The real test of a questionnaire is how it performs under actual conditions of data collection. For this assessment, the questionnaire **pretest** is vital. The questionnaire pretest serves the same role in questionnaire design that test marketing serves in new product development. Even though the product concept, different advertising appeals, alternative packages, and so on, may all have been tested previously in the product development process, test marketing is the first place where they all come together. Test marketing provides the real test of customer reactions to the product and the accompanying marketing program. Similarly, the pretest provides the real test of the questionnaire and the mode of administration.

There are a number of interesting, published examples of unintended implications from questions that could have been avoided with an adequate pretest of the questionnaire. In one life-style study, for example, the following question was asked: "How would you like to be living two years from now?" While the question was intended to get at hoped-for life-styles, a large group of the respondents simply replied "yes." In another study, a question about brands of deodorant was used on a self-administered questionnaire. It was only when a number of replies came back with the written response "AirWick" that the researchers realized that putting the word *personal* in front of deodorant would have eliminated the confusion caused by the question.[36] *Data collection should never begin without an adequate pretest of the instrument.* Research Realities 8.7, for example, describes the procedures used by the Bureau of the Census to pretest the questionnaire used in the 1990 Census of Population and Housing.

---

[35]Payne's book is particularly good in this regard. Chapter 13, for example, is devoted to the development of a passable question. When one considers that an entire chapter can be devoted to the development of one passable question (not a great question, mind you), one can appreciate the need for reexamining each question under a microscope for its potential implications. A condensed treatment of the things to be avoided in a question is to be found in Lyndon O. Brown and Leland L. Beik, *Marketing Research and Analysis,* 4th ed. (New York: Ronald, 1969), pp. 242–262. Sudman and Bradburn, *Asking Questions,* have recommendations specific to the type of question being asked (e.g., opinions versus demographic characteristics).

[36]Linda Kirby, "Bloopers," *Newspaper Research Council* (January/February 1989), p. 1.

Research Realities 8.7

Procedures Used by the Bureau of the Census to Pretest the Questionnaire for the 1990 Census of Population and Housing

When you only get one chance every ten years to send out a questionnaire, it's best to leave nothing to chance. That's why the U.S. Census Bureau carefully pretests all of the questions included in its decennial surveys of the entire U.S. population. For the 1990 Census, the Bureau gave itself more than a five-year head start, launching the National Content Survey to pretest the form and content of the 1990 questionnaire.

Forty-eight thousand scientifically selected households were chosen to participate in the study, and seven different versions of the census questionnaire were tested. Two different types of envelopes were tested as well. Questionnaires were mailed either in an attractive "commercial" envelope with a red, white, and blue flag or in a plain "official business" envelope to determine whether return rates were affected by envelope type.

Most of the topics covered in the questionnaires were familiar from past censuses, but the Census Bureau concentrated on improving the wording or place-

ment of the questions. Several new topics were also included: more questions about Americans with long-term disabilities, the addition of "solar" to possible answers about home heating fuel, the number of smoke detectors in the home, and queries about second jobs, to name just a few.

Families in the representative sample were asked to answer the questions and mail their completed forms back to the Census Bureau. Those who did not respond initially were sent a second questionnaire. Persistent nonresponders were then visited by Census Bureau interviewers.

Forty percent of the families included in the National Content Survey were asked to participate in a further phase of the study. After completing their census "sneak preview," these families were visited by experienced interviewers determined to assess how well respondents understood the various survey questions.

Data gathered from the National Content Survey were then analyzed and used to develop the final questionnaires for the 1990 Census. Once the millions of completed surveys are analyzed and the data made public, it will be time again for the Census Bureau to begin pretesting the 2000 Census.

Source: " 'Sneak Preview' of the 1990 Census Questions Mailed to 48,000 Households Nationwide," *Data User News,* 21 (June 1986), pp. 1, 3.

The pretest can be used to assess both individual questions and their sequence.[37] It is best if there are two pretests. The first pretest should be done by personal interview, regardless of the actual mode of administration that will be used. An interviewer can watch to see if people actually remember data requested of them, or if some questions seem confusing, or if some questions produce respondent resistance or hesitancy for one reason or another. The pretest interviews should be conducted by the firm's most

---

[37]An empirical examination of the usefulness of the pretest in uncovering various problems can be found in Shelby D. Hunt, Richard D. Sparkman, Jr., and James B. Wilcox, "The Pretest in Survey Research: Issues and Preliminary Findings," *Journal of Marketing Research,* 19 (May 1982), pp. 265–275; Ruth N. Bolton, Randall G. Chapman, and John M. Zych, "Pretesting Alternative Survey Administration Design," *Applied Marketing Research,* 30 (No. 3, 1990), pp. 8–13; Lois Oksenberg, Charles Cannell, and Graham Kalton, "New Strategies of Pretesting Survey Questions," *Journal of Official Statistics,* 7 (No. 3, 1991), pp. 349–365.

ETHICAL DILEMMA 8.3

A candy manufacturer tells you that he wants to raise the price of his gourmet chocolates and he needs you to establish the maximum price increase that shoppers will stand. He suggests that you interview patrons of gourmet candy shops without informing them of the sponsor or purpose of the research, describe the candy to them in general terms, and suggest prices that they might find acceptable, starting with the highest price.

- Is it ethical to ask people questions when their answer may be detrimental to their self-interest?
- Is it ethical not to reveal the purpose or sponsor of the research? If you did reveal the purpose of the research, would survey respondents give the same answer as otherwise?

experienced interviewers among respondents similar to those who will be used in the actual study.

The personal interview pretest should reveal some questions in which the wording could be improved or the sequence changed. If the changes are major, the revised questionnaire should again be pretested employing personal interviews. If the changes are minor, the questionnaire can be pretested a second time using mail, telephone, or personal interviews, whichever method is going to be used for the full-scale study. This time, though, less experienced interviewers should also be used in order to determine if typical interviewers will have any special problems with the questionnaire. The purpose of the second pretest is to uncover problems unique to the mode of administration.

Finally, the responses that result from the pretest should be coded and tabulated. The code book to be used when processing the questionnaires needs to be determined.[38] We have previously discussed the need for the preparation of dummy tables prior to the development of the questionnaire. The tabulation of pretest responses can check on our conceptualization of the problem and the data and method of analysis necessary to answer it.

> . . . the tables will confirm the need for various sets of data. If we have no place to put the responses to a question, either the data are superfluous or we omitted some contemplated analysis. If some part of a table remains empty, we may have omitted a necessary question. Trial tabulations show us, as no previous method can, that all data collected will be put to use, and that we will obtain all necessary data.[39]

The researcher who avoids a questionnaire pretest and tabulation of replies is either naive or a fool. The pretest is the most inexpensive insurance the researcher can buy to ensure the success of the questionnaire and the research project. A careful pretest, along with proper attention to the do's and don'ts presented in this chapter and summarized in Table 8.3, should make the questionnaire development process successful.

---

[38]See Chapter 13 for discussion of how to code data, which should be decided before the final questionnaires are administered.

[39]Brown and Beik, *Marketing Research and Analysis,* pp. 265–266.

TABLE 8.3 **Some Do's and Don'ts When Preparing Questionnaires**

Step 1: Specify What Information Will Be Sought

1. Make sure that you have a clear understanding of the issue and what it is that you want to know (expect to learn). Frame your research questions, but refrain from writing questions for the questionnaire at this time.
2. Make a list of your research questions. Review them periodically as you are working on the questionnaire.
3. Use the "dummy tables" that were set up to guide the data analysis to suggest questions for the questionnaire.
4. Conduct a search for existing questions on the issue.
5. Revise existing questions on the issue, and prepare new questions that address the issues you plan to research.

Step 2: Determine Type of Questionnaire and Method of Administration

1. Use the type of data to be collected as a basis for deciding on the type of questionnaire.
2. Use degree of structure and disguise as well as cost factors to determine the method of administration.
3. Compare the special capabilities and limitations of each method of administration and the value of the data collected from each with the needs of the survey.

Step 3: Determine Content of Individual Questions

1. For each research question ask yourself, "Why do I want to know this?" Answer it in terms of how it will help your research. "It would be interesting to know" is not an acceptable answer.
2. Make sure each question is specific and addresses only one important issue.
3. Ask yourself whether the question applies to all respondents; it should, or provision should be made for skipping it.
4. Split questions that can be answered from different frames of reference into multiple questions, one corresponding to each frame of reference.
5. Ask yourself whether respondents will be informed about and can remember the issue that the question is dealing with.
6. Make sure the time period of the question is related to the importance of the topic. Consider using aided-recall techniques like diaries, records, or bounded recall.

7. Avoid questions that require excessive effort, that have hard-to-articulate answers, and that deal with embarrassing or threatening issues.
8. If threatening questions are necessary,
   a. hide the questions among more innocuous ones.
   b. make use of a counterbiasing statement.
   c. phrase the question in terms of others and how they might feel or act.
   d. ask respondents if they have ever engaged in the undesirable activity, and then ask if they are presently engaging in such an activity.
   e. use categories or ranges rather than specific numbers.
   f. use the randomized response model.

Step 4: Determine Form of Response to Each Question

1. Determine which type of question — open-ended, dichotomous, or multichotomous — provides data that fit the information needs of the project.
2. Use structured questions whenever possible.
3. Use open-ended questions that require short answers to begin a questionnaire.
4. Try to convert open-ended questions to closed (fixed) response questions to reduce respondent work load and coding effort for descriptive and causal studies.
5. If open-ended questions are necessary, make the questions sufficiently directed to give respondents a frame of reference when answering.
6. When using dichotomous questions, state the negative or alternative side in detail.
7. Provide for "don't know," "no opinion," and "both" answers.
8. Be aware that there may be a middle ground.
9. Be sensitive to the mildness or harshness of the alternatives.
10. When using multichotomous questions, be sure that the choices are exhaustive and mutually exclusive, and if combinations are possible, include them.
11. Be sure that the range of alternatives is clear and that all reasonable alternative answers are included.

(continued)

TABLE 8.3   *Continued*

12. If the possible responses are very numerous, consider using more than one question to reduce the potential for information overload.
13. When using dichotomous or multichotomous questions, consider the use of a split ballot procedure to reduce order bias.
14. Clearly indicate if items are to be ranked or if only one item on the list is to be chosen.

Step 5:   Determine Wording of Each Question
1. Use simple words.
2. Avoid ambiguous words and questions.
3. Avoid leading questions.
4. Avoid implicit alternatives.
5. Avoid implicit assumptions.
6. Avoid generalizations and estimates.
7. Use simple sentences, and avoid compound sentences.
8. Change long, dependent clauses to words or short phrases.
9. Avoid double-barreled questions.
10. Make sure each question is as specific as possible.

Step 6:   Determine Question Sequence
1. Use simple, interesting questions for openers.
2. Use the funnel-approach, first asking broad questions and then narrowing them down.
3. Ask difficult or sensitive questions late in the questionnaire when rapport is better.
4. Follow chronological order when collecting historical information.
5. Complete questions about one topic before moving on to the next.
6. Prepare a flow chart whenever filter questions are being considered.
7. Ask filter questions before asking detailed questions.
8. Ask demographic questions last so that if respondent refuses, the other data are still usable.

Step 7:   Determine Physical Characteristics of Questionnaire
1. Make sure that the questionnaire looks professional and is relatively easy to answer.

2. Use quality paper and print; do not photocopy the questionnaire.
3. Attempt to make the questionnaire as short as possible while avoiding a crowded appearance.
4. Use a booklet format for ease of analysis and to prevent lost pages.
5. List the name of the organization conducting the survey on the first page.
6. Number the questions to ease data processing.
7. If the respondent must skip more than one question, use a "go to."
8. If the respondent must skip an entire section, consider color coding the sections.
9. State how the responses are to be reported, such as a check mark, number, circle, etc.

Step 8:   Reexamine Steps 1–7 and Revise If Necessary
1. Examine each word of every question to ensure the question is not confusing, ambiguous, offensive, or leading.
2. Get peer evaluations of the draft questionnaire.

Step 9:   Pretest Questionnaire and Revise If Necessary
1. Pretest the questionnaire first by personal interviews among respondents similar to those to be used in the actual study.
2. Obtain comments from the interviewers and respondents to discover any problems with the questionnaire, and revise it if necessary. When the revisions are substantial, repeat Steps 1 and 2 of the pretest.
3. Pretest the questionnaire by mail or telephone to uncover problems unique to the mode of administration.
4. Code and tabulate the pretest responses in dummy tables to determine if questions are providing adequate information.
5. Eliminate questions that do not provide adequate information, and revise questions that cause problems.

OBSERVATIONAL FORMS

There are generally fewer problems in constructing observational forms than question-naires, because the researcher is no longer concerned with the fact that the question and the way it is asked will affect the response. Through proper training of observers, the researcher can create the necessary expertise so that the data-collection instrument is handled consistently. Alternatively, the researcher may simply use a mechanical device to measure the behavior of interest and secure complete consistency in measurement. This is not to imply that observational forms offer no problems of construction. Rather, the researcher needs to make very explicit decisions about what is to be observed and the categories and units that will be used to record this behavior. Figure 8.6, which is the observation form used by a bank to evaluate the service provided by its employees having extensive customer contact, shows how detailed some of these decisions can be. In this case, the observers acted as shoppers.

The statement that "One needs to determine what is to be observed before one can make a scientific observation" seems trite indeed. Yet this is exactly the case. Almost any event can be described in a number of ways. When we watch someone making a

FIGURE 8.6   Form Used by Observer Acting as Shopper to Evaluate Service Provided by Bank Employees

Bank _____

Date _____ Time _____ Shopper's Name _____

Nature of Transaction: ☐ Personal   ☐ Telephone

        Details _____

                _____

                _____

                _____

- -

A. For Personal Transactions:

    Bank Employee's Name _____

How was name obtained?   ☐ Employee had name tag
                       ☐ Name plate on counter or desk
                       ☐ Employee gave name
                       ☐ Shopper had to ask for name
                       ☐ Name provided by other employee
                       ☐ Other _____

                       _____

(continued)

FIGURE **8.6**   *Continued*

B. For Telephone Transactions:

Bank Employee's Name _____

How was name obtained?   ☐ Employee gave name upon answering the telephone
☐ Name provided by other employee
☐ Shopper had to ask for name
☐ Employee gave name during conversation
☐ Other _____

C. Customer Relations Skills	**Yes**	**No**	**Does Not Apply**
1. Did the employee notice and greet you immediately?	☐	☐	☐
2. Did the employee speak pleasantly and smile?	☐	☐	☐
3. Did the employee answer the telephone promptly?	☐	☐	☐
4. Did the employee find out your name?	☐	☐	☐
5. Did the employee use your name during the transaction?	☐	☐	☐
6. Did the employee ask you to be seated?	☐	☐	☐
7. Was the employee helpful?	☐	☐	☐
8. Was the employee's desk or work area neat and uncluttered?	☐	☐	☐
9. Did the employee show a genuine interest in you as a customer?	☐	☐	☐
10. Did the employee thank you for coming in?	☐	☐	☐
11. Did the employee enthusiastically support the bank and its services?	☐	☐	☐
12. Did the employee handle any interruptions effectively? (phone calls, etc.)	☐	☐	☐

Comment on any positive or negative details of the transaction that you found particularly noticeable.

_____

_____

_____

_____

_____

FIGURE 8.6   *Continued*

D. Sales Skills	Yes	No	Does Not Apply
1. Did the employee determine if you had any accounts with this bank?	☐	☐	☐
2. Did the employee use "open-ended" questions in obtaining information about you?	☐	☐	☐
3. Did the employee listen to what you had to say?	☐	☐	☐
4. Did the employee sell you on the bank services by showing you what the service could do for you?	☐	☐	☐
5. Did the employee ask you to open the service which you inquired about?	☐	☐	☐
6. Did the employee ask you to bank with this particular bank?	☐	☐	☐
7. Did the employee ask you to contact him/her when visiting the bank?	☐	☐	☐
8. Did the employee ask you if you had any questions or if you understood the service at the end of the transaction?	☐	☐	☐
9. Did the employee give you brochures about other services?	☐	☐	☐
10. Did the employee give you his/her calling card?	☐	☐	☐
11. Did the employee indicate that you might be contacted by telephone, engraved card, or letter as a means of follow-up?	☐	☐	☐
12. Did the employee ask you to open or use other services? Check the following if they were mentioned.	☐	☐	☐

☐ savings account
☐ checking account
☐ automatic savings
☐ Mastercharge
☐ Master Checking
☐ safe deposit box
☐ loan services
☐ trust services
☐ automatic loan payment
☐ bank hours
☐ other_____

(continued)

FIGURE **8.6**   *Continued*

Comment on the overall effectiveness of the employee's sales skills.

_____

_____

_____

_____

Source: Courtesy of Neil M. Ford.

---

cigarette purchase, we might report that (1) the person purchased one package of cigarettes; (2) the woman purchased one package of cigarettes; (3) the woman purchased a package of Tareyton cigarettes; (4) the woman purchased a package of Tareyton 100's; (5) the woman, after asking for and finding that the store was out of Virginia Slims, purchased a package of Tareyton 100's, and so on.

A great many additional variations are possible (for example, the type, name, or location of the store where this behavior occurred). In order for this observation to be productive for scientific inquiry, we must predetermine which aspects of this behavior are relevant. The decision about what to observe requires that the researcher specify the following:

- Who should be observed? Anyone entering the store? Anyone making a purchase? Anyone making a cigarette purchase?
- What aspects of the purchase should be reported? Which brand they purchased? Which brand they asked for first? Whether the purchase was of king size or regular cigarettes? What about the purchaser? Is the person's sex to be recorded? Is the individual's age to be estimated? Does it make any difference if the person was alone or in a group?
- When should the observation be made? On what day of the week? At what time of the day? Should day and time be reported? Should the observation be recorded only after a purchase occurs or should a customer approaching a salesclerk also be recorded, even if it does not result in a sale?
- Where should the observation be made? In what kind of store? How should the store be selected? How should it be noted on the observational form — by type, by location, by name? Should vending-machine purchases also be noted?

The careful reader will note that these are the same kinds of who, what, when, and where decisions that need to be made in selecting the research design. The ''why'' and ''how'' are also implicit. The research problem should dictate the why of the observa-

ETHICAL DILEMMA 8.4

As you supervise the sending out of a mail survey from a client's place of business, you notice some numbers printed on the inside of the return envelopes. You point out to the client that the cover letter promises survey respondents anonymity, which is not consistent with a policy of coding the return envelopes. She replies that she needs to identify those respondents who have not replied so that she can send a follow-up mailing. She also suggests the information might be useful in the future in identifying those who might react favorably to a sales call for the product.

- Is it ethical to promise anonymity and then not adhere to your promise?
- Is it healthy for the marketing research profession if legitimate research becomes associated with subsequent sales tactics?

tion, whereas the how involves choosing the observation device or form that will be used. A paper-and-pencil form should be very simple to use. It should parallel the logical sequence of the purchase act (for example, a male approaches the clerk, asks for a package of cigarettes, and so on, if these behaviors are relevant) and should permit the recording of observations by a simple check mark if possible. Again, careful attention to detail, exacting examination of the preliminary form, and an adequate pretest should return handsome dividends with respect to the quality of the observations made.

SUMMARY

A researcher wishing to collect primary data will need to tackle the task of designing the data collection device sooner or later. Most typically this will mean designing a questionnaire, although it may mean framing an observational form.

Questionnaire design is still very much of an art rather than a science, and there are many admonitions of things to avoid when doing the designing. Nevertheless, a nine-step procedure was offered as a guide. This guide indicates that researchers need to ask and answer some specific questions when designing questionnaires, including "What information will be sought? What type of questionnaire will be used? How will that questionnaire be administered? What will be the content of the individual questions? What will be the form of response — dichotomous, multichotomous, or open-ended — to each question? How will each question be phrased? How will the questions be sequenced? What will the questionnaire look like physically?" Researchers should not be surprised to find themselves repeating the various steps when designing a questionnaire. Further, although the temptation is sometimes great, one should never omit a pretest of the questionnaire. Regardless of how well it looks in the abstract, the pretest provides the real test of the questionnaire and its mode of administration. Actually, at least two pretests should be conducted. The first should use personal interviews, and after all the troublesome spots have been smoothed over, a second pretest using the normal mode of administration should be conducted. The data collected in the pretest should then be subjected to the analyses planned for the full data set, as this will reveal serious omissions or other shortcomings while it is still possible to correct these deficiencies.

Observational forms generally present fewer problems of construction than questionnaires, because the researcher no longer needs to be concerned with the fact that the question and the way it is asked will affect the response. Observational forms do, however, require a precise statement of who or what is to be observed, what actions or characteristics are relevant, and when and where the observations will be made.

Questions

1. What role do the research hypotheses play in determining the information that will be sought?

2. Suppose you were interested in determining the proportion of men in a geographic area who use hair sprays. How could the necessary information be obtained by open-ended question, by multiple-choice question, and by dichotomous question? Which would be preferable?

3. How does the method of administration of a questionnaire affect the type of question to be employed?

4. What criteria can a researcher use to determine whether a specific question should be included in a questionnaire?

5. What is telescoping error? What does it suggest about the period to be used when asking respondents to recall past events?

6. What are some recommended ways by which one can ask for sensitive information?

7. What is an open-ended question? A multichotomous question? A dichotomous question? What are some of the key things researchers must be careful to avoid in framing multichotomous and dichotomous questions?

8. What is a split ballot, and why is it employed?

9. What is an ambiguous question? A leading question? A question with implicit alternatives? A question with implied assumptions? A double-barreled question?

10. What is the proper sequence when asking for basic information and classification information?

11. What is the funnel approach to question sequencing?

12. What is a branching question? Why are such questions used?

13. Where should one ask for sensitive information in the questionnaire?

14. How can the physical features of a questionnaire affect its acceptance by respondents? Its handling and control by the researcher?

15. What is the overriding principle guiding questionnaire construction?

16. What decisions must the researcher make when developing an observational form for data collection?

Applications and Problems

1. Evaluate the following questions:

   a. *Which of the following magazines do you read regularly?*
      _____ Time
      _____ Newsweek
      _____ Business Week

b. *Are you a frequent purchaser of Birds Eye Frozen vegetables?*

_____ Yes   _____ No

c. *Do you agree that the government should impose import restrictions?*

_____ Strongly agree
_____ Agree
_____ Neither agree nor disagree
_____ Disagree
_____ Strongly disagree

d. *How often do you buy detergent?*

_____ Once a week
_____ Once in two weeks
_____ Once in three weeks
_____ Once a month

e. *Rank the following in order of preference:*

_____ Kellogg's Corn Flakes
_____ Quaker's Life
_____ Post Bran Flakes
_____ Kellogg's Bran Flakes
_____ Instant Quaker Oat Meal
_____ Post Rice Krinkles

f. *Where do you usually purchase your school supplies?*

g. *When you are watching television, do you also watch most of the advertisements?*

h. *Which of the following brands of tea are most similar?*

_____ Lipton's Orange Pekoe
_____ Turnings Orange Pekoe
_____ Bigelow Orange Pekoe
_____ Salada Orange Pekoe

i. *Do you think that the present policy of cutting taxes and reducing government spending should be continued?*

_____ Yes   _____ No

j. *In a seven-day week, how often do you eat breakfast?*

_____ Every day of the week
_____ 5–6 times a week
_____ 2–4 times a week
_____ Once a week
_____ Never

2. Make the necessary corrections to the preceding questions.

3. Evaluate the following multichotomous questions. Would dichotomous or open-ended questions be more appropriate?

a. *Which one of the following reasons is most important in your choice of stereo equipment?*

_____ Price
_____ In-store service
_____ Brand name
_____ Level of distortion
_____ Guarantee/warranty

b. Please indicate your education level.

_____ Less than high school

_____ Some high school

_____ High school graduate

_____ Technical or vocational school

_____ Some college

_____ College graduate

_____ Some graduate or professional school

c. Which of the following reflects your views toward the issues raised by ecologists?

_____ Have received attention

_____ Have not received attention

_____ Should receive more attention

_____ Should receive less attention

d. Which of the following statements do you most strongly agree with?

_____ Eastern Airlines has better service than Republic Airlines.

_____ Republic Airlines has better service than United Airlines.

_____ United Airlines has better service than Eastern Airlines.

_____ United Airlines has better service than Republic Airlines.

_____ Republic Airlines has better service than Eastern Airlines.

_____ Eastern Airlines has better service than United Airlines.

4. Evaluate the following open-ended questions. Rephrase them as multichotomous or dichotomous questions if you think it would be appropriate.

   a. Do you go to the movies often?

   b. Approximately how much do you spend per week on groceries?

   c. What brands of cheese did you purchase during the last week?

5. Discuss how each of the following respondent groups would influence the development of the questionnaire form.
   a. Medical doctors
   b. Welfare recipients
   c. Air Force commanders
   d. Cuban refugees

6. Your employer, a commercial marketing research firm, has contracted you to perform a study whose objective is the investigation of usage patterns and brand preferences for infant diapers among migrant farm workers in the southeastern United States. You have been assigned to develop a suitable questionnaire and method of administration to collect the desired information. What potential problems might arise in the design and administration due to the nature of the population in question? List these problems and provide solutions. What method of administration would you recommend?

7. Campus Cookery, the local burger spot, has asked you to comment on some of the questions that have been developed for a survey they are conducting on a new sandwich offering. What is wrong (if anything) with each of the following questions?

   a. Why haven't you tried our new sandwich at Campus Cookery?

   b. Don't you think that Campus Cookery's products are of the highest quality?

   c. Would you say that our new sandwich tastes good, is priced correctly, is attractive, and is healthy?

   ☐ Yes   ☐ No

d. Have you tried our new sandwich at Campus Cookery?

Very Infrequently	Infrequently	Average	Very Frequently
_____	_____	_____	_____

8. Analyze the following questions. What (if anything) is wrong with each question?

   a. How do you like the flavor of this high-quality, top-bean coffee?

   b. What do you think of the taste and texture of this Danish Treat coffee cake?

   c. We are conducting a study for Guess watches. What do you think of the quality of Guess watches?

   d. How far do you live from the closest mall?

   e. Who in your family shops for clothes?

   f. Where do you buy most of your clothes?

9. A small brokerage firm was concerned with the declining number of customers and decided to do a quick survey. The major objective was to find out the reasons for patronizing a particular brokerage firm and to find out the importance of customer service. The following questionnaire was to be administered by telephone.

Good Afternoon Sir/Madam:

We are doing a survey on attitudes toward brokerage firms. Could you please answer the following questions? Thank you.

1. Have you invested any money in the stock market?
   ____ Yes   ____ No

If respondent replies *yes*, continue; otherwise terminate interview.

2. Do you manage your own investments or do you go to a brokerage firm?
   ____ Manage own investments   ____ Go to a brokerage firm

If respondent replies "go to a brokerage firm" continue, otherwise terminate interview.

3. How satisfied are you with your brokerage firm?

Very Satisfied	Satisfied	Neither Satisfied nor Dissatisfied	Dissatisfied	Very Dissatisfied
____	____	____	____	____

4. How important is personal service to you?

Very Important	Important	Not Particularly Important	Not at All Important
____	____	____	____

(continued)

---

5. *Which of the following reasons is the most important in patronizing a particular firm?*

_____ the commission charged by the firm
_____ the personal service
_____ the return on investment
_____ the investment counseling

6. *Approximately how long have you been investing through the brokerage firm you are currently using?*

_____ about 3 months   _____ about 9 months
_____ about 6 months   _____ about 1 year or more

7. *How much capital do you have invested?*

_____ $500–$750   _____ $1,000–$1,500
_____ $750–$1,000   _____ $1,500 or more

Good-bye and thank you for your cooperation.

Evaluate the preceding questionnaire.

10. Suppose that the Nuclear Regulatory Commission is considering a proposal made by a California utility company to build a nuclear reactor in a small town located in southern California. According to the proposal, the new reactor could provide energy for a good portion of southern California at considerable savings over conventional sources of energy. Ultimately, substantial savings would be passed along to the consumer, according to the utility company. Opponents of the project, primarily anti-nuclear groups and environmental organizations, claim that such a project would needlessly put people who reside in the area, as well as the environment, at risk while the utility company makes a handsome profit. The proponents respond that no other suitable site can be found in southern California and that the benefits of less expensive energy sources far outweigh any potential risks associated with the project — particularly for individuals and families at or below the poverty line. Both sides, citing statistics from various public opinion polls, claim to have public opinion on their side.

   a. Write a question for a public opinion survey that is likely to produce results in favor of building the nuclear reactor (i.e., results that support the utility's position).

   b. Write a question for a public opinion survey that is likely to produce results showing that most people are not in favor of building the new nuclear facility (i.e., results that support the opposition's viewpoint).

   c. Write an appropriate survey question that attempts to accurately measure public opinion about whether or not the nuclear reactor should be built.

 Thorndike Sports Equipment Video Case

1. Ted needs help writing questions for his questionnaire. What questions would you suggest are necessary?

2. What are the advantages of using close-ended questions? List some drawbacks.

3. What are the advantages of open-ended questions? What are the disadvantages?

9

ATTITUDE MEASUREMENT

Attitude is one of the most pervasive notions in all of marketing. It plays a pivotal role in the major models describing consumer behavior, as well as in many, if not most, investigations of consumer behavior that do not rely on a formal integrated model.[1] The main reason attitude plays this central role is because it is believed to strongly influence behavior. "Attitudes *directly affect* purchase decisions and these, in turn, *directly affect* attitudes through experience in using the product or service selected. In a broad sense, purchase decisions are based *almost solely* upon attitudes existing at the time of purchase, however these attitudes might have been formed"[2] (emphasis added). Academic researchers, therefore, use attitude as an important explanatory variable in creating models of behavior.

Practitioners are also interested in people's attitudes and use them for a variety of purposes, including determining the amount to pay employees. For example, the guiding premise for AT&T when it developed its credit-card service was quality. Quality was defined as delighting the customer — exceeding his or her expectations in every way. To make sure it is succeeding in this endeavor, AT&T measures customers' reactions to its service in several ways, including surveying customers every month to determine the features of its service that matter most and how AT&T is performing on these features. It uses these measurements of customer attitudes along with more than 150 measurements of the performance of its vendors and its own internal operations to determine employee pay, since employees in the credit-card division have their paychecks tied to quality performance.[3]

Another use of attitudes is depicted in Research Realities 9.1, which describes the results of a study conducted by Ogilvy & Mather to help the agency pick media in

---

[1]See, for example, James F. Engel, Roger D. Blackwell, and Paul Miniard, *Consumer Behavior,* 7th ed. (Hinsdale, Ill.: Dryden Press 1993).

[2]James H. Myers and William H. Reynolds, *Consumer Behavior and Marketing Management* (Boston: Houghton Mifflin, © 1967), p. 146. For discussion of the role of attitudes and their effect on consumer behavior, see Robert A. Peterson, Wayne D. Hoyer, and William R. Wilson, eds., *The Role of Affect in Consumer Behavior: Emerging Theories and Applications* (Lexington, Mass.: D. C. Heath, 1986).

[3]Kevin T. Keleghan, "Quality of Service: Dancing to the Customer's Tune," *Retail Control,* 60 (March 1992), pp. 3–8.

Research Realities 9.1

Opinions in Various Countries about Advertising in Different Media

	Hong Kong, % Agree	Brazil, % Agree	Colombia, % Agree	UK, % Agree	US, % Agree	West Germany, % Agree
Newspapers						
Informative	32	71	74	45	57	46
Entertaining	39	11	11	8	10	14
Boring	22	13	15	34	25	35
Irritating	7	5	—	13	8	5
Radio						
Informative	23	51	19	23	33	17
Entertaining	39	21	30	18	28	31
Boring	22	19	32	30	23	45
Irritating	16	9	19	29	16	7
TV						
Informative	26	48	18	19	29	18
Entertaining	61	32	75	51	29	39
Boring	6	15	5	13	22	38
Irritating	7	5	2	17	20	5
Billboards						
Informative	24	51	36	33	32	21
Entertaining	50	20	43	33	21	21
Boring	22	20	15	26	26	52
Irritating	24	9	6	8	21	6

various countries. Still other common uses include the following: (1) The appliance manufacturer's interest in present dealer and prospective dealer attitudes toward the company's warranty policy. If the dealers embrace the policy, the company believes that they are more likely to give adequate, courteous service and, in the process, produce more satisfied customers. (2) The cosmetic manufacturer's interest in the early assessment of the attitudes of consumers in the test market toward the company's new shampoo. If the attitudes are unfavorable, the company will consider changing the introductory marketing strategy.(3) The industrial marketer's interest in the general job satisfaction (an attitude)

	Hong Kong, % Agree	Brazil, % Agree	Colombia, % Agree	UK, % Agree	US, % Agree	West Germany, % Agree
Magazines						
Informative	33	71	31	41	52	32
Entertaining	40	14	62	22	19	21
Boring	23	10	6	25	18	40
Irritating	4	5	1	12	11	7
Direct Mail						
Informative	24	62	60	10	16	19
Entertaining	18	2	17	3	5	7
Boring	24	26	19	23	35	57
Irritating	34	10	4	64	44	17

Informative, entertaining, boring, or irritating — pick *one* to describe advertising in each medium: newspapers, magazines, radio, TV, billboards, and direct mail.

If you're American, you're most likely to say newspaper and magazine advertising is "informative," and direct mail is "irritating." After that you can't decide. If you're British, you feel much the same, except you do also grant that TV advertising is "entertaining." For the West Germans, though, it's *all* pretty "boring." By complete contrast, unless you're talking about direct mail, it's all "entertaining" in Hong Kong; and in Brazil, advertising, no matter where you find it, is likely to be "informative." The Colombians are more discriminating — newspaper and direct mail advertising is "informative"; TV, billboards, and magazine advertising is "entertaining"; and radio advertising in Colombia is just as likely to be "boring" as "entertaining."

Source: *Listening Post, Number 64* (New York: Ogilvy & Mather, 1987), pp. 3 and 5. Reprinted with permission from Ogilvy & Mather.

of its highly trained, highly skilled field staff of sales engineers. These few examples indicate some of the many groups of people in whose attitudes the marketer is typically interested: the company's employees, its intermediaries, and its customers. Their posture, stance, or predisposition to act can be important determinants of the company's success, and the marketer needs devices for measuring these postures. This chapter reviews some of the many techniques for assessing a person's posture on an issue.

Researchers and practitioners share some common problems as well as a common interest in attitude. For one thing, although attitude is one of the most widely used notions in all of social psychology, it is also one of the most inconsistently used concepts. There are a variety of interpretations, but there does seem to be substantial agreement about the following:

1. Attitude represents a predisposition to respond to an object, not actual behavior toward the object. Attitude thus possesses the quality of readiness.
2. Attitude is persistent over time. It can change, to be sure, but alteration of an attitude that is strongly held requires substantial pressure.
3. Attitude is a latent variable that produces consistency in behavior, either verbal or physical.
4. Attitude has a directional quality. It connotes a preference regarding the outcomes involving the object, evaluations of the object, or positive/neutral/negative feelings for the object.[4]

These consistencies led to our definition of attitude as representing a person's ideas, convictions, or liking with regard to a specific object or idea, presented in Chapter 7.

SCALES OF MEASUREMENT

To properly address the subject of attitude measurement, it is necessary to define measurement and to briefly review the types of scales that can be used in measurement.

Measurement consists of "rules for assigning numbers to objects in such a way as to represent quantities of attributes."[5] Note two things about the definition. First, it indicates that we measure the attributes of objects and not the objects themselves. We do not measure a person, for example, but may choose to measure the individual's income, social class, education, height, weight, attitudes, or whatever, all of which are attributes of this person. Second, the definition is broad in that it does not specify how the numbers are to be assigned. In this sense, the rule is too simplistic and conveys a false sense of security, because there is a great temptation to read more meaning into the numbers than they actually contain. We often incorrectly attribute all the properties of the scale of numbers to the assigned numerals.

Consider the properties of the scale of numbers for a minute. Take the numbers 1, 2, 3, and 4. Now let the number "1" stand for one object, "2" for two objects, and so on. The scale of numbers possesses a number of properties. For example, we can say that "2" is larger than "1" and "3" is larger than "2," and so on. Also, we can say that the interval between "1" and "2" is the same size as the interval between "3" and "4," which is the same as that between "2" and "3," and so on. We can say still further that "3" is three times greater than "1," while "4" is four times greater than

---

[4]Adapted from the introduction by Gene F. Summers, ed., *Attitude Measurement* (Chicago: Rand McNally, 1970), p. 370. See also J. Paul Peter and Jerry C. Olson, *Consumer Behavior: Marketing Strategy Perspectives,* 3rd ed. (Homewood, Ill.: Richard D. Irwin, Inc. 1993). One of the reasons for the many definitions of attitude is the age-old scientific problem of going from construct to operational definition, a problem that is reviewed in Appendix 9C.

[5]Jum C. Nunnally, *Psychometric Theory,* 2nd ed. (New York: McGraw-Hill, 1978), p. 3.

TABLE **9.1**   **Scales of Measurement**

Scale	Basic Comparisons[a]	Typical Examples	Measures of Average[b]
Nominal	Identity	Male–female User–nonuser Occupations Uniform numbers	Mode
Ordinal	Order	Preference for brands Social class Hardness of minerals Graded quality of lumber	Median
Interval	Comparison of intervals	Temperature scale Grade point average Attitude toward brands	Mean
Ratio	Comparison of absolute magnitudes	Units sold Number of purchasers Probability of purchase Weight	Geometric mean Harmonic mean

[a]All the comparisons applicable to a given scale are permissible with all scales above it in the table. For example, the ratio scale allows the comparison of intervals and the investigation of order and identity, in addition to the comparison of absolute magnitudes.

[b]The measures of average applicable to a given scale are also appropriate for all scales below it in the table; that is, the mode is also a meaningful measure of the average when measurement is on an ordinal, interval, or ratio scale.

"1" and two times greater than "2," and so on. However, when we assign numerals to attributes of objects, these relations do not necessarily hold. Rather, we have to determine which properties of the scale of numbers actually apply. "This problem has nothing to do with determining the properties of the number; rather, we must determine the *properties of the attribute itself,* and then be sure that the numerals are assigned so that the *numerals properly reflect the properties of the attribute*" (emphasis added).[6] Consider the different types of scales on which attributes can be measured — namely, nominal, ordinal, interval, and ratio.[7] Table 9.1 summarizes some of the more important features of these scales, which are elaborated in the following sections.

---

[6]Wendell R. Garner and C. D. Creelman, "Problems and Methods of Psychological Scaling," in Harry Helson and William Bevan, eds., *Contemporary Approaches to Psychology* (New York: Van Nostrand, 1967), p. 3. The following discussion relies heavily on this excellent article. See also Earl R. Babbie, *The Practice of Social Research,* 6th ed. (Belmont, Calif.: Wadsworth Publishing Company, 1992).

[7]Our classification follows that of Stanley S. Stevens, "Mathematics, Measurement and Psychophysics," in Stanley S. Stevens, ed., *Handbook of Experimental Psychology* (New York: John Wiley, 1951), the most accepted classification in the social sciences.

Nominal Scale

One of the simplest properties of the scale of numbers is *identity*. A person's social security number is a **nominal scale,** as are the numbers on football jerseys, lockers, and so on. These numbers simply *identify* the individual assigned the number. Similarly, if in a given study males are coded ''1'' and females ''2,'' we have again made use of a nominal scale. The individuals are uniquely identified as male or female. All we need to determine an individual's sex is to know whether the person is coded as a ''1'' or as a ''2.'' Note further that there is nothing implied by the numerals other than identification of the sex of the person. Females, although they bear a higher number, are not necessarily ''superior'' to males, or ''more'' than males, or twice as many as males as the numbers 2 and 1 indicate, or vice versa. We could just as easily reverse our coding procedure so that each female is a ''1'' and each male a ''2.''

The reason we could reverse our codes is that the only property conveyed by the numbers is identity. With a nominal scale, the only permissible operation is counting. Thus, the mode is the only legitimate measure of central tendency. It does not make sense in a sample consisting of 60 men and 40 women to say that the average sex is 1.4, given males were coded ''1'' and females ''2'' [0.6(1) + 0.4(2)]. All we can say is that there were more males in the sample than females, or that 60 percent of the sample was male.

Ordinal Scale

A second property of the scale of numbers is that of *order*. Thus, we could say that the number ''2'' was greater than the number ''1,'' and that ''3'' was greater than both ''2'' and ''1,'' and that ''4'' was greater than all three of these numbers. The numbers 1, 2, 3, and 4 are ordered, and the larger the number, the greater the property. Note that the **ordinal scale** implies identity, since the same number would be used for all objects that are the same. An example would be the assignment of the number ''1'' to denote freshmen, ''2'' to denote sophomores, ''3'' juniors, and ''4'' seniors. Note that we could have just as well used the numbers ''10'' for freshmen, ''20'' for sophomores, ''25'' for juniors, and ''30'' for seniors. This assignment would still indicate the class level of each person and the *relative standing* of two persons when compared in terms of who is further along in the academic program. Note further that this is all that is conveyed by an ordinal scale. The difference in rank says nothing about the difference in academic achievement between two ranks. This is perhaps easier to see if we talk about the three top people in a graduating class. The fact that one person was ranked number one while the second was ranked number two tells us nothing about the difference in academic achievement between the two. Nor can we say that the difference in academic achievement between the first- and second-ranked people equals the difference between the second- and third-ranked people, even though the difference between ''1'' and ''2'' equals the difference between ''2'' and ''3.''

As suggested, we can transform an ordinal scale in any way that we wish as long as we maintain the basic ordering of the objects. The ordinal scale is thus said to allow any monotonic positive transformation of the assigned numerals, because the differences in numerals are void of meaning other than order.

Again, whether we can use the ordinal scale to assign numerals to objects depends on the attribute in question. The attribute itself must possess the ordinal property to allow ordinal scaling that is meaningful.

With ordinal scales, both the median and mode are permissible or meaningful measures of average. Thus, if twenty people ranked Product A, say, first in comparison with Products B and C, while ten ranked it second and five ranked it third, we could say that (1) the average rank of Product A as judged by the median response was one (with thirty-five subjects, the median is given by the eighteenth response when ranked from lowest to highest) and that (2) the modal rank was also one.

Interval Scale

A third property of the scale of numbers is that the *intervals* between the numbers are meaningful in the sense that the numbers tell us how far apart the objects are with respect to the attribute. This means that the *differences* can be compared. The difference between "1" and "2" is equal to the difference between "2" and "3." Further, the difference between "2" and "4" is twice the difference that exists between "1" and "2."

One classic example of an **interval scale** is the temperature scale, as it indicates what we can and cannot say when we have measured an attribute on an interval scale. Suppose that the low temperature for the day was 40°F and the high was 80°F. Can we say that the high temperature was twice as hot (that is, represented twice the heat) as the low temperature? The answer is an unequivocal no. To see the folly in claiming 80°F is twice as warm as 40°F, one simply needs to convert these temperatures to their centigrade equivalents where $C = (5F - 160)/9$. Now we see that the low was 4.4°C and the high was 26.6°C, a much different ratio between low and high than was indicated by the Fahrenheit scale.

The example serves to illustrate that we cannot compare the absolute magnitude of numbers when measurement is made on the basis of an interval scale. The reason is that in an interval scale, the zero point is established arbitrarily.[8] This means that any positive linear transformation of the form $y = a + bx$, where b is positive, x is the original number, and y is the transformed number, will preserve the properties of the scale.

What, then, can we say when measurement is made on an interval scale? First, we can say that 80°F is warmer than 40°F. Second, given a third temperature, we *can compare the intervals;* that is, we can say the difference in "heat" between 80°F and 120°F is the same as the difference between 40°F and 80°F, and that the difference between 40°F and 120°F is twice the difference between 40°F and 80°F. To see that this conclusion is legitimate, we can simply resort to the centigrade equivalents; 120°F represents 48.8°C, and the difference between 4.4°C (40°F) and 26.6°C (80°F) is the same as that between 26.6°C (80°F) and 48.8°C (120°F) — namely, 22.2°. Further, the difference of 44.4°C between 4.4°C and 48.8°C is twice as large as that between 4.4°C and 26.6°C, as it was when the Fahrenheit scale was used. The comparison of intervals is legitimate with an interval scale because the relationships among the differences hold

---

[8]The zero point on the Fahrenheit scale was originally established by mixing equal weights of snow and salt.

regardless of the particular constants chosen for *a* and *b* when transforming an interval set of numbers. With an interval scale, the mean, median, and mode are all meaningful measures of average.

Ratio Scale

The **ratio scale** differs from an interval scale in that it possesses a *natural* or *absolute* zero, one for which there is universal agreement about its location. Height and weight are obvious examples.

With a ratio scale, the comparison of the *absolute magnitude* of the numbers is legitimate. Thus, a person weighing 200 pounds is said to be twice as heavy as one weighing 100 pounds, and a person weighing 300 pounds is three times as heavy. Further, we have already seen that the more powerful scales include the properties possessed by the less powerful ones. This means that with a ratio scale we can compare intervals, rank objects according to magnitude, or use the numbers to identify the objects.

Ratio scales only allow the proportionate transformation of the scale values and not the addition of an arbitrary constant as do interval scales. A proportionate transformation is of the form $y = bx$, where x again represents the original values and y the transformed values and b is some positive constant. The conversion of feet to inches ($b = 12$) is an obvious example. All the relationships among the objects are preserved whether the comparison is made in feet or inches.

The geometric mean as well as the more usual arithmetic mean, median, and mode are meaningful measures of average when attributes are measured on a ratio scale.

SCALING OF PSYCHOLOGICAL ATTRIBUTES

The attribute determines the most powerful scale that can be used to measure the characteristic. That is always the way it is in measurement. The characteristic and its qualities set the upper limit for the assignment of numerals to objects. Because of the procedures used in generating the instrument, it is always possible to end up with what we might call a less powerful measure of the attribute (for example, a nominal rather than an ordinal scale). However, we can never exceed the basic nature of the attribute with our measure; for example, we can never generate an interval scale for an attribute that is only ordinal in nature. Thus, it is critical to know something about the attribute itself before we assign numbers to it using some measurement procedure. For instance, there are few psychological constructs that can reasonably be assumed to have a natural or absolute zero.

> For example, what would an absolute zero of intelligence be? Or what is the absolute zero of attitude toward the Republican Party? There can be neutrality of feeling, and neutral position is often used as the zero point on the scale, but it does not represent an absolute lack of the attitude.[9]

[9]Garner and Creelman, "Problems and Methods," p. 4.

The problem is no less real in marketing. Many of our constructs, borrowed from psychology and sociology, possess no more than interval measurement and some even less. We have to be very careful in conceptualizing the construct or characteristic so as not to delude ourselves or mislead others with our measures and (more importantly) *with our interpretation of those measures.*

Further, the procedure used in constructing the scale determines the type of scale actually generated. The more powerful scales allow stronger comparisons and conclusions to be made. Thus, we can make certain types of comparisons that allow particular conclusions when measurement is on a ratio scale, for example, that we cannot make when measurement is on an interval, ordinal, or nominal scale. There is a great temptation to *assume* that our measures have the properties of the ratio or at least the interval scale. Whether they do in fact is another question, and the simple condition that the attributes of the objects have been assigned numbers should not delude us. Rather, we should critically ask: What is the basic nature of the attribute? Have we captured this basic nature by our measurement procedure?

Moreover, while ratio scales allow stronger comparisons, they are also more demanding on subjects. For example, Figure 9.1 uses the issue of a respondent's preferences for six different soft drinks to illustrate how questions about this issue might be framed to secure reactions on a nominal, ordinal, interval, and ratio scale. Readers are encouraged to complete the exercise in light of their own preferences. Did you find it more difficult to complete the ''more powerful'' scales at the bottom of the figure than the nominal scale at the top? Thus, while we might like to capture a respondent's reaction on a ratio scale, there is often a question as to whether our measurement procedure will allow it.

ATTITUDE-SCALING PROCEDURES

There are a number of ways in which attitudes have been measured, including self reports, observation of overt behavior, indirect techniques, performance of ''objective'' tasks, and physiological reactions.[10] By far the most common approach has been **self reports,** in which people are asked directly for their beliefs or feelings toward an object, activity, or class of objects. For example, Research Realities 9.2 depicts the results of a study conducted by the Gallup Organization that used self reports to investigate how people of various ages felt about the use of older people in advertisements. A number of scales and scaling methods have been devised to secure these feelings. The main types will be reviewed in the next section. For the moment we will consider very briefly the other approaches to attitude determination.

Observation of Behavior   The observation approach to attitude determination rests on the presumption that a subject's behavior is conditioned by his or her attitudes and, thus, that we can use the observed behavior to infer these attitudes. What is often done is to

---

[10]This classification of approaches is taken from Stuart W. Cook and Claire Selltiz, ''A Multiple Indicator Approach to Attitude Measurement,'' *Psychological Bulletin,* 62 (1964), pp. 36–55.

Nominal Scale

Which of the soft drinks on the following list do you like? Check all that apply.

_____ Coke
_____ Dr Pepper
_____ Mountain Dew
_____ Pepsi
_____ Seven Up
_____ Sprite

Ordinal Scale

Please rank the soft drinks on the following list according to your degree of liking for each, assigning your most preferred drink rank = 1 and your least preferred drink rank = 6.

_____ Coke
_____ Dr Pepper
_____ Mountain Dew
_____ Pepsi
_____ Seven Up
_____ Sprite

Interval Scale

Please indicate your degree of liking of each of the soft drinks on the following list by checking the appropriate position on the scale.

	Dislike A Lot	Dislike	Like	Like A Lot
Coke	_____	_____	_____	_____
Dr Pepper	_____	_____	_____	_____
Mountain Dew	_____	_____	_____	_____
Pepsi	_____	_____	_____	_____
Seven Up	_____	_____	_____	_____
Sprite	_____	_____	_____	_____

Ratio Scale

Please divide 100 points among each of the following soft drinks according to your degree of liking for each.

_____ Coke
_____ Dr Pepper
_____ Mountain Dew
_____ Pepsi
_____ Seven Up
_____ Sprite
  100

Research Realities 9.2

How People in Various Age Groups Feel about Older People in Ads

Percentage of respondents who:

Feel advertisers don't use people over age 50 enough in advertising.

React positively to advertising with older adults.

Feel those over age 50 are not accurately portrayed in advertising.

Feel advertisers are obsessed with youth.

Ages 18-34 35-44 45-54 55-64 65 and over

Source: Adapted from Yvonne Dodd, "Those Old People Are Not Me," *Advertising Age*, 60 (May 22, 1989), p. S–2.

create an artificial situation and see how the individual behaves. For example, to assess a person's attitude toward antipollution legislation, the subject might be asked to sign a "strong" petition prohibiting pollution. The individual's attitude toward pollution would be inferred on the basis of whether or not he or she signed. Alternatively, subjects might be thrust into a group discussing the issue of pollution and their behavior observed. Did the persons oppose or support antipollution legislation in the discussion?

Indirect Techniques   The indirect techniques of attitude assessment use some unstructured or partially structured stimuli as discussed in Chapter 7, such as word association tests, sentence completion tests, storytelling, and so on. Because the arguments concerning the use of these devices were detailed previously, they will not be repeated here.

Performance of "Objective" Task   These approaches rest on the presumption that a subject's **performance of objective tasks** will depend on the person's attitude. Thus, to assess a person's pollution posture, we might ask him or her to memorize a number of facts about the extent of pollution, the magnitude of the cleanup task, and pending antipollution legislation. This material would reflect both sides of the issue. The researcher would then attempt to determine what facts the person assimilated. The assumption is that subjects would be more apt to remember those arguments that are most consistent with their own position.

Physiological Reactions   The physiological reaction approach to attitude measurement was also detailed in Chapter 7. Here, through electrical or mechanical means such as the galvanic skin response technique, the researcher monitors the subject's response to the controlled introduction of some stimuli. One problem that arises in using these measures to assess attitude is that the individual's physiological response only provides an indication of the intensity of the individual's feelings and not whether they are negative or positive.

Multiple Measures   Although self-report techniques for attitude assessment are the most widely used in marketing research studies because they are easy to administer, one should be aware of these other approaches, particularly when one is attempting to establish the validity of a self-report measure. They can provide useful insight into how the method of measurement, and not the differences in the basic attitudes of subjects, caused the scores to vary. This is consistent with the notion of using multiple indicators to establish the convergent and discriminant validity of a measure.[11]

SELF-REPORT ATTITUDE SCALES

Given that attitude is one of the most pervasive concepts in all of sociopsychology, it should not prove surprising to find that there have been many methods advanced to

---

[11]The arguments are elaborated in Cook and Selltiz, "A Multiple Indicator Approach." The ideas of convergent and discriminant validity are discussed in Appendix 9C. Evidence of the convergent validity of a measure is provided by the extent to which it correlates highly with other measures designed to assess the same construct. Evidence of the discriminant validity of a measure is indicated by low correlations between the measure of interest and other measures that are supposedly not measuring the same variable or construct.

measure it. While the self-report technique is common to many of the methods, they still differ in terms of the way the scales are constructed and used. In this section, we shall review some of these self-report scales, particularly those that have novel features or have been used extensively in marketing studies. The discussion should give you an appreciation of the main types and their construction and use. Incidentally, in following the arguments, you will find it helpful to distinguish between how a scale is constructed and how it is used.

Equal-Appearing Intervals

Suppose that one of the banks in town is interested in comparing its image to the images of its competitors and has developed a list of statements that can be employed to describe each of the banks. Now suppose that, when presented with a list of characteristics, a respondent describes Bank A, the sponsor of the research, as having convenient hours and a convenient location but generally discourteous service and higher service charges on personal checking accounts. Does this respondent have a favorable or unfavorable attitude toward Bank A? Suppose that the respondent describes Bank B as just the opposite. To which bank is the individual more favorably disposed? We cannot say without knowing what the individual statements imply about the person's overall attitude. It is the purpose of **equal-appearing interval** scaling to develop values for the statements (characteristics) so that we can assess a person's attitude toward Bank A or any other bank by analyzing the statements with which the individual describes each bank.[12]

Scale Construction   The general procedure for constructing a scale using equal-appearing intervals is first to generate a large number of statements concerning the psychological object of interest. The statements are then edited to remove obviously ambiguous, irrelevant, and awkward statements, as well as statements that are matters of fact rather than opinion. A relatively large sample of judges is then asked to sort the statements by their degree of favorableness, and a scale value is determined for each statement by the frequency with which the statement is placed in each of the piles. The statements are then screened on the basis of two criteria: the scale values and the dispersion in judgments exhibited by the subjects. A final scale is formed from those statements that span the range of scale values and that display relatively good interjudge reliability. Let us illustrate the procedure using our bank example.

The first task would be to generate a large number of statements. These statements could be generated from a search of the literature, discussions with knowledgeable people, personal experience, or in any of the other ways one uses to develop insight into a phenomenon. The important thing at this stage is that the statements be as exhaustive as

---

[12]The equal-appearing interval technique was developed by L. L. Thurstone and E. J. Chave, *The Measurement of Attitude* (Chicago: University of Chicago Press, 1929). The procedure provided an alternative to the paired comparison method of determining statement scale values when the number of statements was large. The paired comparison method, which was also devised by Thurstone, was a forerunner of much modern-day psychological measurement. See L. L. Thurstone, "A Law of Comparative Judgement," *Psychological Review,* 34 (1927), pp. 273–286, and "Psychological Analysis," *American Journal of Psychology,* 38 (1927), pp. 368–389.

possible; that is, they reflect all the attributes of the object that may lead to formation of attitudes about it. Thus, we would want to incorporate statements about a bank's level of service, convenience, interest paid on savings accounts, interest required on loans, and so on.[13] Further, it is often productive at this stage to include several statements that apply to the same attribute but that are worded differently. The following would be examples.

1. The bank offers courteous service.
2. The bank has a convenient location.
3. The bank has convenient hours.
4. The bank offers low interest rates on loans.
5. The bank pays low interest on its savings accounts.

.

.

.

m. The bank's service is friendly.

Ideally, *m* would be in the neighborhood of 100 to 200, and each statement would be presented on a separate card.

After editing the statements, a large sample of subjects would be recruited as judges.[14] Each judge would be instructed to sort the statements into one of eleven piles based on the "degree of favorableness" of the statement. Note this. The judges are not asked whether they agree or disagree with a statement, but rather they are asked to evaluate the statement on its own merits. For example, they would be asked to place (1) those statements that seem to express the *most unfavorable* things one could say about the object in the *A* pile of Figure 9.2, (2) those statements that express the *most favorable* things one could say in the *K* pile, and (3) those statements that are neither positive nor negative in the *F* pile. Those statements that express some intermediate level of favorableness or unfavorableness would, of course, be placed in one of the other piles. The piles are most typically formed by arranging a set of cards with letters on them in front of the judge. Only the two end points and the middle position are anchored with word descriptions in addition to the letter. The presumption is that each judge will perceive the categories as representing equal increments of favorableness, and thus the name *equal-appearing intervals.*

---

[13]See Neil M. Ford, *How to Measure Your Bank's Personality* (Chicago: Bank Marketing Association, 1973), p. 19, for a list of some of the attributes of a bank one might wish to inquire about. See also Sid C. Dudley, Gary F. Young, and Richard L. Powers, "A Study of Factors Affecting Individuals' Banking Preferences," *Journal of Professional Services Marketing,* 1 (1985), pp. 163–168; R. Kenneth Teas and John Wong, "Measurement of Customer Perceptions of the Retail Bank Delivery System," *Journal of Professional Services Marketing,* 7 (No. 1, 1991), pp. 147–167.

[14]Thurstone and Chave used 300 judges. Edwards summarizes a number of studies, however, in which fewer judges have been used to produce reliable scales. See Allen L. Edwards, *Techniques of Attitude Scale Construction* (New York: Appleton-Century-Crofts, 1957), pp. 94–95. The serious student of attitude measurement would be well advised to read Edwards' good little book.

FIGURE **9.2**   **Thurstone Equal-Appearing Interval Continuum**

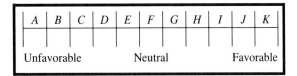

Suppose that 200 judges sorted the *m*-statements according to their favorableness and that Table 9.2 contains the resulting distribution for the first four statements. The right-hand columns of the table contain the scale and *Q* values for each statement. The scale value represents the ''average'' value of the statement, given the scores assigned each sorting category. The scale values locate each statement on the favorability continuum in Figure 9.2. The median is typically used as the measure of average. The *Q* value is the interquartile range, which provides a measure of spread or dispersion in where each statement is placed.

The scale values and measures of dispersion are used to select a subset of statements to serve as the final instrument. Typically, the researcher selects 20 to 22 statements that span the scale of favorableness; that is, some of the statements in the final list would have low scale values, some intermediate values, and some high values. Ideally, the scale values would be equally spaced. One can see from the limited example that several, if not many, of the initial statements will have approximately equal scale values. How does one then choose among them? This is where the interquartile range enters. We would like to have items in our final scale that are likely to be interpreted consistently by those responding. Thus, we do not want to include a statement that could be agreed to by those with both positive and negative attitudes toward the object. Large values of *Q* indicate that, at least in our judgment sample, there was wide disagreement among the judges as to the degree of favorableness expressed in the statement, and, therefore, the statement is ambiguous. Given that two statements have approximately equal values, we

TABLE **9.2**   **Equal-Appearing Interval Sort of the Statements into Categories**

Statement	A 1	B 2	C 3	D 4	E 5	F 6	G 7	H 8	I 9	J 10	K 11	Scale Value	Q Value
					Sorting Categories								
1	0	8	10	30	60	60	14	12	6	0	0	5.4	1.7
2	0	0	0	0	0	6	16	28	44	66	40	9.6	1.8
3	0	0	0	0	10	10	14	32	84	34	16	8.9	1.5
4	0	0	8	16	36	58	48	24	10	0	0	6.2	2.0

choose the one that has the smallest Q. In sum, the scale and Q values serve as filters for reducing the total stimuli to a more manageable number.

Scale Use   Assume that some 20 to 22 statements have been selected from the larger list of *m* statements using the procedure detailed previously. The statements are randomly placed in the final instrument so that there is no order to the scale values. The instrument is then ready to be administered to one or more samples of subjects whose attitudes we are interested in assessing.

When the instrument is administered, subjects are asked to indicate those statements with which they agree or disagree. For example, subjects would be asked to select those statements from the total list that reflect their feelings toward Bank A. A subject's attitude score is considered to be the average of the scale scores for the statements with which the person agrees. Thus, if the subject agreed with three statements with the scale scores 8.2, 8.7, and 9.8, the person's attitude score would be 8.9. Since the scale value 6 represents a neutral attitude, the conclusion would be that the subject had a favorable attitude toward Bank A.

Several criticisms have been leveled at the method of scoring. One centers on subjects' only being asked to select those statements with which they agree and not being asked to respond to each of the statements. This makes it possible for two subjects who respond quite differently to have the same attitude score. Thus, a subject agreeing with statements with scale scores 4, 6, and 8 would have the same attitude score as another person who only agreed with the statement having a scale score of 6. But do they, in fact, have the same attitude? There is still considerable controversy on this point.

Another frequent criticism is that the method does not allow subjects to express the intensity of their feelings. For example, a subject could feel quite strongly that the bank had very convenient hours or he might feel that although basically convenient, the hours could be improved. In either case, all that the subject would be able to do would be to indicate that he agrees with the statement. Yet, are not the two attitudes basically different?

As you might suspect, the equal-appearing interval scale is relatively expensive and time consuming to construct. Once constructed, though, it is very easy to administer and is easy for respondents to complete. It can further be used to assess attitudes toward a variety of objects (for example, each bank in town). The technique can also be employed to scale other things besides attitude, such as the amount of perceived puffery in each of a series of advertising claims or the consistency in the favorableness of various adjectives across groups of people.[15] The effort involved in its construction and the limited diagnostic information it provides have tended to limit its use in assessing attitudes. The evidence indicates, for example, that it is used less than the other self-report techniques for assessing attitudes. Nonetheless, its other potential uses still make the equal-interval technique a valuable component in the marketing researcher's measurement arsenal.

---

[15]Used in this way, the method is helpful in developing anchors for scales that are perceived by respondents to be equally spaced.

FIGURE **9.3** **Example of Likert Summated Rating Form**

	Strongly Disagree	Disagree	Neither Agree Nor Disagree	Agree	Strongly Agree
1. The bank offers courteous service.	____	____	____	____	____
2. The bank has a convenient location.	____	____	____	____	____
3. The bank has convenient hours.	____	____	____	____	____
4. The bank offers low interest rate loans.	____	____	____	____	____

Summated Ratings

The Likert method of **summated ratings** overcomes the previous criticisms about scoring and allowing an expression of intensity of feeling.[16] The method is both constructed and used in a slightly different way than equal-appearing intervals.

Scale Construction   The basic format of the scale for the summated ratings method is the same in both construction and use. Subjects are asked to indicate their degree of agreement or disagreement with each and every statement in a series by checking the appropriate cell. Figure 9.3 serves as an example. Again, the researcher attempts to develop a great many statements that reflect qualities of things about the object that possibly influence a person's attitude toward it. In this respect, the procedure is no different from that used in the method of equal-appearing intervals. The method is quite different, though, in terms of the judgment sample and what is asked of the subjects.

It is often argued that those judging the statements need not represent the population on which an equal-appearing interval scale will be used, because the judges are only asked to indicate the degree of favorableness of each statement.[17] With a Likert scale, there is no question that the screening sample should be representative of the larger group, because of both the different task assigned the subjects and the method by which the total set of statements is reduced to a smaller, more consistent subset. It must be pointed out that a screening sample has not always been used in the published marketing applications of the summated rating scale. This is unfortunate, because omitting refinement of a scale is likely to result in a more ambiguous, less reliable, less valid instrument.

Once again, assume that there are 200 subjects in the screening sample. First, each statement is classified *a priori* as favorable or unfavorable. Subjects are then asked to

---

[16]The scale was first proposed by Rensis Likert, "A Technique for the Measurement of Attitudes," *Archives of Psychology,* No. 140 (1932).

[17]There is some empirical evidence that tends to refute this argument. Even though the judges are supposed to evaluate each statement on its own merits, there does seem to be some tendency for a judge's own attitudes to influence his or her placement of the statements. Edwards, *Techniques,* pp. 106–116, summarizes these studies.

indicate their degree of agreement or disagreement with each statement with respect to a specific bank (or banks).[18] The various degrees of agreement are assigned scale values, although the particular values differ from researcher to researcher. Sometimes the values $-2, -1, 0, 1, 2$ are employed, whereas the values 1, 2, 3, 4, 5 are preferred by other researchers for the respective response categories. It makes no difference in the conclusions we can draw, since the decision is completely arbitrary. Suppose that we decide to use the values 1 through 5. Now, a subject could be considered to feel positively about the bank if he or she either agreed with a favorable statement or disagreed with an unfavorable statement. Therefore, it is necessary to reverse the scaling with negative statements. Thus, a *strongly agree* response to a favorable statement and a *strongly disagree* response to an unfavorable statement would both receive scores of 5.

A total attitude score can be calculated for each subject using the same scoring procedure. The distribution of total scores is then used to refine the original list of m statements. The procedure, known as item analysis, rests on the proposition that there should be consistency in the response pattern of any individual. If the individual has a very favorable attitude toward the object, he or she should basically agree with the favorable statements and disagree with the unfavorable ones and vice versa. If we should happen to have a statement that generates a very mixed response, we would tend to question it on the grounds that it must be ambiguous or at the very least not discriminating of attitude. A parallel example would be the problem $2 + 2 = 4$ for a college math course. The problem tells us little about a person's math ability because both poor and good students could be expected to answer the problem correctly. Thus, the problem would be unsuitable for scaling the students on their math ability.

The same argument holds for attitude scales. We do not want to clutter up the scale with irrelevant statements but rather wish to include only those statements that discriminate among subjects with respect to their attitude. Although you embrace the premise, you may be wondering about the procedure. After all, did we not just say that those with a "very favorable" attitude could be expected to respond favorably to positive statements? How does one determine who has a favorable or unfavorable attitude, though? After all, aren't we developing the scale so that we are in a position to measure a person's attitude, and thus aren't we engaged in circular reasoning of "using a person's basic attitude to select statements by which that attitude can be measured"? You would be right, of course. Yet there is a way out of the circle. The trick is to assume that the total score generated by the response to all m statements serves as a proxy for the person's true attitude. One can then relate each statement in turn to this total score to ascertain which statements are nondiscriminating.

One can relate individual statement scores to total scores by several methods. The most conceptually appealing approach calculates the product moment correlation of each item with the total score.[19] Those items that have the highest correlation with the total

---

[18]Paul E. Spector, "Choosing Response Categories for Summated Rating Scales," *Journal of Applied Psychology,* 61 (June 1976), pp. 374–375, contains a list of typical category descriptors and their numerical values.

[19]Nunnally, *Psychometric Theory,* Chaps. 6–8, has a rather compelling argument as to why correlation coefficients should be used to refine scales. The correlation coefficient is discussed in Chapter 16.

TABLE **9.3** **Difference in Means for One Statement for the Two Groups with the Most Favorable and the Least Favorable Attitudes**

Response Category	Scale Value x	High Group f	High Group fx	Low Group f	Low Group fx
Strongly agree	5	28	140	2	10
Agree	4	14	56	6	24
Neither agree nor disagree	3	6	18	18	54
Disagree	2	2	4	20	40
Strongly disagree	1	0	0	4	4
Sums		50	218	50	132

$$\bar{x}_H = \frac{218}{50} = 4.36, \quad \bar{x}_L = \frac{132}{50} = 2.64, \quad d = \bar{x}_H - \bar{x}_L = 4.36 - 2.64 = 1.72$$

are the best. Those with correlations near zero are suspect and should be eliminated. By ranking the correlations, one can use this method to devise a final scale of any length desired. One simply selects those 25, 50, or however many statements having the highest correlations with the total score, although there usually is some attempt to include negative as well as positive statements.

An alternative way of performing an item analysis involves the division of subjects into some arbitrarily defined groups. For example, those subjects with the top 25 percent of all total scores would be considered to have the most favorable attitudes, whereas those with the lowest 25 percent of all total scores would be considered to have the least favorable attitudes. If the item is a good one, it would seem reasonable that after correcting for the scoring direction, the mean score for each statement for the favorable attitude group should exceed the mean score for the unfavorable attitude group. The statements can then be ranked according to their difference in mean scores. Those with mean differences near zero are poor statements and should be eliminated. Sometimes the researcher will go one step further and will test for the statistical significance of the difference in mean scores for the two groups, in which case only those statements that show a statistically significant difference would be retained.[20] Table 9.3 displays a comparison of means, without testing for the statistical significance of the difference, for a sample statement ''The bank has a convenient location'' and assumed responses for the 50 subjects with the most favorable and the 50 subjects with the least favorable attitudes. The calculation indicates that the statement is a discriminating one, because the difference in mean scores is indeed positive.

Scale Use One advantage of the Likert scale of summated ratings is that directions for its use are the same as the directions employed to generate scores by which to screen statements. The statements remaining after purification of the original list are randomly

---

[20]The statistical test would be the t test for the difference in two means described in Chapter 15.

ordered on the scale form so as to mix positive and negative ones, and subjects are asked to indicate their degree of agreement with each statement. Subjects generally find it easy to respond, because the response categories do allow the expression of the intensity of the feeling. The subject's total score is generated as the simple sum of the scores on each statement.[21]

A problem of interpretation arises with the summated rating scale that did not exist with the equal-appearing interval scale. With the latter, a score of 9.2, say, represented a favorable attitude toward Bank A, but what does a score of 78 on a 20-item Likert scale indicate? Because the maximum is $20 \times 5 = 100$, can we assume that the person's attitude toward the bank is favorable? We cannot, since the raw scores only assume meaning when we compare them to some standard. This problem is not unique to psychological scaling but arises every day of our lives in a variety of ways. We are always making judgments on the basis of comparisons with some standard. Most typically the standard is established through our experiences and rarely is rigorously defined. Thus, when we say ''The man sure is tall,'' we are in effect saying that on the basis of the experience we have, the man is taller than average.

In psychological scaling, this is formalized somewhat by clearly specifying the standard. Very often the standard is taken as the average score for all subjects, although averages are also computed for certain predefined subgroups. The procedure is called developing norms. Comparisons can then be made against the norms to determine whether the person has a positive or negative attitude toward the object. Norms are not, of course, necessary for comparing subjects to determine which person has the more favorable attitude. Here one can simply compare the subjects' raw scores. Nor are norms necessary when attempting to determine whether an individual's attitude has changed over time or whether a person likes one object better than another. One can simply compare the later and earlier scores or the difference in scores for the two objects.

Semantic Differential

The **semantic differential** scale grew out of some research at the University of Illinois designed to investigate the underlying structure of words.[22] The technique has been adapted, however, to measure attitudes.

The original semantic differential scale consisted of a great many bipolar adjectives, which were employed to secure people's reactions to the objects of interest. It was found that the reactions to the bipolar scales tended to be correlated and that three basic uncor-

---

[21]For an example, see William C. Lundstrom and Lawrence M. Lamont, ''The Development of a Scale to Measure Consumer Discontent,'' *Journal of Marketing Research*, 13 (November 1976), pp. 373–381, which reports the procedures used and the results obtained in the development of a Likert scale to measure consumer discontent. For a generalizable procedure on how to go about constructing scales, see Gilbert A. Churchill, Jr., ''A Paradigm for Developing Better Measures of Marketing Constructs,'' *Journal of Marketing Research*, 16 (February 1979), pp. 64–73. See also Paul E. Spector, *Summated Rating Scale Construction* (Newbury Park, CA.: Sage Publications, Inc., 1992).

[22]Charles E. Osgood, George J. Suci, and Percy H. Tannenbaum, *The Measurement of Meaning* (Champaign, Ill.: University of Illinois Press, 1957).

related dimensions could be found to account for most of the variation in ratings: an *evaluation* dimension represented by adjective pairs such as good–bad, sweet–sour, helpful–unhelpful; a *potency* dimension represented by bipolar items such as powerful–powerless, strong–weak, deep–shallow; and an *activity* dimension captured by adjective pairs such as fast–slow, alive–dead, noisy–quiet. The same three dimensions tended to emerge regardless of the object being evaluated.[23] Thus, the general thrust in using the semantic differential technique to form scales has been to select an appropriate sample of adjective pairs so that a score could be generated for the object for each of the evaluation, potency, and activity dimensions. The object could then be compared to other objects using these scores.

The approach in marketing has been somewhat different from the general thrust. First, instead of applying the *basic* adjective pairs to the objects of interest, marketers have generated items of their own. These items have not always been antonyms, nor have they been single words. Rather, marketers have used phrases to anchor the ends of the scale, and some of these phrases have been attributes possessed by the product. Since a negative amount of the attribute is often a meaningless notion, lack of the attribute has been used as one end of the scale and a great deal of the attribute as the other.[24] Second, instead of attempting to generate evaluation, potency, and activity scores, marketers have been more interested in developing profiles for the brands, stores, companies, or whatever is being compared, as well as total scores by which the objects could be compared. In this respect, the use of the semantic differential approach in marketing studies has tended to follow the Likert approach to scale construction rather than the semantic differential tradition. Unfortunately, marketers have often failed to engage in the recommended scale purification procedures that should accompany this switch in emphasis, thus raising questions about the validity of the resulting semantic differential scales.[25]

Let us again use the bank attitude scaling problem to illustrate the semantic differential method. First, a researcher would generate a large list of bipolar adjectives or phrases. Figure 9.4 parallels Figure 9.3 in terms of the attributes used to describe the bank, but it is arranged in a semantic differential format. All we have done in Figure 9.4 is to try to express the things that could be used to describe a bank, and thus serve as a basis for attitude formation, in terms of positive and negative statements. Note that the negative phrase sometimes appears at the left side of the scale and other times at the

---

[23]See David R. Heise, "The Semantic Differential and Attitude Research," in Summers, ed., *Attitude Measurement*, pp. 235–253, for an overview of the many studies in which the three dimensions were found. Factor analysis is the basic procedure employed to reduce a number of bipolar adjective pairs to basic dimensions. The rudiments of factor analysis are presented in Chapter 17.

[24]Much of the impetus for these practices seems to have been provided by W. A. Mindak, "Fitting the Semantic Differential to the Marketing Problem," *Journal of Marketing*, 25 (April 1961), pp. 28–33.

[25]After a sample of subjects uses the scale to evaluate an attitude object, the scale should be purified in the same manner as was the summated rating scale. The total score for each subject would be calculated and the ambiguous or nondiscriminating items eliminated by calculating item to total correlations or by looking at the mean scores by item of the high and low total scores. While this is rarely done with semantic differential scales, it is an important step in ensuring that the scale is really measuring what it was designed to measure.

FIGURE 9.4   **Example of Semantic Differential Scaling Form**

Service is discourteous   :__:__:__:__:__:__:__: Service is courteous
Location is convenient   :__:__:__:__:__:__:__: Location is inconvenient
Hours are inconvenient   :__:__:__:__:__:__:__: Hours are convenient
Loan interest rates are high   :__:__:__:__:__:__:__: Loan interest rates are low

right. This is to prevent a respondent with a positive attitude from simply checking either the right- or left-hand sides without even bothering to read the descriptions.

The scale would then be administered to a sample of subjects. Each respondent would be asked to read each set of bipolar phrases and to check the cell that best described her feelings toward the object. The end positions are usually defined for the respondent in the instructions as being *very closely descriptive* of the object, the center position as being *neutral,* and the intermediate positions as *slightly descriptive* and *quite closely descriptive.* Thus, for example, if the subject thought that Bank A's service was courteous but only moderately so, she would check the sixth position reading from left to right.

The subject could be asked to evaluate two or more banks using the same scale.[26] When several banks are rated, the different profiles can be compared. Figure 9.5, for example (which is sometimes referred to as a **snake diagram** because of its shape), illustrates that Bank A is perceived as having more courteous service and a more convenient location and as offering lower interest rates on loans, but also as having more inconvenient hours than Bank B. Note that in constructing these profiles, the customary practice of placing all positive descriptors on the right, to facilitate communication, has been followed. The plotted values simply represent the average score of all subjects on each descriptor. Although the mean is most often used, there is some controversy about whether the seven scale increments can be treated as an interval scale. If not, as critics contend, then the median scores should be used to develop the profiles. In either case, the plotted profiles readily communicate the perceived positions of Banks A and B by the sample respondents.

When a total score by which objects can be compared is desired (for example, which alternative package design is preferred by customers), the score is generated by summing the scores for the individual descriptors. The individual items may be scored $-3, -2, -1, 0, 1, 2, 3,$ or $1, 2, 3, 4, 5, 6, 7.$ Again, even though the decision is arbitrary because of the arbitrary nature of the zero point, these scores are simply

---

[26]The most popular form of the semantic differential scale places the objects being evaluated at the top and the descriptors used for the evaluation along the sides as the rows. One somewhat popular variation lists the descriptors at the top and the objects being evaluated along the side. For an empirical comparison of the two approaches, see Eugene D. Jaffe and Israel D. Nebenzahl, "Alternative Questionnaire Formats for Country Image Studies," *Journal of Marketing Research,* 21 (November 1984), pp. 463–471. See also Linda L. Golden, Gerald Albaum, and Mary Zimmer, 'The Numerical Comparative Scale: An Economical Format for Retail Image Measurement," *Journal of Retailing,* 63 (Winter 1987), pp. 393–410; Ron Garland, "A Comparison of Three Forms of the Semantic Differential," *Marketing Bulletin,* 1 (May 1990), pp. 19–24.

FIGURE **9.5**   **Contrasting Profiles of Banks A and B**

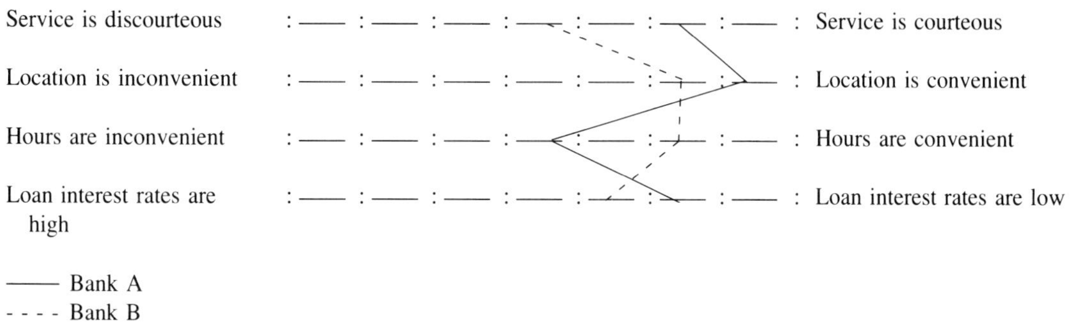

Service is discourteous	: — : — : — : — : — : — : — :	Service is courteous
Location is inconvenient	: — : — : — : — : — : — : — :	Location is convenient
Hours are inconvenient	: — : — : — : — : — : — : — :	Hours are convenient
Loan interest rates are high	: — : — : — : — : — : — : — :	Loan interest rates are low

—— Bank A
- - - - Bank B

summed in the same way as they were in the Likert procedure. It is unfortunate that few marketing studies employ a screening sample with semantic differential scales by which an original sample of items could be refined. While not extremely important in an item-by-item profile comparison, the lack of a rudimentary item analysis is critical when comparing total scores to determine which subject had the most favorable attitude or which object was evaluated most favorably by a given subject. The total scores may be meaningless if the items used in generating the scores are inappropriate, as they very well can be when simply made up but not analyzed for their internal consistency of meaning. The argument and the procedure for accomplishing an item analysis here parallel that for the Likert scale.

Perhaps it is the ease with which semantic differential scales can be developed or the ease with which the findings can be communicated or accumulated experience of their value that accounts for the semantic differential scale's great popularity in marketing. The technique does allow subjects to express the intensity of their feelings toward company, product, package, advertisement, or whatever. When combined with proper item analysis techniques, the semantic differential seems to offer the marketing researcher a most valuable research tool.

Stapel Scale

A modification of the semantic differential scale that has received some attention in marketing literature is the **Stapel scale.** It differs from the semantic differential scale in that (1) adjectives or descriptive phrases are tested separately instead of simultaneously as bipolar pairs; (2) points on the scale are identified by number; and (3) there are ten scale positions rather than seven. Figure 9.6 casts the same four attributes previously used to measure attitudes toward banks in a Stapel scale format. Respondents are told to rate how accurately each statement describes the object of interest (Bank A, for example). Instructions such as the following are given to respondents:

> You would select a *plus* number for words that you think describe (Bank A) accurately. The more accurately you think the word describes it, the larger the *plus* number you would

FIGURE **9.6** **Example of a Stapel Scale**

	−5	−4	−3	−2	−1	+1	+2	+3	+4	+5
Service is courteous	☐	☐	☐	☐	☐	☐	☐	☐	☐	☐
Location is convenient	☐	☐	☐	☐	☐	☐	☐	☐	☐	☐
Hours are convenient	☐	☐	☐	☐	☐	☐	☐	☐	☐	☐
Loan interest rates are high	☐	☐	☐	☐	☐	☐	☐	☐	☐	☐

choose. You would select a *minus* number for words you think do not describe it accurately. The less accurately you think a word describes it, the larger the *minus* number you would choose. Therefore, you can select any number from +5, for words that you think are very accurate, all the way to −5, for words that you think are very inaccurate.[27]

The advantage claimed for the Stapel scale is that it frees the researcher from the need to develop bipolar adjectives for the many items affecting attitudes, which can indeed be a formidable task. Despite this advantage, the Stapel scale has not been as warmly embraced as the semantic differential form, judging by the number of published marketing studies using each.[28] One problem with using it is that many of the descriptors used to evaluate an object can be phrased one of three ways — positively, negatively, or neutrally — and the phrasing chosen seems to affect the results as well as subjects' ability to respond.[29] Nevertheless, it is a useful addition to the researcher's equipment arsenal, and it does lend itself to administration by telephone.[30]

It should be pointed out that a total score on both the semantic differential and Stapel scales is like a total score on a Likert scale. The score 48, for example, is meaningless by itself but takes on meaning when compared to some norm or other score. There is a good deal of controversy about whether semantic differential, Stapel, or even Likert-generated total scores represent interval scaling or, in actuality, reflect ordinal scaling. While the controversy rages, marketers have been inclined to assume the posture of many psychological scaling specialists, who assume interval scaling of their constructs not because they believe that they have necessarily measured them on an

---

[27]Irving Crespi, "Use of a Scaling Technique in Surveys," *Journal of Marketing,* 25 (July 1961), p. 71.

[28]One study that compared the performance of the Stapel scale to the semantic differential found basically no difference between the results produced by, or respondents ability to use, each. See Del I. Hawkins, Gerald Albaum, and Roger Best, "Stapel Scale or Semantic Differential in Marketing Research," *Journal of Marketing Research,* 11 (August 1974), pp. 318–322. See also Grahame R. Dowling, "Measuring Corporate Images: A Review of Alternative Approaches," *Journal of Business Research,* 17 (August 1988), pp. 27–34.

[29]Michael J. Etzel, Terrell G. Williams, John C. Rogers, and Douglas J. Lincoln, "The Comparability of Three Stapel Scale Forms in a Marketing Setting," in Ronald F. Bush and Shelby D. Hunt, eds., *Marketing Theory: Philosophy of Science Perspectives* (Chicago: American Marketing Association, 1982), pp. 303–306.

[30]Gregory D. Upah and Steven C. Cosmas, "The Use of Telephone Dials as Attitude Scales," *Journal of the Academy of Marketing Science* (Fall 1980), pp. 416–426; and Barbara Loken, *et al.,* "The Use of 0–10 Scales in Telephone Surveys," *Journal of the Market Research Society,* 29 (July 1987), pp. 353–362.

interval scale but because interval scaling allows more powerful methods of analysis to be brought to bear. The persistence of this posture in psychological scaling attests to its general fruitfulness, and it seems reasonable that marketers have also found the assumption of interval scaling productive if not entirely correct. There is also a logical justification for this assumption.

> By assuming interval measurement where only ordinal measurement exists, some measurement errors will occur. The result of errors generally is the attenuation of relations among variables. That is, one's apparent results will be more attenuated than they are in reality. Thus it is unlikely that the decision to assume interval measurement when it does not exist will lead to the spurious overestimation of results.[31]

Further, from a statistical point of view, the assumption of intervality often makes sense. Statistical tests of significance, for example, "do not care from where the numbers come." The key criterion in choosing a statistical test is that the assumptions underlying the use of a particular statistical test must be satisfied.[32] It is not necessary,

---

ETHICAL DILEMMA 9.1

An independent researcher was hired by a national chain of department stores to develop a scale by which the chain could measure the image of each of its stores. The researcher thought that the best way to do this was through a semantic differential scale. Since she was interested in establishing her credentials as an expert on store-image research, however, she decided to also develop items for a Likert scale and to administer both of the scales to designated participants. She realized that this might induce greater respondent fatigue and perhaps lower-quality responses, but she was willing to take the chance because she knew that the client would not sanction or pay for administering the second survey to an independent sample of respondents.

- Is it ethical for the researcher to accept the risk of lowering the quality of the data addressing the client's issue so that she can further her own goals and career?

- What if the data collected by the two instruments provided stronger evidence that store image had indeed been measured adequately than that collected through the sole use of the semantic differential scale?

- Would it make any difference if there was a reasonable chance that the Likert format would produce a better instrument for measuring retail image than a semantic differential format?

---

[31]George W. Bohrnstedt, "Reliability and Validity Assessment in Attitude Measurement," in Summers, ed., *Attitude Measurement,* pp. 81–82.

[32]There is evidence that demonstrates, for example, that there is little difference in results when ordinal data are analyzed by procedures appropriate to interval data. See Sanford Labovitz, "Some Observations on Measurement and Statistics," *Social Forces,* 46 (1967), pp. 151–160; Sanford Labovitz, "The Assignment of Numbers to Rank Order Categories," *American Sociological Review,* 35 (1970), pp. 515–524; and John Gaito, "Measurement Scales and Statistics: Resurgence of an Old Misconception," *Psychological Bulletin,* 87 (1980), pp. 564–567. We will have more to say on the relationship between scales of measurements and statistical techniques in Chapter 14.

FIGURE 9.7   **Forced Distribution of *Q*-Sort Items**

Number of statements	4	8	16	24	28	40	28	24	16	8	4	
Least desirable	0	1	2	3	4	5	6	7	8	9	10	Most desirable

therefore, to be *overly* concerned about the level of measurement from a *statistical* point of view. What we must be careful about is the *interpretation* of the results (for example, arguing that a person with a score of 80 has twice as favorable an attitude toward an object as a person with a score of 40 unless the measurement scale is ratio).

Q-*Sort*

The **Q-sort technique** is a general methodology for gathering data and processing the information collected. The task of the subjects in *Q*-sort analysis parallels that for the judgment sample in developing a Thurstone equal-appearing interval scale except (1) the subjects respond to each stimulus in terms of their attitudes toward it and not in terms of its degree of favorableness; and (2) the subjects are instructed to place a specific number of statements in each category — that is, a distribution of responses is forced on the subject. Very often the specified distribution is normal or quasi-normal.

For the bank scaling example, the subject might be asked to sort the *m*-statements into "piles representing the degree of desirability of each characteristic for him specifically." For example, each subject would be asked to place the number of statements in each category indicated in Figure 9.7. To implement, each characteristic of interest would be printed on a separate card, and the subject would be told to place the four characteristics he finds most desirable or preferable in the tenth pile, the four characteristics he finds least desirable in the zero pile, and so on. *Q*-sort scaling is then used to determine the relative ranking of stimuli by individuals and to derive clusters of individuals who display similar preferences, thus perhaps representing unique market segments. Factor analysis, detailed in a later chapter, is used to analyze the responses to identify these clusters of individuals. The objective of *Q*-sort analysis is, then, the intensive study of individuals, a task much different from the scaling of objects or institutions, such as banks.[33]

RATING SCALES

The previous discussion dealt with some of the main scaling methods that have been used to measure attitudes. The treatment was by no means exhaustive. Particularly conspicuous by its absence was a discussion of the importance of the various attributes to

---

[33]See Bruce McKeown and Dan Thomas, *Q Methodology* (Beverly Hills, Calif.: Sage Publications, 1988), for a fuller description of the *Q* methodology.

the individual. That is, in each scaling method discussed, we attempted to determine the individual's perceptions of Bank A. This may not be enough. Even though the individual believes that the bank has convenient hours, the person may not value this attribute, and, therefore, it may not affect her attitude toward the bank. On the other hand, suppose the individual values location convenience; if she perceives the bank as being inconveniently located, this will have a negative, and perhaps a strong negative, effect on her feeling towards the bank. To capture the differing emphases people place on specific attributes, researchers often try to measure their importance. Research Realities 9.3, for example, depicts the importance of various attributes to people who are shopping for microwave ovens, console color televisions, and portable video cameras or camcorders.

Admittedly, there is a good deal of controversy about how the importance of various attributes should be incorporated in determining a person's attitude toward an object. The controversy involves some very complex arguments as to how one determines which attributes are salient (that is, used in forming an attitude) and how they should be measured. For example, when asked about importance directly, many respondents usually believe that most, if not all, of the characteristics that are listed are more than moderately important. Researchers have attempted to get around this measurement problem in a number of ways, including changing the type of scale (e.g., asking respondents how concerned they are about each attribute rather than how important each attribute is to them)[34] and by determining attribute importance indirectly rather than through self reports.[35] We shall not delve into the controversy. Rather, we shall simply use importance values to focus a discussion of general types of rating scales. Some of these scales were employed previously, but now we wish to describe the basic rating scales in one place, using importance values as a vehicle to make the differences between them more vivid. Knowledge of the basic types should facilitate the development of special scales for particular purposes.

There is one feature that is common to all rating scales: "The rater places the person or object being rated at some point along a continuum or in one of an ordered series of categories; a numerical value is attached to the point or the category."[36] The scales differ, though, in the fineness of the distinctions they allow and in the procedures involved in assigning objects to positions. Three of the most common rating scales are the graphic, the itemized, and the comparative.[37]

---

[34]For empirical comparisons involving various forms of self-report scales of attribute importance, see "Measuring the Importance of Attributes," *Research on Research, No. 28* (Chicago: Market Facts, Inc., undated); and "The Use of Concern Scales as an Alternative to Importance Ratings," *Research on Research, No. 44* (Chicago: Market Facts, Inc., undated).

[35]Three indirect ways are through conjoint analysis, information display boards, or statistical derivation of them for groups of respondents. For examples of these approaches, see Roger M. Heeler, Chike Okechuku, and Stan Reid, "Attribute Importance: Contrasting Measurements," *Journal of Marketing Research,* 16 (February 1979), pp. 60–63; Scott A. Neslin, "Linking Product Features to Perceptions: Self-Stated versus Statistically Revealed Importance Weights," *Journal of Marketing Research,* 18 (February 1981), pp. 80–86; Steven A. Sinclair and Edward C. Stalling, "How to Identify Differences Between Market Segments With Attribute Analysis," *Industrial Marketing Management,* 19 (February 1990), pp. 31–40.

[36]Claire Selltiz, Lawrence S. Wrightsman, and Stuart W. Cook, *Research Methods in Social Relations,* 3rd ed. (New York: Holt, Rinehart and Winston, 1976), pp. 403–404.

[37]*Ibid.,* pp. 404–406.

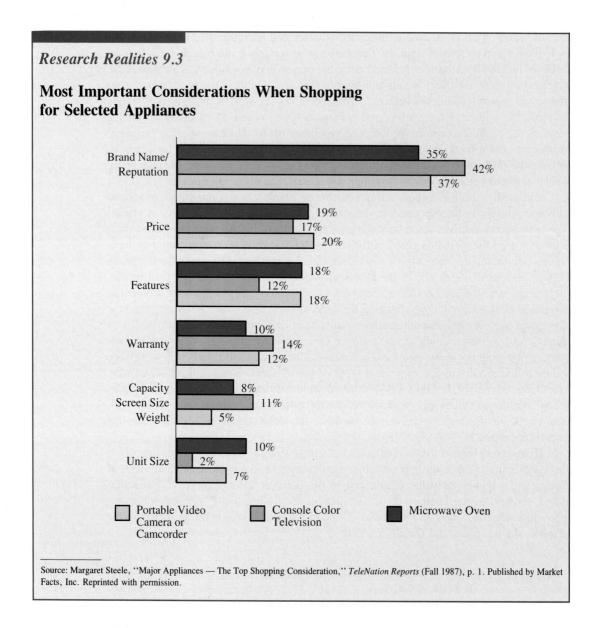

Research Realities 9.3

Most Important Considerations When Shopping for Selected Appliances

Brand Name/Reputation
- 35%
- 42%
- 37%

Price
- 19%
- 17%
- 20%

Features
- 18%
- 12%
- 18%

Warranty
- 10%
- 14%
- 12%

Capacity / Screen Size / Weight
- 8%
- 11%
- 5%

Unit Size
- 10%
- 2%
- 7%

☐ Portable Video Camera or Camcorder   ☐ Console Color Television   ■ Microwave Oven

Source: Margaret Steele, "Major Appliances — The Top Shopping Consideration," *TeleNation Reports* (Fall 1987), p. 1. Published by Market Facts, Inc. Reprinted with permission.

Graphic

When using **graphic rating scales,** individuals indicate their rating by placing a check at the appropriate point on a line that runs from one extreme of the attribute to the other. Many variations are possible. The line may be vertical or horizontal; it may be unmarked or marked; if marked, the divisions may be few or many, as in the case of a thermometer scale, so called because it looks like a thermometer. Figure 9.8 is an example of a horizontal, end-anchored-only, graphic rating scale. Each individual would be instructed

FIGURE **9.8**   **Graphic Rating Scale**

Please evaluate each attribute in terms of how important the attribute is to you personally by placing an ''X'' at the position on the horizontal line that most reflects your feelings.

Attribute	**Not Important**	**Very Important**
Courteous service		
Convenient location		
Convenient hours		
Low interest rate loans		

to indicate the importance of the attribute by checking the appropriate position on the scale. The importance value would then be inferred by measuring the length of the line from the left origin to the marked position.

One of the great advantages of graphic rating scales is the ease with which they can be constructed and used. They provide an opportunity to make fine distinctions and are limited in this regard only by the discrimination abilities of the rater.[38] Yet, for their most effective use, the researcher is well advised to avoid end statements that are so extreme that they are unlikely to be used and to place descriptive statements as close as possible to their numerical points on the scale.[39]

Itemized

The **itemized rating scale** is similar to the graphic in that individuals make their judgments independently — that is, without the benefit of direct comparison. The itemized rating scale is distinguished by the fact that the rater must select from a limited number of categories. In general, five to nine categories work well, because they permit fine distinctions and yet seem to be readily understood by respondents, although ten or more can be used.[40] There are a number of possible variations with itemized scales. Figure 9.9, for example, depicts three different forms of itemized rating scales that have been used to measure customer satisfaction. Note that the categories are ordered in terms of their scale positions. Note further that in some cases the categories have verbal

---

[38]While easy to construct, there is some evidence that suggests graphic rating scales are not as reliable as itemized scales. See A. O. Gregg, ''Some Problems Concerning the Use of Rating Scales for Visual Assessment,'' *Journal of the Market Research Society,* 8 (January 1980), pp. 29–43.

[39]Selltiz, Wrightsman, and Cook, *Research Methods,* p. 204.

[40]Eli P. Cox III, ''The Optimal Number of Response Alternatives for a Scale: A Review,'' *Journal of Marketing Research,* 17 (November 1980), pp. 407–422. For discussion of procedures for determining the optimal number of response categories and appropriate category descriptors, see Madhubalan Viswanathon, Mark Bergen, Shantanu Dutta, and Terry Childers, ''Response Categories as Fuzzy Sets: A Fuzzy Set Theoretic Perspective on Issues in Scale Development,'' unpublished working paper, Department of Business Administration, University of Illinois, Champaign, Illinois.

Figure 9.9 Three Different Forms of Itemized Rating Scales Used to Measure Satisfaction

Measure	Description
Delighted–Terrible Scale	*How do you feel about _____ ? I feel:*

```
    7        6         5          4           3           2          1
    |        |         |          |           |           |          |
Delighted Pleased  Mostly     Mixed       Mostly      Unhappy    Terrible
                   Satisfied  (About      Dissatisfied
                              Equally
                              Satisfied and
                              Dissatisfied)

A = Neutral (neither satisfied nor dissatisfied)
B = I never thought about it
```

Measure	Description
Percentage Scale	*Overall, how satisfied have you been with this _____ ?*

```
100%     90    80    70    60    50    40    30    20    10    0%
Completely                                          Not at All Satisfied
Satisfied
```

Measure	Description
Need Satisfaction–Dissatisfaction	*To what extent does this _____ meet your needs at this time?*

```
Extremely Well: ___ : ___ : ___ : ___ : ___ : ___ : ___ : Extremely Poorly
                (7)                   (1)
```

Source: Adapted from Robert A. Westbrook, "A Rating Scale for Measuring Product/Service Satisfaction," *Journal of Marketing*, 44 (Fall 1980), p. 69. Published by the American Marketing Association.

FIGURE 9.10   Itemized Rating Scale

Please evaluate each attribute in terms of how important the attribute is to you personally by placing an "X" in the appropriate box.

Attribute	Not Important	Somewhat Important	Fairly Important	Very Important
Courteous service	☐	☐	☐	☐
Convenient location	☐	☐	☐	☐
Convenient hours	☐	☐	☐	☐
Low interest rate loans	☐	☐	☐	☐

descriptions attached, and in other cases they do not. Category descriptions are not absolutely necessary in itemized rating scales, although their presence and nature do seem to affect the responses.[41] When they are used, it is important to ensure that the descriptors mean similar things to those responding.[42] When they are not used, it is tempting to conclude that a graphic rating scale is being used. That is an erroneous conclusion, however. The distinguishing feature of an itemized scale is that the possible response categories are limited in number. Thus, a set of faces varying systematically in terms of whether they are frowning or smiling used to capture a person's satisfaction or preference (appropriately called a faces scale) would be considered an itemized scale, even when no descriptions are attached to the face categories.

A Likert statement serves as an example of a five-point itemized rating scale, whereas a semantic differential adjective pair is an example of a seven-point scale. Figure 9.10 is an itemized rating scale used to ascertain importance values; this four-point scale has the descriptor labels attached to the categories.

The itemized rating scale is also easy to construct and use, and although it does not permit the fine distinctions possible with the graphic rating scale, the clear definition of categories generally produces more reliable ratings.

---

[41]Albert R. Wildt and Michael B. Mazis, "Determinants of Scale Response: Label versus Position," *Journal of Marketing Research,* 15 (May 1978), pp. 261–267; H. H. Friedman and J. R. Liefer, "Label versus Position in Rating Scales," *Journal of the Academy of Marketing Science* (Spring 1981), pp. 88–92; "Variations in Semantic Differential Scales," *Research on Research, No. 3* (Chicago: Market Facts, Inc., undated); Norbert Schwarz, *et al.,* "Rating Scales: Numeric Values May Change the Meanings of Scale Labels," *Public Opinion Quarterly,* 55 (Winter 1991), pp. 570–582.

[42]For lists of category descriptors and their numerical values, see James H. Myers and W. Gregory Warner, "Selected Properties of Selected Evaluation Adjectives," *Journal of Marketing Research,* 5 (November 1968), pp. 409–412; Spector, "Choosing Response Categories for Summated Rating Scales"; Robert A. Mittelstaedt, "Semantic Properties of Selected Adjectives: Other Evidence," *Journal of Marketing Research,* 8 (May 1971), pp. 236–237; Melvin R. Crask and Richard J. Fox, "An Exploration of the Interval Properties of Three Commonly Used Marketing Research Scales: A Magnitude Estimation Approach," *Journal of the Market Research Society,* 29 (July 1987), pp. 317–339.

FIGURE **9.11   Comparative Rating Scale**

Please divide 100 points between the two following attributes in terms
of each attribute's relative importance to you.

Courteous service   _____

Convenient location   _____

Comparative

Unlike graphic and itemized scales, **comparative rating scales** involve relative judgments because raters make their judgments of each attribute with direct reference to the other attributes being evaluated. The Q-sort method of scale construction is an example; each attribute is compared to all other m attributes when making judgments.

An example of a comparative rating scale used for securing importance values is the constant sum scaling method. In the **constant sum method,** the individual is instructed to divide some given sum among two or more attributes on the basis of their importance to him or her. Thus, in Figure 9.11, if the subject assigned 50 points to courteous service and 50 points to convenient location, the attributes would be judged to be equally important; if the individual assigned 80 to courteous service and 20 to convenient location, courteous service would be considered to be four times as important.[43] Note the difference in emphasis with this method. All judgments are now made in comparison to some other alternative, and all possible pairs of the m stimuli would be presented to the individual for rating.

Comparison of two attributes is not mandatory in the constant sum method, although it is the most common. The individual could also be asked to divide 100 points among three or more attributes; again all possible combinations would be presented to the individual for judgment.[44]

Although comparative scales require more judgments from the individual than either graphic or itemized scales, they do tend to eliminate **halo effects** that so often manifest themselves in scaling. Halo effects occur when there is carryover from one judgment to another.

---

[43]By considering all possible pairs of attributes in combination, one is able to construct scale values to reflect the importance ratings of each attribute to each individual. See Joy P. Guilford, *Psychometric Methods,* 2nd ed. (New York: McGraw-Hill, 1954), pp. 214–220, or Warren S. Torgerson, *Theory and Methods of Scaling* (New York: John Wiley, 1958), pp. 104–116, for a discussion of the procedure. Another comparative rating scale method is that of magnitude estimation, in which respondents are asked to judge directly the ''magnitude'' of each stimulus versus a reference stimulus. For a general treatment of magnitude scaling, see Milton Lodge, *Magnitude Scaling: Quantitative Measurement of Opinions* (Beverly Hills, Calif.: Sage Publications, 1981). For specific examples of its use, see Crask and Fox, ''An Exploration of the Interval Properties,'' Bruno Neibecker, ''The Validity of Computer-Controlled Magnitude Scaling to Measure Emotional Impact of Stimuli,'' *Journal of Marketing Research,* 21 (August 1984), pp. 325–331.

[44]For empirical examples based on the use of constant sum scales, see Valentine Appel and Babette Jackson, ''Copy Testing in a Competitive Environment,'' *Journal of Marketing,* 39 (January 1975), pp. 84–86, Clyde E. Harris, Jr., Richard R. Still, and Melvin R. Crask, ''Stability or Change in Marketing Methods,'' *Business Horizons,* 21 (October 1978), pp. 32–40.

The great temptation in securing importance values by either the graphic or itemized scaling methods is for the individual to indicate that all, or nearly all, of the attributes are important. Yet empirical research indicates that when individuals are confronted by decisions that are complex because many alternatives or attributes are involved, they tend to simplify the decision by reducing the number of alternatives or attributes they actually consider.[45] This is consistent with the notion that only certain attributes are salient when forming attitudes. The comparative scaling methods do allow more insight into the relative ranking, if not the absolute importance, of the attributes to each individual.

WHICH SCALE TO USE

For some readers, the discussion in this chapter might beg the question of which scale they should use when faced with a problem of measuring attitudes. When making the choice among scale types, number of scale points to use, whether or not to reverse some of the items, and so on, readers might find comfort in the findings of a very extensive study of the marketing measurement literature that examined these questions and more with respect to their effect on the reliability of measures. Reviewing the marketing literature over a 20-year period, the study examined measures for which at least two indicants of their quality were reported, and then quantitatively assessed the effect of a measure's features on its reliability.[46] **Reliability** assesses the issue of the similarity of results provided by independent but comparable measures of the same object, trait, or construct; it is an important indicator of a measure's quality because it determines the impact of inconsistencies in measurement on the results. Reliability is a necessary, but not a sufficient, condition for ensuring the validity of a measure.[47]

Table 9.4 reports the study's findings with respect to some of the major questions surrounding the construction of attitude scales. The general conclusion emerging from Table 9.4 is that many of the choices do not seem to materially affect the quality of the measure that results. The exceptions are the number of items and the number of scale points. For both of these characteristics, the reliability of the measure increases as they increase. For the other characteristics, though, there are no choices that are superior in all instances. Many of the choices are and will probably remain in the domain of researcher judgment, including the choice among semantic differential, Likert, or other rating scales. All the scales have proved to be useful at one time or another. All rightly belong in the researcher's measurement tool kit.

The nature of the problem and the planned mode of administration will affect the final choice. So will the characteristics of the respondents, their commitment to the task,

---

[45]Jerome S. Bruner, Jacqueline J. Goodnow, and George R. Austin, *A Study of Thinking* (New York: John Wiley, 1956); James G. Miller, ''Sensory Overloading,'' in Bernard E. Flaherty, ed., *Psychophysiological Aspects of Space Flight* (New York: Columbia University Press, 1961), pp. 215–224; and Jacob Jacoby, ''Perspectives on Information Overload,'' *Journal of Consumer Research,* 10 (March 1984), pp. 432–435.

[46]Gilbert A. Churchill, Jr., and J. Paul Peter, ''Research Design Effects on the Reliability of Rating Scales: A Meta-Analysis,'' *Journal of Marketing Research,* 21 (November 1984), pp. 360–375.

[47]The issue of reliability and its relationship to the validity of a measure are discussed in Appendix 9C.

TABLE **9.4**   **Impact of Selected Measure Characteristics on Reliability Estimates**

Measure Characteristic	Conclusion
Number of items in final scale	The hypothesis that there is a positive relationship between the number of items used in the scales and the reliability of the measure is supported.
Difficulty of items	The hypothesis that a negative relationship exists between the difficulty of the items and the reliability of the measure is not supported.
Reverse scoring	The hypothesis that scales with reverse-scored items will have lower reliability than scales without them is not supported.
Type of scale	No *a priori* prediction was made that one of the scale types is superior, and no relationship was found between scale types and the reliability of the measure.
Number of scale points	The hypothesis that a positive relationship exists between the number of scale points over the normal range and the reliability of the measure is supported.
Type of labels	No *a priori* prediction was made that numerical and verbal labels are superior to verbal labels only, or vice versa, and no relationship was found between type of labels and the reliability of the measure.
Extent of scale points description	The hypothesis that scales for which all points are labeled have higher reliability than scales for which only polar points are labeled is not supported.
Respondent uncertainty or ignorance	The hypothesis that scales with neutral points have higher reliability than forced-choice scales is not supported.

Source: Adapted from Gilbert A. Churchill, Jr., and J. Paul Peter, "Research Design Effects on the Reliability of Rating Scales: A Meta-Analysis," *Journal of Marketing Research,* 21 (November 1984), pp. 365–366. Published by the American Marketing Association.

and their experience and ability to respond.[48] In some cultures, graphic rating scales may be unknown, and respondents with low levels of education may not even be able to conceptualize a continuous scale from extreme dissatisfaction to extreme satisfaction, say, that is divided into equal increments of satisfaction. In other cultures, such as Eastern Europe, the use of these scales may be a very new experience for most research participants, and interviewers may need to spend considerable time explaining the scale. In still other situations, it might be necessary to develop new scales. For example, the "sad-to-happy faces" scale that works in the United States does not work in Africa; rather, their culture requires some different-looking faces to depict the various stages of happiness. See Figure 9.12.

---

[48]John R. Hauser and Steven M. Shugan, "Intensity Measures of Consumer Preference," *Operations Research,* 28 (March–April 1980), pp. 278–320; Duane F. Alwin and Jon A. Krosnick, "The Reliability of Survey Attitude Measurement: The Influence of Question and Respondent Attributes," *Sociological Methodology and Research,* 20 (August 1991), pp. 139–181.

FIGURE 9.12   Examples of "Sad-to-Happy Faces" Scales That Work in the United States versus Those That Work in Africa

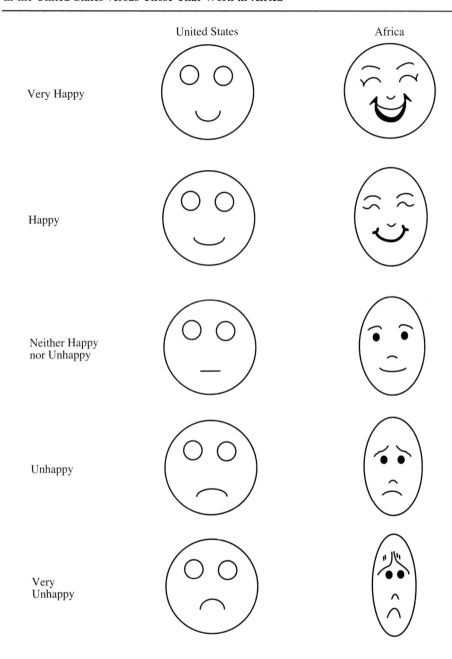

Source: The African faces can be found in C. K. Corder, "Problems and Pitfalls in Conducting Marketing Research in Africa," in Betsy Gelb, ed., *Marketing Expansion in a Shrinking World,* Proceedings of American Marketing Association Business Conference (Chicago: American Marketing Association, 1978), pp. 86–90. Reprinted with permission of American Marketing Association.

ETHICAL DILEMMA 9.2

The Samuelson Research Firm was contacted by Larkin Electronics, a manufacturer of small electronic radio parts, to conduct a survey of Larkin's employees. The purpose of the research was to determine the state of worker morale and the importance of certain employee grievances so that Larkin's management could gauge the strength of its position in collective bargaining with the employee union. Samuelson Research agreed to conduct the study.

- What are the consequences of participating in such a survey for the employees?
- Is this research detrimental to the employee's immediate self-interest?
- Do researchers have the right to ask questions concerning this issue?
- Does this research undercut the position of labor's representatives inasmuch as they have no corresponding way of gauging the intensity of management's opinions?
- If you were director of the research, what kind of questions might you ask of Larkin's management?
- Would you have agreed to conduct such a survey?
- In general, should a researcher be concerned with the uses of the research that he or she conducts or its effects on the research participants?

SUMMARY

This chapter reviewed the methods suggested for measuring attitudes, which were defined as representations of the person's ideas of, or liking for, a specific object or idea. Typically, marketers are concerned with objects such as companies, brands, advertisements, packages, and the like.

Measurement was defined as the assignment of numbers to objects to represent quantities of attributes. Measurement can occur on either a nominal, ordinal, interval, or ratio scale. The properties of these scales were distinguished, and it was pointed out that a controversy exists over whether the measurement of attitudes has been accomplished with ordinal or interval scales. The scales certainly are not ratio, since the origin is not natural, and they are definitely something more than nominal, because they possess more than the identity property. The debate focuses on whether the differences in scores convey meaning other than relative ranking of individuals. The prevailing posture in marketing seems to agree with that of the psychologists — that many of the scales are interval.

Historically, attitudes have been measured by observing behavior, by indirect questioning, by the performance of objective tasks, and by physiological reactions, although direct assessment by means of self-report devices has been the most common. The main self-report techniques were reviewed, including the methods of equal-appearing intervals, summated ratings, semantic differential, Stapel scale, and Q-sort.

As typically constructed, these scales attempt to measure what individuals believe and like about specific objects. Many would argue that simply measuring beliefs about the attributes possessed by the object is not sufficient if we want to assess a person's attitude toward the object. Rather, we must somehow ascertain the importance of the various attributes to the individual. The methods for securing importance values — the graphic, itemized, or comparative rating scales — were thus reviewed. The itemized scale is most commonly used, but there is a good deal of controversy about which rating scale can more accurately measure an individual's importance values.

The empirical evidence indicates that none of the attitude scaling devices is superior in all instances. Each one has its place. Nor is there one single optimal number of scale positions or single optimal condition for other measure characteristics. The nature of the problem, the characteristics of the respondents, and the planned mode of administration will and should affect the choice of which technique should be used in a particular instance and what features the scale should possess.

Questions

1. What is an attitude?
2. What is measurement? What are the scales of measurement, and what information is provided by each?
3. What is a Thurstone equal-appearing interval scale?
4. In an equal-appearing interval scale, what is the scale value for a statement?
5. How does one construct a Likert summated rating scale?
6. How are subjects scaled with a Likert scale? What must be done to give meaning to the scales?
7. What is a semantic differential scale? How is a person's overall attitude assessed with a semantic differential scale?
8. How does a Stapel scale differ from a semantic differential scale? Which is more commonly used?
9. What is the task assigned subjects and what is the thrust or emphasis of *Q*-sort methodology?
10. What is a graphic rating scale? An itemized scale? A constant sum scale?

Applications and Problems

1. Identify the type of scale (nominal, ordinal, interval, or ratio) being used in each of the following questions. Justify your answer.

   a. *During which season of the year were you born?*

   _____ Winter _____ Spring _____ Summer _____ Fall

   b. *What is your total household income?* _____

   c. *Which are your three most preferred brands of cigarettes? Rank them from 1 to 3 according to your preference, with 1 as most preferred.*

_____ Marlboro		_____ Salem	
_____ Kent		_____ Kool	
_____ Benson and Hedges		_____ Vantage	

   d. *How much time do you spend traveling to school every day?*

_____ Under 5 minutes		_____ 16–20 minutes
_____ 5–10 minutes		_____ 30 minutes and over
_____ 11–15 minutes		

e. How satisfied are you with Newsweek magazine?

_____ very satisfied   _____ dissatisfied

_____ satisfied   _____ very dissatisfied

_____ neither satisfied nor dissatisfied

f. On an average, how many cigarettes do you smoke in a day?

_____ over 1 pack   _____ less than 1/2 pack

_____ 1/2 to 1 pack

g. Which one of the following courses have you taken?

_____ marketing research   _____ sales management

_____ advertising management   _____ consumer behavior

h. What is the level of education for the head of the household?

_____ some high school   _____ some college

_____ high school graduate   _____ college graduate and/or graduate work

2. The analysis for each of the preceding questions is given below. Is the analysis appropriate for the scale used?

   a. About 50 percent of the sample was born in the fall, 25 percent of the sample was born in the spring, and the remaining 25 percent was born in the winter. It can be concluded that the fall is twice as popular as the spring and the summer seasons.

   b. The average income is $25,000. There are twice as many individuals with an income of less than $9,999 than individuals with an income of $40,000 and over.

   c. Marlboro is the most preferred brand. The mean preference is 3.52.

   d. The median time spent traveling to school is 8.5 minutes. There are three times as many respondents traveling less than 5 minutes than respondents traveling 16–20 minutes.

   e. The average satisfaction score is 4.5, which seems to indicate a high level of satisfaction with *Newsweek* magazine.

   f. Ten percent of the respondents smoke less than 1/2 pack of cigarettes a day, whereas three times as many respondents smoke over one pack of cigarettes a day.

   g. Sales management is the most frequently taken course because the median is 3.2.

   h. The responses indicate that 40 percent of the sample have some high school education, 25 percent of the sample are high school graduates, 20 percent have some college education, and 10 percent are college graduates. The mean education level is 2.6.

3. **a.** Assume that a manufacturer of a line of packaged meat products wanted to evaluate customer attitudes towards the brand. A panel of 500 regular consumers of the brand responded to a questionnaire that was sent to them and that included several attitude scales. The questionnaire produced the following results:

   (i) the average score for the sample on a 20-item Likert scale was 105.

   (ii) the average score for the sample on a 20-item semantic differential scale was 106.

   (iii) the average score for the sample on a 15-item Stapel scale was 52.

   The vice-president has asked you to indicate whether these customers have a favorable or unfavorable attitude towards the brand. What would you tell him? Please be specific.

   b. Following your initial report, the vice-president has provided you with some more information. The following memo is given to you: "The company has been using the same attitude measures over the past eight years. The results of the previous studies are as follows:

	Likert	Semantic Differential	Stapel
1986	86	95	43
1987	93	95	48
1988	97	98	51
1989	104	101	55
1990	110	122	62
1991	106	112	57
1992	104	106	53
1993	105	106	52

We realize that there may not be any connection between attitude and behavior, but it must be pointed out that sales peaked in 1990 and since then have been gradually declining.'' With this information, do your results change? Can anything more be said about customer attitudes?

4. A leading manufacturer of electric guitars routinely attempts to measure consumer attitudes toward its products, generally by asking a consumer to examine a product and then to complete a brief questionnaire about several of the product's attributes. Over the years, the research manager for the company has decided that scale items related to five attributes have high correlations with total scale scores. The attributes are tone quality, appearance, durability, price, and ease of playing. The following scale is thus used to assess attitudes toward a product:

	Strongly Disagree	Disagree	Neither Agree nor Disagree	Agree	Strongly Agree
1. Tone quality is good.	___	___	___	___	X
2. The guitar is attractive.	___	___	___	X	___
3. The design is durable.	___	___	___	X	___
4. The price is appropriate.	___	X	___	___	___
5. The guitar is easy to play.	___	___	___	___	X
	(1)	(2)	(3)	(4)	(5)

a. Suppose that a consumer has examined a guitar and provided the responses shown in the preceding table. Determine the total score. Would you say that the consumer has a favorable attitude toward the guitar?

b. The particular model of guitar that the respondent examined has been available for five years. The average total scores using this scale for each of these years are as follows:

First year	18
Second year	17
Third year	18
Fourth year	16
Fifth year	17

Would you conclude that the consumer has a favorable attitude toward the guitar?

    c. Assume that the respondent had also completed a comparative rating scale by dividing 100 points between the five attributes according to their importance to her. How could this information be useful in assessing the respondent's attitude toward the electric guitar?

    d. Following are the results of the comparative rating task completed by the respondent:

Tone quality	10
Appearance	25
Durability	10
Price	40
Ease of playing	15

What can you now conclude about the respondent's attitudes toward the guitar?

APPENDIX 9A

Perceptual Mapping

The discussion in the chapter emphasized the measurement of people's attitudes toward objects. A related issue to marketing managers is how people *perceive* various objects, whether they be products or brands. In its constant quest for a differential advantage, the firm needs to correctly position its products against competitive offerings. To do this, the product manager needs to identify the following:

1. the number of dimensions consumers use to distinguish products;
2. the names of these dimensions;
3. the positioning of existing products along these dimensions;
4. the location where consumers prefer a product to be on the dimensions.[1]

    One way in which managers can grasp the positioning of their brand versus competing brands is through the study of perceptual maps. In a perceptual map, each product or brand occupies a specific point. Products or brands that are similar lie close together, and those that are different lie far apart. Perceptual maps provide managers with meaningful pictures of how their products and brands compare to other products and brands. Research Realities 9A.1, for example, depicts the situation in the automobile industry.

    There are several ways by which perceptual maps can be created. As Figure 9A.1 indicates, they can be created using nonattribute-based or attribute-based approaches. The attribute-based approaches use procedures similar to those discussed in the chapter, in that they rely on characteristic-by-characteristic assessments of the various objects using, for example, Likert-type or semantic differential scales. The ratings of the objects

---

[1]Glen L. Urban and John R. Hauser, *Design and Marketing of New Products* (Englewood Cliffs, N.J.: Prentice-Hall, 1980), p. 195. See also Glen L. Urban, John R. Hauser, and Nikhilesh Dholakia, *Essentials of New Product Management* (Englewood Cliffs, N.J.: Prentice-Hall, Inc., 1987), especially Chapter 6, pp. 103–120.

FIGURE 9A.1   Alternative Approaches to the Development of Perceptual Maps

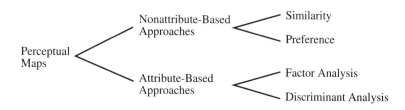

on each of the items are subsequently analyzed using typically either factor or discriminant analysis to identify the key dimensions that consumers use to distinguish the objects.[2]

The nonattribute-based approaches use different methods in determining how individuals perceive the relationships among objects. Instead of asking a subject to rate objects on designated attributes, they ask individuals to make some *summary* judgments about the similarity of objects. When making these judgments, individuals are free to use their own characteristics. An attempt is then made to locate the objects in a multidimensional space in which the number of dimensions corresponds to the number of characteristics the individual used in forming the judgments. **Multidimensional scaling** analysis is the label typically used to describe the nonattribute-based approaches that use similarity judgments to develop perceptual maps.[3]

EXAMPLE

The purpose and nature of multidimensional scaling are best illustrated by example. Consider, therefore, that our interest is in developing a multidimensional map to characterize the perceived relationships among a set of cameras. Label the brands or models A, B, C, D, E, F, G, H, I, and J. A factor of critical interest in multidimensional scaling is the perceived similarity of the objects of study. For example, are certain models seen to be alike while others are viewed as being very dissimilar? Are they all alike? All dissimilar? Just how close are they perceived to be in psychological space? The notion of

---

[2]An alternative to having respondents rate each brand according to specific attributes is to have them simply check which brands possess each of a given list of attributes. Data of this type can be analyzed using correspondence analysis, which is a general exploratory data-analysis technique for graphically displaying categorical data. For an expository treatment of correspondence analysis, see Donna L. Hoffman and George R. Franke, ''Correspondence Analysis: Graphical Representation of Categorical Data in Marketing Research,'' *Journal of Marketing Research,* 23 (August 1986), pp. 213–227. See also Susan C. Weller and A. Kimball Romney, *Metric Scaling: Correspondence Analysis* (Newbury Park, CA: Sage Publications, Inc., 1990).

[3]There are actually three basic types of techniques: fully metric, fully nonmetric, and nonmetric multidimensional scaling. They differ according to the kind of input data and output information used. *Fully metric* methods have metric input (interval- or ratio-scaled data) and metric output, whereas *fully nonmetric* methods have ordinal input and generate ranked output. By far the most interesting from the marketing researcher's vantage point, at least as judged by the relative emphasis in the literature, are the *nonmetric methods,* which generate metric output from ordinal input. The nonmetric methods are emphasized here.

Research Realities 9A.1

Product Positioning in the Automobile Industry

Exasperated by the growing similarity of cars on the road, a former Detroit auto executive recently remarked that if all of today's models were lined up end to end, even the top officers of the Big Three car makers would have a hard time telling them apart at a respectable distance.

The comment addresses an increasing challenge for automotive stylists and marketers. As fuel-effi-

ciency requirements have narrowed design and performance characteristics, the auto companies have turned to subtler distinctions between different models. An example of how that is done is the ''brand image'' map shown in the figure.

According to Mr. R. N. Harper, Jr., manager of product marketing plans and research, Chrysler draws up a series of such maps about three times a year,

---

Perceptual Map—Brand Images

Cadillac •   • Lincoln

          Has a Touch of Class
          a Car I'd Be Proud to Own
          Distinctive Looking

  Mercedes •

                   • Porsche

            • BMW

       • Chrysler
         • Buick   • Pontiac
      • Oldsmobile

Conservative
Looking   Ford •   • Chevrolet   **Has Spirited**
Appeals to   • Datsun   **Performance**
Older People   **Appeals to**
               • Toyota   **Young People**
                         Fun to Drive
      Dodge •   **Sporty Looking**

Plymouth •

          • VW

          Very Practical
          Provides Good Gas Mileage
Source: Chrylser Corp.   **Affordable**

---

psychological proximity plays a central role in the technique of multidimensional scaling, and the technique is sometimes referred to as the *analysis of proximities* data.[4]

---

[4]Psychological proximity may be defined on the basis of the psychological distance between the perceptions of two objects or between a person's preference and perception of an object, resulting in the scaling of similarities and preferences, respectively.

using responses to customer surveys. The surveys ask owners of different makes to rank their autos on a scale of one to 10 for such qualities as "youthfulness," "luxury" and "practicality." The answers are then worked into a mathematical score for each model and plotted on a graph that shows broad criteria for evaluating customer appeal.

The illustration below uses the technique to measure the images of the major divisions of U.S. auto makers, plus a few import companies. Using it, Chrysler would conclude, for instance, that the position of its Plymouth division in the lower left-hand quadrant means that cars carrying the Plymouth name generally have a practical, though somewhat stodgy, image. The Chrysler nameplate, by contrast, is perceived as more luxurious — though not nearly as luxurious as its principal competitors — Cadillac and Lincoln.

The map has other strategic significance, as well. By plotting on the map strong areas of customer demand, an auto maker can calculate whether its cars are on target. It can also tell from the concentration of dots representing competing models how much opposition it is likely to get in a specific territory on the map. Presumably, cars higher up on the graph should also fetch a higher price than models ranked toward the bottom, where the stress is on economy and practicality.

Source: John Koten, "Car Makers Use 'Image' Map as Tool to Position Products," *The Wall Street Journal* (March 22, 1984), p. 31. Reprinted by permission of *The Wall Street Journal*, © Dow Jones & Company, Inc., 1984. All Rights Reserved Worldwide.

After viewing the results for its divisions, Chrysler concluded that Plymouth, Dodge, and Chrysler all needed to present a more youthful image. It also decided that Plymouth and Dodge needed to move up sharply on the luxury scale.

Similarly, General Motors Corp. might find after looking at the map that its Chevrolet division, traditionally for entry-level buyers, ought to move down in practicality and more to the right in youthfulness. Another problem for GM on the map: the close proximity of its Buick and Oldsmobile divisions, almost on top of each other in the upper left-hand quadrant. That would suggest the two divisions are waging a marketing war more against each other than the competition.

Chrysler also uses its marketing map to plot individual models — both those it sells currently and those it plans for the future. By trying to move a model into an unoccupied space on the map through changes in styling, price, or advertising, the company believes it can better hope to carve out a distinctive niche in the market.

"The real advantage of the map," says Mr. Harper, "is that it looks at cars from a consumer perspective while also retaining some sort of tangible product orientation." He says, for example, that his bosses were delighted when, on a recent map, Chrysler's forthcoming Lancer and Commander models showed up on the map next to the Honda Accord. (The two new Chrysler compacts are due out this fall.) "That told us that consumers think of our two new cars exactly the way we hoped they would," says Mr. Harper. "It was tangible evidence of where the car would compete in the market. And frankly, that can be hard to get these days."

Suppose that we were to ask a single respondent for that person's perceptions of the *similarities* among the ten cameras by asking for his or her judgments about all possible *pairs* of cameras. For instance, we might form all possible pairs of the ten cameras, 45 pairs in all. We could then place each pair of cameras on a separate card and ask the individual to rank the cards by increasing dissimilarity of the camera pairs using whatever criteria he or she normally employs to distinguish cameras. Initially the individual could be instructed to sort the cards into four piles, for example, with the piles labeled

TABLE 9A.1   **Respondent Similarity Judgments**

Camera	A	B	C	D	E	F	G	H	I	J
A										
B	28									
C	5	29								
D	24	21	17							
E	32	1	26	18						
F	37	3	34	25	4					
G	31	36	22	7	35	41				
H	27	43	20	13	42	45	9			
I	16	40	23	12	39	44	10	6		
J	7	30	2	15	33	38	19	14	11	

extremely similar, somewhat similar, somewhat dissimilar, and *extremely dissimilar.* After placing each of the 45 cards in one of the piles, the individual would then be asked to order those within each pile from most similar to least similar. Suppose Table 9A.1 resulted from this process. Table 9A.1 indicates that the respondent perceived Cameras *B* and *E* as the most similar, Cameras *C* and *J* as the next most similar, and Cameras *F* and *H* as the least similar.

Given the ranking contained in Table 9A.1, there are at least three questions of concern: (1) How many dimensions underlie this respondent's judgments about the similarity–dissimilarity of the ten cameras? (2) What does the configuration look like — which cameras are perceived as most similar and which are perceived as most dissimilar when all ten cameras are considered simultaneously? (3) What attributes is the individual using in making his or her judgments?

Multidimensional scaling can be used to generate answers to the first two questions, although the identification of the attributes underlying the judgments requires the collection of additional information or an intuitive assessment on the part of someone connected with the research. Note this: nonmetric multidimensional scaling can take this ordinal or rank order input data and can indicate the dimensionality and shape of the configuration needed to reflect the perceived relationships among the banks. How this is accomplished is a technical subject, to which we cannot do justice in a limited space, although we will try to develop a conceptual feel for the approach.

CONCEPTUAL OPERATION OF COMPUTER PROGRAM

There are many computer programs for performing a multidimensional scaling analysis, although they all owe their existence to the early work done by Shepard.[5] Fundamen-

---

[5]Roger N. Shepard, "The Analysis of Proximities: Multidimensional Scaling with an Unknown Distance Function, I," *Psychometrika,* 27 (June 1962), pp. 125–140, and "The Analysis of Proximities: Multidimensional Scaling with an Unknown Distance Function, II," *Psychometrika,* 27 (September 1962), pp. 219–246.

tally, the programs operate by finding the "best" fit in several dimensions where quality of fit is determined by how well the distance between the points matches the input judgments. Thus, if the distances between the points in a two-dimensional configuration, say, when ordered for smallest to largest perfectly matched the order of the input judgments of similarity, the fit would be perfect. To the extent the ordering of the distances is inconsistent with the judged similarities, the fit is imperfect.

The computer programs operate by starting with an arbitrary configuration in each of several dimensions. Given the arbitrary configuration, they move the points or objects around in systematic fashion via a series of iterations to improve the fit until that is no longer possible, at which time they stop. In essence, they determine the best fit for each dimensionality and report how good or bad the fit is.

The number of dimensions that are "actually required" is determined by looking at the quality of fit in each dimension, recognizing that is easier to get a better fit in more dimensions because there is more latitude in how the points can be moved.[6] The basic aim is to find the lowest dimensionality in which the fit is good, that is, where the ordered distances between the objects "closely match" the similarity judgments.

EXAMPLE SOLUTION

Figure 9A.2 displays the computer-determined two-space solution for the rank-order data of Table 9A.1. As Figure 9A.2 shows, the cameras are seen to be relatively heterogeneous, although Cameras B, E, and F appear similar to the respondent, and Cameras A, C, and J seem to form another cluster. One can immediately see how a picture like this could help a firm or product manager quickly identify the company's or product's major competitors as well as how the picture could be used to formulate a repositioning strategy.

Why two dimensions? As mentioned, the basic objective in multidimensional scaling (MDS) is to find the lowest space solution in which there is good correspondence between the input judgments and the distances between the objects. As suggested, the lower space solutions will rarely provide a perfect fit. Rather, it is to be expected that there will always be some differences between the rank orders of the plotted distances and the rank orders of the judged similarities. Thus, one can compute a measure of the lack of fit for each dimension. The lower the lack-of-fit index, the better the computer configuration matches the original configuration.

Different MDS programs (and there are a great many) employ different lack-of-fit indices.[7] The particular configuration displayed in Figure 9A.2 was developed using

---

[6]When the number of objects or stimuli is small (less than seven or eight), it is relatively easy to get a "good fit" in three dimensions or less. However, when the number of objects being compared gets beyond ten, one will not get a "good fit" in a few dimensions unless the model has validity.

[7]The great many multidimensional scaling programs are discussed and compared in A.P.M. Coxon, *The User's Guide to Multidimensional Scaling* (London: Heinemann Educational Books, 1982). For a review of personal computer–based (PC-based) software for multidimensional scaling analysis, see Thomas L. Pilon, "A Review of PC-Based Software for Marketing Research," paper presented at 9th Annual Marketing Research Conference of the American Marketing Association, October 9–12, 1988, Arlington, Virginia.

FIGURE 9A.2   **Multidimensional Scaling Map of Similarity Judgments for Table 9A.1**

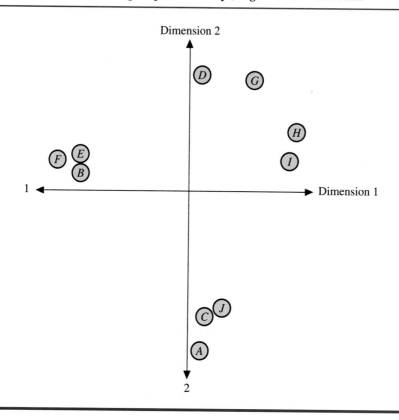

Kruskal's stress for its lack-of-fit index.[8] Figure 9A.3 displays the plot of the stress value as a function of the number of dimensions employed to represent the solution. The fit in one dimension is fair-to-poor using Kruskal's own verbal evaluations.[9]

Stress	Goodness of Fit
20.0%	Poor
10.0%	Fair
5.0%	Good
2.5%	Excellent
0.0%	Perfect

---

[8]Kruskal's stress is probably the most commonly used measure for lack of fit. See J. B. Kruskal, "Multidimensional Scaling by Optimizing Goodness of Fit to a Nonmetric Hypothesis," *Psychometrika*, 29 (March 1964), pp. 1–27.

[9]*Ibid.*, p. 3. These descriptions of what is "good" stress depend on the use of Formula 1 to calculate stress.

FIGURE 9A.3 **Stress Index for Camera Similarity Judgments**

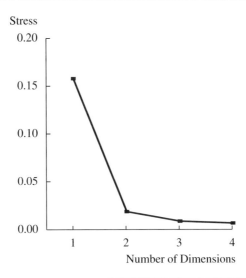

The fit in two dimensions appears adequate enough, though, to conclude that the two-space solution is appropriate. The stress value of .019 is excellent, and there is an elbow in the stress function. The elbow indicates that there is substantial improvement in the goodness of fit with an increase in the number of dimensions from one to two, but only slight additional improvement in fit as the number of dimensions is increased to three or even to four. The two-space solution seems most consistent with the objective of minimum dimensionality, because it reproduces the original rankings just as efficiently as do the three- and four-space solutions.

Accepting the two-space solution as adequately capturing the individual's similarity judgments is one thing; naming the dimensions that serve as a basis for these judgments is quite another, and this output is not provided by the computer program. Rather, the names of the dimensions are supplied by someone associated with the research effort.

There are several approaches that can be used. First, the individual can be asked to evaluate the objects (in this case, cameras) in terms of several defined attributes, such as automatic flash, automatic focus, and so on. The researcher then correlates the attribute scale scores for each object with the coordinates for each object in the plot. In this scheme, the size of the respective correlation coefficients between attributes and dimensions is used to attach labels. Another approach is to have the manager or researcher interpret the dimensions using his or her own experience and the visual configuration of points. Still, a third approach is to attempt to relate the dimensions to physical characteristics of the cameras, such as physical size or price.

Suppose that the dimensions were named using one of these schemes, that Dimension 1 turned out to be an "easy-to-use" dimension while Dimension 2 turned out to be a "good value" dimension, and that you were the manager for Brand J. The perceptual map in Figure 9A.2 indicates that your brand is perceived as being difficult to use and only an average value by our single respondent. If a large enough number of respondents felt this way, and you are suffering market share problems, it might behoove you to examine how ease of use and value can be increased.

Even though the example demonstrates only the placement of stimuli (that is, cameras), it also is possible to locate preferences in the same geometric space. For example, the individual's "ideal" camera is a hypothetical camera possessing just the perfect combination of the two attributes, ease of use and value. The individual's ideal point is located from the preference data that he or she supplies. Once again the objective is to locate the ideal so that the distance between the subject's ideal and each of the objects corresponds as closely as possible to the individual's preferences for the objects.

KEY DECISIONS

The example provides some appreciation for the conceptual underpinnings of multidimensional scaling analysis, but it does not capture the various decisions an analyst has to make to complete a multidimensional scaling analysis. Several of the more basic of these are pictured in Figure 9A.4.

FIGURE 9A.4 **Key Decisions When Conducting a Multidimensional Scaling Analysis**

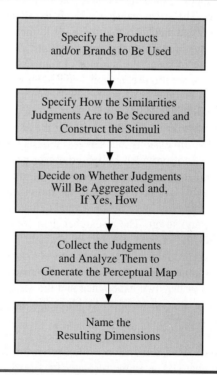

The first decision an analyst has to make is to specify the products or brands at issue. Although they will be partly determined by the purpose of the study, they will not be completely specified by it, and analysts will have some discretion in choosing products or brands to use. When exercising this discretion, analysts need to recognize that the dimensions that appear in the perceptual map will be a direct function of the stimulus set that was used to secure the judgments.[10] Suppose that the study was being conducted to determine respondents' perceptions of various soft drinks. If no unsweetened or low-calorie soft drinks were included in the stimulus set, this very important dimension might not appear in the results. In order to not run such a risk, analysts may be tempted to include every conceivable product or brand in the stimulus set. This strategy, though, can place such a burden on respondents that their answers may be meaningless.

The burden on respondents is going to depend partly on the number of judgments each has to make and partly on the difficulty of each judgment. Both of these issues, in turn, depend on how the similarity judgments are to be secured.[11] There are two main alternatives and a number of options under each alternative. The two major options are direct or indirect similarity judgments, two terms that are relatively self-explanatory. The direct methods rely on data collection mechanisms in which respondents compare stimuli using whatever criteria they desire and, on the basis of that comparison, state which of the stimuli are most similar, least similar, and so on. All possible pairs of the brands being evaluated could be formed, for example, and respondents could be asked to rank-order the various pairs from most similar to least similar. Alternatively, a brand could be singled out as a focal brand, and respondents could be asked to rank-order each of the other brands in terms of their similarity to the focal brand. Each brand could serve in turn as the focal brand. There are a number of alternative ways of collecting these judgments, but they all have one thing in common: the respondents are asked to judge directly how similar the various alternatives are using criteria that they choose. The indirect methods operate differently. Instead of respondents selecting the criteria on which to compare the alternatives, they are asked to evaluate each brand using prespecified criteria. Some kind of measure of similarity is then calculated for each pair of brands (for example, the correlation between the ratings of the brands).

The third decision analysts have to make is whether the judgments of individual respondents will be aggregated so that group perceptual maps can be developed or whether individual maps will be generated. The problem with individual maps is that they become very difficult for the marketing manager to use to develop marketing strategy. Managers typically look at marketing planning questions in terms of segments, not

---

[10]Naresh K. Malhotra, "Validity and Structural Reliability of Multidimensional Scaling," *Journal of Marketing Research*, 24 (May 1987), pp. 164–173. See also Melvin Prince, "How Consistent Is the Information in Positioning Studies?" *Journal of Advertising Research*, 30 (June/July 1990), pp. 25–30.

[11]For discussion of some of the main ways by which similarity judgments can be secured, see M. L. Davison, *Multidimensional Scaling* (New York: Wiley-Interscience, 1983); T. Deutscher, "Issues in Data Collection and Reliability in Multidimensional Scaling Studies — Implication for Large Stimulus Sets," in R. G. Golledge and J. N. Rayner, eds., *Proximity and Preference: Problems in the Multidimensional Scaling Analysis of Large Data Sets* (Minneapolis: University of Minnesota Press, 1982); or S. S. Schiffman, M. L. Reynolds, and F. W. Young, *Introduction to Multidimensional Scaling: Theory, Methods, and Applications* (New York: Academic Press, 1981).

individuals. Yet, as soon as the segment issue is raised, the question becomes one of deciding how the individual judgments will be aggregated. Is it likely that individuals used the same number of criteria when evaluating the various brands? Even if they used the same number, are the criteria themselves likely to be the same? If they are not, what criteria should be used to group respondents? One of the most popular algorithms, INDSCAL, for example, assumes that all subjects use the same criteria to judge the similarity of objects but that they weight the dimensions differently when forming their judgments.[12]

Step 4 in Figure 9A.4 involves the actual collection of the judgments and their processing. The processing involves two steps. First, an initial configuration must be determined for each of the dimensions. Different programs use different routines to generate an initial solution. Second, the points must be moved around until the fit is the best it can be in that dimensionality, using the criterion under which the program operates. The output of this analysis is the **stress,** or other goodness-of-fit diagram alluded to earlier, which analysts use to decide on the "proper number" of dimensions.

The last decision analysts have to make when conducting a nonmetric multidimensional scaling analysis involves what to call the dimensions. As suggested before, there are several procedures that are used to help name the dimensions. The practical fact, though, is that difficulty in naming the dimensions is one of management's major concerns with nonmetric multidimensional scaling analysis.

ATTRIBUTE-BASED APPROACHES

One of the advantages of the attribute-based approaches to the development of perceptual maps is that they do make the naming of dimensions easier. They also seem to be easier for respondents to use.[13] As mentioned earlier, the attribute-based approaches rely on having individuals rate various brands, typically using either semantic differential or Likert scales. These judgments are then usually input to either discriminant analysis or factor analysis.

The emphasis in discriminant analysis is on determining the combinations of attributes that best discriminate between the objects or brands. The dependent measures are the products rated, and the predictor variables are the attribute ratings. The analysis

---

[12]For an overview of some marketing studies that have used various algorithms, see Lee G. Cooper, "A Review of Multidimensional Scaling in Marketing Research," *Applied Psychological Measurement,* 7 (Fall 1983), pp. 427–450. For a review of algorithms generally available on microcomputers, including INDSCAL, see Paul E. Green, Frank J. Carmone, Jr., and Scott M. Smith, *Multidimensional Scaling: Concepts and Applications* (Boston: Allyn and Bacon, 1989).

[13]For general discussions on the use of attribute-based approaches for developing perceptual maps, see John R. Hauser and Frank S. Koppelman, "Alternative Perceptual Mapping Techniques: Relative Accuracy and Usefulness," *Journal of Marketing Research,* 16 (November 1979), pp. 495–506; Joel Huber and Morris B. Holbrook, "Using Attribute Ratings for Product Positioning: Some Distinctions among Compositional Approaches," *Journal of Marketing Research,* 16 (November 1979), pp. 507–516; and William R. Dillon, Donald G. Frederick, and Vanchai Tangpanichdee, "Decision Issues in Building Perceptual Product Spaces with Multiattribute Rating Data," *Journal of Consumer Research,* 12 (June 1985), pp. 47–63.

is typically run across groups of respondents to find a common structure. The dimensions are named by examining the weightings of the attributes that make up a discriminant dimension or by computing the correlations between the attributes and each of the discriminant scores.

Factor analysis relies on the assumption that there are only a few basic dimensions that underlie the attribute ratings. It examines the correlations among the attributes to identify these basic dimensions. The correlations are typically computed across brands and groups of consumers. The dimensions usually are named by examining the factor loadings, which represent the correlations between each attribute and each factor.

COMPARISON OF APPROACHES

The advantages of the attribute-based versus the nonattribute-based approaches to multidimensional scaling analysis are summarized in Table 9A.2.[14] Most of the nonattribute-based applications in marketing use similarity judgments. Similarity measurement has the advantage of not depending on a predefined attribute set. This is a two-edged sword. Although it allows respondents to use only those dimensions that they normally use in making judgments among objects, it creates difficulties in naming the dimensions. Further, different consumers can use different dimensions, and one then has to grapple with how best to combine consumers when forming maps. Constructing a separate map for each individual is prohibitively costly. Aggregating all of the responses and then developing one map distorts reality because it implies a homogeneity in perceptions that probably does not exist. The middle ground of grouping consumers into segments raises the whole issue of how the aggregation should be effected. Even individual consumers have been known to vary the criteria they are using when making a series of judgments, indicating that the criteria depend on the products or brands in the stimulus set. The fact that the criteria can change as a series of similarity judgments are made makes an already difficult problem of naming the dimensions even harder. One has to be especially careful when using the similarity-based programs if the number of objects being judged is less than eight, as it is then very easy to secure an oversimplified picture of the competitive environment.

As previously mentioned, the attribute-based approaches facilitate naming the dimensions, and they also make the task of clustering respondents into groups with similar perceptions easier to deal with. They presume, however, that the list of attributes used to secure the ratings are relatively accurate and complete. They contain the implicit assumption that a person's perception or evaluation of a stimulus is some combination of the individual's reactions to the attributes making up the stimulus. Yet, people may not perceive or evaluate objects in terms of underlying attributes, but may perceive them as some kind of whole that is not decomposable in terms of separate attributes. Further, the

---

[14]For additional discussion of the advantages and the disadvantages of the nonattribute- and attribute-based approaches for the development of perceptual maps, see Hauser and Koppelman, ''Alternative Perceptual Mapping Techniques''; Huber and Holbrook, ''Using Attribute Ratings''; or Urban and Hauser, *Design and Marketing of New Products,* pp. 185–234.

TABLE 9A.2 **Comparison of the Nonattribute- and Attribute-Based Approaches for Developing Perceptual Maps**

Technique	Respondent Measures	Advantages	Disadvantages
Nonattribute-based similarity judgments	Judged similarity of various products and/or brands	Does not depend on a predefined attribute set. Allows respondents to use their normal criteria when judging objects. Allows for condition that perception of the whole may not be simply the sum of the perceptions of the parts.	Difficult to name dimensions. Difficult to determine if, and how, the judgments of individual respondents should be combined. Criteria that respondents use depend on the stimuli being compared. Requires special programs. Provides oversimplified view of perceptions when few objects are used.
Attribute-based discriminant or factor analysis	Ratings on various products and/or brands on prespecified attributes	Facilitates naming the dimensions. Easier to cluster respondents into groups with similar perceptions. Easy and inexpensive to use. Computer programs are readily available.	Requires a relatively complete set of attributes. Rests on assumption that overall perception of a stimulus is made of the individual's reactions to the attributes making up the stimulus.

measures used to group people imply some assumptions about how consumers' reactions to the various attribute scales should be combined. Yet the attribute-based approaches are easier to use than the similarity method, since the programs employed are more readily available and less expensive to run.

Regardless of the approach taken, the appeal of multidimensional scaling analysis lies in the maps produced by the technique. These maps can be used to provide insight into some very basic questions about markets, including the following for product markets:

1. the salient product attributes perceived by buyers in the market;
2. the combination of attributes buyers most prefer;
3. the products that are viewed as substitutes and those that are differentiated from one another;
4. the viable segments that exist in a market;
5. those "holes" in a market that can support a new product venture.

Further, the technique also appears suited for product life-cycle analysis, market segmentation, vendor evaluation, the evaluation of advertisements, test marketing, sales representative and store image research, brand-switching research, and attitude scaling.[15]

■

Applications and Problems

1. Assume that you are a staff researcher for a manufacturer of three nationally branded breakfast cereals. The research and development department has formulated a new type of cereal that the company has decided to introduce under a new brand name. The product manager for the breakfast cereal line has expressed concern that the new brand, unless it is carefully positioned, may cannibalize sales of the firm's current brands. You have been assigned to provide research-based information that will assist management in properly positioning the new brand in order to minimize the possibility of cannibalization. What method of analysis should you employ and why? Given your choice of method, what are some fundamental decisions that you must make?

2. Crystal Clear Beverage Company, a medium-sized manufacturer of bottled water, wanted to expand its line of clear beverages by the introduction of a clear cola. Five major brands served the market. The marketing research department decided to use multidimensional scaling to determine the viable "holes" in the market. Perceptions of the similarities among the five brands resulted in the following similarity judgments.

TABLE **1**   **Respondent Similarity Judgments**

Brand	A	B	C	D	E
A		5	9	10	8
B			1	2	7
C				6	4
D					3
E					

The computer-determined two-space solution for the preceding rank order data is shown in Figure 1.

a. In Figure 1 the computer has located the five brands in two-dimensional space. How are the distances between the objects ordered?

Figure 2 displays the plot of the stress value as a function of the number of dimensions employed.

b. Do you think that the similarity judgments between the brands can be captured by one dimension? Give three reasons to support your decision.

c. The marketing research department has identified the Y axis in Figure 1 as "price." How would you advise management to position its brand?

---

[15]For a review of these applications, see Cooper, "A Review of Multidimensional Scaling in Marketing Research."

FIGURE 1   **Multidimensional Scaling Map of Similarity Judgments**

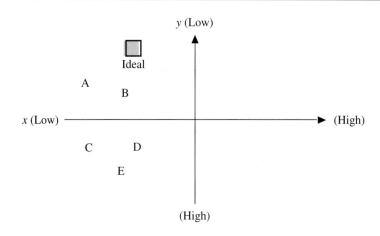

3. Refer to Figure 9A.2 in this appendix. Suppose that objects A–J represent ten fast-food restaurants in a city, each of which is attempting to attract the same market segment. Dimension 1 represents the perceived price of a meal, and Dimension 2 represents the perceived quality of service. Further suppose that an ideal fast-food restaurant would feature very high-quality service and moderate to moderately high prices and that restaurant G is in exactly such a position on the map.
   a. Using this information, briefly describe restaurants F and E and give managerial implications for these restaurants.
   b. Briefly describe and provide managerial implications for restaurant J.
   c. Briefly describe and provide managerial implications for restaurant D.

FIGURE 2   **Stress Index for Brand Similarity Judgments**

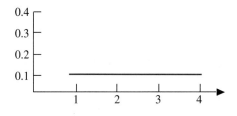

Conjoint Measurement

Like multidimensional scaling analysis, **conjoint analysis** relies on the ability of respondents to make judgments about stimuli. In multidimensional scaling analysis, the stimuli are products or brands, and respondents are asked to make judgments about their relative *similarity*. In conjoint analysis, the stimuli represent some *predetermined combinations of attributes,* and respondents are asked to make judgments about their *preference* for these various attribute combinations. The basic aim is to determine the features respondents most prefer. Respondents might use, for example, such attributes as miles per gallon, seating capacity, price, length of warranty, and so on in making judgments about which automobile they most prefer. Yet, if asked to do so directly, many respondents might find it very difficult to state which attributes they were using and how they were combining them to form overall judgments. Conjoint analysis attempts to handle this problem by estimating how much each of the attributes is valued on the basis of the choices respondents make along product concepts that are varied in systematic ways. In essence, respondents' value systems are inferred from their behaviors as reflected in their choices rather than from self reports about how important each of the various attributes are to them. Research Realities 9B.1, for example, describes how conjoint analysis was used in combination with perceptual mapping to determine the appeal of various state-sponsored lottery games.

The word ''conjoint'' has to do with the notion that the relative values of things considered jointly can be measured when they might not be measurable if taken one at a time. Quite often respondents are asked to express the relative value to them of various alternatives by ordering the alternatives from most desirable to least desirable. The attempt in a conjoint analysis solution, then, is to assign values to the levels of each of the attributes so that the resulting values or utilities are as monotonic as possible with the input rank-order judgments.

EXAMPLE

Suppose that we were considering introducing a new drip coffee maker and wished to assess how consumers evaluated the following levels of each of these product attributes:

* Capacity — 4, 8, and 10 cups
* Price — $18, $22, and $28
* Brewing time — 3, 6, 9, and 12 minutes

All three of these attributes are ''motherhood'' attributes in the sense that, other things being equal, most consumers would prefer either the most or least of each property — in this instance, the largest capacity maker with the shortest brewing time and the lowest price. Unfortunately, life is not that simple. The larger coffee maker will cost more; faster brewing means a larger heating element for the same pot capacity, which also raises the cost; a larger capacity maker with no change in the heating element will

Research Realities 9B.1

Use of Conjoint Analysis and Perceptual Mapping in Combination

Developing a New Lottery Game An "on-line" lottery game is one where the player buys a ticket generated by a lotto terminal and a drawing is held at a later time. Our client was contemplating the launch of a new on-line game, but wasn't sure what combination of game attributes would maximize appeal. They needed to understand the varying "contributions" of the game attributes, which included such things as game theme, prize structure, frequency of drawing, and prize payment. Clearly, conjoint analysis could provide this sort of information.

In addition, past experience had shown that two lottery games, identical in every way but theme, could have very different levels of appeal. This meant, of course, very different levels of profit for the state. To understand *why* certain game themes were preferred, we needed more than utility scores; we needed information on how different types of games

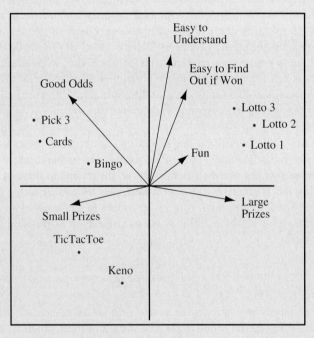

require increased brewing time. In sum, a consumer is going to have to trade off some of one property to secure more of another. What the manufacturer is interested in determining is how consumers value these specific attributes. Is low price most valued, or are consumers willing to pay a higher price to secure some of the other properties? What price? What properties? One thing we might do to answer these questions would be to form all possible combinations of these product attributes, 36 combinations in all, taking one feature from each set and placing that on an index card.

were perceived by potential players. People play lottery games because they are entertaining and fun; would the new game concepts be perceived as "the same old thing," or as something new and exciting? Also, were the reasons for the appeal of the new games the same as the reasons for the appeal of existing games? This was of great concern since the new games would likely cannibalize players from existing games.

Methodology   We decided that perceptual mapping in conjunction with conjoint analysis could answer these important questions. We interviewed recent lottery players in three cities at central location mall facilities. Using Sawtooth Software's ACA and APM Systems, we presented each respondent with a computer interview with both a conjoint and a perceptual mapping component. In the perceptual mapping section of the interview, respondents evaluated nine different game themes on 18 different attributes. Total interview length was 50 minutes — longer than we would have liked — but respondents seemed willing and able to participate.

"Bingo" a Clear Winner   Our analysis of the conjoint portion of the study indicated that a game with a

Bingo theme would be a clear winner across all market segments. The perceptual mapping data confirmed and expanded on these results: Bingo games are perceived to be entertaining and easy to play. Players see this sort of game as a "small prize" game, but like the fact that there are many chances to win.

Another game concept was a lotto game with a smaller-than-usual top prize, but with better odds and a cash payment (with most lotto games, the top prize is paid out over 20–25 years). The conjoint results showed that this particular lotto concept did not have the strong overall appeal of the Bingo concept. Analysis of the perceptual mapping data led us to the reason why: the concept was not different enough from existing lotto games. Although its prize structure was similar to the highly preferred Bingo game, the map shows that respondents grouped it with the other lotto games — the cash prize and better odds were not enough of a differentiator in the minds of respondents.

The conjoint results showed that the least preferred game concept was KENO, a fairly complicated game where the player has to match numbers to a larger set chosen by the lottery. The client thought this game theme had potential because it offered an option that let players, in effect, choose their own odds. The perceptual map showed that, in fact, KENO is perceived as extremely difficult to play. This negative perception overwhelmed the effect of the increased control given to the player.

Source: Katie Klopfenstein, "Combining Conjoint Analysis and Perceptual Mapping," *Sawtooth News*, 7 (Fall 1991), pp. 3–4. Reprinted by Permission, *Sawtooth News*, Suzanne Weiss, Editor.

Suppose that we then asked a respondent to order these product descriptions or cards from least desirable (rank = 1) to most desirable (rank = 36), with higher numbers reflecting greater preference. The respondent could be instructed, for example, to sort the cards first into four categories, labeled "very undesirable," "somewhat undesirable," "somewhat desirable," and "very desirable," and then, after completing the sorting task, to order the cards in each category from least to most desirable. Suppose that the ordering contained in Table 9B.1 resulted from this process.

TABLE 9B.1   **Respondent Ordering of Various Product Descriptions**

Capacity:	4 cup			8 cup			10 cup		
Price:	$18	$22	$28	$18	$22	$28	$18	$22	$28
Brewing Time:									
3 minutes	17	15	6	30	26	24	36	34	28
6 minutes	16	12	5	29	25	22	35	33	27
9 minutes	9	8	3	21	20	8	32	31	23
12 minutes	4	2	1	14	13	7	19	18	11

Note several things about these entries. First, the respondent least preferred the $28 maker with 4-cup capacity and 12 minutes brewing time (rank = 1) and most preferred the 10-cup maker with 3 minutes brewing time priced at $18 (rank = 36). Second, if the respondent cannot have her first choice, she is willing to "suffer" with a longer brewing time so that she could still get the 10-cup maker for $18 (rank = 35). She is not willing to suffer too much, though, as reflected by her third choice (rank = 34). Rather, she is willing to pay a little more to secure the faster 3-minute brewing time rather than having to endure an even slower 9-minute brewing time. In effect, she is willing to trade off price for brewing time.

The type of question that conjoint analysis attempts to answer is: What are the individual's utilities for price, brewing time, and pot capacity in determining her choices?

Procedure

The procedure for determining the individual's utilities for each of several product attributes followed in conjoint analysis is quite similar to that followed in multidimensional scaling analysis. Again the technique is quite dependent on the availability of a high-speed computer. Just as in multidimensional scaling, the computer program emphasis is on generating an initial solution and, subsequently, on modifying that solution through a series of iterations to improve the goodness of fit.[1] More specifically, given a set of input judgments, the computer program will:

1.   assign arbitrary utilities to each level of each attribute;

---

[1]There are several programs available. One of the historically more popular is MONANOVA. See J. B. Kruskal, "Analysis of Factorial Experiments by Estimating Monotone Transformations of the Data," *Journal of the Royal Statistical Society,* Series B, 27 (1965), pp. 251–263; and J. B. Kruskal and F. Carmone, "Use and Theory of MONANOVA, a Program to Analyze Factorial Experiments by Estimating Monotone Transformations of the Data," unpublished paper, Bell Laboratories, 1968. For empirical comparisons involving MONANOVA versus other prediction schemes, see Dick R. Wittink and Philippe Cattin, "Alternative Estimation Methods for Conjoint Analysis: A Monte Carlo Study," *Journal of Marketing Research,* 18 (February 1981), pp. 101–106. René Darmon and Dominique Rouzies, "Internal Validity Assessment of Conjoint Estimated Attribute Importance Weights," *Journal of the Academy of Marketing Science,* 19 (Fall 1991), pp. 315–322.

2. calculate the utilities for each alternative by somehow combining (most typically adding) the individual utility values;
3. calculate the goodness of fit between the ranking of the alternatives using these derived utility values and the original ordering of the input judgments;
4. modify the utility values in a systematic way until the derived utilities produce evaluations that, when ordered, correspond as closely as possible to the order of the input judgments.

For example, suppose that at the first iteration, the computer assigned the following utilities to each level of each attribute:

Capacity		Price		Brewing Time	
4 cup	0.2	$18	0.6	3 minutes	0.5
8 cup	0.3	$22	0.3	6 minutes	0.3
10 cup	0.5	$28	0.1	9 minutes	0.1
				12 minutes	0.1

Suppose further that an additive function is being used so that the utility of any combination of features is given simply by the sum of the utilities of the attribute levels making up the combination. Thus, a 4-cup, 12-minute brewing time, $28 pot would have a utility of 0.4 (0.2 + 0.1 + 0.1). The utilities for each of the other alternatives are shown in Table 9B.2.

An easy way of finding whether the assigned utilities produce an ordering of the product alternatives that corresponds to the original order of the input judgments is by plotting one against the other. For example, the least preferred alternative (rank = 1) was the 4-cup, $28 maker that took 12 minutes. The estimated utility for this combination in Table 9B.2 is 0.4. These two numbers (0.4, 1) serve as coordinates for the point in the lower left-hand corner in Figure 9B.1. Figure 9B.1 shows the relationship that results when each of the derived cell values is plotted against the corresponding preference judgment. If there was a perfect ordering of the derived cell values, the curve would, of course, always increase, since the higher cell values would be associated with higher stated preference. Clearly, the function in Figure 9B.1 does not. The derived cell

TABLE 9B.2   **Utilities for the Feature Combinations Given the Assumed Values**

Capacity	4 cup			8 cup			10 cup		
Price	$18	$22	$28	$18	$22	$28	$18	$22	$28
Brewing Time:									
3 minutes	1.3	1.0	0.8	1.4	1.1	0.9	1.6	1.3	1.1
6 minutes	1.1	0.3	0.6	1.2	0.9	0.7	1.4	1.1	0.9
9 minutes	0.9	0.6	0.4	1.0	0.7	0.5	1.2	0.9	0.7
12 minutes	0.9	0.6	0.4	1.0	0.7	0.5	1.2	0.9	0.7

FIGURE 9B.1   **Input Ranks versus Derived Cell Values**

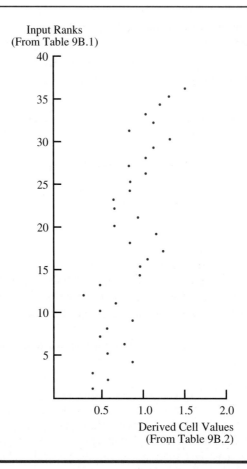

Input Ranks
(From Table 9B.1)

Derived Cell Values
(From Table 9B.2)

values are not monotonic with the original judgments. The computer program would recognize this by computing some measure of goodness of fit between the two orderings. The computer program would also take corrective action and would change the values assigned to the attribute levels in a systematic way in order to improve the correspondence between the two orders. The computer would continue this process of calculating the goodness of fit, changing the assigned values in a systematic way to improve the fit, until it was no longer possible to improve the fit between the two. The program would report the goodness of fit for the final iteration and would also report the utility values assigned to each level of each attribute at this final iteration.

The utilities or part-worth functions for our single subject that resulted from such a process are captured in Figure 9B.2. These utilities suggest several things about our respondent. In the first place, they indicate that our respondent's preferences for price and size are monotonic; other things being equal, she prefers the least costly and largest coffee maker, and her utility function for each attribute declines with increasing price and decreasing size. Her preference function for brewing time is not monotonic, though: she has a higher utility for a 6-minute maker than for a faster or slower one.

FIGURE 9B.2   **Utilities for Various Coffee Maker Attributes**

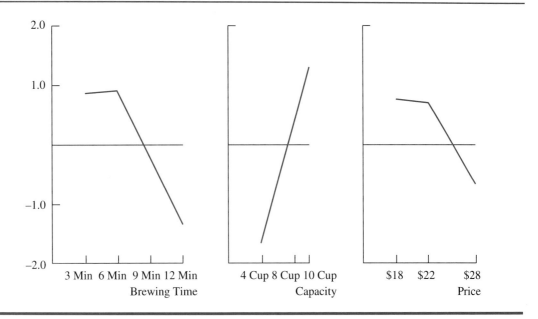

Second, these utilities can be used to determine the relative *importance* of each of these attributes; these are provided by the *spread* in utilities between the highest- and lowest-rated levels of the attribute. The rationale is that, if all levels of an attribute have the same utility to an individual, the attribute is unimportant to the person. Conversely, if different levels of an attribute produce widely differing utilities, the individual is sensitive to the level, implying the attribute is important to her. In interpreting these importance values, one has to remain cognizant that they depend on the level of the attributes used to structure the stimuli. Thus, if price levels of $18, $28, and $38 were used instead of $18, $22, and $28, the differences in utilities for the various price levels would have been greater, suggesting that price was relatively more important to the individual than other attributes. Given the attribute levels used, capacity is most important and price is least important to the subject.

The real pay-off from the preceding analysis comes from the fact that one can use the results to identify the optimal levels and importance of each attribute in structuring a new product offering. Further, by aggregating consumers who have similar preferences or utility functions, products can be designed that come closer to satisfying particular market segments. Thus, conjoint analysis is quite useful at the concept-evaluation stage of the product development process.[2]

[2]See Paul E. Green, J. Douglas Carroll, and Stephen M. Goldberg, "A General Approach to Product Design Optimization via Conjoint Analysis," *Journal of Marketing,* 45 (Summer 1981), pp. 17–37; Paul E. Green and Abba M. Krieger, "Models and Heuristics for Product Line Selection," *Marketing Science,* 21 (Winter 1985), pp. 1–19; Paul E. Green and Abba M. Krieger, "Product Design Strategies for Target-Market Positioning," *Journal of Product Innovation Management,* 8 (September 1991), pp. 189–202, for discussions of the use of conjoint analysis in product design.

KEY DECISIONS

The example illustrates the essential thrust in a conjoint analysis study, but it also provides a somewhat oversimplified picture of the situation, because it does not convey a proper appreciation for the many decisions analysts have to make to conduct such a study. Figure 9B.3 highlights the more critical decision points.[3]

Select Attributes

The first step in the process involves deciding on the attributes to be used when constructing the stimuli. These will stem primarily from the purpose of the investigation, but the analyst will have some discretion in this regard. When choosing, analysts should be guided by the principles that the attributes used should be both actionable and important to individuals. Actionable attributes are those that the company can do something about, in that the company has the technology or other resources to make the changes that might be indicated by consumer preferences. Important attributes are those that actually affect consumer choice. The attributes actually used can be determined by managerial judgment or by any of the other techniques that are typically productive at the exploratory research stage of an investigation, including depth interviews with individual subjects, focus groups, analysis of insight-stimulating examples, and so on. In any single conjoint analysis study, only a handful of all the attributes that could be used will be used, so it is important that they be selected with care. When the number of attributes that need to be varied exceed reasonable limits with respect to data collection problems, a series of conjoint analysis studies can be conducted. The number of attributes actually used in a typical conjoint analysis study averages six or seven.[4]

Determine Attribute Levels

Step 2 in the process involves specifying the actual levels for each attribute. The number of levels for each attribute has a direct bearing on the number of stimuli respondents will be asked to judge and consequently on the burden placed on each subject. In general, we would like to minimize that burden. At the same time, we would like to end up with good estimates of the utility of each attribute level. Our ability to generate good estimates requires that the number of stimuli be relatively large versus the number of parameters that need to be estimated, and the number of parameters in turn depends on the preference model being embraced. Is the model linear in the sense that more or less of

---

[3]The article by Paul E. Green and V. Srinivasan, "Conjoint Analysis in Consumer Research: Issues and Outlook," *Journal of Consumer Research*, 5 (September 1978), pp. 103–123, discusses a number of issues in the implementation of conjoint analysis. The articles by Philippe Cattin and Dick R. Wittink, "Commercial Use of Conjoint Analysis: A Survey," *Journal of Marketing*, 46 (Summer 1982), pp. 44–53; and Dick R. Wittink and Philippe Cattin, "Commercial Use of Conjoint Analysis: An Update," *Journal of Marketing*, 53 (July 1989), pp. 91–96, describe the more common practices among those who use conjoint analysis on a regular basis. See also Paul E. Green and V. Srinivasan, "Conjoint Analysis in Marketing: New Developments with Implications for Research and Practice," *Journal of Marketing*, 54 (October 1990), pp. 3–19.

[4]Cattin and Wittink, "Commercial Use of Conjoint Analysis," p. 47.

FIGURE **9B.3   Key Decisions When Conducting a Conjoint Analysis**

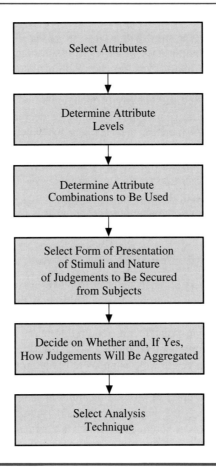

the attribute can be expected to be most desired, or is it nonlinear in a systematic way, or could there be a very nonsystematic relationship between preference and attribute levels? Most subjects may prefer the lowest price or the highest quality when choosing a ballpoint pen, suggesting a linear relationship between their utilities and the attribute levels. At the same time, many may prefer a medium point to a fine or broad point, suggesting that a smooth nonlinear relationship may be appropriate. The nonlinear model requires the estimation of more parameters than the linear model, and, other things being equal, we would like more stimuli when estimating it than when estimating the parameters of the linear model. A very irregular and nonsystematic relationship between utilities and attribute levels would require even more stimuli for good estimation.

When creating stimuli for a conjoint judgment task, analysts also need to be aware that there is a relationship between the number of levels used to measure an attribute and the inferred importance of the attribute to the respondent. More specifically, the empirical evidence suggests that the more levels one uses for an attribute, the more important the attribute is estimated to be in a conjoint analysis.[5] While analysts might want to include more levels for those attributes expected to produce nonlinear versus linear utility functions, they also need to be aware of the erroneous conclusion this can produce about the importance of each of the attributes.

Another factor that affects the choice of attribute levels is their effect on consumer choice. Using levels that are similar to those in existence increases respondents' believability in the task and the validity of their preference judgments. Using attribute levels that are outside the range normally encountered decreases the believability of the task for respondents but can increase the accuracy by which the parameters can be estimated statistically. Similarly, decreasing the intercorrelations among the attributes being varied (such as by combining a very low price with very high quality) decreases the believability of the options for respondents but also increases the accuracy with which the parameters can be estimated. The general recommendation seems to be to make the ranges for the various attributes somewhat larger than what is normally found but not so large as to make the options unbelievable.[6]

Determine Attribute Combinations

The third major decision analysts have to make to conduct a conjoint analysis involves deciding on the specific combinations of attributes that will be used — that is, what the full set of stimuli will look like. In our example, there were only three attributes being considered, but the respondent was required to make 36 judgments. Since the number of possible combinations is given by the product of the number of levels of the attributes, one can readily appreciate what happens to the judgment task if the number of attributes or the number of levels for any attribute is increased. Can we reasonably expect the respondent, for example, to provide meaningful judgments if there are five attributes at three levels each (not an unusual case) requiring then $3 \times 3 \times 3 \times 3 \times 3 = 243$ rank-order judgments? In such a situation, analysts might be tempted to reduce the number of attributes that are varied or the number of levels at which individual attributes are set. An alternative scheme is to use only select combinations of the attributes. For example, it is possible to use orthogonal designs to select only a very small subset of the total number of stimuli if the analyst is willing to assume that there are no interactions among the attributes.[7] This simply means that a person's utility for

---

[5]Dick R. Wittink, Lakshman Krishnamurthi, and David J. Reibstein, "The Effect of Differences in the Number of Attribute Levels on Conjoint Results," *Marketing Letters,* 1 (No. 2, 1990), pp. 113–129; Dick R. Wittink, Joel C. Huber, John A. Fiedler, and Richard L. Miller, "Attribute Level Effects in Conjoint Revisited: ACA versus Full Profile," paper presented at 2nd Annual Advanced Research Techniques Forum, Beaver Creek, Colorado, June 16–19, 1991.

[6]Green and Srinivasan, "Conjoint Analysis in Consumer Research," p. 109.

[7]The use of orthogonal designs to select combinations of the stimuli can produce significant economies in the number of stimuli that respondents need to evaluate. See Sidney Addleman, "Orthogonal Main-Effect Plans for Asymetrical Factorial Experiments," *Technometrics,* 4 (February 1962), pp. 21–46, which is an excellent general source on orthogonal designs. See also Paul E. Green, "On the Design of Choice Experiments Involving Multifactor Alternatives," *Journal of Consumer Research,* 1 (September 1974), pp. 61–68, or David R. Rink, "An Improved Preference Data Collection Method: Balanced Incomplete Block Designs," *Journal of the Academy of Marketing Science,* 15 (Spring 1987), pp. 54–61, which discuss the notions involved more from the perspective of designing choice experiments.

FIGURE 9B.4 **Pairwise Approach to Data Collection in Conjoint Analysis**

		Price		
		$18	$22	$28
Capacity	4 Cup			
	8 Cup			
	10 Cup			

		Brewing Time			
		3 Min	6 Min	9 Min	12 Min
Capacity	4 Cup				
	8 Cup				
	10 Cup				

		Brewing Time			
		3 Min	6 Min	9 Min	12 Min
Price	$18				
	$22				
	$28				

various width tips on a ballpoint pen, for example, is independent of the person's utility for various prices. It is possible to augment the stimuli that are suggested by an orthogonal array with some particularly interesting combinations or ones that allow the estimation of certain select interactions suspected of affecting choice.[8]

The example used the **full profile** approach to collect the judgments; that is, each stimulus was made up of a combination of each of the attributes. One can simplify the judgment task by using the **trade-off matrix** to structure the stimuli instead of the full profile approach. The trade-off matrix, or pairwise procedure, treats two attributes at a time but considers all possible pairs. Thus, in the example, the subject would be asked to indicate her preference ordering for each combination of brewing time and price, brewing time and capacity, and price and capacity by independently completing each of the matrices contained in Figure 9B.4.

It is typically easier for subjects to supply pairwise judgments than full profile judgments. On the other hand, they typically need to make more judgments, and there is a danger of missing some important trade-offs among attributes when the pairwise approach to data collection is used. There can also be a potential loss in realism when only two attributes are considered at a time, because respondents are then forced to make some implicit assumptions about the levels of the other attributes not explicitly varied.[9] Not only is the full profile approach more popular than the pairwise approach, but its popularity is increasing. See Panel A in Research Realities 9B.2.

Another approach that is increasing in popularity is that of paired comparisons. There are several reasons. One reason is that the paired-comparison approach allows one to check how consistent respondents are in their judgments. This means that unmotivated or uninterested respondents (i.e., those whose answers display a great deal of inconsistency, which suggests that the respondents are not taking the task seriously) can be

---

[8]See, for example, Frank J. Carmone and Paul E. Green, "Model Misspecification in Multiattribute Parameter Estimation," *Journal of Marketing Research,* 18 (February 1981), pp. 69–74; Joel H. Steckel, Wayne S. DeSarbo, and Vijay Mahajan, "On the Creation of Acceptable Conjoint Analysis Experimental Designs," *Decision Sciences,* 22 (Spring 1991), pp. 435–442.

[9]See, for example, Madhav N. Segal, "Reliability of Conjoint Analysis: Contrasting Data Collection Procedures," *Journal of Marketing Research,* 19 (February 1982), pp. 139–143; M. Hossein Safizadoh, "The Internal Validity of the Trade-Off Method of Conjoint Analysis," *Decision Sciences,* 20 (Summer 1989), pp. 451–461, for empirical assessments of the performance of the two approaches.

Research Realities 9B.2

Relative Frequency of Usage of Various Techniques in Conjoint Analysis

	Percentage of Projects on Which Used	
	1981–1985	**1971–1980**
Panel A: Data Collection Methods		
Full profile (concept evaluation)	61	56
Paired comparisons	10	NR
Two factors at a time (trade-off matrices)	6	27
Combination of the preceding methods	10	14
Other	13	3
Panel B: Methods of Presenting Stimuli		
Verbal descriptions	NR	50
Paragraph descriptions	NR	20
Pictorial descriptions	NR	19
Actual products	NR	7
Other, including models or pseudoproducts	NR	4
Panel C: Nature of the Judgments		
Preference	NR	33
Liking	NR	10
Intention to buy	NR	54
Other, including actual purchase or order placement	NR	3
Panel D: Nature of Task		
Rank order	36	45
Paired comparison	9	11
Rating scale	49	34
Other	6	10
Total number of projects	1,062 (100%)	698 (100%)

NR = Not Reported.

Source: Developed from the tables in Philippe Cattin and Dick R. Wittink, "Commercial Use of Conjoint Analysis: A Survey," *Journal of Marketing,* 56 (Summer 1982), pp. 44–53, and Dick R. Wittink and Philippe Cattin, "Commercial Use of Conjoint Analysis: An Update," *Journal of Marketing,* 53 (July 1989), pp. 91–96.

FIGURE 9B.5   **Computer-Administered Paired-Comparison Choice**

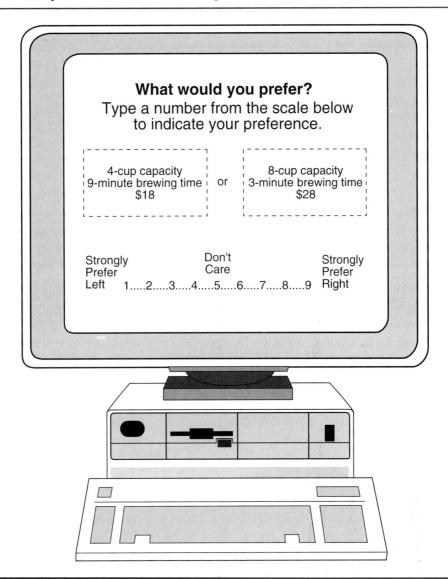

removed from the analysis. Probably a more important reason, though, is that the paired-comparison approach lends itself nicely to computer-interactive interviewing procedures. Respondents simply need to indicate which stimulus they prefer and by how much. Figure 9B.5, for example, depicts a choice pair for the coffee maker. Computer administration of the choice produces several advantages:

1. The judgments requested from a respondent can be made individual-specific, in that different attributes and different attribute levels can be used. Thus, respondents can

be interviewed in detail about only those attribute levels that would be acceptable to them and about only those attributes that they regard as relatively important.

2. The number of judgments required from an individual can be reduced because the parameters can be estimated as soon as a sufficient number of judgments are obtained. Further, the number and kind of additional judgments required from a respondent can be structured to provide the most incremental information, taking into account what is already known about the respondent's utilities.

3. Results can be shown to respondents immediately at the end of the exercise. They can thus be given the opportunity to comment on how realistically the estimates mirror their preferences. The results can also be given to management more quickly.[10]

Select Form of Presentation of Stimuli and Nature of Judgments

Step 4 in the process involves selecting the form of presentation of the stimuli and the nature of the judgments to be secured from subjects. The full profile approach has used variations and combinations of three basic approaches — verbal description, paragraph description, and pictorial representation. Verbal description relies on presenting the cues in list form, typically one stimulus per card, much as was assumed in the example. Paragraph description operates just as the name implies; a paragraph is used to describe each stimulus. Pictorial description relies on some kind of visual prop or three-dimensional model. When visual aids are used, they are typically used in combination with verbal descriptions. As Panel B of Research Realities 9B.2 indicates, verbal descriptions are the most popular.

Related to the issue of the form of presentation of the stimuli is the issue of the nature of the judgments that will be secured from respondents. The two most common approaches measure respondents' preferences for each alternative or their intention to buy each alternative. See Panel C in Research Realities 9B.2. Historically, this information has been secured most often by asking respondents to rank-order the alternatives according to preference or intention to buy. Rating scales have recently become much more popular, though, for securing the needed judgments. Some of the main reasons advanced by those using rank-order judgments are their ease of use by subjects, ease of administration, and a desire to keep the judgment task as close as possible to a consumer's behavior while actually shopping. Those using rating scales believe that they are less time consuming, are more convenient for respondents to use, and are easier to analyze.[11] The nature of the task is different in the two schemes. When the rank-order method is used, subjects are asked to make relative judgments with respect to their

---

[10]For more detailed discussion of the advantages of computer administration of the conjoint task, see Wittink and Cattin, "Commercial Use of Conjoint Analysis: An Update," and Richard M. Johnson, *Adaptive Conjoint Analysis* (Ketchum, Id.: Sawtooth Software, 1987), which also describes how the popular Sawtooth conjoint analysis program works. See also Manoj K. Agarwal and Paul E. Green, "Adaptive Conjoint Analysis Versus Self-Explicated Models: Some Empirical Results," *International Journal of Research in Marketing,* 8 (June 1991), pp. 141–146.

[11]Cattin and Wittink, "Commercial Use of Conjoint Analysis," pp. 48–49.

preference for one alternative over another. When the rating method is used, the judgments are typically made independently; that is, subjects are asked to indicate their degree of liking of each stimulus by checking the appropriate location along the preference or intention-to-buy scale as the alternative is presented. As Panel D of Research Realities 9B.2 indicates, rank order originally was the preferred procedure, but the use of rating scales has now surpassed it in popularity. When the paired-comparison data collection method is used, respondents can be asked either to simply choose which alternative in each pair they prefer or to indicate how much more they prefer it, as in Figure 9B.5.

Decide on Aggregation of Judgments

Step 5 in the process involves deciding if the responses from individual subjects will be aggregated and, if so, how? Although it is possible to derive the utilities for each level of each attribute at the individual level, much as we did in the example, individual-level results are very difficult for marketing managers to use for developing marketing strategy. The other extreme is to pool the results across all respondents and then to estimate one overall utility function. This option fails to recognize any heterogeneity in preference that might exist among respondents, which in turn reduces the predictive power of the model. The middle ground is to form segments from groups of respondents in such a way that the models for the groups will have predictive power close to that found for the individual-level models while having some clear marketing strategy implications for managers. This raises the question, of course, of how these groups should be formed.[12] Most typically it is done by forming segments that are homogeneous with respect to the benefits that the respondents want from the product or service. Operationally, this often translates into estimating utilities for the individual-level models and then clustering respondents into groups that are homogeneous with respect to the utilities assigned to the various levels of the individual attributes.

An attractive feature of conjoint analysis is that it allows market share predictions for selected product alternatives. For example, a common choice rule is the first choice rule, which assumes that each respondent chooses the object with the highest predicted preference. Given the estimated utilities for each level of each attribute, the analyst can investigate which of several product options being considered is likely to appeal most to respondents and what may also be the share of preference for each of the other options. The analyst can also attempt to link individual part-worth utilities with selected consumer characteristics — for example, do high-income households have a higher utility

---

[12]For additional discussion of the aggregation issue, see William L. Moore, ''Levels of Aggregation in Conjoint Analysis: An Empirical Comparison,'' *Journal of Marketing Research*, 17 (November 1980), pp. 516–523; Michael R. Hagerty, ''Improving the Predictive Power of Conjoint Analysis: The Use of Factor Analysis and Cluster Analysis,'' *Journal of Marketing Research*, 22 (May 1985), pp. 168–184; Paul E. Green, Abba M. Krieger, and J. Douglas Carroll, ''Conjoint Analysis and Multidimensional Scaling: A Complementary Approach,'' *Journal of Advertising Research*, 27 (October/November 1987), pp. 21–27; J. Douglas Carroll, Paul E. Green, and Jinko Kim, ''Preference Mapping of Conjoint-Based Profiles: An INDSCAL Approach,'' *Journal of the Academy of Marketing Sciences*, 17 (Fall 1989), pp. 273–281.

for after-the-sale service than low-income households.[13] Research Realities 9B.3, for example, describes how Sunbeam Corporation used conjoint analysis to help design food processors that would appeal to various consumer segments.

Select Analysis Technique

Step 6 in the execution of a conjoint analysis study involves selecting the technique by which the input data will be analyzed. The choice depends in part, but not exclusively, on the type of preference model embraced and the method that was used to secure the input judgments. When linear or smooth nonlinear models are hypothesized to capture preference, one of the constrained parameter estimation models can be used to estimate the functions.[14] When an irregular model is assumed, utilities or **part-worth functions** need to be estimated for each level of each attribute. There are several methods used to estimate the individual part-worths. When rank-order data have been secured from respondents, the nonmetric MONANOVA model (the essential operation of which was described in the example) is most often used to estimate the utilities. Dummy variable regression can be, and is, increasingly being used for this purpose, however, because regression programs are much more readily available than MONANOVA, and the results from the two approaches are highly correlated.[15] When dummy variable regression is used, the rank ordering of the alternatives is the dependent variable and each of the independent variables is coded into a series of 0–1 alternatives.[16] When the preference judgments are collected using rating scales, it is most typical to use either analysis-of-variance techniques or, again, dummy variable regression analysis to estimate the part-worth utilities.[17] In both of these instances, the ratings of each alternative serve as the criterion variable.

---

[13]See, for example, Saul Sands and Kenneth Warwick, "What Product Benefits to Offer to Whom: An Application of Conjoint Segmentation," *California Management Review*, 24 (Fall 1981), pp. 69–74; Kohsuke Ogawa, "An Approach to Simultaneous Estimation and Segmentation in Conjoint Analysis," *Marketing Science*, 6 (Winter 1987), pp. 66–81; Paul E. Green and Abba M. Krieger, "Segmenting Markets with Conjoint Analysis," *Journal of Marketing*, 55 (October 1991), pp. 20–31.

[14]For discussion of the philosophy and some of the more popular techniques for constrained parameter estimation, see V. Srinivasan, Arun K. Jain, and Naresh K. Malhotra, "Improving Predictive Power of Conjoint Analysis by Constrained Parameter Estimation," *Journal of Marketing Research*, 20 (November 1983), pp. 433–438.

[15]For empirical comparisons of the *predictive* accuracy of several of the more popular estimation techniques, see Franklin Acito and Arun K. Jain, "Evaluation of Conjoint Analysis Results: A Comparison of Methods," *Journal of Marketing Research*, 17 (February 1980), pp. 106–112; Wittink and Cattin, "Alternative Estimation Methods for Conjoint Analysis: A Monte Carlo Study," and Ishmael Akaah and Pradeep K. Korgaonkar, "An Empirical Comparison of the Predictive Validity of Self-Explicated, Huber-Hybrid, Traditional Conjoint, and Hybrid-Conjoint Models," *Journal of Marketing Research*, 20 (May 1983), pp. 187–197. For a general discussion of conjoint analysis with metric data, see Jordan J. Louviere, *Analyzing Decision Making: Metric Conjoint Analysis* (Newbury Park, Calif.: Sage Publications, 1988).

[16]The essential notions underlying dummy variable regression are described in Chapter 16.

[17]Analysis of variance is described in Appendix 15A.

GENERAL COMMENTS

It is only after the analyst has made decisions about each of the steps listed in Figure 9B.3 that he or she is in a position to actually collect data for a conjoint analysis study. Unfortunately, there seems to be some propensity among beginning researchers to hurry into the data collection task. This can be a mistake, because there are a great many interrelationships among the many decisions that need to be made, as Figure 9B.3 and the surrounding discussion point out. Rushing into the data collection effort before the interrelated choices are all spelled out can only result in suboptimizing some of the choices. For example, one technique that has become popular in recent years is obtaining conjoint responses to a limited set (usually three to nine) of full profiles drawn for a larger master set and combining that information with other information that respondents directly provide about the relative importance to them of each of the attributes and which levels of each attribute they prefer. Called hybrid models, the essential purpose is to combine the simplicity of the self-explicated approach to attribute measurement with the greater generality of conjoint models.[18]

One can see that vital marketing questions in product design are being addressed by conjoint analysis. Further, the technique is not restricted to product evaluations. It can be used whenever one is making a choice among multiattribute alternatives. With multiattribute alternatives, one typically does not have the option of having more of everything that is desirable and less of everything that is not desirable. Instead, most decisions involve trading off part of something in order to get more of something else. Conjoint analysis attempts to mirror the trade-offs one is willing to make. Thus, while it has most often been used for product design issues, including concept evaluation, it is also used quite regularly as an aid in pricing decisions, market segmentation questions, or advertising decisions. Conjoint analysis has been used less frequently for making distribution decisions, to evaluate vendors, to determine the rewards that salespeople value, and to determine consumer preferences for various attributes of health organizations, among other things.

---

[18]For an exposition of hybrid models and a review of their comparative performance in cross-validation tests, see Paul E. Green, "Hybrid Models for Conjoint Analysis: An Expository Review," *Journal of Marketing Research,* 21 (May 1984), pp. 155–169; Paul E. Green, Abba M. Krieger, and Manoj K. Agarwal, "Adaptive Conjoint Analysis: Some Caveats and Suggestions," *Journal of Marketing Research,* 28 (May 1991), pp. 215–225; Michael J. Dorsch and R. Kenneth Teas, "A Test of the Convergent Validity of Self-Explicated and Decompositional Conjoint Measurement," *Journal of the Academy of Marketing Science,* 20 (Winter 1992), pp. 37–48. For empirical investigations of the reliability of conjoint analysis results, see Thomas W. Leigh, David B. MacKay, and John O. Summers, "Reliability and Validity of Conjoint Analysis and Self-Explicated Weights: A Comparison," *Journal of Marketing Research,* 21 (November 1984), pp. 456–462; R. Kenneth Teas, "An Analysis of the Temporal Stability and Structural Reliability of Metric Conjoint Analysis Procedures," *Journal of Academy of Marketing Science,* 13 (Winter/Spring 1985), pp. 122–142; David Reibstein, John E. G. Bateson, and William Boulding, "Conjoint Analysis Reliability: Empirical Findings," *Marketing Science,* 7 (Summer 1988), pp. 271–286.

Research Realities 9B.3

Using Conjoint Analysis to Redesign Products

Several years ago, the people at the Sunbeam Company's small appliance division (SAC) took a look at some of their mature product lines and decided that a major facelift was in order. But redesigning an entire line of appliances is a tricky proposition because all the products are interrelated in their demand, cost, or both. Therefore, decisions made about one model affect the sales or costs of all the others. SAC decided to tackle the problem by using conjoint analysis to develop the product line.

Because of their strategic position in SAC's product portfolio, food processors were chosen as the first product line to which the conjoint-based redesign procedure would be applied. First, a series of group interviews was conducted to learn consumers' thoughts and feelings about food processors, their attributes and benefits, the uses consumers made of food processors, and their preferences about features.

The interviews also provided an opportunity for SAC's research people to learn the vocabulary that consumers use when they talk and think about food processors. This enabled the researchers to frame questionnaires and interviews to be used in the conjoint analysis study in language that the consumers could understand and find familiar.

Using the group interview results, the attributes and levels to be used in the conjoint study were determined. The 12 attributes of food processors and their levels produced 69,984 possible food processor configurations. SAC decided to use 27 of the possible configurations to assess consumer preferences for the various levels of the 12 attributes.

SAC's industrial designers produced sketches of the 27 food processor designs implied by each of the specific combinations of the attribute levels. The respondents were shown and had to rank in order of preference all 27 of these sketches (see Figure).

More than 500 women were interviewed in four geographically dispersed shopping malls. To be included in the survey, the women had to be the female

head of their household and own and use, on a regular basis, three or more portable cooking or heating appliances. Each completed interview took approximately 40 minutes, most of which was spent ranking the 27 food processor configuration sketches. The actual ranking was done in two stages to reduce the difficulty of respondents' task.

The intitial results from the survey were used to develop the respondents' overall preference for the food processor features. The set of 12 utility functions was estimated from the composite rankings of the attributes by the entire sample. They revealed that appliance buyers preferred the following levels of each of the 12 attributes:

- A standard cylindrical bowl shape
- Two, rather than one or seven, speeds
- A medium-sized bowl capacity
- The ability to use the processor as a mixer but not as a blender
- The maximum number of blades (7)
- A low-profile rear motor design
- A bowl rather than side discharge
- A heavy-duty motor
- A solid rather than three-piece pusher
- A pouring spout
- A larger rather than regular-sized feed tube
- The lowest possible price ($49.99).

Thus, if SAC were to create a new food processor to match the preferences of the average food processor buyer in the study, it would have these attributes. But although all of these attributes were preferred, the intensity of preference varied from attribute to attribute. For example, price, motor power, and number of blades were some of the features that were most important to consumers, whereas number of speeds, type of feed-tube pusher, and type of pouring spout were of little importance.

The next step in the analysis was conjoint utility segmentation by which the 12 utility functions were computed and analyzed for the more than 500 respondents. Using this technique, four clusters of respondents having similar preferences were identified. These clusters fell naturally into two main segments.

One of these segments was labeled the Cheap and Large segment because of the particular preferences for food processor features of buyers in this segment.

Source: Reprinted by permission of the publisher from "Redesigning Product Lines with Conjoint Analysis: How Sunbeam Does It," by Albert L. Page and Harold F. Rosenbaum, *The Journal of Product Innovation Management,* 4 (June 1987), pp. 120–137. Copyright 1987 by Elsevier Science Publishing Co., Inc. For a critical evaluation of the process Sunbeam used, see Dick R. Wittink, "Redesigning Product Lines with Conjoint Analysis: A Comment," *Journal of Product Innovation Management,* 6 (December 1989), pp. 289–296.

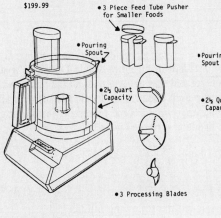

$199.99

- 3 Piece Feed Tube Pusher for Smaller Foods
- Pouring Spout
- 2½ Quart Capacity
- 3 Processing Blades

OTHER FEATURES
- Touch On/Off Pulse Control Switch
- Heavy Duty Motor
- Two Speeds (High/Low)

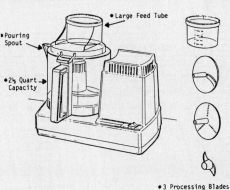

$199.99

- Large Feed Tube
- Pouring Spout
- 2½ Quart Capacity
- 3 Processing Blades

OTHER FEATURES
- Touch On/Off Pulse Control Switch
- Heavy Duty Motor
- Seven Speeds
- Use as a Blender

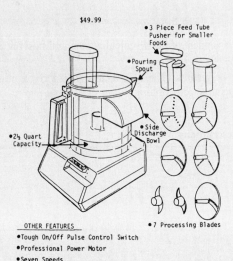

$49.99

- 3 Piece Feed Tube Pusher for Smaller Foods
- Pouring Spout
- 2½ Quart Capacity
- Side Discharge Bowl
- 7 Processing Blades

OTHER FEATURES
- Tough On/Off Pulse Control Switch
- Professional Power Motor
- Seven Speeds
- Use as a Blender and Mixer

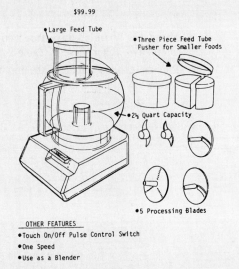

$99.99

- Large Feed Tube
- Three Piece Feed Tube Pusher for Smaller Foods
- 2½ Quart Capacity
- 5 Processing Blades

OTHER FEATURES
- Touch On/Off Pulse Control Switch
- One Speed
- Use as a Blender

The consumers in this group wanted a cheap food processor with the largest possible bowl. They were the least likely of the consumers surveyed to already own a food processor and as a group were older, had midrange incomes, and were most likely to give a food processor as a gift.

The second segment was labeled the Multiple Speeds and Uses segment, because its members' preference for a food processor increased as the number of speeds increased and as the uses of the appliance increased to include mixing and blending. This group seemed to distrust a low price of $49.99 for a food processor but was very sensitive to any price above $99.99.

The two profiles were so different that it seemed unlikely that members of both segments would buy the same food processor. The Cheap and Large segment called for a basic low-end machine whereas the Multiple Speeds and Uses segment called for a more sophisticated and expensive machine.

The overall conjoint results, along with those from the segmentation, demonstrated to SAC which features should be stressed and which could be de-emphasized in the product-line redesign. Even more importantly, these results led SAC's product-line managers to believe that they could greatly increase demand for the food processor line by changing the configuration and the number of models in the line.

Applications and Problems

1. The management of XYZ Company decided to introduce Apple-Down, a frozen concentrated apple juice. However, the management was uncertain about the price and size of the product to introduce. The marketing research department decided to use conjoint analysis to determine the level of each attribute that would come closest to satisfying consumers. The following levels of each of the product attributes were used:

Price	$0.70	$1.10	$1.50
Size	4 fl. oz.	8 fl. oz.	16 fl. oz.

A respondent's rank ordering of the various product descriptions are noted in Table 1:
At the first iteration, the computer assigned the following utilities:

Price	Utility	Size	Utility
$0.70	0.7	4 fl. oz.	0.6
$1.10	0.4	8 fl. oz.	0.2
$1.50	0.1	16 fl. oz.	0.1

   a. Using the linear additive rule and assigned utilities, calculate the utilities for each alternative. Enter these in Table 2.
   b. Plot the original order of the input judgments (Table 1) against the derived utilities for each alternative from Table 2. Discuss your findings.

TABLE 1   **Respondent Ordering of Various Product Descriptions**

	Size		
Price	**4 fl. oz.**	**8 fl. oz.**	**16 fl. oz.**
$0.70	4	1	2
$1.10	6	5	3
$1.50	9	8	7

TABLE 2   **Utilities for the Feature Combinations Given the Assumed Utilities**

	Size		
Price	**4 fl. oz.**	**8 fl. oz.**	**16 fl. oz.**
$0.70			
$1.10			
$1.50			

Psychological Measurement

A problem that marketers have in common with scientists is how to go about measuring the variables in which they have an interest. Research Realities 9C.1, for example, discusses the controversy over measuring something as basic to advertisers as newspaper readership. The problem is particularly acute when the variables represent psychological notions (e.g., attitudes).

The essence of the measurement problem is captured in Figure 9C.1.[1] The basic researcher or scientist uses theories in an attempt to explain phenomena. These theories or models consist of constructs (denoted by the circles with Cs in them), linkages among and between the constructs (single lines connecting the Cs), and data that connect the constructs with the empirical world (double lines). The single lines represent **constitutive** or **conceptual definitions,** in that a given construct is defined in terms of other constructs in the set. The definition may take the form of an equation that precisely expresses the interrelationship of the construct to the other constructs, such as the equation in mechanics that suggests that force equals mass times acceleration. Alternatively, the relationship may be only imprecisely stated, which is typically the case in the social sciences.

The double lines represent operational definitions. An **operational definition** describes how the construct is to be measured. It specifies the activities that the researcher must complete in order to assign a value to the construct (e.g., sum the scores on the ten Likert-type statements to generate a total score). In essence, the operational definition tells the investigator what to do and how to measure the concept. Table 9C.1, for example, shows how consumer sentiment toward marketing was assessed in one large study using Market Facts' mail panel. The measurement assessed respondents' reactions to product quality, product prices, advertising, and retailing and personal selling support. Conceptual definitions logically precede operational definitions and guide their development, for we must specify what a construct is before we can develop rules for assessing its magnitude.

The role of scientific inquiry is to establish the relationships that exist among the constructs of the model. Some of the constructs must be related to observable data if scientists are to accomplish their task. Otherwise, the model will be circular, with given unobservable constructs being defined in terms of other unobservable constructs. Because a circular model cannot be supported or refuted by empirical data, it is not legitimately considered a theory. Rather, a theory or system of explanation rests on the condition that at least some of the constructs can be operationalized sufficiently to allow their measurement. Recall that measurement is defined as ''rules for assigning numbers to objects to represent quantities of attributes.'' The rigor with which these rules are

---

[1]Figure 9C.1 and the discussion surrounding it are adapted from the classic book by Warren S. Torgerson, *Theory and Methods of Scaling* (New York: John Wiley, 1958), pp. 1–11.

Research Realities 9C.1

Controversy Surrounding the Measurement of Newspaper Readership

Roy Megarry, publisher of the *Toronto Globe and Mail,* has had beefs for years with the Audit Bureau of Circulations (ABC), the agency that verifies newspaper circulation figures. Finally last October, he got so fed up that he pulled his paper out of the ABC. The last straw? The ABC's decision to count sales to juvenile detention centers as regular paid circulation.

Mr. Megarry, who describes the ABC as "a dinosaur," also quibbles with rules that permit publishers to include as paid circulation some of the copies stolen from vending boxes and papers distributed to children in classroom reading programs. "And yet," he complains, "the ABC refuses to count bulk sales to hotels that hand out newspapers free to their guests. Somehow I think advertisers would rather reach travelers in first-class hotels than inmates and school kids."

The *Globe and Mail's* surprising defection from the audit bureau, followed by the resignations of 14 Gannett Co. newspapers, brings to the forefront a long-simmering debate about how papers should be measured for advertising purposes. Both publishers and advertisers question audit bureau rules on what qualifies as honest-to-goodness paid circulation. Critics also believe that much more attention should be given to the total number of readers rather than simply the tally of papers sold.

Many advertisers argue that bulk sales should continue to be listed separately because people are less inclined to read a paper they receive as a freebie. "Readers who seek out a publication become more engrossed in its stories and advertising," says Stephen Fajen, media director at the Saatchi & Saatchi Compton ad agency.

More important than bulk sales is the issue of audience data. Audience figures make a publication look better than circulation because, typically, more than one person reads a single copy of a newspaper or magazine.

Marketers are leery, however, of much audience research because it is based on interviews with relatively small samples of readers. Depending on who is counting, there can be great discrepancies. Consider *Newsweek,* which last year became the first major magazine to base ad rates on audience rather than circulation. It says one syndicated research firm estimates that it has more than 20 million readers, whereas another puts the total at 16.9 million.

"I look at audience research but prefer audited circulation figures to projections based on consumer's recollections," says George Mahrlig, director of media services at Campbell Soup Co. Understandably so. Campbell learned from its research that some people consider a quick skim of the paper reading, others devote 20 minutes or more to the paper, and still others page through it just to clip coupons. "It kept us mindful," Mr. Mahrlig says, "that the noses being counted are real people with real distractions."

defined and the skill with which they are implemented determine whether the construct has been captured by the measure.

You would undoubtedly scoff at the following measurement procedure. John has blue eyes and Bill has brown eyes and, therefore, John is taller than Bill. You might reply that "the color of a person's eyes has nothing to do with the person's height and, therefore, you have not in fact measured their height, if that is indeed your purpose. Further, if you wanted to see who was taller, the best procedure would be to measure

FIGURE 9C.1   **Schematic Diagram Illustrating the Structure of Science and the Problem of Measurement**

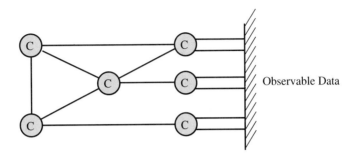

Observable Data

them with a yardstick or to stand them side by side and compare their heights.'' You would be right on both counts. If I measured both John and Bill by asking them how tall they were, you would have probably voiced less objection to my procedure, unless I concluded that John was taller if Bill was definitely the bigger man on observation of the two together. Now the interesting thing about most psychological constructs is that we cannot rely on visual comparisons to either confirm or refute a measure. We cannot see an attitude, a personality characteristic, a person's knowledge about or awareness of a particular product, or other psychological characteristics such as intelligence, mental anxiety, or whatever. These characteristics are all part of the consumer's black box. Their magnitude must be inferred from our measurements. Since we cannot resort to a visual check on the accuracy of our measures, we must rely on assessing the procedures employed to derive the measure. Eye color is certainly not height, but have we captured the sales representatives' satisfaction with their job if we directly ask them how satisfied they are? Probably not, for reasons that will become obvious later.

Note that the problem of establishing operational definitions for constructs (measuring the constructs) is not unique to the researcher interested in scientific explanation. The practitioner shares this concern. Consider the examples in the introductory paragraphs of Chapter 9. The shampoo manufacturer needs to know that the company is in fact measuring consumer attitudes toward the new product and not the many other factors with which the research must contend. The appliance manufacturer must be sure that the full spectrum of dealer attitudes has been correctly tapped and not a small segment of them. The industrial marketer must be certain that the research has not only assessed the sales representative's satisfaction with the obvious dimensions of the work itself, pay, and promotion opportunities, but also has correctly gauged the sales representative's attitudes toward the company, fellow workers, top management, sales supervisor, and customers. The ability to make these assessments relies heavily on an understanding of measurement, measurement error, and the notions of reliability and validity. Understanding these notions is the task to which we now turn.

TABLE 9C.1   **Illustration of Operational Definitions**

Concept	Measurement[a]
	Sum of responses to following items, each measured on five-point disagree–agree scale:
Product Quality	The quality of most products I buy today is as good as can be expected. I am satisfied with most of the products I buy. Most products I buy wear out too quickly. (R) Products are not made as well as they used to be. (R) Too many of the products I buy are defective in some way. (R) The companies that make products I buy don't care enough about how well they perform. (R) The quality of products I buy has consistently improved over the years.
Price of Products	Most products I buy are overpriced. (R) Business could charge lower prices and still be profitable. (R) Most prices are reasonable considering the high cost of doing business. Competition between companies keeps prices reasonable. Companies are unjustified in charging the prices they charge. Most prices are fair. In general, I am satisfied with the prices I pay.
Advertising for Products	Most advertising provides consumers with essential information. Most advertising is annoying. (R) Most advertising makes false claims. (R) If most advertising was eliminated, consumers would be better off. (R) I enjoy most ads. Advertising should be more closely regulated. Most advertising is intended to deceive rather than to inform consumers. (R)
Retailing or Selling	Most retail stores serve their customers well. Because of the way retailers treat me, most of my shopping is unpleasant. (R) I find most retail salespeople to be very helpful. Most retail stores provide an adequate selection of merchandise. In general, most middlemen make excessive profits. (R) When I need assistance in a store, I am usually *not* able to get it. (R) Most retailers provide adequate service.

[a]An (R) indicates scoring of the item needs to be reversed so that higher scores indicate more positive attitudes.

Source: Developed from the information in John F. Gaski and Michael J. Etzel, "The Index of Consumer Sentiment Toward Marketing," *Journal of Marketing*, 50 (July 1986), pp. 71–81.

VARIATIONS IN MEASURED SCORES

Recall that the definition of measurement states that it is the attributes of objects we measure and not the objects themselves. Now, measurement, particularly psychological measurement, always takes place in a rather complex situation in which there are a great many factors that affect the attribute or characteristic being measured, including the process of measurement itself. Consider, for example, during the peak of the energy crisis, the oil companies' interest in measuring people's attitudes toward the energy crisis and particularly their feelings about the role played by the oil companies in deliberately precipitating such a crisis. Suppose that one of the procedures described in the chapter was used to develop an attitude scale to measure these feelings and that the scale was administered to a sample of respondents. A high score means that the respondent believed the oil companies had little to do with precipitating the crisis, whereas a low score indicates just the opposite and, therefore, reflects a poor attitude toward the petroleum producers. Suppose that Mary had a score of 75 and Jane had a score of 40 on the instrument and that the minimum and maximum scores possible were 25 and 100. Conclusion: Mary has a much more favorable attitude toward the oil companies than does Jane. Ideally, yes; practically, maybe. It depends on the quality of the measurement.

Consider some of the potential sources of differences in these two scores of 75 and 40.[2]

1. *True differences in the characteristic that one is attempting to measure.* In the ideal situation, the difference in scores would reflect true differences in the attitudes of Mary and Jane and nothing else. This situation will rarely, if ever, occur. Rather, the difference will also reflect the factors that follow.

2. *True differences in other relatively stable characteristics of the individual that affect the score.* Not only does a person's position on an issue affect the score, but other characteristics can also be expected to have an effect. For example, Research Realities 9C.2 illustrates the impact culture has on people's response styles. Perhaps the difference between Mary's and Jane's scores is simply due to the greater willingness of Jane to express her negative feelings. Mary, by contrast, follows the adage, "If you can't say something nice, don't say anything at all." Her cooperation in the study has been requested and so she responds, but not truthfully.

3. *Differences caused by transient personal factors.* A person's mood, state of health, fatigue, and so on, may all affect the individual's responses. Yet these factors are temporary and can vary. Thus, if Jane had just returned from an IRS audit of her tax return, her responses may be decidedly different than if she were interviewed after receiving a sizable tax refund.

4. *Differences caused by situational factors.* The situation surrounding the measurement also can affect the score. Mary's score might be different if her husband were there while the scale was being administered. Incidentally, this problem is the bane

---

[2]These differences are adapted from Claire Selltiz, Lawrence L. Wrightsman, and Stuart W. Cook, *Research Methods in Social Relations,* 3rd ed. (New York: Holt, Rinehart and Winston, 1976), pp. 164–168. See also Duane F. Alwin and David J. Jackson, "Measurement Models for Response Errors in Surveys: Issues and Applications," in Karl F. Schuessler, ed., *Sociological Methodology 1980* (San Francisco: Jossey-Bass, 1979), pp. 69–119; Frank E. Saal, Ronald G. Downey, and Mary Anne Lakey, "Rating the Ratings: Assessing the Psychometric Quality of Ratings Data," *Psychological Bulletin,* 88 (September 1980), pp. 413–428; Polly A. Phipps and Alan R. Tupek, "Assessing Measurement Errors in a Touchtone Recognition Survey," *Survey Methodology,* 17 (June 1991), pp. 15–26.

Research Realities 9C.2

Impact of Culture on Response Styles

One of the most important and dramatic ways culture impacts multi-country research is in the different ways people in various countries respond to survey questions and use questionnaire scales. In a carefully controlled experiment, Custom Research, Inc., (CRI) explored the use of different kinds of scales in new

Source: Jeffrey Pope, *How Cultural Differences Affect Multi-Country Research,* (Minneapolis, Minn.: Custom Research, Inc., 1991).

product research. The result: *We found extraordinary differences from country to country in the way respondents use common survey scales.* For example: Survey respondents in the Philippines and Italy are four times more likely than respondents in Hong Kong or Japan to use the "top box" of a buying intent scale.

And these differences are clearly the result of culture, not economic levels. Japan and the United States, two of the most affluent countries in the world, are dramatically different on these measures.

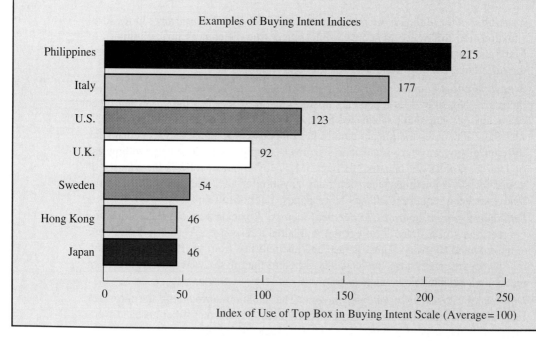

Examples of Buying Intent Indices

Index of Use of Top Box in Buying Intent Scale (Average=100)

of researchers studying the decision-making process of married couples. When the husband is asked for the respective roles of husband and wife in purchasing a new automobile, for instance, one set of responses is secured; when the wife is asked, the responses are different; when the two are asked together, still a third set is obtained. Which is correct? It is hard to say, but the fact remains that the situation surrounding a measurement can affect the scores that are obtained.

5. *Differences because of variations in administration.* Much measurement in marketing involves the use of questionnaires administered by phone or in person. Since

These differences must be understood and taken into account in analyzing multi-country studies. In the CRI experiment across 18 countries, here are a few of the differences we found on use of the buying intent scale:

But the effect of cultural differences on scale use is even more complex: Differences even exist within the same country from one scale to another.

That is illustrated by comparing the example below, showing use of the uniqueness scale, with the previous example on buying intent. Italians are less bullish in their use of the uniqueness scale, while respondents in the United Kingdom are more aggressive in using the uniqueness scale than in stating buying intent.

This means there is no single, simple way to adjust for country-to-country differences. It requires experience across countries and a thorough understanding of how each scale is used differently country by country.

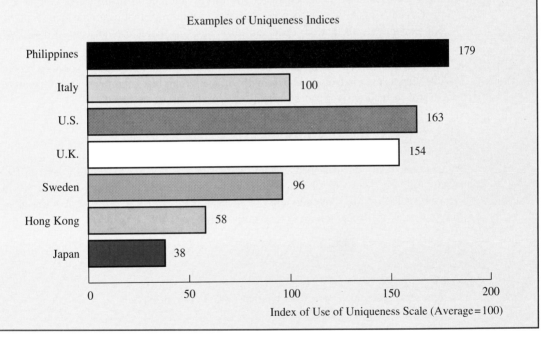

Examples of Uniqueness Indices

interviewers can vary in the way they ask questions, the responses also may vary as a function of the interviewer. The same interviewer may even handle two interviews differently enough to trigger a variance in recorded answers, although the respondents do not really differ on the characteristic.

6. *Differences resulting from sampling of items.* When we measure any construct, we tap only a sample of items relevant to the characteristic being measured. Thus, our attitude scale for the petroleum companies will contain only a sample of all the items or statements that we could possibly have included. If we added, deleted, or

changed the wording of some items, we would undoubtedly change the absolute score achieved by Mary and Jane and could conceivably even change their relative scores so that Jane came out with the more positive attitude. Thus, we must constantly be aware that our measurement represents a narrow conception of the construct and that the resulting score will vary as a function of the items included to capture the construct. A man's height can serve as an indicator of his ''size,'' but so can his weight, the size of his waistline, his chest size, and so on. We certainly could expect to have a better measure of a man's size if we included all these items. So it is with psychological measurements. Other things being equal, a one-item scale is a less adequate sample of the universe of items relevant to a characteristic than is a twenty-five–item scale.

7. *Differences caused by lack of clarity of the measuring instrument.* Sometimes a difference in response to a questionnaire or an item on a scale may represent differences in interpretation of an ambiguous or complex question rather than any fundamental differences in the characteristic one is attempting to measure. One of the researcher's main tasks is to generate items or questions that mean the same thing to all respondents so that the observed differences in scores are not caused by differences in interpretation.

8. *Differences caused by mechanical factors.* Such things as a lack of space to record the responses, inadvertent check marks in the wrong box, improper interpretation of a hard-to-read answer can all affect the scores that are assigned.

CLASSIFICATION AND ASSESSMENT OF ERROR

As mentioned, the ideal in measurement is to generate a score that reflects true differences in the characteristic one is attempting to measure and nothing else. What we in fact obtain, though, is something else. A measurement, call it X_O, for what is observed can be written as a function of several components:

$$X_O = X_T + X_S + X_R,$$

where
X_T represents the true score of the characteristic being measured;
X_S represents systematic error; and
X_R represents random error.

The total error of a measurement is given, of course, by the sum of X_S and X_R; it is important to note that it has two components. **Systematic error** is also known as constant error, because it affects the measurement in a constant way. An example would be the measurement of a man's height with a poorly calibrated wooden yardstick. Differences in other stable characteristics of the individual, which affect the person's score, are a source of systematic error. **Random error** is not constant error but, rather, is due to transient aspects of the person or measurement situation. A random error manifests itself in the lack of consistency of repeated or equivalent measurements when the measurements are made on the same object or person. An example would be the use of an elastic ruler to measure a man's height. It is unlikely that on two successive measurements the observer would stretch the elastic ruler to the same degree of tautness, and, therefore, the two measures would not agree although the man's height had not changed. Differences resulting from transient personal factors are an example of this type of error in psychological measurement.

The distinction between systematic error and random error is critical because of the way the validity of a measure is assessed. **Validity** is synonymous with accuracy or correctness. The validity of a measuring instrument is defined as "the extent to which differences in scores on it reflect true differences among individuals on the characteristic we seek to measure, rather than constant or random errors".[3] When a measurement is valid, $X_O = X_T$, since there is no error. The problem is to develop measures in which the score we observe and record actually represents the true score of the object on the characteristic we are attempting to measure. This is much harder to do than to say. It is not accomplished by simply making up a set of questions or statements to measure the construct (for example, a person's attitude toward the petroleum companies' precipitation of the environmental crisis). Rather, the burden is on the researcher to establish that the measure accurately captures the characteristic of interest. This relationship between measured score and true score is never established unequivocally but is always inferred. The bases for the inference are two: (1) direct assessment employing validity and (2) indirect assessment via reliability.[4] Let us consider each of these sources of evidence in turn.

Pragmatic Validity

As mentioned, a measuring instrument is valid to the extent that differences in scores among objects reflect the objects' true differences on the characteristic that the instrument tries to measure. We normally do not know the true score of an object with respect to a given characteristic. If we did know it, there would be no need to measure the object on that characteristic. What we do, therefore, is infer the validity of the measure by looking for evidence of its pragmatic, content, and construct validity.

The pragmatic approach to validation focuses on the usefulness of the measuring instrument as a predictor of some other characteristic or behavior of the individual; it is thus sometimes called predictive validity or criterion-related validity. **Pragmatic validity** is ascertained by how well the measure predicts the criterion, be it another characteristic or a specific behavior. An example would be the Graduate Management Admissions Test. The fact that this test is required by most of the major schools of business attests to its pragmatic validity; it has proved to be useful in predicting how well a student with a particular score on the exam will do in an accredited MBA program. The test score is used to predict the criterion of performance. An example of an attitude scale

---

[3]Selltiz, Wrightsman, and Cook, *Research Methods,* p. 169.

[4]For detailed discussion of the conceptual relationships that should exist among the various indicants of reliability and validity and an empirical assessment of the evidence, see J. Paul Peter and Gilbert A. Churchill, Jr., "The Relationship among Research Design Choices and Psychometric Properties of Rating Scales: A Meta-Analysis," *Journal of Marketing Research,* 23 (February 1986), pp. 1–10.

might be using scores that sales representatives achieved on an instrument designed to assess their job satisfaction to predict who might quit. The attitude score would again be used to predict a behavior — the likelihood of quitting. Both of these examples illustrate predictive validity in the true sense of the word — that is, use of the score to predict some future occurrence. There is, however, another type of pragmatic validity — concurrent validity. **Concurrent validity** is concerned with the relationship between the predictor variable and the criterion variable when both are assessed at the same point in time. For example, a pregnancy test administered to women to ascertain whether they are pregnant provides an example of concurrent validity. The interest here is not in forecasting whether the woman will become pregnant in the future but in determining if she is pregnant now.

Pragmatic validity is determined strictly by the correlation between the two measures; if the correlation is high, the measure is said to have pragmatic validity.

> Thus if it were found that accuracy in horseshoe pitching correlated highly with success in college, horseshoe pitching would be a valid measure for predicting success in college. This is not meant to imply that sound theory and common sense are not useful in selecting predictor instruments for investigation, but after the investigations are done, the entire proof of the pudding is in the correlations.[5]

Pragmatic validity is relatively easy to assess. It requires, to be sure, a reasonably valid measure of the criterion with which the scores on the measuring instrument are to be compared. Given that such scores are available (for example, the grades the student actually achieves in an MBA program, the sales representative's quitting or not), all that the researcher needs to do is to establish the degree of relationship, usually in the form of some kind of correlation coefficient, between the scores on the measuring instrument and the criterion variable. Although easy to assess, pragmatic validity is rarely the most important kind of validity. We are often concerned with "what the measure in fact measures" rather than simply whether it predicts accurately or not.

Content Validity

Content validity focuses on the adequacy with which the domain of the characteristic is captured by the measure. Consider, for example, the characteristic "spelling ability" and suppose that the following list of words was used to assess an individual's spelling ability: strike, shortstop, foul, inning, catcher, pitcher, ball, umpire, bullpen, dugout. Now, you would probably take issue with this spelling test. Further, the basis for your objection probably would be the fact that all the words relate to the sport of baseball. Therefore, you could argue that an individual who is basically a very poor speller could do well on this test simply because he or she is a baseball enthusiast. You would be right, of course. A person with a basic capacity for spelling but with little interest in baseball might, in fact, do worse on this spelling test than one with less native ability but a good deal more interest in baseball. The test could be said to lack content validity, since it does not properly sample the domain of all possible words that could be used but is very selective in its emphasis.

---

[5]Jum C. Nunnally, *Psychometric Theory,* 2nd ed. (New York: McGraw-Hill, 1978), p. 88.

The preceding example illustrates how content validity is assessed, although not how it is established. Content validity is sometimes known as ''face validity'' because it is assessed by examining the measure with an eye toward ascertaining the domain being sampled. If the included domain is decidedly different from the domain of the variable as conceived, the measure is said to lack content validity. Theoretically, to capture a person's spelling ability, we should administer all words in the English language. The person who spelled the greatest number of these words correctly would be said to have the most spelling ability. This is a completely unrealistic procedure. It would take much of a person's lifetime to complete. Therefore, we resort to sampling the domain of the characteristic by constructing spelling tests that consist of samples of all the possible words that could be used. Different samplings of items can produce different comparative performances by individuals. We need to recognize that whether we have assessed the true characteristic depends on how well we have sampled the domain of the characteristic. This is not only true for spelling ability, but also holds for psychological characteristics in which we have an interest.

How can we ensure that our measure will possess content validity? We can never guarantee it because it is partly a matter of judgment. We may feel quite comfortable with the items included in a measure, for example, while a critic may argue that we have failed to sample from some relevant domain of the characteristic. Although we can never guarantee the content validity of a measure, we can severely diminish the objections of the critics. The key to content validity lies in the *procedures* that are used to develop the instrument.

One of the most critical elements in generating a content valid instrument is conceptually defining the domain of the characteristic. The researcher has to specify what the variable is and what it is not. The task of definition is expedited by examining the literature to determine how the variable has been defined and used. Because it is unlikely that all the definitions will agree, the researcher must specify which elements in the definition underlie his or her use of the term. The researcher's next step is to formulate a large collection of items that broadly represent the variable as defined. The researcher needs to be quite careful to include items from all the relevant dimensions of the variable. Again, a literature search may be productive in indicating the various dimensions or strata of a variable. At this stage, the researcher may wish to include items with slightly different shades of meaning, since the original list of items will be refined to produce the final measure.

The collection of items must be large so that after refinement the measure still contains enough items to adequately sample each of the variable's domains. In the example cited previously, a measure of a sales representative's job satisfaction would need to include items about each of the components of the job (duties, fellow workers, top management, sales supervisor, customers, pay, and promotion opportunities) if it is to be content valid. The process of refinement, the essence of which is the internal consistency exhibited by the items within the test, is statistical in nature.

Construct Validity

Construct validity is most directly concerned with the question of what the instrument is, in fact, measuring. What construct, concept, or trait underlies the performance or score achieved on that test? Does the measure of attitude measure attitude or some other underlying characteristic of the individual that affects his or her score? Construct validity lies at the very heart of scientific progress. Scientists need constructs with which to communicate. So do you and I. Thus, in marketing we speak of people's socioeconomic class, their personality, their attitudes, and so on. These are all constructs that we use as we try to explain marketing behavior. And although vital, they are also unobservable. We can observe behavior related to these constructs, but we cannot observe the constructs themselves. Rather, we operationally define the constructs in terms of a set of observables. When we agree on the operational definitions, precision in communication is advanced. Instead of saying that what is measured by these 75 items is the person's brand loyalty, we can speak of the notion of brand loyalty.

While the measurement of constructs is vital to scientific progress, construct validity is the most difficult type of validity to establish.[6] Research Realities 9C.3, for example, discusses the problems encountered historically when measuring the construct "discretionary income" and a proposed new measure. We need to ensure, through the plans and procedures used in constructing the instrument, that we have adequately sampled the domain of the construct and that there is internal consistency among the items of the domain. The assumption about the internal consistency of a set of items is that "if a set of items is really measuring some underlying trait or attitude, then the underlying trait causes the covariation among the items. The higher the correlations, the better the items are measuring the same underlying construct."[7] We saw that internal consistency was also at issue in determining content validity, and as a matter of fact, negative evidence of the content validity of a measure also provides negative evidence about its construct validity. A measure possessing construct validity must be internally consistent insofar as the construct is internally consistent. On the other hand, it is not true that a consistent measure is a construct-valid measure. "To the extent that the elements of . . . a domain show . . . consistency, it can be said that *some* construct may be employed to account for the data, but it is by no means sure that it is legitimate to employ the construct name which motivated the research. In other words, consistency is a *necessary* but not *sufficient* condition for construct validity."[8]

Given that the domain of the construct has been specified, a set of items relevant to the breadth of the domain has been generated, the items have been refined, and the remaining items have been shown to be internally consistent, the remaining step is to see

---

[6]See Gilbert A. Churchill, Jr., "A Paradigm for Developing Better Measures of Marketing Constructs," *Journal of Marketing Research,* 16 (February 1979), pp. 64–73, for a procedure that can be used to construct scales having construct validity. See J. Paul Peter, "Construct Validity: A Review of Basic Issues and Marketing Practices," *Journal of Marketing Research,* 18 (May 1981), pp. 133–145, for an in-depth discussion of the notion of construct validity. See also Ronald K. Hambleton, H. Swaminathan, and H. Jane Rogers, *Fundamentals of Item Response Theory* (Newbury Park, Ca.: Sage Publications, Inc., 1991).

[7]George W. Bohrnstedt, "Reliability and Validity Assessment in Attitude Measurement," in Gene F. Summers, ed., *Attitude Measurement* (Chicago: Rand McNally, 1970), p. 93. See also George W. Bohrnstedt, "Measurement," in Peter H. Rossi, James D. Wright, and Andy B. Anderson, eds., *Handbook of Survey Research* (Orlando: Academic Press Inc., 1983), pp. 69–121; Robert F. DeVellis, *Scale Development: Theories and Applications* (Newbury Park, Ca.: Sage Publications, Inc., 1991).

[8]Nunnally, *Psychometric Theory,* p. 103.

Research Realities 9C.3

Measuring the Construct "Discretionary Income"

Along with sex and age, family income is among the most often collected and most effective predictors of consumer behavior. Virtually all marketing research instruments include an income question, and the answers to that question are used in many ways. Income describes consumers, segments markets, predicts or explains purchases, and provides reasons for purchasing pattern changes.

Although family income is a useful predictor, it is far from complete. Consumers with low incomes sometimes behave like consumers with high incomes and vice versa. Among the many reasons for such contradictions is that consumers differ greatly in their financial obligations and in their ability to manage the funds they have. When two families have exactly the same income, the amount remaining after the essentials have been purchased may leave one family relatively well off and the other relatively poor. Families with more "discretionary" income have more opportunity to purchase extras or luxury and convenience items, or to put the money away for future use. Knowledge of discretionary income, therefore, would be of considerable value in marketing research.

Despite its obvious benefits, the discretionary income concept has not been used much over the years. One author ascribed this neglect to the fact that consumers cannot determine and report their discretionary income objectively and precisely. Other scholars have cited the generally ambiguous way in which consumers employ economic ideas. They have been especially bothered by the fact that what is "discretionary" and what is "essential" are to some degree a matter of individual taste.

Source: Thomas C. O'Guinn and William D. Wells, "Subjective Discretionary Income," *Marketing Research: A Magazine of Management and Applications*, 1 (March 1989), pp. 32–41.

One way to avoid such problems is to use a psychological approach in determining discretionary income. Instead of trying to get consumers to provide hard, objective economic data, the psychological approach focuses on an entirely subjective variable: how people think about what they have.

Our measure of subjective discretionary income (SDI) was created from three items already present on the DDB Needham advertising agency Life-style Questionnaire:

1. No matter how fast our income goes up, we never seem to get ahead.
2. We have more to spend on extras than most of our neighbors do.
3. Our family income is high enough to satisfy nearly all our important desires.

The statements are answered on a 6-point scale with definitely disagree (1) and definitely agree (6) as the anchor points. When the responses to the three items are summed, with the first item being reverse coded, the result is a score with a range from 3 to 18. Respondents who score high on this scale are indicating that they have enough money to buy what they think they need and then some. Respondents who score low are saying that they have a tough time simply making ends meet.

Each item taps an important aspect of the SDI construct. The first item measures an aspect of SDI very close to perceived economic well-being and also probably related closely to ability to manage money. The second item speaks of "extras" in relation to neighbors, an important reference group. The third item pertains to feelings of having enough income for things that are considered to be important but are still termed "desires." This item gets at the very essence of what "discretionary" means.

how well the measure relates to measures of other constructs to which the construct is theoretically related. Does it behave as expected? Does it fit the theory or model relating this construct to other constructs? The diagram showing the relationships among a set of constructs is often referred to as the *nomological net*. Determining if the construct behaves as expected with respect to the other constructs to which it is theoretically related is consequently referred to as *establishing its nomological validity*.

For example, consider Figure 9C.2, which depicts the relationship between the constructs "job satisfaction" and "job turnover," and suppose that we had developed the measure X to assess a sales representative's job satisfaction. Now, the construct validity of the measure could be assessed by ascertaining the relationship between job satisfaction as measured by X and company turnover as measured by Y. Those companies in which the X-scores are low, indicating less job satisfaction, should experience more turnover than those with high scores. If they do not, one would question the construct validity of the job satisfaction measure. In other words, the construct validity of a measure is assessed by whether the measure confirms or denies the hypotheses predicted from the theory based on the constructs. Is the evidence consistent with the hypothesized linkages among the constructs as captured in a model like Figure 9C.2? The fallacy, of course, is that the failure of the hypothesized relationship to obtain among the observables may be due to a lack of construct validity or incorrect theory. We often try to establish the construct validity of a measure, therefore, by relating it to a number of other constructs rather than simply one, and we also try to use those theories and hypotheses that are sufficiently well founded to inspire confidence in their probable correctness.

If the trait or construct exists, it is also true that it should be measurable by several different methods. Otherwise the trait could be considered to be nothing more than an artifact of the measurement procedure. Moreover, the methods should be independent insofar as possible. If they are all measuring the same construct, though, the measures

FIGURE 9C.2   Diagram Relating the Constructs "Job Satisfaction" and "Job Turnover"

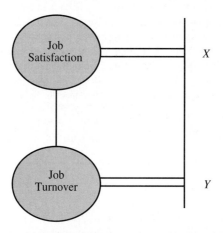

should be highly correlated, which provides evidence of their **convergent validity.** Discriminant validity is also required to establish the construct validity of a measure. **Discriminant validity** requires that a measure does not correlate too highly with measures from which it is supposed to differ.[9] If the correlations are too high, this suggests that the measure is not actually capturing a distinct or isolated trait.

INDIRECT ASSESSMENT THROUGH RELIABILITY

The similarity of results provided by independent but comparable measures of the same object, trait, or construct is called **reliability**. It is distinguished from validity in that validity is represented in the agreement between two attempts to measure the same trait through *maximally different* methods, whereas reliability is the agreement between two efforts to measure the same trait through *maximally similar* methods.[10] If a measure were valid, there would be little need to worry about its reliability. If a measure is valid, it reflects the characteristic that it is supposed to measure and is not distorted by other factors, either systematic or transitory.

Evaluating the reliability of any measuring instrument consists of determining how much of the variation in scores is due to inconsistencies in measurement.[11] The reliability of the instrument should be established before it is used for a substantive study and not after.

Before discussing how this evidence is generated, one point needs emphasis. Reliability involves determining the consistency of independent or comparable measures of the same object, group, or situation. To the extent that a measure is reliable, it is not influenced by transitory factors. In other words, the more reliable the measure, the lower is X_R in the equation for observed scores. Note what this implies. A measure could be reliable and still not be valid, since even if X_R equals zero, $X_O = X_T + X_S$. The converse is, of course, not true. If the measure is valid, $X_O = X_T$, because the measure is simply reflecting true scores without error. Thus, it is often said that (1) if a measure is valid, it is reliable; (2) if it is not reliable, it cannot be valid, since at a very minimum

---

[9]One convenient way of establishing the convergent and discriminant validity of a measure is through the multitrait–multimethod matrix of Campbell and Fiske. See Donald T. Campbell and Donald W. Fiske, "Convergent and Discriminant Validation by the Multitrait–Multimethod Matrix," *Psychological Bulletin,* 56 (1959), pp. 81–105. See also Neal Schmitt, Bryan W. Coyle, and Bruce B. Saari, "A Review and Critique of Analyses of Multitrait–Multimethod Matrices," *Multivariate Behavioral Research,* 12 (October 1977), pp. 447–478; Joseph A. Cote and M. Ronald Buckley, "Estimating Trait, Method, and Error Variance: Generalizing Across To Construct Validation Studies," *Journal of Marketing Research,* 24 (August 1987), pp. 315–318. For an example of its use, see Ronald E. Goldsmith and Janelle Emmert, "Measuring Product Category Involvement: A Multitrait-Multimethod Study," *Journal of Business Research,* 23 (December 1991), pp. 363–371.

[10]Campbell and Fiske, "Convergent and Discriminant Validation," p. 83.

[11]See J. Paul Peter, "Reliability: A Review of Psychometric Basics and Recent Marketing Practices," *Journal of Marketing Research,* 16 (February 1979), pp. 6–17, for a detailed treatment of the issue of reliability in measurement. See Gilbert A. Churchill, Jr., and J. Paul Peter, "Research Design Effects on the Reliability of Rating Scales: A Meta-Analysis," *Journal of Marketing Research,* 21 (February 1984), pp. 360–375, for an empirical assessment of the factors that seem to affect the reliability of rating scales.

TABLE 9C.2   **Relative Frequency with Which Various Psychometric Properties of Measures Are Investigated**

Reliability	95%
Convergent validity	25
Discriminant validity	17
Construct validity	83

Source: Developed from the information in J. Paul Peter and Gilbert A. Churchill, Jr., "The Relationship among Research Design Choices and Psychometric Properties of Rating Scales: A Meta-Analysis," *Journal of Marketing Research, 23* (February 1986), pp. 1–10.

$X_O = X_T + X_R$; and (3) if it is reliable, then it may or may not be valid, because reliability does not account for systematic error. In other words, although lack of reliability provides negative evidence of the validity of a measure, the mere presence of reliability does not mean that the measure is valid. Reliability is a necessary, but not a sufficient, condition for validity. Reliability is more easily measured than validity, though, and this accounts for the emphasis on it over the years. Table 9C.2 indicates that even among studies in which a major thrust is the assessment of the psychometric quality of the measures, reliability is the most frequently investigated property.

Stability

One of the more popular ways of establishing the reliability of a measure is to measure the same objects or individuals at two different points in time and to correlate the obtained scores. Assuming that the objects or individuals have not changed in the interim, the two scores should correlate perfectly. To the extent that they do not, random disturbances were operating in either one or both of the test situations to produce random error in the measurement. The procedure is known as test–retest reliability assessment.

One of the critical decisions the researcher must face in determining the **stability** of a measure is how long to wait between successive administrations of the instrument. Suppose that the researcher's instrument is an attitude scale. If the researcher waits too long, the person's attitude may change, thus producing a low correlation between the two scores. On the other hand, a short wait is likely to produce test bias — people may remember how they responded the first time and be more consistent in their responses than is warranted by their attitudes. To handle this problem, many researchers will use alternate forms for the two administrations. Instead of putting all the items in one form, the researcher generates two instruments that are as identical as possible in content. That is, each form should contain items from the same domains, and each domain of content should receive approximately the same emphasis in each form. Ideally, there would be a one-to-one correspondence between items on each of the two forms so that the means and standard deviations of the two forms would be identical and the intercorrelations among the items would be the same in both versions.[12] Even though it is next to impos-

---

[12]Bohrnstedt, "Reliability and Validity," p. 85.

sible to achieve the ideal, it is possible to construct forms that are roughly parallel, and the parallel forms are correlated across time as the measure of test–retest reliability. The recommended time interval between administrations is two weeks.[13]

Equivalence

The basic assumption in constructing an attitude scale is that when several items are summed into a single attitude score, the items are measuring the same underlying attitude. Each item can, in one sense, be considered a measure of the attitude, and the items should be consistent (or equivalent) in what they indicate about the attitude. Within a given scale, then, the **equivalence** measure of reliability focuses on the internal consistency or internal homogeneity of the set of items forming the scale.

The earliest measure of the internal consistency of a set of items was the split-half reliability of the scale. In assessing split-half reliability, the total set of items is divided into two equivalent halves; the total scores for the two halves are correlated, and this is taken as the measure of reliability of the instrument. Sometimes the division of items is made randomly, whereas at other times the even items are assumed to form one-half and the odd the other half of the instrument. The total score on the even items is then correlated with the total score obtained from the odd items.

Pointed criticism is increasingly being directed at split-half reliability as the measure of a scale's internal consistency. The criticism focuses on the necessarily arbitrary division of the items into equivalent halves. Each of the many possible divisions can produce different correlations between the two forms or different reliabilities. Which division is correct or, alternatively, what is then the reliability of the instrument? For example, a ten-item scale has 126 possible splits or 126 possible reliability coefficients.[14]

A more appropriate way to assess the internal homogeneity of a set of items is to look at all of the items simultaneously, using coefficient alpha. One reason is that coefficient alpha has a direct relationship to the most accepted and conceptually appealing measurement model, the **domain sampling model.** The domain sampling model holds that the purpose of any particular measurement is to estimate the score that would be obtained if *all* the items in the domain were used. The score that any subject would obtain over the whole sample domain is the person's true score, X_T.

In practice, one typically does not use all of the items that could be used, but only a sample of them. To the extent that the sample of items correlates with true scores, it is good. According to the domain sampling model, then, a primary source of measurement error is the inadequate sampling of the domain of relevant items.

Basic to the domain sampling model is the concept of a very large correlation matrix showing all correlations among the items in the domain. No single item is likely to provide a perfect representation of the concept, just as no single word can be used to test

---

[13]Nunnally, *Psychometric Theory,* p. 234, presents a rather scathing argument against test–retest reliability when alternative forms of the instrument are not available. See pages 232–236 in particular.

[14]In general, for a scale with $2n$ items, the total number of possible splits of the items into two halves is $(2n)!/2(n!)(n!)$. See Bohrnstedt, "Reliability and Validity," p. 86.

for differences in subjects' spelling abilities and no single question can measure a person's intelligence.

The average correlation among the items in this large matrix, $\bar{r}$, indicates the extent to which some common core is present in the items. The dispersion of correlations about the average indicates the extent to which items vary in sharing the common core. The key assumption in the domain sampling model is that all items, *if they belong to the domain of the concept,* have an equal amount of common core. This statement implies that the average correlation in each column of the hypothetical matrix is the same, and in turn equals the average correlation in the whole matrix. That is, if all the items in a measure are drawn from the domain of a single construct, responses to those items should be highly intercorrelated. Low inter-item correlations, in contrast, indicate that some items are not drawn from the appropriate domain and are producing error and unreliability.

Coefficient alpha provides a summary measure of the intercorrelations that exist among a set of items. Alpha is calculated as:[15]

$$\alpha = \left(\frac{k}{k-1}\right)\left(1 - \frac{\sum_{i=1}^{k}\sigma_i^2}{\sigma_t^2}\right)$$

where
   k = number of items in the scale
   σ_i^2 = variance of scores on item i across subjects, and
   σ_t^2 = variance of total scores across subjects where the total score for each
       respondent represents the sum of the individual item scores.

Coefficient alpha routinely should be calculated to assess the quality of measure. It is pregnant with meaning because the *square root* of coefficient alpha is the *estimated correlation of the* k-*item test with errorless true scores.*

If alpha is low, what should the analyst do? If the item pool is sufficiently large, this outcome suggests that some items do not share equally in the common core and should be eliminated. The easiest way to find them is to calculate the correlation of each item with the total score and to plot these correlations by decreasing order of magnitude. Items with correlations near zero would be eliminated. Further, items that produce a substantial or sudden drop in the item-to-total correlations would also be deleted.

If the construct had, say, five identifiable dimensions or components, coefficient alpha would be calculated for each dimension. The item-to-total correlations used to delete items would also be based on the items in the component and the total score for that dimension.

---

[15]See Nunnally, *Psychometric Theory,* Chaps. 6 and 7, pp. 190–255, for the rationale behind coefficient alpha and more detailed discussion of the formula for computing it.

The preceding discussion dealt with the equivalence of reliability when applied to a *single* instrument. An alternate equivalence measure is used when different observers or different instruments measure the same individuals or objects at the same point in time. Do these methods produce consistent results? Are they equivalent as measured by the correlations among the total scores? An example would be a beauty contest. Do the judges, using the established criteria of beauty, talent, poise, and so on, rank the contestants in the same order in terms of winner, first runner-up, second runner-up, and so on? The reliability of the measure is greater to the extent that the judges agree.[16] This type of equivalence is the basis of convergent validation when the measures are independent.

DEVELOPING MEASURES

As a beginning researcher, it is easy to become confused about how one goes about developing measures of marketing constructs. How does one contend with the basic issues of reliability and validity, and how does one choose among the various coefficients that can be computed? Figure 9C.3 diagrams a sequence of steps that can be followed to develop valid measures of marketing constructs.[17]

Step 1 in the process involves specifying the domain of the construct that is to be measured. Consider, for example, measuring customer satisfaction with a recently purchased space heater. What attributes of the product and the purchase should be measured to accurately assess the family's satisfaction? Certainly one would want to be reasonably exhaustive in the list of product features to be included, incorporating such facets as cost, durability, quality, operating performance, and aesthetic features. But what about purchaser's reaction to the sales assistance received? What about the family members' reactions to subsequent advertising for a competitor's product offering the same features at lower cost? Or what about the family's reactions to news of some negative environmental effects resulting from use of the product? To detail which of these factors should be included or how customer satisfaction should be operationalized is beyond the scope of this book. Obviously, however, researchers need to be very careful about specifying what is to be included in the domain of the construct being measured and what is to be excluded.

Step 2 in the process is to generate items that capture the domain as specified. Those techniques that are typically productive in exploratory research, including literature searches, experience surveys, and insight-stimulating examples, are generally productive here. The literature should indicate how the variable has been defined previously and how many dimensions or components it has. The search for ways to measure customer

---

[16]For a general discussion of the measurement of interjudge reliability, see William D. Perreault, Jr., and Laurence E. Leigh, ''Reliability of Nominal Data Based on Qualitative Judgments,'' *Journal of Marketing Research,* 26 (May 1989), pp. 135–148; Marie Adele Hughes and Dennis E. Garrett, ''Intercoder Reliability Estimation Approaches in Marketing: A Generalizability Theory Framework for Quantitative Data,'' *Journal of Marketing Research,* 27 (May 1990), pp. 185–195.

[17]The procedure is adapted from Gilbert A. Churchill, Jr., ''A Paradigm for Developing Better Measures of Marketing Constructs,'' *Journal of Marketing Research,* 16 (February 1979), pp. 64–73.

FIGURE 9C.3   **Suggested Procedure for Developing Measures**

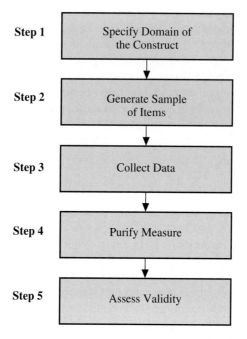

Step 1   Specify Domain of the Construct

Step 2   Generate Sample of Items

Step 3   Collect Data

Step 4   Purify Measure

Step 5   Assess Validity

Source: Adapted from the procedure suggested by Gilbert A. Churchill, Jr., ''A Paradigm for Developing Better Measures of Marketing Constructs,'' *Journal of Marketing Research,* 16 (February 1979), p. 66.

satisfaction would include product brochures, articles in trade magazines and newspapers, or results of product tests such as those published by *Consumer Reports.* The experience survey might include discussions with people in the product group responsible for the product, sales representatives, dealers, persons in marketing research, consumers, and outsiders who have a special expertise in heating equipment. The insight-stimulating examples could involve a comparison of competitors' products or a detailed examination of some particularly vehement complaints in unsolicited letters about the performance of the product. Examples that reveal sharp contrasts or have striking features would be most productive. Focus groups also could be used to advantage at the item-generation state.

Another potential source of items involves having respondents focus on the interactions that were crucial or critical in shaping their reactions to the phenomenon. For example, the following questions were asked of all respondents in an attempt to identify the features of service encounters that make them satisfactory or unsatisfactory:[18]

---

[18]Mary Jo Bitner, Bernard H. Booms, and Mary Stanfield Tetreault, ''The Service Encounter: Diagnosing Favorable and Unfavorable Incidents,'' *Journal of Marketing,* 54 (January 1990), pp. 71–84.

- Think of a time when, as a customer, you had a particularly *satisfying (dissatisfying)* interaction with an employee of an airline, hotel, or restaurant.
- When did the incident happen?
- What specific circumstances led up to this situation?
- Exactly what did the employee say or do?
- What resulted that made you feel the interaction was *satisfying (dissatisfying)*?

Note the emphasis of having respondents describe a specific instance in which a good or poor service interaction occurred. A similar procedure could be used among a sample of purchasers of the space heater to generate items.

Step 3 involves collecting data about the concept from a relevant sample of the target population — for example, all those who have purchased a space heater within the last six months.

Step 4 uses the data collection in Step 3 to purify the original set of items. The purification involves eliminating items that seemed to create confusion among respondents and items that do not discriminate between subjects with fundamentally different positions on the construct. The fundamental criterion that is used to eliminate items is how each item goes together with the other items. If all of the items in a measure are drawn from the domain of a single construct, responses to those items should be highly correlated. If they are not, that is an indication that some of the items are not drawn from the appropriate domain and are producing error and unreliability, and those items should be eliminated. Several of the equivalence reliability coefficients mentioned earlier can be used to make this assessment, as can other statistical techniques.[19]

Step 5 in the process involves determining the validity of the purified measure. Primarily, this involves assessing its convergent, discriminant, and construct validity, because its content validity will have largely been addressed in Steps 1 through 4. The assessment of its construct validity involves determining whether it behaves as expected, which in turn involves determining its pragmatic validity.

Applications and Problems

1. Discuss the notion that a particular measure could be reliable and still not be valid. In your discussion, distinguish between reliability and validity.

2. One construct of general interest involves how "well-off" people are. However, the measurement of this construct is not an easy task, as the following passage from *The Wall Street Journal* attests:

> In the economics sphere, no question is more central. Yet, gauges that bear on how things stand seem often to point in opposite directions. Anyone seeking to determine whether Americans in general are better or worse off now than years ago can find evidence to support either conclusion.
>
> An illustration is the behavior of two statistical series designed to pinpoint how incomes are holding up. Each is produced by a division of the Commerce Department. One, issued by the Census Bureau, traces the average income of families, and the other, put out by the Bureau of Economic

---

[19]See Churchill, "A Paradigm," for detailed discussion of which coefficients should be used and the rationale for their use.

Analysis, tracks the average income of people generally. Both are expressed in "real" terms to eliminate gains due to inflation.

There the similarity ends. Since the early 1970s, the family-income series has climbed from record high to record high.

Between 1973 and 1984, for example, average family income, measured in terms of the dollar's 1984 buying power, dropped $787 to $31,052. No wonder a recent cover story in *U.S. News & World Report* depicts a typical American family "slipping and sliding" on "downhill income." In the same period, however, average per-capita income, again in real terms, rose $1,669 to $12,149.[20]

What goes on? Are people better or worse off? Which series tells it like it is? Discuss the differences in these two measures that purportedly measure the same construct with respect to content validity. What factors do you believe might account for the differences in the two measures?

3. Discuss the use of IQ tests (or similar tests, such as the Graduate Management Admissions Test) in measuring intelligence, an often-used construct. In particular, do you believe that these tests adequately measure a person's abilities? If not, what traits, abilities, or types of intelligence do the tests fail to measure?

4. You have developed a questionnaire designed to measure attitudes toward a set of television ads for a new snack-food product. The respondents, as a group, will view the ads on a television set and then complete the questionnaire. Due to logistical circumstances beyond your control, you must split your sample of respondents into three groups and collect data on three separate days. What steps might you take in an effort to minimize possible variance in scores caused by the three separate administrations?

5. Many areas of marketing research rely heavily on measures of psychological constructs. What characteristics inherent in these constructs make them so difficult to measure? What tools can the marketing researcher bring to bear when evaluating the "correctness" of his or her measure? In other words, what things can we do that allow us to state with some degree of confidence that we are indeed measuring the construct of interest?

6. You are the national sales manager for Perry Pharmaceutical, Inc. You have been concerned with trying to determine the most important characteristics a salesperson must possess in order to be successful. Much of the current research suggests that salesperson adaptiveness is a key component of success. You would like to determine if this is indeed the case. In order to assess this, you need to develop a scale to measure salesperson adaptiveness, collect data with your sales force, and then compare the results to each individual's sales record. At this time, you are asked only to develop a scale to measure salesperson adaptiveness. What kinds of questions would you include? Are there general areas that you think must be measured with a number of different questions?

---

[20]Alfred L. Malabre, Jr., "The Outlook: A Good Statistic Tells of Good Times," *The Wall Street Journal* (September 8, 1986), p. 1.

CASE 3.1
Suchomel Chemical Company

Suchomel Chemical Company was an old-line chemical company that was still managed and directed by its founder, Jeff Suchomel, and his wife, Carol. Jeff served as president and Carol as chief research chemist. The company, which was located in Savannah, Georgia, manufactured a number of products that were used by consumers in and around their homes. The products included waxes, polishes, tile grout, tile cement, spray cleaners for both windows and other surfaces, aerosol room sprays, and insecticides. The company distributed its products regionally. It had a particularly strong consumer following in the northern Florida and southern Georgia areas.

The company had not only managed to maintain but had increased its market share in several of its key lines in the past half dozen years in spite of increased competition from the national brands. Suchomel Chemical had done this largely through product innovation, particularly innovation that emphasized modest product alterations rather than new technologies or dramatically new products. Jeff and Carol both believed that the company should stick to the things it knew best rather than trying to be all things to all people and in the process getting the company's resources spread too thin, particularly given its regional nature. One innovation the company was now considering was a new scent for its insect spray, which was rubbed or sprayed on a person's body. The new scent had undergone extensive testing in both the laboratory and in the field. The tests indicated that it repelled insects, particularly mosquitos, as well as or even better than the two leading national brands. One of the things that the company was particularly concerned about as it considered the introduction of the new brand was what to call it.

THE INSECTICIDE MARKET

The insecticide market had become a somewhat tricky one to figure out over the past several years. Although there had been growth in the purchase of insecticides in general, much of this growth had occurred in the tank liquid market. The household spray market had decreased slightly during the same time span. Suchomel Chemical had not suffered from the general sales decline, however, but had managed to increase its sales of spray insecticides slightly over the past three years. The company was hoping that the new scent formulation might allow it to make even greater market share gains.

The company's past experience in the industry led it to believe that the name that was given to the new product would be a very important element in the product's success, because there seemed to be some complex interactions between purchase and usage characteristics among repellent users. Most purchases were made by married women for their families. Yet repeat purchase was dependent on support by the husband that the product worked well. Therefore, the name must appeal to both the buyer and the end user, but the two people are not typically together at the time of purchase. To complicate matters further, past research indicated that a product with a name that appeals to both purchaser and end user will be rejected if the product's name and scent do not match. In sum, naming a product like this that is used on a person's body is a complex task.

RESEARCH ALTERNATIVES

The company followed its typical procedures in developing possible names for the new product. First, it asked those who had been involved in the product's development to suggest names. It also scheduled some informal brainstorming sessions among potential customers. Subjects in the brainstorming sessions were simply asked to throw out all the names they could possibly think of with respect to what a spray insecticide could or should be called. A panel of executives, mostly those from the product group but a few from corporate management as well, then went through the names and reduced the large list down to a more manageable subset based on their personal reactions to the names and subsequent discussion about what the names connoted to them. The subset of names was then submitted to the corporate legal staff, who checked them for possible copyright infringement. Those that survived this check were discussed again by the panel, and a list of 20 possible names was generated. Those in the product group were charged with the responsibility of developing a research design by which the final name could be chosen.

The people in the product group charged with the name test were considering two different alternatives for finding out which name was preferred. Both alternatives involved personal interviews at shopping malls. More specifically, the group was planning to conduct a set of interviews at one randomly determined mall in Atlanta, Savannah, Tallahassee, and Orlando. Each set of interviews would involve 100 respondents. The target respondents were married females, ages 21 to 54, who purchased the product category during the past year. Likely-looking respondents were to be approached at random and asked if they used any insect spray at all over the past year and then asked their age. Those that qualified would be asked to complete the insecticide-naming exercise using one of the two alternatives being considered.

Alternative 1 involved a sort of the 20 tentative names by the respondents. The sort would be conducted in the following way. First, respondents would be asked to sort the 20 names into two groups based on their appropriateness for an insect repellent. Group 1 was to consist of the ten best names and Group 2 the ten worst. Next, respondents would be asked to select the four best from Group 1 and the four worst from Group 2. Then they would be asked to pick the one best from the subset of the four best and the one worst from the subset of the four worst. Finally, all respondents would be asked why they picked the specific names they did as the best and the worst.

Alternative 2 also had several stages. All respondents would first be asked to rate each of the 20 names on a seven-point semantic differential scale with end anchors "Extremely inappropriate name for an insect repellent" and "Extremely appropriate name for an insect repellent." After completing this rating task, they would be asked to spray the back of their hands or arm with the product. They would then be asked to repeat the rating task using a similar scale, but this time it was one in which the polar descriptors referred to the appropriateness of the name with respect to the specific scent. Next they would be asked to indicate their interest in buying the product by again checking one of the seven positions on a scale that ranged from "Definitely would not buy it" to "Definitely would buy it." Finally, each respondent would be asked why she selected each of the names she did as being most appropriate for insect repellents in general and the specific scent in particular.

Questions

1. Evaluate each of the two methods being considered for collecting the data. Which would you recommend and why?

2. How would you use the data from each method to decide what the brand name should be?

3. Do you think that personal interviews in shopping malls are a useful way to collect these data? If not, what would you recommend as an alternative?

CASE 3.2
Wisconsin Power & Light (B)[1]

In response to the current consumer trend towards increased environmental sensitivity, Wisconsin Power & Light (WP&L) adopted several high-visibility environmental initiatives. These environmental programs fell under the BuySmart umbrella of WP&L's Demand-Side Management Programs and were intended to foster the conservation of energy among WP&L's residential, commercial, and industrial customers. Examples of specific programs include: Appliance Rebates, Energy Analysis, Weatherization Help, and the Home Energy Improvement Loan (HEIL) program. All previous marketing

[1]The contributions of Kavita Maini and Paul Metz to the development of this case are gratefully acknowledged as is the permission of Wisconsin Power & Light to use the material included.

research and information gathering focused primarily on issues from the customers' perspective such as an evaluation of net program impacts in terms of energy and demand savings, and an estimation of the levels of free ridership (individuals who would have undertaken the conservation actions promoted by the program, even if there was no program in place). In addition, a study has been designed and is currently being conducted to evaluate and identify customer attitudes and opinions concerning the design, implementation, features, and delivery of the residential programs. Having examined the consumer perspective, WP&L's next objective is to focus on obtaining information from other participants in the programs, namely employees and lenders.

WP&L's first step in shifting the focus of its research is to undertake a study of the Home Energy Improvement Loan (HEIL) program of the BuySmart umbrella. The HEIL program was introduced in 1987 and was designed to make low-interest-rate financing available to residential gas and electric WP&L customers for conservation and weatherization measures. The low-interest guaranteed loans are delivered through WP&L account representatives in conjunction with participating financial institutions and trade allies. The procedures for obtaining a loan begin with an energy "audit" of the interested customer's residence to determine the appropriate conservation measures. Once the customer decides on which measures to have installed, the WP&L representative assists in arranging low-interest-rate financing through one of the participating local banking institutions. At the completion of the projects, WP&L representatives conduct an inspection of the work by checking a random sample of participants. Conservation measures eligible under the HEIL program include the installation of natural gas furnaces/boilers, automatic vent dampers, intermittent ignition devices, heat pumps, and heat pump water heaters. Eligible structural improvements include the addition of attic/wall/basement insulation, storm windows and doors, sillbox insulation, window weather-stripping, and caulking.

PURPOSE

The primary goal of the current study is to identify ways of improving the HEIL program from the lenders' point of view. Specifically, the following issues need to be addressed:

- Identify the lenders' motivation for participating in the program.
- Determine how lenders get their information regarding various changes/updates in the program.
- Identify how lenders promote the program.
- Assess the current program with respect to administrative and program features.
- Determine the type of credit analysis conducted by the lenders.
- Identify ways of minimizing the default rate from the lenders' point of view.
- Assess the lenders' commitment to the program.
- Identify lenders' opinions of the overall program.
- Identify if the reason for loan inactivity in some lending institutions is due to lack of a customer base.

METHODOLOGY

WP&L decided to use a telephone survey of participating lending institutions to collect the data for its study. WP&L referenced two lists of lending institutions, which were supplied by its resident marketing staff, in order to select the sample for the survey. A total of 124 participating lending institutions were identified with the lists. However, it was found that one of the lists was shorter than the other by 15 names. Specifically, the names of some of the branches of major banks were not enumerated on one of the lists. Nevertheless, all 124 institutions, including the 15 discrepant ones, were included in the pool of names from which the sample was drawn.

The sample pool was classified into three groups based on loan activity in the 1991 calendar year. The groups fell out as follows:

Group	Number of Lenders	Loan Activity, 1991
1	44	0 loans
2	40	1 to 7 loans
3	40	8 to 54 loans

The rationale for the classification strategy was to allow analysis of key variables by three key groups: no loan activity, "light" loan activity, and "heavy" loan activity. The delineation between "light" and "heavy" activity was determined by the median number of loans issued by "active" participants.

The final sample for the survey consisted of 20 randomly chosen institutions from Groups 2 and 3, and 10 from Group 1. The samples of 20 lenders from both Groups 2 and 3 were identified by selecting every other listed respondent after a randomly determined starting point in each list. The 40 institutions selected from among Groups 2 and 3 formed the sample base in which WP&L was most interested (this was because each of these 40 institutions demonstrated loan activity in the past year). The sample size ($n = 40$) was based on judgment. The 10 randomly selected institutions from Group 1 were chosen primarily to explore the hypothesized reasons for zero-loan activity. These 10 zero-loan lenders received a shortened version of the telephone survey that focused only on their lack of activity.

All of the districts within WP&L's service territory were notified two weeks in advance that a survey was going to be conducted. The survey was pre-tested and modified prior to final administration. All interviewing was conducted over a one-week period by a project manager and research assistant, both employees of WP&L's marketing department.

Questions

1. Given the project's objectives, describe the best way to proceed in terms of data collection. Provide support for your conclusion.
2. What kind of sample was used by Wisconsin Power & Light in their research effort? What advantages did WP&L gain by using the sampling method they used? What were the disadvantages? Suggest possible sampling alternatives that WP&L could have used.

CASE 3.3
Rumstad Decorating Centers (B)

Rumstad Decorating Centers was an old-line Rockford, Illinois, business. The company was originally founded as a small paint and wallpaper supply store in 1929 by Joseph Rumstad, who managed the store until his retirement in 1970, at which time Jack Rumstad, his son, took over. In 1974, the original downtown store was closed and a new outlet was opened on the city's rapidly expanding west side. In 1992, a second store was opened on the east side of the city, and the name of the business was changed to Rumstad Decorating Centers.

Jack Rumstad's review of 1993 operations proved disconcerting. Both stores had suffered losses for the year [see Rumstad Decorating Centers (A)]. The picture was far more dismal at the west side store. Losses at the east side store were 80 percent less than the previous year's, which was partially due to some major organizational changes. Further, the east side store had experienced a 25 percent increase in net sales and a 25 percent increase in gross profits over 1992. The west side store, in contrast, had shown a 21 percent decrease in net sales and a 31 percent decrease in gross profit.

Some preliminary research by Rumstad suggested that the problem at the west side store might be traced to the store's location or its advertising. Was the location perceived as convenient? Were potential customers aware of Rumstad Decorating Centers, the products they carried, and where they were located? Did people have favorable impressions of Rumstad? How did attitudes towards Rumstad compare with those towards Rumstad's major competitors?

Rumstad realized that he did not have the expertise to answer these questions. Consequently, he called in Sandra Parrett, who owned and managed her own marketing research service in the Rockford area. Parrett handled all liaison work with the client and assisted in the research design. In addition to Parrett, Lisa Parrett, her daughter, supervised the field staff of four, analyzed data, and prepared research reports. Although the company was small, it had an excellent reputation within the business community.

RESEARCH DESIGN

Rumstad agreed with Sandra Parrett's suggestion that the best way to investigate Rumstad's concerns would be to use a structured, somewhat disguised questionnaire (see Figure 1). The sponsor of the research was to be hidden from the respondents to prevent them from answering "correctly" instead of honestly, so questions about two of Rumstad's main competitors, the Nina Emerson Decorating Center and the Wallpaper Shop, were introduced. Both of these stores offered products and services similar to those carried by Rumstad, and they were located in the same area as Rumstad's west side store. The study was to be confined to the west side store because of cost; loss of profits for the last several years had severely constrained Rumstad's ability to engage in research of this sort. However, the west side store was so critical to the very survival of Rumstad Decorating Centers that Rumstad was willing to commit funds to this

FIGURE 1   **Sample Questionnaire — Rumstad Decorating Centers**

Section I

For Questions 1–8, please indicate your opinion about the importance of the following factors in choosing a decorating center. Place an X in the appropriate blank.

	Not Important	Slightly Important	Fairly Important	Very Important
1. Saw or heard an advertisement	_____	_____	_____	_____
2. Special sale	_____	_____	_____	_____
3. Convenient location	_____	_____	_____	_____
4. Convenient hours	_____	_____	_____	_____
5. Knowledgeable sales personnel	_____	_____	_____	_____
6. Good quality products	_____	_____	_____	_____
7. Additional services (e.g., matching paints, decorator services, etc.)	_____	_____	_____	_____
8. Reasonable prices in relation to quality	_____	_____	_____	_____

Below is a list of abbreviations for the three west side stores that will be referred to throughout the questionnaire:

Emerson Decorating Center — "Emerson"
Rumstad Decorating Center — "Rumstad"
Wallpaper Shop — "Wallpaper Shop"

Please indicate your response with an X in the appropriate blank.

9. *Do you know where any of the following west side stores are located? (i.e., could you find any of these stores without referring to another source?)*

	Yes	No
Emerson	____	____
Rumstad	____	____
Wallpaper Shop	____	____

10. *When was the last time you heard or saw any advertisements for the following stores?*

	Never	Within the Last Month	1–6 Months	More than 6 Months
Emerson	____	____	____	____
Rumstad	____	____	____	____
Wallpaper Shop	____	____	____	____

(continued)

FIGURE 1 *Continued*

11. *Please indicate the source(s) of any advertisements you have seen or heard.*

	Have Not Seen/Heard	Shopper's World	Rockford Morning Star	Radio	TV	Other	Don't Recall
Emerson	___	___	___	___	___	___	___
Rumstad	___	___	___	___	___	___	___
Wallpaper Shop	___	___	___	___	___	___	___

12. *Do you know which of the following items are available in these stores? If so, check the item(s) that apply.*

	Don't Know	Paint	Paneling	Carpeting	Draperies	Other
Emerson	___	___	___	___	___	___
Rumstad	___	___	___	___	___	___
Wallpaper Shop	___	___	___	___	___	___

13. *Which name brands of paint, if any, do you associate with the following stores?*

	Benjamin Moore	Dutch Boy	Glidden	Pittsburgh	Do Not Associate Any Listed
Emerson	___	___	___	___	___
Rumstad	___	___	___	___	___
Wallpaper Shop	___	___	___	___	___

14. *Have you ever visited any of these west side stores?*

	Never	Within Last Year	1–5 Yrs. Ago	More than 5 Yrs. Ago
Emerson	___	___	___	___
Rumstad	___	___	___	___
Wallpaper Shop	___	___	___	___

Section II

If you have visited or have knowledge of *one or more* of the stores listed below, please indicate the extent to which you agree or disagree with the following statements for each store(s). For instance, if you have knowledge of only one store, please answer each question for that particular store. If you have not visited or have no knowledge of any of these stores, omit this section and proceed to Section III.

FIGURE 1 *Continued*

	Strongly Agree	Agree	Neither Agree nor Disagree	Disagree	Strongly Disagree
15. *The location of the store is convenient.*					
Emerson	_____	_____	_____	_____	_____
Rumstad	_____	_____	_____	_____	_____
Wallpaper Store	_____	_____	_____	_____	_____
16. *The sales personnel are knowledgeable.*					
Emerson	_____	_____	_____	_____	_____
Rumstad	_____	_____	_____	_____	_____
Wallpaper Store	_____	_____	_____	_____	_____
17. *The store lacks additional services* (e.g., matching paint, decorator services, etc.).					
Emerson	_____	_____	_____	_____	_____
Rumstad	_____	_____	_____	_____	_____
Wallpaper Store	_____	_____	_____	_____	_____
18. *The store carries good-quality products.*					
Emerson	_____	_____	_____	_____	_____
Rumstad	_____	_____	_____	_____	_____
Wallpaper Store	_____	_____	_____	_____	_____
19. *The prices are reasonable in relation to the quality of the products.*					
Emerson	_____	_____	_____	_____	_____
Rumstad	_____	_____	_____	_____	_____
Wallpaper Store	_____	_____	_____	_____	_____
20. *The store hours are inconvenient.*					
Emerson	_____	_____	_____	_____	_____
Rumstad	_____	_____	_____	_____	_____
Wallpaper Store	_____	_____	_____	_____	_____

Section III

1. Your sex: ____ Male   ____ Female

2. Your age: ____ Under 25 ____ 25–29 years ____ 30–39 years
         ____ 40–54 years ____ 55 or over

(continued)

FIGURE 1   *Continued*

---

3. *How long have you lived in Rockford?*
   ____ Less than 1 year   ____ 1–3 years   ____ 4 or more years

4. *Do you:* ____ Own a home or condominium   ____ Rent a house
   ____ Rent an apartment   ____ Other

5. *When was the last time you painted or remodeled your residence?*
   ____ Never   ____ Within past year   ____ 1–5 years ago
   ____ More than 5 years ago

6. *Approximately how many times have you received the weekly* **Shopper's World** *in the past 3 months?*
   ____ Never   ____ 1–5 times   ____ 6–12 times

7. *Do you read or page through the* **Shopper's World?**
   ____ Do not receive it   ____ Never   ____ Less than ½ the time
   ____ About ½ the time   ____ More than ½ the time

---

investigation, although he repeatedly stressed to Parrett the need to keep the cost as low as possible.

Even though the Emerson Decorating Center and the Wallpaper Shop were similar to Rumstad, there were differences in their marketing strategies. Both stores seemed to advertise more than Rumstad, for example, although the exact amounts of their advertising budgets were not available. Emerson advertised in the *Shopper's World* (a weekly paper devoted exclusively to advertising that is distributed free), ran ads four times a year in the *Rockford Morning Star*, and did a small amount of radio and outdoor advertising. The Wallpaper Shop also advertised regularly in the *Shopper's World* but ran small ads daily in the *Morning Star* and had daily radio commercials as well. Rumstad had formerly advertised in the *Morning Star* but now relied exclusively on the *Shopper's World*.

SAMPLE

Because of the financial constraints imposed on the study by Jack Rumstad, it was decided to limit the study to households within a two-mile radius of Rumstad, Emerson, and the Wallpaper Shop. Aldermanic districts within the two-mile radius were identified; there were four in all, and the wards within each district were listed. Two of the 12 wards were then excluded because they were outside of the specified area. Blocks within each of the 10 remaining wards were enumerated, and 5 blocks were randomly selected from each ward. An initial starting point for each block was determined, and the questionnaires were then administered by the Parrett field staff at every sixth house on the block. All interviews were conducted on Saturday and Sunday. If there was no one at home or if the respondent refused to cooperate, the next house on the block was substituted; there was no one at home at 39 households, and 18 others refused to participate. The field work was completed within one weekend and produced a total sample of 123 responses.

Questions

1. Evaluate the questionnaire. Do you think the questionnaire adequately addresses the concerns raised by Rumstad?

2. How would you suggest the data collected be analyzed to best solve Rumstad's problem?

3. Do you think personal administration of the questionnaires was called for in this study, or would you suggest an alternative scheme? Why or why not?

CASE 3.4
Premium Pizza Inc.[1]

The 1980s saw a sharp increase in the use of promotions (coupons, cents-off deals marked on the package, free gifts, etc.) because of their manifest success at increasing short-term purchase behavior. In fact, sales promotion is now estimated to represent 66 percent of the typical marketing budget compared with 34 percent for advertising.[2] In many industries, however, the initial benefit of increased sales has resulted in long-term escalation of competition. As firms are forced to "fight fire with fire," special offer follows special offer in a never-ending spiral of promotional deals.

The fast-food industry has been one of the most strongly affected by this trend. Pizzas come two for the price of one; burgers are promoted in the context of a double-deal involving cuddly toys for the kids; tacos are reduced in price some days—but not others. It is within this fiercely competitive, erratic environment that Premium Pizza Corporation has grown from a small local chain into an extensive midwestern network with national aspirations. Over the past few years, Jim Battaglia, vice-president of marketing, has introduced a number of promotional offers, and Premium Pizza parlors have continued to flourish. Nevertheless, as the company comtemplates further expansion, Jim is concerned that he knows very little about how his customers respond to his promotional deals. He believes that he needs a long-term strategy aimed at maximizing the effectiveness of dollars spent on promotions. And, as a first step, he thinks that it is important to assess the effectiveness of his existing offers.

---

[1]The contributions of Jacqueline C. Hitchon to this case are gratefully acknowledged.

[2]Courtland L. Bovee and William F. Arens, *Contemporary Advertising,* 4th ed., (Homewood, Ill.: Richard D. Irwin, Inc., 1992), p. 597.

Coupon A:	Get a medium soft drink for 5 cents with the purchase of any slice.
Coupon B:	Buy a slice and get a second slice of comparable value free.
Coupon C:	Save 50 cents on the purchase of any slice and receive one free trip to the salad bar.
Coupon D:	Buy a slice and a large soft drink and get a second slice free.
Coupon E:	Get a single-topping slice for only 99 cents.

SPECIFIC OBJECTIVES

In the past, Jim has favored the use of five types of coupons, and he now wishes to determine their independent appeal, together with their relation to several identifiable characteristics of fast-food consumers. The five promotional concepts are listed in Table 1. The consumer characteristics that Jim's experience tells him warrant investigation include number of children living at home, age of youngest child, propensity to eat fast food, propensity to eat Premium Pizza in particular, preference for slices over pies, propensity to use coupons, and occupation.

The specific objectives of the research study can therefore be summarized as follows:

1. To evaluate the independent appeal of the five promotional deals to determine which deals are most preferred;
2. To gain insight into the reasons that certain deals are preferred; and
3. To examine the relationships between the appeal of each promotional concept and various consumer characteristics.

PROPOSED METHODOLOGY

After much discussion, Jim's research team finally decided that the desired information could best be gathered by means of personal interviews, using a combination of open-ended and close-ended questions. A medium-sized shopping mall on the outskirts of a metropolitan area in the midwest was selected as the research site. Shoppers were intercepted by professional interviewers while walking in the mall and asked to participate in a survey requiring five minutes of their time.

The sampling procedure employed a convenience sample in which interviewers were instructed to approach anyone passing by, provided that they met certain criteria (see Figure 1). In sum, the sample of respondents was restricted to adult men and women between the ages of 18 and 49 who had both purchased lunch, dinner, or carry-out food at a fast-food restaurant in the past seven days and had eaten restaurant pizza within the last thirty days, either at a restaurant or delivered to the home. In addition, interviewers were warned not to exercise any bias during the selection process, as they would do, for example, if they approached only those people who looked particularly agreeable or attractive. Finally, interviewers were asked to obtain as close as possible to a 50-50 split of male and female participants.

FIGURE 1   **Interviewer Instructions**

Below are suggestions for addressing each question. Please read all of the instructions before you begin questioning people.

Interviewer Instructions

Approach shoppers who appear to be between 18–49 years of age. Since we would like equal numbers of respondents in each age category and a 50 percent male-female ratio, please do not select respondents based on their appeal to you. The interview should take approximately five minutes. When reading questions, read answer choices *if indicated*.

Question 1:   Terminate any respondent who has not eaten lunch or dinner from any fast-food restaurant in the last seven days.

Question 2:   Terminate any respondent who has not eaten pizza within the last thirty days. This includes carry-out, drive-thru, or dining in.

Question 3:   Terminate respondent if not between 18–49 years of age. If between 18–49, circle the appropriate number answer. For this question, please read the question and the answer choices.

After completing questions 1 through 3, hand respondent the coupon booklet. *Make sure that the booklet and the response sheets are the same color.* Also check to see that the coupon booklet number indicated on the upper right-hand corner of the response sheet matches the coupon book number.

Question 4:   Ask the respondent to open the coupon booklet and read the first coupon concept. Read the first section of Question 4 showing the respondent that the scales are provided on the page above the coupon concept. Enter his or her answer in the box provided.

Read the second section of the question and enter respondent's answer in the second box provided.

When asking the respondent, "Why did you respond as you did for use," please record the first reason mentioned and use the lines provided to probe and clarify the reasons.

This set of instructions applies to Questions 5 through 8. Periodically remind the respondent to look at the scales provided on the page above the coupon concept that he or she is looking at.

Question 9:   Enter number of children living at home. If none, enter the number zero and proceed to Question 11.

Question 10:   Enter age of *youngest* child living at home in the box provided.

Question 11:   Read the question and each answer slowly. Circle the number corresponding to the appropriate answer.

Question 12:   Read the question and each answer slowly. Circle the number corresponding to the appropriate answer. If answer is never, proceed to Question 14. Otherwise, continue to Question 13.

(continued)

Figure 1   *Continued*

Question 13:   Circle the number corresponding to the appropriate answer. Do not read answer choices.

Question 14:   Circle the number corresponding to the appropriate answer. Do not read answer choices.

Question 15:   Read the question and each answer slowly. Circle the number corresponding to the appropriate answer.

Question 16:   Read the question and each answer slowly. Circle the number corresponding to the appropriate answer.

Question 17:   If an explanation is requested for occupation, please tell respondent that we are looking for a broad category or title. "No occupation" is not an acceptable answer. If this should happen, please probe to see if the person is a student, homemaker, retired, unemployed, etc.

At the end of the questionnaire, you are asked to indicate whether the respondent was male or female. Please circle the appropriate answer. This is not a question for the respondent.

The questionnaire was organized into three sections (see Figure 2). The first section contained the screening questions aimed at ensuring that respondents qualified for the sample. In the second section, respondents were asked to evaluate on ten-point scales the appeal of each of the five promotional concepts based on two factors: perceived value and likelihood of use. After they had evaluated a concept, interviewees were asked to give reasons for their likelihood-of-use rating. The third and final section consisted of the questions on consumer characteristics that Jim believed to be pertinent.

Figure 2   **Questionnaire**

	Response Number	_____
	Coupon Book #	_____

(Approach shoppers who appear to be between the ages of 18–49 and say . . .)

Hi, I'm _____ from Midwest Research Services. Many companies like to know your preferences and opinions about new products and promotions. If you have about 5 minutes, I'd like to have your opinions in this marketing research study.

(If refused, terminate)

1. *Have you eaten lunch or dinner in, or carried food away from, a fast-food restaurant in the last seven days?*

   . . . **(must answer yes to continue)**

FIGURE 2 *Continued*

2. *Have you eaten restaurant pizza within the last thirty days, either at the restaurant or by having it delivered?*

. . . **(must answer yes to continue)**

3. *Which age group are you in?* **(read answers, circle number)**
   1 18–24   2 25–34   3 35–49   4 Other — Terminate interview

I am now going to show you five different coupon concepts and ask you three questions for each. Please respond to each coupon independently of the others. Look at the next coupon only when I ask you to.

4. *Please read the first coupon concept. Using a ten-point scale as shown on the page above, how would you rate this concept if one represents very poor value and ten represents very good value?*

☐ enter value

   Looking at the second scale, how would you rate this concept if one represents definitely would **not** *use and ten represents definitely would use?*

☐ enter value

   Why did you respond as you did for use? _____

   _____

5. *Please turn the page and read the next coupon concept. Ignoring the last coupon and using the same scale, how would you rate this concept in terms of value?*

☐ enter value

   Referring to the second scale, how would you rate this concept in terms of your level of use?

☐ enter value

   Why did you respond as you did for use? _____

   _____

6. *Please turn the page and read the next coupon concept. Ignoring the last coupon and using the same scale, how would you rate this concept in terms of value?*

☐ enter value

   Referring to the second scale, how would you rate this concept in terms of your level of use?

☐ enter value

   Why did you respond as you did for use? _____

   _____

(continued)

Figure 2   *Continued*

7. *Please turn the page and read the next coupon concept.
   Ignoring the last coupon and using the same scale, how would
   you rate this concept in terms of value?*

   enter value

   *Referring to the second scale, how would you rate this concept
   in terms of your level of use?*

   enter value

   *Why did you respond as you did for use?*_____

   _____

   _____

8. *Please turn the page and read the next coupon concept.
   Ignoring the last coupon and using the same scale, how would
   you rate this concept in terms of value?*

   enter value

   *Referring to the second scale, how would you rate this concept
   in terms of your level of use?*

   enter value

   *Why did you respond as you did for use?*_____

   _____

   _____

Thank you. The following questions will help us classify the preceding information.

9. *How many children do you have living at home?*
   If answer is none, proceed to question 11.

   enter number
   none = 0

10. *What is the age of your youngest child?*

11. *How often do you eat fast food for lunch or dinner?*
    (read answers, circle number) 1 Once per month or less
                                       2 Two to three times per month
                                       3 Once or twice a week
                                       4 More than twice a week

12. *How often do you eat at Premium Pizza?*
    (read answers, circle number) 1 Never visited Premium Pizza
                                       2 Once per month or less
                                       3 Two to three times per month
                                       4 Once a week or more
    If answer is never, proceed to question 14.

13. *Do you yourself usually buy whole pies or slices at Premium
    Pizza?*

    1 whole pies
    2 slices
    (circle one)

FIGURE 2 *Continued*

14. **Have you used fast-food or restaurant coupons in the last 30 days?**

 1 yes
 2 no
 (circle one)

15. **Have you ever used coupons for Premium Pizzas?**
 (read answers, circle number) 1 Never
   2 I sometimes use them when I have them.
   3 I always use them when I have them.

16. **What is your marital status:**
 (read answers, circle number) 1 Single
   2 Married
   3 Divorced, separated, widowed

17. **What is your occupation?**_____
 This is *not* a question for the respondent.
 Please circle appropriate answer — respondent was: 1 male
   2 female
   (circle number)

Thank you for your participation — **Terminate interview at this time.**

The questionnaire was to be completed by the interviewer based on the respondent's comments. In other words, the interviewer read the questions aloud and wrote down the answer given in each case by the interviewee. It was decided to show respondents an example of each coupon before they rated it. For this purpose, enlarged photographs of each coupon were produced. It was also thought necessary to depict the ten-point scales that consumers should use to evaluate the promotional offer. Coupons and scales were therefore assembled in a booklet so that, as the interviewer showed each double-page spread, the respondent would see the scales on the top page and the coupon in question on the bottom page (see Figure 3).

Because the researcher wished to counterbalance the order in which the coupons were viewed and rated, the five coupons were organized into booklets of six different sequences. Each sequence was subsequently bound in one of six distinctly colored binders. A total of 96 questionnaires were then printed in six different colors to match the binder. In this way, there were 16 questionnaires of each color, and the color of the respondent's questionnaire indicated the sequence that he or she had seen.

The questionnaire and procedure were pretested at a mall similar to the target mall and were found to be satisfactory.

FIGURE 3 **Stimuli**

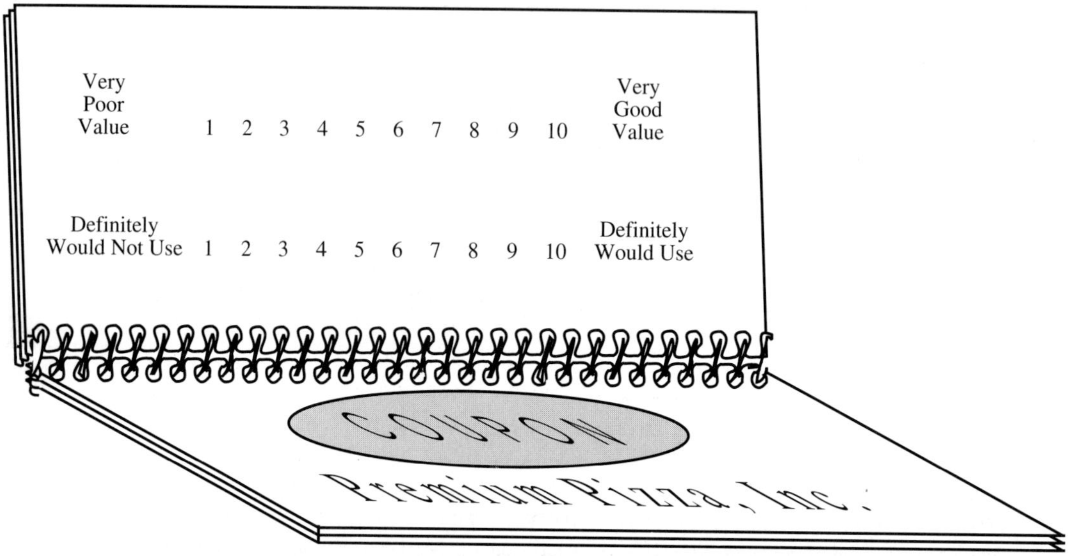
Very Poor Value
1 2 3 4 5 6 7 8 9 10
Very Good Value
Definitely Would Not Use
1 2 3 4 5 6 7 8 9 10
Definitely Would Use
COUPON
Premium Pizza, Inc.

Questions

1. Is the choice of mall intercept interviews an appropriate data collection method given the research objectives?
2. Do you think that there are any specific criteria that the choice of shopping mall should satisfy?
3. Evaluate the instructions to interviewers (Figure 1).
4. Evaluate the questionnaire (Figure 2).
5. Do you think that it is worthwhile to present the coupons in a binder, separate from the questionnaire? Why or why not?
6. Do you consider it advisable to rotate the order of presentation of coupons? Why or why not?

Case 3.5
CTM Productions (A)[1]

CTM Productions, formerly Children's Theatre of Madison, was formed in 1965 to "produce theater of the highest quality." CTM's mission is to "ensure that our [CTM's] efforts are inclusive of all the human family, rather than parts of it." In order to measure its present and future achievement of this goal, CTM must learn who its audience actually is.

CTM's research team decided to study the audience of CTM's production *To Kill a Mockingbird*. The study had three major objectives: (1) to develop an audience profile including demographic and media exposure data; (2) to provide a framework and data collection instrument for future marketing research; and (3) to supply a list of potential season subscribers. Since CTM had never undertaken any marketing research prior to this study, internal secondary information did not exist. External secondary information provided guidance as to the types of questions to be asked on this type of questionnaire and the appropriate phrasing for such questions. The questionnaire is shown in Figure 1.

CTM's volunteer ushers distributed the survey at each of the performances of *To Kill a Mockingbird*. The volunteers gave the survey and a pencil to all adults attending the performances (for the purpose of this survey, adults were defined as anyone sixteen years or older). Respondents were instructed to complete the questionnaire and hand it back to the ushers during the intermission. In addition, collection boxes were placed next to all the exits. While the survey was intended for all adult members of the audience, it is unclear as to whether these instructions were followed at every performance.

Figure 1 **CTM Questionnaire**

Introduce Yourself to CTM

Welcome to CTM's production of *To Kill a Mockingbird*. CTM Productions has been around for a long time — since 1965. And in this time we have had over 33,000 people in our audience. People to whom we have never been introduced. Real people like you that presently exist as numbers in our records. Now you have a chance to change your status. Introduce yourself to us by taking two minutes to answer the following questions to help us understand who you really are.

*Let's start out with the basics. Your name is*_____
*and you live at (please include mailing address with zip code)*_____
_____

(continued)

[1]The contributions of Sara L. Pitterle to this case are gratefully acknowledged.

FIGURE 1   *Continued*

How many CTM productions have you attended?   [   ] this is my first CTM production

1993–1994 Season	**1992–1993 Season**	**1991–1992 Season**
[ ] season subscriber	[ ] season subscriber	[ ] season subscriber
[ ] *Wind in the Willows*	[ ] *Red Shoes*	[ ] *Beauty and the Beast*
[ ] *A Christmas Carol*	[ ] *A Christmas Carol*	[ ] *A Christmas Carol*
[X] *To Kill a Mockingbird*	[ ] *Anne of Green Gables*	[ ] *I Remember Mama*
[ ] *Babar II* (plan to attend)	[ ] *Narnia*	[ ] *Babar the Elephant*

Who is with you today? (check all that apply)

[   ] myself   [   ] my spouse/partner   [   ] my kids

[   ] adult friend(s)   [   ] unrelated kids   [   ] other families

Who have you attended with in the past? (again, check all that apply)

[   ] myself   [   ] my spouse/partner   [   ] my kids

[   ] adult friend(s)   [   ] unrelated kids   [   ] other families

Have you or any of your family particpated in any of these CTM activities? (check all that apply)

[   ] after-school drama classes [   ] auditions   [   ] have not participated

[   ] summer school   [   ] performances   [   ] did not know I could

How did you find out about our production of To Kill a Mockingbird? (check all that apply)

[   ] season brochure   [   ] poster

Read story in:

[   ] *State Journal*   [   ] *Capitol Times*   [   ] *Isthmus*   [   ] other

Saw ad in:

[   ] *State Journal*   [   ] *Capitol Times*   [   ] *Isthmus*   [   ] other

[   ] radio (which station)_____

[   ] television (which station)_____

[   ] magazine (which one)_____

[   ] word of mouth   [   ] other

Did you come to this performance because you knew someone in the cast?   [   ] yes   [   ] no

What other events have you attended in the last six months? (check all that apply)

With your family or friends:

[   ] sports   [   ] movies   [   ] live musical performances

[   ] museums   [   ] lectures   [   ] other live theatrical performances

FIGURE 1 *Continued*

Alone:

[ ] sports   [ ] movies   [ ] live musical performances
[ ] museums   [ ] lectures   [ ] other live theatrical performances

Your answers to the following demographic questions will help us understand who you are.

Are you a female or male?   [ ] female   [ ] male

Which age category do you belong to?
[ ] 16–20   [ ] 31–40   [ ] 51–60   [ ] 71–80
[ ] 21–30   [ ] 41–50   [ ] 61–70   [ ] 81–100

How did you get here today?
[ ] walked   [ ] car   [ ] bus   [ ] other

From how far away did you come?
[ ] within Madison   [ ] less than 5 miles   [ ] 6–10 miles   [ ] over 10 miles

How long have you lived in the Madison/south-central Wisconsin area?
[ ] do not live here   [ ] just arrived   [ ] 1–3 years   [ ] 4–7 years   [ ] more

What is your highest level of education?
[ ] some high school   [ ] some college   [ ] some graduate school   [ ] more
[ ] high school graduate [ ] college graduate [ ] graduate school graduate

What is your annual household income?
[ ] below $20,000 [ ] $31–40,000 [ ] more than $50,000 [ ] do not wish to reply
[ ] $21–30,000   [ ] $41–50,000 [ ] not sure

Does this represent a dual income household?   [ ] yes   [ ] no

How many people live in your household? **(circle only one, include yourself)**
1   2   3   4   5   6   more

If you have children, how many are in each grade category?
[ ] not in school yet   [ ] 4th–5th grade   [ ] high school   [ ] other
[ ] kindergarten–3rd grade   [ ] 6th–8th grade   [ ] college

Would you like to be on our mailing list to keep informed of CTM activities?   [ ] yes   [ ] no

---

(continued)

Are you a CTM member?   [ ] yes   [ ] no

Now here's your chance to share your thoughts with us.

I wish I had known that CTM _____

I'm glad CTM _____

I wish CTM would _____

I want CTM to know _____

It was a real pleasure meeting you. CTM looks forward to seeing you again very soon.

CTM Productions held five shows each weekend for three weekends. Surveys were distributed at each of the fifteen performances; however, the number of completed surveys varied with the size of the audience for each show. A total of 1,016 usable surveys were collected during the course of the study.

Questions

1. The CTM research term used secondary data for question types and wording of specific questions. Did the research team utilize secondary information effectively in this study?

2. Read through the questionnaire shown in Figure 1. Does the questionnaire provide CTM with the information necessary to meet the stated objectives? Explain.

3. Considering CTM's objectives, does the sampling plan used for the study provide the necessary information? Does the sampling plan bias the results?

C<small>ASE</small> 3.6
Calamity-Casualty Insurance Company[1]

Calamity-Casualty is an insurance company located in Dallas, Texas, that deals exclusively with automobile coverage. Its policy offerings include the standard features offered by most insurers, such as collision, comprehensive, emergency road service, med-

---

[1]The contributions of David M. Szymanski to the development of this case are gratefully acknowledged.

ical, and uninsured motorist. The unique aspect of Calamity-Casualty Insurance is that all policies are sold through the mail. Agents do not make personal calls on clients, and the company does not operate district offices. As a result, Calamity-Casualty's capital/labor requirements are greatly reduced at a substantial cost savings to the company. A great portion of these savings are passed on to the consumer in the form of lower prices. The data indicate that Calamity-Casualty offers its policies at 20 to 25 percent below the average market rate.

The company's strategy of selling automobile insurance by mail at low prices has been very successful. Calamity-Casualty has traditionally been the third largest seller of automobile insurance in the Southwest. During the past five years, the company has consistently achieved an average market share of some 14 percent in the four states it serves: Arizona, New Mexico, Nevada, and Texas. This compares favorably to the 19 percent and 17 percent market shares realized by the two leading firms in the region. However, Calamity-Casualty has never been highly successful in Arizona. The largest market share gained by Calamity-Casualty in Arizona for any one year was 4 percent, which placed the company seventh among firms competing in that state.

The company's poor performance in Arizona greatly concerns Calamity-Casualty's board of executives. Demographic experts estimate that during the next six to ten years, the population in Arizona will increase some 10 to 15 percent, the largest projected growth rate of any state in the Southwest. Thus, for Calamity-Casualty to remain a major market force in the area, the company needs to improve its sales performance in Arizona.

In response to this matter, Calamity-Casualty sponsored a study that was conducted by the Automobile Insurance Association of America (AIAA), the national association of automobile insurance executives, to determine Arizona residents' attitudes toward and perception of the various insurance companies selling policies in that state. The results of the AIAA research showed that Calamity-Casualty was favorably perceived across most categories measured. Calamity-Casualty received the highest ratings with respect to service, pricing, policy offering, and image. Although these findings were well received by the company's board of executives, they provided little strategic insight into how Calamity-Casualty might increase sales in Arizona.

Since the company was committed to obtaining information useful for developing a more effective Arizona sales campaign, the executive board sought the services of Aminbane, Pedrone, and Associates, a marketing research firm specializing in insurance consulting, to help with the matter. After many discussions between members of the research team and executives at Calamity-Casualty, it was decided that the most beneficial approach toward designing a more appropriate sales campaign would be to ascertain the psychographic profiles of nonpurchasers and direct-mail purchasers of Calamity-Casualty insurance. This would help the company better understand the personal factors influencing people's decision to respond or not to respond to direct-mail solicitation.

RESEARCH DESIGN

To learn more about which psychographic factors are important in describing purchasers of automobile insurance, some exploratory research was undertaken. In-depth interviews were held with two insurance salespersons, who offered various insights on the subject.

These experience interviews were followed by a focus group meeting with Arizona residents who had received a direct-mail offer from Calamity-Casualty. Finally, the research team consulted university professors in both psychology and mass communications to uncover other determinants of buyer behavior. Output from these procedures revealed three primary factors that could be used to describe purchasers of insurance by mail — namely, risk aversion, powerlessness, and convenience orientation. It was believed that people who were risk averse, had a low sense of powerlessness, and were convenience-oriented would be more favorably disposed toward direct-mail marketing efforts and thus would be more likely to purchase Calamity-Casualty automobile insurance.

TABLE 1 **Calamity-Casualty Marketing Research Questionnaire Items**

Risk Aversion

1. It is always better to buy a used car from a dealer than from an individual.
2. Generally speaking, I avoid buying generic drugs at the drug store.
3. It would be a disaster to be stranded on the road due to a breakdown.
4. It would be important to me to plan a long road trip very carefully and in great detail.
5. I would like to try parachute jumping sometime.
6. Before buying a new product, I would first discuss it with someone who had already used it.
7. Before deciding to see a new movie in a theater, it is important to read the critical reviews.
8. If my car needed even a minor repair, I would first get cost estimates from several garages.

Powerlessness

1. Persons like myself have little chance of protecting our personal interests when they conflict with those of strong pressure groups.
2. A lasting world peace can be achieved by those of us who work toward it.
3. I think each of us can do a great deal to improve world opinion of the United States.
4. This world is run by the few people in power, and there is not much the little guy can do about it.
5. People like me can change the course of world events if we make ourselves heard.
6. More and more, I feel helpless in the face of what's happening in the world today.

Convenience Orientation

1. I like to buy things by mail or catalog because it saves time.
2. I think that it is not worth the extra effort to clip coupons for groceries.
3. I would rather wash my own car than pay to have it washed at a car wash.
4. I would prefer to have an automatic transmission rather than a stick shift in my car.
5. When choosing a bank, I believe that location is the most important factor.
6. When shopping for groceries, I would be willing to drive a longer distance in order to buy at lower prices.

Note: Each item requires one of the following responses:

Responses	Code
S.A. — Strongly Agree	5
A. — Agree	4
N. — Neither Agree nor Disagree	3
D. — Disagree	2
S.D. — Strongly Disagree	1

METHOD OF DATA COLLECTION

Given these factors of interest, the list of the items contained in Table 1 was generated to form the basis of a questionnaire to be administered to Arizona residents. Two samples of subjects were to be used — one of direct-mail buyers and one of nonbuyers. The research team estimated that 175 subjects would be required from both samples to adequately assess the three constructs. Because a mail questionnaire dealing with psychographic subject matter might have a very low response rate, and because attitude toward direct mail was one of the attributes being measured, a telephone interview was believed to be best suited to the needs at hand.

Questions

1. Conceptually, what are the constructs risk aversion, convenience, and powerlessness?
2. Do you think that the sample of items adequately assesses each construct? Can you think of any additional items that could or should be used?

SAMPLE DESIGN AND DATA COLLECTION

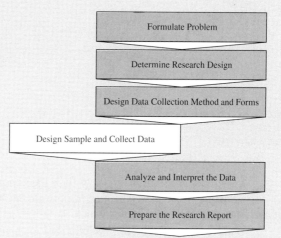

Formulate Problem

Determine Research Design

Design Data Collection Method and Forms

Design Sample and Collect Data

Analyze and Interpret the Data

Prepare the Research Report

Part 4 is concerned with the actual collection of data needed to answer a problem. Chapter 10 discusses the various types of sampling plans that can be employed to determine the population elements from which the data should be collected; Chapter 11 treats the question of how many of these elements are needed to answer the problem with precision and confidence in the results; and Chapter 12 discusses the many errors that can arise in completing this data collection task.

10

C H A P T E R

Sampling Procedures

Once the researcher has clearly specified the problem and developed an appropriate research design and data collection instrument, the next step in the research process is to select those elements from which the information will be collected. One way to do this would be to collect information from each member of the population of interest by completely canvassing this population. A complete canvass of a population is called a **census.** Another way would be to collect information from a portion of the population by taking a **sample** of elements from the larger group, and, on the basis of the information collected from the subset, to infer something about the larger group. One's ability to make this inference from subset to larger group depends on the method by which the sample of elements was chosen. A major part of this chapter is devoted to the ''why'' and ''how'' of taking a sample.

Incidentally, *population* here refers not only to people but also to manufacturing firms, retail or wholesale institutions, or even inanimate objects such as parts produced in a manufacturing plant. **Population** is defined as the totality of cases that conform to some designated specifications. The specifications define the elements that belong to the target group and those that are to be excluded. A study aimed at establishing a demographic profile of frozen-pizza eaters requires specifying who is to be considered a frozen-pizza eater. Anyone who has ever eaten a frozen pizza? Those who eat at least one such pizza a month? A week? Those who eat a certain minimum number of frozen pizzas per month? Researchers need to be very explicit in defining the target group of interest and most careful that they have actually sampled the target population and not some other population because an inappropriate or incomplete sampling frame was used.

One might choose a sample to infer something about a population rather than canvassing the population itself for several reasons. First, complete counts on populations of moderate size are very costly. Also, few marketing research studies warrant complete counts, because the information will often be obsolete by the time the census is completed and the information processed. Further, sometimes a census is impossible, such as when testing the life of electric light bulbs. A 100 percent inspection using the bulbs until they burned out would reveal the average bulb life but would leave no product to sell. Finally (and, to novice researchers, surprisingly), one might choose a sample over a census for purposes of accuracy. Censuses involve larger field staffs, which, in turn,

FIGURE 10.1   **Six-Step Procedure for Drawing a Sample**

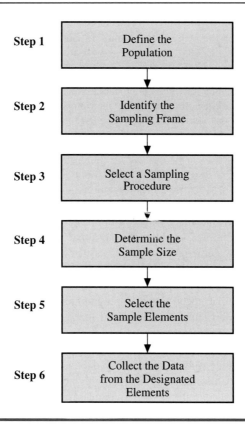

introduce greater potential for nonsampling error. This is one of the reasons the Bureau of the Census uses sample surveys to check the accuracy of various censuses. That is correct; samples are used to infer the accuracy of the census.[1]

REQUIRED STEPS

Figure 10.1 outlines a useful six-step procedure that researchers can follow when drawing a sample of a population. Note that it is first necessary to define the population or the

---

[1]The fact that sample information is used to gauge the accuracy of the census has embroiled the Census Bureau in a debate about whether census counts should be adjusted on the basis of the sample results. For discussion of the controversy surrounding adjustment, see Eugene Carlson, "Census Debate: Is an Estimate More Accurate than a Count?" *The Wall Street Journal* (August 4, 1987), p. 35; "Census Bureau Will Not Adjust '90 Census Data," *Data User News,* 22 (December 1987), p. 3; Timothy Noah, "Census Bureau Says It Missed 2% of Population," *The Wall Street Journal* (April 19, 1991), p. 1; Cyndee Miller, "Census Decision Seen as Unlikely to Hurt Marketing Researchers," *Marketing News,* 25 (August 19, 1991), pp. 16, 22.

collection of elements about which the researcher wishes to make an inference. Relevant elements thus are the objects on which measurements are taken. For example, when the preferences of children are involved, researchers have to decide whether the population to be measured is the kids, their parents, or both.

> One company tested its slotless road racing sets only with children. Kids loved 'em. But moms said they didn't like the sets because they were teaching children to crash cars, and dads didn't like the fact that the product was made into a toy.
>
> It can work the other way, too. One company introduced a food product with a national ad campaign that starred a rather precocious child. The company tested the campaign only with mothers, who thought it was great. Kids thought the precocious child was obnoxious — and the product, too. End of product.[2]

The researcher must decide whether the relevant population consists of individuals, households, business firms, other institutions, credit-card transactions, or what. In making this specification, the researcher also has to be careful to specify what units are to be excluded. This means specifying at a minimum both the geographic boundaries and the time period for the study, although additional restrictions are often placed on the elements. When the elements are individuals, for example, the relevant population may be defined as all those over 18, or females only, or those with a high school education only. A combination of age, sex, education, race, and other restrictions could also be used.

The problem of specifying the geographic boundaries for the target population is sometimes more difficult in international marketing research studies because of the additional complexity an international perspective introduces. For example, urban versus rural areas may be significantly different from each other in various countries. Also, the composition of the population can vary depending on the location within the country. For example, in Chile, the north has a highly centralized Indian population, whereas the south has high concentrations of individuals of European descent.

In general, the simpler the definition of the target population, the higher the incidence and the easier and less costly it is to find the sample.[3] **Incidence** refers to the percentage of the population or group that qualifies for inclusion in the sample using some criteria. Incidence has a direct bearing on the time and cost it takes to complete studies. When incidence is high (i.e., most population elements qualify for the study because only one or very few, easily satisfied criteria are used to screen potential respondents), the cost and time to collect data are minimized. Alternatively, as the number of criteria used to describe what constitutes eligible respondents for the study increases, so does the cost and time necessary to find them. Figure 10.2, for example, shows the percentage of adults who are estimated to participate in various sports. The data in Figure 10.2 suggest that it would be more difficult and costly to focus a study on people who motorcycle, only 3.6 percent of all adults, than people who walk for health, 27.4 percent of all adults. The most important thing in defining the target population is that

---

[2]Cyndee Miller, "Researching Children Isn't Kids Stuff Anymore," *Marketing News,* 24 (September 3, 1990), p. 32.

[3]Seymour Sudman, "Applied Sampling," in Peter H. Rossi, James D. Wright, and Andy B. Anderson, eds., *Handbook of Survey Research* (Orlando: Academic Press, 1983), pp. 145–194. See also, "SSI-LITe™: Low Incidence Targeted Sampling (Fairfield, CT.: Survey Sampling, Inc., 1994).

FIGURE 10.2   **Percentage of Adults Estimated to Participate in Various Sports**

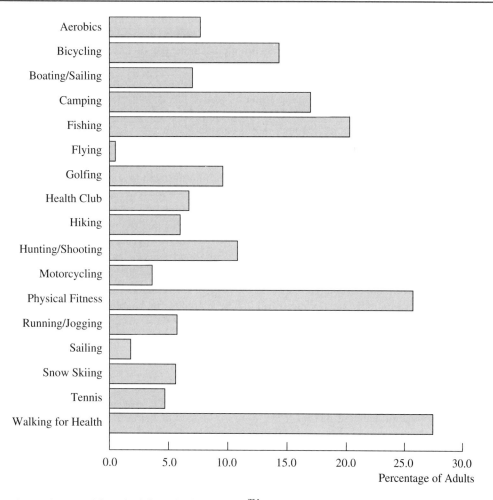

Source: Developed from the information in "SSI-*LITe*™: *Low Incidence Targeted Sampling* (Fairfield, CT.: Survey Sampling, Inc., 1994).

the researcher is precise in specifying exactly what elements are of interest and what elements are to be excluded. A clear statement of research objectives helps immeasurably in determining the appropriate elements of interest.

The second step in the sample selection process is identifying the **sampling frame,** which is the listing of the elements from which the actual sample will be drawn. A telephone book is an obvious example of a sampling frame, which also illustrates the condition that there is rarely a perfect correspondence between the sampling frame and the target population of interest. Even though the target population may be all households living in a particular metropolitan area, the telephone directory provides an inaccurate listing of these households, omitting some without phones and unlisted numbers and double counting others that have multiple listings. One of the researcher's more creative tasks in sampling is developing an appropriate sampling frame when the list of population elements is not readily available. Sometimes this means sampling geographic areas or institutions and then subsampling within these units when, say, the target population is individuals but a current, accurate list of appropriate individuals is not available.

The third step of selecting a sample procedure is inextricably intertwined with the identification of the sampling frame, because the choice of sampling method depends largely on what the researcher can develop for a sampling frame. A simple random sample, for example, requires that a complete, accurate list of population elements by name or other identification code be available. The rest of this chapter reviews the main types of nonprobability and probability samples employed in marketing research. The connection between sampling frame and sampling method should become obvious from this discussion.

Step 4 in the sample selection process requires the sample size to be determined. Chapter 11 discusses this question. Step 5 indicates that the researcher needs to actually pick the elements that will be included in the study. How this is done depends on the type of sample being used, and consequently the discussion of sample selection is woven into the discussion of sampling methods. Finally, the researcher needs to actually collect data from the designated respondents. A great many things can go wrong with this task. These problems are reviewed, and some methods for handling them are discussed, in Chapter 12.

TYPES OF SAMPLING PLANS

Sampling techniques can be divided into the two broad categories of probability and nonprobability samples. **Probability samples** are distinguished by the fact that each population element has a *known, nonzero* chance of being included in the sample. It is not necessary that the probabilities of selection be equal, only that one can specify the probability with which each element of the population will be included in the sample. With **nonprobability samples,** in contrast, there is no way of estimating the probability that any population element will be included in the sample, and thus there is no way of ensuring that the sample is representative of the population. All nonprobability samples rely on personal judgment somewhere in the process, and although these judgment samples may indeed yield good estimates of a population characteristic, they do not permit an objective evaluation of the adequacy of the sample. It is only when the elements have been selected with known probabilities that one is able to evaluate the precision of a sample result.

Samples can also be distinguished by whether they are fixed or sequential. **Fixed samples** imply an *a priori* determination of sample size and the collection of needed information from the designated elements. The question of sample size for fixed samples is discussed in the next chapter. Fixed samples are the most commonly employed types in marketing research and the kind we shall emphasize. Nevertheless, you should be aware that sequential samples can also be taken and that they can be employed with each of the basic sampling plans to be discussed. **Sequential samples** are distinguished by the

FIGURE 10.3   **Classification of Sampling Techniques**

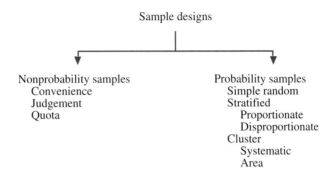

successive decisions they imply. They aim at answering the research question on the basis of accumulated evidence. If the evidence is not conclusive after a small sample is taken, more observations are made; if still inconclusive, still more population elements are designated for inclusion in the sample, and so on. At each stage a decision is made about whether more information should be collected or whether the evidence is now sufficient to permit a conclusion. The sequential sample allows trends in the data to be evaluated as the data are being collected, and this affords an opportunity to reduce costs when additional observations show diminishing usefulness.

Both probability and nonprobability sampling plans can be further divided by type. Nonprobability samples, for instance, can be classified as convenience, judgment, or quota, whereas probability samples can be simple random, stratified, or cluster, and some of these can be further divided. Figure 10.3 shows the types of samples we shall discuss in this chapter. You should be aware that the basic sample types can be combined into more complex sampling plans. If you understand the basic types, though, you should be able to appreciate the more complex designs.

NONPROBABILITY SAMPLES

Nonprobability samples involve personal judgment somewhere in the selection process. Sometimes this judgment is imposed by the researcher, and in other cases the selection of population elements to be included is left to individual field workers. The fact that the elements are not selected probabilistically precludes an assessment of ''sampling error.'' Without some knowledge of the error that can be attributed to sampling procedures, we cannot place bounds on the precision of our estimates.

Convenience Samples

Sometimes, **convenience samples** are called *accidental samples* because those composing the sample enter by ''accident'' — they just happen to be where the information for the study is being collected. Examples of convenience samples abound in our everyday lives. We talk to a few friends, and on the basis of their reactions, we infer the political sentiment of the country; our local radio station asks people to call in and express their reactions to some controversial issue, and the opinions expressed are interpreted as prevailing sentiment; we ask for volunteers in a research study and use those who come forward.

The problem with convenience samples, of course, is that we have no way of knowing if those included are representative of the target population. And while we might be hesitant to infer that the reactions of a few friends indicate prevailing political sentiment, there does seem to be some temptation to conclude that large samples, even though selected conveniently, are representative. The fallacy of this assumption is illustrated by a personal incident.

One of the local television stations in the city where the author resides conducted a daily public opinion poll several years ago on topics of interest to the local community. The polls were labeled the "Pulse of Madison" and were conducted in the following way. During the six o'clock news every evening, the station would ask a question about some controversial issue to which people could reply with a yes or no. Persons in favor would call one number; persons opposed would call another. The number of viewers calling each number was recorded electronically. Percentages of those in favor and opposed would then be reported on the 10:00 p.m. news. With some 500 to 1,000 people calling in their opinions each night, the local TV commentator seemed to interpret these results as reflecting the true state of opinion in the community.

On one 6:00 p.m. broadcast, the following question was posed: "Do you think the drinking age in Madison should be lowered to 18?" The existing legal limit was 21. Would you believe that almost 4,000 people called in that night and that 78 percent were in favor of lowering the age requirement! Clearly, 4,000 responses in a community of 180,000 people "must be representative!" Wrong. As you may have suspected, certain segments of the population were more vitally interested in the issue than others. Thus, it was no surprise, when discussing the issue in class a few weeks later, to find that students took one-half hour phone shifts on an arranged basis. Each person would call the yes number, hang up, call again, hang up, and so on, until it was the next person's turn. Thus neither the size of the sample nor the proportion favoring the age change was surprising. The sample was simply not representative. Further, increasing its size would not make it so.

The representativeness of a sample must be ensured by the sampling procedure. When participation is voluntary or sample elements are selected because they are convenient, the sampling plan provides no assurance that the sample is representative. Empirical evidence, as a matter of fact, is much to the contrary. Rarely do samples selected on a convenience basis, regardless of size, prove to be representative. Research Realities 10.1, for example, depicts what can be wrong with convenience samples, even when they are large. Telephone polls using 800 and 900 numbers represent a particularly common example of large, but unrepresentative samples. What is especially unfortunate is that a great many people believe the results of these polls are accurate.[4]

---

[4]Kathy Gardner Chadwick, "Some Caveats Regarding the Interpretation of Data from 800 Number Callers," *Journal of Services Marketing,* 5 (Summer 1991), pp. 55–61; Jack Honomichl, "It's Time to 86 the 900-Number Poll Plague," *Marketing News,* 25 (September 2, 1991), p. 33.

Research Realities 10.1

The Problem of Representativeness of Convenience Samples

So, what's the best rock radio station in the country?

Don't even try to guess. For the *ninth* consecutive year, Cleveland's WMMS has been voted No. 1 by *Rolling Stone* magazine readers. That's quite a coup, considering that Cleveland is only the country's 11th largest radio market.

What is WMMS's secret? Its with-it disk jockeys? Its mix of hard rock with the top-40 hits? How about its ballot-box stuffing?

The truth is in the stuffing.

Management at WMMS, a Malrite Communications Group station, says that it bought some 800 copies of the magazine that contained the poll and distributed many of them to fans and station employees. "We urge employees to fill them out, but we don't know who they voted for," says station manager Lonnie Gronek. He says the station has done this for many years.

WMMS won this year's contest with 1,000 votes, beating New York's WNEW by 30 votes. About 23,000 votes were cast.

Source: Gregory Stricharchuk, "Repeat After Me: I Like WMMS, I Like WMMS, I Like WMMS," *The Wall Street Journal*, March 2, 1988, p. 25. Reprinted by permission of *The Wall Street Journal*, © Dow Jones & Company, Inc., 1988. All Rights Reserved Worldwide. See also Martha Brannigan, "Pseudo Polls: More Surveys Draw Criticisms for Motives and Methods," *The Wall Street Journal*, January 29, 1987, p. 27; and Jack Honomichl, "It's Time to 86 the 900-Number Poll Plague," *Marketing News*, 25 (September 2, 1991), p. 33, which discuss the use of phone-in polls using AT&T's 900 area code.

Rolling Stone probably wouldn't have uncovered the ploy if the Cleveland *Plain Dealer's* rock editor hadn't gotten a tip. The paper published a station memo to employees asking them to pick up the hundreds of copies at a local store.

"WMMS has always urged its own employees to participate in the balloting — all at the station's expense," WMMS responded in a full-page ad in the Cleveland paper. Besides, it added, "positive recognition of the station translated as a source of pride for Cleveland."

So far WMMS's admission has rocked its hometown more than it has New York. Mark D. Chernoff, WNEW's program director, says he won't insist that his station be declared the winner. "That's up to *Rolling Stone*," he says, quickly adding, "But we'd gladly accept it."

Cleveland broadcasters aren't so kind. John Lanigan, disk jockey at competing station WMJI, suggests that WMMS "should buy a billboard that says: 'We bought more *Rolling Stone* magazines than any other station.' " He also maintains that WMMS's actions "tell kids it's right to lie and cheat to be No. 1."

At *Rolling Stone,* managing editor James Henke says the annual contest hasn't barred stations from voting for themselves. "Obviously they went against the spirit of the contest," he says.

For its part, the magazine is considering stripping WMMS of the once-coveted award. And it has pulled the plug on future radio-popularity votes.

An all too common use of convenience samples in international marketing research is to use foreigners from the countries being studied who are currently residing in the country where the study is being conducted (e.g., Scandinavians currently residing in the United States). Even though such convenience samples can shed some light on certain country conditions, it must be recognized that these individuals typically represent the elite class, often are already "westernized," and may not be in touch with current developments in their own country. Convenience samples are not recommended for descriptive or causal research. They may be used with exploratory designs in which the emphasis is on generating ideas and insights, but even here the judgment sample seems superior.

Judgment Samples

Judgment samples are often called *purposive samples;* the sample elements are hand-picked because it is expected that they can serve the research purpose. Most typically, the sample elements are selected because it is believed that they are representative of the population of interest. One example of a judgment sample is seen every four years at presidential election time, when television viewers are treated to in-depth analyses of the swing communities. These communities are handpicked because they are "representative" in that historically the winner there has been the next president. Thus, by monitoring these pivotal communities, election analysts are able to offer an early prediction of the eventual winner, and even though election analysis and prediction have become much more sophisticated in recent years, the judgment sample of representative communities is still used.

As mentioned, the key feature of judgment sampling is that population elements are purposively selected. This selection may not be made on the basis that they are representative, but rather because they can offer the contributions sought. When the courts rely on expert testimony, they are in a sense using judgment samples, and the same kind of philosophy prevails in creating exploratory designs. When searching for ideas and insights, the researcher is not interested in sampling a cross section of opinion but rather in sampling those who can offer some perspective on the research question.

The **snowball sample** is a judgment sample that is sometimes used to sample special populations.[5] This sample relies on the researcher's ability to locate an initial set of respondents with the desired characteristics. These individuals are then used as informants to identify others with the desired characteristics. Thus, if one were doing a study among the deaf investigating the desirability of various product configurations that would allow deaf people to communicate over telephone lines, one might attempt to initially identify some key people in the deaf community and then ask them for names of other deaf people who might be used in the study. Those initially asked to participate would also be asked for names of others whose cooperation would be solicited.[6] Thus, the sample "snowballs" by getting larger as participants identify still other possible respondents.

---

[5]The technique was originally suggested by Leo A. Goodman, "Snowball Sampling," *Annals of Mathematical Statistics,* 32 (1961), pp. 148–170.

[6]AT&T used such a process for this communications problem, according to Robert Whitelaw, Division Manager for Market Research, in a speech "Research Solutions and New High Technology Service Concepts," which was delivered at the American Marketing Association's 1981 Annual Conference held in San Francisco, California, June 14–17, 1981. When certain very strict procedures are followed when listing members of the rare population, the snowball sample can be treated as a probability sample. For discussion of the requirements, see Martin R. Frankel and Lester R. Frankel, "Some Recent Developments in Sample Survey Design," *Journal of Marketing Research,* 14 (August 1977), pp. 280–293; or Patrick Biernacki and Dan Waldorf, "Snowball Sampling: Problems and Techniques of Chain Referred Sampling," *Sociological Methods and Research,* 10 (November 1981),pp. 141–163. For an example, see George S. Rothbart, Michelle Fine, and Seymour Sudman, "On Finding and Interviewing the Needles in the Haystack: The Use of Multiplicity Sampling," *Public Opinion Quarterly,* 46 (Fall 1982), pp. 408–421. See also Ronald F. Czaja, Deborah H. Trunzo, and Patricia N. Royston, "Response Effects in a Network Survey," *Sociological Methods and Research,* 20 (February, 1992), pp. 340–366.

As long as the researcher is at the early stages of research when ideas or insights are being sought or when the researcher realizes its limitations, the judgment sample can be used productively. It becomes dangerous, though, when it is employed in descriptive or causal studies and its weaknesses are conveniently forgotten. The Consumer Price Index (CPI) provides a classic example of this. As Sudman points out, "the CPI is in only 56 cities and metropolitan areas selected judgmentally and to some extent on the basis of political pressure. In reality, these cities *represent only themselves* although the index is called the *Consumer Price Index for Urban Wage Earners and Clerical Workers,* and most people believe the index reflects prices everywhere in the United States. Within cities, the selection of retail outlets is done judgmentally, so that the *possible size of sample bias is unknown* (emphasis added)."[7]

Quota Samples

A third type of nonprobability sample is the quota sample. **Quota samples** attempt to ensure that the sample is representative by selecting sample elements in such a way that the proportion of the sample elements possessing a certain characteristic is approximately the same as the proportion of the elements with the characteristic in the population. Consider, for example, an attempt to select a representative sample of undergraduate students on a college campus. If the eventual sample of 500 contained no seniors, one would have serious reservations about the representativeness of the sample and the generalizability of the conclusions beyond the immediate sample group. With a quota sample, the researcher could ensure that seniors would be included and in the same proportion as they occur in the entire undergraduate student body.

Suppose that a researcher was interested in sampling the undergraduate student body in such a way that the sample would reflect the composition of the student body by class and sex. Suppose further that there were 10,000 undergraduate students in total and that 3,200 were freshmen, 2,600 sophomores, 2,200 juniors, and 2,000 seniors, and further that 7,000 were males and 3,000 females. In a sample of 1,000, the quota sampling plan would require that 320 sample elements be freshmen, 260 sophomores, 220 juniors, and 200 seniors, and further that 700 of the sample elements be male and 300 be female. The researcher would accomplish this by giving each field worker a quota — thus the name *quota sample* — specifying the types of undergraduates he or she is to contact. Thus, one field worker assigned 20 interviews might be instructed to find and collect data from

- 6 freshmen — 5 male and 1 female
- 6 sophomores — 4 male and 2 female
- 4 juniors — 3 male and 1 female
- 4 seniors — 2 male and 2 female

---

[7]Seymour Sudman, *Applied Sampling* (San Francisco: Academic Press, 1976), p. 10. For discussion of the make-up of the CPI, see John R. Dorfman, "U.S. to Give More Emphasis to Costs of Housing in the Consumer Price Index," *The Wall Street Journal* (February 26, 1987), p. 8; and for discussion of its sample composition, see Richard Valliant, "Variance Estimation for Price Indexes from a Two-Stage Sample with Rotating Panels," *Journal of Business and Economic Statistics,* 9 (October 1991), pp. 409–422.

Note that the specific sample elements to be used would not be specified by the research plan but would be left to the discretion of the individual field worker. The field worker's personal judgment would govern the choice of specific students to be interviewed. The only requirement would be that the interviewer diligently follow the established quota and interview five male freshmen, one female freshman, and so on.

The quota for this field worker accurately reflects the sex composition of the student population, but it does not completely parallel the class composition; 70 percent (14 of 20) of the field worker's interviews are with males but only 30 percent (6 of 20) are with freshmen, whereas freshmen represent 32 percent of the undergraduate student body. It is not necessary or even usual with a quota sample for the quotas per field worker to accurately mirror the distribution of the control characteristics in the population; usually only the total sample has the same proportions as the population.

Note finally that quota samples still rely on personal, subjective judgment rather than objective procedures for the selection of sample elements. Here the personal judgment is that of the field worker rather than the designer of the research, as it might be in the case of a judgment sample. This raises the question of whether quota samples can indeed be considered "representative" even though they accurately reflect the population with respect to the proportion of the sample possessing each control characteristic. Three points need to be made in this regard.

First, the sample could be quite far off with respect to some other important characteristic likely to influence the result. Thus, if the campus study is concerned with racial prejudice existing on campus, it may very well make a difference whether field workers interview students from urban or rural areas. Since a quota for the urban–rural characteristic was not specified, it is unlikely that those participating will accurately reflect this characteristic. The alternative, of course, is to specify quotas for all potentially important characteristics. The problem is that increasing the number of control characteristics makes specifications more complex and makes the location of sample elements more difficult (perhaps even impossible) and certainly more expensive. It is a much more difficult task, assuming that geographic origin and socioeconomic status are important characteristics, for a field worker to locate an upper middle-class male freshman from an urban area than to locate a male freshman.

Second, it is difficult to verify whether a quota sample is indeed representative. Certainly one can check the distribution of characteristics in the sample not used as controls to ascertain whether the distribution parallels that of the population. However, this type of comparison only provides negative evidence. It can indicate that the sample does not reflect the population if the distributions on some characteristics are different. If the sample and population distributions are similar for each of these characteristics, it is still possible for the sample to be vastly different from the population on some characteristic not explicitly compared.

Finally, interviewers left to their own devices are prone to follow certain practices. They tend to interview their friends in excessive proportion. Because their friends are often similar to themselves, this can introduce bias. The empirical evidence from England, for example, indicates that quota samples are biased (1) toward the accessible, (2) against small households, (3) toward households with children, (4) against workers in manufacturing, (5) against extremes of income, (6) against the less educated, and

(7) against low-status individuals.[8] Interviewers who fill their quotas by stopping passers-by are likely to concentrate on areas where there are large numbers of potential respondents, such as business districts, railway and airline terminals, and the entrances to large department stores. This practice tends to overrepresent the particular kinds of people that frequent these areas. When home visits are used, interviewers display a propensity for convenience and appearance, concentrating their interviews at certain times of the day so that working people are underrepresented; avoiding upper stories of buildings without elevator service; and selecting corner buildings and avoiding dilapidated ones.

Depending on the subject of the study, all of these tendencies have the potential for bias. They may or may not in fact actually bias the result, but it is difficult to correct them when analyzing the data. When the sample elements are selected objectively, on the other hand, researchers have certain tools they can rely on to make the question of whether a particular sample is representative less difficult. In these probability samples, one relies on the sampling procedure and not the composition of the specific sample to solve the problem of representation.

ETHICAL DILEMMA 10.1

You are designing an experiment to compare the effectiveness of different types of commercials and need to recruit a large group of subjects of varying ages to watch television for an hour every night for a week. You approach your local church minister and tell her that you will make a donation to the church restoration fund for every member of the congregation who agrees to participate.

- When might incentives be coercive?
- Is it ethical to coerce people to participate in research?
- Will the quality of the data suffer from the coercive recruitment of participants?

PROBABILITY SAMPLES

One can calculate the likelihood that any given population element will be included in a probability sample because the final sample elements are selected objectively by a specific process and not according to the whims of the researcher or field worker. The objective selection of elements, in turn, allows the objective assessment of the reliability of the sample results, something not possible with nonprobability samples regardless of the careful judgment exercised in selecting individuals.

This is not to say that probability samples will always be more representative than nonprobability samples. Far from it. A nonprobability sample may indeed be more representative. What probability samples allow, though, is an assessment of the amount of

---

[8]Catherine Marsh and Elinor Scarbrough, ''Testing Nine Hypotheses About Quota Sampling,'' *Journal of the Market Research Society,* 32 (October 1990), pp. 485–506.

TABLE 10.1   **Hypothetical Population**

Element	Income (Dollars)	Education (Years)	Newspaper Subscription
1 A	5,600	8	X
2 B	6,000	9	Y
3 C	6,400	11	X
4 D	6,800	11	Y
5 E	7,200	11	X
6 F	7,600	12	Y
7 G	8,000	12	X
8 H	8,400	12	Y
9 I	8,800	12	X
10 J	9,200	12	Y
11 K	9,600	13	X
12 L	10,000	13	Y
13 M	10,400	14	X
14 N	10,800	14	Y
15 O	11,200	15	X
16 P	11,600	16	Y
17 Q	12,000	16	X
18 R	12,400	17	Y
19 S	12,800	18	X
20 T	13,200	18	Y

"sampling error" likely to occur because a sample rather than a census was employed when gathering the data. Nonprobability samples allow the investigator no objective method for evaluating the adequacy of the sample.

Simple Random Sampling

By far the probability samples best known to beginning researchers are **simple random samples,** because they are used to frame the concepts and arguments in beginning statistics courses. Simple random samples are distinguished by the fact that each population element has not only a known but an equal chance of being selected and, further, that every combination of *n* population elements is a sample possibility and is just as likely to occur as any other combination of *n* units.

Parent Population   In discussing the various probability sampling plans and the objective assessment of sampling error that they allow, it will prove useful to explore the notion of sampling distribution in some detail.[9] Consider the hypothetical population of 20 individuals shown in Table 10.1. This population can be described by certain param-

---

[9] The notion of a sampling distribution is treated in detail in most introductory statistics texts. The reader who understands the notion of sampling distribution should consider these next few pages an elementary review that will return dividends when discussing the more complex sample designs.

eters. A **parameter** is simply a characteristic or measure of a parent or target population; it is a fixed quantity that distinguishes one population from another. We can calculate a number of parameters to describe this hypothetical population. We could calculate the average income, the dispersion in educational levels, the proportion of the population subscribing to each newspaper, and so on. Note that these quantities are fixed in value. Given a census of this population, we can readily calculate them. Rather than relying on a census, we usually select a sample and use the values calculated from the sample observations to estimate the required population values.

Suppose that our task was one of estimating the average income in this population from a sample of two elements selected randomly. Let μ denote the mean population income and σ^2 the variance of incomes. Both μ and σ are population parameters, one measuring central tendency and the other spread; that is, μ and σ^2 are defined as

$$\mu = \frac{\sum_{i=1}^{N} X_i}{N} = \frac{5,600 + 6,000 + \ldots + 13,200}{20} = 9,400, \text{ and}$$

$$\sigma^2 = \frac{\sum_{i=1}^{N} (X_i - \mu)^2}{N}$$

$$= \frac{(5,600 - 9,400)^2 + (6,000 - 9,400)^2 + \ldots + (13,200 - 9,400)^2}{20}$$

$$= 5,320,000,$$

where X_i is the value of the ith observation and N is the number of population elements. Thus, to compute the population mean, we divide the sum of all the values by the number of values making up the sum. To compute the population variance, we calculate the deviation of each value from the mean, square these deviations, sum them, and divide by the number of values making up the sum.

Derived Population   It seems logical that our estimates of these population parameters would rest on similar calculations. A **statistic** is a characteristic or measure of a sample. We typically use the similarly calculated statistic to estimate the parameter, but we need to recognize that the value of the statistic depends on the particular sample selected from the parent population under the specified sampling plan. Different samples yield different statistics and different estimates.

Consider the **derived population** of *all* possible distinguishable samples that can be drawn from this parent population under a given sampling plan, which specifies that a sample of Size $n = 2$ is to be drawn by simple random sampling without replacement.[10] Assume, for example, that the information for each element, including its identity, is to

---

[10]The term "sample space" is also used for the notion of derived population. See Martin Frankel, "Sampling Theory," in Peter H. Rossi, James D. Wright, and Andy B. Anderson, eds., *Handbook of Survey Research* (Orlando: Academic Press, 1983), pp. 21–67.

TABLE 10.2   **Derived Population of All Possible Samples of Size $n = 2$ with Simple Random Selection**

k	Sample Identity	Mean	k	Sample Identity	Mean	k	Sample Identity	Mean	k	Sample Identity	Mean
1	AB	5,800	26	BI	7,400	51	CQ	9,200	76	EK	8,400
2	AC	6,000	27	BJ	7,600	52	CR	9,400	77	EL	8,600
3	AD	6,200	28	BK	7,800	53	CS	9,600	78	EM	8,800
4	AE	6,400	29	BL	8,000	54	CT	9,800	79	EN	9,000
5	AF	6,600	30	BM	8,200	55	DE	7,000	80	EO	9,200
6	AG	6,800	31	BN	8,400	56	DF	7,200	81	EP	9,400
7	AH	7,000	32	BO	8,600	57	DG	7,400	82	EQ	9,600
8	AI	7,200	33	BP	8,800	58	DH	7,600	83	ER	9,800
9	AJ	7,400	34	BQ	9,000	59	DI	7,800	84	ES	10,000
10	AK	7,600	35	BR	9,200	60	DJ	8,000	85	ET	10,200
11	AL	7,800	36	BS	9,400	61	DK	8,200	86	FG	7,800
12	AM	8,000	37	BT	9,600	62	DL	8,400	87	FH	8,000
13	AN	8,200	38	CD	6,600	63	DM	8,600	88	FI	8,200
14	AO	8,400	39	CE	6,800	64	DN	8,800	89	FJ	8,400
15	AP	8,600	40	CF	7,000	65	DO	9,000	90	FK	8,600
16	AQ	8,800	41	CG	7,200	66	DP	9,200	91	FL	8,800
17	AR	9,000	42	CH	7,400	67	DQ	9,400	92	FM	9,000
18	AS	9,200	43	CI	7,600	68	DR	9,600	93	FN	9,200
19	AT	9,400	44	CJ	7,800	69	DS	9,800	94	FO	9,400
20	BC	6,200	45	CK	8,000	70	DT	10,000	95	FP	9,600
21	BD	6,400	46	CL	8,200	71	EF	7,400	96	FQ	9,800
22	BE	6,600	47	CM	8,400	72	EG	7,600	97	FR	10,000
23	BF	6,800	48	CN	8,600	73	EH	7,800	98	FS	10,200
24	BG	7,000	49	CO	8,800	74	EI	8,000	99	FT	10,400
25	BH	7,200	50	CP	9,000	75	EJ	8,200	100	GH	8,200

be placed on a disk and that these elements are to be placed in an urn and mixed thoroughly. The investigator will reach in the urn, pull out one disk, record the identity and the income of the person and then, without replacing the first disk, will draw a second disk from the urn and record the identity and income. Table 10.2 displays the derived population of all possible samples from following this procedure. There are 190 combinations of the 20 disks possible. For each combination, one can calculate the sample mean income. Thus, for the sample AB, the sample mean income $\bar{x}_1 =$ ($\$5,600 + \$6,000$)/2 $= \$5,800$, and, in general,

$$\bar{x}_k = \sum_{i=1}^{n} \frac{X_i}{n},$$

where k refers to the sample number, $\bar{x}$ to the sample average, and n to the sample size. Figure 10.4 displays the estimates of population mean income and the amount of error in each estimate when samples $k = 25, 62, 108, 147,$ and 189 are drawn.

TABLE **10.2** *Continued*

k	Sample Identity	Mean	k	Sample Identity	Mean	k	Sample Identity	Mean	k	Sample Identity	Mean
101	GI	8,400	126	IK	9,200	151	KQ	10,800	176	OP	11,400
102	GJ	8,600	127	IL	9,400	152	KR	11,000	177	OQ	11,600
103	GK	8,800	128	IM	9,600	153	KS	11,200	178	OR	11,800
104	GL	9,000	129	IN	9,800	154	KT	11,400	179	OS	12,000
105	GM	9,200	130	IO	10,000	155	LM	10,200	180	OT	12,200
106	GN	9,400	131	IP	10,200	156	LN	10,400	181	PQ	11,800
107	GO	9,600	132	IQ	10,400	157	LO	10,600	182	PR	12,000
108	GP	9,800	133	IR	10,600	158	LP	10,800	183	PS	12,200
109	GQ	10,000	134	IS	10,800	159	LQ	11,000	184	PT	12,400
110	GR	10,200	135	IT	11,000	160	LR	11,200	185	QR	12,200
111	GS	10,400	136	JK	9,400	161	LS	11,400	186	QS	12,400
112	GT	10,600	137	JL	9,600	162	LT	11,600	187	QT	12,600
113	HI	8,600	138	JM	9,800	163	MN	10,600	188	RS	12,600
114	HJ	8,800	139	JN	10,000	164	MO	10,800	189	RT	12,800
115	HK	9,000	140	JO	10,200	165	MP	11,000	190	ST	13,000
116	HL	9,200	141	JP	10,400	166	MQ	11,200			
117	HM	9,400	142	JQ	10,600	167	MR	11,400			
118	HN	9,600	143	JR	10,800	168	MS	11,600			
119	HO	9,800	144	JS	11,000	169	MT	11,800			
120	HP	10,000	145	JT	11,200	170	NO	11,000			
121	HQ	10,200	146	KL	9,800	171	NP	11,200			
122	HR	10,400	147	KM	10,000	172	NQ	11,400			
123	HS	10,600	148	KN	10,200	173	NR	11,600			
124	HT	10,800	149	KO	10,400	174	NS	11,800			
125	IJ	9,000	150	KP	10,600	175	NT	12,000			

Before discussing the relationship between the sample mean income (a statistic) and population mean income (the parameter to be estimated), a few words are in order about the notion of derived population. First, note that in practice, we do not actually generate the derived population. This would be extremely wasteful of time and data. Rather, all that the practitioner will do is to generate one sample of the needed size. But the researcher will make use of the *concept* "derived population" and the associated notion of sampling distribution in making inferences. We shall see how in just a moment. Second, note that the derived population is defined as the population of all possible distinguishable samples that can be drawn under a *given sampling plan*. Change any part of the sampling plan and the derived population will also change. Thus, when selecting disks, if the researcher is to replace the first disk drawn, the derived population will include the sample possibilities AA, BB, and so on. With samples of Size 3 instead of 2, drawn without replacement, ABC is a sample possibility, and there are a number of additional possibilities as well — 1,140 versus

FIGURE 10.4   **Several Possible Samples and Their Respective Errors When Estimating the Population Mean**

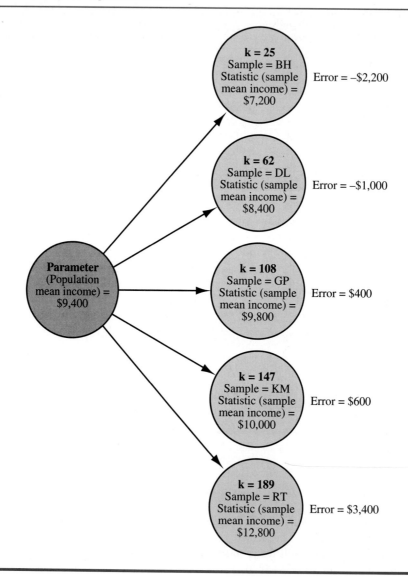

the 190 with samples of Size 2. Change the method of selecting elements by using something other than simple random sampling and the derived population will also change. Finally, note that picking a sample of a given size from a parent population is equivalent to picking a single element (one of the 190 disks) out of the derived population. This fact is basic in making statistical inferences.

Sample Mean versus Population Mean Now consider the relationship between the sample means and the population mean. We wish to make three points. First, suppose that we add up all the sample means in Table 10.2 and divide by the number of samples — in other words, average the averages. By sheer doing, this yields

$$\frac{5,800 + 6,000 \ . \ . \ . \ + 13,000}{190} = 9,400,$$

which is the mean of the population. This is what is meant by an unbiased statistic. A statistic is **unbiased** when its average value equals the population parameter it is supposed to estimate. Note that the fact it is unbiased says nothing about any particular value of the statistic. Even though unbiased, a particular estimate may be very far from the true population value — as for example, if either sample AB or sample ST were selected. In some cases, the true population value may even be *impossible* to achieve with any possible sample even though the statistic is unbiased; this is not true in the example, though, since a number of sample possibilities (for example, AT) yield a sample mean that equals the population average.

Second, consider the spread of these sample estimates and particularly the relationship between this spread of estimates and the dispersion of incomes in the population. We saw previously that the population variance $\sigma^2 = 5,320,000$. We can calculate the *variance of mean incomes* similarly — that is, by taking the deviation of each mean around its overall mean, squaring and summing these deviations, and then dividing by the number of cases.

$$\frac{(5,800 - 9,400)^2 + (6,000 - 9,400)^2 + \ . \ . \ . \ + (13,000 - 9,400)^2}{190} = 2,520,000.$$

Now note the relationship between σ^2 (the variance or spread of the variable in the original population) and the spread of the estimates in the derived population (call it $\sigma_{\bar{x}}^2$ to denote the variance of means). Instead of direct calculations using the 190 sample estimates, $\sigma_{\bar{x}}^2$ could have also been calculated by the following expression:

$$\sigma_{\bar{x}}^2 = \frac{\sigma^2}{n} \frac{N-n}{N-1} = \frac{5,320,000}{2} \frac{20-2}{20-1} = 2,520,000.$$

This result is not unique but is true in general, although the expression relating the two variances is typically modified slightly when the sample size is only a small proportion of the population.[11]

Third, consider the distribution of the estimates in contrast to the distribution of the variable in the parent population. Figure 10.5 indicates that the parent population distri-

---

[11]The expression $(N - n)/(N - 1)$ is known as the finite population correction factor. Whenever the sample size is less than 10 percent of the population size, the finite population correction factor is ignored, since $(N - n)/(N - 1)$ is very close to 1 and the more complex form $\sigma_{\bar{x}}^2 = (\sigma^2/n)(N - n)/(N - 1)$ reduces to $\sigma_{\bar{x}}^2 = \sigma^2/n$.

FIGURE 10.5   **Distribution of Variable in Parent Population and Distribution of Estimates in Derived Population**

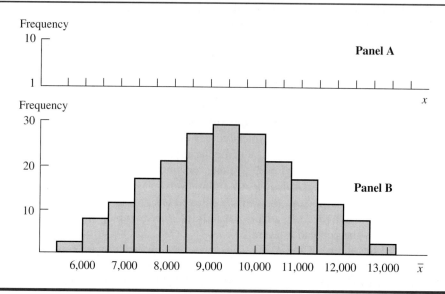

bution depicted by Panel A is spiked (each of the 20 values occurs once) and is symmetrical about the population mean value of 9,400. The distribution of estimates displayed in Panel B was constructed by placing each of the estimates in categories according to size and then counting the number contained in each category (Table 10.3). Panel B is the traditional histogram discussed in beginning statistics courses and represents the

TABLE 10.3   **Classification of Estimates by Size**

Sample Mean	Number of Samples
$6,000 or less	2
$6,100 to 6,600	7
$6,700 to 7,200	11
$7,300 to 7,800	16
$7,900 to 8,400	20
$8,500 to 9,000	25
$9,100 to 9,600	28
$9,700 to 10,200	25
$10,300 to 10,800	20
$10,900 to 11,400	16
$11,500 to 12,000	11
$12,100 to 12,600	7
$12,700 or more	2

sampling distribution of the statistic. Note this: The notion of **sampling distribution** is the single most important notion in statistics; it is the cornerstone of statistical inference procedures. If one knows the sampling distribution for the statistic in question, one is in a position to make an inference about the corresponding population parameter. If, on the other hand, one knows only that a particular sample estimate will vary with repeated sampling and has no information about *how* it will vary, then it will be impossible to devise a measure of the sampling error associated with that estimate. Because the sampling distribution of an estimate describes how that estimate will vary with repeated sampling, it provides a basis for determining the reliability of the sample estimate. This is why probability sampling plans are so important to statistical inference. With known probabilities of inclusion of any population element in the sample, statisticians are able to derive the sampling distribution of various statistics. Researchers then rely on these distributions — whether they are for a sample mean, sample proportion, sample variance, or some other statistic — in making their inferences from single samples to population values. Note that the distribution of sample means is mound shaped and symmetrical about the population mean with samples of size 2.

Recapitulating, we have shown that

1. the mean of all possible sample means is equal to the population mean;
2. the variance of sample means is related to the population variance by the expression

$$\sigma_{\bar{x}}^2 = \frac{\sigma^2}{n} \frac{N - n}{N - 1};$$

3. the distribution of sample means is mound shaped, whereas the population distribution is spiked.

This first result is true in general for simple random sampling. The mean of the sample means is equal to the population mean if sampling is with or without replacement of the elements and sampling is from a finite or infinite parent population. The second result is true only when sampling is from a finite population without replacement. If sampling from an infinite population or when sampling from a finite population with replacement, the simpler expression $\sigma_{\bar{x}}^2 = \sigma^2/n$ holds.

The simpler expression derives from the fact that when the size of the sample is small in *comparison* to the size of the population, the term on the far right in the exact equation for the variance of sample means is approximately equal to one and can be ignored. For many, if not most, problems in marketing, the simpler expression $\sigma_{\bar{x}}^2 = \sigma^2/n$ is used to relate the variance of sample means to the variance of the variable.

Central-Limit Theorem   The third result of a mound-shaped distribution of estimates provides preliminary evidence of the operation of the Central-Limit Theorem. The **Central-Limit Theorem** holds that if simple random samples of Size n are drawn from a parent population with mean μ and variance σ^2, then when n is large, the sample mean $\bar{x}$ will be approximately normally distributed with the mean equal to μ and variance equal to σ^2/n. The approximation will become more and more accurate as n becomes larger. Note the impact of this. It means that *regardless* of the shape of the parent population, the distribution of sample means *will be normal* if the sample is large enough. How large is large enough? If the distribution of the variable in the parent population is normal, the means of samples of Size $n = 1$ will be normally distributed. If the distribution of the variable is symmetrical but not normal, samples of very small size will produce a distribution in which the means are normally distributed. If the distribution of the variable is highly skewed in the parent population, samples of a larger size will be needed. The fact remains, however, that the distribution of the statistic, sample mean, can be assumed to be normal if only we work with a sample of sufficient size. We do not need to rely on the assumption that the variable is normally distributed in the parent population to make inferences using the normal curve. Rather, we rely on the Central-Limit Theorem and adjust the sample size according to the population distribution so that the normal curve can be assumed to hold. Fortunately, the normal distribution of the statistic occurs with samples of relatively small size, as Figure 10.6 indicates.

Confidence Interval Estimates   How does all of the preceding information help us in making inferences about the parent population mean? After all, in practice we do not draw all possible samples of a given size but only one, and we use the results obtained in it to infer something about the target group. It all ties together in the following way.

It is known that with any normal distribution, a specific percentage of all observations is within a certain number of standard deviations of the mean, for example, 95 percent of the values are within ± 1.96 standard deviations of the mean. The distribution of sample means is normal if the Central-Limit Theorem holds and thus is no exception. Now, the mean of this sampling distribution is the population mean μ, and its standard deviation is given by the standard error of the mean $\sigma_{\bar{x}} = \sigma/\sqrt{n}$. Therefore, it is true that:

- 68.26 percent of the sample means will be within $\pm 1 \, \sigma_{\bar{x}}$ of the population mean,
- 95.45 percent of the sample means will be within $\pm 2 \, \sigma_{\bar{x}}$ of the population mean, and
- 99.73 percent of the sample means will be within $\pm 3\sigma_{\bar{x}}$ of the population mean,

and, in general, that $\mu \pm z\sigma_{\bar{x}}$ will contain some certain proportion of all sample means, depending on the selected value of z. This expression can be rewritten as an inequality relation:

$$\mu - z\sigma_{\bar{x}} \leq \bar{x} \leq \mu + z\sigma_{\bar{x}}, \qquad (10.1)$$

which is held to be true a certain percentage of the time and which implies that the sample mean will be in the interval formed by adding and subtracting a certain number of standard deviations to the mean value of the distribution. This inequality can be transferred to the equivalent inequality,

$$\bar{x} - z\sigma_{\bar{x}} \leq \mu \leq \bar{x} + z\sigma_{\bar{x}}, \qquad (10.2)$$

and if Equation 10.1 was true, say, 95 percent of the time ($z = 1.96$), Equation 10.2 is also true 95 percent of the time. *When we make an inference on the basis of a single sample mean, we make use of Equation 10.2.*

FIGURE 10.6 **Distribution of Sample Means for Samples of Various Sizes and Different Population Distributions**

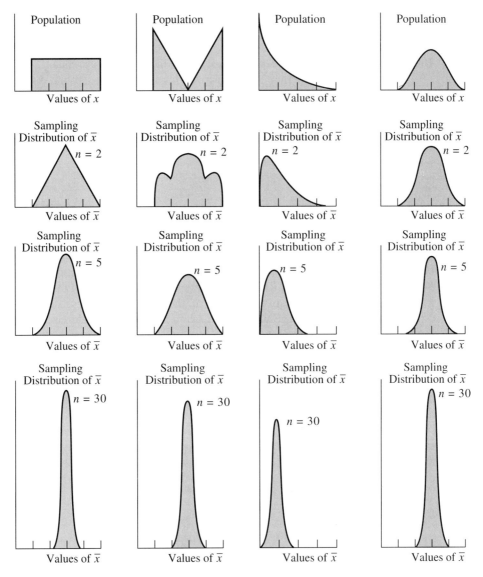

Source: Ernest Kurnow, Gerald J. Glasser, and Frederick R. Ottman, *Statistics for Business Decisions* (Homewood, Ill.: Richard D. Irwin, Inc., 1959), pp. 182–183. Copyright 1959, reprinted with permission.

It is important to note that Equation 10.2 says *nothing about the interval constructed from a particular sample as including the population mean.* Rather, the interval addresses the *sampling procedure.* The interval around a single sample mean may or may not contain the true population mean. Our confidence in our inference rests on the property that 95 percent of all the intervals we could construct under that sampling plan would contain the true value. We trust or hope that our sample is one of those 95 out of 100 that does (when we are 95 percent confident) include the true value.[12]

To illustrate this important point, suppose for the moment that the distribution of sample means of Size $n = 2$ for our hypothetical example was normal. Suppose further that by chance the sampling process yielded sample AB, in which the mean income was 5,800. The 95 percent confidence interval ($z = 1.96$) using Equation 10.2 would then be ($\sigma_{\bar{x}} = \sqrt{\sigma_{\bar{x}}^2} = \sqrt{2,520,000} = 1,587$):

$$5,800 - 1.96(1,587) \leq \mu \leq 5,800 + 1.96(1,587) = 2,689 \leq \mu \leq 8,911.$$

The confidence interval would not include the true (in this case, known) population value, and an inferential error would have been made. The example illustrates that after the sample has been drawn, it is a matter of fact whether or not the particular interval estimate covers the universe mean. Table 10.4 illustrates the outcome pictorially for the first 10 out of the possible 190 samples that could be drawn under the specified sampling plan. Note that only 7 of the 10 intervals contain the true population mean. Confidence in the estimate arises because of the *procedure,* therefore, and not because of a particular estimate. The procedure suggests that with, say, a 95 percent confidence interval, if 100 samples were to be drawn and the sample mean and the confidence interval computed for each, 95 of the constructed intervals would include the true population value. The accuracy of a specific sample is evaluated only by reference to the procedure by which the sample was obtained. A sampling plan that is representative does not guarantee that a particular sample is representative. Statistical inference procedures rest on the representativeness of the sampling plan, and this is why probability samples are so critical to those procedures. Probability samples allow an estimate of the **precision** of the results in terms of how closely the estimates will tend to cluster around the true value. The greater the standard error of the statistic, the more variable the estimates and the less precise the procedure.

---

[12]The argument expressed here on the interpretation of a confidence interval is the traditional or classical statistics argument, which holds that the parameter being estimated is fixed in value. Thus, it is meaningless to interpret the statement probabilistically, because a given interval will or will not contain the population parameter. Bayesian analysts adopt a different perspective, however. Bayesians hold that it is legitimate to assign personal probabilities to the states of nature, values of the unknown parameter in this case. One can then combine these judgments with sample information to produce posterior probabilities regarding the value of the unknown parameter. The confidence interval formed for a population mean is the same under the two approaches if one adopts the Bayesian assumption that the initial probabilities for each of the possible values of the unknown parameter are equal. The difference in perspectives, though, allows Bayesian analysts to interpret the resulting interval as a probability statement; that is, there is a 95 percent probability that the interval $\bar{x} \pm z\sigma_{\bar{x}}$ contains the true population mean. This interpretation tends to be much more satisfying to decision makers. For a discussion of the difference in the two perspectives, see Frankel, "Sampling Theory."

TABLE 10.4   **Confidence Intervals for First Ten Samples Assuming the Distribution of Sample Means Was Normal**

Sample Number	Sample Identity	Mean	Confidence Interval Lower Limit	Confidence Interval Upper Limit	Pictorial True $\mu = 9,400$
1	AB	5,800	2,689	8,911	
2	AC	6,000	2,889	9,111	
3	AD	6,200	3,089	9,311	
4	AE	6,400	3,289	9,511	
5	AF	6,600	3,489	9,711	
6	AG	6,800	3,689	9,911	
7	AH	7,000	3,889	10,111	
8	AI	7,200	4,089	10,311	
9	AJ	7,400	4,289	10,511	
10	AK	7,600	4,489	10,711	

If it disturbs you that the confidence level applies to the procedure and not to a particular sample result, you can take refuge in the fact that you can control the level of confidence with which the population value is estimated. Thus, if you do not wish to take the risk that you might have 1 of the 5 sample intervals in 100 that does not contain the population value, you might employ a 99 percent confidence interval, in which the risk is that only 1 in 100 sample intervals will not contain the population mean. Further, if you are willing to increase the size of the sample, you can increase your confidence and at the same time maintain the precision with which the population value is estimated. This will be explored more fully in the next chapter.

Population Variance Unknown   There is one other perhaps disturbing ingredient in our procedure. The confidence interval estimate made use of three values: $\bar{x}$, z, and $\sigma_{\bar{x}}$. Now $\bar{x}$ is computed from the selected sample, and z is specified to produce the desired level of confidence. But what about $\sigma_{\bar{x}}$? It is equal to $\sigma_{\bar{x}} = \sigma/\sqrt{n}$, and thus to calculate it, we need to know the standard deviation of the variable in the population. What do we do if σ is unknown? There is no problem for two reasons. First, variation typically changes much more slowly than level for most variables of interest in marketing. Thus, if the study is a repeat, we can use the previously discovered value for σ. Second, once the sample is selected and the information gathered, we can calculate the sample variance to estimate the population variance. The unbiased sample variance $\hat{s}^2$ is calculated as

$$\hat{s}^2 = \frac{\sum\limits_{i=1}^{n} (X_i - \bar{x})^2}{n - 1},$$

where $\bar{x}$ is the sample mean and n the sample size.[13] To compute the sample variance, then, we first calculate the sample mean. We then calculate the differences between each of our sample values and the sample mean, square them, sum them, and divide the sum by one less than the number of sample observations. The sample variance not only provides an estimate of the population variance, but it can also be used to secure an estimate of the standard error of the mean. When the population variance, σ^2, is known, the standard error of the mean, $\sigma_{\bar{x}}$, is also known because $\sigma_{\bar{x}} = \sigma/\sqrt{n}$. When the population variance is unknown, the standard error of the mean can only be estimated. The estimate is given by $s_{\bar{x}}$, which equals $\hat{s}/\sqrt{n}$. The estimate calculation parallels that for the true value, with the sample standard deviation substituted for the population standard deviation. Thus if we draw sample AB, with mean of 5,800,

$$\hat{s}^2 = \frac{(5,600 - 5,800)^2 + (6,000 - 5,800)^2}{1} = 80,000,$$

thus $\hat{s} = 283$ and $s_{\bar{x}} = \hat{s}/\sqrt{n} = 283/\sqrt{2} = 200$ and the 95 percent confidence interval is now

$$5,800 - 1.96(200) \leq \mu \leq 5,800 + 1.96(200) = 5,408 \leq \mu \leq 6,192,$$

which is somewhat smaller than before.[14]

Drawing the Simple Random Sample   Although it was useful for illustrating the concepts ''derived population'' and ''sampling distribution,'' the selection of sample elements from an urn containing all the population elements is not particularly recommended because of its great potential for bias. It is unlikely that the disks would be exactly uniform in size or feel, and slight differences here could affect the likelihood that any single element would be drawn. The national draft during the Vietnam war using a lottery serves as an example. Draft priorities were determined by drawing disks with birth dates stamped on them from a large container in full view of a TV audience. Unfortunately, the dates of the year had initially been poured into the bowl systematically, January first and December last. Although the bowl was then stirred vigorously,

---

[13]Division by n, the sample size, is more intuitive because it produces the normal conception of average, which here is the average of the deviations squared. However, the sample variance, when defined as

$$\hat{s}^2 = \frac{\sum_{i=1}^{n} (X_i - \bar{x})^2}{n},$$

produces a biased estimate of the population variance. Thus it is customary to use either the unbiased definition of the sample variance or to generate an estimate of σ^2, denoted by $\hat{\sigma}^2$, by the formula $\hat{\sigma}^2 [n/(n - 1)]s^2$.

[14]The t distribution would strictly be used when σ was unknown. We shall say more about this in Chapter 15.

December dates tended to be chosen first and January dates last. The procedure was later revised to produce a more random selection process.

The preferred way of drawing a simple random sample is through the use of a table of random numbers. Using a random number table involves the following sequence of steps. First, the elements of parent population would be numbered serially from 1 to N; for the hypothetical population, the element A would be numbered as 1, B as 2, and so on. Next, the numbers in the table would be treated to have the same number of digits as N. With $N = 20$, two-digit numbers would be used; if N was between 100 and 999, three-digit numbers would be required, and so on. Third, a starting point would be determined randomly. We might simply open the table to some arbitrary place and point to a position on the page with our eyes closed. Since the numbers in a random number table are in fact random (that is, without order), it makes little difference where we begin.[15] Finally, we would proceed in some arbitrary direction (for example, up, down, or across) and would select those elements for the sample for which there is a match of serial number and random number.

To illustrate, consider the partial list of random numbers contained in Table 10.5. Since $N = 20$, we need work with only two digits, and therefore we can use the entries in Table 10.5 as is, instead of having to combine columns to produce numbers covering the range of serial numbers. Suppose that we had previously decided to read down and that our arbitrary start indicated the eleventh row, the fourth column, and specifically the number 77. This number is too high and would be discarded. The next two numbers would also be discarded, but the fourth entry 02 would be used, because 2 corresponds to one of the serial numbers in the list, Element B. The next five numbers would also be passed over as too large, but the number 05 would designate the inclusion of Element E. Elements B and E would thus represent the sample of two from whom we would seek information on income.

An alternative strategy would be to use a computer program to generate the random numbers. Although there is some recent evidence that suggests the numbers generated by computer programs are not as random as is commonly believed, their accuracy is sufficient for most applied marketing research studies, although perhaps not for complex mathematical model building. See Research Realities 10.2.

You should note that a simple random sample requires a serial numbered list of population elements. This means that the identity of each member of the population must be known. For some populations this is no problem—for example, if the study is to be conducted among *Fortune* magazine's list of the 500 largest corporations in the United States. The list is readily available, and a simple random sample of these firms could be selected easily. For many other populations of interest, the list of universe elements is much harder to come by (for example, all families living in a particular city), and applied researchers often resort to other sampling schemes.

---

[15]There are two major errors to avoid when using random number tables: (1) starting at a given place because one knows the distribution of numbers at that place; and (2) discarding a sample because it does not "look right" in some sense and continuing to use random numbers until a "likely looking" sample is selected. Sudman, "Applied Sampling," p. 165.

T<small>ABLE</small> **10.5   Abridged List of Random Numbers**

10 09 73 25 33	76 52 01 35 86	34 67 35 48 76	80 95 90 91 17	39 29 27 49 45
37 54 20 48 05	64 89 47 42 96	24 80 52 40 37	20 63 61 04 02	00 82 29 16 65
08 42 26 89 53	19 64 50 93 03	23 20 90 25 60	15 95 33 47 64	35 08 03 36 06
99 01 90 25 29	09 37 67 07 15	38 31 13 11 65	88 67 67 43 97	04 43 62 76 59
12 80 79 99 70	80 15 73 61 47	64 03 23 66 53	98 95 11 68 77	12 17 17 68 33
66 06 57 47 17	34 07 27 68 50	36 69 73 61 70	65 81 33 98 85	11 19 92 91 70
31 06 01 08 05	45 57 18 24 06	35 30 34 26 14	86 79 90 74 39	23 40 30 97 32
85 26 97 76 02	02 05 16 56 92	68 66 57 48 18	73 05 38 52 47	18 62 38 85 79
63 57 33 21 35	05 32 54 70 48	90 55 35 75 48	28 46 82 87 09	83 49 12 56 24
73 79 64 57 53	03 52 96 47 78	35 80 83 42 82	60 93 52 03 44	35 27 38 84 35
98 52 01 77 67	14 90 56 86 07	22 10 94 05 58	60 97 09 34 33	50 50 07 39 98
11 80 50 54 31	39 80 82 77 32	50 72 56 82 48	29 40 52 42 01	52 77 56 78 51
83 45 29 96 34	06 28 89 80 83	13 74 67 00 78	18 47 54 06 10	68 71 17 78 17
88 68 54 02 00	86 50 75 84 01	36 76 66 79 51	90 36 47 64 93	29 60 91 10 62
99 59 46 73 48	87 51 76 49 69	91 82 60 89 28	93 78 56 13 68	23 47 83 41 13
65 48 11 76 74	17 46 85 90 50	58 04 77 69 74	73 03 95 71 86	40 21 81 65 44
80 12 43 56 35	17 72 70 80 15	45 31 82 23 74	21 11 57 82 53	14 38 55 37 63
74 35 09 98 17	77 40 27 72 14	43 23 60 02 10	45 52 16 42 37	96 28 60 26 55
69 91 62 68 03	66 25 22 91 48	36 93 68 72 03	76 62 11 39 90	94 40 05 64 18
09 89 32 05 05	14 22 56 85 14	46 42 75 67 88	96 29 77 88 22	54 38 21 45 98
91 49 91 45 23	68 47 92 76 86	46 16 28 35 54	94 75 08 99 23	37 08 92 00 48
80 33 69 45 98	26 94 03 68 58	70 29 73 41 35	53 14 03 33 40	42 05 08 23 41
44 10 48 19 49	85 15 74 79 54	32 97 92 65 75	57 60 04 08 81	22 22 20 64 13
12 55 07 37 42	11 10 00 20 40	12 86 07 46 97	96 64 48 94 39	28 70 72 58 15
63 60 64 93 29	16 50 53 44 84	40 21 95 25 63	43 65 17 70 82	07 20 73 17 90
61 19 69 04 46	26 45 74 77 74	51 92 43 37 29	65 39 45 95 93	42 58 26 05 27
15 47 44 52 66	95 27 07 99 53	59 36 78 38 48	82 39 61 01 18	33 21 15 94 66
94 55 72 85 72	67 89 75 43 87	54 62 24 44 31	91 19 04 25 92	92 92 74 59 73
42 48 11 62 13	97 34 40 81 21	16 86 84 87 67	03 07 11 20 59	25 70 14 66 70
23 52 37 83 17	73 20 88 98 37	68 93 59 14 16	26 25 22 96 63	05 52 28 25 62
04 49 35 24 94	75 24 63 38 24	45 86 25 10 25	61 96 27 93 35	65 33 71 24 72
00 54 99 76 54	64 05 18 81 59	96 11 96 38 96	54 69 28 23 91	23 28 72 95 29
35 96 31 53 07	26 89 80 93 54	33 35 13 54 62	77 97 45 00 24	90 10 33 93 33
59 80 80 83 91	45 42 72 68 42	83 60 94 97 00	13 02 12 48 92	78 56 52 01 06
46 06 88 52 36	01 39 09 22 86	77 28 14 40 77	93 91 08 36 47	70 61 74 29 41
32 17 90 05 97	87 37 92 52 41	05 56 70 70 07	86 74 31 71 57	85 39 41 18 38
69 43 26 14 06	20 11 74 52 04	15 95 66 00 00	18 74 39 24 23	97 11 89 63 38
19 56 54 14 30	01 75 87 53 79	40 41 92 15 85	66 67 43 68 06	84 96 28 52 07
45 15 51 49 38	19 47 60 72 46	43 66 79 45 43	59 04 79 00 33	20 82 66 95 41
94 86 43 19 94	36 16 81 08 51	34 88 88 15 51	01 54 03 54 56	05 01 45 11 76
98 08 62 48 26	45 24 02 84 04	44 99 90 88 96	39 09 47 34 07	35 44 13 18 80
33 18 51 62 32	41 94 15 09 49	89 43 54 85 81	88 69 54 19 94	37 54 87 30 43
80 95 10 04 06	96 38 27 07 74	20 15 12 33 87	25 01 62 52 98	94 62 46 11 71

TABLE **10.5** *Continued*

79 75 24 91 40	71 96 12 82 96	69 86 10 25 91	74 85 22 05 39	00 38 75 95 79
18 63 33 25 37	98 14 50 65 71	31 01 02 46 74	05 45 56 14 27	77 93 89 19 36
74 02 94 39 02	77 55 73 22 70	97 79 01 71 19	52 52 75 80 21	80 81 45 17 48
54 17 84 56 11	80 99 33 71 43	05 33 51 29 69	56 12 71 92 55	36 04 09 03 24
11 66 44 98 83	52 07 98 48 27	59 38 17 15 39	09 97 33 34 40	88 46 12 33 56
48 32 47 79 28	31 24 96 47 10	02 29 53 68 70	32 30 75 75 46	15 02 00 99 94
69 07 49 41 38	87 63 79 19 76	35 58 40 44 01	10 51 82 16 15	01 84 87 69 38

Source: This table is reproduced from page 1 of The Rand Corporation, *A Million Random Digits with 100,000 Normal Deviates* (New York: The Free Press, 1955). Copyright © 1955 and 1983 by The Rand Corporation. Used by permission.

Stratified Sampling

A **stratified sample** is a probability sample that is distinguished by the following two-step procedure:

1. The parent population is divided into mutually exclusive and exhaustive subsets.
2. A simple random sample of elements is chosen independently from each group or subset.

Note these features. The defining characteristics say nothing about the criterion or criteria that may be used to separate the universe elements into subsets. Admittedly, they will make a difference with respect to the advantages obtained in stratified sampling, but the criteria do not determine whether or not a stratified sample has been drawn. As long as the sample reflects the two-stage process, it is a stratified sample. This argument will be of assistance later when distinguishing cluster samples from stratified samples.

The subsets into which the universe elements are divided are called *strata* or *sub-populations*. Note that the division is mutually exclusive and exhaustive. This means that every population element must be assigned to one and only one stratum and that no population elements are omitted in the assignment procedure. To illustrate the process, assume that we will divide our hypothetical population of Table 10.1 into two strata on the basis of educational level. In particular, suppose that all those with a high school education or less are to be considered as forming one stratum and those with more than a high school education as forming another. Table 10.6 displays the results of this stratification procedure; Elements A through J form what is labeled the *first stratum* and Elements K through T form the *second stratum*. There is no magic in the choice of two strata. The parent population can be divided into any number of strata. Two were chosen for purposes of convenience in illustrating the technique.

Stage 2 in the process then requires that a simple random sample be drawn independently *from each* stratum. Suppose that we again work with samples of Size 2, formed this time by selecting one element from each stratum. The number of elements from

Research Realities 10.2

A Problem of Bias in Computer-Generated Random Numbers

When scientists use computers to try to predict complex trends and events, they often apply a type of calculation that requires long series of random numbers. But instructing a computer to produce acceptably random strings of digits is proving maddeningly difficult.

In deciding which team kicks off a football game, the toss of a real coin is random enough to satisfy all concerned. But the cost of even a slightly nonrandom string of electronic coin tosses can be devastating to both practical problem-solving and pure theory, and a new investigation has revealed that nonrandom computer tosses are much more common than many scientists had assumed.

Mathematical "models" designed to predict stock prices, atmospheric warming, airplane skin friction, chemical reactions, epidemics, population growth, the outcome of battles, the locations of oil deposits, and hundreds of other complex matters increasingly depend on a statistical technique called Monte Carlo Simulation, which in turn depends on reliable and inexhaustible sources of random numbers.

Monte Carlo Simulation, named for Monaco's famous gambling casino, can help to represent very complex interactions in physics, chemistry, engineering, economics, and environmental dynamics mathematically. Mathematicians call such a representation a "model," and if a model is accurate enough, it produces the same responses to manipulations that the real thing would do. But Monte Carlo modeling contains a dangerous flaw: if the supposedly random numbers that must be pumped into a simulation actually form some subtle, nonrandom pattern, the entire simulation (and its predictions) may be wrong.

The danger was highlighted in a recent report from Dr. Alan M. Ferrenberg and Dr. D. P. Landau of the University of Georgia at Athens and Dr. Y. Joanna Wong of the I.B.M. Corporation's Supercomputing center at Kingston, N.Y. In a December 7, 1992, article in the journal *Physical Review Letters,* the scientists showed that five of the most popular computer programs for generating streams of random numbers produced errors when they were used in a simple mathematical model of the behavior of atoms in a magnetic crystal.

The reason for the errors, the scientists found, was that the numbers produced by all five programs were not random at all, despite the fact that they passed several statistical tests for randomness. Beneath their apparent randomness, the sequences actually concealed correlations and patterns, revealed only when the subtle nonrandomness skewed the known properties of the crystal model.

All five of these systems for producing random numbers have long been used by scientists and statisticians with generally satisfactory results, Dr. Ferrenberg said. Major flaws turned up only recently when Dr. Ferrenberg and his colleagues were testing an ultra-powerful network of computers operating in parallel. Unlike ordinary sequential computer operations that execute programs one step at a time, parallel computing systems break up tasks into separate parts, which can be attacked simultaneously, with enormous savings in time. Parallel computers are so much faster and more powerful than the conventional kind that subtle problems in the programs they are executing come to light relatively quickly.

Source: Malcolm W. Browne, "Coin-Tossing Computers Found to Show Subtle Bias," *The New York Times* (January 12, 1993), pp. B5–B6.

each stratum does not have to be equal, but again the assumption is made simply for exposition purposes. The procedure that would be used to select two elements for the stratified sample would now parallel that for the simple random sample. Within each stratum, the population elements would be serially numbered from 1 to 10. A table of random numbers would be consulted. The first number encountered between 1 and 10

Table 10.6 Stratification of Hypothetical Population by Education

Stratum I Elements	Stratum II Elements
A	K
B	L
C	M
D	N
E	O
F	P
G	Q
H	R
I	S
J	T

would designate the element from the first stratum. The element from the second stratum could be selected after another independent start or by continuing from the first randomly determined start. In either case it would again be designated by the first encounter with a number between 1 and 10.

Derived Population Although only one sample of Size 2 will in fact be selected, let us look briefly at the derived population of all possible samples of Size 2 that could be selected under this sampling plan. This derived population, along with the mean of each sample, is displayed in Table 10.7.

Note first that every possible combination of sample elements is no longer a possibility, since every combination of two elements from the same stratum is precluded. There are now only 100 possible sample combinations of elements, whereas with simple random sampling there were 190 possible combinations. In this sense, stratified sampling is always more restrictive than simple random sampling. Note further that every element has an equal chance of being included in the sample — 1 in 10 — because each can be the single element selected from the stratum. This explains why we specified an additional requirement to define a simple random sample. Although simple random samples provide each element an equal chance of selection, other techniques can also. Thus, equal probability of selection is a necessary but not a sufficient condition for simple random sampling; in addition, each combination of *n* elements must be a sample possibility and as likely to occur as any other combination of *n* elements.

Sampling Distribution Table 10.8 contains the classification of sample means by size, and Figure 10.7 displays the plot of this sample statistic. Note that in relation to Figure 10.5 for simple random sampling, stratified sampling can produce a more concentrated distribution of estimates. This suggests one reason that we might choose a stratified sample: stratified samples can produce sample statistics that are more precise or that have smaller error as a result of sampling than simple random samples. With education as a stratification variable, there is a marked reduction in the number of sample means that deviate widely from the population mean.

TABLE 10.7   **Derived Population of All Possible Samples of Size *n* = 2 with Stratified Sampling**

k	Sample Identity	Mean	k	Sample Identity	Mean	k	Sample Identity	Mean	k	Sample Identity	Mean
1	AK	7,600	26	CP	9,000	51	FK	8,600	76	HP	10,000
2	AL	7,800	27	CQ	9,200	52	FL	8,800	77	HQ	10,200
3	AM	8,000	28	CR	9,400	53	FM	9,000	78	HR	10,400
4	AN	8,200	29	CS	9,600	54	FN	9,200	79	HS	10,600
5	AO	8,400	30	CT	9,800	55	FO	9,400	80	HT	10,800
6	AP	8,600	31	DK	8,200	56	FP	9,600	81	IK	9,200
7	AQ	8,800	32	DL	8,400	57	FQ	9,800	82	IL	9,400
8	AR	9,000	33	DM	8,600	58	FR	10,000	83	IM	9,600
9	AS	9,200	34	DN	8,800	59	FS	10,200	84	IN	9,800
10	AT	9,400	35	DO	9,000	60	FT	10,400	85	IO	10,000
11	BK	7,800	36	DP	9,200	61	GK	8,800	86	IP	10,200
12	BL	8,000	37	DQ	9,400	62	GL	9,000	87	IQ	10,400
13	BM	8,200	38	DR	9,600	63	GM	9,200	88	IR	10,600
14	BN	8,400	39	DS	9,800	64	GN	9,400	89	IS	10,800
15	BO	8,600	40	DT	10,000	65	GO	9,600	90	IT	11,000
16	BP	8,800	41	EK	8,400	66	GP	9,800	91	JK	9,400
17	BQ	9,000	42	EL	8,600	67	GQ	10,000	92	JL	9,600
18	BR	9,200	43	EM	8,800	68	GR	10,200	93	JM	9,800
19	BS	9,400	44	EN	9,000	69	GS	10,400	94	JN	10,000
20	BT	9,600	45	EO	9,200	70	GT	10,600	95	JO	10,200
21	CK	8,000	46	EP	9,400	71	HK	9,000	96	JP	10,400
22	CL	8,200	47	EQ	9,600	72	HL	9,200	97	JQ	10,600
23	CM	8,400	48	ER	9,800	73	HM	9,400	98	JR	10,800
24	CN	8,600	49	ES	10,000	74	HN	9,600	99	JS	11,000
25	CO	8,800	50	ET	10,200	75	HO	9,800	100	JT	11,200

TABLE 10.8   **Classification of Sample Means by Size with Stratified Sampling**

Sample Mean	Number of Samples
7,300 to 7,800	3
7,900 to 8,400	12
8,500 to 9,000	21
9,100 to 9,600	28
9,700 to 10,200	21
10,300 to 10,800	12
10,900 to 11,400	3

FIGURE 10.7 **Distribution of Sample Means with Stratified Sampling**

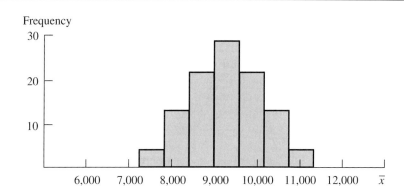

A second reason for drawing a stratified sample is that stratification allows the investigation of the characteristic of interest for particular subgroups. Thus, by stratifying, one is able to guarantee representation of those with a high school education or less and those with more than a high school education. This can be extremely important when sampling from populations with rare segments. If a manufacturer of diamond rings is conducting a study of sales of the product by social class, for example, it is likely that unless special precautions are taken, the upper class will not be represented at all or will be represented by so few cases as to defy conclusion, because it is estimated to represent only 3 percent of the total population. Yet this can be an extremely important segment to the ring manufacturer. It is often true of many populations of interest in marketing that a small subset will account for a large proportion of the behavior of interest (for example, consumption of the product). It then becomes imperative that this subgroup be adequately represented in the sample. Stratified sampling is one way of ensuring adequate representation from each subgroup of interest.

Confidence Interval Estimate In establishing a confidence interval with a simple random sample, we saw that we needed three things to complete the confidence interval specifications given by $\bar{x} - zs_{\bar{x}} \le \mu \le \bar{x} + zs_{\bar{x}}$:

1. the degree of confidence desired so that a z value can be selected;
2. a point estimate of the population mean given by the sample mean $\bar{x}$;
3. an estimate of the amount of sampling error associated with the sample mean, which was given by $s_{\bar{x}} = \hat{s}/\sqrt{n}$ when the population variance was unknown.

The same three quantities are required for making inferences with a stratified sample. The only difference in the procedure occurs in the way Items 2 and 3 are generated. With stratified sampling, the sample estimate of the population mean and the standard error of estimate associated with this statistic are determined by "appropriately weight-ing" the individual strata results.[16]

What are the appropriate weights? They are related to the stratum population size as compared to the total population size. Consider, for example, because of the need to make one specific point that a sample of Size 2 was to be selected from each stratum, producing a total sample of Size 4. In particular, suppose that Elements B and E were randomly selected from the first stratum and Elements N and S from the second stratum. Table 10.9 contains the sample means, sample variances, and estimated standard errors of estimate for each stratum. *These quantities are calculated for each stratum in exactly the same way as they were calculated for the sample as a whole with simple random sampling.*

Consider first the combination of strata sample means to produce a point estimate of the population mean. The weights here are the relative proportions of the population in each of the strata, that is,

$$\bar{x}_{st} = \sum_{h=1}^{L} \frac{N_h}{N} \bar{x}_h \tag{10.3}$$

where
N_h is the number of elements in the population in stratum h,
N is the total size of the population,
$\bar{x}_h$ is the sample mean for stratum h,
$\bar{x}_{st}$ is the sample mean for a stratified sample,

and where summation is across all L strata. In the Table 10.9 example, $L = 2$; there are 10 elements in each stratum, 20 in all; and the overall point estimate of the population mean is

$$\bar{x}_{st} = \frac{N_1}{N} \bar{x}_1 + \frac{N_2}{N} \bar{x}_2 = \frac{10}{20} (6{,}600) + \frac{10}{20} (11{,}800) = 9{,}200.$$

The combined standard error of estimate also employs the relative sizes of the strata in the population; however, it is calculated using the relative proportions squared, be-cause the linear combination holds with respect to *variances* and *not* standard deviations. That is, one must compute the variance of the overall estimate and take the square root. The formula for the variance of the estimate is

$$s_{\bar{x}_{st}}^{2} = \sum_{h=1}^{L} \left(\frac{N_h}{N} \right)^2 s_{\bar{x}_h}^{2}, \tag{10.4}$$

---

[16]For general discussion of the analysis of data gathered through complex sampling schemes, see Eun Sul Lee, Ronald N. Forthofer, and Ronald J. Lorimar, *Analyzing Complex Survey Data* (Newbury Park, CA.: Sage Publications, Inc., 1989).

TABLE 10.9 **Sample Means, Sample Variances, and Estimated Standard Errors of Estimate for Each Stratum**

	Stratum I			Stratum II	
Element	Income		Element	Income	
B	6,000		N	10,800	
E	7,200		S	12,800	

Mean:

$$\bar{x}_1 = \frac{\sum\limits_{i=1}^{n_1} X_i}{n_1} = \frac{6,000 + 7,200}{2}$$

$$= 6,600$$

$$\bar{x}_2 = \frac{\sum\limits_{i=1}^{n_2} X_i}{n_2} = \frac{10,800 + 12,800}{2}$$

$$= 11,800$$

Variance:

$$\hat{s}_1^{\,2} = \frac{\sum\limits_{i=1}^{n_1} (X_i - \bar{x}_1)^2}{n_1 - 1}$$

$$= \frac{(6,000 - 6,600)^2 + (7,200 - 6,600)^2}{2 - 1}$$

$$= 720,000$$

$$\hat{s}_2^{\,2} = \frac{\sum\limits_{i=1}^{n_2} (X_i - \bar{x}_2)^2}{n_2 - 1}$$

$$= \frac{(10,800 - 11,800)^2 + (12,800 - 11,800)^2}{2 - 1}$$

$$= 2,000,000$$

Standard error of estimate:

$$s_{\bar{x}_1} = \frac{\hat{s}_1}{\sqrt{n_1}} = \frac{\sqrt{720,000}}{\sqrt{2}}$$

$$= 600$$

$$s_{\bar{x}_2} = \frac{\hat{s}_2}{\sqrt{n_2}} = \frac{\sqrt{2,000,000}}{\sqrt{2}}$$

$$= 1,000$$

Variance of estimate:

$$s_{\bar{x}_1}^{\,2} = 360,000$$

$$s_{\bar{x}_2}^{\,2} = 1,000,000$$

and for the example

$$s_{\bar{x}_{st}}^{\,2} = \left(\frac{N_1}{N}\right)^2 s_{\bar{x}_1}^{\,2} + \left(\frac{N_2}{N}\right)^2 s_{\bar{x}_2}^{\,2} = \left(\frac{10}{20}\right)^2 (360,000) + \left(\frac{10}{20}\right)^2 (1,000,000)$$

$$= 90,000 + 250,000 = 340,000,$$

so that

$$s_{\bar{x}_{st}} = \sqrt{340,000} = 583.$$

The 95 percent confidence interval for this sample would then be

$$\bar{x}_{st} - zs_{\bar{x}_{st}} \leq \mu \leq \bar{x}_{st} + zs_{\bar{x}_{st}}$$

$$9,200 - 1.96(583) \leq \mu \leq 9,200 + 1.96(583)$$

$$8,057 \leq \mu \leq 10,343.$$

This interval is interpreted as before. The true mean may or may not be in the interval, but since 95 of 100 intervals constructed by this process will contain the true mean, we are 95 percent confident that the true population mean income is between \$8,057 and \$10,343.[17]

Increased Precision of Stratified Samples   We mentioned previously that one of the reasons one might choose a stratified sample is that such samples offer an opportunity for reducing sampling error or increasing precision. When estimating a mean, sampling error is given by the size of $s_{\bar{x}}$; the smaller $s_{\bar{x}}$, the less the sampling error and the more precise the estimate as indicated by the narrower confidence interval associated with a specified degree of confidence.

Consider Equation 10.4 again. The total size of the population and the population within each stratum are fixed. The only way for total sampling error to be reduced, therefore, is for the variance of the estimate within each stratum to be made smaller. Now, the variance of the estimate by strata, in turn, depends on the variability of the characteristic within the strata, because $s_{\bar{x}_h}^2 = \hat{s}_h^2/n_h$, where $\hat{s}_h^2$ is the sample variance within the hth stratum and n_h is the size of the sample selected from the hth stratum. Thus, the estimate of the mean can be made more precise to the extent that the population can be partitioned so that there is little variability within each stratum — that is, to the extent the strata can be made internally homogeneous.

A characteristic of interest will display a certain amount of variation in the population. The investigator can do nothing about this total variation because it is a fixed characteristic of the population. But he or she can do something when dividing the elements of the population into strata to increase the precision with which the average value of the characteristic can be estimated. Specifically, the investigator should divide the population into strata so that the elements within any given stratum are as similar in value as possible and the values between any two strata are as disparate as possible. In the limit, if the investigator is successful in partitioning the population so that the elements in each stratum are exactly equal, there will be no error associated with the estimate of the population mean. That is right! The population mean could then be estimated without error because the *variability that exists between strata does not enter into the calculation of the standard error of estimate with stratified sampling.*

---

[17]We are again assuming that the normal distribution applies in making this inference. Although this assumption is not strictly correct in this instance because of the size of the sample taken from each stratum, we are making it to allow more direct comparison with the interval constructed using simple random sampling. In most situations, the normal distribution would hold because the Central-Limit Theorem also applies to the individual strata means, and the linear combination of these means produces a normally distributed $\bar{x}_{st}$.

One can see this readily in a simple case with a limited number of values. Suppose that in a population of 1,000 elements, 200 had the value 5, 300 had the value 10, and 500 had the value 20. Now, the mean of this population $\mu = 14$ and the variance $\sigma^2 = 39$. If a simple random sample of Size $n = 3$ was to be employed to estimate this mean, then the standard error of estimate would be

$$\sigma_{\bar{x}} = \frac{\sigma}{\sqrt{n}} = \frac{\sqrt{39}}{\sqrt{3}} = 3.61,$$

and the width of confidence interval would be $\pm z$ times this value 3.61. Suppose, on the other hand, that a researcher employed a stratified sample and was successful in partitioning the total population so that all the elements with a value of 5 on the characteristic were in one stratum, those with the value of 10 were in the second stratum, and those with the value 20 were in the third stratum. To generate a completely precise description of the mean of each stratum, the researcher would then need to take a sample of only one from each stratum. Further, when the investigator combined these individual results into a global estimate of the overall mean, the standard error of the estimate would be zero, because each stratum's standard error of estimate is zero. The population mean value would be determined exactly.

Bases for Stratification The fact that variation among strata does not enter into the calculation of the standard error of estimate suggests two things. First, it indicates the kinds of criteria that should be used to partition the population. The values assumed by the characteristic will be unknown, for if they were known, there would be no need to take a sample to estimate their mean level. What the investigator attempts to do, therefore, is to partition the population according to one or more criteria that are expected to be related to the characteristic of interest. Thus it was no accident that in the hypothetical example, education was employed to divide the population elements into strata. As Table 10.1 indicates, there is a relation between education level and income level: the more years of school, the higher the income. Newspaper subscriptions, on the other hand, would have made a poor variable for partitioning the population into segments, because there is almost no relation between the paper to which a person subscribes and the individual's income. Whether one selects a "good" or a "bad" variable for partitioning the population does not affect whether or not a stratified sample is selected. It is important in determining whether a good or poor sample is selected, but the two features defining a stratified sample are still (1) the partitioning of the population into subgroups and (2) the random selection of elements from each subgroup.

Second, the calculation of the standard error of estimate provides some clue to the number of strata that should be employed. Since the standard error of estimate depends only on variability within strata, the various strata should be made as homogeneous as possible. One way of doing this is to employ many very small strata. There are practical limits, however, to the number of strata that should be and are used in actual research studies. First, the creation of additional strata is often expensive in terms of sample design, data collection, and analysis. Second, there is an upper limit to the amount of variation that can be accounted for by any practical stratification. Regardless of the criteria by which the population is partitioned, a certain amount of variation is likely to remain unaccounted for, and the additional strata will serve no productive purpose.

Proportionate and Disproportionate Stratified Sampling   Whether one chooses a stratified sample over a simple random sample depends in part on the trade-off between cost and precision. Although stratified samples typically produce more precise estimates, they also usually cost more than simple random samples. If the decision is made in favor of a stratified sample, the researcher must still decide whether to select a proportionate stratified sample or a disproportionate stratified sample.

With a **proportionate stratified sample,** the number of observations in the total sample is allocated among the strata in proportion to the *relative* number of elements in each stratum in the population. A stratum containing one-fifth of all the population elements would account for one-fifth of the total sample observations and so on. Proportionate sampling was employed in the example; each stratum contained one-half of the population and thus was sampled equally.[18]

One advantage of proportionate allocation is that the investigator needs to know only the relative sizes of each stratum to determine the number of sample observations to select from each stratum with a given sample size.

There is an alternative allocation scheme, however, that can produce still more efficient estimates. **Disproportionate stratified sampling** involves balancing the two criteria of strata size and strata variability. With a fixed sample size, strata exhibiting more variability are sampled more than proportionately to their relative size. Conversely, those strata that are very homogeneous are sampled less than proportionately. Research Realities 10.3, for example, describes the disproportionate stratified sampling scheme used by Nielsen in developing the National Retail Index described in Chapter 6.[19]

Although a full discussion of how the sample size for each stratum should be determined would take us too far afield and would be much too technical for our purpose, some feel for the rationale behind disproportionate sampling is useful. Consider at the extreme a stratum with zero variability. Because all the elements are identical in value, a single observation tells all. In contrast, a stratum that is characterized by great variability will require a large number of observations to produce a precise estimate of the stratum mean (recall that $s_{\bar{x}_h}^2 = \hat{s}_h^2/n_h$). One can expect greater precision when the various strata are sampled proportionate to the relative variability of the characteristic under study rather than proportionate to their relative size in the population.

A disproportionate stratified sample requires more knowledge about the population of interest than does a proportionate stratified sample. To sample the strata in relation to their variability, one needs knowledge of relative variability. Sampling theory is a peculiar phenomenon in that knowledge begets more knowledge. Disproportionate sampling

---

[18]For an example of the use of proportionate stratified sampling, see William C. Moncrief III, "Selling Activity and Sales Position Taxonomies for Industrial Salesforces," *Journal of Marketing Research,* 23 (August 1986), pp. 261–270.

[19]The Census Bureau also uses disproportionate stratified sampling in its surveys. For descriptions of the strata and the sampling rates, see "Eighteen Million Households Will Receive Sample Questionnaire in '90 Census," *Census and You,* 24 (January 1989), p. 2.

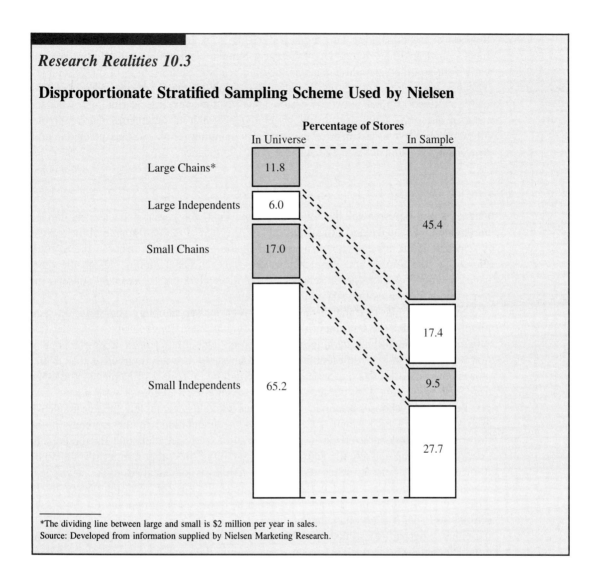

Research Realities 10.3

Disproportionate Stratified Sampling Scheme Used by Nielsen

Percentage of Stores

In Universe

In Sample

Large Chains*	11.8		
Large Independents	6.0		45.4
Small Chains	17.0		
			17.4
			9.5
Small Independents	65.2		27.7

*The dividing line between large and small is $2 million per year in sales.
Source: Developed from information supplied by Nielsen Marketing Research.

can produce more efficient estimates than proportionate sampling, but the former method also requires that some estimate of the relative variation within strata be known. One can sometimes anticipate the relative homogeneity likely to exist within a stratum on the basis of past studies and experience. Sometimes the investigator may have to rely on logic and intuition in establishing sample sizes for each stratum. For example, it might reasonably be expected that large retail stores would show greater variation in sales of some product than would small stores. That is one reason that the large stores would be sampled more heavily in the Nielsen Retail Index.

Stratified versus Quota Samples Stratified samples are sometimes confused with quota samples by the inexperienced researcher. There are similarities. Both involve the division of the population into segments and the selection of elements from each segment. However, there is one key difference. Sample elements are selected probabilistically with stratified samples, whereas they are selected judgmentally in quota samples. This has important implications. Because the sample elements are selected probabilistically, stratified samples allow the establishment of the sampling distribution of the statistic in question, which in turn allows confidence interval judgments. Quota samples allow no objective assessment of the degree of sampling error and thus preclude confidence interval estimates and statistical tests of significance.

Cluster Sampling

Cluster sampling involves the following steps. First, the parent population is divided into mutually exclusive and exhaustive subsets. Second, a random sample of the subsets is selected. If the investigator then uses all of the population elements in the selected subsets for the sample, the procedure is one-stage cluster sampling. If, on the other hand, a sample of elements is selected probabilistically from the selected subsets, the procedure is known as two-stage cluster sampling.

Note the similarities and differences between cluster sampling and stratified sampling. Both involve the division of the population into mutually exclusive and exhaustive subgroups, although the criteria used are different. The criteria for dividing the population are not the key in differentiating the techniques. The key ingredient that distinguishes the procedures is that with stratified sampling, a sample of elements is selected *from each subgroup*. With cluster sampling, one chooses a *sample of subgroups*.

Because one chooses a sample of subgroups with cluster sampling, it is desirable for each subgroup to be a small scale model of the population. At the extreme, if the distribution of the characteristic in each subgroup exactly parallels that for the population, one subgroup can tell all. Thus in cluster sampling, the subgroups ideally should be formed to be as heterogeneous as possible. In the hypothetical example, newspaper subscription would be a good basis for forming subgroups for a cluster sample. If all those subscribing to Paper X were considered to form one subgroup and all those subscribing to Paper Y a second subgroup, one could be relatively safe in randomly selecting either subgroup to estimate the mean income in the population. While the distribution of incomes within each subgroup is not exactly the same as it is in the population, the range of incomes is such that there would be only a slight error if one were to estimate the mean income and variance of incomes of the population with the elements from either subset.

Admittedly, in practice, clusters are not always formed to be as heterogeneous as possible. Because of the way cluster samples are often drawn, the defined clusters are homogeneous rather than heterogeneous in regard to the characteristic of interest. Beginning researchers display a proclivity for then calling the procedure stratified sampling, since it involves the construction of homogeneous subgroups of population elements. As long as subgroups are selected for investigation randomly, the procedure is cluster sampling, regardless of how the subgroups are formed. Admittedly, homogeneous subgroups produce fewer ideal cluster samples from a statistical efficiency viewpoint than do heterogeneous subgroups.

Statistical efficiency is a relative notion by which sampling plans can be compared. One sampling plan is said to be more statistically efficient than another if, for the same size sample, it produces a smaller standard error of estimate. When the characteristic of interest is the mean, for example, the sampling plan that produces the smallest value of $s_{\bar{x}}$ for a given size sample is most statistically efficient. Cluster samples are typically much less statistically efficient than comparable stratified samples or even simple random samples, because the probable margin of error with a fixed size sample is often greatest with cluster sampling.

Even with its typically lower statistical efficiency, cluster sampling is probably the most widely used sampling procedure in large-scale field surveys, particularly those involving in-home personal interviews. Why? Simply because it is often more *economically efficient* since the cost per observation is less. The economies permit the selection of a larger sample at a smaller cost. Often, so many more observations can be secured for a given cost that the margin of error associated with the estimate is smaller for cluster sampling than it is for stratified sampling with the smaller number of observations. That is, cluster sampling is often more *efficient overall* than the other forms of sampling; although it requires a large sample for the same degree of precision and is thus less statistically efficient, the smaller cost per observation allows samples so much larger that estimates with a smaller standard error can be produced for the same cost.

Systematic Sampling   The **systematic sample** offers one of the easiest ways of sampling many populations of interest. A systematic sample involves selecting every *k*th element after a random start.

Consider again the hypothetical population of 20 individuals and suppose that a sample of 5 is to be selected from this population. Number the elements from 1 to 20. With 20 population elements and a sample size of 5, the sampling fraction is $f = n/N = 5/20 = 1/4$, meaning that one element in four will be selected. The sampling interval $i = 1/f$ will be 4. This means that after a random start, every fourth element will be chosen. The random start, which must be some number between 1 and 4 (1 and i in general), is determined from a random number table. Thus, if the random start were 1, the first, fifth, ninth, thirteenth, and seventeenth items would be the sample; if it were 2, the second, sixth, tenth, fourteenth, and eighteenth items would be the sample; and so on.

Systematic sampling is one-stage cluster sampling, because rather than the subgroups being sampled, all of the elements in the selected clusters are used. The subgroups or clusters in this case are

Cluster I	A, E, I, M, Q
Cluster II	B, F, J, N, R
Cluster III	C, G, K, O, S
Cluster IV	D, H, L, P, T

and one of these clusters is selected randomly for investigation. The random start, of course, determines the cluster that is to be used.

One can readily see the ease with which a systematic sample can be drawn. It is much easier to draw a systematic sample than it is to select a simple random sample of the same size, for example. With a systematic sample one needs to enter the random number table only once. The problem of checking for the duplication of elements, which is cumbersome with simple random samples, does not occur with systematic samples. All the elements are uniquely determined by the selection of the random start.[20]

A systematic sample can often be made more representative than a simple random sample. With our hypothetical population, for example, we are guaranteed representation from the low-income segment and the high-income segment. Regardless of which of the four clusters is chosen, one element must have an income of $6,800 or less; another must have an income of $12,000 or more; and the remaining three elements must have incomes between these two values. A simple random sample of Size 5 might or might not include low-income or high-income people.

The same is true when sampling from other populations. Thus, if we are sampling retail stores, we can guarantee representation of both small and large stores by employing a systematic sample, if the stores can be arrayed from smallest to largest according to some criteria such as annual sales or square footage. The ability to guarantee representation from each size segment depends on the availability of knowledge about the size of each store so that the stores can be arrayed from smallest to largest and numbered serially. A simple random sample of stores will probably contain inadequate representation from the large stores, since there are fewer large stores than small stores. Yet the fewer large stores account for a great proportion of all sales.

The degree to which the systematic sample will be more representative than a simple random sample thus depends on the clustering of objects within the list from which the sample will be drawn. The ideal list for a systematic sample will have elements similar in value on the characteristic close together and elements diverse in value spread apart.

There is at least one danger with systematic samples. If there is a natural periodicity in the list of elements, the systematic sample can produce estimates seriously in error. For example, suppose that we have the annual ticket sales of an airline by day and that we wish to analyze these sales in terms of length of trip. To analyze all 365 days may be prohibitively costly, but perhaps the research budget allows the investigation of 52 days of sales. A systematic sample of days using a sampling interval of 7 ($365 \div 52$) would obviously produce some misleading conclusions, because the day's sales will reflect all Monday trips, Friday trips, or Sunday trips, for example.[21] Any other sampling interval will be acceptable, and in general, an enlightened choice of the sampling interval can do much to eliminate the problems associated with natural periodicities in the data. The

---

[20]For an example of the use of systematic sampling, see Mark E. Slama and Armen Tashchian, "Selected Socioeconomic and Demographic Characteristics Associated with Purchasing Involvement," *Journal of Marketing*, 49 (Winter 1985), pp. 72–82; or Richard A. Moore, "A Cross Cultural Research Project — Using the Mail Questionnaire," *Quarterly Review of Marketing*, 41 (Spring 1989), pp. 14–17.

[21]Sudman suggests that when the "sampling interval i is not a whole number, the easiest solution is to use as the interval the whole number just below or above i. Usually, this will result in a selected sample that is only slightly larger or smaller than the initial sample required, and this new sample size will have no noticeable effect on either the accuracy of the results or the budget. For samples in which the interval i is small (generally for i less than 10), so that the rounding has too great an effect on the sample size, it is possible to add or delete the extra cases . . . it is usually easier to round down in computing i so that the sample is larger, and then to delete systematically." Sudman, *Applied Sampling*, p. 54.

enlightened choice of sampling interval, of course, depends on knowledge of the phenomenon and nature of the periodicity.

Area Sampling   In every probability sampling plan discussed so far, the investigator needed a list of population elements in order to draw the sample. A list identifying each population element was a necessary requirement for simple random samples, stratified samples, and systematic samples. The latter two procedures also required knowledge about some other characteristic of the population if they were to be designed optimally. For many populations of interest, these detailed lists will be unavailable. Further, it often will prove to be prohibitively costly to construct them. When this condition arises, the cluster sample offers the researcher another distinct benefit — he or she only needs the list of population elements for the selected clusters.

Suppose, for example, that an investigator wished to measure certain characteristics of industrial sales representatives such as their earnings, attitudes toward the job, hours worked, and so on. It would be extremely difficult (if not impossible) and certainly costly to develop an up-to-date roster listing each industrial sales representative. Yet such a list would be required for a simple random sample. A stratified sample would further require the investigator to possess knowledge about some additional characteristics of each sales representative (for example, education or employer) so that the population could be divided into mutually exclusive and exhaustive subsets. With a cluster sample, on the other hand, one could use companies as sampling units. The investigator would generate a sample of business firms from the population of firms of interest. The business firms would be *primary sampling units* with a **sampling unit** being defined as "that element or set of elements considered for selection in some stage of sampling."[22] The investigator could then get a list of sales representatives working for each of the selected firms — a much more plausible assignment. If the investigator studied each of the sales representatives in each of the selected firms, it would be one-stage cluster sampling. If the researcher subsampled sales representatives from each company's list, it would be two-stage cluster sampling.

The same principle underlies **area sampling.** Current, accurate lists of population elements are rarely available. Directories of all those living in a city at a particular moment simply do not exist for many cities, and when they do exist, they are obsolete when published; people move, others die, and new households are constantly being formed.[23] Although lists of families are nonexistent, relatively accurate lists of primary sampling units are available in the form of city maps, if the areal divisions of the city serve as the primary sampling units. The details of area sampling are much too complex

---

[22]Earl R. Babbie, *The Practice of Social Research,* 6th ed. (Belmont, Calif.: Wadsworth Publishing, 1992), p. 198.

[23]R. L. Polk and Company in Taylor, Michigan, publishes some 1,400 directories for most medium-sized cities in the range of 50,000–800,000 people. The directories contain both an alphabetical list of names and businesses and a street address directory of households. Even though the alphabetic list can contain a reasonably large percentage of inaccurate listings at any one time, the address directory is reasonably accurate since it omits new construction only after the directory is published and the directories are revised every two or three years.

for our purposes, but an appreciation for the rationale underlying the various approaches can be gathered by considering some of the basic types of area sampling.

One-Stage Area Sampling   Suppose that the investigator is interested in estimating the amount of wine consumed per household in the city of Chicago and how consumption is related to family income. An accurate listing of all households is unavailable for the Chicago area. A phone book when published is already somewhat obsolete, in addition to the other inadequacies previously mentioned. One approach to this problem would be to do the following:

1. choose a simple random sample of n city blocks from the population of N blocks;
2. determine wine consumption and income for all households in the selected blocks and generalize the sample relationships to the larger population.

The probability of any household being included in the sample can be calculated. It is given simply as n/N, because it equals the probability that the block on which it is located will be selected. Since the probabilities are known, the procedure is indeed probability sampling. Here, though, blocks have been substituted for households when selecting primary sampling units. The substitution is made because the list of blocks in the Chicago area can be developed from city maps. Each block can be identified, and the existence of this universe of blocks permits the calculation of the necessary probabilities.

Because each household on the selected blocks is included in the sample, the procedure is one-stage area sampling. Note that the blocks serve to divide the parent population into mutually exclusive and exhaustive subsets. Note further that the blocks do not serve very well as ideal subsets statistically for cluster samples; households on a given block can be expected to be somewhat similar with respect to their income and wine consumption rather than heterogeneous as desired.[24] On the other hand, the data collection costs will be very low because of the concentration of households within each block.

Two-Stage Area Sampling   The distinguishing feature of the one-stage area sample is that all of the households in the selected blocks (or other areas) are enumerated and studied. It is not necessary to employ all items in a selected cluster; the selected areas themselves can be subsampled, and it is often quite advantageous to do so. Two types of two-stage sampling need to be distinguished:

1. simple, two-stage area sampling;
2. probability-proportional-to-size area sampling.

---

[24]When geographic clustering of rare populations occurs, it can be used to advantage when designing the sample. See, for example, Seymour Sudman, "Efficient Screening Methods for the Sampling of Geographically Clustered Special Populations," *Journal of Marketing Research,* 22 (February 1985), pp. 20–29. For other discussions of techniques for sampling rare populations, see Roger Tourangeau and A. Wade Smith, "Finding Subgroups for Surveys," *Public Opinion Quarterly,* 49 (Fall 1985), pp. 351–365; Seymour Sudman and Graham Kalton, "New Developments in the Sampling of Special Populations," *Annual Review of Sociology,* 12 (1986), pp. 401–429; Seymour Sudman, Monroe G. Sirken, and Charles D. Cowan, "Sampling Rare and Elusive Populations," *Science,* 240 (May 20, 1988), pp. 991–996; Leslie Kish, "Taxonomy of Elusive Populations," *Journal of Official Statistics,* 7 (No. 3, 1991), pp. 339–347.

With simple, two-stage area sampling, a certain proportion of second-stage sampling units (for example, households) is selected from each first-stage unit (for example, blocks). Consider a universe of 100 blocks; suppose that there are 20 households per block; assume that a sample of 80 households is required from this total population of 2,000 households. The overall sampling fraction is thus $80/2,000 = 1/25$. There are a number of ways by which the sample can be completed: by (1) selecting 10 blocks and 8 households per block; (2) selecting 8 blocks and 10 households per block; (3) selecting 20 blocks and 4 households per block; or (4) selecting 4 blocks and 20 households per block. The last alternative would, of course, be one-stage area sampling, whereas the first three would be two-stage area sampling.

The probability with which the blocks are selected is called the block or first-stage sampling fraction and is given as the ratio of n_B/N_B, where n_B and N_B are the number of blocks in the sample and in the population, respectively. For the first three schemes illustrated previously, the first-stage sampling fractions would be, in order, 1 in 10, 1 in 12.5, and 1 in 5. The probability with which the households are selected is the household or second-stage sampling fraction. Since there must be a total of 80 households in the sample, the second-stage sampling fraction differs for each alternative. The second-stage sampling fraction is given as $n_{H/B}/N_{H/B}$, where $n_{H/B}$ and $N_{H/B}$ are the number of households per block in the sample and in the population. For Sampling Scheme 1, the household sampling fraction is calculated to be $8/20 = 2/5$, for Scheme 2 it is $10/20 = 1/2$, and for Scheme 3 it is $4/20 = 1/5$. Note that the product of the first-stage and second-stage sampling fractions in each case equals the overall sampling fraction of $1/25$.

Which scheme would be preferable? Although we do not wish to get into the detailed calculation of what would be optimal, we would like to illustrate the general principle. Economies of data collection dictate that the second-stage sampling fraction should be high. This means that a great many households would be selected from each designated block, as with Scheme 2. Statistical efficiency would dictate a small second-stage sampling fraction, because one can expect that the blocks would be relatively homogeneous, and thus it would be desirable to have very few households from any one block. Scheme 3 would be preferred on statistical grounds. Statistical sampling theory would suggest the balancing of these two criteria. There are formulas for this purpose that essentially reflect the cost of data collection and the variability of the characteristic within and between clusters, although a useful rule of thumb is that clusters of three to eight households per block or segment are near optimum for most social science variables.[25]

Simple two-stage area sampling is quite effective when there is approximately the same number of second-stage units per first-stage unit. When the second-stage units are decidedly unequal, simple two-stage area sampling can cause bias in the estimate. Sometimes the number of second-stage units per first-stage unit can be made approximately equal by combining areas. When this option is not available or is cumbersome to implement, probability-proportional-to-size sampling can be employed.

---

[25]Sudman, *Applied Sampling*, p. 81.

Consider, for example, the data in Table 10.10, and suppose that a sample of 20 elements is to be selected from this population of 2,000 households. With **probability-proportional-to-size sampling,** a *fixed* number of second-stage units is selected from each first-stage unit. After balancing economic and statistical considerations, suppose that the number of second-stage units per first-stage unit is determined to be ten. Two first-stage units must be selected to produce a total sample of 20. The procedure gets its name from the way these first-stage units are selected. The probability of selection is variable because it depends on the size of the first-stage unit. In particular, a table of four-digit random numbers would be consulted. The first two numbers encountered between 1 and 2,000 are employed to indicate the blocks that will be used. All numbers between 1 and 800 indicate the inclusion of Block 1, those from 801 to 1,200 indicate Block 2, those from 1,201 to 1,400 indicate Block 3, and so on.

The probability that any particular household will be included in the sample is equal, since the unequal first-stage selection probabilities are balanced by unequal second-stage selection probabilities. Consider, for example, Blocks 1 and 10, the two extremes. The first-stage selection probability for Block 1 is 800/2,000 = 1/2.5, since 800 of the permissible 2,000 random numbers correspond to Block 1. In contrast, only 25 of the permissible random numbers (1,976 to 2,000) correspond to Block 10, and thus the first-stage sampling fraction for Block 10 is 25/2,000 = 1/80. Because ten households are to be selected from each block, the second-stage sampling fraction for Block 1 is 10/800 = 1/80, while for Block 10 it is 10/25 = 1/2.5. The products of the first- and second-stage sampling thus compensate, since

$$\frac{800}{2,000} \times \frac{10}{800} = \frac{25}{2,000} \times \frac{10}{25},$$

which is also true for the remaining blocks.

Probability-proportional-to-size sampling is another illustration of how information begets information with applied sampling problems. One can avoid the bias of simple

TABLE 10.10   Illustration of Probability-Proportional-to-Size Sampling

Block	Households	Cumulative Number of Households
1	800	800
2	400	1,200
3	200	1,400
4	200	1,600
5	100	1,700
6	100	1,800
7	100	1,900
8	50	1,950
9	25	1,975
10	25	2,000

two-stage area sampling and can also produce estimates that are more precise when there is great variation in the number of second-stage units per first-stage unit. The price one pays, of course, is that probability-proportional-to-size sampling requires one to have detailed knowledge about the size of each first-stage unit. This is not quite as high a price as it might be, because the Census Bureau has reported the number of households per block for all cities of over 50,000 in population as well as for many other urbanized areas.[26] Maps are included in each report. Even though they are somewhat obsolete when published, these map and block statistics can be updated. The local electrical utility will have records of connections current to the day and so will the telephone company. In many cases, these statistics will be broken down by blocks.

SUMMARY COMMENTS ON PROBABILITY SAMPLING

As you can probably begin to appreciate, sample design is a very detailed subject. Our discussion has concentrated on only a few of the fundamentals and, in particular, the basic types of probability samples. You should be aware that the basic types can be, and are, combined in large-scale field studies to produce some complex designs.

The Gallup poll, for example, is probably one of the best known of all the polls. The sample for the Gallup poll for each survey "consists of 1,500 adults selected from 320 locations, using area sampling methods. At each location the interviewer is given a map with an indicated starting point and is required to follow a specified direction. At each occupied dwelling unit, the interviewer must attempt to meet sex quotas."[27] Thus, the Gallup poll uses a combination of area and quota sampling.

It is not uncommon to have several levels of stratification, such as by geographic area and density of population, precede several stages of cluster sampling. You cannot expect to be a sampling expert with the brief exposure to the subject contained here.[28] But you should be able to communicate effectively about sample design and to use the available microcomputer software effectively to select samples.[29] Further, although you may not completely understand, say, why n_1 observations were taken from one stratum

---

[26]*U.S. Census of Housing: 1990, Vol. III City Blocks,* HC(3) — No. (city number).

[27]Sudman, *Applied Sampling,* p. 71.

[28]Those interested in pursuing the subject further should see one of the excellent books on the subject, such as F. J. Chaudhary and Daroga Singh, *Theory and Analysis of Sample Survey Design* (New York: John Wiley, 1986); William G. Cochran, *Sampling Techniques,* 3rd ed. (New York: John Wiley, 1977); Morris H. Hansen, William N. Hurwitz, and William G. Madow, *Sample Survey Methods and Theory, Vol. I, Methods and Applications* (New York: John Wiley, 1953); Gary T. Henry, *Practical Sampling* (Newbury Park, CA.: Sage Publications, Inc., 1990); Graham Kalton, *Introduction to Survey Sampling* (Beverly Hills, Calif.: Sage Publications, 1982); Leslie Kish, *Survey Sampling* (New York: John Wiley, 1965); Paul S. Levy and Stanley Lemeshow, *Sampling of Populations: Methods and Applications* (New York: John Wiley and Sons, Inc., 1991); Richard L. Schaeffer, William Mendenhall, and Lyman Ott, *Elementary Survey Sampling,* 4th ed. (Boston: PWS-Kent Publishing Co., 1990).

[29]For discussion of the available software, see Thomas L. Pilon, "A Review of PC-Based Software for Marketing Research," paper presented at the 9th Annual Marketing Research Conference in Arlington, Virginia, October 9–12, 1988.

and n_2 from another, you should appreciate the basic considerations determining the choice.

ETHICAL DILEMMA 10.2

Raphael is investigating conflict development and resolution in channels of distribution. Because of the difficulty of accessing actual channel members, he decides to run an experiment on a convenience sample of undergraduate students. Student samples are tolerated in consumer behavior but have met with more severe criticism in channels research because although a student is also a consumer, a student is not also a channel member. However, determined to present his research endeavor in the best possible light, Raphael ignores the large fraction of art students included in his sample of introductory marketing students and refers to his sample as "business students with an average of three years' work experience in jobs in which bargaining and interpersonal skills were required and developed to a level comparable with most channel members."

- Is it ethical to misrepresent an inappropriate sample as an appropriate sample?

SUMMARY

This chapter reviewed the basic types of samples that may be used to infer something about a population. A sample might be preferred to a census on grounds of cost or impossibility of taking a census or because of its greater accuracy.

A practical procedure to use when drawing a sample includes the following steps:

1. define the population;
2. identify the sampling frame;
3. select a sampling procedure;
4. determine the sample size;
5. select the sample elements; and
6. collect the data from the designated elements.

Probability samples are distinguished by the fact that every population element has a known, nonzero chance of being included in the sample. With nonprobability samples, the chance of inclusion is noncalculable because personal judgment is involved somewhere in the actual selection process. Thus, nonprobability samples do not allow the construction of the sampling distribution of the statistic in question. This, in turn, means that the traditional tools of statistical inference are not legitimately employed with nonprobability samples.

The basic types of nonprobability samples are convenience, judgment, and quota samples. Convenience samples are also known as accidental samples, because those elements included just happen to be at the study site at the right time. Population elements are handpicked to serve a specific purpose with judgment samples, whereas with quota samples, the interviewers personally select subjects with specified characteristics in order to fulfill their quota.

Simple random samples are probability samples in which each population element has an equal chance of being included and every combination of sample elements is just as likely as any other combination of *n* sample elements. Simple random samples were used to illustrate the basis of statistical inference, in which a parameter (a fixed characteristic of the population) is estimated from a statistic (a characteristic of a sample). The value of the statistic depends on the sample actually selected, since it varies from sample to sample. The derived population is the set of all possible distinguishable samples that could be drawn from a parent population under a given sampling plan, and the distribution of some sample statistic's values is the sampling distribution of the statistic. The concept of the sampling distribution is the cornerstone of statistical inference, since statistical inferential procedures rely on the sampling distribution of the specific statistic in question. The sampling distributions of a number of statistics of interest to the applied researcher are known from the work of theoretical statisticians.

A stratified sample is a probability sample in which the parent population is divided into mutually exclusive and exhaustive subsets and a sample of elements is drawn from each subset. Stratified samples are typically the most statistically efficient (that is, they have the smallest standard error of estimate for a given size), and they also allow the investigation of the characteristic of interest for particular subgroups within the population. The most statistically efficient stratified samples result when the strata are made as homogeneous as possible. Thus, variables expected to be correlated to the characteristic of interest, and whose values are known, are often employed when establishing the strata. In proportionate stratified sampling, the size of the sample taken from each stratum depends only on the relative size of the stratum in the population, whereas with disproportionate stratified sampling, sample size depends on the variability within the stratum as well.

A cluster sample is a probability sample in which the parent population is divided into mutually exclusive and exhaustive subsets and then a random sample of subsets is selected. If each of the elements within the selected subsets is studied, it is one-stage cluster sampling; if the selected subsets are also subsampled, the procedure represents two-stage cluster sampling. Since only a sample of subsets is selected for analysis, statistical efficiency considerations suggest that the subsets be established to be as heterogeneous as possible. A systematic sample is a form of cluster sample in which every *k*th element is selected after a randomly determined start.

An area sample is one of the most important types of cluster samples (or any kind of probability sample for that matter) in applied, large-scale studies. Area samples make use of one very desirable feature of cluster samples — one only needs the list of population elements for the selected clusters. By defining areas as clusters and then randomly selecting areas, the investigator needs to develop lists of population elements only for the selected areas. Even here the researcher can use dwelling units and select them systematically. Thus, area samples permit probability samples to be drawn when current lists of population elements are unavailable. In drawing area samples, the researcher typically attempts to balance statistical and economic considerations. Because small areas are basically homogeneous, statistical considerations suggest that a great many areas should be used. However, the economies of data collection dictate that few areas be used and a great many observations be collected within each area.

Many applied sample designs represent combinations of the basic types reviewed here.

Questions

1. What is a census? What is a sample?
2. Is a sample ever preferred to a census? Why?
3. What distinguishes a probability sample from a nonprobability sample?
4. What is a convenience sample?
5. What is a judgment sample?
6. Explain the operation of a quota sample. Why is a quota sample a nonprobability sample? What kinds of comparisons should one make with the data from quota samples to check their representativeness, and what kinds of conclusions can one legitimately draw?
7. What are the distinguishing features of a simple random sample?
8. What is a derived population? How is it distinguished from a parent population?
9. Consider the estimation of a population mean. What is the relation between the mean of the parent population and the mean of the derived population? Between the variance of the parent population and the variance of the derived population?
10. What is the Central-Limit Theorem? What role does it play in making inferences about a population mean?
11. What procedure is followed in constructing a confidence interval for a population mean when the population variance is known? When the population variance is unknown? What does such an interval mean?
12. How should a simple random sample be selected? Describe the procedure.
13. What is a stratified sample? How is a stratified sample selected?
14. Is a stratified sample a probability or nonprobability sample? Why?
15. What principle should be followed in establishing the strata for a stratified sample? Why? How can this principle be implemented in practice?
16. Describe the procedure that is followed in developing a confidence interval estimate for a population mean with a stratified sample. Be specific.
17. Which sampling method typically produces more precise estimates of a population mean — simple random sampling or stratified sampling? Why?
18. What is a proportionate stratified sample? What is a disproportionate stratified sample? What must be known about the parent population to select each?
19. What is a cluster sample? How is a cluster sample selected?
20. What are the similarities and differences between a cluster sample and a stratified sample?

21. What is statistical efficiency? What is economic efficiency? What is overall efficiency?

22. Which sampling method is typically most statistically efficient? Which method is typically most economically efficient? Which method is typically most efficient overall? Why?

23. What is a systematic sample? How are the random start and sampling interval determined with a systematic sample?

24. What are the advantages and disadvantages associated with systematic samples?

25. What is an area sample? Why are area samples used?

26. How does a two-stage area sample differ from a one-stage area sample?

27. Illustrate the selection of a simple, two-stage area sample using hypothetical data of your own choosing.

28. Illustrate probability-proportional-to-size two-stage area sampling using an example of your own choosing.

29. What information is needed to effectively draw
    a. a simple, two-stage area sample?
    b. a probability-proportional-to-size area sample?

Applications and Problems

1. For each of the following situations, identify the appropriate target population and sampling frame.
    a. The National Head Injury Foundation, Inc., wants to test the effectiveness of a brochure soliciting volunteers for its local chapter in Indianapolis, Indiana.
    b. A regional manufacturer of yogurt selling primary in the Pacific Northwest wants to test market three new flavors of yogurt.
    c. A national manufacturer wants to assess whether adequate inventories are being held by wholesalers in order to prevent shortages by retailers.
    d. A large wholesaler dealing in electronic office products in Chicago wants to evaluate dealer reaction to a new discount policy.
    e. Your school cafeteria system wants to test a carbonated milk product manufactured in the Food Science department and sold by the cafeteria system.
    f. A local cheese manufacturer wants to assess the satisfaction with a new credit policy offered to mail-order customers.
    g. A regional manufacturer of hog feed wants to conduct an on-farm test of a new type of hog feed in Carroll Count, Indiana.

2. A leisure-wear manufacturer wants to determine consumer preference for several varieties of t-shirts. Respondents will participate in a touch test; that is, they will touch several different t-shirts and then state their preferences. Some aspects of the t-shirts that will be compared are armbands, neckbands, and shirt material. The marketing researcher conducting the study has recommended that the touch tests be conducted by mall intercepts.
    a. What problems, if any, do you see in trying to use the results of this study to estimate the population of consumers who buy t-shirts?
    b. Suggest an alternative to a mall intercept study for determining consumer preferences for t-shirts. Why is this a better method?

3. A leading film-processing company wishes to investigate the market potential for a new line of digital-processing equipment. Because this is a completely new technology, it is felt that industry leaders might offer insights into the desires of customers and consumers. However, a list of industry leaders does not exist. Discuss possible methods of generating a sampling frame for the influential people in the digital-processing industry.

4. The My-Size Company, a manufacturer of clothing for large-sized consumers, was in the process of evaluating its product and advertising strategy. Initial efforts consisted of a number of focus-group interviews. Each focus group consisted of 10 to 12 large men and women of different demographic characteristics who were selected by the company's research department using on-the-street observations of physical characteristics.
   a. What type of sampling method was used?
   b. Critically evaluate the method used.

5. The owners of a popular bed and breakfast inn in Door County, Wisconsin, had noticed a decline in the number of tourists and length of stay during the past three years. An overview of industry trends indicated that the overall tourist trade was expanding and growing rapidly. The managers decided to conduct a study to determine people's attitudes towards the particular activities that were available at the inn. Because they wanted to cause the minimum amount of inconvenience to their guests, the owners devised the following plan. Interview request cards, which were available at the Chamber of Commerce office, the Visitor Information Center, and three of the more popular restaurants in Sturgeon Bay, indicated the nature of the study and encouraged visitors to participate. Visitors were asked to report to a separate room at either the Chamber of Commerce office or the Visitor Information Center. Personal interviews, lasting 20 minutes, were conducted at these locations.
   a. What type of sampling method was used?
   b. Critically evaluate the method used.

6. A national manufacturer of processed meats was planning to enter the Japanese market. Before the final decision about launching its product, management decided to test market the products in two cities. After reviewing the various cities in terms of external criteria such as demographics, shopping characteristics, and so on, the research department settled on the cities of Yokohama and Hiroshima.
   a. What type of sampling method was used?
   b. Critically evaluate the method used.

7. The Now-You-See-Now-You-Don't Credit Union of Wichita, Kansas, has witnessed a sharp increase in the number of branches it operates and in the company's gross sales and net profit margin in the past five years. Management plans to offer free retirement planning and consultation, a service for which other competing credit unions, banks, and brokerage firms charge a substantial price. To offset the increase in operating expenses, management plans to raise the rates on other services by 7 percent. Before introducing this new service and increasing rates, management decides to do a survey using customers as a sample and employing the method of quota sampling. Your assistance is required in planning the study.
   a. On what variables would you suggest the quotas be based? Why? List the variables with their respective levels.
   b. Management has kept close track of the demographic characteristics of customers during the five-year period and decides that these would be most relevant in identifying the sample elements to be used.

Variable	Level	Percentage of Customers
Age	0–15 years	5%
	16–30 years	30
	31–45 years	30
	46–60 years	15
	61–75 years	15
	76 years or over	5
Sex	Male	42
	Female	58
Income	$0–$9,999	10
	$10,000–$19,999	20
	$20,000–$29,999	30
	$30,000–$39,999	20
	Over $40,000	20

Based on these three quota variables, indicate the characteristics of a sample of 200 subjects.

c. Discuss the possible sources of bias with the sampling method.

8. The following table lists the results of one question taken from a survey conducted for Joe's Bar and Grill. The Grill has recently undergone renovations, and with the new look, management has decided to change the menu. They are interested in knowing how well customers like the new menus. Calculate the mean, standard deviation, and confidence interval for menu preference assuming simple random sampling was used.

Respondent	Meal Eaten at Joe's Bar and Grill	Menu Preference on a Five-Point Scale
1	Breakfast	3
2	Breakfast	5
3	Breakfast	4
4	Breakfast	5
5	Breakfast	5
6	Lunch	10
7	Lunch	9
8	Lunch	8
9	Lunch	10
10	Lunch	9
11	Dinner	14
12	Dinner	15
13	Dinner	15
14	Dinner	14
15	Dinner	16

9. The Wisconsin National Bank, headquartered in Milwaukee, Wisconsin, has some 400,000 users of its credit card scattered throughout the state of Wisconsin. The application forms for the credit card ask for the usual information about name, address,

phone, income, education, and so on that is typical of such applications. The bank is now very interested in determining if there is any relationship between the uses to which the card is put and the socioeconomic characteristics of the using party; for example, is there a difference in the characteristics of those people who use the credit card for major purchases only (for example, appliances) and those who use it for minor as well as major purchases.

a. Identify the population and sampling frame that would be used by Wisconsin National Bank.

b. Indicate how you would draw a simple random sample from the sampling frame identified in Part a.

c. Indicate how you would draw a stratified sample from the sampling frame.

d. Indicate how you would draw a cluster sample from the sampling frame.

e. Which method would be preferred? Why?

10. Howdy Supermarkets is considering entering the Cleveland market. However, before doing so, management wishes to estimate the average square feet of selling space among potential competitors' stores to plan better the size of the proposed new outlet. A stratified sample of supermarkets in Cleveland produced the following results:

Size	Total Number in City	Number of This Size in Sample	Mean Size of Stores in Sample (sq. ft.)	Standard Deviation of Stores in Sample (sq. ft.)
Small supermarkets	490	24	4,000	2,000
Medium supermarkets	280	14	27,000	4,000
Large supermarkets	40	2	60,000	5,000

a. Estimate the average-size supermarket in Cleveland. Show your calculations.

b. Develop a 95 percent confidence interval around this estimate. Show your calculations.

c. Was a proportionate or a disproportionate stratified sample design used in determining the number of sample observations for each stratum? Explain.

11. A long-distance telephone company wants to investigate the needs of its customers. Propose a stratification scheme for the sample and discuss the benefits of your scheme.

12. Use the table in Question 8 to calculate the mean, standard deviation, and confidence interval for menu preference assuming stratified sampling based on the meal eaten was used (that is, the strata were breakfast, lunch, and dinner customers). How do the results obtained from assuming a stratified sampling technique compare with the results you obtained using simple random sampling? Why?

13. Andy Smith, the owner of a local hotel, is interested in assessing customer satisfaction with his hotel. Andy's hotel does not accept reservations. Because all of his customers are walk-ins, Andy has no way of knowing how many people will stay in his hotel on any given night. All of the hotel guests must check in with the front-desk clerk; due to the small size of the hotel, there is only one check-in terminal. Andy has decided to distribute a survey to every tenth room that checks in.

a. What type of sampling is to be used?

b. Critically evaluate this method.

Thorndike Sports Equipment Video Case

1. What does the distribution of racquet weights tell Ted? How is the distribution of weights important to the research question?

2. Does the variation in racquet weights explain the increasing number of complaints?

3. With the distribution information, is Ted able to solve Thorndike's racquet problem?

4. A new machine to keep racquetball racquets a consistent weight is not feasible. What would you do next?

5. With the results of Luke's test, can Thorndike Sports Equipment now claim that its racquets can withstand 240 pounds without breaking? Identify the problems in Luke's research design.

6. If Luke truly feels there is strategic advantage to advertising the resiliency of the Thorndike Graphite Pro racquets, design a test that will provide a valid and reliable answer to how much weight the racquets can withstand before breaking.

7. What are the current legal restrictions on making claims of this sort in advertising copy?

11

Sample Size

Thus far, our discussion of sampling has concentrated on sample type. Another important consideration is sample size. Unless the researcher is going to use a sequential sample, he or she needs some means of determining the necessary size of the sample before collecting data.

The question of sample size is complex because it depends on (among other things) the type of sample; the statistic in question; the homogeneity of the population; and the time, money, and personnel available for the study. There is no way we can do all of these issues justice in one chapter. Rather, our objective will be to illustrate the statistical principles determining sample size, using only simple random samples and a few of the more popular statistics. The reader interested in the determination of sample size for stratified or cluster samples should consult one of the standard references on sampling theory. The reader using a simple random sample to estimate a population variance, for example, should consult an intermediate-level statistics text to determine the proper sample size. The principles will remain the same in each case, but the formulas differ, since they depend on the sampling plan and the statistic in question.

BASIC CONSIDERATIONS

It should not be surprising to find that the sampling distribution of the statistic underlies the determination of sample size. Recall that the sampling distribution of the statistic indicates how the sample estimates vary as a function of the particular sample selected. The spread of the sampling distribution thus indicates the error that can be associated with any estimate. For instance, the error associated with the estimation of a population mean by a sample mean was given by the standard error of the mean $\sigma_{\bar{x}} = \sigma/\sqrt{n}$ when the population variance was known, and $s_{\bar{x}} = \hat{s}/\sqrt{n}$ when the population variance was unknown. The first factor that one must consider in estimating sample size, then, is the standard error of the estimate obtained from the known sampling distribution of the statistic.

A second consideration is the precision desired from the estimate. Precision is the size of the estimating interval when the problem is one of estimating a population parameter. For example, a researcher investigating mean income might want the sample estimate to be within ±$100 of the true population value. This is a more precise estimate than one required to be within ±$500 of the true value.

ETHICAL DILEMMA 11.1

Researchers in the laboratory of a regional food manufacturer recently developed a new dessert topping. This topping was more versatile than those currently on the market because it came in a variety of flavors and thus had more potential uses than a product like Dream Whip, for instance. Although the manufacturer believed that the product had great promise, management also thought it would be necessary to convince the trade of its sales potential in order to get wholesalers and retailers to handle it. The manufacturer consequently decided to test market the product in a couple of areas where it had especially strong distribution. It selected several stores with which it had a long working relationship to carry the product. During the planned two-month test period, product sales did not begin to compare to sales of other dessert toppings. Feeling that such evidence would make it very difficult to gain distribution, the manufacturer decided to do two things: (1) run the test for a longer period, and (2) increase the number of accounts handling the test product. Four months later, the results were much more convincing and management felt more comfortable in approaching the trade with the test market results.

- Is it ethical to conduct a test market in an area where a firm's distribution or reputation are especially strong?
- Is it ethical not to report this fact to the trade, thereby causing it to misinterpret the market response to the item?
- Is it ethical to increase the size of the sample until one secures a result one wants? What if the argument for increasing sample size was that the product was so novel that two months simply was not enough time for consumers to become sufficiently familiar with it?
- Would it have been more ethical to plan initially for a larger and longer test than to adjust the length and scope of the test on the basis of early results? Why or why not?

A third factor that must be considered is the desired degree of confidence associated with the estimate. There is a trade-off between degree of confidence and degree of precision with a sample of fixed size; one can specify either the degree of confidence or the degree of precision but not both. It is only when sample size is allowed to vary that one can achieve both a specified precision and a specified degree of confidence in the result, and, as a matter of fact, the determination of sample size involves balancing the two considerations against each other.[1]

---

[1]Bayesian analysts also consider the cost of wrong decisions when determining sample size. See, for example, Robert Schlaifer, *Probability and Statistics for Business Decisions* (New York: McGraw-Hill, 1959), pp. 536–552. For a comparison of classical and Bayesian procedures for determining sample size, see Seymour Sudman, *Applied Sampling* (New York: Academic Press, 1976), pp. 85–105. For an application of Bayesian procedures, see Hugh M. Cannon, David L. Williams, and Ishmael P. Akaah, "A Technique for Increasing the Reliability of Syndicated Product-Media Research," *Journal of Advertising Research,* 30 (June/July 1990), pp. 31–37.

To illustrate the distinction between confidence and precision, consider a point estimate of a population parameter — say, mean income. A point estimate is a precise estimate in that there are no associated bounds of error; for example, the sample mean indicates that the population mean income is $19,243. This point estimate is also most assuredly wrong, and thus we can have no confidence in it. On the other hand, we can have complete confidence in the following statement: The population mean income is between zero and $1 million. Although we're completely confident about the accuracy of the statement, we must admit that the statement is not particularly helpful, because it tells us next to nothing about mean income. The statement is simply too imprecise to be of value.

SAMPLE SIZE DETERMINATION WHEN ESTIMATING MEANS

The interrelation of the basic factors affecting the determination of sample size is best illustrated through example. Consider a simple random sample to estimate the mean annual expenditures of licensed fishermen on food and lodging while on fishing trips within a given state.[2] Now, the Central-Limit Theorem suggests that the distribution of sample means will be normal for samples of reasonable size regardless of the distribution of expenditures in the population of fishermen. Consider, then, the sampling distribution of sample means in Figure 11.1 and distinguish two cases: Case I, in which the population variance is known, and Case II, in which the population variance is unknown.

Case I: Population Variance Known   The population variance might be known from past studies, even though the average expenditures for food and lodging might be unknown, since variation typically changes much more slowly than level.[3] This means that the spread of the distribution given by $\sigma_{\bar{x}}$, as shown in Figure 11.1, is also known up to a proportionality constant, the square root of the sample size, because $\sigma_{\bar{x}} = \sigma/\sqrt{n}$. Thus, we have some idea of the first ingredient in sample size determination, the standard error of estimate.

Suppose that the decision maker desired the estimate to be within $\pm\$25$ of the true population value. Total precision is thus $50, and half precision (call it *H)* is $25. The reason we work with *H* instead of the full length of the interval is that the normal curve is symmetrical about the true population mean, and it simplifies the calculations to work with only one-half of the curve.

The remaining item that needs to be specified is the degree of confidence desired in the result. Suppose the decision maker further wishes to be 95 percent confident that the

---

[2]The problem would be of interest to the tourist industry, and it also could be of interest to the division of state government concerned with economic development. The problem was chosen because the availability of a list of population elements allows a simple random sample to be selected.

[3]Morris H. Hansen, William N. Hurwitz, and William G. Madow, *Sample Survey Methods and Theory: Vol. 1: Methods and Applications* (New York: John Wiley, 1953). One of the best treatments on securing variance estimates from past data is to be found on pages 450–455.

FIGURE 11.1   **Sampling Distribution of Sample Means**

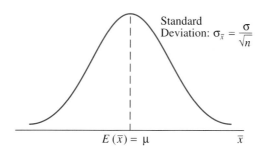

interval the researcher constructs will contain the true population mean. This implies that z is approximately equal to 2.[4]

Now we have all we need for determining sample size, because it is known that a number of standard deviations on each side of the mean will include a certain proportion of all observations with a normal curve and, in particular, that two standard deviations will include 95 percent of all observations. In Figure 11.1, each observation is a sample mean; the distribution of these sample means is centered about the population mean, and two standard deviations are $2\sigma_{\bar{x}}$, or $z\sigma_{\bar{x}}$ in the general case. We want our estimate to be no more than \$25 removed from the true population value, so we can simply equate the size of the specified half interval with the number of standard deviations to yield

$$H = z\sigma_{\bar{x}} \qquad\qquad (11.1)$$

$$= z\,\frac{\sigma}{\sqrt{n}}.$$

This equation can be solved for n, since H and z have been specified and σ is known from past studies. Specifically, n can be shown to be equal to

$$n = \frac{z^2}{H^2}\,\sigma^2. \qquad\qquad (11.2)$$

To illustrate, suppose that the historic variation in expenditures on food and lodging as measured by σ was \$100. Then

$$n = \frac{(2)^2}{(25)^2}\,(100)^2$$

and $n = 64$. Thus, only a relatively small sample needs to be taken to estimate the mean expenditure level when the population standard deviation is \$100 and the allowed precision is \$50.

---

[4]z more correctly equals 1.96 for a 95 percent confidence interval. The approximation $z = 2$ is used because it simplifies the calculations.

Note what happens, though, if the estimate must be twice as precise; that is, $25 is the total width of the desired interval and $H = 12.5$. Substituting in Equation 11.2,

$$n = \frac{(2)^2}{(12.5)^2}(100)^2$$

and $n = 256$. Doubling the precision (halving the total width of the interval) increased the required sample size by a factor of four. This is the basic trade-off between precision and sample size. Whenever precision is increased by a factor c, sample size is increased by a factor c^2. Thus, if the desired precision were $10 instead of $50— in other words, the estimate must be five times more precise ($c = 5$)—the sample size would be 1,600 instead of 64 ($c^2 = 25$).

One also pays dearly for increases in the degree of confidence. For example, what if one wished to be 99 percent confident in one's estimate rather than 95 percent confident. Using the integer approximations for z means that $z = 3$ instead of 2 as before. Suppose that $H = 25$ and $\sigma = 100$ as originally. Then

$$n = \frac{(3)^2}{(25)^2}(100)^2$$

and $n = 144$, whereas $n = 64$ when $z = 2$. When z was increased by a factor of $d(d = \frac{3}{2}$ in the example), sample size increased by a factor of $d^2(d^2 = \frac{9}{4}$ in the example).

The point of all these gyrations is that you should be well aware of the price that must be paid for increased precision and confidence. Although we might constantly strive for very precise estimates in which we can have a great deal of confidence, one can see why applied researchers often learn to live with risky, somewhat imprecise estimates. The degree of precision and lack of confidence that can be tolerated is, of course, a function of the consequences of the decision associated with the result. The more dire the consequences, the more precise and confident the results must be.

Case II: Population Variance Unknown   The previous examples were all framed employing a known population variance. What happens in the more typical case when the population variance is unknown? The procedure for estimating the sample size is the same except that an estimated value of σ is used in place of the previously known value of σ. Once the sample is selected, however, the variance calculated from the sample is used in place of the originally estimated variance when establishing confidence intervals.

Suppose that there were no past studies on which to base an estimate of σ. How does one then generate an estimate of the population standard deviation? One could do a pilot study.[5] Alternatively, sometimes the variance can be estimated from the conditions surrounding the approach to the problem. Research Realities 11.1, for example, dis-

---

[5]See Raphael Gillett, "Confidence Interval Construction by Stein's Method: A Practical and Economical Approach to Sample Size Determination," *Journal of Marketing Research*, 26 (May 1989), pp. 237–240, for discussion of how the pilot study results can be used not only to develop an estimate of the population variance but also to produce an estimate of the population mean corresponding to the specified confidence level and desired interval size.

Research Realities 11.1

Guidelines for Estimating Variance for Data Obtained Using Rating Scales

Rating scales are doubly-bounded: on a 5-point scale, for instance, responses cannot be less than 1 or greater than 5. This constraint leads to a relationship between the mean and the variance. For example, if a sample mean is 4.6 on a 5-point scale, there must be a large proportion of responses of 5, and it follows that the variance must be relatively small. On the other hand, if the mean is near 3.0, the variance can be potentially much greater. The nature of the relationship between the mean and the variance depends on the number of scale points and on the "shape" of the distribution of responses (e.g., approximately normal or symmetrically clustered around some central scale value, or skewed, or uniformly spread among the scale values). By considering the types of distribution shapes typically encountered in practice, it is possible to estimate variances for use in calculating sample size requirements for a given number of scale points.

Table 1 lists ranges of variances likely to be encountered for various numbers of scale points. The low end of the range is the approximate variance when data values tend to be concentrated around some middle point of the scale, as in a normal distribution. The high end of the range is the variance that would be obtained if responses were uniformly spread across the scale points. Although it is possible to encounter distributions with larger variances than those listed (such as distributions with modes at both ends of the scale), such data are rare.

In most cases, data obtained using rating scales tend to be more uniformly spread out than in a normal distribution. Hence, to arrive at conservative sample-size estimates (i.e., sample sizes that are *at least* large enough to accomplish the stated objectives), it is advisable to use a variance estimate at or near the high end of the range listed.

TABLE 1

Number of Scale Points	Typical Range of Variances
4	0.7–1.3
5	1.2–2
6	2–3
7	2.5–4
10	3–7

Source: *Research on Research,* No. 37 (Chicago: Market Facts, Inc., undated).

cusses the estimation of the variance when rating scales are used to measure the important variables. Still a third possibility is to take into account the fact that for a normally distributed variable, the range of the variable is approximately equal to plus or minus three standard deviations. Thus, if one can estimate the range of variation, one can estimate the standard deviation by dividing by six. A little *a priori* knowledge of the phenomenon is often enough to estimate the range. If the estimate is in error, the consequence is a confidence interval more or less precise than desired. Let us illustrate.

Certainly there would be some licensed fishermen who would spend zero dollars on food and lodging while on fishing trips since they would be making only one-day trips. Some might also be expected to go on several one-week trips a year. Suppose that 15 days a year were considered typical of the upper limit, and food and lodging expenses were calculated at $30 per day; the total dollar upper limit would be $450. The range would also be 450, and the estimated standard deviation would then be 450/6 = 75.

With desired precision of $\pm\$25$ and a 95 percent confidence interval, the calculation of sample size is now

$$n = \frac{z^2}{H^2} (\text{est. } \sigma)^2$$

$$= \frac{(2)^2}{(25)^2} (75)^2$$

and $n = 36$.

A sample of Size 36 would then be selected and the information collected. Suppose that these observations generated a sample mean, $\bar{x} = 35$, and a sample standard deviation, $\hat{s} = 60$. The confidence interval is then, as before,[6]

$$\bar{x} \pm z s_{\bar{x}}$$

or

$$35 \pm 2 \frac{\hat{s}}{\sqrt{n}} = 35 \pm 2 \frac{60}{\sqrt{36}} = 35 \pm 20$$

or

$$15 \leq \mu \leq 55.$$

Note what has happened. The desired precision was $\pm \$25$; the obtained precision is $\pm\$20$. The interval is narrower than planned (a bonus) because we overestimated the population standard deviation as judged by the sample standard deviation. If we had underestimated the standard deviation, the situation would have been reversed, and we would have ended up with a wider confidence interval than desired.

Relative Precision

The preceding examples were all framed employing **absolute precision.** The estimates were to be within plus or minus so many units (dollars). It is also possible to frame the calculations of sample size employing **relative precision,** meaning that precision is expressed relative to level. When level is measured by the mean, relative precision suggests that the estimate should be within plus or minus so many percentage points of the mean regardless of its value. Thus, it may be that an estimate within $\pm$ 10 percent of the mean is required; if the mean is 50, the interval will be from 45 to 55, whereas if the mean is 100, the interval will be from 90 to 110.

Relative precision presents few new problems for the calculation of sample size. The measure of absolute precision H is simply replaced by the measure of relative precision in Equation 11.1. That is,

---

[6]One would more strictly use the t distribution to establish the interval, since the population variance was unknown. The example was framed using the approximate $z = 2$ value for a 95 percent confidence interval so as to better illustrate the consequences of a poor initial estimate of σ.

$$H = z \frac{\sigma}{\sqrt{n}}$$

is changed to

$$r\mu = z \frac{\sigma}{\sqrt{n}},$$

where r is the measure of relative precision and μ is the unknown parent population mean. This formula can be transformed so that sample size can be read directly. Simply divide both sides of the equation by $r\mu$ and multiply both sides by n^2 to yield

$$n = \frac{z^2}{r^2} \left(\frac{\sigma}{\mu}\right)^2. \qquad (11.3)$$

Recall from your beginning statistics course that σ/μ is the coefficient of variation C, and thus the formula for sample size reduces to

$$n = \frac{z^2}{r^2} C^2.$$

Here z^2 would be known because z is determined by the desired level of confidence, and r^2 would also be known because r is determined by the expressed level of precision. C would have to be estimated. This would entail making a judgment about the size of the population standard deviation relative to the size of the population mean. Again, there might be past studies to guide the judgment. If prior studies are unavailable or prove to be in error, the interval will be wider or narrower to the extent that the estimate of C is larger or smaller than that actually produced by the ratio of the sample standard deviation to the sample mean.

Multiple Objectives

A study is rarely conducted to estimate a single parameter. It is much more typical for a study to involve multiple objectives. Let us assume more realistically, therefore, that the researcher is also interested in estimating the annual mean level of expenditures on tackle and equipment by licensed fishermen and the number of miles traveled in a year on fishing trips. There are now three means to be estimated. Suppose that each is to be estimated with 95 percent confidence and that the desired absolute precision and estimated standard deviation are as given in Table 11.1. Table 11.1 also contains the sample sizes (which were calculated using Equation 11.2) needed to estimate each variable.

The three requirements produce conflicting sample sizes; n should equal 36, 16, or 100, depending on the variable being estimated. The researcher must somehow reconcile these values to come up with a sample size suitable for the study as a whole. The most conservative approach would be to choose $n = 100$, the largest value. This would ensure that each variable is estimated with the required precision, assuming that the estimates of the standard deviations are accurate.

TABLE 11.1   **Sample Size Needed to Estimate Each of Three Means**

	Variable		
	Expenditures on Food and Lodging	**Expenditures on Tackle and Equipment**	**Miles Traveled**
Confidence level	95 percent ($z = 2$)	95 percent ($z = 2$)	95 percent ($z = 2$)
Desired precision	± $25	± $10	± 100 miles
Estimated standard deviation	± $75	± $20	± 500 miles
Required sample size	36	16	100

If the estimate of miles traveled were less critical than the others, however, the use of a sample of Size 100 would be wasteful of resources. A preferred approach would be to focus on those variables that are most critical and to select a sample sufficient in size to estimate them with the required precision and confidence. Those variables indicating that a larger sample needed to be taken would then be estimated with either a lower degree of confidence or less precision than planned. Suppose in this case that the expenditure data were most critical and that the analyst, therefore, decided on a sample size of 36. Suppose also that the information from this sample of 36 fishermen produced a sample mean of $\bar{x} = 300$ and a sample standard deviation of $s = 500$ miles traveled. The estimate of the population standard deviation is thus seen to agree with the sample result, so the confidence interval estimate will not be affected by inaccuracies here.

The confidence interval for miles traveled is then calculated as

$$\bar{x} \pm z s_{\bar{x}} = \bar{x} \pm z \frac{\hat{s}}{\sqrt{n}} = 300 \pm 2 \frac{500}{\sqrt{36}},$$

or $133.3 \leq \mu \leq 466.7$. Whereas the desired precision was ± 100 miles, the obtained precision is ± 166.7 miles. In order to produce an estimate with the desired precision, the degree of confidence would have to be lowered from its present 95 percent level.

SAMPLE SIZE DETERMINATION WHEN ESTIMATING PROPORTIONS

Absolute Precision

The examples considered previously all concern determining sample size to estimate mean values. The population proportion π is often another parameter of interest in marketing. Thus, the researcher might be interested in determining the proportion of licensed fishermen who are from out of state, or from rural areas, or who took at least

FIGURE 11.2   **Approximate Sampling Distribution of the Sample Proportion**

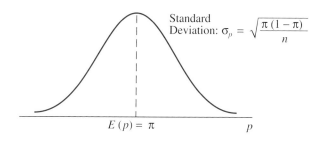

one overnight trip. This section focuses on the determination of sample size necessary to estimate a population proportion.

At the beginning of this chapter we suggested that three things were needed to determine sample size: a specified degree of confidence, specified precision, and knowledge of the sampling distribution of the statistic. The first two items are specified to reflect the requirements of the research problem. Precision can again be expressed absolutely or relatively. With percentages, absolute precision means that the estimate will be within plus or minus so many percentage points of the true value, as, for example, within ± 5 percentage points of the true value.

The remaining consideration, then, is the sampling distribution of the sample proportion. If the sample elements are selected independently, as can reasonably be assumed if the sample size is small relative to the population size, then the *theoretically correct distribution of the sample proportion is the binomial*. But the binomial becomes indistinguishable from the normal with large-size samples or when the population proportion is close to one-half.[7] It is *convenient* to use the normal approximation when estimating sample size. After the sample is drawn and the sample proportion determined, the researcher can always fall back on the binomial distribution to determine the confidence interval if the normal approximation proves to be in error.

The distribution of sample proportions is centered about the population proportion (Figure 11.2). The sample proportion is an unbiased estimate of the population proportion. The standard deviation of the normal distribution of sample proportions (that is, the standard error of the proportion, denoted by σ_p) is equal to $\sqrt{\pi(1-\pi)/n}$. Because we are working again with the normal curve, the level of precision is equated to the number of standard deviations the estimate can be removed from the mean value. But now the mean value is the population proportion, while the standard deviation is the standard error of the proportion; that is,

$$H = z\sigma_p. \tag{11.4}$$

[7]The strict requirement is that $n\pi$ must be above a certain level if the normal curve is to provide a good approximation to the binomial. Some hold that $n\pi$ must be greater than 5, whereas others suggest that the product must be greater than 10.

Substituting $\sqrt{\pi(1 - \pi)/n}$ for σ_p and solving for n yields

$$n = \frac{z^2}{H^2} \pi(1 - \pi). \tag{11.5}$$

Let's say that the researcher is interested in estimating the proportion of all fishermen who took at least one overnight fishing trip in the past year. The researcher wants this estimate within $\pm$ 2 percentage points and he or she wishes to be 95 percent confident in the result. Substitution in Equation 11.5 yields

$$n = \frac{(2)^2}{(0.02)^2} \pi(1 - \pi).$$

This equation contains two unknowns — the population proportion being estimated and the sample size, and is thus not solvable as it stands. In order to determine sample size, the researcher needs to estimate the population proportion. That is right! *The researcher must estimate the very quantity the study is being designed to get at in order to determine sample size.*

This fact is often bewildering and certainly disconcerting to decision makers and beginning researchers alike. Nevertheless, it is true that with proportions one is forced to make some judgment about the approximate value of the parameter in order to determine sample size. This is another example of how information begets information in sample design. One might use past studies or published data to generate an initial estimate. Alternately, one might conduct a pilot study. In the absence of both of these options, one might simply use informed judgment about the probable approximate value of the parameter.

A poor estimate will make the confidence interval more or less precise than desired. Suppose, for example, that the best considered judgment was that 20 percent of all licensed fishermen could be expected to take an overnight fishing trip during the year. Sample size is then calculated to be

$$n = \frac{(2)^2}{(0.02)^2} (0.20)(1 - 0.20)$$

and $n = 1,600$. On receipt of the information from the 1,600 designated fishermen, suppose that the sample proportion p actually turned out to be equal to 0.40. The confidence interval then would be established, employing s_p to estimate the unknown σ_p where $s_p = \sqrt{p(1 - p)/n}$; that is,

$$s_p = \sqrt{\frac{0.40(0.60)}{1,600}} = \sqrt{\frac{0.24}{1,600}} = 0.012.$$

The confidence interval is then

$$p \pm z s_p = 0.40 \pm 2(0.012)$$

or

$$0.376 \leq \pi \leq 0.424.$$

The interval is wider than desired, since the sample proportion was larger than the estimated population proportion.

Suppose that a wider interval than planned was unacceptable. One way of preventing it is to choose the sample size to reflect the "worst of worlds." Note from the formula that the largest sample size will be obtained when the product $\pi(1 - \pi)$ is greatest, because sample size is directly proportional to this quantity. This product is, in turn, greatest when $\pi = 0.5$, as might be intuitively expected, since if one-half of the population behaves one way and the other half the other way, one would require more evidence for a valid inference than if the situation were more clear-cut and a substantial proportion all behaved in the same way.

In the absence of any other information about the population proportion, then, one can always conservatively assume that π is equal to 0.5. The established confidence interval will simply be more precise to the extent that the sample estimate deviates from the assumed 0.5 value.

Relative Precision

The sample size necessary to estimate a population proportion also can be based on a specification of the relative precision to be provided by the estimate. Relative precision means that the size of the interval will be a function of the value — that is, within a certain percentage of the value regardless of its level. Thus, if the relative precision were to be specified to be within $\pm$ 10 percent, this would mean that if the sample proportion were 0.20, the interval would be from 0.18 to 0.22, and if the sample proportion were 0.30, the interval would be from 0.27 to 0.33.

When the interval is specified employing relative precision, the following differences in the calculation of sample size result from the basic formula contained in Equation 11.4. Whereas before

$$H = z\sigma_p,$$

now

$$r\pi = z\sigma_p,$$

where r is the specified relative precision. The formula can be manipulated to express sample size directly, since

$$r\pi = z \sqrt{\frac{\pi(1 - \pi)}{n}}$$

upon substituting the value of σ_p. Simplifying, we obtain

$$n = \frac{z^2}{r^2} \frac{(1 - \pi)}{\pi}. \tag{11.6}$$

Once again some initial estimate of the population proportion is needed to determine the size of sample necessary to estimate that proportion.

To illustrate the calculation, suppose that the population proportion was estimated to be 0.2, the level of confidence was specified at 95 percent ($z = 2$), and the desired level of relative precision $r = 0.10$. Then

$$n = \frac{(2)^2}{(0.10)^2} \frac{(0.8)}{(0.2)} = 1,600.$$

After the information is collected from the sample respondents,

$$s_p = \sqrt{p\,(1 - p)/n}$$

would again be used in calculating the confidence interval.

POPULATION SIZE AND SAMPLE SIZE

Although you may not have noticed it before, consider it now: *The size of the population did not enter into the calculation of the size of sample.* That is right! Except for one slight modification to be discussed shortly, the size of the population has *no direct effect* on the size of the sample.

Although perhaps contrary to your expectations at first, consider this statement for a minute. When estimating a mean, if all population elements have exactly the same value of the characteristic, then a sample of one is all that is needed to determine the mean. This is true whether there are 1,000, 10,000, or 100,000 elements in the population. The thing that directly affects the size of the sample is the variability of the characteristic in the population. The more variable the characteristic, the larger the sample needed to estimate it with some specified level of precision. This not only makes intuitive sense, but it can be seen directly in the formulas for determining sample size to estimate a population mean; for example, $n = z^2\,\sigma^2/H^2$ with absolute precision and $n = (z^2/r^2)C^2$ with relative precision. Thus, population size affects sample size only indirectly through its impact on variability. The larger the population, the greater the potential for variation of the characteristic.

It is perhaps less startling to find that population size does not affect sample size when estimating a proportion than when estimating a mean. With a proportion, the determining factor, as we have seen, is the estimated proportion of the population possessing the characteristic; the closer the proportion is to 0.5, the larger the sample that will be needed, regardless of the size of the population. A value of 0.5 signifies greatest variability, because one-half of the population possesses the characteristic and one-half does not.

The slight modification alluded to earlier arises through the finite population correction. We saw previously that many of our results hold when the sample elements are drawn independently of one another. When the sample is small relative to the population, the independence assumption is justified. However, when the sample represents a large portion of the population, the independence assumption is no longer warranted, and the formulas derived under this assumption must be altered accordingly. Thus, for example, we saw in Chapter 10 that the formula for the standard error of the mean was $\sigma_{\bar{x}} = \sigma/\sqrt{n}$ under the independence assumption, whereas it was

$$\sigma_{\bar{x}} = \frac{\sigma}{\sqrt{n}} \sqrt{\frac{N-n}{N-1}}$$

when the sample elements were not independent of one another. The factor $(N - n)/(N - 1)$ is the finite population correction factor.

When the estimated sample represents more than 5 percent of the population, the calculated size should be reduced by the finite population correction factor.[8] Thus, for example, if the population contained 100 elements and the calculation of sample size indicated a sample of 20 needed to be taken, less than 20 observations would, in fact, be taken to reflect the dependency that existed among the observations. The required sample would be given as $n' = nN/(N + n - 1)$, where n was the originally determined size and n' was the revised size. Thus, with $N = 100$ and $n = 20$, only 17 sample elements would need to be employed.

OTHER PROBABILITY SAMPLING PLANS

So far, the discussions of sample size were based on simple random samples. You should be aware, though, that there are also formulas for determining sample size when other probability sampling plans are used. The formulas are more complex, to be sure, but the same underlying principles still apply. One still needs a knowledge of the sampling distribution of the statistic in addition to the research specifications regarding level of precision and degree of confidence.

The issue of sample size is compounded, however, by the fact that one now has a number of strata or a number of clusters with which to work. This means that one has to deal with within-strata variability and within- and between-cluster variability in calculating sample size, whereas with simple random sampling, only total population variability entered the picture. As before, the more variable the strata or cluster, the larger the sample that needs to be taken from it, other things being equal. This is precisely the basis for disproportionate stratified sampling discussed in Chapter 10. One of the other things that must be equal is cost. Cost did not enter directly into the calculation of sample size with simple random sampling, although it does affect sample size. Perhaps the costs of data collection with a sample of the calculated size would simply exceed the research budget, in which case cost would act to constrain sample size below that indicated by the formulas. Of course, with a simple random sample one could also base the

---

[8]The 5 percent correction factor is not a hard-and-fast rule. Some contend that the finite population correction factor should be ignored if the sample includes no more than 10 percent of the population. Cochran suggests that the finite population correction can be ignored whenever the "sampling fraction does not exceed 5 percent and for many purposes even if it is as high as 10 percent." William G. Cochran, *Sampling Techniques,* 3rd ed. (New York: John Wiley, 1977), p. 25. See also Richard L. Schaeffer, William Mendenhall, and Lymann Ott, *Elementary Survey Sampling,* 4th ed., (Boston: PWS-Kent Publishing Co., 1990). Ignoring the finite population correction will result in overestimating the standard error of estimate.

calculation of sample size directly on cost per observation and the size of the data collection budget. The fact remains, though, that cost per observation did not enter into the formulas for calculating sample size with simple random samples.

With stratified or cluster samples, cost exerts a direct impact. In calculating sample size, one has to allow for unequal costs per observation by strata or by cluster, and in implementing the sample size calculation, one has to have some initial estimate of these costs. The task then becomes one of balancing variability against costs and assessing the trade-off function relating the two. With a stratified sample, for example, one would want to sample most heavily that stratum which was most variable if cost was the same by strata, or which had the lowest cost per observation if the variability was the same within strata. Since the cost per observation or variability probably will not be the same for each stratum, the challenge becomes one of determining sample size by considering the precision likely to result from sampling each stratum at a given rate. Formulas are available for this purpose, as they are for cluster samples. We shall not go into these formulas here, as they are readily available in the standard works on sampling theory and fall largely in the domain of the sampling specialist.[9] You should be aware, though, that when dealing with stratified or cluster samples, cost per observation by subgroup directly enters the calculation of sample size.

You should also know that there are formulas for determining sample size when the problem is one of hypothesis testing and not confidence interval estimation. Once again, the principles are the same, although there are some additional considerations such as the levels of Type I and Type II errors to be tolerated and the issue of whether it is necessary to detect subtle differences or only obvious differences. We shall not deal with these formulas, because they are readily available in standard statistical works and their discussion would take us too far afield.[10]

USING ANTICIPATED CROSS CLASSIFICATIONS TO DETERMINE SAMPLE SIZE

The discussion thus far has focused on the determination of sample size using only statistical principles, particularly the trade-off between degree of confidence and degree of precision while considering only sampling error. The arguments were framed this way to cast them into bold relief. In applied problems, the size of the sample is also going to be affected by certain practical considerations, such as the total size of the budget for the study and the anticipated cost per observation, the size of the sample that may be needed

---

[9]See, for example, Cochran, *Sampling Techniques;* Hansen, Hurwitz, and Madow, *Sample Survey Methods;* Leslie Kish, *Survey Sampling* (New York: John Wiley, 1965); R. L. Jensen, *Statistical Survey Techniques* (New York: John Wiley, 1978); Schaeffer, Mendenhall, and Ott, *Elementary Survey Sampling;* Paul S. Levy and Stanley Lemeshaw, *Sampling of Populations: Methods and Applications* (New York: John Wiley and Sons, Inc., 1991).

[10]Computer-based expert systems that rely on artificial intelligence techniques also exist for determining sample size. These systems guide the researcher through a series of questions about the needed degree of confidence, precision, variability, and so on and, based on the answers, perform the tedious computations concerning the needed sample size. See, for example, Ex-Sample,™ which is available from The Idea Works in Columbia, Missouri.

TABLE 11.2   **Number and Proportion of Fishermen Staying Overnight as a Function of Age and Income**

Income	Age				
	Less than 20	**20–29**	**30–39**	**40–49**	**50 and over**
Less than $10,000					
$10,000–$19,999					
$20,000–$29,999					
$30,000–$39,999					
$40,000 and over					

to convince skeptical executives who do not understand statistical notions that they indeed can have confidence in the results, and so on. One of the more important practical bases for determining the size of sample that will be needed is the anticipated cross classifications to which the data will be subjected.

Suppose, for example, that in our problem of estimating the proportion of all fishermen who took at least one overnight fishing trip in the past year, we were also interested in assessing whether the likelihood of engaging in this behavior is somehow related to an individual's age and income. Suppose further that the age categories of interest were less than 20, 20–29, 30–39, 40–49, and 50 and over, while the income categories of interest were less than $10,000, $10,000–$19,999, $20,000–$29,999, $30,000–$39,999, and over $40,000. There are thus five age categories and five income categories for which the proportion of fishermen taking an overnight trip would be estimated. Although we might reasonably estimate these proportions for each variable considered separately, we should also recognize that the two variables are interrelated, in that increases in incomes are typically related to increases in age. To allow for this interdependence, we need to consider the effect of the two variables simultaneously. The way to do this is through a cross-classification table in which age and income jointly define the cells.[11]

Table 11.2, for instance, is a cross-classification table that could be used for the example at hand. Note that this dummy table is complete in all respects except for the numbers that actually go in each of the cells.[12] These would, of course, be determined by the data actually collected on the number and proportion of all those sampled who actually made at least one overnight trip. In the table there are 25 cells that need estimation. It is unlikely that the decision maker is going to be very comfortable with an estimate of the proportion staying overnight that is based on only a few cases of the phenomenon. Yet even with a sample of, say, 500 fishermen, there is only a potential of 20 cases per cell if the sample is evenly divided with respect to the age and income

---

[11]In Chapter 13 the procedures for setting up and analyzing cross-classification tables so that the proper inferences can be drawn are discussed.

[12]Refer again to Chapter 4 for a discussion of the notion of dummy tables and how they should be set up so that they are most productive.

levels considered. Further, it is very unlikely that the sample would split this way, which would put the researcher in the awkward position of estimating the proportion in a cell engaging in this behavior on the basis of less than 20 cases.

ETHICAL DILEMMA 11.2

A recent discussion between the account manager for an independent research agency and the marketing people for the client left the account manager feeling perplexed. After numerous discussions, the account manager believed that she had a good handle on the client's problem and major concerns. On the basis of this understanding, she had developed a set of dummy tables by which the client's concerns could be investigated. During the most recent meeting, she had presented these to the client. The client had completely accepted the account manager's recommendation about how the data would be viewed; she closed the meeting by asking how large a sample the account manager would recommend and how much the study would cost. The account manager's anxiety was caused by the fact that she believed from the earlier discussions and some preliminary investigation that two of the seven hypotheses were especially promising. The sample size that was needed to investigate these two hypotheses was almost 60 percent smaller than that needed to address some of the other hypotheses because of the fewer cells in the cross-classification table. The account manager was in a dilemma about whether she should take the safe route and recommend the larger sample size to the client and thereby ensure that all of the planned cross-classifications could be completed or whether she should go with her instinct and recommend the smaller sample size and save the client some money.

- What would you recommend that the account manager do?
- Is it ethical for the account manager to recommend the larger sample size when she is fairly certain that the smaller one will provide the answers the client needs? Is it ethical to do the reverse and recommend the smaller sample when there is some risk that the smaller sample will not adequately answer the problem that the firm was hired to solve?
- What are the account manager's responsibilities to the client in a case like this?

One can reverse this argument to estimate how large a sample should be taken. One simply computes the number of cells in the intended cross classifications. It is given by the *product* of the number of levels of the characteristics forming the cross classification. One then allows for the likely distribution of the variables and estimates the sample size so that the important cells can be estimated with a sufficient number of cases to inspire confidence in the results. One general rule of thumb is that "the sample should be large enough so that there are 100 or more units in each category of the major breakdowns and a minimum of 20 to 50 in the minor breakdowns."[13] *Major breakdown* refers here to the cells in the most critical cross tabulations for the study and *minor breakdown* to the cells in the less important cross classifications. Through all of this, one has to make due allowance for nonresponses, because some individuals designated for inclusion in the sample will be unavailable and others will refuse to participate.[14] The researcher "builds

---

[13]Sudman, *Applied Sampling*, p. 30.

[14]Nonresponse and other nonsampling errors and what can be done about them are discussed in Chapter 12.

up'' the sample, so to speak, from the size of the cross-classification table with due allowance for these considerations.

Perhaps cross classification will not be the basic method used to analyze the data. Perhaps, instead, the main technique will be regression or discriminant analysis or one of the other statistical methods discussed in Part 5. If so, the same arguments for determining sample size apply. That is, one needs a sufficient number of cases to satisfy the requirements of the technique in order to inspire confidence in the results.[15] Different techniques have different sample size requirements, often expressed by the degrees of freedom required for the analysis. Some of these requirements should become obvious when the techniques are discussed. For now, we merely wish to reiterate the important point made earlier when introducing the research process — that the stages are very much related and a decision about one stage can affect all of the other stages. Here a decision about Stage 5 regarding the method of analysis can have an important effect on Stage 4, which precedes it, with respect to the size of the sample that should be selected. Thus, the researcher needs to think through the entire research problem, including how the data will be analyzed, before commencing the data collection process.

USING HISTORIC EVIDENCE TO DETERMINE SAMPLE SIZE

A final method by which an analyst can determine the size of sample to employ is simply to use what others have used for similar studies in the past. Even though this may be different from the optimal size in a given problem, the fact that the contemplated sample size is in line with that used for other similar studies is psychologically comforting, particularly to inexperienced researchers. Research Realities 11.2 summarizes the evi-

---

Research Realities 11.2

Typical Sample Sizes for Studies of Human and Institutional Populations

Number of Subgroup Analyses	People or Households		Institutions	
	National	**Regional or Special**	**National**	**Regional or Special**
None or few	1,000–1,500	200–500	200–500	50–200
Average	1,500–2,500	500–1,000	500–1,000	200–500
Many	2,500+	1,000+	1,000+	500+

Source: Seymour Sudman, *Applied Sampling* (Orlando, Fla.: Academic Press, 1976), p. 87.

---

[15]See, for example, Sande Milton, ''A Sample Size Formula for Multiple Regression Studies,'' *Public Opinion Quarterly,* 50 (Spring 1986), pp. 112–118, for discussion of the procedure for estimating sample size for regression analysis. See also Mark Eakin, Lawrence L. Schkade, and Mary Whiteside, ''Optimal Cost Sampling for Decision Making Models with Multiple Regression Models,'' *Decision Sciences* 20 (Winter 1989), pp. 14–26.

dence. It provides a crude yardstick for evaluating the size of sample determined by other means. Note that national studies typically involve larger samples than regional or special studies. Note further that the number of subgroup analyses has a direct effect on sample size.

SUMMARY

In this chapter we reviewed the basic statistical principles involved in determining the size of a sample. The principles were used to develop confidence interval estimates for either a population mean or a population proportion using simple random samples. The examples demonstrated the influence of the sampling distribution of the statistic, the degree of confidence, and the level of precision on sample size. Both absolute and relative precision were discussed. The general conclusion was that sample size must be increased whenever population variability, degree of confidence, or the precision required of the estimate are increased. The size of the parent population does not affect the size of the sample except indirectly, through its impact on variability or through the finite population correction. Sample size can also be determined using the anticipated cross classifications. One simply multiplies the number of cells by the number of observations required in each cell to inspire confidence in the conclusions. A similar argument applies when other data analysis techniques are to be used; the size of the sample must be large enough to satisfy the requirements of the technique.

■

Questions

1. In determining sample size, what factors must an analyst consider?
2. When estimating a population mean, what is meant by absolute precision? What is meant by relative precision?
3. What is the difference between degree of confidence and degree of precision?
4. Suppose that the population variance is known. How does one then determine the sample size necessary to estimate a population mean with some desired degree of precision and confidence? Given that the sample has been selected, how does one generate the desired confidence interval?
5. How does the procedure in Question 4 differ when the population variance is unknown?
6. What effect would relaxing the absolute precision with which a population mean is estimated by 25 percent have on sample size? Decreasing the degree of confidence from 95 percent to 90 percent? ($z = 1.64$)?
7. Suppose that one wanted to estimate a population mean within ± 10 percent at the 95 percent level of confidence. How would one proceed and what quantities would one need to estimate?
8. What is the difference between absolute precision and relative precision in the estimation of a population proportion?
9. Suppose that one wanted to estimate a population proportion within ± 3 percentage points at the 95 percent level of confidence. How would one proceed and what quantities would one need to estimate?

10. Suppose in Question 9 that the researcher wanted the estimate to be within ± 3 percent of the population value. What would be the procedure now and what quantities would she or he need to estimate?

11. What happens if the sample proportion is larger than the estimated population proportion used to determine sample size? If it is smaller? What value of the population proportion should be assumed if one wishes to take no chance that the generated interval will be larger than the desired interval?

12. What is the correct procedure for treating multiple study objectives when calculating sample size?

13. How does one determine sample size based on anticipated cross classifications of the data?

■

Applications and Problems

1. A survey was being designed by the marketing research department of Conner Peripherals, Inc., a large ($2 billion plus) manufacturer of advanced disk drives for portable computers. The general aim was to assess customer satisfaction with the company's disk drives. As part of this general objective, management wished to measure the average maintenance expenditure per year per computer, the average number of malfunctions or breakdowns per year, and the length of service contracts purchased with new portable computers. Management wished to be 95 percent confident in the results. Further, the magnitude of the error was not to exceed ± $20 for maintenance expenditures, ± 1 malfunction, and ± 3 months. The research department noted that although some individuals and businesses would spend nothing on maintenance expenditures per year, others might spend as much as $400. Also, although some portable computers would experience no breakdowns within a year, the maximum expected would be no more than three. Finally, although some portable computers might not be purchased with a service contract, others might be purchased with up to a 36-month contract.
   a. How large a sample would you recommend if each of the three variables is considered separately? Show all your calculations.
   b. What size sample would you recommend *overall* given that management thought that accurate knowledge of the expenditure on repairs was most important and the service contract length least important?
   c. The survey indicated that the average maintenance expenditure is $100 and the standard deviation is $60. Estimate the confidence interval for the population parameter μ. What can you say about the degree of precision?

2. The management of a major brewery wanted to determine the average ounces of beer consumed per resident in the state of Washington. Past trends indicated that the variation in beer consumption (σ) was 4 ounces. A 95 percent confidence level is required, and the error is not to exceed ± ½ ounce.
   a. What sample size would you recommend? Show your calculations.
   b. Management wanted an estimate twice as precise as the initial precision level and an increase in the level of confidence to 99 percent. What sample size would you recommend? Show your calculations. Comment on your results.

3. The director of a state park recreational center wanted to determine the average amount of money that each customer spent traveling to and from the park. On the basis of the findings, the director was planning on raising the entrance fee. The park director noted

that visitors living near the center had no travel expenses but that visitors living in other parts of the state or out of state traveled upwards of 250 miles and spent about 24 cents per mile. The director wanted to be 95 percent confident of the findings and did not want the error to exceed ± 50 cents.

   a. What sample size should the park director use to determine the average travel expenditure? Show your calculations.

   b. After the survey was conducted, the park director found that the average expenditure was $12.00 and the standard deviation was $7.50. Construct a 95 percent confidence interval. What can you say about the level of precision?

4. A large manufacturer of corrugated paper products recently came under severe criticism from various environmentalists for its disposal of industrial effluent and waste. In response, management launched a campaign to counter the bad publicity it was receiving. A study of the effectiveness of the campaign indicated that about 20 percent of the residents of the city were aware of the campaign and the company's position. In conducting the study, a sample of 480 was used and a 95 percent confidence interval was specified. Six months later, it was believed that 40 percent of the residents were aware of the campaign. However, management decided to do another survey and specified a 99 percent confidence level and a margin of error of ± 3 percentage points.

   a. What sample size would you recommend for this study? Show all your calculations.

   b. After doing the survey, it was found that 35 percent of the population was aware of the campaign. Construct a 99 percent confidence interval for the population parameter.

5. Pac-Trac, Inc., is a large manufacturer of video games. The marketing research department is designing a survey to determine attitudes toward the products. In addition, the percentage of households owning video games and the average usage rate per week are to be determined. The research department wants to be 95 percent confident of the results and does not want the error to exceed ± 3 percentage points for video game ownership and ± 1 hour for average usage rate. Previous reports indicate that about 20 percent of the households own video games and that the average usage rate is 15 hours with a standard deviation of 5 hours.

   a. What sample size would you recommend assuming that only the percentage of households owning video games is to be determined? Show all your calculations.

   b. What sample size would you recommend assuming that only the average usage rate per week is to be determined? Show all your calculations.

   c. What sample size would you recommend assuming that *both* of the preceding variables are to be determined? Why?

After the survey was conducted, the results indicated that 30 percent of the households own video games and that the average usage rate is 13 hours with a standard deviation of 4.

   d. Compute the 95 percent confidence interval for the percentage of individuals owning video games. Comment on the degree of precision.

   e. Compute the 95 percent confidence interval for the average usage rate. Comment on the degree of precision.

6. The local bus company in a southwest city of the United States recently started a campaign to encourage people to increase car pooling or use of public transportation. To assess the effectiveness of the campaign, management wanted to do a survey to determine the proportion of people who had adopted the recommended energy-saving measures.

    a. What sample size would you recommend if the error is not to exceed ± 5 percentage points and the confidence level is to be 90 percent? Show your calculations.

    b. The survey indicated that the proportion adopting the measures was 20 percent. Estimate the 90 percent confidence interval. Comment on the level of precision. Show your calculations.

7. A large meat producer recently developed a new brand of hot dogs. The manufacturer wanted to assess the taste preferences of children under the age of seven for its new brand verses its competitor's leading brand. The manufacturer also wanted to assess the average number of hot dogs that a child under seven eats in a month. The director of marketing research wants to be 95 percent confident in the results of the study and does not want the error to exceed 1 percent on any of the estimates. The director believes that 75 percent of children under seven will prefer the new brand to the competitor's leading brand. Past research has shown that children eat approximately five hot dogs each month with a standard deviation of 1.

    a. What sample size would you recommend assuming that only the percentage of children under seven preferring the manufacturer's new brand of hot dogs is to be determined?

    b. What sample size would you recommend assuming that the average number of hot dogs consumed by a child under seven is to be determined?

    c. The manufacturer decided to use a sample halfway between the two estimates. What is the consequence of doing so?

    d. The actual results of the survey showed that 63 percent of children under seven prefer the manufacturer's new brand of hot dogs to the competitor's hot dogs. Compute the 95 percent confidence interval for this point estimate.

    e. The actual results of the survey showed that a child under seven eats an average of seven hot dogs in a month with a sample standard deviation of 2. Compute the 95 percent confidence interval for this point estimate.

8. The transit system of a major metropolitan area was interested in determining the average number of miles a commuter drives to work. Past studies have shown that the variation (σ) in commuting distances was 5 miles. The managers of the transit system want to be 95 percent confident in the result and do not want the error to exceed .75 mile.

    a. What sample size would you recommend?

    b. The results of the survey showed that commuters actually drive an average of 20 miles to work with a standard deviation of 10. Compute the 95 percent confidence interval.

    c. Compute the 95 percent confidence interval if the mean was found to be 20 miles but the standard deviation was found to be 5 miles.

9. Andy Kendel, the owner of a local record store specializing in disco music from the 1970s, wanted to determine the average age of his customers. Andy estimated a 25-year range from his youngest customer to his oldest customer. He wanted to be 95 percent confident in the results of the survey, and he did not want the error to exceed 9 months.

    a. What sample size would you recommend?

    b. The results of Andy's survey indicated that his customers' average age is 35 with a standard deviation of 15. Construct a 95 percent confidence interval.

10. Mary Scott has just been assigned to do a customer satisfaction study for one of her firm's clients. Mary needs to estimate the sample size required for 95 percent confidence and error not to exceed 5 percent; however, Mary is missing one vital piece of information — the standard error. Suggest to Mary several possible methods of estimating the standard error.

11. Tom Johnson, the owner of a local pizzeria, wanted to conduct a survey to find out local residents' favorite pizza toppings. However, he only had enough funds to have a sample of 100 local residents. Based on the sales of toppings in his pizzeria, Tom expected 40 percent of the residents to like pepperoni the best.

   a. If Tom wanted to be 95 percent confident in the results of this survey, what corresponding level of precision would he be able to achieve?

   b. If Tom instead wanted to not exceed an error rate of 5 percent, what corresponding level of confidence would he be able to achieve?

   c. Relate your results in Parts a and b to the concept that one cannot increase both confidence and precision with a fixed sample size.

12. Worldly Travels is a large travel agency located in Indianapolis, Indiana. Management was concerned about its declining leisure travel-tour business. It believed that the profile of those engaging in leisure travel had changed during the past few years. To determine if that was indeed the case, management decided to conduct a survey to determine the profile of the current leisure travel-tour customer. Three variables were identified that required particular attention. Prior to conducting the survey, the three following dummy tables were developed.

	Age			
Income	**18–24**	**25–34**	**35–54**	**55+**
0–$9,999				
$10,000–$19,999				
$20,000–$29,999				
$30,000–$39,999				
Over $40,000				

	Education			
Age	**Some High School**	**High School Graduate**	**Some College**	**College Graduate**
18–24				
25–34				
35–54				
55+				

	Education			
Income	**Some High School**	**High School Graduate**	**Some College**	**College Graduate**
0–$9,999				
$10,000–$19,999				
$20,000–$29,999				
$30,000–$39,999				
Over $40,000				

a. How large a sample would you recommend be taken? Justify your answer.

b. The survey produced the following incomplete table for the variables of age and education. Complete the table on the basis of the assumption that the two characteristics are independent (even though that assumption is wrong). On the basis of the completed table, do you think that an appropriate sample size was used? If yes, why? If not, why not?

	Education				
Age	**Some High School**	**High School Graduate**	**Some College**	**College Graduate**	**Total**
18–24					100
25–34					200
35–54					350
55+					350
Total	200	400	300	100	1,000

13. Jim Stark, managing partner of Askren Monuments in Indianapolis, wants to know consumer attitudes towards the price of markers. Jim wants to be 99 percent confident of the survey results and within a $30 range of error. Customers can spend between $225 and $1,000 on granite markers, depending on size and intricateness of the marker.

a. What sample size should Jim use to determine the average expenditure on markers? Show your calculations.

b. After performing the survey, Jim found the average expenditure to be $375, with a standard deviation of $95. Construct Jim's 99 percent confidence interval. What can you say about the level of precision?

c. If Jim had been willing to accept 90 percent confidence in his results, what sample size would he have needed? What is Jim's 90 percent confidence interval?

12
CHAPTER

COLLECTING THE DATA:
FIELD PROCEDURES AND
NONSAMPLING ERRORS

The step that follows sample design in the research process is data collection. Data collection entails the use of some kind of field force operating either in the field or from an office, as in a phone or mail survey. This, in turn, raises the questions of selection, training, and control of the field staff. This chapter investigates these issues from the perspective of what can go wrong when conducting a field study. The emphasis will be on those sources of error not previously dealt with. An understanding of the various sources of error in data collection should give much insight into the selection, training, and control questions and should also assist in evaluating the research information on which decisions must be based.

IMPACT AND IMPORTANCE OF NONSAMPLING ERRORS

Two basic types of errors arise in research studies: sampling errors and nonsampling errors. The concept of sampling error underlay much of the discussion in Chapters 10 and 11. Basic to that discussion was the concept of the sampling distribution of some statistic, be it the sample mean, sample proportion, or whatever. The sampling distribution arises because of sampling error. The sampling distribution reflects the fact that the different possible samples that could be drawn under the sampling plan will produce different estimates of the parameter. The statistic simply varies from sample to sample because we are sampling only part of the population in each case. **Sampling error,** then, is "the difference between the observed values of a variable and the long-run average of the observed values in repetitions of the measurement."[1] As we saw, sam-

---

[1] Frederick Mosteller, "Nonsampling Errors," *Encyclopedia of Social Sciences* (New York: Macmillan, 1968), p. 113. See also the special issue of the *Journal of Official Statistics,* 4 (No. 3, 1987), edited by Lars Lyberg, which is devoted to nonsampling errors; Elizabeth Hervey Stephen and Beth J. Soldo, "How to Judge the Quality of a Survey," *American Demographics,* 12 (April 1990), pp. 42–43.

pling errors can be reduced by increasing sample size. The distribution of the sample statistic becomes more and more concentrated about the long-run average value, because the sample statistic is more equal from sample to sample when it is based on a larger number of observations.

Nonsampling errors reflect the many other kinds of error that arise in research, even when the survey is not based on a sample. They can be random or nonrandom. Nonrandom nonsampling errors are the more troublesome of the two. Random errors produce estimates that vary from the true value; sometimes these estimates are above and sometimes below the true value, but they vary on a random basis. The result is that, in the absence of sampling errors, the sample estimate will equal the population value. Nonrandom nonsampling errors, on the other hand, tend to produce mistakes only in one direction. They tend to bias the sample value away from the population parameter. Nonsampling errors can occur because of errors in conception, logic, misinterpretation of replies, statistics, or arithmetic; errors in tabulation or coding; or errors in reporting the results. They are so pervasive that they have caused one writer to lament:

> The roster of possible troubles seems only to grow with increasing knowledge. By participating in the work of a specific field, one can, in a few years, work up considerable methodological expertise, much of which has not been and is not likely to be written down. *To attempt to discuss every way a study can go wrong would be a hopeless venture.*[2] (emphasis added)

Not only are nonsampling errors pervasive, but they are not as well-behaved as sampling errors. Sampling errors decrease with increases in sample size. Nonsampling errors do not necessarily decrease with increases in sample size; they may, in fact, increase. Sampling errors can be estimated if probability sampling procedures are used. The direction, much less the magnitude, of nonsampling errors is often unknown. True, they bias the sample value away from the population parameter, but in many studies it is hard to see whether they cause underestimation or overestimation of the parameter. Nonsampling errors also distort the reliability of sample estimates; the bias resulting from them serves to increase the standard error of estimates of particular statistics to such an extent that the confidence interval estimates turn out to be faulty. Some of the most striking evidence in this regard was gathered in the Consumer Savings Project conducted at the University of Illinois, which specifically investigated the reliability of consumer reports of financial assets and debts by contrasting these reports with known data.

> The empirical studies presented . . . indicate in striking fashion that nonsampling errors are not simply a matter of theory, but do in fact exist and are mainly responsible for the pronounced tendency of survey data to understate aggregates. . . . Not only was this bias present in the survey data, but in many instances the contribution of nonsampling errors to the total variance in the data was so large as to *render meaningless confidence intervals computed*

---

[2]Mosteller, "Nonsampling Errors," p. 113.

Research Realities 12.1

Nonsampling Errors Can Have Disastrous Consequences

The latest survey of what Americans eat was so badly bungled federal agencies may not have the data they need to regulate everything from school lunches and food stamps to food labels and pesticide exposures, a new congressional report concluded.

The flawed survey, for which a private contractor was paid $6.2 million, could present a problem for federal agencies, the food industry, nutritionists, and scientists. All of them rely on the survey, conducted every 10 years, for up-to-date numbers on who is eating what.

For instance, the Environmental Protection Agency uses the survey to find out how much of a particular fruit or vegetable Americans eat when setting its rules on safe levels of pesticide residues. USDA uses data on consumption and income to decide how much and which foods to provide through the Food Stamp and school lunch programs.

And the Food and Drug Administration uses information on how much Americans eat to figure out the "average serving size" on a food label.

"I'm very disappointed to see all these questions and doubts raised about the survey because these are extremely important policy decisions involving bil-lions of dollars relying on supposedly scientific guidance," said Rep. George Brown, D-Calif., who asked the GAO (General Accounting Office) to conduct the study.

The GAO, the non-partisan investigative arm of Congress, criticized both the contractor, National Analysts of Philadelphia, and the USDA for mismanagement of the survey.

National Analysts scientifically selected a sample group of 6,000 households of all incomes and 3,600 low-income households. Surveyors were supposed to return with answers to overall household consumption, as well as individual intake.

But information on the individuals came in from only 34 percent of the households — "a response rate so low that it is questionable whether the data are representative of the U.S. population," the report said.

GAO blamed part of the problem on the survey's long, complicated questionnaire. Researchers found it took up to three hours just to answer questions about foods the household ate. Despite the time demanded, participants received only $2.

The report also lambasted National Analysts' quality control, saying that some interviewers weren't trained well, too many interviewers quit, and that the company did not adequately distribute interviews through the year to minimize seasonal differences in food consumption.

Source: Angelina Herrin, "Food Survey Called Flawed," *The Wisconsin State Journal*, (September 11, 1991), p. 3A.

---

by the usual statistical formulas . . . the magnitude of this type of error *tends,* if anything, *to increase with sample size.*[3] (emphasis added)

Further, more sophisticated samples are not the answer to eliminating nonsampling errors.

If the findings of this project are any indication, increasing attention must be given to the detection and correction of nonsampling errors. Such attention will be needed particularly in

---

[3]Robert Ferber, *The Reliability of Consumer Reports of Financial Assets and Debts* (Urbana, Ill.: Bureau of Economic and Business Research, University of Illinois, 1966), p. 261. There was a series of studies with respect to the single objective. Ferber's monograph provides an overview of the studies and results, although there are six monographs in all. See also Gary Lilien, Rex Brown, and Kate Searls, "Cut Errors, Improve Estimates to Bridge Biz-to-Biz Info Gap," *Marketing News,* 25 (January 7, 1991), pp. 20–21.

the conduct of large-scale, well-designed probability samples, for as the efficiency of a sample design increases and the size of sampling variances decreases, the effect of nonsampling errors becomes progressively more important. Since nonsampling variances are virtually unaffected by sample size, we are faced with the paradoxical situation that the more efficient is the sample design, the more important are nonsampling errors likely to be and the more meaningless are confidence interval computations based on the usual error formulas.[4]

Nonsampling errors are frequently the most important errors that arise in research. No responses from some targeted for inclusion in a study, and poor responses from others — two types of nonsampling errors — can literally wreck havoc with survey results, as Research Realities 12.1 indicates. In special Census Bureau investigations of their size, nonsampling errors were found to be ten times the magnitude of sampling errors.[5] This is not an unusual finding. Rather, a consistent finding is that nonsampling error is the major contributor to total survey error, whereas random sampling error has minimal impact.[6] Nonsampling errors can be reduced, but their reduction depends on improving method rather than increasing sample size. By understanding the sources of nonsampling errors, the analyst is in a better position to reduce them.

TYPES OF NONSAMPLING ERRORS

Figure 12.1 offers a general overview of nonsampling errors. They are of two basic types — errors that are due to nonobservation or to observation. **Nonobservation errors** result from a failure to obtain data from parts of the survey population. Nonobservation errors can happen because part of the population of interest was not included or because some elements designated for inclusion in the sample did not respond.[7] **Observation errors** occur because inaccurate information is secured from the sample elements or because errors are introduced in the processing of the data or in reporting the findings. In many ways, they are more troublesome than nonobservation errors. With nonobservation errors, we at least know we have a problem because of noncoverage or nonresponse.

---

[4]Ferber, ''The Reliability of Consumer Reports,'' p. 266. Wiseman and McDonald make a similar point with the comment, ''The use of very sophisticated sampling schemes when other aspects of the data collection effort are much less sophisticated may result in higher costs than are justified for the resultant data quality.'' See Frederick Wiseman and Philip McDonald, ''Noncontact and Refusal Rates in Consumer Telephone Surveys,'' *Journal of Marketing Research,* 16 (November 1979), p. 483. See also Robert Groves, *Survey Errors and Survey Costs* (New York: John Wiley and Sons, Inc., 1989).

[5]W. H. Williams, ''How Bad Can 'Good' Data Really Be?,'' *The American Statistician,* 32 (May 1978), p. 61. See also Henry Assael and John Keon, ''Nonsampling vs. Sampling Errors in Survey Research,'' *Journal of Marketing,* 46 (Spring 1982), pp. 114–123; Judith T. Lessler and William D. Kalsbeek, *Nonsampling Errors in Surveys* (New York: John Wiley and Sons, Inc., 1992).

[6]See, for example, Ronald Andersen, Judith Kasper, Martin R. Frankel, and Associates, *Total Survey Error* (San Francisco: Jossey Bass, 1979); Paul B. Biemer, *et al., Measurement Errors in Surveys* (New York: John Wiley and Sons, Inc., 1991).

[7]Chapter 13, ''Biases and Nonsampling Errors,'' in the book by Leslie Kish, *Survey Sampling* (New York: John Wiley and Sons, Inc., 1965), is particularly recommended for discussion of the biases arising from nonobservation. See also Eleanor Singer and Stanley Presser, eds., *Survey Research Methods: A Reader* (Chicago: The University of Chicago Press, 1989).

FIGURE **12.1**   **Overview of Nonsampling Errors**

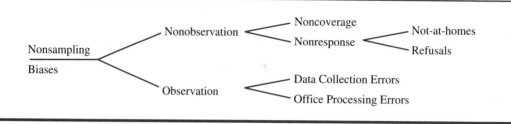

With observation errors, we may not even be aware that a problem exists. The very notion of an observation error rests on the presumption that there is indeed some "true" value for the variable or variables. An observation error, then, is simply the difference between the reported value and the true value. You can readily see that detection of an observation error places the researcher in the awkward position of needing to know the very quantity the study is designed to estimate.

Studies have been specifically designed to estimate the direction and magnitude of data collection errors. Generally, they have

1. relied on the actual availability of bias-free information, which then served as a validity check;
2. used split-run comparisons in which the respondent received different forms of the same questions, say, so that the person's consistency in responding could be measured; or
3. measured the consistency of replies over time from the same respondent.

These methods, while useful, cannot always be applied in substantive as opposed to method studies, and it becomes difficult to adjust the obtained information for response error. Instead this information is taken at face value. Thus, it is vital that researchers understand the sources of response bias so that they can better anticipate and prevent it.

Noncoverage Errors

Noncoverage denotes failure to include some units, or entire sections, of the defined survey population in the actual operational sampling frame. Because of the actual (though unplanned and usually unknown) zero probability of selection for these units, they are in effect excluded from the survey result. We do *not* refer here to any deliberate and explicit exclusion of sections of a larger population from the survey population. Survey objectives and practical difficulties determine such deliberate exclusions. For example, many surveys of attitudes are confined to adults, deliberately excluding persons under 21 years; residents of institutions are often excluded because of practical survey difficulties. These explicit exclusions differ both in intent and result from noncoverage caused by failures in the procedures. When computing noncoverage rates, members of the deliberately and explicitly excluded sections should not be counted either in the survey population or in the noncoverage. Defining the survey population should be part of the stated *essential survey conditions*.[8]

---

[8]Kish, *Survey Sampling*, p. 528.

Noncoverage error is essentially a sampling-frame problem. Research Realities 12.2, for example, describes several of the steps the Census Bureau took to ensure accurate coverage for the 1990 Census. Researchers realize that the telephone directory, for instance, does not provide a complete sampling frame for most general surveys. Not every family has a phone, and not all those people who have telephones have them listed in the directory.[9] Further, there is some variation between those having and not having phones in terms of some important demographic characteristics.

ETHICAL DILEMMA 12.1

During the introduction in a telephone interview, interviewers introduce themselves, provide the research company's name, and then assure potential respondents that the client will be unable to link their responses back to them. However, the interviewer notes the respondents' first names and phone numbers on the completed survey so that the supervisor can randomly select a sample of questionnaires for verification. The possibility of a verification call is explained to the respondents.

   Once the fieldwork has been completed, the research supplier bundles all of the questionnaires and sends them to the client for coding, entry, and analysis. The questionnaires are sent with respondents' names and phone numbers attached.

- Is there a problem with providing the names and phone numbers of respondents to the client company?

- If the client has signed a confidentiality agreement with the field company, is this problem avoided?

Noncoverage is also a problem in mail surveys. The mailing list here dictates the sampling frame. If the mailing list inadequately represents segments of the population, the survey will also suffer from the bias of noncoverage, and rare is the mailing list that exactly captures the population that the researcher wishes to study.

   When the data are to be collected by personal interviews in the home, some form of area sample is typically used to pinpoint respondents. The sampling frame is one of areas and blocks and dwelling units rather than a list of respondents. However, this does not eliminate the incomplete frame problem. Maps of the city may not be totally current, so the newest areas may not have a proper chance of being included in the sample. The instructions to the interviewer may not be sufficiently rigorous. Thus, the direction "Start at the northwest corner of the selected blocks, generate a random start, and take

---

[9]Randolph M. Grossman and Douglas K. Weiland, "The Use of Telephone Directories as a Sample Frame: Patterns of Bias Revisited," *Journal of Advertising,* 7 (Summer 1978), pp. 31–35; Patricia E. Moberg, "Biases in Unlisted Phone Numbers," *Journal of Advertising Research,* 22 (August–September 1982), pp. 51–55. The use of sophisticated sampling schemes is one way in which researchers are trying to deal with the biases in inadequate sampling frames. See, for example, Michael W. Traugott, Robert M. Groves, and James M. Lepkowski, "Using Dual Frame Designs to Reduce Nonresponse in Telephone Surveys," *Public Opinion Quarterly,* 51 (Winter 1987), pp. 522–539; Charles D. Cowan, "Using Multiple Sample Frames to Improve Survey Coverage, Quality, and Costs," *Marketing Research: A Magazine of Management and Applications,* 3 (December 1991), pp. 66–69.

Research Realities 12.2

Steps the Census Bureau Took to Count the Undercounted

The goal of the U.S. census is to count every single American every ten years. But not all Americans have a home, speak English, can read, or are eager to cooperate with the government. To make the 1990 census the most comprehensive ever, the Census Bureau conducted several small-scale "dry runs." During one of these, the 1988 St. Louis Dress Rehearsal Census, several ethnographic studies were carried out to help tackle the specific problems faced by census enumerators in counting those Americans who have traditionally been undercounted.

Ethnography is a social research method that relies on the researcher's participation in the daily lives of the persons or culture being studied. The ethnographer participates over an extended period of time, watching, listening, and asking questions. Ethnographic behavioral research differs from traditional behavioral research by placing the researcher inside the communities being studied. Rather than studying hard-to-count populations as independent observers, the researchers try to understand them by joining in community life.

As part of the St. Louis Dress Rehearsal Census, a group of sociologists at the University of Missouri at St. Louis, who were engaged in long-term ethnographic study of the homeless, attempted to measure how successful the Dress Rehearsal Census was at counting the homeless. The sociologists observed census operations from 6 p.m. to 6 a.m. on three nights when enumerators tried to accurately count homeless people at various shelters. The St. Louis researchers placed participant observers among the homeless population to observe and evaluate the census takers. The group also conducted its own independent count of the street population.

The St. Louis study helped the Census Bureau gain an understanding of the problems census enumerators are likely to experience when trying to count the homeless. As a result of the study and in order to prepare for the 1990 census, census awareness specialists in the regional offices are boosting their efforts to ensure that every community has good lists of shelters and street locations where homeless people congregate.

Although the inability to read and understand Census Bureau forms is an additional obstacle to measuring the homeless, illiteracy and language barriers are problems that plague many other segments of the population as well. During the St. Louis Dress Rehearsal, a study was conducted to evaluate census coverage of the Laotian community. What the researchers discovered was that when many Laotian families received the census form, they had no idea what it was; many thought it was a magazine subscription offer, and they threw it out. Others recognized that it was a government form and sought out translators in social service agencies and churches to assist them in responding. The report recommended community "drop in" assistance centers where Lao speakers would be available to help.

Several Census Bureau studies deal with the problem of underreporting of household residents among African-Americans and Hispanics. Since the early 1970s, researchers have found that African-Americans and Hispanics as groups tend to report not the actual number of people living in any one household but the number who "officially" live there. There are several possible explanations for this. For example, there may be more people actually living in a public housing unit than the housing authority allows, or private housing leases may specify who is supposed to live in the house.

The Census Bureau is conducting three simultaneous studies of nonsampling errors of this kind. One focuses on African-American and Hispanic households in New York City, another examines participation of African-Americans and Hispanics in "underground economies" (business dealings outside the law) and public assistance economies, and a third looks at recidivism among African-American, Hispanic, and Native American parolees and focuses on the difficulty of counting them when they are outside of prison.

Source: "Behavior Studies Look at Groups Traditionally Undercounted," *Census and You,* 24 (July 1989), pp. 3–4. See also David Wessel, "Counting the Homeless Will Tax the Ingenuity of 1990 Census Takers," *The Wall Street Journal* (November 14, 1989), pp. A1, A16.

every fifth dwelling unit thereafter'' would not be sufficiently precise to handle those blocks, say, with a number of apartment units. The evidence indicates, for example, that lower-income households are avoided when the selection of households is made by the field staff rather than by someone in the home office. Further, interviewers typically select the most accessible individuals within the household, contrary to instructions for random selection. This again means that a portion of the intended population is under-represented in the study, while the accessible segment is overrepresented.

There are also sampling-frame problems when personal interviews in shopping malls are used to collect the data. For one thing, there is no list of population elements. Rather, only those people who shop in a particular mall have a chance of being included in the study, and their chances of being included depend on how often they shop there. That is why quota samples are often used in mall-intercept studies.

Noncoverage bias is not eliminated in quota samples, however, whether the interview is conducted in a mall or elsewhere. Rather, the interviewers' flexibility in choosing respondents can introduce substantial noncoverage bias. Interviewers typically underselect in both the high- and low-income classes. This bias is not always discovered, because there is also a tendency for interviewers to falsify characteristics so that the appropriate number of cases per cell is achieved. Further, the more elaborate and complex the quota sample, the more critical this ''forcing'' problem becomes. With three or four variables defining the individual cells, the interviewer finds it difficult to locate respondents who have all the prescribed characteristics.

Overcoverage error can also be a source of bias. It can arise because of duplication in the list of sampling units. Units with multiple entries in the sampling frame (for example, families with several phone listings) have a higher probability of being included in the sample than do sampling units with one listing. For most surveys, however, noncoverage is much more common and troublesome.

Noncoverage bias is not a problem in every survey. For some studies, clear, convenient, and complete sampling frames exist. Thus the department store wishing to conduct a study among its charge-account customers should have little trouble with frame bias. The sampling frame is simply those with charge accounts. There might be some difficulty in distinguishing active accounts from inactive accounts, but this is essentially a definitional problem that should be dictated by the purpose of the study. Similarly, the credit union in a firm should experience little noncoverage bias in conducting a study among its potential clientele. The population of interest here would be the firm's employees, and it could be expected that the list of employees would be current and accurate since it is needed to generate the payroll.

Noncoverage bias raises two questions for the researcher: (1) How pervasive is it likely to be? (2) What can be done to reduce it? One difficulty is that its magnitude can only be estimated by comparing the sample survey results with some outside criterion. The outside criterion can, in turn, be established through an auxiliary quality check of a portion of the results, or it may be available from another reliable and current study, such as the population census. Comparison with the census or another large sample, however, means that the basic sampling units must be similar in terms of operational definitions. The choice of a base, then (for example, dwellings or persons), becomes crucial in effecting such comparisons.

Given that noncoverage bias is likely, what can the researcher do to lessen its effect? The most obvious thing, of course, is to improve the quality of the sampling frame. This may mean taking the time to bring available city maps up to date, or it may mean taking a sample to check the quality and representativeness of a mailing list with respect to a target population. The unlisted number problem common to telephone surveys can be handled by random digit or plus-one dialing, although this will not provide adequate sample representation for those without phones.[10]

There are usually limits to the degree to which an imperfect sampling frame can be improved. Once they are encountered, the researcher's main opportunities for reducing noncoverage bias are through the selection of sampling units and the adjustment of the results, often through weighting subsample results, to account for the remaining imperfections in the frame and sampling procedure. When sampling from lists, for example, three problems are commonly encountered: both ineligibles and duplicates are included on the list, and some members of the target population are excluded. The first thing an analyst would want to do would be to update the list, using supplementary sources if possible. Although this would help reduce the third problem, it might do little to correct the problems of ineligibles and duplicates. These problems can be corrected, though. When the sample is drawn, all ineligibles are ignored. There is a great temptation when doing so to substitute the next name on the list. This is incorrect procedure that introduces a bias, because the probability of selection is higher for those elements that follow ineligible listings. Rather, the correct procedure is to draw another element randomly if simple random selection procedures are being used. If systematic sampling procedures are being used, the sampling interval should be adjusted before the fact to allow for the percentage of ineligibles.[11] The problem of duplicates is then handled by adjustment. Specifically, the results are weighted by the inverse of the probability of selection. In a study using a list of car registrations, for example, each contacted respondent would be asked, "How many cars do you own?" The response of someone who said two would be weighted $\frac{1}{2}$, whereas that of someone who said three would be weighted $\frac{1}{3}$.[12]

The appropriate sampling and adjustment procedures to account for inadequate sampling frames can become quite technical in complex sample designs and fall largely in the domain of the sampling specialist. Consequently, we shall not delve into these processes but shall simply note the following:

1. Noncoverage bias is a nonsampling error and is therefore not dealt with in our standard statistical formulas;

---

[10]E. Laird Landon, Jr., and Sharon K. Banks, "Relative Efficiency and Bias of Plus-One Telephone Sampling," *Journal of Marketing Research,* 14 (August 1977), pp. 294–299; Jane Foreman and Martin Collins, "The Viability of Random Digit Dialing in the UK," *Journal of the Market Research Society,* 33 (June 1991), pp. 219–227.

[11]The correct sampling interval is $i = Np/n$, where N is the total size of the list, p is the estimated percentage ineligible, and n is the desired sample size. Seymour Sudman, *Applied Sampling* (New York: Academic Press, 1976), p. 60.

[12]The general adjustment procedure for dealing with the problem of duplicates on a list is to weight sample elements discovered to have been listed k times by $1/k$. Sudman, *Applied Sampling,* p. 63. Most of the standard computer packages for statistically analyzing the data contain mechanisms by which the analyst can specify the weight to be applied to each sample observation.

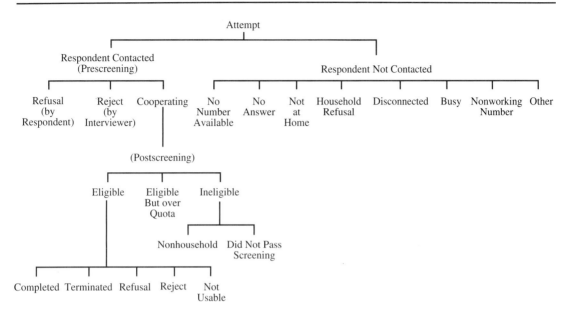

Source: Frederick Wiseman and Philip McDonald, *Toward the Development of Industry Standards for Response and Nonresponse Rates* (Cambridge, Mass.: Marketing Science Institute, 1980), p. 29. Reprinted with permission.

2. Noncoverage bias is *not* likely to be eliminated by increasing the sample size;

3. It can be of considerable magnitude; and

4. It can be reduced, but not necessarily eliminated, by recognizing its existence, working to improve the sampling frame, and employing a sampling specialist to help reduce, through the sampling procedure, and adjust, through analysis, the remaining frame imperfections.[13]

Nonresponse Errors

Another source of nonobservation bias is **nonresponse error,** which represents a failure to obtain information from some elements of the population that were selected and designated for the sample. One problem in dealing with nonresponse error is simply appreciating all of the many things that can go wrong with an attempt to contact a designated respondent. Figure 12.2, for example, depicts the various outcomes of an attempted telephone contact. There is such a bewildering array of alternatives that even the calculation of a measure of the extent of the nonresponse problem becomes difficult.

Spurred by the concern that the absence of standard, industry-wide definitions and methods of calculation for rates of response and nonresponse had prevented an accurate assessment of the potential magnitude of the nonresponse problem, a study was

---

[13]Kish, *Survey Sampling,* pp. 530–531, offers a number of suggestions about what can be done to decrease the effect of noncoverage, as well as some general comments regarding the extent of noncoverage bias.

conducted among a sample of members of the Council of American Survey Research Organizations (CASRO) and leading user companies. The study involved mailing questionnaires that displayed actual contact and response data from three different telephone surveys, a telephone directory sample, a random digit sample, and a list sample. Respondents were asked to calculate the response, contact, completion, and refusal rates for each of the three surveys.[14] The difference in results was rather startling. Panel A of Table 12.1, for example, displays the raw data from the telephone directory sample. Using the very same data, one responding organization reported the response rate as 12 percent while another suggested it was 90 percent. Further, there was little agreement among the other firms. No more than three firms out of forty agreed on any single definition of the response rate, and that occurred with respect to three different definitions. Panel B of Table 12.1 displays the three most frequently used definitions, as well as the definitions producing the minimum and maximum response rates.

Not only does the variation in definitions cause confusion when nonresponse rates are reported for a survey, but it also makes the treatment of the nonresponse error problem more difficult. It becomes hard to discern, for instance, whether a particular method proved to be effective or whether a different definition was responsible for a lower nonresponse error in a particular study. Because of the need to generalize findings in order to improve the practice of survey research, a special CASRO task force developed a definition of response rate that the industry is being encouraged to embrace as the standard definition — namely that[15]

$$\text{Response rate} = \frac{\text{Number of completed interviews with responding units}}{\text{Number of eligible responding units in the sample}}.$$

The key requirement in accurately calculating the response rate is properly handling eligibles. Table 12.2 displays the proper calculation when there is not an eligibility requirement (Example 1), as well as the calculation when there is an eligibility requirement for inclusion in the sample (Example 2).

Nonresponse is a problem in any survey in which it occurs, because it raises the question of whether those who did respond are different in some important way from those who did not respond. This is, of course, something we do not know, although study after study have indicated that the assumption that those who did not respond were in fact equal to those who did is risky.

The two main sources of nonresponse bias are not-at-homes and refusals. Nonresponse bias can arise with studies using personal interviews or telephone or mail surveys to secure the data. However, with mail surveys, the not-at-home problem becomes one of nonreceipt of the questionnaire. The questionnaire may simply have been lost in the mail, in which case the nonsampling error could be considered random and nonbiasing, or there may be more fundamental reasons for nonreceipt: the addressee may have moved or died. These latter conditions would be a source of systematic nonsampling error.

---

[14]Frederick Wiseman and Philip McDonald, *Toward the Development of Industry Standards for Response and Nonresponse Rates* (Cambridge, Mass.: Marketing Science Institute, 1980).

[15]"On the Definition of Response Rates," *CASRO Special Report* (Port Jefferson, N.Y.: The Council of American Survey Research Organizations, 1982).

TABLE 12.1   Response Rate Calculations for Telephone Directory Sample

Panel A: Outcome of Telephone Call

Disconnected/nonworking telephone number	426
Household refusal	153
No answer, busy, not at home	1,757
Interviewer reject (language barrier, hard of hearing, . . .)	187
Respondent refusal	711
Ineligible respondent	366
Termination by respondent	74
Completed interview	501
Total	4,175

Panel B: Most Frequent, Minimum, and Maximum Response Rates

Most frequent:

$$\frac{\text{Household refusals + Rejects + Refusals + Ineligibles + Terminations + Completed interviews}}{\text{All}} = \quad (1)$$

$$\frac{153+187+711+366+74+501}{4,175} = 48\%$$

$$\frac{\text{Rejects + Refusals + Ineligibles + Terminations + Completed interviews}}{\text{All}} = \quad (2)$$

$$\frac{187 + 711 + 366 + 74 + 501}{4,175} = 44\%$$

$$\frac{\text{Completed interviews}}{\text{All}} = \frac{501}{4,175} = 12\% \; (3)$$

Minimum:

$$\frac{\text{Completed interviews}}{\text{All}} = \frac{501}{4,175} = 12\%$$

Maximum:

$$\frac{\text{Refusals + Ineligibles + Termination + Completed Interviews}}{\text{Rejects + Refusals + Ineligibles + Termination + Completed interviews}} =$$

$$\frac{711 + 366 + 74 + 501}{187 + 711 + 366 + 74 + 501} = 90\%$$

Source: Frederick Wiseman and Philip McDonald, *Toward the Development of Industry Standards for Response and Nonresponse Rates* (Cambridge, Mass.: Marketing Science Institute, 1980), pp. 12 and 19. Reprinted with permission.

TABLE **12.2**   **The Impact of an Eligibility Requirement on the Calculation of the Response Rate**

Example 1.   ***Single-stage Sample, No Eligibility Requirement***
Suppose a survey is conducted to obtain 1,000 interviews with subscribers of a particular magazine. A random sample of $n = 1,000$ is selected, and the initial data collection effort produces the following results.

$$
\begin{aligned}
\text{Completed interviews} \quad &= 660 \\
\text{Refusals} \quad &= 115 \\
\text{Respondents not contacted} &= 225
\end{aligned}
$$

For each of the 340 nonrespondents, substitute subscribers are selected until a completed interview is obtained. Assume that in this follow-up data collection effort 600 substitute names are required to secure the 340 interviews. The recommended response rate is

$$660/1{,}000 = 66.0\%$$

and not

$$1{,}000/1{,}600 = 62.5\%$$

Example 2.   ***Single-stage Sampling, Eligibility Requirement***
From a list of registered voters, a sample of $n = 900$ names is selected. Eligible respondents are defined as those planning to vote in an upcoming election. Assume the data collection effort produces the following results.

$$
\begin{aligned}
\text{Completed interviews} \quad &= 300 \\
\text{Not contacted} \quad &= 250 \\
\text{Refused, eligibility not determined} &= 150 \\
\text{Ineligible} \quad &= 200
\end{aligned}
$$

The recommended response rate is

$$
\frac{300}{300 + \left[\dfrac{300}{300 + 200}\right](250 + 150)} = \frac{300}{300 + 240} = 55.5\%.
$$

As indicated, when using an eligibility requirement one first must estimate the number of eligibles among the nonrespondents. This is done by using the eligibility percentage, $(300/500) = 60\%$, obtained among persons successfully screened and applying this percentage to the nonrespondents. Thus, of the 400 nonrespondents, 60% (240) are estimated to have been eligible and the estimated response rate becomes (300/540) or 55.5%.

Not-at-Homes Replies will not be secured from some designated sampling units because the respondent will not be at home when the interviewer calls. The empirical evidence indicates that there is a long upward trend in the **not-at-homes.** The percentage of not-at-homes depends on the nature of the designated respondent and the time of the call. Married women with young children are more likely to be at home during the day on weekdays than are men, married women without children, or single women. The probability of finding someone at home is also greater for low-income families and for rural families. Seasonal variations, particularly during the holidays, do occur, as do weekday-to-weekend variations.[16] Further, it is much easier to find a "responsible adult" at home than a specified respondent, and thus the choice of the elementary sampling unit is key in the not-at-home problem.

Several things can be done to reduce the incidence of not-at-homes. For example, the interviewer might make an appointment in advance by telephone with the respondent. This approach is particularly valuable in surveys of busy executives, but it may not be justifiable in an ordinary consumer survey. A commonly used technique in the latter instance is the callback, which is particularly effective if the callback (preferably callbacks) is made at a different time than the original call. As a matter of fact, the nonresponse problem due to not-at-homes is so acute and so important to the accuracy of most surveys that one leading expert has suggested that small samples with four to six callbacks are more efficient than large samples without callbacks, unless the percentage of initial response can be increased considerably above normal levels.[17] There are data that indicate, for example, that four to five calls are often needed to reach three-fourths of the sample of households.[18]

---

[16]There are several studies that contain data about when particular types of individuals are likely to be home. See, for example, M. F. Weeks, B. L. Jones, R. E. Folsum, Jr., and C. H. Benrud, "Optimal Times to Contact Sample Households," *Public Opinion Quarterly,* 44 (Spring 1980), pp. 101–114; Michael F. Weeks, Richard A. Kulka, and Stephanie A. Pierson, "Optimal Call Scheduling for a Telephone Survey," *Public Opinion Quarterly,* 51 (Winter 1987), pp. 540–549; Gideon Vigderhaus, "Scheduling Telephone Interviews: A Study of Seasonal Patterns," *Public Opinion Quarterly,* 45 (Summer 1981), pp. 250–259. The article by Ed Swires Hennessy and Marc Drake, "The Optimum Time at Which to Conduct Survey Interviews," *Journal of the Market Research Society,* 34 (January 1992), pp. 61–72, discusses optimal calling times in Wales, while the article by Betsy S. Greenberg and S. Lynn Stokes, "Developing an Optimal Call Scheduling Strategy for a Telephone Survey," 6 (No. 4, 1990), pp. 421–435, develops a conceptual model that can be used to minimize the expected number of telephone calls needed to make contacts. The report "Identifying Monthly Response Rates Aids in Mail Planning," *Specialty Advertising Report,* 15 (4th Quarter, 1979), contains a useful table for scheduling mail studies to coincide with the months in which people are most likely to respond.

[17]W. Edwards Deming, "On a Probability Mechanism to Attain an Economic Balance between the Resultant Error of Response and the Bias of Nonresponse," *Journal of the American Statistical Association,* 48 (December 1953), pp. 766–767. See also Benjamin Lipstein, "In Defense of Small Samples," *Journal of Advertising Research,* 15 (February 1975), pp. 33–40; and William C. Dunkelburg and George S. Day, "Nonresponse Bias and Callbacks in Sample Surveys," *Journal of Marketing Research,* 10 (May 1973), pp. 160–168, a study that provides "evidence on the rate at which sample values converge on their population distribution as the number of callbacks increases." See also Frederick Wiseman and Maryann Billington, "Comment on a Standard Definition of Response Rates," *Journal of Marketing Research,* 21 (August 1984), p. 337. Published by the American Marketing Association. See also Lorna Opatow, "Some Thoughts About How Interview Attempts Affect Survey Results," *Journal of Advertising Research,* 31 (February/March 1991), pp. RC6–RC9.

[18]Robert M. Groves and Robert L. Kahn, *Surveys by Telephone* (New York: Academic Press, 1979), pp. 56–58.

An alternative to the "straight" callback is the "modified" callback. If the initial contact attempt and first few callbacks were made by an interviewer and a contact was not established, the interviewer might simply leave a self-administered questionnaire with a stamped, self-addressed envelope behind. If the not-at-home is simply a "designated respondent absent" rather than a "nobody-at-home," the interviewer can use the opportunity to inquire about the respondent's hours of availability.

One technique that is sometimes naively suggested for handling the not-at-homes is substituting the neighboring dwelling unit, or in a telephone survey, calling the next name on the list. This is a very poor way of handling the not-at-home condition. All it does is substitute more at-homes (who may be different from the not-at-homes in a number of important characteristics) for the population segment the researcher is in fact trying to reach. This increases the proportion of at-homes in the sample and, in effect, aggravates the problem instead of solving it.

The proportion of reported not-at-homes is likely to depend on the interviewer and the judgment used in scheduling initial contacts and callbacks. This suggests that one way of reducing not-at-home nonresponse bias is by better interviewer training with particular emphasis on how to schedule callbacks more efficiently.

The fact that interviewer effectiveness affects the number of not-at-homes also suggests one measure by which interviewers can be compared and evaluated. This is the **contact rate (K),** defined as the percentage of eligible assignments in which the interviewer makes contact with the designated respondent; that is,

$$K = \frac{\text{Number of eligible sample units contacted}}{\text{Total number of eligible sample units approached}}.$$

The contact rate measures the interviewer's persistence. Interviewers can be compared with respect to their contact rate, and corrective measures can often be taken. Those with low contact rates can be checked as to why. Perhaps these interviewers are operating in traditionally high not-at-home areas, such as high-income sections of an urban area. Alternatively, by examining the call reports for time of each call, the trouble may be traced to poor follow-up procedures. This condition would suggest that additional training is necessary, which might then be provided by the field supervisor while the study is still in progress. The contact rate can also be used to evaluate an entire study in terms of the potential nonresponse caused by not-at-homes.

Not-at-home nonresponse bias can also be addressed by statistical adjustment of the results using a scheme developed by Politz and Simmons.[19] Rather than relying on

---

[19]The technique can be used with telephone interviews, although it was designed for personal interviews because of the tremendous expense of personal interview callbacks. Moreover, probing on the phone about when a respondent was home during the last five days can cause mistrust. See Alfred Politz and Willard Simmons, "An Attempt to Get the Not-at-Homes into the Sample Without Callbacks," *Journal of the American Statistical Association,* 44 (March 1949), pp. 9–32, for explanation of the technique. For an empirical investigation of the effect of weighting on bias, see James Ward, Bertram Russick, and William Rudelius, "A Test of Reducing Callbacks and Not-At-Home Bias in Personal Interviews by Weighting At-Home Respondents," *Journal of Marketing Research,* 22 (February 1985), pp. 66–73. See also Charles H. Alexander, "A Class of Methods for Using Personal Controls in Household Weighting," *Survey Methodology,* 13 (December 1987), pp. 183–198.

callbacks, their scheme depends on a single attempted contact with each sample member at a randomly determined time. During this contact, the respondent is asked if he or she was home at the time of the interview for the five preceding days. These five answers and the time of the interview provide information on the time the respondent was at home for six different days. The responses from each informant are then weighted by the reciprocal of their self-reported probability of being at home; for example, the answers of a respondent who was home one out of six times would receive a weight of six. The basic rationale is that people who are usually not at home are more difficult to catch for an interview and therefore will tend to be underrepresented in the survey. Consequently, the less a subject reports being at home, the more that subject's responses should be weighted.

Refusals   In almost every study, some respondents will refuse to participate. In one of the most extensive investigations of the magnitude of the problem, 46 field research companies sponsored a study called "Your Opinion Counts," which involved almost 1.4 million phone and personal interviews. The study indicated that 38 percent of the people asked to participate declined to do so, with 86 percent of those refusing to participate before or during the introduction. The rest broke away before the survey was completed.[20] Research Realities 12.3 depicts what is happening to refusal rates in general and presents some of the major reasons respondents give for having refused to participate in surveys.

The rate of **refusals** depends, among other things, on the nature of the respondent, the auspices of the research, the circumstances surrounding the contact, the nature of the subject, and the interviewer. Even the culture of the country can affect the refusal rate. For example, in some cultures (such as Saudi Arabia), it is nearly impossible to interview women. The method used to collect the data also makes a difference. The empirical evidence indicates, for example, that personal interviews are most effective and mail questionnaires least effective in generating response. Telephone interviews are somewhat less successful on average than personal interviews in getting target respondents to cooperate.

Although it is hard to generalize across data collection techniques about the types of people likely to cooperate in a survey, there does seem to be some tendency for females, nonwhites, those who are less well-educated, those who have lower incomes, and those who are older to be more likely to refuse to participate.[21] The auspices of the research can also make a difference in the number of refusals. People not only report differently to different sponsors, but the sponsor can also affect whether or not they report at all. Sometimes the condition surrounding the contact can cause a refusal. A respondent may be too busy or tired or may be sick when contacted and thus refuse to participate. The subject of the research also affects refusal rate. Those who typically respond are those

---

[20]*Your Opinion Counts: 1986 Refusal Rate Study* (Chicago: Marketing Research Association, 1986). See also Erhard Meier, "Response Rate Trends in Britain," *Marketing and Research Today,* 19 (June 1991), pp. 120–123.

[21]T. De Maio, "Refusals: Who, Where, and Why," *Public Opinion Quarterly,* 44 (Summer 1980), pp. 223–233. See also Jolene M. Strubbe, Jerome B. Kernan, and Thomas J. Grogan, "The Refusal Problem in Telephone Surveys," *Journal of Advertising Research,* 26 (June/July 1986), pp. 29–37.

Research Realities 12.3

Trends in Refusal Rates and Reasons Given for Refusing to Participate

Panel A: Percentage of Those Contacted Who Had Refused to Participate in a Survey in the Past Year

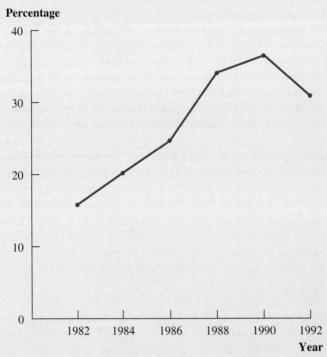

Percentage

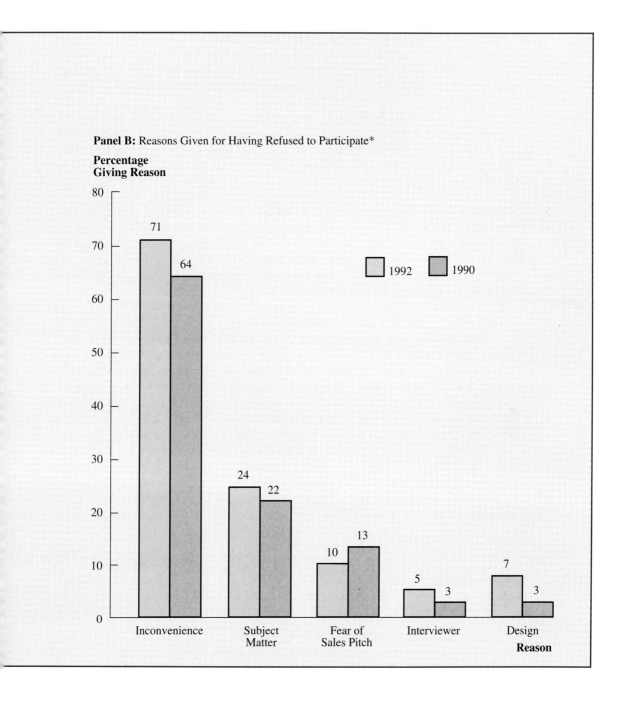

Panel B: Reasons Given for Having Refused to Participate*

who are most interested in the subject. Also, nonresponse errors tend to increase with the sensitivity of the information being sought. Finally, interviewers themselves can have an important effect on the number of refusals they obtain. Their approach, their manner, and even their own demographic characteristics can affect a respondent's willingness to participate.

What can be done to correct the nonresponse bias introduced when designated respondents refuse their participation? There seem to be three available strategies. One, the initial response rate can be increased. Two, the impact of refusals can be reduced through follow-up. Three, the obtained information can be extrapolated to allow for nonresponse.

Increasing Initial Response Rate   It would appear that the nature of the respondent is beyond the researcher's control. The problem dictates the target population, and this population is likely to contain households with different educational levels, income levels, cultural and occupational backgrounds, and so forth. The task is not as hopeless as it might seem, though. A model for interviewer–interviewee interaction will be offered when discussing errors of observation. Granted that the nature of the respondent can affect the refusal rate, the interviewee's cooperation can be encouraged by an "appropriate choice" of interviewer. But more on this later.

There are also some more traditional things that can be done to ensure respondents' participation. One thing, of course, is to sell respondents on the value of the research and the importance of their participation. Advance notice may help. Interviewers can be trained in useful approaches. The evidence suggests, for example, that the more information interviewers provide about the content and purpose of the survey, the higher the response rate in both personal and telephone interviews.[22] Some individuals refuse to participate because they do not wish to be identified with their responses. A guarantee that the replies will be held in confidence (if they truly will be) is often effective in calming such fears. Sometimes money or some other incentive is offered; monetary incentives seem to be most effective in increasing response rates in mail surveys.[23]

Nonresponse attributable to identification of the sponsor can be overcome by hiding the sponsor; this can be accomplished by hiring a professional research organization to

---

[22]Eleanor Singer, "Informed Consent: Consequences for Response Rate and Response Quality in Social Surveys," *American Sociological Review,* 43 (April 1978), pp. 144–162; Eleanor Singer and Martin R. Frankel, "Informed Consent Procedures in Telephone Interviews," *American Sociological Review,* 47 (June 1982), pp. 416–427; and Jean Morton-Williams and Penny Young, "Obtaining the Survey Interview — An Analysis of Tape Recorded Doorstep Introductions," *Journal of the Market Research Society,* 29 (January 1987), pp. 35–54.

[23]James R. Chromy and Daniel G. Horowitz, "The Use of Monetary Incentives in National Assessment Household Surveys," *Journal of the American Statistical Association,* 73 (September 1978), pp. 473–478; *The Use of Monetary and Other Gift Incentives in Mail Surveys: An Annotated Bibliography* (Monticello, Ill.: Vance Bibliographies, 1979); Lee Harvey, "Factors Affecting Response Rates to Mailed Questionnaires: A Comprehensive Literature Review," *Journal of the Market Research Society,* 29 (July 1987), pp. 341–353; Thomas J. Bergmann, William J. Hannaford, and James Wenner, "Amount, Timing, and Value of Financial Incentives in Mail Surveys: Does It Make a Difference," *Marketing Research: A Magazine of Management and Applications,* 2 (September 1990), pp. 30–36; Mike Brennan, "The Effect of a Monetary Incentive on Mail Survey Response Rates: New Data," *Journal of the Market Research Society,* 34 (April 1992), pp. 173–177.

conduct the field study.[24] This is one reason why companies with established, sophisticated research departments do, in fact, employ research firms to collect data.

The ability to generalize what might happen if a particular inducement technique is used to increase the cooperation rate in a survey is clouded by the fact that the effects are different from survey to survey. When one looks across surveys, the picture becomes somewhat clearer, even though the many review articles do not completely agree on the impact of various response inducement techniques. This is due partially to the articles and time periods included in their reviews.[25] The results of one of the most recent and extensive reviews of mail-survey response involvement techniques are shown in Figure 12.3. The average effect of the facilitation technique is shown by the weighted correlation coefficient across studies where the weights reflect the size of the various samples on which the individual correlations were based. The larger the weighted mean correlation, the more impact the particular facilitation technique has. The results in Figure 12.3 indicate that, on average, the most successful response inducement techniques in mail surveys are the use of incentives, preliminary notification that the survey is coming, and follow-ups or repeated mailings.

Follow-up   Because many of the circumstances surrounding a contact are temporary and changeable, this source of bias introduced through refusals can often be reduced. If a respondent declined participation because he or she was busy or sick, a callback at a different time or employing a different approach may be sufficient to secure cooperation. In a mail survey, this may mean a follow-up mailing at a more convenient time. Thus, one means of reducing this source of bias seems to be the training and control of the field staff.

It would seem that very little can be done with the subject of the research as a source of nonresponse bias, since it is dictated by the problem to be solved. A sensitive research subject or one of little interest to the respondents is likely to elicit a high rate of refusals. The researcher should not overlook the opportunity to make the study as interesting as possible, though. This often means that "questions that are interesting but not vital" should be avoided. The development of the measuring instrument thus becomes essential in reducing this source of refusals.

---

[24]Wesley H. Jones and James R. Lang, "Sample Composition Bias and Response Bias in a Mail Survey: A Comparison of Inducement Methods," *Journal of Marketing Research,* 17 (February 1980), pp. 69–76; Wesley H. Jones and James R. Lang, "Reliability and Validity Effects Under Mail Survey Conditions," *Journal of Business Research,* 10 (September 1982), pp. 339–353; Gerald Albaum, "Do Source and Anonymity Affect Mail Survey Results," *Journal of the Academy of Marketing Science,* 15 (Fall 1987), pp. 64–71; A. J. Faria and John R. Dickinson, "Mail Survey Response, Speed, and Cost," *Industrial Marketing Management,* 21 (February 1992), pp. 51–60.

[25]Leslie Kanuk and Conrad Berenson, "Mail Surveys and Response Rates: A Literature Review," *Journal of Marketing Research,* 12 (November 1975), pp. 440–453; T. A. Heberlein and R. A. Baumgartner, "Factors Affecting Response Rates to Mailed Questionnaires: A Quantitative Analysis of the Published Literature," *American Sociological Review,* 43 (August 1978), pp. 447–462; Julie Yu and Harris Cooper, "A Quantitative Review of Research Design Effects on Response Rates to Questionnaires," *Journal of Marketing Research,* 20 (February 1983), pp. 36–44; Richard J. Fox, Melvin R. Crask, Jonghoon Kim, "Mail Survey Response Rate: A Meta-Analysis of Selected Techniques for Inducing Response," *Public Opinion Quarterly,* 52 (Winter 1989), pp. 467–491; Francis J. Yammarino, Steven J. Skinner, and Terry L. Childers, "Understanding Mail Survey Response Behavior: A Meta-Analysis," *Public Opinion Quarterly,* 55 (Winter 1991), pp. 613–639.

FIGURE 12.3   Impact of Selected Response Inducement Techniques on Mail Survey Response Rates

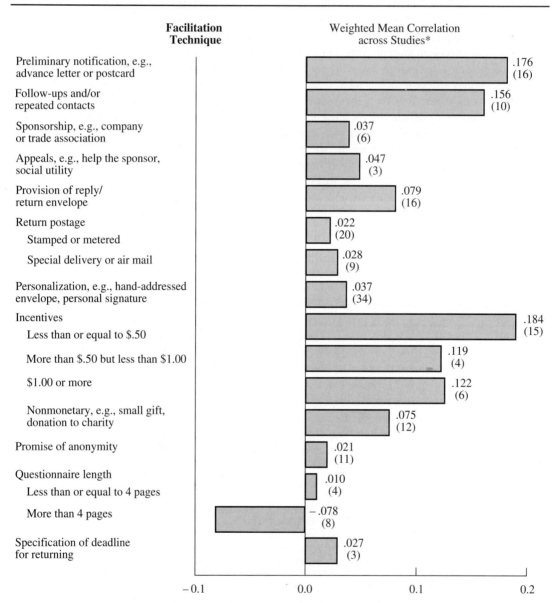

*The numbers shown in brackets indicate the number of correlations on which the average correlation is based.

Source: Developed from the information in Frances J. Yammarino, Steven J. Skinner, and Terry L. Childers, "Understanding Mail Survey Response Behavior: A Meta-Analysis," *Public Opinion Quarterly,* 55 (Winter 1991), pp. 613–639. Reprinted with permission University of Chicago Press.

Generally, other than for refusals because of circumstances, callbacks will be less successful in personal interviews and telephone surveys for reducing the incidence of refusals than they are for treating the not-at-home condition. This is not so with mail surveys. Frequently, responses are obtained with the second and third mailings from those who did not respond to earlier mailings. Of course, follow-up in a mail survey requires identification of those not responding earlier. This means that those who did respond need to be identified. However, as we have already seen, respondents who know that they can be identified may refuse to participate. Thus, identification of the respondents, which may serve to decrease one source of nonresponse, may actually increase another. The alternative of sending each mailing to each designated sample member, without screening those who have responded previously, can be expensive for the research organization and frustrating for the respondent.

Adjusting the Results   A third strategy for treating nonresponse bias involves estimating its effects and then adjusting the results.[26] Suppose, for instance, that the problem was one of estimating the mean income for some population and that responses were secured from only a portion (p_r) of some designated sample. The proportion not responding could then be denoted p_{nr}. If $\bar{x}_r$ is the mean income of those *responding* and $\bar{x}_{nr}$ the mean income of those *not* responding, then the overall mean would be

$$\bar{x} = p_r\bar{x}_r + p_{nr}\bar{x}_{nr}.$$

This computation, of course, assumes that $\bar{x}_{nr}$ is known or at least can be estimated. An intensive follow-up of a *sample* of the *nonrespondents* is sometimes used to generate this estimate. The follow-up may be a modified callback. Although this rarely generates a response from each nonrespondent designated for the follow-up, it does allow a crude adjustment of the initial results. Ignoring the initial nonresponse is equivalent to assuming that $\bar{x}_{nr}$ is equal to $\bar{x}_r$, which is usually incorrect.

A second way by which the adjustment is sometimes made involves keeping track of those responding to the initial contact, the first follow-up, the second follow-up, and so on. The mean of the variable (or other appropriate statistic) is then calculated, and each subgroup is compared to determine whether any statistically significant differences emerge as a function of the difficulty experienced in making contact. If not, the variable mean for the nonrespondents is assumed to be equal to the mean for those responding. If

---

[26]*Statistical Adjustment for Nonresponse in Sample Surveys: A Selected Bibliography with Annotations* (Monticello, Ill.: Vance Bibliographies, 1979); J. Scott Armstrong and Terry S. Overton, "Estimating Nonresponse Bias in Mail Surveys," *Journal of Marketing Research,* 14 (August 1977), pp. 396–402; Michael J. O'Neil, "Estimating the Nonresponse Bias Due to Refusals in Telephone Surveys," *Public Opinion Quarterly,* 40 (Summer 1976), pp. 218–232; David Elliot and Roger Thomas, "Further Thoughts on Weighting Survey Results to Compensate for Nonresponse," *Survey Methodology Bulletin,* 15 (February 1983), pp. 2–11; Juha M. Alho, "Adjusting for Nonresponse Bias Using Logistic Regression," *Biometrika,* 77 (No. 3, 1990), pp. 617–624; Linda Robinson and Donald Lifton, "Reducing Market Research Costs: Deciding When to Eliminate Expensive Survey Follow-Up," *Journal of the Market Research Society,* 33 (October 1991), pp. 301–308; Valentine Uppel and Julian Baim, "Predicting and Correcting Response Rate Problems Using Geodemography," *Marketing Research: A Magazine of Management and Applications,* 4 (March 1992), pp. 22–28.

a discernible trend is evident, the trend is extrapolated to allow for nonrespondents. This method is particularly valuable in mail surveys, where it is an easy task to identify those responding to the first mailing, the second mailing, and so on.

Evidence accumulated in past surveys also sometimes serves as the basis of the adjustment for nonresponse. This approach is particularly well-suited to organizations that frequently conduct surveys involving similar sampling procedures. While no method of adjustment is perfect, the assumption that nonrespondents are similar to respondents on the characteristic of interest is risky. Yet this is the very assumption we make if no attempt is made to correct for nonresponse.

The preceding discussions all deal with total nonresponse. Item nonresponse, which can also be a problem, occurs when the respondent agrees to the total interview but refuses, or is unable, to answer some specific questions because of the content, form, or sequence of the questions or the amount of work required to produce the requested information. The primary mechanisms for treating these problems lie in the development of the questionnaire and methods for administering it, issues discussed earlier. Suppose that item nonresponses occur in spite of our best efforts on these tasks. Whether anything can then be done about item nonresponse depends on its magnitude. Here we must distinguish between flagrant item nonresponse and isolated or sporadic nonresponse. If too many questions are left unanswered, the reply becomes unusable, and the treatment, or at least adjustment, is the same as that for a complete nonresponse. On the other hand, if only a few items are left unanswered on any questionnaire, the reply can often be made usable. At the very minimum, the "don't know" and "no answers" can be treated as separate categories when reporting the results. In many ways this is the best strategy, because the little evidence that is available on item nonresponse suggests that the problem is extensive and nonrandom.[27] Alternatively, the information from the missing item or items can sometimes be inferred from other information in the questionnaire.[28] This works if there are other questions on the questionnaire that relate to the same issue. The other questions are checked, and a consistent answer is formulated for the unanswered item. In the absence of such consistency checks, regression analysis is sometimes used. The missing item is treated as the criterion variable, and the functional

---

[27]J. Frances and L. Busch, "What We Know about 'I Don't Knows'," *Public Opinion Quarterly,* 39 (Summer 1975), pp. 207–218; Herbert Schuman and Stanley Presser, "The Assessment of 'No Opinion' in Attitude Surveys," in Karl F. Schuessler, ed., *Sociological Methodology 1979* (San Francisco: Jossey-Bass, 1979), pp. 241–275; C. Coombs and L. Coombs, " 'Don't Know': Item Ambiguity or Respondent Uncertainty," *Public Opinion Quarterly,* 40 (Winter 1976), pp. 497–514; Glenn S. Omura, "Correlates of Item Nonresponse," *Journal of the Market Research Society,* 25 (October 1983), pp. 321–330; Richard M. Durand, Hugh J. Guffey, Jr., and John M. Planchon, "An Examination of the Random versus Nonrandom Nature of Item Omissions," *Journal of Marketing Research,* 20 (August 1983), pp. 305–313; James H. Leigh and Claude R. Martin, Jr., " 'Don't Know' Item Nonresponse in a Telephone Survey: Effects of Question Form and Respondent Characteristics," *Journal of Marketing Research,* 24 (November 1987), pp. 418–424.

[28]Graham Kalton, *Compensating for Missing Survey Data* (Ann Arbor: Institute for Social Research, University of Michigan, 1983); R. L. Hinde and R. L. Chambers, "Nonresponse Imputation with Multiple Sources of Nonresponse,"*Journal of Official Statistics,* 7 (No. 2, 1991), pp. 167–179; Otis W. Gilley and Robert P. Leone, "A Two-State Imputation Procedure for Item Nonresponse in Surveys," *Journal of Business Research,* 22 (June 1991), pp. 281–291; Paul S. Levy and Stanley Lemeshow, *Sampling of Populations: Methods and Applications* (New York: John Wiley and Sons, Inc., 1991), especially Chapter 13.

relationship is established between it and *a priori* related questions through regression analysis for those cases for which the item was answered. The equation is then used to estimate a response for the remaining questionnaires given the information that they contain on the predictor variables. Finally, a third way by which item nonresponse is handled is by substituting the average response for the item of those who did respond. This technique, of course, carries the assumption that those who did not respond to the item are similar to those who did. As we have suggested many times, this assumption may be risky, and, therefore, substituting the average should be done with caution.

Just as the contact rate can be used to compare and evaluate interviewers with respect to not-at-homes, at least two ratios have been suggested for comparing interviewers with respect to refusals: the **response rate *R*** and the **completeness rate *C*.** The response rate was discussed previously. It equals the ratio of the number of completed interviews with responding units divided by the number of eligible responding units in the sample. The response rate reflects the interviewer's effectiveness at the door or on the phone.

The completeness rate applies to the individual items in the study. Most typically it will be used to evaluate interviewers with respect to the crucial questions involved in the study (for example, a respondent's income, debt, or asset position), although it can also be used to evaluate the whole contact. The completeness rate simply determines whether or not the response is complete, either in terms of the crucial questions or the whole questionnaire.

ETHICAL DILEMMA 12.2

During a telephone survey, the names of respondents who refuse to answer the survey are placed in a special bin. All of these respondents are recontacted 24 hours later and asked again for their answers. The person making these follow-up calls receives special training in converting these refusals to completions. If the respondent refuses again, the interviewer attempts to ''sell'' the respondent on cooperating in the study. If the respondent remains unwilling to complete the survey, the interviewer terminates the call and notes this as a refusal.

- List the implications arising from increased refusals, as the number of telephone surveys increases.
- List the implications for marketing research if research companies make follow-up calls to refusals the industry standard.
- Should an initial refusal be taken as a refusal? Explain.

Field Errors

Field errors are by far the most prevalent type of observation error. **Field errors** arise after the individual has agreed to participate in a study. Instead of cooperating fully, the individual refuses to answer specific questions or provides a response that somehow differs from what is actually true or correct. Such errors have been referred to, respectively, as

FIGURE 12.4   **A Model of Bias in the Interview**

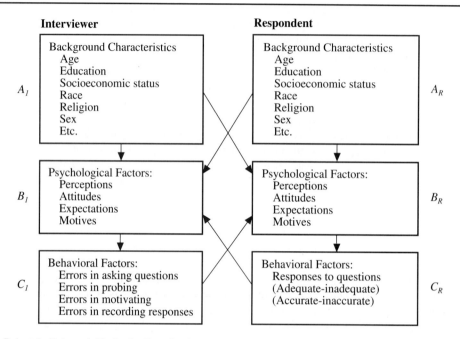

Source: Robert L. Kahn and Charles L. Cannell, *The Dynamics of Interviewing* (New York: John Wiley & Sons, Inc., © 1957), p. 193. Reprinted by permission of John Wiley & Sons, Inc. See also Wendy Sykes and Martin Collins, "Anatomy of the Survey Interview," *Journal of Official Statistics,* 8 (No. 3, 1992), pp. 277–291.

errors of omission and errors of commission.[29] It was convenient to discuss errors of omission or item nonresponse in the last section. Now we wish to turn our attention to errors of commission, which are most typically referred to as *response errors.*

When considering response errors, it is useful to keep in mind what needs to occur for respondents to answer questions put to them. First, the respondent needs to understand what is being asked. Second, the individual needs to engage in some cognitive processing to arrive at an answer. That cognitive processing will typically include an assessment of the information needed for an accurate answer, retrieval of the pertinent attitudes, facts, or experiences, and the organization of the retrieved cognitions and the formulation of the response on this basis. Third, the person needs to evaluate the response in terms of its accuracy. Fourth, the subject needs to evaluate the response in

---

[29]Robert A. Peterson and Roger A. Kerin, "The Quality of Self-Report Data: Review and Synthesis," in Ben Enis and Kenneth Roering, eds., *Annual Review of Marketing 1981* (Chicago: American Marketing Association, 1981), pp. 5–20. See also C. A. Muircheartaigh, "Response Errors," in C. A. Muircheartaigh and Clive Payne, eds., *The Analysis of Survey Data: Model Fitting* (London: John Wiley and Sons, 1977), pp. 193–239; Duane F. Alwin and David J. Jackson, "Measurement Models for Response Errors in Surveys: Issues and Applications," in Karl F. Schuessler, *Sociological Methodology 1980* (San Francisco: Jossey-Bass, 1980), pp. 68–119.

terms of other goals he or she might have, such as preserving one's self-image or attempting to please the interviewer. Finally, the subject needs to give the response that results from all this mental processing. Reaching the final step is the object of the survey process. Breakdowns can occur at any of the preceding steps, however, resulting in an inaccurate answer or a response error.

The number of factors that can cause response errors is so large that the factors almost defy categorization. One seemingly useful scheme for dealing with data collection errors, though, is the **interviewer–interviewee interaction model,** proposed by Kahn and Cannell and shown in Figure 12.4.[30]

The model suggests several things. First, each person brings certain background characteristics and psychological predispositions to the interview. Although some of the background characteristics are readily observable, others are not, nor can the psychological state of the other person be seen. Yet both interviewer and interviewee will form some attitudes toward and expectations of the other person on the basis of their initial perceptions. Second, the interview is an interactive process, and both interviewer and interviewee are important determinants of the process. Each party perceives and reacts to the specific behaviors of the other. Note, though, that there is no direct link between the boxes labeled "behavioral factors." Rather, the linkage is more complicated, "involving a behavior on the part of the interviewer or respondent, the perception of this behavior by the other principal in the interview, a cognitive or attitudinal development from that perception, and finally a resultant motivation to behave in a certain way. Only at this point is a behavioral act carried out, which in turn may be perceived by and reacted to by the other participant in the interview."[31] The perceptions of this behavior may not be correct, just as the initial perceptions of each party may be in error. Nevertheless, such inferences will inevitably be made as both interviewer and respondent search for cues to help them understand each other and carry out the requirements imposed by the interview situation. In sum, not only do the specific behaviors of each party to the interaction affect the outcome, but so do the background characteristics and psychological predispositions of both interviewer and respondent.

The interviewer–interviewee interaction model is appealing for several reasons. One, it is consistent with the empirical evidence. Two, it offers some valuable insight on how response errors (as well as nonresponse errors due to refusals) can be potentially reduced. The model partly applies to telephone and mail surveys, thereby further increasing its value. For example, the respondents' perceptions of the background characteristics and behavior of a telephone interviewer are likely to affect the answers he or she provides. The respondent's background is certainly going to affect the person's reported responses. So will the person's suspicions about the true purpose of the study, or the individual's assumption of how confidential his or her responses will truly be. These

---

[30]Robert L. Kahn and Charles L. Cannell, *The Dynamics of Interviewing* (New York: John Wiley, 1957), p. 193. The figure is used by permission of John Wiley & Sons, Inc. See also Floyd J. Fowler, Jr., and Thomas W. Mangione, *Standardized Survey Interviewing: Minimized Interviewer-Related Error* (Newbury Park, CA.: Sage Publications, Inc., 1989); Wendy Sykes and Martin Collins, "Anatomy of the Survey Interview," *Journal of Official Statistics,* 8 (No. 3, 1992), pp. 277–291.

[31]Kahn and Cannell, *The Dynamics of Interviewing,* p. 194.

factors can distort the respondent's answers regardless of the manner used to collect the data, and it is unlikely that these distortions would be random. At any rate, the model suggests certain things that the researcher can do to generate accurate information.

Background Factors   The empirical evidence is consistent with the supposition that background factors affect reported responses. More particularly, the evidence suggests that better cooperation and more information are obtained when the backgrounds of the interviewer and respondent are similar than when they are different. This is particularly true for readily observable characteristics, such as race, age, and sex, but it applies as well to more unobservable characteristics, such as social class and income.[32] This suggests that it is productive to match the background characteristics of the interviewer and respondent as closely as possible, as the more characteristics the two have in common, the greater the probability of a successful interview.

Unfortunately, the research is somewhat constrained in this regard. Most interviewers are housewives who use interviewing as a mechanism to supplement their family income. Although the profession also attracts some part-time workers such as students or school teachers, interviewing by no means attracts a balanced demographic cross section of people.[33] Nevertheless, the researcher needs to recognize that the interviewer's background can affect the results, and thus investigators should do what they can to minimize such biases. This may simply mean computing a measure of interviewer variability while analyzing the results. Alternatively, a slight modification of interviewer schedules may be made in a specific project to improve background matches. It certainly seems that recruiting should be aimed at securing interviewers with diverse socioeconomic backgrounds, if other things are equal.

Psychological Factors   The evidence regarding the impact of psychological factors on responses tends to support the notion that interviewers' opinions, perceptions, expectations, and attitudes affect the responses they receive.[34] Now certainly, the interviewers'

---

[32]Barbara Bailor, Leroy Bailey, and Joyce Stevens, "Measures of Interviewer Bias and Variance," *Journal of Marketing Research,* 14 (August 1977), pp. 337–343; Shirley Hatchett and Howard Schuman, "White Respondents and Race-of-Interviewer Effects," *Public Opinion Quarterly,* 39 (Winter 1975), pp. 523–528; Patrick R. Cotter, Jeffrey Cohen, and Philip B. Coulter, "Race of Interviewer Effects on Telephone Interviews," *Public Opinion Quarterly,* 46 (Summer 1982), pp. 278–284; Robert M. Groves and Nancy H. Fultz, "Gender Effects among Telephone Interviewers in a Study of Economic Attitudes," *Sociological Methods & Research,* 14 (August 1985), pp. 31–52; Louis G. Pol and Thomas G. Ponzurick, "Gender of Interviewee/ Gender of Respondent Bias in Telephone Surveys," *Applied Marketing Research,* 29 (Spring 1989), pp. 9–13.

[33]Raymond F. Barker, "Demographic Profile of Marketing Research Interviewers," *Journal of the Market Research Society,* 29 (July 1987), pp. 279–292.

[34]Seymour Sudman, Norman Bradburn, Ed Blair, and Carol Stocking, "Modest Expectations: The Effects of Interviewers' Prior Expectations and Response," *Sociological Methods and Research,* 6 (November 1977), pp. 177–182; Eleanor Singer and Luanne Kohnke-Aguirre, "Interviewer Expectation Effects: A Replication and Extension," *Public Opinion Quarterly,* 43 (Summer 1979), pp. 245–260; Eleanor Singer, Martin R. Frankel, and Marc B. Glassman, "The Effect of Interviewer Characteristics and Expectations on Response," *Public Opinion Quarterly,* 47 (Spring 1983), pp. 68–83; Robert M. Groves and Lou J. Magilavy, "Measuring and Explaining Interviewer Effects in Centralized Telephone Surveys," *Public Opinion Quarterly,* 50 (Summer 1986), pp. 251–266; Stanley Presser and Shanyang Zhao, "Attributes of Questions and Interviewers as Correlates of Interviewing Performance," *Public Opinion Quarterly,* 56 (Summer 1992), pp. 236–240.

attitudes, opinions, expectations, and so on are going to be conditioned by the interviewers' backgrounds, and since that is something we cannot control, how are we to control for these psychological factors? The primary way is through training. The fact that interviewers will have psychological predispositions is not critical, because these psychological factors are not observed by the respondent. What is critical, however, is that these factors not be allowed to affect interviewers' behavior during the interview and thereby contaminate the response.

Most surveys, therefore, are conducted using a rather rigid set of procedures that interviewers must follow. The instructions should be clear and should be written. Further, they should state the purpose of the study clearly. They should describe the materials to be used, such as questionnaires, maps, time forms, and so on. They should describe how each question should be asked, the kinds of answers that are acceptable, and the kinds and timing of probes that are to be used, if any. The instructions should also specify the number and identity of respondents that interviewers need to contact and the time constraints under which they will be operating. It is also important that the instructions are well-organized and unambiguous.

The instructions must be clearly articulated; however, it is even more important that interviewers understand and can follow them. This suggests that practice training sessions will be necessary. It might also be necessary to actually examine the interviewers with respect to study purposes and procedures. Finally, interviewers might also be required to complete the questionnaire so that, if there is a pattern between the interviewers' answers and the answers they get when administering the questionnaire, it can be determined.

Behavioral Factors   The respondents' background, attitudes, motives, expectations, and so on are also potentially biasing. Whether they actually do introduce bias depends on how the interviewer and respondent interact. In other words, the predisposition to bias only becomes operative in behavior.

Unfortunately the evidence indicates that even when the rules are rigid and the questionnaires relatively simple and structured, interviewers do not follow the rules. They thereby introduce bias. In one classic study, 15 college-educated interviewers interviewed the same respondent, who had previously been instructed to give identical answers to all 15.[35] All the interviews were recorded and were later analyzed for the incidence of errors by type and frequency. One of the most startling findings of the study was the sheer number of errors. For example, there were 66 failures to ask supplementary questions when inadequate responses were given, and the number of errors per interviewer varied from 12 to 36. In another study, it was found that ". . . one-third of the . . . interviewers deviated frequently and markedly from their instructions, sometimes failing to explain the key terms or to repeat them as required, sometimes leaving

---

[35]L. L. Guest, "A Study of Interviewer Competence," *International Journal of Opinion and Attitude Research,* 1 (March 1947), pp. 17–30. See also Wil Dijkstra, "Interviewing Style and Respondent Behavior: An Experimental Study of the Survey Interview," *Sociological Methods & Research,* 16 (November 1987), pp. 309–334.

them out altogether, shortening questions, or failing to follow up certain ambiguous answers in the manner required."[36]

At least three interviewer behaviors lead to response bias: (1) errors in asking questions and in probing when additional information is required, (2) errors in recording the answer, and (3) errors due to cheating.

Even though errors in asking questions can arise with any of the basic question types, the problem is particularly acute with open-ended questions where probing follows the initial response. No two interviewers are likely to employ the same probes. The content as well as the timing of the probes may differ. This raises the possibility that the differences in answers may be due to the probes that are used rather than any "true" differences in the position of the respondents.

The manner in which the initial question is phrased can also introduce error. Two of the more common errors here are for interviewers to reword the question to fit their perceptions of what the respondent is capable of understanding or in a way that incorporates their own opinions of what constitutes an appropriate answer. Surprisingly, questions that include alternative answers possess great potential for interviewer bias. This bias occurs because the interviewer places undue emphasis on one of the alternatives in stating the question. Slight changes in tone can change the meaning of the entire question. In one of the most comprehensive studies that investigated interviewer error in asking questions, it was found, for example, that the *average number of errors per question by type* was:[37]

Reading error	0.293
Speech variations	0.116
Probes	0.140
Feedbacks to respondents	0.161

One of an interviewer's main tasks is keeping the respondent interested and motivated. At the same time, the interviewer tries to record what the respondent is saying by dutifully writing down the person's answers to open-ended questions or checking the appropriate box with closed questions. These dual, sometimes incompatible, responsibilities can also be a source of error. Interviewers may not correctly "hear" what the respondent is actually saying. This may be because the respondent is inarticulate and the response is garbled or because an interviewer's selective processes are operating. Interviewers may hear what they want to hear and retain what they want to retain. This is a common failing with all of us, and, in spite of interviewer training, recording errors in the interview are all too common.[38]

---

[36]W. A. Belson, "Increasing the Power of Research to Guide Advertising Decisions," *Journal of Marketing*, 29 (April 1965), p. 38. See also Martin Collins and Bob Butcher, "Interviewer and Clustering Effects in an Attitude Survey," *Journal of the Market Research Society*, 25 (January 1983), pp. 39–58.

[37]Norman M. Bradburn and Seymour Sudman, *Improving Interview Method and Questionnaire Design* (San Francisco: Jossey-Bass, 1979), p. 29.

[38]Martin Collins, "Interviewing Variability: A Review of the Problem," *Journal of the Market Research Society*, 22 (April 1980), pp. 77–95. For ways of investigating interviewer errors, see Jean Morton-Williams and Wendy Sykes, "The Use of Interaction Coding and Follow-up Interviews to Investigate Comprehension of Survey Questions," *Journal of the Market Research Society*, 26 (April 1984), pp. 109–127. See also Jacques Billiet and Geert Loosveldt, "Improvement of the Quality of Responses to Factual Survey Questions by Interviewer Training," *Public Opinion Quarterly*, 52 (Summer 1988), pp. 190–211.

Lest we be too hard on interviewers, we need to recognize that their job is a difficult one. It demands a good deal of ingenuity, creativity, and dogged determination. Research Realities 12.4 highlights what an interviewer for the Census Bureau must do to complete the work assigned.

Interviewer cheating can also be a source of response error. Cheating may range from the fabrication of a whole interview to the fabrication of one or two answers to make the response complete. The Advertising Research Foundation (ARF), for example, conducts validation studies for its members upon request by reinterviewing a sample of those who were reported to have been interviewed previously. This is done to verify that the interview actually took place and that the designated questions were asked. In one of its studies, ARF found that 5.4 percent of the interviews across 33 separate studies could not be verified, and that an additional 7.9 percent contained at least two performance errors.[39] What was especially disturbing about these results is that it is generally believed that the surveys submitted for verification are among the best executed in the advertising area. Even the Census Bureau, commonly recognized as the most sophisticated and careful collector of data in the world, must contend with the fabrication of interviews. See Research Realities 12.5.

Most commercial research firms validate 10 to 20 percent of the completed interviews through follow-up telephone calls or by sending postcards to a sample of "respondents" to verify that they have in fact been contacted. The validation usually covers such general areas as:

1. Method of contact — to be sure a personal interview wasn't actually handled on the telephone, for example.
2. Questions asked — to verify that no important questions, such as qualifying or demographic questions, were skipped.
3. Exhibits/products shown — to make sure people saw any concept boards or products that they were supposed to see.
4. Respondent's familiarity with interviewer — to determine that the interviewer did not contact friends or acquaintances.
5. General reactions to the interview — to check on the general quality of the contact.[40]

Another form of cheating, which is not exactly response error but which has a strong effect on all nonsampling errors, is padding bills. The interviewer may falsify the number of hours worked or the number of miles traveled. The problem is widespread because of the nature of the interviewing situation. The interviewer works without direct supervision in a basically low-paying job. Further, the supervisor's pay is normally geared to the interviewer's charges, so the higher the interviewer's bills, the higher the supervisor's compensation. Bill padding drains resources from other parts of the study and thereby decreases the efficiency (value) of the information because it is obtained at higher cost.

---

[39]Lipstein, "In Defense of Small Samples."

[40]Jeffrey L. Pope, *Practical Marketing Research* (New York: American Management Association, 1993), p. 57. See also pages 56–59 for some effective validation questions for getting at these issues.

Research Realities 12.4

Adventures of a Census Interviewer

Allie Sanborn held up the questionnaire. "You go in as information, but come out as a statistic," she said and then launched into the questions that make up the Census Bureau's Survey of Income and Program Participation (SIPP). Allie is one of the Census Bureau's 3,000 field representatives, a hardy band of adventurers who scour the streets for their target households and conduct the interviews that give us the data we release.

On this day, Allie was visiting three households. In two cases, she was meeting her respondents for the first time. She would tell them she would be visiting them every four months over the next two and one-half years to ask about their income and employment.

In one household, she interviewed a single parent living on disability. The householder fought off weakness to answer Allie's questions and expressed pleasure at participating in the survey. Here Allie asked the basic SIPP questions on income and labor force participation. In future interviews, she would be asking questions on these and other subjects.

Allie arrived at the second household and managed to persuade the woman of the house to answer questions while frying salmon cakes for dinner. This interview proved to be more difficult since the household consisted of several adults.

No, the woman told Allie, she couldn't give her all the information needed. She gave what she could and called her son-in-law to complete his portion of the interview. None of her daughters were home. Allie tried unsuccessfully to interview the woman's hus-

band, but agreed to come back two days hence to continue the interview.

"I have a feeling," Allie said as she left. Sure enough, when Allie returned two days later, no one was home. Missed appointments are a way of life.

"The larger households are tough," Allie explained. "Some of the respondents may be out, and those you talk to may not be able to answer for those who aren't there, especially if the people aren't related. Over the two and one-half year interviewing cycle, people will come and go, move out of state — and we make an attempt to follow them. We have to question each adult about recent work and income. We ask what's happened over the past four months. The more adults, the more difficult it is to get all the information from everyone.

"We become a part of the family history. We see births, deaths, divorces; we see children grow up and leave. I had one respondent tell me that I knew the family better than anyone else in the world.

"We walk in as a stranger but after two and one-half years we leave practically a member of the family."

The third household Allie visited that day had been in the survey for two years. It housed an older couple with grown children away at school. In this household, Allie asked the basic SIPP questions on income and several supplemental questions on assets, work disability, and other topics. (After the first interview, households are asked additional questions on various topics ranging from family background to taxes.)

Allie finally returned home at 10 p.m.; even so, she still wasn't finished. She had to review the questionnaires to see if she conducted the interviews properly. The next day she shipped the questionnaires off to the Philadelphia regional office.

Source: "Census Field Representatives Meet Statistics Face to Face," *Census and You,* 24 (April 1989), pp. 6–8.

As suggested previously, it is much more difficult to adjust for response errors than for nonresponse errors. Their direction, much less their magnitude, is unknown, because in order to estimate their effects, the true value must be known. The researcher's main hope lies in prevention rather than subsequent adjustment of the results. The various sources of errors themselves suggest preventives. For example, training can help reduce

"Interviewer's Interviewer"

Allie is a supervisory field representative, the interviewer's interviewer. She trains new field representatives, rates them, handles problem cases, and in general provides on-the-spot support for the army of field representatives.

Most representatives work in their own counties. Supervisory field representatives have a much larger territory; Allie's is particularly large. She generally works in Baltimore and Annapolis but routinely drives to Delaware and Pennsylvania.

The first two weeks of the month she works on SIPP. She sees 10–15 households. In this survey, the representative must contact all households in person. The third week she works on the Current Population Survey; the workload is heavier, about 35 households. Many of these are telephoned. The last week of the month is used for reinterviews or solving other problems.

The representatives are on the road a good bit and work odd hours — nights and weekends. "We have to go when people are most likely to be home," Allie explains.

Allie receives her assignments from the Philadelphia regional office. After that, it's up to her. She sends new households a standard introductory letter to break the ice. "I always try to add a personal note," she says.

Occasionally one household member may be cooperative, another much less so. "In one case, the wife greeted me and we proceeded into the living room where the husband was sprawled out in his recliner. He was a steelworker who had just lost his job. And he wasn't feeling kindly towards the Government.

"He refused the interview and made me leave. I arranged to call the wife at work in order to continue. But that didn't work and when I stopped by to see her again, he came out and became very abusive. I tried to explain the value of the survey, but he got angrier and louder. I was afraid he'd become violent. It was quite frightening. About 90 to 95 percent of the people I meet are cooperative. It takes some ingenuity and persistence to deal with the others. But I take it as a real challenge to get the interview."

Tales from the Trenches

Calling at a rural address, one field representative found a locked gate. The house was out of sight up an entrance road behind a nearby hill. No one came to the gate to let her in, and there were no neighbors nearby. She wrote a note explaining her visit and setting a time at which she would return later that day.

When she returned, the note was gone, the gate was ajar, and there was a horse standing just inside the gate. There was also a note addressed to "Census representative." The note instructed our field representative to mount the horse, which would carry her up to the house where the owner would be happy to see her.

Without hesitation, the interviewer, who had never ridden a horse before, clambered up on the horse, which then plodded up the hill and delivered her to the door of the house.

Sure enough, the respondent, gracious and congenial, was waiting, and the interview was completed.

At the end of the interview, the Census Bureau worker thanked the respondent and again mounted the horse, which plodding carefully, delivered her to the gate.

errors in asking questions and recording answers. Similarly, the way interviewers are selected, paid, and controlled could reduce cheating. Overall interviewer performance can be assessed by rating the quality of the work in terms of appropriate characteristics such as costs, types of errors, ability to follow instructions, and so on. We shall not detail the established procedures in this regard, since that would be a book in its own

Even the Census Bureau Must Contend with Interviewer Cheating

Terry Ghazey and Mary Beth Scully used to believe in the census. They started working in the district office here last winter. Ghazey at one point made three visits after dark to a motel for the homeless to try and count everyone. In time she was promoted to supervise 100 enumerators.

Scully led a quality-control team of 25. "If I thought people in the field were making things up, we'd fight it," she said.

Then came the weekend of June 22. Hackensack was under pressure from the Philadelphia regional census office to finish its count. Of the 45,000 district households that hadn't mailed in forms, enumerators still had no data for 4,500.

Scully, Ghazey, and six others interviewed said that on Friday, June 22, the Hackensack district manager, Michael Rodak, ordered the staff to begin making up numbers, alternating "one, two, and three" occupants on questionnaires.

"Everyone was sitting around falsifying questionnaires," Scully said. "They were laughing. People were being paid overtime to work all weekend making up forms. They'd say, 'We need 300 more to finish this section' and they'd fill out 300."

"It went on for days," said Ghazey, who estimates that 3,500 forms were falsified. "There were piles and piles."

Kristin Veleber said she was one of 50 workers Rodak told to do the "one-two-three" forms. "Everybody available did them," she said. "I did a big stack, probably 300 in two days." She was asked to work overtime to do more, but refused. "When I realized what was going on, I was disturbed."

The Census Bureau began an inquiry two weeks ago, after *The Record of Hackensack* reported some of these events. John Connelly, a Census Bureau spokesman, said there could be "no legitimate explanation for a one-two-three rotation. No way you could authorize that."

Scully was so upset on that Friday in June that she tracked down the regional manager for central New Jersey, Medell Ford. "I was livid," she said. "I had just spent three months doing quality control and here they were falsifying data. I told Medell I had refused to take part. He said the Bureau appreciated my concern, but it was fine, other offices were doing the same thing. He acted as if it was common practice in the region."

Ford refused to comment, saying he had been told not to speak to reporters. Rodak would say only, "I followed procedures and I did nothing wrong."

There had been considerable turmoil in the central New Jersey operation. Directors of three of the area's four district offices — Hackensack, Bergenfield, and Wayne — resigned in the midst of the count last spring. Rodak, who is 24 years old and had been the sixth ranking person in Hackensack, was promoted to run the office in April. With much of the census over, he now works part-time for a local state assemblyman and is a substitute teacher.

Former supervisors say much of the problem was lack of experience from top to bottom. Hackensack is one of the more urban areas of this largely suburban district. "It was hard to find adult enumerators to do Hackensack," Ghazey said. "They wound up with almost all high school students."

Murray Rubenstein, who was a crew leader, said questionnaires were constantly being lost. "Some forms were misplaced twice. We don't know how much was lost." He said at the end of the count the office was training hundreds of new enumerators at a time when there wasn't enough work for existing enumerators.

"So much tax money was wasted," Scully said.

Ghazey said that even as office workers were falsifying questionnaires in June, enumerators were out trying to count households legitimately. "They'd bring in the correct forms and we tried to process them. But the computer would reject them because there was already a falsified form for that address."

Bob Fuchs, a former supervisor, said that when he tried to enter accurate forms, "they were rejected as duplicates." What happened to the correct forms? "They were taken outside and thrown away," Ghazey said.

Source: Michael Winerip, "How to Finish a Census: Just Make It Up," *New York Times*, (November 19, 1990), p. A18. Copyright © 1990/93 by the New York Times Company. Reprinted by permission.

right.[41] For our part we need to recognize the existence of response errors, their sources, and their potentially devastating effect. The interviewer–interviewee interaction model is helpful in visualizing these sources and in indicating some methods of prevention.

Office Errors

Our problems with nonsampling errors do not end with data collection. Errors can and do arise in the editing, coding, tabulation, and analysis of the data.[42] For the most part, these errors can be reduced, if not eliminated, through the exercise of proper controls in data processing. These questions are discussed in the chapter dealing with analysis.

TOTAL ERROR IS KEY

By this time we hope that the reader understands the admonition that total error, rather than any single type of error, is the key in designing a research investigation. The admonition particularly applies to sampling error, because there is a general tendency for beginning students of research method to argue for the "largest possible sample." After all, training in statistical method suggests that a large sample is much more likely to produce a statistic close to the population parameter being estimated than a small sample. What the student fails to appreciate, though, is that the argument applies only to sampling error. Increasing the sample size does, in fact, decrease sampling error. It may also increase nonsampling error, however, because the larger sample requires more interviewers, for instance, and this creates additional burdens in selection, training, and control. Further, nonsampling error is a much more insidious and troublesome error than sampling error. Sampling error can be estimated; many forms of nonsampling error cannot. Sampling error can be reduced through more sophisticated sample design or by using a larger sample. The path is clear and relatively well-traveled, so the researcher should have little difficulty constraining sampling error within desired bounds. Not so with nonsampling errors. The path is not paved. New sources of nonsampling error are

---

[41]Some useful general sources are: Ronald Anderson, Judith Kasper, Martin R. Frankel *et al., Total Survey Error* (San Francisco: Jossey-Bass, 1979); Bradburn and Sudman, *Improving Interview Method and Questionnaire Design;* Donald Dillman, *Mail and Telephone Surveys* (New York: John Wiley and Sons, 1978); Paul L. Erdos, *Professional Mail Surveys* (Malabar, Fla.: Robert E. Kreiger, 1983); Robert Ferber, ed., *Handbook of Marketing Research* (New York: McGraw-Hill, 1974), particularly Section II-B; Robert M. Groves and Robert L. Kahn, *Surveys by Telephone* (New York: Academic Press, 1979); J. Rothman, "Acceptance Checks for Ensuring Quality in Research," *Journal of the Market Research Society,* 22 (July 1980), pp. 192–204; and James E. Nelson and Pamela L. Kiecker, "Some Causes and Consequences of Interviewer Cheating Behavior," in Stanley Shapiro and A. H. Walle, eds., *Marketing: A Return to the Broader Dimensions* (Chicago: American Marketing Association, 1988), pp. 498–503.

[42]The reader who believes that analysis errors should be no problem should see Mosteller, "Nonsampling Errors," in which he devotes 9 of 19 pages to the discussion of potential errors in analysis. See also John G. Keane, "Questionable Statistics," *American Demographics,* 7 (June 1985), pp. 18–21. For an empirical example illustrating the potential extent of the problem, see David Elliot, "A Study of Variation in Occupation and Social Class Coding — Summary of Results," *Survey Methodology Bulletin,* 14 (May 1982), pp. 48–49.

ETHICAL DILEMMA 12.3

A well-known car agency needed to make a decision about whether or not to import a relatively unknown line of foreign cars to complement its domestic line. To aid in its decision making, the agency contracted a research firm to conduct a study to determine potential consumer interest and demand for this foreign car line. The results indicated that substantial awareness and interest existed, and consequently the decision was made to take on the new line.

To publicize the new line, a special preview was arranged for interested community members such as local newspaper and radio people, executives in related automotive industries, filling stations and repair shop owners, and leaders of men's and women's clubs. The agency's owners also wanted to invite the survey participants who had expressed an interest in the car; consequently, they asked the research firm to make known to them the respondents' names. The research firm refused to comply with this request, arguing that to do so would be a violation of the respondents' promised anonymity.

- Should the research firm comply with the agency's request?
- Does the car agency have the right to receive the participants' names since it has paid for the research?
- Would it have made a difference if the study had not been one to determine sales potential?
- What are some of the consequences of making the respondents' names known to the car agency?
- If the question had been anticipated before the survey was begun, could the interview structure have avoided the dilemma in which the company and the agency now find themselves?

ETHICAL DILEMMA 12.4

"These new computer-voiced telephone surveys are wonderful!" your friend enthuses over lunch. "Because we don't have to pay telephone interviewers, we can afford to have target numbers automatically redialed until someone answers. Of course, the public finds the computer's voice irritating and the whole notion of being interviewed by a machine rather humiliating. Nevertheless, we can overcome most people's reluctance to participate by repeatedly calling them until they give in and complete the questionnaire."

- Is it ethical to contact respondents repeatedly until they agree to participate in a research study? How many contacts are legitimate?
- If an industry is unable to constrain its members to behave ethically, should the government step in with regulations?
- If the public reacts against this kind of telephone survey, what are the results likely to be for researchers using traditional, more considerate telephone surveys?

being discovered all the time, and even though known, many of these sources defy reduction by any automatic procedure. ''Improved method'' is critical, but what these methods should be is sometimes unknown, although the chapter has attempted to highlight some of the better known sources of nonsampling error and ways of dealing with them.

Table 12.3 attempts to summarize what we have been saying about nonsampling errors and how they can be reduced or controlled. The table can be used as a sort of checklist for marketing managers and other users of research to evaluate the quality of the research before making substantive decisions on the basis of the research results. Although not all of the methods for handling nonsampling errors will be applicable in every study, a systematic analysis of the research effort using the suggested approaches should provide the proper appreciation for the quality of research information that is obtained.

TABLE **12.3 Overview of Nonsampling Errors and Some Methods for Handling Them**

Type	Definition	Methods for Handling
Noncoverage	Failure to include some units or entire sections of the defined survey population in the sampling frame.	1. Improve basic sampling frame using other sources. 2. Select sample in such a way as to reduce incidence, such as by ignoring ineligibles on a list. 3. Adjust the results by appropriately weighting the subsample results.
Nonresponse	Failure to obtain information from some elements of the population that were selected for the sample.	
Not-at-homes:	Designated respondent is not home when the interviewer calls.	1. Have interviewers make advance appointments. 2. Call back at another time, preferably at a different time of day. 3. Attempt to contact the designated respondent using another approach (i.e., use a modified callback).
Refusals:	Respondent refuses to cooperate in the survey.	1. Attempt to convince the respondent of the value of the research and the importance of his or her participation. 2. Provide advance notice that the survey is coming. 3. Guarantee anonymity. 4. Provide an incentive for participating. 5. Hide the identification of the sponsor by using an independent research organization. 6. Try to get a ''foot in the door'' by getting the respondent to comply with some small task before getting the survey.

(continued)

TABLE **12.3**   *Continued*

Type	Definition	Methods for Handling
		7. Use personalized cover letters. 8. Use a follow-up contact at a more convenient time. 9. Avoid interesting but not vital questions. 10. Adjust the results to account for the nonresponse.
Field	Although the individual participates in the study, he or she refuses to answer specific questions or provides incorrect answers to them.	1. Match the background characteristics of the interviewer and respondent as closely as possible. 2. Make sure interviewer instructions are clear and written down. 3. Conduct practice training sessions with interviewers. 4. Examine the interviewers' understanding of the study's purposes and procedures. 5. Have interviewers complete the questionnaire and examine the replies they secure to see if there is any relationship between these answers and their own answers. 6. Verify a sample of each interviewer's interviews.
Office*	Errors that arise when coding, tabulating, or analyzing the data.	1. Use field edit to detect the most glaring omissions and inaccuracies in the data. 2. Use a second edit in the office to decide how data collection instruments containing incomplete answers, obviously wrong answers, and answers that reflect a lack of interest are to be handled. 3. Use closed questions to simplify the coding, but when open-ended questions need to be used, specify the appropriate codes that will be allowed before collecting the data. 4. When open-ended questions are being coded and multiple coders are being used, divide the task by questions and not by data collection forms. 5. Have each coder code a sample of the other's work to ensure a consistent set of coding criteria is being employed. 6. Follow established conventions; for example, use numeric codes and not letters of the alphabet when coding the data for computer analysis. 7. Prepare a code book that lists the codes for each variable and the categories included in each code. 8. Use appropriate methods to analyze the data.

*Note: Steps that can be taken to reduce the incidence of office errors are discussed in more detail in the analysis chapters.

SUMMARY

This chapter concentrated on the data collection phase of the research process. The emphasis was on sources of error, because it was thought that an understanding of sources is more fundamental than a how-to-do-it approach. Practitioners need to be aware of the many potential sources of error so that they can better evaluate research proposals and can place research results in a proper perspective. Researchers need an understanding of error sources so that they can design studies with proper controls and allowances.

The main distinction in errors is that between sampling error and nonsampling error. Sampling error represents the difference between the observed values of a variable and the long-run average of the observed values in repetitions of the measurement. Nonsampling errors include everything else. They may arise because of errors in conception, logic, analysis, data gathering, and so forth and are divided into the two major categories of errors of nonobservation and errors of observation. Errors of nonobservation can, in turn, be divided into errors of noncoverage and errors of nonresponse. Errors of observation can arise while collecting the data or while processing the information collected.

Noncoverage errors are essentially sampling frame problems. The list of population elements is rarely complete. Nonresponse errors reflect a failure to obtain information from certain elements of the population that were designated for inclusion in the sample. They can arise because the designated respondent was not at home or refused to participate. Empirical evidence indicates that the not-at-homes and the refusals often differ from respondents, and thus a systematic bias is introduced when they are excluded.

The interviewer–interviewee interaction model was offered as a useful vehicle for conceptualizing the errors that can arise while collecting the data. This model presents the interview as an interactive process between interviewer and respondent. Each principal brings different background and psychological factors to the interview. These affect each person's behavior and the way he or she perceives the other principal's behavior.

Finally, office errors occur because of weaknesses in the procedures for editing, coding, tabulating, and analyzing the collected data.

The research objective of minimization of total error was reiterated. Total error in conjunction with cost determines the value of any research effort.

Questions

1. Distinguish between sampling error and nonsampling error. Why is the distinction important?
2. What are noncoverage errors? Are they a problem with telephone surveys? How? With mail surveys? How? With personal interview studies? How?
3. How can noncoverage bias be assessed? What can be done to reduce it?
4. What is nonresponse error?
5. What are the basic types of nonresponse error? Are they equally serious for mail, telephone, or personal interview studies? Explain.

6. What can be done to reduce the incidence of not-at-homes in the final sample?

7. What is the contact rate? What role does it play in evaluating the results?

8. What are the typical reasons why designated respondents refuse to participate in a study? What can be done to reduce the incidence of refusals? Do refusals generally introduce random error or systematic biases into studies?

9. What is item nonresponse? What alternatives are available to the researcher for treating item nonresponse?

10. What is the response rate? What is the completeness rate? Is there any relation between the two?

11. What are observation errors? What are the basic types of observation errors?

12. Are observation errors likely to be a more serious or less serious problem than nonobservation errors? Explain.

13. Describe the interviewer–interviewee interaction model, including its basic propositions.

14. What does the interviewer–interviewee interaction model suggest with respect to the background characteristics of interviewers? With respect to their psychological characteristics?

15. What basic types of interviewer behavior can lead to response bias?

16. Explain the statement, "Total error is key."

Applications and Problems

1. Discuss some of the potential problems with each of the following sampling frames. For each potential problem you list, indicate whether it would result in a non-coverage or over-coverage error.
   a. Phone book
   b. Mailing list
   c. Maps

2. Sue Candleshoe, a manager of marketing research at a large over-the-counter drug manufacturer, wanted to investigate consumers' reactions to a recent poisoning scare in one of her brands. She needed the results quickly. However, Sue was familiar with some of the faults of using a phone book for a sampling frame. Recommend another option that would allow Sue to get the results quickly by telephone but would not introduce as much bias as using a phone book. Discuss which biases, if any, your suggested solution might still have.

3. Henry Brown owns a sailboat rental yard located in Sister Bay, Wisconsin. He has been considering altering the services that his business offers to customers. He would like to offer sailboards for rental as well as add a convenience store so that customers could picnic at the state park adjacent to his rental yard. Before making these changes, he has decided to administer a short questionnaire in the store to a random sample of customers. For a period of one month, clerks have been instructed to conduct personal interviews with every fourth customer. Henry gave specific instructions that on no account were customers to be harassed or offended. Identify the major sources of noncoverage and nonresponse errors. Explain.

4. Deal-A-Wheel, a large manufacturer of radial tires located in Pittsburgh, Pennsylvania, was experiencing a problem common to tire manufacturers. The poor performance of the

auto industry was having a severe negative impact on the tire industry. To maintain sales and competitive positions, the various manufacturers were offering wholesalers additional credit and discount opportunities. Deal-A-Wheel's management was particularly concerned about wholesaler reaction to a new discount policy they were considering. The first survey the company conducted to explore these reactions was unsatisfactory to top management. Management thought that it was conducted in a haphazard manner and contained numerous nonsampling errors. Deal-A-Wheel's management decided to conduct another study containing the following changes:

- The sampling frame was defined as a list of 1,000 of the largest wholesalers that stocked Deal-A-Wheel tires, and the sample elements were to be randomly selected from this list.
- A callback technique was to be employed, with the callbacks being made at different times than the original attempted contact.
- The sample size was to be doubled from 200 to 400 respondents.
- The sample elements that were ineligible or refused to cooperate were to be substituted for by the next element from the list.
- An incentive of $1.00 was to be offered to respondents.

Critically evaluate the steps that were being considered to prevent the occurrence of nonsampling errors. Do you think they are appropriate? Be specific.

5. Bingham Seeds is a local, commercial producer of agricultural seed products located in McGraw, New York. Bingham has developed a new variety of field oats that in university field trials has out-performed the industry leaders by 15 to 20 percent during the last three years. Robert Arthur, Bingham's sales and marketing vice-president, wants to conduct a survey to determine farmers' interest in the new variety. Robert has contacted a market research agency in Syracuse, New York, to conduct the survey for Bingham Seeds. The research agency has suggested the following study:

- The population is defined as the 100 largest grain crop farms in the United States.
- The sampling frame will be the list of the 400 largest U.S. farms according to *Successful Farming* magazine.
- A telephone survey will be conducted by the agency's interviewing staff, which consists of women and Syracuse University students.
- The next phone number from the list will be used if selected elements are ineligible or refuse to be interviewed.
- Ten questions will be added to the questionnaire for a farm equipment manufacturer.
- In order to keep costs down, the survey will be run without a training session.

Critically evaluate the steps that are being considered by the marketing research agency. Do they control or prevent nonsampling errors? Do you think that they are appropriate? What recommendations would you make to improve the proposed study? Why?

6. In a recent survey conducted for a large tire manufacturer, the marketing research firm intended to obtain 1,400 interviews with recent purchasers of the company's premier brand. Eight hundred completed surveys were obtained. Two hundred people were found to be ineligible, and another 300 people refused to participate in the study even before their eligibility could be determined. Furthermore, 100 respondents were not even contacted. Compute the response rate for this survey including any information given regarding eligibility.

7. Andrew Blake is a new employee at S and S Research. He has just been instructed to write an introduction to a survey for a mail study. Andrew has been told that the survey will evaluate long-distance customers' reasons for calling long distance. He has also been told that the respondents will each receive $20 after the survey has been completed and returned to S and S Research. Andrew is having a difficult time remembering what he should include in an introduction in order to persuade respondents to complete the questionnaire. First, list several persuasive techniques that Andrew should include in his introduction, then write an introduction to this study that you think will increase the response rate.

8. Sharon Klein, the owner of a local furniture-store chain, has recently hired you as her research analyst. Sharon has little experience in research and is expecting you to lead her in the right direction. She wants to conduct a study to determine the buying cycle for living room furniture. Sharon feels that the best approach in conducting this study is to use the largest possible sample that her budget allows. Try to convince Sharon why increasing the sample size may not be the best research strategy. Be sure to include specific strategies that Sharon might want to spend some of her money on rather than spending it all on increasing the sample size.

9. A major publisher of diverse magazines was interested in determining customer satisfaction with three of the company's leading publications: *TrendSetter, BusWhizz,* and *CompuTech*. The three magazines dealt respectively with women's fashions, business trends, and computer technology developments. Three sampling frames, consisting of lists of subscribers residing in New York, were formulated. Three random samples were to be chosen from these lists. Personal interviews using an unstructured–undisguised questionnaire were to be conducted. The publishing company had a regular pool of interviewers that it called on whenever interviews were to be conducted. The interviewers had varying educational backgrounds, although 95 percent were high school graduates and the remaining 5 percent had some college education. In terms of age and sex, the range varied from 18 years to 45 years, with 70 percent female and 30 percent male. The majority of interviewers were housewives and students. Before conducting a survey, the company sent the necessary information in the mail and asked interviewers to indicate whether they were interested. The questionnaires, addresses, and other detailed information were then sent to those interviewers replying affirmatively. After the interviewer completed his or her quota of interviews, the replies were sent back to the company. The company then mailed the interviewer's remuneration.
   a. Using the guidelines in Table 12.3, critically evaluate the selection, training, and instructions given to the field interviewers.
   b. Using Kahn and Cannell's model, identify the major sources of bias that would affect the interviews.

 Thorndike Sports Equipment Video Case

1. Ted mentions that his grandfather tended to drift off the questionnaire when collecting information. Is this acceptable for interviewers? Why? Why not?

2. If you were hiring interviewers to present this survey to respondents, what type of people would you hire? What would you stress during interviewer briefing sessions?

CASE 4.1
Young Ideas Publishing Company (A)[1]

How does a company go about marketing products to a specified niche of the teenage market? That is the question confronting Linda Halley, co-owner of Young Ideas Publishing Company. Halley is convinced that her unconventional novels for young people would be very attractive to at least a segment of the teenage market. She is unsure, however, about how to reach this "nonconformist" segment of the market.

BACKGROUND

Three years ago, Halley wrote her first novel, a youth-oriented book (ages 15–18) entitled *Illusions of Summer*. None of the major publishers would publish the book, however, primarily because it dealt with several controversial social and political concerns. Most publishers simply felt that such topics would not be of interest to enough high school teenagers to justify publication, although many agreed that the novel was of publication quality in other respects.

Frustrated in her efforts to publish her novel, Halley and a business partner, Teresa Martinez, decided to form their own publishing company and publish the book themselves. Both believed that teenagers would be interested in social and political topics and would buy the book. Thus, Young Ideas Publishing Company was born. Halley hoped that effective marketing of the books on a local basis by the company might encourage national distributors to alter their positions toward the novel.

When *Illusions of Summer* was released, it was very well-received by several literary critics, winning promising reviews and awards. Despite its critical success, however, commercial acceptance has been much harder to find. During the first 24 months after publication, only about 1,500 copies of the book have been sold, mostly through local bookstores and mail-order. Most distributors have been unwilling to handle the book because it is not from an established publisher. With few channels through which to market the product, it remains virtually unknown outside of a limited local market.

[1]The contributions of Tom J. Brown to the development of this case are gratefully acknowledged.

Even with this poor showing from a commercial standpoint, Halley continued to believe that so-called "nonconformist" teenagers would be willing to buy books of this nature. Accordingly, she wrote and published a second novel, *Ultimate Choices*. Once again, the novel dealt with several controversial issues for teens and social and political concerns; once again, the critics reacted favorably. Initial sales for *Ultimate Choices* have been better than they were for *Illusions of Summer;* currently (two months after publication), about 250 copies have been sold. By talking to clerks in local bookstores, Halley has learned that most of the books are being sold to teenagers.

NATURE OF THE PROBLEM

Although encouraged by the good reviews and increased sales of the second book, Halley and Martinez are concerned about the future of Young Ideas Publishing Company. Even though the company has managed to break even during the past two years by contracting for outside printing jobs, Martinez has indicated that the survival of the company may well depend on the success of the new novel.

Both partners are still convinced that a market exists for the novels. They now recognize, however, that they may not know enough about the teenage market to effectively market the novels. For example, they believe that insights are needed in the following areas:

- Will high school teenagers specifically select young adult novels, or do they think that these are written for younger teens?
- Are teenagers interested in social and political issues?
- Where do high school teenagers usually obtain books for pleasure reading?
- Do teens purchase books for themselves, or do parents purchase books for them?
- What types of promotional items do high school teens enjoy most?
- What advertising media are most effective in reaching teens?
- How do "nonconformist" teens differ on these issues from other teens?

You have been hired by Young Ideas Publishing Company to develop and implement a research project to investigate these ideas. Resources are limited; Halley would like the results of the research within 60 days.

Questions

1. Based on the information provided and your knowledge of marketing and marketing research, define the research problem.
2. What is the target population for your study?
3. Discuss your proposed sampling plan, including the implications for the implementation of the project.

CASE 4.2
St. Andrews Medical Center[1]

The Eating Disorders Clinic of the St. Andrews Medical Center has been operating since 1985 to treat patients with anorexia nervosa and bulimia. Anorexia nervosa, often characterized by intense obsession with dieting and weight loss, and bulimia, also known as the "binge and purge syndrome," typically afflict young women between the ages of 14 and 22 years. Both conditions can result in very serious health problems (or even death) if left untreated.

In recent years, the clinic has experienced a dramatic decline in patients, while, officials believe, a competing program offered by City Hospital has continued to grow. The programs are comparable in terms of staffing and cost of treatment. Patients are normally referred to an eating disorders program by their primary care physician or other healthcare professional.

Officials at St. Andrews were very concerned about the downward trend in the number of patients being referred to and treated at the Eating Disorders Clinic. Initially, they believed that the decrease might simply be a reflection of a decrease in the prevalence of anorexia nervosa and bulimia in the population. However, a review of the medical literature and discussions with administrators of eating disorders programs from across the country strongly suggested that this was not the case. Furthermore, conversations with the medical director at City Hospital confirmed that the number of cases of the disorders treated by the City Hospital program has continued to increase during recent years.

St. Andrews' officials next turned to the marketing department for the development and implementation of some type of research designed to uncover the reasons behind the decreasing enrollment in the eating disorders program.

SAMPLING PLAN

Because more than 80 percent of the cases treated at the Eating Disorders Clinic are referred to the program by other healthcare providers, St. Andrews' marketing staff believed that the research should be directed at these healthcare providers. In particular, they wanted to obtain attitudes and opinions about the St. Andrews program specifically and about eating disorders programs in general.

The population for which a sample frame was to be developed included all healthcare professionals in the market area of St. Andrews Medical Center who may treat female patients between the ages of 14 and 22 years.

A review of admittance records showed that referrals were most likely to come from primary care practitioners, including physicians in general medicine, family medicine, internal medicine, and gastroenterology. In addition, referrals have been received from pediatricians, obstetricians/gynecologists, psychiatrists, and psychologists. Although the

---

[1]The contributions of Tom J. Brown to the development of this case are gratefully acknowledged.

TABLE 1   **Sampling Frame**

Specialty	Number of Practitioners
Pediatricians	63
Obstetricians/Gynecologists	63
Psychiatrists	124
Psychologists	128
Primary Care Practitioners*	321
Total	699

*Includes specialists in family medicine, general medicine, internal medicine, and gastroenterology.

names and addresses of physicians in these specialties were available from several sources, the marketing staff believed that the telephone directory provided the easiest and least expensive listing. The sampling frame thus included all physicians (or psychologists) from each of these specialties and was drawn from the Yellow Pages of the current telephone directory. Table 1 provides the breakdown of the number of professionals of each type included in the sampling frame. All healthcare providers on the list were to be contacted.

ADMINISTRATION

The marketing department staff decided to conduct a mail survey and constructed a three-page structured questionnaire that was sent to the 699 healthcare providers on the list using the addresses obtained from the telephone directory. An appropriate cover letter was also included. Although neither the cover letter nor the questionnaire identified St. Andrews Medical Center as the sponsor of the survey, no attempt was made to disguise the purpose of the survey. In addition to questions related specifically to the St. Andrews' program, the marketing staff included questions about City Hospital's competing program and about eating disorders programs in general.

Of the 699 questionnaires distributed, 56 (8 percent) were returned as undeliverable by the postal service, while 119 were completed and returned by respondents (a 17 percent response rate). Although St. Andrews' officials were displeased with the low response rate — they had anticipated at least a 25 percent return rate — they thought that the data would provide useful information for the management of the Eating Disorders Clinic.

Questions

1. What is the appropriate target population given the hospital's interest?
2. Evaluate the sampling frame given the target population chosen by the hospital staff. What other sources might exist for use in developing the sampling frame?
3. Evaluate the use of a mail questionnaire for this research.

CASE 4.3
PartyTime, Inc.[1]

Andrew Todd, chief executive officer of PartyTime, Inc., a manufacturer of specialty paper products, is preparing to make an important decision. In the 14 years since he founded the company, sales and profits have increased over tenfold to all-time highs of $7,000,000 and $1,150,000, respectively, during the current year. Industry analysts predict continued stable growth during the upcoming year. Despite his firm belief in the adage, "If it's not broken, don't fix it," Todd thinks that it might be time for the addition of a new channel of distribution, based on information he has recently received.

ABOUT THE COMPANY

PartyTime manufactures a variety of specialty paper products that can be grouped into three basic categories: gift wrap (all types), party goods (printed plates, cups, napkins, party favors, etc.), and other paper goods (specialty advertising, calendars, etc.). When Todd founded the company, he purchased and renovated an existing paper mill located in the Pacific Northwest. Today, company headquarters and production facilities remain at the original location. During the heavy production season, the company employs approximately 200 people.

As shown in Table 1, gift wrap accounts for about 60 percent of revenues (50 percent of profits), and party goods amount to about 30 percent of sales (40 percent of profits). All other paper products sold by the company produce about 10 percent of revenues and an equivalent percentage of profits. Sales of gift wrap and other paper goods have been stable, increasing 3 to 4 percent per year during the previous five years. Interestingly (and as Todd is pleased to note), total sales of party goods have been increasing at about a 9 percent annual rate.

TABLE 1   **Current-Year Sales and Profit Breakdown by Category**

Category	Sales	Percentage	Profit	Percentage
Gift wrap	$4,302,300	61	$564,700	49
Party goods	2,045,500	29	472,300	41
Other paper goods	705,200	10	115,000	10
Total	$7,053,000	100	$1,152,000	100

[1]The contributions of Tom J. Brown to the development of this case are gratefully acknowledged.

THE DISTRIBUTION DECISION

Given the profitability of the party-goods line and its substantial sales growth in recent years, Todd is very interested in further increasing sales of specialty party goods. A recent publication of the National Association of Paper and Party Retailers (NAPPR) indicated that industry-wide sales of party goods are expected to increase some 10 to 20 percent during the upcoming year. Of particular interest is the projection that sales of party goods through independent party goods (IPG) shops will increase more than 25 percent. Currently, PartyTime party goods are distributed only through mass merchandisers and chain drug stores.

Although sales have been increasing steadily using existing channels, Todd wondered if the time was right to add the IPG channel. Any decision to include the new channel would have to be made early in the year, however, before orders for the holiday season begin arriving (a large percentage of total sales of party goods at the retail level occur during the holiday season).

INDEPENDENT PARTY GOODS (IPG) SHOPS

IPG retailers typically operate small- to moderate-sized stores that are often located in malls or strip shopping centers. The label "independent" indicates that the stores are not owned or franchised by major manufacturers such as Hallmark. In recent years, the number of IPG shops has grown tremendously, to the point where it is not unusual to have 15 to 20 shops in larger cities. Growth has been particularly strong in California, Florida, the upper Midwest, and the East.

COMPETITIVE ISSUES

Competition within traditional channels of distribution for party goods is intense. Within these channels, PartyTime must compete against major producers such as C.A. Reed, Beach Products, Unique, Hallmark, and Ambassador. The major competitors within the IPG channel, in contrast, are fewer in number; only AMSCAM, Contempo, and Paper Art serve as primary suppliers. Competition within the IPG channel is thought to be much less intense than that in the traditional channels.

(December 13)   Todd is leaning strongly toward committing the resources necessary to enter the IPG channel and has called a meeting of his managers to discuss the proposed move. He believes that there is room for at least one more supplier, because the competition is less intense than in the traditional distribution channels. In addition, he regards this as an opportunity to further expand the most profitable area of PartyTime's business.

At the meeting, most of PartyTime's managers seem to agree with Todd, although Kim Shinoda, the company's chief accountant, suggests that the company should learn more about IPG retailers before a decision is made. In a memorandum distributed at the meeting, she details the following areas in which more information is needed before a decision is reached:

- *Competitive Products*   Are IPG retailers satisfied with current product offerings on the market? Do they receive a satisfactory level of service from the current suppliers?
- *Purchase Criteria*   In addition to price and product considerations, what other characteristics of suppliers and product lines do retailers think are important?
- *Supplier Loyalty*   To what extent are retailers willing to carry product lines of more than one supplier?

Todd agrees that more information would be useful in making a decision, but he realizes that time constraints will force him to make a decision within the next few weeks. Along with his managers, he decides to bring in a marketing research team.

(January 16)   The marketing research team is now ready to share the results of the research project with the managers at PartyTime. To implement the research, they had developed an undisguised, semi-structured telephone questionnaire designed to obtain the information that Shinoda had suggested, as well as other information pertaining to the decision problem. The survey document used by the interviewers is shown in Figure 1.

Officials at PartyTime are particularly interested in the responses of retailers located in those geographic areas in which growth is expected to be strongest over the next year; therefore, a sampling frame was developed using telephone directories in the major cities within these geographic regions. Because many types of stores could conceivably be considered IPG shops, two criteria were established for inclusion in the sampling frame: (1) the shop must devote more than 50 percent of its shelf space to paper and party goods, and (2) the shop must carry products from more than one supplier. A total of 110 shops were identified using the telephone directories. Although attempts were made to contact each of these shops during business hours, only 82 could be reached. Thirty-two of these met the two criteria, and 23 agreed to participate in the interview.

FIGURE 1   **Survey Form**

Location:

Hello, may I speak with the store owner or purchasing agent, please?
My name is _____ . My company is doing a study of the Independent Party Shop channel for a private firm; and I would like to take a few minutes of your time to have you answer some questions. Any information you provide will be treated confidentially, and your name will not be used.

Do not pause.

Is this a convenient time? **(If yes, continue)**
(If, no) *Is there another time when you could be reached that would be more convenient for you, Mr./Ms. _____ ?*

Day and Time

(continued)

Figure 1 *Continued*

1. *In what category would your store fit?*
   [ ] Gift shop
   [ ] Card shop
   [ ] Party-goods shop
   [ ] Combination. Please describe _____
   [ ] Other _____

If not a party-goods shop or combination with party goods, stop, thank respondent for willingness to cooperate, and go on to the next call.

2. *What is the appropriate percentage of shelf space that your store devotes to paper and party goods?*

   Do not read off the categories.
   [ ] 0–20%
   [ ] 21–49%
   [ ] 50% or more

If less than 50%, stop survey here. Thank respondent for willingness to cooperate, and go on to the next call.

3. *Approximately how many suppliers of paper and party goods does your store deal with?* _____

If it carries only one line, stop survey here. Again, thank respondent for willingness to cooperate, and go on to the next call.

4. *Which of the following lines do you carry?*
   [ ] C.A. Reed   [ ] Contempo
   [ ] AMSCAM   Others?_____
   [ ] Paper Art

   The remaining questions refer to paper and party goods and the suppliers of these products.

5. *Concerning the suppliers of paper and party goods that you carry, how would you rate your satisfaction with the following (on a scale of 1 to 5, 5 being very satisfied and 1 being very dissatisfied):*
   a. Pricing, and in particular, discounts and mark-up capabilities _____
   b. Sales representative service _____
   c. Distribution (timeliness and completeness) _____
   d. Product line _____

6. *Based on what you just said, you seem to be satisfied/dissatisfied with* _____ .
   What aspects of the suppliers' products or service have caused this? **[Probe for reasons]** _____
   _____

FIGURE 1 *Continued*

Is there anything else that you think is important about your relationship with your suppliers? _____

_____

7. *For each manufacturer, how would you rate the following in terms of importance? (1 being most important and 4 being least important.)*

	C.A. Reed	AMSCAM	Paper Art	Contempo
Pricing	_____	_____	_____	_____
Promotion	_____	_____	_____	_____
Product line	_____	_____	_____	_____
Distribution	_____	_____	_____	_____

Repeat remaining options after each selection, if necessary.
Starting with most important and working down to least important, probe for reasons. Put responses for each supplier on the separate sheets that are attached.

Pricing:
   a. Wholesale pricing (discounts and allowances)
   b. Suggested retail prices
   c. Do you get credit for leftover seasonal merchandise?
Promotion:
   a. Display vehicles
   b. Manufacturer-sponsored consumer promotions
Product Line:
   a. Quality
   b. Dynamic product line (changing designs)
   c. Number of items/product categories
   d. Style
Distribution:
   a. Sales rep. service (service calls, assistance)
   b. Timeliness of delivery
   c. Completeness of the delivery (out of stocks)
   d. Ease of ordering

8. *Do any of your present suppliers offer a 1-800 telephone number to process orders?*
   ☐ Yes   ☐ No   *If yes, which ones?*_____

9. *Do you get advertising support from your suppliers?*
   ☐ Yes   ☐ No   *If yes, which ones?* _____

10. *Does a representative from your store attend paper and party goods trade shows regularly? How often? Which ones?* _____

_____

11. *In general, do you feel that there is loyalty to suppliers from stores such as yours?*

_____

_____

12. *What do you think is necessary for capturing loyalty?* _____

_____

(continued)

FIGURE 1   *Continued*

---

13. How would your store react to additional suppliers attempting to enter the market?

_____

_____

14. What could a new supplier do to make your store aware of its existence and offerings? _____

_____

15. Other than party goods, what are the best selling products in your store now? ____

_____

16. What are the worst selling products in your store? _____

_____

Demographics

Now I'd like to ask you some general questions that will be used to help us classify the information given by all the people who have participated in this survey.

17. In what type of area is your store located?

[ ]   Mall   [ ]   Free-standing
[ ]   Strip shopping center   [ ]   Outlet center
[ ]   Downtown

18. How many stores do you have?

[ ]   One
[ ]   Two
[ ]   Three to five
[ ]   Six to ten
[ ]   More

19. What is the approximate size of your store in square feet?
Do not read off the categories.

[ ]   Less than 1,999   [ ]   5,000–5,999
[ ]   2,000–2,999   [ ]   6,000–20,000
[ ]   3,000–3,999   [ ]   over 20,000
[ ]   4,000–4,999

20. What is your store's approximate level of annual sales? Is it

[ ]   under $100,000?
[ ]   under $250,000?
[ ]   under $500,000?
[ ]   under $1,000,000?
[ ]   over $1,000,000 **[don't ask]**

FIGURE 1   *Continued*

---

21. **How many years has this particular store been in business?**
    - [ ]   0–2 years
    - [ ]   3–4 years
    - [ ]   5–7 years
    - [ ]   8–10 years
    - [ ]   More than 10 years

22. **Compared to 1993, have sales in 1994 been up, down, or the same? (percentage)**

    _____

    Thank you Mr./Ms. _____ for your time and consideration. You have been very helpful.

(**January 19**)   Based on the results of the marketing research project and the input of his managers, Todd has decided to increase production of party goods and market these products through the IPG channel.

Questions

1. Evaluate the research team's development of the sample of store owners. How would you have recommended the research team develop the sampling frame?
2. Do you think that a telephone survey was the best way to collect the needed information?
3. Evaluate the questionnaire used in the research project.

CASE 4.4
Hart Machine Company[1]

Hart Machine Company of Newberry, South Carolina, is one of five major manufacturers of textile equipment in the country. It is also the only firm that *specializes* in the design and production of textile machinery rollers. Confining its distribution to the three-state area of Georgia, North Carolina, and South Carolina, company sales have been lucrative, averaging some $50 million annually. Part of Hart's success is due to the company being the only roller manufacturer headquartered in the Southeast, an area where 40 percent of the nation's textile mills are located. This location advantage allows

---

[1]The contributions of David M. Szymanski to the development of this case are gratefully acknowledged.

TABLE 1   Total Number of Textile Mills by SIC Code Located in Georgia, North Carolina, and South Carolina

SIC Code	Type of Textile Mill	State			Total
		Georgia	North Carolina	South Carolina	
221	Weaving mills, cotton	27	43	42	112
222	Weaving mills, synthetics	26	71	90	187
223	Weaving & finishing mills, wool	8	7	3	18
224	Narrow fabric mills	7	44	13	64
225	Knitting mills	39	604	63	706
226	Textile finishing	46	98	52	196
227	Floor covering mills	218	29	16	263
228	Yarn & thread mills	107	221	66	394
229	Miscellaneous textile goods	55	98	44	197
	Total	533	1,215	389	2,137

Source: U.S. Bureau of the Census, *County Business Patterns 1992,* for each of the states of Georgia, North Carolina, and South Carolina. U.S. Government Printing Office, Washington, D.C., 1984.

Hart to offer customers both prompt shipment and service at low prices (because of lower transportation costs), factors that have helped catapult Hart Machine Company to the number three position in the textile equipment industry.

In an effort to determine how to best allocate sales personnel and to appraise the performance of current members of the selling team, Thomas Stein, the sales manager, decided to develop estimates of the sales potential for each state served by (1) measuring

TABLE 2   Number of Textile Mills Employing 20 or More Persons by SIC Code for Georgia, North Carolina, and South Carolina between 1988 and 1990

Type of Textile Mill	Year = 1990			
	Georgia	North Carolina	South Carolina	Total
Weaving mills, cotton	24	31	33	88
Weaving mills, synthetics	22	56	83	161
Weaving & finishing mills, wool	8	3	3	14
Narrow fabric mills	2	33	13	48
Knitting mills	33	438	47	518
Textile finishing	28	70	41	139
Floor covering mills	136	11	14	161
Yarn & thread mills	92	199	59	350
Miscellaneous textile goods	30	61	22	113
Total	375	902	315	1,592

the inventory of rollers currently used by textile mills and (2) obtaining estimates of manufacturers' future needs. He hoped to develop a feel for new product demand by first-time users and potential entrants into the textile mill industry as well as an indication of the replacement demand for Hart rollers by current users of the firm's products.

A search of the Standard Industrial Classification (SIC) codes identified nine three-digit textile mill industries that were candidates for Hart rollers. Fortunately, there was a good deal of published data available on these industries, and much of the data was broken down by geographic region, state, and county. Stein also had access to data on individual textile mills that employed 20 or more individuals. Stein thought that this information was especially useful because only the larger mills possessed the scale of operations necessary to have textile machinery requiring Hart rollers. The published data (see Tables 1 and 2) also indicated that most of the mills (74 percent) in Georgia, North Carolina, and South Carolina qualified as likely prospects for Hart equipment, in that they employed more than 20 people.

Because of limited research funds, the Hart Company decided to survey only a sample of textile plants in Georgia, North Carolina, and South Carolina. For each firm surveyed, Hart would attempt to ascertain the number of milling machines owned and operated, their age, and the number and brand of rollers used in each piece of equipment. The researchers also hoped to gain information on each mill's performance — including plans for expansion or curtailment of different operations — and brand preferences for roller supplies. From this information it would be possible to estimate the number of machines per textile mill type as well as the new and replacement demand for Hart rollers in the three-state market area. This data would aid Stein in the allocation of sales personnel to different sectors and industries in relation to the demand for rollers. Currently, according to the overall number of textile mills in each sector, Hart's sales force is assigned to seven geographic districts: the northern and southern sections of Georgia; the northeast, southeast, and western sections of North Carolina; and the eastern and western sections of South Carolina (see Table 3).

TABLE 2   *Continued*

	Year = 1989				Year = 1988		
Georgia	North Carolina	South Carolina	Total	Georgia	North Carolina	South Carolina	Total
24	34	34	92	24	34	34	92
22	58	86	166	23	56	82	161
8	3	3	14	9	3	3	15
2	36	13	51	2	32	13	47
33	437	45	515	32	442	45	519
29	70	38	137	30	70	38	138
133	11	14	158	136	10	14	160
90	194	60	344	89	194	58	341
34	58	23	115	40	60	26	126
375	901	316	1,592	385	901	313	1,599

TABLE 3   **Total Number of Textile Mills Employing More Than 20 Persons in Each of Hart Machine Company's Seven Sales Regions, 1990**

Georgia		
North sales region	317	
South sales region	58	
Total		375*
North Carolina		
Northeast sales region	305	
Southeast sales region	111	
Western sales region	485	
Total		901*
South Carolina		
East sales region	70	
West sales region	244	
Total		314*

*Due to differences in methods of reporting, totals differ slightly from those in Table 2.

Industry figures indicate that the number of mills in each of the three states is stabilizing across most industry types (see Table 2). Therefore, estimating the demand for rollers by each textile industry in each state could be crucial to optimal allocation of current sales personnel and to the determination of Hart's future sales force needs.

Having obtained a detailed listing of the addresses of the textile mills located in Georgia, North Carolina, and South Carolina by industry type, company officials tried to decide on the sampling plan that would best enable them to calculate the sales for Hart rollers quickly and inexpensively. Three plans were being considered for determining the mills at which production personnel were to be interviewed:

- Plan A, in which textile mills in each of the seven sales regions would be sampled in proportion to the district's size. For example, given that the northeast sales region in the North Carolina district accounts for approximately 19 percent (305/1,590 × 100) of the textile mills in the three-state area, 19 percent of the sample would come from the northeast sales region. Interviewers would be allowed to pick the mills in which the interviews would be conducted.

- Plan B, in which after the total number of textile mills of each type in each sales region was determined, each of the 63 groups (9 SIC types × 7 regions) would be sampled in proportion to its size, and the plants at which the interviews would take place would be determined randomly.

- Plan C, in which two of the regions would be randomly selected, and production personnel at all of the plants in each of the two randomly selected regions would be interviewed.

Questions

1. What type of sampling plan is being proposed in each case?
2. What are the strengths and weaknesses of each plan? Which of the three plans would you recommend and why?
3. What other plans might the company consider?

CASE 4.5
HotStuff Computer Software (B)[1]

Simpson, Edwards and Associates, encouraged by its success with a computer software package for government agencies, is developing a second software product, HotStuff, which is tailored specifically for use in the firefighting industry. In the normal course of affairs, fire departments need to handle and store a considerable amount of information: building layouts, hazardous material characteristics and locations, equipment inventories, and so on. Further, although some exploratory research has suggested that some fire departments already own computers, it was generally recognized that the information-processing needs of the industry rendered computerization a future necessity. Based on preliminary inquiries into the composition of the industry, Simpson, Edwards and Associates decided to restrict its marketing efforts to volunteer fire departments only, at least initially, and planned a national survey to determine the market potential of HotStuff (see Case 2.2 for more background).

SAMPLING PLAN

The key issue in executing a national survey turned on sampling control: how could the research select and contract volunteer fire departments in a reliable, systematic fashion? After much deliberation and a few false starts, Craig Simpson's research staff finally presented him with two cohesive sampling plans.

Option 1 The first option that Craig and his staff considered was a mail survey based on a sample drawn from a list of volunteer fire departments nationwide. The National Fire Protection Agency, like other national fire safety organizations, had a comprehensive mailing list of all 30,000 U.S. fire departments, but it did not distinguish between volunteer and municipal fire departments. Fortunately, the research team discovered that Alvin B. Zeller Inc. of New York sells listings of population groups. Moreover, the company could provide Craig's team with an exhaustive mailing list of volunteer fire departments, organized by the state in which they are located. The total number of

---

[1]The contributions of Jacqueline C. Hitchon to the development of this case are gratefully acknowledged.

volunteer fire departments included on the recently updated list was almost 20,000, and the cost of sampling names from the list was $40 per 1,000 departments sampled. The names could be drawn according to whatever scheme Simpson, Edwards and Associates preferred.

The research team believed that a viable way to proceed to sample from the Zeller list would be to order the 48 states in the United States (excluding Alaska and Hawaii) according to the number of volunteer fire departments in each state. Once the states were ordered from smallest to largest in terms of incidence of volunteer fire departments, a sample could be drawn from all the departments on the list by selecting every kth department after a random beginning. If it adopted a pessimistic perspective, expected only a 20 percent response rate, and were satisfied with only 100 completed surveys, Simpson, Edwards and Associates calculated that it would need to mail 500 questionnaires. With 20,000 population elements and a sample of 500, every 40th volunteer fire station on the list would need to be selected, after a random start between 1 and 40.

Option 2   The second sampling plan being considered was founded on information received from the local state fire marshall and two assumptions. The marshall informed the researchers that most volunteer fire departments were located in communities with populations under 25,000. Based on the assumption that towns with a population under 5,000 would be too small to productively use a computer, the team decided that it should concentrate on two categories of towns: those with populations between 5,000 and 15,000, and those with populations between 15,000 and 25,000. In addition, it seemed logical to assume that volunteer fire departments located near large cities would be more progressive than those in more isolated areas and thus that they would be more likely to own or plan to purchase a computer.

Consistent with the preceding reasoning, the research team also considered drawing a sample in the following way:

- Step 1: Randomly select two cities of over 10,000 inhabitants from every state in the continental United States.
- Step 2: Randomly select a town of population 5,000–15,000 within 20 miles of one city, and a town of population 15,000–25,000 within 20 miles of the second city.
- Step 3: Obtain telephone numbers of the volunteer fire departments in each of the two towns selected in each state from Directory Assistance.

This strategy would provide a sample size of 96 volunteer fire departments from the 48 states.

After some discussion, Craig decided to adopt the second option to use in conjunction with a telephone survey.

Questions

1. What kind of sampling plan was considered for sampling from the mailing list?
2. What kind of sampling plan was actually used to sample volunteer fire departments?
3. Evaluate the sampling plans.

Case 4.6
First Federal Bank of Bakersfield

The Equal Credit Opportunity Act, which was passed in 1974, was partially designed to protect women from discriminatory banking practices. It forbade, for example, the use of credit evaluations based on gender or marital status. While adherence to the law has changed the way many bankers do business, women's perception that there is a bias against them by a particular financial institution often remains unless some specific steps are taken by the institution to counter that perception.

Close to a dozen ''women's banks'' — that is, banks owned and operated by and for women — opened their doors during the 1980s with the specific purpose of targeting and promoting their services to this otherwise underdeveloped market. Today, although women's banks are evolving into full-service banks serving a wide range of clients, a number of traditional banks are moving in the other direction by attempting to develop services that are targeted specifically toward women. Many of these institutions see such a strategy as a viable way to attract valuable customers and to increase their market share in the short term while gaining a competitive advantage by which they can compete in the long term as the roles of women in the labor force gain in importance. One can find, with even the most cursory examination of the trade press, examples of credit card advertising that depicts single, affluent, and head-of-the-household female card holders; financial seminar programs for wives of affluent professional men; informational literature that details how newly divorced and separated women can obtain credit; and entire packages of counseling, educational opportunities, and special services for women.

The First Federal Bank of Bakersfield was interested in developing its own program of this kind. The executives were curious about a number of issues. Were women's financial needs being adequately met in the Bakersfield area? What additional financial services would women especially like to have? How do Bakersfield's women feel about banks and bankers? Was First Federal in a good position to take advantage of the needs of women? What channels of communication might be best to reach women who may be interested in the services that First Federal had to offer?

The executives believed that First Federal might have some special advantages if it did try to appeal to women. For one thing, the Bakersfield community seemed to be quite sensitive to the issues being raised by the feminist movement. For another, First Federal was a small, personal bank. The executives thought that women might be more comfortable in dealing with a smaller, more personalized institution and that the bank might not have the traditional ''image problem'' among women that larger banks might have.

RESEARCH OBJECTIVES

One program the bank executives were considering that they believed might be particularly attractive to women was a series of financial seminars. The seminars could cover a number of topics, including money management, wills, trusts, estate planning, taxes, insurance, investments, financial services, and establishing a credit rating. The executives were interested in determining women's reactions to each of these potential topics. They were also interested to know what the best format might be in terms of location, frequency, length of each program, and so on, if there were a high level of interest. Consequently, they decided that the bank should conduct a research study that had the assessment of the financial seminar series as its main objective but that also shed some light on the other issues they had been debating. More specifically, the objectives of the research were as follows:

1. to determine the interest that exists among women in the Bakersfield area for seminars on financial matters;

2. to identify the reasons why Bakersfield women would change, or have changed, their banking affiliations;

3. to examine the attitudes of Bakersfield women toward financial institutions and the people who run them;

4. to determine if there was any correlation between the demographic characteristics of women in the Bakersfield area and the services they might like to have; and

5. to analyze the media usage habits of Bakersfield-area women.

METHOD

The assignment to develop a research strategy by which these objectives could be assessed was given to the bank's internal marketing research department. The department consisted of only five members — Beth Anchurch, the research director, and four project analysts. As Anchurch pondered the assignment, she was concerned about the best way to proceed. She was particularly concerned with the relatively short time horizon she was given for the project. Top executives thought that there was promise in the seminar idea. If they were right, they wanted to get on with designing and offering the seminars before any of their competitors came up with a similar idea. Thus, they specified that they would like the results of the research department's investigation to be available within 45 to 50 days.

As Anchurch began to contemplate the data collection, she became particularly concerned with whether the study should use mail questionnaires or telephone interviews. She had tentatively ruled out personal interviews because of the short deadline that had been imposed. After several days of contemplating the alternatives, she finally decided that it would be best to collect the information by telephone. Further, she decided that it would be better to hire out the telephone interviewing than to use her four project analysts to make the calls.

Anchurch believed that the multiple objectives of the project required a reasonably large sample of women so that the various characteristics of interest would be sufficiently represented to enable some conclusions to be drawn about the population of Bakersfield as a whole. After pondering the various cross tabulations in which the bank executives would be interested, she finally decided that a sample of 500 to 600 adult women would be sufficient. The sample was to be drawn from the white pages of the Bakersfield telephone directory by the Bakersfield Interviewing Service, the firm that First Federal had hired to complete the interviews.

The sample was to be drawn using a scheme in which two names were selected from each page of the directory, first by selecting two of the four columns on the page at random and then by selecting the fifteenth name in each of the selected columns. The decision to sample names from each page was made so that each interviewer could operate with certain designated pages of the directory, since each was operating independently out of her home.

The decision to sample every fifteenth name in the selected columns was determined in the following way. First, there were 328 pages in the directory with four columns of names per page. There were 80 entries per column on average, or approximately 26,240 listings. Using Bureau of the Census data on household composition, it was estimated that 20 percent of all households would be ineligible for the study because they did not contain an adult female resident. This meant that only 20,992 ($0.80 \times 26,240$) of the listings would probably qualify. Since 500 to 600 names were needed, it seemed easiest to select two columns on each page at random and to take the same numbered entry from each column. The interviewer could then simply count or measure down from the top of the column. The number 15 was determined randomly; thus, the fifteenth listing in the randomly selected columns on each page was called. If the household did not answer or if the women of the house refused to participate, the interviewers were instructed to

TABLE 1   **Selected Demographic Comparison of Survey Respondents with Bureau of Census Data**

	Percentage of Women	
Characteristic/Category	**Survey**	**Census**
Marital Status		
Married	53	42
Single	30	40
Separated	1	2
Widowed	9	9
Divorced	7	7
Age		
18–24	23	23
25–34	30	28
35–44	16	14
45–64	18	21
65+	13	14
Income		
Less than $10,000	9	29
$10,000–$19,999	19	29
$20,000–$50,000	58	36
More than $50,000	2	6
Refused	12	

Table 2   **Results of Calls by Interviewer**

Interviewer	Number of Nonresponses			Number of Refusals		Number of Completions
	Line Busy	No Answer	Ineligibles*	Initial	After Partial Completion	
1	7	101	36	15	0	30
2	2	45	13	16	0	30
3	11	71	23	17	7	30
4	14	56	47	35	6	39
5	9	93	10	23	13	30
6	5	102	28	63	14	35
7	6	36	17	16	0	18
8	7	107	23	13	0	30
9	11	106	36	47	0	30
10	10	55	6	35	9	30
11	38	83	48	92	0	30
12	5	22	3	8	0	9
13	23	453	102	65	7	99
14	12	102	27	31	0	19
15	7	173	29	66	0	34
16	2	65	9	33	0	22
Total	169	1,670	457	575	56	515
		1,839			631	

*No adult female resident.

select another number from that column through the use of an abbreviated table of random numbers that each was given. They were to use a similar procedure if the household that was called did not have an adult woman living there.

First Federal decided to operate without callbacks because the interviewing service charged heavily for them. Anchurch did think it would be useful to follow up with a sample of those interviewed to make sure that they indeed had been called, since the interviewers for Bakersfield Interviewing Service operated out of their own homes and it was impossible to supervise them more directly. She did this by selecting at random a handful of the surveys completed by each interviewer. She then had one of her project assistants call that respondent, verify that the interview had taken place, and check the accuracy of the responses of a few of the most important questions. This audit revealed absolutely no instances of interviewer cheating.

The completed interview forms were turned over to First Federal for its own internal analysis. As part of this analysis, the project analyst compared the demographic characteristics of those contacted to the demographic characteristics of the population in the Bakersfield area as reported in the 1990 Census. The comparison is shown in Table 1 (page 711). The analyst also prepared a summary of the nonresponses and refusals by interviewer. This comparison is shown in Table 2.

Questions

1. Compare the advantages and disadvantages of using telephone interviews as compared to personal interviews or mail questionnaires to collect the needed data.

2. Compare the advantages and disadvantages of using in-house staff versus a professional interviewing service to collect the data.

3. Do you think that the telephone directory provided a good sampling frame given the purposes of the study, or would you recommend an alternative sampling frame?

4. What type of sample is being used here? Still using the white pages of the telephone directory as the sampling frame, would you recommend some other sampling scheme? Why or why not?

5. If you were Anchurch, would you be happy with the performance of the Bakersfield Interviewing Service? Why or why not?

CASE 4.7
Holzem Business Systems

Holzem Business Systems serviced a number of small business accounts in the immediate area surrounding its Madison, Wisconsin, location. The company, which was headed by Claude Holzem, a certified public accountant, specialized in the preparation of financial statements, tax forms, and other reports required by various governmental units. Since its founding in 1962, the company had experienced steady, and sometimes spectacular, growth. Holzem, whose policy was high-quality service at competitive rates, was so successful in Dane County that it was far and away the dominant firm serving small businesses in the area. Further growth seemed to depend more on expansion into new areas than on further penetration of the Madison market.

Faced with such a prospect, Holzem conceived a plan that would capitalize on the substantial talent at the company's main office. What he envisioned was an operation in which area field representatives would secure raw data from clients. At the end of each day, they would transmit this information to headquarters using microcomputers with modems. There it would be coded and processed and the necessary forms prepared. These income statements, balance sheets, or tax forms would then be returned to the area representative. The field person would go over them with clients and would answer any question that clients might have.

In Holzem's mind, the system had a number of advantages. First, it allowed Holzem Business Systems to capitalize on the substantial expertise it had in its Madison office. The quality control for which the company had become noted could be maintained, as could the company's record of quick service. Second, the company would not need to hire CPAs as field representatives, because these area managers would not actually be preparing financial statements. The prospect of using general business-college graduates who understood financial statements and could explain their significance to clients had cost advantages for Holzem since CPAs were commanding higher salaries.

The big question confronting Holzem was whether there would be a demand for such a service. There was no question in his mind that there was a need for accounting services among small businesses. His Madison experience had demonstrated this. But he was concerned that the physical distance between the client and the office might prove to be a psychological barrier for clients. If it proved to be necessary to establish full-service branches in each area, then geographic expansion was less attractive to him.

To help him decide whether to go ahead, Holzem commissioned a research study that had as its objectives identifying the perceived problems and the need for CPA services in general and, in particular, potential client attitudes toward the type of service arrangement he envisioned.

Hathaway Research Associates, headed by James and Nancy Hathaway, was retained to do the study. It was to be conducted using personal interviews among a representative sample of small businesses within the state. For purposes of the study, a small business was defined as one employing fewer than 50 people. The study was to be confined to small businesses in the industries designated contract construction, manufacturing, wholesale trade, retail trade, and commercial services. These categories represented approximately 95 percent of all Holzem accounts, 85 percent of the total small businesses, and 81 percent of all businesses in the state.

SAMPLING PLAN

The businesses serving as the sample were to be selected in the following way. First, the state was to be divided into the three regions depicted in Figure 1. Next, five counties were to be selected from each region by the following scheme.

1. The cumulative number of businesses was to be calculated from Table 1. The accumulation for the first ten counties in Region 1, for example, is as follows:

County	Number of Businesses	Cumulative Number of Businesses
Douglas	668	668
Burnett	147	815
Polk	488	1,303
Washburn	282	1,585
Barron	565	2,150
Bayfield	178	2,328
Sawyer	324	2,652
Rusk	229	2,881
Ashland	307	3,188
Iron	122	3,310

2. A table of random numbers would be employed to determine which five counties would be selected. For example, if a number between 816 and 1,303 came up, Polk county would be used.

FIGURE 1   **Regional Breakdown of Wisconsin Counties**

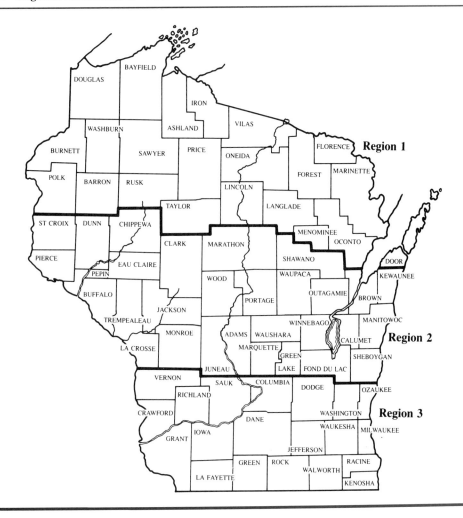

Hathaway Research Associates then planned to contact the state Department of Industry, Labor, and Human Relations (DILHR) for a list of individual firms within each county. DILHR used the unemployment computer tape to prepare such lists. This tape was compiled each year and reflected payments by firms into the state's unemployment compensation system. The records within the tape were maintained county by county, by SIC (Standard Industrial Classification) code within county, and in alphabetical order within the SIC code. Since the number of employees of each firm was indicated, DILHR could screen the master list and print out only those firms that satisfied the location, industry, and geographic criteria Hathaway Research Associates specified. DILHR would sell these lists of firms to interested clients, but they would only provide the name, address, and phone number of the selected businesses.

TABLE 1   **Number of Small Businesses by Major Industry Category**

County	Contract Construction	Manufacturing	Wholesale Trade	Retail Trade	Commercial Services	Total
Adams	14	10	3	49	27	103
Ashland	26	37	26	127	91	307
Barron	88	52	82	295	48	565
Bayfield	20	25	8	85	40	178
Brown	387	187	330	871	804	2,579
Buffalo	23	14	22	92	47	198
Burnett	22	12	7	82	24	147
Calumet	62	47	48	162	128	447
Chippewa	105	67	94	300	216	782
Clark	60	76	82	203	101	522
Columbia	98	55	84	360	208	805
Crawford	33	25	32	119	64	273
Dane	638	314	493	1,800	1,705	4,950
Dodge	143	98	119	370	258	988
Door	76	27	27	206	168	504
Douglas	49	30	43	339	207	668
Dunn	37	21	55	187	110	410
Eau Claire	122	39	113	415	331	1,020
Florence	4	6	1	29	6	46
Fond du Lac	178	94	131	546	374	1,323
Forrest	9	25	8	116	27	185
Grant	88	60	125	341	200	814
Green	71	49	82	234	122	558
Green Lake	60	28	28	150	84	350
Iowa	41	23	55	135	65	319
Iron	11	15	10	60	26	122
Jackson	27	14	29	120	49	239
Jefferson	120	88	111	400	283	1,002
Juneau	38	28	27	172	79	344
Kenosha	159	75	105	624	167	1,130
Kewaunee	44	35	32	112	76	299
La Crosse	167	91	159	573	450	1,440
Lafayette	31	29	50	106	58	274
Langlade	29	53	59	135	92	368
Lincoln	50	43	38	184	109	424
Manitowoc	161	102	119	464	338	1,184
Marathon	244	148	196	520	432	1,540

Table 1   *Continued*

County	Contract Construction	Manufacturing	Wholesale Trade	Retail Trade	Commercial Services	Total
Marinette	63	75	56	253	153	600
Marquette	27	11	9	68	34	149
Menominee	1	5	2	4	6	18
Milwaukee	1,200	1,238	1,711	4,914	5,708	14,771
Monroe	49	37	67	235	115	503
Oconto	49	43	50	143	97	382
Oneida	101	40	45	305	180	671
Outagamie	273	117	227	697	568	1,882
Ozaukee	151	109	95	313	245	915
Pepin	12	7	18	61	31	129
Pierce	50	27	29	206	104	416
Polk	59	44	51	234	100	488
Portage	83	42	71	280	171	647
Price	19	44	32	92	59	246
Racine	292	285	178	853	738	2,346
Richland	29	20	35	108	67	259
Rock	236	118	148	811	570	1,883
Rusk	24	34	34	95	42	229
St. Croix	80	44	61	225	144	554
Sauk	104	58	91	376	223	852
Sawyer	36	25	16	128	119	324
Shawano	65	58	61	232	110	526
Sheboygan	204	151	118	523	433	1,429
Taylor	29	28	36	93	57	243
Trempeleau	51	43	60	192	98	444
Vernon	37	39	52	154	85	367
Vilas	72	30	17	175	113	407
Walworth	144	106	90	522	345	1,207
Washburn	41	27	18	136	60	282
Washington	173	110	97	369	262	1,011
Waukesha	694	506	501	1,147	1,097	3,945
Waupaca	81	70	72	328	201	752
Waushara	26	22	30	114	71	263
Winnebago	244	157	151	759	632	1,943
Wood	141	83	104	427	303	1,058
Totals	8,475	5,995	7,466	26,655	20,957	69,548

Source: County Business Patterns.

Hathaway Research Associates proposed to select 40 businesses from each county by the following procedure:

1. The total number of businesses within the county was to be divided by 40 to get a sampling interval. The sampling interval would be different, of course, for each county.

2. A random start was to be generated for each county, using a table of random numbers. The random number was to be some number between one and the sampling interval, and this number was to be used to designate the first business to be included in the sample.

3. The sampling interval was to be added repeatedly to the random start, and every number generated in this manner was to designate a business to be included in the sample.

This procedure was to be followed for all counties except Milwaukee and Dane. Holzem believed that if he were to expand into the Milwaukee market at all, he wanted to do it with a completely self-sufficient branch and not with a satellite office tied to the Madison headquarters. He consequently instructed Hathaway Research Associates to exclude Milwaukee County from this part of the research investigation. Dane County was to be excluded because of the company's already successful penetration of this market.

Once the total sample of 600 businesses had been specified, Hathaway Research Associates would contact each firm by phone to set up an appointment for a personal interview with one of its highly trained field interviewers.

Questions

1. What kind of sample is being proposed by Hathaway Research Associates? Is this a good choice?

2. Is the sample a true probability sample (i.e., does every small business in Wisconsin have a known chance of selection)?

3. What is the probability that a small business in Menominee County (the county with the fewest small businesses) will be included in the sample? What is the probability that a small business in Waukesha County (of those counties eligible, the one with the most small businesses) will be included in the sample? Will this discrepancy cause any problems in analysis?

4. Are businesses within each of the Standard Industrial Classifications likely to be represented properly in the sample?

CASE 4.8
The Dryden Press

The Dryden Press was established in the mid-1960s by Holt, Rinehart and Winston, which had traditionally been a strong social science publisher, as a response to the growth in enrollments that business schools were experiencing and the explosion in enrollments that was predicted they would experience in the future. The venture represented one of the first forays by a traditional nonbusiness text publisher into the college business market. The experiment turned out to be very successful, and by the mid-1980s The Dryden Press was one of the top six publishers in the business area in sales. Company executives believed that one of the key reasons for Dryden's success was its ability to target books for specific market segments. The company was one of the first to recognize the potential growth in courses in consumer behavior and managerial economics, for example, and introduced the successful texts by Engel, Kollat, and Blackwell in consumer behavior and by Brigham and Pappas in managerial economics in response. Through careful management of the revisions, these books still maintained strong market positions more than 25 years after they had been introduced.

The Dryden Press editorial staff tried to maintain a posture of extreme sensitivity to changing market conditions brought about by the publication of new research findings or the changing demands placed on students as a result of changes in the environment and the needs of businesses. The editors made it a point to keep up with these changes so that the company would be prepared with new products when the situation demanded it. This was no small task, because the lead time on a book typically ran from three to four years from the time the author was first signed to a contract to when the book was actually published. It seemed to take most authors almost two years to develop a first draft of a book manuscript. The typical manuscript was then reviewed by a sample of experts in the field. Based on their reactions, most manuscripts would undergo some revision before being placed in production. The production process, which included such things as copyediting the manuscript, setting type, drawing all figures, preparing promotional materials, proofreading, and so on, usually took about a year.

RESEARCH QUESTIONS AND OBJECTIVES

So that it would not be caught short if the needs and desires of the market in consumer behavior texts changed, the editorial staff decided to find out the current level of use of the various texts in consumer behavior and the directions in which the market was moving. What were the market shares of the respective texts? What features of the various books were liked and disliked? Did the use of the various texts and the preference for the certain features vary by class of school? Did four-year colleges have different requirements for consumer behavior texts than two-year schools? After a good deal of discussion among the members of the editorial staff, these general concerns were translated into specific research objectives. More specifically, the staff decided to conduct a research investigation that attempted to determine the following:

1. the importance of various topical areas in the teaching of consumer behavior within the next two to five years;

2. the importance and treatment of managerial applications in consumer behavior courses;

3. the level of satisfaction with the textbooks currently in use;

4. the relative market shares of the major consumer behavior textbooks;

5. the degree of switching of texts that goes on in consumer behavior courses from year to year;

6. the importance of various pedagogical aids such as glossaries, cases, learning objectives, and so on, in the textbook selection decision; and

7. the importance of supplementary teaching tools such as student study guides, overhead transparency masters, or an instructor's manual, among others, in the consumer textbook selection decision.

The editorial staff thought it was important that the needed information be obtained from those who were actively involved in teaching consumer behavior courses. The staff also thought it imperative that only one respondent be used from any given school, even though the editors realized that some schools had multiple sections of the consumer behavior course and that different books might be used in different sections. For the most part, however, the editors believed that the same book would be used across sections, though not across courses, in the sense that the introductory courses at the undergraduate and graduate levels would use different books. The editors decided that it would be better to target the questionnaires to one individual at each of the selected institutions and to simply have that person indicate on the questionnaire whether he or she normally taught a graduate or undergraduate course. Dryden could then analyze the responses to determine if there were any differences in them that could be attributed to the level at which the course was taught.

METHOD

There were several reasons why the editorial staff decided to use a mail questionnaire to collect the data. For one thing, the target population was geographically dispersed. Even though it was decided to limit the study only to those actively involved in teaching consumer behavior domestically, that still meant respondents could come from all over the United States, which in turn meant that it could be prohibitive to collect this information by personal interview. At the same time, professors had no standard working schedule. Some might teach in the morning and some in the evening. When they were not teaching, some might work in their offices while others might work elsewhere. This variety of schedules and work conditions required that the questionnaires be available when the professors might be inclined to fill them out. Also, the objectives finally decided on allowed the use of a relatively structured and undisguised questionnaire.

The big question facing the Dryden staff was how to draw a sample from the target population of those actively teaching the consumer behavior course, either at the undergraduate or graduate levels. For purposes of the study, "actively teaching" was operationally defined as having taught a consumer behavior course at least once in the last two years or being scheduled to teach one within the next year.

The company was considering drawing the sample from one of two lists that it had at its disposal. One of the lists was an internal list consisting of all those professors whom the salespeople's reports indicated were interested in teaching specific courses such as financial planning, introductory accounting, marketing management, or consumer behavior. This meant that the salesperson had indicated on his or her reports that the professor was to receive sample copies of all those books in, say, consumer behavior that The Dryden Press publishes. Most of the entries on the list were developed from salespeople's calls, although some of them arose at the national association meetings at which Dryden displayed its list of titles. Professors would often request sample copies of selected titles at the meetings so that they could review them before making an adoption decision. All requests for complimentary copies were sent for authorization to the salesperson serving the school. By approving the request, the salesperson was aware of the professor's interest and could follow it up in an attempt to get the adoption. Because of how it was developed and used, the internal list paralleled the salesperson territory structure.

Although most salespeople operated within one state and often within only part of a state, some operated across several states. Each salesperson was responsible for all the schools in his or her territory, including the universities with graduate programs, four-year colleges without graduate programs, and two-year institutions. The schools were listed alphabetically by salesperson, and each school had a computer code associated with it, designating its type. Each professor on the list had a set of computer codes associated with the name that identified his or her interest areas.

The alternate list The Dryden Press considered using was the printed membership directory of the Association for Consumer Research (ACR). ACR is an organization formed in the late 1960s that was designed for the pursuit of knowledge in the area of consumer behavior. Its membership is dominated by marketing professors (almost 80 percent of the total), although it also includes interested members from business and government as well as members representing other academic disciplines, such as sociology and psychology. The ACR directory was organized alphabetically by name of the member. Along with each member's name, the directory provided either the office or home address, depending on which the individual preferred to use, and both the office and home phone numbers. While about one-half of the addresses listed only the college at which the individual worked, the other 50 percent also listed the department. There were 64 pages in the directory, and all pages except the last one had 16 names. A small percentage of the addresses were international.

Questions

1. Given the purposes of the study, how would you recommend a sample be drawn from:
   a. Dryden's internal computer list?
   b. the ACR printed membership directory?
2. Which approach would you recommend and why?

CASE 4.9
Canopy of Care (A)[1]

Canopy of Care is a nonprofit institution that raises money from the public and then allocates the funds to programs run by charitable agencies endeavoring to serve the human-care needs of the community. In this way, it functions as an umbrella or canopy for specialized charities, relieving them in large part of the need to market themselves and solicit donations. The campaign area encompasses a city with a population of half a million and its suburbs. In 1993, for example, Canopy of Care raised almost $17 million, which it distributed to 341 local health and social service programs. An efficient system for giving has been developed with the help of companies and government agencies, who solicit their employees on behalf of Canopy of Care and deduct donations corresponding to the employees' pledges directly out of their wages or salaries.

Despite the relative ease of administration, however, the percentage of solicited employees contributing to Canopy of Care has been decreasing. In 1993, for example, only 50 percent of the employees at companies that agreed to participate contributed. Economic downturns in the area are thought to be partially responsible for the reduction in employee contributions. The manufacturing industry, for example, one of Canopy of Care's largest targets, has recently experienced plant closings leading to employee cutbacks and wage freezes. Although Canopy of Care cannot control the effects of changes in the economy, its officials believe that the agency may be able to compensate for them by becoming more efficient in its approach to potential donors.

STUDY OBJECTIVES

Based on this reasoning, three broad research objectives were developed:

1. To determine why a large percentage of employees in companies solicited by Canopy of Care do not choose to contribute.
2. To assess both the information and attitudes that givers and non-givers in solicited companies have about Canopy of Care.
3. To obtain general information that Canopy of Care can use in better planning its campaigns.

A local marketing research firm was asked to develop a study to investigate these issues.

DATA COLLECTION PROCEDURE

The target population consisted of individuals employed in firms solicited by Canopy of Care. The marketing researcher advised Canopy of Care that there were two principal ways to access the population for research purposes:

---

[1]The contributions of Jacqueline C. Hitchon to the development of this case are gratefully acknowledged.

A. Sample companies solicited by Canopy of Care, and then select a sample of employees within each selected company from a list of employees provided by the company. Once they were identified, the employees could be surveyed by mail or telephone. Since the desired information could be obtained through fixed-alternative questions without probing, personal interviews did not seem warranted.

B. Broaden the population of potential respondents to include all adults who were employed in the campaign area. This sample could be accessed by telephone, using plus-one sampling based on the local white-pages telephone directory and screening out unemployed respondents by means of an introductory question about employment. The survey could be administered either by volunteers from Canopy of Care staff or by professional telephone interviewers.

After some deliberation, Canopy of Care selected the second option and decided to employ trained telephone interviewers to conduct the survey, although the budget for the project was very small and the sample size needed to be drastically reduced.

Plus-one dialing was used to generate a random sample that included unlisted numbers. Because of time and budget constraints, callbacks were not made; instead, new numbers were generated and dialed until a valid response was obtained. The telephone interviewers were instructed in the correct manner to administer the survey and were monitored by supervisors both during a pretest and during the actual survey. The research took place between April 21 and April 25, 1994. Calls were placed between the hours of 4:00 p.m. and 9:00 p.m. in order to find a greater number of people at home. A total of 260 completed questionnaires was obtained.

Initial Results

As an initial step in analyzing the results of this survey, the researchers undertook two tasks. First, they examined the statistics on completed and uncompleted contacts (see Table 1). Second, they compared the demographic profile of their sample with projected 1994 census data, based on the 1990 census of the area, to evaluate the representativeness of their sample (see Tables 2, 3, and 4).

TABLE 1 **Numbers of Completed and Uncompleted Contacts**

Classification	Number of Individuals
Completed contacts	260
Contacts unemployed last year	271
Mid-survey terminations	22
Answering machine contacts	61
Refusals	235
No answers and busy signals	132
Nonworking numbers	419
Businesses contacted	90
Contacts with language/hearing barrier	13
No adult at home	30
Total dialings	1,533

TABLE 2   **Comparison of Household Income**

Income Category	Sample Percentage	1994 Projected Census Percentage
Less than $10,000	12.7	25.7
$10,000–$14,999	17.3	14.3
$15,000–$24,999	31.9	27.8
$25,000–$39,999	26.9	23.0
More than $40,000	11.2	9.2

TABLE 3   **Comparison of Race**

Racial Classification	Sample Percentage	1994 Projected Census Percentage
White	91.1	82.3
African-American	6.5	13.9
Hispanic	0.8	2.4
Asian	0.4	0.8
Native American	1.2	0.6

TABLE 4   **Comparison of Occupation**

Type of Organization	Sample Percentage	1994 Projected Census Percentage
Manufacturing	22.4	28.5
Government	9.9	12.0
Wholesale/Retail	16.5	19.2
Service Industry	51.2	40.3

All in all, the sample demographic profiles were similar to the 1994 population projections based on the 1990 census with one or two differences. Both the nonwhite and lower-income groups were underrepresented in the sample (Tables 2 and 3). Further, all occupational categories were underrepresented except the service category, which appeared to be overrepresented (Table 4). Nevertheless, the researchers were reasonably happy with these initial results.

Questions

1. What was the response rate?

2. Was the choice of plus-one telephone interviews judicious? Compare its advantages and disadvantages with those of the rejected sampling option.

3. Would you have selected professional interviewers over Canopy of Care volunteers, given the time and budget constraints? Why or why not?

4. Does the evidence indicate that the data collection effort was of high quality?

CASE 4.10
Management Institute Video-Based Training

The Management Institute (MI) is a division of the University of Wisconsin-Extension, an outreach arm of the University of Wisconsin System. Primarily, MI develops and organizes management-training seminars for all levels of management. In particular, MI has developed the Basic Management Certificate Program, a successful series of seminars for first-level managers designed to enhance these managers' leadership, supervisory, administrative, and communication skills.

Recently, a large client approached MI about the possibility of developing a series of videotape seminars. The video-based training would include most of the information provided with the Basic Management Certificate Program but would be customized toward the specific applications of the client. The videos would then be available to the client's affiliates nationwide. MI agreed to undertake the project.

Officials at MI liked the concept so much that they decided to produce an additional "generic" set of videos that could be used by a wide variety of companies. The tapes would be of the same high quality as the customized tapes; however, the programs would not be directed to any specific industry. They felt that this concept would be especially attractive to companies that planned to hold in-house training sessions for first-level managers.

At this early stage, MI officials recognized that several important decisions were still pending:

- Should the program be offered for purchase, rental, or both?
- Which target markets should be selected?
- What would be the final program content?
- How would the product be distributed?
- How should the new product be promoted?

THE MARKETING RESEARCH PROJECT

At this point, it was decided that a marketing research project should be undertaken to help generate information useful in the decision process. An outside research team was brought in and briefed on the new concept, including specific information about the areas where management felt more information was needed.

Officials at MI considered companies in the private sector to provide better sales or rental opportunities than public organizations. Further, they felt that the key areas for research involved the identification of potential target markets and the review of competitive products. These objectives were presented to the research team, who immediately began work on the project.

Initially, the team began to formulate questions useful for uncovering attitudes toward the training process within organizations and the usefulness of video-based training. Questions were also formulated dealing with companies' past use of video-based training and opinions of such programs. In addition, they began collecting secondary data useful for analyzing competitive offerings. For example, product brochures were obtained for other video-based training programs. Competitors were identified through a review of trade journals and data-base searches.

SAMPLING FRAME, METHOD, AND IMPLEMENTATION

The Management Institute considered the primary geographic market for the new product to be the upper midwestern portion of the United States, although a secondary market would likely exist nationwide. Due in part to time and cost constraints, however, the research team included in the sampling frame only businesses with 50 or more employees that were headquartered within the same county as MI. (Companies with fewer than 50 employees were felt to be too small to effectively utilize the video-training programs.) The sampling frame was developed from a list of businesses obtained through the local Chamber of Commerce and was verified by a listing provided by the Wisconsin Department of Industry, Labor, and Human Relations. A total of 395 private-sector companies with 50 or more employees were included in the sampling frame.

The research team felt that a sample of 200 of these companies would provide sufficient information and used a stratified random-sampling procedure based on company size to develop the size. Table 1 provides a summary of the sampling plan.

TABLE 1   **Sampling Plan**

Number of Employees	Total Number of Companies	Number of Sampled Companies	Proportion Sampled
50–99	190	57	30%
100–149	88	26	30
150–249	54	54	100
250–499	40	40	100
500–999	15	15	100
1,000+	8	8	100
Total	395	200	51%

The telephone interview method was selected for this project, primarily because of the ability to quickly implement the project and because of available telephoning resources. In addition, the researchers felt that the use of the telephone interview method allowed more control over the research project, particularly compared with the mail questionnaire method. The appropriate respondents — people involved with the training process — could be reached and more accurate information could be gathered through probing questions and two-way interaction.

A structured and undisguised questionnaire consisting of 35 total questions was developed (Figure 1). With the approval of MI, the project was implemented; the interviewing process was completed within a two-week period.

FIGURE 1   **Telephone Interview Guide**

No.____

Pre-Recorded Information

Company name: _____

City/Phone #: _____

# of employees: _____

Industry: _____

Name of respondent: _____

Position: _____

ASTD-member in company: ____ YES ____ NO

Identifying the Appropriate Respondent

Call the company and say:

I would like to speak with the person who is responsible for personnel training.

If you have a name, add:

Would that be _____?

If the target respondent is not available, ask:

Who else could I speak with about personnel training?

Or/if not, ask:

When is the best time to call back? **(Record on call-back sheet.)**

Figure 1   *Continued*

Interviewing the Appropriate Respondent

Good morning/afternoon/evening. My name is _____ , and I am working on a research project. I would like to ask you a few questions about your management training practices. These questions are purely for research, and your responses will be kept strictly confidential.

I am interested in discussing the training of your **first-level** *managers. By this, I mean those managers who have no other managers working under them.*

(**Start interview.**)

1. *How important do you think it is for your company/division to provide management training for first-level managers?*

   Is it of high, medium, or low importance?
   High importance   ____
   Medium importance   ____
   Low importance   ____
   Do not know   ____

2. *Can you give me one or more titles that are used in your company for first-level managers?*

   _____

3. *a. During the last year, did your company/division provide any training for first-level managers?*
   YES   ____
   NO   ____
   Do not know ____

   If NO or Do not know, go to Question #8.

   b. Did this training include basic management skills, such as supervision and leadership?
   YES   ____
   NO   ____
   Do not know ____

   If NO or Do not know, go to Question #8.

FIGURE 1   *Continued*

4. *During the last year, did your company/division send any first-level managers to a basic management-training program outside the office?*
   YES   ____
   NO   ____
   Do not know   ____

5. *During the last year, did your company/division hire an outside consultant to conduct in-house basic management training for first-level managers?*
   YES   ____
   NO   ____
   Do not know   ____

6. a. *Does your company/division have printed management-training materials that are currently used by first-level managers?*
   YES   ____
   NO   ____
   Do not know   ____

   If YES, go to Question #6b.

   b. *Are most of these materials developed in-house, or are they purchased from an outside supplier?*
   In-house   ____
   Outside supplier   ____
   Both equally   ____
   Do not know   ____

7. a. *During the last year, did your company/division use any kind of videotape in connection with first-level management training?*
   YES   ____
   NO   ____
   Do not know   ____

   If NO or Do not know, go to Question #8.

   b. *Were any of these videotapes part of a training package that also included things like reading materials and an instructor's guide?*
   YES   ____
   NO   ____
   Do not know   ____

   If NO or Do not know, go to Question #8.

FIGURE 1 *Continued*

c. **What do you like about these video training packages?**

_____

_____

_____

d. **What do you not like about these video training packages?**

_____

_____

_____

e. **What is your overall satisfaction level with these video training packages?**

Is your satisfaction level high, medium, or low?

High satisfaction _____
Medium satisfaction _____
Low satisfaction _____
Do not know _____

8. *Now I would like to ask you a few* **general** *questions about management-training packages that include* **videotapes.** *I want you to think about how such packages might apply to your own company/division.*

Consider a training package for a group of first-level managers that covers issues like supervision or leadership. The package includes the following:

• Study guide and reading materials
• Detailed leader guide
• An interactive videotape with cases and role plays

a. **How valuable do you think that such a video training package would be for your first-level managers?**

Would it be of high, medium, or low value?

High value _____
Medium value _____
Low value _____
Do not know _____

FIGURE **1**   *Continued*

b. ***Do you think that this kind of a video training package would work in your company/division?***

NO ____

YES ____

Do not know ____

c. **(Probe)** *Why/Why not?*

_____

_____

_____

d. ***For this kind of video training package, which of these session lengths would you prefer?*** **(Read list)**

1–2 hour(s) ____

Half-day ____

Full-day ____

Do not know ____

e. ***How important is it to* you *that such a package is flexible, allowing you to adjust the length of the training session?***

Is it of high, medium, or low importance?

High importance ____

Medium importance ____

Low importance ____

Do not know ____

f. ***Would you be more likely to purchase or rent such a video training package?***

Purchase ____

Rent ____

Do not know ____

9. a. ***Does your company/division have room facilities available for management training sessions?***

YES ____

NO ____

Do not know ____

FIGURE 1   *Continued*

---

b. **Does your company/division have both a TV and a VCR available?**
   YES   ____
   NO   ____
   Do not know ____

10. a. **How many first-level managers does your company/division have?**
    4 or less   ____
    5–9   ____
    10–19   ____
    20–29   ____
    30–39   ____
    40 or more   ____
    Do not know ____

b. **During the last year, approximately how much did your company/division spend on employee training, excluding tuition?**
   Less than $500   ____
   $501–$1,000   ____
   $1,001–$1,500   ____
   $1,501–$2,000   ____
   More than $2,000   ____
   Do not know/refused to answer ____

That is all the questions I have for you. Thank you very much for your participation.

RESULTS

A total of 200 firms were contacted, and 148 questionnaires were completed (a 74 percent response rate). The researchers coded and tabulated the information from the surveys and prepared a summary report for MI. They felt that the research appropriately addressed the two major objectives set for the study.

Questions

1. What seems to be the target population for MI's video-based training?
2. How would you recommend sampling from this target population?

Case 4.11
Rockway Publishing Company, Inc.

THE PROBLEM

Rockway Publishing Company publishes telephone directories for suburban and rural communities. Headquartered in a large midwestern metropolitan area, Rockway publishes directories for over 80 markets, mostly in the midwestern and southern parts of the United States. The telephone directories are published as an alternative to, and in competition with, directories published by the local telephone company serving these markets. Rockway has been very successful in offering yellow-page advertisers a quality product at competitive rates. However, there have been some problems with distribution.

The distribution of the directories is handled in one of two ways. Winston Delivery Company has been under contract for the past two years to hand deliver directories in suburban areas and small cities. Winston hires college students, at minimum wage plus car expenses, to make the deliveries. Each student is given an assigned area of streets and rural routes to cover. For some locations, particularly where the households are heavily rural, the directories are sent through the mail. Recently, Rockway's salespeople have been receiving complaints from advertisers that some of their customers have not received a directory. It is believed by some of the salespeople that as much as 10 to 15 percent of households, in an given market, are not receiving a directory.

SURVEY METHOD

Faced with the prospect that not all of the directories intended for households are being delivered, Ron Combs, president of Rockway, instituted a plan for measuring the discrepancy. Approximately three weeks after a directory is delivered in an area, a sample of households is telephoned, and respondents are asked if the directory has been received. The results are tabulated according to whether the household has a city or rural address. To be counted, the respondent must be sure that the book has been received or has not been received. Respondents who are uncertain or don't know are given more information about the time of delivery, what the face of the book looks like, and how it was delivered (by mail or by hand). If they are still uncertain, they are replaced in the sample and not included in the tally. The respondent may be anyone in the household who answers the phone or is available at the time of the call. Combs wants to ensure that sampling error is not greater than plus or minus two percentage points.

Source: This case was prepared by Paul D. Boughton, Ph.D., Associate Professor of Marketing, Saint Louis University, 3674 Lindell Blvd., St. Louis, MO 63108. Reprinted with permission.

TABLE 1   **Survey Results**

	Hand Delivered			Mail Delivered	
	Area 1	**Area 2**	**Area 3**	**Area 4**	**Area 5**
Total area population	35,000	50,000	69,000	85,000	155,000
City	24,000	45,700	52,000	43,000	100,000
Rural	11,000	4,300	17,000	42,000	55,000
Total sample	525	750	1,035	1,275	2,325
City	325	650	775	685	1,325
Rural	200	100	260	590	1,000
Overall percentage receiving directory	88%	90%	95%	85%	92%

THE SAMPLING PLAN

The sampling frame is an internally produced cross directory of white-page listings by street. The interviewer goes through the pages, arbitrarily pulling names from the listings. If a respondent says a directory has not been received, additional calls are made on that street to determine if the entire street was missed. However, these additional calls are not included in the survey results.

Table 1 shows the results of the survey for areas distributed to in the most recent months.

The total sample size for each area was determined by taking 1.5 percent of the area population. The breakdown between city and rural sample is arbitrary and the result of actual calls completed.

Combs wants to determine three things: (1) the overall soundness of the sampling plan; (2) the amount of sampling error in the results; and (3) the amount of response error by respondents.

Questions

1. What type of sample is being taken? Are city and rural residents being represented adequately? What other approach would you recommend and why?

2. What is the range of sampling error experienced from Area 1 to Area 5? (Assume 95 percent level of confidence.) How can Combs' error goal of plus or minus two percentage points be achieved?

3. What would you recommend as a sample size for each of the five areas?

4. Does Combs have enough information to determine respondent error? What would you recommend he do to obtain this information?

5

ANALYSIS AND INTERPRETATION OF DATA

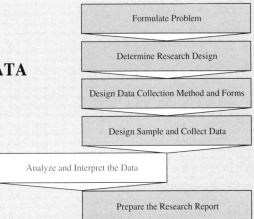

Formulate Problem
Determine Research Design
Design Data Collection Method and Forms
Design Sample and Collect Data
Analyze and Interpret the Data
Prepare the Research Report

Once data have been collected, emphasis in the research process logically turns to analysis, which amounts to the search for meaning in the collected information. This search involves many questions and several steps. Chapter 13 is a review of the preliminary steps of editing, coding, and tabulating the data. Chapter 14 is a discussion of the main questions that need to be resolved before statistical examination of the data can begin. Chapters 15, 16, and 17 review the statistical techniques that are most useful in the analysis of marketing data. Chapter 15 is a discussion of the procedures appropriate for examining group differences; Chapter 16 examines the assessment of associations; and Chapter 17 covers the multivariate techniques of discriminant, factor, and cluster analysis.

DATA ANALYSIS: PRELIMINARY STEPS

The purpose of analysis is to obtain meaning from the collected data. All previous steps in the research process have been undertaken to support the search for meaning. The specific analytical procedures to be used are closely related to the preceding steps, and the careful analyst will remember this when designing the other steps. Hopefully, the analyst will go so far as to develop dummy tables, indicating how each item of information will be used, before beginning data collection. Thorough preparatory work should reveal undesirable data gaps and should also pinpoint items that are ''interesting'' but that do not relate to the problem being examined.

The search for meaning can take many forms. However, the preliminary analytical steps of editing, coding, and tabulation are common to most studies. Research Realities 13.1, for example, describes what happens to the census forms once we complete them. Given their pervasiveness and value, a review of what editing, coding, and tabulation entail and how they are used is desirable.

EDITING

The basic purpose of editing is to impose some minimum quality standards on the raw data. Editing involves the inspection and, if necessary, correction of each questionnaire or observation form. Inspection and correction are often done in two stages: the field edit and the central office edit.

Field Edit

The **field edit** is a preliminary edit, designed to detect the most glaring omissions and inaccuracies in the data. It is also useful in helping to control the field force and to clear up their misunderstandings about directions, procedures, specific questions, and so on. For example, in a Roper survey conducted in the Ukraine, the field edit revealed that an employee had left the questionnaire with the respondents instead of interviewing them as instructed. The tip-off was the different ways in which the answers were circled.[1]

---

[1] Lourdes Lee Valeriano, ''Marketing: Western Firms Poll Eastern Europeans to Discern Tastes of Nascent Consumers,'' *The Wall Street Journal* (April 27, 1992), p. B1.

Ideally, the field edit is done as soon as possible after the questionnaire (or other data collection form) has been administered, so that problems can be corrected before the interviewing or observation staff is disbanded and while the particular contacts that were the source of trouble are still fresh in the interviewer's or observer's mind. The preliminary edit will more than likely be conducted by a field supervisor. Some of the things that will be checked are described in Research Realities 13.2.[2]

Central Office Edit

The field edit is typically followed by a **central office edit.** This involves more complete and exacting scrutiny and correction of the completed returns. The work calls for the keen eye of a person well-versed in the objectives and procedures of the study. To ensure consistency of treatment, it is best if one individual handles all completed instruments. If this is impossible because of length and time considerations, the work can be divided. However, the division should be by parts of the data collection instruments rather than by respondents. That is, one editor would be concerned with editing Part A of all questionnaires, while the other would edit Part B.

Unlike the field edit, the central office edit depends less on follow-up procedures and more on deciding just what to do with the data. Accurate follow-up is now more difficult because of the time that has elapsed. In deciding what to do with the data, the editor will usually have to decide how data collection instruments containing incomplete answers, obviously wrong answers, and answers that reflect a lack of interest will be handled. Since such problems are more prevalent with questionnaires than observational forms, we will discuss these difficulties from that perspective, although the discussion applies generally to all types of data collection forms.

The study in which all the returned questionnaires are completely filled out is rare. Some will have complete sections omitted; others will reflect sporadic item nonresponse. The editor's decision on how to handle these incomplete questionnaires depends on the severity of the problem. Questionnaires that omit complete sections are obviously suspect, yet they should not automatically be thrown out. It might be, for example, that the omitted section refers to the influence of the spouse in some major durable purchase and the respondent is not married. This type of reply is certainly usable in spite of the incomplete section. Alternatively, there might not be a logical justification for the large number of questions that were not answered. In this case, the total reply would probably be thrown out, increasing the nonresponse rate for the study. Questionnaires containing only isolated instances of item nonresponse would be retained, although they might undergo some data cleaning after coding, a subject discussed later in this chapter.

Careful editing of the questionnaire will sometimes show that an answer to a question is obviously incorrect. For example, respondents might be asked for the type of store in which they purchased a camera in one part of the questionnaire and the name of the store in another. If the person responded ''department store'' whereas the name of the store indicated a discount store, one of the answers is incorrect. The editor may be

---

[2]The classification of items to be checked in the field edit is taken from Claire Selltiz, Lawrence S. Wrightsman, and Stuart W. Cook, *Research Methods in Social Relations,* 3rd ed. (New York: Holt, Rinehart and Winston, 1976), pp. 475–476.

Research Realities 13.1

Preliminary Processing of Census Forms

On April 1, 1990, we as a nation will officially stand up to be counted. We'll take the census questionnaire we've just completed and drop it into a mailbox. Some of us will give the questionnaire to an enumerator who comes to call. For most of us, the census ends here; we've done our part for another ten years.

But, for the Census Bureau, the job is only half complete.

Within the ten days that follow Census Day, some 70 million questionnaires are expected to come flooding back to the Bureau, courtesy of the U.S. Postal Service, creating a tidal wave of paper. When all the questionnaires are in, we expect to have about 106 million questionnaires — approximately 94 million for occupied housing units and another 12 million for vacant units.

As the questionnaires come back, we won't just stand there watching them accumulate into mountains. For years, we have been carefully preparing for flow processing.

Flow Processing Is the Key

Flow processing will let us use computers in monitoring each questionnaire from the moment we receive

the form from the respondent. We'll edit each questionnaire, earmark it for any follow-up action, and submit it for the capture of data.

This is, in brief, how flow processing will work:

Check-In   Most questionnaires will arrive in their mailback envelopes at a census field office. We will read the bar-coded number on the envelope by manually passing a laser wand over it, automatically recording the arrival. For several highly populated areas of the country, however, questionnaires will be delivered to high-tech processing offices where high-speed, automated sorters will be pressed into service. All the questionnaires then will be taken from their envelopes, unfolded, and placed in stacks.

Filming   The stacks will be sent to a processing office where they will be filmed by a machine that is a combination camera and page turner.

Data Capture   The film will be developed and forwarded to a FOSDIC (Film Optical Sensing Device for Input to Computer), which will scan respondents' answers and transmit the information to the processing office computers.

FOSDIC does not record the names shown on the questionnaires; no names go into the computer files.

Source: "Next Year You Answer the Census and We'll Do the Rest," *Census and You*, 24 (April 1989), pp. 1–2.

able to determine which from other information in the questionnaire. Alternatively, the editor may need to establish policies concerning which answer will be treated as correct, if either, when these inconsistencies or other types of inaccuracies arise. These policies will reflect the purposes of the study. As an example, consider the quandary of Susan Hooper, the Eastern Europe marketing director for Pepsi Cola International, who recently was given results of a survey conducted in Hungary that said drug stores are an outlet for soft drinks. Susan cannot take this information at face value for she knows full well that drug stores don't exist in Hungary and that the information has been forced into a structure developed in the west.[3]

[3]Valeriano, "Marketing: Western Firms Poll," p. B1.

The Census Bureau will use a clerical or computer edit to quickly spot questionnaires that have been incorrectly filled out so that a processing office or an enumerator can follow up.

"Heavy Artillery"

How many people and how much equipment will flow processing take? The Census Bureau describes the upcoming census as the biggest national effort since World War II's D-Day. The front lines of the data gathering and collection effort will consist of the following:

- A field force of some 300,000 workers at the peak of the census.
- A complex of 484 temporary field offices, 13 regional census centers, and 7 processing centers.
- "Artillery" consisting of some 530 minicomputers and microcomputers, 12 laser sorters, 72 camera/page turners, 21 microfilm processors, and 21 FOSDICs — not to mention thousands of telephones, telecommunications modems, typewriters, temporary cardboard desks, and tons of other supplies.

Total Cost: $2.6 Billion

Total cost for the years of planning (beginning in 1984), actual decennial census activities, and production of the results (to be completed in 1993) will be an estimated $2.6 billion, or about $10.40 per U.S. resident.

Deadlines to Meet

Throughout the spring, summer, and fall of 1990, Census Bureau flow processing will be in high gear so that the Secretary of Commerce can deliver the population count of each state to the White House by the December 31 legal deadline.

By that time, the vast army assembled by the Bureau will largely have been dispersed, not to be assembled again until the next decennial census.

The larger minicomputer systems will be returned to headquarters to upgrade the central computer facility, while the majority of smaller computers, which will be leased, will be returned to the vendors.

But the early 1990s will not be a time of rest for the Census Bureau. We will begin releasing the more detailed information from the census. At the same time, we will begin looking forward to the year 2000 — when the whole process begins again.

Indications that the completed questionnaire reflects a lack of interest on the part of the subject are sometimes subtle and sometimes obvious. For example, a subject who checked the "5" position on a five-point scale for each of the 40 items in an attitude questionnaire in which some items were expressed negatively and some positively is obviously not taking the study very seriously. An editor would probably throw out such a response. A discerning editor might also be able to pick up more subtle indications of disinterest, such as check marks that are not within the boxes provided, scribbles, spills on the questionnaire, and so on. An editor may not want to throw out these responses, but they should be coded so that it is later possible to run separate tabulations for both questionable instruments and obviously good questionnaires, to see if that makes any difference in the results and conclusions.

Research Realities 13.2

Items Checked in the Field Edit

1. **Completeness:** This check for completeness involves scrutinizing the data form to ensure that no sections or pages were omitted, and it also involves checking individual items. A blank for a specific question could mean that the respondent refused to answer; alternatively, it may simply reflect an oversight on the respondent's part or show that she or he did not know the answer. It may be important for the purposes of the study to know which reason is correct. Hopefully, by contacting the field worker while the interview is fresh in her or his mind, the needed clarification will be provided.

2. **Legibility:** It is impossible to code a questionnaire that cannot be deciphered because the interviewer's handwriting is unintelligible or because abbreviations were used that are not understood by others. It is a simple matter to correct this now, whereas it is often extremely time-consuming later.

3. **Comprehensibility:** Sometimes a recorded response is incomprehensible to all but the field interviewer. By detecting this now, the necessary clarification can be easily provided.

4. **Consistency:** Marked inconsistencies within an interview or observation schedule typically indicate errors in collecting or recording the data and may indicate ambiguity in the instrument or carelessness in its administration. For instance, if a respondent indicated that she or he saw a particular commercial on TV last night on one part of the questionnaire and later indicated that she or he did not watch TV last night, the analyst would indeed be in a dilemma. Hopefully, such inconsistencies would be detected and corrected in the field edit.

5. **Uniformity:** It is very important that the responses be recorded in uniform units. For instance, if the study is aimed at determining the number of magazines read per week per individual, and the respondent indicates the number of magazines for which she or he has monthly subscriptions, the response base is not uniform, and the result could cause no small amount of confusion in the later stages of analysis. If detected now, perhaps the interviewer can recontact the respondent and get the correct answer.

CODING

"**Coding** is the technical procedure by which data are categorized. Through coding, the raw data are transformed into symbols — usually numerals — that may be tabulated and counted. The transformation is not automatic, however; it involves judgment on the part of the coder."[4]

The first step in coding is specifying the categories or classes into which the responses are to be placed.[5] There is no magic number of categories. Rather, the number will depend on the research problem being investigated and the specific items used to generate the information. Nevertheless, several rules for specifying the classes can be

---

[4]Selltiz, Wrightsman, and Cook, *Research Methods,* p. 473.

[5]Some writers would make the specification of categories part of the editing rather than the coding function. Its placement in one or the other function is not nearly as important as the recognition that it is an extremely critical step with important ramifications for the whole research effort.

stated. First, the classes should be mutually exclusive and exhaustive. Every response should logically fall into one and only one category. Multiple responses are legitimate, of course, if the question is "For what purposes do you use JELL-O?" and the responses include such things as "a dessert item," "an evening snack," "an afternoon snack," and so on. If the question focuses on the person's age, then only one age category is, of course, acceptable, and the code should indicate unequivocally which category.

Coding closed questions and most scaling devices is simple because the coding is established, for all practical purposes, when the data collection instrument is designed. Respondents then code themselves with their responses, or the interviewer effectively codes them when he or she records the response on the checklist provided.

Coding open-ended questions can be very difficult and is often much more expensive than coding closed questions. The coder has to determine appropriate categories on the basis of answers that are not always anticipated.[6]

International studies can create their own special coding problems because different labels may mean different things. For example, a conservative in the former Soviet Union is someone who wishes to adhere to or return to the "old Communism," which in turn might be seen as very left wing in Western countries. Liberal Russians, in turn, are the ones who wish to introduce market perspectives into economics and politics, a perspective which usually will be held by conservatives in the West.

The coding of open-ended questions can create the additional problem of inconsistent treatment when the number of questionnaires necessitates the use of several coders. To ensure consistency of treatment, the work should again be divided by task and not by apportioning the questionnaires equally among the coders. The result of allowing coders to concentrate their energies on one or a few questions is that a consistent set of standards is applied to each question. This approach is also more efficient because coders can learn the codes and do not have to consult the code book for each instrument. When several persons do, in fact, code the same question on different batches of questionnaires, it is important that they also code a sample of the other's work to ensure that a consistent set of coding criteria is being employed.[7]

---

[6]In one study that explicitly compared the responses to open and closed questions, marked differences were found in the response distributions to the two types of questions. The authors concluded that the responses to closed questions were the more valid, because the responses to open questions are often so vague that they are misclassified by coders. See H. Schuman and S. Presser, "The Open and Closed Question," *American Sociological Review,* 44 (1979), pp. 692–712. To improve the consistency with which similar answers are coded, some researchers have attempted to develop systems by which computers can code open-ended responses. For an illustration, see Colin McDonald, "Coding Open-Ended Answers With the Help of a Computer," *Journal of the Market Research Society,* 24 (January 1982), pp. 9–27. For discussion of the problems and available methods for coding open-ended questions, see Rodger Knaus, "Methods and Problems in Coding Natural Language Survey Data," *Journal of Official Statistics,* 3 (No. 1, 1987), pp. 45–67; Wesley H. Jones, "Quantitative Analysis of Qualitative Data: Field Experience," paper presented at Marketing Science Institute conference on New Tools and New Rules for Marketing Research, Cambridge, Massachusetts, June 23, 1992.

[7]For discussion of a set of indices that can be used to investigate coder reliability as well as to determine which questions might prove to be particularly troublesome, see Martin Collins and Graham Kalton, "Coding Verbatim Answers to Open Questions," *Journal of the Market Research Society,* 22 (October 1980), pp. 239–247; William D. Perreault, Jr., and Laurence E. Leigh, "Reliability of Nominal Data Based on Qualitative Judgments," *Journal of Marketing Research,* 26 (May 1989), pp. 135–148.

The second step in coding involves assigning code numbers to the classes. For example, sex might be assigned the letters M for male and F for female. Alternatively, the classes could be denoted by 1 for male and 2 for female. Generally, it is better to use numbers than letters to denote the classes. It also is better to treat numerical data in their reported form at this stage rather than collapsing interval or ratio scale data into categories. For example, it is not advisable to code age in years as 1 = under 20, 2 = 20 to 29, 3 = 30 to 39, and so on. This would entail some unnecessary sacrifice of information in the original measurement and can just as easily be done at later stages in the analysis.

When the analysis of data is to be done by computer, it is necessary to code the data so that they can readily be put into the machine. Regardless of how that input will be effected, whether by mark-sense forms, by mouse-activated optical readers, or directly through a keyboard on a terminal, it is helpful to visualize the input in terms of a multiple-column record. Further, it is advisable to follow certain conventions when coding the data:

1. Use only one character per column. Most computer programs cannot read multiple characters per column. When the question allows multiple responses, spread or spray the answers by allowing separate columns in the coding for each answer. Thus, the question on JELL-O usage would dictate that a separate column be provided in the coding form to indicate whether the respondent used it as a dessert item, another column for use as an evening snack, and so on.

2. Use only numeric codes and not letters of the alphabet, special characters like @, or blanks. Most computer statistical programs have severe difficulty in manipulating anything but numbers.

3. The field or portion of the record assigned to a variable should consist of as many columns as are necessary to capture the variable. Thus, if the variable is such that the ten codes from 0 to 9 are not sufficient to exhaust the categories, then one should use two columns in the record, which provides 100 codes from 00 through 99. Moreover, no more than one variable should be assigned to any field.

4. Use standard codes for "No information." Thus, all "Don't know" responses might be coded "8," "No answers" as "9," and "Does not apply" as "0." It is best if the same code is used throughout the study for each of these types of "No information."[8]

5. Code in a respondent identification number on each record. This number need not, and typically will not, identify the respondent by name. Rather, the number simply ties the questionnaire to the coded data. This is often useful information in data cleaning. If the questionnaire will not fit on one record, then code the respondent identification number and a sequence number into each record. Column 10 in the first record might then indicate how the respondent answered Question 2, whereas

---

[8]For discussion of the analysis of "Don't know" responses, see Richard M. Durand and Zarrell V. Lambert, "Don't Know Responses in Surveys: Analysis and Interpretational Consequences," *Journal of Business Research,* 16 (March 1988), pp. 169–188.

Column 10 in the second record might indicate whether the person is male or female.[9]

The final step in the coding process is to prepare a **code book.** The code book contains the general instructions indicating how each item of data was coded. It lists the codes for each variable and the categories included in each code. It further indicates where on the computer record the variable is located, and how the variable should be read — for example, with a decimal point or as a whole number. The latter information is provided by the format specifications. Figure 13A.1 (in Appendix 13A) contains a sample questionnaire and the code book for the questionnaire is shown in Table 13A.1.

TABULATION

Tabulation consists simply of counting the number of cases that fall into the various categories. The tabulation may take the form of a simple tabulation or a cross tabulation. **Simple tabulation** involves counting a single variable. It may be repeated for each of the variables in the study, but the tabulation for each variable is independent of the tabulation for the other variables. In **cross tabulation,** two or more of the variables are treated simultaneously; the number of cases that have the joint characteristics are counted (for example, the number of people who bought Campbell's soup at a Kroger store).

The tabulations may be done entirely by hand, entirely by machine, or some by machine and some by hand. Which method is more efficient depends partly on the number of tabulations necessary and partly on the number of cases in each tabulation. The number of tabulations is a direct function of the number of variables, whereas the number of cases is a direct function of the size of the sample. The fewer the number of tabulations required and the smaller the sample, the more attractive hand methods become. However, the attractiveness of either alternative is also highly dependent on the complexity of the tabulations. Complexity increases as the number of variables receiving simultaneous treatment in a cross tabulation increases. Complexity also increases as the number of categories per variable increases.

Although the hand tabulation might be useful in very simple studies involving a few questions and a limited number of responses, most studies rely on computer tabulation using packaged programs. Many such programs are available.[10] Some will calculate summary statistics and will plot a histogram of the values in addition to reporting the number of cases in each category. The basic input to these statistical analyses will be the data array. The data array lists the value of each variable for each sample unit. Each

---

[9]Philip S. Siedl, "Coding," in Robert Ferber, ed., *Handbook of Marketing Research* (New York: McGraw-Hill, 1974), pp. 2–178 to 2–199. This article provides an excellent overview of the issues that arise in coding data and how they can be handled. See also Linda B. Bourque and Virginia A. Clark, *Processing Data: The Survey Example* (Newbury Park, CA: Sage Publications, Inc., 1992).

[10]For a review of the features contained in the most popular statistical packages for microcomputers, see Robin Raskin, "Statistical Software for the PC: Testing for Significance," *PC Magazine,* 8 (March 14, 1989), pp. 103–255.

variable occupies a specific place in the record for a sample unit, thereby making it easy to pick off the values for it from all of the cases. The location of each variable is given in the code book. Table 13A.2 in the appendix to this chapter provides an example of a data array, and Table 13A.1 describes what is contained in each column. Note that only one line had to be devoted to each sample unit or observation. If the amount of information sought from each sample unit had been greater, so that it would not fit as a single record, additional lines would have been devoted to each observation. The code book would still indicate where the information for any particular variable was located.

There are a number of important questions concerning the analysis of data that can be illustrated, using one-way tabulations and cross tabulations as vehicles. Consider, therefore, the data in Table 13.1. Suppose that the data were collected for a study focusing on car ownership, particularly on the following questions:

- What characteristics distinguish families owning two or more cars from families owning one car?

- What are the distinguishing characteristics of those who buy station wagons? Foreign economy cars? Vans?

- Are there differences in the characteristics of families who financed their automobile purchase and those who did not?

Suppose that the data were collected from a probability sample of respondents using mailed questionnaires and that the 100 people to whom the questionnaire was sent all replied. Thus, there are no problems of nonresponse with which to contend.

One-Way Tabulation

The one-way tabulation, in addition to communicating the results of a study, can be used for several other purposes: (1) to determine the degree of item nonresponse, (2) to locate blunders, (3) to locate outliers, (4) to determine the empirical distribution of the variable in question, and (5) to calculate summary statistics. The first three of these are often referred to as "data cleaning."

What to do about item nonresponse is an aggravating problem in most surveys. It seems that some percentage of the survey instruments invariably suffer from item nonresponse. As a matter of fact, the degree of item nonresponse often serves as a useful indicator of the quality of the research. When it is excessive, it calls the whole research effort into question and suggests that a critical examination of the research objectives and procedures should be undertaken. When it is in bounds, it still demands that decisions be made with respect to what to do about the missing items before analyzing the data. There are several possible strategies:

1. Leave the items blank and report the number as a separate category. While this procedure works well for simple one-way and cross tabulations, it does not work very well at all for some statistical techniques.

2. Eliminate the case with the missing item in analyses using the variable. When using this approach, the analyst must continually report the number of cases on which the analysis is based, because the sample size is not constant across analyses. This

approach also ignores the fact that a significant incidence of no information on any item might in itself be insightful; it signals that respondents do not care very deeply about the issue being addressed by the question.

3. Substitute values for the missing items. Typically, the substitution will involve some measure of central tendency such as the mean, median, or mode. Alternatively, sometimes the analyst attempts to estimate the answer using other information contained in the questionnaire. The substitution of values makes maximum use of the data, since all the reasonably good cases are used. At the same time, it is more work, and it does contain some potential for bias. It also raises the question of which statistical technique should be used to generate the estimate.[11]

There is no single "right" answer for how missing items should be handled. It all depends on the purposes of the study, the incidence of missing items, and the methods that will be used to analyze the data. Research Realities 13.3, for example, describes how Nielsen estimates missing store sales data for its SCANTRACK service, previously discussed in Chapter 6.

A **blunder** is simply an error. It can happen during editing, during coding, or when entering the data on the computer. Consider the one-way tabulation of the number of cars owned per family in Table 13.2. A check of the original questionnaire indicates that the family having nine cars had, in fact, one car. The nine is a blunder. The simple one-way tabulation has revealed the error, and it can now be corrected at a very early stage in the analysis with a minimum of difficulty and expense.

An interesting example of the use of the one-way tabulation to locate blunders occurred in a series of articles *The Boston Globe* was working on concerning money laundering using government-developed data. In this case, the tabulations produced large and unexplainable swings in cash transactions in certain cities. "Ultimately, the discrepancies were traced to a clerk in Detroit, who occasionally added five zeros to actual figures to ease boredom."[12]

---

[11]David W. Stewart, "Filling the Gap: A Review of the Missing Data Problem," unpublished manuscript, provides an excellent review of the literature on the missing data problem, including various methods for eliminating cases and estimating answers. On the basis of this review, he concludes several things: missing data points should be estimated regardless of whether the data are missing randomly or nonrandomly; for very small amounts of missing data, almost any of the estimation procedures work reasonably well; when larger amounts of data are missing and the average intercorrelation of variables is .20 or less, the substitution of the mean seems to work best; and when the average intercorrelation of the variables exceeds .20, a regression or principal components procedure is the preferred choice when linearity among the variables may be assumed. For a study that empirically examines the question of whether or not missing items are random, see Richard M. Durand, Hugh J. Guffey, Jr., and John M. Planchon, "An Examination of the Random versus Nonrandom Nature of Item Omissions," *Journal of Marketing Research,* 20 (August 1983), pp. 305–313. See also Roderick J. A. Little and Philip J. Smith, "Editing and Imputation for Quantitative Survey Data," *Journal of the American Statistical Association,* 82 (March 1987), pp. 58–68; Roderick J. Little and Donald B. Rubin, "The Analysis of Social Science Data with Missing Values," *Sociological Methods and Research,* 18 (November 1989), pp. 292–326, Paul S. Levy and Stanley Lemeshaw, *Sampling of Populations: Methods and Applications* (New York: John Wiley and Sons, Inc., 1991), Chapter 13.

[12]Gregory Stricharchuk, "Computer Records Become Powerful Tool for Investigative Reporters and Editors," *The Wall Street Journal* (February 3, 1988), p. 23.

TABLE 13.1 Raw Data for Car Ownership Study

Family Ident. No.	(1) Income in Dollars	(2) Number of Members in Family	(3) Education of Household Head in Yrs.	(4) Region Where Live N = North S = South	(5) Lifestyle Orientation L = Liberal C = Conservative	(6) Number of Cars Family Owns	(7) Did Family Finance the Car Purchase?	(8) Does Family Own Station Wagon?	(9) Does Family Own Foreign Economy Car?	(10) Does Family Own Van?	(11) Does Family Own Some Other Kind of Car?
1001	26,800	3	12	N	L	1	N	N	N	Y	N
1002	17,400	4	12	N	L	1	N	N	N	N	Y
1003	14,300	2	10	N	L	1	N	N	N	N	Y
1004	35,400	4	9	N	L	1	N	N	N	N	Y
1005	24,000	3	8	N	L	1	N	N	N	N	Y
1006	17,200	2	12	N	L	1	N	N	N	N	N
1007	27,000	4	12	N	L	1	N	N	Y	N	Y
1008	16,900	3	10	N	L	1	N	N	N	N	N
1009	26,700	2	12	N	L	1	N	N	N	N	Y
1010	13,800	4	6	N	C	1	Y	N	N	N	Y
1011	34,100	3	8	N	C	1	N	N	N	N	Y
1012	16,300	3	11	N	C	1	N	N	N	N	Y
1013	14,700	2	12	N	C	1	N	N	N	N	Y
1014	25,400	4	12	N	C	1	N	N	N	N	Y
1015	15,400	4	12	N	C	1	N	N	N	N	Y
1016	25,900	3	11	N	C	1	N	N	N	N	Y
1017	36,300	3	12	N	C	1	Y	N	N	N	Y
1018	27,400	2	12	N	C	1	N	N	N	N	Y
1019	17,300	2	12	N	C	2	N	N	N	N	Y
1020	13,700	3	8	N	C	1	N	N	N	N	Y
1021	26,100	2	12	N	C	1	N	N	Y	N	N
1022	16,300	4	12	N	C	1	Y	N	N	N	Y
1023	33,800	3	6	N	C	1	N	N	N	N	Y
1024	34,400	4	8	N	C	1	N	N	N	N	Y
1025	15,300	2	9	N	C	1	Y	N	N	N	Y
1026	35,900	3	12	S	C	1	N	N	N	N	Y
1027	15,100	4	12	S	L	1	N	N	N	N	Y
1028	17,200	2	12	S	L	1	N	N	N	N	N
1029	35,400	4	10	S	L	1	N	N	N	N	Y
1030	15,600	3	12	S	L	1	N	N	N	N	Y
1031	24,900	3	12	S	C	1	N	N	N	N	Y
1032	34,800	3	11	S	C	1	N	N	N	Y	N
1033	14,600	4	12	S	C	1	N	N	N	N	Y
1034	23,100	3	9	S	C	1	N	N	N	Y	N
1035	15,900	3	12	S	C	1	N	N	N	Y	Y
1036	26,700	3	12	S	C	1	N	N	N	N	Y
1037	17,300	4	12	S	C	1	N	N	N	Y	N
1038	37,100	3	12	S	C	1	N	N	N	N	Y
1039	14,000	3	10	S	C	1	N	N	N	N	Y
1040	23,600	3	10	S	C	1	N	N	N	N	N
1041	16,200	3	12	S	C	1	N	N	N	N	Y
1042	24,100	4	10	N	C	1	N	Y	N	Y	N
1043	12,700	2	8	S	C	1	N	Y	N	N	Y
1044	26,000	4	13	N	L	1	N	Y	Y	N	N
1045	15,400	3	16	N	L	2	N	Y	Y	N	N
1046	16,900	4	16	N	L	1	N	N	N	N	Y

Z	Z	Z	Y	Y	1	C	S	10	6	23,800	1047
Y	Z	Y	Z	Y	2	L	N	16	8	37,100	1048
Y	Y	Z	Y	Y	1	L	S	15	5	16,800	1049
Z	Z	Z	Y	Z	1	L	N	8	6	22,900	1050
Y	Z	Z	Y	Y	2	L	S	8	8	13,700	1051
Z	Z	Z	Y	Z	1	C	N	12	8	26,800	1052
Y	Z	Z	Z	Z	1	L	N	12	6	16,100	1053
Y	Z	Z	Z	Z	1	L	N	12	2	25,700	1054
Y	Z	Z	Z	Z	1	L	N	12	3	38,200	1055
Y	Z	Z	Z	Z	1	L	N	12	4	49,800	1056
Y	Z	Z	Z	Y	1	L	N	12	2	60,400	1057
Y	Z	Z	Z	Z	1	L	N	12	4	39,000	1058
Z	Y	Z	Z	Y	1	L	N	12	3	57,600	1059
Y	Z	Y	Z	Z	1	L	N	12	3	42,000	1060
Y	Z	Z	Z	Y	2	C	N	12	4	38,600	1061
Y	Z	Z	Z	Z	1	C	N	12	2	66,400	1062
Y	Z	Z	Z	Z	1	C	N	10	4	71,200	1063
Y	Y	Y	Z	Z	1	L	N	10	4	49,300	1064
Y	Z	Z	Z	Y	2	L	N	12	3	37,700	1065
Y	Y	Z	Z	Y	1	L	N	12	3	72,400	1066
Y	Z	Y	Z	Z	1	C	N	12	2	88,700	1067
Y	Y	Z	Z	Y	2	C	S	12	4	44,200	1068
Z	Z	Z	Z	Z	1	C	S	12	2	55,100	1069
Y	Z	Z	Z	Y	1	L	S	10	3	73,300	1070
Y	Z	Z	Y	Z	2	L	S	16	4	80,200	1071
Z	Z	Z	Z	Z	1	L	S	14	3	39,300	1072
Y	Z	Z	Z	Z	1	L	S	17	4	48,200	1073
Y	Y	Z	Z	Y	2	L	S	13	2	57,800	1074
Y	Z	Z	Z	Z	1	L	N	14	3	38,000	1075
Y	Z	Z	Z	Z	1	L	N	16	4	81,300	1076
Y	Z	Z	Z	Z	1	L	N	13	4	96,900	1077
Y	Z	Z	Z	Y	2	L	N	16	3	44,700	1078
Z	Z	Z	Z	Z	1	L	N	16	3	107,300	1079
Y	Y	Z	Z	Z	1	L	N	14	2	38,100	1080
Y	Z	Z	Z	Z	1	L	N	10	2	304,200	1081
Y	Z	Z	Z	Y	9	L	S	8	3	46,100	1082
Y	Y	Z	Z	Z	1	L	S	12	4	49,300	1083
Y	Y	Z	Z	Z	1	L	S	10	4	160,800	1084
Y	Z	Z	Y	Y	2	C	S	12	4	39,100	1085
Y	Z	Z	Z	Z	2	L	S	10	2	46,400	1086
Y	Z	Z	Z	Y	2	L	S	12	4	58,300	1087
Z	Z	Z	Z	Z	2	L	N	12	6	47,800	1088
Z	Z	Z	Z	Z	3	L	N	16	5	58,000	1089
Y	Y	Y	Z	Z	2	L	N	18	7	69,600	1090
Z	Z	Z	Y	Y	2	L	N	15	9	44,200	1091
Z	Y	Y	Y	Y	2	C	N	16	11	62,100	1092
Y	Y	Z	Y	Y	3	L	S	12	6	99,000	1093
Y	Z	Z	Z	Y	2	L	S	10	5	53,300	1094
Z	Y	Z	Y	Z	2	L	S	12	6	72,200	1095
Z	Z	Y	Y	Y	3	C	N	10	9	64,700	1096
Y	Y	Z	Z	Y	1	C	N	12	7	77,300	1097
Z	Y	Z	Y	Z	3	L	S	16	6	116,900	1098
Z	Z	Y	Y	Z	1	L	S	18	10	71,200	1099
Y	Z	Y	Y	Y	2	C	S	15	7	103,800	1100

Research Realities 13.3

Handling of Missing Data in Nielsen's SCANTRACK Service

When a sample store does not provide usable scanning data in a given week, the missing data must be estimated in some fashion. There are two general methods for handling missing data: weighting adjustments and imputation. The weighting-adjustment procedure merely reweights the usable stores in the sample. Implicit estimates are made using this procedure. The imputation procedure, in contrast, inserts values for the missing stores. In this case, explicit estimates are made. Procedures commonly used to impute missing data in continuous long-term surveys of retail trade include reprojection, time-series estimates, and matrix projection.

For any given week, the Nielsen SCANTRACK® sample can be divided into two groups: a response

Source: William B. Owens, "Missing Data," *The Nielsen Researcher*, 2 (Spring 1989), pp. 15–17. Reprinted with permission from Nielsen Marketing Research.

group, made up of all stores that provide usable information for that week; and a nonresponse group, which contains all stores that have not provided information or whose information is judged, after quality edits, to be unusable for that week.

Which group better represents the universe of all stores? Reweighting and reprojection methods use only the response group for the current week; the assumption is that the response group represents the nonresponse group. Time-series estimating procedures use only the nonresponse group; the assumption is that the nonresponse group is not like the response group and must be estimated using its own data. The matrix projection system uses both the response and the nonresponse groups.

Within the Nielsen SCANTRACK sample, major chain organizations are sampled and projected individually. A comparison of the three methods of estimating missing values is shown in Figure A. With

FIGURE A   **Treatments of Missing Data Assuming that Store #4 Is Missing in the Current Week**

	Store No.	Previous Weeks	Current Week	
A. Reprojection	1		10	
	2		8	
	3		12	
	4		X_t	10
B. Time Series	4	10 ... 10	X_t	10
C. Matrix Projection	1	5 ... 5	10	
	2	4 ... 4	8	
	3	6 ... 6	12	
	4	10 ... 10	X_t	20

four sample stores from the same organization in a given market, the reprojection methodology would assume that Store #4's sales in period t were similar to sales in Stores #1, #2, and #3. Projected sales for the chain would be based in period t on three stores of data rather than four. The resulting assumption is that Store #4 sold the average for the three other sample stores in the chain; in this example, that would be 10 units.

The time-series approach, which assumes that Store #4 is not like its sister stores, requires the estimate for Store #4 in time period t to be made by looking at past sales activity for that store. In the simplest case, if Store #4 had constant sales for a given item in past periods, the estimate of sales in time period t would be a continuation of the constant sales pattern, 10 units in this example.

The matrix projection method combines the logic of both the reprojection and time-series methods. Current and past sales activities are examined in a subset of the response group known as "sister" stores, allowing an estimate of the sales trend in the missing store that is based on the sales trend in the sister stores. The trend then can be applied to the time-series estimate of the missing store. In this example, current-period sales jumped by 100 percent from the previous week's sales in the sister stores. This trend was applied to the missing store to give a matrix projection estimate of 20 units.

The matrix projection method was designed to minimize the effect of sample fluctuation caused by missing data. In any given SCANTRACK report, this procedure ensures that the following information will be included for the missing store:

1. The product group and brand mix within the store;
2. All special prices, displays, and retail advertisements associated with the store;
3. The effect of weekly promotions on sales in the sister stores; and
4. Any holiday or seasonal effects on sales.

The matrix projection method provides explicit UPC-by-UPC estimates of sales for missing stores. Each sample store is grouped with similar sister stores, which are used to obtain week effect and causal effect projection factors. These factors, which are computed for each Nielsen product group, quantify the effect on weekly sales of various market conditions such as seasonality and key pay weeks, as well as the effect on weekly sales of in-store conditions such as displays, retail ads, and price cuts.

Figure B displays the data components used in matrix projection. For the sister stores, the week effects are established using current and previous weeks' information on sales, prices, and promotions for each UPC. The same information is available for the missing store's previous week, as are promotions and special prices for the current week. Data on causal sales activity such as special price and promotional activity are collected weekly within all SCANTRACK stores. Thus, although an individual store may not provide usable scanning data for a given week, the special price and in-store causal conditions are known and can be incorporated into the matrix projection method.

FIGURE B   Data Components Used in Matrix Projection

Sister Stores	Missing Stores
Current Week's	Current Week's
Sales	—
Prices	Special Prices Only
Promotions	Promotions
Previous Week's	Previous Week's
Sales	Sales
Prices	Prices
Promotions	Promotions

TABLE 13.2   **Cars per Family**

Number of Cars per Family	Number of Families
1	74
2	23
3	2
9	1

TABLE 13.3   **Cars per Family**

Number of Cars per Family	Number of Families	Percentage of Families
1	75	75
2	23	23
3	2	2
	100	100

The number of cases serving as a base for the one-way tabulation in Table 13.2 is 100, and thus the number entries are readily converted to percentages. Conversion will rarely be this easy, but it is good practice to indicate percentages in the table. Percentages facilitate communication, and a more typical presentation of the preceding result, corrected for blunders, is found in Table 13.3. Note that the *percentages are presented to zero decimal places*. Though in this case it is because the sample size was 100, in most cases it would be done *deliberately*. The sample is small, and with small samples one has to be particularly careful not to convey a greater accuracy than the figures can support. They also are easier to read when rounded off. On some occasions the analyst might wish to report percentages to one decimal place.[13] Rarely, if ever, would they be reported to two decimal places, because this would typically introduce a spurious sense of accuracy and might seriously impair the analysis by lulling the reader into assuming that the data are more accurate than they actually are. The general rule in reporting percentages is: *Unless decimals serve a special purpose, they should be omitted.*

Sometimes the percentages also are presented in parentheses (see Table 13.4) immediately to the right or below the actual count entry in the table. Sometimes only the percentages are presented. In this case it is imperative that the total number of cases on which the percentages are based is provided.

---

[13]See the classic book by Hans Zeisel, *Say It with Figures,* 5th ed. (New York: Harper & Row, 1968), pp. 16–17, for conditions that would support reporting percentages with decimal-place accuracy.

TABLE 13.4   **Income Distribution of Respondents in Car Ownership Study**

Income	Number of Families		Cumulative Number of Families	
Less than $15,000	8	(8.0)	8	(8.0)
$15,000 to $24,900	25	(25.0)	33	(33.0)
$25,000 to $34,900	15	(15.0)	48	(48.0)
$35,000 to $44,900	18	(18.0)	66	(66.0)
$45,000 to $54,900	8	(8.0)	74	(74.0)
$55,000 to $64,900	8	(8.0)	82	(82.0)
$65,000 to $74,900	7	(7.0)	89	(89.0)
$75,000 to $84,900	3	(3.0)	92	(92.0)
$85,000 to $94,900	1	(1.0)	93	(93.0)
$95,000 to $104,900	3	(3.0)	96	(96.0)
More than $105,000	4	(4.0)	100	(100.0)
Total number of families	100	(100.0)		

The third use of the one-way tabulation is to locate **outliers.** An outlier is not an error. Rather, it is an observation so different in magnitude from the rest of the observations that the analyst chooses to treat it as a special case. This may mean eliminating the observation from the analysis or determining the specific factors that generate this unique observation.[14] Consider, for example, the tabulation of incomes contained in Table 13.4, but ignore the right-hand column for the moment. The tabulation indicates there are only four families with incomes greater than $105,000, and Table 13.1 indicates that only one family had an annual income greater than $161,000, namely Number 1081 with an income of $304,200. This is clearly out of line with the rest of the sample and is properly considered an outlier. What the analyst chooses to do with this observation depends on the objectives of the study. In this case, it is not unreasonable for a family to have such an income, so the observation will be retained in the analysis.

The fourth use of the one-way frequency tabulation is to determine the *empirical distribution* of the characteristic in question. Some analysts ignore the distribution of the variables and automatically calculate summary statistics such as the mean. Ignoring the distribution of the variables can be a serious mistake. Consider the case of a new sauce product.

> On the average, consumers wanted it neither really hot nor really mild. The mean rating of the test participants was quite close to the middle of the scale, which had "very mild" and "very hot" as its bipolar adjectives. This happened to fit the client's preconceived notion.
>
> However, examination of the distribution of the ratings revealed the existence of a large proportion of consumers who wanted the sauce to be mild and an equally large proportion

---

[14]For discussion of the treatment of outliers, see Terry Clark, "Managing Outliers: Qualitative Issues in the Handling of Extreme Observations in Marketing Research," *Marketing Research: A Magazine of Management and Applications,* 1 (June 1989), pp. 31–48.

FIGURE 13.1   **Histogram and Frequency Polygon of Incomes of Families in Car Ownership Study**

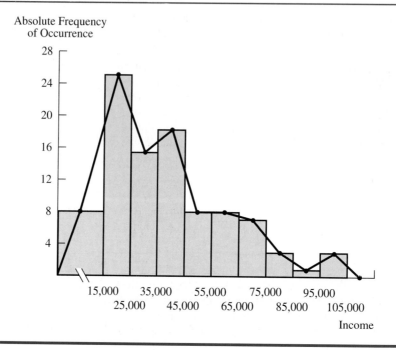

who wanted it to be hot. Relatively few wanted the in-between product, which would have been suggested by looking at the mean rating alone.[15]

It is always a good idea to get a sense of a variable's distribution before performing any analysis with it.

The distribution of a variable often is best visualized through a histogram. A **histogram** is a form of bar chart in which successive values of the variable are placed along the abscissa, or *X* axis, and the absolute frequency or relative frequency of occurrence of the values is indicated along the *Y* axis, or ordinate. The histogram for the income data in Table 13.4 appears as Figure 13.1, with the incomes over $105,000 omitted because their inclusion would have required an undue extension of the income axis. It is readily apparent that the distribution of incomes is skewed to the right. The actual distribution can be compared to some theoretical distribution to determine whether the data are consistent with some *a priori* model. Further insight into the empirical distribution of income can be obtained by constructing the **frequency polygon.** The frequency polygon is obtained from the histogram by connecting the midpoints of the bars with

---

[15]Robert J. Lavidge, "How to Keep Well-Intentioned Research from Misleading New-Product Planners," *Marketing News,* 18 (January 6, 1984), p. 8. Recent evidence suggests consumers want their sauces hot. See Kathleen Deveny, "Rival Hot Sauces Are Breathing Fire at Market Leader Tabasco," *The Wall Street Journal* (January 7, 1993), pp. B1, B6.

straight lines. The frequency polygon for incomes is superimposed on the histogram in Figure 13.1.

An alternative way of gaining insight into empirical distribution is through the empirical **cumulative distribution function.** The one-way tabulation is again the source. In this case, though, the number of observations with a value less than or equal to a specified quantity is determined; that is, the cumulative frequencies are generated. Thus, in the right-hand column of Table 13.4, we see that there are eight families with incomes less than $15,000, 33 families (8 + 25) with incomes of $24,900 or less, and 48 families (8 + 25 + 15) with incomes of $34,900 or less. These cumulative frequencies are denoted along the ordinate in Figure 13.2, while the abscissa again contains incomes. The empirical cumulative distribution function is generated by connecting the points representing the given combinations of Xs (values) and Ys (cumulative frequencies) with straight lines.

The cumulative distribution function can also be used to determine whether the distribution of observed incomes is consistent with some theoretical or assumed distribution. In addition, it can be used to calculate some of the commonly used measures of location such as the median, quartiles, and percentiles. These can simply be read from the plot once the cumulative relative frequencies are entered. In our case, the cumulative relative frequencies are equal to the cumulative absolute frequencies divided by 100, since there are 100 cases.

FIGURE 13.2   **Cumulative Distribution of Incomes of Families in Car Ownership Study**

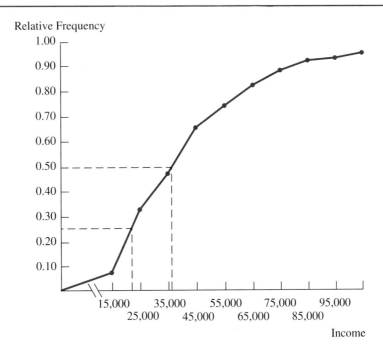

By definition, the sample median is that value at which 50 percent of the values lie below it and 50 percent are above it. To read the sample median from the plot of the cumulative distribution, simply extend a horizontal line from 0.50 on the relative frequency ordinate until it intersects the graph, and then drop a vertical line from the point of intersection to the X axis. The point of intersection with the X axis is the approximate sample median. In the case at hand, the sample median equals $35,700. The quality of the approximation could be checked by actually determining the median using the detailed data.

Sample quartiles could be determined in similar fashion. The first sample quartile (also known as the twenty-fifth percentile) is that value at which 25 percent of the observations are below it. This first sample quartile is determined by drawing a horizontal line from 0.25 on the relative frequency ordinate until it intersects the graph, dropping a vertical line from the point of intersection to the horizontal axis, and reading off the value of the first quartile at the point of intersection with the X axis. The first quartile is thus found to be $21,800. The procedure for the third quartile (seventy-fifth percentile) or any other percentile would be the same as that for the median or first quartile. The only change would be where the horizontal line commenced.

The one-way tabulation is also useful in calculating other summary measures, such as the mode, mean, and standard deviation. The mode, or the most frequently occurring item, can be read directly from the one-way tabulation. Thus, Table 13.3 suggests that most families own one car. The mean, or "average" response, can be calculated from a one-way tabulation by weighting each value by its frequency of occurrence, summing these products, and dividing by the number of cases. The average number of cars per family given the data in Table 13.3 would thus be estimated to be the following:

Value	Frequency	Value × Frequency
1	75	75
2	23	46
3	2	6
	100	127

or

$$\frac{127}{100} = 1.27 \text{ cars per family.}$$

The standard deviation provides a measure of spread in the data. It is calculated from the one-way tabulation by taking the deviation of each value from the mean, and squaring these deviations. The squared deviations are then multiplied by the frequency with which each occurs, these products are summed, and the sum is divided by one less than the number of cases to yield the sample variance. The square root of the sample variance then yields the sample standard deviation. The calculation of the standard deviation is thus very similar to that for ungrouped data, except that each value is weighted by the frequency with which it occurs. The standard deviation for the data in Table 13.3 is thus calculated to be the following:

Value	Value-Mean	(Value-Mean)^2	Frequency	Frequency Times Difference Squared
1	−0.27	0.0729	75	5.4675
2	0.73	0.5329	23	12.2567
3	1.73	2.9929	2	5.9858
				23.7100

yielding a variance of

$$\frac{23.7100}{99} = 0.2395$$

and a standard deviation of $\sqrt{0.2395} = 0.4894$.

The one-way tabulation as a communication vehicle for the results has not been discussed. The reader only needs to look at Table 13.1 to see how much insight can be gathered about the variable income and then compare that with the insight generated in the one-way tabulation contained in Table 13.4. When one realizes that they also serve as a basic input to the histogram, frequency polygon, and empirical cumulative distribution function, and that they are also used in calculating summary statistics, it is an unwise analyst indeed who does not take the time to develop the one-way tabulations of the variables in the study and to plot the results in order to get a sense of how they are distributed.[16]

Cross Tabulation

Although the one-way tabulation is useful for examining the variables of the study separately, **cross tabulation** is a most important mechanism for studying the relationships among and between variables. In cross tabulation, the sample is divided into subgroups in order to learn how the dependent variable varies from subgroup to subgroup. It is clearly the most widely used data analysis technique in marketing research. Some would call it the "bread and butter" of applied research. Most marketing research studies go no further than cross tabulation, and many of the studies that do use more sophisticated analytical methods still contain cross tabulation as an important component. Thus, the analyst and decision maker both need to understand how cross tabulations are developed and interpreted.

---

[16]Box and whisker plots can also be used to get a sense for the distribution of the variable. They possess the attractive feature of including information about the variable mean, median, 25th and 75th percentiles, and outliers. For discussion of how they are constructed, see "Graphic Displays of Data: Box and Whisker Plots," *Research on Research,* No. 17 (Chicago: Market Facts, Inc., undated).

TABLE **13.5**   **Family Income and Number of Cars Family Owns**

Income	Number of Cars		
	1 or None	2 or More	Total
Less than $37,500	48	6	54
More than $37,500	27	19	46
Total	75	25	100

Consider, for example, the question of the relationship, if any, between the number of cars that the family owns and family income. To keep the example simple, suppose that the analyst was only interested in determining if a family with above-average income was more likely to own two or more cars than a family with below-average income. Suppose further that $37,500 was the median income in the population and that this figure was to be used to split the families in the sample into two groups, those with below-average and those with above-average incomes.

Table 13.5 presents the two-way classification of the sample families by income and number of cars. Looking at the marginal totals, we see that 75 families have one car or less, while 25 families have two cars or more. We also see that the sample is not unrepresentative of the population, at least as far as income is concerned: 54 families fall into the lower-than-average income group using the $37,500 cutoff.

Does the number of cars depend on income? It certainly seems so on the basis of Table 13.5, since 19 of the families owning two or more cars are in the upper income group. Is there anything that can be done to shed additional light on the relationship? The answer is *yes. Compute percentages.* Tables 13.6 and 13.7 are mathematically equivalent to Table 13.5 but are based on percentages calculated in different directions: horizontally in Table 13.6 and vertically in Table 13.7. The tables contain quite different messages. Table 13.6 suggests that multiple car ownership is affected by family income; 41 percent of the families with above-average incomes had two or more automobiles, but only 11 percent of the below-average-income families did so. This is a clear, interesting finding. Table 13.7, on the other hand, conveys a different story. It suggests that 64 percent of those who owned one car had below average incomes, while only 24 percent of those who owned two or more cars were below average in income. Does this mean that multiple car ownership paves the way to higher incomes? Definitely not. Rather, it simply illustrates a fundamental rule of percentage calculations: Always calculate percentages in the direction of the causal factor, or across the effect factor.[17] In this case, income is logically considered to be the cause, or independent variable, and multiple car ownership to be the effect, or dependent variable. The percentages are correctly calculated, therefore, in the direction of income as in Table 13.6.

[17]See Zeisel, *Say It with Figures*, p. 28, for a slightly modified statement of the percentage-direction–calculation rule, which takes into account the representativeness of the sample.

TABLE 13.6   **Number of Cars by Family Income**

| Income | Number of Cars | | | |
	1 or None	2 or More	Total	Number of Cases
Less than $37,500	89%	11%	100%	54
More than $37,500	59%	41%	100%	46

TABLE 13.7   **Family Income by Number of Cars**

Income	1 or None	2 or More
Less than $37,500	64%	24%
More than $37,500	36%	76%
Total	100%	100%
(Number of cases)	(75)	(25)

One very useful way to think about the direction in which to calculate percentages is to conceptualize the problem in terms of **conditional probability,** or the probability of one event occurring given that another event has occurred or will occur. Thus, the notion of the probability that the family has two or more cars *given* that they are high income makes sense, whereas the notion that the family is high income *given* that they have two or more cars does not.

Although it provides some insight into a dependency relationship, the two-way cross tabulation is not the final answer. Rather, it represents a start. Consider now, for example, the relationship between multiple car ownership and size of family. Table 13.8 indicates the number of small and large (five or more members) families that possess two or more cars. Now, size of family is logically considered a cause of multiple car ownership and not vice versa. Thus, the percentages would properly be computed in the

TABLE 13.8   **Number of Cars and Size of Family**

| Size of Family | Number of Cars | | |
	1 or None	2 or More	Total
4 or less	70	8	78
5 or more	5	17	22
Total	75	25	100

TABLE 13.9   **Number of Cars by Size of Family**

Size of Family	Number of Cars			Number of Cases
	1 or None	2 or More	Total	
4 or less	90%	10%	100%	(78)
5 or more	23%	77%	100%	(22)

direction of size of family or *across number of cars*. Table 13.9 presents these percentages and suggests that the number of cars a family owns is affected by the size of the family — 77 percent of the large families have two or more cars, while only 10 percent of the small families do.

This result raises the question: Does multiple car ownership depend on family size or, as previously suggested, on family income? The proper way to answer this question is through the *simultaneous* treatment of income and family size. In effect, the two-way cross-classification table needs to be partitioned and a three-way table of income, family size, and multiple car ownership formed. One way of doing this is illustrated in Table 13.10. This table is, in one sense, two cross-classification tables of multiple car ownership versus income — one for small families of four or fewer members and one for large families of five or more members.

Once again we would want to compute percentages in the direction of income within each table. Table 13.11 contains these percentages, which indicate that multiple car ownership depends on both income and family size. For small families of four or less, 19 percent of those with above-average incomes have two or more cars, while only 4 percent of those with below-average incomes have more than one automobile. For large families, 93 percent of the above-average-income and 50 percent of the below-average-income families have more than one vehicle.

The preceding comparisons highlight the effect of income on multiple car ownership, holding family size constant. We could also compare the effect of family size on

TABLE 13.10   **Number of Cars by Income and Size of Family**

Income	Four Members or Less: Number of Cars			Five Members or More: Number of Cars			Total Number of Cars		
	1 or None	2 or More	Total	1 or None	2 or More	Total	1 or None	2 or More	Total
Less than $37,500	44	2	46	4	4	8	48	6	54
More than $37,500	26	6	32	1	13	14	27	19	46
Total	70	8	78	5	17	22	75	25	100

TABLE 13.11 **Number of Cars by Income and Size of Family**

Income	Four Members or Less: Number of Cars			Five Members or More: Number of Cars			Total Number of Cars		
	1 or None	2 or More	Total	1 or None	2 or More	Total	1 or None	2 or More	Total
Less than $37,500	96%	4%	100% (46)	50%	50%	100% (8)	89%	11%	100% (54)
More than $37,500	81%	19%	100% (32)	7%	93%	100% (14)	59%	41%	100% (46)

multiple car ownership, holding income constant. We would still find that each provides a partial explanation for multiple car ownership. Now, you may have felt a bit uncomfortable with the presentation of the data in Tables 13.10 and 13.11. The information is there to be mined, but perhaps you may have wondered whether it could not have been presented in a more revealing manner. It can, if you are willing to accept a couple of refinements in the manner of presentation. Look specifically at the first row of the first section of Table 13.11, reproducing it as Table 13.12. All of the information contained in this table can be condensed into one figure, 4 percent. This is the percentage of small, below-average-income families that have two or more cars. It follows that the complementary percentage, 96 percent, represents those that have one automobile or none.

Table 13.13 shows the rest of the data in Table 13.11 treated in the same way. The entry in each case is the percentage of families in that category that own two or more automobiles. Table 13.13 conveys the same information as Table 13.11, but it delivers the message with much greater clarity. The separate effect of income on multiple car ownership, holding family size constant, can be determined by reading down the columns, while the effect of family size, holding income constant, can be determined by reading across the rows. Omitting the complementary percentages has helped reveal the structure of the data. Therefore, let us agree to use this form of presentation whenever we attempt to determine the effect of several explanatory variables, considered simultaneously, in the pages that follow.

The original association between number of cars and family income reflected in Table 13.6 is called the **total** (or **zero order**) association between the variables. Table 13.13, which depicts the association between the two variables within categories of

TABLE 13.12 **Car Ownership for Small, Below-Average-Income Families**

Income	Number of Cars		
	1 or None	2 or More	Total
Less than $37,500	96%	4%	100% (46)

TABLE 13.13   **Percentage of Families Owning Two or More Cars by Income and Size of Family**

Income	Size of Family		
	4 or Less	**5 or More**	**Total**
Less than $37,500	4%	50%	11%
More than $37,500	19%	93%	41%

family size, is called a *conditional table* that reveals the **conditional association** between the variables. Family size here is a *control variable*. Conditional tables that are developed on the basis of one control variable are called *first-order* conditional tables, those developed using two control variables are called *second-order* conditional tables, and so on.

Which variable has the greater effect on multiple car ownership — income or family size? A useful method for addressing this question is to calculate the *difference in proportions* as a function of the level of the variable.[18] This can be done for the zero-order tables as well as the conditional tables of higher order. Consider again Table 13.6 and concentrate on the effect of income on the probability of the family having multiple cars. The proportion of low-income families that have two or more cars is 0.11, while the proportion of high-income families is 0.41. The probability of having multiple cars is clearly different depending on the family's income; specifically, high income increases the probability of having two or more cars by 0.30 (0.41 − 0.11) over low income. A similar analysis applied to Table 13.9 suggests that the probability of multiple car ownership is clearly different depending on family size. Whereas 0.10 of the small families have multiple cars, 0.77 of the large families do. Thus, being a large family increases the probability of having two or more cars by 0.67 (0.77 − 0.10) over small families.

To determine whether income or family size has the greater impact, it is necessary to consider the factors simultaneously using a similar analysis. Table 13.13 contains the data that are necessary for this analysis. Let us first consider the effect of income. The proper way to determine income's effect is to hold family size constant, which means in essence that we must investigate the relationship between income and multiple car ownership for small families and then again for large families. Among small families, having high income increases the probability of having multiple cars by 0.15 (0.19 − 0.04). Among large families, having high income increases the probability of having multiple cars by 0.43 (0.93 − 0.50) compared to low income. The size of the associations between income and multiple car ownership are different for different family sizes. This means that there is a statistical interaction between the independent variables, and in order to generate a single estimate of the effect of income on car ownership, some kind of average of the separate effects needs to be computed. The appropriate average is a

---

[18]See Ottar Hellevik, *Introduction to Causal Analysis: Exploring Survey Data by Crosstabulation* (London: George Allen & Unwin, 1984).

weighted average that takes account of the sizes of the groups on which the individual effects were calculated. There were 78 small families in the sample of 100 cases and 22 large families; the weight for small families is thus 0.78 and for large families 0.22. The weighted average is

$$0.15(0.78) + 0.43(0.22) = 0.21,$$

which suggests that, on average, high versus low income increases the probability of owning multiple cars by 0.21.

To investigate the effect of family size, it is necessary to hold income constant or, alternatively, to investigate the impact of family size on multiple car ownership for low-income families, then for high-income families, and then to generate a weighted average of the two results if they are not the same. Among low-income families, being large increases the probability of having multiple cars by 0.46 (0.50 − 0.04) compared to small families. Among high-income families, large size increases the probability by 0.74 (0.93 − 0.19) versus small size. Since there were 54 low-income families and 46 high-income families, the appropriate weights for weighting the two effects are 0.54 and 0.46, respectively. The calculation yields

$$0.46(0.54) + 0.74(0.46) = 0.59$$

as the estimate of the impact of family size on multiple car ownership.

Family size has a more pronounced effect on multiple car ownership than does income. It increases the probability of having two or more cars by 0.59, whereas income increases it by 0.21.

The previous example highlighted an important application of cross tabulation — the use of an additional variable to refine an initial cross tabulation. In this case, family size

ETHICAL DILEMMA 13.1

After collecting the data for a study that is being repeated with the use of an updated questionnaire, an analyst is instructed to complete the analysis and report for the project. The fieldwork took longer than expected to complete, leaving the analyst with very little time to complete the analysis for the project. So that the project can be completed on time, the analyst follows the analysis plan used for the previous project. For the final report, the analyst decides simply to update the tables from the previous report to reflect the new data and to alter wording only where required by the table information.

- Is it acceptable to charge the new client for a full analysis on this project when the researcher has not completed a full analysis?
- What are the risks associated with this short-cut in data analysis?
- Under the same constraints, what would you have done in this situation?

TABLE 13.14   Conditions That Can Arise with the Introduction
of an Additional Variable into a Cross Tabulation

| Initial Conclusion | With the Additional Variable | |
	Change Conclusion	Retain Conclusion
Some relationship	I A. Refine explanation B. Reveal spurious explanation C. Provide limiting conditions	II
No relationship	III	IV

was used to refine the relationship between multiple car ownership and income. This is only one of the many applications of successive cross tabulation of variables, and, in fact, a number of conditions can occur when additional variables are introduced into a cross tabulation, as shown in the various panels of Table 13.14. The two-way tabulation may initially indicate the existence or nonexistence of a relationship between the variables. The introduction of a third variable may occasion no change in the initial conclusion, or it may indicate that a substantial change is in order. We have considered Panel I–A. Let us now turn to an analysis of examples of these alternative conditions.

Panel I: An Initial Relationship Is Modified by the Introduction of a Third Variable

Case I–B: Initial Relationship Is Spurious   One of the purposes of the automobile purchase study was to determine the kinds of families that purchase specific kinds of automobiles. Consider vans. It was expected that van ownership would be related to life-style and, in particular, that those with a liberal orientation would be more likely to own vans than would those who are conservative by nature. Table 13.15 was constructed, employing the raw data on car ownership in Table 13.1, to test this hypothesis. Contrary to expectation, conservatives are more apt than liberals to own vans; 24 percent of the conservatives but only 16 percent of the liberals in the sample owned vans.

TABLE 13.15   Van Ownership by Life-style

| Life-style | Own Van? | | Total |
	Yes	No	
Liberal	9(16%)	46(84%)	55(100%)
Conservative	11(24%)	34(76%)	45(100%)

Is there some logical explanation for this unexpected happening? Consider the addition of a third variable, region of the country in which the family resides, to the analysis. A clear picture of the relationship among the three variables considered simultaneously can be developed employing our previously agreed-upon convention; that is, simply report the percentage in each category. The complement, 100 minus the percentage, then indicates the proportion not owning vans.

As Table 13.16 indicates, van ownership is not related to life-style. Rather, it depends on the region of the country in which the family resides. When region is held constant, there is no difference in van ownership between liberals and conservatives. Families living in the South are much more likely to own a van than are families who live in the northern states. It just so happens that people in the South tend to be more conservative in their life-style than people in the North. The original relationship is, therefore, said to be spurious.

Although it seems counterproductive to calculate the difference in proportions to determine the effect of each variable for each of the potential conditions in Table 13.14, it does seem useful to do it for this case to demonstrate what is meant by a main effect without a statistical interaction. The example is also useful in reinforcing how the difference-in-proportions calculation can be used to isolate the causal relationships that exist in cross-tabulation data. Consider first the zero order association between van ownership and life-style contained in Table 13.15. Being conservative increases the probability of van ownership by 0.08 (0.24 − 0.16) compared to being liberal. Yet Table 13.16 shows that this is a spurious effect that is due to region of the country, since it disappears when region is held constant. Among those living in the North, the partial association between van ownership and life-style is 0.00 (0.05 − 0.05). Among those living in the South, there is a slightly higher probability of van ownership among conservatives, namely 0.02 (0.43 − 0.41). This effect is so small that it can be attributed to rounding error, particularly since the proportions were carried only to two decimal places and the number of cases is so small. Regardless of the region of the country in which the family resides, its liberal/conservative orientation has no effect on whether or not it owns a van.

Note to the contrary that the effect of region is pronounced and consistent. Among liberal families, living in the South increases the probability of van ownership by 0.36 (0.41 − 0.05) compared to living in the North. Among conservative families, living in the South increases the probability by 0.38 (0.43 − 0.05). Within rounding error, the

TABLE **13.16**   **Van Ownership by Life-style and Region of Country**

Life-style	Region of Country		Total
	North	South	
Liberal	5%	41%	16%
Conservative	5%	43%	24%

TABLE **13.17** **Foreign Economy Car Ownership by Family Size**

Size of Family	Own Foreign Economy Car?		Total
	Yes	No	
4 or less	6 (8%)	72(92%)	78(100%)
More than 4	6(27%)	16(73%)	22(100%)

effect is the same for families with both philosophical orientations, which means that there is no interaction among the two predictor variables. Rather, there is only a main effect of region on van ownership, and the best estimate of its size is given by either of these estimates or their average.

Case I–C: Limiting Conditions Are Revealed Consider now the question of owner-ship of foreign economy cars. Does it depend on the size of the family? Table 13.17 suggests that it does. *Smaller* families are *less* likely to own a foreign economy car than are larger families! Only 8 percent of the small families but 27 percent of the large families have such automobiles. Can this counter-intuitive finding be accounted for?

Consider the expansion of this cross classification by adding a variable for the number of cars the family owns. Table 13.18 presents the percentage data, which indi-cate that it is only when large families have two or more cars that they own a foreign economy car. No large families with one car own such an automobile. The introduction of the third variable has revealed a condition that limits foreign economy car owner-ship — multiple car ownership where large families are concerned.

Panel II: Initial Conclusion of a Relationship Is Retained

Consider now the analysis of station wagon ownership based on the data in Table 13.1. *A priori*, it would seem to be related to family size. A case could be made that larger families have a greater need for station wagons than smaller families.

The cross tabulation of these two variables in Table 13.19 suggests that larger families do display a higher propensity to own station wagons; 68 percent of the large families and only 4 percent of the small families own wagons.

TABLE **13.18** **Foreign Economy Car Ownership by Family Size and Number of Cars**

Size of Family	Number of Cars		Total
	1 or None	2 or More	
4 or less	4%	38%	8%
More than 4	0%	35%	27%

TABLE 13.19   **Station Wagon Ownership by Family Size**

	Own Station Wagon		
Size of Family	**Yes**	**No**	**Total**
4 or less	3 (4%)	75(96%)	78(100%)
More than 4	15(68%)	7(32%)	22(100%)

Consider, however, whether income might also affect station wagon ownership. As Table 13.20 indicates, income has an effect over and above family size. As one goes from a small to a large family, there is a substantial increase in the propensity to own a station wagon. With larger families, though, the increase is larger. Alternatively, if one focuses solely on large families, there is an increase in station wagon ownership from below-average-income to above-average-income families. The initial conclusion is retained: large families do display a greater tendency to purchase station wagons. Further, the effect of family size on station wagon ownership is much larger than the effect of income.

Panel III: A Relationship Is Established with the Introduction of a Third Variable

Suppose that one of the purposes of the study was to determine the characteristics of families who financed the purchase of their automobile. Consider the cross tabulation of installment debt compared with education of the household head. Table 13.21 results when the families included in Table 13.1 are classified into one of two educational categories — those with a high school education or less and those with some college training. As is evident, there is no relationship between education and installment debt; the percentage of families with outstanding car debt is 30 percent in each case.

Table 13.22 illustrates the situation when income is also considered in the analysis. For below-average-income families, the presence of installment debt increases with education. For above-average-income families, installment debt decreases with education. The effect of education was obscured in the original analysis because the effects canceled each other. When income is also considered, the relationship of installment debt to education is quite pronounced.

TABLE 13.20   **Station Wagon Ownership by Family Size and Income**

	Income		
Size of Family	**Less than $37,500**	**More than $37,500**	**Total**
4 or less	4%	3%	4%
More than 4	63%	71%	68%

TABLE 13.21   **Financed Car Purchase by Education of Household Head**

Education of Household Head	Financed Car Purchase		Total
	Yes	No	
High school or less	24(30%)	56(70%)	80(100%)
Some college	6(30%)	14(70%)	20(100%)

TABLE 13.22   **Financed Car Purchase by Education of Household Head and Income**

Education of Household Head	Income		Total
	Less than $37,500	More than $37,500	
High school or less	12%	58%	30%
Some college	40%	27%	30%

Panel IV: The Conclusion of No Relationship Is Retained with the Addition of a Third Variable

Consider once again the question of station wagon ownership. We have seen previously that it is related to family size. Let us forget this result for a minute and begin the analysis with the question: Is station wagon ownership affected by region of the country in which the family lives? Table 13.23 provides an initial answer. Station wagon ownership does not depend on region; 18 percent of the sample families living in both the North and the South own wagons.

Let us now consider the relationship when family size is again taken into account. Table 13.24 presents the data. Once again the percentages are constant across regions. There is minor variation, but this is due to round-off accuracy. Small families display a low propensity to purchase station wagons, regardless of whether they live in the North or the South. Large families have a high propensity, and this, too, is independent of

TABLE 13.23   **Station Wagon Ownership by Region**

Region	Own Station Wagon		Total
	Yes	No	
North	11(18%)	49(82%)	60(100%)
South	7(18%)	33(82%)	40(100%)

TABLE 13.24   **Station Wagon Ownership by Region and Family Size**

	Size of Family		
Region	**4 or Less**	**More than 4**	**Total**
North	4%	69%	18%
South	3%	67%	18%

where they live. The original lack of relationship between station wagon ownership and region of residence is confirmed with the addition of the third variable, family size.

Summary Comments on Cross Tabulation

The previous examples certainly should highlight the tremendous usefulness of cross tabulation as a tool in analysis. We have seen an application in which a third variable helped to uncover a relationship not immediately discernible, as well as applications in which a third variable triggered the modification of conclusions drawn on the basis of a two-variable classification. You may have paused to ask yourself: Why stop with three variables? Would the conclusion change with the addition of a fourth variable? A fifth? Indeed it might. The problem is that one never knows for sure when to stop introducing variables. The conclusion is always susceptible to change with the introduction of the ''right'' variable or variables. For example, there is currently a great deal of concern about the disappearance of the middle class and what that portends for the United States economically and socially. Yet there is a very real question as to whether the nation's middle class is in fact disappearing. Research Realities 13.4 overviews the concern and highlights what happens when other factors, such as age and marital status, are taken into account. Thus, the analyst is always in the position of ''inferring'' that a relationship exists. Later research may demonstrate that the inference was incorrect. This is why the accumulation of studies, rather than a single study, supporting a particular relationship is so vital to the advancement of knowledge.

Table 13.25 is an overview of the dilemma that the researcher faces. The true situation is always unknown. If it were known, there would be no need to research it. The analyst may conclude that there is no relationship, or that there is some relationship between two or more variables when in fact there is none or there is some. Only one of these four possibilities in Table 13.25 *necessarily* corresponds to a correct conclusion — when the analyst concludes that there is no relationship and in fact there is no relationship. Two of the other possibilities are necessarily incorrect, while one contains the possibility for error. That is, suppose the true situation is one of some relationship between or among the variables. The analyst has reached a correct conclusion *only* if he or she concludes that there is some relationship and has discovered its correct form.

Spurious noncorrelation results whenever the analyst concludes that there is no relationship when, in fact, there is. Spurious correlation occurs when the true state of

Research Realities 13.4

The Disappearance of the Middle Class: Fact or Fancy?

In recent years, there has been a growing and uncritical acceptance of the view that the United States is becoming an increasingly polarized society — with rich and poor growing more numerous, and the middle class becoming an endangered species.

The proponents of this thesis maintain that those developments are the consequence of significant structural changes in our economy and hence will become increasingly aggravated. We are warned that this will eventually have alarming political and social consequences as the middle class — "the glue that holds society together" — continues to wither away.

But this bleak outlook is curiously inconsistent with many of the nation's principal economic indicators. Over the past decade and a half alone, the U.S. economy generated more than 30 million new jobs, an increase of an imposing third in the size of the labor force. Today, close to 80 percent of all working-age men and women are earning a paycheck, up from about 70 percent 20 years ago. Over those years, real per capita income rose at an average annual pace of 1.9 percent — which has added up to almost a 50 percent increase in the real living standards of the average American. Certainly, this is not arithmetic that lends credibility to the notion that the poor are growing poorer, and that the middle class is shrinking.

Precisely how the fortunes of the nation's middle class have changed over the years varies according to which earning brackets are selected to define middle income. But whatever the definition selected, the middle class is clearly not "disappearing." It has, in fact, been growing — but less rapidly than the nation's total household population and hence has declined in relative importance.

The affluent earning brackets have increased significantly over the years, as millions of families moved up from the middle class. Contributing powerfully to this process has been the growing prevalence of working wives. In fact, over the past two decades, the entire increase in the number of families in the highest fifth of the income scale was accounted for by working-wife families. As of last year, two thirds of all wives in that bracket brought home a paycheck, up from only one in two 20 years ago.

With millions of families moving from the middle to the affluent brackets, the pertinent issue is why so many households have crowded into the lower brackets. Again, demographic and related social developments provide the answer.

By the early 1970s, the baby-boom generation began to come of age, which made for an extraordinary surge in the number of young adults. That generation has been inclined to marry late. Today, more than two out of every five women aged 20 to 30 are still single, compared with only one in four in 1970. Thus, over the past two decades, the number of husband-wife families in the nation increased by a mere 15 percent, but the number of single-person homes increased by an awesome 90 percent, and young singles by considerably more than that.

Not surprisingly, of the entire increase in the number of households in the lower-income brackets, a large proportion was accounted for by single-person households, and because the young are more likely to divorce than those further along in age, the nation also experienced a sharp rise in the number of single-parent families.

Clearly, it's been primarily demographic and social currents, not structural changes in the nation's economy, that have made for some polarization of income in recent years. In fact, over the longer run, we

Source: Fabian Linden, "How We Live," *Across the Board*, 27 (December 1990), pp. 9–10. Reprinted with permission of The Conference Board, Inc., New York.

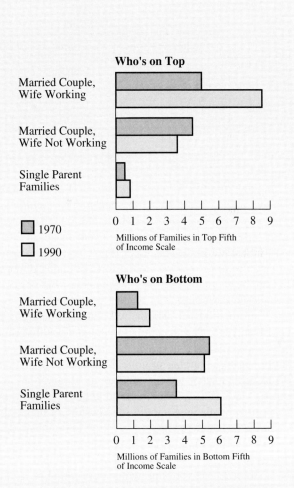

Who's on Top

Married Couple,
Wife Working

Married Couple,
Wife Not Working

Single Parent
Families

☐ 1970
☐ 1990

0 1 2 3 4 5 6 7 8 9
Millions of Families in Top Fifth
of Income Scale

Who's on Bottom

Married Couple,
Wife Working

Married Couple,
Wife Not Working

Single Parent
Families

0 1 2 3 4 5 6 7 8 9
Millions of Families in Bottom Fifth
of Income Scale

have experienced a continous upward trend in earnings at all levels of the income scale. Many in the lower brackets moved into the middle, and those in the middle into the upper. Since the mid-1970s, however, while many middle-class homes swelled into the upper-income tiers, the proportion of households with marginal earnings remained stubbornly high. The latter development was not due to a polarization of jobs and wages, as alleged, but principally to the increase in the number of young homes and the rapid growth in the number of single-parent families.

In summary, then, what the proponents of the income-polarization thesis have demonstrated is that the young earn less than at later stages in life, that single-parent families experience financial stress, and that two people working earn more than one.

TABLE 13.25   **The Researcher's Dilemma**

Researcher's Conclusion	True Situation	
	No Relationship	**Some Relationship**
No relationship	Correct decision	Spurious noncorrelation
Some relationship	Spurious correlation	Correct decision if concluded relationship is of proper form

affairs is one of no relationship among the variables, and the analyst concludes that a relationship exists.

Thus, the opportunities for error are great. This necessarily gives rise to a temptation to continue adding variables to the analysis *ad infinitum*. Fortunately, the analyst will be constrained in this regard by theory and by data. Theory will constrain him or her, because certain tabulations simply will not make any sense. The analyst will be constrained by the data in several ways. First, note that he or she will wish to successively add variables to the analysis in the form of higher dimensional cross-classification tables. This can be accomplished only if the analyst has correctly anticipated the tabulations that would be desirable. This is most important. It is too late to say, "If only we had collected information on Variable X!" once the analysis has begun. The relationships to be investigated, and thus the cross tabulations that should be appropriate, must be specified before the data are collected. Ideally, the analyst would have constructed dummy tables before beginning to collect the data. The dummy tables would be complete in all respects except for the number of observations falling in each cell. As a practical matter, it is usually impossible to anticipate all the cross tabulations one will want to develop. Nevertheless, careful specification of these tables at problem-definition time can return substantial benefits.

The analyst also is going to be limited by the size of the sample. In the example, since we started with 100 observations, the two-way tables were not particularly troublesome. Yet as soon as we introduced the third variable, cell sizes became extremely small. This occurred even though we treated all variables as dichotomies. Families were either below average or above average in income; they were either small or large; they lived either in the North or in the South, and so on. This was done purposely to simplify the presentation. Yet even here the three-way tabulation offers 8 cells ($2 \times 2 \times 2$) into which the observations may be placed. Assuming an even allocation of the cases to the cells, this allows only 12.5 cases per cell. This is clearly a small number on which to base any kind of conclusion. The problem, of course, would have been compounded if a greater number of levels had been used for any of the variables — for example, if families had been divided into four income groups rather than two — since the number of cells is the product of the number of levels for the variables being considered. For example, four income levels, three educational levels, and four family-size levels would generate a cross-tabulation table with 48 separate cells ($4 \times 3 \times 4$). One would need a much larger sample than 100 to have any confidence in the suggested relationships.

A manufacturer of aspirin had its marketing research department conduct a national survey among doctors to investigate what common household remedies doctors would be most likely to recommend when treating a patient with a cold. The question asked doctors to pick the one product they would most likely prescribe for their patients from among the choices Advil, Tylenol, aspirin, or none of the above. The distribution of responses was as follows:

Advil	100
Tylenol	100
Aspirin	200
None of the three	600
Total	1,000

The firm used the results of the survey as a basis for an extensive ad campaign that claimed: "In a national survey, doctors recommended aspirin two to one over Advil and Tylenol as the medicine they would most likely recommend to their patients suffering from colds."

- Is the firm's claim legitimate?
- Is it ethical for the firm to omit reporting the number of doctors that expressed no preference?
- What would be the fairest way to state the ad claim? Do you think stating the claim in this way would be as effective as stating it in the way the firm did?

PRESENTING TABULAR DATA

Tabular results for commercial marketing-research studies are seldom presented using the tabulation and cross-tabulation procedures discussed so far in this chapter. Rather, the use of banners has become increasingly popular. A **banner** is a series of cross tabulations between a criterion or dependent variable and several (sometimes many) explanatory variables in a single table on a single page. The dependent variable, or phenomenon to be explained, typically serves as the row variable, which is also known as the *stub*. The predictor or explanatory variables serve as the column variables, with each category of these variables serving as a banner point. Table 13.26, for example, shows what the banner format might look like for the car ownership study. Although only two explanatory variables are shown, many more could be. The top line in each row of the table indicates the absolute number possessing the characteristic, whereas the second line indicates the percentage. All percentages have been rounded to zero decimal places in keeping with recommended practice.

The advantages of banner tables are several. In the first place, they allow a great amount of information to be conveyed in a very limited space. Second, their display format makes it easy for nonresearch managers to understand. Managers simply need to look at how the responses to the actual questions that were asked are distributed. A

TABLE 13.26   **Banner Format for Car Ownership Data**

	Total Sample	Income		Family Size	
		Less than $37,500	More than $37,500	Four or Less	Five or More
Question: How many cars does your family own?					
Total	100	54	46	78	22
	100	100	100	100	100
One	75	48	27	70	5
	75.	89.	59.	90.	23.
Two	23	6	17	8	15
	23.	11.	37.	10.	68.
Three or more	2	0	2	0	2
	2.	0.	4.	0.	9.

difficulty with these tables is that they tend to hide relationships in which it is necessary to consider several variables simultaneously (e.g., the joint effect of income and family size on multiple car ownership). They consequently make it more difficult to probe alternative explanations for what is producing the results. Banners also make it more difficult to detect data errors caused by improper coding or editing. Although popular, they should not be considered as a substitute for careful cross-tabulation analysis but more as an efficient form of data presentation.

ETHICAL DILEMMA 13.3

Sarah is very happy on the whole with the project that she has just completed for the Crumbly Cookie Company. Most of her hypotheses were supported by the survey data. There were two hypotheses that did not work out, but she thought that she would just leave them out of the report.

- Is it ethical to omit information that does not tally with your beliefs?
- Can valuable information be lost through the omission?

SUMMARY

This chapter reviewed the common analysis functions of editing, coding, and tabulation. Editing involves the inspection and correction, if necessary, of each questionnaire or observation form. The field edit, a preliminary edit most often conducted by the field supervisor, is aimed at correcting the most glaring omissions and inaccuracies while the field staff is still intact. The central office edit follows and involves a more careful scrutiny and correction of the completed data collection instruments. In the central office edit, particular attention is given to such things as incomplete answers, obviously wrong answers, and answers that reflect a lack of interest.

Coding is the procedure by which data are categorized. It involves the three-step process of (1) specifying the categories or classes into which the responses are to be placed, (2) assigning code numbers to the classes, and (3) preparing a code book. If the data are to be analyzed by computer, a number of conventions should be followed in assigning the code numbers, including the following:

1. Use only one character per column;
2. Use only numeric codes;
3. Assign as many columns as are necessary to capture the variable;
4. Use the same standard codes throughout for "No information"; and
5. Code in a respondent identification number on each record.

Tabulation consists of counting the number of cases that fall into the various categories. The simple, or one-way, tabulation involves the count for a single variable, whereas cross tabulation involves counting the number of cases that have the characteristics described by two or more variables considered simultaneously. The one-way tabulation is useful for communicating the results of a study, and it can also be employed to locate blunders or errors, to determine the degree of item nonresponse, to locate outliers (observations very different in value from the rest), and to determine the empirical distribution of the variable in question. It also serves as basic input to the calculation of measures such as the mean, median, and standard deviation, which provide a summary picture of the distribution of the variable. Cross tabulation is one of the more useful devices for studying the relationships among and between variables because the results are easily communicated. Further, cross tabulation can provide insight into the nature of a relationship, since the addition of one or more variables to a two-way cross-classification analysis is equivalent to holding each of the variables constant.

A useful method for determining the effect that one variable has on another variable in a cross-tabulation table is to compute the difference in proportions with which the dependent variable occurs as a function of the levels of the independent variable. This can be done for zero order tables as well as conditional tables of higher order. The higher order tables are used to remove the effects of other variables that might be influencing the dependent variable.

In commercial studies, tabular results are often presented using banners, which represent a series of cross tabulations between a dependent variable and several explanatory variables in a single table.

Questions

1. Distinguish among the preliminary data analysis steps of editing, coding, and tabulation.
2. What are the differences in emphasis between a field edit and a central office edit?

3. What should an editor do with incomplete answers? Obviously wrong answers? Answers that reflect a lack of interest?

4. What are the principles that underlie the establishment of categories so that collected data may be properly coded?

5. Suppose that you have a large number of very long questionnaires, making it impossible for one person to handle the entire coding task. How should the work be divided?

6. What is the difference between a one-way tabulation and a cross tabulation? Illustrate through an example.

7. When should you use machine tabulation? Manual tabulation?

8. What are the possible ways for treating item nonresponse? Which strategy would you recommend?

9. What is a blunder?

10. What is an outlier?

11. With how many digits should percentages be reported?

12. What is a histogram? A frequency polygon? What information do they provide?

13. What is the cumulative distribution function? Of what value is it?

14. How is the mean calculated from the one-way tabulation? The standard deviation?

15. What is the proper procedure for investigating the following hypotheses using cross-tabulation analysis?
   a. Consumption of Product X depends on a person's income.
   b. Consumption of Product X depends on a person's education.
   c. Consumption of Product X depends on both.

16. How would you determine whether income or education had the greater effect on the consumption of Product X?

17. Illustrate the procedure from Questions 15 and 16 with data of your own choosing; that is, develop the tables, fill in the assumed numbers, and indicate the conclusions to be drawn from each table.

18. What is meant by the statement: the introduction of an additional variable
   a. refined the original explanation?
   b. revealed a spurious explanation?
   c. provided limiting conditions?

19. How do you explain the condition in which a two-way cross tabulation of Variables X and Y revealed no relationship between X and Y but the introduction of Z revealed a definite relationship between X and Y?

20. What is the researcher's dilemma with respect to cross-tabulation analysis?

21. What constraints operate on researchers that prevent them from adding variables to cross-classification tables *ad infinitum?*

22. What are banners?

Applications and Problems

1. A marketing research supplier has five employees in its coding department. The firm has just received 10,000 completed mail questionnaires. The survey contains 175 questions.

How would you recommend that the company handle the editing and coding process? What would you instruct them to look for in the edit, and how would you recommend they handle each of these problems if found?

2. The WITT TV station was conducting research in order to develop programs that would be well-received by the viewing audience and would be considered a dependable source of information. A two-part questionnaire was administered by personal interviews to a panel of 3,000 respondents residing in the city of Chicago. The field and office edits were done simultaneously so that the deadline of May 1st could be met. A senior supervisor, Mr. Z, was placed in charge of the editing tasks and was assisted by two junior supervisors and two field workers. The two field workers were instructed to discard instruments that were illegible or incomplete. Both the junior supervisors were instructed to scrutinize 1,500 of the instruments each for incomplete answers, wrong answers, and responses that indicated a lack of interest. They were instructed to discard instruments that had greater than five incomplete or wrong answers (the questionnaire contained 30 questions). In addition, they were asked to use their judgment in assessing whether the respondent showed a lack of interest, in which case they should also discard the questionnaire.
   a. Critically evaluate the preceding editing tasks. Please be specific.
   b. Make specific recommendations to Mr. D. Witt, the owner of the WITT TV station, about how the editing should be done.

3. a. Establish response categories and codes for the question, "What do you like about this new brand of cereal?"
   b. Code the following responses using your categories and codes.
      (1) "$1.50 is a reasonable price to pay for the cereal."
      (2) "The raisins and nuts add a nice flavor."
      (3) "The sizes of the packages are convenient."
      (4) "I like the sugar coating on the cereal."
      (5) "The container does not tear and fall apart easily."
      (6) "My kids like the cartoons on the back of the package."
      (7) "It is reasonably priced compared to other brands."
      (8) "The package is attractive and easy to spot in the store."
      (9) "I like the price; it is not so low that I doubt the quality and at the same time it is not so high as to be unaffordable."
      (10) "The crispness and lightness of the cereal improve the taste."

4. a. Establish response categories and codes for the following question that was asked to a sample of business executives. "In your opinion, which types of companies have not been affected by the present economic climate?"
   b. Code the following responses using your categories and codes.

(1) *Washington Post*	(6) Prentice-Hall	(11) Holiday Inns
(2) Colgate Palmolive	(7) Hoover	(12) Dryden Press
(3) Gillette	(8) Fabergé	(13) Singer
(4) Hilton Hotels	(9) Marine Midlands Banks	(14) Saga
(5) Chase Manhattan	(10) Zenith Radio	(15) Bank America

5. A large manufacturer of electronic components for automobiles recently conducted a study to determine the average value of electronic components per automobile. Personal interviews were conducted with a random sample of 400 respondents. The following information was secured with respect to each subject's "main" vehicle when he or she had more than one.

Average Dollar Value of Electronic Equipment per Automobile

Dollar Value of Electronic Equipment	Number of Automobiles
Less than $50	35
$ 51 to $100	40
$101 to $150	55
$151 to $200	65
$201 to $250	65
$251 to $300	75
$301 to $350	40
$351 to $400	20
More than $401	5
Total number of automobiles	400

a. Convert the preceding information into percentages.
b. Compute the cumulative absolute frequencies.
c. Compute the cumulative relative frequencies.
d. Prepare a histogram and frequency polygon with the average value of electronic equipment on the x-axis and the absolute frequency on the y-axis.
e. Graph the empirical cumulative distribution function with the average value on the x-axis and the relative frequency on the y-axis.
f. Locate the median, first sample quartile, and third sample quartile on the cumulative distribution function in Part e.
g. Calculate the mean, standard deviation, and variance for the frequency distribution. (Hint: Use the midpoint of each class interval and multiply that by the appropriate frequency. For the interval starting at $401, assume the midpoint is 425.5.)

6. An analyst for a leading Fortune 500 company demanded that all percentages be reported to one decimal place on graphs being presented to upper management. Several of the cross-tabulation cells had sample sizes of less than 30. Discuss why you feel it is or is not necessary to record all of the percentages to one decimal place.

7. A office-products retailer recently conducted a study. One of the questions asked of those interviewed was the following: "In an average month, how many times does your company purchase office supplies from an office-products retailer?" The following table lists the results of this question. Calculate the mean and standard deviation.

Value	Frequency
0	25
1	10
2	15
3	5
4	20

8. A manufacturer was interested in assessing how children ages four, five, and six play with one of the manufacturer's toys. Each child was asked 15 questions. Following the child's completed interview, the parent was asked the same 15 questions to validate the child's answers. The following table lists the number of responses to selected items from the survey. One hundred interviews were conducted with both the parent and the child.

Notice that item response rates varied from question to question. For each question, state at least one method that could be used to attempt to correct for this item nonresponse bias.

Question	Number of Children Responding	Number of Parents Responding
Age of child	95	100
Location of play	80	85
Preference for color or black and white slides	30	50

9. A large financial institution wanted to know which options were most important to small businesses. The financial institution hypothesized that the options that businesses found to be important would vary as annual sales of the businesses varied. The financial organization set up a cross-tabulation to investigate if any changes in importance were occurring between the groups of businesses. The following table lists the number of businesses that reported each of the options as most important. Calculate the percentages. Interpret your calculations.

Option	Annual Sales	
	Under $2 Million	$2 to $10 Million
Checking account	50	30
Mutual fund	10	70
Savings account	40	50

10. A social organization was interested in determining if there were various demographic characteristics that might be related to people's propensity to contribute to charities. The organization was particularly interested in determining whether individuals above age 40 were more likely to contribute larger amounts than individuals below age 40. The average contribution in the population was $1,500, and this figure was used to divide the individuals in the sample into two groups, those who contributed large amounts or more than average versus those who contributed less than average. The following table presents a two-way classification of the sample of individuals by contributions and age.

TABLE 1 **Personal Contributions and Age**

Personal Contribution	Age		Total
	39 or Less	40 or More	
Less than or equal to $1,500	79	50	129
More than $1,500	11	60	71
Total	90	110	200

In addition, the social organization wanted to determine if contributions depended on income, age, or both. The following table presents the simultaneous treatment of age and income. The median income in the population was $18,200, and this figure was used to split the sample into two groups.

TABLE 2   **Personal Contributions by Age and Income**

Personal Contributions	Income					
	Less than or Equal to $18,200		**More than $18,200**		**Total**	
	Age		Age		Age	
	39 or Less	**40 or More**	**39 or Less**	**40 or More**	**39 or Less**	**40 or More**
Less than or equal to $1,500	63	22	16	28	79	50
More than $1,500	7	18	4	42	11	60
Total	70	40	20	70	90	110

a. Does the amount of personal contributions depend on age? Generate the necessary tables to justify your answer.

b. Does the amount of personal contributions depend on age alone? Generate the necessary tables to justify your answer.

c. Present the percentage of contributions that are more than $1,500 by age and income in tabular form. Interpret the table.

11. Suppose that the following exhibit was prepared to present a portion of the results of a national survey aimed at identifying demographic and socioeconomic differences between individuals with published telephone numbers and individuals with nonpublished telephone numbers.

	Published Telephone Numbers	Nonpublished Telephone Numbers
Sex		
Male	43%	40%
Female	57	60
Age		
Under 25	8%	6%
25–34	21	26
35–44	13	27
45–54	14	17
55–64	19	15
65 and Over	25	9

	Published Telephone Numbers	Nonpublished Telephone Numbers
Ethnic Background		
White	95%	87%
Nonwhite (including Hispanic)	5	13
Household Income		
Under $5,000	10%	12%
$5,000–9,999	16	14
$10,000–14,999	15	16
$15,000–19,999	15	16
$20,000–24,999	16	15
$25,000–39,999	18	21
$40,000 or More	10	6

a. Describe the type of analysis represented in the exhibit. Is this an appropriate representation of the information on which the exhibit is based? Why or why not?

b. Suppose that the exhibit is based on 4,060 responses; 3,586 respondents indicated that they had a published telephone number and 474 indicated that they did not publish their number. Complete the exhibit below:

	Published Telephone Numbers	Nonpublished Telephone Numbers	Total
	Frequency (%)	Frequency (%)	Frequency (%)

Sex
Male
Female

Age
Under 25
25–34
35–44
45–54
55–64
65 and Over

Ethnic Background
White
Nonwhite (including Hispanic)

(continued)

	Published Telephone Numbers	Nonpublished Telephone Numbers	Total
	Frequency (%)	Frequency (%)	Frequency (%)

Household Income
Under $5,000
$5,000–9,999
$10,000–14,999
$15,000–19,999
$20,000–24,999
$25,000–39,999
$40,000 or More

NFO Applications   NFO Research, Inc. (NFO), recently conducted a study of the ground caffeinated coffee market because several of its clients operate in this market. The study was undertaken with several objectives in mind, including the identification of benefits that consumers seek and the comparison of consumer opinions regarding several of the brands offered in the market.

The questionnaire in Figure 8.3 (page 403) was designed to accomplish these objectives. This questionnaire was mailed to 400 individuals previously identified as consumers of ground caffeinated coffee (personally drinking at least one cup per day). Of those mailed out, 328 were returned; 299 of these were judged to be usable responses.

The data collected from these consumers are stored in a free-field format (space delimited) ASCII file named ''coffee.dat'' that is available from your instructor. The coding format for the data follows. Missing data are coded −99 for all items and should be disregarded for all analyses. While the data included are basically the data collected, some items or responses were generated to complete the data set.

Coding Format for NFO Coffee Study

Question Number	Variable (Variable Number)	Coding Specification
—	Questionnaire ID (VAR1)	—
1	Usual Method of Preparation (VAR2)	1 = automatic drip 2 = electric percolator 3 = stove-top percolator 4 = stove-top dripolator
2a	Ever Use: Folgers (VAR3) Hills Bros. (VAR4) Maxwell House Regular (VAR5) Maxwell House Master Blend (VAR6) Yuban (VAR7) Other (VAR8)	0 = no 1 = yes

Question Number	Variable (Variable Number)	Coding Specification
2b	Brand Used Most Often (VAR9)	1 = Folgers 2 = Hills Bros. 3 = Maxwell House Regular 4 = Maxwell House Master Blend 5 = Yuban 6 = Other

2c	On Hand:
	    Folgers (VAR10)
	    Hills Bros. (VAR11)
	    Maxwell House Regular (VAR12)
	    Maxwell House Master Blend (VAR13)
	    Yuban (VAR14)
	    Other (VAR15)
		0 = no
		1 = yes

2d	Brand Will Buy Next (VAR16)	1 = Folgers 2 = Hills Bros. 3 = Maxwell House Regular 4 = Maxwell House Master Blend 5 = Yuban 6 = Other

2e	Overall Rating:
	    Folgers (VAR17)
	    Hills Bros. (VAR18)
	    Maxwell House Regular (VAR19)
	    Maxwell House Master Blend (VAR20)
	    Yuban (VAR21)
	    Other (VAR22)
		Rating 1–10, where
		  1 = dislike it extremely
		  10 = like it extremely

3	Add Nothing (VAR23) Add Dairy Creamer (VAR24) Add Nondairy Creamer (VAR25) Add Sugar (VAR26) Add Artificial Sweetener (VAR27) Add Something Else (VAR28)	0 = no 1 = yes
4	Are You Primary Coffee Purchaser (VAR29)	0 = no 1 = yes

5	Rich Taste (VAR30)
	Always Fresh (VAR31)
	Gets Day Off to Good Start (VAR32)
	Full-Bodied Taste (VAR33)
		Importance Ratings, 0–10, where
		  0 = not at all important
		  10 = extremely important

(continued)

Question Number	Variable (Variable Number)	Coding Specification
	Rich Aroma in the Cup (VAR34)	
	Good Value for the Money (VAR35)	
	Best Coffee in the Morning (VAR36)	
	Rich Aroma in the Can/Bag (VAR37)	
	Smooth Taste (VAR38)	
	Highest Quality Coffee (VAR39)	
	Premium Brand (VAR40)	
	Not Bitter (VAR41)	
	Coffee That Brightens Day Most (VAR42)	
	Costs More Than Other Brands (VAR43)	
	Strong Taste (VAR44)	
	Has No Aftertaste (VAR45)	
	Economy Brand (VAR46)	
	Rich Aroma While Brewing (VAR47)	
	Best Ground Coffee Available (VAR48)	
	Enjoy Drinking with Meal (VAR49)	
	Costs Less Than Other Brands (VAR50)	

Special Coding Instructions, Question 6:

All variables are rating scales coded 0–10, where

   0 = does not describe at all
  10 = describes completely

Variable	Folgers Var. No.	Hills Bros. Var. No.	Maxwell House Regular Var. No.	Maxwell House Master Blend Var. No.	Yuban Var. No.
Rich Taste	VAR51	VAR72	VAR93	VAR114	VAR135
Always Fresh	VAR52	VAR73	VAR94	VAR115	VAR136
Good Start	VAR53	VAR74	VAR95	VAR116	VAR137
Full-Bodied Taste	VAR54	VAR75	VAR96	VAR117	VAR138
Rich Aroma/Cup	VAR55	VAR76	VAR97	VAR118	VAR139
Good Value	VAR56	VAR77	VAR98	VAR119	VAR140
Best Coffee in AM	VAR57	VAR78	VAR99	VAR120	VAR141
Rich Aroma/Can	VAR58	VAR79	VAR100	VAR121	VAR142
Smooth Taste	VAR59	VAR80	VAR101	VAR122	VAR143
Highest Quality	VAR60	VAR81	VAR102	VAR123	VAR144
Premium Brand	VAR61	VAR82	VAR103	VAR124	VAR145
Not Bitter	VAR62	VAR83	VAR104	VAR125	VAR146
Brightens Day Most	VAR63	VAR84	VAR105	VAR126	VAR147
Costs More	VAR64	VAR85	VAR106	VAR127	VAR148
Strong Taste	VAR65	VAR86	VAR107	VAR128	VAR149

Variable	Folgers Var. No.	Hills Bros. Var. No.	Maxwell House Regular Var. No.	Maxwell House Master Blend Var. No.	Yuban Var. No.
No Aftertaste	VAR66	VAR87	VAR108	VAR129	VAR150
Economy Brand	VAR67	VAR88	VAR109	VAR130	VAR151
Rich Aroma/Brewing	VAR68	VAR89	VAR110	VAR131	VAR152
Best Available	VAR69	VAR90	VAR111	VAR132	VAR153
Enjoy with Meal	VAR70	VAR91	VAR112	VAR133	VAR154
Costs Less	VAR71	VAR92	VAR113	VAR134	VAR155

Question Number	Variable (Variable Number)	Coding Specification
7a	Gender (VAR156)	1 = male 2 = female
7b	Age (VAR157)	Actual Age Coded

Because this is a relatively large data file (103,168 bytes), it will probably be useful to conduct the analyses necessary to complete the following application problems using a personal computer with a hard disk drive or on a mainframe computer.

12. a. Produce a histogram for the age variable. Does it appear that anything has been obviously miscoded? If so, explain.

   b. Produce a histogram for the variable "brand used most often." Determine an estimate of market share for the various brands based on this data set.

13. a. Cross tabulate "brand used most often" with "age," when the age variable has been recoded into the following categories:

   35 years or less
   36–45 years
   46–59 years
   60 years or more

   Generate percentages as well as frequency counts for each cell. What general conclusions might be drawn based on this information?

   b. How is the perceived relationship between "brand used most often" and "age" affected by the addition of a third variable, "sex of the respondent," to the analysis? Explain.

14. Suppose that it is your job to compare Folgers with Maxwell House Regular. Produce a snake diagram profiling these brands on the 21 attributes included in Question 6 of the questionnaire. What do your results indicate?

Thorndike Sports Equipment Video Case

1. If Ted's suggestion to use the sample mean in the body of the print ad was followed, what message would the majority of consumers take away from the advertisement? Why?

2. Would you feel comfortable applying Ted's solution to this problem knowing that a proportion of consumers would believe that their racquet would withstand 230 pounds of pressure? Why or why not?

APPENDIX 13A

Avery Sporting Goods

To provide some hands-on experience to the coding, tabulating, and analysis functions, this appendix and some of the remaining appendices discuss the results of a study on catalog buying. A portion of the data set is included as part of this appendix so that those who are interested can duplicate the analyses to check the results, thereby increasing their understanding of the various analysis techniques. The data are also rich enough to allow interested parties to investigate other questions not addressed in these appendices.

STUDY BACKGROUND

The primary purpose of the study was to gain insight into people who are likely to buy from catalogs. Avery's management was stimulated to conduct the study by published research investigating the characteristics of in-home (mail order or catalog) shoppers versus store shoppers. This research had indicated that there were differences in the demographic characteristics of those likely to buy in-home from those likely to buy in a store.[1] These studies had also indicated that those who shop in-home are motivated by convenience. Further, the product "is not necessarily the most important determinant of the success or failure of an in-home sale; prior shopping experience, the quality of the product description, its price, delivery, and guarantee policies also interact to influence the degree of perceived shopping risk."[2] The evidence also indicated that the perceived risk in buying in-home was higher than it was with in-store buying. Those who purchased in-home had higher tolerances for perceived risk. Also important was the fact that the degree of risk varied by product. It was highest for high-priced and personalized items.

Background Information

Through the years, Avery Sporting Goods had been one of the leading catalog sellers of sporting equipment in the country. Known for its wide assortment and colorful print

---

[1] See Peter L. Gillet, "In Home Shoppers — An Overview," *Journal of Marketing*, 40 (October 1976), pp. 81–88, for a review of the evidence on in-home shopping behavior.

[2] *Ibid.*, p. 85.

displays, the company's catalogs had been very popular with customers and employees, and workers had prided themselves on the high number of orders filled correctly. Still, management was considering expanding company operations by opening retail sporting goods stores. The three stores that the company had recently opened on the east side of Buffalo, New York, had met with tremendous sales success, far surpassing company expectations. Filled with growing optimism, management had developed plans to open three other stores during the next six to eight months in other areas of western New York. However, executives were not sure what to do with the company's catalog sales division.

Although catalog sales had been substantial, the level of growth had begun to taper off. This appeared to be an industry trend, as other sporting equipment enterprises (as well as major department stores) offering catalog sales and services had experienced similar low rates of growth in sales revenues. Although current income from catalog sales was adequate to financially support Avery's plan to develop retail stores, company management had no desire to de-emphasize its catalog operation. In fact, given the catalog's ability to reach a national market at relatively low costs, Avery believed that a large portion of its future success resided in catalog customers. Hence, the company was extremely interested in revitalizing this market segment. As a first step toward the formulation of a long-term strategy for ensuring the continued viability of catalog sales, Avery management decided to have its marketing research department survey a sample of past, present, and potential catalog customers, operationally defined as all those who had been sent catalogs in the past three years, to get a better feel for the catalog market. The issues that were to be addressed included the following:

- customer perceptions of buying merchandise, in particular sporting equipment, through catalogs;
- people's evaluation of Avery's offerings and services; and
- characteristics of Avery customers.

Randomly sampling individuals from company records and geographic areas served, the questionnaire shown in Figure 13A.1 was mailed to 225 subjects after it was found to

FIGURE 13A.1 **Questionnaire for Avery Sporting Goods**

The following questions are designed to give the Avery Sporting Goods Company a better idea of people's perceptions of buying sporting goods and other general merchandise through catalogs. Please read each question carefully and indicate your response by putting an X next to the appropriate statement. (Answer each question with a single response.) Thank you for your cooperation in completing the questionnaire.

1. During the past year, what percentage of the sporting goods you purchased was ordered through a catalog?

_____ 0 percent

_____ 1–10 percent

(continued)

_____ 11–15 percent
_____ 16–20 percent
_____ 21+ percent

2. *How willing are you to purchase merchandise offered through the Avery Sporting Goods catalog?*
    _____ Not at all willing
    _____ Somewhat willing
    _____ Very willing

3. *Have you ever ordered any merchandise from the Avery Sporting Goods catalog?*
    _____ Never
    _____ Ordered before, but not within the last year
    _____ Ordered within the last year

	Not at All Confident	Slightly Confident	Somewhat Confident	Confident	Very Confident
4. *How confident are you that the following sporting goods purchased through a catalog would be of high quality?*					
a. Athletic clothing (shirts, warm-up suits, etc.)	___	___	___	___	___
b. Athletic shoes	___	___	___	___	___
c. Fishing equipment	___	___	___	___	___
d. Balls (basketballs, footballs, etc.)	___	___	___	___	___
e. Skiing equipment	___	___	___	___	___
5. *How confident are you that the following sporting goods would be of high quality if purchased in a retail sporting goods store?*					
a. Athletic clothing (shirts, warm-up suits, etc.)	___	___	___	___	___
b. Athletic shoes	___	___	___	___	___
c. Fishing equipment	___	___	___	___	___
d. Balls (basketballs, footballs, etc.)	___	___	___	___	___
e. Skiing equipment	___	___	___	___	___

6. *Approximately how many items of sporting equipment did you purchase during the past year?*
    _____ 0–1
    _____ 2–3
    _____ 4–5
    _____ 6–7
    _____ 8 or more

	Strongly Disagree	Disagree	Neither Agree nor Disagree	Agree	Strongly Agree
7. In general, Avery Sporting Goods sells a high-quality line of merchandise.	____	____	____	____	____
8. Avery Sporting Goods carries all of the most popular name brands of sporting equipment.	____	____	____	____	____
9. Avery Sporting Goods has a very high-quality catalog.	____	____	____	____	____
10. The descriptions of the products shown in the Avery catalog are very accurate.	____	____	____	____	____
11. The selection of sporting goods available through the Avery catalog is very broad.	____	____	____	____	____
12. When buying from a catalog, there is a low probability that the merchandise will get lost in the mail.	____	____	____	____	____
13. Before purchasing merchandise through a catalog, people do not need to discuss the product with someone who has already purchased it.	____	____	____	____	____
14. Most catalog merchandising companies can be trusted to deliver the product pictured in the catalog.	____	____	____	____	____
15. I enjoy purchasing merchandise through a catalog because it saves time.	____	____	____	____	____
16. When buying from a catalog, it is not difficult to negotiate the price.	____	____	____	____	____
17. If given a choice, I would purchase merchandise from the catalog company that has the easiest form to fill out.	____	____	____	____	____
18. Merchandise purchased from a catalog is less expensive than merchandise purchased in a retail store.	____	____	____	____	____
19. I prefer ordering merchandise from a catalog because the product is delivered to your door.	____	____	____	____	____
20. Catalogs have lower prices because the company does not have to pay salespeople.	____	____	____	____	____

(continued)

	Very Unimportant	Unimportant	Neither Important nor Unimportant	Important	Very Important
21. How important are the following factors in your decision to purchase sporting goods through a catalog?					
a. Availability of a toll-free number for placing orders	____	____	____	____	____
b. Availability of quantity discounts	____	____	____	____	____
c. Shipping time	____	____	____	____	____
d. The company's policy on returning merchandise	____	____	____	____	____
e. The provision of a trial period	____	____	____	____	____
f. Number of years the company has been in business	____	____	____	____	____
g. Reputation of the company	____	____	____	____	____
h. Guarantees	____	____	____	____	____
i. Company endorsements by celebrities, sports teams, etc.	____	____	____	____	____

22. In general, do you prefer to do your shopping:

____ in a retail store
____ in a discount outlet store
____ through a catalog
____ over the phone
____ by having salespeople call on you at home

23. What was your approximate before-tax family income during the past year?

____ $0–$14,999   ____ $25,000–$34,999
____ $15,000–$24,999   ____ $35,000–$44,999
                         ____ $45,000 or more

24. Is your current occupation best described as blue collar? ____ white collar? ____

---

25. *How long have you been working (in years)?*____

26. *What is your current marital status?*
    ____ single   ____ separated
    ____ married   ____ divorced
                    ____ widowed

27. *Are you male?* ____ *female?*____

---

work well when pretested on a sample of 25 customers. A three-dollar coupon toward the next item purchased through Avery's catalog was enclosed with each questionnaire; 124 usable surveys were returned, for a 55 percent response rate. The responses to the individual questions were converted to the codes indicated in Table 13A.1. Unanswered

Tᴀʙʟᴇ **13A.1**   **Coding Format for Avery Sporting Goods Questionnaire**

Column(s)	Question Number	Variable (Variable Number)	Coding Specification
1–3	—	Questionnaire identification number (V1)	—
4	1	Percentage of products purchased through a catalog (V2)	1 = 0 percent 2 = 1–10 percent 3 = 11–15 percent 4 = 16–20 percent 5 = 21+ percent
5	2	Willingness to purchase merchandise from the Avery Sporting Goods catalog (V3)	1 = Unwilling 2 = Somewhat willing 3 = Very willing
6	3	Ever ordered from the Avery Sporting Goods catalog (V4)	1 = Never ordered 2 = Ordered before, but not within the last year 3 = Ordered within the last year
			Coding Specifications 4a–5e 1 = Not at all confident 2 = Slightly confident 3 = Somewhat confident 4 = Confident 5 = Very confident

(continued)

TABLE **13A.1**   *Continued*

Column(s)	Question Number	Variable (Variable Number)	Coding Specification
7	4a	Confidence in buying athletic clothing through a catalog (V5)	
8	4b	Confidence in buying athletic shoes through a catalog (V6)	
9	4c	Confidence in buying fishing equipment through a catalog (V7)	
10	4d	Confidence in buying balls through a catalog (V8)	
11	4e	Confidence in buying skiing equipment through a catalog (V9)	
12	5a	Confidence in buying athletic clothing in a retail store (V10)	
13	5b	Confidence in buying athletic shoes in a retail store (V11)	
14	5c	Confidence in buying fishing equipment in a retail store (V12)	
15	5d	Confidence in buying balls in a retail store (V13)	
16	5e	Confidence in buying skiing equipment in a retail store (V14)	
17	6	Number of sporting equipment items purchased (V15)	$1 = 0-1$ $2 = 2-3$ $3 = 4-5$ $4 = 6-7$ $5 = 8$ or more
			Coding Specifications 7–20 $1 = $ Strongly disagree $2 = $ Disagree $3 = $ Neither agree nor disagree $4 = $ Agree $5 = $ Strongly agree
18	7	Avery sells a high-quality line of merchandise (V16)	
19	8	Avery carries the most popular name brands of sporting equipment (V17)	
20	9	Avery has a high-quality catalog (V18)	
21	10	Descriptions of products in the Avery catalog are accurate (V19)	
22	11	Selection of goods available through Avery is very broad (V20)	

TABLE **13A.1** *Continued*

Column(s)	Question Number	Variable (Variable Number)	Coding Specification
23	12	Low probability that merchandise will get lost in the mail (V21)	
24	13	No need to discuss product with someone who has purchased it before buying through a catalog (V22)	
25	14	Can be trusted to deliver product that's pictured in the catalog (V23)	
26	15	Catalog purchasing saves time (V24)	
27	16	Not difficult to negotiate the price (V25)	
28	17	Purchase from catalog with easiest form to fill out (V26)	
29	18	Catalog merchandise is less expensive (V27)	
30	19	Catalogs deliver the product to door (V28)	
31	20	Catalogs have lower prices because the company does not have to pay salespeople (V29)	
			Coding Specification 21a–21i 1 = Very unimportant 2 = Unimportant 3 = Neither important nor unimportant 4 = Important 5 = Very important
32	21a	Availability of a toll-free number for placing orders (V30)	
33	21b	Availability of quantity discounts (V31)	
34	21c	Shipping time (V32)	
35	21d	Company policy on returning merchandise (V33)	
36	21e	Provision of a trial period (V34)	
37	21f	Number of years company has been in business (V35)	
38	21g	Reputation of the company (V36)	
39	21h	Guarantees (V37)	
40	21i	Company endorsements (V38)	
41	22	Prefer to do shopping (V39)	1 = in a retail store 2 = in a discount outlet store 3 = through a catalog 4 = over the phone 5 = by having salespeople call at home

(continued)

Column(s)	Question Number	Variable (Variable Number)	Coding Specification
42	23	Before-tax family income during the past year (V40)	1 = $0–$14,999 2 = $15,000–$24,999 3 = $25,000–$34,999 4 = $35,000–$44,999 5 = $45,000 or more
43	24	Current occupation (V41)	0 = blue collar 1 = white collar
44–45	25	Years worked (V42)	Actual years recorded
46	26	Current marital status (V43)	5 = single 4 = married 3 = separated 2 = divorced 1 = widowed
47	27	Sex (V44)	1 = male 2 = female

Note: Except for variables V1, V41, and V42, zeroes represent nonresponses.

questions were coded with a ''0'' (except for Question 24, in which ''blue collar'' was coded as ''0,'' and Question 25 in which a ''0'' is a valid partial response for the subject's years worked). The first three columns of the data listed in Table 13A.2 contain the customer's survey identification number.

ONE-WAY TABULATION

As pointed out in the chapter, one-way tabulation is useful for locating blunders and outliers, for determining the empirical distribution of the variable, and for communicating results. Thus, an analyst would normally construct the one-way tabulations for each variable in the study. This is not done here because of space limitations. Rather, only the one-way tabulation of the percentage of sporting goods purchased from a catalog during the past year is shown in Table 13A.3. This, incidentally, will be a general strategy followed throughout the appendices investigating catalog buying behavior. Even though a number of relationships might be analyzed using a particular technique, only one is used in each case to illustrate the technique.

Table 13A.3 was constructed using the SPSS/PC+ frequencies program. *SPSS (Statistical Package for the Social Sciences)* is a widely distributed system of computer programs for data management and statistical analysis. It is used whenever possible in the appendices that follow, which analyze the catalog buying data, because of its general

T<small>ABLE</small> **13A.2   Listing of Raw Data**

```
0011115555434443434445554454545544554444445 3112551      06311144444543513123134543424244455444425101121
0021214455545453545444454545445324254431421 2551         06412345533245313122223555555515442433313301421
0034135544245321455554555455555503030504232 14051        06533145555254135321224555454544444444403401231
0043225543554324535454111555555242423243321 2551         06621155554154535444524435543544504044343212551
0052115355453542454444545450535455555503412551           06741235455154324345551215442521414441434102551
0061335543452435455534434425342444444440231 3651         06822355525541235355555555555555555555554351 02751
0071314453545354544445344324321444445341511 2451         06951244444254313553345454434444434355432111 2441
0085235543535454543555455525513355555355114 513651       07013254355254135454444443325324444444435512551
0093123555523555544554453555555424355224232 13651        07113345555543555325555424414141444444415511531
0101324451553423345444324254242224343331141 2551         07213144444545353445444423545454352535143341 2551
0111335353524555325254454534544233333343421 512351       07311245355543544355445554545400455240551 2551
0122315445335554345455324555455224344435315 15641        07413345444354444454235355525243345334413112541
0132335555544444555554334225243444243321140 51           07513155552355553555533355555555555555455511113651
0144115355541455534445433555555424442333322 12341        07621344544235455444545455555454554541111 2431
0151334444255444255554455555555325455353332 214051       07723154355235555155543455452544233445213112451
0163225551533554544453322555532525544544313 212341       07823355544235455555553445555533443344444333 14051
0175134455355545453544234341143443344443311 2551         07921144455324554354554444555454444441421 2531
0182225354535454444444444353234204040400411 2451         08052244454355555555554444442421332444341521 3851
0193115554435555454354552432554424040505033 412551       08113155453251435355454255353543144252533112551
0203324444543255454454535353333445343254124 51           08211254325215454544546333443234344321113651
0211235354554245555555334445545455454543455 14041        08312354354543213355545332445452424342531113651
0221315243455555325554532454545223345451435 312421       08432235455245513544444544252515534344021 2441
0231335435432154435554122542255455253525321 3651         08521155555442515355540005451544403050402221 2441
0241315453535124555444555555325525545553525 413651       08623255553541235444543424554542443352432212441
0251135455532123554445433525252254523253541 2541         08741344441222134354543452515255354435332 12531
0262215325521453444533315554534352511321154 1             08813354353541234445532535345443354331321 2551
0272115244435412445454342535352445555541231 3641         08911255555215355335553335555524343434343421 2441
0282135555533333535554444153325342434342221 3641         09012153421451232455553444545454525454534213651
0292125435523544554553434545555503050501311 2551         09131211212543253444524545555535353545525125 42
0301214554354241555544244555532242444341113 951          09223312222255541555555533443332335523331112552
0311112541235545333554543435442243333443314 212551       09311322111344451111214442334424344442441310051 2
0325225545324453444114441114311232251424214 34432 12551  09412132211354451231110455454544444035314200922
0331115354421453444454343434355453444453511 2541         09521115221355552222235435353423344442502401232
0343222544535455255444354445151403050401541 3651         09623121351214553121114445545454545454513400512
0352122455455334355453544455554544444353534 312541       09722322222235555522225344243533335343335511232
0362231321254154144455324455544334323342321 2542         09851211114554451311222223353425544545514500932
0371113212135432424444545354535233445333444 12432         09913122111355541123223345554545433334313201232
0381321234354354254555545455554525252525112 13752        10011323111544331212220033222245324525323 00922
0391231242354354253555555242525525302523011 403652       10151223222254352111145545252545444442120 0412
0401121242355555235545444555353434343434314 212742       10252211121255551212233425151515555444551 20 0922
0413331241235435344444444323252424234343421 2742         10322222115435422223000504455202020201320 1232
0424332131154354255555221444455252524143331 4052         10431132112354532123211152515154535255 13301232
0432231111145435112321544555555534453541310 1222         10541112112344442121400033113300000000004 400822
0441111222154354111114553233444555552550001 22           10612351132551150002233500000000000540 00922
0451322222223545221212435555252355551352440 0812         10732311111244441112222555353535555555555 15500927
0461333111145435122222331542525243434141435 401222       10851233211555453231113145251513533543 43545 01032
0471232122233545551123135553225153355554223 200922       10921212123354555211111225545222424242 311245 01432
0482332311154555121222322525252435555453133 00922        11043111112355444123111434515253030303 023100922
0491111221335423123112222535455405050401220 0922         11112322211234551222240005151005355555 1301232
0502233332245325231111444354535435155252210 0512         11213131114554512112325353534343544413 200822
0511112222225555552111324434455453344333332 500812       11351221122325554121121210351524454545 4512200522
0521221411254333111214555454534444535414400 512           11432111114545411245354555545454555555 12201832
0531112423152224555512411335223344555552534 100922       11511122224255551241133324354543424242313101232
0541231232154555112222423142533444243335200 922          11623332222453552321115445544430405050402300922
0551132222254355211111454222334433244532400 412          11742312121435541222214443525153050505023501232
0561223111225445122223030050505500050050143 01232        11811212311531552351114324555342322431124501432
0571112131153334122133455555545334443432440 1232         11923222431155555321412342455455445455443 442 15501232
0582311111244444111132545555555533554555155 00822        12043321321354352212334334435454444444 4551201232
0592231232154354121222355555452543455555323 300922       12111124511354532142433325215243445254 14401332
0602122222555555222212222544434332422323350 0922         12222133311545452111115344151544455354 533200412
0614314535512455411111424545342332444231220 0411         12341132131235555122221434212524432423433 1501232
0621325555454532152111133244423333314332234 110511       12431221311145354135555534444524243435302 55513652
```

TABLE **13A.3   One-Way Tabulation Showing Percentage of Sporting Goods Purchased from a Catalog during the Past Year**

Percent Category Label	Code	Absolute Frequency	Relative Frequency (Percent)	Adjusted Frequency (Percent)	Cumulative Frequency (Percent)
0%	1	56	45.2	45.2	45.2
1–10%	2	33	26.6	26.6	71.8
11–15%	3	14	11.3	11.3	83.1
16–20%	4	11	8.9	8.9	91.9
21+%	5	10	8.1	8.1	100.0
Missing Values	0	0	0.0	0.0	
Total		124	100.0	100.0	
Valid cases 124 Missing cases 0					

availability.[3] The program that will produce the computer output needed for constructing Table 13A.3 is listed in Table 13A.4.

The use of statistical and data management packages to analyze marketing research data is very efficient. Once the control language for a package is learned, almost all of the most popular statistical analyses can be conducted using it.[4]

Table 13A.3 indicates that most people receiving Avery catalogs buy only a small portion of their sporting goods through catalogs; 56, or 45 percent, of the respondents bought no sporting goods at all from catalogs in the previous year. Further, more than 83 percent of the catalog recipients satisfied 15 percent or less of their sporting goods purchases through catalogs. Only 8 percent purchased more than 20 percent of their sporting goods through catalogs.

CROSS TABULATION

Table 13A.5 is offered as an illustration of the makeup of the two-way tabulation output by SPSS. It depicts the relationship between willingness to purchase merchandise offered through the Avery sporting goods catalog and whether respondents have previously ordered from the catalog. The cross tabulation can be used to assess the extent to which catalog customers are satisfied and are likely to be repeat buyers in the sense that they

---

[3]SPSS is really a family of compatible systems depending on whether the data are to be analyzed in a batch mode, an interactive mode, or on a microcomputer. See, for example, Marija J. Norusis, *SPSS/PC+ Advanced Statistics V4.0* (Chicago: SPSS, Inc., 1990); and Marija J. Norusis, *SPSS/PC+ V4.0 Update Manual* (Chicago: SPSS, Inc., 1990).

[4]Other powerful and popular systems are BMDP and SAS. See W. J. Dixan *et al.*, eds., *BMDP Statistical Software Manual,* Vol. 2 (Berkeley: University of California Press, 1988); SAS Language, Refrence Version 6 *Additional SAS/STAT* (Cary, N.C.: SAS Institute, 1990). A powerful microcomputer statistical package is SYSTAT. Leland Wilkinson, *SYSTAT: The System for Statistics* (Evanston, Ill.: SYSTAT, Inc., 1992).

A. Program Structure

```
DATA LIST FILE='A:AVERY.DAT'
      /V1 1-3 V2 to V41 4-43 V42 44-45 V43 to V44 46-47.
MISSING VALUE V2 to V40 V43 V44 (0).
SAVE OUTFILE='AVERY.SYS'.
FREQUENCIES VAR=V2
      /STATISTICS=ALL.
FINISH.
```

B. Explanation of Commands

DATA LIST

In this example, the DATA LIST command causes the data to be read from an ASCII file named "AVERY.DAT" located on a floppy disk that has been inserted in disk drive A. On the following line, the command continues by naming and locating the variables in the file. For example, "V42" represents the number of years that a respondent has been working; this information is contained in columns 44 and 45 in the data file for each respondent. Note that the program allows the use of a shortcut for variables held in single columns: the TO command. For example, variables 2 through 41 ("V2 to V41") are located in column 4 through 43, respectively.

MISSING VALUE

The MISSING VALUE command advises the software program of what values it should treat as missing values. In the example, missing values have been coded "0" at the time the data were input into the ASCII file. Therefore, this command tells the program that a value of "0" really represents missing responses for all variables except V1, V41, and V42. A review of the coding format in Table 13A.1 shows that a value of "0" has definite meaning for V41 and V42. V1 is simply the subject identification number; a missing value would not be expected for this variable since it is researcher-defined.

SAVE

The SAVE command tells the program to save the newly created SPSS/PC+ system file on the hard drive in a file named "AVERY.SYS." The original data are stored along with information about the data including variable names, location, and any missing values that have been defined. Once a system file has been saved, it can be easily retrieved at a later time by using the GET command. In this situation, the appropriate command line to retrieve the system file would be:

GET FILE='AVERY.SYS'.

If the file were saved on a floppy disk, then the drive specification would be used with the file name.

FREQUENCIES

This command activates the FREQUENCIES subprogram of the SPSS/PC+ system. The variable for which a frequency table is to be formed, V2, follows the FREQUENCIES command.

STATISTICS

The STATISTICS command enables the user to select among a number of available statistics to accompany the calculations and to be reported in the output. The command ALL causes all the available statistics to be reported.

FINISH

The FINISH command always terminates the processing of the current computer run. It is always the last command in the command structure.

TABLE 13A.5   Cross Tabulation of Willingness to Purchase from Avery's Catalog (V3) with Whether Respondent Has Purchased from It Before (V4)

Count Row Percent Column Percent Total Percent	V4	Never Ordered 1	Ordered Before but Not within Past Year 2	Ordered within Past Year 3	Row Total
V3					
Unwilling	1	20	20	10	50
		40.0	40.0	20.0	40.3
		46.5	51.3	23.8	
		16.1	16.1	8.1	
Somewhat Willing	2	7	11	17	35
		20.0	31.4	48.6	28.2
		16.3	28.2	40.5	
		5.6	8.9	13.7	
Very Willing	3	16	8	15	39
		41.0	20.5	38.5	31.5
		37.2	20.5	35.7	
		12.9	6.5	12.1	
Column Total		43	39	42	124
		34.7	31.5	33.9	100.0

A Raw chi square = 10.997 with 4 degrees of freedom. Significance = 0.027, Cramer's V = 0.211.

B Contingency coefficient = 0.285.

C Lambda (asymmetric) = 0.095 with V3 dependent = 0.123 with V4 dependent. Lambda (symmetric) = 0.110. Uncertainty coefficient (asymmetric) = 0.043 with V3 dependent = 0.043 with V4 dependent. Uncertainty coefficient (asymmetric) = 0.043. Kendall's Tau B = 0.103. Significance = 0.101. Kendall's Tau C = 0.102. Significance = 0.101. Gamma = 0.151. Somer's D (asymmetric) = 0.102 with V3 dependent = 0.103 with V4 dependent. Somer's D (symmetric) = 0.102. Eta = 0.205 with V3 dependent = 0.239 with V4 dependent. Pearson's r = 0.103. Significance = 0.127.

have ordered before and are willing to order again. The cross tabulation also provides some insight into the size of an untapped market, defined as those who have received Avery catalogs in the past and have not purchased from them but are willing to do so.

Note that percentages based on row totals, column totals, and overall totals are reported in the table in addition to the raw frequencies. Willingness to buy through the Avery Sporting Goods catalog is the dependent variable that we are interested in explaining. The percentages we should logically focus on, then, are those based on the column totals. These percentages suggest that the "most willing" group of catalog recipients are those who ordered from Avery within the past year. Over three-fourths of these people (40.5 + 35.7 percent) are somewhat willing or very willing to order from Avery again. At the same time, almost one-fourth of those who bought within the last year are not willing to place another order. This relatively large proportion of potentially dissatisfied customers would certainly deserve further investigation by Avery management.

The column percentages also suggest that there may be a sizable untapped segment of people receiving Avery catalogs who might become customers if the right inducement can be found. Over 50 percent (16.3 + 37.2) of the people who have never placed an order with Avery said that they were willing to place an order.

Note finally the statistics located at the bottom of Table 13A.5, which are output by the SPSS cross-tabulation program. Most of these assess the degree of association between the two variables. Three of the more important for our purposes are the chi-squared statistic, the contingency coefficient, and the index of predictive association, which are labeled A, B, and C, respectively, on the output and are described in Appendix 16A. Their interpretations, which you will appreciate after reading that appendix, are as follows:

A The chi-square value of $\chi^2 = 10.997$ with 4 degrees of freedom is significant at the .027 level. This indicates that the null hypothesis of independence between the two variables should be rejected in favor of the alternative that willingness to purchase from Avery's catalog is a function of having purchased from it before.

B The contingency coefficient value of $C = .285$ suggests that there is only moderate association between the variables, given that the maximum value for C in a table with three rows and three columns is .816.

C The index of predictive association $\lambda_{3.4} = .095$ indicates that errors in predicting Variable 3 (willingness to purchase through Avery's catalog) are only reduced by 9.5 percent by taking account of Variable 4 (whether or not the respondent has ordered from the Avery catalog before). This again suggests that, although statistically significant, the strength of the relationship between the two variables is low.

14

C H A P T E R

Data Analysis: Basic Questions

Chapter 13 discussed the preliminary data analysis steps of editing, coding, and tabulation. The chapter was intended to convey the importance and potential value of these preliminary procedures, which are common to almost all research studies. Some studies stop with tabulation and cross tabulation. Many involve additional analyses, though, particularly the search for statistical significance. A recurring problem in this search is the determination of the appropriate statistical procedure. This chapter will highlight the basic considerations that dictate a choice of method.

CHOICE OF ANALYSIS TECHNIQUE: AN EXAMPLE

The considerations that underlie a choice of analysis method and the interpretation of the results are best demonstrated through example. Assume that the following hypothetical study was completed by a consumer products firm that manufactures the dishwashing liquid Sheen. The study was designed to determine homemakers' perceptions of the gentleness of Sheen and its nearest competitor, Glitter. Assume that the study used a scientifically determined probability sample and that the data were collected by administering a rating scale to each respondent. The respondents were specifically asked to locate each brand on a five-point mildness scale with the descriptors

- very rough (VR)
- rough (R)
- neither rough nor gentle (N)
- mild (M)
- very mild (VM)

according to how they thought the brand affected their hands. The basic considerations underlying the choice of method can be easily illustrated using a small sample, so assume that the analysis was to be based on the ten responses contained in Table 14.1, which also contains some alternative ways of analyzing the data. Not all of these methods are correct, nor are all the conclusions that can be drawn from the data. As a matter

TABLE 14.1 **Homemakers' Perceptions of Dishwashing Liquids**

Respondent	Perception of VR R N M VM — S	G	A −2 −1 0 1 2 — S	G	B 1 2 3 4 5 — S	G	C 5 4 3 2 1 — S	G	D −1 0 1 — S	G	E Higher-Rated Alternative*
1	VM	VM	2	2	5	5	1	1	1	1	T
2	M	VM	1	2	4	5	2	1	1	1	G
3	N	VM	0	2	3	5	3	1	0	1	G
4	M	VM	1	2	4	5	2	1	1	1	G
5	M	VM	1	2	4	5	2	1	1	1	G
6	M	VM	1	2	4	5	2	1	1	1	G
7	M	M	1	1	4	4	2	2	1	1	T
8	M	R	1	−1	4	2	2	4	1	−1	S
9	N	R	0	−1	3	2	3	4	0	−1	S
10	N	M	0	1	3	4	3	2	0	1	G
Sums			8	12	38	42	22	18	7	6	
Averages			0.8	1.2	3.8	4.2	2.2	1.8	0.7	0.6	

*A "T" indicates a tie, in that both brands received the same rating.

of fact, it is the purpose of this section to demonstrate how the conclusion depends on the method. There is no problem in most studies in deciding, "What ways *can* the analysis be done?" There is an acute problem in deciding, "What way *should* the analysis be conducted?"

The methods reported in Table 14.1 vary according to how values (numbers) were assigned to each of the scale locations. Consider Method A, for instance. Underlying Method A is the assumption that mildness is desirable and roughness undesirable in dishwashing liquids. Thus, if the respondent believed that the dishwashing soap was very mild on one's hands, that response received a positive score of +2. A response of "very rough" received a negative score of −2, a response of "rough" a score of −1, and so on. The scores are totaled and averaged at the bottom of Table 14.1.

Look at the average scores for Method A; Sheen had an average score of 0.8, and Glitter had an average score of 1.2. Both soaps are thus "mild." Now let us search for the milder product, looking at the average score differences between the products and converting them to a percentage mildness difference. With Sheen as the comparative yardstick, we find that

$$\frac{\bar{x}_G - \bar{x}_S}{\bar{x}_S}(100) = \frac{1.2 - 0.8}{0.8}(100) = 50 \text{ percent},$$

and the conclusion is that Glitter is 50 percent milder on the hands.

With Glitter as the basis of comparison, the result is

$$\frac{\bar{x}_G - \bar{x}_S}{\bar{x}_G}(100) = \frac{1.2 - 0.8}{1.2}(100) = 33 \text{ percent},$$

and the conclusion is that Glitter is 33 percent milder on your hands. Similar calculations underlie each of the comparisons reflected in Table 14.1 except for Method E, the conclusions for which are summarized in Table 14.2. Methods B and C, for example, employ assignments of numbers to response categories similar to those used in Method A, except that Method B uses all positive numbers, with "very mild" receiving a score of 5. Method C reverses the scoring so that a score of 5 represents a "very rough" evaluation. Method D assigns negative values to "rough" evaluations and positive values to "mild" evaluations, but the "rough" and "very rough" evaluations receive the same score (-1), as do the "mild" and "very mild" evaluations ($+1$). Method E, in contrast, does not rely on average scores for all respondents but focuses on the alterna-

TABLE 14.2 Comparison of Dishwashing Liquids

Method	Base in Comparison	Calculation	Conclusion
A	Sheen	$\dfrac{\bar{x}_G - \bar{x}_S}{\bar{x}_S}(100) = \dfrac{1.2 - 0.8}{0.8}(100) = 50.0\%$	Glitter is 50% milder on the hands.
	Glitter	$\dfrac{\bar{x}_G - \bar{x}_S}{\bar{x}_G}(100) = \dfrac{1.2 - 0.8}{1.2}(100) = 33.3\%$	Glitter is 33% milder on the hands.
B	Sheen	$\dfrac{\bar{x}_G - \bar{x}_S}{\bar{x}_S}(100) = \dfrac{4.2 - 3.8}{3.8}(100) = 10.5\%$	Glitter is 11% milder on the hands.
	Glitter	$\dfrac{\bar{x}_G - \bar{x}_S}{\bar{x}_G}(100) = \dfrac{4.2 - 3.8}{4.2}(100) = 9.5\%$	Glitter is 10% milder on the hands.
C	Sheen	$\dfrac{\bar{x}_S - \bar{x}_G}{\bar{x}_S}(100) = \dfrac{2.2 - 1.8}{2.2}(100) = 18.2\%$	Glitter is 18% milder on the hands.
	Glitter	$\dfrac{\bar{x}_S - \bar{x}_G}{\bar{x}_G}(100) = \dfrac{2.2 - 1.8}{1.8}(100) = 22.2\%$	Glitter is 22% milder on the hands.
D	Sheen	$\dfrac{\bar{x}_S - \bar{x}_G}{\bar{x}_S}(100) = \dfrac{0.7 - 0.6}{0.7}(100) = 14.3\%$	Sheen is 14% milder on the hands.
	Glitter	$\dfrac{\bar{x}_S - \bar{x}_G}{\bar{x}_G}(100) = \dfrac{0.7 - 0.6}{0.6}(100) = 16.7\%$	Sheen is 17% milder on the hands.
E	....		60% of the respondents thought Glitter was milder on the hands, while 20% thought Sheen was milder.

tive rated higher by each respondent. In particular, the conclusions in Method E reflect the facts that Respondents 1 and 7 perceived Glitter and Sheen to be of equal mildness, six of the ten respondents perceived Glitter as milder, and two perceived Sheen as milder.

The right-hand column of Table 14.2 suggests a number of conclusions about which is the preferred detergent. Which of these conflicting statements is correct and why? The answer is the last one, corresponding to Method E, and the reasons are intimately associated with the considerations that dictate the choice of analysis method. These considerations include the type of data, the research design, and the assumptions underlying the test statistic.

Before discussing these considerations, let us indicate why the last statement is correct and, in the process, reveal some of the caveats associated with these data. First, some analysts would hold that the response categories reflect ordinal measurements, in that the difference between ''very rough'' and ''rough'' is not the same as the difference between ''rough'' and ''neither rough nor gentle.'' Further, we saw previously that the assignment of scale values is completely arbitrary with order data as long as the order relationships are preserved, but that the calculation of means is misleading. Thus, these analysts would argue that Methods A to D are inappropriate, *not because of the values that were assigned to the categories but rather because the values were averaged.*

ETHICAL DILEMMA 14.1

A beer producer conducted a study to determine whether consumers perceive an actual or psychological difference in the taste of beer. As part of the experiment, each subject was asked to taste three unmarked cans of beer and to order them according to preference. Although they were led to believe that the three cans of beer were different beers, the participants discovered when the beers were unmasked that the three cans were, in fact, the same beer. A fair proportion of participants had stated that the three beers tasted quite different.

- It is argued that such an experiment may induce stress in some participants inasmuch as it may lead them to doubt their competence as shoppers. Comment on this argument.
- Should the investigator offer some sort of psychic support (i.e., debriefing) upon completion of the experiment to counteract any possible negative effects?
- Under what conditions might debriefing be problematic?

Second, even if the data had interval properties, Methods A to D would still be incorrect for two reasons. First, the comparisons in Table 14.2 involve absolute magnitudes, because each difference is compared to a mean and the result is interpreted as a certain percentage of the mean. Such comparisons are inappropriate unless the variables have a natural zero. The comparisons involving Methods A through D would be meaningful, then, if the variables were on a ratio scale but not when the zero position is so arbitrary, as it is in the rating scales. Further, the evaluations of Sheen and Glitter are not independent and cannot be treated as such statistically. Instead, they represent multiple responses from the same individual. They are related or dependent samples, and the appropriate procedure involves an analysis of the difference in the evaluations per individual. Method E is the only procedure that correctly deals with these differences.

Third, the conclusion was that "60 percent of the people thought Glitter was milder on the hands." The question has not been raised about whether this is a statistically significant result. The question of statistical significance involves the size of the sample employed to generate the percentage. In this case, the result is not significant. Yet if 60 out of 100 people thought that Glitter was milder on the hands than Sheen, the result would be statistically significant, although the percentage "preferring" Glitter would remain the same. Sample size is an important barometer in determining

---

Research Realities 14.1

Comparative Ad Legal Battle in Which Type of Data and Research Design Were Central Issues

One tactic in the continuing battle over comparative advertising claims is to attack the validity of statements about the marketing research on the product rather than complaining about statements directed at the product itself.

Philip Morris and R. J. Reynolds pioneered this line of attack in 1980 when they separately challenged references to consumer surveys in a Triumph cigarette ad campaign. One ad claimed that "an amazing 60%" said Triumph tasted as good or better than Merit. The court ruled this ad was misleading because it failed to disclose that, on the same basis, Merit had obtained a score of 64% compared to Triumph.

Another lawsuit in 1980 was decided by the influential federal court of appeals in New York City. Vidal Sassoon Inc. took legal action against Bristol-Myers over a series of TV commercials and print ads for a shampoo named Body on Tap because of its beer content. The prototype commercial featured a well-known high-fashion model saying "In shampoo tests with over 900 women like me, Body on Tap got

higher ratings than Prell for body. Higher than Flex, for conditioning. Higher than Sassoon for strong, healthy looking hair."

The evidence showed that several groups of approximately 200 women each tested just one shampoo. They rated it on a six-step qualitative scale, from "outstanding" to "poor," for 27 separate attributes, such as body and conditioning. It became clear that 900 women did not, after trying both shampoos, make product-to-product comparisons between Body on Tap and Sassoon or between Body on Tap and any of the other brands mentioned. In fact, no woman in the tests tried more than one shampoo.

The basis for the claim that the women preferred Body on Tap to Sassoon for "strong, healthy looking hair" was to combine the data for the "outstanding" and "excellent" ratings and discard the lower four ratings on the scale. The figures then were 36% for Body on Tap and 24% (of a separate group of women) for Sassoon. When the "very good" and "good" ratings were combined with the "outstanding" and "excellent" ratings, however, there was only a statistically insignificant difference of 1% between the two products in the category of "strong, healthy looking hair."

Source: Sidney A. Diamond, "Market Research Latest Target in Ad Claims," *Advertising Age,* 53 (January 25, 1982), p. 52.

whether a research finding is due to chance or represents an underlying condition in the population.

BASIC CONSIDERATIONS

The example has highlighted some of the considerations involved in the choice of analysis method. One useful classification of these considerations is that the appropriate technique depends on the type of data, the research design, and the assumptions underlying the test statistic and its related consideration, the power of the test. Research Realities 14.1, which overviews the legal arguments between Vidal Sassoon and Bristol-Myers regarding some comparative ad claims, highlights the importance careful specification and interpretation of these features can make.

The research was conducted for Bristol-Myers by Marketing Information Systems Inc. (MISI), using a technique known as blind monadic testing. The president of MISI testified that this method typically is employed when what is wanted is an absolute response to a product "without reference to another specific product." Although he testified that blind monadic testing was used in connection with comparative advertising, that was not the purpose for which Bristol-Myers retained MISI. Rather, they wished to determine consumer reaction to the introduction of Body on Tap. And Sassoon's in-house research expert stated flatly that blind monadic testing cannot support comparative advertising claims.

Sassoon also found some other things wrong with the tests and the way they were represented in the Bristol-Myers advertisements. The fashion model said 900 women "like me" tried the shampoos. Actually, one-third of the women were aged 13 to 18. This was significant because Body on Tap appealed disproportionately to teenagers, and the advertising executive who created the campaign for Bristol-Myers testified that its purpose was to attract a larger portion of the adult women's shampoo market. A study by Bristol-Myers, shortly after the campaign was launched, showed that for women in the 18 to 34 age group, awareness and purchases of Body on Tap did increase.

Finally, Sassoon charged that the methodology of the tests was flawed. There was evidence that the women who tested Sassoon shampoo were told to use it contrary to Sassoon's own instructions. Also, these women were allowed to use other brands while they were testing Sassoon. As a result, their responses might not have accurately reflected their reaction to Sassoon as distinct from other shampoo products.

Sassoon obtained an order for a preliminary injunction from the federal district court ordering a stop to the campaign. The preliminary injunction order then was affirmed by the three-judge court of appeals.

The court of appeals was careful to point out that not every misrepresentation concerning consumer tests results will result automatically in legal liability. But a lawsuit like the one Sassoon filed is appropriate, in the words of the published opinion, "where depictions of consumer test results or methodology are so significantly misleading that the reasonably intelligent consumer would be deceived about the product's inherent quality or characteristics."

Type of Data

The level at which attributes can be measured was discussed earlier. At that time it was pointed out that a useful classification involves nominal, ordinal, interval, and ratio scales of measurement. Consider again some of the main differences in the application of these scales. The nominal scale is used when categorizing objects. A letter or numeral is assigned to each category so that each number represents a distinct category. For instance, if individuals are to be classified by sex, the numbers 1 and 2 serve equally as well as the letters M and F for denoting males and females. The nominal scale remains undistorted under a one-to-one substitution of the numerals. Thus, the number 2 could be used to denote males and the number 1 to denote females without a loss of information. The mean and median are not appropriate measures of central tendency. The appropriate measure of central tendency is the mode. Only it remains unchanged under a one-to-one substitution of the numerals. Thus, if there are more females than males, the mode describes the category ''female'' regardless of whether we choose to call it 1, 2, or F.

The ordinal scale represents a higher level of measurement than the nominal because the numerals assigned are reflecting order as well as serving to identify the objects. For example, we might wish to classify students into three categories, such as good, average, and poor. We might simply choose to call the categories A, B, and C. Alternatively, we might use the numbers 1 = good, 2 = average, and 3 = poor, or perhaps the reverse, in which good = 3 and poor = 1. The schemes are equally fruitful as long as the numeral assignment is understood by all. The structure of an ordinal scale is undistorted by any one-to-one substitution that preserves the order, since only order is implied by the assignment of numerals. The median and the mode are now both legitimate measures of central tendency.

The assignment of numerals to objects using an interval scale conveys information about the magnitude of the differences between the objects. We can determine how much more one category is than another. We *cannot,* however, *compare the ratio of absolute magnitudes* of the objects; for example, A is five times larger than B. All comparisons must be made using differences between objects. The reason is that the interval scale contains an arbitrary zero. An interval scale is undistorted under linear transformations — that is, transformations of the form $y = b + cx$. The effect of this transformation is to shift the origin b units and multiply the unit of measurement by c, as in going from a Fahrenheit scale to a centigrade scale. The mean, the median, and the mode are all appropriate measures of central tendency.

The ratio scale is similar to the interval scale except that it has a natural zero point. Thus, it makes sense to say that A is twice as heavy or twice as tall as B, since both of the scales possess a natural zero. The ratio scale is undistorted under proportionate or scalar transformations — that is, transformations of the form $y = cx$. The effect of such a transformation is to change the scale of measurement by the factor c. The conversion of feet to inches is an example; c in this case would equal 12. All statistics appropriate for the interval scale are also appropriate for a ratio scale.

The analyst has to be very careful in interpreting numerical relationships to properly reflect the properties of the measurement scale. The user of information has to be equally cautious. Consider the following hypothetical ad claim, which is not too different from what one sees on television and in magazines.

> New Lustre gets your clothes 20 percent brighter and you need 50 percent less detergent compared to old Lustre. Furthermore, even for linens you can use water temperatures 30 percent lower than that required for old Lustre.

Probably, the "brighter" claim in this ad is based on homemakers' reactions to clothes washed with old Lustre. It is also likely that these perceptions were determined by having the respondents complete "dingy" to "bright" rating scales. Suppose, indeed, that a seven-point scale was employed and that old Lustre received an average score of five and new Lustre an average score of six; thus, the 20 percent brighter claim results from the calculation

$$\frac{\bar{x}_{new} - \bar{x}_{old}}{\bar{x}_{old}} (100) = \frac{6 - 5}{5} = 20 \text{ percent.}$$

The use of adjective scales like this highlights the disagreement between those who insist that most marketing measurements reflect ordinal measurement and those who argue that such scales can be treated as interval measures. There is some evidence to support each position. On the one hand, there have been several empirical studies demonstrating that descriptors that might appear to the scale developer to reflect equal increments of the characteristic are often not interpreted that way by those responding.[1] Research Realities 14.2, for example, depicts how sensitive the distribution of responses can be to the descriptors used to label the various categories. Of the two versions of each questionnaire that were administered to different samples of respondents, the main difference in each case was how the second highest and middle positions on the scales were described. Yet, the percentage responding "good" was different, as was the total distribution of the responses for the two versions in each case. The evidence also indicates that it is possible to develop questions in which the descriptors do reflect equal increments of the characteristic by the proper choice of descriptors — that is, by carefully choosing descriptors on the basis of their scale positions. The descriptors "remarkably good," "good," "neutral," "reasonably poor," and "extremely poor" could be used, for example, to approximate a five-point interval scale. While the debate rages, a reasonably balanced argument suggests the following:

1. It is very safe, and certainly productive, to treat the total score summed over a number of items as an interval scale;

2. It is sometimes safe to treat individual items as interval scales, such as when specific steps have been taken to ensure the intervality of the response categories; and

---

[1]James H. Myers and W. Gregory Warner, "Semantic Properties of Selected Evaluation Adjectives," *Journal of Marketing Research,* 5 (November 1968), pp. 409–412; Paul E. Spector, "Choosing Response Categories for Summated Rating Scales," *Journal of Applied Psychology,* 61 (September 1976), pp. 374–375; and Melvin R. Crask and Richard J. Fox, "An Exploration of the Interval Properties of Three Commonly Used Marketing Research Scales: A Magnitude Estimation Approach," *Journal of the Market Research Society,* 29 (July 1987), pp. 317–339.

It Depends on How It's Asked

Panel A: How would you rate the quality of your telephone service? Would you say it's (read scale)?

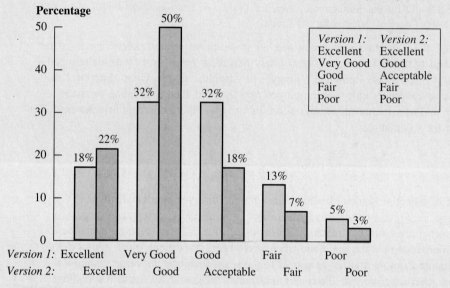

Version 1:	Version 2:
Excellent	Excellent
Very Good	Good
Good	Acceptable
Fair	Fair
Poor	Poor

Panel B: How would you rate the service of the U.S. Postal Service? Would you say it's (read scale)?

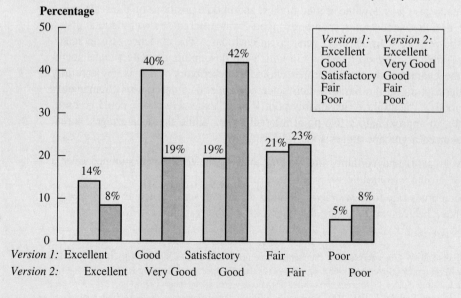

Version 1:	Version 2:
Excellent	Excellent
Good	Very Good
Satisfactory	Good
Fair	Fair
Poor	Poor

Source: Omar J. Bendikas, ''A Lot Depends on How It's Asked,'' *Telenation Reports* (Summer 1987), p. 4; and Lisa Lainer, ''It All Depends on How It's Asked,'' *Telenation Reports* (Spring 1988), p. 2, for the examples in Panels A and B, respectively.

3. It is always legitimate to treat the scale as ordinal when neither Condition 1 nor 2 is satisfied. Suppose that Condition 3 applied to the "dingy" to "bright" rating scale so that the descriptors anchoring the categories did not reflect equal increments of "brightness." The calculation and comparison of the difference in means would then be suspect.

Suppose, on the other hand, that appropriate procedures were employed, that the evaluation scale did reflect interval measurement, and that the calculation of means was appropriate. The "brighter" claim would still be in error, and for the same reason that the temperature claim is also probably erroneous. More likely than not, the temperature claim would be based on the fact that whereas old Lustre required 200°F water to be effective, new Lustre requires only 140° F water; that is, new Lustre can operate effectively with temperatures

$$\frac{200 - 140}{200} (100) = 30 \text{ percent}$$

lower. We have previously seen, however, that the Fahrenheit scale is an interval scale because it possesses an arbitrary zero and that the calculation of ratios with such scales is meaningless. To see the folly in this exercise, simply convert the 200°F and 140°F temperatures to their centigrade equivalents of 93.3°C and 60.0°C, respectively. Now you can use 36 percent lower temperatures with new Lustre. The same argument applies to the brightness comparison. Unless the "dingy" to "bright" scale was ratio, it would be incorrect to divide the difference in mean ratings for the two formulations by the original rating.

Thus, only one of the three ad claims is probably legitimate — the claim that 50 percent less detergent is needed with new Lustre. The scale here is of the ratio variety, and if one uses, say, ½ cup of new Lustre whereas one used 1 cup of old Lustre, then indeed one needs 50 percent less detergent. This is not to say that the claims could not be supported with data. For instance, the temperature claim follows if all measurements were made on a Kelvin scale, which possesses an absolute zero. Similarly, the brightness claim would follow if measurements were made using the integrating sphere.[2] The brightness claim does not follow, though, from the aggregation of consumer perceptions.

An understanding of the level of measurement underlying data is crucial to proper interpretation. Incidentally, this comment is equally valid for day-to-day living. For instance, the other night on the news, a meteorologist reported that the month of December was 38 percent colder than normal. The statement was based on the fact that, although the average mean temperature in December is 40°F, this past December it was 25°F or 38 percent colder. In fact, using the proper Kelvin scale, it was only 3 percent colder than normal. Fortunately the meteorologist did not translate this into a 38 percent increase in fuel consumption.

---

[2]The integrating sphere measures the amount of light reflected from an object placed in the sphere. Black objects do not reflect any of the light directed at them, while white objects reflect 100 percent of the light directed into the sphere. See, for instance, K. S. Gibson, *Spectrophotometry,* National Bureau of Standards, Circular Number 484, 1949.

Research Design

A second consideration that affects the choice of analysis technique is the research design used to generate the data. Some of the more important questions the analyst has to face involve the dependency of observations, the number of observations per object, the number of groups being analyzed, and the control exercised over the variables of interest. Consider several hypothetical cases.

Sample Independence   Consider first the question of dependent or independent samples. Without worrying at this point about the details of the research design (and whether it was good or poor), suppose that you were interested in determining the effectiveness of a mailed brochure. Suppose, too, that the measure of effectiveness was attitudes toward a product, that the scale used to measure attitudes was interval, and in particular that the research design was

$$X \qquad O_1$$
$$O_2,$$

where O_1 represents the attitudes of those who received the brochure and O_2 the attitudes of those who did not receive the brochure. In this case, the samples are independent. The O_2 measures do not depend on the O_1 measures. An appropriate test of significance would allow for the independence of the samples. In this case, the t test for the difference in two means would be appropriate.[3]

Consider another research design that could be diagrammed thus:

$$O_1 \qquad X \qquad O_2.$$

There are again two sets of observations, O_1 and O_2. Now, however, they are made on the same individuals, before and after receiving the brochure. The measurements are not independent, and a t test of the difference between two means is inappropriate. The observations must be analyzed in pairs. The focus is on differences in attitudes per individual before and after exposure to the brochure. A paired difference test for statistical significance should be used in this case.[4]

Number of Groups   Consider next the question of number of groups being compared. Suppose that you were interested in the relative effectiveness of two different brochures and you decided to explore the question through a controlled experiment. In the experiment, some respondents receive X_1, others get X_2, and a third group receives neither. The design can be diagrammed:

$$X_1 \qquad O_1$$
$$X_2 \qquad O_2$$
$$O_3.$$

---

[3] The t test for the difference in means is discussed in Chapter 15.
[4] The paired difference statistical test is discussed in Chapter 15.

This design parallels that for the single brochure, except for the addition of the alternative brochure X_2. Now, however, there are three groups (two experimental and one control) whereas previously there were two (one experimental and one control). The t test for the difference in two means is no longer applicable; the problem is best handled through analysis-of-variance procedures.[5]

Number of Variables Let us return to the one-brochure design to illustrate how the number of measurements per object affects the analysis procedure. Previously we have used attitudes toward the advertised product as the measure of effectiveness of the brochure; specifically, we contrasted the attitudes of the "receivers" with those of the "nonreceivers." Suppose that we believe this attitude to be a legitimate measure of effectiveness, but the sales impact of the brochure must also be considered. That is, we now wish to contrast the "exposed" and "unexposed" groups not only in terms of their differences in attitude but also in terms of the sales of the product to each group. The design has not changed. It is still diagrammed

$$X \quad O_1$$
$$O_2,$$

only now O_1 and O_2 represent measures of both sales and attitudes.

Of course, one way to proceed would be to test separately for the differences in attitudes and the differences in sales to the two groups. What happens, though, if the two groups differ only slightly on each criterion so that neither of the univariate tests detects a significant difference? Would we conclude that the brochure had no impact even though the average attitude score and average sales were higher for the experimental group? Or do we conclude that the small, nonsignificant differences, taken together, indicate a real difference? On the other hand, let's say that the individual tests are statistically significant but inconsistent; that is, one result is more favorable to the control group and the other to the experimental group. Do we take the favorable and unfavorable results at their face value, or do we take the position that one of them represents a Type I error and in reality is attributable to chance?[6] To answer this question (and it becomes much more conceptually difficult as the number of measurements per object increases), we need to have some means of looking at the differences among groups when several characteristics are considered simultaneously. This type of problem is handled using multivariate statistical procedures.

Variable Control Another important question in analysis involves the control of variables that can affect the result. Return to the one-brochure design

$$X \quad O_1$$
$$O_2,$$

---

[5]Analysis of variance is discussed in the appendix to Chapter 15.

[6]Type I error is discussed in the appendix to this chapter.

in which the emphasis is on the differences in attitudes between the two groups. One variable that would certainly seem to determine attitudes is previous usage of the product. If so, in the experimental design, the analyst would like to control for prior usage to minimize its effect. A good way of doing this would be to make the experimental and control groups equal with respect to prior usage by matching, by randomization, or by some combination of these approaches. If this control procedure is followed, the t test for analyzing the difference in two means can legitimately be employed. If the control is not affected but attitudes do depend on prior use of the product, the conclusions produced using the t test will be in error to the extent that the two groups differ in their previous use of the product. One way to adjust for these differences is by allowing prior use to be a covariate — that is, by regressing attitudes on use and adjusting the attitude scores represented by O_1 and O_2 by the resulting regression equation.[7] The adjusted scores for the experimental and control groups would then be compared.

Assumptions Underlying Test Statistic

Also underlying the choice of a statistical method of analysis is a consideration of the assumptions supporting the various test statistics. Examine once again (you will be glad to know for the last time) the test for the differences in attitudes toward the product of those who received the brochure and those who did not. The t test for the difference in two means was deemed appropriate for this analysis. Therefore, let us look at the assumptions implicit in the choice of this statistical test.

The samples are assumed to have been drawn independently of each other. Further, it is assumed that the individuals composing the experimental group come from a population with unknown mean μ_1 and unknown variance σ_1^2, that those in the control group come from a population with unknown mean μ_2 and unknown variance σ_2^2, and that attitudes toward the product are *normally distributed* in each of these populations. It is also assumed that the variances of the two populations are equal — that is, $\sigma_1^2 = \sigma_2^2$; thus, a pooled estimator for the overall variance is warranted.[8] In sum, the assumptions

1. are independent samples;
2. have normal distribution of the characteristic of interest in each population; and
3. have equal variances in the two populations.

The t test is more sensitive to certain violations of these assumptions than others. For example, it still works well with respect to violations of the normality assumption but is quite sensitive to violations of the equal-variance assumption. When the violation

---

[7]See Paul E. Green and Donald S. Tull, "Covariance Analysis in Marketing Experimentation," *Journal of Advertising Research,* 6 (June 1966), pp. 45–53, for a discussion of some of the uncontrolled but measurable influences common to marketing experiments as well as a discussion of some other useful outputs of covariance analysis. See Geoffrey Keppel, *Design and Analyses: A Researcher's Handbook,* 2nd ed. (Englewood Cliffs, N.J.: Prentice-Hall, Inc., 1982), pp. 481–515, for a general discussion of the method of covariance analysis. For an example using it, see Marjorie Wall, John Liefeld, and Louise A. Heslop, "Impact of Country-of-Origin Cues on Consumer Judgments in Multi-Cue Situations: A Covariance Analysis," *Journal of the Academy of Marketing Science,* 19 (Spring 1991), pp. 105–113.

[8]The assumption of equality of variances is not mandatory. When the variances cannot be assumed to be equal, though, the "proper procedure" is shrouded in controversy. There is a vast statistical literature on this condition, which is known as the Behrens-Fisher problem.

is "too severe," the conclusions drawn are inappropriate. Yet it is surprising how little attention is paid to these underlying conditions in published research. At least little mention is made of the tests used to verify that the assumptions were satisfied. This is surprising in view of the availability of such checks. For instance, the independent-samples assumption can be checked by analyzing the sampling plan employed. The normality assumption can be investigated through a χ^2 goodness-of-fit test or Kolmogorov-Smirnov test, and the equality of the variances can be examined through an F test for homogeneity of variances.[9]

This is not the time or the place to discuss how such analyses would be conducted, nor to criticize the t test for differences in two means. Our purpose is simply to illustrate the basic fact that statistical tests depend on certain assumptions for their validity. If the assumptions are not met, there are several things that analysts can do. Perhaps the assumptions can be satisfied through some transformation (for example, change from actual units to log units). If not, analysts can perhaps choose a different test statistic that employs different assumptions. Perhaps they might even employ a distribution-free statistical test.[10] In any case, careful analysts will not neglect the assumptions that underlie the technique, nor will they blindly assume that all the conditions for a valid test are satisfied. Analysts will be too concerned about the correctness of the results to neglect a check of assumptions.

ETHICAL DILEMMA 14.2

A member of your research staff has submitted the results of an experiment to you, and you note with pleasure that all the hypotheses are fulfilled at $p \leq 0.05$. The fact that they are all fulfilled at exactly $p \leq 0.05$ eventually arouses your suspicions, however. When challenged, your staff member happily explains: "Oh, yes, I rounded down some 0.06s and 0.07s. Do you remember how you explained to me that measurement is by convention? And how $p \leq 0.05$ is an arbitrary number selected to be significant by general agreement, although it is not very logical to have $p \leq 0.05$ be significant but $p \leq 0.06$ be insignificant? Well, I agree that it's not logical, so I decided that p levels close to 0.05 could be rounded to 0.05 without any harm being done."

- Is your researcher's position reasonable?
- If you do not agree with a standard, does that mean that you can cheat to meet it?

---

[9]The chi-square goodness-of-fit test and the Kolmogorov-Smirnov test are discussed in Chapter 15. Most introductory statistics books discuss the F test for the equality of variances.

[10]A *distribution-free statistical test* is one that involves minimal assumptions. The somewhat misleading nomenclature **nonparametric test** is often used interchangeably to distinguish such techniques from the **parametric tests**. The parametric tests include such tests as the t, z, or F and typically involve a greater number of and more rigorous assumptions. The nonparametric label is inappropriate for distribution-free tests because the researcher does, in fact, try to generate statements about population parameters with these tests. The emphasis is still on parameters, although the specific parameter in question may change; for example, the median rather than the mean is used as the measure of central tendency. For discussion of some of the more popular nonparametric tests, see Jean Dickinson Gibbons and Subhabrata Chakraborti, *Nonparametric Statistical Inference,* 3rd ed. (New York: Marcel Dekker, Inc., 1992).

OVERVIEW OF STATISTICAL PROCEDURES

In the previous section some of the more important considerations in the choice of analysis technique were highlighted. Perhaps the section raised more questions than answers. This section will introduce some of the answers by overviewing the statistical techniques discussed in Chapters 15 to 17. Such an overview must necessarily be brief. However, it should serve to direct you to the section or sections that discuss the techniques appropriate for a given problem. Figures 14.1 and 14.2 should assist in this regard. The figures illustrate the sequence of questions an analyst needs to ask and answer in order to determine the appropriate statistical technique.[11]

The most important task in preparing to run the maze of statistical methods is deciding whether the problem is of a univariate or multivariate nature. The problem is **univariate** if there is a single measurement of each of the *n* sample objects, or if there are several measurements of each of the *n* observations but each variable is to be analyzed in isolation. In a **multivariate** problem, there are two or more measures of each observation (e.g., number of new accounts generated and total sales by salesperson), and the variables are to be analyzed simultaneously. Given that there are multiple measures per sample observation, we find ourselves dealing with two distinct emphases: the search for differences and the investigation of association. The search for group differences is the multivariate extension of much univariate analysis. These techniques are not discussed in this book,[12] although techniques for investigating association are.

Univariate Analysis

Figure 14.1 overviews the subsequent decisions that must be made given that the problem is univariate. Let us review several of the questions that an analyst can ask in deciding among the procedures.

A useful first question involves the level of measurement of the data. Is the variable nominal, ordinal, interval, or ratio scaled? If it is nominal or ordinal, distribution-free (nonparametric) statistical procedures are appropriate. If the data are either interval or ratio scaled, the variable is metric, and parametric procedures apply. Actually, from a *statistical theory perspective,* the level of measurement is *not* important when selecting techniques. As Lord said so elegantly 30 years ago, "the numbers do not know where they come from"[13] — meaning that statistical techniques do not "know" what the level

---

[11]There are computer programs available that guide analysts through a sequence of decisions to the proper choice of statistical technique. See, for example, *Statistical Navigator Professional*®.

[12]See P. J. Rulon and W. D. Brooks, "On Statistical Tests of Group Differences," in Dean K. Whittla, ed., *Handbook of Measurement and Assessment in Behavioral Sciences* (Reading, Mass.: Addison-Wesley, 1968), pp. 60–99, for a succinct overview of the issues and procedures.

[13]F. M. Lord, "On the Statistical Treatment of Football Numbers," *American Psychologist,* 8 (1953), p. 751. While Lord was one of the first to contradict Stevens' assertion that his four levels of measurement had important implications for choosing statistical techniques, a number of authors later made the same point. Gaito points out, for example, that "Scale properties do not enter into any of the mathematical requirements for the various statistical procedures. I have not known of any mathematical statistician who agreed with the Stevens' misconception. A number have indicated in print that this suggestion is erroneous." John Gaito, "Measurement Scales and Statistics: Resurgence of an Old Misconception," *Psychological Bulletin,* 87 (1980), p. 564. See also J. Paul Peter and Peter A. Dacin, "Measurement Scales, Permissible Statistics, and Marketing Research" in Terry L. Childers and Scott B. MacKenzie, eds., *Marketing Theory and Applications,* Vol. 2 (Chicago: American Marketing Association, 1991), pp. 275–283.

FIGURE 14.1 Flow Diagram for Choosing a Univariate Statistical Test

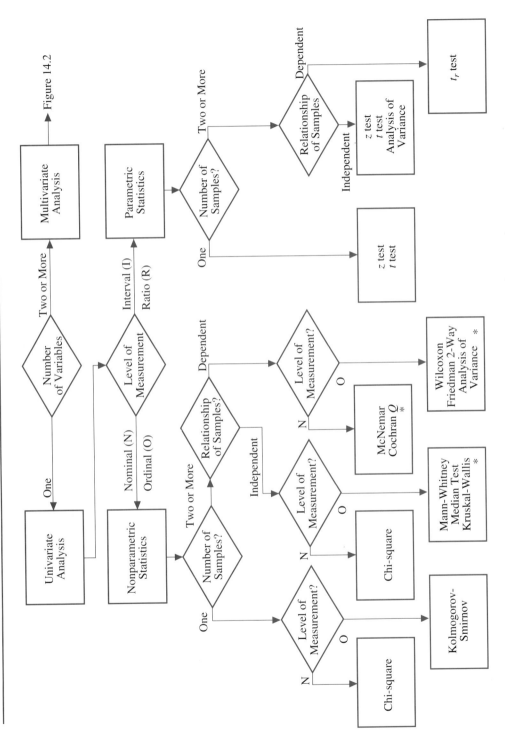

*These tests are not discussed in this book, although they are useful for some problems in marketing research.

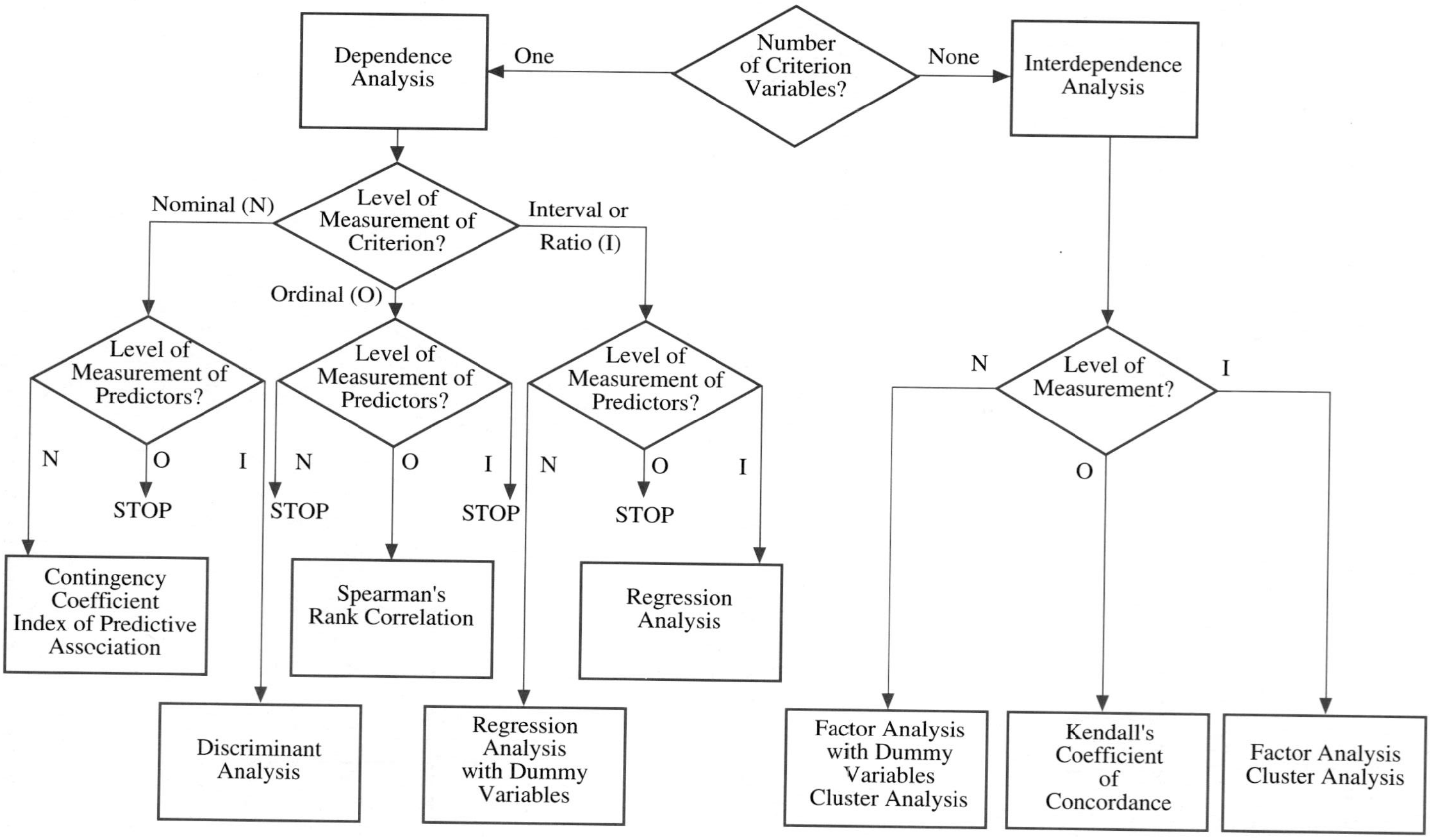

FIGURE 14.2   Flow Diagram for Choosing a Multivariate Statistical Test

of measurement of the input data is. Rather, it is the *assumptions* that are *key* in determining whether a particular statistical technique is appropriate for analyzing a particular set of data. If the assumptions are satisfied, or if the statistical technique is robust (works well anyway) to violations of the assumptions, the technique can be used. Although scale of measurement may not be important from a statistical theory perspective, it is important from a *measurement theory perspective*. In this sense, it is important that the numbers assigned be meaningful given the attributes of concern, that we are careful in interpreting what the numbers imply with respect to the "amount of the attribute" possessed by the object, and that we take care in how we manipulate the numbers when generating meaning from the data. Further, it is difficult even to address the topic of how to choose a statistical test without considering the level of measurement, because the level of measurement often provides important clues about statistical assumptions. In sum, level of measurement provides a useful heuristic or map for getting an analyst in the right ball park. Consequently, the heuristic is employed to organize the discussion on choosing a statistical test, although one needs to be conscious of the fact that it may be perfectly appropriate to apply a parametric test, say, to data that are only ordinal.[14]

The analyst must then determine whether a single sample or multiple samples are involved. An hypothesis about the mean income of residents of Chicago is a single-sample analysis. If we were interested in determining how the mean income of Chicago residents compares with that of New York residents, two independent samples are involved — that is, the population of Chicago and the population of New York. Suppose that we were interested in comparing the mean income in Chicago now with the mean income five years ago; again, two samples are involved. Whether the samples are dependent or independent depends on the specifics of the sampling procedure employed. Let's assume that the recent sample was selected without considering the sample five years ago. The samples are then independent. Suppose, instead, that the study's emphasis was one of determining the income changes that occurred among the families composing the first sample. The samples are then dependent; the latest income measurements are related to the earlier incomes, and those statistical methods that treat dependent samples should be used.

Suppose that we are interested in how average income and average educational levels compare in Chicago and New York. Now there are two (multiple) measures —

---

[14]The product moment correlation coefficient, for example, has been found to be quite robust to violations of the "continuous variable" assumption on which it is based. Thus, it can be used to assess the degree of association between two variables when the data are intervally scaled or ordinally scaled, or even when one or both of the variables are dichotomies. See, for example, Donald G. Morrison, "Regression with Discrete Random Variables: The Effect on R^2," *Journal of Marketing Research,* 9 (August 1972), pp. 338–340; or Jum Nunnally, *Psychometric Theory,* 2nd ed. (New York: McGraw-Hill, 1978), especially pp. 117–150. A number of other parametric techniques using the *t* and *F* distributions have also been found to be quite robust to violations of their assumptions and work particularly well with ordinal data. See, for example, Sanford Lobovitz, "Some Observations on Measurement and Statistics," *Social Forces,* 46 (1967), pp. 151–160; Sanford Lobovitz, "The Assignment of Numbers to Rank Order Categories," *American Sociological Review,* 35 (1970), pp. 515–524; B. O. Baker, C. D. Hardyck, and L. F. Petrinovich, "Weak Measurement vs. Strong Statistics: An Empirical Critique of S. S. Stevens' Proscriptions on Statistics," *Educational and Psychological Measurement,* 26 (1966), pp. 291–309; John Gaito, "Scale Classification and Statistics," *Psychological Review,* 67 (1960), pp. 277–278; Mark Traylor, "Ordinal and Interval Scaling," *Journal of the Market Research Society,* 25 (October 1983), pp. 297–303.

income and education — for two independent samples — residents of Chicago and New York. One of the multivariate tests for group differences could be used.

Multivariate Analysis

As was stated previously, multivariate procedures are distinguished by the fact that each of n sample observations bears the value of p different variates. The p variate condition means that additional considerations must be dealt with in choosing from among available procedures. One of these considerations, previously mentioned, was the investigation of association and the determination of group differences, and this latter condition was categorized with univariate techniques. The following discussion will, therefore, emphasize association.

Two considerations dictate a choice of technique here: the type of scale used in making the measurements and the role the individual variables will play in the specific model being discussed. The most common distinction is the one between independent (antecedent or predictor) variables and dependent (consequent or criterion) variables. The distinction suggests a division of the subject into two parts: dependence and interdependence. In dependence analysis, one (or more) of the variables is selected to serve as a dependent or criterion variable, and the analyst seeks to investigate how it depends on the other variables. In interdependence analysis, none of the variables is selected as special in the sense of serving as a dependent or criterion variable. Rather, the emphasis in the analysis is on the relationships among the whole set of variables as a set.

Unfortunately, these dual considerations of scale and role of each variable interact to generate a somewhat complex classification scheme. The problem is particularly acute because there may be a great many variables involved, and they may represent different levels of measurement. One has to simultaneously entertain the following questions in order to determine the appropriate method:

1. Are one or more of the variables to be singled out for separate treatment as dependent or criterion variables? If so, how many and what level of measurement do they reflect?

2. How many independent variables are there? What level of measurement does each of these variables reflect?

Figure 14.2 illustrates the sequence of decisions involved in the choice of multivariate statistical techniques. The techniques were chosen because they represent the most useful procedures for the marketing research analyst, although all cases to which they are applicable are not shown in the figure. For instance, one could convert nominal or ordinal variables to dummy variables and then run a multivariate regression analysis.[15] The figure is designed to clearly indicate the types of problems for which multivariate techniques of association are appropriate. The chapters on analysis should place some flesh on the skeleton so that you will be able to picture some of the modifications that are possible.

---

[15] Dummy variables are discussed in Chapter 16.

Note in the figure that technique is highly dependent on the number and scaling of the variables. Change either of these and the technique typically changes. For instance, consider factor analysis and multiple regression analysis. In multiple regression analysis, one of the variables is singled out for special treatment as a criterion variable, and the relationship between the single criterion variable and the predictor variables is investigated. If the emphasis were on determining the relationships that exist among all the variables considered at once, the problem would be dealt with using factor analysis procedures.

Similarly, suppose that the variable singled out as the criterion variable reflected a nominal scale of measurement involving two categories (for example, purchase of Product A or B). It would then be appropriate to use linear discriminant analysis rather than multivariate regression.

SUMMARY

The basic considerations involved in choosing a statistical method with which to analyze the collected data were discussed in this chapter. Scale of measurement, the research design, and the assumptions underlying the test statistic all affect this choice.

When considering the scale of measurement, an analyst must be careful to distinguish between ideas of measurement theory and statistical theory. The origin of the numbers is important from the standpoint of the interpretation of the results. That is, from a measurement theory perspective, it makes a difference whether the level of measurement is nominal, ordinal, interval, or ratio. The level of measurement does not make a difference from a statistical theory perspective, however. The key in dictating a choice of technique in that case is the assumptions underlying the technique. The assumptions should be satisfied or the technique should be robust to violations of the assumptions at issue if the technique is to be used to analyze the data. Even here, though, scale of measurement provides a useful heuristic for identifying statistical techniques for which the assumptions are likely to be satisfied.

Several questions in the research design affect choice of method, including the independence of the sample observations, the number of groups, the number of variables, and the control exercised over those variables likely to affect the results.

In choosing from among the many available tests, the analyst needs to ask a number of questions, the first of which is whether the problem is univariate or multivariate. If univariate, the next questions are whether the variable reflects nonmetric or metric measurement, whether a single sample or multiple samples are involved, and if multiple, whether the samples are dependent or independent.

In multivariate analysis, there are two or more variables to be analyzed simultaneously. If one (or more) of these variables is considered a criterion variable that is to be related to some other variables, the problem is one of dependence analysis. If we are solely concerned with the relationships within and among the set of variables considered together, the problem is one of interdependence analysis. The role of each variable in the analysis and the level of measurement reflected by each variable interact to produce a complex classification scheme of multivariate techniques.

Questions

1. What basic considerations underlie the choice of a statistical test? Explain.
2. What are the basic levels of measurement? How does the type of data affect the choice of a statistical test?
3. Discuss the difference between independent and dependent samples, and indicate how sample independence/dependence affects the choice of a statistical test.
4. Discuss the difference between one-, two-, and three-group analyses, and indicate how the number of groups affects the choice of a statistical test.
5. Discuss the difference between a univariate analysis and a multivariate analysis. What are the problems inherent in treating a multivariate problem as a number of univariate problems?
6. What is the distinction between a multivariate test of group differences and a multivariate test of the association among the variables?
7. Discuss the difference between dependence and interdependence analysis.

Applications and Problems

1. Evaluate the two following hypothetical advertising claims. Do you think the claims are legitimate?
   a. "Con-Air gives you twice as much satisfaction while traveling — at a price 50% lower than other major airlines."
   b. "In blind taste tests, the majority of people preferred our beer twice as much as any other major brand of beer. Is it any wonder we sell one and one-half times more beer than our nearest competitor?"
2. Discuss whether the use of adjective scales reflects ordinal or interval measurement.
3. Discuss the importance of the level of measurement from a statistical theory perspective and measurement theory perspective.
4. The Tobacco Institute wanted to test the effectiveness of two booklets that discuss the issue of whether advertising causes children to start smoking. A random sample of 1,200 was selected from a mailing list of 10,000 people. The sample was randomly divided into three groups of size 400 each; one group received one version of the booklet, the second received the other version, and the third group received neither booklet. One week later the attitudes of all three groups about whether advertising causes children to smoke were measured on an interval scale.
   a. Present the experimental design in diagrammatic form.
   b. What analysis technique would you recommend? Why?
5. A large national chain of department stores wanted to test the effectiveness of a promotional display for a new brand of household appliances. Fifty stores were randomly selected from a total of 263 stores. The sample of 50 stores was randomly divided into two groups of 25 stores each. Only one group used the promotional display. For three weeks, sales of the new brand of appliances were monitored for both groups.
   a. Present the experimental design in diagrammatic form.
   b. What analysis technique would you recommend? Why?

6. A medium-sized life insurance company was concerned about its poor public image resulting from a major lawsuit. The public relations department designed a 20-page bulletin that was to be mailed to all existing and prospective clients and shareholders in order to allay any negative feelings that might have resulted from the bad publicity. Prior to incurring the expenses of the complete mailing, the department randomly selected 300 clients and shareholders and mailed the 20-page bulletin to them. Attitudes toward the company were measured on an interval scale before and after sending the bulletin. However, top management was dissatisfied with this experiment and requested that another random sample of 500 clients and shareholders be generated. This sample was to be randomly divided into two groups of 250 respondents each. The bulletin was to be mailed to one group of respondents. Attitudes towards the company were to be measured for both groups on an interval scale two weeks after mailing the bulletin.

  a. Present the experimental designs in diagrammatic form.

  b. What analysis technique would you recommend for each? Why?

7. A large national automobile manufacturer wanted to relate sales of its latest models by area to the demographic composition of each area as measured by such variables as average income, average size of household, average age of head of household, and so on.

  a. Is this dependence or interdependence analysis? Why?

  b. Are there any criterion or predictor variables? If so, what are they? Identify the level of measurement of each.

  c. On the basis of the preceding information, what multivariate procedure would you recommend?

8. A medium-sized department store wanted to determine its customers' attitudes, opinions, interests, and so on using a five-point Likert scale.

  a. Is this dependence or interdependence analysis? Why?

  b. Are there any criterion or predictor variables? If so, what are they? Identify the level of measurement of each.

  c. On the basis of the preceding information, what multivariate procedure would you recommend?

9. A large soft-drink manufacturer conducted a survey to determine customers' likes and dislikes about a new diet soft drink. The "lightness" of the soft drink was perceived as being one of the three most important soft drink attributes. The "low calorie" attribute was not ranked as high as "lightness." The company was wondering if most consumers believed that low calorie content of the soft drink was associated with lightness.

  a. Is this dependence or interdependence analysis? Why?

  b. Are there any criterion or predictor variables? If so, what are they? Identify the level of measurement of each.

  c. On the basis of the preceding information, what multivariate procedure would you recommend?

10. Discuss the advantages of Design a over Design b. Does Design a also have advantages over Design c? Explain.

  a. $O_1 \quad X_1 \quad O_2$
       $O_3 \qquad\quad O_4$

  b. $O_1 \quad X_1 \quad O_2$

  c. $X_1 \quad O_1$
           O_2

11. A survey asked users of a new deodorant product how satisfied they were with the product's performance using the following scale:

Very Satisfied	Satisfied	Neither Satisfied nor Dissatisfied	Satisfied	Very Dissatisfied
1	2	3	4	5

A research analyst noticed an interesting difference between male and female respondents. The mean satisfaction score for this product was 30 percent higher for women than men. Given the scale, is this a valid calculation? What are valid calculations? Can any comparison between men and women be made with these data?

12. A political opinion poll was conducted concerning the performance of two presidential candidates. Two hundred respondents were asked to rate Candidates A and B on a seven-point scale. In summarizing the results, a pooled sample t test was used to show that there existed significant differences in the mean scores at $p \leq 0.05$ for Candidates A and B. Discuss whether the t test is an appropriate test to use in this circumstance. Have any of the underlying assumptions of the test been violated in this example?

13. On a product-tracking survey, the following three categories were used to capture consumers' knowledge and trial of different products: "Never heard of the product," "heard of the product but have never bought the product," and "have bought the product." These categories were coded 1, 3, 6. The research team leader changed the codes to 1, 2, 3 so that the scores reflected equal intervals. Explain why the team leader's correction is unnecessary and unwarranted.

14. With the introduction of grocery-store scanners, elaborate marketing experiments can be run in the field. For example, a company wishing to test the effects of a new advertising campaign on its breakfast cereal sales designed the following test to determine which campaign was the most effective. Six cities were chosen for this experiment. In three cities, viewers saw the new advertisement, and in the other three cities, viewers continued to see the traditional advertising campaign.
    a. Present the experimental design in diagrammatic form.
    b. What analysis technique would you recommend? What assumptions underlie the recommended test?
    c. Given the company's research objective, discuss alternative designs.

15. The following figure shows the satisfaction scores obtained from a survey on a new car model. Looking at the plot, can the t test be used to check for statistically significant differences in the satisfaction scores between these two groups? Explain.

**Degree of
Satisfaction**

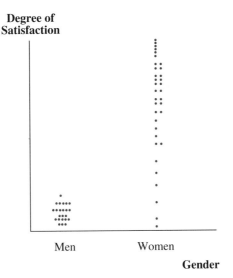

Men   Women

Gender

 Thorndike Sports Equipment Video Case

1. What are the benefits of sponsoring a player in the racquetball tournament?

2. Is it possible to quantify the benefits received from sponsoring a player in the racquetball tournament?

3. Is it possible to measure the exposure Thorndike receives from sponsoring a player in this racquetball tournament?

4. What other promotions would allow Thorndike to fully capitalize on the racquetball tournament as a marketing opportunity? Along with your proposals for promotions, design means of tracking the exposure that resulted from these promotions.

APPENDIX 14A

Hypothesis Testing

Many procedures discussed in the next few chapters are used to test specific hypotheses. Therefore, it seems useful to review some basic concepts that underlie hypothesis testing in classical statistical theory, such as framing the null hypothesis or setting the risk of error in making a wrong decision, as well as the general steps involved in testing the hypothesis.[1]

---

[1]With respect to hypothesis testing, Bayesian statistical theory assumes a different posture than classical statistics. Because classical statistical-significance testing procedures are more commonly used in marketing research, only the basic elements underlying classical statistical theory are presented here.

NULL HYPOTHESIS

One simple fact underlies the statistical test of a hypothesis: A hypothesis may be rejected but can never be accepted except tentatively, because further evidence may prove it wrong. In other words, one rejects the hypothesis or does not reject the hypothesis on the basis of the evidence at hand. It is wrong to conclude, though, that since the hypothesis was not rejected, it can necessarily be accepted as valid.

A naive qualitative example should illustrate the issue.[2] Let's say we are testing the hypothesis that "John Doe is a poor man." We observe that Doe dines in cheap restaurants, lives in the slum area of the city in a run-down building, wears worn and tattered clothes, and so on. Although his behavior is certainly consistent with that of a poor man, we cannot "accept" the hypothesis that he is poor. It is possible that Doe may, in fact, be rich but extremely tight in his spending. We can continue gathering information about him, but for the moment we must decide not to reject the hypothesis. One single observation, for example, that indicates he has a six-figure bank account or that he owns 100,000 shares of AT&T stock would allow the immediate rejection of the hypothesis and the conclusion that "John Doe is rich."

Thus, researchers need to recognize that in the absence of perfect information (such as is the case when sampling), the best they can do is form hypotheses or conjectures about what is true. Further, their conclusions about these conjectures can be wrong, and thus there is always some probability of error in accepting any hypothesis. Statistical parlance holds that researchers commit a Type I error when they reject a true null hypothesis and thereby accept the alternative; they commit a Type II error when they do not reject a false null hypothesis, which they should given that it is false. The null hypothesis is assumed to be *true* for the purpose of the test. Such an assumption is used to generate knowledge about how the various sample estimates produced under the sampling plan might vary. Further, researchers need to be aware that Type I errors can be specified to be no more than some specific amount (e.g., ≤ 0.05), whereas Type II errors are functions.[3]

The upshot of these considerations is that the researcher needs to frame the null hypothesis in such a way that its rejection leads to the acceptance of the desired conclusion — that is, the statement or condition that the researcher wishes to verify. For example, suppose that a firm was considering introducing a new product if it could be expected to secure more than 10 percent of the market. The proper way to frame the hypotheses then would be

$$H_0 : \pi \leq 0.10,$$

$$H_a : \pi > 0.10.$$

If the evidence leads to the rejection of H_0, the researcher would then be able to

---

[2] The author expresses his appreciation to Dr. B. Venkatesh of Burke Marketing Institute for suggesting this example to illustrate the rationale behind the framing of hypotheses.

[3] We will have more to say about Type I and Type II errors later.

"accept" the alternative — that the product could be expected to secure more than 10 percent of the market — and the product would be introduced, since such a result would have been unlikely to occur if the null was indeed true. If H_0 cannot be rejected, though, the product should not be introduced unless more evidence to the contrary becomes available. The example as framed involves the use of a "one-tailed" statistical test; the alternate hypothesis is expressed directionally — that is, as being greater than 0.10. The one-tailed test is most commonly used in marketing research, although there are research problems that warrant a "two-tailed" test. For example, the market share achieved by the new formulation of Product X is no different from that achieved by the old formulation, which was 10 percent. A two-tailed test would be expressed as

$$H_0 : \pi = 0.10,$$
$$H_a : \pi \neq 0.10.$$

There is no direction implied with the alternate hypothesis; the proportion is simply expressed as not being equal to 0.10.

The one-tailed test is more commonly used than the two-tailed test in marketing research for two reasons. First, there is typically some preferred direction to the outcome — for example, the greater the market share, the higher the product quality, or the lower the expenses, the better. The two-tailed alternative is used when there is no preferred direction in the outcome or when the research is meant to demonstrate the existence of a difference but not its direction. Second, the one-tailed test, when it is appropriate, is more powerful statistically than the two-tailed alternative.

TYPES OF ERRORS

Because the result of statistically testing a null hypothesis would be to reject it or not reject it, two types of errors may occur. First, the null hypothesis may be rejected when it is true. Second, it may not be rejected when it is false and, therefore, should be rejected. These two errors are, respectively, termed **Type I error** and **Type II error** (or **α error** and **β error,** which are the probabilities associated with their occurrence). The two types of errors are not complementary, in that $\alpha + \beta \neq 1$.

To illustrate each type of error and to demonstrate that they are not complementary, consider a judicial analogy.[4] Since under U.S. criminal law, a person is innocent until proven guilty, the judge and jury are always testing the hypothesis of innocence. The defendant may, in fact, be either innocent or guilty, but based on the evidence the court may reach either verdict regardless of the true situation. Table 14A.1 displays the possibilities. If the defendant is innocent and the jury finds the person innocent, or if the defendant is guilty and the jury finds him or her guilty, the jury has made a correct decision. If, however, the defendant truly is innocent and the jury finds the person guilty, or if the defendant is guilty and the jury finds him or her innocent, they have

---

[4]R. W. Jastram, *Elements of Statistical Inference* (Berkeley, Calif.: Book Company, 1947), p. 44.

Table **14A.1**   **Judicial Analogy Illustrating Decision Error**

	True Situation: Defendant Is	
Verdict	**Innocent**	**Guilty**
Innocent	Correct decision: probability $= 1 - \alpha$	Error: probability $= \beta$
Guilty	Error: probability $= \alpha$	Correct decision: probability $= 1 - \beta$

made an error. The jury must decide one way or the other, and thus the probabilities of the jury's decision must sum vertically to 1. If we let α represent the probability of incorrectly finding the person guilty when he or she is innocent, then $1 - \alpha$ must be the probability of correctly finding him or her innocent. Similarly, β and $1 - \beta$ represent the probabilities of findings of innocence and guilt when the person is guilty. It is intuitively obvious that $\alpha + \beta$ is not equal to 1, although later discussion will indicate that β must increase when α is reduced if other things remain the same. Since our society generally holds that finding an innocent person guilty is more serious than finding a guilty person innocent, α error is reduced as much as possible in our legal system by requiring proof of guilt "beyond any reasonable doubt."

Table 14A.2 contains the analogous research situation. Just as the defendant's true status is unknown to the jury, the true situation regarding the null hypothesis is unknown to the researcher. The researcher's dilemma parallels that of the jury in that he or she has limited information with which to work. Suppose that the null hypothesis is true. If the researcher concludes it is false, he or she has made a Type I error. The significance level associated with a statistical test indicates the probability with which this error may be made. Because sample information will always be somewhat incomplete, there will always be some α error. The only way it can be avoided is by never rejecting the null hypothesis (never finding anyone guilty, in the judicial analogy). The *confidence level* of a statistical test is $1 - \alpha$, and the more confident we want to be of a statistical result, the

Table **14A.2**   **Types of Errors in Hypothesis Testing**

	True Situation: Null Hypothesis Is	
Research Conclusion	**True**	**False**
Do not reject H_0	Correct decision Confidence level Probability $= 1 - \alpha$	Error: Type II Probability $= \beta$
Reject H_0	Error: Type I Significance level Probability $= \alpha$	Correct decision Power of test Probability $= 1 - \beta$

lower we must set α error. The **power** associated with a statistical test is the probability of correctly rejecting a false null hypothesis. One-tailed tests are more powerful than two-tailed tests because, for the same α error, they are simply more likely to lead to a rejection of a false null hypothesis. β error represents the probability of not rejecting a false null hypothesis. There is no unique value associated with β error.

PROCEDURE

The relationship between the two types of errors is best illustrated through example, and the example would be most productive if developed following the general format of hypothesis testing. Research Realities 14A.1 overviews the typical sequence of steps that is followed. Assume the problem is indeed one of investigating the potential for a new product and the research involves the preferences of consumers. Suppose that, in the judgment of management, the product should not be introduced unless at least 20 percent of the population could be expected to prefer it and that the research calls for 625 respondents to be interviewed for their preferences.

Step 1   The null and alternate hypotheses would be

$$H_0 : \pi \leq 0.20,$$
$$H_a : \pi > 0.20.$$

The hypotheses are framed so that if the null hypothesis is rejected, the product should be introduced.

Step 2   The appropriate sample statistic is the sample proportion, and the distribution of all possible sample proportions under the sampling plan is based on the assumption that the null hyothesis is true. Although the distribution of sample proportions is theoretically binomially distributed, the large sample size permits the use of the normal approximation.[5] The z test therefore applies. The z statistic in this case equals

$$z = \frac{p - \pi}{\sigma_p},$$

---

[5]The binomial distribution tends toward the normal distribution for a fixed π as sample size increases. The tendency is most rapid when $\pi = 0.5$. With sufficiently large samples, normal probabilities may be used to approximate binomial probabilities with πs in this range. As π departs from 0.5 in either direction, the normal approximation becomes less adequate, although it is generally held that the normal approximation may be used safely if the smaller of $n\pi$ or $n(1 - \pi)$ is 10 or more. If this condition is not satisfied, binomial probabilities can either be calculated directly or found in tables that are readily available. In the example, $n\pi = 625(0.2) = 125$, and $n(1 - \pi) = 500$, and thus there is little question about the adequacy of the normal approximation to binomial probabilities.

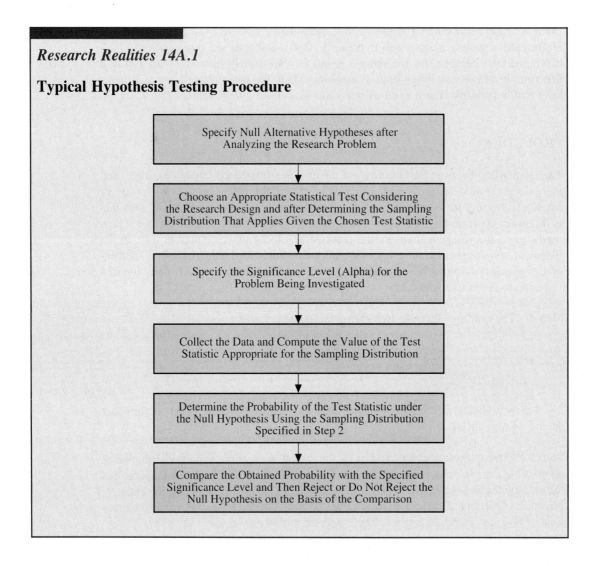

Research Realities 14A.1

Typical Hypothesis Testing Procedure

Specify Null Alternative Hypotheses after Analyzing the Research Problem

Choose an Appropriate Statistical Test Considering the Research Design and after Determining the Sampling Distribution That Applies Given the Chosen Test Statistic

Specify the Significance Level (Alpha) for the Problem Being Investigated

Collect the Data and Compute the Value of the Test Statistic Appropriate for the Sampling Distribution

Determine the Probability of the Test Statistic under the Null Hypothesis Using the Sampling Distribution Specified in Step 2

Compare the Obtained Probability with the Specified Significance Level and Then Reject or Do Not Reject the Null Hypothesis on the Basis of the Comparison

where p is the sample proportion preferring the product and σ_p is the standard error of the proportion, or the standard deviation of the distribution of sample ps. In turn, σ_p equals

$$\sqrt{\frac{\pi(1 - \pi)}{n}} = \sqrt{\frac{0.20(0.80)}{625}} = 0.0160,$$

where n is the sample size. Note this peculiarity of proportions. As soon as we have hypothesized a population value, we have said something about the standard error of the estimate. The proportion is the most clear-cut case of "known variance," since the variance is specified automatically with an assumed π. The researcher thus knows all of the values for calculating z except p before ever taking the sample and further knows *a priori* the distribution to which the calculated statistic will be related. This is true in general, and the researcher should have these conditions clearly in mind before taking the sample.

Step 3   The researcher selects a significance level (α) using the following reasoning. In this situation, α error is the probability of rejecting H_0 and concluding that $\pi > 0.2$, when in reality $\pi \leq 0.2$. This conclusion will lead the company to market the new product. However, because the venture will only be profitable if $\pi > 0.2$, a wrong decision to market would be financially unprofitable and possibly disastrous. The probability of Type I error should, therefore, be minimized as much as possible. The researcher recognizes, though, that the probability of a Type II error increases as α is decreased, other things being equal. Type II error in this case implies concluding that $\pi \leq 0.2$ when in fact $\pi > 0.2$, which in turn suggests that the company would table the decision to introduce the product when it could be profitable. The opportunity loss from making such an error could be quite serious. Although, as explained later, the researcher does not know what β would be, he or she knows that α and β are interrelated and that an extremely low value of α (say, $\alpha = 0.01$ or 0.001) would produce intolerable β errors. Therefore, the researcher decides on an α level of 0.05 as an acceptable compromise.[6]

Step 4   Since Step 4 involves the computation of the test statistic, it can be completed only after the sample is drawn and the information collected. Suppose 140 of the 625 sample respondents preferred the product. The sample proportion is thus $p = 140/625 = 0.224$. The basic question that needs to be answered is conceptually simple: "Is this value of p too large to have occurred by chance from a population with π assumed to be equal to 0.2?" or, in other words, "What is the probability of getting $p = 0.224$ when $\pi = 0.2$?"

$$z = \frac{p - \pi}{\sigma_p} = \frac{0.224 - 0.20}{0.0160} = 1.500.$$

Step 5   The probability of occurrence of a z value of 1.500 can be found from standard tabled values of areas under the normal curve. (See Appendix A at the end of the book.) Figure 14A.1 shows the procedure. The shaded area between $-\infty$ and 1.500 equals 0.9332; this means that the area to the right of $z = 1.500$ is $1.000 - 0.9332$, or 0.0668. This is the probability of securing a z value of 1.500 under a true situation of $\pi = 0.2$.

Step 6   Since the calculated probability of occurrence is higher than the specified significance level of $\alpha = 0.05$, the null hypothesis is not rejected. The product would not

---

[6]We shall have more to say about the choice of $\alpha = 0.05$ and its interpretation after we have introduced the notion of power.

Figure 14A.1   **Probability of $z = 1.500$ with a One-Tailed Test**

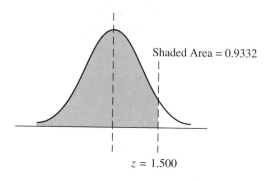

Shaded Area = 0.9332

$z = 1.500$

be introduced because, although the evidence is in the right direction, it is not sufficient to conclude beyond "any reasonable doubt" that $\pi > 0.2$. If the decision maker had been able to tolerate a 10 percent chance of committing a Type I error, the null hypothesis would have been rejected and the product marketed, since the probability of getting a sample $p = 0.224$ when the true $\pi = 0.20$ is, as we have seen, 0.0668.

POWER

The example illustrates the importance of correctly specifying the risk of error. If a 10 percent chance of an α error were tolerable and the researcher specified $\alpha = 0.05$, a potentially profitable opportunity would have been bypassed. The choice of the proper significance level involves weighing the costs associated with the two types of error — unfortunately a procedure that most researchers ignore, choosing out of habit $\alpha = 0.10$ or 0.05. Perhaps this lapse is due to the difficulty encountered in specifying β error, or Type II error.[7]

The difficulty arises because β error is not a constant. Recall that it is the probability of not rejecting a false null hypothesis. Therefore, the probability of committing a Type II error depends on the size of the difference between the *true*, but unknown, population value and the value *assumed to be true* under the null hypothesis. Other things being equal, we would prefer a test that minimized such errors. Alternatively, since the power of a test equals $1 - \beta$, we would prefer the test with the greatest power so that we would have the best chance of rejecting a false null hypothesis.[8] Clearly, our ability to do this

---

[7]See Robert Hooke, *How to Tell the Liars from the Statisticians* (New York: Dekker, 1983), for several interesting analogies highlighting the trade-offs between Type I and Type II errors.

[8]See Alan G. Sawyer and A. Dwayne Ball, "Statistical Power and Effect Size in Marketing Research," *Journal of Marketing Research*, 18 (August 1981), pp. 275–290, for a persuasive argument about why marketing researchers need to pay more attention to power in their research designs. The article also offers some suggestions on how to improve statistical power. For a general discussion, see Jacob Cohen, *Statistical Power Analysis for the Behavioral Sciences*, 2nd ed. (New York: Academic Press, 1988).

depends on how false H_0 truly is. It could be just a little bit false or way off the mark, and the probability of an incorrect conclusion would certainly be higher in the first case. The difference between the assumed value under the null hypothesis and the true, but unknown, value is known as the effect size. As intuition suggests, large effects are easier to distinguish than small effects.

Consider again the hypotheses

$$H_0 : \pi \leq 0.2,$$

$$H_a : \pi > 0.2,$$

where $\sigma_p = 0.0160$ and $\alpha = 0.05$, as before. Any calculated z value greater than 1.645 will cause us to reject this hypothesis, since this is the z value that cuts off 5 percent of the normal curve. The z value can be equated to the *critical* sample proportion through the formula

$$z = \frac{p - \pi}{\sigma_p},$$

$$1.645 = \frac{p - 0.20}{0.0160},$$

or $p = 0.2263$. Thus, any sample proportion greater than $p = 0.2263$ will lead to the rejection of the null hypothesis that $\pi \leq 0.2$. This means that if 142 or more [$0.2263(625) = 141.4$] of the sample respondents prefer the new product, the null hypothesis will be rejected and the product introduced, while if 141 or less of the sample respondents prefer it, the null hypothesis will not be rejected and the new product will not be introduced.

The likelihood of a sample proportion of $p = 0.2263$ is much greater for certain values of π than for others. Suppose, for instance, that the true but unknown value of π was 0.22. The sampling distribution of the sample proportions is again normal, but now it is centered about 0.22. The probability of obtaining the critical sample proportion $p = 0.2263$ under this condition is found again from the normal curve table, where[9]

$$z = \frac{p - \pi}{\sigma_p} = \frac{0.2263 - 0.22}{0.0166} = 0.380.$$

The shaded area between $-\infty$ and $z = 0.380$ is given in Appendix A at the end of the book as 0.6480, and thus the area to the right of $z = 0.380$ is equal to $1.000 - 0.6480 = 0.3520$ (see Panel B in Figure 14A.2). This is the probability that a value as

[9]Note that σ_p is now $\sqrt{0.22(0.78)/625} = 0.0166$, because a different specification of π implies a different standard error of estimate.

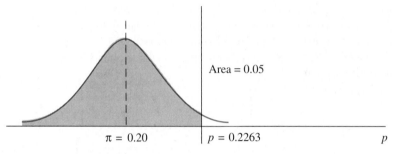

$\pi = 0.20 \qquad p = 0.2263 \qquad\qquad p$

Area = 0.05

Panel A: Critical Proportion under Null Hypothesis

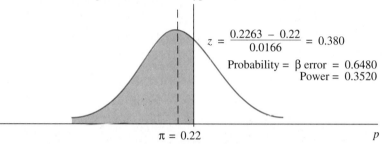

$$z = \frac{0.2263 - 0.22}{0.0166} = 0.380$$

Probability = β error = 0.6480
Power = 0.3520

$\pi = 0.22 \qquad\qquad\qquad p$

Panel B: Probability of Realizing Critical Proportion When π = 0.22,
Which Means Null Hypothesis Is False

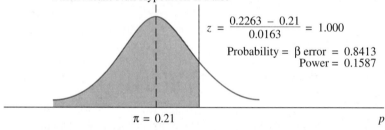

$$z = \frac{0.2263 - 0.21}{0.0163} = 1.000$$

Probability = β error = 0.8413
Power = 0.1587

$\pi = 0.21 \qquad\qquad\qquad p$

Panel C: Probability of Realizing Critical Proportion When π = 0.21,
Which Means Null Hypothesis Is False

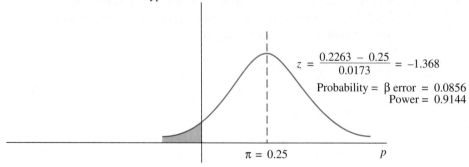

$$z = \frac{0.2263 - 0.25}{0.0173} = -1.368$$

Probability = β error = 0.0856
Power = 0.9144

$\pi = 0.25 \qquad\qquad p$

Panel D: Probability of Realizing Critical Proportion When π = 0.25,
Which Means Null Hypothesis Is False

large or larger than $p = 0.2263$ would be obtained if the true population proportion was $\pi = 0.22$. It is also the power of the test in that, if π is truly equal to 0.22, the null hypothesis is false and 0.3520 is the probability that the null will be rejected. Conversely, the probability that $p < 0.2263$ equals $1 - 0.3520 = 0.6480$, which is β error. The null hypothesis is false and yet the false null hypothesis is not rejected for any sample proportions $p < 0.2263$.

Suppose that the true population condition was $\pi = 0.21$ instead of $\pi = 0.22$, and the null hypothesis was again $H_0: \pi \le 0.20$. Since the null hypothesis is less false in this second case, we would expect power to be lower and the risk of β error to be higher because the null hypothesis is less likely to be rejected. Let us see if that is indeed the case. The z value corresponding to the critical $p = 0.2263$ is 1.000. Power given by the area to the right of $z = 1.000$ is 0.1587 (the β error is 0.8413), and the expected result does obtain. (See Figure 14A.2, Panel C.)

Consider one final value, true $\pi = 0.25$. The null hypothesis of $\pi = 0.20$ would be way off the mark in this case, and we would expect there would only be a small chance that it would not be rejected and a Type II error would be committed. The calculations are displayed in Figure 14A.2, Panel D; $z = -1.368$, and the area to the right of $z = -1.368$ is 0.9144. The probability of β error is 0.0856, and the *a priori* expectation is confirmed.

Table 14A.3 contains the power of the test for other selected population states, and Figure 14A.3 shows these values graphically.

Figure 14A.3 is essentially the power curve for the hypothesis

$$H_0: \pi \le 0.20,$$
$$H_a: \pi > 0.20,$$

TABLE 14A.3   **β Error and Power for Different Assumed True Values of π and the Hypotheses $H_0 : \pi \le 0.20$ and $H_a : \pi > 0.20$**

Value of π	Probability of Type II or β Error	Power of the Test: $1 - \beta$
0.20	$(0.950) = 1 - \alpha$	$(0.05) = \alpha$
0.21	0.8413	0.1587
0.22	0.6480	0.3520
0.23	0.4133	0.5867
0.24	0.2133	0.7867
0.25	0.0856	0.9144
0.26	0.0273	0.9727
0.27	0.0069	0.9931
0.28	0.0014	0.9986
0.29	0.0005	0.9995
0.30	0.0000	1.0000

FIGURE 14A.3   **Power Function for Data in Table 14A.3**

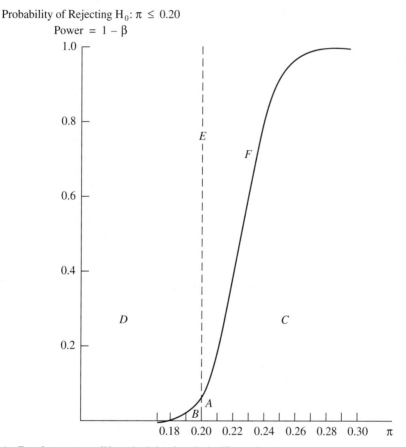

Probability of Rejecting H_0: $\pi \leq 0.20$

Power $= 1 - \beta$

A—Type I error; true null hypothesis is rejected; significance level.
B—Type I error; true null hypothesis is rejected.
C—No error; false null hypothesis is rejected.
D—No error; true null hypothesis is not rejected.
E—No error; true null hypothesis is not rejected; confidence level.
F—Type II error; false null hypothesis is not rejected.

and it confirms that the farther away the true π from the hypothesized value in the direction indicated by the alternate hypothesis, the higher the power. Note that power is not defined for the hypothesized value because if the true value in fact equals the hypothesized value, a β error cannot be committed.

Because power is a function rather than a single value, the researcher attempting to balance Type I and Type II errors logically needs to ask how false the null hypothesis is likely to be and to establish the decision rule accordingly. The way to control both errors within predetermined bounds for a given size effect is to vary the sample size.[10] The need to specify all three items — α error (or degree of confidence), β error (or power), and the size of the effect it is necessary to detect — possibly explains why so many researchers content themselves with the specification of Type I or α error and allow β error to fall where it may. The failure to even worry about, much less explicitly take into account, the power of the statistical test represents one of the fundamental problems with the classical statistics hypothesis-testing approach as it is commonly practiced in marketing research. Moreover, Type II errors are often more costly than Type I errors. Another common problem is the misinterpretation of what a "statistically significant result" really means. There are several common misinterpretations.[11]

One of the most frequent misinterpretations is to view a *p* value as representing the probability that the results occurred because of sampling error. Thus, the commonly used $p = 0.05$ is taken to mean that there is a probability of only 0.05 that the results were caused by chance and thus there must be something fundamental causing them. In actuality, a *p* value of 0.05 means that *if* (and this is a big if) the null hypothesis is indeed true as assumed, the odds are only 1 in 20 of getting a sample result of the magnitude that was observed. Unfortunately, there is no way in classical statistical significance testing to determine whether the null hypothesis is true.

> A *p* value reached by classical methods is not a summary of the data. Nor does the *p* value attached to a result tell how strong or dependable the particular result is . . . Writers and readers are all too likely to read .05 as *p(H/E)* "the probability that the Hypothesis is true, given the Evidence." As textbooks on statistics reiterate almost in vain, *p* is *p(E/H)*, the probability that this Evidence would arise if the (null) hypothesis is true.[12]

Another common misinterpretation is to equate statistical significance with practical significance. Many fail to realize that a difference can be of practical importance and not statistically significant if the power of the test is weak. Conversely, a result may be of no practical importance, even if highly significant, if the sample size is very large.

A third frequent misinterpretation is to hold that the α or *p* level chosen is in some way related to the probability that the research hypothesis captured in the alternative hypothesis is true. Most typically, this probability is taken as the complement of the α level. Thus, a *p* value of 0.05 is interpreted to mean that its complement, $1 - 0.05 = 0.95$, is the probability that the research hypothesis is true. "Related to this misinterpretation is the practice of interpreting *p* values as a measure or the degree of validity of research results, i.e., a *p* value such as $p < .0001$ is 'highly statistically significant' or

---

[10]See Helena Chumura Kraemer and Sue Thiemann, *How Many Subjects?* (Newbury Park, Calif.: Sage Publications, 1988), for discussion of the use of power to determine sample size.

[11]For an excellent discussion of some of the most common misinterpretations of classical significance tests and some recommendations on how to surmount the problems, see Alan G. Sawyer and J. Paul Peter, "The Significance of Statistical Significance Tests in Marketing Research," *Journal of Marketing Research,* 20 (May 1983), pp. 122–133. See also Jacob Cohen, "Things I Have Learned (So Far)," *American Psychologist,* 45 (December 1990), pp. 1304–1312.

[12]Lee J. Cronbach and R. E. Snow, *Aptitudes and Instructional Methods: A Handbook for Research on Interactions* (New York: Irvington, 1977), p. 52.

'highly significant' and therefore much more valid than a *p* value of, say, 0.05.''[13] Both of these related interpretations are wrong.

The only logical conclusion that can be drawn when a null hypothesis is rejected at some predetermined *p* level is that sampling error is an unlikely explanation of the results *given* that the null hypothesis is true. In many ways that is not saying very much, because, as was argued previously, the null hypothesis is set up to be false. The null, as typically stated, holds that there is no relationship between two certain variables, say, or that the groups are equal with respect to some particular variable. Yet, we do not really believe that. Rather, we investigate the relationship between variables because we believe there is some association between them, and we contrast the groups because we believe they are different with respect to the variable. Further, we can control our ability to reject the null hypothesis simply by the power we build into the statistical test, primarily through the size of the sample used to test it. "Given sufficiently high statistical power, one would expect virtually *always* to conclude the exact null hypothesis is false."[14]

Marketing researchers then need to be wary when interpreting the results of their hypothesis testing procedures so that they do not mislead themselves and others. They constantly need to keep in mind both types of errors that are possible to make. Further, they need to make certain that they do not misinterpret what a test of significance reveals. It represents no more than a test against the null hypothesis. One useful way of avoiding misinterpretation is to calculate confidence intervals when possible, because this gives decision makers a much better feel for how much faith they can have in the results. A test of significance is very much a yes–no situation: either the sample result is statistically significant or it is not. In contrast, "the confidence interval not only gives a yes or no answer, but also, by its width, gives an indication of whether the answer should be whispered or shouted."[15] Although not every test of significance can be put in the form of a confidence interval estimate, many of them can, and it is advisable to do so when the opportunity arises.[16]

■

Questions

1. Comment on the statement: "A hypothesis can never be accepted, only rejected." Is the statement true? Why or why not?

---

[13]Sawyer and Peter, "The Significance," p. 123. For other useful discussions of what statistical tests of significance mean, see Mick Alt and Malcolm Brighton, "Analyzing Data or Telling Stories?" *Journal of the Market Research Society,* 23 (October 1981), pp. 209–219; and Norval D. Glenn, "Replications, Significance Tests and Confidence in Findings in Survey Research," *Public Opinion Quarterly,* 47 (Summer 1983), pp. 261–269.

[14]*Ibid.,* p. 125.

[15]Mary G. Natrella, "The Relation between Confidence Intervals and Tests of Significance," *American Statistician,* 14 (1960), p. 22. See also G. R. Dawling and P. K. Walsh, "Estimating and Reporting Confidence Intervals for Market and Opinion Research," *European Research,* 13 (July 1985), pp. 130–133; Charles Cowan, "Testing Versus Description: Confidence Intervals and Hypothesis Testing," *Marketing Research: A Magazine of Management and Application,* 2 (September 1990), pp. 59–61.

[16]For an excellent discussion of the relationship between tests of significance and confidence interval estimates, see Natrella, "The Relation between Confidence Intervals," pp. 20–22, 33.

2. What is the basic scientific proposition that guides the framing of hypotheses? Illustrate the principle with a research question of your own choosing.

3. When is a two-tailed test preferred to a one-tailed test, and vice versa?

4. What is a Type I error? What is a Type II error? What is the relationship between these two types of error?

5. What is meant by the statistical notion of power?

6. Illustrate the steps involved in the statistical testing of hypotheses with your own example.

7. Explain the comment, "The farther away the true population parameter is from the hypothesized population value in the direction indicated by the alternate hypothesis, the higher the power." Is power not a constant? Why?

8. Using your own example, construct the power function.

9. What does it mean when the null hypothesis is rejected at the $\alpha = 0.10$ level?

Applications and Problems

1. Assume that the brand manager of a medium-sized manufacturer of consumer products decides to introduce a new brand of breakfast cereal if the company can initially acquire 1.5 percent of the market. The following hypotheses are to be tested:

$$H_0 : \pi \leq 0.015$$
$$H_a : \pi > 0.015$$

   Explain and discuss the Type I and Type II errors that could occur while testing these hypotheses. What are the implications for the company?

2. Discuss the danger of specifying Type I or α error and allowing β error to fall where it may.

3. Bentley Foods, Inc., a large manufacturer of frozen foods, has developed a new line of frozen pizza. Management has agreed to begin production and marketing of the new line if at least 15 percent of the population would prefer the pizza over other frozen pizzas currently available. To determine preferences, a sample of 1,000 consumers was obtained; 172 indicated that they would prefer the new product over existing brands.
   a. State the null and alternative hypotheses.
   b. Compute the standard error of the proportion.
   c. Calculate the z statistic. What is the probability of obtaining this value of the z statistic if the null hypothesis is true?
   d. The research manager for Bentley Foods is comfortable using the 0.05 significance level. Should the null hypothesis be rejected?
   e. At this significance level, what is the critical sample proportion?

4. A computer company is considering a nationwide introduction of a new type of personal computer. In order to test whether the product would be successful, the company is contemplating a nationwide survey to assess people's intentions to purchase the new model instead of existing models. The research team has framed the hypotheses as follows:

$$H_0 : \pi_N \leq \pi_O$$
$$H_a : \pi_N > \pi_O$$

where N and O refer to the new and old models, respectively. If people do not prefer the new model, introducing it would be extremely costly for the company. Under this scenario, does the research team need to be more concerned about a Type I or Type II error? What should α be set at to minimize the company's risk?

5. A research team tested new batteries to see if they lasted significantly longer than the company's existing battery. Traditionally, all experiments have been run at $\alpha = 0.05$. After testing 100 old batteries as well as 100 new batteries, the mean life for the new battery was found to be greater than that of the old, at $\alpha = .05$ significance level; however, a new analyst became greatly excited when it was discovered that the difference was significant at $\alpha = 0.001$. He commented, "This product is much better than we thought; the difference is highly significant!"

   a. Is this a correct interpretation of the test results? Explain.

   b. Is it appropriate for the research team to announce that the difference in mean life is significant at $\alpha = 0.001$ instead of $\alpha = 0.05$?

6. Before analyzing a set of scores, a researcher decides to test whether the assumption of a normal distibution is appropriate for the data. When testing to verify assumptions, does the researcher need to be more concerned about Type I or Type II error? What should α be set at under these circumstances?

15

Data Analysis: Examination of Differences

A question that arises regularly in the analysis of research data is, "Are the research results statistically significant? Could the result have occurred by chance due to the fact that only a sample of the population was contacted, or does it indicate an underlying condition in the population?" To answer, we use some kind of test of statistical significance.

This chapter reviews some of the more important tests for examining the statistical significance of differences. The difference at issue might be between some sample result and some expected population value, or it might be between two or more sample results. The intent is to indicate the types of tests that are available and the types of problems to which they apply. The first part of the chapter reviews the χ^2 goodness-of-fit test, which is especially useful with nominal data, and the second part reviews the Kolmogorov-Smirnov test, which is useful with ordinal data. The latter sections focus on the parametric tests that are applicable when examining differences in means or proportions.

GOODNESS OF FIT

In a number of marketing situations, it is necessary to determine whether some observed pattern of frequencies corresponds to an "expected" pattern. Consider a breakfast food manufacturer who has recently developed a new cereal called Score. The cereal will be packaged in the three standard sizes: small, large, and family size. The manufacturer's past experience suggests that for every one small package, three of the large and two of the family size are also sold. The manufacturer wishes to see if this same tendency would hold with this new cereal, since a change in consumption patterns could have important production implications. Therefore, the manufacturer decides to conduct a market test to determine the relative frequencies with which the various sizes would be purchased.

Suppose that, in an appropriate test market over a one-week period, 1,200 boxes of the new cereal were sold and that the distribution of sales by size was as follows:

	Number Buying		
Small	**Large**	**Family**	**Total**
240	575	385	1,200

Does this preliminary evidence indicate that the firm should expect a change in the purchase patterns of the various sized packages with Score?

This is the type of problem for which the **chi-square goodness-of-fit test** is ideally suited. The variable of interest has been broken into k mutually exclusive categories ($k = 3$ in the example), and each observation logically falls into one of the k classes or cells. The trials (purchases) are independent, and the sample size is large.

All that is necessary to employ the test is to calculate the *expected* number of cases that would fall in each category and to compare that with the *observed* number actually falling in the category using the statistic

$$\chi^2 = \sum_{i=1}^{k} \frac{[O_i - E_i]^2}{E_i},$$

where

O_i is the observed number of cases falling in the ith category;
E_i is the expected number of cases falling in the ith category; and
k is the number of categories.

The expected number falling into a category is generated from the null hypothesis that the composition of sales of Score by package size would follow the manufacturer's normal sales; that is, for every small package, three large and two family sizes would be sold. In terms of proportions, $\pi_1 = 1/(1 + 3 + 2) = \frac{1}{6}$, $\pi_2 = \frac{3}{6}$, and $\pi_3 = \frac{2}{6}$. Thus the expected sales would be $E_1 = n\pi_1 = 1,200(\frac{1}{6}) = 200$ of the small size, $E_2 = n\pi_2 = 1,200(\frac{3}{6}) = 600$ of the large size, and $E_3 = n\pi_3 = 1,200(\frac{2}{6}) = 400$ of the family size. The appropriate χ^2 statistic is computed as

$$\chi^2 = \frac{(240 - 200)^2}{200} + \frac{(575 - 600)^2}{600} + \frac{(385 - 400)^2}{400} = 9.60.$$

The chi-square distribution is one of the statistical distributions that is completely determined by its degrees of freedom v. The mean of the chi-square distribution is equal to the number of degrees of freedom v, and its variance is equal to $2v$. For large values of v, the chi-square distribution is approximately normally distributed.

In the example, the number of degrees of freedom is one less than the number of categories k; that is, $v = k - 1 = 2$. This is because the sum of the differences between the observed and expected frequencies is zero. Both the expected and observed frequencies must sum to the total number of cases. Given any $k - 1$ differences, the remaining difference is thus fixed, and this results in the loss of one degree of freedom.

Suppose that the researcher has chosen a significance level of $\alpha = 0.05$ for this test. The tabled value of χ^2 for two degrees of freedom and $\alpha = 0.05$ is 5.99 (see Appendix B at the end of the book). Since the calculated value ($\chi^2 = 9.60$) is larger, the conclusion is that the sample result would be unlikely to occur by chance alone. Rather, the preliminary market test results suggest that sales of Score will follow a different pattern than is typical. The null hypothesis of sales in the ratio of $1:3:2$ is rejected.

The chi-square test just outlined is an approximate test.[1] The approximation is relatively good if, as a rule of thumb, the *expected* number of cases in each category is five or more, although this value can be as low as one for some situations.[2]

The previous example illustrated the use of the chi-square distribution to test a null hypothesis concerning k population proportions, $\pi_1, \pi_2, \ldots, \pi_k$. The proportions were needed to generate the expected number of cases in each of the k categories. Viewed in this light, the test of a single proportion discussed when reviewing the logic of hypothesis testing in the appendix to Chapter 14 is a special case; in the goodness-of-fit test, the single parameter π is replaced by the k parameters $\pi_1, \pi_2, \ldots, \pi_k$.

Another use of the chi-square goodness-of-fit test is in determining whether a population distribution has a particular form. For instance, we might be interested in finding out whether a sample distribution of scores might have arisen from a normal distribution of scores. To investigate, we could construct the sample frequency histogram. The intervals would correspond to the k cells of the goodness-of-fit test. The observed cell frequencies would be the number of observations falling in each interval. The expected cell frequencies would be the number falling in each interval, if indeed the sample came from a normal distribution with mean μ and variance σ^2. If the population mean and variance were unknown, the sample mean and variance could be used as estimates. This would result in the loss of two additional degrees of freedom, but the basic test procedure would remain unchanged.

ETHICAL DILEMMA 15.1

A marketing researcher is perplexed at the results of his experiment — they do not tally at all with his *a priori* hypotheses. He immediately starts hunting through the literature for alternative hypotheses that will account for the findings. Halfway through the stack of journal articles on his desk, he stops reading and leans back in his chair with a whistle of relief. "Thank goodness! That idea fits my findings pretty well." He reaches for a pad of paper to write his final report, in which his new hypothesis is presented *a priori* and is neatly upheld in the experiment.

- Is it ethical to select the first explanation that fits the existing data without considering all alternative explanations *and* without further testing?
- Is it ethical to present a *post hoc* explanation as an *a priori* hypothesis?
- How often, in fact, are theories abandoned in the face of disconfirming evidence?

---

[1]The correct distribution to test the hypothesis is the hypergeometric. The hypergeometric distribution, however, is unwieldy for anything but very small samples. The chi-square distribution approximates the hypergeometric for large sample sizes. For a discussion of this point, as well as the other conditions surrounding a goodness-of-fit test, see Leonard A. Marascuilo and Maryellen McSweeney, *Nonparametric and Distribution Free Methods for the Social Sciences* (Belmont, Calif.: Brooks/Cole, 1977), pp. 243–248. See also Wayne W. Daniel, *Applied Nonparametric Statistics,* 2nd ed. (Boston: PWS-Kent Publishing, 1990).

[2]W. G. Cochran, "The χ^2 Test of Goodness of Fit," *Annuals of Mathematical Statistics,* 23 (1952), pp. 315–345.

KOLMOGOROV-SMIRNOV TEST

The **Kolmogorov-Smirnov test** is similar to the chi-square goodness-of-fit test because it uses a comparison between observed and expected frequencies to determine whether observed results are in accord with a stated null hypothesis. But the Kolmogorov-Smirnov test takes advantage of the ordinal nature of the data.

Consider, for example, a manufacturer of cosmetics who is testing four different shades of a foundation compound — very light, light, medium, and dark. The company has hired a marketing research firm to determine whether any distinct preference exists toward either extreme. If so, the company will manufacture only the preferred shades. Otherwise, it is planning to market all shades. Suppose that in a sample of 100, 50 persons preferred the ''very light'' shade, 30 the ''light'' shade, 15 the ''medium'' shade, and 5 the ''dark'' shade. Do these results indicate some kind of preference?

Since shade represents a natural ordering, the Kolmogorov-Smirnov test can be used to test the preference hypothesis. The test involves specifying the cumulative distribution function that would occur under the null hypothesis and comparing that with the observed cumulative distribution function. The point at which the two functions show the maximum deviation is determined, and the value of this deviation is the test statistic.

The null hypothesis for the cosmetic manufacturer would be that there is no preference for the various shades. Thus, it would be expected that 25 percent of the sample would prefer each shade. The cumulative distribution function resulting from this assumption is presented as the last column of Table 15.1.

Kolmogorov-Smirnov D, which is equal to the *absolute value of the maximum deviation* between the observed cumulative proportion and the theoretical cumulative proportion, is $0.80 - 0.50 = 0.30$. If the researcher chooses an $\alpha = 0.05$, the critical value of D for large samples is given by $1.36/\sqrt{n}$, where n is the sample size. In our case, the critical value is 0.136. Calculated D exceeds the critical value, and thus the null hypothesis of no preference among shades is rejected. The data indicate a statistically significant preference for the lighter shades.

The careful reader will have noticed that the hypothesis of no preference could also have been tested with the chi-square goodness-of-fit test. When the data are ordinal, though, the Kolmogorov-Smirnov test is the preferred procedure. It is more powerful

TABLE **15.1   Observed and Theoretical Cumulative Distributions of Foundation Compound Preference**

Shade	Observed Number	Observed Proportion	Observed Cumulative Proportion	Theoretical Proportion	Theoretical Cumulative Proportion
Very light	50	0.50	0.50	0.25	0.25
Light	30	0.30	0.80	0.25	0.50
Medium	15	0.15	0.95	0.25	0.75
Dark	5	0.05	1.00	0.25	1.00

than chi-square in almost all cases, is easier to compute, and does not require a certain minimum expected frequency in each cell as the chi-square test does.

The Kolmogorov-Smirnov test can also be used to determine whether two independent samples have been drawn from the same population or from populations with the same distribution. An example would be a manufacturer interested in determining whether consumer preference among sizes for a new brand of laundry detergent was the same as for the old brand. To apply the test, we would simply need to create a cumulative frequency distribution for each sample of observations using the same intervals. The test statistic would be the value of the maximum deviation between the two observed cumulative frequencies.[3]

HYPOTHESES ABOUT ONE MEAN

A recurring problem in marketing research studies is the need to make some statement about the parent population mean. Recall that the distribution of sample means is normal, with the mean of the sample means equal to the population mean and the variance of the sample means, $\sigma_{\bar{x}}^2$, equal to the population variance divided by the sample size — that is, $\sigma_{\bar{x}}^2 = \sigma^2/n$. Thus, it should not be surprising to find that the appropriate statistic for testing a hypothesis about a mean when the population variance is known is

$$z = \frac{\bar{x} - \mu}{\sigma_{\bar{x}}}$$

where

$\bar{x}$ is the sample mean;
μ is the population mean; and
$\sigma_{\bar{x}}$ is the standard error of the mean, which is equal to $\sigma/\sqrt{n}$, where n is the sample size.

The z statistic is appropriate if the sample comes from a normal population, or if the variable is not normally distributed in the population but the sample is large enough for the Central-Limit Theorem to be operative. What happens, though, in the more realistic case in which the population variance is unknown?

When the parent population variance is unknown, then, of course, the standard error of the mean, $\sigma_{\bar{x}}$, is unknown since it is equal to $\sigma/\sqrt{n}$. The standard error of the mean must then be estimated from the sample data. The estimate is $s_{\bar{x}} = \hat{s}/\sqrt{n}$, where $\hat{s}$ is the unbiased sample standard deviation; that is,

$$\hat{s} = \sqrt{\frac{\sum_{i=1}^{n} (X_i - \bar{x})^2}{n - 1}}.$$

---

[3]See Marascuilo and McSweeney, *Nonparametric and Distribution Free Methods*, pp. 250–251. See also Jean Dickinson Gibbons and Subhabrata Chakraborti, *Nonparametric Statistical Inference*, 3rd ed. (New York: Marcel Dekker, Inc., 1992).

The test statistic now becomes $(\bar{x} - \mu)/s_{\bar{x}}$, which is t distributed with $n - 1$ degrees of freedom if the conditions for the t test are satisfied.

To use the t statistic appropriately for making inferences about the mean, two basic questions need to be answered:

- Is the distribution of the variable in the parent population normal or is it asymmetrical?
- Is the sample size large or small?

If the variable of interest is normally distributed in the parent population, then the test statistic $(\bar{x} - \mu)/s_{\bar{x}}$ is t distributed with $n - 1$ degrees of freedom. This is true whether the sample size is large or small. For small samples, we actually use t with $n - 1$ degrees of freedom when making an inference. Although t with $n - 1$ degrees of freedom is also the theoretically correct distribution for large n, the distribution approaches and becomes indistinguishable from the normal distribution for samples of 30 or more observations. The test statistic $(\bar{x} - \mu)/s_{\bar{x}}$ is therefore referred to a table of normal deviates when making inferences with large samples. Note, though, that this is because the theoretically correct t distribution (since σ is unknown) has become indistinguishable from the normal curve, which is somewhat easier to use.

What happens if the variable is not normally distributed in the parent population when σ is unknown? If the distribution of the variable is symmetrical or displays only moderate skew, there is no problem. The t test is quite robust to departures from normality. However, if the variable is highly skewed in the parent population, the appropriate procedure depends on the sample size. If the sample is small, the t test is inappropriate. Either the variable has to be transformed so that it is normally distributed, or one of the distribution-free statistical tests must be used. If the sample is large, the normal curve could be used for making the inference, provided that the two following assumptions are satisfied:

1. The sample size is large enough so that the sample mean $\bar{x}$ is normally distributed because of the operation of the Central-Limit Theorem. The greater the degree of asymmetry in the distribution of the variable, the larger the sample size needed to satisfy this assumption.

2. The sample standard deviation $\hat{s}$ is a close estimate of the parent population standard deviation σ. The higher the degree of variability in the parent population, the larger the size of the sample that is needed to justify this assumption.

Research Realities 15.1 summarizes the situation for making inferences about a mean for known and unknown σ and normally distributed and asymmetrical parent population distributions.

To illustrate the application of the t test, consider a supermarket chain investigating the desirability of adding a new product to the shelves of its associated stores. Suppose that 100 units must be sold per week in each store for the item to be sufficiently profitable to warrant handling it in lieu of the many products competing for the limited shelf space. The research department decides to investigate the item's turnover by putting it in a random sample of ten stores for a limited period of time. Suppose that the average sales per store per week are as shown in Table 15.2.

Research Realities 15.1

Testing Hypotheses about a Single Mean

	σ Known	σ Unknown
Distribution of variable in parent population is normal or symmetrical.	Small *n:* Use $z = \dfrac{\bar{x} - \mu}{\sigma_{\bar{x}}} \sim N(0,1)$ Large *n:* Use $z = \dfrac{\bar{x} - \mu}{\sigma_{\bar{x}}} \sim N(0,1)$	Small *n:* Use $$t = \dfrac{\bar{x} - \mu}{s_{\bar{x}}}$$ where $s_{\bar{x}} = \hat{s}/\sqrt{n}$ and $$\hat{s} = \sqrt{\dfrac{\displaystyle\sum_{i=1}^{n} (X_i - \bar{x})^2}{n - 1}}$$ and refer to *t* table for $n - 1$ degrees of freedom. Large *n:* Since the *t* distribution approaches the normal as *n* increases, use $$z = \dfrac{\bar{x} - \mu}{s_{\bar{x}}}$$ for $n > 30$.
Distribution of variable in parent population is asymmetrical.	Small *n:* There is no theory to support the parametric test. One must either transform the variate so that it is normally distributed and then use the *z* test, or one must use a distribution-free statistical test. Large *n:* If the sample is large enough so that the Central-Limit Theorem is operative, use $$z = \dfrac{\bar{x} - \mu}{\sigma_{\bar{x}}} \sim N(0,1)$$	Small *n:* There is no theory to support the parametric test. One must either transform the variate so that it is normally distributed and then use the *t* test, or one must use a distribution-free statistical test. Large *n:* If sample is large enough so that 1. the Central-Limit Theorem is operative, 2. $\hat{s}$ is a close estimate of σ, use $$z = \dfrac{\bar{x} - \mu}{s_{\bar{x}}} \sim N(0,1)$$

TABLE 15.2   **Store Sales of Trial Product per Week**

Store i	Sales X_i	Store i	Sales X_i
1	86	6	93
2	97	7	132
3	114	8	116
4	108	9	105
5	123	10	120

Since the variance of sales per store is unknown and has to be estimated, the *t* test is the correct parametric test if the distribution of sales is normal. The normality assumption seems reasonable and could be checked using one of the goodness-of-fit tests. The little sales evidence that is available does not indicate any real asymmetry, so let us assume that the normality assumption is satisfied.

A one-tailed test is appropriate, because it is only when the sales per store per week are at least 100 that the product will be introduced on a national scale. The null and alternate hypotheses are

$$H_0 : \mu \leq 100,$$
$$H_a : \mu > 100.$$

Assume that the significance level is to be $\alpha = 0.05$. From the data in Table 15.2,

$$\bar{x} = \frac{\sum_{i=1}^{n} X_i}{n} = 109.4,$$

and

$$\hat{s} = \sqrt{\frac{\sum_{i=1}^{n} (X_i - \bar{x})^2}{(n-1)}} = 14.40.$$

Therefore, the standard error of the mean $s_{\bar{x}} = \hat{s}/\sqrt{n} = 4.55$. Calculations yield

$$t = \frac{\bar{x} - \mu}{s_{\bar{x}}} = \frac{109.4 - 100}{4.55} = 2.07.$$

Critical t as read from the t table with $v = n - 1 = 9$ degrees of freedom is 1.833 ($\alpha = 0.05$). (See Appendix C at the end of the book.) It is unlikely that the calculated value would have occurred by chance if the sales per store in the population were indeed less than or equal to 100 units per week.

Some insight into the sales per store per week that might be expected if the product was introduced on a national scale can be achieved by calculating the confidence interval. The appropriate formula is $\bar{x} \pm ts_{\bar{x}}$. For a 95 percent confidence interval and 9 degrees of freedom, $t = 1.833$, as we have already seen. The 95 percent confidence interval is thus $109.4 \pm (1.833)(4.55)$, or 109.4 ± 8.3, or, alternatively, $101.1 \le \mu \le 117.7$.

Suppose that the product was placed in 50 stores and that the sample mean and standard deviation were the same; that is, $\bar{x} = 109.4$ and $\hat{s} = 14.40$. The test statistic would now be $z = 4.62$, which would be referred to a normal table since the t is indistinguishable from the normal for samples of this size. Calculated z is greater than critical $z = 1.645$ for $\alpha = 0.05$, and, as expected, the same conclusion is warranted. The evidence is stronger now because of the larger sample of stores; the product could be expected to sell at a rate greater than 100 units per store per week.

The effect of the larger sample and the opportunity it provides to use the normal curve can also be seen in the smaller confidence interval that the larger sample produces. When the normal curve rather than t distribution applies, the formula $\bar{x} \pm ts_{\bar{x}}$ for calculating the confidence interval changes to $\bar{x} \pm zs_{\bar{x}}$, where the appropriate z value is read from the normal-curve table. Since for a 95 percent confidence interval $z = 1.645$, the interval is $109.4 \pm (1.645)(4.55)$, or 109.4 ± 7.5, which yields the estimate $101.9 \le \mu \le 108.6$, a slightly narrower interval than that produced when 10 stores instead of 50 were in the sample.

HYPOTHESES ABOUT TWO MEANS

Consider testing a hypothesis about the difference between two population means. Assuming that the samples are independent, there are three cases to consider:

- The two parent population variances are known.
- The parent population variances are unknown but can be assumed equal.
- The parent population variances are unknown and cannot be assumed equal.

Variances Are Known Experience has shown that the population variance usually changes much more slowly than the population mean. This means that the ''old'' variance can often be used as the ''known'' population variance for studies that are being repeated. For example, we may have annually checked the per capita soft-drink consumption of people living in different regions of the United States. If we were now to test an hypothesis about the differences in per capita consumption of a new soft drink, we could use the previously determined variances as known variances for our new soft drink. Consider that our problem is indeed one of determining whether there are any differences between Northerners and Southerners in their consumption of a new soft drink that our company has recently introduced, called Spark. Further, past data indicate that per capita variation in the consumption of soft drinks is 10 ounces per day for Northerners and 14 ounces per day for Southerners as measured by the standard deviation; that is, $\sigma_N = 10$ and $\sigma_S = 14$.

The null hypothesis is that there is no difference between Northerners and Southerners in their consumption of Spark ($H_0 : \mu_N = \mu_S$), whereas the alternate hypothesis is that there is a difference ($H_a : \mu_N \neq \mu_S$). It so happens that if $\bar{x}_N$ and $\bar{x}_S$, the sample means, are normally distributed random variables, their sum or difference is also normally distributed. The two sample means could be normally distributed because per capita consumption is normally distributed in each region or because the two samples are large enough that the Central-Limit Theorem is operative. In either case, the test statistic is

$$z = \frac{(\bar{x}_1 - \bar{x}_2) - (\mu_1 - \mu_2)}{\sigma_{\bar{x}_1 - \bar{x}_2}}$$

where
$\bar{x}_1$ is the sample mean for the first (northern) sample;
$\bar{x}_2$ is the sample mean for the second (southern) sample;
μ_1 and μ_2 are the unknown population means for the northern and southern samples; and
$\sigma_{\bar{x}_1 - \bar{x}_2}$ is the standard error of estimate for the difference in means and is equal to
$\sqrt{\sigma_{\bar{x}_1}^2 + \sigma_{\bar{x}_2}^2}$, where, in turn, $\sigma_{\bar{x}_1}^2 = \sigma_1^2/n_1$ and $\sigma_{\bar{x}_2}^2 = \sigma_2^2/n_2$.

Now, σ_1^2 and σ_2^2 are the "known" population variances of $\sigma_1^2 = (10)^2 = 100$ and $\sigma_2^2 = (14)^2 = 196$. Suppose that a random sample of 100 people from the North and South, respectively, was taken and that $\bar{x}_1 = 20$ ounces per day and $\bar{x}_2 = 25$ ounces per day. Does this result indicate a real difference in consumption rates? The standard error of estimate is

$$\sigma_{\bar{x}_1 - \bar{x}_2} = \sqrt{\frac{100}{100} + \frac{196}{100}} = \sqrt{2.96} = 1.720,$$

and the calculated z is

$$z = \frac{(20 - 25) - (\mu_N - \mu_S)}{1.720} = \frac{-5 - 0}{1.720} = -2.906.$$

Calculated z exceeds the critical tabled value of -1.96 for $\alpha = 0.05$, and the null hypothesis is rejected. There is a statistically significant difference in the per capita consumption of Spark by Northerners and Southerners.

The confidence interval for the difference in the two means is given by the formula

$$(\bar{x}_1 - \bar{x}_2) \pm z\sigma_{\bar{x}_1 - \bar{x}_2}.$$

For a 95 percent confidence interval, $z = 1.96$, and the interval estimate of the difference in consumption of Spark by the two groups is $-5 \pm (1.96)(1.720) = -5 \pm 3.4$. Southerners on average are estimated to drink 1.6 to 8.4 ounces less of Spark per day than Northerners.

Variances Are Unknown   When the two parent population variances are unknown, the standard error of the test statistic $\sigma_{\bar{x}_1 - \bar{x}_2}$ is also unknown, since $\sigma_{\bar{x}_1}$ and $\sigma_{\bar{x}_2}$ are unknown and have to be estimated. As was true with one sample, the sample standard deviations are used to estimate the population standard deviations;

$$\hat{s}_1^2 = \frac{\sum\limits_{i=1}^{n_1} (X_{i1} - \bar{x}_1)^2}{(n_1 - 1)}$$

is used to estimate σ_1^2 and

$$\hat{s}_2^2 = \frac{\sum\limits_{i=1}^{n_2} (X_{i2} - \bar{x}_2)^2}{(n_2 - 1)}$$

is used to estimate σ_2^2. Thus the estimates of the standard error of the means become $s_{\bar{x}_1} = \hat{s}_1/\sqrt{n_1}$ and $s_{\bar{x}_2} = \hat{s}_2/\sqrt{n_2}$. The general estimate of $\sigma_{\bar{x}_1 - \bar{x}_2}$ is then

$$s_{\bar{x}_1 - \bar{x}_2} = \sqrt{s_{\bar{x}_1}^2 + s_{\bar{x}_2}^2} = \sqrt{\frac{\hat{s}_1^2}{n_1} + \frac{\hat{s}_2^2}{n_2}}.$$

Although unknown, if the two parent population variances *can be assumed to be equal*, a better estimate of the common population variance can be generated by *pooling* the samples to calculate

$$\hat{s}^2 = \frac{\sum\limits_{i=1}^{n_1} (X_{i1} - \bar{x}_1)^2 + \sum\limits_{i=1}^{n_2} (X_{i2} - \bar{x}_2)^2}{n_1 + n_2 - 2},$$

where $\hat{s}^2$ is the pooled sample variance used to estimate the common population variance. In this case the estimated standard error of the test statistic $s_{\bar{x}_1 - \bar{x}_2}$ reduces to

$$s_{\bar{x}_1 - \bar{x}_2} = \sqrt{\frac{\hat{s}_1^2}{n_1} + \frac{\hat{s}_2^2}{n_2}} = \sqrt{\frac{\hat{s}^2}{n_1} + \frac{\hat{s}^2}{n_2}} = \sqrt{\hat{s}^2 \left(\frac{1}{n_1} + \frac{1}{n_2}\right)}.$$

If the distribution of the variable in each population can further be assumed to be normal, the appropriate test statistic is

$$t = \frac{(\bar{x}_1 - \bar{x}_2) - (\mu_1 - \mu_2)}{s_{\bar{x}_1 - \bar{x}_2}},$$

which is t distributed with $\nu = n_1 + n_2 - 2$ degrees of freedom.

Let's say, for example, that a manufacturer of floor waxes has recently developed a new wax. The company is considering designs for two different containers for the wax, one plastic and one metal. The company decides to make the final determination on the basis of a limited sales test in which the plastic containers are introduced in a random sample of ten stores and the metal containers are introduced in an *independent* random sample of ten stores. The test results are contained in Table 15.3.

$$\text{Calculated } t = \frac{(\bar{x}_1 - \bar{x}_2) - (\mu_1 - \mu_2)}{s_{\bar{x}_1 - \bar{x}_2}}$$

$$= \frac{(403.0 - 390.3) - (0)}{8.15} = 1.56.$$

This value is referred to a t table for $\nu = n_1 + n_2 - 2 = 18$ degrees of freedom. The test is two-tailed because the null hypothesis is that the containers were equal; there was no *a priori* statement that one was expected to sell better than the other. For $\alpha = 0.05$, say, and 18 degrees of freedom, critical $t = 2.101$. (One needs to look in the column headed $1 - \alpha = .975$ rather than .95 in Appendix C at the end of the text, because this is a two-tailed test.) Since calculated t is less than critical t, the null hypothesis of no difference would not be rejected. The sample data do *not* indicate that the plastic container could be expected to outsell the metal container in the total population, even though it did so in this limited experiment.

The example again demonstrates the importance of explicitly determining the statistical significance level by appropriately balancing Type I and Type II errors. Here α

TABLE 15.3   **Store Sales of Floor Wax in Units**

Store	Plastic Container	Metal Container	Store	Plastic Container	Metal Container
1	432	365	6	380	372
2	360	405	7	422	378
3	397	396	8	406	410
4	408	390	9	400	383
5	417	404	10	408	400

error was arbitrarily set equal to 0.05. This led to nonrejection of the null hypothesis and the conclusion that the plastic container would not be expected to outsell the metal container in the total population. Yet if the decision maker had been able to tolerate an α error of, say, 0.20, just the opposite conclusion would have been warranted, since interpolating in the table in Appendix C for 18 degrees of freedom indicates that the probability of getting calculated $t = 1.56$ under an assumption of no difference in the population means is approximately 15 percent. Assuming that the production and other costs associated with each container were the same, it would clearly seem that the final packaging decision should favor the plastic container. If the production and other costs were not the same, these costs should clearly be reflected in the statistical decision rule.[4]

One of the assumptions underlying the previous procedure was that the variances in sales of the plastic and metal containers were equal in the population. The assumption could be checked using an F test for the equality of variances, and indeed, the sample evidence does not contradict the assumption.[5] Suppose, though, that the assumption was not justified. Then the pooling of the variances is also no longer warranted, and the estimated standard error of the test statistic becomes

$$s_{\bar{x}_1 - \bar{x}_2} = \sqrt{\frac{\hat{s}_1^{\,2}}{n_1} + \frac{\hat{s}_2^{\,2}}{n_2}}$$

instead of

$$s_{\bar{x}_1 - \bar{x}_2} = \sqrt{\hat{s}^2 \left(\frac{1}{n_1} + \frac{1}{n_2} \right)}.$$

A real question now arises about the appropriate degrees of freedom for the test statistic. A large amount of controversial literature deals with this condition, known as the Behrens-Fisher problem. One suggested approach is the Aspin-Welch test, in which the degrees of freedom is a kind of weighted average of the degrees of freedom in each of the independent samples.[6] If the samples are both large so that $\hat{s}_1^{\,2}$ and $\hat{s}_2^{\,2}$ provide good estimates of their respective population variances $\sigma_1^{\,2}$ and $\sigma_2^{\,2}$, then the problem becomes less acute, as the normal z statistic can be used to examine the hypothesis.

---

[4]The Bayesian posture would be to introduce the plastic container even with the obtained sample results if the opportunity costs associated with each alternative were the same. If they were not the same, then the Bayesian approach would incorporate these costs directly into the decision rule regarding which container should be produced.

[5]Most introductory statistics books detail the procedure for testing the equality of two parent population variances. See, for example, William L. Hays, *Statistics*, 4th ed. (Forth Worth: Holt, Rinehart and Winston, Inc., 1988), pp. 332–335.

[6]See Acheson J. Duncan, *Quality Control and Industrial Statistics*, rev. ed. (Homewood, Ill.: Richard D. Irwin, 1959), pp. 476–478, for one of the better discussions of the Aspin-Welch test. See also Samuel Kotz and Norman L. Johnson, *Encyclopedia of Statistical Sciences*, Vol. 9 (New York: John Wiley, 1988), pp. 586–589, for discussion of some of the alternatives that have been proposed for handling the problem.

The preceding discussion assumed that the samples are independent and that the variable of interest is normally distributed in each of the parent populations. The normality assumption was again necessary to justify the use of the t distribution. What happens, though, if the variable is not normally distributed or the samples are not independent? The lower half of Research Realities 15.2 summarizes the approach for nonnormal parent distributions for known and unknown σ, and the next section treats the case of dependent samples.

Samples Are Related   A manufacturer of camping equipment wished to study consumer color preferences for a sleeping bag it had recently developed. The bag was of medium quality and price. Traditionally, the high-quality, high-priced sleeping bags used by serious campers and backpackers came in the earth colors, such as green and brown. Previous research indicated that the low-quality, low-priced sleeping bags were frequently purchased for children, for use at slumber parties. The vivid colors were preferred by this market segment, with bright reds and oranges leading the way. Production capacity restrictions would not allow the company to produce both sets of colors. To make the comparison, the company selected a random sample of five stores into which it introduced bags of both types. The sales per store are indicated in Table 15.4. Do the data present sufficient evidence to indicate a difference in the average sales for the different colored bags?

An analysis of the data indicates a difference in the two means of $(\bar{x}_1 - \bar{x}_2) = (50.2 - 45.2) = 5.0$. This is a rather small difference, considering the variability in sales that exists across the five stores. Further, application of the procedures of the last section suggests that the difference is not statistically significant. The pooled estimate of the common variance is

$$\hat{s}^2 = \frac{\sum\limits_{i=1}^{n_1} (X_{i1} - \bar{x}_1)^2 + \sum\limits_{i=1}^{n_2} (X_{i2} - \bar{x}_2)^2}{n_1 + n_2 - 2}$$

$$= \frac{1{,}512.8 + 1{,}222.8}{8} = 341.95,$$

and

$$s_{\bar{x}_1 - \bar{x}_2} = \sqrt{\hat{s}^2 \left(\frac{1}{n_1} + \frac{1}{n_2} \right)} = \sqrt{341.95 \left(\frac{1}{5} + \frac{1}{5} \right)} = 11.70.$$

Calculated t is thus

$$t = \frac{(\bar{x}_1 - \bar{x}_2) - (\mu_1 - \mu_2)}{s_{\bar{x}_1 - \bar{x}_2}} = \frac{(50.2 - 45.2) - 0}{11.70} = 0.427,$$

Testing Hypotheses about the Difference in Two Means

	σ's Known	σ's Unknown
Distribution of variables in parent populations is normal or symmetrical.	Small *n*: Use $z = \dfrac{(\bar{x}_1 - \bar{x}_2) - (\mu_1 - \mu_2)}{\sigma_{\bar{x}_1 - \bar{x}_2}} \sim N(0,1)$ where $\sigma_{\bar{x}_1 - \bar{x}_2} = \sqrt{\dfrac{\sigma_1^2}{n_1} + \dfrac{\sigma_2^2}{n_2}}$	Small *n*: Can you assume $\sigma_1 = \sigma_2$? 1. Yes: Use pooled variance *t* test where $t = \dfrac{(\bar{x}_1 - \bar{x}_2) - (\mu_1 - \mu_2)}{s_{\bar{x}_1 - \bar{x}_2}}$ and $s_{\bar{x}_1 - \bar{x}_2} =$ $\sqrt{\dfrac{\sum\limits_{i=1}^{n_1}(X_{i1} - \bar{x}_1)^2 + \sum\limits_{i=1}^{n_2}(X_{i2} - \bar{x}_2)^2}{n_1 + n_2 - 2}\left(\dfrac{1}{n_1} + \dfrac{1}{n_2}\right)}$ with $(n_1 + n_2 - 2)$ degrees of freedom. 2. No: Approach is shrouded in controversy. Might use Aspin-Welch test.
	Large *n*: Use $z = \dfrac{(\bar{x}_1 - \bar{x}_2) - (\mu_1 - \mu_2)}{\sigma_{\bar{x}_1 - \bar{x}_2}} \sim N(0,1)$	Large *n*: Use $z = \dfrac{(\bar{x}_1 - \bar{x}_2) - (\mu_1 - \mu_2)}{s_{\bar{x}_1 - \bar{x}_2}}$ and use pooled variance if variances can be assumed to be equal and unpooled variance if equality assumption is not warranted.
Distribution of variables in parent populations is asymmetrical.	Small *n*: There is no theory to support the parametric test. One must either transform the variates so that they are normally distributed and then use the *z* test, or one must use a distribution-free statistical test.	Small *n*: There is no theory to support the parametric test. One must either transform the variates so that they are normally distributed and then use the *t* test, or one must use a distribution-free statistical test.
	Large *n*: If the individual samples are large enough so that the Central-Limit Theorem is operative for them separately, it will also apply to their sum or difference. Use $z = \dfrac{(\bar{x}_1 - \bar{x}_2) - (\mu_1 - \mu_2)}{\sigma_{\bar{x}_1 - \bar{x}_2}} \sim N(0,1)$	Large *n*: One must assume that n_1 and n_2 are large enough so that the Central-Limit Theorem applies to the individual sample means. Then it can also be assumed to apply to their sum or difference. Use $z = \dfrac{(\bar{x}_1 - \bar{x}_2) - (\mu_1 - \mu_2)}{s_{\bar{x}_1 - \bar{x}_2}},$ employing a pooled variance if the unknown parent population variances can be assumed to be equal and unpooled variance if the equality assumption is not warranted.

TABLE 15.4   **Per-store Sales of Sleeping Bags**

Store	Bright Colors	Earth Colors
1	64	56
2	72	66
3	43	39
4	22	20
5	50	45

which is less than the critical value $t = 2.306$ found in the table for $\alpha = 0.05$ and $v = n_1 + n_2 - 2 = 8$ degrees of freedom. The null hypothesis of no difference in sales of the two types of colors cannot be rejected on the basis of the sample data.

But wait a minute! A closer look at the data indicates a marked inconsistency with this conclusion. The bright-colored sleeping bags outsold the earth-colored ones in each store, and, indeed, an analysis of the per-store differences (the procedure is detailed below) indicates that there is a statistically significant difference in the sales of the two bags. The reason for the seeming difference in conclusions (the difference is not significant versus it is significant) arises because the *t* test for the difference in two means is *not appropriate* for the problem. The difference-in-means test assumes that the samples are independent. These samples are not. Sales of bright-colored and earth-colored bags are definitely related, since they are both found in the same stores. Note how this example differs from the floor wax example, in which the metal containers were placed in one sample of stores and the plastic containers were located in an independent sample of stores. We need a procedure that takes into account the fact that the observations are related.

The appropriate procedure is the *t* test for related samples. The procedure is as follows. Define a new variable d_i, where d_i is the difference between sales of the bright-colored bags and the earth-colored bags for the *i*th store. Thus,

$$d_1 = 64 - 56 = 8,$$
$$d_2 = 72 - 66 = 6,$$
$$d_3 = 43 - 39 = 4,$$
$$d_4 = 22 - 20 = 2,$$
$$d_5 = 50 - 45 = 5.$$

Now calculate the mean difference

$$\bar{d} = \frac{\sum_{i=1}^{n} d_i}{n} = \frac{8 + 6 + 4 + 2 + 5}{5} = 5.0,$$

and the standard error of the difference

$$s_d = \sqrt{\frac{\sum\limits_{i=1}^{n}(d_i - \bar{d})^2}{n - 1}} = \sqrt{\frac{20}{4}} = 2.24.$$

The test statistic is

$$t = \frac{\bar{d} - D}{s_d/\sqrt{n}},$$

where D is the difference that is expected under the null hypothesis. Since there is no *a priori* reason why one color would be expected to sell better than the other, the appropriate null hypothesis is that there is no difference, while the alternate hypothesis is that there is:

$$H_0 : D = 0,$$
$$H_a : D \neq 0.$$

Calculated t is thus

$$t = \frac{5.0 - 0}{2.24/\sqrt{5}} = 5.0.$$

This value is referred to a t table for $\nu =$ (number of differences -1) degrees of freedom; in this case, there are five paired differences, and thus $\nu = 4$. Critical t for $\nu = 4$ and $\alpha = 0.05$ is 2.776, and, therefore, the hypothesis of no difference is rejected. The sample evidence indicates that the bright-colored sleeping bags are likely to outsell the earth-colored ones.

An estimate of how much sales per store of the vivid-colored sleeping bags would exceed those of the earth-colored bags can be calculated from the confidence interval formula $\bar{d} \pm t(s_d/\sqrt{n})$. The 95 percent confidence interval is $5.0 \pm (2.776)$ $(2.24/\sqrt{5}) = 5.0 \pm 2.8$, suggesting that sales of the vivid-colored bags would be in the range of 2.2 to 7.8 bags greater per store on average.

HYPOTHESES ABOUT TWO PROPORTIONS

The appendix to Chapter 14 reviewed the essential nature of hypothesis testing, employing as an example the testing of a hypothesis about a single population proportion. In this section, we want to illustrate the procedure for testing for the difference between two population proportions.[7]

The test for the difference between two population proportions is basically a large sample problem. The samples from each population must be large enough so that the normal approximation to the exact binomial distribution of sample proportions can be used. As a practical matter, this means that np and nq should be greater than 10 for each sample, where p is the proportion of "successes" and q is the proportion of "failures" in the sample, and n is the sample size.

To illustrate, consider a cosmetics manufacturer that was interested in comparing male college students and nonstudents in terms of their use of hair spray. Random samples of 100 male students and 100 male nonstudents in Austin, Texas, were selected, and their use of hair spray during the last three months was determined. Suppose that 30 students and 20 nonstudents had used hair spray within this period. Does this evidence indicate that a significantly higher percentage of college students than nonstudents use hair spray?

Because we are interested in determining whether the two parent population proportions are different, the null hypothesis is that they are the same; that is,

$$H_0 : \pi_1 = \pi_2,$$

$$H_a : \pi_1 \neq \pi_2,$$

where Population 1 is the population of college students, and Population 2 is the population of nonstudents. The sample proportions are $p_1 = 0.30$ and $p_2 = 0.20$, and, therefore, $n_1 p_1 = 30$, $n_1 q_1 = 70$, $n_2 p_2 = 20$, $n_2 q_2 = 80$, and the normal approximation to the binomial distribution can be used. The test statistic is

$$z = \frac{(p_1 - p_2) - (\pi_1 - \pi_2)}{\sigma_{p_1 - p_2}},$$

where $\sigma_{p_1 - p_2}$ is the standard error of the difference in the two sample proportions. The one question that still remains in the calculation of z is what does $\sigma_{p_1 - p_2}$ equal.

A general statistical result that is useful for understanding the calculation of $\sigma_{p_1 - p_2}$ is that the *variance of the sum or difference of two independent random variables is equal to the sum of the individual variances.* For a single proportion, the variance is $\pi(1 - \pi)/n$, and thus the variance of the difference is.

---

[7]The tests for population proportions are logically considered with nominal data because they apply in situations in which the variable being studied can be divided into those cases *possessing* the characteristic and those cases lacking it, and the emphasis is on the number or proportion of cases falling into each category. Marketing examples abound: "prefer A" versus "do not prefer A"; "buy" versus "do not buy"; "brand loyal" versus "not brand loyal"; "sales representatives meeting quota" versus "sales representatives not meeting quota." The test for the significance of the difference between two proportions is treated here because the hypothesis is examined using the z test, and the procedure relies on an "automatic pooled sample variance" estimate. It was thought that these notions would be better appreciated after the discussion of the test of means rather than before.

$$\sigma^2_{p_1 - p_2} = \sigma^2_{p_1} + \sigma^2_{p_2} = \frac{\pi_1(1 - \pi_1)}{n_1} + \frac{\pi_2(1 - \pi_2)}{n_2}.$$

Note that the variance of the difference is given in terms of the two unknown population proportions π_1 and π_2. Although unknown, the two population proportions have been assumed to be equal, and thus we have a "natural" case of a *pooled variance* estimate; $s^2_{p_1 - p_2}$ is logically used to estimate $\sigma^2_{p_1 - p_2}$, where

$$s^2_{p_1 - p_2} = pq\left(\frac{1}{n_1} + \frac{1}{n_2}\right)$$

and

$$p = \frac{\text{Total number of successes in the two samples}}{\text{Total number of observations in the two samples}},$$

$$q = 1 - p.$$

For the example

$$p = \frac{30 + 20}{100 + 100} = \frac{50}{200} = 0.25,$$

$$s^2_{p_1 - p_2} = (0.25)(0.75)\left(\frac{1}{100} + \frac{1}{100}\right) = 0.00375,$$

and

$$s_{p_1 - p_2} = 0.061.$$

Calculated z is found as follows:

$$z = \frac{(0.30 - 0.20) - (0)}{0.061} = \frac{0.10}{0.061} = 1.64,$$

whereas critical $z = 1.96$ for $\alpha = 0.05$. The sample evidence does not indicate that there is a difference in the proportion of college students and nonstudents using hair spray.

The 95 percent confidence interval calculated by the formula $(p_1 - p_2) \pm zs_{p_1 - p_2}$, which is $(0.30 - 0.20) \pm 1.96 (0.061) = 0.10 \pm 0.12$ yields a similar conclusion. The interval includes zero, suggesting that there is no difference in the proportions of males using hair spray in the two groups.

ETHICAL DILEMMA 15.2

A field experiment was conducted to determine the most effective advertising appeal for an immunization program for a serious flu epidemic, one in which people had a chance of dying if they contracted the flu. The control communities received no appeal at all, whereas the experimental communities received varying appeals in different strengths. An analysis of the differences in the proportion of people with respiratory problems getting immunization shots clearly indicated the level of advertising that would be most cost effective for a national campaign.

• Is it ethical to withhold benefits (i.e., knowledge of an immunization program) from participants in the control group?

• What participant rights are being violated?

• How can this research be justified? Do the long-term benefits of the research outweigh the costs?

SUMMARY

Several statistical tests that are useful to marketing researchers for examining differences were discussed in this chapter. The difference at issue might be between some sample result and some expected population value or between two sample results.

The chi-square goodness-of-fit test is appropriate when a nominally scaled variable falls naturally into two or more categories and the analyst wishes to determine whether the observed number of cases in each cell corresponds to the expected number.

The Kolmogorov-Smirnov test is the ordinal counterpart to the chi-square goodness-of-fit test in that it focuses on the comparison of observed and expected frequencies. It can be employed to test whether a set of observations could have come from some theoretical population distribution, such as a normal distribution, or whether two independent samples could have come from the same population distribution.

In testing a hypothesis about a single mean, the z test is appropriate if the variance is known, whereas the t test applies with unknown variance. A similar situation arises in the analysis of two means from independent samples. If the variances are known, the z test is used. If the variances are unknown but assumed to be equal, a t test using a pooled sample variance estimate applies. If unknown and probably unequal, there is controversy surrounding the correct procedure. If the samples are related instead of independent, the t test for paired differences is appropriate.

The test of the equality of proportions from two independent samples involves a "natural" pooling of the sample variances. The z test applies.

Questions

1. What is the basic use of a chi-square goodness-of-fit test? How is the value of the test statistic calculated? How are the expected frequencies determined?

2. If the data are ordinal and the analyst wishes to determine whether the observed frequencies correspond to some expected pattern, what statistical test is appropriate? What is the basic procedure to follow in implementing this test?

3. What is the appropriate test statistic for making inferences about a population mean when the population variance is known? When the population variance is unknown? Suppose that the population variance is unknown, but the sample is large. What is the appropriate procedure then?

4. Suppose one is testing for the statistical significance of the observed difference between the sample means from two independent samples. What is the appropriate procedure when the two parent population variances are
  a. known;
  b. unknown but can be assumed to be equal;
  c. unknown and cannot be assumed to be equal?

  What conditions must occur in each case regarding the distribution of the variable?

5. Would your response to Question 4 change if the samples were related? Explain.

6. How do you test whether two parent population proportions differ?

Applications and Problems

1. A large publishing house recently conducted a survey to assess the reading habits of teenagers. The company publishes four magazines specifically tailored to suit the interests of teenagers. Management hypothesized that there were no differences in the preferences for the magazines. A sample of 1,600 teenagers interviewed in the city of Buffalo, New York, indicated the following preferences for the four magazines.

Publication	Frequency of Preference
1. Rock-Town	350
2. Rappin'	500
3. Teen-Tips	450
4. R.A.D.	300
Total	1,600

Management needs your expertise to determine whether there are differences in teenager preferences for the magazines.
  a. State the null and alternate hypotheses.
  b. How many degrees of freedom are there?
  c. What is the chi-square critical table value at the 5 percent significance level?
  d. What is the calculated χ^2 value? Show all your calculations.
  e. Should the null hypothesis be rejected or not? Explain.

2. Moon Shine Company is a medium-sized manufacturer of shampoo. During the past years the company has increased the number of product variations of Moon Shine shampoo from three to five to increase its market share. Management conducted a survey to compare sales of Moon Shine shampoo with sales of Sun Shine and Star Shine, the brand's two major competitors. A sample of 1,800 housewives indicated the following frequencies with respect to most recent shampoo purchased:

Shampoo	Number Buying
1. Moon Shine	425
2. Sun Shine	1,175
3. Star Shine	200
Total	1,800

Past experience had indicated that three times as many households preferred Sun Shine to Moon Shine and that, in turn, twice as many households preferred Moon Shine to Star Shine. Management wants to determine if the historic tendency still holds, considering that Moon Shine Company has increased the range of shampoos available.

a. State the null and alternate hypotheses.

b. How many degrees of freedom are there?

c. What is the chi-square critical table value at the 5 percent level?

d. What is the calculated χ^2 value? Show all your calculations.

e. Should the null hypothesis be rejected or not? Explain.

3. A manufacturer of music cassettes wants to test four different cassettes varying in tape length: 30 minutes, 60 minutes, 90 minutes, and 120 minutes. The company has hired you to determine whether customers show any distinct preference toward either extreme. If there is a preference toward any extreme, the company would manufacture only cassettes of the preferred length; otherwise, the company is planning to market cassettes of all four lengths. A sample of 1,000 customers indicated the following preferences.

Tape Length	Frequency of Preference
30 minutes	150
60 minutes	250
90 minutes	425
120 minutes	175
Total	1,000

a. State the null and alternate hypotheses.

b. Compute Kolmogorov-Smirnov *D* by completing the following table.

Tape Length	Observed Number	Observed Proportion	Observed Cumulative Proportion	Theoretical Proportion	Theoretical Cumulative Proportion
30 min.					
60 min.					
90 min.					
120 min.					

c. Compute the critical value of D at $\alpha = 0.05$. Show your calculations.

d. Would you reject the null hypothesis? Explain.

e. What are the implications for management?

f. Explain why the Kolmogorov-Smirnov test would be used in this situation.

4. A medium-sized manufacturer of paper products was planning to introduce a new line of tissues, hand towels, and toilet paper. However, management had stipulated that the new products should be introduced only if average monthly purchases per household were $2.50 or more. The product was market tested and the diaries of the 100 panel households living in the test market area were checked. They indicated that average monthly purchases were $3.10 per household with a standard deviation of $0.50. Management is wondering what decision it should make and has asked for your recommendation.

a. State the null and alternate hypotheses.

b. Is the sample size considered large or small?

c. Which test should be used? Why?

d. At the 5 percent level of significance, would you reject the null hypothesis? Support your answer with the necessary calculations.

5. The president of a chain of department stores had promised the managers of the various stores a bonus of 8 percent if the average monthly sales per store increased $300,000 or more. A random sample of 12 stores yielded the following sales increases:

Store	Sales Increase	Store	Sales Increase
1	$320,000	7	$380,000
2	$230,000	8	$280,000
3	$400,000	9	$420,000
4	$450,000	10	$360,000
5	$280,000	11	$440,000
6	$320,000	12	$320,000

The president is wondering whether this random sample of stores indicates that the population of stores has reached the goal. (Assume that the distribution of the variable in the parent population is normal.)

a. State the null and alternate hypotheses.

b. Is the sample size considered small or large?

c. Which test should be used? Why?

d. Would you reject the null hypothesis at the 5 percent level of significance? Support your conclusion with the necessary calculations.

6. Ruby Gem is the owner of two jewelry stores located in Los Angeles and San Francisco. During the past year, the San Francisco store spent a considerable amount on in-store displays compared to the Los Angeles store. Ruby Gem wants to determine if the in-store displays resulted in increased sales. The average sales for a sample of 100 days for the San Francisco and Los Angeles stores were $21.8 million and $15.3 million, respectively. (Past experience has shown that $\sigma_{SF} = 8$ and $\sigma_{LA} = 9$, where σ_{SF} is the standard deviation in sales for the San Francisco store and σ_{LA} is the standard deviation for the Los Angeles store.)

a. State the null and alternate hypotheses.

b. What test would you use? Why?

    c. What is the calculated value of the test statistic? Show your calculations.
    d. What is the critical tabled value at 5 percent significance level?
    e. Would you reject the null hypothesis? Explain.
    f. What can Ruby Gem conclude?

7. Travel Time Company, a large travel agency located in Baltimore, Maryland, wanted to study consumer preferences for its package tours to the East. For the past five years, Travel Time had offered two similarly priced packaged tours to the East that differed only in the places included in the tour. A random sample of five months' purchases from the past five years was selected. The number of consumers that purchased the tours during these five months is as follows:

Month	Packaged Tour I	Packaged Tour II
1	90	100
2	70	60
3	120	80
4	110	90
5	60	80

The management of Travel Time needs your assistance to determine whether there is a difference in preferences for the two tours.
    a. State the null and alternate hypotheses.
    b. What test would you use? Why?
    c. What is the calculated value of the test statistic? Show your calculations.
    d. What is the critical tabled value at the 5 percent significance level?
    e. Would you reject the null hypothesis? Explain.
    f. What can the management of Travel Time Company conclude about preferences for the two tours?

8. A manufacturer of exercise equipment for health clubs is interested in comparing usage of exercise equipment at health clubs by men and women. Random samples of 250 women and 250 men in Oklahoma City were selected and the usage of health club facilities was determined. The results indicated that 87 men and 51 women from the samples had been to a health club and had used exercise equipment at least once during the previous six weeks. The manufacturer is interested in determining whether or not this evidence indicates that a significantly higher percentage of men than women use exercise equipment at health clubs.
    a. State the null and alternate hypotheses.
    b. Which test would you use? Why?
    c. Calculate the test statistic. Show all your calculations.
    d. Assuming that $\alpha = 0.05$, can you conclude that a higher proportion of men use exercise equipment at health clubs? Since the discovery that a larger proportion of women than men use such equipment would be just as important a finding, use a two-tailed test.
    e. Construct a 90 percent confidence interval for the difference between the proportion of men and the proportion of women using exercise equipment at health clubs. What conclusions can you draw from the confidence interval?

9. A local charity wanted to run an advertisement encouraging people to donate their old winter coats for the organization to redistribute to the city's homeless people. The charity is able to obtain some free commercial time on both local TV and radio stations. However, the charity wants to use the medium that provides the greatest recall. A short pilot was conducted to test whether there was a difference in recall between spots run on the radio and those on TV. The table that follows provides the results.

	Radio	TV
Number of people who were able to recall the charity's commercials	25	29
Number of people who did not recall the charity's commercials	50	46
Total number of people surveyed	75	75

   a. State the null and alternative hypotheses for the test.
   b. At $\alpha = 0.10$, use an appropriate test and interpret the results for the charity.
   c. If the research objective had been to determine whether TV advertisements resulted in greater recall, do the null and alternative hypotheses change? State and test the new hypotheses. Do the results change?

10. A large manufacturer of healthy snacks wants to test whether the sales of a health-food snack bar follow the same pattern with respect to package size in both Los Angeles and New York. The company has equal distribution in both cities and sells the following package sizes: packages of 6 bars, packages of 8 bars, packages of 12 bars, and econopacks of 24 bars. In Los Angeles, sales of these package types are in the following ratio: $3:1:2:5$. In New York during the same period, 4,880 bars are sold; specifically, sales for the four package types are as follows: 1,500, 475, 925, 1,980.
   a. State the null and alternative hypotheses for the test.
   b. What is the appropriate test in this situation? How many degrees of freedom are there? At $\alpha = 0.05$, can the null hypothesis be rejected?

11. The Spazi Italian food company is considering introducing a new extra-spicy spaghetti sauce. Before introducing the new sauce, however, the company wants to test it against its major competitor's spicy sauce. In a mall test, shoppers were stopped at random and asked to taste the two sauces. Shoppers were then asked to rate the sauces on a scale of 1 to 10, with 1 being awful and 10 being excellent. The table that follows shows the ratings given to the two sauces by ten shoppers.

Shopper	Spazi's Sauce	Other Sauce	Shopper	Spazi's Sauce	Other Sauce
1	1	7	6	8	10
2	7	10	7	10	7
3	5	7	8	2	8
4	6	10	9	3	8
5	2	9	10	9	10

   a. What is the appropriate test to use for analyzing these scores? Explain.
   b. At $\alpha = 0.05$, is there a significant difference in ratings for these two sauces?
   c. Is this an appropriate design to use for this situation? Explain. What are alternative designs that may be more appropriate for this situation?

d. After looking at Spazi's scores, do you think that additional research is warranted? Why?

Refer to the NFO Research, Inc., coffee study described on pages 780–783 in Chapter 13 for the next two problems.

12. Compare the overall ratings (from Question 2) of Folgers and Yuban. Is there a difference in the ratings for the two brands of coffee ($\alpha = .05$)? If so, which brand is rated more highly?

13. Compute a "taste" index score on the following features of Question 6 for Maxwell House Regular: rich taste, always fresh, full-bodied taste, smooth taste, not bitter, has no aftertaste. Is there a difference in this overall score for individuals who add nothing to their coffee versus those who do add something ($\alpha = .05$)?

APPENDIX 15A

Analysis of Variance

In Chapter 15 we used the example of packaging floor wax in plastic and metal containers to examine that statistical test of the difference in two population means. Let us now reconsider the data of Table 15.3 to demonstrate an alternate approach to the problem. Known as the **analysis of variance (ANOVA),** it has the distinct advantage of being applicable when there are more than two means being compared. ANOVA is a moderately popular analysis technique among practitioners. As Research Realities 15A.1 indicates, it is used most by consumer goods manufacturers and finance and insurance companies. Its use by 26 percent of the total firms surveyed ranks it sixth out of the 12 statistical analysis techniques studied. While ANOVA would not normally be applied when there are only two means, it is best illustrated using a familiar example.

Although not necessary for this simple example, a little additional notation at this time will pay dividends when more complex examples are introduced. Therefore, let:
x_{ij} = the ith observation on the jth treatment or group. There are two treatments in the example: $j = 1$ refers to plastic containers and $j = 2$ to metal containers. For each treatment there are ten stores. Thus, for the first treatment $X_{11} = 432$, $X_{21} = 360$, . . . , $X_{10,1} = 408$ and for the second treatment $X_{12} = 365$, $X_{22} = 405$, and $X_{10,2} = 400$.

n_j = the number of observations on the jth treatment; $n_1 = 10$ and $n_2 = 10$.

n = the total number of observations in all treatments combined: $n = n_1 + n_2 = 20$.

$\bar{x}_{.j}$ = the mean of the jth treatment:

$$\bar{x}_{.j} = \frac{\sum_{i=1}^{n_j} X_{ij}}{n}.$$

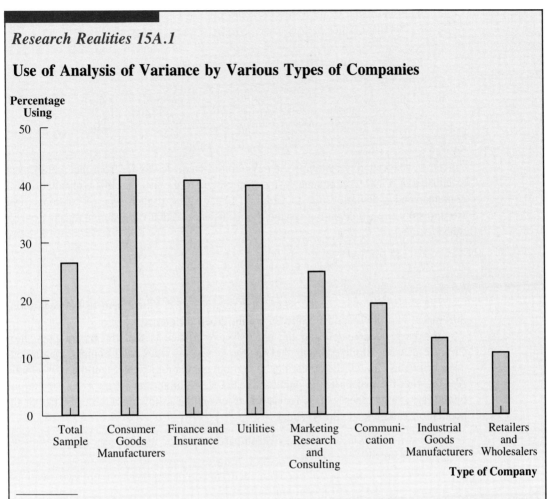

Research Realities 15A.1

Use of Analysis of Variance by Various Types of Companies

Source: Developed from the information in Barnett A. Greenberg, Jac L. Goldstucker, and Danny W. Bellenger, ''What Techniques Are Used by Marketing Researchers in Business?'' *Journal of Marketing*, 41 (April 1977), pp. 64–65.

Thus,

$$\bar{x}_{.1} = \frac{432 + 360 + \ldots + 408}{10} = 403.0,$$

and

$$\bar{x}_{.2} = \frac{365 + 405 + \ldots + 400}{10} = 390.3.$$

$\cdot \; \bar{x}_{..}$ = the grand mean of all n observations:

$$\bar{x}_{..} = \frac{\displaystyle\sum_{j=1}^{2} \sum_{i=1}^{n_j} X_{ij}}{n}$$

$$= \frac{432 + \ldots + 408 + 365 + \ldots + 400}{20} = 396.7.$$

Now, one can conceptualize the deviation of any sales figure from the overall mean as consisting of two components — a deviation due to the fact that it is a plastic or metal container and a deviation due to variation in the sales of each type of container from store to store (i.e., a deviation around the mean sales of that type of container). Conceptually,

$$(X_{ij} - \bar{x}_{..}) = (\bar{x}_{.j} - \bar{x}_{..}) + (X_{ij} - x_{.j}).$$

The first difference on the right-hand side is called a treatment or between-group difference, and the second is called a within-group difference.

The basic idea underlying the analysis of variance is that the parent population variance can be estimated from the sample in several ways, and comparisons among these estimates can tell us a great deal about the population. Recall that the null hypothesis was that the two parent population means were equal; that is, $\mu_1 = \mu_2$. If the null hypothesis is true, then except for sampling error, the following three estimates of the population variance should be equal:

1. the *total variation,* computed by comparing each of the 20 sales figures with the grand mean;

2. the *between-group variation,* computed by comparing each of the two treatment means with the grand mean; and

3. the *within-group variation,* computed by comparing each of the individual sales figures with the mean of its own group.

If, however, the hypothesis is not true and there is a difference in the means, then the between-group variation should produce a higher estimate than the within-group variation, which only considers the variation within groups and is independent of differences between groups.

These three separate estimates of the population variation are computed in the following way when there are k treatments or groups.

1. Total variation — sum of squares total SS_T:

$$SS_T = \sum_{j=1}^{k} \sum_{i=1}^{n_j} (X_{ij} - \bar{x}_{..})^2$$

$$= (432 - 396.7)^2 + \ldots + (408 - 396.7)^2$$
$$+ (365 - 396.7)^2 + \ldots + (400 - 396.7)^2.$$

The difference between *each observation* and the *grand mean* is determined; the differences are squared and then summed.

2. Between-group variation — sum of squares between groups SS_B:

$$SS_B = \sum_{j=1}^{k} n_j (\bar{x}_{.j} - \bar{x}_{..})^2$$
$$= 10(403.0 - 396.7)^2 + 10(390.3 - 396.7)^2.$$

The difference between each *group mean* and the *overall mean* is determined, the difference is squared, each squared difference is weighted by the number of observations making up the group, and the results are summed.

3. Within-group variation — sum of squares within groups SS_W:

$$SS_W = \sum_{j=1}^{k} \sum_{i=1}^{n_j} (X_{ij} - \bar{x}_{.j})^2$$
$$= (432 - 403.0)^2 + \ldots + (408 - 403.0)^2$$
$$+ (365 - 390.3)^2 + \ldots + (400 - 390.3)^2.$$

The difference between *each observation* and its *group mean* is determined; the differences are squared and then summed.

Let us take a closer look at the behavior of these three sources of variation. First, SS_T measures the overall variation of the n observations. The more variable the n observations, the larger SS_T becomes. Second, SS_B reflects the total variability of the means. The more nearly alike the k means are, the smaller SS_B becomes. If they differ greatly, SS_B will be large. Third, SS_W measures the amount of variation within each column or treatment. If there is little variation among the observations making up a group, SS_W is small. When there is great variability, SS_W is large.

It can be shown that $SS_T = SS_B + SS_W$ and that each of these sums of squares, when divided by the *appropriate number of degrees of freedom,* generates a mean square, which is essentially an unbiased estimate of the population variance.[1] Further, if the null

---

[1]See Geoffrey Keppel, *Design and Analysis: A Researcher's Handbook,* 2nd ed. (Englewood Cliffs, N.J.: Prentice-Hall, 1982), pp. 24–64, for the derivation. See also William L. Hays, *Statistics,* 4th ed. (Fort Worth: Holt, Rinehart and Winston, Inc., 1988), pp. 355–365. For a more complete discussion of the various designs discussed in this appendix, see B. J. Winer, Donald R. Brown, and Kenneth M. Michels, *Statistical Principles in Experimental Design,* 3rd ed. (New York: McGraw Hill, Inc., 1991).

hypothesis of no difference among population means is true, they are all estimates of the same variance and should not differ more than would be expected because of chance. If the variance between groups is significantly greater than the variance within groups, the hypothesis of equality of population means will be rejected.

In other words, we can view the variance within groups as a measure of the amount of variation in sales of containers that may be expected on the basis of chance. It is the *error variance* or *chance variance*. The between-group variance reflects error variance *plus* any group-to-group differences occasioned by differences in popularity of the two containers. Therefore, if it is found to be significantly larger than the within-group variance, this difference may be attributed to group-to-group variation, and the hypothesis of equality of means is discredited.

But what are these degrees of freedom? The total number of degrees of freedom is equal to $n - 1$, since there is only a single constraint $\bar{x}$ in the computation of SS_T. For the within-group sum of squares, there are n observations and k constraints, one constraint for each treatment mean. Hence, the degrees of freedom for the within-group sum of squares equals $n - k$. There are k values, one corresponding to each treatment mean, in the calculation of SS_B, and there is one constraint imposed by $\bar{x}$; hence the degrees of freedom for the between-group sum of squares is $k - 1$.

The separate estimates of the population variance or the associated mean squares are

$$MS_T = \frac{SS_T}{df_T} = \frac{SS_T}{n - 1},$$

$$MS_B = \frac{SS_B}{df_B} = \frac{SS_B}{k - 1},$$

$$MS_W = \frac{SS_W}{df_W} = \frac{SS_W}{n - k}.$$

The mean squares computed from the sample data are estimates of the true mean squares. The true mean squares are, in turn, given by the expected values of the corresponding sample mean squares. Given that the samples are independent, the population variances are equal, and the variable is normally distributed in the parent population, it can be shown that these expected values, E, are

$$E(MS_W) = \sigma^2 = \text{Error variance or chance variance,}$$

and

$$E(MS_B) = \sigma^2 + \text{Treatment effect.}$$

The ratio $E(MS_B)/E(MS_W)$ will equal 1 if there is no treatment effect. It will be greater than 1 if there is a difference in the sample means. Because the two expected values are not known, the sample mean squares are used instead to yield the ratio

TABLE 15A.1   **Analysis of Variance of Sales of Plastic versus Metal Containers**

Source of Variation	Sum of Squares	Degrees of Freedom	Mean Square	*F* Ratio
Between group	806.5	1	806.5	2.43
Within group	5,978.1	18	332.1	
Total	6,784.6	19		

$$\frac{MS_B}{MS_W} = F,$$

which follows the F distribution. Unlike the t or χ^2 distributions, the F distribution depends on two degrees of freedom: one corresponding to the mean square in the numerator and one corresponding to the mean square in the denominator. Since MS_B and MS_W are only sample estimates of the true variances, one should not expect the ratio MS_B/MS_W to be exactly 1 when the treatment effect is zero, and one should not immediately conclude that there is a difference among the group means when the ratio is greater than 1. Rather, given a significance level and the respective degrees of freedom for the numerator and denominator, a critical value of F may be read from standard tables. The critical value indicates the magnitude of the ratio that can occur because of random sampling fluctuations, even when there is no difference in the group means; that is, $E(MS_B)/E(MS_W) = 1$. The entire analysis is conveniently handled in an analysis-of-variance table.

Table 15A.1 is the analysis-of-variance table for the plastic and metal container sales data. The calculated F value is referred to an F table for 1 and 18 degrees of freedom (see Appendix D at the end of the book). Using the same α as before, $\alpha = 0.05$, critical F is found to be 4.41, and again the sample evidence is not sufficient to reject the hypothesis of the equality of the two means. This should not be surprising, since it can be shown that when the comparison is between two means (the degrees of freedom in the numerator of the F ratio are then $\nu_1 = k - 1 = 1$), $F = t^2 = (1.56)^2 = 2.43$.[2] Both tests are identical in this special case, and if one test does not indicate a significant difference between the two means, neither will the other.

The plastic and metal container sales example is the simplest type of what is known as a **completely randomized design,** since there were only two treatments. The distinguishing feature of the completely randomized design is that experimental treatments are assigned to the stores on a random basis. In this case, the container types were assigned to the stores at random, with no attempt to match stores or make the test units equal in any way.

---

[2]It can be shown mathematically that if a random variable is t distributed with ν degrees of freedom, then t^2 is F distributed with $\nu_1 = 1$, $\nu_2 = \nu$ degrees of freedom; that is, if $t \sim t_\nu$, then $t^2 \sim F_{1,\nu}$.

An alternative statement of the hypothesis of equality of means can be generated from the model of a completely randomized design. The model statement has the added advantage of facilitating discussion when more complex models are introduced. The model for a completely randomized design is

$$X_{ij} = \mu + \tau_j + \epsilon_{ij}.$$

This means that an observation, X_{ij}, is conceived of as being made up of three components: the overall mean μ; the effect of the jth treatment, τ_j; and the random error associated with the ith observation on the jth treatment, ϵ_{ij}. The null hypothesis of equality of population means is equivalent to the hypothesis that the treatment effects are all zero, since $\mu_1 = \mu_2$ implies that $\tau_1 = \mu_1 - \mu_2 = 0$. The alternate hypothesis, when there are k treatments, is that at least one of the treatment effects is not zero; this is equivalent to the statement that at least one mean differs from the others. The symbolic statement of the hypotheses is[3]

$$H_0 : \tau_j = 0 \qquad \text{for all } j = 1, \ldots, k,$$
$$H_a : \tau_j \neq 0 \qquad \text{for at least one } j \text{ where } j = 1, \ldots, k.$$

The assumptions underlying the model and the test are that the samples are independent, the variable is normally distributed, and the variance is the same for each treatment. The last assumption is necessary to justify the pooling of variances and, in this respect, is similar to the t test for two means.

RANDOMIZED BLOCKS

The reader can readily appreciate the difficulty that can arise in the preceding situation if, by chance, the stores selected to handle one type of container were, say, systematically larger than the stores chosen to distribute the other type. If a significant difference had been observed, it could have been because the plastic container was sold in the large stores, which have greater sales potential because they have more traffic.

When, in fact, there is one source of extraneous variation distorting the results of an experiment, a **randomized-block design** can be employed. This design involves the grouping of "similar" test units into blocks and the random assignment of treatments to test units in each block. Similarity is determined by matching the test units on the expected extraneous source of variation (for example, store size in the container example). The hope is that the units within each block will be more alike than units selected completely at random. Since the differences between blocks can be taken into account in the variance analysis, for the same number of observations the error mean square should

---

[3]For an insightful discussion of how one should set up hypotheses for analysis of variance, see Richard K. Burdick, "Statement of Hypotheses in the Analysis of Variance," *Journal of Marketing Research*, 20 (August 1983), pp. 320–324.

TABLE 15A.2   **Sales Generated by Various Call Plans (in thousands of dollars)**

	Plan				Plan		
Block	A	B	C	Block	A	B	C
1	42	51	43	6	29	35	30
2	36	35	36	7	52	50	54
3	40	52	44	8	46	49	44
4	38	47	42	9	40	44	40
5	32	38	36	10	38	36	35

be smaller than it would be if a completely randomized design had been used. Therefore, the test should be more efficient.

Consider, for example, an investigation of the effectiveness of alternative sales representatives' call-frequency plans made by a manufacturer that sells primarily to industrial distributors. There are three plans: A, B, and C. The plans differ in the frequency with which the various sized accounts are called on, and the manufacturer is interested in determining which of the three would produce the most sales. The firm employs some 500 sales representatives. Rather than choose one of the schemes arbitrarily, it was believed that it would be worthwhile to employ each on a trial basis before making a decision. The firm's management selected a sample of 30 sales representatives who were to try the new call plans. Management was concerned that differences in sales ability might affect the results of the test. Consequently, it decided to match the sales representatives in terms of their ability, employing their past sales as the matching criterion. Thus, ten blocks with three sales representatives having relatively equal sales records within a block were formed, resulting in a randomized-block design.

The sales that resulted are given in Table 15A.2. The model that underlies the randomized-block experiment is given by[4]

$$X_{ij} = \mu + \tau_j + \beta_i + \epsilon_{ij},$$

where
X_{ij} is the ith observation (ith block) on the jth treatment;
μ is the overall mean;
τ_j is the effect attributable to the jth treatment or call plan, $j = 1,2, \ldots, k$;
β_i is the effect attributable to the ith block, $i = 1,2, \ldots, r$; and
ϵ_{ij} is the random error associated with the ith observation on the jth treatment.

[4]The example is an illustration of a mixed model. The treatments are fixed; only the three call plans being investigated are of interest. The test units are a random sample from the population of sales representatives, and thus a random-effects model would apply. The combination of fixed treatments and the random sample of test units creates the conditions for a mixed model.

The assumptions are that a random sample of Size 1 is drawn from each of the kr (k treatments times r blocks) populations; X is normally distributed in each of the kr populations; the variance of each is the same; and the block and treatment effects are additive. Except for the last assumption, these are the same assumptions that were made in the completely randomized design. But now there are kr populations, whereas there were k populations with the completely randomized design.

Let $j = 1$ be Call Plan A, $j = 2$ Call Plan B, and $j = 3$ Call Plan C. The average sales under each call plan are

$$\bar{x}_{.1} = \frac{\sum\limits_{i=1}^{r} X_{i1}}{r} = \frac{42 + 36 + \ldots + 38}{10} = 39.3,$$

$$\bar{x}_{.2} = \frac{\sum\limits_{i=1}^{r} X_{i2}}{r} = \frac{51 + 35 + \ldots + 36}{10} = 43.7,$$

$$\bar{x}_{.3} = \frac{\sum\limits_{i=1}^{r} X_{i3}}{r} = \frac{43 + 36 + \ldots + 35}{10} = 40.4,$$

while the overall mean is

$$\bar{x}_{..} = \sum_{j=1}^{k} \sum_{i=1}^{r} \frac{X_{ij}}{n}$$

$$= \frac{(42 + \ldots + 38) + (51 + \ldots + 36) + (43 + \ldots + 35)}{30} = 41.1$$

In addition to the total, treatment, and error sum of squares, the sum of squares corresponding to blocks must now be computed. The block means are helpful in determining this sum of squares. They are given by the formula

$$\bar{x}_{i.} = \frac{\sum\limits_{j=1}^{k} X_{ij}}{k},$$

where $\bar{x}_{i.}$ refers to the mean of the ith block. Thus for the first block, $i = 1$,

$$\bar{x}_{1.} = \frac{\sum\limits_{j=1}^{k} X_{1j}}{k} = \frac{(42 + 51 + 43)}{3} = 45.3.$$

The remaining block means, which are calculated similarly, are

$$\bar{x}_{2.} = 35.7 \qquad \bar{x}_{5.} = 35.3 \qquad \bar{x}_{8.} = 46.3$$

$$\bar{x}_{3.} = 45.3 \qquad \bar{x}_{6.} = 31.3 \qquad \bar{x}_{9.} = 41.3$$

$$\bar{x}_{4.} = 42.3 \qquad \bar{x}_{7.} = 52.0 \qquad \bar{x}_{10.} = 36.3.$$

The sums of squares are

$$SS_T = \sum_{j=1}^{k} \sum_{i=1}^{r} (X_{ij} - \bar{x}_{..})^2$$

$$= (42 - 41.1)^2 + (36 - 41.1)^2 + \ldots + (35 - 41.1)^2$$

$$= 1{,}333.5.$$

$$SS_{TR} = \sum_{j=1}^{k} r(\bar{x}_{.j} - \bar{x}_{..})^2$$

$$= 10(39.3 - 41.1)^2 + 10(43.7 - 41.1)^2 + 10(40.4 - 41.1)^2$$

$$= 104.9.$$

$$SS_B = \sum_{i=1}^{r} k(\bar{x}_{i.} - \bar{x}_{..})^2$$

$$= 3(45.3 - 41.1)^2 + 3(35.7 - 41.1)^2 + \ldots + 3(36.3 - 41.1)^2$$

$$= 1{,}093.5.$$

$$SS_E = SS_T - SS_{TR} - SS_B = 1{,}333.5 - 104.9 - 1{,}093.5$$

$$= 135.1.$$

As mentioned, the model underlying the randomized-block design suggests that any sample response can be written as the sum of four additive factors: the overall mean, the effect of the jth treatment, the effect of the ith block, and the error term. It may happen that the effect of an individual treatment will vary according to the type of test unit to which it is applied; for example, Call Plan A works best for the better sales representatives, whereas Call Plan B works better for the average sales representatives. Interaction between the treatment and the blocks is said to be present when this condition occurs, and the additive model is no longer applicable. The reasonableness of the additivity assumption can be checked with Tukey's test for nonadditivity.[5] If the additivity assumption is rejected, the interpretation of the results becomes difficult, because it is then hard to say which call plan is best.

---

[5]See Keppel, *Design and Analysis*, pp. 155–156, for a discussion and calculation formulas for Tukey's test of nonadditivity.

TABLE 15A.3   **Analysis of Variance of Randomized-Block Design Investigating Sales Call Plans**

Source of Variation	Sum of Squares	Degrees of Freedom	Mean Square	F Ratio
Blocks	1,093.5	$(r - 1) = 9$	121.50	16.18
Treatments	104.9	$(k - 1) = 2$	52.45	6.98
Error	135.1	$(r - 1)(k - 1) = 18$	7.51	
Total	1,333.5	$rk - 1 = 29$		

The additivity assumption is not rejected in the sample at hand. Table 15A.3 is the analysis-of-variance table for the applicable linear model. There are now two F ratios of interest — one corresponding to blocks and one corresponding to treatments. Calculated F for the treatment mean square is 6.98; critical F for $\alpha = 0.05$ and $v_1 = 2$ and $v_2 = 18$ is 3.55. Calculated F exceeds critical F, and the null hypothesis of equal means is rejected. There is a difference in the effectiveness of at least one of the call plans. Call Plan B, in particular, produces significantly better sales.[6]

Calculated F for the block effect is 16.18. Critical F for $\alpha = 0.05$ and $v_1 = 9$ and $v_2 = 18$ is 2.46. Since calculated F exceeds critical F, the block variation is statistically significant. This means that the grouping of sales representatives according to ability before assigning the call plans has eliminated a source of variation in the results. The blocking was indeed worthwhile. The randomized-block design was more efficient than a completely randomized design would have been.

LATIN SQUARE

The **Latin-square design** is appropriate when there are two extraneous factors that can cause serious distortion in the results. Suppose in the previous example that we wanted to conduct the investigation not only with sales representatives of different ability but also among sales representatives having different sized territories. Suppose, in fact, that we had divided the sales representatives into three classes on the basis of ability — outstanding, good, and average — and the territories into the three classes — large, average, and small. There are thus nine different conditions with which to cope. One way of proceeding would be to use randomized blocks and test each of the three call plans under each of the nine conditions. This would require a sample of 27 sales representatives. An alternative approach would be to try each call plan only once with each size territory and each level of ability. This would require a sample of only nine test units or sales representatives. The primary gain in this case would be administrative control. In

---

[6]If the null hypothesis of equality of means is rejected, then it is reasonable to look for the means or other possible linear contrasts that are responsible. For discussion of the tests for determining which means are statistically significantly different, see *Ibid.*, pp. 144–156.

other cases, there may be cost advantages associated with the use of fewer test units. The interesting point is that if differences in territory size do indeed have an effect, the Latin-square design with nine test units could be as efficient as the randomized-block design with many more test units.

The Latin-square design requires that the number of categories for each of the extraneous variables we wish to control be equal to the number of treatments. With three call plans to investigate, it was no accident that we divided the sales representatives into three ability levels and the territories into three size categories. The Latin-square design also requires that the treatments be randomly assigned to the resulting categories. This is typically accomplished by selecting one of the published squares at random and then randomizing the rows, columns, and treatments using this square.[7]

As an example of the analysis of a Latin square, consider the supermarket chain interested in the effect of an in-store promotion on sales of its private-label cola. Suppose that the three promotional plans being considered were

- A — no promotion
- B — free samples with demonstrator
- C — special end display

and that the company decided to run a controlled experiment to test the effectiveness of the choices. The company's management was concerned that the timing of the experiment could affect the results because of changes in weather and also that the size of the store might influence the outcome. Since there are two potentially serious distorting factors, a Latin-square design is appropriate. Further, since there are three treatments, there also must be three categories for each extraneous variable. Let the stores, therefore, be divided into three size classes: 1, 2, and 3; and assume that one had been selected at random from each class. Let the time for the experiment also be broken into three segments, and suppose that randomization of rows, columns, and treatments yielded the 3×3 design reported in Table 15A.4.

The underlying model for a Latin-square design is

$$X_{ijk} = \mu + \alpha_i + \beta_j + \tau_k + \epsilon_{ijk},$$

where
X_{ijk} is the result when the kth treatment is applied to cell ij;
μ is the overall mean;
α is the effect attributable to the ith block (say, time period), $i = 1, 2, \ldots, r$;
β_j is the effect attributable to the jth block (say, store size), $j = 1, 2, \ldots, r$;
τ_k is the effect attributable to the kth treatment (promotional plan), $k = 1, \ldots, r$;
ϵ_{ijk} is the random error associated with the ijk observation.

We have already remarked that the number of categories for each of the extraneous variables must equal the number of treatments in a Latin-square experiment. Thus, the

---

[7]See R. A. Fisher and F. Yates, *Statistical Tables* (Edinburgh: Oliver and Boyd, 1948) for Latin squares from 4×4 to 12×12.

Table 15A.4   **Latin-Square Design and Results for Experiment on Effect of Promotion on Cola Sales**

	Design				Sales		
	Store:				**Store:**		
Time Period	**1**	**2**	**3**		**1**	**2**	**3**
1	B	C	A		69	63	72
2	C	A	B		63	63	72
3	A	B	C		48	66	51

Time Period (rows)   **Mean Sales**

1

$$\bar{x}_{1..} = \sum_{j,k=1}^{3} \frac{X_{1jk}}{3} = \frac{69 + 63 + 72}{3} = 68.0$$

2

$$\bar{x}_{2..} = \sum_{j,k=1}^{3} \frac{X_{2jk}}{3} = \frac{63 + 63 + 72}{3} = 66.0$$

3

$$\bar{x}_{3..} = \sum_{j,k=1}^{3} \frac{X_{3jk}}{3} = \frac{48 + 66 + 51}{3} = 55.0$$

Store (columns)

1

$$\bar{x}_{.1.} = \sum_{i,k=1}^{3} \frac{X_{i1k}}{3} = \frac{69 + 63 + 48}{3} = 60.0$$

2

$$\bar{x}_{.2.} = \sum_{i,k=1}^{3} \frac{X_{i2k}}{3} = \frac{63 + 63 + 66}{3} = 64.0$$

3

$$\bar{x}_{.3.} = \sum_{i,k=1}^{3} \frac{X_{i3k}}{3} = \frac{72 + 72 + 51}{3} = 65.0$$

Treatment

A

$$\bar{x}_{..1} = \sum_{i,j=1}^{3} \frac{X_{ij1}}{3} = \frac{48 + 63 + 72}{3} = 61.0$$

B

$$\bar{x}_{..2} = \sum_{i,j=1}^{3} \frac{X_{ij2}}{3} = \frac{69 + 72 + 66}{3} = 69.0$$

C

$$\bar{x}_{..3} = \sum_{i,j=1}^{3} \frac{X_{ij3}}{3} = \frac{63 + 63 + 51}{3} = 59.0$$

Overall

$$\bar{x}_{...} = \sum_{i,j,k=1}^{3} \frac{X_{ijk}}{9} = \frac{(69 + 63 + \ldots + 51)}{9} = 63.0$$

ranges of i, j, and k are all the same, 1 to r in the general case and 1 to 3 in the example at hand. There are now r^2 populations — r populations for each blocking factor or $r \times r$ populations in all. The assumptions of the Latin-square experiment are that a random sample of Size 1 is drawn from each of the r^2 populations; X is normally distributed in each of the r^2 populations; the variance of each of the r^2 populations is the same; and the row, column, and treatment effects are additive. These are the same assumptions made in the randomized-block design, with two minor modifications: (1) There are r^2 populations, whereas there are rk populations in the randomized-block design; (2) there is an additional additive effect, that resulting from the second blocking factor.

The null hypothesis in a Latin-square experiment is that the means are equal or that sales are the same under the three treatments. This is equivalent to testing the hypothesis

$$H_0 : \tau_k = 0 \text{ for } k = 1, 2, 3,$$

$$H_a : \text{not all the } \tau_k \text{ are zero.}$$

The sales reported in Table 15A.4 resulted from the experiment. The overall mean and the mean sales for each time period, store, and treatment must be determined so that the sums of the squares can be calculated. These means are presented in the lower portion of Table 15A.4, where it is understood that i, j, k are summed over the proper values. The various sums of squares are

$$SS_T = \sum_{i=1}^{r} \sum_{j=1}^{r} (X_{ijk} - \bar{x}_{...})^2$$
$$= (69 - 63)^2 + (63 - 63)^2 + \ldots + (51 - 63)^2 = 576.$$

$$SS_R = r \sum_{i=1}^{r} (\bar{x}_{i..} - \bar{x}_{...})^2$$
$$= 3 \left[(68 - 63)^2 + (66 - 63)^2 + (55 - 63)^2 \right] = 294.$$

$$SS_C = r \sum_{j=1}^{r} (\bar{x}_{.j.} - \bar{x}_{...})^2$$
$$= 3 \left[(60 - 63)^2 + (64 - 63)^2 + (65 - 63)^2 \right] = 42.$$

$$SS_{TR} = r \sum_{k=1}^{r} (\bar{x}_{..k} - \bar{x}_{...})^2$$
$$= 3 \left[(61 - 63)^2 + (69 - 63)^2 + (59 - 63)^2 \right] = 168.$$

$$SS_E = SS_T - SS_R - SS_C - SS_{TR}$$
$$= 576 - 294 - 42 - 168 = 72.$$

Table 15A.5 contains the resulting mean squares and F ratios. Assuming that $\alpha = 0.05$, critical F for $v_1 = 2$ and $v_2 = 2$ is 19.0. None of the calculated F ratios is statistically significant. The hypothesis of equal means is not rejected. The sample evidence does not indicate that the promotions significantly affected sales nor that stores or time periods significantly affected the results.

TABLE 15A.5   **Analysis-of-Variance Table for Latin-Square Experiment on Effect of Promotion of Cola Sales**

Source of Variation	Sum of Squares	Degrees of Freedom	Mean Square	F Ratio
Rows (time periods)	294	$r - 1 = 2$	147	4.083
Columns (stores)	42	$r - 1 = 2$	21	0.583
Treatments	168	$r - 1 = 2$	84	2.333
Error	72	$(r - 1)(r - 2) = 2$	36	
Total	576	$r^2 - 1 = 8$		

FACTORIAL DESIGNS

So far we have considered designs that involve only one experimental variable, although it may have had multiple levels (for example, three different call plans). It is often desirable to investigate the effects of two or more factors in the same experiment. For instance, it might be desirable to investigate the sales impact of the shape as well as the construction material of containers for floor wax. Suppose that in addition to packaging a new floor wax in metal or plastic containers, two shapes, A and B, were being considered for the containers. Package shape and package type would both be called factors. There would be two different levels of each factor, four different treatments in all since they can be used in combination, and a factorial design would be used. A **factorial design** is one in which the effects of two or more independent treatment variables are considered simultaneously.

There are three very good reasons why one might want to use a factorial design.[8] First, it allows the interaction of the factors to be studied. The plastic container might sell better in Shape A, whereas the metal container might sell better in Shape B. This type of effect can only be investigated if the factors are considered simultaneously. Second, a factorial design allows a saving of time and effort, because all the observations are employed to study the effects of each of the factors. Suppose that separate experiments were conducted, one to study the effect of container type and another to study the effect of container shape. Some of the observations would yield information about type and some about shape. By combining the two factors in one experiment, all the observations bear on both factors. "Hence one two-factor experiment is more economical than two one-factor experiments."[9] Third, the conclusions reached have

---

[8]William C. Guenther, *Analysis of Variance* (Englewood Cliffs, N.J.: Prentice-Hall, 1964), pp. 99–100; and John Neter, William Wasserman, and Michael H. Kutner, *Applied Linear Statistical Models,* 3rd ed. (Homewood, Ill.: Richard D. Irwin, Inc., 1990), pp. 673–677.

[9]Guenther, *Analysis of Variance,* p. 100. For examples of factorial experiments, see J. B. Wilkinson, J. Barry Mason, and Christie H. Paksoy, "Assessing the Impact of Short-Term Supermarket Strategy Variables," *Journal of Marketing Research,* 19 (February 1982), pp. 72–86; and Susan M. Petroshius and Kent B. Monroe, "Effect of Product-Line Pricing Characteristics on Product Evaluations," *Journal of Consumer Research,* 13 (March 1987), pp. 511–519; Paul M. Herr, Frank R. Kardes, and John Kim, "Effects of Word-of-Mouth and Product Attribute Information on Persuasion: An Accessibility-Diagnosticity Perspective," *Journal of Consumer Research,* 17 (March 1991), pp. 454–462.

broader application, since each factor is studied with varying combinations of the other factors.[10] This result is much more useful than it would be if everything else had been held constant.

The factorial design may be used with any of the single-factor designs previously discussed — completely randomized, randomized block, and Latin square. The underlying model changes, as does the analysis-of-variance table, but the principle remains the same. Consequently, let us illustrate the method with the simplest case, a completely randomized design.

Consider again the sales representatives' call plan example. Suppose that the company's managers were thinking of revising both the method and frequency of customer contact by supplementing sales representatives' personal contacts with office telephone contacts. Two phone contact plans, which differed in the frequency with which customers were contacted, were being considered. Call the telephone contact Plan A and the personal contact Plan B, and consider the 2×3 factorial experiment in which each of the two levels of A occurs with each of the three levels of B to yield six treatments. Suppose that the treatments were randomly assigned to each of five sales representatives. Thus, there would be five replications for each treatment.

	Personal Call Plan		
Telephone Call Plan	B_1	B_2	B_3
A_1	A_1B_1	A_1B_2	A_1B_3
A_2	A_2B_1	A_2B_2	A_2B_3

Suppose that the results were as contained in Table 15A.6. Let:

α_i = the effect of the ith level of the A factor (telephone call plan), $i = 1, \ldots, a$;
β_j = the effect of the jth level of the B factor (personal call plan), $j = 1, \ldots, b$;
$(\alpha\beta)_{ij}$ = the effect of the ith level of the A factor and jth level of the B factor;
X_{ijk} = the kth observation on the ith level of the A factor and the jth level of the B factor;
μ = the grand mean; and
ϵ_{ijk} = the error associated with the kth observation on the ith level of A and jth level of B.

The underlying model for this completely randomized design suggests that any observation X_{ijk} can be written as the sum of the grand mean, treatment effects, and an error term; that is,

$$X_{ijk} = \mu + \alpha_i + \beta_j + (\alpha\beta)_{ij} + \epsilon_{ijk}.$$

---

[10]One can often use select combinations of factor levels rather than every possible combination, which greatly simplifies the experiment. See Charles W. Holland and David W. Cravens, "Fractional Factorial Experimental Designs in Marketing Research," *Journal of Marketing Research,* 10 (August 1973), pp. 270–276. See also Raghu N. Kacker and Kwock-Leung Tsui, "Interaction Graphs: Graphical Aids for Planning Experiments," *Journal of Quality Technology,* 22 (January 1990), pp. 1–14, for discussion of graphical aids to plan fractional factorial experiments.

TABLE 15A.6   **Sales Generated by Various Personal and Telephone Call Plans**

Telephone Call Plan	Personal Call Plan			Total	Mean
	B_1	B_2	B_3		
A_1	42 40 52 46 40	51 52 50 49 44	43 44 54 44 40	691	46.1
A_2	36 38 32 29 38	35 47 38 35 36	36 42 36 30 35	543	36.2
Total	393	437	404	1,234	41.1
Mean	39.3	43.7	40.4		

Cell	A_1B_1	A_1B_2	A_1B_3	A_2B_1	A_2B_2	A_2B_3
Total	220	246	225	173	191	179
Mean	44.0	49.2	45.0	34.6	38.2	35.8

The assumptions are the same as for a completely randomized design except there are now $r = ab$ populations, whereas in the completely randomized design there were k populations — one for each treatment. Otherwise, though, it is still assumed that the distribution of the variable in each of the populations is normal and that the populations have the same variance.

There are three main hypotheses, all of which essentially state that the treatment effects are zero (the cell means are equal). The alternate hypotheses are that at least some of the cell means differ. The hypotheses can be written as follows:

$$H_0^{(1)}: \alpha_i = 0 \quad i = 1, \ldots, a,$$

$$H_a^{(1)}: \text{not all } \alpha_i \text{ are zero.}$$

$$H_0^{(2)}: \beta_j = 0 \quad j = 1, \ldots, b,$$

$$H_a^{(2)}: \text{not all } \beta_j \text{ are zero.}$$

$$H_0^{(3)}: (\alpha\beta)_{ij} = 0 \quad i = 1, \ldots, a \quad j = 1, \ldots, b,$$

$$H_a^{(3)}: \text{not all } (\alpha\beta)_{ij} \text{ are zero.}$$

The first two hypotheses state that there are no differences caused, respectively, by the levels of the A and B factors; the third says that the effects caused by Factors A and

B are additive. To test these hypotheses, the following sums of squares are needed ($n = 5$ replications):

$$SS_T = \sum_{i=1}^{a} \sum_{j=1}^{b} \sum_{k=1}^{n} (X_{ijk} - \bar{x}_{...})^2$$
$$= (42 - 41.1)^2 + (40 - 41.1)^2 + \ldots + (35 - 41.1)^2$$
$$= 1{,}333.5.$$

$$SS_{TR} = n \sum_{i=1}^{a} \sum_{j=1}^{b} (\bar{x}_{ij.} - \bar{x}_{...})^2$$
$$= 5 [(44.0 - 41.1)^2 + (49.2 - 41.1)^2 + (45.0 - 41.1)^2$$
$$+ (34.6 - 41.1)^2 + (38.2 - 41.1)^2 + (35.8 - 41.1)^2]$$
$$= 839.9.$$

$$SS_A = bn \sum_{i=1}^{a} (\bar{x}_{i..} - \bar{x}_{...})^2$$
$$= 3 (5) [(46.1 - 41.1)^2 + (36.2 - 41.1)^2] = 735.1.$$

$$SS_B = an \sum_{j=1}^{b} (\bar{x}_{.j.} - \bar{x}_{...})^2$$
$$= 2 (5) [(39.3 - 41.1)^2 + (43.7 - 41.1)^2 + (40.4 - 41.1)^2]$$
$$= 104.8.$$

$$SS_{AB} = SS_{TR} - SS_A - SS_B$$
$$= 839.9 - 735.1 - 104.8 = 0.0.$$

$$SS_E = SS_T - SS_{TR}$$
$$= 1.333.5 - 839.9 = 493.6.$$

Table 15A.7 contains the various mean squares and F ratios. Consider the interaction term first. Calculated F is zero. Critical F for $\alpha = 0.05$ and $v_1 = 2$, $v_2 = 24$ is 3.40. Calculated F is less than critical F, and the null hypothesis is not rejected. The effects are additive. The effectiveness of the telephone call plan is not dependent on the personal sales call plan, and vice versa. Consider next the effectiveness of the sales representative personal call plan. Calculated F is again less than critical F, and the null hypothesis of equality of means is not rejected. The data do not indicate that there is any difference in the effectiveness of the three personal call plans. Consider finally the telephone call plan. Calculated F is 35.86. Critical F for $v_1 = 1$, $v_2 = 24$ and $\alpha = 0.05$ is 4.26. Since calculated F exceeds critical F, the null hypothesis is rejected. There is a difference in effectiveness of the two telephone call plans. An examination of the cell means in Table 15A.6 indicates that telephone call Plan A_1 is much better than Plan A_2. If the company were to make a change, this would be the plan it would adopt.

TABLE 15A.7   **Analysis-of-Variance Table for 2 × 3 Factorial Experiment of Telephone and Personal Call Plans**

Source of Variation	Sum of Squares	Degrees of Freedom	Mean Square	F Ratio
A (telephone)	735.1	$(a - 1) = 1$	735.1	35.86
B (personal)	104.8	$(b - 1) = 2$	52.4	2.56
AB (interaction)	0.0	$(a - 1)(b - 1) = 2$	0.0	0.00
Error	493.6	$ab(n - 1) = 24$	20.5	
Total	1,333.5	$abn - 1 = 29$		

Suppose that the interaction term had tested significantly. We would not have bothered to check for the significance of the A and B factors by themselves. Rather, we would have looked for the best combination of a telephone call plan with a personal call plan, because a significant interaction term would have indicated that the effects were not additive; a significant interaction term would have implied that the effects of A were different for some levels of B or vice versa.

Questions

1. What is the basic idea underlying the analysis-of-variance procedure? In general, how are these sources of variation computed? What is the basic statistic used to test for the differences among means in analysis of variance?

2. When is a randomized-block design preferred over a completely randomized design? How does the underlying model change? How do the calculations change?

3. When is a Latin square the preferred experimental design? What is its basic nature? What is the underlying model for a Latin-square design? What is the basic test procedure?

4. When is a factorial design appropriate? What is the basic model of a completely randomized factorial design? What sums of squares are calculated? What are the basic comparisons among the various mean squares?

Applications and Problems

1. Mr. Z, the advertising manager of a medium-sized manufacturer of rug and room deodorizers, has developed three preliminary advertising campaigns for the company's line of deodorizers. The three campaigns are tested in an independent sample of 24 cities across the United States, and the sales in each city are monitored. (Note: (1) cities are randomly assigned to each treatment or campaign, and (2) the 24 cities are comparable in terms of various socioeconomic and demographic variables.) The results of this test market are as follows:

Sales (in thousands of dollars)

City	Advertising Campaign 1	City	Advertising Campaign 2	City	Advertising Campaign 3
1	10	9	9	17	12
2	6	10	7	18	10
3	8	11	6	19	8
4	12	12	10	20	13
5	6	13	6	21	11
6	8	14	4	22	10
7	9	15	5	23	9
8	7	16	5	24	7

Mr. Z wants to determine if there is a difference in sales as a result of the three advertising campaigns. He requires your assistance in analyzing the preceding information.

a. State the null and alternate hypotheses.

b. What statistical test is appropriate in this situation? Identify the assumptions underlying the test of the hypotheses.

c. Compute the grand mean and the mean of the *j*th treatment ($j = 1, 2, 3$). Show your calculations.

d. Compute the total variation (the sum of squares total). Show your calculations.

e. Compute the between-group variation (sum of squares between groups). Show your calculations.

f. Compute the within-group variation (sum of squares within groups). Show your calculations.

g. What are the degrees of freedom associated with each of these sums of squares?

h. Compute the mean squares associated with each of the sums of squares. Show your calculations.

i. Complete the following analysis of variance table.

Source of Variation	Sum of Squares	Degrees of Freedom	Mean Square	F Ratio
Between-group				
Within-group				
Total				

j. Discuss your findings on the basis of the preceding calculations. (Note: Assume that $\alpha = 0.05$ to find the critical *F* value.)

2. The training coordinator of a Fortune 500 company is considering different training approaches for a course to be offered the following year for new managers in entry-level positions. The course is intended to teach managers with no technical background the basic electrical engineering skills necessary to understand the company's products. The coordinator believes that the course can be offered in two ways: the traditional lecture format, in which an instructor provides the necessary information to the new managers with minimal interaction between the instructor and the managers; and the group discussion format, in which interaction between the managers and the instructor is encouraged.

In addition, the training coordinator is considering two types of instructional materials for the new course — one using a standard electrical engineering textbook, and one using a series of workbooks, or training modules.

To determine how the course should be conducted and what materials to use to maximize the amount of information learned by new managers, the coordinator has decided to conduct a simple experiment using 20 new managers who were scheduled to take the course. Based on experience and college coursework and grades, there were no obvious differences between the 20 managers. Using a factorial design, the 20 managers were randomly assigned to one of four training groups. Managers in the first group were taught using a standard lecture format and a current electrical engineering textbook. A second group also used a textbook, but sessions were held using the group discussion format. The third group used a series of workbooks rather than a textbook and was taught by the instructor in the lecture format. Finally, the fourth group also used the workbooks, but it was taught in the group discussion format. The same instructor was used for each of the four experimental groups.

At the conclusion of the course, the managers were given a comprehensive test to determine how much of the material each retained from the coursework. The training coordinator plans to use this information to determine how the new course should be implemented in the future. The test scores for each of the participants are as follows:

Group 1: Lecture-Textbook	Group 2: Discussion-Textbook	Group 3: Lecture-Workbook	Group 4: Discussion-Workbook
62	74	84	94
78	86	72	84
86	76	72	88
64	88	66	78
70	84	88	86

a. State the null and alternate hypotheses.

b. Complete the following table:

Source of Variation	Sum of Squares	Degrees of Freedom	Mean Square	F Ratio
A (instruction format)				
B (instruction materials)				
AB (interaction)				
Error				
Total				

c. What recommendations can you make based on the findings of the experiment? (Note: Assume that $\alpha = 0.05$ to find the critical F value.)

3. What are the underlying assumptions for the ANOVA model? Which assumption is necessary to allow the pooling of variances? What happens if this assumption is violated and the variances are still pooled?

4. A beverage company is testing different point-of-purchase displays. The marketing manager selects 12 stores in a market area and assigns them at random to the following

treatment conditions: Control group (no change in display), end-of-aisle display, and store shelf flyer with tear-away coupon. The manager will measure the sales occurring in each treatment condition and analyze the figures using ANOVA. The sales for each store are shown in the following table:

Control Stores (No change)				Experimental Group I (End-of-aisle display)				Experimental Group II (Shelf display with coupon)			
6	14	19	17	18	11	20	23	7	11	18	10

a. List the sources of variation for this test. What are the corresponding degrees of freedom for each source?

b. Considering the underlying assumptions for ANOVA, which of these assumptions may be violated? Is there a more appropriate design for this experiment? Discuss the advantages and disadvantages of your proposed design.

c. Assume that all assumptions are valid for the experiment. Using the data, perform a one-way analysis of variance. What is the calculated F statistic? At $\alpha = 0.05$, can we reject the null hypothesis of no difference in sales between the treatment groups?

Refer to the NFO Research, Inc., coffee study described on pages 780–783 in Chapter 13 for the next problem.

5. Is there a difference in the importance rating of the attribute "premium brand" for people who prefer the various brands ($\alpha = .05$)? Conduct an analysis of variance using the importance rating as the dependent variable to determine your answer.

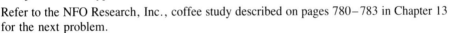

APPENDIX 15B

Analysis of Catalog-Buying Data

DIFFERENCES IN MEANS

One question of major interest in the catalog-buying study (Appendix 13A) is the amount of confidence people have when purchasing products from a catalog. The CATCON "catalog confidence" index was formed to address this question. The CATCON index is the summed score for the responses to Questions 4a through 4e in the survey.

Table 15B.1 investigates whether the CATCON index depends on the person's sex. The table indicates that the mean score for males is higher than that for females. The difference is also statistically significant, indicating that males are more confident when buying from catalogs than females. The variance in CATCON scores is the same for males and females, suggesting that it is better to use the pooled sample variance when checking the statistical significance of the difference in the two means.

PAIRED DIFFERENCE TEST

To investigate whether there was a difference in confidence when purchasing sporting goods from retail stores rather than from catalogs, a second index was formed to go

TABLE 15B.1 Difference in Means for CATCON Index between Males and Females

Variable/Group	Number of Cases	Mean	Standard Deviation	Standard Error	Pooled Variance Estimate			Separate Variance Estimate		
					t Value	Degrees of Freedom	2-Tail Probability	t Value	Degrees of Freedom	2-Tail Probability
CATCON										
1. Males	65	21.462	2.001	0.248						
2. Females	58	9.224	2.000	0.263	33.87	121	0.000	33.87	119.42	0.000

TABLE 15B.2 Paired Difference Test for the CATCON and RETCON Indices

Variable/Group	Number of Cases	Mean	Standard Deviation	Standard Error	(Difference) Mean	Standard Deviation	Standard Error	t Value	Degrees of Freedom	2-Tail Probability
CATCON	124	15.605	6.494	0.583						
RETCON		19.395	3.154	0.283	-3.790	8.402	0.755	-5.02	123	0.000

along with the CATCON index described above. Called RETCON for "retail store confidence," this index was formed by summing the numerical responses to Questions 5a through 5e in the survey. Note that each of these questions involving retail stores has an exact parallel for purchases made through a catalog. Thus, it makes sense to look at the difference in the two summed scores for each person, a comparison contained in Table 15B.2. The comparison indicates that there is indeed a statistically significant difference in the two summed scores. Subjects are more confident when buying sporting goods from retailers as compared to buying from catalogs, at least with respect to the five items contained in the questionnaire.

ANALYSIS OF VARIANCE

Table 15B.3 contains the analysis investigating whether the CATCON index varies as a function of the number of sporting goods items purchased in the past year. The analysis-of-variance portion of the table (the top portion) indicates that the differences among the

TABLE 15B.3   **Analysis of Variance of CATCON Index as a Function of Number of Sporting Goods Items (V15) Purchased in Past Year**

Source of Variation	Sum of Squares	DF	Mean Square	F	Significance of F
Main effects (V15)	4320.278	4	1080.069	148.184	0.000
Explained	4320.278	4	1080.069	148.184	0.000
Residual	867.358	119	7.289		
Total	5187.635	123	42.176		

124 cases were processed
  0 cases were missing

Grand Mean = 15.60
Variable + Category

V15	N	Unadjusted Deviation	Eta	Adjusted for Independents Deviation	Eta
1	29	−7.85		−7.85	
2	27	−4.35		−4.35	
3	18	1.84		1.84	
4	15	5.26		5.26	
5	35	6.65		6.65	
			0.91		0.91
Multiple R squared					0.833
Multiple R					0.913

cell means are statistically significant; there is less than 1 chance in 1,000 that the differences in mean squares would have been as large as they were under the null hypothesis of no differences in the CATCON index as a function of the number of sporting goods items purchased in the past year. The cell means in the lower portion of the table (the cell means are expressed as deviations from the grand mean) suggest that as the number of items purchased goes up, so does the CATCON index.

16

DATA ANALYSIS:
INVESTIGATION OF ASSOCIATION

In the discussion of data analysis so far, we have been primarily concerned with testing for the significance of *differences* obtained under various research conditions. It may have been a difference between a sample result and an assumed population condition, or between two or more sample results. Quite often, however, the researcher has the different assignment of determining whether there is any association between two or more variables and, if so, the strength and functional form of the relationship.

Typically, we try to predict the value of one variable (for example, consumption of a specific product by a family) on the basis of one or more other variables (for example, income and number of family members). The variable being predicted is called the dependent or, more aptly, the criterion variable. The variables that form the basis of the prediction are called the independent, or predictor, variables.

SIMPLE REGRESSION AND CORRELATION ANALYSIS

Regression and correlation analysis are terms referring to techniques for studying the relationship between two or more variables. Although the two terms are often used interchangeably, there is a difference in purpose. **Correlation analysis** involves measuring the *closeness* of the relationship between two or more variables; it considers the joint variation of two measures, neither of which is restricted by the experimenter. **Regression analysis** refers to the techniques used to derive an *equation* that relates the criterion variable to one or more predictor variables; it considers the frequency distribution of the criterion variable, when one or more predictor variables are held fixed at various levels.[1]

---

[1] Although the regression model theoretically applies to fixed levels of the predictor variables (Xs), it can also be shown to apply when the Xs themselves are random variables, assuming that certain conditions are satisfied. See John Neter, William Wasserman, and Michael H. Kutner, *Applied Linear Regression Models,* 2nd ed. (Homewood, Ill.: Richard D. Irwin, 1989), pp. 86–87; or Thomas H. Wonnacott and Ronald J. Wonnacott, *Regression: A Second Course in Statistics* (Malabar, Florida: Robert E. Krieger Publishing Co., 1986), pp. 49–50.

It is perfectly legitimate to measure the closeness of the relationship between variables without deriving an estimating equation. Similarly, one can perform a regression analysis without investigating the closeness of the relationship between the variables. But, since it is common to do both, the body of techniques is usually referred to as either regression or correlation analysis.

Before introducing simple correlation analysis, a comment on the distinction between correlation and causation is in order. The use of the terms *dependent* (criterion) and *independent* (predictor) variables to describe the measures in correlation analysis stems from the mathematical functional relationship between the variates and is in no way related to dependence of one variable on another in a *causal* sense. There is nothing in correlation analysis, or any other mathematical procedure, that can be used to establish causality. All these procedures can do is measure the nature and degree of *association* or *covariation* between variables. Statements of causality must spring from underlying knowledge and theories about the phenomena under investigation. They categorically do *not* spring from the mathematics.[2] Research Realities 16.1, for example, highlights what Lawrence Gibson, former director of marketing research at General Mills, has to say about the important role of theory in directing marketing inquiry.

The subject of regression and correlation analysis is best discussed through example. Consider, therefore, the national manufacturer of a ballpoint pen, Click, who is interested in investigating the effectiveness of the firm's marketing efforts.[3] The company uses regional wholesalers to distribute Click and supplements its efforts with company sales representatives and spot TV advertising. The company intends to use annual territory sales as its measure of effectiveness. These data and information on the number of sales representatives serving a territory are readily available in company records. The other characteristics to which they desire to relate sales — TV spot advertising and wholesaler efficiency — are more difficult to determine. Obtaining information on TV spot advertising in a territory requires analysis of advertising schedules and a study of area coverage by channel to determine which areas each broadcast could be considered to be reaching. Wholesaler efficiency requires rating the wholesalers on a number of criteria and aggregating the ratings into an overall measure of wholesaler efficiency, where 4 = outstanding, 3 = good, 2 = average, and 1 = poor. Because of the time and expense required to generate these advertising and distribution characteristics, the company has decided to carry out its analysis employing only a sample of sales territories. The data for a simple random sample of 40 territories are contained in Table 16.1.

The effect of each of the marketing-mix variables on sales can be investigated in several ways. One obvious way is simply to plot sales as a function of each of the variables. Figure 16.1 contains these plots, which are called scatter diagrams. Panel A suggests that sales increase as the number of TV spots per month increases. Panel B suggests that sales increase as the number of sales representatives serving the territory increases. Finally, Panel C suggests that there is little relationship between sales in a

---

[2]See Darrell Huff, *How to Lie with Statistics* (New York: Norton, 1954), pp. 87–99, for a discussion of this point using some rather humorous anecdotes.

[3]Many of the results contained in the discussion were determined by computer and thus may differ slightly from those generated using hand calculations because of the rounding errors associated with the latter method.

Research Realities 16.1

Role of Theory in Directing Marketing Inquiry

If marketing researchers want to acquire true marketing "knowledge" they should devote more time and effort to developing and validating marketing theories, according to Lawrence D. Gibson, director of marketing research, General Mills Inc., Minneapolis.

"There's a funny notion around that theories are vague, ephemeral, and useless, and data are nice, hard, real things. And that somehow knowledge is associated with facts and data. This is nonsense.

"Knowledge is an interrelated set of validated theories and established facts, not just facts. In marketing, we are profoundly ignorant of what we're doing because we're woefully short on theory while we're drowning in data."

Deploring the lack of validated marketing theories and overabundance of marketing "facts," Gibson quoted the scientist R. B. Braithwaite. "The world is not made up of empirical facts with the addition of the laws of nature. What we call the laws of nature are simply theories, the conceptual devices by which we organize our empirical knowledge and predict the future."

And he quoted Albert Einstein: "The grand aim of all science is to cover the maximum number of empirical facts, by logical deduction, into the smallest number of axioms, axioms which represent that remainder which is not comprehended."

In other words, Gibson said, "the axioms and theories are not our knowledge, they are our ignorance. They're part of the problem we assume away." A

theory, he said, is how "scientists choose to organize their knowledge and perceptions of the world. Theories are pretty well laid out, simplistic, general, have predicted usefulness, and fit the facts.

"Theory is basic to what data you choose to collect," he said, "You can't observe all the veins of all the leaves of all the branches of all the trees of all the forests in the world. You've got to choose what facts you choose to observe, and you're going to be guided in some sense by some kind of theory.

"And when you turn around to use the data, you're also going to be guided by theory. It will have a profound effect on what you do."

This shows up in the way researchers go about analyzing different kinds of data. For example, when working with observational data, people simply don't realize the weak theoretical ground on which they stand. They wander around the data, happily and merrily, trying to find out what makes sense.

"Perhaps you've seen some fairly typical versions of this. The creative analyst looks at the data and the survey and they don't make sense. 'Make sense' means the findings are congenial to his prior judgment. But the world isn't working the way he thought it was supposed to be working.

"So he cross-tabs by big cities vs. little cities. Still doesn't make sense. But he is very creative, and observes there are more outer-directed people in big cities than in little cities, so he now cross-tabs by inner-directed vs. outer-directed by city size, and — lo and behold — he finds out he was right all along!"

"Now, obviously, as long as you keep analyzing when you don't like what you see, and stop analyzing when you do like what you see, the world always will look to you the way it's supposed to look. You'll never learn anything."

Source: Larry Gibson, "Marketing Research Needs Validated Theories," *Marketing News*, 17 (January 21, 1983), p. 14. Reprinted with permission from Marketing News, published by the American Marketing Association.

---

territory and the efficiency of the wholesaler serving the territory. Panels A and B further suggest that the relationship between sales and each of the predictor variables could be adequately captured with a straight line. One way to generate the relationship between sales and either TV spots or number of sales representatives would be to "eyeball" it;

TABLE **16.1**   **Territory Data for Click Ballpoint Pens**

Territory	Sales (in thousands) Y	Advertising (TV spots per month) X_1	Number of Sales Representatives X_2	Wholesaler Efficiency Index X_3
005	260.3	5	3	4
019	286.1	7	5	2
033	279.4	6	3	3
039	410.8	9	4	4
061	438.2	12	6	1
082	315.3	8	3	4
091	565.1	11	7	3
101	570.0	16	8	2
115	426.1	13	4	3
118	315.0	7	3	4
133	403.6	10	6	1
149	220.5	4	4	1
162	343.6	9	4	3
164	644.6	17	8	4
178	520.4	19	7	2
187	329.5	9	3	2
189	426.0	11	6	4
205	343.2	8	3	3
222	450.4	13	5	4
237	421.8	14	5	2
242	245.6	7	4	4
251	503.3	16	6	3
260	375.7	9	5	3
266	265.5	5	3	3
279	620.6	18	6	4
298	450.5	18	5	3
306	270.1	5	3	2
332	368.0	7	6	2
347	556.1	12	7	1
358	570.0	13	6	4
362	318.5	8	4	3
370	260.2	6	3	2
391	667.0	16	8	2
408	618.3	19	8	2
412	525.3	17	7	4
430	332.2	10	4	3
442	393.2	12	5	3
467	283.5	8	3	3
471	376.2	10	5	4
488	481.8	12	5	2

FIGURE **16.1** **Scatter Diagrams of Sales versus Marketing-Mix Variables**

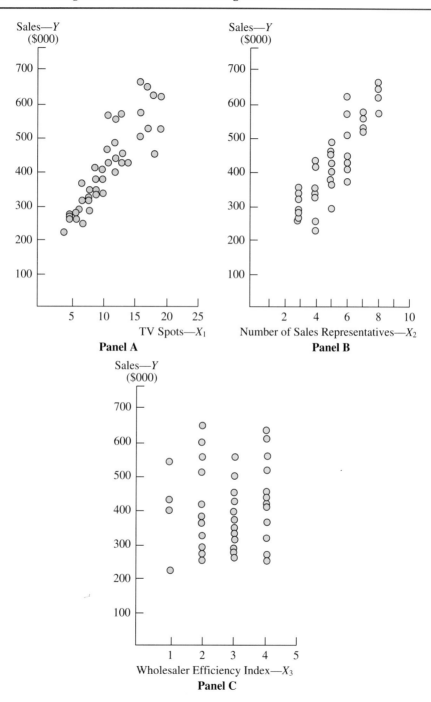

that is, one could draw a straight line through the points in the graphs. Such a line would represent the line of "average" relationship. It would indicate the average value of the criterion variable, sales, for given values of either of the predictor variables, TV spots or number of sales representatives. One could then enter the graph with, say, the number of TV spots in a territory and could read off the average level of sales expected in the territory. The difficulty with the graphic approach is that two analysts might generate different lines to describe the relationship. This simply raises the question of which line is more correct or fits the data better.

An alternative approach is to mathematically fit a line to the data. The general equation of a straight line is $Y = \alpha + \beta X$, where α is the Y intercept and β is the slope coefficient. In the case of sales Y and TV spots X_1, the equation could be written as $Y = \alpha_1 + \beta_1 X_1$. For the relationship between sales Y and number of sales representatives X_2, it could be written as $Y = \alpha_2 + \beta_2 X_2$, where the subscripts indicate the predictor variable being considered. As written, each of these models is a *deterministic model*. When a value of the predictor variable is substituted in the equation with specified α and β, a unique value for Y is determined and no allowance is made for error.

When investigating social phenomena, there is rarely, if ever, zero error. Thus, in place of the deterministic model, we might substitute a *probabilistic model* and make some assumptions about the error. For example, let us work with the relationship between sales and the number of TV spots and consider the model

$$Y_i = \alpha_1 + \beta_1 X_{i1} + \epsilon_i,$$

where Y_i is the level of sales in the ith territory, X_{i1} is the level of advertising in the ith territory, and ϵ_i is the error associated with the ith observation. This is the form of the model that is used for regression analysis. The error term is part and parcel of the model. It represents a failure to include all factors in the model, the fact that there is an unpredictable element in human behavior, and the condition that there are errors of measurement.[4] The probabilistic model allows for the fact that the Y value is not uniquely determined for a given X_i value. Rather, all that is determined for a given X_i value is the "average value" of Y. Individual values can be expected to fluctuate above and below this average.

The mathematical solution for finding the line of "best fit" for the probabilistic model requires that some assumptions be made about the distribution of the error term. The line of best fit could be defined in several ways. The typical way is in terms of the line that minimizes the sum of the deviations squared about the line (the least-squares solution). Consider Figure 16.2 and suppose that the line drawn in the figure is the estimated equation. Employing a caret to indicate an estimated value, the error for the ith observation is the difference between the actual Y value, Y_i, and the estimated Y value,

---

[4]Strictly speaking, the regression model requires that errors of measurement be associated only with the criterion variable and that the predictor variables be measured without error. See Wonnacott and Wonnacott, *Regression*, pp. 293–299, for a discussion of the problems and solutions when the predictor variables also have an error component.

F$_{\text{IGURE}}$ 16.2   **Relationship between Y and X_1 in the Probabilistic Model**

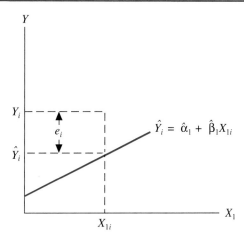

$\hat{Y}_i$; that is, $e_i = Y_i - \hat{Y}_i$. The least-squares solution is based on the principle that the sum of these squared errors should be made as small as possible; that is, $\sum_i^n = e_i^2$ should be minimized. The sample estimates $\hat{\alpha}_1$ and $\hat{\beta}_1$ of the true population parameters α_1 and β_1 are determined so that this condition is satisfied.

There are three simplifying assumptions made about the error term in the least-squares solution:

1. The mean or average value of the disturbance term is zero.
2. The variance of the disturbance term is constant and is independent of the values of the predictor variable.
3. The values of the error term are independent of one another.

Given these assumptions, the sample estimates of the intercept and slope population parameters, α and β in the general case, can be shown to be[5]

$$\hat{\alpha} = \bar{y} - \hat{\beta}\bar{x},$$

$$\hat{\beta} = \frac{n \sum_{i=1}^{n} X_i Y_i - \left(\sum_{i=1}^{n} X_i \right) \left(\sum_{i=1}^{n} Y_i \right)}{n \sum_{i=1}^{n} X_i^2 - \left(\sum_{i=1}^{n} X_i \right)^2}$$

---

[5]See Neter, Wasserman, and Kutner, *Applied Linear Regression Models*, Chapter 2, for the derivation.

where

$$\bar{y} = \sum_{i=1}^{n} \frac{Y_i}{n} \quad \text{and} \quad \bar{x} = \sum_{i=1}^{n} \frac{X_i}{n}.$$

Thus, one needs various sums, sums of squares, and sums of cross products to generate the least-squares estimates.

Consider only the sales Y and TV spots per month X_1 data provided in Table 16.1. It turns out that

$$\sum_{i=1}^{40} Y_i = (260.3 + 286.1 + \ldots + 481.8) = 16{,}451.5,$$

$$\sum_{i=1}^{40} X_{i1} = (5 + 7 + \ldots + 12) = 436.0,$$

$$\sum_{i=1}^{40} X_{i1}\, Y_i = 5(260.3) + 7(286.1) + \ldots + 12(481.8) = 197{,}634,$$

$$\sum_{i=1}^{40} X_{i1}{}^2 = (5)^2 + (7)^2 + \ldots + (12)^2 = 5{,}476,$$

$$\bar{y} = \frac{\sum_{i=1}^{40} Y_i}{n} = \frac{16{,}451.5}{40} = 411.3,$$

$$\bar{x}_1 = \frac{\sum_{i=1}^{40} X_{i1}}{n} = \frac{436}{40} = 10.9.$$

Therefore,

$$\hat{\beta}_1 = \frac{n \sum_{i=1}^{n} X_{i1} Y_i - \left(\sum_{i=1}^{n} X_{i1} \right) \left(\sum_{i=1}^{n} Y_i \right)}{n \sum_{i=1}^{n} X_{i1}{}^2 - \left(\sum_{i=1}^{n} X_i \right)^2}$$

$$= \frac{40(197{,}634) - (436)\,(16{,}451.5)}{40(5{,}476) - (436)^2} = 25.3,$$

$$\hat{\alpha} = \bar{y} - \hat{\beta}_1 \bar{x}_1 = 411.3 - (25.3)\,(10.9) = 135.4.$$

The equation is plotted in Figure 16.3. The slope of the line is given by β_1. The value 25.3 of β_1 suggests that sales increase by \$25,300 for every unit increase in TV

FIGURE 16.3   **Plot of Equation Relating Sales to TV Spots**

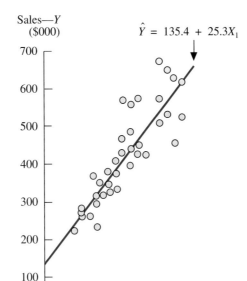

spots. As mentioned previously, this is an estimate of the true population condition based on our particular sample of 40 observations. A different sample would most assuredly generate a different estimate. Further, we have not yet asked whether this is a statistically significant result or whether it could have occurred by chance. Nevertheless, it is a most vital item of information that helps in determining whether advertising expense is worth the estimated return. The estimate of the intercept parameter is $\hat{\alpha}_1 = 135.4$; this indicates where the line crosses the Y axis because it represents the estimated value of Y when the predictor variable equals zero.

Standard Error of Estimate

An examination of Figure 16.3 shows that, while the line seems to fit the points fairly well, there is still some deviation in the points about the line. The size of these deviations measures the goodness of the fit, and a numerical measure of the variation of the points about the line may be computed in much the same way as we compute the standard deviation of a frequency distribution.

Just as the sample mean is an estimate of the true parent population mean, the line given by $Y_i = \hat{\alpha}_1 + \hat{\beta}_1 X_{i1} + e_i$ is an estimate of the true regression line $Y_i = \alpha_1 + \beta_1 X_{i1} + \epsilon_i$. Consider the variance of the random error ϵ around the true line of regression; that is, σ_ϵ^2 or $\sigma_{Y/X}^2$. When the population variance σ^2 is unknown, an unbiased estimate is given by

$$\hat{s}^2 = \frac{\sum\limits_{i=1}^{n} (X_i - \bar{x})^2}{(n-1)}.$$

Similarly, let $s_{Y/X}^2$ be an unbiased estimate of $\sigma_{Y/X}^2$. Now it can be shown that

$$s_{Y/X^2} = \frac{\sum\limits_{i=1}^{n} e_i^2}{(n-2)} = \frac{\sum\limits_{i=1}^{n} (Y_i - \hat{Y}_i)^2}{(n-2)}$$

is an unbiased estimator of $\sigma_{Y/X}^2$, where Y_i and $\hat{Y}_i$ are, respectively, the observed and estimated values of Y for the ith observation. The square root of the quantity $s_{Y/X}$ is often called the **standard error of estimate,** although the term *standard deviation from regression* is more meaningful.

The interpretation of the standard error of estimate parallels that for the standard deviation. Consider any X_{i1} value. What the standard error of estimate means is that for any such value of TV spots X_{i1}, Y_i (sales) tends to be distributed about the corresponding $\hat{Y}_i$ value—the point on the line—with a standard deviation equal to the standard error of estimate. Further, the variation about the line is the same throughout the entire length of the line. The point on the line (the arithmetic mean) changes as X_{i1} changes, but the distribution of Y_i values around the line does not change with changes in the number of TV spots. Figure 16.4 depicts the situation under the assumption that the error term is rectangularly distributed, for example.[6] Note that the assumption of constant $s_{Y/X}$, irrespective of the value of X_{i1}, produces parallel bands around the regression line.

The smaller the standard error of estimate, the better the line fits the data. For the line relating sales to TV spots, it is $s_{Y/X} = 59.6$.

Inferences about the Slope Coefficient

The value of the slope coefficient, $\hat{\beta}_1 = 25.3$, was previously calculated, although at that time the question of whether the result could have been due to chance was not raised. To deal with that question requires an additional assumption—namely, that the errors are normally distributed rather than rectangularly distributed as previously assumed. However, before proceeding, let us emphasize that the least-squares estimators of the parent population parameters are BLUE; that is, they are the *b*est, *l*inear, *u*nbiased

---

[6]This assumption will be modified shortly to that of normally distributed errors. It is made this way now in order to make more vivid the fact that the assumption of normally distributed errors is only necessary if statistical inferences are to be made about the coefficients.

FIGURE 16.4   **Rectangular Distribution of Error Term**

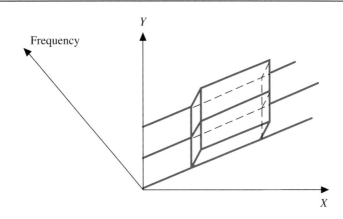

estimators of the true population parameters regardless of the shape of the distribution of the error term. All that is necessary is that the previous assumptions be satisfied. This is the remarkable result of the Gauss-Markov theorem. It is only if we wish to make statistical inferences about the regression coefficients that the assumption of normally distributed errors is required.

It can be shown that if the ϵ_i are normally distributed random variables, then $\hat{\beta}_1$ is also normally distributed. In other words, if we were to take repeated samples from our population of sales territories and calculate a $\hat{\beta}_1$ for each sample, the distribution of these estimates would be normal and *centered* around the *true population* parameter β_1. Further, the variance of the distribution of $\hat{\beta}_1$s can be shown to be equal to

$$\sigma_{\hat{\beta}_1}^2 = \frac{\sigma^2_{Y/X_1}}{\sum_{i=1}^{n} (X_{i1} - \bar{x}_1)^2}.$$

Because the population $\sigma_{Y/X}^2$ is unknown, $\sigma_{\hat{\beta}_1}^2$ is also unknown and has to be estimated. The estimate is generated by substituting the standard error of estimate $s_{Y/X}$ for $\sigma_{Y/X}$:

$$s_{\hat{\beta}_1}^2 = \frac{s_{Y/X_1}^2}{\sum_{i=1}^{n} (X_{i1} - \bar{x}_1)^2}.$$

The situation so far is as follows: Given the assumption of normally distributed errors, $\hat{\beta}_1$ is also normally distributed with a mean of β_1 and unknown variance $\sigma_{\hat{\beta}_1}^2$.

The situation thus parallels that of making an inference about the mean when the population variance is unknown. That set of conditions requires a t test to examine statistical significance, and the test for the significance of β_1 has a similar requirement.

The null hypothesis is that there is no linear relationship between the variables, whereas the alternate hypothesis is that a linear relationship does exist; that is,

$$H_0:\beta_1 = 0,$$
$$H_a:\beta_1 \neq 0.$$

The test statistic is $t = (\hat{\beta}_1 - \beta_1)/s_{\hat{\beta}_1}$, which is t distributed with $n - 2$ degrees of freedom. In the example,

$$s_{\hat{\beta}_1}^2 = \frac{s^2_{Y/X_1}}{\displaystyle\sum_{i=1}^{n}(X_{i1} - \bar{x}_1)^2} = \frac{(59.6)^2}{723.6} = 4.91,$$

$$s_{\hat{\beta}_1} = \sqrt{4.91} = 2.22,$$

$$t = \frac{\hat{\beta}_1 - \beta_1}{s_{\hat{\beta}_1}} = \frac{25.3 - 0}{2.22} = 11.4.$$

For a 0.05 level of significance, the tabled t value for $v = n - 2 = 38$ degrees of freedom is 2.02. Since calculated t exceeds critical t, the null hypothesis is rejected; $\hat{\beta}_1$ is sufficiently different from zero to warrant the assumption of a linear relationship between sales and TV spots. Now, this does not mean that the true relationship between sales and TV spots is *necessarily* linear, only that the evidence indicates that Y (sales) changes as X_1 (TV spots) changes and that we may obtain a better prediction of Y using X_1 and the linear equation than if we simply ignored X_1.

What if the null hypothesis is not rejected? As we have noted, β_1 is the slope of the assumed line over the region of observation and indicates the linear change in Y for a one-unit change in X_1. If we do not reject the null hypothesis that β_1 equals zero, it *does not mean* that Y and X_1 are unrelated. There are two possibilities. First, we may simply be committing a Type II error by not rejecting a false null hypothesis. Second, it is possible that Y and X_1 might be perfectly related in some curvilinear manner, and we have simply chosen the wrong model to describe the physical situation.

Prediction of Y

Having established that the regression is not attributable to chance, let us use it to predict sales from given values of TV spots. There are two cases to consider:

1. predicting the average value of Y for a given X_1,
2. predicting an individual value of Y for a given X_1.

Let us consider these cases in order.

For a given X_1 value, say X_{01}, the Y value predicted by the regression equation is the *average* value of Y given X_1. Thus, in a territory with ten TV spots per month, the expected sales $\hat{Y}_0$ are

$$\hat{Y}_0 = \hat{\alpha}_1 + \hat{\beta}_1 X_{01} = 135.4 + 25.3 \ (10) = 388.4.$$

This is an unbiased estimate of the true *average* value of sales to be expected when there are indeed ten TV spots per month in a territory. Individual territories may, of course, exhibit sales above or below the average, just as there are observations above and below a true population mean. Further, just as a sample mean may not exactly equal the population mean it is estimating, $\hat{Y}_0$ may not exactly equal Y_0, the population mean it is estimating for the given X_1 value. It would, therefore, seem useful to place bounds of error on the estimate.

To determine the bounds of error, it is necessary to know the variance of the distribution of Y_0 given X_{01}. This variance can be estimated, and in particular it is given by

$$s^2_{\hat{Y}_0/X_{01}} = s^2_{Y/X_1} \left[\frac{1}{n} + \frac{(X_{01} - \bar{x}_1)^2}{\displaystyle\sum_{i=1}^{n} (X_{i1} - \bar{x}_1)^2} \right].$$

Note that this variance depends on the particular X_1 value in question. When X_1 equals the mean of the X_1s, the variance is smallest, since $(X_{01} - \bar{x}_1)$ is then equal to zero. As X_1 moves away from the mean, the variance increases. For ten TV spots per day,

$$s^2_{\hat{Y}_0/X_{01}} = (59.6)^2 \left[\frac{1}{40} + \frac{(10) - 10.9)^2}{723.6} \right] = 92.8.$$

The confidence interval for the estimate is given by

$$\hat{Y}_0 \pm t s_{\hat{Y}_0/X_{01}},$$

where t is the tabled t value for the assumed level of significance and $\nu = n - 2$ degrees of freedom. We have already mentioned that for a 0.05 level of significance and $\nu = 38$, $t = 2.02$. Thus, the confidence interval for the average value of sales when there are ten TV spots per month is

$$\hat{Y}_0 \pm t s_{\hat{Y}_0/X_{01}} = 388.4 \pm (2.02) \ (\sqrt{92.8}) = 388.4 \pm 19.5.$$

Although the preceding equation enables us to predict the average level of sales for all sales territories with ten TV spots per month, we might wish to predict the sales that could be expected in some particular territory. This prediction contains an additional element of error, the amount by which the particular territory could be expected to deviate from the average. Thus, the error in predicting a specific value is larger than that for predicting the average value. Specifically, it equals

$$s^2_{Y_0/X_{01}} = s^2_{\hat{Y}/X_1} \left[1 + \frac{1}{n} + \frac{(X_{01} - \bar{x}_1)^2}{\displaystyle\sum_{i=1}^{n} (X_{i1} - x_1)^2} \right],$$

where the caret is removed from Y_0 to indicate that we are now talking about a specific value of Y_0 rather than an average value. Note that $s^2_{Y_0/X_{01}}$ also equals $s^2_{\hat{Y}_0/X_{01}} + s^2_{Y/X_1}$. This alternate expression shows why the confidence interval is wider when the prediction involves a specific value of Y_0 instead of the average value. The second term in this expression, s^2_{Y/X_1}, represents the estimated amount by which the particular value deviates from the average value. For ten TV spots per month,

$$s^2_{Y_0/X_{01}} = (59.6)^2 \left[1 + \frac{1}{40} + \frac{(10 - 10.9)^2}{723.6} \right] = 3{,}645,$$

and the confidence interval is

$$Y_0 \pm t s_{Y_0/X_{01}} = 388.4 \pm (2.02) (\sqrt{3{,}645}) = 388.4 \pm 122.0.$$

Note that the bounds of error are much wider when a particular Y value is being predicted.

Even though the regression equation can be used to develop predictions about the average or likely value of Y for a given X, those doing so must be mindful of the dangers in all such predictions. It is particularly risky to predict outside of the range of values on which the equation was developed. In Research Realities 16.2, for example, a well-known writer of the precomputer era points out the hazards inherent in forecasting the future based on data collected in the past.

Correlation Coefficient

So far we have been concerned with the functional relationship of Y to X. Suppose that we were also concerned with the *strength of the linear relationship* between Y and X. This leads to the notion of the correlation coefficient.

Two additional assumptions are made when discussing the correlation model. First, X_i is also assumed to be a random variable. A sample observation yields both an X_i and Y_i value. Second, it is assumed that the observations come from a bivariate normal distribution — that is, one in which the X variable is normally distributed and the Y variable is also normally distributed.

Now consider the drawing of a sample of n observations from a bivariate normal distribution. Let ρ represent the strength of the linear association between the two variables in the parent population. Let r represent the sample estimate of ρ. Assume that the sample of n observations yielded the scatter of points down in Figure 16.5, and consider

---

Research Realities 16.2

Life on the Mississippi—742 Years from Now

Mark Twain may not have been a statistician, but he knew enough about the tricks numbers can play to write this little spoof for those who would predict "logical" outcomes based on past data.

"In the space of one hundred and seventy-six years the Lower Mississippi has shortened itself two hundred and forty-two miles. This is an average of a trifle over one mile and a third per year. Therefore, any calm person, who is not blind or idiotic, can see that in the Old Oölitic Silurian Period, just a million years ago next November, the Lower Mississippi River was upward of one million three hundred thousand miles long, and stuck out over the Gulf of Mexico like a fishing-rod. And by the same token any person can see that seven hundred and forty-two years from now the Lower Mississippi will be only a mile and three-quarters long, and Cairo and New Orleans will have joined their streets together, and be plodding comfortably along under a single mayor and a mutual board of aldermen. There is something fascinating about science. One gets such wholesale returns of conjecture out of such a trifling investment of fact."

Source: Mark Twain, *Life on the Mississippi.*

---

the division of the figure into the four quadrants formed by erecting perpendiculars to the two axes at $\bar{x}$ and $\bar{y}$.

Consider the deviations from these bisectors. Take any point P with coordinates (X_i, Y_i) and define the deviations

$$x_i = X_i - \bar{x},$$

$$y_i = Y_i - \bar{y},$$

FIGURE 16.5 **Scatter of Points for Sample of *n* Observations**

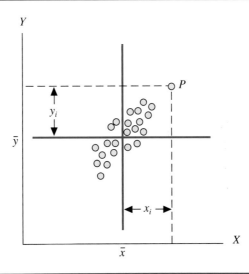

where the small letters indicate deviations around a mean. It is clear from an inspection of Figure 16.5 that the product $x_i y_i$ is

- positive for all points in Quadrant I,
- negative for all points in Quadrant II,
- positive for all points in Quadrant III,
- negative for all points in Quadrant IV.

Hence, it would seem that the quantity $\sum_{i=1}^{n} x_i y_i$ could be used as a measure of the linear association between X and Y, for

- if the association is positive so that most points lie in Quadrants I and III, $\sum_{i=1}^{n} x_i y_i$ tends to be positive,
- if the association is negative so that most points lie in Quadrants II and IV, $\sum_{i=1}^{n} x_i y_i$ tends to be negative, and
- if no relation exists between X and Y, the points will be scattered over all four quadrants and $\sum_{i=1}^{n} x_i y_i$ will tend to be very small.

The quantity $\sum_{i=1}^{n} x_i y_i$ has two defects, however, as a measure of linear association between X and Y. First, it can be increased arbitrarily by adding further observations — that is, by increasing the sample size. Second, it can also be arbitrarily influenced by changing the units of measurement for either X or Y or both (for example, by changing feet to inches). These defects can be removed by making the measure of the strength of linear association a dimensionless quantity and dividing by n. The result is the Pearsonian, or product-moment, coefficient of correlation; that is,

$$r = \frac{\sum\limits_{i=1}^{n} x_i y_i}{n s_X s_Y},$$

where s_X is the standard deviation of the X variable and s_Y is the standard deviation of the Y variable.

The correlation coefficient computed from the sample data is an estimate of the parent population parameter ρ, and part of the job of the researcher is to use r to test hypotheses about ρ. It is unnecessary to do so for the example at hand, because the test of the null hypothesis $H_0: \rho = 0$ is equivalent to the test of the null hypothesis $H_0: \beta_1 = 0$. Since we have already performed the latter test, we know that the sample evidence leads to the rejection of the hypothesis that there is no linear relationship between sales and TV spots; that is, it leads to the rejection of $H_0: \rho = 0$.

The product-moment coefficient of correlation may vary from -1 to $+1$. Perfect positive correlation, where an increase in X determines exactly an increase in Y, yields a coefficient of $+1$. Perfect negative correlation, where an increase in X determines exactly a decrease in Y, yields a coefficient of -1. Figure 16.6 depicts these situations and several other scatter diagrams and their resulting correlation coefficients. An examination of these diagrams will provide some appreciation of the size of the correlation coefficient associated with a particular degree of scatter. The square of the correlation

FIGURE 16.6 Sample Scatter Diagrams and Associated Correlation Coefficients

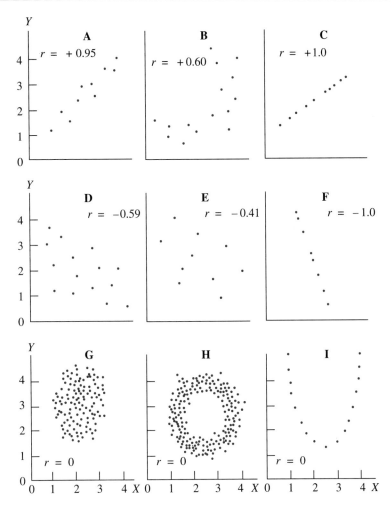

Source: Ronald E. Frank, Alfred A. Kuehn, and William F. Massy, *Quantitative Techniques in Marketing Analysis* (Homewood, Ill.: Richard D. Irwin, Inc., 1962), p. 71. Copyright 1962, reprinted with permission.

coefficient is the **coefficient of determination.** By some algebraic manipulation, it can be shown to be equal to

$$r^2 = 1 - \frac{s_{Y/X}^2}{s_Y^2}.$$

In the absence of the predictor variable, our best estimate of the criterion variable would be the sample mean. If there was low variability in sales from territory to

ETHICAL DILEMMA 16.1

The newly appointed analyst in the firm's marketing research department was given the responsibility of developing a method by which market potential for the firm's products could be estimated by small geographic areas. The analyst went about the task by gathering as much secondary data as he could. He then ran a series of regression analyses using the firm's sales as the criterion and the demographic factors as predictors. He realized that several of the predictors were highly correlated (e.g., average income in the area and average educational level), but he chose to ignore this fact when presenting the results to management.

- What is the consequence when the predictors in a regression equation are highly correlated?
- Is a research analyst ethically obliged to learn all he or she can about a particular technique before applying it to a problem in order to avoid incorrectly interpreting the results?
- Is a research analyst ethically obliged to advise those involved to be cautious in interpreting results because of violations of the assumptions in the method used to produce the results?
- What are the researcher's responsibilities if management has no interest in the technical details by which the results are achieved?

territory, the sample mean would be a good estimate of the expected sales in any territory. High variability would render it a poor estimate, however. Thus, the variance in sales s_Y^2 is a measure of the "badness" of such an estimating procedure. The introduction of the covariate X might produce an improvement in the territory sales estimates. It depends on how well the equation fits the data. Since $s_{Y/X}^2$ measures the scatter of the points about the regression line, $s_{Y/X}^2$ can be considered a measure of the "badness" of an estimating procedure that takes account of the covariate. Now, if $s_{Y/X}^2$ is small in relation to s_Y^2, the introduction of the covariate by means of the regression equation can be said to have substantially improved the predictions of the criterion variable, sales. Conversely, if $s_{Y/X}^2$ is approximately equal to s_Y^2, the introduction of the covariate X can be considered not to have helped in improving the predictions of Y. Thus, the ratio $s_{Y/X}^2/s_Y^2$ can be considered to be the ratio of variation left unexplained by the regression line divided by the total variation; that is,

$$r^2 = 1 - \frac{\text{Unexplained variation}}{\text{Total variation}}.$$

The right side of the equation can be combined in a single fraction to yield

$$r^2 = \frac{\text{Total variation} - \text{Unexplained variation}}{\text{Total variation}}.$$

Total variation minus unexplained variation leaves "explained variation," or the variation in Y that is accounted for or explained by the introduction of X. Thus, the coefficient of determination can be considered to equal

$$r^2 = \frac{\text{Explained variation}}{\text{Total variation}},$$

where it is understood that total variation is measured by the variance in Y. For the sales and TV spot example, $r^2 = 0.77$. This means that 77 percent of the variation in sales from territory to territory is accounted for, or can be explained, by the variation in TV spot advertising across territories. Thus, we can do a better job of estimating sales in a territory if we take account of TV spots than if we neglect this advertising effort.

MULTIPLE-REGRESSION ANALYSIS

So far we have considered only two variables in our analysis: sales and TV spot advertising. We now want to deal with the introduction of additional variables by considering multiple-regression analysis. The purposes will remain the same. We still want to construct an equation that will enable us to estimate values of the criterion variable, but now from given values of *several* predictor variables. And we still wish to measure the closeness of the estimated relationship. Our objective in introducing additional variables is basic — to improve our predictions of the criterion variable.

Revised Nomenclature

A more formal, revised notational framework is valuable for discussing multiple-regression analysis. Consider the general regression model with three predictor variables. The regression equation is

$$Y = \alpha + \beta_1 X_1 + \beta_2 X_2 + \beta_3 X_3 + \epsilon,$$

which is a simplified statement of the more elaborate and precise equation

$$Y_{(123)} = \alpha_{(123)} + \beta_{Y1.23} X_1 + \beta_{Y2.13} X_2 + \beta_{Y3.12} X_3 + \epsilon_{(123)}.$$

In this more precise system:

$Y_{(123)}$ is the value of Y that is estimated from the regression equation, in which Y is the criterion variable and X_1, X_2, and X_3 are the predictor variables.

$\alpha_{(123)}$ is the intercept parameter in the multiple-regression equation, in which Y is the criterion variable and X_1, X_2, and X_3 are the predictor variables.

$\beta_{Y1.23}$ is the coefficient of X_1 in the regression equation, in which Y is the criterion variable and X_1, X_2, and X_3 are the predictor variables. It is called the **coefficient of partial (or net) regression.** Note the subscripts. The two subscripts to the left of the decimal point are called primary subscripts. The first identifies the criterion variable, and the second identifies the predictor variable of which this β value is the coefficient. There are always two primary subscripts. The two subscripts to the right of the decimal point are called secondary subscripts. They indicate which other predictor variables are in the regression equation. The number of secondary subscripts varies from zero for simple regression to any number $k - 1$, where there are k predictor variables in the problem. In this case, the model contains three predictor variables ($k = 3$), and there are two secondary subscripts throughout.

$\epsilon_{(123)}$ is the error associated with the prediction of Y when X_1, X_2, and X_3 are the predictor variables.

When the identity of the variables is clear, it is common practice to use the simplified statement of the model. The more elaborate statement is helpful, though, in interpreting the solution to the regression problem.

Multicollinearity Assumption

The assumptions that we made about the error term for the simple regression model also apply to the multiple-regression equation. The multiple-regression model also requires the additional assumption that the predictor variables are not correlated among themselves. When the levels of the predictor variables can be set by the researcher, the assumption is easily satisfied. When the observations result from a survey rather than an experiment, the assumption is often violated because many variables of interest in marketing vary together. For instance, higher incomes are typically associated with higher education levels. Thus, the prediction of purchase behavior employing both income and education would violate the assumption that the predictor variables are independent of one another. **Multicollinearity** is said to be present in a multiple-regression problem when the predictor variables are correlated among themselves.

Coefficients of Partial Regression

Consider the introduction of number of sales representatives into our problem of predicting territory sales. We could investigate the two-variable relationship between sales and the number of sales representatives. This would involve, of course, the calculation of the simple-regression equation relating sales to number of sales representatives. The calculations would parallel those for the sales and TV spot relationship. Alternatively, we could consider the simultaneous influence of TV spots and number of sales representatives on sales using multiple-regression analysis. If we assume that that is indeed the research problem, the regression model would be written

$$Y_{(12)} = \alpha_{(12)} + \beta_{Y1.2} X_1 + \beta_{Y2.1} X_2 + \epsilon_{(12)},$$

indicating that the criterion variable, sales in a territory, is to be predicted employing two predictor variables, X_1 (TV spots per month) and X_2 (number of sales representatives).

Once again the parameters of the model could be estimated from sample data employing least-squares procedures. Let us again distinguish the sample estimates from the true, but unknown, population values by using a caret to denote an estimated value. Let us not worry about the formulas for calculating the regression coefficients. They typically will be calculated on a computer anyway and can be found in almost any introductory statistics book. The marketing analyst's need is how to interpret the results provided by the computer.

For this problem, the equation turns out to be

$$\hat{Y} = \hat{\alpha}_{(12)} + \hat{\beta}_{Y1.2} X_1 + \hat{\beta}_{Y2.1} X_2 = 69.3 + 14.2X_1 + 37.5X_2.$$

This regression equation may be used to estimate the level of sales to be expected in a territory, given the number of TV spots and the number of sales representatives serving the territory. Like any other least-squares equation, the line (a plane in this case because three dimensions are involved) fits the points in such a way that the sum of the deviations about the line is zero. In other words, if sales for each of the 40 sales territories were to be estimated from this equation, the positive and negative deviations about the line would exactly balance.

The level at which the plane intercepts the Y axis is given by $\hat{\alpha}_{(12)} = 69.3$. Consider now the coefficients of partial regression, $\hat{\beta}_{Y1.2}$ and $\hat{\beta}_{Y2.1}$. *Assuming that the multicollinearity assumption is satisfied,* these coefficients of partial regression can be interpreted as the *average change* in the criterion variable associated with a *unit change* in the appropriate predictor variable while holding the other predictor variable constant. Thus, assuming that there is no multicollinearity, $\hat{\beta}_{Y1.2} = 14.2$ indicates that on the average, an increase of \$14,200 in sales can be expected with each additional TV spot in the territory if the number of sales representatives is not changed. Similarly, $\hat{\beta}_{Y2.1} = 37.5$ suggests that each additional sales representative in a territory can be expected to produce \$37,500 in sales, on the average, if the number of TV spots is held constant.

In simple-regression analysis, we tested the significance of the regression equation by examining the significance of the slope coefficient employing the t test. Calculated t was 11.4 for the sales and TV spot relationship. The significance of the regression could also have been checked with an F test. In the case of a two-variable regression, calculated F is equal to calculated t squared; that is, $F = t^2 = (11.4)^2 = 130.6$. In general, calculated F is equal to the ratio of the mean square due to regression to the mean square due to residuals. In simple regression, the calculated F value would be referred to an F table for $v_1 = n - 2$ degrees of freedom. The conclusion would be exactly equivalent to that derived by testing the significance of the slope coefficient employing the t test.

In the multiple-regression case, it is *mandatory that the significance of the overall regression* be examined using an F test. The appropriate degrees of freedom are $v_1 = k$ and $v_2 = n - k - 1$, where there are k predictor variables. Critical F for $v_1 = 2$ and $v_2 = 40 - 2 - 1 = 37$ degrees of freedom and a 0.05 level of significance is 3.25. Calculated F for the regression relating sales to TV spots and the number of sales representatives is 128.1. Since calculated F exceeds critical F, the null hypothesis of no relationship is rejected. There is a statistically significant linear relationship between sales and the predictor variables (number of TV spots and number of sales representatives).

The slope coefficients can also be tested individually for their statistical significance in a multiple-regression problem, given that the overall function is significant. The t test is again used, although the validity of the procedure is highly dependent on multicollinearity that exists within the data. If the data are highly multicollinear, there will be a tendency to commit Type II errors; that is, many of the predictor variables will be judged as not being related to the criterion variable when in fact they are. It is even possible to have a high R^2 value and to conclude that the overall regression is statistically significant but that none of the coefficients are significant. The difficulty with the t tests for the significance of the individual slope coefficients arises because the standard error of estimate of the least-squares coefficients, s_{β_i}, increases as the dependence among the predictor variables increases. And, of course, as the denominator of calculated t gets larger, t itself decreases, occasioning the conclusion of no relationship between the criterion variable and the predictor variable in question.

Is multicollinearity a problem in our example? Consider again the simple regression of sales on TV spots; $\hat{\beta}_1$ ($\hat{\beta}_{Y1}$ in our more formal notational system) was equal to 25.3. Thus, when the number of sales representatives in a territory was not considered, the average change in sales associated with an additional TV spot was $25,300. Yet when the number of sales representatives is considered, the average change in sales associated with an additional TV spot was $14,200 ($\hat{\beta}_{Y1.2} = 14.2$). Part of the sales effect that we were attributing to TV spots was in fact due to the number of sales representatives in the territory. We were thus overstating the effect of the TV spot advertising because of the way decisions have historically been made in the company. Specifically, those territories with the greater number of sales representatives have received more TV advertising support (or vice versa). Perhaps this was logical, as they contained a larger proportion of the consuming public. Nevertheless, the fact that the two predictor variables are not independent (the coefficient of simple correlation between TV spots and number of sales representatives is 0.78) has caused a violation of the assumption of independent predictors. Multicollinearity is present within this data set.

A multicollinear condition within a data set *reduces the efficiency* of the estimates for the regression parameters. This is because the amount of information about the effect of each predictor variable on the criterion variable declines as the correlation among the predictor variables increases. The reduction in efficiency can easily be seen in the limiting case as the correlation between the predictor variables approaches 1 for a two-predictor model. Such a situation is depicted in Figure 16.7, where it is assumed that there is a perfect linear relationship between the two predictor variables, TV spots and number of sales representatives, and also that there is a strong linear relationship between the criterion variable sales and TV spots. Consider the change in sales from $75,000 to $100,000. This change is associated with a change in the number of TV spots, from three to four. This change in TV spots is also associated with a change in the number of sales representatives, from four to five. What is the effect of a TV spot on sales? Can we say it is $100 - 75 = 25$, or $25,000? Most assuredly not, for historically a sales representative has been added to a territory whenever the number of TV spots has been increased by one (or vice versa). The number of TV spots and sales representatives varies in perfect proportion, and it is impossible to distinguish their separate influences on sales — that is, their influence when the other predictor variable is held constant.

Very little meaning can be attached to the coefficients of partial regression when multicollinearity is present, as it is in our example. The "normal" interpretation of the coefficients of partial regression as "the average change in the criterion variable associated with a unit change in the appropriate predictor variable while holding the other predictor variables constant" simply does not hold.[7] The equation may be quite useful for prediction, assuming that conditions are stable; it still may be used to predict sales in the various territories for given levels of TV spots and number of sales representatives *if*

---

[7]M. G. Kendall, *A Course in Multivariate Analysis* (London: Charles Griffin, 1957), p. 74. See also Douglas C. Montgomery and Elizabeth A. Peck, *Introduction to Linear Regression Analysis* 2nd ed. (New York: Wiley, 1992).

FIGURE 16.7   Hypothetical Relationship between Sales and TV Spots and between TV Spots and Number of Sales Representatives

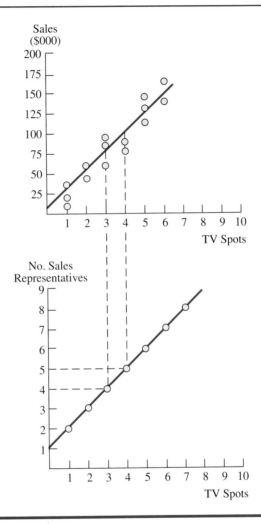

the historical relationship between sales and each of the predictor variables, and between or among the predictor variables themselves, can be expected to continue.[8] The partial-

[8]There are some things that the analyst faced with multicollinear data can do. See R. R. Hocking, "Developments in Linear Regression Methodology: 1959–1982," *Technometrics,* 25 (August 1983), pp. 219–230, and Ronald D. Snee, "Discussion," *Technometrics,* 25 (August 1983), pp. 230–237, for a discussion of the problem and some alternative ways of handling it. See also Chezy Ofir and Andre Khuri, "Multicollinearity in Marketing Models: Diagnostics and Remedial Measures," *International Journal of Research in Marketing,* 3 (No. 3, 1986), pp. 181–205; Charlotte H. Mason and William D. Perreault, Jr., "Collinearity, Power, and Interpretation of Multiple Regression Analysis," *Journal of Marketing Research,* 28 (August 1991), pp. 268–280; R. Carter Hill, Phillip A. Cartwright, and Julia F. Arbaugh, "The Use of Biased Predictors in Marketing Research," *International Journal of Forecasting,* 7 (November 1991), pp. 271–282.

regression coefficients should not be used, though, as the basis for making marketing strategy decisions when significant multicollinearity is present.[9]

Coefficients of Multiple Correlation and Determination

One item of considerable importance in simple-regression analysis was the measure of the *closeness* of the relationship between the criterion and predictor variables. The coefficient of correlation and its square, the coefficient of multiple determination, were used for this purpose. In multiple regression, there are similar coefficients for the identical purpose.

The coefficient of multiple correlation is formally denoted by $R_{Y.123}$, where the primary subscript identifies the criterion variable and the secondary subscripts identify the predictor variables. When the variables entering into the relationship are obvious, the abbreviated form, R, is used. The **coefficient of multiple determination** is denoted formally by $R_{Y.123}^2$ and informally by R^2. It represents the proportion of variation in the criterion variable that is accounted for by the covariation in the predictor variables. In the investigation of the relationship between sales and TV spots and number of sales representatives, $R_{Y.12}^2 = 0.874$. This means that 87.4 percent of the variation in sales is associated with variation in TV spots and number of sales representatives. The introduction of the number of sales representatives has improved the fit of the regression line; 87.4 percent of the variation in sales is accounted for by the two-predictor variable model, whereas only 77.5 percent was accounted for by the one-predictor model. The square root of this quantity, $R_{Y.12} = 0.935$, is the **coefficient of multiple correlation.** It is always expressed as a positive number.

Coefficients of Partial Correlation

There are two additional quantities to consider when interpreting the results of a multiple-regression analysis that were not present in simple-regression analysis: the coefficient of partial correlation and its square, the coefficient of partial determination.

Recall that in the simple-regression analysis relating sales Y to TV spots X_1, the coefficient of simple determination could be written

$$r_{Y.1}{}^2 = 1 - \frac{\text{Unexplained variation}}{\text{Total variation}},$$

and recall also that the unexplained variation was given by the square of standard error of estimate, $s_{Y.1}{}^2$, since the standard error of estimate measures the variation in the

---

[9] There is another interpretation danger in the example that was not discussed. It is not unreasonable to assume that both the number of sales representatives serving a territory and the number of TV spots per month were both determined on the basis of territorial potential. If this is the case, the implied causality is reversed or at least confused; instead of the number of sales representatives and number of TV spots determining sales, sales in a sense (potential sales anyway) determine the former quantities, and they in turn could be expected to affect realized sales. If this is actually the case, the coefficient-estimating procedure needs to take into account the two-way "causation" among the variables. See Wonnacott, *Regression,* pp. 284–292, for a discussion of the problems and the logic underlying the estimation of simultaneous equation systems.

criterion variable that was unaccounted for by the predictor variable X_1. Total variation, of course, was given by the variance in the criterion variable s_Y^2. Thus,

$$r_{Y.1}^2 = 1 - \frac{s_{Y.1}^2}{s_Y^2}.$$

The last term in this formula is the ratio of the variation *remaining* in the criterion variable, after taking account of the predictor variable X_1, to the total variation in the criterion variable. It measures the *relative degree* to which the association between the two variables can be used to provide information about the criterion variable.

Now consider the multiple-regression case with two predictor variables, X_1 and X_2. Denote the standard error of estimate by $s_{Y.12}$ and its square by $s_{Y.12}^2$. The standard error of estimate measures the variation *still remaining* in the criterion variable Y after the two predictor variables X_1 and X_2 have been taken into account. Since $s_{Y.1}^2$ measures the variation in the criterion variable that remains after the first predictor variable has been taken into account, the ratio $s_{Y.12}^2/s_{Y.1}^2$ can be interpreted as measuring the relative degree to which the association among the three variables Y, X_1, and X_2 provides information about Y over and above that provided by the association between the criterion variable and the first predictor variable alone. In other words, the ratio $s_{Y.12}^2/s_{Y.1}^2$ measures the *relative degree* to which X_2 adds to the knowledge about Y after X_1 has already been fully utilized. The ratio is the basis for the **coefficient of partial determination,** which in the sales (Y) versus TV spots (X_1) and number of sales representatives (X_2) example is

$$r_{Y2.1}^2 = 1 - \frac{s_{Y.12}^2}{s_{Y.1}^2} = 1 - \frac{(45.2)^2}{(59.6)^2} = 1 - 0.576 = 0.424.$$

This means that 42.4 percent of the variation in sales that is not associated with TV spots is incrementally associated with the number of sales representatives. Alternatively, the errors made in estimating sales from TV spots are, as measured by the variance, reduced by 42.4 percent when the number of sales representatives X_2 is added to X_1 as an additional predictor variable. The square root of the coefficient of partial determination is the **coefficient of partial correlation.**

In our example there were two predictors. Thus, we defined the coefficient of partial determination for the number of sales representatives X_2 as $r_{Y2.1}^2$. We could similarly define a coefficient of partial determination for TV spots. It would be denoted as $r_{Y1.2}^2$, and it would represent the percentage of the variation in sales not associated with X_2 that is incrementally associated with X_1; this latter coefficient would show the incremental contribution of X_1 after the association between Y and X_2 had already been considered.

When there are more than two predictors, we could define many more coefficients of partial determination. Each would have two primary subscripts indicating the criterion variable and the newly added predictor variable. There could be a great many secondary subscripts, as they always indicate which predictor variables have already been considered. Thus, if we had three predictor variables, we could calculate $r_{Y2.1}$, $r_{Y3.1}$, $r_{Y1.2}$, $r_{Y3.2}$, $r_{Y1.3}$, and $r_{Y2.3}$. These would all be *first-order* partial correlation coefficients, because they have one secondary subscript indicating that one other predictor variable is taken into account. We could also calculate $r_{Y1.23}$, $r_{Y2.13}$, and $r_{Y3.12}$. These are all *second-order* partial correlation coefficients. Each has two secondary subscripts, indicating that the incremental contribution of the variable is being considered after two other predictor variables have already been taken into account. Simple correlation coefficients, of course, have no secondary coefficients; they are, therefore, often referred to as *zero-order* partial correlation coefficients.

Dummy Variables

The analysis in the sales data in Table 16.1 is still not complete. No attention has yet been given to the effect of distribution on sales, particularly as measured by the wholesaler efficiency index. One way of considering the effect of wholesaler efficiency on sales would be to introduce the index directly; that is, the X_3 value for each observation would simply be the value recorded in the last column of Table 16.1. Letting X_3 represent the wholesaler efficiency index, the multiple-regression equation, using the informal notational scheme, would be

$$Y = \alpha + \beta_1 X_1 + \beta_2 X_2 + \beta_3 X_3 + \epsilon.$$

The least-squares estimate of β_3 in this equation turns out to be $\hat{\beta}_3 = 11.5$. Note what this number implies if the predictor variables are independent. It means that the estimated average change in sales is \$11,500 for each unit change in the wholesaler efficiency index. This means that a fair distributor could be expected to sell \$11,500 more on the average than a poor one; a good one could be expected to average \$11,500 more than a fair one; and an excellent one could be expected to sell \$11,500 more on the average than a good one. The sales increments are assumed to be constant for each change in wholesaler rating. The implication is that the wholesaler efficiency index is an interval scaled variable and that the difference between a poor and a fair wholesaler is the same as the difference between a fair one and a good one. This is a questionable assumption with an index that reflects ratings.

An alternative way of proceeding would be to convert the index into a set of **dummy variables** or, more appropriately, *binary variables*. A binary variable is one that takes on one of two values, 0 or 1. Thus, it can be represented by a single binary digit. Binary variables are used mainly because of the flexibility one has in defining them. They can provide a numerical representation for attributes or characteristics that are not essentially quantitative. For example, one could introduce gender into a regression equation using the dummy variable X_i, where

$$X_i = 0 \quad \text{if the person is female,}$$
$$X_i = 1 \quad \text{if the person is male.}$$

The technique is readily extended to handle multichotomous as well as dichotomous classifications. For instance, suppose that one wanted to introduce the variable social class into a regression equation, and there were three distinct class levels: upper class, middle class, and lower class. This could be handled using two dummy variables, say X_1 and X_2, where

	X_1	X_2
• if a person belongs to the upper class	1	0
• if a person belongs to the middle class	0	1
• if a person belongs to the lower class	0	0

There are several other logically equivalent coding schemes; for example,

	X_1	X_2
• if a person belongs to the upper class	0	0
• if a person belongs to the middle class	1	0
• if a person belongs to the lower class	0	1

It is, therefore, most important that the analyst interpreting the output from a regression run employing dummy variables pays close attention to the coding of the variables. It should be clear that an m category classification is capable of unambiguous representation by a set of $m - 1$ binary variables and that an mth binary would be entirely superfluous. As a matter of fact, the use of m variables to code an m-way classification variable would render most regression programs inoperative.

Suppose that we were to employ three dummy variables to represent the four-category wholesaler efficiency index in the Click ballpoint pen example and that

	X_3	X_4	X_5
• if a wholesaler is poor	0	0	0
• if a wholesaler is fair	1	0	0
• if a wholesaler is góod	0	1	0
• if a wholesaler is excellent	0	0	1

The regression model is

$$Y = \alpha + \beta_1 X_1 + \beta_2 X_2 + \beta_3 X_3 + \beta_4 X_4 + \beta_5 X_5 + \epsilon.$$

The least-squares estimates of the wholesaler efficiency parameters are[10]

$$\hat{\beta}_3 = 9.2,$$
$$\hat{\beta}_4 = 20.3,$$
$$\hat{\beta}_5 = 33.3.$$

These coefficients indicate that on the average, a fair wholesaler could be expected to sell \$9,200 more than a poor one, a good wholesaler could be expected to sell \$20,300 more than a poor one, and an excellent wholesaler could sell \$33,300 more than

---

[10]The data were artificially created employing specified parameter values and a random error term in a linear equation. The parameters were actually $\beta_3 = 2.0$, $\beta_4 = 22.0$, and $\beta_5 = 32.0$.

a poor one. Note that all of these coefficients are interpreted with respect to the "null" state — that is, with respect to the classification "poor" in this case.[11]

The analyst wishing to determine the difference in sales effectiveness between other classifications must look at coefficient differences. Thus, if the researcher wanted to calculate the estimated difference in expected sales from a good wholesaler and a fair wholesaler, the appropriate difference would be $\hat{\beta}_4 - \hat{\beta}_3 = 20.3 - 9.2 = 11.1$ thousand dollars ($11,100). Similarly, an excellent wholesaler could be expected on the average to sell $\hat{\beta}_5 - \hat{\beta}_4 = 33.3 - 20.3 = 13.0$ thousand dollars ($13,000) more than a good one.

The use of dummy variables indicates that the relationship between sales and the wholesaler efficiency index is not linear as was assumed when the index was introduced as an interval scaled variable. Instead of an across-the-board increase of $11,500 with each rating change, the respective increases are 9.2 ($9,200) from poor to fair, 11.1 ($11,100) from fair to good, and 13.0 ($13,000) from good to excellent.

Variable Transformations

The use of dummy variables greatly expands the scope of the regression model. Dummy variables allow the introduction of classificatory and rank-order variables in regression problems. As we have seen, they also allow nonlinear criterion variable/predictor variable relationships to be dealt with. Another technique that expands the obvious scope of the regression model involves variable transformations.

A **variable transformation** is simply a change in the scale in which the given variable is expressed. Consider the model

$$Y = \alpha X_1^{\beta_1} X_2^{\beta_2} X_3^{\beta_3} \epsilon$$

in which the relationship among the predictors and between the predictors and the error is assumed to be multiplicative. At first glance, it seems that it would be impossible to estimate the parameters α, β_1, β_2, and β_3 using our normal least-squares procedures. Now consider the model

$$W = \alpha' + \beta_1 Z_1 + \beta_2 Z_2 + \beta_3 Z_3 + \epsilon'.$$

This is a linear model, so it can be fitted by the standard least-squares procedures. But consider the fact that it is exactly equivalent to our multiplicative model if we simply let

$$W = \ln Y \qquad Z_2 = \ln X_2$$
$$\alpha' = \ln \alpha \qquad Z_3 = \ln X_3$$
$$Z_1 = \ln X_1 \qquad \epsilon' = \ln \epsilon$$

---

[11]For a useful discussion of some alternative ways to code dummy variables and the different insights that can be provided by the various alternatives, see Jacob Cohen and Patricia Cohen, *Applied Multiple Regression/ Correlation Analysis for the Behavioral Sciences,* 2nd ed. (Hillsdale, N.J.: Lawrence Erlbaum Associates, 1983), pp. 181–222.

Thus, we have converted a nonlinear model to a linear model using variable transformations. To solve for the parameters of our multiplicative model, we simply (1) take the natural log of Y and each of the Xs; (2) solve the resulting equation by the normal least-squares procedures; (3) take the antilog of α' to derive an estimate of α; and (4) read the values of the $\hat{\beta}_i$, since they are the same in both models.

The transformation to natural logarithms involved the transformation of both the criterion and predictor variables. It is also possible to change the scale of either the criterion or predictor variables. Transformations to the exponential and logarithmic are some of the most useful, since they serve to relax the constraints imposed by the assumptions that[12]

- the relationship between the criterion variable and the predictor variables is additive,
- the relationship between the criterion variable and the predictor variables is linear, and
- the errors are homoscedastic (equal to a constant for all values of the predictors).

Dummy variables are one form of transformation, and we have already seen how they allow the treatment of nonlinear relationships.

ETHICAL DILEMMA 16.2

Sarah was absolutely convinced that there was a relationship between the firm's product sales to a household and the household's total disposable personal income. Consequently, she was very disappointed when her first pass through the diary panel data that she had convinced her superior to purchase revealed virtually no relationship between household purchases of the product and household income in the simple regression of one on the other. A series of additional passes in which a variety of transformations were tried proved equally disappointing. Finally, Sarah decided to break the income variable into classes through a series of dummy variables. When she regressed household purchases of the product against the income categories, she found a very irregular but strong relationship as measured by R^2. Purchases rose as income increased up to $25,000, then decreased as income went from $25,000 to $59,999, increased again for income between $60,000 and $104,999, and seemed to be unaffected by incomes greater than $105,000.

- How would you evaluate Sarah's approach?
- Do you think it is good procedure to continue searching data for support for a hypothesis that you absolutely believe is true, or would you recommend a single pass through the data with the procedure that *a priori* you thought was best?
- What are Sarah's ethical responsibilities when reporting the results of her analysis? Is she obliged to discuss all the analyses she ran, or is it satisfactory for her to report only the results of the dummy variable regression?

---

[12]See Ronald E. Frank, "Use of Transformations," *Journal of Marketing Research,* 3 (August 1966), pp. 247–253, for a discussion of these conditions and how the proper transformation can serve to fulfill them. See also James G. MacKinnon and Lonnie Magee, "Transforming the Dependent Variable in Regression Models," *International Economic Review,* 31 (May 1990), pp. 315–339.

SUMMARY

This chapter examined the question of association or covariation between (among) variables when one of the variables is in some sense considered a criterion variable. Simple regression and correlation analysis is the primary statistical device for analyzing the association between a single predictor and a single criterion variable. This model allows the estimation of a functional equation relating the variables as well as an estimate of the strength of the association between them. Some of the more useful outputs from a simple regression analysis are the following:

1. the functional equation, which allows the prediction of the criterion variable for assumed values of the predictor variable,
2. the standard error of estimate, which provides an absolute measure of the lack of fit of the equation to the data,
3. the coefficient of determination, which provides a relative assessment of the goodness of fit of the equation, and
4. the slope coefficient, which indicates how much the criterion variable changes, on the average, per unit of change in the predictor variable.

The regression model is readily extended to incorporate multiple predictor variables to estimate a single criterion variable. If the predictor variables are not correlated among themselves, each partial regression coefficient indicates the average change in the criterion variable per unit change in the predictor variable in question, holding the other predictor variables constant. If the predictor variables are correlated among themselves, little substantive meaning can be attached to the slope coefficients, although the regression equation often can still be used successfully to predict values of the criterion variable for assumed values of the predictor variables. The coefficient of multiple determination measures the proportion of the variation in the criterion variable accounted for or "explained" by all the predictor variables. The coefficient of partial determination measures the relative degree to which a given variable adds to our knowledge of the criterion variable over and above that provided by other predictor variables. Dummy or binary variables allow the introduction of classificatory or nominally scaled variables in the regression equation, whereas variable transformations considerably increase the scope of the regression model, because they allow certain nonlinear relationships to be considered.

■

Questions

1. What is the basic nature of the distinction between tests for group differences and tests to investigate association?
2. What is the difference between regression analysis and correlation analysis?
3. What is the difference between a deterministic model and a probabilistic model? Which type of model underlies regression analysis? Explain.
4. What assumptions are made about the error term in the least-squares solution to the regression problem? What is the effect of the assumption; that is, what is the Gauss-Markov theorem? When the analyst wishes to make an inference about a regression population parameter, what additional assumption is necessary?

5. What is the standard error of estimate?

6. Suppose that an analyst wished to make an inference about the slope coefficient in a regression model. What is the appropriate procedure? What does it mean if the null hypothesis is rejected? If it is not rejected?

7. What is the difference in procedure when one is predicting an individual value of Y for a given X_i and when one is predicting an average value of Y for a given X_i?

8. What is the correlation coefficient, and what does it measure? What is the coefficient of determination, and what does it measure?

9. What is a coefficient of partial or net regression, and what does it measure? What condition must occur for the usual interpretation to apply? What happens if this condition is not satisfied?

10. What is the coefficient of multiple determination?

11. What is a coefficient of partial determination? What does it measure?

12. What is a dummy variable? When is it used? How is it interpreted?

13. What is a variable transformation? Why is it employed?

Applications and Problems

1. The quality of public school education has become a major political issue in the 1990s. In many states, dissatisfied parents are voting for school-choice legislation that allows them to use public money to send their children to the school they deem most appropriate. Under some school-choice legislation, parents can even choose to send their children to private schools and pay only the difference between the amount charged by the private school and the amount it would have cost to send the child to a public school.

   One local school district in which parents were calling for school-choice reform hired a marketing research company to assess customer satisfaction and relate this satisfaction to demographic variables. The school district had hypothesized that satisfaction was related to income levels, with those earning more money being more dissatisfied with the public school system. The research company found that the variable income explained only 10 percent of the total variance in school satisfaction; thus, the company stated that there was no relationship between income and school satisfaction. Given the analysis described, is this a valid conclusion for the research company to make? Why?

2. A cereal manufacturer believes that there is an association between cereal sales and the number of facings the cereal has on each store's shelves. Eight stores were surveyed to test this hypothesis. The data are as follows:

Facings	Sales
5	45
6	50
6	52
7	53
5	44
7	57
6	49
8	56

a. Is there an association between shelf facings and sales?

b. Based on this data, is it appropriate to state that increased shelf facings produce additional sales? Why or why not?

c. What other variables can you think of that may be correlated with cereal sales?

3. The Brite-Lite Bottling Company, which provides glass bottles to various soft-drink manufacturers, has the following information pertaining to the number of cases per shipment, size of cartons, and the corresponding transportation cost:

Number of Cases per Shipment (in hundreds)	Size of Carton (in cubic inches)	Transportation Costs (in dollars)
15	12	200
22	16	260
35	20	310
43	24	360
58	28	420
65	32	480
73	36	540
82	40	630
85	44	710
98	48	730

The marketing manager is interested in studying the relationship between the number of cases per shipment and the transportation costs. Your assistance is required in performing a simple regression analysis.

a. Plot the transportation costs as a function of the number of cases per shipment.

b. Interpret the scatter diagram.

c. Calculate the coefficients $\hat{\alpha}$ and $\hat{\beta}$ and develop the regression equation.

d. What is the interpretation of the coefficients $\hat{\alpha}$ and $\hat{\beta}$?

e. Calculate the standard error of estimate.

f. What is the interpretation of the standard error of estimate that you calculated?

g. Compute the t value with $n - 2$ degrees of freedom with the use of the following formula for the square root of the variance of the distribution of βs:

$$s_{\hat{\beta}} = \sqrt{\frac{s_{Y/X^2}}{\sum_{i=1}^{10} (X_i - \bar{x})^2}}$$

$$t = \frac{\hat{\beta}_1 - \beta_1}{s_{\hat{\beta}_1}},$$

where β is assumed to be zero under the null hypothesis of no relationship; that is:

$$H_0 : \beta_1 = 0,$$

$$H_a : \beta_1 \neq 0.$$

h. What is the tabled t value at a 0.05 significance level?

i. What can you conclude about the relationship between transportation costs and number of cases shipped?

j. The marketing manager wants to estimate the transportation costs for 18 cases.
   (1) Use the regression model to derive the average value of Y_0.
   (2) Provide a confidence interval for the estimate.

$$s_{\hat{Y}_0/X_{01^2}} = s_{Y/X_1^2}\left[\frac{1}{n} + \frac{(X_{01} - \bar{x})^2}{\displaystyle\sum_{i=1}^{10}(X_{i1} - \bar{x})^2}\right],$$

$$\hat{Y}_0 \pm t \, s_{\hat{Y}_0/X_{01}} = \qquad .$$

4. The marketing manager of Brite-Lite Company wanted to determine if there was an association between the size of carton and the transportation cost per shipment. (The company followed a policy of including the same sized cartons for any particular shipment.) Refer to the previous question for information on the transportation costs per shipment and size of carton.
   a. Calculate the correlation coefficient.
   b. Interpret the correlation coefficient.
   c. Determine the coefficient of determination.
   d. Interpret the coefficient of determination.

5. The marketing manager of Brite-Lite Company is considering multiple regression analysis with number of cartons per shipment and size of cartons as predictor variables and transportation costs as the criterion variable (refer to the previous problem). The manager has devised the following regression equation:

$$\hat{Y} = \hat{\alpha}_{(12)} + \hat{\beta}_{Y_{1.2}} X_1 + \hat{\beta}_{Y_{2.1}} X_2 = -41.44 - 3.95 \, X_1 + 24.44 \, X_2,$$

where X_1 is the number of cartons per shipment and X_2 is the size of the carton.
   a. Interpret $\hat{\alpha}_{(12)}$, $\hat{\beta}_{Y_{1.2}}$, and $\hat{\beta}_{Y_{2.1}}$.
   b. Is multiple regression appropriate in this situation? If yes, why? If no, why not?

6. An analyst for a large shoe manufacturer had developed a formal linear regression model to predict sales of the firm's 122 retail stores located in different SMSAs in the United States.
   The model is:

$$Y_{(123)} = \alpha_{(123)} + \beta_{1.23}X_1 + \beta_{2.13}X_2 + \beta_{3.12}X_3,$$

where
X_1 = population in surrounding area in thousands;
X_2 = marginal propensity to consume;
X_3 = median personal income in surrounding area in thousands of dollars;
Y = sales in thousands of dollars.

   Some empirical results were as follows:

Variable	Regression Coefficient	Coefficient Standard Errors ($s_{\hat{\beta}_i}$)
X_1	$\hat{\beta}_{1.23} = 0.49$	0.24
X_2	$\hat{\beta}_{2.13} = -0.40$	95
X_3	$\hat{\beta}_{3.12} = 225$	105
$R^2 = 0.47$	$\hat{\alpha} = -40$	225

a. Interpret each of the regression coefficients.
b. Are X_1, X_2, and X_3 significant at the 0.05 level? Show your calculations.
c. Which independent variable seems to be the most significant predictor?
d. Provide an interpretation of the R^2 value.
e. The marketing research department of the shoe manufacturer wants to include an index that indicates whether the service in each store is poor, fair, or good. The coding scheme is as follows:

1 = poor service
2 = fair service
3 = good service

(1) Indicate how you would transform this index so that it could be included in the model. Be specific.
(2) Write out the regression model including the transformation that you developed.
(3) Suppose that two of the parameters for the index are 4.6 and 10.3. Interpret these values in light of the scheme you adopted.

7. Carol Lynne and K. C. Lee are leaders of a popular local country and western band. Each week during the summer, the band played an outdoor concert at a different park located in the city. Advertising for the concerts consisted of handbills posted around the city on public billboards, at supermarkets, and so on. During some weeks, Carol, K. C., and the other band members were able to distribute many handbills; during other weeks, fewer were distributed. Similarly, many people attended some concerts, and only a few attended others. At the end of the summer, the band wanted to know if there was any relationship between the number of handouts that were distributed and the number of people attending its concerts. Following are the approximate number of handbills distributed each week along with the number of people attending that week's concert:

Number of Handbills	Number of People
900	625
550	400
750	450
300	200
600	500
1,000	650
400	375
325	350
675	400
200	200
500	500
150	125
500	300
700	550
600	400

a. Develop and interpret a scatter diagram showing number of people as a function of number of handbills.

b. Calculate the coefficients $\hat{\alpha}$ and $\hat{\beta}$, and develop the regression equation using a statistical software package.

c. Interpret the coefficients $\hat{\alpha}$ and $\hat{\beta}$. Be specific about the meaning of the terms in this situation.

d. What is the standard error of estimate, and what is its interpretation in this situation?

e. What is the t value associated with $\hat{\beta}$? Is this value significant at the 0.05 level? If so, what can be concluded about the relationship between the number of handbills distributed and the number of people attending the concerts?

f. How much of the variance in the number of people attending the concerts can be explained by the number of handbills delivered?

g. What are some other factors that might be included in a multiple regression model to explain the number of people attending the concerts?

Refer to the NFO Research, Inc. coffee study described on pages 780–783 in Chapter 13 for the next three problems.

8. Use simple linear regression to investigate the association between the predictor variable age (as a continuous variable) and the criterion variable "value" index score composed of the following attributes from Question 6 for Folgers: good value for the money, economy brand, costs less than other brands.

9. Repeat the previous analysis using dummy codes for age in the following categories:

35 years or more
36–45 years
46–59 years
60 years or more

Compare these results with those obtained previously.

10. Investigate the association between the "taste" index score for Yuban and the use (or nonuse) of the various additives from Question 3 using multiple regression. The "taste" index will serve as the dependent variable and is composed of the following items from Question 6: rich taste, always fresh, full-bodied taste, smooth taste, not bitter, has no aftertaste.

APPENDIX 16A

Nonparametric Measures of Association

Chapter 16 focused on the product-moment correlation as the measure of association. Although the product-moment correlation coefficient was originally developed to deal with continuous variables, it has proved to be quite robust to scale type and can handle variables that are ordinal or dichotomous as well as those that are interval.[1] It is, therefore, a rather general measure of association although it is not universally applicable.

---

[1]Jum Nunnally, *Psychometric Theory,* 2nd ed. (New York: McGraw-Hill, 1978), especially pp. 117–150. For an empirical comparison of how various correlation coefficients perform with rating scale data, see Emin Babakus and Carl E. Ferguson, Jr., "On Choosing the Appropriate Measure of Association When Analyzing Rating Scale Data," *Journal of the Academy of Marketing Science,* 16 (Spring 1988), pp. 95–102.

This appendix treats some alternate measures of association — namely, the contingency table and coefficient and the index of predictive association, which are appropriate for nominal data, and Spearman's rank-order correlation coefficient and the coefficient of concordance, which are suited to the analysis of rank-order data.

CONTINGENCY TABLE

A problem frequently encountered in the analysis of nominal data is the independence of variables of classification. In Chapter 13, for example, a number of research questions involving the relationship between auto purchase and family characteristics were dealt with. No statistical tests of significance were computed at that time. The question of whether the results reflected sample aberrations or represented true population conditions was thus avoided. If statistical tests had been run at that time, they would have been primarily of the chi-square **contingency table** type, which is ideally suited for investigating the independence of variables in cross classifications.

Consider, for example, a consumer study involving the preferences of families for different sizes of washing machines. *A priori,* it would seem that larger families would be more likely to buy the larger units and that smaller families would tend to buy smaller washing machines. To investigate this question, suppose that the manufacturer checked a random sample of those purchasers who returned their warranty cards. Included on the warranty cards was a question on the size of the family. Although not a perfect population for analysis, the manufacturer believed it was good enough for this purpose, because some 85 percent of all warranty cards are returned. Furthermore, it was a relatively economical way to proceed, since the data were internal. The study could be carried out by checking a random sample of warranty cards for family size and machine purchased.

A random sample of 300 of these cards provided the data in Table 16A.1. The assignment is to determine if family size affects the size of the machine that is purchased. The null hypothesis is that the variables are independent; the alternate is that they are not. A significance level of $\alpha = 0.10$ was chosen for the test. To calculate a χ^2 statistic, one needs to generate the expected number of cases likely to fall into each category. *The expected number is generated by assuming that the null hypothesis is*

TABLE 16A.1   Size of Washing Machine versus Size of Family

Size of Washing Machine Purchased	Size of Family in Members			Total
	1 to 2	3 to 4	5 or More	
8-lb. load	25	37	8	70
10-lb. load	10	62	53	125
12-lb. load	5	41	59	105
Total	40	140	120	300

indeed true — that is, that there is no relationship between size of machine purchased and family size. Suppose that size of machine purchased is denoted by the variable A and size of family by the variable B and that

- A_1 — purchase of an 8-lb. load washing machine,
- A_2 — purchase of a 10-lb. load washing machine,
- A_3 — purchase of a 12-lb. load washing machine,
- B_1 — family of one to two members,
- B_2 — family of three to four members,
- B_3 — family of five or more members.

If variables A and B are indeed independent, then the probability of occurrence of the event $A_1 B_1$ (a family of one to two members purchased an 8-lb. load machine) is given as the product of the separate probabilities for A_1 and B_1; that is,

$$P(A_1 B_1) = P(A_1)P(B_1)$$

by the multiplication law of probabilities for independent events. Now $P(A)$ is given by the number of cases possessing the characteristic A_1, n_{A_1}, over the total number of cases n. $P(A_1)$ is thus

$$\frac{n_{A_1}}{n} = \frac{70}{300} = \frac{7}{30}.$$

Similarly, $P(B_1)$ is given by the number of cases having the characteristic B_1, n_{B_1}, over the total number of cases, or $P(B_1) = n_{B1}/n = 40/300 = 2/15$. The joint probability $P(A_1 B_1)$ is

$$P(A_1 B_1) = P(A_1)P(B_1) = \left(\frac{7}{30}\right)\left(\frac{2}{15}\right) = \frac{7}{225}.$$

Given a total of 300 cases, the number expected to fall in the cell $A_1 B_1$, E_{11}, is given as the product of the total number of cases and the probability of any one of these cases falling into the $A_1 B_1$ cell; that is,

$$E_{11} = nP(A_1 B_1) = 300(7/225) = 9.33.$$

Although this is the underlying rationale for generating the expected frequencies, there is an easier computational form. Recall that $P(A_1) = n_{A_1}/n$, that $P(B) = n_{B_1}/n$, and that $P(A_1 B_1) = P(A_1)P(B_1)$. The formula for E_{11}, on substitution, then reduces to

$$E_{11} = nP(A_1 B_1) = nP(A_1)P(B_1)$$

$$= n \frac{n_{A_1}}{n} \frac{n_{B_1}}{n} = \frac{n_{A_1} n_{B_1}}{n}$$

$$= \frac{70 \times 40}{300} = 9.33.$$

Thus, to generate the expected frequencies for each cell, one merely needs to multiply the marginal frequencies and divide by the total. The remaining expected frequencies, which are calculated in like manner, are entered below the cell diagonals in Table 16A.2. The calculated χ^2 value is thus

$$\chi^2 = \sum_{i=1}^{3} \sum_{j=1}^{3} \frac{[O_{ij} - E_{ij}]^2}{E_{ij}}$$

$$= \frac{(25 - 9.33)^2}{9.33} + \frac{(37 - 32.67)^2}{32.67} + \frac{(8 - 28.00)^2}{28.00}$$

$$+ \frac{(10 - 16.67)^2}{16.67} + \frac{(62 - 58.33)^2}{58.33} + \frac{(53 - 50.00)^2}{50.00}$$

$$+ \frac{(5 - 14.00)^2}{14.00} + \frac{(41 - 49.00)^2}{49.00} + \frac{(59 - 42.00)^2}{42.00}$$

$$= 26.318 + 0.574 + 14.286 + 2.669 + 0.231 + 0.180 + 5.786$$
$$+ 1.306 + 6.881$$

$$= 58.231,$$

where O_{ij} and E_{ij}, respectively, denote the actual number and expected number of observations that fall in the ij cell. Now, the expected frequencies in any row add to the marginal total. This must be true because of the way the expected frequencies were calculated. Thus, as soon as we know any two expected frequencies in a row (say

TABLE 16A.2   Size of Washing Machine versus Size of Family: Observed and Expected Frequencies

Size of Washing Machine Purchased	Size of Family in Members			Total
	B_1 1 to 2	B_2 3 to 4	B_3 5 to more	
A_1—8-lb load	25 / 9.33	37 / 32.67	8 / 28.00	70
A_2—10-lb load	10 / 16.67	62 / 58.33	53 / 50.00	125
A_3—12-lb load	5 / 14.00	41 / 49.00	59 / 42.00	105
Total	40	140	120	300

9.33 and 32.67 in Row A_1, for example), the third expected frequency is fixed because the three must add to the marginal total. This means that there are only $(c - 1)$ degrees of freedom in a row, where c is the number of columns. A similar argument applies to the columns; that is, there are $(r - 1)$ degrees of freedom per column, where r is the number of rows. The degrees of freedom in total in a two-way contingency table are thus given by

$$\nu = (r - 1)(c - 1).$$

In our problem, $\nu = (3 - 1)(3 - 1) = 4$. Using our assumed $\alpha = 0.10$, the tabled critical value of χ^2 for four degrees of freedom is 7.78 (see Appendix B at the back of the book). Computed $\chi^2 = 58.231$ thus falls in the critical region. The null hypothesis of independence is rejected. Family size is a factor in determining size of washing machine purchased.

In one form or another, the chi-square test is probably the most widely used test in marketing research, and the serious student is well advised to become familiar with its requirements. Research Realities 16A.1 summarizes them.

Research Realities 16A.1

Requirements for the Chi-Square Test

1. The test deals with frequencies. Percentage values need to be converted to counts of the number of cases in each cell.
2. The chi-square distribution, although continuous, is being used to approximate the distribution of a discrete variable. This results in the computed value being proportionately inflated if too many of the expected frequencies are small. It is generally agreed that only a few cells (less than 20 percent) should be permitted to have expected frequencies less than 5, and none should have expected frequencies less than 1. Categories may be meaningfully combined to conform to this rule.
3. Multiple answers per respondent should not be analyzed with chi-square contingency table analysis, because the normal tabled critical values of the chi-square statistic for a specified alpha error no longer apply when more than one cross-tabulation analysis is conducted with the same data. If multiple answers per respondent are to be analyzed, special tables should be used for testing the statistical significance of the results.
4. Each observation should be independent of the others. The chi-square test would not be appropriate, for example, for analyzing observations on the same individuals in a pretest–posttest experiment.

CONTINGENCY COEFFICIENT

While the χ^2 contingency table test indicates whether two variables are independent, it does not measure the strength of association when they are dependent. The **contingency coefficient** can be used for this latter purpose. Because the contingency coefficient is directly related to the χ^2 test, it can be generated by the researcher with relatively little additional computational effort. The formula for the contingency coefficient (call it C) is

$$C = \sqrt{\frac{\chi^2}{n + \chi^2}},$$

where n is the sample size and χ^2 is calculated in the normal way.

Recall that calculated χ^2 for the data in Table 16A.1 was 58.23, and that since the calculated value was larger than the critical tabled value, the null hypothesis of independence was rejected. The conclusion that naturally follows, that family size affects the size of washing machine purchased, is an interesting finding, but it is only part of the story. Although the variables are dependent, what is the strength of the association between them? The contingency coefficient helps answer this question. The contingency coefficient is

$$C = \sqrt{\frac{58.23}{300 + 58.23}} = 0.403.$$

Does this value indicate strong or weak association between the variables? We cannot say without comparing the calculated value against its limits. When there is no association between the variables, the contingency coefficient will be zero. Unfortunately, the contingency coefficient does not possess the other attractive property of the Pearsonian product-moment correlation coefficient of being equal to one when the variables are completely dependent or perfectly correlated. Rather, its upper limit is a function of the number of categories. When the number of categories is the same for each variable (that is, when the number of rows r equals the number of columns c), the upper limit on the contingency coefficient for two perfectly correlated variables is

$$\sqrt{(r - 1)/r}.$$

In the example at hand, $r = c = 3$, and thus the upper limit for the contingency coefficient is

$$\sqrt{\frac{2}{3}} = 0.816.$$

The calculated value is approximately halfway between the limits of zero for no association and 0.816 for perfect association, suggesting that there is moderate association between size of family and size of washing machine purchased.

INDEX OF PREDICTIVE ASSOCIATION

One of the difficulties associated with the contingency coefficient is interpreting the strength of the association between the variables as judged by the calculated value. For instance, even though we were able to say that there was moderate association between the variables of cross classification, the interpretation was not as straightforward as it would have been if the Pearsonian r had been calculated. Recall that the square of r is the coefficient of determination, which indicates the proportion of the variance in one variable that is accounted for by covariation in the other. This is a clear measure of the strength of the association between the variables. The contingency coefficient has no such standard to assist the analyst in interpreting the results. The index of predictive association is "more directly interpretable" in this regard.[2]

The **index of predictive association** is appropriate for nominally scaled variables. Consider for a moment a hypothetical example with the following conditions. First, there is one criterion and one predictor variable, and both are divisible into three classes: A_1, A_2, and A_3 and B_1, B_2, and B_3, respectively. Second, the 100 observations are as arrayed in Table 16A.3. Third, the purpose is to predict the A classification of an object chosen at random; that is, should it be predicted as falling into category A_1, A_2, or A_3. Assume initially that we have no knowledge of the B classification. The best estimate for the randomly chosen object is classification A_2, because one-half of all the observations of the A variate fall in this category. Proceeding on this basis, we would make 50 percent of all assignments correctly, since we would assign them all to A_2. Conversely, we would be wrong half of the time. Suppose now that we know the B classification of the object chosen at random. If the B classification is B_1, the best guess is A_1, since two-thirds of all cases possessing B_1 fall in the A_1 classification. Similarly, if it is B_2, the best guess is A_2, and if it is B_3, the best guess is A_3.

The **index of predictive association**, $\lambda_{A.B}$, measures the relative decrease in the probability of error by taking account of the B classification in predicting the A classification, over the error of prediction when the B classification is unknown. In the example, $\lambda_{A.B} = 0.400$. The errors in predicting the A classification are reduced by 40 percent by taking account of the B classification. The original classification error rate is 50 percent; these errors are decreased by 20 percent (50 percent times 0.400 equals 20 percent). In effect, one should now make 70 percent of the A classification predictions correctly (the original 50 percent plus the additional 20 percent) by taking account of B.

TABLE 16A.3   Hypothetical Data: Some Relationship — $\lambda_{A.B} = 0.400$

	A_1	A_2	A_3	Total
B_1	10	5	0	15
B_2	10	35	5	50
B_3	0	10	25	35
Total	20	50	30	100

---

[2]The index was originally proposed by Leo A. Goodman and William H. Kruskal, "Measures of Association for Cross-Classifications," *Journal of the American Statistical Association*, 49 (December 1954), pp. 732–764. See also Lawrence J. Feick, "Analyzing Marketing Research Data with Association Models," *Journal of Marketing Research*, 21 (November 1984), pp. 376–386, for a discussion of a number of other association coefficients that can be used with categorical or nominal data.

The index of predictive association varies from 0 to 1. It is zero if the B classification is of no help in predicting the A classification. In Table 16A.4, without any knowledge of the B classification, the logical guess for the A classification is A_2. Given that the randomly drawn element is in any of the three B classifications, B_1, B_2, or B_3, the best assignment for the element on the criterion variable is still A_2. The B classification is of no assistance in predicting the A classification.

Table 16A.5 illustrates the case in which B is a perfect predictor of A. Given no information about B, A_2 is the best classification estimate; 50 percent of the time this assignment is in error. Given the knowledge that the element drawn at random possesses characteristic B_1, the proper prediction of the criterion variable is classification A_1. For B_2, it is A_2, and for B_3, it is A_3. The B classification allows the A classification estimates to be made without error. That is, the errors in estimating A have been reduced 100 percent by taking account of B. The index of predictive association, $\lambda_{A.B.}$, equals 1.0.

The index of predictive association is calculated as follows. Assume that we are indeed predicting the A classification from the B classification. Let

$n_{.m}$ be the *largest* marginal frequency among the A classes, and
n_{bm} be the *largest* frequency in the bth row (or column) of the table.

Then

$$\lambda_{A.B} = \frac{\sum_b n_{bm} - n_{.m}}{n - n_{.m}},$$

TABLE 16A.4   **Hypothetical Data: No Relationship — $\lambda_{A.B} = 0$**

	A_1	A_2	A_3	Total
B_1	5	10	0	15
B_2	15	20	15	50
B_3	0	20	15	35
Total	20	50	30	100

TABLE 16A.5   **Hypothetical Data: Perfect Relationship — $\lambda_{A.B} = 1.0$**

	A_1	A_2	A_3	Total
B_1	20	0	0	20
B_2	0	50	0	50
B_3	0	0	30	30
Total	20	50	30	100

where $\Sigma_b n_{bm}$ is taken across all the *B* classes. Now, for the washing machine and family size example, $n = 300$. Considering that size of machine purchased is to be predicted from family size, the largest marginal frequency among the *A* classes, $n_{.m}$, is 125, corresponding to the 10-lb. load machines. Given that the family is one to two members, the largest frequency in the first column of the cross-classification table, n_{1m}, is 25; similarly, $n_{2m} = 62$, and $n_{3m} = 59$. Thus, the index of predictive association is

$$\lambda_{A.B} = \frac{n_{1m} + n_{2m} + n_{3m} - n_{.m}}{n - n_{.m}} = \frac{25 + 62 + 59 - 125}{300 - 125} = 0.12.$$

Given no information about family size, the best estimate of the size of the washing machine that would be purchased by a family chosen at random would be the 10-lb. load machine. Some 41.7 percent, or 125 out of 300 families, purchased these machines. In 41.7 percent of the cases we would be right, and in 58.3 percent we would be wrong, if we predicted that a family chosen at random would purchase a 10-lb. load washing machine. This error is reduced by 12 percent by taking account of family size. Since 12 percent of 58.3 is 7.0, this means that $41.7 + 7.0 = 48.7$ percent of the predictions would be made correctly if family size is considered.

The improvement in predictive accuracy is slight, even though by using the contingency-table test for independence of the variables of classification we convincingly rejected the notion of independence between the variables. This demonstrates the two important questions in association analysis. First, is there association between the criterion and predictor variables, or are they independent? Second, if they are dependent, by how much are predictions about the criterion variable improved by taking into account the important predictor variables? The index of predictive association, as well as the other measures of association, is used to answer the latter question. The tests of their statistical significance answer the former.[3]

SPEARMAN'S RANK CORRELATION COEFFICIENT

One of the best known coefficients of association for rank-order data is **Spearman's rank correlation coefficient,** denoted r_s. The coefficient is appropriate when there are two variables per object, both of which are measured on an ordinal scale so that the objects may be ranked in two ordered series.[4]

---

[3]It is also possible to attempt to isolate the *sources of dependence* in a cross-classification table. See David L. Rados, "Two-Way Analysis of Tables in Marketing Research," *Journal of the Market Research Society,* 22 (October 1980), pp. 248–262, and Ottar Hellevik, *Introduction to Causal Analysis* (London: George Allen & Unwin, 1984), for discussion of techniques for doing so. Log-linear models can also be used to analyze the data. See Thomas D. Wickens, *Multiway Contingency Tables Analysis for the Social Sciences* (Hillsdale, N.J.: Lawrence Erlbaum Associates, Inc., 1989).

[4]The Spearman rank correlation coefficient is a shortcut version of the product-moment correlation coefficient, in that both coefficients produce the same estimates of the strength of association between two sets of ranks. The rank correlation coefficient is easy to conceptualize and calculate, so it is often used when the data are ranked. See Nunnally, *Psychometric Theory,* pp. 134–135.

Suppose, for instance, that a company wished to determine whether there was any association between the overall performance of a distributor and the distributor's level of service. Again, there are many measures of overall performance: sales, market share, sales growth, profit, and so on. The company's management thought that no single measure adequately defined distributor performance but that overall performance was a composite of all of these measures. Thus, the marketing research department was assigned the task of developing an index of performance that effectively incorporated all of these characteristics. The department was also assigned the responsibility of evaluating each distributor in terms of the service provided. This evaluation was to be based on customer complaints, customer compliments, service turnaround records, and so on. The research department believed that the indices it developed to measure these characteristics could be employed to rank-order the distributors in terms of overall performance and service.

Table 16A.6 contains the ranks of the company's 15 distributors with respect to each of the performance criteria. One way to determine whether there is any association between service and overall performance would be to look at the differences in ranks based on each of the two variables. Let X_i be the rank of the ith distributor in terms of service and Y_i be the rank of the ith distributor with regard to overall performance.

TABLE 16A.6   Distributor Performance

Distributor	Service Ranking X_i	Overall Performance Ranking Y_i	Ranking Difference $d_i = X_i - Y_i$	Difference Squared d_i^2
1	6	8	−2	4
2	2	4	+2	4
3	13	12	+1	1
4	1	2	−1	1
5	7	10	−3	9
6	4	5	−1	1
7	11	9	+2	4
8	15	13	+2	4
9	3	1	+2	4
10	9	6	+3	9
11	12	14	−2	4
12	5	3	+2	4
13	14	15	−1	1
14	8	7	+1	1
15	10	11	−1	1

$$\sum_{i=1}^{15} d_i^2 = 52$$

Further, let $d_i = X_i - Y_i$ be the difference in rankings for the ith distributor. Now, if the rankings on the two variables are exactly the same, each d_i will be zero. If there is some discrepancy in ranks, some of the d_is will not be zero. Further, the greater the discrepancy, the larger some of the d_is would be. Thus, one way of looking at the association between the variables would be to examine the sum of the d_is. The difficulty with this measure is that some of the negative d_is would cancel some of the positive ones. To circumvent this difficulty, the differences are squared in calculating the Spearman rank-order correlation coefficient. The calculation formula is[5]

$$r_s = 1 - \frac{6 \sum_{i=1}^{n} d_i^2}{n(n^2 - 1)}.$$

In the example at hand

$$\sum_{i=1}^{15} d_i^2 = 52,$$

and

$$r_s = 1 - \frac{6(52)}{15(15^2 - 1)} = 1 - \frac{312}{3,360} = 0.907.$$

Now the null hypothesis for the example would be that there is no association between service level and overall distributor performance, whereas the alternate hypothesis would suggest that there is a relationship. The null hypothesis that $r_s = 0$ can be tested by referring directly to tables of critical values of r_s or, when the number of sample objects is greater than ten, by calculating the t statistic,

$$t = r_s \sqrt{\frac{n - 2}{1 - r_s^2}},$$

which is referred to a t table for $v = n - 2$ degrees of freedom. Calculated t is

$$t = 0.907 \sqrt{\frac{15 - 2}{1 - (0.907)^2}} = 7.77,$$

---

[5]See Leonard A. Marascuilo and Maryellen McSweeney, *Nonparametric and Distribution-Free Methods for the Social Sciences* (Belmont, Calif.: Brooks/Cole, 1977), pp. 429–439, for the development of the logic underlying the computational formula. An alternate measure of rank correlation is provided by Kendall's tau coefficient. See M. G. Kendall, *Rank Correlation Methods* (London: Griffin, 1948), pp. 47–48, for a discussion of the rationale behind the tau coefficient. See also Wayne N. Daniel, *Applied Nonparametric Statistics,* 2nd ed. (Boston: PWS-Kent Publishing, 1990); Jean Dickinson Gibbons and Subhabrata Chakraborti, *Nonparametric Statistical Inference,* 3rd ed. (New York: Marcel Dekker, 1992).

while critical t for $\alpha = 0.05$ and $\nu = 13$ degrees of freedom is 2.16. Calculated t exceeds critical t, and the null hypothesis of no relationship is rejected. Overall distributor performance is related to service level. The upper limit for the Spearman rank correlation coefficient is one, since if there were perfect agreement in the ranks, $\Sigma_{i=1}^{n} d_i^2$ would be zero. Thus, the relationship is significant and relatively strong.

COEFFICIENT OF CONCORDANCE

So far we have been concerned with the correlation between *two* sets of rankings of n objects. There has been an X and Y measure in the form of ranks for each object. There will be cases in which we will wish to analyze the association among three or more rankings of n objects or individuals. When there are k sets of rankings, Kendall's coefficient of concordance (W) can be employed to examine the association among the k variables.

One particularly important use of the coefficient of concordance is in examining interjudge reliability. Consider the computer equipment manufacturer interested in evaluating its domestic sales branch managers. Many criteria could be used: sales from the branch office, sales in relation to the branch's potential, sales growth, and sales representative turnover are just a few. It was believed that different executives in the company would place different emphasis on the various criteria and that a consensus about how the criteria should be weighted would be hard to achieve. It was decided, therefore, that the vice-president in charge of marketing, the general sales manager, and the marketing research department should all attempt to rank the ten branch managers from best to worst. Table 16A.7 contains these rankings. The company wished to determine whether there was agreement among these rankings.

TABLE 16A.7   **Branch Manager Rankings**

Branch Manager	Rank Advocated by			Sum of Ranks R_i
	Vice-President, Marketing	General Sales Manager	Marketing Research Department	
A	4	4	5	13
B	3	2	2	7
C	9	10	10	29
D	10	9	9	28
E	2	3	3	8
F	1	1	1	3
G	6	5	4	15
H	8	7	7	22
I	5	6	6	17
J	7	8	8	23

The right-hand column of Table 16A.7 contains the sum of ranks assigned to each branch manager. Now, if there was *perfect agreement* among the three rankings, the sum of ranks, R_i, for the top-rated branch manager would be $1 + 1 + 1 = k$, where $k = 3$. The second-rated branch manager would have sum of ranks $2 + 2 + 2 = 2k$, and the nth-rated branch manager would have sum of ranks $n + n + n = nk$. Thus, when there is perfect agreement among the k sets of rankings, the R_i would be k, $2k$, $3k$, . . . , nk. If there is little agreement among the k rankings, the R_i would be approximately equal. Thus, the degree of agreement among the k rankings could be measured by the variance of the n sums of ranks; the greater the agreement, the larger the variance in the n sums would be.

The **coefficient of concordance** (W) is a function of the variance in the sums of ranks. It is calculated in the following way. First, the sum of the R_i for each of the n rows is determined. Second, the average R_i, $\overline{R}$, is calculated by dividing the sum of the R_i by the number of objects. Third, the sum of the squared deviations is determined; call this quantity s, where

$$s = \sum_{i=1}^{n} (R_i - \overline{R})^2.$$

The coefficient of concordance is then computed as

$$W = \frac{s}{\frac{1}{12} k^2(n^3 - n)}.$$

The denominator of the coefficient represents the maximum possible variation in sums of ranks if there was perfect agreement in the rankings. The numerator, of course, reflects the actual variation in ranks. The larger the ratio, the greater the agreement among the evaluations.

$$\overline{R} = \frac{\sum_{i=1}^{n} R_i}{n} = \frac{13 + 7 + \cdots + 23}{10} = \frac{165}{10} = 16.5,$$

$$s = (13 - 16.5)^2 + (7 - 16.5)^2 + \cdots + (23 - 16.5)^2$$
$$= 720.5,$$

and

$$\frac{1}{12} k^2(n^3 - n) = \frac{1}{12} (3)^2(10^3 - 10) = 742.5.$$

Thus,

$$W = \frac{720.5}{742.5} = 0.970.$$

The significance of W can be examined by using special tables when the number of objects being ranked is small, in particular when $n \leq 7$. When there are more than seven objects, the coefficient of concordance is approximately chi-square distributed where $\chi^2 = k(n - 1)\, W$ with $v = n - 1$ degrees of freedom. The null hypothesis is that there is no agreement among the rankings, and the alternate hypothesis is that there is some agreement. For an assumed $\alpha = 0.05$, critical χ^2 for $v = n - 1 = 9$ degrees of freedom is 16.92, whereas calculated χ^2 is

$$\chi^2 = k(n - 1)\, W = 3\ (9)(0.970) = 26.2.$$

Calculated χ^2 exceeds critical χ^2, and the null hypothesis of no agreement is rejected. There is agreement. Further, the agreement is good, as is evidenced by the calculated coefficient of concordance. The limits of W are zero with no agreement and one with perfect agreement among the ranks. The calculated value of W of 0.970 suggests that although the agreement in the ranks is not perfect, it is certainly good. The marketing vice-president, the general sales manager, and the marketing research department are applying essentially the same standards in ranking the branch managers.

Kendall has suggested that the best estimate of the true ranking of n objects is provided by the order of the various sums of ranks, R_i, when W is significant.[6] Thus, the best estimate of the true ranking of the sales managers is that F is doing the best job and B the next best job, and that C is doing the poorest job.

Questions

1. What is the basic question at issue in a contingency-table test? What is the null hypothesis for this test? How are the expected frequencies determined?
2. What is the contingency coefficient, and to what types of situations does it apply? How does one determine whether the association between the variables indicated by the calculated value of the contingency coefficient is ''strong'' or ''weak''?
3. What is the index of predictive association? When is it properly used? What is meant by an index of predictive association of $\lambda_{A.B} = 0.750$?
4. What is the Spearman rank correlation coefficient? To what types of situations does it apply? How is it calculated and interpreted?
5. What is the coefficient of concordance? When is it used? What is the rationale underlying its computation?

Applications and Problems

1. A large publishing house wants to determine if there is an association between newspaper-publication choice and the education level of the customer. A random sample of 400 customers provided the data in Table 1:

---

[6]Kendall, *Rank Correlation Methods*, p. 87.

TABLE 1   **Education Level versus Newspaper Choice: Observed Frequencies**

Newspaper Publication	Level of Education			Total
	High School Diploma	**Undergraduate Degree**	**Graduate Degree**	
A	75	45	5	125
B	35	10	30	75
C	50	35	10	95
D	65	35	5	105
Total	225	125	50	400

a. State the null and alternate hypotheses.
b. Generate the expected frequencies for each cell of Table 1. Enter the observed and expected frequencies next to each other in Table 2.

TABLE 2   **Education Level versus Newspaper Choice: Observed and Expected Frequencies**

Newspaper Publication	Level of Education			Total
	High School Diploma	**Undergraduate Degree**	**Graduate Degree**	
A				
B				
C				
D				
Total				

c. Is there an association between newspaper-publication choice and level of education at $\alpha = 0.05$? Show all your calculations.
d. What is the strength of association as measured by the contingency coefficient between education level and newspaper choice? Show your calculations.

2. A marketing researcher from the publishing company in Problem 1 stated that the best estimate of newspaper choice by a customer chosen at random would be the "A" publication, since 31.25 percent (or 125 out of 400) customers purchased this publication. The researcher further stated that 68.75 percent of the time the company would be wrong and decided to discard the previous study.
   a. How could the predictive accuracy be improved? Show your calculations.
   b. The index of predictive association is "more directly interpretable" than the contingency coefficient. Discuss.

3. Katherine Martin is the newly hired marketing director for the Alpine Bottling Company (ABC). ABC produces a premium line of soft drink products made with all-natural ingredients. ABC soft drinks are typically about 20 percent more expensive than other soft drinks, including the industry leaders.

Convinced that ABC soft drinks would appeal to a large segment of the market (be-yond just the health-conscious consumers) if moved into nationwide distribution, Martin decided that the best way to introduce the product would be to show that it tastes better than other soft drinks. This could be accomplished by using the "blind taste test" approach and showing the results in ABC's television advertising. Before proceeding, however, she decided to conduct a very limited taste test to get a rough idea of how ABC ranked with other soft drinks. Five subjects each sampled eight brands of soft drinks, including one of the ABC products and the industry leaders. None of the soft drinks were identified. The subjects then ranked the eight soft drinks according to their taste prefer-ences (the most preferred was given a ranking of 1). The results of this limited test are as follows:

	Subject				
Brand	**1**	**2**	**3**	**4**	**5**
ABC Brand	2	3	1	1	1
Brand A	7	8	7	6	7
Brand B	3	2	3	2	3
Brand C	5	5	5	5	6
Brand D	8	7	8	8	8
Brand E	1	1	2	3	2
Brand F	6	6	6	7	5
Brand G	4	4	4	4	4

a. Calculate the coefficient of concordance to determine the five subjects' degree of agreement with respect to their taste preferences.

b. Assuming a 0.05 significance level, is there evidence of agreement among the sub-jects?

c. What is the best estimate of the true ranking of the soft drinks based on this analysis?

d. What are the managerial implications for Martin?

4. For what types of variables was the product moment correlation coefficient originally developed? Can this coefficient be used reliably with other types of variables?

5. When should one use the coefficient of concordance instead of Spearman's rank correla-tion coefficient? What is the null hypothesis for this test? What are the limits of this test and what do these limits mean?

6. The Spazi Italian food company invited six world-renowned chefs to try its new spicy tomato sauce along with four other tomato sauces. Each of the six chefs ranked the five tomato sauces from most preferred (1) to least preferred (5). The rankings are shown in the following table:

Chef	Spazi's Sauce	Competitor 1	Competitor 2	Competitor 3	Competitor 4
1	3	2	4	5	1
2	1	2	4	5	3
3	2	1	5	4	3
4	1	4	3	5	2
5	3	2	4	5	1
6	1	3	4	5	2

Using an appropriate nonparametric test, determine whether there is agreement between the chefs as to the most preferred tomato sauce.

Analysis of Catalog-Buying Data

SIMPLE REGRESSION

One of the questions of concern was the attitude of catalog recipients toward buying from Avery Sporting Goods and whether that attitude was related in any way to the person's demographic characteristics. To address this issue, an "attitude toward Avery" index, called ATTAVRY, was formed from the responses to Questions 7 through 11 of the questionnaire (the questionnaire appears in Appendix 13A). ATTAVRY was formed in such a way that higher scores implied more favorable attitudes about buying from Avery. The responses to the five questions were summed to produce the ATTAVRY score for each subject.

Table 16B.1 investigates whether the ATTAVRY index varies as a function of the person's occupation. Recall that blue-collar workers were coded as 0 and white-collar workers as 1. Instead of the t value discussed in the text, the statistical significance of the equation is assessed in the program using analysis-of-variance techniques discussed in Appendix 15A. The calculated F value of 374.512 is statistically significant at the 0.01 level, since the tabled F value for 1 and 122 degrees of freedom is approximately 2.75. The relationship is also practically significant. The adjusted R square value of 0.752 indicates that approximately 75 percent of the variation in the ATTAVRY index can be accounted for or explained by the variation in occupation. There is a positive relationship between the two variables ($B = 11.534$); white-collar workers have more favorable attitudes toward Avery than blue-collar workers.

TABLE 16B.1   Simple Regression Analysis of ATTAVRY Index versus Occupation

Dependent Variable . . . ATTAVRY
Variable(s) Entered on Step Number 1. V41

		Analysis of Variance	DF	Sum of Squares	Mean Square	F
Multiple R	0.869	Regression	1	4071.174	4071.174	374.512
R square	0.754	Residual	122	1326.213	10.871	
Adjusted R square	0.752					
Standard error	3.297					

Variables in the Equation

Variable	B	Beta	Standard Error B	F
V41	11.534	0.869	0.596	374.512
(Constant)	9.727			

MULTIPLE REGRESSION

In an attempt to determine if the ATTAVRY index was related to other demographic characteristics, a multiple-regression analysis was conducted in which the ATTAVRY index was regressed on the catalog recipient's age and marital status in addition to the person's occupation. Since marital status was categorical, it was necessary to convert it to a series of dummy variables before proceeding. More specifically, the five marital status categories were converted to four dummy variables with the following equivalences using SPSS's recode ability.

V43 =	Implying	D2	D3	D4	D5
1	Widowed	0	0	0	0
2	Divorced	1	0	0	0
3	Separated	0	1	0	0
4	Married	0	0	1	0
5	Single	0	0	0	1

Table 16B.2 contains the output. Note first that the overall regression equation is statistically significant; the calculated F value of 277.036 compares with a tabled F value of approximately 1.82 for 6 and 117 degrees of freedom for $\alpha = 0.01$. Further, the variables as a set account for 93 percent of the variation in the ATTAVRY index as witnessed by the adjusted R square value of 0.931.

The results also provide an interesting opportunity to interpret a dummy variable coding. Note that the respective values for the dummy variables D2 through D5 referring to the marital status categories are

$$D2 = 2.851,$$
$$D3 = 4.387,$$
$$D4 = 7.006,$$
$$D5 = 7.577.$$

The four positive values all indicate that in comparison to the null state (defined as widowed), divorced, separated, married, and single people all have more favorable attitudes toward Avery. The D2 value indicates that there is an increase in the ATTAVRY index of 2.85 on average if the person is divorced rather than widowed. The differential resulting from comparisons with other than widowed people is found by looking at appropriate differences in the dummy variable values. Thus, for example, married people have an ATTAVRY index approximately 2.62 higher on average than separated people, since $D4 - D3 = 2.619$.

TABLE 16B.2   Multiple-Regression Analysis of ATTAVRY Index versus Several Demographic Characteristics

Dependent Variable . . . ATTAVRY
Variable(s) Entered on Step Number 1 . .D2
V41
V42
D5
D4
D3

		Analysis of Variance	DF	Sum of Squares	Mean Square	F
Multiple R	0.967	Regression	6	5042.459	840.410	277.036
R square	0.934	Residual	117	354.928	3.034	
Adjusted R square	0.931					
Standard error	1.742					

Variables in the Equation

Variable	B	Beta	Standard Error B	F
D2	2.851	0.165	0.627	20.668
V41	3.753	0.283	0.600	39.081
V42	0.213	0.368	0.029	55.626
D5	7.577	0.550	0.935	65.625
D4	7.006	0.391	0.948	54.618
D3	4.387	0.267	0.646	46.076
(Constant)	4.491			

DATA ANALYSIS: DISCRIMINANT, FACTOR, AND CLUSTER ANALYSIS

The best known and most commonly used multivariate data-analysis technique is multiple-regression analysis. In Chapter 16, multiple regression's purpose and key interpretive quantities were discussed. In this chapter, three multivariate techniques that have historically been used less often in the analysis of marketing problems — discriminant analysis, factor analysis, and cluster analysis — are discussed. Discriminant analysis is similar to multiple-regression analysis in that it involves the investigation of a criterion variable/predictor variable relationship. Only now the criterion variable is a dichotomy or multichotomy, whereas with regression analysis it is interval scaled. Factor analysis and cluster analysis are both methods of interdependence analysis, as no variable is singled out for special treatment as a criterion variable. While factor analysis is the most frequently used technique of the three, popularity varies by industry, and the magnitude of the usage differences are not great, either in total or within specific industries. See Research Realities 17.1.

DISCRIMINANT ANALYSIS

Many marketing problems naturally involve the investigation of group differences. Two or more groups may be compared, but the problem is essentially one of determining whether they differ from one another and understanding the nature of these differences. For example, we might be interested in determining the characteristics that differentiate between (or among) the following:

- light and heavy users of the product;
- purchasers of our brand and those of competing brands;
- brand-loyal and nonloyal customers;
- customers who patronize one type of retail outlet and those who patronize others;
- good, mediocre, and poor sales representatives.

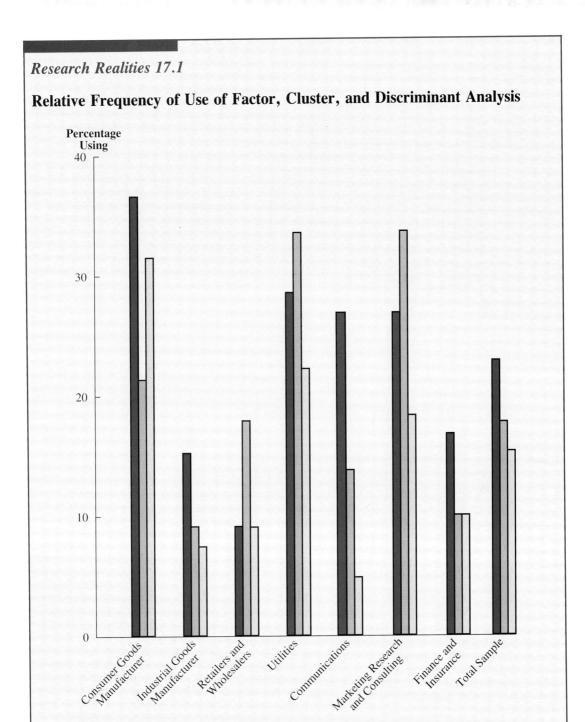

Research Realities 17.1

Relative Frequency of Use of Factor, Cluster, and Discriminant Analysis

Percentage
Using

Factor Analysis   Cluster Analysis   Discriminant Analysis

Source: Developed from the information in Barnett A. Greenberg, Jac L. Goldstucker, and Danny N. Bellenger, *"What Techniques Are Used by Marketing Researchers in Business?" Journal of Marketing,* 41 (April 1977), pp. 64–65.

Suppose that the comparisons for any of these problems were to be made along demographic-socioeconomic lines. One way to proceed would be simply to calculate the mean income, age, education level, and so on for the comparison groups to determine which group is higher.

While such an approach might be interesting with respect to the individual variables, it would tell us little about their respective impacts when used in combination, in that it is unlikely that all the variables will have independent effects. Suppose, for example, that we were investigating the characteristics that distinguish light users from heavy users of our product. If the groups showed a difference with respect to mean income levels, it is also likely that they would show a difference with respect to mean educational levels, because these two variables are fairly highly correlated. Yet if we were interested in segmenting the market using income and educational level as segmentation variables, we would be interested in the total effect of the two variables in combination, not their separate effects. Further, we would be interested in determining which of the variables was more important or had the greater impact. In essence, we need a mechanism that allows us to consider the variables *simultaneously* so as to take into account their interrelationship and partially overlapping information.

One alternative is to construct a *linear combination* of the variables — that is, a weighted sum — in such a way that the linear combination will *best discriminate* among the groups in some sense. We can then assess how the groups differ with respect to this new linear combination score and can also look at the relative weights assigned to each of the variables when forming the linear combination to get some idea as to their relative importance.

Discriminant analysis is the method by which such linear combinations are determined. It was first proposed by R. A. Fisher for the analysis of two-group situations.[1] When two groups are being compared, one linear combination, or discriminant function, results. The technique was later extended to the analysis of three or more groups (for example, light, medium, and heavy users), in which case several discriminant functions can result.[2]

Two-Group Case

The essential purpose and key interpretive output of discriminant analysis are best illustrated by example. Consider, in particular, the experience of the manufacturing firm that conducted a ''new account world series'' sales contest among its salespeople in an attempt to increase the number of distributors handling the firm's products. The contest

---

[1]R. A. Fisher, ''The Use of Multiple Measurements in Taxonomic Problems,'' *Annuals of Eugenics,* 8 (1936), pp. 376–386.

[2]The extension is customarily attributed to Rao, although it seems to have been accomplished by several researchers working independently. See J. G. Bryan, ''A Method for the Exact Determination of the Characteristic Equation and Latent Vectors of a Matrix with Applications to the Discriminant Function for More than Two Groups,'' unpublished doctoral dissertation, Harvard University, 1950; C. P. Rao, ''The Utilization of Multiple Measurements in Problems of Biological Classification, *Journal of the Royal Statistical Society, Series B,* 10 (1948), pp. 159–193; J. W. Tukey, ''Dyadic Anova, An Analysis of Variance for Vectors,'' *Human Biology,* 21 (1949), pp. 65–110.

ran for three months. Each salesperson was assigned a quota for the number of new accounts he or she was expected to generate in that period. The quotas were determined by the sales analysis department and were based on a detailed examination of the segments the company served as defined by SIC codes. More specifically, the sales analysis department based the quotas on the historic penetration of the various segments and the number of accounts of each type that were not current customers in each salesperson's territory. All salespeople who had 15 or more new accounts place an order in the contest period received an all-expense-paid vacation for two to Hawaii. Salespeople who had at least five new accounts place an order received a lesser prize — the choice of a new color TV set or VCR. Those converting less than five new accounts received nothing. As it turned out, 15 salespeople won the grand prize and another 15 the consolation prize, while a third of the salespeople won nothing.[3] The sales analysis department was interested in determining what salesperson activities made a difference in terms of whether a salesperson was a prizewinner or not.

There are a number of ways to proceed with the analysis. The sales department could compare those who were grand prize winners against the others. Alternatively, it might compare those who won any kind of prize against those who won nothing. Still further, it might compare each group against each of the other two. For the moment, let us just consider the two prizewinning groups in order to throw the basic thrust of discriminant analysis into bold relief. Specifically, let us see if we can determine what activities tended to have the greatest impact on whether a salesperson won a grand prize or only a consolation prize. We will take up the question of what activities tend to discriminate among all three groups later.

Table 17.1 contains the data that the sales analysis department collected on each salesperson's new account activities. One way to proceed would be to plot the salespeople according to their activities while maintaining the identity of the group to which each salesperson belongs. Figure 17.1 contains several such plots comparing the grand prize and consolation prize winners. Consider Panel A, which displays the plot of the percentage of calls for which the salesperson had advance appointments against the total number of calls the salesperson made on new accounts. Panel A indicates that, in general, both of these variables were positively related to success, because the more calls on new accounts the salesperson made and the greater the percentage of these calls for which the representative had advance appointments, the more likely the salesperson was to be a grand prize winner than a consolation prize winner. There were exceptions, though. Some consolation prize winners made more calls on new accounts than did grand prize winners. Similarly, some grand prize winners made a smaller percentage of advance appointments than did consolation prize winners. Overall, however, the mean number of calls on new accounts and the mean percentage with advance appointments were higher for grand prize winners as compared to consolation prize winners. A similar type of analysis, conducted with respect to Panels B and C of Figure 17.1, indicates that grand

---

[3]The contest had a number of the ingredients that are generally recommended for sales contests, including a specific objective, a theme, and a reasonable percentage of contest winners. See Gilbert A. Churchill, Jr., Neil M. Ford, and Orville C. Walker, Jr., *Sales Force Management,* 4th ed. (Homewood, Ill.: Richard D. Irwin, 1993), pages 590–596, for a general discussion of the purposes and structure of sales contests.

TABLE 17.1   Salespeople's New Account Activities

		Number of Calls on New Accounts X_1	Percentage of Calls with Advance Appointments X_2	Telephone Calls Made to Prospects X_3	Number of New Accounts Visited X_4
Grand Prize Winner (W)					
1	RMB	130	62	148	42
2	ALB	122	70	186	44
3	BCC	89	68	171	32
4	JJC	104	58	135	40
5	EDC	116	40	160	36
6	WPD	100	65	151	30
7	RHH	85	66	183	42
8	BEK	113	59	130	25
9	DAK	108	52	163	41
10	JJN	116	48	154	48
11	MYS	99	57	188	32
12	PJS	78	70	190	40
13	CET	106	61	157	38
14	LLV	94	58	173	29
15	LMW	98	64	137	36
	Mean	103.9	59.9	161.7	37.0
Consolation Prize Winner (C)					
1	JGB	105	39	155	45
2	RAB	86	60	140	33
3	HAF	64	48	132	36
4	PPD	104	36	119	29
5	BCE	102	53	143	41
6	ASG	73	62	128	30
7	WLH	94	51	152	36
8	LHL	59	64	130	28
9	RJL	84	31	102	32
10	WFM	91	47	96	35
11	JRP	83	40	87	30

prize winners made more telephone calls to prospects and called on more new accounts on average than did consolation prize winners.

The graphical approach for determining which activities seemed to make the most difference in terms of whether a salesperson was a grand prize or consolation prize winner is intuitively insightful, but it has its problems. In the first place, it is difficult and time-consuming to anticipate and then construct all the graphs that might be useful in a given situation. Even for our four-variable example, Figure 17.1 contains only three of the six possible combinations of the variables from which separate graphs could be

TABLE **17.1**   *Continued*

	Number of Calls on New Accounts X_1	Percentage of Calls with Advance Appointments X_2	Telephone Calls Made to Prospects X_3	Number of New Accounts Visited X_4
Consolation Prize Winner (C)				
12 EJS	95	42	114	28
13 VES	68	52	123	26
14 HMT	101	51	98	24
15 BMT	89	39	117	33
Mean	86.5	47.7	122.4	32.4
Unsuccessful Salespeople (U)				
1 RBB	80	23	69	32
2 GEB	47	42	74	33
3 ADC	26	37	132	20
4 JFC	94	24	68	26
5 LDE	57	32	94	23
6 JFH	38	41	83	28
7 JCH	29	52	96	22
8 RPF	48	24	73	26
9 APL	57	36	82	28
10 HAL	39	37	98	21
11 ERM	51	38	117	24
12 WRR	40	42	112	22
13 JTS	64	21	67	29
14 JMV	35	32	78	25
15 HEY	51	29	81	26
Mean	50.4	34.0	88.3	25.7
Overall				
Mean	80.3	47.2	124.1	31.7
Standard Deviation	15.91	8.97	19.99	5.37

constructed when the variables are taken two at a time.[4] Although we might consider more variables at one time to reduce the number of potential graphs, higher dimensional

---

[4]The number of possible two-way graphs is given by the standard combinatorial formula

$$C_2^m = \frac{m!}{(m-2)!2!}$$

where m is the number of variables.

FIGURE 17.1 Scatter Plots of Selected Two-Variable Combinations

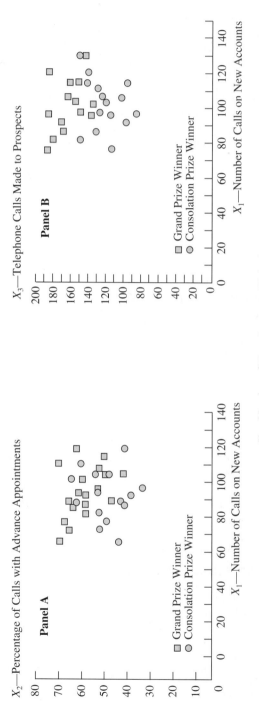

X_2—Percentage of Calls with Advance Appointments

Panel A

■ Grand Prize Winner
○ Consolation Prize Winner

X_1—Number of Calls on New Accounts

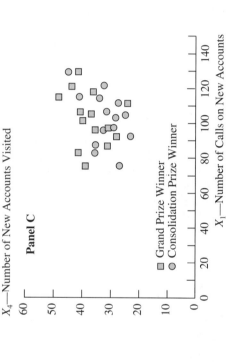

X_3—Telephone Calls Made to Prospects

Panel B

■ Grand Prize Winner
○ Consolation Prize Winner

X_1—Number of Calls on New Accounts

X_4—Number of New Accounts Visited

Panel C

■ Grand Prize Winner
○ Consolidation Prize Winner

X_1—Number of Calls on New Accounts

graphs become exceedingly difficult to interpret. At the same time, two-dimensional graphs are limited in the amount of information they convey, since they allow us to consider only two independent variables at once. What is needed is a mechanism that allows us to assess the effect of each factor, taking into account the factors' partially overlapping information.

Determining the Coefficients One effective way to determine which variables discriminate between the two types of contest winners is to build an index that separates the two groups on the basis of their values on the measured characteristics. In other words, consider when forming the index an arbitrary linear combination of number of calls on new accounts X_1, percentage of calls with advance appointments X_2, telephone calls made to prospects X_3, and number of new accounts visited X_4,

$$Y = v_1X_1 + v_2X_2 + v_3X_3 + v_4X_4,$$

where v_1, v_2, v_3, and v_4 are the arbitrary weights. Given values for v_1 through v_4, we can readily calculate a Y or index score for each of the 30 prize winners. The question at issue, however, is what criterion should be satisfied in deriving values for v_1 through v_4, or how should the Y scores behave?

   In discriminant analysis, the weights are derived so that the *variation in Y scores between the two groups is as large as possible, while the variation in Y scores within the groups is as small as possible*. That is, the weights are derived so that the ratio

$$\frac{\text{Between-group variation}}{\text{Within-group variation}}$$

is maximized. This makes the groups as distinct as possible with respect to the new index scores.

   The operation of the index score is seen most easily in the two-variable case, so let us consider for the moment only the two predictors number of calls on new accounts X_1 and percentage of calls with advance appointments X_2. Given values for v_1 and v_2, we can readily calculate an index score for each of the 30 prize winners using the linear combination

$$Y = v_1X_1 + v_2X_2.$$

   It turns out that the values for v_1 and v_2 that maximize the ratio of the between-group to within-group variation with respect to the new index scores are $v_1 = .064$ and $v_2 = .106$ — that is, the linear combination

$$Y = .064X_1 + .106X_2.$$

   Not only can we calculate each salesperson's score on the new index but we can graphically visualize what is happening, since a linear combination of variables essentially produces a new axis on which the scores in the original plot can be projected. The axis is constructed so that the perpendicular from each point to the Y axis meets the axis

Figure **17.2**   **Scatter Plot Containing New Axis**

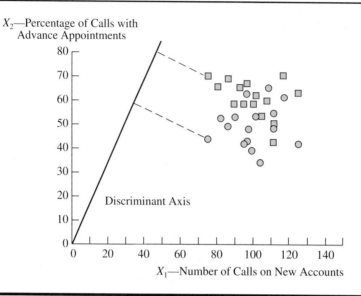

at the scale value equal to the appropriate *Y* score. Figure 17.2, which displays this plot, is equivalent to Panel A of Figure 17.1 except for the inclusion of the new axis representing the linear combination.[5] Using the index score, we can now classify each of the salespeople as a grand prize winner or a consolation prize winner. If the salesperson's index score is closer to the mean of the grand prize winners' index scores, we would classify him or her as a grand prize winner, and vice versa.

The basic approach in discriminant analysis is, therefore, similar to that employed in regression analysis. In each case, the analyst uses a weighted linear combination of independent variables to predict a dependent variable. In regression analysis, the dependent variable is continuous. In discriminant analysis, the dependent variable is group membership. In fact, one can transform a two-group discriminant analysis problem into a regression problem by using a dummy code for the dependent variable (for example, $Y = 0$ if a consolation prize winner and $Y = 1$ if a grand prize winner). The resulting regression coefficients will be proportional to those obtained using standard discriminant analysis procedures.

---

[5]The linear combination is easily located, since the weights assigned each of the variables, when divided by the square root of the sum of the squared weights, equals the cosine of the angle between each of the variables and the new axis. That is, $(.064)^2 + (.106)^2 = .015$, and $\sqrt{.015} = .122$. Since $.064/.122 = .525$, the angle θ between the X_1 and the new discriminant axis is given by $\text{Cos } \theta = .525$, or $\theta = 58°$. The axis can also be located by first plotting the point that corresponds to the coefficients or some multiple of the coefficients in the function — that is, .064 and .106 or some fixed multiple of these values. Next, a line is drawn from the origin through this point.

For the original four-variable problem, the discriminant weights are $v_1 = .058$, $v_2 = .063$, $v_3 = .034$, and $v_4 = -.032$, so the linear combination that maximally differentiates between the groups is[6]

$$Y = .058X_1 + .063X_2 + .034X_3 - .032X_4.$$

The function presents the weights to be applied to X_1 through X_4 so that the distribution of Y scores will show the largest separation between grand prize and consolation prize winners among all possible linear combinations that could have been formed. These Y scores, which are known as discriminant scores, are presented for each sample member in Table 17.2. Note that the discriminant scores of grand prize winners are similar in magnitude, as are those of consolation prize winners, and that the two sets of scores are very different from each other. As a matter of fact, the members within the groups are as much alike as possible on these generated scores consistent with the fact that the groups themselves are as different as possible on these generated scores.

Note what we have done. We have taken a four-variable problem (the groups could be compared in terms of each of the salespeople's new account activities) and have reduced it to a univariate problem by forming a linear combination of X_1 through X_4, simplifying it in the process. We now need to compare only the discriminant scores of the groups rather than comparing the groups on all four variables. Further, we are secure in the knowledge that the groups are as different as possible with respect to these discriminant scores. But how does that help us in determining how grand prize winners differ from consolation prize winners in terms of their new account activities? Further, how does that help the sales analysis department isolate those factors that were most critical to salespeople's success? In effect, what can we do with this discriminant function now that we have it? These questions are answered by

- looking at the interpretation of the discriminant function, and
- employing the discriminant function to classify individuals in groups.

Interpreting the Discriminant Function Before attempting to interpret the discriminant function, the careful analyst will check on its statistical significance. A statistically significant function means that there is a meaningful differentiation of the groups on the discriminant scores. This implies that the investigation of the discriminant function can be worthwhile. The investigation is typically carried out by checking the statistical significance of Mahalanobis' D^2 statistic, which is a squared distance measure that is similar to the standard Euclidian distance measure. More particularly, it measures the distance from each case to the group mean while allowing for correlated axes and different

---

[6]The weights themselves are given by the eigenvector in the solution of the eigenvalue equation

$$(\mathbf{W}^{-1}\mathbf{B} - \lambda\mathbf{I})\mathbf{v} = \mathbf{0},$$

where $\mathbf{W}$ is the pooled sample variance-covariance matrix and $\mathbf{B}$ is the between-group sum-of-squares cross-products matrix.

TABLE 17.2   **Calculated Discriminant Scores for Grand Prize and Consolation Prize Winners Using the Discriminant Function** $Y = .058X_1 + .063X_2 + .034X_3 - .032X_4$

		X_1	X_2	X_3	X_4	Y
Grand Prize Winners						
1	RMB	130	62	148	42	15.2
2	ALB	122	70	186	44	16.5
3	BCC	89	68	171	32	14.3
4	JJC	104	58	135	40	13.0
5	EDC	116	40	160	36	13.6
6	WPD	100	65	151	30	14.1
7	RHH	85	66	183	42	14.0
8	BEK	113	59	130	25	13.9
9	DAK	108	52	163	41	13.8
10	JJN	116	48	154	48	13.5
11	MYS	99	57	188	32	14.8
12	PJS	78	70	190	40	14.2
13	CET	106	61	157	38	14.2
14	LLV	94	58	173	29	14.1
15	LMW	98	64	137	36	13.3
	Mean	103.9	59.9	161.7	37.0	
Consolation Prize Winners						
1	JGB	105	39	155	45	12.4
2	RAB	86	60	140	33	12.5
3	HAF	64	48	132	36	10.1
4	PPD	104	36	119	29	11.4
5	BCE	102	53	143	41	12.8
6	ASG	73	62	128	30	11.6
7	WLH	94	51	152	36	12.7
8	LHL	59	64	130	28	11.0
9	RJL	84	31	102	32	9.3
10	WFM	91	47	96	35	10.4
11	JRP	83	40	87	30	9.4
12	EJS	95	42	114	28	11.2
13	VES	68	52	123	26	10.6
14	HMT	101	51	98	24	11.7
15	BMT	89	39	117	33	10.6
	Mean	86.5	47.7	122.4	32.4	

measurement units for the variables. Fortunately, the F statistic for testing the significance of the D^2 statistic is routinely printed out by most canned computer programs.[7] It turns out that the discriminant function is statistically significant, and the interpretation of the function can proceed.

Discriminant Coefficients Discriminant coefficients are interpreted in much the same way as regression coefficients, in that each coefficient reflects the relative contribution of a unit change of each of the independent variables on the discriminant function. A small coefficient means that a one-unit change in that particular variable produces a small change in the discriminant function score, and vice versa. Like regression coefficients, discriminant coefficients are affected by the scale of the independent variables. That is, the original function $Y = .058X_1 + .063X_2 + .034X_3 - .032X_4$ contains the weights to be applied to the variables in raw-score scales. The problem with this is that if the unit of measurement for one or more variables were to be changed — for example, variable X_2 reflecting calls with advance appointments was measured as a proportion (a decimal) rather than as a percentage (a whole number) — the discriminant function would also change. To remove arbitrary scale-of-measurement effects, the discriminant weights that would be applied to the predictors in *standardized form* are employed when comparing the contributions of the individual variables. The relative magnitudes of these standardized weights are determined by multiplying each raw score weight by the *pooled standard deviation* of the corresponding variable. Define $v_k{}^*$ as the standardized weight; $v_k{}^*$ is related to the raw score weight v_k by the formula

$$v_k{}^* = v_k s_k,$$

where s_k is the pooled sample standard deviation of the kth variable. Considering only the grand and consolation prize winners, the pooled sample standard deviations are $s_1 = 16.76$, $s_2 = 10.89$, $s_3 = 28.16$, and $s_4 = 6.33$. Therefore

$$v_1{}^* = v_1 s_1 = .058(16.76) = .972,$$
$$v_2{}^* = v_2 s_2 = .063(10.89) = .686,$$
$$v_3{}^* = v_3 s_3 = .034(28.16) = .957,$$
$$v_4{}^* = v_4 s_4 = -.032(6.33) = -.203.$$

The absolute size of the standardized weights can be compared to determine the relative contribution of the variables. They indicate that the variables number of calls on new accounts (X_1) and telephone calls made to prospects (X_3) are the most important and that number of new accounts visited (X_4) is the least important in differentiating grand prize from consolation prize winners. Further, variables X_1 through X_3 exert a positive

---

[7]See William R. Dillon and Matthew Goldstein, *Multivariate Analysis: Methods and Applications* (New York: John Wiley & Sons, 1984), pp. 366–369, for the details of how the significance of a discriminant function can be tested. See also Geoffrey J. McLachlan, *Discriminant Analysis and Statistical Pattern Recognition*, (New York: John Wiley & Sons, 1992).

effect because the greater the number of calls, the higher the percentage of calls with advance appointments, and the greater the number of telephone calls made to prospects, the more likely it is the salesperson was a grand prize instead of a consolation prize winner. In contrast, the number of new accounts the salesperson visited has a negative impact on the likelihood that the representative was a grand prize winner.

The standardized weights agree with what intuition might suggest about the importance of the variables when there is relatively little correlation among the predictors. For example, one very common intuitive assessment of the relative importance of the various variables in distinguishing between the groups is a comparison of their means. Large differences in the means on a particular variable suggest that the variable is an important discriminator between the groups, and vice versa. When there is little correlation among the predictors, the relative size of the coefficients in the discriminant function will yield the same ranking of importance of each variable in discriminating between the groups as ranking the size of their mean differences. When there is a high degree of correlation among the predictors, the ordering is not necessarily the same; and, in fact, the coefficients in the discriminant function need to be interpreted with a good deal more caution. Just as in regression analysis, a small standardized weight may then mean either that the variable is irrelevant in discriminating between the groups or, alternatively, that its effect has been partialed out of the relationship because of the high degree of multicollinearity in the data.

Discriminant Loadings   Also used to assess the importance of the variables in discriminating between groups, a discriminant loading gives the simple pairwise correlation between the variable and the discriminant score.[8] For example, we can easily calculate the simple correlations between the discriminant scores Y and each of the predictors X_1 through X_4 in Table 17.2. It turns out that these correlations or loadings are as follows:

$$\text{Between } Y \text{ and } X_1 : 0.627,$$

$$\text{Between } Y \text{ and } X_2 : 0.679,$$

$$\text{Between } Y \text{ and } X_3 : 0.847,$$

$$\text{Between } Y \text{ and } X_4 : 0.441.$$

The loadings suggest that variable X_3, reflecting the telephone calls made to prospects, is now the most important and that variable X_4, reflecting the number of new accounts visited, is still the least important in discriminating between grand prize and consolation prize winners. The difference in the ordering of the variables in comparison to the standardized weights is due to the correlations among the predictors. Like any correlation coefficient, the discriminant loadings can be squared, and the interpretation is similar to r^2 when they are. That is, the squared value for any loading indicates the amount of variance that the discriminant score shares with the variable.

In sum, there are three quantities that are typically used to assess the relative importance of variables in discriminating between groups: the mean differences of the groups

---

[8]We will have more to say about the notion of a loading later in this chapter when discussing factor analysis.

on each variable, the standardized coefficients, and the discriminant loadings. All three will produce similar conclusions about the relative importance of the variables in discriminating between the groups when there is little intercorrelation among the predictors. When multicollinearity is a problem, their conclusions will differ, and the same caveats that apply when interpreting the coefficients in a regression analysis when the predictors are correlated apply here. The best posture is to display a good deal of caution.

Classifying Individuals Using the Discriminant Function   To assist in interpretation, we could also calculate the mean discriminant score for each group. To do this, it is simply necessary to substitute the mean values of the variables for each group into the calculated discriminant function. For the grand prize winners, $\bar{x}_1 = 103.9$, $\bar{x}_2 = 59.9$, $\bar{x}_3 = 161.7$, and $\bar{x}_4 = 37.0$, and thus the mean discriminant score for grand prize winners, $\bar{Y}_W$, is

$$\bar{Y}_W = v_1\bar{x}_1 + v_2\bar{x}_2 + v_3\bar{x}_3 + v_4\bar{x}_4$$

$$= .058(103.9) + .063(59.9) + .034(161.7) - .032(37.0) = 14.2.$$

For consolation prize winners, $\bar{x}_1 = 86.5$, $\bar{x}_2 = 47.7$, $\bar{x}_3 = 122.4$, and $\bar{x}_4 = 32.4$, and the mean discriminant score, $\bar{Y}_C$, is similarly calculated as

$$\bar{Y}_C = .058(86.5) + .063(47.7) + .034(122.4) - .032(32.4)$$

$$= 11.2.$$

This calculation indicates that on the average, grand prize winners have higher discriminant scores than consolation prize winners. (The same result would be obtained if the discriminant scores in Table 17.2 had been averaged.)

To determine whether the discriminant function provides meaningful practical differentiation (versus statistical differentiation) between the two groups, it is possible to apply the discriminant function to each individual to predict the person's score and, on the basis of the generated score, to classify the salesperson as a grand prize or consolation prize winner. We could then compare this prediction with the individual's known actual classification to determine whether the function provides meaningful discrimination. Since we have already calculated the discriminant scores, let us create a predicted classification for each sample member using the very simple decision rule: *If a salesperson's discriminant score is closer to the mean score for grand prize winners than for consolation prize winners, classify the salesperson as a grand prize winner; otherwise, classify him or her as a consolation prize winner.* An alternative, but equivalent, procedure is to compute the score that divides the mean discriminant scores. This "cutting score" is then used to assign objects to groups in the following way: *If the individual's score is above the cutting score, classify the salesperson as a grand prize winner; if it is below, classify the salesperson as a consolation prize winner.* When the groups are equal in size, the **cutting score,** Y_{cs}, is given as the simple average of the mean discriminant scores for the groups — that is, by the calculation

$$Y_{cs} = (\bar{Y}_W + \bar{Y}_C)/2 = (14.2 + 11.2)/2 = 12.7.$$

When the groups are not equal, the formula needs to be modified to take the size of each group into account. The appropriate formula is then

$$Y_{cs} = \frac{n_2\overline{Y}_1 + n_1\overline{Y}_2}{n_1 + n_2},$$

where $\overline{Y}_1$ and $\overline{Y}_2$ are the mean discriminant scores and n_1 and n_2 the sizes of Groups 1 and 2, respectively.[9]

Either decision rule essentially defines the group to which the individual is most similar. The rules' application suggests the predicted classifications contained in the right-hand column of Table 17.3. Table 17.4, which is commonly referred to as a **confusion matrix,** summarizes the accuracy of this predictive classification decision rule.

The entries on the diagonal of Table 17.4 represent the **hit rate,** or the proportion correctly classified, P_{cc}. This proportion is

$$P_{cc} = \frac{28}{30} = 0.933.$$

Approximately 93 percent of the salespeople are correctly classified as grand prize or consolation prize winners on the basis of their new account activities.

Assessing Classification Accuracy   A question that logically arises with any hit rate is assessing how good it is. One would probably argue for the example at hand that an approximate 93 percent hit rate is very good, given that one would only expect a 50 percent hit rate by chance alone, considering that there were as many consolation as grand prize winners in the sample of salespeople. How would you assess the hit rate, though, if the two groups were not equal in size? Suppose that in a sample of 100, 20 won grand prizes and 80 won consolation prizes, which could easily be the case if the quota requirements for the grand prize were changed. What is then a good hit rate? At least two criteria can be used: the maximum chance criterion and the proportional chance criterion.[10]

The **maximum chance criterion** holds that any object chosen at random should be classified as belonging to the larger group, as that will maximize the proportion of cases correctly classified. In the sample of 100, we would thus classify anyone chosen at random as   consolation prize winner, because that would make 80 percent of all the classificatio s correct.

---

[9]See Joseph F. Hair, Jr., Rolph E. Anderson, Ronald L. Tatham, and William C. Black, *Multivariate Data Analysis with Readings,* 3rd ed. (New York: Macmillan, 1992), especially pp. 100–102, for a graphic portrayal of what happens to the optimal cutting score when the groups are not equal in size.

[10]Donald G. Morrison, "On the Interpretation of Discriminant Analysis," *Journal of Marketing Research,* 6 (May 1969), pp. 156–163. For a general discussion of the issues surrounding linear discriminant analysis and linear classification analysis, as well as an extensive bibliography, see Carl J. Huberty, "Issues in the Use and Interpretation of Discriminant Analysis," *Psychological Bulletin,* 95 (1984), pp. 156–171.

TABLE **17.3** **Predicted Group Membership Using the Simple Classification Rule**

	Discriminant Score Y_i	Differences from Mean of		Predicted Group Membership
		First Group $Y_i - \bar{Y}_W = Y_i - 14.2$	Second Group $Y_i - \bar{Y}_C = Y_i - 11.2$	
Grand Prize Winners (W)				
1	15.2	1.0	4.0	W
2	16.5	2.3	5.3	W
3	14.3	0.1	3.1	W
4	13.0	−1.2	1.8	W
5	13.6	−0.6	2.4	W
6	14.1	−0.1	2.9	W
7	14.0	−0.2	2.8	W
8	13.9	−0.3	2.7	W
9	13.8	−0.4	2.6	W
10	13.5	−0.7	2.3	W
11	14.8	0.6	3.6	W
12	14.2	0.0	3.0	W
13	14.2	0.0	3.0	W
14	14.1	−0.1	2.9	W
15	13.3	−0.9	2.1	W
Consolation Prize Winners (C)				
1	12.4	−1.8	1.2	C
2	12.5	−1.7	1.3	C
3	10.1	−4.1	−1.1	C
4	11.4	−2.8	0.2	C
5	12.8	−1.4	1.6	W
6	11.6	−2.6	0.4	C
7	12.7	−1.5	1.5	W*
8	11.0	−3.2	−0.2	C
9	9.3	−4.9	−1.9	C
10	10.4	−3.8	−0.8	C
11	9.4	−4.8	−1.8	C
12	11.2	−3.0	0.0	C
13	10.6	−3.6	−0.6	C
14	11.7	−2.5	0.5	C
15	10.6	−3.6	−0.6	C

*The assignments were actually carried out using more significant digits in the calculations of discriminant scores. While the calculations to one decimal place suggest this case is equidistant from the two group means, it actually is slightly closer to the mean for the grand prize winners.

TABLE 17.4   **Confusion Matrix of Actual versus Predicted Group Membership**

| | Predicted Classification | | |
Actual Classification	Grand Prize Winner	Consolation Prize Winner	Total
Grand prize winner	15	0	15
Consolation prize winner	2	13	15

The maximum chance classification rule is not very helpful from a marketing viewpoint, though, because we wish to identify the two types of winners. Thus, we would like to classify some salespeople chosen at random as grand prize winners and thereby defy the *a priori* odds. In such instances, the **proportional chance criterion, C_{pro},** applies as the standard of evaluation, in which

$$C_{pro} = \alpha^2 + (1 - \alpha)^2,$$

where
    α = the proportion of individuals in Group 1;
$1 - \alpha$ = the proportion of individuals in Group 2.

Suppose in the sample of 100 with unequal size groups that there were indeed 20 grand prize winners (Group 1) and 80 consolation prize winners (Group 2). The proportional chance criterion would then equal $C_{pro} = (0.20)^2 + (0.80)^2 = 0.68$. Thus, a classification accuracy of, say, 85 percent through the use of the discriminant function would represent a good improvement over chance alone, but 85 percent classification accuracy would not look very impressive against the maximum chance criterion. When the two groups are equal in size, as they are in the original example, the proportional chance criterion equals the maximum chance criterion.

A couple of comments must be made about the original classification procedure summarized in Table 17.4. First, there is an upward bias in the procedure because the proportion of correct hits is somewhat overstated.[11] This upward bias results because the data that were used to develop the discriminant model are also used to test the model. Since the criterion used to fit the model generates an equation that provides an optimal fit to the data at hand, the actual predictive accuracy of the model should be tested on a new sample of data. In many problems, this means that the original sample of observations is split into two subsamples. The one subsample, called the *analysis sample,* is used to

---

[11]See R. E. Frank, W. F. Massy, and D. G. Morrison, "Bias in Multiple Discriminant Analysis," *Journal of Marketing Research,* 2 (August 1965), pp. 250–258, for the development of the bias argument. See also Robert A. Eisenbeis, "Pitfalls in the Application of Discriminant Analysis in Business, Finance, and Economics," *Journal of Finance,* 23 (June 1977), pp. 875–900, for a general discussion of the problems encountered in applying discriminant analysis to business problems.

develop the equation, while the other, called the *holdout sample,* is employed to examine how well the equation predicts group membership.[12]

Second, the particular decision rule we used to classify grand prize and consolation prize winners will minimize the costs of misclassification (that is, will be optimal) when: (1) the costs of misclassifying a grand prize winner as a consolation prize winner, and vice versa, are equal; (2) the *a priori* probabilities of winning each prize are equal; and (3) the distribution of the variables in the two populations is multinormal with equal and known covariance matrices. When these conditions are not satisfied, the decision rule for classifying objects must be revised.[13]

Three-Group Case

We now want to entertain the question of $k \geq 3$ groups. The biggest change that occurs when we move beyond two groups is that there can be more than one discriminant function.[14] As a matter of fact, when there are k groups and p variables, the maximum number of discriminant functions will be given by the following rules:

- If there are more variables p than groups k (the typical case), there will be at most $k - 1$ discriminant functions.

- If the number of variables p is less than the number of groups k, there will be no more than p discriminant functions.

---

[12]With small samples one often cannot afford the luxury of setting aside some of the observations for later use because all are needed to develop the equation. In such instances, one can systematically delete one case in turn from a sample of size n and fit the equation to each of the remaining $n - 1$ observations. The process, which is repeated n times with each observation left out in turn, provides useful estimates of the coefficients and prediction accuracy of the equation. See Melvin R. Crask and William D. Perreault, Jr., "Validation of Discriminant Analysis in Marketing Research," *Journal of Marketing Research,* 14 (February 1977), pp. 60–68, for details of the procedure, which is technically called "jackknifing the estimates." See Panel on Discriminant Analysis, Classification, and Clustering, "Discriminant Analysis and Clustering," *Statistical Science,* 4 (No. 1, 1989), pp. 34–69, for a review of the empirical evidence on the jackknife and other procedures used to assess the error rates in predicting group membership.

[13]For general discussions about the accuracy of the classification rules under various conditions, see Dillon and Goldstein, *Multivariate Analysis,* pp. 392–393; B. Efron, "Estimating the Error Rate of a Prediction Rule: Improvement and Cross-Validation," *Journal of the American Statistical Association,* 78 (1983), pp. 316–331; William R. Dillon and Stuart Westin, "The Performance of the Linear Discriminant Function in Nonoptimal Situations and the Estimation of Classification Error Rates: A Review of Recent Findings," *Journal of Marketing Research,* 16 (August 1979), pp. 370–381.

[14]There are two variations in discriminant analysis when there are more than two groups: the classical and simultaneous approaches. The classical approach emphasizes the generation of classification functions, one for each group, that maximize the likelihood of correct classifications of the members of the group. The classical approach produces $g(g - 1)/2$ discriminant functions (where g is the number of groups) that separate each pair of groups; the coefficients for each variable in each discriminant function turn out to be equal to the differences in the coefficients for the variable in the respective classification functions. The coefficients for the discriminant function separating Groups 1 and 3, for example, would be equal to the differences in coefficients for the classification functions for Groups 1 and 3. The simultaneous approach, which is also known as the canonical approach, is the one emphasized here. For a very readable discussion of the differences in the two approaches, see Donald R. Lehmann, *Market Research and Analysis,* 3rd ed. (Homewood, Ill.: Richard D. Irwin, 1989), pp. 769–770.

Regardless of which case results, the number of statistically significant discriminant functions can be less than the maximum number possible. It depends on whether the extracted functions provide "meaningful differentiation" among the objects forming the groups.

Consider again the sample of salespeople and their success in securing new accounts. This time, though, consider all three groups. Since the number of groups is less than the number of variables, the number of groups will determine the maximum number of discriminant functions that can be derived, $k - 1 = 2$ in this case.

The two discriminant functions turn out to be

$$Y_1 = .064X_1 + .079X_2 + .027X_3 - .002X_4;$$

$$Y_2 = -.036X_1 - .037X_2 + .041X_3 - .003X_4.$$

The functions have the following interpretation. Of all the linear combinations of the four variables that could be developed, the linear combination given by the first function provides maximum separation. Maximum separation is understood, of course, to be defined on the basis of discriminant scores; the salespeople within a group are very similar with respect to their Y_1 scores, while the salespeople in different groups have very dissimilar Y_1 scores. Given the first linear combination, the second function provides maximum separation among all possible linear combinations that were uncorrelated with the first set of scores. Thus, the second function provides maximum separation on a contingent set of scores, provided that they are uncorrelated with the first set of scores; that is, $r_{Y_1Y_2} = 0$.

Classifying Respondents   The statistical significance of these functions should be checked before they are employed to classify salespeople.[15] It turns out that only the first function is statistically significant. Thus, we can develop a classification rule that depends only on it. Let that rule simply be an extension of the one previously employed; that is, let us simply assign salespeople to the group to which their discriminant score is closest. This rule requires that the mean discriminant scores be known for each group. They can be generated by substituting the means of the variables (number of calls on new accounts, percentage of calls with advance appointments, telephone calls made to prospects, and number of new accounts visited) for each group in the discriminant function.

$$\text{Grand prize winner: } \overline{Y}_W = .064(103.9) + .079(59.9)$$

$$+ .027(161.7) - .002(37.0)$$

$$= 15.67.$$

$$\text{Consolation prize winner: } \overline{Y}_C = .064(86.5) + .079(47.7)$$

$$+ .027(122.4) - .002(32.4)$$

$$= 12.54.$$

[15]See Dillon and Goldstein, *Multivariate Analysis*, pp. 400–406, for a discussion of how to test the statistical significance of each of the discriminant functions that can be generated where there are more than two groups.

Unsuccessful salesperson: $\overline{Y}_U = .064(50.4) + .079(34.0)$

$$+ .027(88.3) - .002(25.7)$$

$$= 9.58.$$

The cutting scores $(15.67 + 12.54)/2 = 14.11$ and $(12.54 + 9.58)/2 = 11.06$ bisect the difference in mean scores between grand prize and consolation prize winners, and between consolation prize winners and unsuccessful salespeople, respectively. Thus, any salesperson with a score less than 11.06 would be considered an unsuccessful contest competitor, whereas all those with discriminant scores greater than 14.11 would be considered grand prize winners. Those with scores between 11.06 and 14.11 would be considered consolation prize winners. The scores and predicted classification of each of the 45 salespeople are contained in Table 17.5. Table 17.6 is the confusion matrix that results from these predicted classifications. The performance of this procedure is quite good; the classification of 91.1 percent of the salespeople is predicted correctly against the chance criterion of 33 percent. All the incorrect predictions involve consolation prize winners, two of whom are predicted to be grand prize winners and two of whom are predicted to be unsuccessful in the sales contest. The function is particularly effective, then, in discriminating between grand prize winners and those who did not win anything in the sales contest. Of course, there is upward bias in the prediction because the data employed to generate the function are also being used to check its predictive validity. A different sample of salespeople who also participated in the sales contest but who are not used to fit the function would be preferred to truly assess predictive accuracy.

TABLE **17.5** **Discriminant Scores for Each Salesperson and Group to Which Salesperson Would Be Predicted to Belong Employing the Function** $Y = .064X_1 + .079X_2 + .027X_3 - .002X_4$

	Grand Prize Winners (W)				Consolation Prize Winners (C)				Unsuccessful Salespeople (U)		
	Person	Score	Prediction		Person	Score	Prediction		Person	Score	Prediction
1	RMB	17.25	W	1	JGB	14.00	C	1	RBB	8.80	U
2	ALB	18.40	W	2	RAB	14.06	C	2	GEB	8.32	U
3	BCC	15.73	W	3	HAF	11.47	C	3	ADC	8.18	U
4	JJC	14.91	W	4	PPD	12.74	C	4	JFC	9.76	U
5	EDC	14.94	W	5	BCE	14.60	W	5	LDE	8.73	U
6	WPD	15.66	W	6	ASG	13.06	C	6	JFH	7.92	U
7	RHH	15.63	W	7	WLH	14.18	W	7	JCH	8.58	U
8	BEK	15.45	W	8	LHL	12.38	C	8	RPF	6.94	U
9	DAK	15.45	W	9	RJL	10.59	U	9	APL	8.71	U
10	JJN	15.39	W	10	WFM	12.14	C	10	HAL	8.08	U
11	MYS	15.97	W	11	JRP	10.83	U	11	ERM	9.45	U
12	PJS	15.69	W	12	EJS	12.50	C	12	WRR	8.93	U
13	CET	15.88	W	13	VES	11.81	C	13	JTS	7.56	U
14	LLV	15.32	W	14	HMT	13.17	C	14	JMV	6.88	U
15	LMW	15.06	W	15	BMT	11.95	C	15	HEY	7.75	U

TABLE 17.6

Actual Classification	Predicted Classification			
	Grand Prize Winner	Consolation Prize Winner	Unsuccessful Salesperson	Total
Grand Prize Winner	15	0	0	15
Consolation Prize Winner	2	11	2	15
Unsuccessful Salesperson	0	0	15	15

Key Variables Disregarding the fact that the accuracy of the estimating procedure is biased, the sales analysis department would be interested in determining the key new account activities that differentiated salespeople's performance. We cannot use the raw-score coefficients for this purpose but must generate the standardized coefficients to negate the effect of the units with which we measure the variables. The standardized weights, which are derived by multiplying the raw-score weights by the pooled standard deviations of the respective variables, are

$$v_1^* = v_1 s_1 = .064(15.91) = 1.018,$$

$$v_2^* = v_2 s_2 = .079(8.97) = .709,$$

$$v_3^* = v_3 s_3 = .027(19.99) = .540,$$

$$v_4^* = v_4 s_4 = -.002(5.37) = -.011,$$

Number of calls on new accounts, X_1, is the most important variable in differentiating among the levels of success in the sales contest, while the number of new accounts visited, X_4, is the least important. However, the relative importance of each predictor should be interpreted with a degree of caution, because there is some intercorrelation among the predictors.

Marketing Applications

Although discriminant analysis has not been applied as often as regression analysis to marketing problems, it has been used for a variety of problems. Some of these uses include attempts to determine those characteristics that distinguish the listening audiences of various radio stations, to discriminate among different types of automobile buyers, to predict adopters and nonadopters of new products, to relate purchase behavior to advertising exposure, to determine the relationship between personality variables and the consumer decision process, to discriminate between those who choose to save at commercial banks and those who choose savings and loan institutions, to develop perceptual maps depicting the relationships among products to determine segmentation opportunities, to identify factors associated with aggressive price behavior, to assess the differences in importance of various attributes where the same products are being purchased in different countries, to assist in retail positioning, and to determine the factors that supermarket buyers use in deciding whether to stock a new product.[16]

ETHICAL DILEMMA 17.1

A marketing research consultant was asked to address a local business group to discuss some of the research methods currently being used in the field. To make the presentation more meaningful, the consultant recounted the details of some recent studies undertaken by her firm. The consultant was particularly explicit in recounting how her company had used discriminant, factor, and cluster analysis at various times to develop perceptual maps. As a consequence of such detail, most of the audience had sufficient information with which to identify the clients for whom the research was conducted.

- What are the clients' rights?
- Is there a tacit agreement between the researcher and clients to uphold the confidentiality of the clients' studies?
- Should the consultant have obtained the clients' consent before revealing the nature of their studies?
- What are the consequences of such a presentation for the client?
- What might be some of the consequences for the researcher and her firm?

FACTOR ANALYSIS

Factor analysis is one of the more popular "analysis of interdependence" techniques. In studies of interdependence, all the variables have equal footing, and the analyst is concerned with the whole set of relationships among the variables that characterize the objects. Table 17.7, for example, shows two hypothetical sets of correlations among nine variables. A **factor analysis** would focus on the whole set of interrelationships displayed by the nine variables; it would not treat one or more of the variables as dependent variables to be predicted by the others, as would, say, regression or discriminant analysis. The focus on the full set of relationships can be looked at in one of two ways — conceptually or mathematically. At the mathematical level, a **factor** is simply a linear combination of variables. The linear combination is not chosen arbitrarily, however, but is selected to capture the "essence" of the data. There are various ways by which linear combinations of variables can be formed; consequently, the term "factor analysis" applies to a *body* of techniques. The various methods of factor analysis are differentiated in terms of how the weights used in forming the linear combinations are determined.

---

[16]For lists of references and some examples summarizing the use of discriminant analysis in marketing, see Dillon and Goldstein, *Multivariate Analysis;* Hair, Anderson, Tatham, and Black, *Multivariate Data Analysis*.

TABLE 17.7   Two Hypothetical Sets of Correlations among Nine Variables

Panel A Variable	Variable								
	1	2	3	4	5	6	7	8	9
1	1.00								
2	.96	1.00							
3	.94	.88	1.00						
4	.91	.95	.89	1.00					
5	.05	.09	.08	.10	1.00				
6	.12	.04	.03	.11	.92	1.00			
7	.07	.14	.06	.03	.86	.91	1.00		
8	.10	.12	.08	.04	.94	.95	.88	1.00	
9	.08	.11	.06	.13	.97	.87	.91	.90	1.00

Panel B Variable	Variable								
	1	2	3	4	5	6	7	8	9
1	1.00								
2	.92	1.00							
3	.95	.98	1.00						
4	.07	.13	.02	1.00					
5	.09	.05	.11	.95	1.00				
6	.06	.09	.07	.90	.89	1.00			
7	.10	.08	.10	.08	.14	.10	1.00		
8	.05	.07	.09	.09	.06	.12	.94	1.00	
9	.13	.04	.08	.13	.09	.06	.91	.92	1.00

An alternative way of looking at factor analysis is conceptual. In this sense, a factor is a qualitative dimension of the data that attempts to depict the "way in which entities differ, much as the length of an object or the flavor of a product defines a qualitative dimension on which objects may or may not differ. A factor does not indicate how much different various entities are, just as knowing that length is an important physical dimension does not indicate how much longer one object is than another."[17] The correlations among the nine variables depicted in Panel A of Table 17.7 suggest, for example, that the objects differ along two dimensions. In particular, Variables 1 through 4 seem to go together, and Variables 5 through 9 also seem to covary because the pairwise correlations between the variables in each set are uniformly high. Note that the two sets of variables seem to behave very differently, though, as the correlations between any two variables in different sets are very low. Panel B of Table 17.7, in contrast, suggests that

---

[17]David W. Stewart, "The Application and Misapplication of Factor Analysis in Marketing Research," *Journal of Marketing Research,* 18 (February 1981), pp. 51–52. For a general bibliography on factor analysis and its use in marketing research, see John R. Dickinson, *The Bibliography of Marketing Research Methods,* 3rd ed. (Lexington, Mass.: Lexington Books, 1990), p. 807–845.

there are three dimensions underlying the interrelation among the nine variables. More particularly, it seems here that Variables 1 through 3, 4 through 6, and 7 through 9 covary or behave similarly.

The purposes of factor analysis are actually two: data reduction and substantive interpretation. The first purpose emphasizes summarizing the important information in a set of observed variables by a new, smaller set of variables expressing that which is common among the original variables. The second purpose concerns the identification of the constructs or dimensions that underlie the observed variables.

Consider the Imaginative Development Company. The company produces a line of highly sophisticated measuring devices, which it sells primarily to research laboratories. Many of the company's products are custom designed to meet the customer's particular measurement needs. Suppose the company was interested in isolating those personality traits that are likely to lead to success in this type of selling situation. Suppose further that no single measure of performance seemed adequate and that the company decided to employ several measures — namely, sales growth, profitability of sales, and new account sales. Further, to compensate for potential differences caused by differences in sales territory, the company converted each sales representative's performance on each of these variables to index form, employing an index of 100 to indicate "average" performance. Table 17.8 contains the data for a sample of 50 sales representatives.

Summarizing Data

Consider the first purpose of factor analysis — summarizing the important information contained in the data by a fewer number of factors. This raises the question of what is "important information." Two quantities are typically highlighted: the variance of each variable, which is the measure of the variability of the variable across objects, and the correlation between variables, which is a measure of the covariation of the variables across objects.[18] Most factor analyses are implemented using standardized variables because in many problems, the raw variables reflect widely differing units of measurement. By standardizing the variables to mean zero and unit standard deviation, the effect of units of measurement on the final solution is removed. In our case, standardization would not be necessary. The variables are measured in the same units. Because standardization is common, however, let us discuss the variability recovery and covariability recovery questions with standardized data.

Table 17.9 contains the simple pairwise correlations among the variables, and Table 17.10 is the factor-loading matrix that results from performing a principal components analysis on the data in Table 17.9.[19] The factor-loading matrix is one of the key outputs of a factor-analytic solution. Let us, therefore, closely examine the entries in Table 17.10.

---

[18]A factor analysis can be based on other measures of covariation. Correlations are most commonly used, though, and the exposition is most easily understood when the correlations between variables are used.

[19]Some would argue that the principal components procedure is not part of factor analysis. The point is controversial, and it would be confusing to illustrate the argument at this time. The argument centers on the communality question, which is discussed later in the chapter.

TABLE 17.8   **Sales Performance Data for Sample of Sales Representatives from Imaginative Development Company**

Sales Representative	Sales Growth X_1	Sales Profitability X_2	New Account Sales X_3
1	93.0	96.0	97.8
2	88.8	91.8	96.8
3	95.0	100.3	99.0
4	101.3	103.8	106.8
5	102.0	107.8	103.0
6	95.8	97.5	99.3
7	95.5	99.5	99.0
8	110.8	122.0	115.3
9	102.8	108.3	103.8
10	106.8	120.5	102.0
11	103.3	109.8	104.0
12	99.5	111.8	100.3
13	103.5	112.5	107.0
14	99.5	105.5	102.3
15	100.0	107.0	102.8
16	81.5	93.5	95.0
17	101.3	105.3	102.8
18	103.3	110.8	103.5
19	95.3	104.3	103.0
20	99.5	105.3	106.3
21	88.5	95.3	95.8
22	99.3	115.0	104.3
23	87.5	92.5	95.8
24	105.3	114.0	105.3
25	107.0	121.0	109.0

Factor Loadings   Consider first the individual row/column entries. These are the *correlations* between the *variables* and the *factors*. For example, 0.976, the entry in the first row and first column, represents the simple correlation between the first variable and the first factor; 0.083 is the correlation between the first variable and the second factor.

TABLE 17.9   **Simple Pairwise Correlations among the Performance Measures**

	X_1	X_2	X_3
X_1	1.000		
X_2	0.926	1.000	
X_3	0.884	0.843	1.000

TABLE 17.8

Sales Representative	Sales Growth X_1	Sales Profitability X_2	New Account Sales X_3
26	93.3	102.0	97.8
27	106.8	118.0	107.3
28	106.8	120.0	104.8
29	92.3	90.8	99.8
30	106.3	121.0	104.5
31	106.0	119.5	110.5
32	88.3	92.8	96.8
33	96.0	103.3	100.5
34	94.3	94.5	99.0
35	106.5	121.5	110.5
36	106.5	115.5	107.0
37	92.0	99.5	103.5
38	102.0	99.8	103.3
39	108.3	122.3	108.5
40	106.8	119.0	106.8
41	102.5	109.3	103.8
42	92.5	102.5	99.3
43	102.8	113.8	106.8
44	83.3	87.3	96.3
45	94.8	101.8	99.8
46	103.5	112.0	110.8
47	89.5	96.0	97.3
48	84.3	89.8	94.3
49	104.3	109.5	106.5
50	106.0	118.5	105.0

TABLE 17.10

Variable	Factor		
	1	2	3
1	0.976	0.083	−0.203
2	0.961	0.232	0.151
3	0.945	−0.321	0.056
	2.769	0.164	0.067

Similarly, 0.961 is the correlation between the second variable and first factor, and so on. These correlations are called **factor loadings.** When we examine the table of loadings, we find that all three variables load heavily on (correlate highly with) Factor F_1.

Since the entries are variable/factor correlations, their square indicates the proportion of variation in the variable that is accounted for by the factor. Thus,

$$(0.976)^2 = 0.952,$$

$$(0.961)^2 = 0.924, \text{ and}$$

$$(0.945)^2 = 0.894$$

are the proportions of variance in Variables 1, 2, and 3, respectively, accounted for by the first factor.[20]

Covariability recovery focuses on how closely the original pairwise correlations between the variables can be estimated. Consider the sum of the products of the respec-

---

[20]The interpretation of these quantities as the proportion of the total variation in each variable accounted for by the factors parallels that for regression analysis. Recall that in regression analysis, the problem is one of predicting the value of a criterion variable, given one or more predictor variables. When the variables are standardized, the parallel problem in factor analysis becomes one of estimating a z score (a standardized criterion variable) from the factor scores (the predictor variables). There are potentially three factor scores for each sales representative, one corresponding to each of the three linear combinations that can be formed from the original variables. In a one-factor model, the question being addressed is how well the original variables can be estimated using only the first of the factor scores. The coefficient of determination employed in assessing the goodness of fit in a regression model provides a useful frame of reference.

The coefficient of determination is expressed as

$$R^2 = \frac{\text{Explained variation}}{\text{Total variation}} = 1 - \frac{\text{Unexplained variation}}{\text{Total variation}}.$$

Total variation, of course, is measured by the variance of the variable. Unexplained variation is conceptualized in the following way. Suppose that the criterion variable was to be estimated for each object. The difference between the estimated value and the actual value could then be determined. If each of these residuals were then squared and the squared results were summed, the calculation would produce a measure of unexplained variation.

The factor-analytic case suggests a similar calculation. The difference between the standardized scores and the scores estimated using the first-factor scores (which do not have to be actually calculated to assess the fit) could be calculated for, say, variable z_1. If these differences were then squared and summed, the result could be considered a measure of the variation in z_1 left unexplained by the one-factor estimating procedure. If this unexplained variation were then to be divided by a measure of the total variation in z_1 and subtracted from 1, a measure of goodness of fit would be obtained. But what is the total variation in z_1? Since the variables are all standardized to unit variance, it is simply 1. Thus, the sum of the residuals squared when subtracted from 1 provides the needed summary measure. It turns out that

- 95.2 percent of the variation in z_1,
- 92.4 percent of the variation in z_2, and
- 89.4 percent of the variation in z_3

are accounted for by the first factor, F_1.

tive column entries of any two rows of Table 17.10. Take Rows 1 and 2, for example. The sum of the products is

$$(0.976)(0.961) + (0.083)(0.232) + (-0.203)(0.151) = 0.926,$$

which is the original correlation, r_{12}, between Variables 1 and 2 displayed in Table 17.9. Any of the correlations in Table 17.9 can be *regenerated exactly* if all three factors extracted by the principal components procedure are used. The general calculation formula is

$$r_{jl} = \sum_{k=1}^{3} a_{jk} a_{lk},$$

where j and l denote the original variables, k denotes the factor, and a_{jk} is the loading or correlation between the jth variable and kth factor or the entry in the jth row and kth column of Table 17.10.

What happens when fewer factors are used? The pairwise correlations are not regenerated but only *estimated*. The estimate is given by the same formula, but now the summation is from 1 to m, where m denotes the number of factors being considered. For a one-factor ($m = 1$) estimating procedure, the estimated correlation between Variables 1 and 2 ($j = 1, l = 2$) is

$$\hat{r}_{12} = \sum_{k=1}^{1} a_{1k} a_{2k} = (0.976)(0.961) = 0.937,$$

an estimate that is quite close to the true value of 0.926. The other estimates are

$$\hat{r}_{13} = (0.976)(0.945) = 0.922, \text{ and}$$
$$\hat{r}_{23} = (0.961)(0.945) = 0.908,$$

compared to actual values of 0.884 and 0.843, respectively. These estimates are quite good.

Is one factor sufficient, or is more than one factor needed to summarize the data adequately? To answer this question, it is helpful to realize that in a principal components solution, the m factors are uncorrelated. This means that the proportion of variance accounted for by m factors is simply the sum of the proportions accounted for by each factor. Take two factors, for example. The proportion of the variation in each variable accounted for by a two-factor solution is

Variable 1: $(0.976)^2 + (0.083)^2 = 0.959;$
Variable 2: $(0.961)^2 + (0.232)^2 = 0.977;$
Variable 3: $(0.945)^2 + (-0.321)^2 = 0.997.$

Communalities These values, which express the proportion of the variance of the variables extracted by m factors, are called the achieved **communalities** of the variables and are typically denoted as h_j^2, where j refers to the variable number. Thus, we see that two factors account for 95.9 $(= h_1^2)$ percent of the variation in X_1, 97.7 $(= h_2^2)$ percent of the variation in X_2, and 99.7 $(= h_3^2)$ percent of the variation in X_3. The two-factor model does a remarkable job in accounting for the variability within the data. Variable 1 is most poorly captured, but even here 95.9 percent of the total variability in Variable 1 is captured by the first two factors in the principal components solution. This result raises the question of whether it would be wise to retain two factors as the ''proper'' factor-analytic solution.

There is no definitive answer, but the column totals in Table 17.10 can assist the analyst in making a decision. As mentioned, the row/column entries represent the correlations between the variables and the factors, and their squares represent the proportions of variation in each variable explained by the factor. Thus, the sum of the squares in a column will provide a measure of the amount of variation accounted for by the factor representing the column. Take Column 1, for example:

$$(0.976)^2 + (0.961)^2 + (0.945)^2 = 2.769,$$

the column total. Now, because the three variables are all standardized to unit variance, total variance equals 3. The proportion of total variance that is accounted for by the first factor is $2.769/3 = 92.3$ percent. The first two factors, however, account for

$$\frac{2.769 + 0.164}{3} = 0.978,$$

or 97.8 percent of the total variance. The second factor accounts for 5.5 percent of the total variance in the three variables. It seems that in the interest of scientific parsimony, a one-factor solution would suffice; there is only a small gain in explained variation with the addition of the second factor.[21]

Conceptual Basis of Principal Components Analysis   Unlike some of the less structured factor-analytic techniques, principal components analysis leads to unique results. The objective of a principal components analysis is to transform a set of interrelated variables into a set of unrelated linear combinations of these variables. The set of linear combinations is chosen so that each of the linear combinations (factors or components) accounts for a *decreasing proportion* of the variance in the original variables, subject to the condition that each linear combination is uncorrelated (geometrically at right angles) to all previous linear combinations.

The physical analogy of a watermelon should help in understanding the conceptual basis of principal components analysis. The watermelon could be considered to have three basic dimensions; call them length, width, and height and conceive of them as being at right angles to one another. Further, let length always refer to the longest

---

[21]One of the points of controversy surrounding factor analysis is when to stop factoring; that is, how many factors should be retained in the final solution. There is no ''correct'' answer, although a number of rules of thumb have been advanced. We discuss two of the more popular rules later in the chapter. All of the criteria suggest that one factor is adequate for the example.

dimension, width to the next longest dimension that is perpendicular to the length axis, and height to the axis perpendicular to the length and width axes. Now, the total size of the watermelon can be indicated by specifying its length, width, and height. Would fewer dimensions provide a reasonably accurate estimate of its size? It all depends on the shape of the watermelon. Suppose that the watermelon was very long and narrow, much like a cigar. Then clearly its size would be closely indicated by simply specifying its length. If the melon was long and wide but rather flat, two dimensions would be needed to accurately portray its size. Finally, if it was long, wide, and high, three dimensions would be needed to describe its size.

The principal components correspond to the axes of the watermelon in this three-dimensional problem. Consider the sales performance data. Each sales representative has three scores, one for each of the performance criteria. The scores could thus be plotted in three space according to the reported values for X_1, X_2, and X_3. Now, the task in principal components analysis is to produce a set of uncorrelated composite scores that measure what the variables have in common and yet account for decreasing proportions of the total variance in the variables. The first component corresponds to the principal axis of the ellipsoid in three space (the length of the watermelon). Of all the linear combinations that could be formed, it possesses maximum variation. Whether it adequately captures the important information contained in the data depends on the shape of the concentration of the swarm of points. If the plot of the data results in a cigar-shaped figure, one factor is enough. If not, more than one factor is needed to summarize the data. The second principal component would be chosen so that it accounts for the maximum variation left unexplained, consistent with the condition that it is uncorrelated with the first component. (The second component would correspond to the width of the watermelon.) Thus, a principal components analysis reveals how several measures of a domain can be combined in a single measure, the first component, to produce maximum discrimination among objects along this single dimension. The variation accounted for by each component also indicates when several independent dimensions or components are needed to adequately define the domain under investigation.

Substantive Interpretation

Principal components analysis provides a useful tool from the standpoint of data reduction, but it generally does not provide the optimal solution from an interpretive point of view. Interpretation of a factor solution focuses on the identification of the construct or constructs that underlie the observed variables. The problem is captured in Figure 17.3. There it is assumed that measures have been obtained for five variables across a set of objects. The question is: Do these variables have something in common? Do they reflect some underlying, unobserved construct or constructs? How many? What are they? Figure 17.3 suggests that the observed variables are really the result of two underlying factors or dimensions, and substantive interpretation in factor analysis would focus on isolating and identifying those factors.

The sales performance data pose little problem for substantive interpretation. One factor effectively summarizes the important information in the data. It could be considered a general performance factor. A factor score could be calculated for each sales representative using this first factor, and the sales representatives could then be ranked

FIGURE 17.3   **Search for Substantive Interpretation in a Factor Analysis Solution**

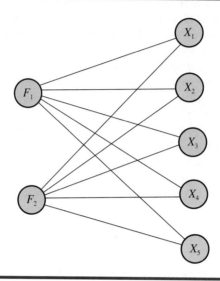

according to these factor scores. The "best" performing sales representative would have the highest score and the "worst" sales representative the lowest score.

Rarely is a factor solution so tidy. In more complex situations, it is useful to rotate the initial principal components solution to facilitate substantive interpretation. Since rotation would be fruitless in the sales performance example, we need another example to illustrate its use, particularly how it can be of assistance in interpreting factors. Consider, for this purpose, a study that was conducted to compare the images of various department stores in a particular city. The data were collected using a semantic differential scale. Figure 17.4 contains a portion of the items that were used. Although the

FIGURE 17.4   **Portion of Items Used to Measure Department-Store Image**

1. Convenient place to shop	:___:___:___:___:___:___:___:	Inconvenient place to shop
2. Fast checkout	:___:___:___:___:___:___:___:	Slow checkout
3. Store is clean	:___:___:___:___:___:___:___:	Store is dirty
4. Store is not well-organized	:___:___:___:___:___:___:___:	Store is well-organized
5. Store is messy, cluttered	:___:___:___:___:___:___:___:	Store is neat, uncluttered
6. Convenient store hours	:___:___:___:___:___:___:___:	Inconvenient store hours
7. Store is far from home, school, or work	:___:___:___:___:___:___:___:	Store is close to home, school, or work
8. Store has bad atmosphere	:___:___:___:___:___:___:___:	Store has good atmosphere
9. Attractive decor inside	:___:___:___:___:___:___:___:	Unattractive decor inside
10. Store is spacious	:___:___:___:___:___:___:___:	Store is crowded

negative or undesirable descriptor sometimes appears on the left and sometimes on the right, the scoring was reversed for those variables where the negative descriptor appeared on the right so that higher scores always reflect more desirable amounts of the property. Table 17.11 shows the correlations among the responses to these specific items.

Determining the Number of Factors   One of the first issues that needs to be addressed is determining the number of factors that are necessary to account for the variation in the data. As was the case previously, we can look at the amount of variation accounted for by each factor in making the decision. That information is contained in Table 17.12. A number of rules have been advanced for deciding how many factors to retain for the

TABLE 17.11

	Question or Variable									
Variable	X_1	X_2	X_3	X_4	X_5	X_6	X_7	X_8	X_9	X_{10}
X_1	1.00	.79	.41	.26	.12	.89	.87	.37	.32	.18
X_2	.79	1.00	.32	.21	.20	.90	.83	.31	.35	.23
X_3	.41	.32	1.00	.80	.76	.34	.40	.82	.78	.72
X_4	.26	.21	.80	1.00	.75	.30	.28	.78	.81	.80
X_5	.12	.20	.76	.75	1.00	.11	.23	.74	.77	.83
X_6	.89	.90	.34	.30	.11	1.00	.78	.30	.39	.16
X_7	.87	.83	.40	.28	.23	.78	1.00	.29	.26	.17
X_8	.37	.31	.82	.78	.74	.30	.29	1.00	.82	.78
X_9	.32	.35	.78	.81	.77	.39	.26	.82	1.00	.77
X_{10}	.18	.23	.72	.80	.83	.16	.17	.78	.77	1.00

TABLE 17.12

Factor (Latent Root)	Variance Explained
1	5.725
2	2.761
3	0.366
4	0.357
5	0.243
6	0.212
7	0.132
8	0.123
9	0.079
10	0.001

FIGURE 17.5   **Variance Explained by Each Factor or Latent Root**

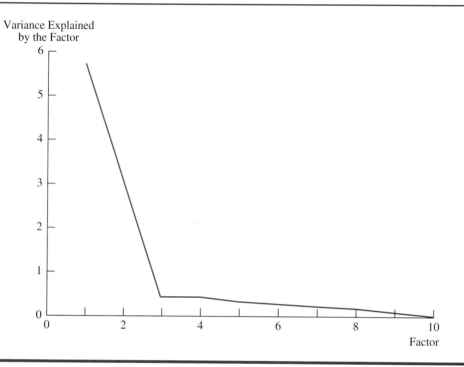

solution. Two of the most popular are (1) the latent roots criterion and (2) the scree test.[22]

The latent roots criterion holds that the amount of variation explained by each factor or latent root must be greater than one.[23] The rationale is that the variation in each variable is one after the variable has been standardized. Thus, each factor should account for the variation in at least one variable if the factor is to be considered useful from a data summarization perspective. Since there are two factors with latent roots greater than one, the latent roots criterion would suggest a two-factor solution for the department store image data.

The scree test employs a plot of the size of the latent roots against the number of factors in their order of extraction. Figure 17.5 contains the plot for the department-store image data. Note how the curve drops sharply at first and then levels off as it approaches the horizontal axis. This is often the case in such plots, and the method actually gets its name because of the resemblance of the plot to a side view of a mountain. Typically such a view will show a sharp drop representing the mountain face. At the foot of the mountain, there will be a straight line or two or even three at a much lesser angle to the

[22]For a discussion of these criteria, plus several others that have been advanced for determining the number of factors, see Stewart, "The Application and Misapplication of Factor Analysis."

[23]The technique actually gets its name from the type of problem in matrix algebra that is solved in generating a factor analytic solution — namely, a latent root or eigenvalue problem. Each eigenvalue equals the amount of variation explained by that factor or latent root.

TABLE **17.13**   **Unrotated Factor-Loading Matrix for Department-Store Image Data Using Two Principal Components**

Variable	Factor 1	Factor 2	Achieved Communality
1	0.633	0.707	0.900
2	0.621	0.695	0.869
3	0.872	−0.241	0.819
4	0.833	−0.366	0.828
5	0.774	−0.469	0.818
6	0.626	0.719	0.908
7	0.619	0.683	0.850
8	0.859	−0.303	0.829
9	0.865	−0.293	0.835
10	0.790	−0.454	0.831
Eigenvalue or latent root	5.725	2.761	

horizontal, where rocks that have fallen off the mountain have piled up. These various piles of stable rocks are called screes. The last real factor is considered to be that point *before the first scree begins.*[24] In the example, the first scree or straight line connects Factors 3 through 6. The scree plot criterion also suggests, therefore, that a two-factor solution is necessary to capture the store image data.

How much of the total variation in the data is explained by the two-factor solution? The total variance of the ten variables when standardized is 10. The first component accounts for $5.725/10 = 57.3$ percent, and the second component accounts for $2.761/10 = 27.6$ percent. The two components together account for 84.9 percent of the total variation in the ten variables.

What about the achieved communalities of each of the variables considered separately? How much of the variation in each variable is accounted for by the two-factor solution? This information can be obtained from the factor-loading matrix contained in Table 17.13. The achieved communalities shown in the right-hand column are again secured by squaring each factor loading and adding the results across factors. Thus, for Variable 1, the achieved communality is

$$(0.633)^2 + (0.707)^2 = 0.900,$$

and it is similarly derived for the other variables. All the variables are captured rather nicely by the two-factor solution. Variable 5 is most poorly captured, but even here 81.8 percent of the variation in Variable 5 is reflected by the first two factors.

---

[24]Cattell and Vogelmann offer very specific instructions for determining the number of factors from a scree plot. See Raymond B. Cattell and S. Vogelmann, "A Comprehensive Trial of the Scree and KG Criteria for Determining the Number of Factors," *The Journal of Multivariate Behavioral Research,* 12 (1977),pp. 289–325.

Rotating the Factors   What are these factors? Their interpretation is obscure. All ten variables correlate highly with or load heavily on the first factor. Variables 1, 2, 6, and 7 also have high positive loadings on the second factor. Figure 17.6, which employs the correlations between the variables and the two factors as coordinates, suggests that the variables do cluster somewhat in two space. Variables 1, 2, 6, and 7 occupy the same general location, and Variables 3, 4, 5, 8, 9, and 10 also occupy the same general two-space location. That some variables do share a common location raises the question of whether the original factor axes can be rotated to still new orientations to facilitate interpretation of the factors. There is no question of whether the axes can be rotated; they can be, since an axis rotation simply amounts to forming linear combinations of the factors. The key question is: *How* should these new linear combinations be selected to best facilitate interpretation?

Several alternatives have been proposed by which the new linear combinations can be formed. Just about all of these methods attempt to produce loadings that are close to either 0 or 1, because such loadings show more clearly what things go together and, in this sense, are more interpretable. The methods differ in the criterion that is satisfied when these modified loadings are produced.[25] For example, both orthogonal and oblique rotations have been proposed. Orthogonal rotations are also called rigid or angle-preserving rotations, because they preserve the right angles that exist among the factor axes. Oblique rotations do not, which means that the factors themselves can be correlated.

Figure 17.7 displays the **varimax** rotation of the original axes. Varimax attempts to "clean up" the factors in the factor-loading table — that is, force the entries in the columns to be near 0 or 1. The main alternative to varimax is quartimax, which attempts to clean up variables or rows in the factor loading table while maintaining the right angles between the factors. The empirical evidence indicates that varimax tends to produce loadings that are more interpretable except when there is a general factor present in the data, in which case quartimax is the preferred orthogonal rotation scheme. Varimax is consequently the most popular orthogonal rotation scheme.[26] In the figure, the original axes are labeled F_1 and F_2, and the rotated axes are labeled F_1' and F_2'.

Note in Figure 17.7 that each of the new axes seems to be purer than the original axes. That is, whereas the variables had high loadings — as represented by the *magnitude* of the *vertical projections* — on both of the original factor axes, they seem to have

---

[25]The earliest axes rotations in factor analysis were done graphically by hand and were aimed at satisfying the five criteria of "simple structure" that Thurstone proposed. While the criteria of simple structure are intuitively appealing, they are mathematically unmanageable. Thus, two analysts working on a rotation of factor axes typically produced two distinct configurations, even though both relied on Thurstone's qualitative rules of simple structure, setting off a controversy about which configuration was more correct. Since the advent of large capacity, high-speed computers, "objective" rotations employing some analytic criteria have been used to transform the initial factor solution so that the variables may be more readily named and understood. One advantage of the objective methods is that two analysts working on the same data set and using the same rotation method should produce similar conclusions. See L. L. Thurstone, *Multiple Factor Analysis* (Chicago: University of Chicago Press, 1947), for the rationale for and the criteria of simple structure.

[26]Whereas the empirical evidence favors varimax when an orthogonal rotation is planned, the evidence concerning which scheme to use is not as clear when an oblique rotation is contemplated. Oblique rotations tend to pass the axes through clusters of points without regard to the angles separating the axes. For a brief discussion of the criteria that the major oblique rotations attempt to satisfy, see Dillon and Goldstein, *Multivariate Analysis*, pp. 91–95.

FIGURE 17.6   Scatter Diagram Using Correlations between Variables and Factors as Coordinates

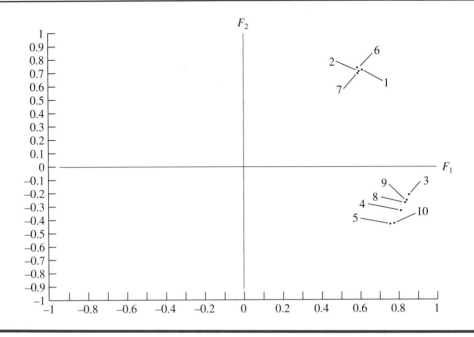

FIGURE 17.7   Scatter Diagram after Orthogonal Rotation of Axes

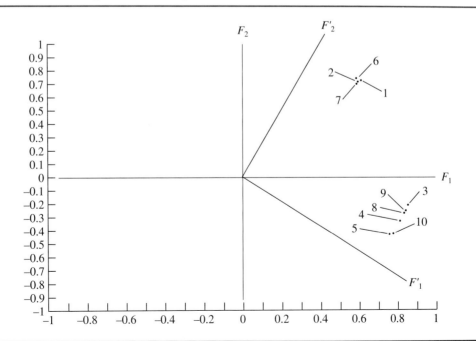

TABLE **17.14**   **Factor-Loading Matrix for Department-Store Image Data after Orthogonal Rotation of Two Principal Components Using Varimax**

	Factor		Achieved
Variable	1	2	Communality
1	0.150	0.937	0.900
2	0.147	0.920	0.869
3	0.864	0.269	0.819
4	0.899	0.142	0.828
5	0.904	0.024	0.818
6	0.138	0.943	0.908
7	0.151	0.909	0.850
8	0.886	0.209	0.829
9	0.887	0.221	0.835
10	0.910	0.045	0.831
Eigenvalue or latent root	4.859	3.628	

high loadings on either one *or* the other of the new axes but not both. Table 17.14 presents the magnitudes of these vertical projections, loadings, or correlations of variables with factors.

Naming the Factors   What are these factors? In order to name them, it is useful to see what variables go with each factor and to name the factors accordingly. The following process is useful for this purpose.

1. Begin with the first variable and first factor and move horizontally from left to right looking for the highest loading. Circle that loading. Repeat this procedure for each of the other variables in turn.

2. Examine each of the circled loadings and assess its significance. The significance of any loading can be judged using either statistical or practical criteria. Statistical criteria mean that the loading is statistically significant at some specified alpha level, typically 0.05. This means that for samples of less than 100, the loading would have to be greater than 0.30 to be considered statistically significant. The practical significance criterion means that the factor must account for a certain percentage of the variation in the variable. In this regard, a loading of 0.30 means that the factor accounts for 9 percent of the variation in the variable. Typically, the cutoff for saying that the loading is significant is somewhere in the neighborhood of 0.30 or 0.35.

3. Underline the other significant loadings using the criteria decided on in Step 2.

4. Examine the loading matrix and identify all those variables that do not have significant loadings on any factor. It is hoped there is none, but if there is, the analyst has two options: (1) interpret the solution as it is and simply ignore those variables without a significant loading, or (2) critically evaluate each of the variables that do

not load significantly on any factor. This evaluation would be in terms of the variable's overall contribution to the research as well as its communality index. If the variable(s) is of minor importance to the study's objective and/or has a low communality index, the analyst may decide to eliminate the variable or variables and derive a new factor solution with the nonloading variables eliminated.[27]

5. Focus on the significant loadings, and attempt to name the factors on the bases of what the variables loading on a given factor seem to have in common. Variables that have significant loadings on more than one factor complicate the naming task and are candidates for elimination, depending on the purpose of the study as well as on whether the mixed pattern of loadings makes sense or indicates there are fundamental problems with the variable or item.[28]

It turns out that when these steps are applied to the loadings in Table 17.13, each variable loads significantly on one and only one factor. Specifically, Variables 3, 4, 5, 8, 9, and 10 load only on Factor 1, whereas Variables 1, 2, 6, and 7 load only on Factor 2. An examination of the wording of the individual items suggests that Factor 1 is a "store atmosphere" factor in that it addresses the issue of whether the store is clean, organized, spacious, and has a nice atmosphere in general. Factor 2 reflects whether the store is a convenient place to shop because of the hours it is open, where it is located, and the speed of the checkouts. Therefore, we would probably want to call it a "convenience" factor. Instead of describing differences in department stores using the ten original variables, there is considerable economy in describing these differences in terms of the two derived factors.

Note that the rotation of a factor solution is contemplated for one reason and one reason only — to facilitate the isolation and identification of the factors underlying a set of observed variables. No additional variation in the observed variables is explained by the factors after an analytic rotation is done. If two factors were originally needed to capture the important information in the data, two factors will also be needed after the rotation, if information is not to be discarded. To see this, one simply has to compare Tables 17.13 and 17.14. First, note that the achieved communality for each variable is the same after rotation as it was before. The contribution of each factor in accounting for the variation in the respective variables has changed, but the total explained variation has not. For Variable 1, the achieved communality before rotation was $(0.633)^2 + (0.707)^2 = 0.900$, while after rotation it is $(0.150)^2 + (0.937)^2 = 0.900$, or still the same. However, whereas before rotation the second factor accounted for 50.0 percent of the total variation in Variable 1, after rotation it accounts for 87.8 percent of this variation.

---

[27]Hair, Anderson, Tatham, and Black, *Multivariate Data Analysis,* p. 241.

[28]Although we cannot go into a discussion of the criteria that are used to judge whether an item is a bad or garbage item because that would take us too far afield, readers should be aware that the criteria are intimately bound up in the psychometric processes that one uses to develop measures of constructs. For a discussion of these processes, see Gilbert A. Churchill, Jr., "A Paradigm for Developing Better Measures of Marketing Constructs," *Journal of Marketing Research,* 16 (February 1979), pp. 64–73. For discussion of how to go about identifying the most influential observations in a factor analysis, see Sangit Chatterjee, Linda Jamieson, and Frederick Wiseman, "Identifying Most Influential Observations in Factor Analysis," *Marketing Science,* 10 (Spring 1991), pp. 145–160.

The contributions of the factors have simply been altered, although no additional variation has been accounted for. The same holds true for the contribution of factors to total explained variation. The total remains constant, although the contribution of each factor in explaining this total variation changes. Initially, the contribution of the first factor was $5.725/10 = 57.3$ percent and the second was $2.761/10 = 27.6$ percent, for a total of 84.9 percent. After rotation, the contribution of the first factor is $4.859/10 = 48.6$ percent and the second is $3.628/10 = 36.3$ percent, so the total remains the same. Once again, rotation is undertaken for the sole purpose of naming the underlying factors. No additional variance is accounted for in any variable, nor in the variables as a set.

The Key Decisions

As one might suspect by now, factor analysis represents a *body of techniques* for studying the interrelation among a set of variables. The method employed to analyze the sales performance data was based on a rather specific assumed underlying model — in particular, the principal components model, which suggests

$$z_j = W_{j1}F_1 + W_{j2}F_2 + \ldots + W_{jm}F_m \qquad j = 1, 2, \ldots, p.$$

That is, it was assumed that any of the p performance variables could be perfectly described by a set of m common factors. Many would argue that this is inaccurate for several reasons.[29] First, if the measures were repeated, it is unlikely that the "new" variables would correlate perfectly with the "old." There would be errors of measurement, and it is unrealistic to expect the underlying model to account for these measurement aberrations. Second, and more important, it is unreasonable to expect all the variance of a variable to be summarized by common factors only; a fraction would certainly seem to be unique. Thus, although income and assets are both manifestations of the underlying trait of "being rich," for example, they are not one and the same.

When these conditions are expected to arise, an alternative model is often suggested:

$$z_1 = W_{11}F_1 + W_{12}F_2 + \ldots + W_{1m}F_m + d_1V_1$$
$$z_2 = W_{21}F_1 + W_{22}F_2 + \ldots + W_{2m}F_m + d_2V_2$$
$$\vdots$$
$$z_p = W_{p1}F_1 + W_{p2}F_2 + \ldots + W_{pm}F_m + d_pV_p.$$

Each variable is described linearly in terms of m common factors and a factor unique to the particular observed variable. This is the *classical model* for factor analysis, and it involves a different approach for its solution. The distinction between the classical model and the principal components model can be best appreciated by again referring to the sales performance data. If we had used all three principal components and the factor loadings displayed in Table 17.10, we would have been able to reproduce *exactly* the

---

[29]The argument is technically known as the communality problem.

value of *each variable* for each of the 50 observations contained in Table 17.8; alternatively, we would have been able to account for all the variation in each variable. Viewed from the vantage point of the variable-by-variable correlation matrix, we would have been able to generate the ones in the diagonal of the correlation matrix from Table 17.9. Under the assumption of the classical factor model, the correlations between variables are reproduced by means of the common factor coefficients alone. Thus, if the estimated correlations are to provide a good fit to the observed correlations, the diagonal elements in the correlation matrix must also be reproduced from the common factor portion of the classical model. If unities are placed on the diagonal of the correlation matrix, then the classical factor model could not possibly apply. There is simply no way in which a variable could be considered to have a unique portion and yet have it reproduced exactly by common factors only. Now, if numbers approximating communalities (measuring what the variable has in common with other variables) are placed in the diagonal of the matrix of observed correlations, the factor solution will involve both common and unique factors. Of course, this raises the question of how these communalities are to be secured.

Generating Communality Estimates   There are at least three popular approaches for securing communality estimates. One approach uses the results from an initial principal component analysis. That is, the correlation matrix with 1s in the diagonal is factor analyzed using the principal components model. The communalities for each variable for a given *m*-factor solution are entered into the diagonal of the correlation matrix, and this matrix is then factor analyzed. A second alternative makes use of the multiple-regression model. Each variable is regressed on each of the other variables in the analysis, and the resulting R^2s are determined. The diagonal of the correlation matrix is replaced by these squared multiple correlations before the correlation matrix is factor analyzed. A third alternative is to determine the largest absolute value of the correlation of the variable with any other variable in the analysis by examining the off-diagonal elements in the correlation matrix. This correlation is then placed on the diagonal before the correlation matrix is factor analyzed. Note that all three of these schemes attempt to assess what the variable in question has in common with the other variables in the analysis. Even though the initial communality estimates are different, depending on which alternative is used, that does not seem to make much difference in the results. All three schemes tend to produce similar solutions in the typical situation of large numbers of observations and variables.

Decision Items   Not only must analysts make decisions about what values to enter into the diagonal of the correlation matrix, but they also need to make decisions about various other issues in order to conduct a factor analysis. Figure 17.8 outlines the sequence of decisions that need to be made. We have already discussed the content of some of these decisions, but let us briefly review the essential questions that need to be addressed at each stage in the process.[30]

---

[30]For a more detailed discussion of these questions and the main options and empirical evidence addressing them, see Stewart, ''The Application and Misapplication of Factor Analysis.''

FIGURE 17.8   **Key Decisions When Factor-Analyzing Data**

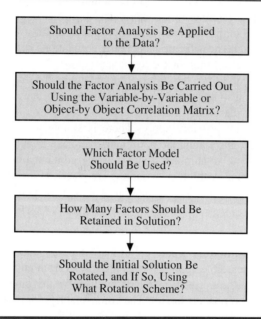

1. Should factor analysis be applied to the data? Although we just went ahead and applied factor analysis to the two examples in this section, analysts would typically want to ask whether it is wise to do so before proceeding. There are several useful methods for deciding whether a factor analysis should be applied to a set of data. Two of the simplest procedures are examining the correlation matrix and plotting the latent roots. Factor analysis is concerned with the homogeneity of items. This means that some of the items in the correlation matrix should be large, indicating that they go together. A pattern of low correlations throughout the matrix indicates a heterogeneous set of items and suggests that the matrix may be inappropriate for factoring. The plot of the latent roots or eigenvalues should indicate a sharp break. If the plot of the original, unrotated roots results in a continuous, unbroken line, factoring may be inappropriate.

2. Should the factor analysis be carried out using the variable-by-variable or object-by-object correlation matrix? Typically, the variable-by-variable correlation matrix is analyzed because most studies aim at determining which variables go together. That is not the only alternative. The object-by-object matrix can also be analyzed, and there are other options as well.

3. Which factor model would be used? We have already discussed whether to use the principal components model, in which ones, or the factor model, in which communalities, are placed in the diagonal of the correlation matrix before it is factor analyzed. Suppose that the analyst decides on the factor model to allow for the unique

components in the variables. The question then becomes one of deciding which of the many factor models to use, as there are a number of choices. Most of the popular statistical packages have a default option that selects one of the more robust alternatives when a choice is not specified.

4. How many factors should be retained in solution? We have already discussed some of the main criteria that can be used to decide on the proper number of factors. The latent roots and scree criteria generally work well, although not always perfectly, and analysts may be uncertain about how many factors they should retain. When too few factors are retained and carried into rotation, the factor output can be very difficult to interpret. Recall that no additional variation can be accounted for by rotation. The amount of variance in each variable accounted for is exactly the same after rotation as it was before. The only thing that changes is how the variance accounted for is distributed among the factors. When too few factors are carried into rotation, the variance in each variable is forced on too few factors, resulting in a number of mid-size loadings rather than loadings near zero and one. This, of course, makes interpretation much more difficult. When too many factors are carried into rotation, some factors come out capturing the variance of a single variable or, at most, two variables. This is counter to the whole notion underlying factor analysis, which suggests that a factor is a latent variable reflecting what a number of observed variables have in common. In general, though, the empirical evidence suggests that over-factoring by one or two factors has less severe consequences for the final solution than does taking too few factors into rotation.[31]

5. Should the initial solution be rotated, and if so, using what rotation scheme? In some ways, ''rotation is something like staining a microscope slide. Just as different stains reveal different structures in the tissue, different rotations reveal different structures in the data, even though in both cases all the structures are always actually there.''[32] It is possible that different rotations will yield results that appear to be entirely different. Rather than being bothered by this, it is useful to keep in mind that all rotations are equivalent from a statistical point of view. They differ only in how they apportion the variation accounted for, which, of course, is what is used to name the factors. Thus, performing several rotations and examining the results to see which rotation produced the ''most interpretable'' structure is often a very productive analysis strategy. The right rotation, just like the right stain on a microscope slide, can be very revealing of the underlying structure in the data or organism.

Marketing Applications

In marketing, factor analysis historically has been employed to ''purify'' original sets of scale items by isolating and then eliminating those items that do not seem to belong with

---

[31]*Ibid.*, p. 59.

[32]William D. Wells and Jagdish N. Sheth, ''Factor Analysis,'' in Robert Ferber, ed., *Handbook of Marketing Research* (New York: McGraw-Hill, 1974), p. 2–462.

Research Realities 17.2

Factors That Make Commercials Likeable

If you like an ad, will you buy the product? According to a study conducted by Ogilvy Mather, when people like a commercial, they are twice as likely to be persuaded by it as people who simply feel neutral toward the ad.

What makes a commercial likeable? Does it need to be entertaining to be liked? Or are consumers content with the more subtle pleasures evoked by a sentimental or nostalgic approach? What role does creativity play? Do clever treatments of old topics make people like the advertising more?

To answer these questions, the Ogilvy Center for Research and Development tackled the problem of what makes a likeable commercial. Researchers studied a representative sample of 80 prime-time commercials using a nationwide sample of target market consumers. The researchers located consumers who had seen the commercials in their own homes and asked them to describe what they had seen, using a well-researched advertising checklist. The consumers were then asked how much they *liked* each commercial, using a five-point scale that ranged from "liked a lot"

to "disliked a lot." Every respondent rated an average of five commercials, and, on average, each commercial was rated by 133 viewers.

To get people to systematically describe the commercials that they had seen, the research team at Ogilvy had them describe the commercials using the following list of adjectives:

Amusing	Irritating
Appealing	Lively
Believable	Original
Clever	Phony
Confusing	Pointless
Convincing	Seen a Lot
Dull	Sensitive
Easy to Forget	Silly
Effective	True to Life
Familiar	Warm
Fast Moving	Well Done
Gentle	Worn Out
Imaginative	Worth Remembering
Informative	

The researchers then used factor analysis to reduce this long list of adjectives to a more manageable set of summary ratings. They found that 26 of the adjectives clustered nicely into five distinct category groupings.

Source: "What Makes a Likeable Commercial?" *Viewpoint*, 19 (March/April 1987), pp. 32–35; Alexander L. Biel and Carol A. Bridgewater, "Attributes of Likeable Television Commercials," *Journal of Advertising Research*, 30 (June/July 1990), pp. 38–44.

the rest of the items, as well as to name the dimensions captured by a measure.[33] Research Realities 17.2, for example, discusses the use of factor analysis by the Ogilvy Center for Research and Development to isolate the features that make commercials likable. Factor analysis has been used in life-style and psychographic research problems to develop consumer profiles reflecting people's attitudes, activities, interests, opinions,

---

[33]The emphasis on factor analysis in scale development is particularly evident in the semantic differential scales. See the original book describing the development of the semantic differential technique by Charles E. Osgood, George J. Suci, and Percy H. Tannenbaum, *The Measurement of Meaning* (Urbana, Ill.: University of Illinois Press, 1957). See also Roger M. Heeler, Thomas W. Whipple, and Thomas P. Hustad, "Maximum Likelihood Factor Analysis of Attitude Data," *Journal of Marketing Research*, 14 (February 1977), pp. 42–51.

For example, if people used the word ''clever'' to describe a commercial, they were also likely to say that the same commercial was imaginative, amusing, and original. The factor analysis allowed the researchers to combine these adjectives, along with ''silly'' and ''not dull,'' into a summary category that measured ingenuity. The five summary categories were as follows:

Ingenuity:	Clever, Imaginative, Amusing, Original, Silly, (not) Dull
Meaningful:	Worth Remembering, Effective, (not) Pointless, (not) Easy to Forget, True to Life, Believable, Convincing, Informative
Energy:	Lively, Fast Moving, Appealing, Well Done
Rubs the Wrong Way:	Seen a Lot, Worn Out, Irritating, Familiar, Phony
Warmth:	Gentle, Warm, Sensitive

Now that the researchers at Ogilvy had a way to summarize people's descriptions of what they say, they sought to relate this to how well the people liked what they saw. The researchers attempted, by means of multiple-regression analysis, to determine which of the five summary labels (or combinations of labels) was most related to commercial liking. Specifically, they regressed the liking scores on the five dimension scores.

The analysis revealed that consumers best liked the commercials that seemed relevant and meaningful to their lives. An energetic and lively execution also contributed to liking, although it was less important than how meaningful the commercial was to consumers. Ingenuity and whether the commercial rubbed people the wrong way were much less important to commercial liking.

Strangely enough, whether or not a commercial was perceived as being warm had little effect on how well the commercial was liked. The glaring exception to this finding was that advertisements featuring animals consistently ranked tops in terms of likeability and warmth.

The researchers point out that their findings apply differently to different categories of products. Growing evidence suggests that the relationship between liking and persuasion is strongest in low-involvement categories such as fast-moving consumer goods, for which the emotional component of persuasion is proportionately more important than the deliberate consideration of product attributes.

perceptions, and preferences in order to better predict their consumption and purchase behavior. It also has been used in marketing to ascertain the key attributes that determine customer preferences for particular products or institutions, to assess a company's image, to isolate those dimensions of printed advertisements that most affect readership, to develop a measure by which the job satisfaction of industrial sales representatives can be assessed, to group objects (typically people) on the basis of their similarities in behavior, and to screen variables before performing a regression analysis to eliminate or at least reduce the problems of correlated predictors.[34]

---

[34]For bibliographies listing some of the major studies in marketing that used factor analysis, see Dillon and Goldstein, *Multivariate Analysis;* Hair, Anderson, Tatham, and Black, *Multivariate Data Analysis;* or Stewart, ''The Application and Misapplication of Factor Analysis.''

ETHICAL DILEMMA 17.2

Clark was feeling very smug. He had just completed the analysis and writeup of a study that involved respondents' completing a lengthy attitude scale about such things as their need for security, their attitudes toward life insurance, their willingness to assume risk, how vulnerable they feel to life's unexpected events, and similar constructs. The purpose of the investigation was to determine if those purchasing his firm's products could somehow be differentiated from those purchasing competitors' products on the basis of the attitude profiles. The first factor analyzed the responses to discover which items belonged to which constructs. This involved a series of iterations. After Clark had purified the items and felt comfortable with the results, he formed a total score for each construct for each respondent by summing the responses to the items making up that construct. He used the total scores thus generated as independent variables in a discriminant analysis in which brand purchased served as the criterion. The results clearly indicated that the attitude profile of those purchasing his firm's insurance differed from that of people purchasing competitors' products and, further, that some of the differences lent themselves to actionable strategies by which the firm might increase its share.

Clark's smugness began to dissipate, however, when a chance conversation with one of his old college buddies caused him to wonder if he had not made a mistake. His college friend pointed out that according to the accepted rules of thumb for factor analysis, Clark did not have a large enough sample in terms of the number of respondents versus the number of items. Consequently, his factor analysis results might be quite unstable.

- What should Clark do? If he admits his error now to his boss, his boss might think less highly of him, particularly since Clark was hired into the marketing research department partially on the basis of his statistical skills. However, not reporting it could cause those in his firm to place more confidence in the results than they should.
- What are Clark's ethical responsibilities here?
- Would the ethical problem be different if Clark knew of the requirement and intentionally overlooked it, knew it but inadvertently forgot it, or never learned it in the first place?

CLUSTER ANALYSIS

In marketing there is keen interest in developing useful ways of classifying objects. Very often the objects to be classified are customers. Consider a firm that is interested in segmenting its market. The objective is to group potential customers into homogeneous groups that are large enough to be profitably cultivated. The segmentation base could involve many characteristics, ranging from the commonly used socioeconomic bases to the more recently advocated buyer behavior and psychological bases. One thing is sure, it would be based on numerous factors and not simply on one or two factors. This, of course, raises a problem for the researcher — how to identify natural groupings of the objects given the multivariate nature of the data. To base the classification on a single factor would be an oversimplification. Yet some means of combining variables must be found if more than one factor is to be used. **Cluster analysis** offers the researcher a way out of the dilemma. It specifically deals with how objects should be assigned to groups so that there will be as much similarity within and difference among groups as possible.

One of the more important uses of cluster analysis has been in identifying aggregates of consumers who behave similarly. By then determining the areas where they live and the demographics of those areas from census data, geodemographic segments of the population can be formed. Research Realities 17.3, for example, lists the twelve major groups, the subgroups forming each group, and a few features of some selected subgroups in the Claritas Prizm system.

As an example, consider the problem faced by firms that wish to test market products, prices, promotional campaigns, and so on. The problem is to select "like" cities so that the results obtained are not attributable to differences in market areas. But how does one determine when cities are "alike"? Consider the situation when similarity is assessed on the basis of two city characteristics — population and median income. This represents an oversimplification of the actual situation, but nevertheless it can be used to illustrate the purposes and procedures of cluster analysis. Since the variables possess vastly different measurement scales, it is advisable to effect the grouping using standardized scores. Otherwise, the grouping would change when the unit in which a variable was measured was altered; for example, population was specified as a number of thousands of people instead of simply number of people. Table 17.15 contains the standardized income and population scores for 15 test cities that a firm is considering grouping into like categories.

TABLE 17.15   **Key Characteristics of Cities to be Grouped Expressed in Standardized Units**

City	Income X_1	Population X_2
A	1.14	1.72
B	−1.25	−1.17
C	1.62	0.89
D	1.64	1.35
E	0.55	0.10
F	−0.94	−1.25
G	0.89	1.32
H	−0.87	−0.63
I	−0.44	−0.07
J	0.08	−0.55
K	−0.18	0.62
L	−1.29	−0.86
M	−1.07	−1.38
N	−0.09	0.02
O	0.21	−0.11

Research Realities 17.3

Characteristics of Selected Subgroups in Prizm Life-Style Clusters

Major Group	Subgroups	Demographic Description	Life-Style/Media/ Financial Preferences
The Suburban Elite	Blue-Blood Estates Money and Brains Furs and Station Wagons	New-money families in suburbs, upwardly mobile white collar, college grads, age 35–54	Own a CD player All-news radio 3+ stock transactions a year
The Affluentials	Pools and Patios Two More Rungs Young Influentials	Upper-middle income, two-income empty nesters, age 45–64, in upscale suburbs	Foreign cruise Epicurean magazines $5,000+ mutual funds
Greenbelt Families	Young Suburbia Blue-Chip Blues	Upper-middle income, traditional suburban families, age 25–44, mixed white/blue collar, single-family houses	Go fishing Watch headline news Interest checking accounts
The Urban Gentry	Urban Gold Coast Bohemian Mix Black Enterprise New Beginnings	Lower-middle income families and singles, age 25–34, low-level white collar and clerical	Jog/run AOR/prog radio Have first mortgage

The boxed subgroup is the largest subgroup in its major group.

Source: *Prizm® Lifestyle Cluster System* (Alexandria, Va.: Claritas, Inc., 1992).

One way of effecting the grouping is simply to plot the results and make a visual assignment. Figure 17.9, which employs income and population as axes, suggests that there are three distinct clusters in the data:

- Cluster 1 consisting of Cities A, C, D, and G;
- Cluster 2 consisting of Cities E, I, J, K, N, and O; and
- Cluster 3 consisting of Cities B, F, H, L, and M.

Major Group	Subgroups	Demographic Description	Life-Style/Media/ Financial Preferences
The Exurban Boom	God's Country New Homesteaders Towns and Gowns	Lower-middle income, town-dwelling, young families, age 18–34, some college, blue/white collar	Ride motorcycles MOR/nostalgia radio Veterans life insurance
Suburban Elders	Levittown, U.S.A. Gray Power Rank and File	Middle-income, suburban, older couples, age 55–65+, tract housing, two income, high school education	Belong to a union Golden oldies radio Christmas Club account
Satellite Blues	Blue-Collar Nursery Middle America Coalburg and Corntown	Lower-middle income, mid-size town families, age 45–64, blue collar, single-unit housing	Woodworking Fishing/hunting magazines Christmas Club account
Mid-City Mix	New Melting Pot Old Yankee Rows Emergent Minorities Single City Blues	Low income, urban singles, age 18–34, some college, mixed blue and white collar	Contribute to public radio Jazz radio Non-interest checking accounts

The visual assignment procedure worked in this example because there were only two dimensions on which the grouping was based. There are potentially many characteristics on which the cities might be grouped, however, and graphic display becomes more difficult as the number of dimensions increases. Thus, it would appear to be useful to have some objective measure of ''similarity'' or ''likeness'' with which to form the natural groupings of the objects in higher space.

FIGURE 17.9   **Two-Dimensional Plot of City Characteristics**

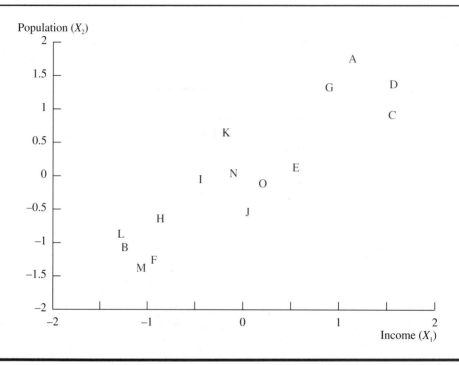

Euclidean Distance to Measure Similarity

A rather obvious measure is the Euclidean distance between the points. In the two-dimensional figure, the distance between, say, Cities A and C would be calculated

$$d_{A,C} = \sqrt{(X_{C1} - X_{A1})^2 + (X_{C2} - X_{A2})^2},$$

where X_{C1}, for example, represents the coordinate of City C on the first dimension, median income. This distance turns out to be

$$d_{A,C} = \sqrt{(1.14 - 1.62)^2 + (1.72 - 0.89)^2} = 0.959.$$

In three dimensions, the expression for distance between A and C would be

$$d_{A,C} = \sqrt{(X_{C1} - X_{A1})^2 + (X_{C2} - X_{A2})^2 + (X_{C3} - X_{A3})^2},$$

while for any two objects, i and j, it would be

$$d_{ij} = \left\{ \sum_{i=1}^{3} (X_{ik} - X_{jk})^2 \right\}^{1/2}$$

The generalization to *n* dimensions to account for *n* characteristics is obvious; the summation is simply taken from *k* equals 1 to *n*.

The distance between all 15 cities is presented in Table 17.16. An examination of Table 17.16 prompts several comments. First, distance is an inverse measure of similarity because the larger the distance, the further apart the objects. Second, one can readily appreciate why cluster analysis is highly dependent on computers.[35] In this simplified example involving 15 objects, there were 15(14)/2 = 105 distances that needed computing. In the general case of *n* objects, there would be $n(n - 1)/2$ separate distances. Third, the specification of the clusters is not as readily apparent as it was when the data were presented graphically. As a matter of fact, without the two-dimensional figure to help us, there is a real question whether we could even specify some appropriate clusters. Clearly we need some alternate way of proceeding.

Clustering Methods

A number of methods have been suggested for forming ''natural groupings'' of objects employing variables. One of the most popular classifications includes:[36]

1. linkage procedures,
2. nodal procedures, and
3. factor procedures.

There are also variations within each method. Keep in mind, however, that the objective underlying each method is the same — to assign objects to groups so that there will be as much similarity within groups and as much difference among groups as possible. Unfortunately, the different methods can produce some widely divergent results with the same data set, and none of the methods is as yet accepted as the ''best'' under all circumstances. The research analyst must, therefore, be familiar with the various methods so that he or she can exercise the proper degree of caution in choosing the method that is most compatible with the desired nature of the classification.

Linkage Methods Various linkage methods have been advanced.[37] We shall discuss the single linkage method in some detail, because an understanding of this method is the key to understanding the other linkage procedures, such as complete linkage and average linkage.

---

[35]The growth in popularity of cluster analysis paralleled the early growth in computer installations. The major stimulus was the classic book by R. Sokal and P. Sneath, *Principles of Numerical Taxonomy* (San Francisco: W. H. Freeman, 1963). The literature on cluster analysis virtually exploded after its publication and continues to show dramatic annual increases even now.

[36]For an alternative seven-category classification, see Mark S. Aldenderfer and Roger K. Blashfield, *Cluster Analysis* (Beverly Hills, Calif.: Sage Publications, 1984).

[37]The linkage methods are sometimes called hierarchical agglomerative methods. For useful introductions to the subject, see Aldenderfer and Blashfield, *Cluster Analysis;* M. Lorr, *Cluster Analysis for Social Sciences* (San Francisco: Jossey-Bass, 1983); Leonard Kaufman and Peter J. Rousseeuw, *Finding Groups in Data: An Introduction to Cluster Analysis* (New York: Wiley, 1990).

TABLE 17.16 Distance between Cities i and j in Two Space

$j =$

$i =$	1 A	2 B	3 C	4 D	5 E	6 F	7 G	8 H	9 I	10 J	11 K	12 L	13 M	14 N	15 O
1. (A)	0.000														
2. (B)	3.750	0.000													
3. (C)	0.959	3.533	0.000												
4. (D)	0.622	3.834	0.460	0.000											
5. (E)	1.724	2.203	1.330	1.658	0.000										
6. (F)	3.626	0.320	3.337	3.663	2.011	0.000									
7. (G)	0.472	3.283	0.847	0.751	1.266	3.155	0.000								
8. (H)	3.092	0.660	2.917	3.197	1.597	0.624	2.627	0.000							
9. (I)	2.388	1.366	2.273	2.518	1.004	1.282	1.924	0.706	0.000						
10. (J)	2.505	1.467	2.108	2.458	0.802	1.237	2.038	0.953	0.708	0.000					
11. (K)	1.718	2.085	1.820	1.961	0.896	2.019	1.279	1.428	0.737	1.199	0.000				
12. (L)	3.544	0.313	3.396	3.670	2.075	0.524	3.083	0.479	1.160	1.405	1.850	0.000			
13. (M)	3.807	0.277	3.520	3.847	2.194	0.184	3.336	0.776	1.454	1.418	2.189	0.565	0.000		
14. (N)	2.098	1.662	1.919	2.182	0.645	1.528	1.628	1.015	0.361	0.595	0.607	1.488	1.709	0.000	
15. (O)	2.053	1.804	1.729	2.044	0.400	1.619	1.583	1.199	0.651	0.459	0.828	1.677	1.803	0.327	0.000

Single Linkage Single linkage computer programs operate in the following way. First, the similarity values are arrayed from most to least similar. Then, those objects with the highest similarity (lowest distance) coefficients are clustered together. The similarity coefficient is then systematically lowered, and the union of objects at each similarity value is recorded. The union of two objects, the admission of an object into a cluster, or the union of two clusters is by the criterion of single linkage. This means that if the similarity level (distance level) in question is, say, 0.20, a *single linkage* of an object at that level with *any member* of a cluster would allow the object to join the cluster. Similarly, *any pair of objects* (one in each of two clusters) related at the criterion level *will make their clusters join*.

Consider, for example, all those similarity values less than 1.000 in Table 17.16. When arrayed from most similar to least similar, the tabulation in Table 17.17 results. The highest reported similarity value is 0.184, the distance between F and M. Starting at a distance of zero, the first computer iteration would be to this value, and objects F and M would be joined to form a cluster. The next table entry is 0.277, the distance between objects B and M. Consider what happens at this second computer iteration value.

Since M has already been joined to F at the first iteration, the situation can be diagrammed as follows:

Will B be allowed to join the cluster consisting of the elements F and M? The answer is yes under the criterion of single linkage. Even though the distance from B to F

TABLE 17.17   All Distances Less Than 1.000 Arrayed in Increasing Order of Dissimilarity

Distance Level	City Pairs	Distance Level	City Pairs	Distance Level	City Pairs
0.184	FM	0.524	FL	0.737	IK
0.277	BM	0.565	LM	0.751	DG
0.313	BL	0.595	JN	0.776	HM
0.320	BF	0.607	KN	0.802	EJ
0.327	NO	0.622	AD	0.828	KO
0.361	IN	0.624	FH	0.847	CG
0.400	EO	0.645	EN	0.896	EK
0.459	JO	0.651	IO	0.953	HJ
0.460	CD	0.660	BH	0.959	AC
0.472	AG	0.706	HI		
0.479	HL	0.708	IJ		

is 0.320, that does not matter under the criterion of single linkage. Rather, the one link between B and M that satisfies the criterion value is sufficient to allow B to join F and M to form the larger group BFM. The next iteration would be to the similarity value 0.313, representing the distance between B and L. Would L be allowed to join the group BFM at this iteration value? Again, the answer would be yes under the criterion of single linkage; even though the distance from F to L, which is 0.524, and the distance from L to M, which is 0.565, are both greater than the criterion value, that would not matter under the criterion of single linkage. Since BFL and M are already joined, nothing further happens at the similarity value 0.320. At the value 0.327, however, N joins O, and I joins this new pair at the iteration value 0.361 to form the larger group INO. E and J are subsequently admitted to this cluster of objects at the iteration values 0.400 and 0.459, respectively. The process would proceed similarly with objects joining to form pairs of objects or objects being admitted to previously formed groups until, after the fifteenth iteration corresponding to a distance of 0.607, the situation would look like this:

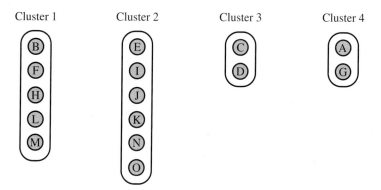

Thus, none of the variables would still be in clusters by themselves. When will the clusters themselves join to form larger groupings? According to the criterion of single linkage, the clusters will join when the distance between *any pair of objects* in the distinct clusters equals the iteration distance value. Consider, for example, the situation between Clusters 3 and 4, which can be diagrammed as follows:

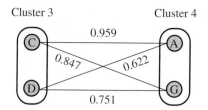

At an iteration value of 0.622, Cluster 3 will be joined with Cluster 4, because the single bond between A and D satisfies the criterion. Note that although the clusters are joined because of the single bond between two members of the respective clusters, some of the members within the newly formed cluster are much further removed from one another; for example, the distance from A to C is 0.959 and the distance from C to G is 0.847, approximately 1½ times larger than the merging distance. Single linkage can thus produce long, "straggling" groups.

Before turning to alternate linkage methods, let us introduce the notion of the **dendrogram** as a way of presenting the results of cluster analysis. A dendrogram is simply a "tree" that indicates the groups of objects forming at various similarity (distance) levels. The dendrogram for the test city data employing the single linkage method is shown in Figure 17.10.

Objects A through O are shown at the top. As we saw, the class FM forms first $(d_{FM} = 0.184)$; B is admitted to this cluster at a distance iteration value of 0.277; and so on. These unions and the values at which they occur are shown by the horizontal lines connecting the objects in Figure 17.10. The levels at which groups join to form even larger groups are depicted similarly in the figure. What are the natural groupings in the data? It all depends on what similarity level one is using. At a distance level of 0.50, there are five separate classes, reading from left to right:

- Group 1 — CD
- Group 2 — AG
- Group 3 — INOEJ
- Group 4 — K
- Group 5 — FMBLH

FIGURE 17.10   **Dendrogram of City Data Using Single Linkage**

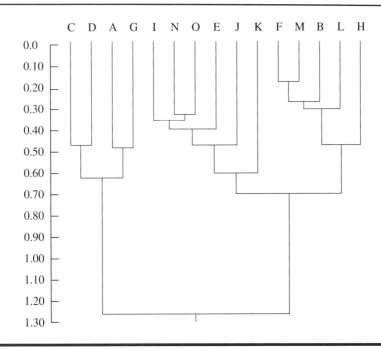

If, on the other hand, a distance level of 0.65 is to be used, then there are three classes:

- Group 1 — CDAG
- Group 2 — INOEJK
- Group 3 — FMBLH

Finally, if one selects a distance level of 0.80, there are only two classes:

- Group 1 — CDAG
- Group 2 — INOEJKFMBLH

Many would probably select a cutoff distance of 0.65, because the two-dimensional portrayal of the data suggests that there are three natural groupings. With p variables, the decision concerning the proper cutoff value must be made without such a visual referent, making the decision much more difficult. The purpose of the analysis would assist the analyst in making the choice. If the researcher simply needed two cities that were very much alike, he or she might use a more stringent criterion level, such as 0.35. The researcher would then have two groups with quite homogeneous cities, one group consisting of the pair of cities N and O and the other group consisting of the four cities F, M, B, and L. If, alternatively, the analyst needed a large number of similar test cities, he or she would use a more relaxed similarity coefficient, such as 0.65, which would produce three groups of four, six, and five members.

An alternative way of deciding the number of clusters is to plot the number of clusters against the **fusion coefficients,** which represent the numerical values at which various cases merge to form clusters. The fusion (or, as they are sometimes called, amalgamation) coefficients can be read directly from the dendrogram. Note, for example, that at a value of 0.184 in the Figure 17.10 dendrogram, where Objects F and M join, there are 14 groups. At the value of 0.277, where objects F, M, and B join, there are 13 groups, and so on. These fusion values and number of groups serve as the coordinates for the two points farthest to the left in Figure 17.11.

Figure 17.11 can be used in much the same way as the plot of the eigenvalues versus the number of factors was used in factor analysis. One can look for ''significant'' jumps in the fusion coefficient, indicating that two relatively dissimilar clusters have been merged. This suggests that the number of clusters before the merger is the most probable solution. Alternatively, one can use a scree-like test by searching where the curve flattens out. The flattening of the graph suggests that no new information is portrayed by the subsequent mergers of the clusters. Note that in Figure 17.11 the curve flattens at two points, once when going from five to four clusters and once when going from two clusters to one, implying that there are five or two clusters in the data. The incremental change in the fusion coefficient also suggests there are either five or two clusters in the data, since there is a substantial jump in the value of the coefficient between five and four and between two and one clusters. As the example indicates, these rules of thumb for determining the number of clusters can be helpful, but they sometimes produce ambiguous results.

FIGURE **17.11**   **Plot of Number of Clusters versus Fusion Coefficient**

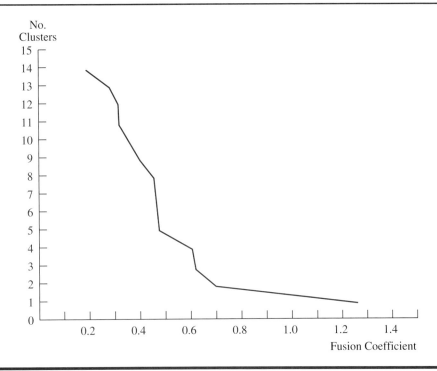

Complete Linkage   In the complete linkage method, an object joining a cluster at a certain similarity coefficient must have relations at that level or above with *every member* of the cluster. Thus, single bonds with just one member of the cluster would not be sufficient to effect the juncture. In practice, this is a fierce condition, with larger groups forming only when the criterion level is lowered considerably. Complete linkage has a tendency to produce very tight, compact clusters.

Consider again the Group ADGC. This group will eventually form under the complete linkage criterion, but consider how. The respective distances are

	A	C	D	G
A	0.000			
C	0.959	0.000		
D	0.622	0.460	0.000	
G	0.472	0.847	0.751	0.000

At a value of 0.460, Objects C and D join. Similarly, Objects A and G join at the value 0.472. When will the two groups join? Under the criterion of complete linkage, they will come together only when *all* the linkages among the objects in the two groups satisfy the criterion level. In other words, the largest distance among the objects in the groups controls the union. This means that the two groups will not join to form the larger group consisting of the elements ACDG until the iteration distance value 0.959 is reached, as that is the distance between Object A in the one group and Object C in the other.

Average Linkage   The average linkage method is an attempt to walk a middle ground between the single linkage and complete linkage methods. As the name implies, the *average* of all similarities between an object and a class of objects or between the members of two classes has to be above the given level for linkage to occur. The average linkage method involves more calculation than either single linkage or complete linkage methods. Both of the latter methods involve using a table look-up procedure. One calculates the distance between objects once. Subsequently, one checks the table of distances to see whether the criterion is satisfied. With average linkage, union is established when the average similarity between objects in distinct groups satisfies the criterion. As the composition of the groups changes, these average distances or similarities must be calculated anew.

Although more computer-intensive in terms of calculations, empirical evidence indicates that the average linkage method generally works well in recovering "known" configurations. It can perform erratically at times, but most of the time it outperforms the complete linkage method. Conversely, the evidence suggests that the single linkage method does not work well. It generally yields poorer cluster recovery than either the complete or average linkage methods. Further, it seems to be adversely affected by even small levels of error in the data.[38]

Nodal Methods   The linkage methods are all considered hierarchical clustering methods. That is, a hierarchy of groupings is formed as the criterion similarity value is altered. The dendrogram captures the resulting hierarchy.

Another main type of clustering method involves selecting an object or objects that will serve as focal objects or nodes for clusters. The remaining objects are then allocated to each cluster on the basis of their similarity to the focal objects. The basic operation of the nodal methods can be illustrated by the following scheme:

- Choose as nodes those objects that have the least similarity or greatest distance.
- Consider these two objects as polar nodes, and allocate all remaining objects to one or the other cluster based on their similarity to the polar nodes.
- Split the two resulting clusters in the same way. Continue the process until the collection of objects is split into its original members.

In the test city example, Cities D and M are most dissimilar ($d_{DM} = 3.847$), and thus they would be considered as the nodes for the two clusters. Each of the remaining

---

[38]Glenn W. Milligan and Martha C. Cooper, "Methodology Review: Clustering Methods," *Applied Psychological Measurement*, 11 (December 1987), pp. 329–354.

objects would then be allocated to each cluster on the basis of the shortest distance to either D or M. Thus, the original clusters would be

- Group 1 — DACEGK
- Group 2 — MBFHIJLNO

In Group 1, the least similar cities are D and K ($d_{DK} = 1.961$). Thus, they would be considered new nodes, and the items in Group 1 would be allocated to each of the new clusters on the basis of their distances to these new nodes. Therefore, the new groups would be

- Group 1A — DACG
- Group 1B — KE

Similarly, Group 2 would be divided (using B and J as new nodes) to yield

- Group 2A — BFHLM
- Group 2B — JINO

At each stage one could check to see if the resulting subgroups should be combined based on, say, some average measure of similarity between the objects within and among subgroups.

An alternative nodal clustering method employs a "prime" node. The prime node is the most "typical" object — that is, the object that has characteristics closest to the average characteristics for all the objects. Because the data have been standardized, the average median income and average population for the 15 cities are zero. City N is most typical, and it would be considered the prime node, and a cluster would be formed around it. Cities would be added to this cluster one at a time. After each addition, a measure of the resulting homogeneity of the cluster would be determined. When the measure of homogeneity — average-within-cluster distance in our case — took a large jump in value, the "natural" limits of the cluster would be considered to have been exceeded, and the last object added to the cluster would be removed.

After the primary clump was determined, it would be removed from the analysis. A new typical object would be determined from the remaining objects, and the process would be repeated. The procedure would continue until all the objects had joined clusters or until only a few residual objects remained. The residual objects could then be attached to those clusters that they seemed to fit best.

The nodal methods are also known as *iterative partitioning methods* because of the way they work; that is, they begin with some initial partition of the data and subsequently change these assignments. The use of polar nodes or a prime node represents just two of the many alternatives that have been proposed for effecting an initial partition of the objects. Two other alternatives are to specify "seed points" by picking certain objects to serve as group centroids or to randomly assign objects to one of a prespecified number of clusters (for example, three).[39] Regardless of how the initial assignment of

---

[39]For a very readable discussion of some of the main options when using iterative partitioning methods, see Aldenderfer and Blashfield, *Cluster Analysis,* especially pp. 45–49.

Operation of the *k*-Means Method

Suppose that the two swarms of x characters in Figure A were two clusters of points in a two-space awaiting discovery. If we want to find the two-cluster solution, we first pick two starting points. As a "bad case," suppose that the starting points are at the A and B in the point swarm on the right.

Figure A

```
   xxxxx                    xxxxx
 xxxxxxxxx                xxxxxxxxx
xxxxxxxxxxxx           xxxxAxxxxxxx
xxxxxxxxxxxxxx         xxxxxxxxxxxxxx
xxxxxxxxxxxxx          xxxxxxxxxBxx
xxxxxxxxxxx               xxxxxxxxx
 xxxxxxx                  xxxxxxx
```

We measure the distance of each x to starting points A and B, classifying each x into the group associated with the closer of those two. In Figure B, each point is identified with an x or a y, depending on whether it is closer to A or B.

Figure B

```
   xxxxx                    xxxxx
 xxxxxxxxx                xxxxxxxxx
xxxxxxxxxxxx           xxxxAxxxxyyyy
xxxxxxxxxxxxxx         xxxxxxxyyyyyyy
xxxxxxxxxxxxx          xxxxyyyyByy
xxxxxxxxxxx               xxxyyyyyy
 xxxxxxx                  xyyyyyy
```

Notice that only the lower right side of the right-hand swarm in Figure C is closer to B than A. Now we compute the averages, or "centers of gravity" of all the x points and all the y points. We indicate those by labels A and B in Figure C.

Source: Richard M. Johnson, *Convergent Cluster Analysis System* (Ketchum, Idaho: Sawtooth Software, 1988), pp. 7–8. Printed with permission.

Figure C

```
   xxxxx                    xxxxx
 xxxxxxxxx                xxxxxxxxy
xxxxxxxxxxxx           xxxxxxxxxyyyy
xxxxxxxxxxxxxA         xxxxxxyyyyyyyy
xxxxxxxxxxxxx          xxxxxyyyByyy
xxxxxxxxxxx               xxxyyyyyy
 xxxxxx                   xyyyyyy
```

In Figure D we have reclassified each point according to whether it is closer to the new A or the B.

Figure D

```
   xxxxx                    yyyyy
 xxxxxxxxx                xyyyyyyyy
xxxxxxxxxxxx           xyyyyyyyyyyy
xxxxxxxxxxxxxxxA       xxyyyyyyyyyyyyy
xxxxxxxxxxxxx          xyyyyyyyByyy
xxxxxxxxxxx               yyyyyyyyy
 xxxxxx                   yyyyyyy
```

Notice that only a few points in the right-hand swarm are still closer to the A than the B. Again, we compute the averages of the points now classified as x and those classified as y, indicating those positions by A and B in Figure E.

Figure E

```
   xxxxx                    yyyyy
 xxxxxxxxx                xyyyyyyyy
xxxxxxxxxxxx           xyyyyyyyyyyy
xxxxxxxxAxxxxx         xxyyyyyByyyyyy
xxxxxxxxxxxxx          xyyyyyyyyyyyy
xxxxxxxxxxx               yyyyyyyyy
 xxxxxxx                  yyyyyyy
```

Finally, we would classify as x all the points closer to A and classify as y all points closer to B.

Because all points on the left would now be identified as x and all on the right identified as y, continuation of this process would result in no further reclassification of points.

This process would have converged even more quickly if our starting points had not been chosen so disadvantageously. For example, if one point had been in the swarm on the left and the other in the swarm on the right, convergence might have been immediate.

objects to groups is determined, the next step is to calculate the centroids, or group means, of each cluster and then to reallocate each data point to the cluster that has the nearest centroid. After all reassignments are made, the centroids of the new clusters are computed, and the process is repeated until no reassignments occur. Thus, iterative partitioning methods make more than one pass through the data, which allows them to recover from a poor initial partition.

Currently, the most popular partitioning method is the ***k*-means** approach, which requires that the number of clusters, *k*, be specified in advance and that *k* starting points be determined somehow, either randomly, by purposively selecting certain objects to serve as nodes, or by some other means. In the first pass through the data, each object is assigned to one of the *k* starting points according to which starting point it is most similar or closest. Then (1) the mean or centroid for each group is calculated, (2) the objects are reassigned on the basis of the mean to which they are closest, and steps (1) and (2) are repeated until no objects are reclassified. The points in each of the *k*-groups are considered to form a cluster. Research Realities 17.4 visually demonstrates the operation of the *k*-means approach; while the example suggests *k*-means can recover quickly from a poor specification of starting points, that is not always true but depends on how clearly separated the groups are.

Factor Analysis A third major way of attacking the clustering problem is through factor analysis. Previously we searched for the latent dimensions of the *variables* by determining which variables go together or measure common characteristics. We could just as easily attempt to determine which *objects* logically belong together. Object-by-object factor analysis is often called *Q* analysis or inverse factor analysis.[40]

Consider again the distance matrix contained in Table 17.16. It has been demonstrated that a distance matrix can be factored and, in particular, that factoring it is equivalent to factoring the raw score cross-products matrix.[41] The starting point for this sort of analysis is then the cross-products matrix computed across objects, which is presented as Table 17.18.[42]

---

[40]Variable-by-variable and object-by-object are just two types of factor analysis. See R. B. Cattell, "The Three Basic Factor Analytic Research Designs — Their Interrelationships and Derivatives," *Psychological Bulletin*, 49 (1952), pp. 449–520, for an extensive discussion of the basic types.

[41]Jum C. Nunnally, "The Analysis of Profile Data," *Psychological Bulletin*, 59 (1962), pp. 313–319.

[42]The entries in Table 17.18 were obtained in the following way. Consider the scores from Table 17.15 as defining the raw score matrix $X = (X_{ik})$, where X_{ik} represents the score of the *i*th city on the *k*th variable and where $i = 1, 2, \ldots, 15$ and $k = 1, 2$. Form the matrix sums of cross-products $S = (S_{ij})$, where

$$S_{ij} = \sum_{k=1}^{2} X_{ik}X_{jk}.$$

Thus, for $i = 1$ (City A) and $j = 2$ (City B),

$$S_{12} = \sum_{k=1}^{2} X_{1k}X_{2k} = X_{11}X_{21} + X_{12}X_{22} = (1.14)(-1.25) + (1.72)(-1.17) = -3.434.$$

The remaining entries in the object-by-object cross-product matrix reported in Table 17.18 were computed in similar fashion.

TABLE 17.18 Object-by-Object Raw Scores Cross-Product Matrix

$j =$

$i =$	1 A	2 B	3 C	4 D	5 E	6 F	7 G	8 H	9 I	10 J	11 K	12 L	13 M	14 N	15 O
1. (A)	4.252														
2. (B)	−3.434	2.932													
3. (C)	3.371	−3.065	3.413												
4. (D)	4.186	−3.626	3.849	4.500											
5. (E)	0.809	−0.813	0.987	1.044	0.316										
6. (F)	−3.218	2.634	−2.626	−3.221	−0.647	2.443									
7. (G)	3.284	−2.654	2.608	3.236	0.626	−2.487	2.537								
8. (H)	−2.083	1.832	−1.976	−2.283	−0.548	1.609	−1.611	1.163							
9. (I)	−0.626	0.636	−0.777	−0.818	−0.250	0.502	−0.485	0.430	0.199						
10. (J)	−0.848	0.538	−0.355	−0.607	−0.013	0.610	−0.653	0.276	0.005	0.305					
11. (K)	0.861	−0.501	0.262	0.546	−0.033	−0.609	0.663	−0.237	0.033	−0.352	0.413				
12. (L)	−2.950	2.621	−2.856	−3.274	−0.803	2.285	−2.281	1.672	0.630	0.367	−0.304	2.407			
13. (M)	−3.595	2.952	−2.956	−3.615	−0.733	2.732	−2.778	1.807	0.570	0.672	−0.668	2.568	3.056		
14. (N)	−0.064	0.087	−0.127	−0.117	−0.048	0.056	−0.050	0.065	0.038	−0.020	0.030	0.098	0.065	0.009	
15. (O)	0.056	−0.139	0.247	0.200	0.105	−0.063	0.044	−0.116	−0.085	0.076	−0.104	−0.180	−0.076	−0.022	0.056

TABLE **17.19**   **Factor Loadings on First Factor**

Object	Loading	Object	Loading
A	2.02	I	−0.36
B	−1.71	J	−0.33
C	1.77	K	0.31
D	2.11	L	−1.52
E	0.46	M	−1.73
F	−1.55	N	−0.05
G	1.56	O	0.07
H	−1.06	λ	26.5

This cross-products matrix can be factored using any of the usual methods. Let us determine what happens when the principal components procedure is used. The sum of the diagonal elements in Table 17.18 yields the total variance in the data, which is 28.0. By again comparing the variance extracted by each factor with this total variance, we are in a position to estimate the number of factors that are needed to satisfactorily recover the data. It turns out that two factors are needed to summarize all of the variance in the data; 95 percent of the variance (26.5 in absolute magnitude) is accounted for by the first factor, and 5 percent (1.5 in absolute magnitude) is accounted for by the second factor. Thus, it would seem that the objects could be clustered along a single dimension. This should not be surprising when you recall the conceptual basis of principal components analysis and apply it to the two-dimensional plot of the data contained in Figure 17.5. The first component is simply the major axis of the ellipse generated by this scatter of points extending from the southwest to the northeast quadrant of the graph.

The resulting factor loadings on this one factor are presented in Table 17.19. There seem to be three levels of magnitude: high positive values, near-zero values, and high negative values. The use of these criteria would generate three clusters:

- Cluster 1 — ACDG
- Cluster 2 — EIJKNO
- Cluster 3 — BFHLM

These are the clusters that we visually distinguished from the scatter of cities in Figure 17.9. This tidy result is not generally to be expected but occurs simply because the objects were aligned rather nicely along the southwest-northeast diagonal of the figure.

If more than one factor were necessary to summarize the basic variation in the data, the original factor solution could be rotated to simple structure. Then the objects that formed natural groupings would be determined by examining the rotated-loadings matrix. The objects that loaded similarly on the same factors would be considered to form clusters.

FIGURE 17.12   **Key Decisions When Cluster-Analyzing Data**

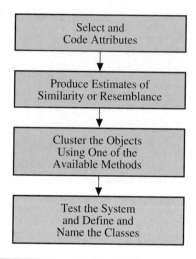

When factor analysis is used to cluster objects, it is important to note that the number of clusters is *not* given by the number of factors. Only two factors are necessary to account for *all* the variation in the sum-of-squares-and-cross-products matrix, and the first factor accounts for the bulk of it. Yet, there are three clusters in the data even when only the first factor is used. Rather than using the number of factors to indicate the number of clusters, analysts need to examine the loading matrix. The *pattern* of loadings determines both the number of clusters and which objects belong to which cluster.

Key Decisions

The discussion so far may suggest that to use cluster analysis, the analyst must make one key decision: which clustering method to use. This is not the case. The topic has simply been presented this way to bring the basic objective of cluster analysis into bold relief. It is time to introduce additional complications.

To perform a cluster analysis, it is actually necessary to make decisions concerning each of the four stages depicted in Figure 17.12. The discussion so far has concentrated on Stage 3 in that process. Let us now look at each of the other stages in turn.

Select and Code Attributes   Stage 1 focuses on the related questions "Which attributes are to be employed to generate the natural groupings?" and "How are these attributes to be coded?" The example assumed that income and population were the characteristics of importance in defining similar test cities. These are both ratio-scaled variables. No additional coding other than standardization was necessary before generating Euclidean distances to assess similarity. The example was artificial in these respects. The selection of attributes is key in its own right; a change in the characteristics used to define similarity will often change the ''natural groupings'' that exist among the objects.

There is not a great deal of guidance in the literature with regard to selecting attributes. Yet the choice of variables used to cluster the objects is one of the most critical decisions analysts make. The best advice seems to be to choose those variables that make sense conceptually rather than using any and all variables simply because they are convenient or accessible.

When coding the attributes, it is necessary to keep their basic nature in mind. Some of them may be continuous in nature (for example, income), whereas others may be categorical (for example, geography). If categorical, they may be dichotomous or multichotomous. In the city example, we could classify the various cities by whether they were located in the southern half of the United States or the northern half. Alternatively, we could use finer geographical divisions. The important thing to note is that the coding decision fundamentally depends on the type of variables that are considered and, again, on what theory suggests about how the variables should affect the natural grouping of objects.

> The basic problem is to find that set of variables that best represents the concept of similarity under which the study operates. Ideally, variables should be chosen within the context of an explicitly stated theory that is used to support the classification. The theory is the basis for the rational choice of the variables to be used in the study . . . .
>
> The importance of using theory to guide the choice of variables should not be underestimated. The temptation to succumb to a naive empiricism in the use of cluster analysis is very strong, since the technique is ostensibly designed to produce ''objective'' groupings of entities. By ''naive empiricism'' we mean the collection and subsequent analysis of as many variables as possible in hope that the ''structure'' will emerge if only enough data are obtained.[43]

Not only is the choice of attributes sometimes difficult to make, but the weights that are to be given to each attribute when producing estimates of similarity can also prove to be troublesome. Again, theory should guide the choice. When theory has little to say on the subject, the prevailing sentiment is to consider all the attributes to be of equal importance and to weight them equally when producing estimates of resemblance.

Produce Estimates of Similarity or Resemblance   The estimates of resemblance that are used to specify how similar the objects are also depend on the level of measurement used to capture the attributes. There was little question in our example about the measures. Both income and population were ratio scaled, and it was natural to define similarity employing Euclidean distance. Consider now a situation in which the analyst's interest is in grouping people into similar groups, as in a market segmentation study. Here a number of variables of interest would be nominally scaled, or ordinally scaled at best (for example, marital status, ethnic background, religious preference, stage in the life cycle). Such variables raise the question of what kind of estimate of resemblance is to be used as input to the cluster algorithm. Are they to be 0–1 (absence–presence of an

---

[43]Aldenderfer and Blashfield, *Cluster Analysis,* pp. 19–20.

attribute), matching coefficients (for example, a family member is black or is not), or are the coefficients to reflect the individual categories (for example, a family member is black, white, yellow), and so on?

Given the input measures, the analyst has several decisions to make in order to produce estimates of resemblance. The decisions are in large part dictated by the scale quality of the measures. They are not completely dictated, however, and the analyst has some latitude. If the input measures reflect cardinal measurement, the analyst's most basic decision is whether to use a distance function or a correlation coefficient to capture resemblance. Further, if the researcher chooses a distance function, should the distance function be Euclidean distance, as in the example, or should it be city-block distance or even perhaps Mahalanobis distance?[44] Euclidean distance is clearly the most popular, yet one of the problems with it is that it is not scale invariant. This means that the relative ordering of the objects in terms of their similarity can be affected by a simple change in the scale by which one or more of the variables are measured. For example, we could have measured income in thousands of dollars rather than in dollars when attempting to determine which cities were most similar, and that could possibly have affected the ordering of the similarity coefficients if the data had not first been standardized to mean zero and standard deviation one. In general, we prefer that the similarity coefficients are not sensitive to the units in which we choose to measure variables. While standardization is one way to remove that sensitivity, standardization carries its own costs, because it can reduce the differences between groups on those variables that may very well be the best discriminators of group differences. Ideally, we would like to standardize variables within groups rather than across all cases.[45] Obviously this cannot be done until the cases have been placed into groups. In sum, the standardization issue is far from settled. The best advice is to decide the standardization issue on a case-by-case basis. If the units in which the variables are measured are roughly of the same magnitude, it might be best not to standardize them. If the variables are measured on widely differing units, standardization is needed to prevent the variables measured in larger units from dominating the cluster solution. Standardization based on division by the range of each variable seems to work better than converting the variables to z scores by subtracting their means and dividing by their standard deviations.[46]

What if the data are dichotomous or multichotomous rather than reflecting cardinal measurement? Rather than using distance or product-moment correlations to measure resemblance, some kind of matching coefficient is called for. A matching coefficient should represent the number of characteristics on which two objects match in relation to

---

[44]Morrison suggests that Mahalanobis distance is best, because it allows for intercorrelations among the variables and also provides for variable weighting by the investigator that is explicit rather than implicit. Implicit weighting occurs, for example, when correlated variables are used to compute a measure of similarity. If four highly correlated variables are used, the effect is the same as using only one variable that has a weight four times greater than any other variable. Donald G. Morrison, "Measurement Problems in Cluster Analysis," *Management Science,* 13 (August 1967), pp. 755–780.

[45]For a discussion of the issues involved in standardization, see B. Everett, *Cluster Analysis* (New York: Halsted Press, 1980).

[46]Glenn W. Milligan and Martha C. Cooper, "A Study of Standardization of Variables in Cluster Analysis," *Journal of Classification,* 5 (No 2, 1988), pp. 181–204.

TABLE **17.20**   **Some Alternative Similarity Coefficients**

A. Attributes Possessed by Each Object

Object	Attributes									
	1	**2**	**3**	**4**	**5**	**6**	**7**	**8**	**9**	**10**
A	1	0	0	0	1	0	0	1	1	1
B	0	1	0	0	1	0	0	1	0	0
C	0	0	1	0	0	1	0	1	1	0

B. Summary of the Number of Positive Matches, Negative Matches, and Mismatches

	Object Pairs		
	AB	**AC**	**BC**
Number of positive matches (a)	2	2	1
Number of negative matches (b)	4	3	4
Number of mismatches (c)	4	5	5

C. Similarity of the Various Pairs Using Alternative Similarity Coefficients

Coefficient	Object Pair	Value
1. $\dfrac{a}{a+b+c}$	AB	.200
	AC	.200
	BC	.100
2. $\dfrac{a}{a+b}$	AB	.333
	AC	.400
	BC	.250
3. $\dfrac{a}{a+c}$	AB	.333
	AC	.286
	BC	.167
4. $\dfrac{a+c}{a+b+c}$	AB	.600
	AC	.700
	BC	.600
5. $\dfrac{c}{a+b}$	AB	.667
	AC	1.000
	BC	1.000

the number of comparisons made. However, this simple notion begs the question of what kind of matches should count: positive matches? negative matches? both kinds?

To illustrate the fundamental dilemma concerning what types of matches to emphasize, consider the hypothetical data for three objects contained in Panel A of Table 17.20. Each object has been measured on ten attributes; a one indicates that the object possesses the attribute and a zero indicates that it does not. The attributes could represent any number of features of the objects. Suppose, for example, that the attributes indicate which of ten magazines these three people read, and we wish to calculate the similarity of reading habits for each of the object pairs AB, AC, and BC. A 1–1 indicates that both people in the pair read the same magazine and represents a positive match; a 0–0 indicates that neither person reads that particular magazine and represents a negative match; a 1–0 means that the first person reads it but the second does not, whereas a 0–1 indicates the opposite, implying there is a mismatch in reading habits in both cases. Panel B of Table 17.20 summarizes the information contained in Panel A concerning the number of positive matches, negative matches, and mismatches for each of the three possible pairs of the three objects.

Panel C of Table 17.20 illustrates the computation of several possible coefficients that could be used to describe the similarity of the three pairs of objects.[47] Formula C1 expresses similarity as a function of the ratio of the number of positive matches versus the number of attributes on which the objects were measured. Formula C2 also emphasizes positive matches, but it is based on the ratio of the number of positive matches to the number of total matches, both positive and negative. Mismatches do not explicitly count in C2. Formula C3 compares the number of positive matches to the number of positive matches plus the number of mismatches; it explicitly deemphasizes negative matches while considering mismatches. Formula C4 also explicitly considers mismatches; it compares the number of positive matches plus the number of mismatches to the total number of comparisons that are made between the objects. Formula C5 looks at the number of features on which the objects are different versus the number on which they are the same.

As suggested, the essential difference among the formulas is how they handle the three types of comparisons. A case could be made for any one of them when deciding which people have more similar reading habits. We could argue that it is the magazines that two people *both* read that determines whether they have similar reading habits and thereby choose a coefficient that emphasizes positive matches. Alternatively, we could argue that it is important to note that *neither* one reads, say, *Sports Illustrated* when determining whether they have similar reading habits and could thereby choose to emphasize negative matches as well. Still further, we could argue that the fact that one of the respondents reads *Sports Illustrated* while the other does not indicates something important about the similarity of their reading habits, and we would therefore want to give some weight to mismatches, although perhaps not as much as to positive or negative matches. The five sample coefficients reflect these types of considerations. The important thing to note about these coefficients is that they produce different orderings in terms of the similarity of the three objects. Coefficient C1 indicates that Object Pairs AB and AC are the most similar. Coefficient C2 suggests that Object Pair AC is more similar

---

[47]A great many coefficients have been proposed for assessing the similarity of objects. One of the most detailed discussions can be found in Sokal and Sneath, *Numerical Taxonomy,* who devote 74 pages to the discussion of the topic and provide formulas for most of the coefficients they discuss. See also H. Clifford and W. Stephenson, *An Introduction to Numerical Taxonomy* (New York: Academic Press, 1975); Maurice Lorr, *Cluster Analysis for the Social Sciences* (San Francisco: Jossey Bass, 1983).

than Object Pair AB, and that, in turn, is more similar than Object Pair BC. A different ordering of similarity is produced by Coefficient C3. Whereas for the first three coefficients Object Pair BC is always less similar than either of the other two pairs, that is not the case with Coefficients C4 and C5; with Coefficient C4 it is tied with Pair AB for being the least similar, and with Coefficient C5 it is tied with Pair AC for being the most similar. In sum, with as few as three objects, the ordering of the pairs in terms of their similarity is affected by the emphasis that is given to positive and negative matches and mismatches. The situation is simply exaggerated when more objects are being grouped. Further, there is no answer as to which emphasis is inherently correct. It all depends on the objectives of the study.

The most popular of the five coefficients highlighted in Table 17.20 are coefficients C1 and C3. Coefficient C1 is known as the simple matching coefficient, whereas Coefficient C3 is known as Jaccards' coefficient. Both coefficients emphasize the importance of positive matches.

Another problem can arise when determining the estimates of resemblance when the attributes reflect different levels of measurement. If they are all interval- or ratio-scaled variables, the correlation coefficient or a distance measure can be, and typically is, used. If they are all categorical, some sort of matching coefficient can be calculated to describe how similar they are. When some are cardinal and others are categorical, the situation is more difficult. Should the continuous variables be converted to categorical variables so that a matching coefficient can be calculated, or should they be left as is? If they are left as is, how are the two types of measures to be combined?

One coefficient that is particularly attractive for this purpose is Gower's coefficient of similarity, which is capable of handling two-state (e.g., gender), multistate (e.g., religious preference), and quantitative (e.g., age) characteristics. The coefficient is calculated by the formula

$$S_{ij} = \frac{\sum_{k=1}^{m} w_k s_{ijk}}{\sum_{k=1}^{m} w_k},$$

where
S_{ij} is the overall similarity of Objects i and j;
s_{ijk} is the similarity of Objects i and j on the kth characteristic and there are m characteristics in all. s_{ijk} must be greater than or equal to zero and less than or equal to one. With qualitative characters, it is one when there is a match and zero with a mismatch. With quantitative characters $s_{ijk} = (|X_{ik} - X_{jk}|/R_k)$, where X_{ik} and X_{jk} are the values of Character k for the ith and jth objects, respectively, and R_k is the range of Character k in the sample;
w_k is the weight attached to the kth character.

Note that the coefficient allows the analyst to specify which of the two types of matches to count with respect to any attribute. The analyst simply sets w_k at one if the comparison is to count and at zero if it is not. Further, the coefficient allows the analyst to weight certain attributes more than others. Consider, for example, the first two rows of Panel A of Table 17.20, and assume that the first five attributes refer to business magazines while the last five refer to general-interest magazines like *Time* and *Newsweek*. Now suppose that the emphasis in the cluster analysis is on determining the similarity of reading habits of executives, particularly in terms of business literature, and that we therefore want to weight matches, *both* positive and negative, twice as much for the first five attributes as for the last five. The situation can be diagrammed as follows:

| | Attribute | | | | | | | | | |
Object	1	2	3	4	5	6	7	8	9	10
A	1	0	0	0	1	0	0	1	1	1
B	0	1	0	0	1	0	0	1	0	0
s_{ijk}	0	0	1	1	1	1	1	1	0	0
w_k	2	2	2	2	2	1	1	1	1	1

This suggests that the overall similarity of Persons 1 and 2 is

$$S_{ij} = \frac{2(0) + 2(0) + 2(1) + 2(1) + 2(1) + 1(1) + 1(1) + 1(1) + 1(0) + 1(0)}{2 + 2 + 2 + 2 + 2 + 1 + 1 + 1 + 1 + 1}$$

$$= \frac{9}{15}$$

$$= 0.600.$$

To illustrate the computation of Gower's coefficient for quantitative characteristics, consider the city data again. For City A, income has a value of 1.14 and population a value of 1.72. For City E, income has a value of 0.55 and population a value of 0.10. The range of population values across all cases is greater than the range of income values; specifically, it is 3.10 for the former compared to 2.93 for the latter. The similarity of Objects A($i = 1$) and E($j = 5$) in terms of income ($k = 1$) would be $s_{151} = (|1.14 - 0.55|/2.93) = 0.201$, whereas in terms of population ($k = 2$) it would be $s_{152} = (|1.72 - 0.10|/3.10) = 0.526$. Assuming that we wanted to weight income and population equally, the overall similarity of Objects A and E would be

$$S_{15} = \frac{1(0.201) + 1(0.526)}{1 + 1} = 0.364.$$

As can be seen, Gower's coefficient offers the analyst a great deal of flexibility in generating similarity values, which is one of the primary reasons for its popularity.

Cluster the Objects Using One of the Available Methods   We have already discussed the issue of clustering methods at some length and have only a few comments to add. One thing that should be pointed out is that all of the methods are heuristical in nature. Although the heuristics that they use seem logical on their face, they are still heuristics, and there is very little statistical theory in the normal sense of the term to back them up.[48] The empirical evidence that is available as to which is best is based on the various methods' ability to recover known configurations. It suggests that the factor-based procedures generally work poorly. The hierarchical methods work somewhat better but tend to have problems when the data contain a high level of error. One problem with them is that what appear to be trivial decisions made early in the clustering tend to have large effects on the final outcome because only one pass is made through the data. The multiple-pass partitioning methods work best, particularly *k* means. However, this method's performance depends on the use of fairly accurate starting points.[49]

Thus, analysts need to display the proper caution when interpreting the output produced by one of the clustering procedures. Equally important, analysts need to recognize that all of the methods have the same aim. They should not be thought of as mutually exclusive alternatives but as complementary procedures to get at the same objective. Sometimes they can be productively used in combination. For example, one way of getting the seed points for a *k*-means approach is to use average linkage and the resulting dendrogram to determine both the number of clusters and which objects to use as the starting points for each cluster.

Test the System and Define and Name the Clusters   Given decisions pertaining to the first three steps, a set of clusters will be obtained. That is right; a set of clusters will be obtained from the application of the methods discussed previously. In fact, one of the problems with cluster analysis methods is that they always produce clusters, even when they should not, because there are no "natural groupings" in the data. The big question concerns what the clusters mean. Do they reflect some natural or compelling structures in the data, or do they simply represent artifacts of the method? To address this issue, analysts have to examine and test the solution and then name the clusters.

The system test focuses on whether the results offer a reasonable summary of the similarity, correlation, or distance matrix. First, are the individual clusters sufficiently homogeneous? Some measure of average similarity is typically useful in this regard.[50] Second, is the system as a whole consistent with the input similarities? Suppose that one of the linkage methods was used to generate object groupings. A dendrogram would

---

[48]For an empirical examination of some of the things that can affect the reliability of a clustering method, see G. Ray Funkhouser, "A Note on the Reliability of Certain Clustering Algorithms," *Journal of Marketing Research,* 20 (February 1983), pp. 99–102. For a summary of some of the main attempts to generate statistical criteria by which the results of a cluster analysis can be assessed, see Dillon and Goldstein, *Multivariate Analysis,* pp. 202–205. For a demonstration of how one can test whether given clusters differ significantly from clusters that are randomly determined, see T. D. Klastorin, "Assessing Cluster Analysis Results," *Journal of Marketing Research,* 20 (February 1983), pp. 92–98.

[49]Milligan and Cooper, "Methodology Review." One strategy for minimizing the problem of accurate starting points is to replicate the analysis using different starting points. See, for example, Kristiaan Helsen and Paul E. Green, "A Computational Study of Replicated Clustering with an Application to Market Segmentation," *Decision Sciences,* 22 (November/December 1991), pp. 1124–1141.

[50]Milligan compared the performance of 30 measures that have been proposed for assessing the internal consistency of clusters. He found six of them that generally outperformed the others. See G. W. Milligan, "A Monte Carlo Study of Thirty Internal Measures for Cluster Analysis," *Psychometrika,* 46 (1981), pp. 187–199.

result. Now, for each pair of objects, the *cophenetic value,* or amalgamation coefficient, could be read from the dendrogram. The **cophenetic value** is the level at which the objects or classes are actually linked. If the dendrogram contained all of the information in the similarity matrix, the cophenetic value for each pair of objects would exactly equal the input similarity value. They will not be equal in practice, of course, because the union of any two objects is affected by their links with the other objects.

Consider again, as an example, the application of the single linkage method to the city data. A comparison of the actual distances between Objects F, M, and H as read from the distance matrix in Table 17.16 and the distances where the objects joined as read from the dendrogram indicates the following differences:

Object Pair	Actual Distance	Distance When Joined
FM	0.184	0.184
FH	0.624	0.479
MH	0.776	0.479

A similar comparison could be made for each of the other 225 pairs of objects, and then some summary measure of the goodness of fit of the actual values with the obtained values could be calculated (for example, the product moment correlation between the two sets of distances).

One problem with the use of the cophenetic correlation is that it can be used only with hierarchical clustering methods. An alternative procedure that can be used with any of the clustering methods is to test whether the variables used to determine the clusters have statistically significant differences across the groups. This is typically done by comparing the mean levels across the groups. Although this scheme is intuitively plausible, it turns out that the results are invariably statistically significant, regardless of whether clusters exist in the data or not, which led one pair of authors to conclude that "the performance of these tests is useless at best and misleading at worst."[51]

Both of these schemes for testing cluster solutions are commonly found in the literature, but neither is particularly recommended by methodologists working in the area. Rather, their general recommendation is to estimate the reliability of a cluster solution across data sets. This typically involves splitting the data into multiple subsets and assessing whether the same sets of objects are produced when the various subsets are analyzed.

Another alternative that is used less often but that has much to recommend it is to perform significance tests comparing the clusters on variables that were not used to generate the cluster solution. We could, for example, compare our 15 test cities in terms of the average age of the population. Those within the same subgroup should be approximately equal in terms of average age, whereas those cities in different subgroups should be different.

---

[51]Aldenderfer and Blashfield, *Cluster Analysis,* p. 65. Pages 62–74 of this book have an excellent discussion of the various alternatives that are used to test the quality of a cluster solution.

If the resulting clusters are acceptable, the analyst must then describe and name them. The researcher's description will typically center on those variables that determine membership in a given class rather than membership in other classes. The example produced (1) a large-size, high-income cluster, (2) a medium-size, middle-income cluster, and (3) a small-size, low-income cluster of cities. In most cases, the names will not be so obvious. The analyst has to be particularly careful that the names do not mislead others.

Marketing Applications

The example of forming homogeneous groups of cities that was employed to develop the purpose and logic of cluster analysis reflects a pervasive marketing problem. The problem of determining homogeneous groupings of objects is a real one in accurately assessing the impact of marketing manipulations. For many kinds of experimental manipulations, we must be sure that the groups of objects being manipulated were equal at some prior time.[52] Thus, when market-testing products or advertisements or packages, it is important that the test cities used be similar so that the results cannot be attributed to idiosyncratic differences in the cities.

Although cluster analysis has not been as widely employed in marketing as factor analysis has, the number of applications continues to increase.[53] For example, it has been used to sort householders' demand patterns for electricity into similar shapes, to group customers according to the product benefits they seek or according to their lifestyle, to group TV programs into similar types on the basis of viewers' reported listening tendencies, to group other kinds of media in terms of the similarity of audiences to which they appeal, to develop homogeneous configurations of census tracts, to construct market segments, to group personality profiles, to group brands and products on the basis of how similar to competitors' products they are perceived to be and also how they serve as substitutes in use, to determine spheres of opinion leadership, and to assess the similarity of world markets.

SUMMARY

Three analysis techniques increasingly being advocated in the marketing literature for the solution of marketing research problems were reviewed in this chapter. The techniques are all multivariate in that they involve the analysis of p measures. Discriminant analysis

---

[52]See George S. Day and Richard M. Heeler, "Using Cluster Analysis to Improve Marketing Experiments," *Journal of Marketing Research,* 8 (August 1971), pp. 340–347, for an example of how cluster analysis can be used to choose samples of stores for test marketing.

[53]For an excellent review of the applications of cluster analysis in marketing, see Girish Punj and David W. Stewart, "Cluster Analysis in Marketing Research: Review and Suggestions for Application," *Journal of Marketing Research,* 20 (May 1983), pp. 134–148. For reviews of the various programs for performing cluster analysis, see R. K. Blashfield and L. Morey, "Cluster Analysis Software," in P. Krishnaiah and L. Kanal, eds., *Handbook of Statistics,* Vol. 2 (Amsterdam: New Holland, 1982), pp. 245–266. See also William D. Neal, "A Comparison of 18 Clustering Algorithms Generally Available to the Marketing Research Professional," *Sawtooth Software Conference Proceedings* (Ketchum, Idaho: Sawtooth Software, 1989).

treats the p measures in a dependency relationship, whereas factor analysis and cluster analysis involve the examination of interdependencies among the variables.

Discriminant analysis shows the relationship between a dichotomous or multichotomous criterion variable and a set of p predictor variables. The emphasis is on determining the variables that are most important in discriminating among the objects falling into the various classes of the criterion variable. With a number of predictor variables and a multichotomous criterion variable, several discriminant functions may be derived. Not all of these functions will necessarily be statistically significant, however. The discriminant function or functions can also be used to predict the classification of new objects.

Factor analysis gives all p variables equal status. The emphasis is on isolating the factors that are common to the interrelated manifest variables in order to summarize the important information in the data and assist in interpreting the data. The initial factor solution and the choice of the number of factors to be retained are key in accomplishing the first task, whereas the rotation of the initial solution is important for accomplishing the latter. Numerous options are open to the researcher in both regards.

Cluster analysis searches for the natural groupings among objects described by the p variables. The emphasis is on placing together those objects that are similar in terms of the p variables. Their similarity is properly captured with a coefficient reflecting the scale of measurement that underlies the variables. The analyst has many choices in this regard, as well as with respect to the clustering algorithm that will be used to generate the groupings.

Questions

1. How does the purpose of discriminant analysis differ from that of regression analysis?

2. What basic criterion is satisfied in determining the weights for a discriminant function?

3. Just as in regression analysis, there are two basic purposes of discriminant analysis: prediction or classification and structural interpretation. How are both of these purposes achieved with the discriminant model?

4. Suppose that there are more than two groups to be discriminated. How many discriminant functions will there be?

5. Describe the basic purpose of factor analysis. What is meant by variability recovery and covariability recovery?

6. What is a factor-loading table? What do the individual entries measure? How does the table help to determine the "appropriate" number of factors?

7. What is the basic principle that underlies the principal components procedure?

8. What is the "substantive interpretation" question in factor analysis? How is such interpretation typically facilitated?

9. What is the essence of the communality question in factor analysis? What is the effect of the communality issue?

10. What is the basic purpose of cluster analysis?

11. Explain the differences among the linkage procedures, nodal procedures, and factor procedures in cluster analysis.

12. What is the difference between single and complete linkage cluster analysis?

13. What is a dendrogram? For what is it used?

14. Discuss what is at issue in each of the cluster analysis decision areas of
  a. selecting and coding attributes;
  b. producing estimates of resemblance;
  c. clustering technique; and
  d. testing the system and defining and naming the clusters.

Applications and Problems

1. List the defining characteristics or parameters of discriminant functions.

2. The management of a large chain of grocery stores wanted to determine the characteristics that differentiated national-brand shoppers and private-label shoppers. In particular, the management wanted to determine how these groups differed with respect to income and the size of household. Personal interviews with a random sample of national-brand shoppers and private-label shoppers generated the following data:

	Annual Income (thousands of dollars) X_1	Household Size (number of persons) X_2
National-Brand Shoppers		
1	16.8	3.0
2	21.4	2.0
3	17.3	4.0
4	18.4	1.0
5	23.2	2.0
6	21.1	5.0
7	14.5	4.0
8	18.9	1.0
9	17.8	2.0
10	19.3	1.0
Private-Label Shoppers		
1	17.3	4.0
2	15.4	3.0
3	14.3	4.0
4	14.5	5.0
5	17.4	2.0
6	16.7	6.0
7	13.9	7.0
8	12.4	7.0
9	15.3	6.0
10	13.3	4.0

A discriminant analysis of the data resulted in the following discriminant function: $Y = 0.333X_1 - 0.315X_2$.

a. Identify the criterion that was satisfied in deriving these weights.

b. On the basis of the preceding function, derive the discriminant scores for the two groups by completing the following table.

National-Brand Shoppers	X_1	X_2	Y	Private-Label Shoppers	X_1	X_2	Y
1							
2							
3							
4							
5							
6							
7							
8							
9							
10							

c. What do the discriminant scores indicate?

d. Compute the pooled standard deviation for X_1 and X_2. (Hint: Refer to Chapter 15 in the text for the formula of the pooled standard deviation.)

e. Convert the original weights of the discriminant function to standardized weights.

f. Interpret the discriminant function by evaluating the standardized weights.

g. Compute the mean values of the variables for each group.

h. Compute the mean discriminant scores for each group.

i. Interpret the mean discriminant scores for each group.

j. Compute the cutting score.

k. Predict the group membership for the entire sample and complete the following table.

Simple Decision Rule

	Discriminant Score Y_i	Difference from Mean of		Predicted Group Membership
		First Group $Y_i - \bar{Y}_1$	Second Group $Y_i - \bar{Y}_2$	
National-Brand Shoppers				
1				
2				
3				
4				
5				
6				
7				
8				
9				
10				

Simple Decision Rule

Difference from Mean of

	Discriminant Score Y_i	First Group $Y_i - \bar{Y}_1$	Second Group $Y_i - \bar{Y}_2$	Predicted Group Membership
Private-Label Shoppers				
1				
2				
3				
4				
5				
6				
7				
8				
9				
10				

l. On the basis of the preceding table, develop the confusion matrix.

m. Compute the hit rate or the proportion correctly classified.

n. Assess the goodness of the hit rate by computing the proportional chance criterion. Interpret your results.

o. Suppose that the management wanted to classify two individuals according to whether they were national-brand shoppers or private-label shoppers. The characteristics are as follows:

Individual I
X_1 — annual income, $18,300
X_2 — household size, 4 persons

Individual II
X_1 — annual income, $21,000
X_2 — household size, 7 persons

How should management classify these individuals? Show your calculations.

p. There is an upward bias in the proportion of correct hits. Why? What can be done to overcome this upward bias?

3. When is factor analysis an appropriate technique? What do the eigenvalues tell you about the amount of variance explained by each factor? How can this be used to determine the number of factors retained in the final solution? Should an analyst ever keep a factor with an eigenvalue less than 1? Explain.

4. In a rotated factor solution, what is the implication if an item has significant loadings on more than one factor?

5. What is the purpose behind rotating the factors?

6. Prefertronics, Inc., is a medium-sized manufacturer of electronic toys. The vice-president of sales has asked Bill Jurkowski, a product manager, to conduct a marketing research study to determine the key attributes that contribute to consumer preferences for the firm's products. Jurkowski employed interviewers to conduct personal interviews with a random sample of 100 customers. The respondents were asked to rate Prefertronics' toys on four attributes (expensive–inexpensive, safe–unsafe, educational–uneducational, and good quality–poor quality) using a seven-point semantic differential scale.

Jurkowski conducted a principal components analysis with the standardized scores, which resulted in the following factor-loading matrix. Jurkowski needs your help in analyzing this information.

The factor-loading matrix was as follows:

		Factors		
Variable	1	2	3	4
X_1	.812	.567	.121	.070
X_2	.532	−.743	.321	.249
X_3	.708	−.640	.205	.217
X_4	.773	.630	.018	.078

where

X_1 = expensive–inexpensive;
X_2 = safe–unsafe;
X_3 = educational–uneducational;
X_4 = good quality–poor quality.

a. What are the individual row/column entries called, and what do they indicate?
b. What does the entry in the second row and first column indicate?
c. What is the proportion of variation in each of the four variables that is accounted for by Factor 1? Show your calculations.
d. What is the proportion of variation in each of the four variables that is accounted for by Factor 2? Show your calculations.
e. The following table is a partially completed correlation matrix derived from the preceding factor-loading matrix. Complete the original correlation matrix using all *four* of the factors. Hint: Use the formula

$$r_{jl} = \sum_{k=1}^{4} a_{jk}a_{lk}.$$

Simple Pairwise Correlations among the Attributes (computed from four factors)

	X_1	X_2	X_3	X_4
X_1	1.000			
X_2	0.067	1.000		
X_3			1.000	
X_4			0.165	1.000

f. Complete the following correlation matrix using only the *first* and *second* factors to estimate the correlations. Comment on your results.

Simple Pairwise Correlations among the Attributes (computed from two factors)

	X_1	X_2	X_3	X_4
X_1	1.000			
X_2		1.000		
X_3			1.000	
X_4				1.000

g. Compute the achieved communalities of the four variables using the *first* and *second* factors. Show your calculations. Comment on your results.

h. Compute the proportion of the total variation in the data that is accounted for by each of the four factors. Show your calculations. Comment on your results.

i. On the basis of the preceding computations, discuss the variability and covariability recovery of two factors as compared to four factors.

j. Construct a scatter diagram using the correlations between the variables and the *first* and *second* factors as coordinates of the points.

k. On the basis of the scatter diagram, would you recommend that the factors be rotated? If yes, why? If no, why not?

l. Assume that the factors were rotated. Provide an interpretation of the factors.

m. Assume that the original factor solution was rotated. Explain the following statement: The contribution of each factor in accounting for the variation in the respective variables has changed; however, the total variation accounted for by the factors has remained constant.

7. A company has decided to cluster respondents based on the four product characteristics that customers have chosen as most important from a list of 18 characteristics. If the company's research analyst finds that a particular product characteristic is important for all customers, how should the analyst proceed? Justify your answer.

8. In the example above, how should the research team proceed if cluster membership changes substantially based on the algorithm being used?

9. Adstar, Inc., is a large-sized advertising agency located in New York City. The market research manager wants to identify the market segments for one of the agency's clients, a manufacturer of caffeine-free soft drinks, so that an effective advertising campaign can be developed. The manufacturer believes that the product would appeal to high-income families with large households. The market research manager has collected information from a probability sample of 500 regular purchasers of the caffeine-free soft drink. The manager has decided to use cluster analysis but is not familiar with the technique. Information pertaining to a sample of ten regular purchasers is given to you. The following table contains the standardized scores for income and household size for the sample of ten respondents.

	Average Ratings on Attributes Expressed in Standardized Units	
Respondents	Income X_1	Household Size X_2
1	−2.75	−2.50
2	3.00	3.00
3	2.50	2.75
4	−1.75	−2.25
5	4.00	3.50
6	−3.50	−2.75
7	2.75	3.25
8	−2.25	−2.50
9	3.50	2.50
10	−3.00	−3.25

a. Plot the individual scores in two dimensions using the two attributes as axes. What does the plot suggest?

b. Determine the similarity of each pair of respondents by computing the Euclidean distance between them.

c. The single linkage clustering method is to be used in developing the clusters. Consider the similarity values less than 1.00 in Part b., and array the distances from most similar to least similar.

d. What clusters exist after the fourth iteration (distance levels of approximately 0.70)?

e. What clusters exist after the eighth iteration (distance levels of approximately 1.12)?

f. Construct a dendrogram for similarity values up to approximately 0.56. Interpret the dendrogram.

g. Suppose that the complete linkage method of clustering is used; indicate at what distance level the results will be the same as Part e.

10. Kay Sealey is the news director for KASI-TV, the local NBC affiliate for a large southwestern city. Sealey believes that the most important quality of an on-air news broadcaster is credibility in the eyes of the viewer. Accordingly, surveys are taken every six months that attempt to evaluate the credibility of the news broadcasters who appear on the local news programs. The following figure shows one of the survey instruments used by the station to measure the credibility of a newscaster:

Evaluate the anchorperson on the news broadcast that you reviewed by completing the following series of scales. Place a check mark on the scale position that most nearly matches your feelings about this anchorperson. For example, if you thought that this anchorperson was extremely likeable, you would place a check mark in the blank nearest "likeable" (in this case, the far left blank).

1.   likeable ____ ____ ____ ____ ____ ____ ____ not likeable
2.   knowledgeable ____ ____ ____ ____ ____ ____ ____ not knowledgeable
3.   unattractive ____ ____ ____ ____ ____ ____ ____ attractive
4.   intelligent ____ ____ ____ ____ ____ ____ ____ not intelligent
5. not similar to you ____ ____ ____ ____ ____ ____ ____ similar to you

---

6.	good looking	___ ___ ___ ___ ___ ___ ___	bad looking
7.	unexciting	___ ___ ___ ___ ___ ___ ___	exciting
8.	confident	___ ___ ___ ___ ___ ___ ___	not confident
9.	friendly	___ ___ ___ ___ ___ ___ ___	not friendly
10.	not believable	___ ___ ___ ___ ___ ___ ___	believable
11.	expert	___ ___ ___ ___ ___ ___ ___	not expert
12.	ugly	___ ___ ___ ___ ___ ___ ___	beautiful
13.	don't identify with	___ ___ ___ ___ ___ ___ ___	identify with
14.	competent	___ ___ ___ ___ ___ ___ ___	not competent
15.	active	___ ___ ___ ___ ___ ___ ___	passive
16.	irritating	___ ___ ___ ___ ___ ___ ___	not irritating
17.	not trustworthy	___ ___ ___ ___ ___ ___ ___	trustworthy
18.	dull	___ ___ ___ ___ ___ ___ ___	interesting
19.	not sincere	___ ___ ___ ___ ___ ___ ___	sincere

Suppose that this questionnaire was administered to a sample of 50 people after they had watched a videotape of a nightly news broadcast that featured the specific broadcaster. The following table contains the responses of the 50 people surveyed:

Items

1	2	3	4	5	6	7	8	9	10	11	12	13	14	15	16	17	18	19
1	2	5	3	3	3	4	3	3	6	3	4	4	3	3	6	6	5	6
1	4	6	3	1	2	4	2	2	6	2	5	7	1	3	5	6	5	5
5	6	5	5	5	5	6	3	3	5	6	4	3	6	2	1	2	2	2
2	2	5	2	4	3	4	3	3	5	3	5	5	3	3	3	5	5	5
2	2	6	2	1	2	6	1	1	6	1	6	5	2	1	7	6	5	6
4	5	3	3	2	5	2	2	2	4	5	4	4	3	2	3	5	2	6
3	3	5	5	2	3	5	2	2	4	3	5	2	3	3	5	5	5	6
1	1	6	1	5	2	5	1	2	7	2	5	6	1	1	7	7	6	7
5	4	3	3	1	5	4	2	2	6	3	4	3	3	6	6	6	4	6
3	3	5	1	4	2	4	1	1	7	4	4	6	1	1	7	7	7	7
3	3	5	4	3	3	4	2	4	5	4	5	4	4	3	3	4	4	5
2	5	6	4	4	3	3	5	2	1	6	5	4	5	3	3	2	4	1
3	5	2	4	1	6	3	3	4	4	5	3	3	4	3	5	4	2	3
3	3	6	2	4	2	4	2	4	5	2	5	4	3	2	6	5	4	4
2	3	6	3	4	3	6	2	2	6	4	5	4	2	2	6	5	5	5
5	4	4	3	2	4	2	3	3	4	5	4	2	4	4	1	4	3	4
3	3	4	4	3	4	4	3	3	4	4	4	3	4	3	4	5	3	4
5	3	3	6	1	3	4	1	1	2	2	4	2	2	2	3	5	3	6
2	3	6	2	1	3	5	1	1	3	5	4	2	1	1	6	5	5	3
2	2	5	2	3	3	4	2	3	6	4	4	4	2	2	3	5	3	4
3	6	1	5	1	7	2	4	1	7	7	2	1	5	4	1	4	1	6
2	2	6	2	4	3	6	2	3	6	4	5	4	2	2	5	6	6	6
2	2	6	3	6	2	5	2	2	6	3	6	6	2	2	6	6	6	6
2	2	4	2	4	4	6	1	1	6	2	4	4	2	4	6	6	6	6

(continued)

Items

1	2	3	4	5	6	7	8	9	10	11	12	13	14	15	16	17	18	19
3	3	4	3	4	4	3	4	2	6	4	4	4	2	3	4	5	5	5
3	3	6	3	5	2	6	4	2	4	3	5	4	3	1	3	4	5	4
5	4	5	3	3	3	2	3	4	2	5	5	2	4	4	3	4	2	1
2	4	5	4	4	3	4	4	3	4	5	5	4	3	3	6	5	4	4
3	5	7	5	2	2	2	2	3	2	6	6	1	5	5	4	2	3	1
2	3	2	3	4	2	5	2	2	6	3	5	5	3	2	6	6	5	6
3	3	5	4	3	4	4	3	3	4	5	4	4	4	3	5	5	4	5
2	2	6	2	4	2	7	1	1	5	2	6	4	2	1	6	5	6	6
1	1	6	1	6	1	6	1	1	7	4	5	6	1	1	7	6	6	7
2	3	6	5	5	2	4	6	2	6	4	5	5	2	2	6	5	4	6
2	3	5	2	1	2	1	3	2	4	6	5	2	2	6	2	4	2	5
2	3	5	4	2	4	6	6	2	6	4	5	4	2	3	6	6	5	5
4	4	4	4	2	3	3	2	3	4	4	5	4	3	2	3	4	3	2
4	5	4	4	2	4	3	3	4	3	4	4	2	3	5	3	3	4	2
3	2	3	2	3	2	4	1	3	7	1	5	4	6	3	3	7	4	5
4	5	7	5	3	2	4	2	2	6	4	4	5	3	4	4	4	3	4
3	3	4	3	1	4	5	2	2	6	4	4	3	2	2	4	6	4	6
2	4	5	5	4	5	3	3	3	5	5	5	4	3	3	5	4	5	5
4	3	4	3	4	4	4	3	2	5	4	4	4	2	3	5	5	4	5
3	2	4	2	2	4	3	1	1	5	6	4	3	2	2	5	4	4	5
2	2	6	3	4	2	4	2	2	6	4	6	4	2	2	6	4	6	6
4	3	3	3	2	4	4	1	2	5	4	4	2	3	5	4	4	3	4
2	3	6	3	4	2	6	2	2	5	4	5	5	3	2	5	5	5	3
5	4	5	4	3	3	3	3	2	4	6	4	3	5	2	2	4	4	3
2	2	5	2	4	3	5	1	1	6	2	5	7	1	2	6	7	6	7
2	2	6	2	4	2	4	1	1	7	2	5	4	1	4	7	7	6	6

Notes:
1. For each item in the survey, the responses are coded 1–7, with 1 representing the left-most position on the scale and 7 representing the right-most position.
2. Items 1, 2, 4, 6, 8, 9, 11, 14, and 15 must be reverse-scaled before any analysis is attempted.

a. Discuss the possible reasons for the use of factor analysis with these data.

b. Produce a correlation matrix for the 19 variables (scale items). Does it appear that factor analysis would be appropriate for these data?

c. Do a principal components factor analysis (with varimax rotation if necessary for interpretation) using these data. How many factors should be retained? What is the percentage of variance accounted for by each factor?

d. Interpret the factors.

Refer to the NFO Research, Inc., coffee study described on pages 780–783 in Chapter 13 for the next three problems.

11. Perform a discriminant analysis using "brand used most often" as the classification, or grouping, variable and the 21 importance ratings as predictors. Is the first discriminant function statistically significant at the .05 level? If so, provide an interpretation of the discriminant function.

12. Perform a factor analysis on the 21 importance ratings of Question 5 to determine the dimensions underlying these data. Provide an interpretation of the factors.

13. Consider the importance ratings from Question 5 for the following items: rich taste, gets day off to good start, good value for the money, premium brand, best ground coffee available, and costs less than other brands. Use these variables to cluster the 66 male respondents into relatively homogeneous market segments. Provide an interpretation or description of the various segments obtained.

APPENDIX 17A

Analysis of Catalog-Buying Data

DISCRIMINANT ANALYSIS

Another question of interest in the Avery Sporting Goods study (found in Appendix 13A) was catalog recipients' feelings toward the breadth of the Avery line. To address this question, two groups were formed from Question 11, "The selection of sporting goods available through the Avery catalog is very broad." Those agreeing or strongly agreeing with this statement were placed in one group, labeled as those perceiving Avery as having a broad product line. Those strongly disagreeing, disagreeing, or neither agreeing nor disagreeing with the statement were placed in the other group, labeled as those perceiving Avery to have a narrow product line.

Table 17A.1 contains the results of the discriminant analysis that relates group membership to the same demographic characteristics that were used in the multiple-regression analysis with the ATTAVRY index — namely, the individual's occupation, age, and marital status. In addition, the gender of the respondent (V44) was included as an additional predictor variable, with females recoded, using the SPSS RECODE command, to 1 and males to 0.

The calculated chi-square value of 133.46 is significant at the 0.001 level, suggesting that these demographic variables can discriminate between those who think Avery has a broad product line and those who think Avery's line is narrow. Note the discriminant function that states the following:

$$
\begin{aligned}
Y = \quad & .502 \times V41 \ (\text{if white collar}) \\
& .085 \times V42 \ (\text{age}) \\
-\, & .042 \times V44 \ (\text{if female}) \\
& .959 \times D5 \ (\text{if single}) \\
& .752 \times D4 \ (\text{if married}) \\
& .468 \times D3 \ (\text{if separated}) \\
& .139 \times D2 \ (\text{if divorced})
\end{aligned}
$$

where Y is the discriminant score.

This function, of course, is constructed in such a way that it maximally discriminates between the two groups. The group centroid for those that think Avery has a broad product line is 1.237, while the group centroid for those who believe that Avery has a narrow product line is −1.657.

TABLE **17A.1   Discriminant Analysis of Those Believing Avery's Product Line Is Narrow or Broad as a Function of Demographic Characteristics**

Number of Cases by Group

		Number of Cases	
V20		**Unweighted**	**Weighted**
1		53	53.0
2		71	71.0
Total		124	124.0

Canonical Discriminant Function

Minimum number of functions . . .	1
Minimum cumulative percent of variance . . .	100.0
Maximum significance of Wilks' lambda . . .	1.0000
Prior probability for each group is .500	

Classification Function Coefficients
(Fisher's Linear Discriminant Functions)

V20 =	1	2
V41	1.525	6.077
V42	0.153	0.184
V44	2.244	2.065
D5	6.168	13.186
D4	6.283	12.418
D3	7.967	11.394
D2	8.056	9.224
(Constant)	−5.625	−12.471

Canonical Discriminant Functions

Function	**Eigenvalue**	**Percent of Variance**	**Cumulative Percent**	**Canonical Correlation**
1	2.084	100.0	100.0	.822

After Function	**Wilks' Lambda**	**Chi-squared**	**DF**	**Significance**
0	.324	133.46	7	.000

TABLE **17A.1**   *Continued*

Standardized Canonical Discriminant Function Coefficients

	Function 1
V41	.502
V42	.085
V44	−.042
D5	.959
D4	.752
D3	.468
D2	.139

Canonical Discriminant Functions Evaluated at Groups' Means (Group Centroids)

Group	Function 1
1	−1.657
2	1.237

Note from the confusion matrix in Table 17A.2 that there were actually 53 people in Group 1 and 71 in Group 2. Using the discriminant function, 48 of the 53 belonging to Group 1 would be predicted to belong there and 65 of the 71 belonging to Group 2 would be predicted to belong there. The overall classification accuracy is approximately 91 percent. Because the proportional chance or C_{pro} criterion is

TABLE **17A.2**   **Confusion Matrix**

		Classification Results	
		Predicted Group Membership	
Actual Group	**Number of Cases**	**1**	**2**
Group 1	53	48 (90.6%)	5 (9.4%)
Group 2	71	6 (8.5%)	65 (91.5%)

Percent of "Grouped" Cases Correctly Classified: 91.13%

$$C_{pro} = \alpha^2 + (1 - \alpha)^2$$
$$= (71/124)^2 + (53/124)^2 = .328 + .182 = .511,$$

there is approximately a 40 percent $(91 - 51)$ improvement in prediction accuracy through the use of the discriminant function.

FACTOR ANALYSIS

Another question of interest in the Avery study is whether people's attitudes toward buying from catalogs is a unidimensional trait or whether it has dimensions to it, just like a person's arithmetic ability is a composite of the individual's addition, subtraction, multiplication, and division abilities. To explore this issue, the responses to Questions 12 through 20, which all deal with what might happen when ordering from catalogs, were factor analyzed.

Table 17A.3 contains the results. The principal factor method was used to generate the initial solution. The eigenvalues suggested that a three-factor solution was appropriate. Consequently, three factors were rotated using the varimax criterion. The achieved communality for each of the variables is high. Further, close to 72 percent of the total variation in the data is explained by the three-factor solution. The factors are, of course, named by looking at the variation in the variables accounted for by each factor. Panel C of Table 17A.3 suggests, for example, that Factor 1 does a particularly good job of accounting for the variation in Variables 24, 26, and 28, Factor 2 for the variation in Variables 21, 22, and 23, and Factor 3 for the variation in Variables 25, 27, and 29. Variables 24, 26, and 28 all address the convenience of ordering through catalogs, and thus Factor 1 might be called a convenience factor or dimension. Similarly, Factor 2 might be labeled a riskiness factor and Factor 3 an economy factor.

TABLE 17A.3   **Factor Analysis of Attitude Statements Concerning Buying from Catalogs**

Panel A: Initial Factor Analysis Solution

Variable	Estimated Communality	Factor	Eigenvalue	Percentage of Variance	Cumulative Percentage
V21	1.000	1	2.917	32.4	32.4
V22	1.000	2	1.935	21.5	53.9
V23	1.000	3	1.608	17.9	71.8
V24	1.000	4	0.621	6.9	78.7
V25	1.000	5	0.537	6.0	84.6
V26	1.000	6	0.478	5.3	89.9
V27	1.000	7	0.388	4.3	94.2
V28	1.000	8	0.298	3.3	97.6
V29	1.000	9	0.220	2.4	100.0

TABLE 17A.3   *Continued*

Panel B: Factor Loadings before Rotation

Variable	Factor 1	Factor 2	Factor 3	Communality
V21	.612	.289	−.550	.760
V22	.594	.412	−.355	.648
V23	.605	.356	−.517	.760
V24	−.502	.615	.104	.641
V25	.364	.433	.609	.691
V26	−.520	.713	−.048	.781
V27	.705	.156	.491	.762
V28	−.575	.632	−.011	.731
V29	.584	.237	.536	.684

Panel C: Varimax-Rotated Factor Matrix

Variable	Factor 1	Factor 2	Factor 3	Communality
V21	−.115	.864	.023	.760
V22	.001	.779	.204	.648
V23	−.055	.867	.068	.760
V24	.793	−.110	.018	.641
V25	.169	.016	.814	.691
V26	.881	.020	−.073	.781
V27	−.254	.184	.815	.762
V28	.846	−.073	−.103	.731
V29	−.119	.114	.811	.684

CLUSTER ANALYSIS

The SPSS/PC+ package was used to cluster the responses to Question 21, which concerned the importance of the various services or features when purchasing through catalogs. The purpose was to determine if various features go together in the sense that there are such things as convenience features, risk-reducing features, and so on. The average linkage method was used.

The program operates by first converting the raw importance scores into a correlation matrix of the nine variables. These correlations, presented in Panel A of Table 17A.4, are then employed in the analysis. Panel B presents the sequence in which variables are combined into clusters along with associated fusion coefficients. For example, at the fusion coefficient .3053, Variable 35 joins the cluster containing Variables 31, 33, and 37. When the fusion coefficient equals −.0302 (which indicates that the clusters to be fused are very dissimilar), all items combine into a single cluster. A dendrogram portraying the information from Panel B provides better insight into what is going on and is presented in Panel C, along with brief descriptions of the nine features under consideration. A glance at this diagram reveals that the nine variables might best be divided into three clusters:

Cluster 1	Cluster 2	Cluster 3
Toll-free number	Quantity discounts	Endorsements
Company reputation	Guarantees	
Shipping time	Return policy	
Trial period	Years in business	

The researcher would then undertake the more subjective task of naming the three clusters.

TABLE 17A.4   Cluster Analysis of Importance Features

Panel A: Similarities (Correlations) between Variables

Variable Name	V31	V32	V33	V34	V35	V36	V37	V38
V30	.0854	.3897	−.0114	.4310	.0069	.6411	.0772	−.3742
V31		.0000	.4403	−.0464	.2574	.0063	.5431	.1992
V32			.1921	.4590	.0767	.6042	.1711	−.1529
V33				.0189	.2881	.0566	.4177	.0781
V34					−.0290	.5548	−.0105	−.3143
V35						−.0100	.3703	.1520
V36							.0473	−.3936
V37								.1115

Panel B: Sequential Combination of Clusters Using Average Linkage Method

Stage	Clusters Combined		Fusion Coefficient*
	Cluster 1	Cluster 2	
1	V30	V36	.6411
2	V31	V37	.5431
3	V30, V36	V32	.4969
4	V30, V36, V32	V34	.4816
5	V31, V37	V33	.4290
6	V31, V37, V33	V35	.3053
7	V31, V37, V33, V35	V38	.1352
8	V30, V36, V32, V34	V31, V37, V33, V35, V38	−.0302

*Note that clusters combined at decreasing fusion coefficients, because the fusion coefficients represent correlation between the clusters. Thus, highly similar (highly correlated) objects or clusters will combine at high fusion coefficients whereas less similar objects or clusters will combine at lower values of the fusion coefficient. Had a measure of dissimilarity been used, this relationship would have been reversed, with increasing dissimilarity between objects or clusters leading to higher fusion coefficients.

TABLE 17A.4   *Continued*

Panel C: Dendrogram

Variable Name	Description	1.00 .95 .90 .85 .75 .70 .65 .60 .55 .50 .45 .40 .35 .30 .25 .20 .15 .10 .05 .00
V30	Toll-free number	
V36	Company Reputation	
V32	Shipping Time	
V34	Trial Period	
V31	Quantity Discounts	
V37	Guarantees	
V33	Return Policy	
V35	Years in Business	
V38	Endorsements	

CASE 5.1

University of Wisconsin-Extension: Engineering Management Program[1]

INTRODUCTION

The University of Wisconsin-Extension is the outreach campus of the University of Wisconsin System. It is responsible for offering high-quality continuing education to adults in a variety of professions from around the country.

The Management Institute is one of the many specialized departments within the UW-Extension. It conducts programs aimed at providing education and training in at least a dozen areas of business management and not-for-profit management. Extension Engineering is another of the specialized departments. Since 1901, it has grown from its summer-school origins into one of the finest organizations of its kind. Extension Engineering has offered institutes and short courses annually since 1949. It has a dedicated full-time faculty of engineering and science professors, most of whom have extensive business and industrial experience.

OPPORTUNITY FOR AN ENGINEERING MANAGEMENT PROGRAM

In the spring of 1994, William Nitzke, the director of Extension Engineering client services, set out to explore the possibility of establishing a certificate program in engineering management. He recognized this opportunity after speaking with attendees of Extension Engineering seminars and reading several articles that made reference to the need for management training for engineers. Nitzke believed it would be feasible to develop a coordinated curriculum in engineering management by combining the strengths of the Management Institute and Extension Engineering. This new program would include a comprehensive series of management courses specifically created to provide engineers with skills to better meet the challenges of management positions.

Background

More than half of the chief executives in major U.S. companies are engineers, and most of the middle-management positions are filled by engineers. Moreover, the American

[1]The contributions of Maria Papas Heide to the development of this case are gratefully acknowledged.

Association of Engineering Societies reports that about two-thirds of all engineers spend two-thirds of their careers in supervisory or management positions. Yet the crowded engineering curricula at major colleges and universities allow little room for courses that prepare engineers for the types of problems they will have to face as managers. Thus, as many engineers evolve in their careers, they find themselves promoted into management positions without formal training, leaving them unprepared to deal with a quite different set of challenges. One estimate suggests that nearly a million engineering supervisors and managers are currently not well-prepared for their positions.

Major corporations throughout the United States are becoming aware that their technically capable engineers are inadequately trained to handle the management-related problems they confront. As a result, the efficiencies of the corporations are affected, and the full potential of the engineers as managers is not realized.

The Management Institute of the UW-Extension does provide programs for the non-management manager. However, neither Extension Engineering nor the Management Institute offers a coordinated or comprehensive series of programs specifically designed for engineers or similar professions. Further, according to secondary data and direct client inquiry, few continuing education opportunities presently exist on a national level for engineers to gain specialized management training. The Extension Engineering department consequently decided that it would attempt to establish itself and the Management Institute as a leading-edge provider of professional development programs in engineering management by being one of the first continuing education institutes to offer a certificate program in Engineering Management.

The original conceptualization of the certificate program held that:

> Engineers would be granted a certificate only after successful completion of 10–12 seminars from the total set available. Each seminar would run 3–5 days. About 5–6 of these seminars would be required and the other 5–6 would be electives.

A study was undertaken to discover the degree of interest in this type of specialized management training among engineers who had previously attended Extension Engineering seminars. The thought was that the original conceptualization described previously could be modified easily enough, depending on the findings from the study.

More specifically, the research was to address the following specific issues:

1. The overall general interest in an engineering management program offered by the UW-Extension;
2. The appeal of earning a certificate in contrast to taking selected seminars on an "as needed" basis;
3. The preferred design of a certificate engineering management program in terms of schedules of attendance, availability of correspondence seminars, and years to complete the certificate requirements;
4. The type of seminar topics that should compose the certificate engineering management curriculum.

Research Method

The study had several stages. In the preliminary stage, letters were sent to 212 recent attendees of UW-Extension engineering seminars, asking them to participate in a telephone interview regarding the proposed engineering management program. Reply postcards were received from 100 of the attendees, providing a response rate of 47 percent. The respondents fit into the following categories:

Percentage

38	agreed to participate in the telephone interview.
49	did not wish to participate in the telephone interview but were willing to complete a written questionnaire and/or were interested in receiving information on the program when it was developed.
13	were not interested in an engineering management program.
100	

The respondents contacted for the telephone interviews were very helpful in designing the written questionnaire, which was subsequently pretested on attendees of a current Extension Engineering seminar. After incorporating the changes suggested from the pretest, a final version of the written questionnaire was mailed to 2,000 randomly selected participants of Extension Engineering seminars within the past two years. A second mailing of the questionnaire to the same 2,000 respondents followed two weeks after the first mailing. The questionnaires for 123 of the names on the mailing list were returned as undeliverable. A total of 502 usable surveys, providing a response rate of 27 percent, was returned from the first and second mailings.

In the second mailing, a reply postcard was included along with the questionnaire. The postcard was provided to induce those contacted who were unwilling to complete an entire questionnaire to at least return a postcard answering the critical question about their interest in an engineering management program. One hundred ninety-one (191) usable postcards were returned. Including both the surveys and the postcards in which the single critical question about interest was answered, the response rate was 35 percent. It was found that 69 percent of all the respondents were interested in a program offering management seminars specifically designed for engineers.

One of the open-ended questions that was asked stated:

What are the three most important management-related problems you (or the engineers you supervise) face at work?

1. _____

2. _____

3. _____

The question was designed to gather some insights into the most common areas of management-related difficulties faced by all types of engineers. The question also specifically addresses the fourth research objective listed earlier — to determine the type of seminar topics that should compose the certificate engineering management curriculum. A representative sample of the responses to this question provided by the engineers are listed in Table 1.

TABLE 1   Sample of Verbatim Responses Regarding the Most Important
Management-Related Problems Engineers Face

1. Increasing productivity
2. Management/union relationships
3. Management does not relate to employees
4. Quality of job performed
5. Dealing with changing priorities
6. Human relations
7. Client/public interactions and manipulation
8. Quality control of projects
9. Getting bogged down on minor items and losing sight of the big picture
10. Keeping employees happy
11. Communicating technical items to nontechnical persons
12. Utilization of time
13. The lack of ability of some to see the big picture
14. Motivation of subordinates to achieve consistent level of performance
15. Quality of workmanship
16. Obtaining appropriate information on a timely basis
17. Contract administration
18. Communications between scattered segments of company
19. Contractor performance
20. Designing job to be motivating
21. Effective sharing of information
22. Managing employees for maximum productivity
23. More efficient use of time
24. Management of information related to many projects in progress simultaneously
25. Personnel management
26. Communicating with other divisions of the company
27. Peer communications
28. Motivating those I supervise
29. Lack of defined career plan
30. Ability to communicate in nonengineering terms
31. Handling below-standard employees with union ties
32. Long-term motivation
33. Data exchange
34. Time constraints
35. Motivation of subordinates
36. Getting the most productivity out of subordinates
37. Information exchange with other departments
38. Cope with upcoming computers
39. Salary management
40. Understanding of contract management
41. Sometimes lack of enthusiasm
42. Correspondence
43. Determining accurate fee estimates
44. Evaluation/selection of "best" applicant for position
45. Satisfying the client
46. Problem identification and solving
47. Bureaucracy
48. Building confidence
49. Market entry/penetration
50. Timely responses from other departments
51. Bolstering morale
52. Lack of salary increases
53. Learning computer-management tools
54. Holding effective meetings
55. Results tracking
56. Contract compliance
57. Interface with other project groups
58. Understanding and setting goals
59. Making sales contacts
60. Gaining recognition and promotion for qualified people
61. Conveying engineering problems to nontechnical management
62. Effective technical writing
63. Cost reduction
64. Follow-through on projects
65. Personal development with respect to career
66. Priority rank of assignments
67. Keeping good relationship with employees
68. Improving work habits
69. Figuring of project costs
70. Researching and compiling information to generate realistic cost proposal
71. Interdepartmental coordination of work efforts
72. Low productivity
73. Seeing the forest through the trees
74. Getting time to do my own work while supervising other workers
75. Dealing with hostile public
76. Lack of devotion of employees

continued

Table 1   *Continued*

77. Accomplish the volume of work in the given time
78. Skill in making sound management decisions
79. Politics with the company (how they affect decisions)
80. Estimating time to perform work
81. Budget control and forecasting
82. In-house cost estimating/tracking
83. Purchasing policies
84. Interpersonal relations
85. Scheduling
86. Motivating others to contribute as a team toward a project goal
87. Data-base optimization and report use
88. Lack of supervisory training
89. Estimating engineering man hours required
90. Knowing what the boss really wants
91. Meeting mandated deadlines
92. Motivating the people who work under you to try to achieve goals set
93. Upward communication
94. Business planning (growth projections, marketing plans, etc.)
95. Lack of initiative and curiosity
96. Understanding other people's work-related problems
97. Communications with upper management
98. Discipline (self and principles of application)
99. Financial management of firm
100. Time management
101. Workload distribution
102. Unions
103. System bureaucracy
104. Sales and marketing of services
105. Work appropriation
106. Performance evaluation
107. Keeping employees interested, enthusiastic, and committed to job
108. Salary adjustments
109. Scheduling individual items in a project so project is completed on time
110. Information collection and dissemination
111. Project management — getting a project to run smoothly
112. Developing people
113. Task prioritization
114. Performance/salary-structure relationship
115. Engineer performance review
116. Selling ideas
117. Politics
118. Effective presentation of the results
119. Cost analysis/control
120. Monitoring jobs in progress
121. Effective communications with associates
122. Providing opportunities for advancement
123. The inability to rate people properly
124. Achieving desired end results
125. Making effective use of computer-based systems
126. Training
127. Lack of coordination of effort
128. Keeping projects within budget
129. Reducing duplication of effort
130. Cost awareness
131. Conveying concise direct ideas to engineers in written form
132. Inefficient budgeting and financial expertise
133. Not getting continual feedback on my performance — feel like a machine expected to do a task
134. Public speaking
135. Distribution of assignments
136. Transfer of knowledge
137. Meeting budgets
138. Correcting those I supervise
139. Written communication
140. Establishing priorities
141. Management at meetings
142. Decision making
143. Application of appropriate disciplinary actions
144. Long-range planning
145. Conducting effective presentations
146. Creating and controlling project budgets
147. Employee handling
148. Making the right decision based on facts
149. Cross-training in other departments
150. Manpower projection
151. Financial control
152. Work flow between departments
153. Getting ideas across
154. Distribution and best use of manpower
155. Communications

TABLE 1 *Continued*

156. Management perception of engineers as people vs. tools	170. Conducting effective meetings
157. Commitment and performance	171. Keeping projects on schedule
158. Rating of subordinates	172. Project administration
159. Convincing top management of your ideas	173. Understanding financial management
160. Preparation and management of budgets	174. Understanding leadership roles
161. Managing people	175. Keeping a project within the cost restrictions
162. Manpower allotment	176. Delegation of authority as well as responsibility
163. Meeting schedules that change rapidly	177. Lack of honest constructive performance appraisal
164. Evaluation of employees	178. Hiring/interviewing
165. Failure of those in management positions to take control	179. Project work staffing
166. To communicate more effectively	180. Counseling employees
167. Clear division of responsibility between groups	181. Controlling employees
168. Negotiating	182. Supervisor does not aid me as he might in helping to pursue and achieve goals set down in annual performance review
169. Documenting	

Questions

1. Establish what you believe would be a relatively exhaustive and useful set of codes that could be used to code the responses to the question and to achieve the fourth objective for the study.

2. Use your *a priori* codes to code the verbatim responses listed in Table 1. Establish additional codes if needed to account for unanticipated categories of responses.

3. Summarize what the sample of data suggests about the problems faced by the engineers who responded to this survey. Recommend the types of seminars that should be included in the engineering management curriculum.

CASE 5.2
Wisconsin Power & Light[1]

In response to the current consumer trend towards increased environmental sensitivity, Wisconsin Power & Light (WP&L) adopted several high-visibility environmental initiatives. These environmental programs fell under the BuySmart umbrella of WP&L's Demand-Side Management Programs and were intended to foster the conservation of energy among WP&L's residential, commercial, and industrial customers. Examples of

---

[1]The contributions of Kavita Maini and Paul Metz to the development of this case are gratefully acknowledged as is the permission of Wisconsin Power & Light to use the material included.

specific programs include: Appliance Rebates, Energy Analysis, Weatherization Help, and the Home Energy Improvement Loan (HEIL) program. All previous marketing research and information gathering focused primarily on issues from the customers' perspective, such as an evaluation of net program impacts in terms of energy and demand savings and an estimation of the levels of free ridership (individuals who would have undertaken the conservation actions promoted by the program, even if there was no program in place). In addition, a study has been designed and is currently being conducted to evaluate and identify customer attitudes and opinions concerning the design, implementation, features, and delivery of the residential programs. Having examined the consumer perspective, WP&L's next objective is to focus on obtaining information from other participants in the programs, namely employees and lenders.

WP&L's immediate research focus is to undertake a study of the Home Energy Improvement Loan (HEIL) program of the BuySmart umbrella. The HEIL program was introduced in 1987 and was designed to make low-interest-rate financing available to residential gas and electric WP&L customers for conservation and weatherization measures. The low-interest guaranteed loans are delivered through WP&L account representatives in conjunction with participating financial institutions and trade allies. The procedures for obtaining a loan begin with an energy "audit" of the interested customer's residence to determine the appropriate conservation measures. Once the customer decides on which measures to have installed, the WP&L representative assists in arranging low-interest-rate financing through one of the participating local banking institutions. At the completion of the projects, WP&L representatives conduct an inspection of the work by checking a random sample of participants. Conservation measures eligible under the HEIL program include the installation of natural gas furnaces/boilers, automatic vent dampers, intermittent ignition devices, heat pumps, and heat pump water heaters. Eligible structural improvements include the addition of attic/wall/basement insulation, storm windows and doors, sillbox insulation, window weather-stripping, and caulking.

PURPOSE

The primary goal of the current study is to identify ways of improving the HEIL program from the lenders' point of view. Specifically, the following issues need to be addressed:

- Identify the lenders' motivation for participating in the program.
- Determine how lenders get their information regarding various changes/updates in the program.
- Identify how lenders promote the program.
- Assess the current program with respect to administrative and program features.
- Determine the type of credit analysis conducted by the lenders.
- Identify ways of minimizing the default rate from the lenders' point of view.
- Assess the lenders' commitment to the program.
- Identify lenders' opinions of the overall program.
- Identify if the reason for loan inactivity in some lending institutions is due to lack of a customer base.

METHODOLOGY

WP&L decided to use a telephone survey of participating lending institutions to collect the data for their study. WP&L referenced two lists of lending institutions, which were supplied by their residential marketing staff, in order to select the sample for the survey. A total of 124 participating lending institutions was identified with the lists. However, it was found that one of the lists was shorter than the other by 15 names. Specifically, the names of some of the branches of major banks were not enumerated on one of the lists. Nevertheless, all 124 institutions, including the 15 discrepant ones, were included in the pool of names from which the sample was drawn.

The sample pool was stratified into three groups based on loan activity in the 1991 calendar year. The groups fell out as follows:

Group	Number of Lenders	Loan Activity, 1991
1	44	0 loans
2	40	1 to 7 loans
3	40	8 to 54 loans

The final sample for the survey consisted of 20 systematically chosen lenders from Groups 2 and 3, and 10 randomly chosen institutions from Group 1. The 40 institutions selected from among Groups 2 and 3 formed the sample base in which WP&L was most interested (this was because each of these 40 institutions demonstrated loan activity in the past year). Consequently, WP&L used a systematic selection procedure for this key group in order to ensure that the sample was representative of the population and to improve the statistical efficiency of the sample. The sample size (n = 40) was based on judgment. The 10 randomly selected institutions from Group 1 were chosen primarily to explore the hypothesized reasons for zero-loan activity. These 10 zero-loan lenders received a shortened version of the telephone survey that focused only on their lack of activity.

All of the districts within WP&L's service territory were notified two weeks in advance that a survey was going to be conducted. A survey was designed to address the research objectives and included both closed and open-ended questions. The survey was pretested and modified prior to final administration. All interviewing was conducted over a one-week period by a project manager and research assistant, both employees of WP&L's marketing department.

One of the open-ended questions in the survey asked lenders to identify the benefits gained by participating in the HEIL program. The actual wording of the question follows:

Q.6   Does your bank benefit in any way by participating in this program?
   1   Yes
   2   No

Q.7   Would you please explain your answer?

Data from this question, it was hypothesized, could be used to address several of the aforementioned research objectives. First, the responses would provide qualitative insights into the lenders' motivation for participating in the program. Second, they would help explain lenders' level of commitment to the program as well as help identify reasons why banks promote (or fail to promote) the HEIL program. Finally, the benefits cited could provide WP&L with an understanding of the lenders' overall opinion of the program. Table 1 contains a list of the verbatim responses to this open-ended question.

TABLE 1   Vertabim Responses Regarding the Benefits Conveyed by Lenders to Participation in the HEIL Program

1. We acquire a new loan customer. The customer likes the fact that the loan is guaranteed.
2. It's good public relations to be associated with WP&L. Also, we have nothing to lose on it. It is a risk-free program.
3. It fulfills the CRA (Credit Reinvestment Act) requirement.
4. We got some new customers. People from other towns cannot get into the HEIL program from their bank.
5. We make some money through the buydown.
6. We have access to more customers and can therefore cross-sell other services. We stay competitive this way. It's also good PR to be associated with WP&L.
7. We provide another service to the customer. It helps us to stay competitive.
8. We improve on customer service by providing an additional service. It helps us stay competitive.
9. We can provide another service. We have also built customer contact a lot more.
10. We earn interest income. Customers look on us more favorably because this program is really good.
11. We got some new customers. In addition, the HEIL program helps us make more loans, which is helping us to make revenue.
12. We get money out of the interest buydowns.
13. Another service to provide our customers.
14. It is an added service that enriches our offerings. People come back for other loans.
15. It fulfills CRA. Also, good public relations to be associated with WP&L.
16. It fulfills CRA. Also, more loans implies more income for the bank and a higher proportion can be reinvested back into the community.
17. Another service to provide our customers.
18. It fulfills CRA.
19. Another service to provide for our customers.
20. Good public relations.
21. We can provide another service to our customers.
22. We got some new customers.
23. It's good for our customers.
24. No benefits anymore. There are so many restrictions. There should be more types of options.
25. We are in it for the CRA.
26. We can provide another service to our customers.
27. No benefits because too many good options are excluded.
28. It fulfills the CRA requirement. We are providing the customers a service that has very good rates.
29. We got some new customers.
30. Financially, we get more money by lending without the program.
31. We provide another service to our customers.
32. We are in it for the CRA.
33. We get money through the buydowns.
34. We gain new customers.
35. Good public relations.
36. We provide another service and it allows us to help people who really need the loan.
37. We provide another service to our clients and community.
38. It helps us provide another service to our clients and community.
39. We don't have a high enough volume to be able to say that there has been a benefit.
40. We provide another service to our customers.

Questions

1. Synthesize the verbatim responses by developing a set of codes and then grouping them into categories that would help WP&L understand the perceived benefits of the HEIL program.

2. What advantages does the researcher gain by coding open-ended data?

3. What recommendations would you make to WP&L about the HEIL program based on what the open-ended data suggest?

CASE 5.3
Star Equipment (A)[1]

Star Equipment is a Fortune 500 company that manufactures technologically advanced equipment for a variety of applications. Star Equipment's office-products division is one of the three largest manufacturers of office equipment in the world. Traditionally, its largest competitor in the office-equipment category has been Vetra — a domestic manufacturer of advanced office equipment. However, beginning in the 1980s and continuing into the 1990s, Calt, a large foreign manufacturer of office equipment, achieved major gains in the U.S. market. Star also faces significant competition from a number of smaller, specialized office-equipment manufacturers.

In order for Star Equipment's office products division to remain profitable with the increased competition, division managers outlined four strategies to promote sales: (1) identify key accounts for Star's office products, (2) examine the purchase decision process within these key accounts, (3) determine the critical vendor services sought by these accounts, and (4) assess the performance of Star and its two main competitors on these critical characteristics.

RESEARCH METHOD

Star's marketing research team designed a two-stage research project involving both secondary and primary research to gather the information identified in the four strategies. The first stage of the project involved exhaustive secondary research along with internal and external depth interviews to identify the vendor attributes important to office-equipment customers. Thirteen vendor characteristics were identified as being of some importance to customers.

The thirteen characteristics were incorporated in a survey in which respondents were asked to select the four most- and four least-important characteristics. Respondents were also asked to rate the vendors considered for their company's most recent office-equipment purchase on each of the attributes. Since Star was interested primarily in its

[1]The contributions of Sara L. Pitterle to this case are gratefully acknowledged.

own performance ratings along with its two major competitors, Calt and Vetra, these three vendors were explicitly specified in Question 3 in the survey; an "other" column was provided to capture the ratings of smaller vendors that may have been considered.

The survey in Figure 1 was mailed to 812 respondents who were either considering an office-equipment purchase or had purchased this type of equipment within the last two years. The sample was drawn from the customer lists of both Star and its office-

FIGURE 1   **Star Office Equipment Questionnaire**

Q1. Thinking specifically about your most recent equipment purchase decision, list all the vendors considered in this decision. By vendor we mean companies that manufacture the equipment.

_____	7–8
_____	9–10
_____	11–12
_____	13–14

Q2. Listed below are vendor characteristics that could be used to make a decision about which equipment to purchase. Thinking about your most recent purchase decision:

A. Check (✔) the four (4) most important vendor characteristics in your purchase decision.

B. Check (✔) the four (4) least important vendor characteristics in your purchase decision.

	A	B
Vendor Characteristics	**Most Important** **(Check 4)**	**Least Important** **(Check 4)**
a. Vendor values a long-term relationship and works to meet my organization's unique needs...........................	01 ☐ 15–16/	01 ☐ 23–24/
b. My relationships with the vendor's sales and support representatives are easy and productive	02 ☐ 17–18/	02 ☐ 25–26/
c. Vendor enables my organization to have a smooth decision process..............	03 ☐ 19–20/	03 ☐ 27–28/
d. The vendor establishes fair pricing policies for products and services........	04 ☐ 21–22/	04 ☐ 29–30/
e. The vendor's service organization is responsive to my organization's needs ...	05 ☐	05 ☐
f. The vendor offers an extensive line of reliable products meeting the needs of my organization	06 ☐	06 ☐

FIGURE 1 *Continued*

	A	B
	Most Important	**Least Important**
Vendor Characteristics	**(Check 4)**	**(Check 4)**
g. The vendor's solutions enable my organization to use people, space, and resources efficiently	07 ☐	07 ☐
h. The vendor offers software to increase the productivity and satisfaction of my department and employees	08 ☐	08 ☐
i. Vendor's products are easy to use	09 ☐	09 ☐
j. The vendor's solutions help my business grow	10 ☐	10 ☐
k. The vendor's solutions give me the ability to offer quick response to my customers' needs	11 ☐	11 ☐
l. The vendor provides my company with solutions that protect the safety and legality of information	12 ☐	12 ☐
m. The vendor provides my firm with technological advantages today that can be leveraged to meet our future requirements	13 ☐	13 ☐

Q3. *Using the following scale, write the number (in each box) that best describes how well each of the vendors fulfilled your expectations during your <u>most recent</u> <u>purchase</u> decision.*

1 = *Completely* *Fulfilled*	*2 =* *Somewhat* *Fulfilled*	*3 =* *Neither* *Fulfilled* *nor Unfulfilled*	*4 =* *Somewhat* *Unfulfilled*	*5 =* *Not at All* *Fulfilled*	*0 =* *Not* *Appropriate*

Vendor Characteristics	**Calt**	**Star**	**Vetra**	**Other**
a. Vendor values a long-term relationship and works to meet my organization's unique needs.........	☐ 31/	☐ 44/	☐ 57/	☐ 70/
b. My relationships with the vendor's sales and support representatives are easy and productive	☐ 32/	☐ 45/	☐ 58/	☐ 71/
c. Vendor enables my organiztion to have a smooth decision process	☐ 33/	☐ 46/	☐ 59/	☐ 72/
d. The vendor establishes fair pricing policies for products and services ...	☐ 34/	☐ 47/	☐ 60/	☐ 73/

continued

FIGURE 1 *Continued*

Vendor Characteristics	Calt	Star	Vetra	Other
e. The vendor's service organization is responsive to my organization's needs	☐ 35/	☐ 48/	☐ 61/	☐ 74/
f. The vendor offers an extensive line of reliable products meeting the needs of my organization	☐ 36/	☐ 49/	☐ 62/	☐ 75/
g. The vendor's solutions enable my organization to use people, space, and resources efficiently	☐ 37/	☐ 50/	☐ 63/	☐ 76/
h. The vendor offers software to increase the productivity and satisfaction of my department and employees.	☐ 38/	☐ 51/	☐ 64/	☐ 77/
i. Vendor's products are easy to use	☐ 39/	☐ 52/	☐ 65/	☐ 78/
j. The vendor's solutions help my business grow	☐ 40/	☐ 53/	☐ 66/	☐ 79/
k. The vendor's solutions give me the ability to offer quick response to my customers' needs.	☐ 41/	☐ 54/	☐ 67/	☐ 80/
l. The vendor provides my company with solutions that protect the safety and legality of information.	☐ 42/	☐ 55/	☐ 68/	☐ 81/
m. The vendor provides my firm with technological advantages today that can be leveraged to meet our future requirements.	☐ 43/	☐ 56/	☐ 69/	☐ 82/

Q4. How often do you acquire new equipment?

1☐ Less than 1 year   3☐ 3 years to less than 6 years   83/
2☐ 1 year to less than 3 years   4☐ 6 years or more

Q5. From whom do you acquire your equipment? (Check all that apply.)

1☐ Directly from manufacturers   3☐ Broker   84–87/
2☐ Dealer   4☐ Other (Specify):_____

Q6. From whom do you acquire your supplies and software? (Check all that apply.)

1☐ Manufacturer   6☐ Small storefront   88–98/
2☐ Mail order   7☐ Super stores
3☐ Contract dealer   8☐ Warehouse club
4☐ Buying group   9☐ Dealer
5☐ Supplies merchant   10☐ Other (Specify):_____

FIGURE 1   *Continued*

Q7. *What are the reasons for using these suppliers and software?* (Check all that apply.)

1☐	Reputation of supplier	5☐	Recommendation	99–106/
2☐	Product-quality	6☐	Delivery time	
3☐	Product-performance/yield	7☐	Price	
4☐	Ease of ordering	8☐	Other (Specify):_____	

Q8. *Do you purchase, rent, and/or lease your equipment?* (Check all that apply.)

1☐	Purchase	3☐	Lease	107–110/
2☐	Rent	4☐	Other (Specify):_____	

Q9. *Which of the following best describes where these types of purchase decisions are made in your company?*

1☐	At corporate headquarters for all locations	111/
2☐	At each company location or branch office	
3☐	Departmental level within each location	
4☐	My company has only one office or location	
5☐	Other (specify):_____	

---

equipment dealers. A $10 incentive was used to encourage responses. The research sponsor was not identified, and data collection was coordinated through an independent research-supply firm. Three hundred usable surveys were returned from the initial mailing. Figure 2 displays the coding of the questionnaires.

FIGURE 2   **Coding Format for Star Office Equipment Questionnaire**

Columns	Contents
1–5	Respondent identification number
6	Current primary equipment manufacturer for respondent: precoded, not a survey question.
	Manufacturers:
	1 = Star
	2 = Vetra
	3 = Calt
	4 = Snap
	5 = Reggies
	Q1. Vendors considered in *most recent* purchase
7–8	Vendor 1 (See vendor code list below)
9–10	Vendor 2
11–12	Vendor 3

continued

Figure 2   *Continued*

Columns	Contents
13–14	Vendor 4
	Vendor codes:
	1 = Calt
	2 = Star
	3 = Reggies
	4 = Snap
	5 = Vetra
	94 = No selection made
	95 = Other vendor
	98 = Don't know
15–22	Q2. Four most important vendor characteristics
	(See Questionnaire for definition of codes 01–13)
23–30	Q2. Four least important vendor characteristics
	(See Questionnaire for definition of codes 01–13)
31	Q3a, Calt rating of how well vendor fulfilled expectations
	(See Questionnaire for definition of characteristics a–m and scale values
32	Q3b
33	Q3c
34	Q3d
35	Q3e
36	Q3f
37	Q3g
38	Q3h
39	Q3i
40	Q3j
41	Q3k
42	Q3l
43	Q3m
44	Q3a, Star rating of how well vendor fulfilled expectations
	(See Questionnaire for definition of characteristis a–m and scale values)
45	Q3b
46	Q3c
47	Q3d
48	Q3e
49	Q3f
50	Q3g
51	Q3h
52	Q3i
53	Q3j
54	Q3k
55	Q3l
56	Q3m
57	Q3a, Vetra rating of how well vendor fulfilled expectations
	(See Questionnaire for definition of characteristics a–m and scale values)
58	Q3b
59	Q3c

FIGURE 2 *Continued*

Columns	Contents
60	Q3d
61	Q3e
62	Q3f
63	Q3g
64	Q3h
65	Q3i
66	Q3j
67	Q3k
68	Q3l
69	Q3m
70	Q3a, ''Other vendor'' rating of how well the vendor fulfilled expectations (See Questionnaire for definition of characteristics a–m and scale)
71	Q3b
72	Q3c
73	Q3d
74	Q3e
75	Q3f
76	Q3g
77	Q3h
78	Q3i
79	Q3j
80	Q3k
81	Q3l
82	Q3m
83	Q4. How often do you purchase this equipment?
84	Q5. Acquire equipment from manufacturers
85	from dealers
86	from brokers
87	from other
88–96	Q6. Where acquire supplies
	1 = Manufacturer
	2 = Mail order
	3 = Contract dealer
	4 = Buying group
	5 = Supplies merchant
	6 = Small storefront
	7 = Super stores
	8 = Warehouse club
	9 = Dealer
97–98	10 = Other
99–106	Q7. Reasons use suppliers
	1 = Reputation of supplier
	2 = Product-quality
	3 = Product-performance/yield
	4 = Ease of ordering

continued

FIGURE 2 *Continued*

Columns	Contents
	5 = Recommendation
	6 = Delivery time
	7 = Price
	8 = Other
107	Q8. Purchase equipment
108	Rent equipment
109	Lease equipment
110	Other
111	Q9. Where purchase decisions made

THE SAMPLE

Star was able to identify the primary office-equipment manufacturer for each of the 300 respondents. This information is contained in Table 1. Table 2 lists the equipment vendors considered by these respondents for their most recent equipment purchase. Table 3

TABLE 1 **Primary Manufacturers**

Manufacturer	Frequency	% Sample
Vetra	98	33
Star	87	29
Calt	61	20
Snap	32	11
Reggies	22	7

TABLE 2 **Vendors Considered in Most Recent Equipment Purchase**

Manufacturer	Frequency	% Sample
Vetra	166	55
Star	109	36
Calt	109	36
Other Vendors	97	32
Snap	57	19
Reggies	46	15

TABLE 3   **Attributes Chosen As Most and Least Important**

Attribute	Most Important				Least Important			
	1	**2**	**3**	**4**	**1**	**2**	**3**	**4**
a	183	0	0	0	33	0	0	0
b	48	75	0	0	44	8	0	0
c	8	13	5	0	110	32	3	0
d	37	101	40	2	4	7	0	0
e	12	71	104	26	1	5	1	1
f	2	16	47	29	26	35	12	0
g	4	6	16	5	37	62	21	1
h	1	10	30	21	9	29	25	8
i	2	3	31	102	4	10	16	4
j	3	2	11	23	13	49	45	5
k	0	3	9	24	4	37	54	11
l	0	0	6	1	0	7	91	130
m	0	0	0	62	0	0	3	104
Total	300	300	299	295	285	281	271	264

summarizes the variables chosen as **Most Important** and **Least Important** by the respondents.

Questions

1. Star wants the questionnaire in Figure 1 to be completed by the person responsible for purchasing office equipment. Is a mail survey the most appropriate way to reach these people? Why or why not?

2. Was conducting secondary research followed by depth interviews an appropriate means of generating the primary vendor characteristics for this survey? Why or why not?

3. Read each of the 13 vendor-characteristic statements carefully. Are these statements appropriate for a mail survey? Are there particular statements that may pose problems for respondents? Why?

4. Star's sample for this study was generated from its own sales lists and those of its dealers. Did the use of these lists as sampling frames lead to a biased sample? Explain.

5. Using the questionnaire and coding format provided in Figures 1 and 2, how many variables are necessary to capture completely the responses to Questions 6 and 7? Identify the problems that may arise from this particular coding format.

6. Using data supplied by your instructor, generate one-way tabulations for Survey Questions 6 and 7 (columns 88–106). How can these frequencies be explained? Is there a better way of coding these questions to avoid these types of problems?

7. Can the data in columns 88–106 still be used in this analysis? Justify your decision.

8. Star's research team wants to group respondents based on the similarity of attributes chosen as either important or not important. Thus, Question 2 is critical to the success of this project. Looking at Table 3, did respondents answer this question correctly? What should be done with those cases that are incorrect? Justify your answer.

9. How would you recode the data from Question 3 to facilitate interpretation? How would you handle the 0 ("Not Appropriate") ratings in this question?

Case 5.4
Canopy of Care (B)[1]

Canopy of Care is a nonprofit organization that solicits donations on behalf of various local charities, thereby relieving them of the need to market themselves and raise funds on an individual basis [see Case 4.9, Canopy of Care (A), for more details]. Fundraising is accomplished with the cooperation of local businesses and government agencies, who approach their employees on behalf of Canopy of Care and, given employee pledges, deduct donations directly out of their wages and salaries.

Recent statistics have shown that only 50 percent of the employees in participating companies agree to contribute. With economic conditions in the community deteriorating, Canopy of Care officials believe that their approach to potential donors needs to be rendered more effective. To determine why solicited employees do not contribute, they decided to investigate differences in knowledge and attitudes about Canopy of Care between givers and nongivers. A marketing research firm was hired to tackle the problem, and based on interviews with Canopy of Care personnel and a review of secondary sources, the following summary of ideas was developed to guide the research:

1. The manner in which a firm conducts its Canopy of Care campaign may negatively affect employee giving. Employee reactions to the following issues could be important in this regard:
   a. Employees are pressured to contribute by management.
   b. Firms participate in Canopy of Care campaigns to enhance their image.
   c. Employees would like to be more involved with their firms' Canopy of Care campaigns.
   d. Employees think that the union should be involved in Canopy of Care campaigns.

2. Employees who have inaccurate information about Canopy of Care's functions and activities are less likely to give. Influential knowledge factors could be the following:
   a. Employees think that Canopy of Care receives government funding.

---

[1]The contributions of Jacqueline C. Hitchon to the development of this case are gratefully acknowledged.

b. Employees don't know about the donor option program.

c. Employees of firms conducting Canopy of Care campaigns have more accurate knowledge about Canopy of Care.

3. Employees who have negative attitudes toward and perceptions about Canopy of Care are less likely to give. Key negative attitudes and perceptions could include the following:

a. Canopy of Care is inefficient.

b. Canopy of Care programs are not useful to employees in general.

c. Canopy of Care funds programs that do not aid an employee and his or her family.

d. Canopy of Care helps only the poor.

METHOD

The previously outlined issues were addressed by means of a questionnaire (see Figure 1). Because lists of employees might be considered confidential by many businesses, it was decided that the research population would be broadened from employees of companies solicited by Canopy of Care to all adult employees in the area. The white pages in the local telephone book could then be used as the sampling frame. Accordingly, professional interviewers were hired to complete the telephone survey using Plus-One dialing. Because the target population was employed adults, the majority of whom are working away from home during the day, phone calls were placed during evening hours.

FIGURE 1

Name of interviewer _____

(Interviewer — fill out for each person:)

First name _____

Time called _____

Date _____

Sex of respondent   M   or   F   {**Do not ask**}

Telephone # _____

Hello, my name is _____

{**If a child answers, ask:**} *Could I please speak to someone over 16 who is employed?*

I am conducting a survey for Canopy of Care. I'd appreciate it if you would answer a few questions. I will not be soliciting donations.

1. *Which of the programs funded by Canopy of Care do you feel is the most important?*_____

---

continued

Figure 1   *Continued*

2. *Have you been employed in the last year?*   Y   or   N

{**If No, stop questionnaire.**}

3. *Does your employer conduct a Canopy of Care campaign?*   Y   or   N

{**If No, go to question #8.**}

4. *How would you describe your company's attitude toward employee giving? Would you say:* {**Read a–c.**}
   a.   The company is against employee giving.
   b.   The company is neutral to the entire issue.
   c.   The company encourages employee giving.
   d.   Don't know.

5. *For the following statements, please indicate whether you Agree, have No opinion, or Disagree.*

The company should support Canopy of Care.	A, N, D
Pressure is put on me to contribute.	A, N, D
The Canopy of Care fund drive should be run by the company's executives.	A, N, D
The company wants to contribute in order to help its image.	A, N, D
More employees at all levels should be involved in the Canopy of Care fund and its fund drive.	A, N, D
Unions should not be involved in the Canopy of Care fund drive.	A, N, D
Canopy of Care should solicit people at home.	A, N, D

6. *Please answer the following question Yes or No.*
   Did you, personally, give money to Canopy of Care last year?   Y   or   N

{**If Yes, go to #8.**}

7. *We are interested in why people do not contribute. The following is a list of answers others have given. Please tell me which, if any, apply to you.*

{**Read each and ask for a yes or a no.**}

   a.   _____   Someone else in my household had already contributed.
   b.   _____   I did not have the money at the time.
   c.   _____   I gave to other charities.
   d.   _____   I volunteered my services to Canopy of Care instead of contributing money.
   e.   _____   I volunteered my services to other charities instead of contributing to Canopy of Care.
   f.   _____   I did not give because Canopy of Care spends its money inefficiently.
   g.   _____   None of the above.

FIGURE 1   *Continued*

8. *To how many different charities do you think Canopy of Care gives money?*

{**Interviewer — Circle the appropriate response.**}

    a. 0–20
    b. 21–40
    c. 41–80
    d. 81–100
    e. More than 100
    f. Don't know.

9. *For the following statements, please indicate whether you Agree, have No opinion, Disagree, or Don't Know.*

The programs funded by Canopy of Care are useful.	A, N, D, DK
The government should be responsible for the type of services Canopy of Care agencies provide.	A, N, D, DK
Canopy of Care programs are not useful to me or my family.	A, N, D, DK
Canopy of Care agencies help only the poor.	A, N, D, DK
Canopy of Care receives government funding.	A, N, D, DK
Canopy of Care can be viewed as a kind of insurance policy for everyone.	A, N, D, DK
Canopy of Care funds programs it should not support.	A, N, D, DK

10. *Respond True or False — You can specify which charity your money goes to when donating to Canopy of Care.*   T   or   F   or   DK

{**If False, or Don't Know, go to #12.**}

11. *Again, True or False — The money donated really goes to the specific charity picked.*   T   or   F   or   DK

12. *I'm going to read to you a list that includes a number of organizations. Please tell me which of these groups, if any, you contributed to last year.*

{**Interviewer — please read the list, and check the appropriate spaces.**}

  _____ American Cancer Society
  _____ Red Cross
  _____ American Heart Association
  _____ March of Dimes
  _____ Easter Seals
  _____ Multiple Sclerosis
  _____ Salvation Army
  _____ MACC Fund
  _____ UPAF (United Performing Arts Funds)
  _____ Other
  _____ Did not contribute

continued

FIGURE 1   *Continued*

13. *How many employees are there in the firm for which you work?*

{Interviewer — Circle the appropriate response.}

    a. Fewer than 100 employees
    b. 100 to 500 employees
    c. More than 500 employees
    d. Don't know

14. *For what type of organization do you work?*

{Interviewer — please read the list.}

    a. Manufacturing
    b. Government
    c. Wholesale/retail
    d. Service industry — includes trades and professions
    e. Other

15. *Are you employed full-time?*   Y or N

16. *In your present company, are you in a managerial position?*   Y or N

17. *Do you presently belong to a union?*   Y or N

18. *How long have you lived in the area?*
    a. Less than 1 year
    b. 1 year up to 3 years
    c. 3 years up to 5 years
    d. More than 5 years

19. *How many children do you have at home?*
    a. None
    b. One
    c. Two
    d. Three
    e. More than three

20. *What is your marital status?*
    a. Married
    b. Single — never married
    c. Separated
    d. Divorced
    e. Widowed
    f. Other

FIGURE 1   *Continued*

---

21. *What is your zip code?*_____

22. *What is your race?* {**Read list.**}
   a.   White
   b.   African-American
   c.   Hispanic
   d.   Native American
   e.   Asian
   f.   Other_____

23. *Please stop me when I come to the category that contains your age.*
   a.   16–24
   b.   25–34
   c.   35–49
   d.   50 and over

24. *Stop me when we get to your annual personal income level before taxes.*
   a.   Less than $10,000
   b. $10,000 to under $15,000
   c. $15,000 to under $25,000
   d. $25,000 to under $40,000
   e.   More than $40,000

Questions

1. Which items in the questionnaire correspond to each of the issues guiding the research?
2. How would you propose to analyze the data to investigate these issues? Be specific.

CASE 5.5
CTM Productions (B)[1]

CTM Productions, formerly Children's Theatre of Madison, was formed in 1965 to "produce theater of the highest quality." CTM's mission is to ensure that the theatre's efforts are inclusive of the entire family. For CTM to fulfill its role in the community,

---

[1]The contributions of Sara L. Pitterle to this case are gratefully acknowledged.

the organization must identify its present audience in terms of demographic, psychographic, and media-exposure characteristics.

The research team decided to study the audience of CTM's production *To Kill a Mockingbird*. The study had three major objectives: (1) to develop an audience profile including demographic and media-exposure data; (2) to provide a framework and data collection instrument for future marketing research; and (3) to supply a list of potential season subscribers.

CTM had never undertaken marketing research prior to this study, so internal secondary information about previous audiences did not exist. External secondary information provided guidance as to the types of questions to be asked in a survey and the appropriate phrasing of these questions. The questionnaire is shown in Figure 1 of CTM Productions (A) — Case 3.5.

CTM's volunteer ushers distributed the survey at each of the 15 performances of *To Kill a Mockingbird*. The number of completed surveys for each show varied with the size of the audience for that show. A total of 1,016 usable surveys were collected during the course of the study. The data coding scheme for the survey is shown in Figure 1. The research team wishes to analyze the data in order to understand the profile of CTM audiences in general as well as how the audience profiles vary between different performances of the same production.

FIGURE 1   Coding Format for CTM Productions Questionnaire

Column(s)	Question Number	Variable	Coding Specification
1	—	Weekend of performance	1 = First weekend
			2 = Second weekend
			3 = Third weekend
2	—	Day and time of performance	1 = Friday, 7:30 P.M.
			2 = Saturday, 3:30 P.M.
			3 = Saturday, 7:30 P.M.
			4 = Sunday, 1:00 P.M.
			5 = Sunday, 3:30 P.M.
3–4	—	Performance in production	1 = Weekend 1, Show 1
			2 = Weekend 1, Show 2
			3 = Weekend 1, Show 3
			4 = Weekend 1, Show 4
			5 = Weekend 1, Show 5
			6 = Weekend 2, Show 1
			7 = Weekend 2, Show 2
			8 = Weekend 2, Show 3
			9 = Weekend 2, Show 4
			10 = Weekend 2, Show 5
			11 = Weekend 3, Show 1
			12 = Weekend 3, Show 2

FIGURE 1 *Continued*

Column(s)	Question Number	Variable	Coding Specification
			13 = Weekend 3, Show 3
			14 = Weekend 3, Show 4
			15 = Weekend 3, Show 5
5–7	1	Zip code — last three digits	999 = No response
			000 = Outside of 53XXX
			XXX = other digit combos
8	2a	Attending first CTM production	1 = Yes, box checked
			2 = No, box checked
9–22		Past Attendance of CTM productions	Questions 2b–2o
9	2b	Season subscriber 91/92	1 = Yes, box checked
10	2c	*Wind in the Willows*	2 = No, box checked
11	2d	*A Christmas Carol 92*	
12	2e	*Babar II* — Plan to attend	
13	2f	Season subscriber 90/91	
14	2g	*Red Shoes*	
15	2h	*A Christmas Carol 91*	
16	2i	*Anne of Green Gables*	
17	2j	*Narnia*	
18	2k	Season subscriber 89/90	
19	2l	*Beauty and the Beast*	
20	2m	*A Christmas Carol 90*	
21	2n	*I Remember Mama*	
22	2o	*Babar the Elephant*	
23–28		Who attending with today	Questions 3a–3f
23	3a	By myself	1 = Yes, box checked
24	3b	Adult friends	2 = No, box checked
25	3c	Partner/spouse	9 = All blank = No response
26	3d	Unrelated kids	
27	3e	My kids	
28	3f	Other families	
29–34		Who attended with in past	Questions 4a–4f
29	4a	By myself	1 = Yes, box checked
30	4b	Adult friends	2 = No, box checked
31	4c	Partner/spouse	9 = All blank = No response
32	4d	Unrelated kids	
33	4e	My kids	
34	4f	Other families	
35–40		CTM activity participation	Questions 5a–5f
35		After-school drama classes	1 = Yes, box checked
36		Summer school	2 = No, box checked
37		Auditions	9 = All blank = No response

continued

FIGURE 1   *Continued*

Column(s)	Question Number	Variable	Coding Specification
38		Performances	
39		Have not participated	
40		Did not know I could	
41–55		Media Exposure for *To Kill a Mockingbird*	Questions 6a–6o
41	6a	Season brochure	1 = Yes, box checked
42	6b	Poster	2 = No, box checked
43	6c	*State Journal* story	9 = All blank = No response
44	6d	*Capital Times* story	
45	6e	*Isthmus* story	
46	6f	Other story	
47	6g	*State Journal* ad	
48	6h	*Capital Times* ad	
49	6i	*Isthmus* ad	
50	6j	Other ad	
51	6k	Radio	
52	6l	Television	
53	6m	Magazine	
54	6n	Word of mouth	
55	6o	Other media/exposure	
56	7	Attending because knew cast member	1 = Yes; 2 = No; 9 = No response
57–62		Events attended in the last 6 months	Questions 8a–8f
57	8a	Sports	1 = Yes, box checked
58	8b	Museums	2 = No, box checked
59	8c	Movies	9 = All blank = No response
60	8d	Lectures	
61	8e	Live musical performances	
62	8f	Other live theatrical performances	
63	9	Gender of survey respondent	1 = Female; 0 = Male; 9 = No response
64	10	Age category of respondent	1 = 16–20 6 = 61–70
			2 = 21–30 7 = 71–80
			3 = 31–40 8 = 81–100
			4 = 41–50 9 = No response
			5 = 51–60
65	11	Method of transport to performance	1 = Walk 4 = Other
			2 = Car 9 = No response
			3 = Bus
66	12	Distance traveled to performance	1 = Within Madison
			2 = Less than 5 miles
			3 = 6–10 miles
			4 = Over 10 miles
			9 = No response

FIGURE 1   *Continued*

Column(s)	Question Number	Variable	Coding Specification
67	13	Time lived in Madison/SC Wis.	1 = Do not live here 2 = Just arrived 3 = 1–3 years 4 = 4–7 years 5 = More 9 = No response
68	14	Level of education	1 = Some high school 2 = High school graduate 3 = Some college 4 = College graduate 5 = Some graduate school 6 = Graduate school graduate 7 = More 9 = No response
69	15	Annual household income	1 = Below $20,000 2 = $21–$30,000 3 = $31–$40,000 4 = $41–$50,000 5 = More than $50,000 6 = Not sure 7 = Do not wish to reply 9 = No response
70	16	Dual-income household	1 = Yes; 2 = No; 9 = No response
71	17	Number of people in household	1 = 1 (person) 5 = 5 2 = 2 6 = 6 3 = 3 7 = More 4 = 4 9 = No response
72–78		Number children in grade categories	Questions 18a–18g
72	18a	Not in school yet	1, 2, . . . = Yes, # = Quantity
73	18b	Kindergarten–3rd grade	0 = None, box not checked
74	18c	4th–5th grade	9 = All blank = No response
75	18d	6th–8th grade	
76	18e	High school	
77	18f	College	
78	18g	Other	
79	19	Like to be on mailing list?	1 = Yes; 0 = No; 9 = No response
80	20	CTM member	1 = Yes; 0 = No; 9 = No response

Questions

1. Discuss the implications for CTM's marketing team if there are significant differences in the demographic profiles of those people attending the afternoon versus evening shows.

2. Generate *a priori* hypotheses about the demographic profiles for the *To Kill a Mockingbird* performances. Identify the cross-tabulations necessary to test your hypotheses. Explain why these particular cross-tabulations are necessary.

3. Using data provided by your instructor, run one-way tabulations on this data. Discuss the general findings from these tabulations.

4. Run the cross-tabulations that you chose. What recommendations would you make to CTM based on these tables? Are the recommendations actionable? Explain.

5. What are the limitations of these profiles? Explain.

CASE 5.6
Young Ideas Publishing Company (B)[1]

Young Ideas Publishing Company was founded three years ago by Linda Halley and her business partner, Teresa Martinez. Thus far, the company has published two novels, *Illusions of Summer* and *Ultimate Choices,* both of which were written by Halley. The novels address several controversial social and political topics and are targeted toward high-school–age teenagers (ages 15 to 18 years). Both books have received critical praise but have not fared well commercially. Distributors have been unwilling to carry the books, believing that no real market demand exists for novels of this type. Halley, however, maintains that her novels would appeal to teens, particularly ''nonconformist'' teens — by her definition, teens who take an interest in social and political issues.

   In an effort to generate insights into the local teen market, Halley has retained the services of a young marketing researcher. A research project has been designed to focus on the potential demand for the product among teens as well as potential marketing-mix elements. A questionnaire has been designed and administered to 166 teens in the target age group. A portion of the questionnaire is shown in Figure 1; note that a scale to measure the nonconformity construct is included.

[1]The contributions of Tom J. Brown to the development of this case are gratefully acknowledged.

FIGURE 1   **Partial Questionnaire/Coding**

The following is a portion of a questionnaire administered to teens ages 15 to 18 years. The questionnaire was designed to gather information and opinions pertaining to reading habits, subject matter preferences, and related issues.

NOTE: Nonresponses were coded as "9" or "99."

For the first group of questions, respondents were asked to check the appropriate box.

1. *On average, how many books do you read for pleasure outside of school in one month?*
   ☐ Less than one   ☐ Four
   ☐ One   ☐ Five
   ☐ Two   ☐ Six
   ☐ Three   ☐ I never read any.

2. *In the last 12 months, where have you usually gotten the books you have read for pleasure?*
   ☐ I never read any.   ☐ Store other than book store
   ☐ Public library   ☐ Book club
   ☐ School library   ☐ Mail order other than book club
   ☐ Home   ☐ Receive as gifts
   ☐ Borrow from another person   ☐ Other
   ☐ Book store

3. *On average, what would you pay for a new paperback book?*
   ☐ Less than $3.00   ☐ $6.00 to $6.99
   ☐ $3.00 to $3.99   ☐ $7.00 to $7.99
   ☐ $4.00 to $4.99   ☐ $8.00 or more
   ☐ $5.00 to $5.99

In the following section, the teens were asked to judge the importance of various features of books in their decision process of purchasing a book.

	Very Important	Somewhat Important	Neither Important nor Unimportant	Somewhat Unimportant	Very Unimportant
4. *The story description*	☐	☐	☐	☐	☐
5. *The author*	☐	☐	☐	☐	☐
6. *The price*	☐	☐	☐	☐	☐

continued

FIGURE 1 *Continued*

Next, respondents were asked to circle the appropriate number corresponding to how likely they were to read books within various subject-matter categories.

	Extremely Likely			Neither Likely nor Unlikely			Extremely Unlikely
7. *Science fiction*	1	2	3	4	5	6	7
8. *Humor/comedy*	1	2	3	4	5	6	7
9. *Mystery/suspense*	1	2	3	4	5	6	7
10. *Political*	1	2	3	4	5	6	7
11. *Romance*	1	2	3	4	5	6	7
12. *Social issues/problems*	1	2	3	4	5	6	7

To determine the degree to which a teen was "nonconformist," he/she was asked to indicate his/her level of agreement with each of the following statements.

	Strongly Agree	Agree	Disagree	Strongly Disagree
13. *When I make decisions, I like to get other people's opinions.*	1	2	3	4
14. *I would lead a demonstration for a social cause if I felt strongly about it.*	1	2	3	4
15. *I fit in well with society.*	1	2	3	4
16. *I respect the opinions of most adults.*	1	2	3	4
17. *I like to try to change society.*	1	2	3	4
18. *It's important to me that I fit in well with other students my age.*	1	2	3	4

FIGURE 1 *Continued*

	Strongly Agree	Agree	Disagree	Strongly Disagree
19. *I would participate in a local/national campaign to promote a candidate who represented my views.*	1	2	3	4
20. *My life-style is different than most students my own age.*	1	2	3	4
21. *I keep up with current events.*	1	2	3	4
22. *I don't like to call attention to myself.*	1	2	3	4
23. *If I feel strongly about something, I need to make my statement even if my friends disagree.*	1	2	3	4
24. *I try to avoid conflict with my parents.*	1	2	3	4
25. *Keeping up with the trends is important to me.*	1	2	3	4

Finally, two of the classification questions from the questionnaire are presented.

26. *What is your age?* _____ *years old.*
    [actual age was coded]

27. *Are you male or female?*
    ☐ Male
    ☐ Female

Questions

1. Items 13 through 25 in Figure 1 attempt to measure nonconformity. Define "non-conformity" based on these items. How well do these items tap into the construct? What other items could (or should) have been included?

2. Analyze the data provided by your instructor using cross-tabulations or other analyses. Summarize your findings and make recommendations. Include descriptions of the student market in general, the most likely student market for books of this nature (if one exists), and the "nonconformist" student market.

CASE 5.7

Madison Gas and Electric Company (B)[1]

Madison Gas and Electric Company (MG&E) is a public utility serving the Madison, Wisconsin, metropolitan area. For a number of years, MG&E had extensively advertised the twin themes of energy conservation and electric and gas safety [see Case 2.6, Madison Gas and Electric Company (A), for more details]. In 1993 the company was compelled to deal with a new Wisconsin law requiring that a public utility could not charge its ratepayers for any expenditure for advertising unless the advertising contained a verbal or written disclaimer that the expenditure would be charged to the utility's ratepayers. MG&E's management thought that the introduction of a disclaimer in the company's advertisements might have a negative impact on viewers' evaluation of the company's ads. As a consequence, a study was commissioned in which the influence of disclaimers on viewers' evaluations of MG&E's advertisements was to be examined.

SELECTION OF RESPONDENTS

The research design to investigate the question of whether the disclaimer affected viewers' reactions to the ads involved exposing people to the ads and assessing their evaluations. More specifically, a sample of 450 subjects was selected, 150 subjects from each of the three main shopping centers serving the Madison area: East Towne, West Towne, and South Towne. All three centers were located on the outskirts of Madison. The West Towne center was located in a higher-income area of the city and served primarily professionals and other white-collar workers. The East Towne center was located in a lower income area and served primarily blue-collar workers. The South Towne center served a mix of the two groups.

Subjects were selected in each mall according to the following procedure. Interviewers were assigned specific spots in the corridors and stopped adults going by at irregular intervals. Each adult was asked whether he or she had heard, seen, or read any utility advertising in the past few months and whether the household was a MG&E customer. Those who said yes to both questions were asked to participate in a study involving customer reactions to some selected commercials.

---

[1]The contributions of Thomas Noordewier to the development of this case are gratefully acknowledged.

TREATMENT CONDITIONS

Each qualified subject was assigned to one of three treatment conditions. In each treatment condition, the subject was exposed to four ads and was asked to rate each commercial immediately after seeing it, using a scale that ran from "high rating" to "worst rating" on each of the attributes "helpful," "informative," "necessary," and "believable." Moreover, after viewing all four commercials, each subject was asked to provide an overall (summary) evaluation of the commercials, using "excellent" to "poor" descriptors. Subjects were also asked to indicate which ad they liked the "best" and the "least" and why. Finally, each subject was asked to respond to a set of demographic and socioeconomic questions. See Figure 1 for a copy of the screening questionnaire and Figure 1 in Case 2.6, Madison Gas and Electric Company (A), for a copy of the viewing questionnaire (South Towne example).

The treatment conditions differed with respect to the presence or absence of the disclaimer; otherwise, the ads in each treatment condition were the same. One ad involved the availability of a free home energy audit, another described a free commercial energy audit, a third was concerned with gas safety, and the fourth offered congratulations for conserving energy. All subjects in Treatment Condition A were shown video-

FIGURE 1   **Screening Questionnaire (asked of all three groups)**

We're conducting research for a local utility company. Have you seen, heard, or read any advertisements from your gas and electric company in the past few months?

Where do you recall having seen, heard, or read the advertisements for your gas and electric company?

1. Radio
2. TV
3. Newspaper
4. Magazines
5. Billboards
6. Bill inserts
7. Other (specify)
8. Don't remember/don't know

Please tell me what those advertisements said. Tell me as many different things as you can remember. **PROBE**

If it is not clear that the person is an MG&E customer, ask if he or she is.

If not an MG&E customer, dismiss. If MG&E customer, but not at all aware of television advertising, dismiss.

TABLE 1 Summary of Treatment Conditions*

| | Shopping Center/Treatment Group | | | | | | | | |
| | South Towne | | | West Towne | | | East Towne | | |
Commercial Number	A	B	C	A	B	C	A	B	C
1	DW/O	DW	FW	EW/O	EW	FW/O	FW/O	FW	FW
2	EW/O	EW	DW/O	GW/O	GW	DW/O	DW/O	DW	DW
3	FW/O	FW	GW	DW/O	DW	GW	GW/O	GW	GW/O
4	GW/O	GW	EW/O	FW/O	FW	EW	EW/O	EW	EW/O

*The various symbols are:
  D: home energy audit ad;
  E: congratulations for conserving energy ad;
  F: gas safety ad;
  G: commercial energy audit ad;
  W: with the disclaimer;
  W/O: without the disclaimer.

taped television commercials without any disclaimers. All those in Treatment Condition B were shown the same four ads with the disclaimer "the cost of this message is included in MG&E's rates" inserted at the end of the message. Those in Treatment Condition C saw two ads with the disclaimer attached and two ads without the disclaimer. The ads to which the disclaimer was attached varied by shopping center, and the order in which the ads were seen also varied by shopping center. The complete design is displayed in Table 1. A complete list of the data is available from your instructor.

Questions

1. What is the effect of the disclaimer?
2. Are there differences in reactions to each of the four commercials by mall?

CASE 5.8
Chestnut Ridge Country Club (B)[1]

For many years, Chestnut Ridge Country Club has been one of the most well-respected country clubs in the Elma, Tennessee, area. It has one of the finest golf courses in the state, and its dining and banquet facilities are highly regarded. In addition, the club provides its members with outdoor tennis courts and a swimming pool. The country club's outstanding reputation is due in part to the commitment by Chestnut Ridge's Board of Directors to keep attuned to the needs of current and potential club members. Recently, the board was concerned that applications for membership to Chestnut Ridge were declining. The board members believed that a similar decline in applications was

[1]The contributions of David M. Szymanski to the development of this case are gratefully acknowledged.

1. *The following is a list of factors that may be influential in the decision to join a
   country club. Please rate the factors according to their importance to you in terms
   of your membership at Chestnut Ridge. Circle the appropriate response, where 1 =
   not at all important and 5 = extremely important.*

Golf facilities	1 2 3 4 5
Tennis facilities	1 2 3 4 5
Pool facilities	1 2 3 4 5
Dining facilities	1 2 3 4 5
Social events	1 2 3 4 5
Family activities	1 2 3 4 5
Number of friends who are members	1 2 3 4 5
Cordiality of members	1 2 3 4 5
Prestige	1 2 3 4 5
Location	1 2 3 4 5

2. *What is the approximate distance of your residence from the club (in miles)?*
   ____ 0–2 miles   ____ 3–5 miles   ____ 6–10 miles   ____ 10+ miles

3. *Age:* ____ 21–30   ____ 31–40   ____ 41–50   ____ 51–60   ____ 61 or over

4. *Sex:* ____ male   ____ female

5. *Marital status:* ____ married   ____ single   ____ widowed   ____ divorced

6. *Number of dependents including yourself:*
   ____ 2 or less   ____ 3–4   ____ 5 or more

not occurring at the other country clubs in the area — Alden, Chalet, and Lancaster. As
a result, the board contracted an outside research firm to survey members of the various
clubs to see how Chestnut Ridge was perceived in comparison to the others [see Case
2.3, Chestnut Ridge Country Club (A), for more background information and some
summary results].

Currently the board is interested in determining what personal characteristics, if any,
differentiate the members of Alden, Chalet, Chestnut Ridge, and Lancaster country
clubs. The board wants to know if demographic factors such as age, sex, income, and so
on, or club features themselves, bear any relation to the decision to join one of the
country clubs in the area.

METHODOLOGY

To ascertain this information, the board surveyed a sample of randomly selected members of Chestnut Ridge. Various questions were asked, including questions concerning
member demographics and features that were influential in the members' decision to join
a country club. The questions used to assess these two issues are shown in Figure 1.

Ninety-three (93) questionnaires were mailed and 63 usable surveys were returned, for a response rate of 68 percent.

The results of the survey of Chestnut Ridge members were to be used in conjunction with the responses to a similar set of questions asked respondents in a related survey. See Figure 1 in Case 2.3, Chestnut Ridge Country Club (A), for a copy of the questionnaire used for Alden, Chalet, and Lancaster members. In that survey, 87 randomly chosen members from each of the three clubs were mailed a questionnaire. Sixty-three (63) surveys from each member group were returned. In all, 252 survey responses were available for analysis, 63 from the Chestnut Ridge survey and 189 from the survey of other country clubs. A list of the data is available from your instructor.

Question

1. Are there any demographic factors or club features deemed influential in the decision to join a country club that differentiate current members of Alden, Chalet, Chestnut Ridge, and Lancaster country clubs?

CASE 5.9
Star Equipment (B)[1]

Star Equipment is a Fortune 500 company manufacturing technologically advanced equipment for numerous purposes. Star's office-products division is one of the three largest manufacturers of office equipment in the world. Traditionally, it's largest competitors in this area have been Vetra and Calt. However, Star has also been facing significant competition in recent years from a number of other smaller, specialized office-equipment manufacturers.

In order to ensure its future competitiveness, Star's office-products division managers developed a four-stage plan to promote sales: (1) identify key accounts for Star's office products, (2) examine the purchase decision process within these key accounts, (3) determine the critical vendor services sought by these accounts, and (4) assess the performance of Star and its two main competitors on these characteristics.

RESEARCH METHOD

Star's marketing research team designed a two-stage research project involving both secondary and primary research to gather the information identified in the four strategies. The first stage of the project involved exhaustive secondary research along with internal and external depth interviews to identify the vendor attributes important to office-

---

[1]The contributions of Sara L. Pitterle to this case are gratefully acknowledged.

T<small>ABLE</small> 1   **Attributes Chosen As Most and Least Important**

Attribute	Most Important				Least Important			
	1	2	3	4	1	2	3	4
a	183	0	0	0	33	0	0	0
b	48	75	0	0	44	8	0	0
c	8	13	5	0	110	32	3	0
d	37	101	40	2	4	7	0	0
e	12	71	104	26	1	5	1	1
f	2	16	47	29	26	35	12	0
g	4	6	16	5	37	62	21	1
h	1	10	30	21	9	29	25	8
i	2	3	31	102	4	10	16	4
j	3	2	11	23	13	49	45	5
k	0	3	9	24	4	37	54	11
l	0	0	6	1	0	7	91	130
m	0	0	0	62	0	0	3	104

equipment customers. Thirteen vendor characteristics were identified as being of some importance to customers.

The thirteen characteristics were incorporated in a survey in which respondents were asked to select the four most- and four least-important characteristics. Respondents were also asked to rate the vendors considered for their company's most recent office-equipment purchase on each of the attributes. Since Star was interested primarily in its own performance ratings along with its two major competitors, Calt and Vetra, these three vendors were explicitly specified in Question 3 in the survey; an "other" column was provided to capture the ratings of smaller vendors that may have been considered. [See Case 5.3, Star Equipment (A), for additional background information and initial results.]

SEGMENTATION BASED ON IMPORTANCE SCORES

Star planned to use cluster analysis to group together these respondents who chose similar vendor characteristics as being most and least important. Specifically, the analysts planned to treat the four characteristics in Question 2 chosen as most important by each respondent as a set and the four characteristics chosen as least important as another set. The remaining five characteristics were to be considered a set of neutral attributes. Table 1 shows the frequency tables for the attributes chosen as least and most important in Question 2. The actual question is shown in Figure 1. [See Case 5.3, Star Equipment (A), for the complete questionnaire.]

After forming clusters based on the importance ratings given to the vendor characteristics by survey respondents, the research team planned to analyze cluster membership to determine Star's performance ratings as well as the demographic characteristics of the

FIGURE 1   **Primary Vendor Characteristics**

Q2. Listed below are vendor characteristics that could be used to make a decision about which equipment to purchase. Thinking about your most recent purchase decision:

A. Check (✔) the four (4) <u>most</u> important vendor characteristics in your purchase decision.

B. Check (✔) the four (4) <u>least</u> important vendor characteristics in your purchase decision.

Vendor Characteristics	A Most Important (Check 4)		B Least Important (Check 4)	
a. Vendor values a long-term relationship and works to meet my organization's unique needs.........................	01 ☐	15–16/	01 ☐	23–24/
b. My relationships with the vendor's sales and support representatives are easy and productive	02 ☐	17–18/	02 ☐	25–26/
c. Vendor enables my organization to have a smooth decision process..............	03 ☐	19–20/	03 ☐	27–28/
d. The vendor establishes fair pricing policies for products and services	04 ☐	21–22/	04 ☐	29–30/
e. The vendor's service organization is responsive to my organization's needs....	05 ☐		05 ☐	
f. The vendor offers an extensive line of reliable products meeting the needs of my organization.........................	06 ☐		06 ☐	
g. The vendor's solutions enable my organization to use people, space, and resources efficiently	07 ☐		07 ☐	
h. The vendor offers software to increase the productivity and satisfaction of my department and employees	08 ☐		08 ☐	
i. Vendor's products are easy to use	09 ☐		09 ☐	
j. The vendor's solutions help my business grow	10 ☐		10 ☐	
k. The vendor's solutions give me the ability to offer quick response to my customers' needs	11 ☐		11 ☐	
l. The vendor provides my company with solutions that protect the safety and legality of information	12 ☐		12 ☐	
m. The vendor provides my firm with technological advantages today that can be leveraged to meet our future requirements	13 ☐		13 ☐	

respondents within each cluster. The results of this analysis were to be used to identify clusters of opportunities for Star as well as clusters in which Star's competitors appear to have an advantage.

Questions

1. Is cluster analysis the most appropriate technique to use in order to meet the objectives of this project? What other analyses may prove helpful in this situation?

2. How must the data be recoded to be appropriate for cluster analysis? How many new variables are necessary in order to recode the data from survey Question 2 so that it can be used in cluster analysis?

3. Using data provided by your instructor, perform a cluster analysis aimed at determining the appropriate number of customer groupings based on the importance of characteristics. Justify your choice of clusters.

4. How do the obtained clusters differ? In which clusters does Star Equipment dominate? In which clusters do Vetra and/or Calt dominate? What general recommendations would you make to Star Equipment based on this analysis?

CASE 5.10
Fabhus, Inc.

Fabhus, Inc., a manufacturer of prefabricated homes located in Atlanta, Georgia, had experienced steady, sometimes spectacular, growth since its founding in the early 1950s. By the early 1990s, however, things were not so rosy. Sales fell off 8 percent from 1991 to 1992 and another 6 percent from 1992 to 1993, in spite of a very attractive interest-rate environment for home building.

In an attempt to offset the decline in sales, company management decided to use marketing research to get a better perspective on their customers so that they could better target their marketing efforts. After much discussion among the members of the executive committee, it was finally determined that the following questions would be important to address in this research effort.

1. What is the demographic profile of the typical Fabhus customer?

2. What initially attracts these customers to a Fabhus home?

3. Do Fabhus home customers consider other factory-built homes when making their purchase decision?

4. Are Fabhus customers satisfied with their homes? If they are not, what particular features are dissatisfactory?

METHOD

The research firm that was called in on the project suggested conducting a mail survey to past owners. Preliminary discussions with management revealed that Fabhus had the greatest market penetration near its factory. As one moved further from the factory, the share of the total new housing business that went to Fabhus declined. The company suspected that this might result from the higher prices of the units due to shipping charges. Fabhus relied on a zone-price system in which prices were based on the product delivered at the construction site.

Local dealers actually supervised construction. Each dealer had pricing latitude and could charge more or less than Fabhus's suggested list price. Individual dealers were responsible for seeing that customers were satisfied with their Fabhus home, although Fabhus also had a toll-free number that customers could call if they were not satisfied with the way their dealer handled the construction or if they had problems moving in.

Considering the potential impact distance and dealers might have, the research team thought it was important to sample purchasers in the various zones as well as customers of the various dealers. Since Fabhus's records of houses sold were kept by zone and by date sold within zone, sample respondents were selected in the following way. First, the registration cards per zone were counted. Second, the sample size per zone was determined so that the number of respondents per zone was proportionate to the number of homes sold in the zones. Third, a sample interval, k, was chosen for each zone, a random start between 1 and k was generated, and every kth record was selected. The mail questionnaire shown in Figure 1 was sent to the 423 households selected.

A cover letter informing Fabhus's customers of the general purpose of the survey accompanied the questionnaire, and a new one-dollar bill was included with each survey

---

FIGURE 1   **Factory-Built Home Owners Survey**

---

1. *How did you first learn of the factory-built home that you bought? (check one, please)*

   ☐ Friend or relative   ☐ Direct mail
   ☐ Another customer   ☐ Newspaper
   ☐ Realtor   ☐ Radio
   ☐ Model home   ☐ TV
   ☐ Yellow pages   ☐ Don't remember
   ☐ National magazine   ☐ Other_____

                                           (please specify)

2. *Did you own the land your home is on before you first visited your home builder?*

   ☐ Yes   ☐ No

3. *How long have you lived in your home?* _____ *years*

FIGURE 1 *Continued*

4. *Where did you live before purchasing your factory-built home? (please check one)*
   ☐ Rented a house, apartment, or mobile home
   ☐ Owned a mobile home
   ☐ Owned a conventionally built home
   ☐ Owned another factory-built home
   ☐ Other_____
         (please specify)

5. *Please rate your overall level of satisfaction with your home. (please check one)*
   ☐ Very satisfied
   ☐ Somewhat satisfied
   ☐ Somewhat dissatisfied
   ☐ Very dissatisfied

6. *How important to you were each of the following considerations in purchasing your factory-built home? (please check a box for each item)*

Considerations	Extremely Important	Important	Slightly Important	Not Important
Investment value	☐	☐	☐	☐
Quality	☐	☐	☐	☐
Price	☐	☐	☐	☐
Energy features	☐	☐	☐	☐
Dealer	☐	☐	☐	☐
Exterior style	☐	☐	☐	☐
Floor plan	☐	☐	☐	☐
Interior features	☐	☐	☐	☐
Delivery schedule	☐	☐	☐	☐

7. *Below, please list any other homes you looked at before purchasing the home you chose. Please state the reason you did not purchase the other home.*

Name of Home	Factory-Built?	Reason for Not Purchasing
_____	☐ Yes ☐ No	_____
_____	☐ Yes ☐ No	_____
_____	☐ Yes ☐ No	_____
_____	☐ Yes ☐ No	_____

Now we would like you to please tell us about yourself and your family.

8. *How many children do you have living at home?* _____ children

continued

Figure 1   *Continued*

9. **What is the age of the head of your household?** *(check one, please)*

☐ Under 20   ☐ 35–44   ☐ 55–64
☐ 20–24   ☐ 45–54   ☐ 65 or over
☐ 25–34

10. **What is the occupation of the head of the household?** *(check one, please)*

☐ Professional or official   ☐ Labor or machine operator
☐ Technical or manager   ☐ Foreman
☐ Proprietor   ☐ Service worker
☐ Farmer   ☐ Retired
☐ Craftsperson   ☐ Other_____
☐ Clerical or sales   (please specify)

11. **Which of the following categories includes your family's total annual income?** *(check one, please)*

☐ $10,000   ☐ $40,000–49,999
☐ $10,000–19,999   ☐ $50,000–59,999
☐ $20,000–29,999   ☐ $60,000–69,999
☐ $30,000–39,999   ☐ $70,000 or over

12. **Is the spouse of the head of the household employed?** *(check one, please)*

☐ Spouse employed full-time
☐ Spouse employed part-time
☐ Spouse not employed
☐ Not married

One final question:

13. **Would you recommend your particular factory-built home to someone interested in building a new home?**

☐ Yes   ☐ No

Thank you very much for completing this survey.
Your help in this study is greatly appreciated.

as an incentive to respond. Further, the anonymity of the respondents was guaranteed by enclosing a self-addressed postage-paid postcard in the survey. Respondents were asked to mail the postcard when they mailed their survey. All of those who had not returned their postcards in two weeks were sent a notice reminding them that their survey had not been returned. The combination of incentives, guaranteed anonymity, and follow-up prompted the return of 342 questionnaires for an overall response rate of 81 percent.

A complete list of the data is available from your instructor.

Questions

1. Using the data provided by your instructor and analytic techniques of your own choosing, address as best you can the objectives that prompted the research effort in the first place.

2. Do you think the research design was adequate for the problems posed? Why or why not?

CASE 5.11

Como Western Bank[1]

Como Western Bank is one of several commercial lending institutions located in the Colorado community of Brentwood Hills. The bank maintains four branch offices with one branch each located in the east, west, north, and south districts of town. Its main office is located in downtown Brentwood Hills.

During the past decade, changes in the banking industry in Brentwood Hills have paralleled those taking place nationally, in that the environment has become increasingly complex and competitive. Deregulation, technological innovation, and changing interest rates have all made it difficult for banks to attract and keep customers. Local banks must now compete with insurance companies, multiservice investment firms, and even the government for clients. As a result, lending institutions are focusing increased attention on meeting consumer needs and developing strategies to increase their client base. Como Western is no exception.

A 1982 study of commercial banking in Brentwood Hills showed Como Western to have an above-average proportion of older households, long-time residents of the community, and middle-income persons as customers. The bank appeared to be less successful in attracting younger households, college graduates, and new residents of Brentwood Hills. In addition, the study found noncustomers of Como Western to have a weak image of the bank, even though customers held a very positive image. Bank officials sensed that these results typified the current situation as well. However, because the officials were in the process of developing a comprehensive marketing plan, they desired more up-to-date and detailed information to aid in formulating an appropriate marketing strategy. Therefore, bank officials contracted with the Mestousis Research Agency to study current bank customers. This small, local agency was led by its founder, Mike Mestousis, and Kathy Rendina, who served as the principal investigator on most projects. In addition, it employed six clerical people. The objectives of the study given to the Mestousis Agency were: (1) to determine the demographic profiles of present bank customers; (2) to determine customer awareness, use, and overall perception of current bank services; and (3) to identify new bank services desired by customers.

[1]The contributions of David M. Szymanski to the development of this case are gratefully acknowledged.

RESEARCH METHOD

The Mestousis Agency proposed and the bank's directors agreed that the study should be conducted in two phases. The first phase was designed to increase the research team's familiarity with Como Western's current clientele and service offerings. Several methods of inquiry were used. They included personal interviews with customers, bank employees, and members of the bank's board of directors, as well as a literature search of studies relating to the banking industry. Based on information gathered through these procedures, a questionnaire was developed to be used in the second portion of the project.

Because the information being sought was general yet personal in nature, the mail survey was deemed appropriate for data collection purposes. To encourage a high response rate, a cover letter describing the research objectives and importance of responding was written by the bank president and mailed with each questionnaire, along with a stamped, self-addressed envelope. Furthermore, those who returned the questionnaire became eligible to participate in a drawing to win one of five $50 bills. To ensure anonymity, the name and address of the respondent was to be sealed in a separate envelope, which was supplied, and returned with the questionnaire.

The questionnaire itself was also designed to encourage high response. The instructions made it clear that the information would be held in strict confidence, and the more sensitive questions were asked last. In addition, the questionnaire was extensively pretested using bank customers of various ages and backgrounds.

Several weeks before the questionnaire was mailed, customers were notified by means of the bank's newsletter of the possibility that they would be receiving the questionnaire.

SAMPLING PLAN

The relevant population for the study was defined as all noncommercial customers of Como Western Bank who lived in Brentwood Hills and who were not employees of the bank. The total number of customers meeting these requirements was 10,300. A printout of bank customers revealed that bank records list customers in blocks according to zip codes.

The researchers were of the opinion that 500 survey responses were required to adequately perform the analysis. Anticipating a 30 to 35 percent response rate, 1,500 to 1,600 surveys needed to be mailed. Given 10,300 population elements and the estimated sample size of 1,600, the researchers decided to send a questionnaire to one of every six names on the list. They generated the first name randomly using a table of random numbers. It was the fourth name on the list. They consequently sent questionnaires to the fourth, tenth, sixteenth, and so on names on the list. In all, 1,547 questionnaires were sent and 673 were returned for a response rate of approximately 44 percent. The questionnaire coding form and listing of the data are available from your instructor.

Questions

1. Evaluate the general research design.
2. Evaluate the sampling plan.

3. What do the results suggest with respect to the following:
   a. The demographic characteristics of Como Western's customers?
   b. Customer awareness, use, and perceptions of the various services provided by Como Western?
   c. The relationship, if any, between age and income of the respondents and their overall evaluation of the services provided by Como Western?
4. What new services, if any, should Como Western offer?

CASE 5.12

Steve's Stereo Shop[1]

Steven Jensen is planning to open a new retail electronics store, Steve's Stereo Shop, in a few months. He is currently in the process of selecting different brands of portable radios to offer for sale. He has been assured by regional distributors that he will be allowed to carry several different brands if he chooses to do so.

Specifically, Steve is considering carrying three or four radios from among eight alternatives that he believes meet a certain minimum standard for quality. These alternatives are presented in Figure 1, as are details on two competitive brands (radios sold by Penney's and Sears). Although Steve would like to carry all eight brands of radios, the new business simply cannot afford to stock more than three or four, at least initially.

Steve has several years of experience as the manager of a major electronics store. Over the years, he has determined that many different factors affect a consumer's overall perceptions of these types of portable radios. Among them are the perceived value for the money spent, the ease of use, the fragility of the design, the sound quality, the stability of performance in different locations, the sensitivity in reception of radio signals, and the perceived status of a particular radio. In addition, Steve's experience tells him that consumers tend to group together brands of radios that are similar to each other; certain products seem to "go together" in a customer's mind.

For this reason, Steve wants to be careful to offer models that are perceived by the consumer as being "different." He does not want to offer radios that are all viewed as being similar, because he wants to appeal to different types of customers. Essentially, he wants to be certain that the radios he carries represent the different groupings of radios based on consumer perceptions.

To determine how he might obtain the information he needs to make a decision about which products to carry, Steve contacted one of his former marketing professors. His professor suggested that cluster analysis would be an appropriate research method in this situation.

To implement cluster analysis, Steve and his professor developed the questionnaire reproduced in Figure 2 and administered it to a group of young adults, the age group that

[1]The contributions of Tom J. Brown to the development of this case are gratefully acknowledged.

FIGURE 1   **Description of Radios under Consideration**

Model:	Aiwa HS-T500
List price:	$185
Dust access to tape chamber:	No
Tape controls positioned conveniently on top:	Yes
Level of performance, stationary:	Excellent
Level of performance, moving:	Average
Ability to pull in distant FM stations:	Excellent
Has autoreverse:	Yes
Model:	Sanyo MG-R99
List price:	$135
Dust access to tape chamber:	No
Tape controls positioned conveniently on top:	No
Level of performance, stationary:	Good
Level of performance, moving:	Good
Ability to pull in distant FM stations:	Good
Has autoreverse:	Yes
Model:	Toshiba KT-4066
List price:	$ 99
Dust access to tape chamber:	Yes
Tape controls positioned conveniently on top:	No
Level of performance, stationary:	Average
Level of performance, moving:	Good
Ability to pull in distant FM stations:	Excellent
Has autoreverse:	Yes
Model:	Sony WM-F41
List price:	$ 45
Dust access to tape chamber:	No
Tape controls positioned conveniently on top:	No
Level of performance, stationary:	Average
Level of performance, moving:	Good
Ability to pull in distant FM stations:	Excellent
Has autoreverse:	No
Model:	J.C. Penney 6090
List price:	$ 80
Dust access to tape chamber:	No
Tape controls positioned conveniently on top:	No
Level of performance, stationary:	Good
Level of performance, moving:	Average
Ability to pull in distant FM stations:	Excellent
Has autoreverse:	Yes

FIGURE 1 *Continued*

Model:	Sansui FX-W51R
List price:	$120
Dust access to tape chamber:	No
Tape controls positioned conveniently on top:	No
Level of performance, stationary:	Good
Level of performance, moving:	Below Average
Ability to pull in distant FM stations:	Excellent
Has autoreverse:	Yes

Model:	Quasar GX3666
List price:	$ 35
Dust access to tape chamber:	No
Tape controls positioned conveniently on top:	No
Level of performance, stationary:	Average
Level of performance, moving:	Average
Ability to pull in distant FM stations:	Excellent
Has autoreverse:	No

Model:	Sharp JC-126
List price:	$ 30
Dust access to tape chamber:	No
Tape controls positioned conveniently on top:	No
Level of performance, stationary:	Average
Level of performance, moving:	Average
Ability to pull in distant FM stations:	Good
Has autoreverse:	No

Model:	Sears Cat. No. 21169
List price:	$ 40
Dust access to tape chamber:	No
Tape controls positioned conveniently on top:	Yes
Level of performance, stationary:	Below Average
Level of performance, moving:	Good
Ability to pull in distant FM stations:	Excellent
Has autoreverse:	Yes

Model:	Panasonic RX-SA77
List price:	$100
Dust access to tape chamber:	No
Tape controls positioned conveniently on top:	No
Level of performance, stationary:	Good
Level of performance, moving:	Average
Ability to pull in distant FM stations:	Good
Has autoreverse:	Yes

FIGURE 2 **Radio Survey**

We are interested in your opinion of the models described in Figure 1. Please fill in the following scales by circling the number that best expresses your views.

Aiwa HS-T500

			Average Scores
easy to use	1 2 3 4 5 6 7	hard to use	2.27
excellent value for money	1 2 3 4 5 6 7	rotten value for money	3.91
bad buy	1 2 3 4 5 6 7	good buy	4.18
robust design	1 2 3 4 5 6 7	fragile design	2.64
good sound quality	1 2 3 4 5 6 7	poor sound quality	2.09
unstable performance	1 2 3 4 5 6 7	stable performance	4.64
sensitive performance	1 2 3 4 5 6 7	insensitive performance	3.18
high-status model	1 2 3 4 5 6 7	low-status model	1.91

Sanyo MG-R99

easy to use	1 2 3 4 5 6 7	hard to use	4.36
excellent value for money	1 2 3 4 5 6 7	rotten value for money	4.18
bad buy	1 2 3 4 5 6 7	good buy	4.18
robust design	1 2 3 4 5 6 7	fragile design	3.73
good sound quality	1 2 3 4 5 6 7	poor sound quality	2.91
unstable performance	1 2 3 4 5 6 7	stable performance	4.82
sensitive performance	1 2 3 4 5 6 7	insensitive performance	3.45
high-status model	1 2 3 4 5 6 7	low-status model	3.09

Toshiba KT-4066

easy to use	1 2 3 4 5 6 7	hard to use	3.91
excellent value for money	1 2 3 4 5 6 7	rotten value for money	3.18
bad buy	1 2 3 4 5 6 7	good buy	5.09
robust design	1 2 3 4 5 6 7	fragile design	3.64
good sound quality	1 2 3 4 5 6 7	poor sound quality	3.09
unstable performance	1 2 3 4 5 6 7	stable performance	4.45
sensitive performance	1 2 3 4 5 6 7	insensitive performance	3.36
high-status model	1 2 3 4 5 6 7	low-status model	3.64

Sony WM-F41

easy to use	1 2 3 4 5 6 7	hard to use	5.00
excellent value for money	1 2 3 4 5 6 7	rotten value for money	3.00
bad buy	1 2 3 4 5 6 7	good buy	4.55
robust design	1 2 3 4 5 6 7	fragile design	4.00
good sound quality	1 2 3 4 5 6 7	poor sound quality	3.73
unstable performance	1 2 3 4 5 6 7	stable performance	4.00
sensitive performance	1 2 3 4 5 6 7	insensitive performance	3.91
high-status model	1 2 3 4 5 6 7	low-status model	4.45

Figure 2   *Continued*

J.C. Penney 6090

easy to use	1 2 3 4 5 6 7	hard to use	4.18
excellent value for money	1 2 3 4 5 6 7	rotten value for money	4.18
bad buy	1 2 3 4 5 6 7	good buy	4.45
robust design	1 2 3 4 5 6 7	fragile design	4.18
good sound quality	1 2 3 4 5 6 7	poor sound quality	3.70
unstable performance	1 2 3 4 5 6 7	stable performance	4.45
sensitive performance	1 2 3 4 5 6 7	insensitive performance	3.82
high-status model	1 2 3 4 5 6 7	low-status model	5.27

Sansui FX-W51R

easy to use	1 2 3 4 5 6 7	hard to use	3.82
excellent value for money	1 2 3 4 5 6 7	rotten value for money	5.73
bad buy	1 2 3 4 5 6 7	good buy	2.55
robust design	1 2 3 4 5 6 7	fragile design	4.27
good sound quality	1 2 3 4 5 6 7	poor sound quality	4.70
unstable performance	1 2 3 4 5 6 7	stable performance	2.82
sensitive performance	1 2 3 4 5 6 7	insensitive performance	3.64
high-status model	1 2 3 4 5 6 7	low-status model	3.64

Quasar GX3666

easy to use	1 2 3 4 5 6 7	hard to use	4.82
excellent value for money	1 2 3 4 5 6 7	rotten value for money	2.91
bad buy	1 2 3 4 5 6 7	good buy	4.82
robust design	1 2 3 4 5 6 7	fragile design	4.30
good sound quality	1 2 3 4 5 6 7	poor sound quality	4.00
unstable performance	1 2 3 4 5 6 7	stable performance	4.45
sensitive performance	1 2 3 4 5 6 7	insensitive performance	4.00
high-status model	1 2 3 4 5 6 7	low-status model	5.82

Sharp JC-126

easy to use	1 2 3 4 5 6 7	hard to use	4.45
excellent value for money	1 2 3 4 5 6 7	rotten value for money	3.27
bad buy	1 2 3 4 5 6 7	good buy	4.55
robust design	1 2 3 4 5 6 7	fragile design	4.82
good sound quality	1 2 3 4 5 6 7	poor sound quality	4.64
unstable performance	1 2 3 4 5 6 7	stable performance	4.09
sensitive performance	1 2 3 4 5 6 7	insensitive performance	4.45
high-status model	1 2 3 4 5 6 7	low-status model	5.64

Sears Cat. No. 21169

easy to use	1 2 3 4 5 6 7	hard to use	2.64
excellent value for money	1 2 3 4 5 6 7	rotten value for money	3.27
bad buy	1 2 3 4 5 6 7	good buy	4.45
robust design	1 2 3 4 5 6 7	fragile design	3.91

continued

Figure 2   *Continued*

Sears Cat. No. 21169

good sound quality	1 2 3 4 5 6 7	poor sound quality	4.55
unstable performance	1 2 3 4 5 6 7	stable performance	3.27
sensitive performance	1 2 3 4 5 6 7	insensitive performance	3.91
high-status model	1 2 3 4 5 6 7	low-status model	5.64

Panasonic RX-SA77

easy to use	1 2 3 4 5 6 7	hard to use	3.55
excellent value for money	1 2 3 4 5 6 7	rotten value for money	5.45
bad buy	1 2 3 4 5 6 7	good buy	3.09
robust design	1 2 3 4 5 6 7	fragile design	4.27
good sound quality	1 2 3 4 5 6 7	poor sound quality	3.64
unstable performance	1 2 3 4 5 6 7	stable performance	4.55
sensitive performance	1 2 3 4 5 6 7	insensitive performance	4.00
high-status model	1 2 3 4 5 6 7	low-status model	3.82

Steve thought composed the primary target market for these types of radios. The scores for each of the items are averaged and are shown in Figure 2. Note that several of the scale items have been reversed.

Questions

1. Is cluster analysis appropriate for this situation? Discuss the use of other types of analysis, such as factor analysis or multidimensional scaling (MDS).

2. Using the data provided, perform a cluster analysis to determine which radios "go together." How do these clusters appear to differ?

3. What general recommendations would you make to Steve Jensen?

6

THE RESEARCH REPORT

Formulate Problem

Determine Research Design

Design Data Collection Method and Forms

Design Sample and Collect Data

Analyze and Interpret the Data

Prepare the Research Report

Part 6 consists of one chapter and an epilogue. The chapter discusses one of the most important parts of the entire research process, the research report. The research report often becomes the standard by which the research effort is assessed. Chapter 18 deals with the criteria a research report should satisfy and the form a research report can follow so that it contributes positively to the research effort. The chapter also discusses oral reports and some of the graphic means that can be used to communicate important findings more forcefully. The epilogue ties together the parts of the research process. It reinforces the points made early that the steps in the research process are highly interrelated and that a decision made at one stage has implications for the others as well.

18

CHAPTER

THE RESEARCH REPORT

A frustrated executive of a large corporation recently remarked that he is convinced reports are devices by which the informed ensure that the uninformed remain that way.[1]

To avoid creating the kind of reports that the executive was thinking of requires considerable skill and attention to detail. If length were the criterion of a chapter's importance, there would be an inverse relationship between this chapter and the criterion. The chapter is short, but its subject is vital to the success of the research effort. Regardless of the sophistication displayed in other portions of the research process, the project is a failure if the research report fails. Empirical evidence indicates, for example, that the research report is one of the five most important variables affecting the use of research information.[2] The preceding research steps determine the content. The research report provides the form, and since the report is all that many executives will see of the project, it becomes the yardstick for evaluation. The writer must ensure that the report informs without misinforming.

The report must tell readers what they need and wish to know. Typically, executives are interested in results and must be convinced of the usefulness of the findings. They must be able to act on the report while recognizing the caveats entailed in the results. This means that they must sufficiently appreciate the method to recognize its weaknesses and bounds of error. The researcher must convey the limitations and necessary details of the method to allow this appreciation. However, the researcher must do it in a way that is understandable and useful, and this is often easier said than done.

---

[1]William J. Gallagher, *Report Writing for Management*, (Reading, Mass.: Addison-Wesley Publishing Company, Inc., 1969), p. 1. Much of this introductory section is also taken from this excellent book. See also Richard Hatch, *Business Communication*, 2nd ed. (Chicago: Science Research Associates, 1983).

[2]The other variables are the extent of interaction that researchers have with managers, the research objectives, the degree of surprise in the results, and the stage of the product or service in its life cycle. See Rohit Deshpande and Gerald Zaltman, "A Comparison of Factors Affecting Researcher and Manager Perceptions of Market Research Use," *Journal of Marketing Research,* 21 (February 1984), pp. 32–38. The understandability of the research report also affects managers' trust in it and that, in turn, affects what they do with the information. See, for example, Christine Moorman, Rohit Deshpande, and Gerald Zaltman, "Factors Affecting Trust in Market Research Relationships," *Journal of Marketing,* 57 (January 1993), pp. 81–101.

This chapter, which is designed to assist the researcher in this regard, is divided into four main sections: (1) the criteria by which research reports are evaluated, (2) the parts and forms of the written research report, (3) the oral report, and (4) some graphic means of presenting the results.

FUNDAMENTAL CRITERION OF RESEARCH REPORTS

Research reports are evaluated by one fundamental criterion — communication with the reader. The "iron law" of marketing research holds that "people would rather live with a problem they cannot solve than accept a solution they cannot understand."[3] The reader is not only the reason that the report is prepared but is also the standard by which its success is measured. This means, purely and simply, that the report must be tailor-made for the reader or readers, with due regard for their technical sophistication, interest in the subject area, the circumstances under which they will read the report, and the use they will make of it.

The technical sophistication of the readers determines their capacity for understanding methodological decisions such as experimental design, measurement device, sampling plan, analysis technique, and so on. Readers with little technical sophistication will probably be offended by the use of unexplained technical jargon. "The readers of your reports are busy people, and very few of them can balance a research report, a cup of coffee, and a dictionary at one time."[4] Unexplained jargon may even make such persons suspicious of the report writer. Researchers must be particularly sensitive to this, because, being technical people, they may fail to realize that they are using technical language and terms.

The readers' capacity establishes the technical upper limit of the report, while their interest, circumstances, and intended use restrict its level. These factors delineate individual preferences, and such preferences must be considered by the report writer.

> Some executives demand a minimum report; they want only the results — not a discussion of how the results were obtained. Others want considerable information on the research methods used in the study. Many executives place a premium on brevity, while others demand complete discussion. Some are interested only in the statistical results and not in the researcher's conclusions and recommendations.

> Thus, *the audience determines the type of report*. Researchers must make every effort to acquaint themselves with the *specific preferences of their audiences*. They should not con-

---

[3]Walter B. Wentz, *Marketing Research: Management, Method, and Cases*, 2nd ed. (New York: Harper & Row, 1979), p. 61. David J. Smallen, director of marketing research at Fisher-Price, similarly argues that research reports must be easy to access, easy to understand, easy to use, and easy to believe. See David J. Smallen, "Little People to Puffalumps: Managing Information in an Emerging Marketing Research Environment," paper presented at the 9th Annual Marketing Research Conference of the American Marketing Association, Arlington, Virginia, October 9–12, 1988. See also Edward P. Bailey, *The Plain English Approach to Business Writing* (New York: Oxford University Press, 1990).

[4]Stewart Henderson Britt, "The Communication of Your Research Findings," in Robert Ferber, ed., *Handbook of Marketing Research* (New York: McGraw-Hill, 1974), pp. 1–90. See also Edward R. Steinberg, ed., *Plain Language: Principles and Practice* (Detroit: Wayne State University Press, 1992).

sider these preferences as unalterable, but *any deviations from them should be made with reason and not from ignorance!*[5] (emphasis added)

The report writer's difficulties in tailoring the report are often compounded by the existence of several audiences. The marketing vice-president might have a different technical capacity and level of interest than the manager responsible for the product discussed in the report. There is no easy solution to this problem of "many masters." The researcher has to recognize the potential differences that may arise and must often use a great deal of ingenuity to reconcile them. This sometimes may require the preparation of several reports, each designed for a specific audience, although it is customary to satisfy the conflicting demands with one report containing both technical and nontechnical sections for different readers.

Writing Criteria

Certain specific criteria that the report should satisfy enhance the likelihood that it will indeed communicate with the reader. In particular, the report should be complete, accurate, clear, and concise.[6] These criteria are intimately related. A clear report is an accurate report. For purposes of exposition, though, it helps to discuss the criteria as if they were distinct.

Completeness

A report is complete when it provides all the information readers need in language they understand. This means that the writer must continually ask whether every question in the original assignment has been addressed. What alternatives were examined? What was found? An incomplete report implies that supplementary reports, which are annoying and delay action, will be forthcoming.

The report may be incomplete because it is too brief or too long. The writer may omit necessary definitions and short explanations. Alternatively, the report may be heavy because it is lengthy but not profound. Report writers tend not to waste collected information. However, presenting information outside the interest of the intended readers may distract them from the main issues. If the report is big, it may discourage readers from even attempting to digest its contents. Readers' interests and abilities thus determine what clarification should be added and what findings should be omitted. In general, the amount of detail should be proportionate to the amount of direct control users can exercise over the areas under discussion.

Accuracy

The previous steps in the research process are not the only determinants of accuracy. They are vital, to be sure, for a report cannot be accurate when the basic input is

---

[5]Harper W. Boyd, Jr., Ralph Westfall, and Stanley F. Stasch, *Marketing Research: Text and Cases,* 7th ed. (Homewood, Ill.: Richard D. Irwin, 1989), p. 657.

[6]Gallagher, *Report Writing,* p. 78.

TABLE **18.1**   **Some Examples of Sources of Inaccuracy in Report Writing**

A. *Simple Errors in Addition or Subtraction*

"In the United States, 14 percent of the population has an elementary school education or less, 51 percent has attended or graduated from high school, and 16 percent has attended college."

An oversight such as this (14 + 51 + 16 do not equal 100 percent) can be easily corrected by the author, but not so easily by the reader because he or she may not know if one or more of the percentage values is incorrect or if a category might have been left out of the tally.

B. *Confusion between Percentages and Percentage Points*

"The company's profits as a percentage of sales were 6.0 percent in 1989 and 8.0 percent in 1994. Therefore, they increased only 2.0 percent in five years."

In this example, the increase is, of course, 2.0 percentage points, or 33 percent.

C. *Inaccuracy Caused by Grammatical Errors*

"The reduction in the government's price supports for dairy products has reduced farm income $600 million to $800 million per year."

To express a range of reduction, the author should have written: "The reduction in the government's price supports for dairy products has reduced farm income $600–$800 million per year."

D. *Confused Terminology Resulting in Fallacious Conclusion*

"The Jones' household and annual income increased from $10,000 in 1964 to $30,000 in 1994, thereby tripling the family's purchasing power."

While the Jones' household annual income may have tripled in the 30 years, the family's purchasing power certainly did not, as the cost of living, as measured by the consumer price index, more than tripled in the same period.

---

inaccurate. But even with accurate input, the research report may generate inaccuracies because of carelessness in handling the data, illogical reasoning, or inept phrasing.[7] Thus, accuracy is another writing criterion. Table 18.1 illustrates some examples of sources of inaccuracy in report writing.

An excellent example of inept phrasing and its consequences is provided in Research Realities 18.1 by the experience of Jock Elliott, the chairman emeritus of the Ogilvy & Mather advertising agency. Elliott makes no bones about the importance of being able to write well in order to advance in a career. "As you sail along on your

---

[7]See Gallagher, *Report Writing*, pp. 80–83, for a number of examples that display some of the inaccuracies that may arise. The examples are particularly interesting because they have been extracted from actual company reports.

Research Realities 18.1

An Example of Inept Phrasing and Its Consequences

Last month I got a letter from a vice-president of a major management consulting firm. Let me read you two paragraphs. The first:

"Recently, the companies of our Marketing Services Group were purchased by one of the largest consumer research firms in the U.S. While this move well fits the basic business purpose and focus of the acquired MSG units, it is personally restrictive. I will rather choose to expand my management opportunities with a career move into industry."

Source: Jock Elliott, "How Hard It Is to Write Easily," *Viewpoint: The Ogilvy & Mather magazine,* 2 (1980), p. 18. Reprinted with permission. The use of jargon and imprecise expression has become so commonplace that computer programs that analyze grammar readability and sentence structure and suggest alternative wordings have been developed to deal with it. See, for example, Suien L. Hwang, "Of Course, Software Instructions Aren't Models of Clarity, Either," *The Wall Street Journal* (February 27, 1991), p. B1. For a comparison of these programs, see John Lombardi, "Grammar Checkers: Keep Your Writing in Line," *InfoWorld,* 13 (October 28, 1991), pp. 64–77.

What he meant was: The deal works fine for my company, but not so fine for me. I'm looking for another job.

Second paragraph:

"The base of managerial and technical accomplishment reflected in my enclosed resumé may suggest an opportunity to meet a management need for one of your clients. Certainly my experience promises a most productive pace to understand the demands and details of any new situation I would choose."

What he meant was: As you can see in my resumé, I've had a lot of good experience. I am a quick study. Do you think any of your clients might be interested in me?

At least, that's what I think he meant.

This fellow's letter reveals him as pompous. He may not be pompous. He may only be a terrible writer. But I haven't the interest or time to find out which. There are so many people looking for jobs who *don't* sound pompous.

Bad writing done him in — with me, at any rate.

---

career, bad writing acts as a sea anchor, pulling you back, good writing as a spinnaker, pulling you ahead."[8]

Examples of inept phrasing abound, often permeating our daily lives. Inaccuracies also arise because of grammatical errors in punctuation, spelling, tense, subject and verb agreement, and so on.[9]

Clarity

Clarity is probably violated more than any other principle of good writing. Clear and logical thinking and precise expression produce clarity. When the underlying logic is fuzzy or the presentation imprecise, readers have difficulty understanding what they

---

[8]Jock Elliott, "How Hard It Is to Write Easily," *Viewpoint: The Ogilvy & Mather Magazine,* 2 (1980), p. 18. Frustrated by writing that is muddled and wastes time, firms are increasingly turning to writing consultants or in-house seminars to improve their employees' writing skills. See Cynthia F. Mitchell, "Firms Seek Cure for Dull Memos; Find Windy Writers Hard to Curb," *The Wall Street Journal* (October 4, 1985), p. 21.

[9]Gallagher, *Report Writing,* Chapter 10, "Reviewing for Accuracy: Grammar," pp. 156–177, has examples of how these inaccuracies can confuse and misinform. See also Gretchen N. Vik, C. W. Wilkinson, and Dorothy C. Wilkinson, *Writing and Speaking in Business,* 10th ed. (Homewood, Ill.: Irwin, 1989).

read. They may be forced to guess, in which case the corollary to Murphy's law applies: "If the reader is offered the slightest opportunity to misunderstand, he probably will."[10]

It is easy to say that the report should be clear, but it is much more difficult to develop such a report. It is essential that the organization of the report is clear.[11] For this to happen, you must know what you want to say. Make an outline of your major points. Order the points logically and place the supporting details in their proper position. Tell the reader where you are going and then do what you said you were going to do. Use short paragraphs and short sentences. Don't mumble; once you have decided what to say, come out and say it. Choose your words carefully. See Research Realities 18.2 for some specific suggestions when choosing words. Don't expect to get it right the first time; expect to rewrite it several times. When rewriting, try to reduce the length by half. That forces you to simplify and remove the clutter. It also forces you to think about every word and its purpose. Jock Elliott has some pointed comments on writing clearly.

> Our written and spoken words reflect what we are. If our words are brilliant, precise, well ordered and human, then that is how we are seen.
>
> When you write, you must constantly ask yourself: What am I trying to say? If you do this religiously, you will be surprised at how often you don't know what you are trying to say.
>
> You have to *think* before you start every sentence, and you have to *think* about every word.
>
> Then you must look at what you have written and ask: Have I said it? Is it clear to someone encountering the subject for the first time? If it's not, it is because some fuzz has worked its way into the machinery. The clear writer is a person clearheaded enough to see this stuff for what it is: fuzz.
>
> It is not easy to write a simple declarative sentence. Here is one way to do it. Think what you want to say. Write your sentence. Then strip it of all adverbs and adjectives. Reduce the sentence to its skeleton. Let the verbs and nouns do the work.
>
> If your skeleton sentence does not express your thought precisely, you've got the wrong verb or noun. Dig for the right one. Nouns and verbs carry the guns in good writing; adjectives and adverbs are decorative camp followers.[12]

Conciseness

Although the report must be complete, it must also be concise. This means that the writer must be selective about what is included. The researcher must avoid trying to impress the reader with all that has been found. If something does not pertain directly to

---

[10]Gallagher, *Report Writing,* p. 83.

[11]Kenneth Roman and Joel Raphaelson, *Writing That Works* (New York: Harper & Row, 1981). This book gives some excellent advice on how to write more effective reports, memos, letters, and speeches. See also Kenneth Roman and Joel Raphaelson, "Don't Mumble and Other Principles of Effective Writing," *Viewpoint: By, For, and About Ogilvy & Mather,* 2 (1980), pp. 19–36; Mary Cross, *Persuasive Business Writing: Creating Better Letters, Memos, Reports, and More* (New York: American Management Association, 1987). The little book by William Strunk, Jr., and E. B. White, *The Elements of Style,* 3rd ed. (New York: Macmillan, 1979), is a classic on how to write clearly.

[12]Elliott, "How Hard It Is to Write Easily," pp. 18–19.

Research Realities 18.2

Some Suggestions When Choosing Words for Marketing Research Reports

1. *Use short words.* Always use short words in preference to long words that mean the same thing.

Use this	Not this
Now	Currently
Start	Initiate
Show	Indicate
Finish	Finalize
Use	Utilize
Place	Position

2. *Avoid vague modifiers.* Avoid lazy adjectives and adverbs and use vigorous ones. Lazy modifiers are so overused in some contexts that they have become clichés. Select only those adjectives and adverbs that make your meaning more precise.

Lazy modifiers	Vigorous modifiers
Very good	Short meeting
Awfully nice	Crisp presentation
Basically accurate	Baffling instructions
Great success	Tiny raise
Richly deserved	Moist handshake
Vitally important	Lucid recommendation

3. *Use specific, concrete language.* Avoid technical jargon. There is always a simple, down-to-earth word that says the same thing as the show-off fad word or the vague abstraction.

Jargon	Down-to-earth English
Implement	Carry out
Viable	Practical, workable
Net net	Conclusion
Suboptimal	Less than ideal
Proactive	Active
Bottom line	Outcome

4. *Write simply and naturally — the way you talk.* Use only those words, phrases, and sentences that you might actually say to your reader if you were face-to-face. If you wouldn't say it, if it doesn't sound like you, don't write it.

Stiff	Natural
The reasons are fourfold	There are four reasons
Importantly	The important point is
Visitation	Visit

5. *Strike out words you don't need.* Certain commonly used expressions contain redundant phrasing. Cut out the extra words.

Don't write	Write
Advance plan	Plan
Take action	Act
Study in depth	Study
Consensus of opinion	Consensus
Until such time as	Until
The overall plan	The plan

Source: Excerpts on pages 7, 9, 10, 15 from *Writing That Works* by Kenneth Roman and Joel Raphaelson. Copyright © 1981 by Kenneth Roman and Joel Raphaelson. Reprinted by permission of Harper & Row, Publishers, Inc.

the subject, it should be omitted. The writer must also avoid lengthy discussions of commonly known methods.

Even if the material is appropriate, conciseness can still be violated by writing style. This commonly occurs when the writer is groping for the phrases and words that capture an idea. Instead of finally coming to terms with the idea, the writer writes around it, restating it several times in different ways, hoping that repetition will overcome poor expression. Concise writing, in contrast, is effective because "it makes maximum use of every word . . . no word in a concise discussion can be removed without impairing or destroying the function of the whole composition. . . . To be concise is to express a thought completely and clearly in the fewest words possible."[13]

One helpful technique for ensuring that the report is concise is reading the draft aloud. This points out sections that should be pruned or rewritten.

> Silent reading allows him [the writer] to skim over the familiar material and thus impose an artificial rapidity and structural simplicity on something that is in reality dense and tangled. The eye can grow accustomed to the appearance of a sentence, but it is much more difficult for the tongue, lips, and jaw to deal with what the eye might accept readily.[14]

ETHICAL DILEMMA 18.1

As a member of an independent research team, it is your job to write the final report for a client. One of your colleagues whispers to you in passing, "Make it sound very technical. Lots of long words and jargon — you know the sort of thing. We want to make it clear that we earned our money on this one."

- Is it ethical to obscure the substance of a report beneath complex language?
- Will some clients be impressed by words that they do not fully understand?

FORMS OF THE REPORT

The organization of the report influences all the criteria of report writing. Good organization cannot guarantee clarity, conciseness, accuracy, and completeness, but poor organization can preclude them. There is no single, acceptable organization for a report. The form chosen depends on the audience. The following format is flexible enough to allow the inclusion or exclusion of elements to satisfy particular needs.

1. Title page
2. Table of contents

---

[13]Gallagher, *Report Writing*, p. 87.

[14]*Ibid.*, p. 84.

3. Summary
   a. Introduction
   b. Results
   c. Conclusions
   d. Recommendations
4. Introduction
5. Body
   a. Methodology
   b. Results
   c. Limitations
6. Conclusions and recommendations
7. Appendix
   a. Copies of data collection forms
   b. Detailed calculations supporting sample size, test statistics, and so on
   c. Tables not included in the body
   d. Bibliography

Title Page

The title page indicates the subject of the report, the name of the organization for whom the report is made, the name of the organization submitting it, and the date. If the report is internal, the names of organizations or companies are replaced by those of individuals. Those for whom the report is intended are listed on the title page, as are the departments or people preparing the report. It is advisable to list those who should receive a confidential report with intended limited distribution.

Table of Contents

The table of contents lists, in order of appearance, the divisions and subdivisions of the report with page references. In short reports, the table of contents may simply contain the main headings. It will also typically include tables and figures and the pages on which they can be found. For most reports, exhibits will be labeled as either tables or figures, with maps, diagrams, and graphs falling into the latter category.

Summary

The summary is the most important part of the report. It is its heart and core. Many executives will read only the summary. Others will read more, but even they will use the summary as a guide to those questions about which they would like more information.

The true summary is not an abstract of the whole report in which everything is restated in condensed form; neither is it a simple restatement of the subject, nor a brief statement of the significant results and conclusions. A true summary gives the high points of the entire body of the report. Properly written, the summary saves busy executives' time without sacrificing their understanding. A good test of a summary is self-sufficiency. Can it stand on its own, or does it collapse without the full report?

A good summary contains the necessary background information, as well as the important results and conclusions. Whether or not it contains recommendations is determined to an extent by the reader. Some managers prefer that the writer suggest appropriate action, while others prefer to draw their own conclusions on the basis of the evidence contained in the study. Although the good summary contains the necessary information, it will rarely be broken down through the use of headings and subheadings. The summary that requires such subdivisions is probably too long.

The introduction in the summary provides the reader with minimal background to appreciate the study's results, conclusions, and recommendations. The introduction should state who authorized the research and for what purpose and should explicitly outline the problem(s) or hypotheses that guided the research. The problems as stated here should also guide the remainder of the report. No subject should be treated in the report if it is not anticipated here.

The results presented in the summary must agree, of course, with those in the body of the report, but only the key findings should be presented here. It is useful to include one or several findings to each problem or objective.

Conclusions and recommendations are not the same. A conclusion is an opinion based on the results. It is a statement of what we know and what it means. A recommendation is a suggestion for appropriate future action. Conclusions should be included in the summary section. The writer is in a better position to base conclusions on the evidence than the readers, as the writer is more familiar with the methods used to generate and analyze the data. The writer is at fault if conclusions are omitted and readers are allowed to draw their own. Recommendations, though, are another matter. Some managers simply prefer to determine the appropriate courses of action themselves and do not want the writer to offer recommendations. Others hold that the writer, being closest to the research, is in the best position to suggest a course of action. For example, the Lipton Company has the philosophy that it is the responsibility of the marketing research people to interpret the findings. As Dolph von Arx, the executive vice-president, comments, "We feel strongly that our market research people must go beyond reporting the facts. We want them to tell us what *they* think the facts mean — both in terms of conclusions, and, if possible, indicated actions. Those who are responsible for making the decisions may or may not accept those conclusions or recommendations, but we want this input from our market research people."[15] The Lipton Company's philosophy is consistent with recent trends in the industry. Increasingly, marketing researchers are being asked to interpret the findings in terms of what they mean to the business and to make recommendations as to appropriate courses of action.

Introduction

Whereas in the summary the readers' interests are taken into account, in the introduction their education and experience are considered. The introduction provides background information that readers need in order to appreciate the discussion in the body of the

---

[15]Dolph von Arx, "The Many Faces of Market Research," paper delivered at meeting of the Association of National Advertisers, Inc., New York, April 3, 1985. See also Arthur Shapiro, "Downsizing and Its Effect on Corporate Marketing Research," *Marketing Research: A Magazine of Management and Applications,* 2 (December 1990), pp. 56–59.

report. Some form of introduction is almost always necessary. Its length and detail, however, depend on the readers' familiarity with the subject, the approach to it, and the treatment of it.[16] As a general rule, the report with wide distribution will require a more extensive introduction than a report for a narrow audience.

The introduction often defines unfamiliar terms or terms that are used in a specific way in the report. For instance, in a study of market penetration of a new product, the introduction might be used to define the market. What products and companies were considered "competitors" in calculating the new product's market share?

The introduction may provide some pertinent history. What similar studies have been conducted? What findings did they produce? What circumstances precipitated the present study? How were its scope and emphasis determined? Clearly, if readers are familiar with the history of this project and related research or the circumstances that inspired the current research, these items can be omitted. A report going to executives with only tangential interest in the particular product or service dealt with would probably have to include them.

The introduction should state the specific objectives of the research. If the project was part of a larger, overall project, this should be mentioned. Each of the subproblems or hypotheses should be explicitly stated. After reading the introduction, readers should know exactly what the report concerns and what it omits. They should appreciate the overall problem and how the subproblems relate to it. They should be aware of the relationship between this study and other related work. And they should appreciate the need for the study and its importance. Through all of this, the introduction should serve to win the readers' confidence and dispel any prejudices they may have.

Body

The details of the research are contained in the body of the report. This includes details of method, results, and limitations.

One of the hardest portions of the report to write is that giving the details of the method. The writer has a real dilemma here. Sufficient information must be presented so that readers can appreciate the research design, data collection methods, sample procedures, and analysis techniques that were used without being bored or overwhelmed. However, technical jargon, which is often a succinct way of communicating a complex idea, should be omitted, because many in the audience will not understand it.

Readers must be told whether the design was exploratory, descriptive, or causal as well as why the particular design was chosen. What are its merits in terms of the problem at hand? Readers should also be told whether the results are based on secondary or primary data. If primary, were they based on observation or questionnaire? And if the latter, were the questionnaires administered in person or by mail or telephone? Again, it is important to mention why the particular method was chosen. What were its perceived advantages over alternative schemes? This may mean *briefly* discussing the perceived weaknesses of the other data collection schemes that were considered.

---

[16]Gallagher, *Report Writing,* p. 54.

Sampling is a technical subject, and the writer cannot hope to convey all the nuances of the sampling plan in the body of the report but must be somewhat selective in this regard. At the minimum, the researcher should answer the following questions:

1. How was the population defined? What were the geographical, age, gender, or other bounds?

2. What sampling units were employed? Were they business organizations or business executives? Were they dwelling units, households, or individuals within a household? Why were these particular sampling units chosen?

3. How was the list of sampling units generated? Did this produce any weaknesses? Why was this method used?

4. Were any difficulties experienced in contacting designated sample elements? How were these difficulties overcome, and was bias introduced in the process?

5. Was a probability or nonprobability sampling plan employed? Why? How was the sample actually selected? How large a sample was selected? Why was this size sample chosen?

Readers need to understand at least three things pertaining to the sample: What was done? How was it done? Why was it done?

Little can be said about the method of analysis when discussing research methods, since the results tend to show what has been done in this regard. It often is quite useful, though, to discuss the method in general before detailing the results. Thus, if statistical significance was established through chi-square analysis, the writer might provide the general rationale and calculation procedure for the chi-square statistic, as well as the assumptions surrounding this test and how well the data supported the assumptions. This enables readers to divorce what was found from how it was determined. This cannot only help their understanding but also prevent repetition. The procedure is outlined with its key components once and for all, and the results are then simply reported in terms of these components.

The results are the findings of the study, and their detailed presentation, with supporting tables and figures, will consume the bulk of the report. The results need to address the specific problems posed, and they must be presented with some logical structure.[17] The first requirement suggests that information that is interesting but irrelevant to the specific problems guiding the research be omitted. The second requirement suggests that the tables and figures should not be a random collection but should reflect some psychological ordering.[18] This may be by subproblem, geographic region, time, or other criterion that served to structure the investigation. Tables and figures should be used liberally when presenting the results. Whereas the tables in the appendix are com-

---

[17]Some of the many structures and the conditions under which they can be used are contained in Jessamon Dawe, *Writing Business and Economic Papers: Theses and Dissertations* (Totowa, N.J.: Littlefield, Adams, 1975), pp. 75–86. See also David Morris and Satish Chandra, *Guidelines for Writing a Research Report* (Chicago: American Marketing Association, 1992).

[18]See Gallagher, *Report Writing,* pp. 50–68, for a discussion of the psychological order of things in research reports.

plex, detailed, and apply to a number of problems, the tables in the body of the report should be simple summaries of this information. Each table should address only a single problem, and it should be especially constructed to shed maximum light on this problem. There are several things that researchers should do to accomplish this, including the following:

1. Order the columns or rows of the table by the marginal averages or some other measure of size. If there are many similar tables, keep the same order in each one.
2. Put the figures to be compared into columns rather than rows, and, if possible, put the larger numbers at the top of the columns.
3. Round the numbers to two effective digits.
4. Give brief verbal summaries of each table that guide the reader to the main patterns and exceptions.[19]

Figure 18.1 shows how these guidelines can yield better tables. The figures should also address one and only one subproblem. Further, they should be chosen carefully for the type of message they can most effectively convey (but more on their choice later).

Although it would be nice to conduct the "perfect" study, this goal is unrealistic. Every study has its limitations. The researcher knows what these limitations are and should not try to hide them from the readers. An open, frank admission of the study's limitations can actually increase, rather than diminish (as is sometimes feared) the readers' opinion of the quality of the research. If some limitations are not stated and readers discover them, they may begin to question the whole report and assume a much more skeptical, critical posture than they would if the limitations were explicitly stated. Stating them also allows the writer to discuss whether, and by how much, the limitations might bias the results. Their exclusion and later discovery allows readers to draw their own conclusions in this regard.

When discussing the limitations, the writer should provide some idea of the research's accuracy. Specifically, the sources of nonsampling error and the suspected direction of their biases should be discussed. This often means that the researcher must provide some limits by which the results were distorted as a result of these inaccuracies. Readers should be informed about how far the results can be generalized. To what populations can they be expected to apply? If the study was done in Miami, readers should be warned not to generalize the results to the southern states or to all the states. The writer should provide the proper caveats for readers and not allow them to discover the weaknesses themselves. However, the writer should not overstate the limitations either but should assume a balanced perspective.

Conclusions and Recommendations

The results precipitate the conclusions and recommendations. In this section, the writer shows the step-by-step development of the conclusions and states them in greater detail

---

[19]See A. S. C. Ehrenberg, "Rudiments of Numeracy," *Journal of the Royal Statistical Society,* Series A, 140 (1977), pp. 277–297, and A. S. C. Ehrenberg, "The Problem of Numeracy," *American Statistician,* 35 (May 1981), pp. 67–71, for particularly informative discusssions using examples of how adherence to these principles can dramatically improve readers' abilities to comprehend the information being presented in tables.

FIGURE 18.1   **Guidelines for Producing Better Tables**

Table A displays some sales figures for a product being sold in ten U.S. cities. At first glance it seems fairly laid out, but look again. How would you summarize the information in the table to someone over the phone?

TABLE A   **Quarterly Sales of Product Y in Ten Cities**

City	Sales in Thousands of Dollars			
	Quarter 1	Quarter 2	Quarter 3	Quarter 4
Atlanta	540.4	507.6	528.4	833.2
Chattanooga	68.9	64.0	55.4	64.5
Des Moines	65.7	61.1	52.9	61.5
Hartford	61.1	71.5	59.0	70.5
Indianapolis	153.2	162.8	122.8	185.7
Los Angeles	700.2	660.3	580.8	662.7
Miami	553.6	517.2	446.0	672.4
Omaha	78.3	72.8	63.0	73.3
Phoenix	196.8	227.6	198.5	235.2
San Antonio	168.2	179.3	166.9	207.1

The table seems to be a jumble when looked at more carefully. It appears that no thought was given to communicating what the numbers really mean. The main difficulty is that the cities for which the numbers are given are listed alphabetically. There is no apparent pattern in each column. Now look at the same information as presented in Table B.

TABLE B   **Quarterly Sales of Product Y in Ten Cities Ordered by Population Size (Rounded and with Averages)**

City	Quarter 1	Quarter 2	Quarter 3	Quarter 4	Average
Los Angeles	700	660	580	660	650
Miami	550	520	450	670	550
Atlanta	540	510	530	830	620
Phoenix	200	230	200	240	220
San Antonio	170	180	170	210	180
Indianapolis	150	160	120	190	160
Hartford	60	70	60	70	70
Omaha	80	70	60	70	70
Chattanooga	70	60	60	60	60
Des Moines	70	60	50	60	60
Average	260	250	230	310	260

continued

Note how ordering the information by following these steps improves the table's readability:

- Order the columns or rows of the table by the marginal averages or some other measure of size. In this case, the cities are ordered by the size of the populations.
- Round the numbers to two effective digits.
- Give brief verbal summaries of each table that guide the reader to the main patterns and exceptions.

Table B's heading informs the reader that the cities are ordered by population size. Having this information and examining the table as it's now laid out, we can begin to see major patterns emerge: the bigger the cities, the higher the sales, as might be expected. The single exception is Atlanta, where sales are relatively high given its population size.

Trends over time are also easier to see. Although not typical, the column averages help us see that sales in each city were relatively steady quarter by quarter, but that they were lower in Quarter 3 and higher in Quarter 4. We can also see that the 4th quarter increases were largest in Miami and Atlanta.

The difference between Tables A and B is the difference between a good table and a poor one. In a good table, the patterns and exceptions should be obvious at a glance, at least once one knows what they are.

Next time you have trouble reading a table, ask yourself if the information could be better ordered. The fault may not be in your ability to comprehend the information but in the table itself.

Source: Adapted from A.S.C. Ehrenberg, "The Problem of Numeracy," *The American Statistician,* 35 (May 1981), pp. 67–71.

---

than in the summary. There should be a conclusion for each study objective or problem. As one book puts it, "readers should be able to read the objectives, turn to the conclusions section, and find specific conclusions relative to each objective."[20] If the study does not provide evidence sufficient to draw a conclusion about a problem, this should be explicitly stated.

Researchers need to be careful that the conclusions drawn reflect an unbiased interpretation of the data. (See Research Realities 18.3.) Researchers' recommendations should follow the conclusions. In developing the recommendations, researchers need to focus on the value of the information that has been gathered. They need to interpret this information in terms of what it means for the business. One of the best ways of doing this is by offering specific recommendations as to the appropriate courses of action — along with reasons why — given the evidence. While not all managers want the researcher's recommendations, many do, and the researcher needs to be prepared to offer and support them.

Appendix

The appendix contains material that is too complex, too detailed, too specialized, or not absolutely necessary for the text. The appendix will typically contain as an exhibit a copy of the questionnaire or observation form used to collect the data. It will also

---

[20]Boyd, Westfall, and Stasch, *Marketing Research,* p. 663.

Research Realities 18.3

Are American Students Really Lost in Math and Science?

A 1989 government-funded study concluded that American students ranked last or near the bottom in an international comparison of mathematics and science skills. Politicians, educators, and journalists expressed concerns about continued American competitiveness in the international marketplace. The U.S. school system seemed to be lagging behind in preparing students for global competition.

However, research experts have questioned the validity of the international comparisons. ''I find it scary when I look at a magazine and see a graph ranking countries with virtually no explanatory material,'' said David Robitaille, a researcher at the University of British Columbia. ''The graph makes it look like the Japanese system is wonderful and the U.S. system is the pits. The actual facts are much more complicated.''

International comparisons have routinely been made since the 1960s. Students in selected countries take tests designed to find out which country has the best system of education. The overall goal is to improve the effectiveness of schools. But as soon as the results are published, people start comparing results of the participating countries.

''Countries have different emphases in different areas so they produce different profiles of achievement,'' according to Richard Wolfe, a Canadian researcher. Consider the question of curriculum. In Hungary, students before the eighth grade study math more extensively than do students in other countries. It should come as no surprise that Hungary scored higher than the United States in math for 13-year-olds. This does not necessarily lead directly to the conclusion that Hungarians teach math more effectively than Americans.

The weighting of the elements of the test also affects the results. The 1989 study placed particular emphasis on numbers and operations, two areas that are not stressed in Great Britain. The British stress logic in the study of math. However, the 1989 study placed little weight on the logic section of the test. Not surprisingly, British students did not place well in the math category.

Sampling can also affect the validity of comparisons. In Hungary, about half of its 12th-graders take advanced math. In Great Britain only 6 percent of its 12th-graders, mostly the math whizzes, do the same. Comparing the results of Hungary's 50 percent with Britain's elite 6 percent is not fair. Ranked near the top in eighth-grade math because of its curriculum, Hungary falls to apparent mediocrity by the 12th grade, largely due to the belief that advanced math should be taught to more than just the select few.

Other factors that can affect the comparisons include cultural differences, educational system setup, and teaching patterns. So where does this leave the United States? ''The public perception that the U.S. is falling behind in science and mathematics . . . is based on a narrow criterion that has serious methodological deficiencies,'' wrote Iris Rotberg, an education specialist with the National Science Foundation, in a recent *Phi Delta Kappan* article. ''Clearly, we have problems in science and mathematics education. But the bottom line is not so grim as the current rhetoric would have us believe.''

Source: Malcolm Gladwell, ''U.S. Education Gap Called Overstated,'' *The Washington Post,* (November 1, 1991), p. A1. © 1991 The Washington Post. Reprinted with permission.

contain any maps used to draw the sample, as well as any detailed calculations used to support the determination of the sample size and sample design. The appendix may include detailed calculations of test statistics and will often include detailed tables from which the summary tables in the body of the report are generated. The writer should recognize that the appendix will be read by only the most technically competent and interested reader. Therefore, the writer should not put material in the appendix if its omission from the body of the report would create gaps in the presentation.

Table 18.2 can serve as a checklist of things to include in reports. The checklist reflects the guidelines that have been developed to evaluate research that is to be put to a

TABLE 18.2   Checklist for Evaluating Research Reports

A. Origin: What Is Behind the Research

Does the report identify the organizations, discussion, or departments that initiated and paid for the research?

Is there a statement of the purpose of the research that says clearly what it was meant to accomplish?

Are the organizations that designed and conducted the research identified?

B. Design: The Concept and the Plan

Is there a full, nontechnical description of the research design?

Is the design consistent with the stated purpose for which the research was conducted?

Is the design evenhanded? That is, is it free of leading questions and other biases?

Have precautions been taken to avoid sequence or timing bias or other factors that might prejudice or distort the findings?

Does it address questions that respondents are capable of answering?

Is there a precise statement of the universe or population that the research is meant to represent?

Does the sampling frame fairly represent the population under study?

Does the report specify the kind of sample used and clearly describe the method of sample selection?

Does the report describe the plan for the analysis of the data?

Are copies of all questionnaire forms, field and sampling instructions, and other study materials available in the appendix or on file?

C. Execution: Collecting and Handling the Information

Does the report describe the data collection and data processing procedures?

Is there an objective report on the care with which the data were collected?

What procedures were used to minimize bias and ensure the quality of the information collected?

D. Stability: Sample Size and Reliability

Was the sample large enough to provide stable findings?

Are sampling error limits shown if they can be computed?

Are methods of calculating the sampling error described, or, if the error cannot be computed, is this stated and explained?

Does the treatment of sampling error limits make clear that they do not cover nonsampling error?

For the major findings, are the reported error tolerances based on direct analysis of the variability of the collected data?

Table 18.2   *Continued*

E. Applicability: Generalizing the Findings

Does the report specify when the data were collected?   _____

Does the report say clearly whether its findings do or do not apply beyond the direct source of the data?   _____

Is it clear who is underrepresented by the research, or not represented at all?   _____

If the research has limited application, is there a statement covering who or what it represents and the times or conditions under which it applies?   _____

F. Meaning: Interpretations and Conclusions

Are the measurements described in simple and direct language?   _____

Does it make logical sense to use such measurements for the purpose to which they are being put?   _____

Are the actual findings clearly differentiated from the interpretation of the findings?   _____

Have rigorous objectivity and sound judgment been exercised in interpreting the research findings?   _____

G. Candor: Open Reporting and Disclosure

Is there a full and forthright disclosure of how the research was done?   _____

Has the research been fairly presented?   _____

Source: Adapted from *Guidelines for the Public Use of Market and Opinion Research,* © 1981 by the Advertising Research Foundation. Adapted with permission.

---

public purpose. Public-purpose research can affect the interests of people and organizations who have had no part in its design, execution, or funding. Consequently, the criteria on which it is evaluated tend to be stricter than those applied to research done for private use. Still, the general issues and questions serve as useful criteria by which all research reports can be judged.

THE ORAL REPORT

In addition to the written report, most marketing research investigations require one or more oral reports. Frequently, they require interim reports regarding progress. Almost always they require a formal oral report at the conclusion of the study. The principles surrounding the preparation and delivery of the oral report parallel those for the written report.

That means report preparers and presenters need to realize that many listeners will not truly understand the technical ramifications involved in research and certainly will not be able to judge whether the research done is "quality research." However, they can judge whether the research was presented in a professional, confidence-inspiring manner or in a disorganized, uninformed one. A quality presentation can disguise poor research, but quality research cannot improve a poor presentation.

ETHICAL DILEMMA 18.2

A colleague confides in you: "I've just run a survey for a restaurant owner who is planning to open a catering service for parties, weddings, and the like. He wanted to know the best way to advertise the new service. In the questionnaire, I asked respondents where they would expect to see advertisements for catering facilities, and the most common source was the newspaper. I now realize that my question only established where people are usually exposed to relevant ads, not where they would like to see relevant ads or where they could most productively be exposed to an ad. All we know is where other caterers advertise! Yet I'm sure my client will interpret my findings as meaning that the newspaper is the most effective media vehicle. Should I make the limitations of the research explicit?"

- What are the costs of making the limitations of the research explicit?
- What are the costs of not doing so?
- Isn't promoting the correct use of the research one of the researcher's prime obligations?

Preparing the Oral Report

The first imperative is to know the audience. What is its technical level of sophistication? What is its members' involvement in the project? Their interest? Once again, oral reports being delivered to those who are heavily involved or have a high degree of technical sophistication can contain more detail than reports to those only tangentially involved or interested. In general, it is better to err on the side of too little technical detail than too much. Executives want to hear and see what the information means to them as managers of marketing activities. What do the data suggest in terms of marketing actions? They can ask for the necessary clarification about the technical details if they want it.

Another important consideration is the organization of the presentation. There are two popular forms. Both begin by stating the general purpose of the study and the specific objectives that were addressed. They differ in terms of when the conclusions are introduced. In the most popular structure, the conclusions are introduced after all of the evidence supporting a particular course of action is presented. This allows the presenter to build a logical case in sequential fashion. By progressively disclosing the facts, the presenter has the opportunity to deal with audience concerns and biases as they arise and thus can lead them to the conclusion that the case builds.

The alternative structure involves presenting the conclusions immediately after the purpose and main objectives. The structure tends to involve managers immediately in the findings. It not only gets them thinking about what actions are called for given the results but also sensitizes them to paying attention to the evidence supporting the conclusions. It places them in the desirable position of wanting to evaluate the strength of the evidence supporting an action, because they know beforehand the conclusions that were drawn from it. The structure a presenter decides to use should depend on what is preferred within the corporate culture as well as the presenter's own comfort level with each organizational form. In either case, the evidence supporting the conclusions must be

TABLE 18.3   Ten Tips for Preparing Effective Presentation Visuals

Keep it simple. Deliver complex ideas in a manner that your audience can understand. Present one point per slide, with as few words and lines as possible.

Use lots of slides as you talk, rather than lots of talk per slide. Less is more when you are speaking.

Use one minute per visual. Slides and overheads should make their impact quickly; then move on. No more than ten words per slide.

Highlight significant points. Bullets work for black and white transparencies; slides are better suited for color and graphics.

Use a graphic on every page. One is usually enough. Take advantage of "white space," and don't over-crowd.

Build complexity. If you have a complicated concept to communicate, start with the ground level and use three or four slides to complete the picture.

Be careful with color. Color can add interest and emphasis. It can also detract if used without planning. Plan your color scheme and use it faithfully throughout.

Prepare copies of overheads or slides. Hand them to the audience before or after your presentation. If people have to take notes, they won't be watching or listening closely.

Number your pages. You will have a better reference for discussion or a question-and-answer period.

Make visuals easy to read. Use large, legible typefaces. You can use up to three sizes of type, but use only one or two typefaces. Bold and italics can be used freely for emphasis. With slides, use light type against a dark background.

Source: Colleen Paul, "You're in Show Biz! 10 Tips for Presenters," *Micro Monitor*, 6 (May 1989), pp. 12–13.

presented systematically, and the conclusions drawn must be consistent with the evidence.

A third important consideration for effective delivery of the oral report is the use of appropriate visual aids. Flip charts, transparencies, slides, and even chalkboards can all be used to advantage. Their use depends on the size of the group and the physical facilities in which the meeting is held. Regardless of which type of visual is used, make sure that it can be read easily by those in the back of the room. The other principles of effective visual-aid design are listed in Table 18.3.

Delivering the Oral Report

Honor the time limit set for the meeting. Use only a portion of the time set aside for the formal presentation, no more than a third to a half. At the same time, don't rush the presentation of the information. Remember that the audience is hearing it for the first time. Reserve the remaining time for questions and discussion. One of the unique benefits of the oral presentation is that it allows interaction. Use this potential benefit to advantage to clear up points of confusion and to highlight points deserving special emphasis. Adapt the presentation so that there is enough time to both present and discuss the most critical findings.

Finally, use the time-honored principles of public speaking when delivering the message. Keep the presentation simple and uncluttered so that the audience does not have to mentally backtrack to think about what has been said. When writing out the presentation, choose simple words and sentences that are naturally spoken and expressed in your usual vocabulary.[21]

GRAPHIC PRESENTATION OF THE RESULTS

The old adage that ''a picture is worth a thousand words'' is equally true for business reports. A picture, called a graphic illustration in the case of the research report, can indeed be worth a thousand words when it is appropriate and a good design form is selected. When inappropriate or poorly designed, such a presentation may actually detract from the value of the written or oral research report. In this section, therefore, we wish to briefly review when graphics are appropriate and to discuss the use of some of the more popular forms.[22]

As used here, graphic illustration refers to the presentation of quantities in graph form. Effective graphic presentation means more than merely converting a set of numbers into a drawing.

> It means presenting a picture that will give the reader an accurate understanding of a particular set of ''figure'' information: a picture of the comparisons or relationships that he would otherwise have to search for — and perhaps fail to see. And if well done, it will give him this understanding more quickly, more forcefully, more completely, and more accurately than could be done in any other way.[23]

Graphic presentation is not the only way to present quantitative information, nor is it always the best. Text and tables can also be used. Graphics should be used only when they serve the purpose better than these other modes. Textual material is generally the most useful in explaining, interpreting, and evaluating results, whereas tables are particularly good for providing emphasis and vivid demonstrations of important findings. Since some readers tend to shy away from graphic presentation because it is ''too technical,'' it should be used with discretion and designed with care.

Graphic presentation used to be expensive and often delayed the presentation of reports because the visuals had to be drawn by graphic artists. Computer graphics are changing that. Trends in the development of computer software for graphically portraying the results of a study now make the preparation of visuals fast and inexpensive.

---

[21]There are a number of excellent books available on making effective oral presentations. See, for example, Dorothy Sarnoff, *Make the Most of Your Best: A Complete Program for Presenting Yourself and Your Ideas with Confidence and Authority* (Garden City, N.Y.: Doubleday, 1983); Sonya Hamlin, *How to Talk So People Listen: The Real Key to Job Success* (New York: Harper & Row, 1988); Jan D'Arcy, *Technically Speaking: Proven Ways to Make Your Next Presentation a Success* (New York: AMACOM, 1992).

[22]The presentation by no means includes all the graph forms that could be used, just some of the more common ones. Those interested in more detail should see Mary E. Spear, *Practical Charting Techniques* (New York: McGraw-Hill, 1969); Edward R. Tufte, *The Visual Display of Quantitative Information* (Cheshire, Conn.: Graphics Press, 1983); Edward R. Tufte, *Envisioning Information* (Cheshire, Conn.: Graphic Press, 1991).

[23]American Management Association, *Making the Most of Charts: An ABC of Graphic Presentation,* Management Bulletin, 28 (New York: American Telephone and Telegraph Company, 1960). See also J.M. Chambers, W.J. Cleveland, B. Kleiner, and P.A. Tukey, *Graphical Methods for Data Analysis* (Boston: Duxbury Press, 1983); William S. Cleveland, *The Elements of Graphing Data* (Monterey, Calif.: Wadsworth Publishing Co., 1985).

FIGURE 18.2   Personal Consumption Expenditures by Major Category for 1992

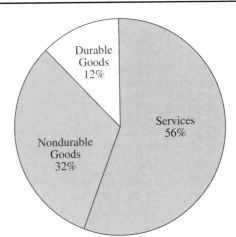

There is no longer any excuse for not using appropriately chosen graphics to emphasize the points being studied.

There are three basic kinds of graphics: charts that show how much, maps that show where, and diagrams that show how. Charts are generally the most useful of the three types, and diagrams the least.[24] The following sections discuss a few of the more common chart types and maps.

Pie Chart

Probably one of the more familiar charts, the **pie chart** is simply a circle divided into sections, with each of the sections representing a portion of the total. Since the sections are presented as part of a whole, the pie chart is particularly effective for depicting relative size or emphasizing static comparisons. Figure 18.2 uses the data from Table 18.4, for instance, to show the breakdown of personal consumption expenditures by major category for 1992. The conclusion is obvious. Expenditures for services account for the largest proportion of total consumption expenditures. Further, expenditures for services and nondurable goods completely dwarf expenditures for durable goods.

Figure 18.2 has three slices, and the interpretation is obvious. With finer consumption classes, a greater number of sections would have been required, and although more

---

[24]Although some general comments are offered about the usefulness of the various types, the serious reader will want to examine the empirical evidence that has been gathered regarding which form communicates best. See, for example, L. E. Sarbaugh, *Comprehension of Graphs* (Washington, D.C.: U.S. Department of Agriculture, Office of Information, 1961); Jacques Bertin, *Graphics and Graphic Information Processing* (New York: Walter de Gruyter, 1977). The graphics portion of the SYSTAT statistical package for microcomputers, SYGRAPH, has some very useful suggestions concerning the best ways to structure graphs so that they communicate accurately. The suggestions are based on the evidence regarding visual processing of information. See Leland Wilkinson, *SYGRAPH* (Evanston, Ill.: Systat, Inc., 1990), especially pp. 38–61.

TABLE 18.4   **Personal Consumption Expenditures for 1970–1992 (billions of dollars)**

		Durable Goods			Nondurable Goods				Services
Year	Total Personal Consumption Expenditures	Total Durable Goods	Motor Vehicles & Parts	Furniture & Household Equipment	Total Nondurable Goods	Food	Clothing and Shoes	Gasoline and Oil	
1970	621.70	85.20	36.20	35.20	265.70	138.90	46.80	22.40	270.80
1971	672.20	97.20	45.40	37.20	278.80	144.20	50.60	23.90	296.20
1972	737.10	111.10	52.40	41.70	300.60	154.90	55.40	25.40	325.30
1973	812.00	123.30	57.10	47.10	333.40	172.10	61.40	28.60	355.20
1974	888.10	121.50	50.40	50.60	373.40	193.70	64.80	36.60	393.20
1975	976.40	132.20	55.80	53.50	407.30	213.60	69.60	40.40	437.00
1976	1,084.30	156.80	72.60	59.10	441.70	230.60	75.30	44.00	485.70
1977	1,204.40	178.20	84.80	65.70	478.80	249.80	82.60	48.10	547.40
1978	1,346.50	200.20	95.70	72.80	528.20	275.90	92.40	51.20	618.00
1979	1,507.20	213.40	96.60	81.80	600.00	311.60	99.10	66.60	693.70
1980	1,668.10	214.70	90.70	86.30	668.80	345.10	104.60	84.80	784.50
1981	1,849.10	235.40	101.90	92.30	730.70	373.90	114.30	94.60	883.00
1982	2,050.70	252.70	108.90	95.70	771.00	398.80	124.40	89.10	1,027.00
1983	2,234.50	289.10	130.40	107.10	816.70	421.90	135.10	90.20	1,128.70
1984	2,430.50	335.50	157.40	118.80	867.30	448.50	146.70	90.00	1,227.60
1985	2,629.00	372.20	179.10	129.90	911.20	471.60	156.40	90.60	1,345.60
1986	2,797.40	406.00	196.20	139.70	942.00	500.00	166.80	73.50	1,449.50
1987	3,009.40	423.40	197.90	148.80	1,001.30	530.70	178.40	75.30	1,584.70
1988	3,238.20	457.50	212.20	161.80	1,060.00	562.60	191.10	77.30	1,720.70
1989	3,450.10	474.60	215.50	171.40	1,130.00	595.30	204.60	83.80	1,845.50
1990	3,659.30	480.30	213.00	176.40	1,193.70	624.70	213.20	93.80	1,983.30
1991	3,887.70	446.10	185.40	170.40	1,251.50	617.70	209.00	105.50	2,190.10
1992	4,095.80	480.40	203.70	180.90	1,290.70	630.90	221.80	105.40	2,324.70

Source: Survey of Current Business (July 1993).

information would have been conveyed, emphasis would have been lost. As a rule of thumb, no more than six slices should be generated; the division of the pie should start at the 12 o'clock position; the sections should be arrayed clockwise in decreasing order of magnitude; and the exact percentages should be provided on the graph.[25]

Line Chart

The pie chart is a one-scale chart, which is why its best use is for static comparisons of the phenomena at a point in time. The **line chart** is a two-dimensional chart that is

---

[25]Jessamon Dawe and William Jackson Lord, Jr., *Functional Business Communication,* 3rd ed. (Englewood Cliffs, N.J.: Prentice-Hall, 1983). See also Gene Zelazny, *Say It With Charts* (Homewood, Ill.: Business One Irwin, 1991).

FIGURE 18.3   **Retail Sales of New Passenger Cars, 1970–1992**

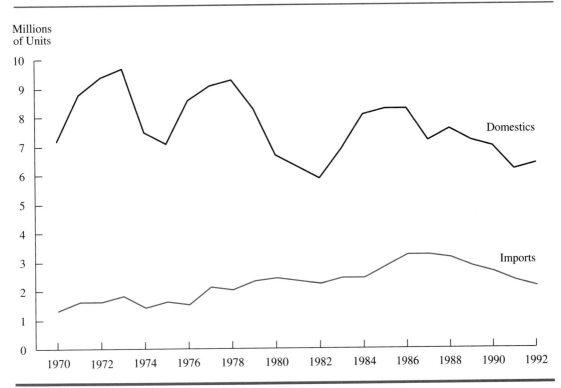

particularly useful in depicting dynamic relationships such as time-series fluctuations of one or more series. For example, Figure 18.3, produced from the data in Table 18.5, shows that, for 1970–1992, new car sales of imports were subject to much less fluctuation than were domestic sales.

The line chart is probably the most commonly used chart. It is typically constructed on graph paper with the X axis representing time and the Y axis representing values of the variable or variables. When more than one variable is presented, it is recommended that the lines for different items be distinctive in color or form (dots and dashes in suitable combinations) with identification of the different forms given in a legend.

Stratum Chart

In some ways, the **stratum chart** is a dynamic pie chart, because it can be used to show relative emphasis by sector (for example, quantity consumed by user class) and change in relative emphasis over time. The stratum chart consists of a set of line charts whose quantities are aggregated (or a total that is disaggregated). It is also called a stacked line chart. For example, Figure 18.4 (again resulting from the data in Table 18.4) shows personal consumption expenditures by major category for the 23-year period 1970–

TABLE **18.5** **Retail Sales of New Passenger Cars (millions of units)**

Year	Domestics	Imports	Total
1970	7.10	1.30	8.40
1971	8.70	1.60	10.30
1972	9.30	1.60	10.90
1973	9.60	1.80	11.40
1974	7.40	1.40	8.80
1975	7.00	1.60	8.60
1976	8.50	1.50	10.00
1977	9.00	2.10	11.10
1978	9.20	2.00	11.20
1979	8.20	2.30	10.50
1980	6.60	2.40	9.00
1981	6.20	2.30	8.50
1982	5.80	2.20	8.00
1983	6.80	2.40	9.20
1984	8.00	2.40	10.40
1985	8.20	2.80	11.00
1986	8.20	3.20	11.40
1987	7.10	3.20	10.30
1988	7.50	3.10	10.60
1989	7.10	2.80	9.90
1990	6.90	2.60	9.50
1991	6.10	2.30	8.40
1992	6.30	2.10	8.40

Source: Economic Indicators.

1992 The lowest line shows the expenditures just for durable goods; the second lowest line shows the total expenditures for durable goods *plus* nondurable goods. Personal consumption expenditures for nondurable goods are thus shown by the area between the two lines. So it is with the remaining areas. We would need 23 pie charts to capture the same information, and the message would not be as obvious.

The X axis typically represents time in the stratum chart, and the Y axis again captures the value of the variables. The use of color or distinctive cross-hatching is strongly recommended to distinguish the various components in the stratum chart. As was true for the pie chart, the number of components distinguished in a stratum chart should not exceed six.

Bar Chart

The **bar chart** can be either a one-scale or two-scale chart. This feature, plus the many other variations that it permits, probably accounts for its wide use. Figure 18.5, for example, is a one-scale chart. It also shows personal consumption expenditures by major

FIGURE 18.4 **Personal Consumption Expenditures by Major Category, 1970–1992**

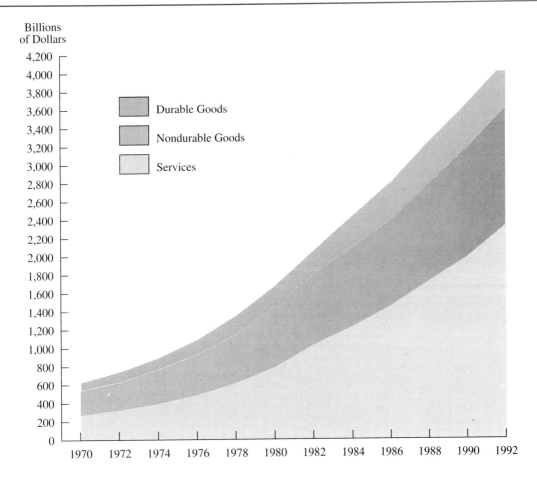

category at a single point in time. Figure 18.5 presents the same information as Figure 18.2 but is, in at least one respect, more revealing; it not only offers some appreciation of the relative expenditures by major category, but it also indicates the magnitude of the expenditures by category. Readers could, of course, generate this information from the pie chart, but it would involve some calculation on their part.

Figure 18.6 is a two-scale bar chart. It uses the data contained in Table 18.5 and shows total automobile sales for the period 1970–1992. The *Y* axis represents quantity, and the *X* axis shows time.

Figures 18.5 and 18.6 should illustrate the fact that the bar chart can be drawn either vertically or horizontally. When emphasis is on the change in the variable through time, the vertical form is preferred, with the *X* axis as the time axis. When time is not a variable, either the vertical or horizontal form is used.

FIGURE 18.5 **Personal Consumption Expenditures by Major Category for 1992**

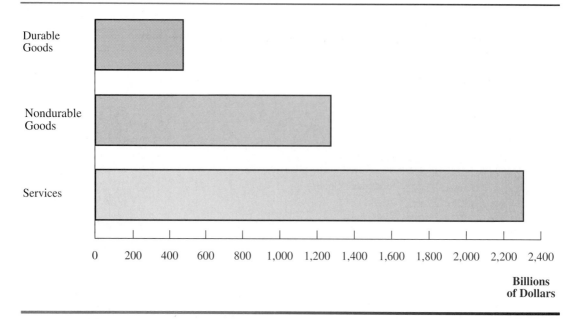

**Billions
of Dollars**

FIGURE 18.6 **Total Automobile Sales, 1970–1992**

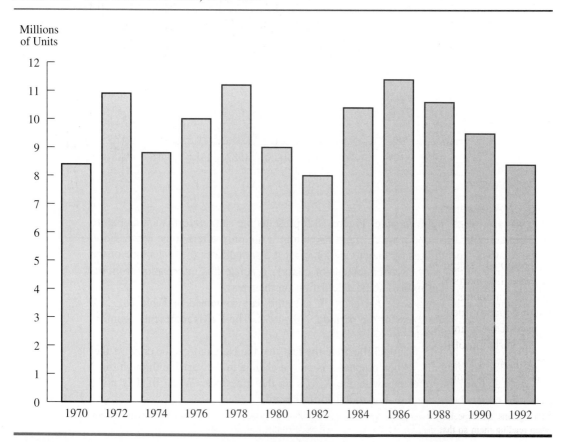

FIGURE 18.7   **Personal Consumption Expenditures by Major Category, 1984–1992**

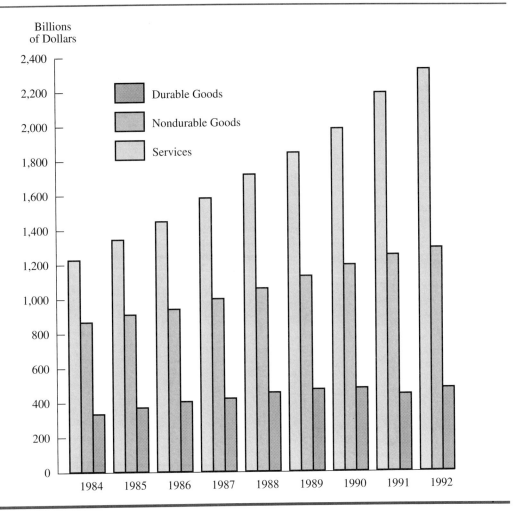

Bar Chart Variations

As previously suggested, great variation is possible with bar charts. One variation is to convert the charts to **pictograms.** Instead of using the length of the bar to capture quantity, amounts are shown by piles of dollars for income, pictures of cars for automobile production, people in a row for population, and so on. This can be a needed change of pace if there are a number of graphs in the report.[26]

A variation of the basic bar chart — the grouped bar chart — can be used to capture the change in two or more series through time. Figure 18.7, for example, shows the change in consumption expenditures by the three major categories for the period 1984–

---

[26]Pictograms are especially susceptible to perceptual distortions. Report users have to be especially careful when reading them so that they are not led to incorrect conclusions.

1992. Just as distinctive symbols are effective in distinguishing the separate series in a line chart, distinctive coloring or cross-hatching is equally helpful in a grouped bar chart.

There is also a bar chart equivalent to the stratum chart — the divided bar chart or stacked bar chart. Its construction and interpretation are similar to those for the stratum chart. Figure 18.8, for example, is a divided or stacked bar chart showing personal consumption expenditures by major category. It shows both total and relative expenditures through time. It, too, makes use of distinctive cross-hatching for each component.

Maps

Maps focus attention on geographic areas. When used for the geographic display of quantitative or statistical information, they are usually called data maps.

Data maps are especially suited to the presentation of rates, ratios, and frequency-distribution data by areas. In constructing data maps, the quantity of interest is typically broken into groups, and cross-hatching, shading, or color is used to display the numerical group in which each area belongs. In general, it is helpful to keep the group intervals approximately equal and to use a limited number of shadings, four to seven and

FIGURE 18.8   Personal Consumption Expenditures by Major Category, 1970–1992

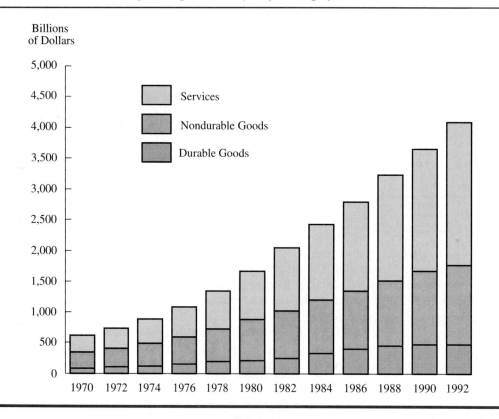

FIGURE 18.9 Growth in Employment, 1982–1991

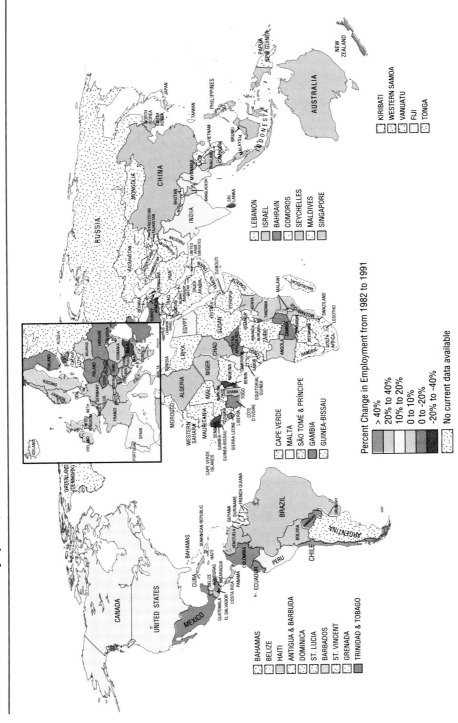

Source: Michael R. Czinkota, Ilkka A. Ronkainen and Michael H. Moffett, *International Business*, 3rd ed. (Fort Worth, Tx: The Dryden Press, 1994), p. 366.

certainly no more than ten. Moreover, the shadings should run progressively from light to dark, and all areas should have some shading. Leaving an area blank or white tends to weaken its importance. For example, Figure 18.9 shows how employment, a sign of economic vitality, grew over a ten year period in various countries.

ETHICAL DILEMMA 18.3

You are writing the final report for top management to make the case that your new advertising campaign has increased sales dramatically in trial areas. Your conceptual arguments on behalf of the new campaign are very convincing, but although there has been a consistent rise in sales in trial areas, the bar charts look rather disappointing: 61,500 units the first month, 61,670 units the next, 61,820 the next. . . . Why, the increase is barely visible! Then you notice how much more exciting your results would look if the Y axis were broken above the origin so that the plots started at 50,000 units.

- Where does salesmanship stop and deception start?

SUMMARY

The research report was discussed in this chapter. Four points were emphasized: the criteria for evaluating research reports, the elements of a written research report, the delivery of an oral report, and the graphic presentation of results.

The fundamental criterion for the development of every research report is the audience. The readers' interests, capabilities, and circumstances determine what goes in the report, what is left out, and how the information included in the report is presented. The other criteria that need to be kept in mind in preparing the report are the following:

1. **Completeness** — does it provide all the information readers need in a language they understand?
2. **Accuracy** — is the reasoning logical and the information correct?
3. **Clarity** — is the phrasing precise?
4. **Conciseness** — is the writing crisp and direct?

There is no standard form for a research report since this, too, depends on the readers' preferences. Nonetheless, a standard report form that can be adapted to suit specific preferences was offered. It included a title page, table of contents, summary, introduction, body, conclusions and recommendations, and appendix. The main items contained in each section were highlighted.

The first rule when preparing an oral report is also to know the audience. It is useful to begin an oral report by stating the general purpose of the study and the specific objectives. The remainder of the presentation needs to systematically build on the evidence so that logical conclusions are drawn. It is better to present too little detail in an oral report than too much. Visual aids used in an oral report should be easily understood and easily seen by those in the back of the room. The time limit set for the meeting should always be honored, and only a portion of the allotted time should be used for the formal presentation. The remainder should be set aside for questions and discussion. The words and sentences used in the oral report should be natural sounding and simple, reflecting the presenter's usual vocabulary.

Graphic presentation is often the best way to communicate those findings that require emphasis. Three main forms are the pie chart, the line chart, and the bar chart. The pie chart is a one-scale chart that is particularly effective in communicating a static comparison. The bar chart can be either a one-scale chart or a two-scale chart, while all the other types are basically two-scale charts. The two-scale chart can show the relationship between two variables and is often used when one of the variables is time, in which case time is captured on the X axis.

Questions

1. What is the fundamental report criterion? Explain.

2. What is meant by the report criteria of completeness, accuracy, clarity, and conciseness?

3. On the one hand, it is argued that the research report must be complete and, on the other, that it must be concise. Are these two objectives incompatible? If so, how do you reconcile them?

4. What is the essential content of each of the following parts of the research report?
   a. title page
   b. table of contents
   c. summary
   d. introduction
   e. body
   f. conclusions and recommendations
   g. appendix

5. What are the key considerations in preparing an oral report?

6. What is a pie chart? For what kinds of information is it particularly effective?

7. What is a line chart? For what kinds of information is it generally employed?

8. What is a stratum chart? For what kinds of information is it particularly appropriate?

9. What is a bar chart? For what kinds of problems is it effective?

10. What is a pictogram?

11. What is a grouped bar chart? When is it used?

Applications and Problems

1. Many marketing research professionals would argue that the summary is the most important part of the research report. Describe the information that should be contained in the summary and why it is so important.

2. The owner of a medium-sized home building center specializing in custom-designed and do-it-yourself kitchen supplies asked the I & J Consulting firm to prepare a customer profile report for the kitchen design segment of the home improvement market. Evaluate the following sections of the report.

The customer market for the company can be defined as the do-it-yourself and kitchen design segments. A brief profile of each follows.

The do-it-yourself (DIY) market consists of individuals in the 25–45 age group living in a single dwelling. DIY customers are predominantly male, although an increasing number of females are becoming active DIY customers. The typical DIY customer has an income in excess of $20,000 and the median income is $22,100 with a standard deviation of 86. The DIY customer has an increasing amount of leisure time, is strongly value and convenience conscious, and displays an increasing desire for self-gratification.

The mean age of the custom-kitchen design customer segment is 41.26, and the annual income is in the range of $25,000 to $35,000. The median income is $29,000 with a standard deviation of 73. Custom-kitchen design customers usually live in a single dwelling. The wife is more influential and is the prime decision maker about kitchen designs and cabinets.

3. The executive director of the Cortland Chamber of Commerce asked the marketing research class of the community college located nearby to prepare a research report on members' attitudes toward the service offerings of the chamber. Evaluate the completeness of the executive summary portion of their report, which follows.

To provide a foundation for a comprehensive marketing plan, the Cortland Chamber of Commerce (CCC) undertook a membership survey in November 1993. Eighty-four usable surveys were returned from a stratified proportionate sampling plan of 172 CCC members.

Results showed that members were familiar with all of the services except National Safety Council materials and employers manuals. Newsletters were found to be the most often used as well as the most important service offered by CCC. Government regulation and mandated employee benefits were thought to be the most threatening issues facing businesses, according to the survey results. Over half of all members responding felt favorably to eleven statements about CCC services.

4. Discuss the difference between conclusions and recommendations in research reports.

5. Your marketing research firm is preparing the final written report on a research project commissioned by a major manufacturer of water ski equipment. One objective of the project was to investigate seasonal variations in sales, both on an aggregate basis and by each of the company's sales regions individually. Your client is particularly interested in the width of the range between maximum and minimum seasonal sales. The following table was submitted by one of your junior analysts. Critique the table and prepare a revision suitable for inclusion in your report.

Seasonal Variations in Sales (thousands of dollars)

Sales Region	Spring	Summer	Fall	Winter
Northeast	120.10	140.59	50.90	30.00
East-Central	118.80	142.70	61.70	25.20
Southeast	142.00	151.80	134.20	100.10
Midwest	100.20	139.42	42.90	20.00
South-Central	80.77	101.00	90.42	78.20
Plains	95.60	120.60	38.50	19.90
Southwest	105.40	110.50	101.60	92.10
Pacific	180.70	202.41	171.54	145.60

6. The management of the Canco Company, a manufacturer of metal cans, presents you with the following information.

THE CANCO COMPANY

Comparative Profit and Loss Statement, Fiscal Years 1989–1993

	1989	1990	1991	1992	1993
Net sales	$40,000,000	$45,000,000	$48,000,000	$53,000,000	$55,000,000
Cost and expenses					
Cost of goods sold					
(COGS)	$28,000,000	$32,850,000	$33,600,000	$39,750,000	$40,150,000
Selling and administrative					
expenses	4,000,000	4,500,000	4,800,000	5,300,000	5,500,000
Depreciation	1,200,000	1,350,000	1,440,000	1,590,000	1,650,000
Interest	800,000	900,000	960,000	1,060,000	1,100,000
	$34,000,000	$39,600,000	$40,800,000	$47,700,000	$48,400,000
Profits from operations	6,000,000	5,400,000	7,200,000	5,300,000	6,600,000
Estimated taxes	$ 2,400,000	$ 2,160,000	$ 2,880,000	$ 2,120,000	$ 2,640,000
Net profits	$ 3,600,000	$ 3,240,000	$ 4,320,000	$ 3,180,000	$ 3,960,000

a. Management has asked that you develop a visual aid to present the company's distribution of sales revenues in 1993.

b. You are asked to develop a visual aid that would compare the change in the net profit level to the change in the net sales level.

c. The management of Canco Company wants you to develop a visual aid that will present the following expenses (excluding COGS) over the five-year period: selling and administration expenses, depreciation, and interest expenses.

d. The management has the following sales data relating to the company's two major competitors:

	1989	1990	1991	1992	1993
The We-Can Co.	$35,000,000	$40,000,000	$42,000,000	$45,000,000	$48,000,000
The You-Can Co.	$41,000,000	$43,000,000	$45,000,000	$46,000,000	$48,000,000

You are required to prepare a visual aid to facilitate the comparison of Canco Company's sales performance with that of its major competitors.

The subject of marketing research can be approached in several ways. The perspective used in this book is primarily a *project emphasis*. We have focused on the definition of a problem and the research needed to answer it. Initially, the whole research process may have appeared to be a number of disconnected bits and pieces because of the necessity of separating it into logical components so that the design issues that arose at each stage could be highlighted. As mentioned early in the book, however, the research process is anything but a set of disconnected parts. All the steps are highly interrelated, and a decision made at one stage has implications for the others as well. To remind us how this functions, the research process and some of the key decisions that must be made will be reviewed in this epilogue.

A research project should not be conceived as the end in itself. Projects arise because managerial problems need solving. The problems themselves may concern the identification of market opportunities, the evaluation of alternative courses of action, or control of marketing operations. Because these activities, in turn, are the essence of the managerial function, research activity can also be viewed from the broader perspective of the firm's marketing intelligence system. Chapter 2, therefore, focused on the nature and present status of the supply of marketing intelligence.

Marketing research was defined as the function that links the consumer, customer, and public to the marketer through information — information used to identify and define marketing opportunities and problems; generate, refine, and evaluate marketing actions; monitor marketing performance; and improve our understanding of marketing as a process. Addressing these issues involves the systematic gathering, recording, and analyzing of data. These tasks are logically viewed as a sequence called the research process, consisting of the following steps:

1. Formulate the problem;
2. Determine the research design;
3. Design data collection methods and forms;
4. Design the sample and collect the data;
5. Analyze and interpret the data;
6. Prepare the research report.

The decision problem logically comes first. It dictates the research problem and the design of the project. However, the transition from problem to project is not an automatic one. There is a good deal of iteration from problem specification to tentative research design to problem respecification to modified research design and back again. This is natural, and one of the researcher's more important roles involves helping to define and redefine the problem so that it can be researched and, more important, so that it answers the decision maker's problem. Although this might appear to be simple in principle, the task can be formidable because it requires a clear specification of objectives, alternatives, and environmental constraints and influences. The decision maker may not readily provide these, and it is up to the researcher to dig them out in order to design effective research. Perhaps research is not even necessary. If the decision maker's views are so strongly held that no amount of information might change them, the research will be wasted. It is up to the researcher to determine this before rather than after conducting the research. This often entails asking ''what if'' questions: What if consumer reaction to the product concept is overwhelmingly favorable? What if it is unfavorable? What if it is only slightly favorable? If the decision maker indicates that the same decision will be made in each case, there are other objectives that have not been explicitly stated. This is a critical finding. Every research project should have one or more objectives, and one should not proceed to other steps in the process until these can be explicitly stated.

Here it is also important to ask whether the contemplated benefits of the research exceed the expected costs. It is a mistake to assume that simply because something might change as a result of the research, the research is called for. It may be that the likelihood of finding something that might warrant a change in the decision is so remote that the research still would be wasted. Researchers constantly need to ask: Why should this research be conducted? What could we possibly find out that we do not already know? Will the expected benefits from the research exceed its costs? If the answers indicate research, then the question logically turns to: What kind?

If the problem cannot be formulated as some specific ''if–then'' conjectural relationship, exploratory research is in order. The primary purpose of exploratory research is to gather some ideas and insights into the phenomenon. The output of an exploratory study will *not* be answers but more specific questions or statements of tentative relationships. The search for insights demands a flexible research design. Structured questionnaires or probability sampling plans are not used in exploratory research, because the emphasis is not on gathering summary statistics but on gaining insight into the problem. The personal interview is much more appropriate than the telephone interview, and that, in turn, is more appropriate than a mail survey, since the unstructured question is most useful in the experience survey. Interviewees should be handpicked because they can provide the wanted information; thus, a convenience or judgment sample is very much in order here, whereas it would be completely out of place in descriptive or causal research. Focus groups can be productive for gaining important insights. A survey of the literature and an analysis of selected cases can also be used to advantage in exploratory research, particularly if the researcher assumes the correct posture of seeking rather than finding. The analysis of sharp contrasts or striking features in published data or selected cases is particularly productive of tentative explanations for the occurrence of the phenomenon.

Given that the exploratory effort has generated one or more specific hypotheses to be investigated, the next research thrust would logically be descriptive or causal research. The design actually selected would depend on the conviction with which the tentative explanation is held to be *the* explanation and the feasibility and cost of conducting an experiment. While experiments typically provide more convincing proof of causal relationships, they also usually cost more than descriptive designs. This is one reason why descriptive designs are the most commonly employed type in marketing research.

Whereas exploratory designs are flexible, descriptive designs are rigid. Descriptive designs demand a clear specification of the who, what, when, where, how, and why of the research before data collection begins. They generally employ structured questionnaires or scales because these forms provide advantages in coding and tabulating. In descriptive designs, the emphasis is on generating an accurate picture of the relationships between and among variables. Probability sampling plans are desirable, but if the sample is to be drawn using nonprobabilistic methods, it is important that a quota sample be used. Descriptive studies typically rely heavily on cross-tabulation analysis or other means of investigating the association among variables, such as regression analysis or discriminant analysis, although the emphasis can also be on the search for differences. The great majority of descriptive studies are cross-sectional, although some do use longitudinal information.

Experiments are the best means we have for making inferences about cause-and-effect relationships, because, if designed properly, they provide the most compelling evidence about concomitant variation, time order of occurrence of variables, and elimination of other factors. A key feature of the experiment is that the researcher is able to control who will be exposed to the experimental stimulus (the presumed cause). This allows the researcher to establish the prior equality of groups by randomization, either with or without matching, which in turn allows the adjustment of the results to eliminate many contaminating influences. Sampling plays little role in experiments other than in selecting objects that are to be assigned randomly to the treatment conditions. Because the emphasis is on testing a specific relationship, causal designs demand a clear specification of what is to be measured and how it is to be measured. Structured data collection instruments should be used, and, although structured questionnaires and scales are often employed, experiments also rely heavily on the observational mode of data collection because of the typically more objective, more accurate information obtained this way. The major thrust in the analysis of experimental results is a test for differences between those exposed to the experimental stimulus and those not exposed; the analysis-of-variance procedure is most often employed, although other techniques (for example, the t test for the difference in means of independent or correlated samples) are used as well.

The previous paragraphs should indicate how intimately the steps are interrelated. In particular, it should be noted how the basic nature of the research design implies various things in terms of the structure of the data collection form, design of the sample, and collection and analysis of the data. A decision about appropriate research design does not completely determine the latter considerations, of course, but simply suggests their basic nature. The analyst still has to determine the specific format. For example, is the structured questionnaire to be disguised or undisguised? Is the probability sample to be simple, stratified, or cluster? How large a sample is needed? These questions, too, will be determined in large part by the way the research question is framed, although the ingenuity displayed by the designer of the research will determine their final form. The researcher will have to balance the various sources of error that can arise in the process when determining this final form. In effecting this balance, the researcher must be concerned with assessing and minimizing total error; this often means assuming additional error in one of the parts of the process so that total error can be diminished.

APPENDIX A   Cumulative Standard Unit Normal Distribution

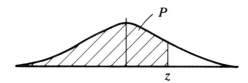

Values of P corresponding to Z for the normal curve. Z is the standard normal variable. The value of P for $-Z$ equals one minus the value of P for $+Z$, (e.g., the P for -1.62 equals $1 - .9474 = .0526$).

Z	.00	.01	.02	.03	.04	.05	.06	.07	.08	.09
.0	.5000	.5040	.5080	.5120	.5160	.5199	.5239	.5279	.5319	.5359
.1	.5398	.5438	.5478	.5517	.5557	.5596	.5636	.5675	.5714	.5753
.2	.5793	.5832	.5871	.5910	.5948	.5987	.6026	.6064	.6103	.6141
.3	.6179	.6217	.6255	.6293	.6331	.6368	.6406	.6443	.6480	.6517
.4	.6554	.6591	.6628	.6664	.6700	.6736	.6772	.6808	.6844	.6879
.5	.6915	.6950	.6985	.7019	.7054	.7088	.7123	.7157	.7190	.7224
.6	.7257	.7291	.7324	.7357	.7389	.7422	.7454	.7486	.7517	.7549
.7	.7580	.7611	.7642	.7673	.7704	.7734	.7764	.7794	.7823	.7852
.8	.7881	.7910	.7939	.7967	.7995	.8023	.8051	.8078	.8106	.8133
.9	.8159	.8186	.8212	.8238	.8264	.8289	.8315	.8340	.8365	.8389
1.0	.8413	.8438	.8461	.8485	.8508	.8531	.8554	.8577	.8599	.8621
1.1	.8643	.8665	.8686	.8708	.8729	.8749	.8770	.8790	.8810	.8830
1.2	.8849	.8869	.8888	.8907	.8925	.8944	.8962	.8980	.8997	.9015
1.3	.9032	.9049	.9066	.9082	.9099	.9115	.9131	.9147	.9162	.9177
1.4	.9192	.9207	.9222	.9236	.9251	.9265	.9279	.9292	.9306	.9319
1.5	.9332	.9345	.9357	.9370	.9382	.9394	.9406	.9418	.9429	.9441
1.6	.9452	.9463	.9474	.9484	.9495	.9505	.9515	.9525	.9535	.9545
1.7	.9554	.9564	.9573	.9582	.9591	.9599	.9608	.9616	.9625	.9633
1.8	.9641	.9649	.9656	.9664	.9671	.9678	.9686	.9693	.9699	.9706
1.9	.9713	.9719	.9726	.9732	.9738	.9744	.9750	.9756	.9761	.9767
2.0	.9772	.9778	.9783	.9788	.9793	.9798	.9803	.9808	.9812	.9817
2.1	.9821	.9826	.9830	.9834	.9838	.9842	.9846	.9850	.9854	.9857
2.2	.9861	.9864	.9868	.9871	.9875	.9878	.9881	.9884	.9887	.9890
2.3	.9893	.9896	.9898	.9901	.9904	.9906	.9909	.9911	.9913	.9916
2.4	.9918	.9920	.9922	.9925	.9927	.9929	.9931	.9932	.9934	.9936
2.5	.9938	.9940	.9941	.9943	.9945	.9946	.9948	.9949	.9951	.9952
2.6	.9953	.9955	.9956	.9957	.9959	.9960	.9961	.9962	.9963	.9964
2.7	.9965	.9966	.9967	.9968	.9969	.9970	.9971	.9972	.9973	.9974
2.8	.9974	.9975	.9976	.9977	.9977	.9978	.9979	.9979	.9980	.9981
2.9	.9981	.9982	.9982	.9983	.9984	.9984	.9985	.9985	.9986	.9986
3.0	.9987	.9987	.9987	.9988	.9988	.9989	.9989	.9989	.9990	.9990
3.1	.9990	.9991	.9991	.9991	.9992	.9992	.9992	.9992	.9993	.9993
3.2	.9993	.9993	.9994	.9994	.9994	.9994	.9994	.9995	.9995	.9995
3.3	.9995	.9995	.9995	.9996	.9996	.9996	.9996	.9996	.9996	.9997
3.4	.9997	.9997	.9997	.9997	.9997	.9997	.9997	.9997	.9997	.9998

Source: Appendix A from *Analyzing Multivariate Data* by Paul E. Green, copyright © 1978 by The Dryden Press. Reprinted by permission of the publisher.

APPENDIX B Selected Percentiles of the χ^2 Distribution

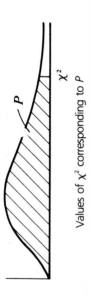

Values of χ^2 corresponding to P

ν	$\chi^2_{.005}$	$\chi^2_{.01}$	$\chi^2_{.025}$	$\chi^2_{.05}$	$\chi^2_{.10}$	$\chi^2_{.90}$	$\chi^2_{.95}$	$\chi^2_{.975}$	$\chi^2_{.99}$	$\chi^2_{.995}$
1	.000039	.00016	.00098	.0039	.0158	2.71	3.84	5.02	6.63	7.88
2	.0100	.0201	.0506	.1026	.2107	4.61	5.99	7.38	9.21	10.60
3	.0717	.115	.216	.352	.584	6.25	7.81	9.35	11.34	12.84
4	.207	.297	.484	.711	1.064	7.78	9.49	11.14	13.28	14.86
5	.412	.554	.831	1.15	1.61	9.24	11.07	12.83	15.09	16.75
6	.676	.872	1.24	1.64	2.20	10.64	12.59	14.45	16.81	18.55
7	.989	1.24	1.69	2.17	2.83	12.02	14.07	16.01	18.48	20.28
8	1.34	1.65	2.18	2.73	3.49	13.36	15.51	17.53	20.09	21.96
9	1.73	2.09	2.70	3.33	4.17	14.68	16.92	19.02	21.67	23.59
10	2.16	2.56	3.25	3.94	4.87	15.99	18.31	20.48	23.21	25.19
11	2.60	3.05	3.82	4.57	5.58	17.28	19.68	21.92	24.73	26.76
12	3.07	3.57	4.40	5.23	6.30	18.55	21.03	23.34	26.22	28.30
13	3.57	4.11	5.01	5.89	7.04	19.81	22.36	24.74	27.69	29.82
14	4.07	4.66	5.63	6.57	7.79	21.06	23.68	26.12	29.14	31.32
15	4.60	5.23	6.26	7.26	8.55	22.31	25.00	27.49	30.58	32.80
16	5.14	5.81	6.91	7.96	9.31	23.54	26.30	28.85	32.00	34.27
18	6.26	7.01	8.23	9.39	10.86	25.99	28.87	31.53	34.81	37.16
20	7.43	8.26	9.59	10.85	12.44	28.41	31.41	34.17	37.57	40.00
24	9.89	10.86	12.40	13.85	15.66	33.20	36.42	39.36	42.98	45.56
30	13.79	14.95	16.79	18.49	20.60	40.26	43.77	46.98	50.89	53.67
40	20.71	22.16	24.43	26.51	29.05	51.81	55.76	59.34	63.69	66.77
60	35.53	37.48	40.48	43.19	46.46	74.40	79.08	83.30	88.38	91.95
120	83.85	86.92	91.58	95.70	100.62	140.23	146.57	152.21	158.95	163.64

Source: Adapted with permission from *Introduction to Statistical Analysis* (2d ed.) by W. J. Dixon and F. J. Massey, Jr., McGraw-Hill Book Company, Inc., copyright 1957.

APPENDIX C   Upper Percentiles of the *t* Distribution

ν	.75	.90	.95	.975	.99	.995	.9995
1	1.000	3.078	6.314	12.706	31.821	63.657	636.619
2	.816	1.886	2.920	4.303	6.965	9.925	31.598
3	.765	1.638	2.353	3.182	4.541	5.841	12.941
4	.741	1.533	2.132	2.776	3.747	4.604	8.610
5	.727	1.476	2.015	2.571	3.365	4.032	6.859
6	.718	1.440	1.943	2.447	3.143	3.707	5.959
7	.711	1.415	1.895	2.365	2.998	3.499	5.405
8	.706	1.397	1.860	2.306	2.896	3.355	5.041
9	.703	1.383	1.833	2.262	2.821	3.250	4.781
10	.700	1.372	1.812	2.228	2.764	3.169	4.587
11	.697	1.363	1.796	2.201	2.718	3.106	4.437
12	.695	1.356	1.782	2.179	2.681	3.055	4.318
13	.694	1.350	1.771	2.160	2.650	3.012	4.221
14	.692	1.345	1.761	2.145	2.624	2.977	4.140
15	.691	1.341	1.753	2.131	2.602	2.947	4.073
16	.690	1.337	1.746	2.120	2.583	2.921	4.015
17	.689	1.333	1.740	2.110	2.567	2.898	3.965
18	.688	1.330	1.734	2.101	2.552	2.878	3.922
19	.688	1.328	1.729	2.093	2.339	2.861	3.883
20	.687	1.325	1.725	2.086	2.528	2.845	3.850
21	.686	1.323	1.721	2.080	2.518	2.831	3.819
22	.686	1.321	1.717	2.074	2.508	2.819	3.792
23	.685	1.319	1.714	2.069	2.500	2.807	3.767
24	.685	1.318	1.711	2.064	2.492	2.797	3.745
25	.684	1.316	1.708	2.060	2.485	2.787	3.725
26	.684	1.315	1.706	2.056	2.479	2.779	3.707
27	.684	1.314	1.703	2.052	2.473	2.771	3.690
28	.683	1.313	1.701	2.048	2.467	2.763	3.674
29	.683	1.311	1.699	2.045	2.462	2.756	3.659
30	.683	1.310	1.697	2.042	2.457	2.750	3.646
40	.681	1.303	1.684	2.021	2.423	2.704	3.551
60	.679	1.296	1.671	2.000	2.390	2.660	3.460
120	.677	1.289	1.658	1.980	2.358	2.617	3.373
∞	.674	1.282	1.645	1.960	2.326	2.576	3.291

Top-left header: $1 - \alpha$; left axis label: ν = degrees of freedom

Source: Table taken form Table III of Fisher and Yates: *Statistical Tables for Biological, Agricultural and Medical Research* (6th Edition 1974) published by Longman Group UK Ltd., London (previously published by Oliver and Boyd Ltd., Edinburgh) and by permission of the authors and publishers.

APPENDIX D Selected Percentiles of the F Distribution

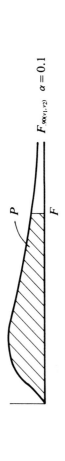

$F_{.90(\nu_1, \nu_2)}$ $\alpha = 0.1$

ν_1 = degrees of freedom for numerator

ν_2 = degrees of freedom for denominator

$\nu_2 \backslash \nu_1$	1	2	3	4	5	6	7	8	9	10	12	15	20	24	30	40	60	120	∞
1	39.86	49.50	53.59	55.83	57.24	58.20	58.91	59.44	59.86	60.19	60.71	61.22	61.74	62.00	62.26	62.53	62.79	63.06	63.33
2	8.53	9.00	9.16	9.24	9.29	9.33	9.35	9.37	9.38	9.39	9.41	9.42	9.44	9.45	9.46	9.47	9.47	9.48	9.49
3	5.54	5.46	5.39	5.34	5.31	5.28	5.27	5.25	5.24	5.23	5.22	5.20	5.18	5.18	5.17	5.16	5.15	5.14	5.13
4	4.54	4.32	4.19	4.11	4.05	4.01	3.98	3.95	3.94	3.92	3.90	3.87	3.84	3.83	3.82	3.80	3.79	3.78	3.76
5	4.06	3.78	3.62	3.52	3.45	3.40	3.37	3.34	3.32	3.30	3.27	3.24	3.21	3.19	3.17	3.16	3.14	3.12	3.10
6	3.78	3.46	3.29	3.18	3.11	3.05	3.01	2.98	2.96	2.94	2.90	2.87	2.84	2.82	2.80	2.78	2.76	2.74	2.72
7	3.59	3.26	3.07	2.96	2.88	2.83	2.78	2.75	2.72	2.70	2.67	2.63	2.59	2.58	2.56	2.54	2.51	2.49	2.47
8	3.46	3.11	2.92	2.81	2.73	2.67	2.62	2.59	2.56	2.50	2.50	2.46	2.42	2.40	2.38	2.36	2.34	2.32	2.29
9	3.36	3.01	2.81	2.69	2.61	2.55	2.51	2.47	2.44	2.42	2.38	2.34	2.30	2.28	2.25	2.23	2.21	2.18	2.16
10	3.29	2.92	2.73	2.61	2.52	2.46	2.41	2.38	2.35	2.32	2.28	2.24	2.20	2.18	2.16	2.13	2.11	2.08	2.06
11	3.23	2.86	2.66	2.54	2.45	2.39	2.34	2.30	2.27	2.25	2.21	2.17	2.12	2.10	2.08	2.05	2.03	2.00	1.97
12	3.18	2.81	2.61	2.48	2.39	2.33	2.28	2.24	2.21	2.19	2.15	2.10	2.06	2.04	2.01	1.99	1.96	1.93	1.90
13	3.14	2.76	2.56	2.43	2.35	2.28	2.23	2.20	2.16	2.14	2.10	2.05	2.01	1.98	1.96	1.93	1.90	1.88	1.85
14	3.10	2.73	2.52	2.39	2.31	2.24	2.19	2.15	2.12	2.10	2.05	2.01	1.96	1.94	1.91	1.89	1.86	1.83	1.80
15	3.07	2.70	2.49	2.36	2.27	2.21	2.16	2.12	2.09	2.06	2.02	1.97	1.92	1.90	1.87	1.85	1.82	1.79	1.76
16	3.05	2.67	2.46	2.33	2.24	2.18	2.13	2.09	2.06	2.03	1.99	1.94	1.89	1.87	1.84	1.81	1.78	1.75	1.72
17	3.03	2.64	2.44	2.31	2.22	2.15	2.10	2.06	2.03	2.00	1.96	1.91	1.86	1.84	1.81	1.78	1.75	1.72	1.69
18	3.01	2.62	2.42	2.29	2.20	2.13	2.08	2.04	2.00	1.98	1.93	1.89	1.84	1.81	1.78	1.75	1.72	1.69	1.66
19	2.99	2.61	2.40	2.27	2.18	2.11	2.06	2.02	1.98	1.96	1.91	1.86	1.81	1.79	1.76	1.73	1.70	1.67	1.63
20	2.97	2.59	2.38	2.25	2.16	2.09	2.04	2.00	1.96	1.94	1.89	1.84	1.79	1.77	1.74	1.71	1.68	1.64	1.61
21	2.96	2.57	2.36	2.23	2.14	2.08	2.02	1.98	1.95	1.92	1.87	1.83	1.78	1.75	1.72	1.69	1.66	1.62	1.59
22	2.95	2.56	2.35	2.22	2.13	2.06	2.01	1.97	1.93	1.90	1.86	1.81	1.76	1.73	1.70	1.67	1.64	1.60	1.57
23	2.94	2.55	2.34	2.21	2.11	2.05	1.99	1.95	1.92	1.89	1.84	1.80	1.74	1.72	1.69	1.66	1.62	1.59	1.55
24	2.93	2.54	2.33	2.19	2.10	2.04	1.98	1.94	1.91	1.88	1.83	1.78	1.73	1.70	1.67	1.64	1.61	1.57	1.53
25	2.92	2.53	2.32	2.18	2.09	2.02	1.97	1.93	1.89	1.87	1.82	1.77	1.72	1.69	1.66	1.63	1.59	1.56	1.52
26	2.91	2.52	2.31	2.17	2.08	2.01	1.96	1.92	1.88	1.86	1.81	1.76	1.71	1.68	1.65	1.61	1.58	1.54	1.50
27	2.90	2.51	2.30	2.17	2.07	2.00	1.95	1.91	1.87	1.85	1.80	1.75	1.70	1.67	1.64	1.60	1.57	1.53	1.49
28	2.89	2.50	2.29	2.16	2.06	2.00	1.94	1.90	1.87	1.84	1.79	1.74	1.69	1.66	1.63	1.59	1.56	1.52	1.48
29	2.89	2.50	2.28	2.15	2.06	1.99	1.93	1.89	1.86	1.83	1.78	1.73	1.68	1.65	1.62	1.58	1.55	1.51	1.47
30	2.88	2.49	2.28	2.14	2.05	1.98	1.93	1.88	1.85	1.82	1.77	1.72	1.67	1.64	1.61	1.57	1.54	1.50	1.46
40	2.84	2.44	2.23	2.09	2.00	1.93	1.87	1.83	1.79	1.76	1.71	1.66	1.61	1.57	1.54	1.51	1.47	1.42	1.38
60	2.79	2.39	2.18	2.04	1.95	1.87	1.82	1.77	1.74	1.71	1.66	1.60	1.54	1.51	1.48	1.44	1.40	1.35	1.29
120	2.75	2.35	2.13	1.99	1.90	1.82	1.77	1.72	1.68	1.65	1.60	1.55	1.48	1.45	1.41	1.37	1.32	1.26	1.19
∞	2.71	2.30	2.08	1.94	1.85	1.77	1.72	1.67	1.63	1.60	1.55	1.49	1.42	1.38	1.34	1.30	1.24	1.17	1.00

$$F_{.95}(v_1, v_2) \qquad \alpha = 0.05$$

v_1 = degrees of freedom for numerator

v_2 \ v_1	1	2	3	4	5	6	7	8	9	10	12	15	20	24	30	40	60	120	∞
1	161.4	199.5	215.7	224.6	230.2	234.0	236.8	238.9	240.5	241.9	243.9	245.9	248.0	249.1	250.1	251.1	252.2	253.3	254.3
2	18.51	19.00	19.16	19.25	19.30	19.33	19.35	19.37	19.38	19.40	19.41	19.43	19.45	19.45	19.46	19.47	19.48	19.49	19.50
3	10.13	9.55	9.28	9.12	9.01	8.94	8.89	8.85	8.81	8.79	8.74	8.70	8.66	8.64	8.62	8.59	8.57	8.55	8.53
4	7.71	6.94	6.59	6.39	6.26	6.16	6.09	6.04	6.00	5.96	5.91	5.86	5.80	5.77	5.75	5.72	5.69	5.66	5.63
5	6.61	5.79	5.41	5.19	5.05	4.95	4.88	4.82	4.77	4.74	4.68	4.62	4.56	4.53	4.50	4.46	4.43	4.40	4.36
6	5.99	5.14	4.76	4.53	4.39	4.28	4.21	4.15	4.10	4.06	4.00	3.94	3.87	3.84	3.81	3.77	3.74	3.70	3.67
7	5.59	4.74	4.35	4.12	3.97	3.87	3.79	3.73	3.68	3.64	3.57	3.51	3.44	3.41	3.38	3.34	3.30	3.27	3.23
8	5.32	4.46	4.07	3.84	3.69	3.58	3.50	3.44	3.39	3.35	3.28	3.22	3.15	3.12	3.08	3.04	3.01	2.97	2.93
9	5.12	4.26	3.86	3.63	3.48	3.37	3.29	3.23	3.18	3.14	3.07	3.01	2.94	2.90	2.86	2.83	2.79	2.75	2.71
10	4.96	4.10	3.71	3.48	3.33	3.22	3.14	3.07	3.02	2.98	2.91	2.85	2.77	2.74	2.70	2.66	2.62	2.58	2.54
11	4.84	3.98	3.59	3.36	3.20	3.09	3.01	2.95	2.90	2.85	2.79	2.72	2.65	2.61	2.57	2.53	2.49	2.45	2.40
12	4.75	3.89	3.49	3.26	3.11	3.00	2.91	2.85	2.80	2.75	2.69	2.62	2.54	2.51	2.47	2.43	2.38	2.34	2.30
13	4.67	3.81	3.41	3.18	3.03	2.92	2.83	2.77	2.71	2.67	2.60	2.53	2.46	2.42	2.38	2.34	2.30	2.25	2.21
14	4.60	3.74	3.34	3.11	2.96	2.85	2.76	2.70	2.65	2.60	2.53	2.46	2.39	2.35	2.31	2.27	2.22	2.18	2.13
15	4.54	3.68	3.29	3.06	2.90	2.79	2.71	2.64	2.59	2.54	2.48	2.40	2.33	2.29	2.25	2.20	2.16	2.11	2.07
16	4.49	3.63	3.24	3.01	2.85	2.74	2.66	2.59	2.54	2.49	2.42	2.35	2.28	2.24	2.19	2.15	2.11	2.06	2.01
17	4.45	3.59	3.20	2.96	2.81	2.70	2.61	2.55	2.49	2.45	2.38	2.31	2.23	2.19	2.15	2.10	2.06	2.01	1.96
18	4.41	3.55	3.16	2.93	2.77	2.66	2.58	2.51	2.46	2.41	2.34	2.27	2.19	2.15	2.11	2.06	2.02	1.97	1.92
19	4.38	3.52	3.13	2.90	2.74	2.63	2.54	2.48	2.42	2.38	2.31	2.23	2.16	2.11	2.07	2.03	1.98	1.93	1.88
20	4.35	3.49	3.10	2.87	2.71	2.60	2.51	2.45	2.39	2.35	2.28	2.20	2.12	2.08	2.04	1.99	1.95	1.90	1.84
21	4.32	3.47	3.07	2.84	2.68	2.57	2.49	2.42	2.37	2.32	2.25	2.18	2.10	2.05	2.01	1.96	1.92	1.87	1.81
22	4.30	3.44	3.05	2.82	2.66	2.55	2.46	2.40	2.34	2.30	2.23	2.15	2.07	2.03	1.98	1.94	1.89	1.84	1.78
23	4.28	3.42	3.03	2.80	2.64	2.53	2.44	2.37	2.32	2.27	2.20	2.13	2.05	2.01	1.96	1.91	1.86	1.81	1.76
24	4.26	3.40	3.01	2.78	2.62	2.51	2.42	2.36	2.30	2.25	2.18	2.11	2.03	1.98	1.94	1.89	1.84	1.79	1.73
25	4.24	3.39	2.99	2.76	2.60	2.49	2.40	2.34	2.28	2.24	2.16	2.09	2.01	1.96	1.92	1.87	1.82	1.77	1.71
26	4.23	3.37	2.98	2.74	2.59	2.47	2.39	2.32	2.27	2.22	2.15	2.07	1.99	1.95	1.90	1.85	1.80	1.75	1.69
27	4.21	3.35	2.96	2.73	2.57	2.46	2.37	2.31	2.25	2.20	2.13	2.06	1.97	1.93	1.88	1.84	1.79	1.73	1.67
28	4.20	3.34	2.95	2.71	2.56	2.45	2.36	2.29	2.24	2.19	2.12	2.04	1.96	1.91	1.87	1.82	1.77	1.71	1.65
29	4.18	3.33	2.93	2.70	2.55	2.43	2.35	2.28	2.22	2.18	2.10	2.03	1.94	1.90	1.85	1.81	1.75	1.70	1.64
30	4.17	3.32	2.92	2.69	2.53	2.42	2.33	2.27	2.21	2.16	2.09	2.01	1.93	1.89	1.84	1.79	1.74	1.68	1.62
40	4.08	3.23	2.84	2.61	2.45	2.34	2.25	2.18	2.12	2.08	2.00	1.92	1.84	1.79	1.74	1.69	1.64	1.58	1.51
60	4.00	3.15	2.76	2.53	2.37	2.25	2.17	2.10	2.04	1.99	1.92	1.84	1.75	1.70	1.65	1.59	1.53	1.47	1.39
120	3.92	3.07	2.68	2.45	2.29	2.17	2.09	2.02	1.96	1.91	1.83	1.75	1.66	1.61	1.55	1.50	1.43	1.35	1.25
∞	3.84	3.00	2.60	2.37	2.21	2.10	2.01	1.94	1.88	1.83	1.75	1.67	1.57	1.52	1.46	1.39	1.32	1.22	1.00

v_2 = degrees of freedom for denominator

APPENDIX D continued

$$F_{.975}(v_1, v_2) \qquad \alpha = 0.025$$

v_1 = degrees of freedom for numerator

v_2	1	2	3	4	5	6	7	8	9	10	12	15	20	24	30	40	60	120	∞
1	647.8	799.5	864.2	899.6	921.8	937.1	948.2	956.7	963.3	968.6	976.7	984.9	993.1	997.2	1001	1006	1010	1014	1018
2	38.51	39.00	39.17	39.25	39.30	39.33	39.36	39.37	39.39	39.40	39.41	39.43	39.45	39.46	39.46	39.47	39.48	39.49	39.50
3	17.44	16.04	15.44	15.10	14.88	14.73	14.62	14.54	14.47	14.42	14.34	14.25	14.17	14.12	14.08	14.04	13.99	13.95	13.90
4	12.22	10.65	9.98	9.60	9.36	9.20	9.07	8.98	8.90	8.84	8.75	8.66	8.56	8.51	8.46	8.41	8.36	8.31	8.26
5	10.01	8.43	7.76	7.39	7.15	6.98	6.85	6.76	6.68	6.62	6.52	6.43	6.33	6.28	6.23	6.18	6.12	6.07	6.02
6	8.81	7.26	6.60	6.23	5.99	5.82	5.70	5.60	5.52	5.46	5.37	5.27	5.17	5.12	5.07	5.01	4.96	4.90	4.85
7	8.07	6.54	5.89	5.52	5.29	5.12	4.99	4.90	4.82	4.76	4.67	4.57	4.47	4.42	4.36	4.31	4.25	4.20	4.14
8	7.57	6.06	5.42	5.05	4.82	4.65	4.53	4.43	4.36	4.30	4.20	4.10	4.00	3.95	3.89	3.84	3.78	3.73	3.67
9	7.21	5.71	5.08	4.72	4.48	4.32	4.20	4.10	4.03	3.96	3.87	3.77	3.67	3.61	3.56	3.51	3.45	3.39	3.33
10	6.94	5.46	4.83	4.47	4.24	4.07	3.95	3.85	3.78	3.72	3.62	3.52	3.42	3.37	3.31	3.26	3.20	3.14	3.08
11	6.72	5.26	4.63	4.28	4.04	3.88	3.76	3.66	3.59	3.53	3.43	3.33	3.23	3.17	3.12	3.06	3.00	2.94	2.88
12	6.55	5.10	4.47	4.12	3.89	3.73	3.61	3.51	3.44	3.37	3.28	3.18	3.07	3.02	2.96	2.91	2.85	2.79	2.72
13	6.41	4.97	4.35	4.00	3.77	3.60	3.48	3.39	3.31	3.25	3.15	3.05	2.95	2.89	2.84	2.78	2.72	2.66	2.60
14	6.30	4.86	4.24	3.89	3.66	3.50	3.38	3.29	3.21	3.15	3.05	2.95	2.84	2.79	2.73	2.67	2.61	2.55	2.49
15	6.20	4.77	4.15	3.80	3.58	3.41	3.29	3.20	3.12	3.06	2.96	2.86	2.76	2.70	2.64	2.59	2.52	2.46	2.40
16	6.12	4.69	4.08	3.73	3.50	3.34	3.22	3.12	3.05	2.99	2.89	2.79	2.68	2.63	2.57	2.51	2.45	2.38	2.32
17	6.04	4.62	4.01	3.66	3.44	3.28	3.16	3.06	2.98	2.92	2.82	2.72	2.62	2.56	2.50	2.44	2.38	2.32	2.25
18	5.98	4.56	3.95	3.61	3.38	3.22	3.10	3.01	2.93	2.87	2.77	2.67	2.56	2.50	2.44	2.38	2.32	2.26	2.19
19	5.92	4.51	3.90	3.56	3.33	3.17	3.05	2.96	2.88	2.82	2.72	2.62	2.51	2.45	2.39	2.33	2.27	2.20	2.13
20	5.87	4.46	3.86	3.51	3.29	3.13	3.01	2.91	2.84	2.77	2.68	2.57	2.46	2.41	2.35	2.29	2.22	2.16	2.09
21	5.83	4.42	3.82	3.48	3.25	3.09	2.97	2.87	2.80	2.73	2.64	2.53	2.42	2.37	2.31	2.25	2.18	2.11	2.04
22	5.79	4.38	3.78	3.44	3.22	3.05	2.93	2.84	2.76	2.70	2.60	2.50	2.39	2.33	2.27	2.21	2.14	2.08	2.00
23	5.75	4.35	3.75	3.41	3.18	3.02	2.90	2.81	2.73	2.67	2.57	2.47	2.36	2.30	2.24	2.18	2.11	2.04	1.97
24	5.72	4.32	3.72	3.38	3.15	2.99	2.87	2.78	2.70	2.64	2.54	2.44	2.33	2.27	2.21	2.15	2.08	2.01	1.94
25	5.69	4.29	3.69	3.35	3.13	2.97	2.85	2.75	2.68	2.61	2.51	2.41	2.30	2.24	2.18	2.12	2.05	1.98	1.91
26	5.66	4.27	3.67	3.33	3.10	2.94	2.82	2.73	2.65	2.59	2.49	2.39	2.28	2.22	2.16	2.09	2.03	1.95	1.88
27	5.63	4.24	3.65	3.31	3.08	2.92	2.80	2.71	2.63	2.57	2.47	2.36	2.25	2.19	2.13	2.07	2.00	1.93	1.85
28	5.61	4.22	3.63	3.29	3.06	2.90	2.78	2.69	2.61	2.55	2.45	2.34	2.23	2.17	2.11	2.05	1.98	1.91	1.83
29	5.59	4.20	3.61	3.27	3.04	2.88	2.76	2.67	2.59	2.53	2.43	2.32	2.21	2.15	2.09	2.03	1.96	1.89	1.81
30	5.57	4.18	3.59	3.25	3.03	2.87	2.75	2.65	2.57	2.51	2.41	2.31	2.20	2.14	2.07	2.01	1.94	1.87	1.79
40	5.42	4.05	3.46	3.13	2.90	2.74	2.62	2.53	2.45	2.39	2.29	2.18	2.07	2.01	1.94	1.88	1.80	1.72	1.64
60	5.29	3.93	3.34	3.01	2.79	2.63	2.51	2.41	2.33	2.27	2.17	2.06	1.94	1.88	1.82	1.74	1.67	1.58	1.48
120	5.15	3.80	3.23	2.89	2.67	2.52	2.39	2.30	2.22	2.16	2.05	1.94	1.82	1.76	1.69	1.61	1.53	1.43	1.31
∞	5.02	3.69	3.12	2.79	2.57	2.41	2.29	2.19	2.11	2.05	1.94	1.83	1.71	1.64	1.57	1.48	1.39	1.27	1.00

v_2 = degrees of freedom for denominator

APPENDIX D *continued*

ν_1 = degrees of freedom for numerator

$F_{.99}(\nu_1, \nu_2)$ $\alpha = 0.01$

ν_2 \ ν_1	1	2	3	4	5	6	7	8	9	10	12	15	20	24	30	40	60	120	∞
1	4052	4999.5	5403	5625	5764	5859	5928	5982	6022	6056	6106	6157	6209	6235	6261	6287	6313	6339	6366
2	98.50	99.00	99.17	99.25	99.30	99.33	99.36	99.37	99.39	99.40	99.42	99.43	99.45	99.46	99.47	99.47	99.48	99.49	99.50
3	34.12	30.82	29.46	28.71	28.24	27.91	27.67	27.49	27.35	27.23	27.05	26.87	26.69	26.60	26.50	26.41	26.32	26.22	26.13
4	21.20	18.00	16.69	15.98	15.52	15.21	14.98	14.80	14.66	14.55	14.37	14.20	14.02	13.93	13.84	13.75	13.65	13.56	13.46
5	16.26	13.27	12.06	11.39	10.97	10.67	10.46	10.29	10.16	10.05	9.89	9.72	9.55	9.47	9.38	9.29	9.20	9.11	9.02
6	13.75	10.92	9.78	9.15	8.75	8.47	8.26	8.10	7.98	7.87	7.72	7.56	7.40	7.31	7.23	7.14	7.06	6.97	6.88
7	12.25	9.55	8.45	7.85	7.46	7.19	6.99	6.84	6.72	6.62	6.47	6.31	6.16	6.07	5.99	5.91	5.82	5.74	5.65
8	11.26	8.65	7.59	7.01	6.63	6.37	6.18	6.03	5.91	5.81	5.67	5.52	5.36	5.28	5.20	5.12	5.03	4.95	4.86
9	10.56	8.02	6.99	6.42	6.06	5.80	5.61	5.47	5.35	5.26	5.11	4.96	4.81	4.73	4.65	4.57	4.48	4.40	4.31
10	10.04	7.56	6.55	5.99	5.64	5.39	5.20	5.06	4.94	4.85	4.71	4.56	4.41	4.33	4.25	4.17	4.08	4.00	3.91
11	9.65	7.21	6.22	5.67	5.32	5.07	4.89	4.74	4.63	4.54	4.40	4.25	4.10	4.02	3.94	3.86	3.78	3.69	3.60
12	9.33	6.93	5.95	5.41	5.06	4.82	4.64	4.50	4.39	4.30	4.16	4.01	3.86	3.78	3.70	3.62	3.54	3.45	3.36
13	9.07	6.70	5.74	5.21	4.86	4.62	4.44	4.30	4.19	4.10	3.96	3.82	3.66	3.59	3.51	3.43	3.34	3.25	3.17
14	8.86	6.51	5.56	5.04	4.69	4.46	4.28	4.14	4.03	3.94	3.80	3.66	3.51	3.43	3.35	3.27	3.18	3.09	3.00
15	8.68	6.36	5.42	4.89	4.56	4.32	4.14	4.00	3.89	3.80	3.67	3.52	3.37	3.29	3.21	3.13	3.05	2.96	2.87
16	8.53	6.23	5.29	4.77	4.44	4.20	4.03	3.89	3.78	3.69	3.55	3.41	3.26	3.18	3.10	3.02	2.93	2.84	2.75
17	8.40	6.11	5.18	4.67	4.34	4.10	3.93	3.79	3.68	3.59	3.46	3.31	3.16	3.08	3.00	2.92	2.83	2.75	2.65
18	8.29	6.01	5.09	4.58	4.25	4.01	3.84	3.71	3.60	3.51	3.37	3.23	3.08	3.00	2.92	2.84	2.75	2.66	2.57
19	8.18	5.93	5.01	4.50	4.17	3.94	3.77	3.63	3.52	3.43	3.30	3.15	3.00	2.92	2.84	2.76	2.67	2.58	2.49
20	8.10	5.85	4.94	4.43	4.10	3.87	3.70	3.56	3.46	3.37	3.23	3.09	2.94	2.86	2.78	2.69	2.61	2.52	2.42
21	8.02	5.78	4.87	4.37	4.04	3.81	3.64	3.51	3.40	3.31	3.17	3.03	2.88	2.80	2.72	2.64	2.55	2.46	2.36
22	7.95	5.72	4.82	4.31	3.99	3.76	3.59	3.45	3.35	3.26	3.12	2.98	2.83	2.75	2.67	2.58	2.50	2.40	2.31
23	7.88	5.66	4.76	4.26	3.94	3.71	3.54	3.41	3.30	3.21	3.07	2.93	2.78	2.70	2.62	2.54	2.45	2.35	2.26
24	7.82	5.61	4.72	4.22	3.90	3.67	3.50	3.36	3.26	3.17	3.03	2.89	2.74	2.66	2.58	2.49	2.40	2.31	2.21
25	7.77	5.57	4.68	4.18	3.85	3.63	3.46	3.32	3.22	3.13	2.99	2.85	2.70	2.62	2.54	2.45	2.36	2.27	2.17
26	7.72	5.53	4.64	4.14	3.82	3.59	3.42	3.29	3.18	3.09	2.96	2.81	2.66	2.58	2.50	2.42	2.33	2.23	2.13
27	7.68	5.49	4.60	4.11	3.78	3.56	3.39	3.26	3.15	3.06	2.93	2.78	2.63	2.55	2.47	2.38	2.29	2.20	2.10
28	7.64	5.45	4.57	4.07	3.75	3.53	3.36	3.23	3.12	3.03	2.90	2.75	2.60	2.52	2.44	2.35	2.26	2.17	2.06
29	7.60	5.42	4.54	4.04	3.73	3.50	3.33	3.20	3.09	3.00	2.87	2.73	2.57	2.49	2.41	2.33	2.23	2.14	2.03
30	7.56	5.39	4.51	4.02	3.70	3.47	3.30	3.17	3.07	2.98	2.84	2.70	2.55	2.47	2.39	2.30	2.21	2.11	2.01
40	7.31	5.18	4.31	3.83	3.51	3.29	3.12	2.99	2.89	2.80	2.66	2.52	2.37	2.29	2.20	2.11	2.02	1.92	1.80
60	7.08	4.98	4.13	3.65	3.34	3.12	2.95	2.82	2.72	2.63	2.50	2.35	2.20	2.12	2.03	1.94	1.84	1.73	1.60
120	6.85	4.79	3.95	3.48	3.17	2.96	2.79	2.66	2.56	2.47	2.34	2.19	2.03	1.95	1.86	1.76	1.66	1.53	1.38
∞	6.63	4.61	3.78	3.32	3.02	2.80	2.64	2.51	2.41	2.32	2.18	2.04	1.88	1.79	1.70	1.59	1.47	1.32	1.00

ν_2 = degrees of freedom for denominator

Source: Adapted from *Biometrika Tables for Statisticians*, Vol. 1 (2nd ed.), edited by E. S. Pearson and H. O. Hartley, 1958. Reproduced by permission of the Biometrika Trustees, the Imperial College of Science and Technology, London, England.

absolute precision Degree of precision in an estimate of a parameter expressed as within plus or minus so many units.

accuracy Criterion used to evaluate a research report according to whether the reasoning in the report is logical and the information correct.

administrative control Term applied to studies relying on questionnaires and referring to the speed, cost, and control of the replies afforded by the mode of administration.

analysis of selected cases Intensive study of selected examples of the phenomenon of interest.

analysis of variance (ANOVA) Statistical test employed with interval data to determine if $k(k \geq 2)$ samples came from populations with equal means.

area sampling Form of cluster sampling in which areas (for example, census tracts, blocks) serve as the primary sampling units. The population is divided into mutually exclusive and exhaustive areas using maps, and a random sample of areas is selected. If all the households in the selected areas are used in the study, it is one-stage area sampling. If the areas themselves are subsampled with respect to households, the procedure is two-stage area sampling.

attitudes/opinions Some preference, liking, or conviction regarding a specific object or idea; a predisposition to act.

awareness/knowledge Insight into or understanding of facts about some object or phenomenon.

banner A series of cross-tabulations between a criterion, or dependent, variable and several (sometimes many) explanatory variables in a single table.

bar chart Chart in which the relative lengths of the bars show relative amounts of variables or objects.

Bayes' rule Formal mechanism for revising prior probabilities in the light of new information.

Bayesian probability Probability based on a person's subjective or personal judgments and experience.

behavior What subjects have done or are doing.

blunder Error that arises when editing, coding, entering, or tabulating the data.

brain wave research Research technique that assesses the stimuli that subjects find arousing or interesting by using electrodes fitted to the subject's head that monitor the electrical impulses emitted by the brain.

branching questions A technique used to direct respondents to different places in a questionnaire based on their response to the question at hand.

brand-switching matrix Two-way table that indicates which brands a sample of people purchased in one period and which brands they purchased in a subsequent period, thus highlighting the switches occurring among and between brands as well as the number of persons that purchased the same brand in both periods.

causal research Research design in which the major emphasis is on determining a cause-and-effect relationship.

census A complete canvass of a population.

Central-Limit Theorem Theorem that holds that if simple random samples of size n are drawn from a parent population with mean μ and variance σ^2, then when n is large, the sample mean $\bar{x}$ will be approximately normally distributed with the mean equal to μ and variance equal to σ^2/n. The approximation will become more and more accurate as n becomes larger.

central office edit   Thorough and exacting scrutiny and correction of completed data collection forms, including a decision about what to do with the data.

chi-square goodness-of-fit test Statistical test to determine whether some observed pattern of frequencies corresponds to an expected pattern.

clarity   Criterion used to evaluate a research report; specifically, whether the phrasing in the report is precise.

classical probability Probability determined by the relative frequency with which an event occurs when an experiment is repeated under controlled conditions.

cluster analysis   Body of techniques concerned with developing natural groupings of objects based on the relationships of the p variables describing the objects.

cluster sample   A probability sample distinguished by a two-step procedure in which (1) the parent population is divided into mutually exclusive and exhaustive subsets, and (2) a random sample of subsets is selected. If the investigator then uses all of the population elements in the selected subsets for the sample, the procedure is one-stage cluster sampling; if a sample of elements is selected

probabilistically from the subsets, the procedure is two-stage cluster sampling.

codebook   A document that describes each variable, gives it a code name, and identifies its location in the record.

coding   Technical procedure by which data are categorized; it involves specifying the alternative categories or classes into which the responses are to be placed and assigning code numbers to the classes.

coefficient alpha   A statistic that summarizes the extent to which a set of k-items making up a measure intercorrelate or go together; the square root of coefficient alpha is the estimated correlation of the k-item test with errorless true scores.

coefficient of concordance Statistic used with ordinal data to measure the extent of association among $k(k \geq 2)$ variables.

coefficient of determination Term used in regression analysis to refer to the relative proportion of the total variation in the criterion variable that can be explained or accounted for by the fitted regression equation.

coefficient of multiple correlation   In multiple-regression analysis, the square root of the coefficient of multiple determination.

coefficient of multiple determination   In multiple-regression analysis, the proportion of variation in the criterion variable that is accounted for by the covariation in the predictor variables.

coefficient of partial correlation In multiple-regression analysis, the square root of the coefficient of partial determination.

coefficient of partial determination   Quantity that results from a multiple-regression analysis, which indicates the proportion of variation in the criterion variable not accounted for by the earlier variables that is accounted for by adding a new variable into the regression equation.

coefficient of partial (or net) regression   Quantity resulting from a multiple-regression analysis, which indicates the average change in the criterion variable per unit change in a predictor variable, holding all other predictor variables constant; the interpretation applies only when the predictor variables are independent, as required for a valid application of the multiple-regression model.

cohort   The aggregate of individuals who experience the same event within the same time interval.

communality   Quantity resulting from a factor analysis that expresses the proportion of the variance of a variable extracted by m factors, where m can vary from one to the total number of variables; the communalities help determine how many factors should be retained in a solution.

communication   Method of data collection involving questioning of respondents to secure the desired information using a data collection instrument called a questionnaire.

comparative rating scale Scale requiring subjects to make their ratings as a series of relative judgments or comparisons rather than as independent assessments.

completely randomized design Experimental design in which the experimental treatments are assigned to the test units completely at random.

completeness Criterion used to evaluate a research report; specifically, whether the report provides all the information readers need in a language they understand.

completeness rate (C) Measure used to evaluate and compare interviewers in terms of their ability to secure needed information from contacted respondents; the completeness rate measures the proportion of complete contacts by interviewer.

computer-assisted interviewing (CAI) The conducting of surveys using computers to manage the sequence of questions in which the answers are recorded electronically through the use of a keyboard.

conciseness Criterion used to evaluate a research report; specifically, whether the writing in the report is crisp and direct.

conditional association Association existing between two variables when the levels of one or more other variables are considered in the analysis; the other variables are called control variables.

conditional probability Probability that is assigned to an Event A when it is known that

another Event B has occurred or that would be assigned to A if it were known that B had occurred.

confusion matrix Device used in discriminant analysis to assess the adequacy of the discriminant function or functions; the confusion matrix is essentially a cross-classification table, in which the variables of cross classification are the actual group membership categories and the predicted group membership categories, and the entries are the number of observations falling into each cell.

conjoint analysis Technique in which respondents' utilities or valuations of attributes are inferred from the preferences they express for various combinations of these attributes.

constant sum method A type of comparative rating scale in which an individual is instructed to divide some given sum among two or more attributes on the basis of their importance to him or her.

constitutive (conceptual) definition Definition in which a given construct is defined in terms of other constructs in the set, sometimes in the form of an equation that expresses the relationship among them.

construct validity Approach to validating a measure by determining what construct, concept, or trait the instrument is in fact measuring.

contact rate (K) Measure used to evaluate and compare the effectiveness of interviewers in making contact with designated

respondents. K = number of sample units contacted/total number of sample units approached.

content validity Approach to validating a measure by determining the adequacy with which the domain of the characteristic is captured by the measure; it is sometimes called face validity.

contingency coefficient Statistic used to measure the extent of association between two nominally scaled attributes.

contingency table Statistical test employing the χ^2 statistic that is used to determine whether the variables in a cross-classification analysis are independent.

controlled test market A market in which an entire marketing test program is conducted by an outside service. Also called a forced distribution test market.

convenience sample Nonprobability sample sometimes called an accidental sample because those included in the sample enter by accident, in that they just happen to be where the study is being conducted when it is being conducted.

convergent validity Confirmation of the existence of a construct determined by the correlations exhibited by independent measures of the construct.

cophenetic value Level at which a pair of objects or classes are actually linked in cluster analyses.

correlation analysis   Statistical technique used to measure the closeness of the linear relationship between two or more intervally scaled variables.

cross-sectional study Investigation involving a sample of elements selected from the population of interest at a single point in time.

cross tabulation   Count of the number of cases that fall into each of several categories when the categories are based on two or more variables considered simultaneously.

cumulative distribution function Function that shows the number of cases having a value less than or equal to a specified quantity; the function is generated by connecting the points representing the given combinations of Xs (values) and Ys (cumulative frequencies) with straight lines.

cutting score   Term used in discriminant analysis to indicate the score that divides the groups in terms of their respective discriminant scores; if the object's score is above the cutting score, the object is assigned to one group, whereas if its score is below the cutting score, it is assigned to the other group.

data system   The part of a decision support system that includes the processes used to capture and the methods used to store data coming from a number of external and internal sources.

decision support system (DSS) A coordinated collection of data, system tools, and techniques with supporting software and hardware

by which an organization gathers and interprets relevant information from business and the environment and turns it into a basis for marketing action.

decision tree   Decision flow diagram in which the problem is structured in chronological order, typically with small squares indicating decision forks and small circles indicating chance forks.

dendrogram   Treelike device employed to interpret the output of a cluster analysis that indicates the groups of objects forming at various similarity levels.

deontology   An ethical or moral reasoning framework that focuses on the welfare of the individual and that uses means, intentions, and features of the act itself in judging its ethicality; sometimes referred to as the rights or entitlements model.

depth interview   Unstructured personal interview in which the interviewer attempts to get subjects to talk freely and to express their true feelings.

derived population   Population of all possible distinguishable samples that could be drawn from a parent population under a specific sampling plan.

descriptive research   Research design in which the major emphasis is on determining the frequency with which something occurs or the extent to which two variables covary.

dialog system   The part of a decision support system that permits users to explore the data bases by employing the system

models to produce reports that satisfy their particular information needs. Also called language systems.

dichotomous question   Fixed-alternative question in which respondents are asked to indicate which of two alternative responses most closely corresponds to their position on a subject.

discriminant analysis Statistical technique employed to model the relationship between a dichotomous or multichotomous criterion variable and a set of p predictor variables.

discriminant validity   Criterion imposed on a measure of a construct requiring that it not correlate too highly with measures from which it is supposed to differ.

disguise   Amount of knowledge about the purpose of a study communicated to the respondent by the data collection method. An undisguised questionnaire, for example, is one in which the purpose of the research is obvious from the questions posed, whereas a disguised questionnaire attempts to hide the purpose of the study.

disproportionate stratified sampling   Stratified sample in which the individual strata or subsets are sampled in relation to both their size and their variability; strata exhibiting more variability are sampled more than proportionately to their relative size, while those that are very homogeneous are sampled less than proportionately.

domain sampling model   A measurement model that holds that the true score of a characteristic is obtained when all of the items in the domain are used to capture it. Since only a sample of items is typically used, a primary source of measurement error is the inadequate sampling of the domain of relevant items; to the extent that the sample of items correlates with true scores, it is good.

double-barreled question   A question that calls for two responses and thereby creates confusion for the respondent.

dummy table   Table that contains a title and headings to denote the categories to be used for each variable making up the table to categorize the data when it is collected.

dummy (or binary) variable Variable that is given one of two values, 0 or 1, and that is used to provide a numerical representation for attributes or characteristics that are not essentially quantitative.

editing   Inspection and correction, if necessary, of each questionnaire or observation form.

electronic test market   Market or geographic area in which a firm tracks purchases made by specific households that are part of its panel, using identification cards held by panel members and the electronic recording of the products they purchase using scanners.

element   Term used in sampling to refer to the objects on which measurements are to be taken, such as individuals, households, business firms, or other institutions.

equal-appearing intervals   Self-report technique for attitude measurement in which subjects are asked to indicate those statements in a larger list of statements (typically 20 to 22) with which they agree and disagree; subjects' attitude scores are the average score of the scale values of the statements with which they agree.

equivalence   Measure of reliability that is applied to both single instruments and measurement situations. When applied to instruments, the equivalence measure of reliability is the internal consistency or internal homogeneity of the set of items forming the scale; when applied to measurement situations, the equivalence measure of reliability focuses on whether different observers or different instruments used to measure the same individuals or objects at the same point in time yield consistent results.

ethics   A concern with the development of moral standards by which situations can be judged; applies to all situations in which there can be actual or potential harm of any kind (e.g., economic, physical, or mental) to an individual or group.

expected value   Value resulting from multiplying each consequence by the probability of that consequence occurring and summing the products.

expected value of perfect information   Difference between the expected value under certainty and the expected value of the optimal act under uncertainty.

expected value of a research procedure   Value determined by multiplying the probability of obtaining the kth research result by the expected value of the preferred decision given the kth research result and summing the products.

expected value under certainty Value derived by multiplying the consequence associated with the optimal act under each possible state of nature by the probability associated with that state of nature and summing the products.

experience survey   Interviews with people knowledgeable about the general subject being investigated.

experiment   Scientific investigation in which an investigator manipulates and controls one or more independent variables and observes the dependent variable for variation concomitant to the manipulation of the independent variables.

experimental design   Research investigation in which the investigator has direct control over at least one independent variable and manipulates at least one independent variable.

experimental mortality Experimental condition in which test units are lost during the course of an experiment.

exploratory research   Research design in which the major emphasis is on gaining ideas and insights; it is particularly helpful in breaking broad, vague problem statements into smaller, more precise subproblem statements.

external data   Data that originate outside the organization for which the research is being done.

external validity   One criterion by which an experiment is evaluated; the extent to which the observed experimental effect can be generalized to other populations and settings.

eye camera   Camera used to study eye movements while the subject reads advertising copy.

factor   Linear combination of variables.

factor analysis   Body of techniques concerned with the study of interrelationships among a set of variables, none of which is given the special status of a criterion variable.

factor loading   Quantity that results from a factor analysis and that indicates the correlation between a variable and a factor.

factorial design   Experimental design that is used when the effects of two or more variables are being studied simultaneously; each level of each factor is used with each level of each other factor.

field edit   Preliminary edit, typically conducted by a field supervisor, that is designed to detect the most glaring omissions and inaccuracies in a completed data collection instrument.

field error   Nonsampling error that arises during the actual collection of the data.

field experiment   Research study in a realistic situation in which one or more independent variables are manipulated by the experimenter under as carefully controlled conditions as the situation will permit.

fixed-alternative questions   Questions in which the responses are limited to stated alternatives.

fixed sample   Sample for which size is determined *a priori* and needed information is collected from the designated elements.

focus group   Personal interview conducted among a small number of individuals simultaneously; the interview relies more on group discussion than on directed questions to generate data.

frequency polygon   Figure obtained from a histogram by connecting the midpoints of the bars of the histogram with straight lines.

full profile   An approach to collecting respondents' judgments in a conjoint analysis in which each stimulus is made up of a combination of each of the attributes.

funnel approach   An approach to question sequencing that gets its name from its shape, starting with broad questions and progressively narrowing the scope.

fusion coefficients   In linkage cluster analysis, the numerical values at which various cases

merge to form clusters. Also called amalgamation coefficients, they can be read directly from a dendrogram.

galvanometer   Device used to measure the emotion induced by exposure to a particular stimulus by recording changes in the electrical resistance of the skin associated with the minute degree of sweating that accompanies emotional arousal; in marketing research, the stimulus is often specific advertising copy.

geodemography   The availability of demographic consumer behavior and life-style data by arbitrary geographic boundaries that are typically quite small.

goodness of fit   Statistical test employing χ^2 to determine whether some observed pattern of frequencies corresponds to an expected pattern.

graphic rating scale   Scale in which individuals indicate their ratings of an attribute by placing a check at the appropriate point on a line that runs from one extreme of the attribute to the other.

halo effect   Problem that arises in data collection when there is carry-over from one judgment to another.

histogram   Form of bar chart on which the values of the variable are placed along the X axis, or abscissa, and the absolute frequency or relative frequency of occurrence of the values is indicated along the Y axis, or ordinate.

history Specific events external to an experiment but occurring at the same time that may affect the criterion or response variable.

hit rate Measure used to assess the results of a discriminant analysis by measuring the proportion of the objects that were correctly classified by the discriminant function(s) in the group to which they actually belong.

hypothesis A statement that specifies how two or more measurable variables are related.

implicit alternative An alternative answer to a question that is not expressed in the options.

implied assumption A problem that occurs when a question is not framed to explicitly state the consequences; thus, it elicits different responses from individuals who *assume* different consequences.

incidence The percentage of the population or group that qualifies for inclusion in the sample using some criteria.

index of predictive association A statistic used to measure the extent of association between two nominally scaled attributes.

information control Term applied to studies using questionnaires and concerning the amount and accuracy of the information that can be obtained from respondents.

instrument variation Any and all changes in the measuring device used in an experiment that might account for differences in two or more measurements.

intention Anticipated or planned future behavior.

interdependence analysis Problem in multivariate analysis to determine the relationship of a set of variates among themselves; no one variate is selected as special in the sense of the dependent variable.

internal data Data that originate within the organization for which the research is being done.

internal validity One criterion by which an experiment is evaluated; the criterion focuses on obtaining evidence demonstrating that the variation in the criterion variable was the result of exposure to the treatment or experimental variable.

interval scale Measurement in which the assigned numbers legitimately allow the comparison of the size of the differences among and between members.

interviewer–interviewee interaction model Model that attempts to describe how an interviewer and a respondent could be expected to respond to each other during the course of an interview; it is helpful in suggesting techniques by which response errors can be potentially reduced.

item nonresponse Source of nonsampling error that arises when a respondent agrees to an interview but refuses or is unable to answer specific questions.

itemized rating scale Scale in which individuals must indicate their ratings of an attribute or object by selecting one from among a limited number of categories that best describes their attitude toward the attribute or object.

judgment sample Nonprobability sample that is often called a purposive sample; the sample elements are handpicked because they are expected to serve the research purpose.

***k*-means** One of the nodal or partitioning methods for cluster analysis; the technique revolves around the selection of k starting points and the assignment of each element to the starting point to which it is most similar. After all points are assigned, the mean or centroid for each group is determined. Then the objects are reassigned on the basis of which mean they are closest to, and the process of computing new centroids and reassigning points is repeated until no objects are reclassified.

Kolmogorov-Smirnov test Statistical test employed with ordinal data to determine whether some observed pattern of frequencies corresponds to some expected pattern; also tests whether two independent samples have been drawn from the same population or from populations with the same distribution.

laboratory experiment Research investigation in which investigators create a situation with exact conditions in order to control some variables and manipulate others.

Latin-square design
Experimental design in which (1) the number of categories for each extraneous variable we wish to control is equal to the number of treatments, and (2) each treatment is randomly assigned to categories according to a specific pattern. The Latin-square design is appropriate when there are two extraneous factors to be explicitly controlled.

leading question   A question framed to give the respondent a clue about how he or she should answer.

line chart   Two-dimensional chart constructed on graph paper in which the X axis represents one variable (typically time) and the Y axis represents another variable.

literature search   Search of statistics, trade journal articles, other articles, magazines, newspapers, and books for data or insight into the problem at hand.

longitudinal study
Investigation involving a fixed sample of elements that is measured repeatedly through time.

mail questionnaire
Questionnaire administered by mail to designated respondents with an accompanying cover letter to be returned by mail by the subject to the research organization.

mall intercept   A method of data collection in which interviewers in a shopping mall stop a sample of those passing by to ask them if they would be willing to participate in a research study; those who agree are typically taken to any interviewing facility that has been set up in the mall, where the interview is conducted.

market test   Controlled experiment, done in a limited but carefully selected sector of the marketplace; its aim is to predict the sales or profit consequences, either in absolute or relative terms, of one or more proposed marketing actions.

marketing information system (MIS)   Set of procedures and methods for the regular, planned collection, analysis, and presentation of information for use in making marketing decisions.

marketing research   Function linking the consumer to the marketer through information used to identify and define marketing opportunities and problems; generate, refine, and evaluate marketing actions; monitor marketing performance; and improve understanding of marketing as a process.

maturation   Processes operating within the test units in an experiment as a function of the passage of time *per se*.

maximum chance criterion
Decision rule used in discriminant analysis to develop a comparison yardstick for assessing the predictive accuracy of the discriminant function; the maximum chance criterion holds that an object chosen at random should be classified as belonging to the largest size group.

measurement   Rules for assigning numbers to objects to represent quantities of attributes.

method variance   The variation in scores attributable to the method of data collection.

model system   The part of a decision support system that includes all the routines that allow the user to manipulate the data in order to conduct the kind of analysis the individual desires.

motive   Need, want, drive, wish, desire, or impulse, or any inner state that energizes, activates, or moves and that directs or channels behavior toward goals.

multichotomous question
Fixed-alternative question in which respondents are asked to choose the alternative that most closely corresponds to their position on the subject.

multicollinearity   Condition said to be present in a multiple-regression analysis when the predictor variables are not independent as required but are correlated among themselves.

multidimensional scaling
Approach to measurement in which people's perceptions of the similarity of objects and their preferences among the objects are measured, and these relationships are plotted in a multidimensional space.

multivariate   Problem of analysis in which there are two or more measures of each of n sample objects, and the variables are to be analyzed simultaneously.

nominal scale Measurement in which numbers are simply assigned to objects or classes of objects solely for the purpose of identification.

noncoverage error
Nonsampling error that arises because of a failure to include some units or entire sections of the defined survey population in the actual sampling frame.

nonobservation error
Nonsampling error that arises because of nonresponse from some elements designated for inclusion in the sample.

nonparametric tests Class of statistical tests, also known as distribution-free tests, that are applicable when the data reflect nominal or ordinal measurement or when the data reflect interval measurement but the assumptions required for the appropriate parametric test are not satisfied.

nonprobability sample Sample that relies on personal judgment somewhere in the element-selection process and therefore prohibits estimating the probability that any population element will be included in the sample.

nonresponse error
Nonsampling error that represents a failure to obtain information from some elements of the population that were selected and designated for the sample.

nonsampling errors Errors that arise in research that are not due to sampling; nonsampling errors can occur because of errors in conception, logic, misinterpretation of replies,

statistics, and arithmetic; errors in tabulating or coding; or errors in reporting the results.

not-at-home Source of nonsampling error that arises when replies are not secured from some designated sampling units because the respondents are not at home when the interviewer calls.

observation Method of data collection in which the situation of interest is watched and the relevant facts, actions, or behaviors are recorded.

observation error Nonsampling error that arises because inaccurate information is secured from the sample elements or because errors are introduced in processing the data or in reporting the findings.

office error Nonsampling error that arises in the processing of the data because of errors in editing, coding, entering, tabulating, or some other part of the analysis.

omnibus panel Panel in which the information collected from the participating panel members varies from study to study.

open-ended question Question characterized by the condition that respondents are free to reply in their own words rather than being limited to choosing from among a set of alternatives.

operational definition
Definition of a construct that describes the operations to be carried out in order for the construct to be measured empirically.

ordinal scale Measurement in which numbers are assigned to data on the basis of some order (for example, more than, greater than) of the objects.

outlier Observation so different in magnitude from the rest of the observations that the analyst chooses to treat it as a special case.

overcoverage error
Nonsampling error that arises because of the duplication of elements in the list of sampling units.

paired comparison A data collection procedure in which respondents indicate which item in each pair of items is preferred; when used in conjoint analysis, the items in each pair represent predetermined combinations of attributes.

panel (omnibus) Fixed sample of respondents who are measured repeatedly over time but on variables that change from measurement to measurement.

panel (true) Fixed sample of respondents who are measured repeatedly over time with respect to the same variables.

parameter Fixed characteristic or measure of a parent or target population.

parametric tests Class of statistical tests used when the variable (variables) is (are) measured on at least an interval scale.

part-worth function Function that describes the relationship between the perceived utilities associated with various levels of an attribute and the objective or physical levels of the attributes (for example, utilities associated with various prices).

payoff table Table containing three elements: alternatives, states of nature, and consequences of each alternative under each state of nature.

people meter A device used to measure when a TV is on, to what channel it is tuned, and who in the household is watching it. Each member in a household is assigned a viewing number, which the individual is supposed to enter into the people meter whenever the set is turned on, the channel is switched, or the person enters or leaves the room.

performance of objective tasks Method of assessing attitudes that rests on the presumption that a subject's performance of a specific assigned task (for example, memorizing a number of facts) will depend on the person's attitude.

personal interview Direct, face-to-face conversation between a representative of the research organization (the interviewer) and a respondent, or interviewee.

personal (or subjective) probability *See* Bayesian probability.

personality Normal patterns of behavior exhibited by an individual; the attributes, traits, and mannerisms that distinguish one individual from another.

physiological reaction technique Method of assessing attitudes in which the researcher, by electrical or mechanical means,

monitors the subject's response to the controlled introduction of some stimuli.

pictogram Bar chart in which pictures represent amounts — for example, piles of dollars for income, pictures of cars for automobile production, people in a row for population.

pie chart Circle, representing a total quantity, divided into sectors, with each sector showing the size of the segment in relation to that total.

plus-one sampling Technique used in studies employing telephone interviews in which a single randomly determined digit is added to numbers selected from the telephone directory.

population Totality of cases that conforms to some designated specifications.

power Function associated with a statistical test indicating the probability of correctly rejecting a false null hypothesis.

pragmatic validity Approach to validation of a measure based on the usefulness of the measuring instrument as a predictor of some other characteristic or behavior of the individual; it is sometimes called predictive validity or criterion-related validity.

precision Desired size of the estimating interval when the problem is one of estimating a population parameter; the notion of degree of precision is useful in determining sample size.

pretest Use of a questionnaire (observation form) on a trial basis in a small pilot study to determine how well the

questionnaire (observation form) works.

primary data Information collected specifically for the purpose of the investigation at hand.

primary source Originating source of secondary data.

probability-proportional-to-size sampling Form of cluster sampling in which a fixed number of second-stage units is selected from each first-stage cluster. The probabilities associated with the selection of each cluster are, in turn, variable because they are directly related to the relative sizes of each cluster.

probability sample Sample in which each population element has a known, nonzero chance of being included in the sample.

projective technique A method of questioning respondents using a vague stimulus that respondents are asked to describe, expand on, or build a structure around; the basic assumption is that an individual's organization of the relatively unstructured stimulus is indicative of the person's basic perceptions of the phenomenon and reactions to it.

proportional chance criterion Decision rule used in discriminant analysis to develop a comparison yardstick for assessing the predictive accuracy of the discriminant function; the proportional chance criterion holds that the percentage of objects likely to be classified correctly by chance alone equals $\alpha^2 + (1 - \alpha)^2$, where α equals the proportion of objects in

Group 1 and $1 - \alpha$ equals the proportion of objects in Group 2.

proportionate stratified sampling Stratified sample in which the number of observations in the total sample is allocated among the strata in proportion to the relative number of elements in each stratum in the population.

psychographic analysis Technique that investigates how people live, what interests them, and what they like; it is also called life-style or AIO analysis, because it relies on a number of statements about a person's *A*ctivities, *I*nterests, and *O*pinions.

Q-sort technique General methodology for gathering data and processing the collected information. The subjects are assigned the task of sorting various statements by placing a specific number of statements in each sorting category; the emphases are on determining the relative ranking of stimuli by individuals and deriving clusters of individuals who display similar preference orderings of stimuli.

quota sample Nonprobability sample chosen in such a way that the proportion of sample elements possessing a certain characteristic is approximately the same as the proportion of the elements with the characteristic in the population; each field worker is assigned a quota that specifies the characteristics of the people he or she is to contact.

random-digit dialing Technique used in studies employing telephone interviews in which the numbers to be called are randomly generated.

random error Error in measurement due to the transient aspects of the person or measurement situation.

randomized-block design Experimental design in which (1) the test units are divided into blocks or homogeneous groups using some external criterion, and (2) the objects in each block are randomly assigned to treatment conditions. The randomized-block design is typically employed when there is one extraneous influence to be explicitly controlled.

randomized response model Interviewing technique in which potentially embarrassing and relatively innocuous questions are paired, and the question the respondent answers is randomly determined.

ratio scale Measurement that has a natural or absolute zero and that therefore allows the comparison of absolute magnitudes of the numbers.

recall loss A type of error caused by a respondent forgetting that an event happened at all.

refusals Nonsampling error that arises because some designated respondents refuse to participate in the study.

regression analysis Statistical technique used to derive an equation that relates a single criterion variable to one or more predictor variables.

relative precision Degree of precision desired in an estimate of a parameter as expressed relative to the level of the estimate of the parameter.

reliability Similarity of results provided by independent but comparable measures of the same object, trait, or construct.

research design Framework or plan for a study that guides the collection and analysis of the data.

research process Sequence of steps in the design and implementation of a research study, including problem formulation, determination of sources of information and research design, determination of data collection method and design of data collection forms, design of the sample and collection of the data, analysis and interpretation of the data, and the research report.

response latency The amount of time a respondent deliberates before answering a question.

response rate (R) Measure used to evaluate and compare interviewers in terms of their ability to induce contacted respondents to participate in the study; R = number of interviews/ number of contacts.

sample Selection of a subset of elements from a larger group of objects.

sample survey Cross-sectional study in which the sample is selected to be representative of the target population and in which the emphasis is on the generation of summary statistics such as averages and percentages. Also called a field survey.

sampling control Term applied to studies relying on questionnaires and concerning the researcher's dual abilities to direct the inquiry to a designated respondent and to secure the desired cooperation from that respondent.

sampling distribution
Distribution of values of some statistic calculated for each possible distinguishable sample that could be drawn from a parent population under a specific sampling plan.

sampling error   Difference between the observed values of a variable and the long-run average of the observed values in repetitions of the measurement.

sampling frame   List of sampling units from which a sample will be drawn; the list could consist of geographic areas, institutions, individuals, or other units.

sampling units   Nonoverlapping collections of elements from the population.

scanner   Electronic device that automatically reads imprinted Universal Product Codes as the product is pulled across the scanner, looks up the price in an attached computer, and instantly prints the price of the item on the cash register tape.

secondary data   Statistics not gathered for the immediate study at hand but for some other purpose.

secondary source   Source of secondary data that did not originate the data but secured them from another source.

selection bias   Contaminating influence in an experiment occurring when there is no way of certifying that groups of test units were equivalent at some previous time.

self report   Method of assessing attitudes in which individuals are asked directly for their beliefs about or feelings toward an object or class of objects.

semantic differential   Self-report technique for attitude measurement in which subjects are asked to check which cell between a set of bipolar adjectives or phrases best describes their feelings toward the object.

sentence completion
Questionnaire containing a number of sentences that subjects are directed to complete with the first words that come to mind.

sequence bias   Distortion in the answers to some questions on a questionnaire because the replies are not independently arrived at but are conditioned by responses to other questions; the problem is particularly acute in mail questionnaires because the respondent can see the whole questionnaire.

sequential sample   Sample formed on the basis of a series of successive decisions. If the evidence is not conclusive after a small sample is taken, more observations are taken; if still inconclusive after these additional observations, still more observations are taken. At each stage, a decision is made about whether more information should be collected or whether the evidence is sufficient to draw a conclusion.

simple random sample
Probability sample in which each population element has a known and equal chance of being included in the sample and in which every combination of n population elements is a sample possibility and is just as likely to occur as any other combination of n units.

simple tabulation   Count of the number of cases that fall into each category when the categories are based on one variable.

simulated test marketing   Test marketing done by firms in shopping malls or consumers' homes as a prelude to a full-scale marketing test for the product.

snake diagram   Diagram (so called because of its shape) that connects with straight lines the average responses to a series of semantic differential statements, thereby depicting the profile of the object or objects being evaluated.

snowball sample   Judgment sample that relies on the researcher's ability to locate an initial set of respondents with the desired characteristics; these individuals are then used as informants to identify still others with the desired characteristics.

Spearman's rank correlation coefficient (r_s) A statistic employed with ordinal data to measure the extent of association between two variables.

spurious correlation   Condition that arises when there is no relationship between two variables but the analyst concludes that a relationship exists.

spurious noncorrelation Condition that arises when the analyst concludes that there is no relationship between two variables but, in fact, there is.

stability A technique for assessing the reliability of a measure by measuring the same objects or individuals at two different points in time and then correlating the scores; the procedure is known as test–retest reliability assessment.

standard error of estimate Term used in regression analysis to refer to the absolute amount of variation in the criterion variable that is left unexplained or unaccounted for by the fitted regression equation.

standard test market A market in which companies sell their products through normal distribution channels.

Stapel scale Self-report technique for attitude measurement in which the respondents are asked to indicate how accurately each of a number of statements describes the object of interest.

statistic Characteristic or measure of a sample.

statistical efficiency Measure used to compare sampling plans; one sampling plan is said to be superior (more statistically efficient) to another if, for the same size sample, it produces a smaller standard error of estimate.

statistical regression Tendency of extreme cases of a

phenomenon to move toward a more central position during the course of an experiment.

storytelling Questionnaire method of data collection relying on a picture stimulus such as a cartoon, photograph, or drawing, about which the subject is asked to tell a story.

stratified sample Probability sample that is distinguished by the two-step procedure in which (1) the parent population is divided into mutually exclusive and exhaustive subsets, and (2) a simple random sample of elements is chosen independently from each group or subset.

stratum chart Set of line charts in which quantities are aggregated or a total is disaggregated so that the distance between two lines represents the amount of some variable.

stress Measure of the "badness of fit" of a configuration determined by multidimensional scaling analysis when compared to the original input data.

structure Degree of standardization imposed on the data collection instrument. A highly structured questionnaire, for example, is one in which the questions to be asked and the responses permitted subjects are completely predetermined; a highly unstructured questionnaire is one in which the questions to be asked are only loosely predetermined and respondents are free to respond in their own words and in any way they see fit.

summated ratings Self-report technique for attitude

measurement in which the subjects are asked to indicate their degree of agreement or disagreement with each of a number of statements; a subject's attitude score is the total obtained by summing the scale values assigned to each category checked.

syndicated research Information collected on a regular basis that is then sold to interested clients (for example, Nielsen Retail Index).

systematic error Error in measurement that is also known as constant error, since it affects the measurement in a systematic way.

systematic sample Probability sample in which every kth element in the population is designated for inclusion in the sample after a random start.

tabulation Procedure by which the number of cases that fall into each of a number of categories are counted.

tachistoscope Device that provides the researcher timing control over a visual stimulus; in marketing research, the visual stimulus is often a specific advertisement.

teleology An ethical or moral reasoning framework that focuses on the net consequences that an action may have. If the net benefits minus all costs are positive, the act is morally acceptable; if the net result is negative, the act is not morally acceptable.

telephone interview Telephone conversation between a

representative of the research organization, the interviewer, and a respondent or interviewee.

telescoping error   A type of error resulting from the fact that most people remember an event as having occurred more recently than in fact is the case.

testing effect   Contaminating effect in an experiment occurring because the process of experimentation itself affected the observed response. The *main testing effect* refers to the impact of a prior observation on a later observation, whereas the *interactive testing effect* refers to the condition when a prior measurement affects the test unit's response to the experimental variable.

Thematic Apperception Test (TAT)   Copyrighted series of pictures about which the subject is asked to tell stories.

total association   Association existing between the variables without regard to the levels of any other variables; also called the zero-order association between the variables.

trade-off matrix   A method of structuring the stimuli that respondents evaluate in a conjoint

analysis that treats two attributes at a time but considers all possible pairs; also known as the pairwise procedure.

turnover table   *See* brand-switching matrix.

Type I error   Rejection of a null hypothesis when it is true; also known as α error.

Type II error   Failure to reject a null hypothesis when it is false; also known as β error.

unbiased   Used to describe a statistic when the average value of the statistic equals the population parameter it is supposed to estimate.

univariate   Problem of analysis in which there is a single measurement on each of n sample objects or there are several measurements on each of the n observations, but each variable is to be analyzed in isolation.

utilitarianism   The most well-known branch of teleological ethics; the utilitarian perspective holds that the correct course of action is the one that promotes the greatest good for the greatest number and that all acts for which the net benefits exceed the net costs are morally acceptable.

validity   Term applied to measuring instruments reflecting the extent to which differences in scores on the measurement reflect true differences among individuals, groups, or situations in the characteristic that it seeks to measure, or reflect true differences in the same individual, group, or situation from one occasion to another, rather than constant or random errors.

variable transformation   Change in scale in which a variable is expressed.

varimax   Angle-preserving rotation of a factor-analytic solution done to facilitate substantive interpretation of the factors.

voice pitch analysis   Type of analysis that examines changes in the relative frequency of the human voice that accompany emotional arousal.

word association   Questionnaire containing a list of words to which respondents are instructed to reply with the first word that comes to mind.

zero-order association   *See* total association.